Why Do You Need this New Edition?

If you're wondering why you should buy this FIFTH edition of *INVITATION TO PSYCHOLOGY*, here are seven good reasons!

❶ Chapter 4 ("Neurons, Hormones, and the Brain") describes new research on teaching monkeys to use brain waves to control a robotic arm; using electric stimulation to restore awareness in patients who are in a minimally conscious state; using brain activity to identify which pictures a person is looking at; and *induced pluripotent stem cells*. In a new discussion of the field of *neuroethics,* this chapter also raises the question of the benefits and potential harm of drugs that produce cognitive enhancement and others that might have the power to delete traumatic memories.

❷ Chapter 8 ("Memory") contains fascinating new research on working memory and its importance for staying on task; recent biological work on the role of the hippocampus not only in memory formation but also recall; research in the Horror Labyrinth of the London Dungeon on the impact of too much arousal on memory; and research on the effectiveness of the *read-recite-review strategy* and retrieval practice for students who want to improve their study skills.

❸ Chapter 12 ("Approaches to Treatment and Therapy") contains an updated and expanded discussion of medications for routine emotional disorders; a critical assessment of new drugs; the increasing use of prescription cocktails; and conflicts of interest, placebo effects, and publication bias in medical research. New material also includes deep brain stimulation and TMS; the use of virtual-reality treatments for Iraq veterans; the next generation of cognitive-behavior therapy, focusing on mindfulness and acceptance; and a new list of unvalidated, potentially harmful therapies.

❹ Every major section within a chapter now opens with learning objectives that highlight key content and alert students to the material that follows.

❺ Each chapter begins with an updated story for "Psychology in the News," and a corresponding revised and updated discussion at the end of the chapter for "Psychology in the News, Revisited."

❻ Explore/Watch/Listen/Simulate/Study and Review icons integrated in the text lead to web-based expansions on topics, allowing instructors and students access to extra information, videos, podcasts, and simulations. Many more resources are available than those highlighted in the book, but the icons do draw attention to some of the most high-interest materials available at **www.mypsychlab.com**.

❼ Easily navigated eBook with highlighting and note-taking features and powerful embedded media is now available including simulations, podcasts, video clips, and an interactive timeline. The online media for *Invitation to Psychology*, 5th edition, includes over 200 video clips, all available in Closed Caption.

INVITATION TO PSYCHOLOGY

Fifth Edition

Carole Wade

Carol Tavris

Prentice Hall

Boston   Columbus   Indianapolis   New York   San Francisco   Upper Saddle River
Amsterdam   Cape Town   Dubai   London   Madrid   Milan   Munich   Paris   Montréal   Toronto
Delhi   Mexico City   São Paulo   Sydney   Hong Kong   Seoul   Singapore   Taipei   Tokyo

Editorial Director: *Craig Campanella*	Art Director: *Kathy Mrozek*
Editor in Chief: *Jessica Mosher*	Text and Cover Designer: *Ximena Tamvakopoulos*
Executive Editor: *Stephen Frail*	Image Lead: *Ben Ferrini/Beth Brenzel*
Editorial Project Manager: *Judy Casillo*	Photo Researcher: *Tim Herzog/Bill Smith Group*
Editorial Assistant: *Kerri Hart-Morris*	Cover Art: © *Paul Fleet/Alamy*
Director of Marketing: *Brandy Dawson*	Media Director: *Brian Hyland*
Executive Marketing Manager: *Jeanette Koskinas*	Lead Media Project Manager: *Paul DeLuca*
Marketing Assistant: *Craig Deming*	Full-Service Project Management: *Jill Traut*
Managing Editor: *Maureen Richardson*	Composition: *MPS Limited, a Macmillan Company*
Project Manager: *Marianne Peters-Riordan*	Printer/Binder: *Courier Companies*
Senior Operations Specialist: *Sherry Lewis*	Cover Printer: *Lehigh/Phoenix Color*
Senior Art Director: *Nancy Wells*	Text Font: *Janson Text/10*

Credits and acknowledgments borrowed from other sources and reproduced, with permission, in this textbook appear on appropriate page within text (or on pages C1–C3).

Library of Congress Cataloging-in-Publication Data
Wade, Carole.
  Invitation to psychology / Carole Wade, Carol Tavris.
      p. cm.
  Includes bibliographical references and index.
  ISBN-13: 978-0-205-03519-9 (student edition)
  ISBN-10: 0-205-03519-1 (student edition)
  ISBN-13: 978-0-205-06610-0 (exam)
  ISBN-10: 0-205-06610-0 (exam)
  [etc.]
  1. Psychology—Textbooks. I. Tavris, Carol. II. Title.

BF121.W265 2010
150—dc22

2010050936

10 9 8 7 6 5 4 3 2 1

Prentice Hall
is an imprint of

www.pearsonhighered.com

Student Edition: ISBN 10: 0-205-035191
ISBN 13: 978-0-205-03519-9
Exam Edition: ISBN 10: 0-205-06610-0
ISBN 13: 978-0-205-06610-0
A La Carte: ISBN 10: 0-205-06636-4
ISBN 13: 978-0-205-06636-0

Contents at a glance

Contents

From the Authors

Every time we revise this textbook, our enthusiasm for psychology is reignited. These are especially exciting times for psychology teachers and students, because the field is bubbling over with many new ideas, possibilities, and controversies inspired by the biomedical revolution in science and society. Biological findings have led to an integration of specialties within psychology as well as collaboration with scholars from other fields: Neuroscientists and behavioral geneticists are working with social psychologists, behaviorists, cognitive therapists, developmental psychologists, economists, and others to better understand human behavior.

It is unwise, however, to jump on any bandwagon uncritically, without thinking about what direction it's headed. When we first wrote this book, psychology was undergoing a different revolution: Researchers were coming to understand the scientific and social importance of making psychology the study of all human beings, not just, as the joke had it at the time, the study of young, white, sophomore, male . . . rats. For us, integrating the burgeoning new research on gender and culture was an invigorating challenge. It was important (and fun!) to show students that "culture" is not merely a thin veneer on human behavior, but a factor that shapes our behavior profoundly in every domain—from how often people think it is appropriate to bathe, to the conditions that make men angry enough to kill for the sake of their honor, to whether a person wants to stand out in a group or fit in. Nonetheless, from the beginning, we maintained a commitment to thinking critically about this research. We rejected the common practice of equating "mainstreaming culture and gender" with simply throwing in a gender or cultural difference wherever one existed, without assessing its significance and explaining its likely causes.

Likewise, we believe it is crucial to assess the biomedical revolution thoughtfully and critically, rather than simply report new findings. PET scans and fMRIs are amazing tools, but like all tools, they can be misused to distort or exaggerate. Evolutionary psychology is extremely interesting, but some people are inclined to apply it unskeptically to any behavior or attribute of interest ("There must be an evolutionarily adaptive reason for baldness, pimples, and collecting ceramic sheep"). The excitement about biological research in general often creates a kind of pop reductionism, in which many people come to think that biology explains nearly everything.

For these reasons, we believe that the original goal of our book—the goal of integrating critical and scientific thinking into the warp and woof of our writing—is more important now than ever. The public in general, and students in particular, need to learn about the astonishing new developments in neuroscience, but they also need to learn to think intelligently about them. Not all of these developments are as dramatic or applicable as they are often made to appear in the popular press. Not all of the findings that are reported are based on good science, no matter how fancy the tools that produce them.

A textbook, in short, is not a laundry list of items, and its writers are not simply reporters. For us, the primary job of an introductory textbook in psychology is to help students learn to think like a psychologist, and to understand why scientific and critical thinking is so important for everything they do: from the decisions they make in their own lives to being wary of Internet scams, hoaxes, and viral panics.

An Invitation to *Invitation to Psychology*

The 14 chapters in this book cover the major topics in introductory psychology but are organized differently from our 16-chapter version. Here, we wanted to do two things: engage students quickly and provide a logical scaffolding for the diverse topics in psychology. The first chapter, which introduces students to the field and to the fundamentals of critical and scientific thinking, is followed by six sections, each consisting of two chapters (in one case, three). The title of each section invites readers to consider how the discipline of psychology can illuminate aspects of their own lives and provides readers with a personal frame of reference for assimilating the information:

- **PART ONE: YOUR SELF** examines major theories of personality (Chapter 2) and development (Chapter 3). These are high-interest topics for students and will draw them into the course right away. Moreover, starting off with these chapters allows us to avoid redundancy in coverage of the major schools of psychology—biological, learning, cognitive, sociocultural, and psychodynamic. Instead of introducing these perspectives in the first chapter and then having to explain them again in a much later personality chapter, we cover them once, in this section.

- **PART TWO: YOUR BODY** explores the many ways in which the brain, neurons, and hormones affect psychological functioning (Chapter 4), body rhythms and states of consciousness (Chapter 5), and the neurological and psychological underpinnings of sensation and perception (Chapter 6).

- **PART THREE: YOUR MIND** discusses the impressive ways in which human beings think and reason—and why, unfortunately, they so often fail to think and reason well (Chapter 7) and, along with other paradoxes of memory, why human recall is not as accurate as a machine's (Chapter 8).

- **PART FOUR: YOUR ENVIRONMENT** covers basic principles of learning (Chapter 9) and the impact of social and cultural contexts on behavior (Chapter 10). Combining learning and social psychology in the same part is a break from convention, but we think it makes good sense, for these two fields share an emphasis on external influences on behavior.

- **PART FIVE: YOUR MENTAL HEALTH** reviews the major mental and emotional disorders (Chapter 11) and evaluates the therapies designed to treat them (Chapter 12).

- **PART SIX: YOUR LIFE** shows how mind, body, and environment influence emotions, stress, and health (Chapter 13) and the fundamental motives that drive people: the biological, social, and cultural factors involved in eating and weight; attachment and love; passion and sex; and work and achievement (Chapter 14).

Naturally, we could not include every topic that might be found in a longer book, but we have retained those that are truly essential in an introductory course. In most cases, you will find these topics in the chapters where you expect them to be, but there are a few exceptions. For example, eating disorders are not discussed in the chapter on psychological disorders; instead, we discuss them in the context of psychological, genetic, and cultural factors in eating, overweight, and dieting (Chapter 14). Cognitive dissonance is discussed not only in social psychology (Chapter 10) but also under "barriers to thinking critically" (Chapter 7). If at first you do not see a topic that interests you, we urge you to look for it in the table of contents or the index.

In the next section of this preface, as an overview for those unfamiliar with our book, we describe the five guiding principles and features of *Invitation to Psychology*: our efforts to ensure liveliness and relevance, promote critical thinking, explore the frontiers of biology and neuroscience, mainstream culture and gender, and help students get involved with the material they are learning. Following that section, for instructors who have taught from the previous edition, we offer some highlights of changes and updated research from the fourth to the new edition. We invite all of you to peruse this *Invitation*!

GUIDING PRINCIPLES AND FEATURES

LIVELINESS AND RELEVANCE

Virginia Woolf once said that fiction is not dropped like a pebble upon the ground but, like a spider's web, is attached to life at all four corners. The same principle applies to good textbook writing. Authors of texts at all levels have a unique opportunity to combine scholarly rigor and authority with warmth and compassion in conveying what psychologists know (and still seek to know) about the predicaments and puzzles of life.

Right from the outset, we want students to see that psychology can deepen our understanding of those predicaments and puzzles. Its lessons apply to the world and to us all as individuals. Each chapter, therefore, begins with a feature called **Psychology in the News** that presents a real news item, including a 70-year-old Indian woman giving birth; a man who had been in a vegetative state for years but seemed to reveal signs of brain activity; a rape victim whose mistaken eyewitness testimony sent an innocent man to prison for years; a little boy expelled on zero-tolerance grounds for bringing a Cub Scout camping utensil to school; celebrities who claim their extramarital adventures were a result of their sex addiction; and the man who crashed his plane into an IRS building in Austin, killing himself and two employees, out of rage and frustration.

We use these stories to raise issues that will be addressed in the chapter. Then, at the end of the chapter, we revisit the opening story to show how concepts and findings that the reader has been studying illuminate the issues raised. We think this device helps promote critical thinking and also helps students appreciate that psychology is indeed "attached to life at all four corners."

THINKING CRITICALLY ABOUT CRITICAL THINKING

In a textbook, true critical thinking cannot be reduced to a set of rhetorical questions, a short boxed feature, or a formula for analyzing studies; it is a process that must be woven seamlessly into the narrative. The primary way we "do" critical and creative thinking is by applying a three-pronged approach: We *define* it, we *model* it, and we give students a chance to *practice* it.

critical thinking The ability and willingness to assess claims and make objective judgments on the basis of well-supported reasons and evidence rather than emotion or anecdote.

One of the greatest benefits of studying psychology is that you learn not only how the brain works in general but also how to use yours in particular—by thinking critically. **Critical thinking** is the ability and willingness to assess claims and make objective judgments on the basis of well-supported reasons and evidence, rather than emotion or anecdote. Critical thinkers are able to look for flaws in arguments and to resist claims that have no support. They realize that criticizing an argument is not the same as criticizing the person making it, and they are willing to engage in vigorous debate about the validity of an idea. Critical thinking, however, is not merely negative thinking. It includes the ability to be creative and constructive—the ability to come up with alternative explanations for events, think of implications of research findings, and apply new knowledge to social and personal problems.

Most people know that you have to exercise the body to keep it in shape, but they may not realize are a conspiracy of the Japanese government," you forfeit the right to have your opinion taken seriously. Your opinion, if it ignores reality, is *not* equal to any other.

Critical thinking is not only indispensable in ordinary life; it is also fundamental to all science, including psychological science. By exercising critical thinking, you will be able to distinguish serious psychology from the psychobabble that clutters the airwaves and bookstores. Critical thinking requires logical skills, but other skills and dispositions are also important (Anderson, 2005; Halpern, 2002; Levy, 2010; Stanovich, 2010). Here are eight essential critical-thinking guidelines that we will be emphasizing throughout this book.

1 Ask Questions; Be Willing to Wonder. What is the one kind of question that most exasperates parents of young children? "Why is the sky blue, Mommy?" "Why doesn't the plane fall?" "Why

The first step is to define what critical thinking is and what it is not. Chapter 1 introduces **Eight Guidelines to Critical Thinking,** which we draw on throughout the text as we evaluate research and popular ideas. These guidelines are also listed and described briefly on the inside front cover of the book.

The second step is to model these guidelines in our evaluations of research and popular ideas. Many, though by no means all, of our critical-thinking discussions in the text itself are signaled by a light bulb symbol in the margin along with the topic: **Thinking Critically about . . .** These signposts serve as pointers to critical analyses in the text and invite readers into the discussion.

exasperatingly, new evidence throws our beliefs into disarray. Critical thinkers are willing to accept this state of uncertainty. They are not afraid to say, "We don't have answers yet" or "I'm not sure."

((•—Listen to
**Science and
Pseudoscience** on
mypsychlab.com

Hypnosis has traditionally been considered a trance state in which people involuntarily do things they ordinarily could not or would not do. But might there be another interpretation of the surprising things that hypnotized people often do? (We will look at competing explanations in Chapter 5.)

poke holes in another person's argument than to critically examine our own position. Yet we think the journey is well worth the mental effort, because the ability to think critically will help you in countless ways, from saving you money to improving your relationships.

As you read this book, keep in mind the eight guidelines we have described. Practice in critical thinking can help you bulk up your "thinking muscles" and understand psychological concepts better, which is why we have given you many opportunities to apply these guidelines to psychological theories and to the personal and social issues that affect us all. From time to time, a tab with a light bulb symbol (like the one shown here) will highlight a discussion where one or more of our critical-thinking guidelines are especially relevant. In Quick Quizzes, the light bulb will indicate questions that give you practice in applying the guidelines yourself. Keep in mind, however, that critical thinking is important throughout the book, not only where the light bulb appears. Finally, at the end of every chapter, a feature called "Taking Psychology with You" will help you apply critical thinking to a topic in the chapter and take its message home with you. ((•—**Listen**

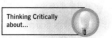

Thinking Critically
about...

The third step is to give students opportunities to practice what we've preached. Throughout each chapter are periodic **Quick Quizzes** that encourage students to check their progress and to go back and review if necessary. These quizzes do more than just test for memorization of definitions; they tell students whether they comprehend the issues. Many of them include critical-thinking items, signaled again with the light bulb icon. These items invite students to reflect on the implications of findings and consider how psychological principles might illuminate real-life issues.

Quick Quiz

Bulk up your own thinking muscles by answering these questions.

1. Describe how the guidelines to critical thinking were violated in each of the following cases:

   a. For years, writer Norman Cousins told how he had cured himself of a rare, life-threatening disease through a combination of humor and vitamins. In a best-selling book, he recommended the same approach to others.

   b. Benjamin Rush, an eighteenth-century physician, believed that yellow fever should be treated by bloodletting. Many of his patients died, but Rush did not lose faith in his approach; he attributed each recovery to his treatment and each death to the severity of the disease (Stanovich, 2010).

2. Amelia and Harold are arguing about the death penalty. "Look, I just feel strongly that it's barbaric, ineffective, and wrong," says Harold. "You're nuts," says Amelia, "I believe in an eye for an eye, and besides, I'm absolutely sure it's a deterrent to further crime." Which lapses of critical thinking might Amelia and Harold be committing?

Answers:

1a. Cousins oversimplified, arguing by anecdote instead of examining evidence from controlled studies that included people who were not helped by humor and vitamins, and he may have been reasoning emotionally because of his own dramatic recovery. *1b.* Rush failed to analyze and test his assumptions; he violated the principle of falsifiability, interpreting a patient's survival as support for his hypothesis and explaining away each death by saying that the person had been too ill for the treatment to work. Thus, there was no possible counterevidence that could refute the theory (which, by the way, was dead wrong; the treatment was actually as dangerous as the disease). *2.* Harold and Amelia are reasoning emotionally ("I feel strongly about this, so I'm right and you're wrong"). They do not cite evidence that supports or contradicts their arguments. What do studies show about the link between the death penalty and crime? How often are innocent people executed? They have not examined their biases. And they may not by clearly defining the problem: What is the purpose of the death penalty? Is it to deter criminals, to satisfy the public desire for revenge, or to keep criminals from being paroled and returned to the streets?

EXPLORING NEW RESEARCH IN BIOLOGY AND NEUROSCIENCE

For examples of how we cover biological research, see our discussions of the following:

- Genetics and personality (pp. 49–54)
- Noncoding DNA (pp. 49–50)
- Stem cells and the production of new neurons (pp. 118–119)
- Schizophrenia (pp. 393–396)
- Sexual desire and behavior (pp. 479–481)
- Weight and body shape (pp. 468–470)

Findings from the Human Genome Project, studies of behavioral genetics, discoveries about the brain, technologies such as PET scans and fMRI, and the proliferation of medications for psychological disorders—all have had a profound influence on our understanding of human behavior and on interventions to help people with chronic problems. This work cannot be confined to a single chapter. Accordingly, we report new findings from the biological front wherever they are relevant throughout the book: in discussions of neurogenesis in the brain, memory, emotion, stress, child development, aging, mental illness, personality, and many other topics.

MAINSTREAMING CULTURE AND GENDER

At the time of our first edition, some considered our goal of incorporating research on gender and culture into introductory psychology to be quite radical, either a sop to political correctness or a fluffy and superficial fad. Today, the issue is no longer whether to include these topics, but how best to do it. From the beginning, our own answer has been to include studies of gender and culture in the main body of the text, wherever they are relevant to the larger discussion, rather than relegating these studies to an intellectual ghetto of separate chapters or boxed features.

For examples of how we treat gender issues, see our discussions of the following:

- Sex differences in the brain (pp. 136–137)
- Gender and emotion (pp. 444–445)
- Gender and heroism (pp. 348–349)
- Gender and transgender identity (pp. 91–93)
- Evolutionary theories of sexual behavior (pp. 481–482)
- Weight and eating disorders in women and men (pp. 471–473)

Over the years, most psychologists have come to appreciate the influence of culture on all aspects of life, from nonverbal behavior to the deepest attitudes about how the world should be. We raise empirical findings about culture and ethnicity as topics warrant, throughout the book. In addition, Chapter 10 highlights the sociocultural perspective in psychology and includes extended discussions of ethnocentrism, prejudice, and cross-cultural relations. The study of culture, in our view, should increase students' understanding of what culture means, how and why ethnic and national groups differ, and why no group is inherently better, kinder, or more moral than another. Thus we try to apply critical thinking to our own coverage of culture, avoiding the twin temptations of ethnocentrism and stereotyping.

For examples of how we treat culture, see our discussions of the following:

- Cultural influences on personality (pp. 58–62)
- Ethnocentrism (pp. 351–352)
- Culture and concepts of control (pp. 335–337)
- Culture and the diagnosis of mental disorder (pp. 370–375)
- Addiction rates and drug abuse (pp. 388–390)
- Attitudes toward achievement (pp. 248–249)

FACING THE CONTROVERSIES

Psychology has always been full of lively, sometimes angry, debates, and we feel that students should not be sheltered from them. They are what make psychology so interesting! In this book, we candidly address controversies in the field of psychology, try to show why they are occurring, and suggest the kinds of questions that might lead to useful answers in each case.

For examples of our in-depth treatment of important controversies in psychology, see our discussions of the following:

- Evolutionary theories of sexuality (pp. 484–485)
- The scientific and legal debates about psychoactive drugs (pp. 408–410)
- Parental influence on children's personalities (pp. 55–56)
- Medication for psychological disorders (pp. 406–408)
- The scientist-practitioner gap (pp. 420–422)
- "Cosmetic neurology" and neuroethics (pp. 139–140)

APPLICATIONS AND ACTIVE LEARNING: GETTING INVOLVED

Throughout this book, we have kept in mind one of the soundest findings about learning: It requires the active encoding of material. Several pedagogical features in particular encourage students to become actively involved in what they are reading.

Get Involved exercises in each chapter make active learning entertaining. They consist of quick demonstrations, mini-studies, or ways to help students relate course material to their own lives. Instructors may want to assign some of these exercises to the entire class and then discuss the results and what they might mean.

observational studies, like other descriptive studies, are more useful for describing behavior than for explaining it. If we observe infants protesting whenever a parent leaves the room, we cannot be sure why they are protesting. Is it because they have become

ings, or behaviors of which an individual is aware; *projective tests* are designed to tap unconscious feelings or motives (see Chapter 11).

At one time or another, you no doubt have taken a personality test, an achievement test, or a

Get Involved! A Study of Personal Space

Try a little naturalistic observation of your own. Go to a public place where people seat themselves, such as a movie theater or a cafeteria with large tables. You might recruit some friends to help you; you can divide the area into sections and assign each observer one section to observe. As individuals and groups sit down, note how many seats they leave between themselves and the next person. On the average, how far do people tend to sit from strangers? Once you have your results, see how many possible explanations you can come up with.

Taking Psychology with You, a feature that concludes each chapter, illustrates the practical implications of psychological research for individuals, groups, and society. For this feature, now with a special focus on thinking critically, we have chosen topics of interest and personal relevance to many students.

Taking Psychology with You

What Psychology Can Do for You—and What it Can't

If you intend to become a psychologist or a mental health professional, you have an obvious reason for taking a course in psychology. But psychology can contribute to your life in many ways, even if you do not plan to work in the field. Here are a few things psychology can do for you:

Make you a more informed person. One purpose of education is to acquaint people with their cultural heritage and with human achievements in literature, the arts, and sci-

customer service. Finally, psychology can be useful to those whose jobs require them to predict people's behavior: labor negotiators, politicians, advertising copywriters, managers, product designers, buyers, market researchers, magicians....

Give you insights into political and social issues. Crime, drug abuse, discrimination, and war are not only social issues but also psychological ones. Psychological knowledge alone cannot solve the complex political

emphasized, psychology will not provide you with simple answers to complex questions.

Yet despite the complexity of behavior and the lack of simple answers to human problems, psychologists have made enormous progress in unraveling the secrets of the human brain, mind, and heart. The study of psychology will provide you with sound information, empirical findings, and the skills of critical thinking, all of which can help guide your thinking and your decisions. At the end

You are about to learn ... consists of a set of learning objectives that cover each major section within a chapter.

 YOU are about to learn...

• how "psychobabble" differs from serious psychology.
• what's wrong with psychologists' nonscientific competitors, such as astrologers and psychics.
• how and when psychology became a formal discipline.
• three early schools of psychology.
• the five major perspectives in psychology.

The Science of Psychology

ogists, promoters of these competing systems try to explain people's problems and predict their behavior. If you are having romantic problems, an astrologer may advise you to choose an Aries instead of an Aquarius as your next love, and a channeler of past lives may say it's because you were jilted in a former life. Belief in these unscientific approaches is widespread. Yet, whenever the predictions of psychics, astrologers, and the like are put to the test, they turn out to be so vague as to be meaningless (for example, "Spirituality will increase next year") or just plain wrong (Radford, 2010; Shaffer & Jadwiszczok, 2010). In 2008, one well-known Canadian psychic predicted that George Clooney would marry and have a child, Sean Penn would be wounded in the Middle East, and John Edwards would win the U.S. presidency after Hillary Clin

CONCEPT MAP

S PSYCHOLOGY?

The Science of Psychology

Psychology is the discipline concerned with behavior and mental processes and how they are affected by an organism's physical state, mental state, and external environment. Unlike pseudoscientific approaches to behavior, it relies on **empirical** data.

The Birth of Modern Psychology

- Wilhelm Wundt founded the first psychology laboratory in Leipzig, Germany, in 1879, and emphasized the analysis of experience through trained introspection.
- American William James emphasized the adaptive nature of behavior, an approach known as **functionalism.**
- Sigmund Freud developed **psychoanalysis,** an early form of psychotherapy, in Vienna, Austria.

Today's Five Major Psychological Perspectives

- The **biological perspective** focuses on how bodily events interact with the external environment to affect behavior, feelings, and thoughts.
- The **learning perspective** emphasizes the environment's effect on behavior.
- The **cognitive perspective** emphasizes mental processes in reasoning, memory, perception, language, problem solving, and beliefs.
- The **sociocultural perspective** focuses on the influence of social and cultural forces on behavior.

Every chapter ends with a two-page spread of **concept maps**, visual summaries that organize the material and show relationships between topics at a glance. Instructors and students have found this way of presenting the material to be a useful study aid. These concept maps follow **chapter summaries** in paragraph form, so students can review material both ways.

Other pedagogical features designed to help students study and learn better include a **running glossary** that defines bold-faced technical terms on the pages where they occur for handy reference and study; a **cumulative glossary** at the back of the book; a list of **key terms** at the end of each chapter that includes page numbers so that students can find the sections where the terms are covered; and, as noted previously, **summaries** in paragraph and conceptual form.

Psychology in the News

Traces of Consciousness Found in Some Patients Diagnosed as "Vegetative"

LIEGE, BELGIUM, February 4, 2010. A 29-year-old man thought to have been in a persistent vegetative state for five years following a car accident has shown signs of brain activity in response to questions from

made headlines when neurological tests indicated that he too had some possible awareness, and a brain scan revealed nearly normal activity in his brain. Therapists provided Houben with a computer touch screen that seemed to allow him to communicate by spelling out words. But skeptics pointed out that all of Houben's messages were typed with the help of an aide who supported and guided his hand. Scientific research has dis-

Psychology in the News REVISITED

Now that you know more about the workings of the brain, let's return to the opening story of the patients who were in vegetative or minimally conscious states but who appeared to have some brain function. Political and religious debates continue over the rights of incapacitated people, the meaning of "death by natural causes," and when life should end if a person has left no written instructions. We cannot resolve these debates here, but the information in this chapter, and an increased understanding of the brain, can help us to separate what we might wish to be true about a patient's mental abilities from what really is true.

Consider the tragic case of Terri Schiavo, whose

any connection to events in the environment. Eventually, a judge gave Terri's husband permission to have her feeding tube removed, and she died peacefully soon thereafter.

What, then, about the man who responded to yes–no questions by imagining scenarios that produced

Finally, we hope that the framing effect of the chapter opening story in **Psychology in the News** and the end-of-chapter feature **Psychology in the News, Revisited** will serve to unify and integrate the material, showing students how the material they just read helps them understand the kinds of real-world events, mysteries, and surprises that they encounter every day.

CHANGES IN THE FIFTH EDITION

In this fifth edition of *Invitation to Psychology*, we have retained the text's approach and pedagogy. We have made no changes just for the sake of making changes. Many of the book's features have been tested by time and student reaction; students and instructors like them.

In every chapter, we have updated the research, deleting findings that did not hold up, adding new ones, and expanding others. Here are **just a few highlights of the new research** we added:

- Chapter 2 ("Theories of Personality") includes information on *noncoding DNA* (formerly thought to be "junk" DNA), the genetic dissimilarities of supposedly identical twins, and other findings from new research in genetics.

- Chapter 4 ("Neurons, Hormones, and the Brain") includes new research on teaching monkeys to use brain waves to control a robotic arm; using electric stimulation to restore awareness in patients who are in a minimally conscious state; using brain activity to identify which pictures a person is looking at; and *induced pluripotent stem cells*. This chapter also discusses drugs that produce cognitive enhancement and methods of possibly deleting memories stored in the brain as an introduction to the field of *neuroethics*.

- Chapter 6 ("Sensation and Perception") introduces fascinating Swedish research on the ultimate illusion—body swapping—and a discussion of a leading explanation of phantom limb pain, along with an exciting new way to treat it, using a simple, inexpensive mirror.

- Chapter 8 ("Memory") includes new research on working memory and its importance for staying on task; recent biological work on the role of the hippocampus not only in memory formation but also recall; research in the Horror Labyrinth of the London Dungeon on the impact of too much arousal on memory; and research on the effectiveness of the *read-recite-review strategy* and retrieval practice for students.

- Chapter 12 ("Approaches to Treatment and Therapy") offers updated and expanded discussion of medications for routine emotional disorders: a critical assessment of new drugs; the increasing use of prescription cocktails; and conflicts of interest, placebo effects, and publication bias in medical research. New material includes deep brain stimulation and transcranial magnetic stimulation (TMS); the use of virtual-reality treatments for Iraq veterans; the next generation of cognitive-behavior therapy, focusing on mindfulness and acceptance; a new list of unvalidated, potentially harmful therapies.

The rest of our content changes are too numerous to mention here, but a detailed explanation of all deletions, additions, and modifications in this edition is available to adopters of the fourth edition, so that no one will have to guess why we made particular changes. We hope this support will make the transition from one edition to the next as painless as possible. You can obtain this description from your Pearson sales representative or by emailing your request to Executive Marketing Manager Jeanette Koskinas at jeanette.koskinas@pearson.com.

From the Publisher

Teaching and Learning: Integrated, Meaningful, Easy-to-Use Activities

As valuable as a good textbook is, it is one element of a comprehensive learning package. We at Pearson Publishers have made every effort to provide high-quality instructor and student supplements that will save you preparation time and will enhance the classroom experience.

For access to all instructor supplements for Wade and Tavris's *INVITATION TO PSYCHOLOGY*, Fifth Edition, simply go to **www.pearsonhighered.com/irc** and follow the directions to register (or log in if you already have a Pearson user name and password). Once you have registered and your status as an instructor is verified, you will be emailed a login name and password. Use your login name and password to access the catalog. Click on the "online catalog" link, click on "psychology" followed by "introductory psychology" and then the Wade/Tavris *Invitation to Psychology*, Fifth Edition text. Under the description of each supplement is a link that allows you to download and save the supplement to your desktop.

You can request hard copies of the supplements through your Pearson sales representative. If you do not know your sales representative, go to **www.pearsonhighered.com/replocator/** and follow the directions. For technical support for any of your Pearson products, you and your students can contact **http://247.pearsoned.com.**

Wade/Tavris's *Invitation to Psychology*, Fifth Edition, is available in these formats:

Paper cover (ISBN 0-205-03519-1)
Books a la Carte (ISBN 0-205-06636-4)
CourseSmart e-Textbook subscription **(www.CourseSmart.com)**

Supplements for Instructors

The Instructor's Resource Center **(www.pearsonhighered.com/irc)** provides information and the following downloadable supplements:

Test Item File This excellent test bank, prepared by David Waxler (Widener University), contains over 3000 multiple-choice, true-false, and essay questions, each referenced to the relevant page in the textbook. An additional feature for the test bank is the inclusion of rationales for the correct answer in the *conceptual and applied* multiple-choice questions. The rationales help instructors to evaluate the questions they are choosing for their tests and give instructors the option to use the rationales as an answer key for their students. Feedback from customers indicates this unique feature is useful for ensuring quality and quick response to student queries.

A two-page Total Assessment Guide chapter overview makes creating tests easier by listing all of the test items in an easy-to-reference grid. The Total Assessment Guide organizes all test items by text section and section learning objectives. All multiple-choice questions are categorized as factual, conceptual, or applied. Many of the test items also include an item analysis indicating how many students answered that question correctly in class testing at both two-year and four-year schools. The Test Item File is available for download from the Instructor's Resource Center at **www.pearsonhighered.com/irc**. It is also avaible on the Instructor's Resource DVD **(ISBN 0-205-06631-3)**

MyTest mypearsontest ☑ **(www.pearsonmytest.com)** The Fifth Edition test bank comes with Pearson MyTest, a powerful assessment-generation program that helps instructors easily create and print quizzes and exams. Instructors can do this online, allowing flexibility and the ability to efficiently manage assessments at any time. Instructors can easily access existing questions and edit, create, and store using simple drag-and-drop and Word-like controls. Each question comes with information on its related page number in the text, and mapped to the appropriate section learning objectives. For more information go to **www.PearsonMyTest.com**.

BlackBoard Test Item File/WebCT Test Item File For instructors who only need the test item file, we offer the complete test item file in BlackBoard and WebCT format. Go to Instructor's Resource Center at **www.pearsonhighered.com/irc**.

Interactive PowerPoint Slides These slides, available on the Instructor's DVD **(ISBN 0-205-06631-3)**, bring the Wade/Tavris design right into the classroom, drawing students into the lecture and providing wonderful interactive activities, visuals, and videos. A video walk-through is available and provides clear guidelines on using and customizing the slides. The slides are built around the text's learning objectives and offer many links between content areas. **Icons** integrated throughout the slides indicate interactive exercises, simulations, and activities that can be accessed directly from the slides if instructors want to use these resources in the classroom.

Lecture PowerPoint Slides, prepared by Jason S. Spiegelman (The Community College of Baltimore County) in a more traditional format with excerpts of the text material, photos, and art work, are available on the

Instructor's DVD (**ISBN 0-205-06631-3**) and also online at **www.pearsonhighered.com/irc.**

Classroom Response System (CRS) Classroom Response questions ("clicker" questions) created by Debra Ahola (SUNY Schenectady County Community College) for *Invitation to Psychology*, Fifth Edition, are intended to be the basis for class discussions as well as lectures. The incorporation of the CRS questions into each chapter's slideshow facilitates the use of clickers—small devices similar to remote controls, which process student responses to questions and interpret and display results in real time. CRS questions are a great way to involve students in what they are learning. These are available on the Instructor's DVD (**ISBN 0-205-06631-3**) and also online at **www.pearsonhighered.com/irc.**

Instructor's Resource Manual In this collection of abundant resources for each chapter prepared by Alan Swinkels (St. Edwards College), instructors will find activities, exercises, assignments, handouts, and demos for in-class use, as well as guidelines for integrating the many Wade/Tavris media resources into the classroom and syllabus. The material for each chapter is organized in an easy-to-use Chapter Lecture Outline. This resource saves prep work and helps you make maximum use of classroom time. A unique hyperlinking system allows for easy reviewing of relevant sections and resources. The IRM is available on the Instructor's DVD (**ISBN 0-205-06631-3**) or online at **www.pearsonhighered.com/irc.**

Instructor's DVD (ISBN 0-205-06631-3) Bringing all of the Fifth Edition's instructor resources together in one place, the Instructor's DVD offers both versions of the PowerPoint presentations, the CRS slides, the electronic files for the Instructor's Resource Manual materials, and the Test Item File to help instructors customize their lecture notes.

Introductory Psychology Teaching Films Boxed Set (ISBN 0-13-175432-7) This multi-DVD set of videos includes 100 short video clips of 5 to 15 minutes in length from many of the most popular video sources for psychology content, such as ABC News, Films for the Humanities series, PBS, and Pennsylvania State Media Sales Video Classics. Annual update volumes are also available (2009 volume **ISBN 0-205-65280-8**; 2010 volume **ISBN 0-13-605401-3**).

Teaching Psychology: A Guide for the New Instructor (ISBN 0-13-194399-5) This guide by Fred W. Whitford (Montana State University) helps new instructors or graduate teaching assistants manage the myriad complex tasks required to teach an introductory course effectively. The author has used his own teaching experience over the past 25 years to help illustrate some of the problems a new instructor may expect to face.

Study Guide (ISBN 0-205-06635-6) for *Invitation to Psychology*, Fifth Edition The Fifth Edition study guide, prepared by Douglas Johnson (Wester Michigan University), contains material to help reinforce students' understanding of the concepts covered in the text. Each chapter provides an overview to introduce students to the chapter; learning-objective exercises to test students' understanding of the main themes; and multiple-choice tests so that students can gauge their progress. Contact a Pearson Education sales representative for a package ISBN of the text and study guide.

Supplementary Texts and Readings

Contact your Pearson Education representative to package any of the following supplementary texts with *Invitation to Psychology*, Fifth Edition. A package ISBN is required for your bookstore order.

***Psychobabble and Biobunk: Using Psychological Science to Think Critically About Popular Psychology*, Third Edition (ISBN 0-205-01591-3)** In this almost entirely new collection of 21 book reviews and essays, Carol Tavris shows how an understanding of psychological science and critical thinking can be brought to bear in evaluating popular arguments in modern culture. Is criminal profiling scientific? Is positive psychology always as beneficial as its proponents maintain? Will sperm that have been donated by alleged geniuses create genius babies? Instructors may find that the questions raised in these essays make for stimulating class discussions and paper topics.

***Current Directions in Introductory Psychology*, Second Edition (ISBN 0-13-714350-8)** The second edition of this reader includes more than 20 articles selected for undergraduates from *Current Directions in Psychological Science*. These timely, cutting-edge articles allow instructors to show students how psychologists go about their research and how they apply it to real-world problems.

***Forty Studies That Changed Psychology*, Sixth Edition (ISBN 0-13-603599-X)** This brief collection of the seminal studies that have shaped modern psychological research, by Roger Hock (Mendocino College), provides an overview of the environment that gave rise to each study, its experimental design, its findings, and its impact on current thinking in the discipline.

***The Psychology Major: Career Options and Strategies for Success*, Fourth Edition (ISBN 0-205-68468-8)** This paperback, by Eric Landrum (Boise State University) and Stephen Davis (Emporia State University), provides valuable information about career options available to psychology majors, tips for improving academic performance, and a guide to the American Psychological Association (APA) style of reporting research.

Online Options for Instructors and Students

mypsychlab For *Invitation To Psychology,* Fifth Edition

Across the country, from small community colleges to large public universities, a trend is emerging: Introductory psychology enrollments are increasing, and available resources can't keep pace. Many instructors are finding that their time is being stretched to the limit. Yet continual feedback to students is an important contributor to successful student progress. For this reason, the APA strongly recommends the use of student self-assessment tools and embedded questions and assignments (see www.apa.org/ed/eval_strategies.html for more information). In response to these demands, Pearson's MyPsychLab (MPL) provides students with useful and engaging self-assessment tools and offers instructors flexibility in assessing and tracking student progress.

MyPsychLab (www.mypsychlab.com) provides instructors with a full suite of tools to assess students' mastery of course material and to hold students accountable for the amount of time they spend with the material out of class. Proven in classrooms big and small across the country, and loved by hundreds of thousands of students, MyPsychLab includes the following:

- **An Interactive eBook** with highlighting and note-taking features and powerful embedded media including over 100 simulations, more than 3,000 video clips (available in closed caption), dozens of podcasts, and an interactive timeline that presents the history of psychology.

- **Customized Study Plans and Assessments** allow students to take a pretest to self-assess how much they already know about the topics in a section of the chapter they're working on. These pretests pair together with posttests on the website to generate customized study plans and ebook self-assessments.

- **New! Concept Mapping Tool:** Students can use the new Concept Mapping Tool to create a variety of personalized graphic study aids using preloaded content from each chapter. Students can use this flexible and customizable tool to create their own unique organizational aids, to produce aids that conform to instructors' guidelines, or to prepare note-taking maps using the *Map It* instructions in the text. The organizers that the Concept Mapping Tool produces can be saved, emailed to you, or printed out to be used as a study tool.

- **New! APA Learning Goals and Outcome Assessments:** For instructors interested in assessing their students' progress against the APA Psychology Learning Goals and Outcomes, we have provided a separate bank of assessment items keyed specifically to those goals in MyPsychLab.

- **Pearson Psychology Experiments Tool** presents a suite of data-generating experiment demonstrations, inventories, and surveys that allow students to experience firsthand some of the main concepts covered in the text. Each item in the Experiments Tool generates anonymous class data that instructors can download and use in class lectures or for homework assignments. With over 50 assignable demonstrations, such as the Implicit Association Test, Roediger Effect, Interhemispheric Transfer Time, IPIP-Neo Personality Inventory, Buss Mate Preference Survey, and general surveys, the Experiments Tool holds students accountable for *doing* psychology.

- **A Gradebook for Instructors** as well as full course management capabilities for instructors teaching online or hybrid courses are included in the instructor version of MyPsychLab.

- **Audio Files of Each Chapter** benefit students who are blind and others who prefer sound-based materials, and conform to Americans with Disabilities Act (ADA) guidelines.

- **New! Podcasting Tool** with preloaded podcasts permits you to easily record and upload podcasts of your own lectures for students to access.

- **Interactive Mobile-Ready Flash Cards** of the key terms from the text can be used by students to build their own stacks, print the cards, or export their flash cards to their cell phones.

You decide the extent of integration, from independent self-assessment for students to total course management. Students benefit from an easy-to-use site at which they can test themselves on key content, track their progress, and create individually tailored study plans. By transferring faculty members' most time-consuming tasks—content delivery, student assessment, and grading—to automated tools, MyPsychLab allows you to spend more quality time with students.

For more information on MyPsychLab, go to **www.mypsychlab.com**.

Additional Course Management Resources:

- **Online Resource MyPsychLab for BlackBoard/ MyPsychLab for WebCT** The customized BlackBoard cartridge and WebCT epack include the complete Test Bank, each chapter's Learning Objectives, Glossary Flash Cards, Chapter Summaries, a link to MyPsychLab, and Chapter Exams.

- Ask your Pearson representative about custom offerings for other learning management systems or visit **www.mypsychlab.com** for more information.

CourseSmart **CourseSmart Textbooks Online** is an exciting new choice for students looking to save money.

Students can subscribe to the same content online and save up to 50 percent off the suggested list price of the print text. With a CourseSmart eTextbook, students can search the text, make notes online, print out reading assignments that incorporate lecture notes, and bookmark important passages for later review. For more information, or to subscribe to the CourseSmart eTextbook, visit **www** **.coursesmart.com/**.

Authors' Acknowledgments

We are indebted to the following reviewers for their many insightful and substantive suggestions during the development and revision of *Invitation to Psychology* and for their work on supplements. (The affiliations of some individuals may have changed since they reviewed our book.)

Paul Ackerman, *Wichita State University*
Nelson Adams, *Winston-Salem State University*
Debra A. Ahola, *SUNY Schenectady County Community College*
Benton E. Allen, *Mt. San Antonio College*
Susan M. Andersen, *University of California, Santa Barbara*
Lloyd Anderson, *Bismarck State College*
Lynn R. Anderson, *Wayne State University*
Susan A. Anderson, *University of South Alabama*
Emir Andrews, *Memorial University of Newfoundland*
Richard Anglin, *Oklahoma City Community College*
Kevin J. Apple, *James Madison University*
Eva Glahn Atkinson, *Brescia University*
Alan Auerbach, *Wilfrid Laurier University*
Lynn Haller Augsbach, *Morehead State University*
Harold Babb, *Binghamton University*
Brian C. Babbitt, *Missouri Southern State College*
MaryAnn Baenninger, *Trenton State College*
Ronald Baenninger, *Temple University*
Judith Barker, *Cuyahoga Community College*
Patricia Barker, *Schenectady County Community College*
Ronald K. Barrett, *Loyola Marymount University*
Nazira Barry, *Miami Dade College*
Allan Basbaum, *University of California, San Francisco*
Linda M. Bastone, *SUNY-Purchase College*
Carol Batt, *Sacred Heart University*
William M. Baum, *University of New Hampshire*
Gordon Bear, *Ramapo College of New Jersey*
Peter A. Beckett, *Youngstown State University*
Bill E. Beckwith, *University of North Dakota*
Helen Bee, *Madison, Wisconsin*
Jim Beers, *John Jay College of Criminal Justice*
Dan Bellack, *Trident Technical College*
David F. Berger, *SUNY at Cortland*
Michael Bergmire, *Jefferson College*
Philip J. Bersh, *Temple University*
Kathleen Bey, *Palm Beach Community College*
Martin Bink, *Western Kentucky University*
Randolph Blake, *Vanderbilt University*

John Bouseman, *Hillsborough Community College*
Richard Bowen, *Loyola University of Chicago*
Laura L. Bowman, *Kent State University*
Edward Brady, *Southwestern Illinois College*
Lynn Brandsma, *Chestnut Hill College*
Ann Brandt-Williams, *Glendale Community College*
John R. Braun, *University of Bridgeport*
Sharon S. Brehm, *SUNY at Binghamton*
Sylvester Briggs, *Kent State University*
Gwen Briscoe, *College of Mt. St. Joseph*
Michael A. Britt, *Marist College*
Barbara L. Brown, *Georgia Perimeter College*
Kimberly Brown, *Ball State University*
Robert C. Brown, *Jr., Georgia State University*
Robert Bruel, *Kean College*
Dan Brunsworth, *Kishwaukee College*
Linda L. Brunton, *Columbia State Community College*
Stephen R. Buchanan, *University of South Carolina, Union*
Peter R. Burzvnski, *Vincennes University*
Cheryl Busbee, *CUNY BMCC*
Frank Calabrese, *Community College of Philadelphia*
Sharon K. Calhoun, *Indiana University–Kokomo*
Jean Caplan, *Concordia University*
Thomas Capo, *University of Maryland*
Bernardo J. Carducci, *Indiana University Southeast*
David N. Carpente, *Southwest Texas State University*
Sally S. Carr, *Lakeland Community College*
Charles Carver, *University of Miami*
Michael Catchpole, *North Island College*
Paul Chance, *Seaford, Delaware*
Alex Chapman, *Simon Fraser University*
Loren Cheney, *Community College of Rhode Island*
Herbert H. Clark, *Stanford University*
Russ Clark, *University of North Texas*
Job B. Clément, *Daytona Beach Community College*
Samuel Clement, *Marianopolis College*
Richard Coelho, *Lansing Community College*
Eva Conrad, *San Bernardino Valley College*
Richard L. Cook, *University of Colorado*
Robert Cormack, *New Mexico Institute of Mining and Technology*
Paul Costa, *National Institutes of Health*
Wendi Cross, *Ohio University*
Norman Culbertson, *Yakima Valley College*
Mark Cummins, *Dason College*
William Curtis, *Camden County College*
Gregory Cutler, *Bay de Noc Community College*
Dean Daniel, *Wayland Baptist University*
Betty Davenport, *Campbell University*
Gerald Davidson, *University of Southern California*
Gaylen Davidson-Podgorny, *Santa Rosa Junior College*
Robert M. Davis, *Purdue University School of Science, IUPUI*
Shawn Davis, *University of Houston, Downtown*
Nat DeAnda, *Los Medanos College*
Michael William Decker, *University of California, Irvine*

Katherine Dernitrakis, *Albuquerque Technical-Vocational Institute*
Virginia Diehl, *Western Illinois University*
Geri Anne Dino, *Frostburg State University*
Lynn Dodson, *Seattle Central Community College*
William Domhoff, *University of California, Santa Cruz*
Evelyn Doody, *Community College of Southern Nevada*
Kimberly Duff, *Cerritos College*
Chris Dula, *University of Memphis*
Laurel End, *Mt. Mary College*
Susan H. Evans, *University of Southern California*
William Fabricius, *Arizona State University*
Fred Fahringer, *Southwest Texas State University*
Bryan Fantie, *American University*
Dan Fawaz, *Georgia Perimeter College*
Vivian Ferry, *Community College of Rhode Island*
Ronald Finke, *SUNY at Stony Brook*
Deborah Finkel, *Indiana University Southeast*
John H. Flowers, *University of Nebraska, Lincoln*
William F. Ford, *Bucks County Community College*
Donald G. Forgays, *University of Vermont*
Sheila Francis, *Creighton University*
Howard S. Friedman, *University of California, Riverside*
Perry Fuchs, *University of Texas at Arlington*
Charles A. Fuller, *University of California, Davis*
Grace Galliano, *Kennesaw State College*
Maryanne Garry, *Victoria University of Wellington*
Mary Gauvain, *Oregon State University*
Andrew Geoghegan, *Longview Community College*
Leonard George, *Capilano College*
Ron Gerrard, *SUNY at Oswego*
David Gersh, *Houston Community College*
Eugene Gilden, *Linfield College*
Jessica B. Gillooly, *Glendale Community College*
Richard Girard, *New Hampshire Community Technical College*
Margaret Gittis, *Youngstown State University*
Randy Gold, *Cuesta College*
Carlos Goldberg, *Indiana University, Purdue University at Indianapolis*
Peter Graham, *Pensacola Junior College*
Carol Grams, *Orange Coast College*
Vincent J. Granito, *Lorain County Community College*
Patricia Greenfield, *University of California, Los Angeles*
Richard A. Griggs, *University of Florida*
David Grilly, *Cleveland State University*
Jed Grodin, *University of Southern California*
Bea Gattuso Grosh, *Millersville University*
Laura Gruntmeir, *Redlands Community College*
Andrew Guest, *University of Portland*
Sarmi Gulgoz, *Auburn University*
Jimmy G. Hale, *McLennan Community College*
Pryor Hale, *Piedmont Virginia Community College*
Len Hamilton, *Rutgers University*
Connie Hammond, *University of California, Los Angeles*
George Hampton, *University of Houston*

Judith Harackiewicz, *University of Wisconsin, Madison*
Eddie Harmon-Jones, University of Wisconsin, *Madison*
Jack Harnett, *Virginia Commonwealth University*
Roger Harnish, *Rochester Institute of Technology*
Algea Harrison, *Oakland University*
James E. Hart, *Edison Community College*
Susan M. Harvey, *Delta College*
Elaine Hatfield, *University of Hawaii*
Neil Helgeson, *The University of Texas at San Antonio*
John E. Hesson, *Metropolitan State College*
Rex Hieser, *University of Wisconsin, Fox Valley*
Robert Higgins, *Oakland Community College*
Peter C. Hill, *Grove City College*
James Horn, *Saint Louis University*
Susan Horton, *Mesa Community College*
John P. Hostetler, *Albion College*
Amy Hotchkin, *Benedictine University*
Kenneth I. Howard, *Northwestern University*
Charles Huffman, *James Madison University*
John Hunsley, *University of Ottawa*
William G. Iacono, *University of Minnesota*
Gene Indenbaum, *SUNY-Farmingdale*
David E. Irwin, *University of Illinois*
Linda A. Jackson, *Michigan State University*
Sherri Jackson, *Jacksonville University*
Craig Johnson, *Towson State University*
Douglas Johnson, *Western Michigan University*
James Johnson, *University of North Carolina at Wilmington*
Robert D. Johnson, *Arkansas State University*
Timothy P. Johnston, *University of North Carolina at Greensboro*
Jim Jokerst, *Aims Community College*
James Jordan, *Lorain County Community College*
Susan Joslyn, *University of Washington*
Chadwick Karr, *Portland State University*
Yoshito Kawahara, *San Diego Mesa College*
Patricia Kemerer, *Ivy Tech Community College*
Michael C. Kennedy, *Allegheny University*
Geoffrey Keppel, *University of California, Berkeley*
Janet E. Keubli, *St. Louis University*
Harold O. Kiess, *Framingham State College*
Steve Kilianski, *Rutgers University*
Gary King, *Rose State College*
Jack Kirschenbaum, *Fullerton College*
David Klein, *Stark State College of Technology*
Donald Kline, *University of Calgary*
Katherine Kocel, *Jackson State University*
Anne Kollath, *Allan Hancock College*
James H. Korn, *Saint Louis University*
Stephen M. Kosslyn, *Harvard University*
Martha Kuehn, *Central Lakes College*
Michael J. Lambert, *Brigham Young University*
Travis Langley, *Henderson State University*
George S. Larimer, *West Liberty State College*
Andrea Lassiter, *Minnesota State University*

Patsy Lawson, *Volunteer State Community College*
Herbert Leff, *University of Vermont*
Patricia Lefler, *Lexington Community College*
S. David Leonard, *University of Georgia*
Gary Levy, *University of Wyoming*
Robert Levy, *Indiana State University*
Lewis Lieberman, *Columbus College*
Scott Lilienfeld, *Emory University*
John F. Lindsay, Jr., *Georgia College and State University*
R. Martin Lobdell, *Pierce College*
Walter J. Lonner, *Western Washington University*
Karsten Look, *Columbia State Community College*
Nina Lott, *National University*
Bonnie Lustigman, *Montclair State College*
James E. Maddux, *George Mason University*
Laura Madson, *New Mexico State University*
Brian Malley, *University of Michigan*
Peter Maneno, *Normandale Community College*
Donna B. Mantooth, *Georgia Highlands College*
G. Alan Marlatt, *University of Washington*
Marc Marschark, *University of North Carolina, Greensboro*
Monique Martin, *Champlain Regional College*
Lyla Maynard, *Des Moines Area Community College*
Debra Moehle McCallum, *University of Alabama, Birmingham*
Jason McCartney, *Salisbury University*
Phil McClung, *West Virginia University at Parkersburg*
Cynthia McCormick, *Armstrong Atlantic State University*
D. F. McCoy, *University of Kentucky*
C. Sue McCullough, *Texas Woman's University*
Elizabeth McDonel, *University of Alabama*
Susanne Wicks McKenzie, *Dawson College*
Mark B. McKinley, *Lorain County Community College*
Judith McLaughlin, *Montana State University, Billings*
Ronald K. McLaughlin, *Juniata College*
Richard J. McNally, *Harvard University*
Holly McQuillan, *Porterville Community College*
Frances K. McSweeney, *Washington State University*
Mary Jo Meadow, *Mankato State University*
Elizabeth Meadows, *Central Michigan University*
Linda Mealey, *College of St. Benedict*
Joseph Melcher, *St. Cloud State University*
Ronald Melzack, *McGill University*
Rafael Mendez, *Bronx Community College*
Dorothy Mercer, *Eastern Kentucky University*
Laura J. Metallo, *Five Towns College*
Judi Misale, *Truman State University*
Denis Mitchell, *University of Southern California*
Timothy H. Monk, *University of Pittsburgh Medical Center*
Maribel Montgomery, *Linn-Benton Community College*
Douglas G. Mook, *University of Virginia*
T. Mark Morey, *SUNY College at Oswego*
Joel Morgovsky, *Brookdale Community College*
Karen Mottarella, *University of Central Florida*
Micah Mukabi, *Essex County College*
Sarah Murray, *Kwantlen University College, Vancouver, BC*

Tamara Musumeci-Szabo, *Rutgers University*
Diana P. Nagel, *Northwest Arkansas Community College*
James S. Nairne, *University of Texas at Arlington*
Michael Nash, *University of Tennessee, Knoxville*
Douglas Navarick, *California State University, Fullerton*
Robert A. Neimever, *Memphis State University*
Todd Nelson, *California State University, Stanislaus*
Benjamin Newberry, *Kent State University*
Nora Newcombe, *Temple University*
J. Ken Nishita, *California State University, Monterey Bay*
Jack Nitschke, *University of Wisconsin, Madison*
Linda Noble, *Kennesaw State College*
Peggy Norwood, *Metro State College of Denver*
Keith Oatley, *Ontario Institute for Studies in Education, Toronto*
Dina Y. Olave, *Washington State University*
Orlando Olivares, *Bridgewater State College*
Peter Oliver, *University of Hartford*
Patricia Owen-Smith, *Oxford College*
Elizabeth Weiss Ozorak, *Allegheny College*
David Page, *Nazareth College*
Kristine R. Palmer, *Richland Community College*
M. Carr Payne Jr., *Georgia Institute of Technology*
Letitia A. Peplau, *University of California, Los Angeles*
Edison Perdomo, *Michigan State University, Mankato*
Dan G. Perkins, *Richland College*
David Perkins, *College of St. Elizabeth*
Gregory Pezzetti, *Rancho Santiago Community College*
Wade Pickren, *Southeastern Oklahoma State University*
Michelle Pilati, *Rio Hondo College*
Tamar Pincus, *Royal Holloway, University of London*
Claire St. Peter Pipkin, *West Virginia University*
Robert Plomin, *Institute of Psychiatry, King's College, London*
Devon Polaschek, *Victoria University of Wellington*
Wayne Poniewaz, *University of Arkansas, Monticello*
Debra Poole, *Central Michigan University*
Paula M. Popovich, *Ohio University*
Lyman Porter, *University of California, Irvine*
Amy Posey, *Benedictine College*
Jack Powell, *University of Hartford*
Judith Pratt, *Longview Community College*
Shirley Pritchett, *Northeast Texas Community College*
Robert Prochnow, *St. Cloud State University*
Janet Proctor, *Purdue University*
Barbara Lane Radigan, *Community College of Allegheny County*
John Ramirez, *Middlesex County College*
Richard Rapson, *University of Hawaii*
Donald Ratcliff, *Vanguard Unviersity*
Jeffery A. Ratliff-Crain, *University of Minnesota, Morris*
Eric Ravussin, *Obesity Research & Clinical Investigation, Lilly Research Laboratories*
Reginald L. Razzi, *Upsala College*
Steven Richman, *Nassau Community College*
Mark P. Rittman, *Cuyahoga Community College*

Sheena Rogers, *University of Wisconsin, Madison*
Jayne Rose, *Augustana State College*
Gary Ross-Reynolds, *Nicholls State University*
Peter J. Rowe, *College of Charleston*
Gerald Rubin, *Central Virginia Community College*
Joe Rubinstein, *Purdue University*
Denis Sabat, *Mary Washington College*
Traci Sachteleben, *Southwestern Illinois College*
Karen P. Saenz, *Houston Community College, Southeast*
Moises Salinas, *Central Connecticut State University*
Nancy Sauerman, *Kirkwood Community College*
Spring Schafer, *Delta College*
Kraig Schell, *Angelo State University*
H. R. Schiffman, *Rutgers University*
Lael Schooler, *Indiana University*
Lee Schrock, *Kankakee Community College*
David A. Schroeder, *University of Arkansas*
Suzanne Schultz, *Umpqua Community College*
Marvin Schwartz, *University of Cincinnati*
Shelley Schwartz, *Vanier College*
Joyce Segreto, *Youngstown State University*
Kimron Shapiro, *University of Calgary*
Phillip R. Shaver, *University of California, Davis*
Arthur Shimamura, *University of California, Berkeley*
Susan A. Shodahl, *San Bernardino Valley College*
Dale Simmons, *Oregon State University*
Angela Simon, *El Camino College*
Christina S. Sinisi, *Charleston Southern University*
Art Skibbe, *Appalachian State University*
Charles Slem, *Cal Poly-San Luis Obispo*
William P. Smotherman, *SUNY at Binghamton*
Samuel Snyder, *North Carolina State University*
Barbara A. Spellman, *University of Texas at Austin*
Larry R. Squire, *University of California, San Diego*
Keith Stanovich, *University of Toronto*
Tina Stern, *Georgia Perimeter College*
A. Stirling, *John Abbott College*
Holly Straub, *University of South Dakota*
Milton E. Strauss, *Johns Hopkins University*
Jutta M. Street, *Barton College*
Judith Sugar, *Colorado State University*
Rose Suggett, *Southeast Community College, Lincoln*
Alan Swinkles, *St. Edwards University*
Granville L. Sydnor, *San Jacinto College North*
Nichole Thomas, *Chesapeake College*
Shelley E. Taylor, *University of California, Los Angeles*
Cheryl Terrance, *University of North Dakota*
Dennis C. Turk, *University of Washington*
Barbara Turpin, *Missouri State University*
Ed Valsi, *Oakland Community College*
Tim VanderGast, *William Paterson University*
Lynda Vannice, *Umpqua Community College*
Ronald J. Venhorst, *Kean University*
Wayne A. Viney, *Colorado State University*

Benjamin Wallace, *Cleveland State University*
Phyllis Walrad, *Macomb Community College*
Charles R. Walsmith, *Bellevue Community College*
Phillip Wann, *Missouri Western State College*
Connie Watson, *Delta College*
Sheree Watson, *University of Southern Mississippi*
David E. Waxler, *Widener University*
Thomas Weatherly, *Georgia Perimeter College*
Mary Wellman, *Rhode Island University*
Gary L. Wells, *University of Alberta*
Matthew Westra, *Longview Community College*
Fred Whitford, *Montana State University*
Todd Wiebers, *Henderson State University*
Warner Wilson, *Wright State University*
Loren Wingblade, *Jackson Community College*
Judith K. Winters, *DeKalb College*
Rita S. Wolpert, *Caldwell College*
James M. Wood, *University of Texas, El Paso*
Jean Wynn, *Manchester Community College*
Karen Yanowitz, *Arkansas State University*
Phyllis Zee, *Northwestern University Medical School*
Edmond Zuromski, *Community College of Rhode Island*

Our superb editorial and production teams at Pearson have unfailingly come through for us on every edition of this complex book. Our deepest thanks to Editor-in-Chief Jessica Mosher and Executive Editor Stephen Frail for their invaluable and creative ideas; Managing Editor Judy Casillo, who brilliantly supervised every detail of the revision from start to finish—and we do mean *every* detail!; and Executive Marketing Manager Jeanette Koskinas for her editorial and marketing contributions. These talented people offered countless good suggestions and provided moral as well as practical support, and we appreciate everything they did for us and for the book. The production team was also spectacular, most especially, at Pearson, Managing Editor Maureen Richardson and Project Manager Marianne Peters-Riordan, and, at Macmillan Publishing Solutions, Project Manager Jill Traut. Between them, Judy Casillo and Jill Traut coordinated all of the details of the editorial and production phases with exceptional efficiency and patience. We send special thanks to Heather McElwain for her excellent copyediting. We are also delighted with the work of the design team, headed by Art Director Ximena Tamvakopoulos, who created the warm, clean text design and cover.

And, as ever, our loving thanks go to Howard Williams and Ronan O'Casey, who for so many years and editions have bolstered us with their love, humor, good cheer, and good coffee.

We hope that you will enjoy reading and using *Invitation to Psychology* and that your students will find it a true invitation to the field we love.

CAROLE WADE
CAROL TAVRIS

About the Authors

Carole Wade earned her Ph.D. in cognitive psychology at Stanford University. She began her academic career at the University of New Mexico, where she taught courses in psycholinguistics and developed the first course at the university on the psychology of gender. She was professor of psychology for ten years at San Diego Mesa College, then taught at College of Marin and Dominican University of California. In addition to this text, she and Carol Tavris have written *Psychology; Psychology in Perspective*; and *The Longest War: Sex Differences in Perspective*. Dr. Wade has a long-standing interest in making psychology accessible to students and the general public. In particular, she has focused her efforts on the teaching and promotion of critical-thinking skills, diversity issues, and the enhancement of undergraduate education in psychology. She chaired the APA Board of Educational Affairs' Task Force on Diversity Issues at the Precollege and Undergraduate Levels of Education in Psychology, as well as the APA's Public Information Committee; has been a G. Stanley Hall lecturer at the APA convention; and served on the steering committee for the National Institute on the Teaching of Psychology. Dr. Wade is a fellow of the American Psychological Association and of the Association for Psychological Science. When she isn't busy with her professional activities, she can be found riding the trails of northern California on her Morgan horse, McGregor, or one of his Arabian stable mates, Condé or Ricochet.

Carol Tavris earned her Ph.D. in the interdisciplinary program in social psychology at the University of Michigan, and as a writer and lecturer, she has sought to educate the public about the importance of critical and scientific thinking in psychology. In addition to this text, she and Carole Wade have written *Psychology; Psychology in Perspective*; and *The Longest War: Sex Differences in Perspective*. Dr. Tavris is also coauthor, with Elliot Aronson, of *Mistakes Were Made (But Not by Me): Why We Justify Foolish Beliefs, Bad Decisions, and Hurtful Acts*; and author of *The Mismeasure of Woman* and *Anger: The Misunderstood Emotion*. She has written on psychological topics for a wide variety of magazines, journals, edited books, and newspapers, some of which have been collected in *Psychobabble and Biobunk: Using Psychological Science to Think Critically about Popular Psychology*. Dr. Tavris lectures widely on topics involving science versus pseudoscience in psychology and psychiatry, on writing about science for the public, and many other subjects of contemporary interest. She has taught in the psychology department at University of California, Los Angeles, and at the Human Relations Center of the New School for Social Research in New York. She is a fellow of the American Psychological Association and a charter fellow of the Association for Psychological Science; a member of the editorial board of the APS journal *Psychological Science in the Public Interest*; and a member of the international advisory board of the Institute for Science and Human Values.

INVITATION
TO PSYCHOLOGY

Psychology in the News

Zaniness on Parade in Pasadena

PASADENA, CA, May 1, 2010. The 33rd Occasional Pasadena Doo Dah Parade, a joyful celebration of wacky weirdness, took place today to the cheers of fans lining the streets. Known as "the other parade" (the more

Anything goes at the Doo Dah Parade.

famous one being Pasadena's Rose Parade on January 1), the event encourages marchers to shed their inhibitions and dress as outrageously as they please. The parade's favorites include the Men of Leisure Synchronized Nap Team, Tequila Mockingbird & the Royal Doo Dah Orchestra, the BBQ & Hibachi Marching Grill Team, and the Clown Doctors from Outer Space.

Brazil Boy Reunited with Father After Five-Year Custody Battle

ORLANDO, FL, December 27, 2009. After a frustrating five-year custody dispute in Brazilian courts, David Goldman has finally prevailed and has brought his son Sean, now 9, back to the United States. The boy's mother had taken him to her native Brazil, but after her unexpected death, her family refused to allow the father to have custody. David said the boy has yet to call him Dad, but, he added, "now we're together and we'll heal."

Mexico City Legalizes Gay Marriage

MEXICO CITY, December 24, 2009. Mexico city has become the first city in Latin America to allow same-sex couples to marry and to have the same rights as spouses in heterosexual unions, in-

Gay couples in Mexico City celebrate.

cluding the right to adopt children. "This is a huge triumph that has followed so many years of struggle," said Kin Castañeda. But the ruling has also sparked hostility from social conservatives and church officials. The Roman Catholic Archbishop of Mexico City described the law as immoral and abhorrent. Belgium, the Netherlands, Spain, and Canada have also legalized gay marriage, but the issue remains divisive and inflammatory in the United States.

Court Finds No Evidence Linking Vaccine to Autism

WASHINGTON, DC, March 13, 2010. A special federal court, headed by judges called "special masters," has sustained an earlier court ruling against three sets of parents who blamed their children's autism on their having gotten the MMR vaccine (which inoculates children against measles, mumps, and rubella, also called German measles). For years, many parents of children with autism have argued that vaccines trigger the devastating condition, but one of the special masters said that the evidence for this claim is "weak, contradictory, and unpersuasive." Nonetheless, some autism advocacy groups expressed disappointment and said that they still believe a link exists.

Man Charged with Failed Attack on Transatlantic Airliner

DETROIT, MI, December 25, 2009. A 23-year-old Nigerian man, Umar Farouk Abdulmutallab, has been charged with attempting to destroy a Northwest Airlines plane on Christmas Eve as it prepared to land in Detroit with 278 passengers and 11 crew members aboard. Abdulmutallab apparently attended University College London until 2008, studying engineering and living in a posh apartment in an upscale neighborhood. He is accused of trying to detonate a bomb with ingredients that he concealed in his clothes. His plans went awry when the bomb failed to detonate and passengers heard popping noises and saw smoke and fire. Passenger Jasper Schuringa, 32, immediately jumped over several seats to reach Abdulmutallab and helped to douse the fire and subdue him. "I didn't hesitate a moment, just wanted to stop it with whatever I can do," said Schuringa.

What Is Psychology?

The news is full of tales of heroism and cowardice, challenges to existing laws and social norms, acts of joyful playfulness and savage terror, human creativity and human folly. What on earth do these stories have to do with psychology?

The answer is: Everything.

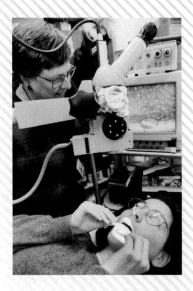

People usually associate psychology with mental and emotional disorders, personal problems, and psychotherapy. But psychologists take as their subject the entire spectrum of beautiful and brutish things that human beings do—the kinds of things you read and hear about every day. They want to know why some people, like the jovial marchers in the Doo Dah Parade, are extroverts, whereas others prefer to blend in quietly. They investigate why people become straight, gay, or bisexual, why many straight people fear or detest homosexuality, and why people differ in their attitudes toward gay marriage. They explore the reasons that some individuals, who grow up in affluence and with every educational opportunity, become willing to sacrifice their lives to commit a terrorist act that will kill hundreds of innocent people, and why some people spontaneously risk their own lives to save others. They study the factors that predict whether a child will emerge from difficult early years as a resilient and healthy adult, or carry the scars of those years forever. And psychologists ask why some parents of autistic children, when given the good news from scientific research that they don't need to beat themselves up for having had their children vaccinated, react not with relief but with anger.

In this book, we will be discussing the psychological issues raised by these stories and many others in the news. But psychology is not only about behavior that is newsworthy. Psychologists are also interested in how ordinary human beings learn, remember, solve problems, perceive, feel, and get along (or fail to get along) with others. They are therefore as likely to study commonplace experiences—rearing children, gossiping, remembering a shopping list, daydreaming, making love, and making a living—as exceptional ones.

If you have ever wondered what makes people tick, or if you want to gain some insight into your own behavior, then you are in the right course. We invite you now to step into the world of psychology, the discipline that dares to explore the most complex topic on earth: you.

 YOU are about to learn...

- how "psychobabble" differs from serious psychology.
- what's wrong with psychologists' nonscientific competitors, such as astrologers and psychics.
- how and when psychology became a formal discipline.
- three early schools of psychology.
- the five major perspectives in psychology.

The Science of Psychology

Psychology can be defined as *the discipline concerned with behavior and mental processes and how they are affected by an organism's physical state, mental state, and external environment*. This definition, however, is a little like defining a car as a vehicle for transporting people from one place to another, without explaining how a car differs from a train or a bus, how a Ford differs from a Ferrari, or how a catalytic converter works. To get a clear picture of what psychology is, you are going to need to know more about its methods, its findings, and its ways of interpreting information.

Psychology, Pseudoscience, and Common Sense

Let's begin by considering what psychology is *not*. First, the psychology that you are about to study bears little relation to the popular psychology ("pop psych") often found in self-help books or on talk shows. In recent years, the public's appetite for psychological information has created a huge market for "psychobabble": pseudoscience and quackery covered by a veneer of psychological language. Pseudoscience (*pseudo* means "false") promises quick fixes to life's problems, such as reliving the supposed trauma of birth to resolve your current unhappiness, or "reprogramming" your brain to make it more creative. Serious psychology is more complex, more informative, and, we think, far more helpful than psychobabble because it is based on rigorous research and **empirical**

evidence—evidence gathered by careful observation, experimentation, and measurement.

Second, serious psychology differs radically from such nonscientific competitors as graphology (handwriting analysis), fortune-telling, numerology, and the most popular, astrology. Like psychologists, promoters of these competing systems try to explain people's problems and predict their behavior. If you are having romantic problems, an astrologer may advise you to choose an Aries instead of an Aquarius as your next love, and a channeler of past lives may say it's because you were jilted in a former life. Belief in these unscientific approaches is widespread. Yet, whenever the predictions of psychics, astrologers, and the like are put to the test, they turn out to be so vague as to be meaningless (for example, "Spirituality will increase next year") or just plain wrong (Radford, 2010; Shaffer & Jadwiszczok, 2010). In 2008, one well-known Canadian psychic predicted that George Clooney would marry and have a child, Sean Penn would be wounded in the Middle East, and John Edwards would win the U.S. presidency after Hillary Clinton dropped out of the race. Obviously, she was wrong on all counts. Moreover, contrary to what you might think from watching TV shows like *Medium* or reading claims on psychic websites, no psychic has ever found a missing child, identified a serial killer, or helped police solve any other crime by using "psychic powers." Their claims merely add to the heartbreak the victim's family feels.

Third, psychology is not just a fancy name for common sense. Often, psychological research produces findings that directly contradict prevailing beliefs, and throughout this book you will be discovering many of them. Are unhappy memories repressed and then accurately recalled years later, as if they had been recorded on videotape? Do most women suffer from PMS? Do policies of abstinence from alcohol reduce rates of alcoholism? If you play Beethoven to your infant, will your baby become smarter? These beliefs are widely held, but as you will learn, they are wrong.

At the start of an introductory psychology course, many students hold beliefs that have been promoted in the popular culture, or are based on personal experience or what seems to be common sense, but which are not scientifically supported. Two instructors gave their 90 introductory psychology students a true–false psychological information questionnaire on the first day of class, a questionnaire consisting entirely of false statements such as "At any point in time, we use only 10 percent of our brains" and "Under hypnosis, you can perform feats that are otherwise impossible." The students

psychology The discipline concerned with behavior and mental processes and how they are affected by an organism's physical state, mental state, and external environment; often represented by Ψ, the Greek letter psi (usually pronounced "sy").

empirical Relying on or derived from observation, experimentation, or measurement.

I see you being less gullible in the future.

were accurate only 38.5 percent of the time, which is actually worse than chance (Taylor & Kowalski, 2004). But by the last week of class, when the students took a test containing all of the earlier items, their overall accuracy was much better: 66.3 percent. Although there was still room for improvement, the students had lost confidence in their remaining misconceptions, suggesting that they were on the way to giving them up. If so, they had learned one of the most important lessons in science: Uncertainty about untested assumptions and beliefs can be a good thing.

Throughout this book and your introductory course, you, too, will repeatedly learn that popular opinion and common sense are not always reliable guides to human behavior. The kind of research you will encounter won't always provide the answers you might have wished for, and sometimes there won't be definite answers. Our goal, however, is to show you why the scientific investigation of even our most cherished beliefs can lead to explanations that are far more sensible than common sense. Of course, psychological findings do not have to be surprising or counterintuitive to be important. Like scientists in other fields, psychological scientists strive not only to discover new phenomena and correct mistaken ideas, but also to deepen our understanding of an already familiar world—as they do by identifying the varieties of love, the origins of violence, the nonsexual motives for sex, or the mysteries of memory.

The Birth of Modern Psychology

Most of the great thinkers of history, from Aristotle to Zoroaster, raised questions that today would be called psychological. They wanted to know how people take in information through their senses, use information to solve problems, and become motivated to act in brave or villainous ways. They wondered about the elusive nature of emotion, and

whether it controls us or is something we can control. Like today's psychologists, they wanted to *describe*, *predict*, *understand*, and *modify* behavior to add to human knowledge and increase human happiness. But unlike modern psychologists, scholars of the past did not rely heavily on empirical evidence. Often, their observations were based simply on anecdotes or descriptions of individual cases.

This does not mean that the forerunners of modern psychology were always wrong. On the contrary, they often had insights and made observations that were verified by later work. Hippocrates (c. 460 B.C.–c. 377 B.C.), the Greek physician known as the founder of modern medicine, observed patients with head injuries and inferred that the brain must be the ultimate source of "our pleasures, joys, laughter, and jests as well as our sorrows, pains, griefs, and tears." And so it is. In the first century A.D., the Stoic philosophers observed that people do not become angry or sad or anxious because of actual events but because of their explanations of those events. And so they do.

Without empirical methods, however, the forerunners of psychology also committed terrible blunders. A good example comes from the early 1800s, when the theory of **phrenology** (Greek for "study of the mind") became wildly popular in Europe and America. Inspired by the writings and lectures of Austrian physician Franz Joseph Gall (1758–1828), phrenologists argued that different brain areas accounted for specific character and personality traits, such as stinginess and religiosity,

phrenology The now-discredited theory that different brain areas account for specific character and personality traits, which can be "read" from bumps on the skull.

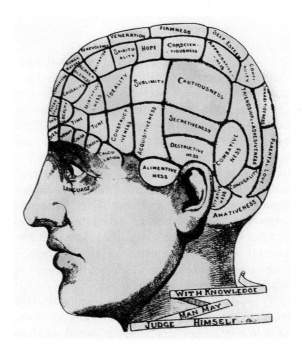

On this nineteenth-century phrenology "map," notice the tiny space allocated to self-esteem and the large one devoted to cautiousness!

functionalism An early psychological approach that emphasized the function or purpose of behavior and consciousness.

psychoanalysis A theory of personality and a method of psychotherapy, originally formulated by Sigmund Freud, that emphasizes unconscious motives and conflicts.

biological perspective A psychological approach that emphasizes bodily events and changes associated with actions, feelings, and thoughts.

evolutionary psychology A field of psychology emphasizing evolutionary mechanisms that may help explain human commonalities in cognition, development, emotion, social practices, and other areas of behavior.

✳ Explore
a time line of important dates in psychology on mypsychlab.com

and that such traits could be read from bumps on the skull. Thieves, for example, supposedly had large bumps above the ears. So how to account for people who had these stealing bumps but who were not thieves? Phrenologists explained away this counterevidence by saying that the person's thieving impulses were being held in check by *other* bumps representing positive traits. In the United States, parents, teachers, and employers flocked to phrenologists for advice and self-improvement (Benjamin, 1998). But phrenology was a classic pseudoscience—sheer nonsense.

At about the time that phrenology was peaking in popularity, several pioneering men and women in Europe and America were starting to study psychological issues using scientific methods. In 1879, Wilhelm Wundt (VIL-helm Voont) officially established the first psychological laboratory in Leipzig, Germany. Wundt (1832–1920), who was trained in medicine and philosophy, promoted a method called *trained introspection*, in which volunteers were taught to carefully observe, analyze, and describe their own sensations, mental images, and emotional reactions. Wundt's introspectors might take as long as 20 minutes to report their inner experiences during a 1.5-second experiment. The goal was to break down behavior into its most basic elements, much as a chemist might analyze water into hydrogen plus oxygen. Most psychologists eventually rejected trained introspection as too subjective, but Wundt still is usually credited for formally initiating the movement to make psychology a science. Many early psychologists in North America were trained in Wundt's laboratory.

Another early approach to scientific psychology, called **functionalism**, emphasized the function or purpose of behavior, as opposed to its analysis and description. One of functionalism's leaders was William James (1842–1910), an American philosopher, physician, and psychologist. Attempting to grasp the nature of the mind through introspection, wrote James (1890/1950), is "like seizing a spinning top to catch its motion, or trying to turn up the gas quickly enough to see how the darkness looks." (He was also a wonderful writer.) Inspired in part by the evolutionary theories of British naturalist Charles Darwin (1809–1882), James and other functionalists instead asked how various actions help a person or animal adapt to the environment. This emphasis on the causes and consequences of behavior was to set the course of psychological science.

Psychology also has roots in Vienna, Austria, where it first developed as a method of psychotherapy. While researchers were at work in their laboratories, struggling to establish psychology as a science, Sigmund Freud (1856–1939), an obscure physician, was in his office listening to his patients' reports of depression, nervousness, and obsessive habits. Freud became convinced that their symptoms had mental, not bodily, causes. His patients' distress was due, he concluded, to conflicts and emotional traumas that had originated in early childhood and were too threatening to be remembered consciously, such as forbidden sexual feelings for a parent. Freud's ideas eventually evolved into a broad theory of personality, and both his theory and his method of treating people with emotional problems became known as **psychoanalysis**.

From its early beginnings in philosophy, natural science, and medicine, psychology eventually grew into a complex discipline encompassing many different specialties, perspectives, and methods. (In other chapters, you will be learning more about the history of psychology and the people who played a prominent role in its development.) Today, the field is like a large, sprawling family. The members of this family have common great-grandparents, and many of the cousins have formed alliances, but some are quarreling and a few are barely speaking to one another. ✳ Explore

Psychology's Present

The early approaches to psychology eventually evolved into five major theoretical perspectives, which now predominate in the field. These approaches reflect different questions that psychologists ask about human behavior, different assumptions about how the mind works, and, most important, different ways of explaining why people do what they do.

1 The **biological perspective** focuses on how bodily events affect behavior, feelings, and thoughts. Electrical impulses shoot along the intricate pathways of the nervous system. Hormones course through the bloodstream, telling internal organs to slow down or speed up. Chemical substances flow across the tiny gaps that separate one microscopic brain cell from another. Biological psychologists study how these physical events interact with events in the external environment to produce perceptions, memories, and behavior. They also investigate the contribution of genes and other biological factors to the development of abilities and personality traits. A popular specialty, **evolutionary psychology**, follows in the tradition of functionalism by focusing on how genetically influenced behavior that was functional or adaptive during our evolutionary past may be reflected in many

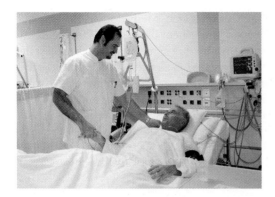

Psychologists study many puzzles of human behavior. Why does human touch reduce anxiety and feel so comforting? Why do some people become champion athletes in spite of physical disabilities? What causes someone to become anorexic, willing even to starve to death? What could motivate ordinary individuals to torture and humiliate prisoners, as soldiers did at the notorious Abu Ghraib prison in Iraq? Psychologists approach these and other questions from five major perspectives: biological, learning, cognitive, sociocultural, and psychodynamic.

of our present behaviors, mental processes, and traits. The message of the biological approach is that we cannot really know ourselves if we do not know our bodies.

2 The **learning perspective** is concerned with how the environment and experience affect a person's (or a nonhuman animal's) actions. Within this perspective, *behaviorists* focus on the environmental rewards and punishers that maintain or discourage specific behaviors. Behaviorists do not invoke the mind to explain behavior; they prefer to stick to what they can observe and measure directly: acts and events taking place in the environment. Do you have trouble sticking to a schedule, focusing on what you are studying, or keeping your temper under control? A behaviorist would analyze the environmental factors that are rewarding your giving in to distractions or that are encouraging your outbursts. *Social-cognitive learning theorists* combine elements of behaviorism with research on thoughts, values, and intentions. They believe that people learn not only by adapting their behavior to the environment, but also by imitating others and by thinking about the events happening around them. As we will see in other chapters, the learning perspective has many practical applications.

3 The **cognitive perspective** emphasizes what goes on in people's heads—how people reason, remember, understand language, solve problems, explain experiences, acquire moral standards, and form beliefs. (The word *cognitive* comes from Latin for "to know.") Using clever methods to infer mental processes from observable behavior, cognitive researchers have been able to study phenomena that were once only the stuff of speculation, such as emotions, motivations, and insight. They are designing computer programs that model how humans perform complex tasks, discovering what goes on in the mind of an infant, and identifying types of intelligence not measured by conventional IQ tests. The cognitive approach is one of the strongest forces in psychology and has inspired an

learning perspective
A psychological approach that emphasizes how the environment and experience affect a person's or animal's actions; it includes behaviorism and social-cognitive learning theories.

cognitive perspective
A psychological approach that emphasizes mental processes in perception, memory, language, problem solving, and other areas of behavior.

sociocultural perspective A psychological approach that emphasizes social and cultural influences on behavior.

psychodynamic perspective A psychological approach that emphasizes unconscious dynamics within the individual, such as inner forces, conflicts, or the movement of instinctual energy.

explosion of research on the intricate workings of the mind.

4 The **sociocultural perspective** focuses on social and cultural forces outside the individual, forces that shape every aspect of behavior, from how we kiss to what and where we eat. Most of us underestimate the impact of other people, the social context, and cultural rules on nearly everything we do: how we perceive the world, express joy or grief, manage our households, and treat our friends and enemies. We are like fish that are unaware they live in water, so obvious is water in their lives. Sociocultural psychologists study the water—the social and cultural environments that people swim in every day. Because human beings are social animals who are profoundly affected by their different cultural worlds, the sociocultural perspective has made psychology a more representative and rigorous discipline.

5 The **psychodynamic perspective** deals with unconscious dynamics within the individual, such as inner forces, conflicts, or instinctual energy. It has its origins in Freud's theory of psychoanalysis, but many other psychodynamic theories now exist. Psychodynamic psychologists try to dig below the surface of a person's behavior to get to the roots of personality; they think of themselves as archeologists of the mind. As we will see in Chapter 2, psychodynamic psychology is the thumb on the hand of

psychology—connected to the other fingers, but also set apart from them because it differs radically from the others in its language, methods, and standards of acceptable evidence. Many psychological scientists believe that psychodynamic approaches belong in philosophy or literature rather than in academic psychology. But psychotherapists and laypeople are often attracted to the psychodynamic perspective's emphasis on such grand psychological issues as the power of sexuality and the universal fear of death.

Of course, not all psychologists feel they must swear allegiance to one approach or another; many draw on what they take to be the best features of diverse schools of thought. In addition, many psychologists have been affected by social movements and intellectual trends, such as humanism and feminism, that do not fit neatly into any of the major perspectives or that cut across all of them.

Despite the diversity of psychological approaches, most psychological scientists agree on basic guidelines about what is and what is not acceptable in their discipline. Nearly all reject supernatural explanations of events—evil spirits, psychic forces, miracles, and so forth. Most believe in the importance of gathering empirical evidence and not relying on hunches or personal belief. This insistence on rigorous standards of proof is what sets psychology apart from nonscientific explanations of human experience.

✔•⎯ **Study** and **Review** on mypsychlab.com

Quick Quiz

Here is your first Quick Quiz. Try it; you won't be graded!

A. See whether psychology's past is still present in your memory.

1. *True or false?* Psychology's forerunners relied heavily on empirical evidence.
2. Credit for founding modern scientific psychology usually goes to _____.
3. Early psychologists who emphasized how behavior helps an organism adapt to its environment were known as _____.

B. To find out whether you understand the five major perspectives in psychology, match each possible explanation of anxiety on the left with a perspective on the right.

1. Anxious people often think about the future in distorted ways.
2. Anxiety is due to forbidden, unconscious desires.
3. Anxiety symptoms often bring hidden rewards, such as being excused from exams.
4. Excessive anxiety can be caused by a chemical imbalance.
5. A national emphasis on competition and success promotes anxiety about failure.

a. learning
b. psychodynamic
c. sociocultural
d. biological
e. cognitive

Answers:

A. 1. false 2. Wilhelm Wundt 3. functionalists B. 1. e 2. b 3. a 4. d 5. c

YOU are about to learn...

- why you can't assume that all therapists are psychologists, or that all psychologists are therapists.

- the three major areas of psychologists' professional activities.

- the difference between a clinical psychologist and a psychiatrist.

What Psychologists Do

Now you know the main viewpoints that guide psychologists in their work. But what do psychologists actually do with their time between breakfast and dinner?

The professional activities of psychologists generally fall into three broad categories: (1) teaching and doing research in colleges and universities; (2) providing mental health services, often referred to as *psychological practice*; and (3) conducting research or applying its findings in nonacademic settings such as business, sports, government, law, and the military (see Table 1.1). Some psychologists move flexibly across these areas. A researcher might also provide counseling services in a mental health setting, such as a clinic or a hospital; a university professor might teach, do research, and serve as a consultant in legal cases. **✳ Explore**

Psychological Research

Most psychologists who do research have doctoral degrees (Ph.D.s or Ed.D.s, doctorates in education). Some, seeking knowledge for its own sake, work in **basic psychology**; others, concerned with the practical uses of knowledge, work in **applied psychology**. A psychologist doing basic research might ask, "How does peer pressure influence people's attitudes and behavior?" An applied psychologist might ask, "How can knowledge about peer pressure be used to reduce binge drinking in colleges?"

Psychologists doing basic and applied research have made important scientific contributions in areas as diverse as health, education, child development, testing, conflict resolution, marketing, industrial design, worker productivity, and urban planning. Their findings are the focus of this book and of your course. Yet scientific research is the aspect of the discipline least recognized and understood by the public (Benjamin, 2003). We hope that by the time you finish this book, you will have a greater understanding of what research psychologists do and of their contributions to human knowledge and welfare.

Psychological Practice

Psychological practitioners, whose goal is to understand and improve people's physical and mental health, work in mental hospitals, general hospitals, clinics, schools, counseling centers, the criminal

basic psychology The study of psychological issues in order to seek knowledge for its own sake rather than for its practical application.

applied psychology The study of psychological issues that have direct practical significance; also, the application of psychological findings.

✳ Explore
Psychologists at Work on mypsychlab.com

TABLE 1.1
What Is a Psychologist?

Not all psychologists do clinical work. Many do research, teach, work in business, or consult. The professional activities of psychologists with doctorates fall into three general categories.

Academic/Research Psychologists	Clinical Psychologists	Psychologists in Industry, Law, or Other Settings
Specialize in areas of basic psychology or applied research, such as:	*Do psychotherapy and sometimes research; may work in any of these settings:*	*Do research or serve as consultants to institutions on, for example:*
Human development	Private practice	Sports
Psychometrics (testing)	Mental health clinics	Consumer issues
Health	General hospitals	Advertising
Education	Mental hospitals	Organizational problems
Industrial/organizational psychology	Research laboratories	Environmental issues
Physiological psychology	Colleges and universities	Public policy
Sensation and perception		Opinion polls
Design and use of technology		Military training
		Animal behavior
		Legal issues

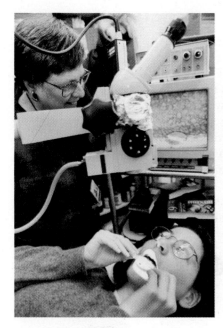

Psychological researchers and practitioners work in all kinds of settings. Here, Linda Bartoshuk (left) uses technology to study how the anatomy of the tongue influences the way we experience different tastes. A clinical psychologist (top right) helps a couple in therapy. And Louis Herman (bottom right) studies a dolphin's ability to understand an artificial language consisting of hand signals. In response to the gestural sequence "person" and "over," the dolphin will leap over the person in the pool.

justice system, and private practice. Since the late 1970s, the proportion of psychologists who are practitioners has steadily increased; practitioners now account for over two-thirds of new psychology doctorates and members of the American Psychological Association (APA), psychology's largest professional organization.

Some practitioners are *counseling psychologists*, who generally help people deal with problems of everyday life, such as test anxiety, family conflicts, or low job motivation. Others are *school psychologists* who work with parents, teachers, and students to enhance students' performance and resolve emotional difficulties. The majority, however, are *clinical psychologists* who diagnose, treat, and study mental or emotional problems. Clinical psychologists are trained to do psychotherapy with severely disturbed people, as well as with those who are simply troubled or unhappy and want to learn to handle their problems better.

In almost all states, a license to practice clinical psychology requires a doctorate. Most clinical psychologists have a Ph.D., some have an Ed.D., and a smaller but growing number have a Psy.D. (doctorate in psychology, pronounced *sy-dee*). Clinical psychologists typically do four or five years of graduate work in psychology, plus at least a year's internship under the direction of a practicing psychologist. Clinical programs leading to a Ph.D. or

Ed.D. are usually designed to prepare a person both as a scientist and as a practitioner; they require completion of a *dissertation*, a major scholarly project (usually involving research) that contributes to knowledge in the field. Programs leading to a Psy.D. focus on professional practice and do not usually require a dissertation, although they typically require the student to complete a major study, theoretical paper, or literature review.

People often confuse *clinical psychologist* with three other terms: *psychotherapist*, *psychoanalyst*, and *psychiatrist*. But these terms mean different things:

- A *psychotherapist* is simply someone who does any kind of psychotherapy. The term is not legally regulated; in fact, in most states, anyone can say that he or she is a therapist of one sort or another without having any training at all.

- A *psychoanalyst* is a person who practices one particular form of therapy, psychoanalysis. To call yourself a psychoanalyst, you must have an advanced degree, get specialized training at a psychoanalytic institute, and undergo extensive psychoanalysis yourself.

- A *psychiatrist* is a medical doctor (M.D.) who has done a three-year residency in psychiatry under the supervision of more experienced physicians to learn to diagnose and treat mental disorders. Like some clinical psychologists, some psychiatrists do research on mental problems, such as depression or schizophrenia, instead of working with patients. Psychiatrists and clinical psychologists do similar work, but psychiatrists, because of their medical training, are more likely to focus on possible biological causes of mental disorders and often treat these problems with medication. Unlike psychiatrists, most clinical psychologists at present cannot write prescriptions. (In the United States, New Mexico and Louisiana have given prescription privileges to psychologists who receive special training.) Psychiatrists, however, are often uneducated in current psychological theories and methods and unfamiliar with current research in psychology (Luhrmann, 2000).

Other mental health professionals include licensed clinical social workers (LCSWs), marriage, family, and child counselors (MFCCs), and counselors with specific specialties. These professionals

TABLE 1.2

Types of Psychotherapists

Just as not all psychologists are psychotherapists, not all psychotherapists are clinical psychologists. Here are the major terms used to refer to mental health professionals:

Psychotherapist	Does any kind of psychotherapy; may have anything from no degree to an advanced professional degree; the term is unregulated.
Clinical psychologist	Diagnoses, treats, and/or studies mental and emotional problems, both mild and severe; has a Ph.D., an Ed.D., or a Psy.D.
Psychoanalyst	Practices psychoanalysis; has specific training in this approach after an advanced degree (usually, but not always, an M.D. or a Ph.D.); may treat any kind of emotional disorder or pathology.
Psychiatrist	Does work similar to that of a clinical psychologist but is likely to take a more biological approach; has a medical degree (M.D.) with a specialty in psychiatry.
Licensed clinical social worker (LCSW); marriage, family, and child counselor (MFCC)	Treats common individual and family problems, but may also deal with more serious problems such as addiction or abuse; generally has at least an M.A. in psychology or social work, though licensing requirements vary.

ordinarily treat general problems in adjustment and family conflicts rather than serious mental disturbance, although their work may bring them into contact with people who have serious problems—violent delinquents, people with drug addictions, sex offenders, and individuals involved in domestic violence or child abuse. Licensing requirements vary from state to state but usually include a master's degree in psychology or social work and one or two years of supervised experience. (For a summary of the types of psychotherapists and the training they receive, see Table 1.2.)

Many research psychologists, and some practitioners, are worried about an increase in the number of counselors and psychotherapists who are unschooled in research methods and the empirical findings of psychology, and who use untested, outdated, or ineffective therapy techniques (Baker, McFall, & Shoham, 2008; Lilienfeld, Lynn, & Lohr, 2003). Such concerns contributed to the formation of the Association for Psychological Science (APS), a national organization devoted to the needs and interests of psychology as a science, and to recent efforts to mandate scientific training for all clinical psychologists before they can be accredited (Bootzin, 2009). Many practitioners, however, argue that psychotherapy is an art and that research findings are largely irrelevant to the work they do with clients. In Chapter 12, we will return to the important issue of the gap in training between scientists and many therapists.

Psychology in the Community

During the second half of the twentieth century, psychology expanded rapidly in terms of scholars, publications, and specialties. The American Psychological Association now has 53 divisions. Some represent major fields such as developmental psychology or physiological psychology. Others represent specific research or professional interests, such as the psychology of women, the psychology of men, ethnic minority issues, sports, the arts, environmental concerns, gay and lesbian issues, peace, psychology and the law, and health.

As psychology has grown, psychologists have found ways to contribute to their communities in about as many fields as you can think of. They consult with companies to improve worker satisfaction and productivity. They establish programs to improve race relations and reduce ethnic tensions. They advise commissions on how pollution and noise affect mental health. They do rehabilitation training for people who are physically or mentally disabled. They educate judges and juries about eyewitness testimony. They assist the police in emergencies involving hostages or disturbed people. They conduct public opinion surveys. They run suicide-prevention hotlines. They advise zoos on the care and training of animals. They help coaches improve the athletic performances of their teams. And those activities are just for starters. Is it any wonder that people are often a little fuzzy about what a psychologist is?

✓ Study and Review on mypsychlab.com

Quick Quiz

Fortunately, you aren't fuzzy about what a student is—so try this quiz.

Can you match the specialties on the left with their defining credentials and approaches on the right?

1. psychotherapist
2. psychiatrist
3. clinical psychologist
4. research psychologist
5. psychoanalyst

a. Trained in a therapeutic approach started by Freud
b. Has a Ph.D., Psy.D., or Ed.D. and does research on, or psychotherapy for, mental health problems
c. May have any credential, or none
d. Has an advanced degree (usually a Ph.D.) and does applied or basic research
e. Has an M.D.; tends to take a medical approach to emotional problems

Answers:

1.c 2.e 3.b 4.d 5.a

YOU are about to learn …

- what it means to think critically.
- why not all opinions are created equal.
- eight guidelines for evaluating psychological claims.
- why a psychological theory is unscientific if it explains anything that could conceivably happen.
- what's wrong with drawing conclusions about behavior from a collection of anecdotes.

Critical and Scientific Thinking in Psychology

One of the greatest benefits of studying psychology is that you learn not only how the brain works in general but also how to use yours in particular—by thinking critically. **Critical thinking** is the ability and willingness to assess claims and make objective judgments on the basis of well-supported reasons and evidence, rather than emotion or anecdote. Critical thinkers are able to look for flaws in arguments and to resist claims that have no support. They realize that criticizing an argument is not the same as criticizing the person making it, and they are willing to engage in vigorous debate about the validity of an idea. Critical thinking, however, is not merely negative thinking. It includes the ability to be creative and constructive—the ability to come up with alternative explanations for events, think of implications of research findings, and apply new knowledge to social and personal problems.

Most people know that you have to exercise the body to keep it in shape, but they may not realize that clear thinking also requires effort and practice. All around us we can see examples of flabby thinking. Sometimes people justify their mental laziness by proudly telling you they are open-minded. It's good to be open-minded, many scientists have countered, but not so open that your brains fall out! If you prefer the look of a Chevy truck to the look of a Honda Accord, no one can argue with your personal taste. But if you say, "The Chevy truck is better than a Honda and gets better mileage, besides," you have uttered more than an opinion. Now you have to support your belief with evidence of the car's reliability, mileage, and safety record (Ruggiero, 2004). And if you say, "Chevy trucks are the best in the world and Hondas do not exist; they are a conspiracy of the Japanese government," you forfeit the right to have your opinion taken seriously. Your opinion, if it ignores reality, is *not* equal to any other.

Critical thinking is not only indispensable in ordinary life; it is also fundamental to all science, including psychological science. By exercising critical thinking, you will be able to distinguish serious psychology from the psychobabble that clutters the airwaves and bookstores. Critical thinking requires logical skills, but other skills and dispositions are also important (Anderson, 2005; Halpern, 2002; Levy, 2010; Stanovich, 2010). Here are eight essential critical-thinking guidelines that we will be emphasizing throughout this book. ✴ Explore

1 Ask Questions; Be Willing to Wonder. What is the one kind of question that most exasperates parents of young children? "Why is the sky blue, Mommy?" "Why doesn't the plane fall?" "Why

✴ Explore
How to Be a Critical Thinker on mypsychlab.com

critical thinking The ability and willingness to assess claims and make objective judgments on the basis of well-supported reasons and evidence rather than emotion or anecdote.

don't pigs have wings?" Unfortunately, as children grow up, they tend to stop asking "why" questions like these. (Why do you think this is?) But critical and creative thinking begins with wondering why. This educational program isn't working; why not? I want to stop smoking and improve my grades but can't seem to do it; why? Is my way of doing things the best way, or just the most familiar way? Critical thinkers are willing to question received wisdom— "We do it this way because this is the way we've always done things around here"—and ask, in essence, "Oh, yeah? Why?"

In science, knowledge advances by asking questions. What is the biological basis of consciousness? How are memories stored and retrieved? Why do we sleep and dream? Why are there critical periods for language learning? What causes schizophrenia? What are the cultural influences on addiction? Critical thinkers are not discouraged by the fact that questions like these have not yet been fully answered; they see them as an exciting challenge.

2 Define Your Terms. Once you have raised a general question, the next step is to frame it in clear and concrete terms. "What makes people happy?" is a fine question for midnight reveries, but it will not lead to answers until you have defined what you mean by "happy." Do you mean being in a state of euphoria most of the time? Do you mean feeling pleasantly contented with life? Do you mean being free of serious problems or pain? Vague or poorly defined terms can lead to misleading or incomplete answers or even to terrible misunderstandings. For example, is prejudice declining? The answer depends on how you define prejudice. Is conscious dislike the same as discomfort with a group's rules and beliefs? What if a person is unaware of having any prejudiced beliefs or feelings, yet a test suggests that he or she has an unconscious prejudice; what does that mean? (We will discuss this issue further in Chapter 10.)

For scientists, defining terms means being precise about just what it is that they're studying. Researchers often start out with a **hypothesis**, a statement that attempts to describe or explain a given behavior. Initially, this hypothesis may be stated quite generally, as in, say, "Misery loves company." But before any research can be done, the hypothesis must be made more precise. "Misery loves company" might be rephrased as "People who are anxious about a threatening situation tend to seek out others facing the same threat."

A hypothesis, in turn, leads to explicit predictions about what will happen in a particular situation. In a prediction, terms such as *anxiety* or

We often hear that all viewpoints should be taught to students in the name of "fairness" and "open-mindedness," but not all viewpoints, theories, and opinions are equally valid or supported by the evidence.

threatening situation are given **operational definitions**, which specify how the phenomena in question are to be observed and measured. "Anxiety" might be defined operationally as a score on an anxiety questionnaire; "threatening situation" might be defined as the threat of an electric shock. The prediction might be, "If you raise people's anxiety scores by telling them they are going to receive electric shocks, and then you give them the choice of waiting alone or with others in the same situation, they will be more likely to choose to wait with others than they would be if they were not anxious." The prediction can then be tested, using systematic methods.

3 Examine the Evidence. Have you ever heard someone in the heat of argument exclaim, "I just know it's true, no matter what you say" or "That's my opinion; nothing's going to change it"? Have you ever made such statements yourself? Accepting a conclusion without evidence, or expecting others to do so, is a sure sign of lazy thinking. A critical thinker asks, "What evidence supports or refutes this argument and its opposition? How reliable is the evidence?" Have you ever received some dire warning or funny "I swear it's true" story emailed by a friend, and then forwarded it to your entire address book or posted it on Facebook, only to learn later that it was a hoax or an urban folktale? A critical thinker would ask, "Is this story something I'd better check out on snopes.com

hypothesis A statement that attempts to predict or to account for a set of phenomena; scientific hypotheses specify relationships among events or variables and are empirically tested.

operational definition A precise definition of a term in a hypothesis, which specifies the operations for observing and measuring the process or phenomenon being defined.

When demonstrating "levitation" and other supposedly magical phenomena, illusionists such as André Kole exploit people's tendency to trust the evidence of their own eyes even when such evidence is misleading. Critical thinkers ask about the nature and reliability of the evidence for a phenomenon.

principle of falsifiability The principle that a scientific theory must make predictions that are specific enough to expose the theory to the possibility of disconfirmation.

confirmation bias The tendency to look for or pay attention only to information that confirms one's own belief, and ignore, trivialize, or forget information that disconfirms that belief.

before I tell my closest 90,000 friends?"

In scientific research, an idea may initially generate excitement because it is plausible, imaginative, or appealing, but eventually it must be backed by empirical evidence if it is to be taken seriously. A collection of anecdotes or an appeal to authority will not do. Sometimes, of course, checking the reliability of the evidence directly is not practical. In those cases, critical thinkers consider whether it came from a reliable source. Sources who are reliable exercise critical thinking themselves. They have education or experience in the field in which they claim expertise. They do not pressure people to agree with them. They are trusted by other experts in the field. They share their evidence openly. Their research has been published in professional journals where it has been reviewed by other experts on the subject, rather than merely announced to the public in a press release or blog.

4 Analyze Assumptions and Biases. *Assumptions* are beliefs that are taken for granted, and *biases* are assumptions that keep us from considering the evidence fairly or that cause us to ignore the evidence entirely. Critical thinkers try to identify and evaluate the unspoken assumptions on which claims and arguments may rest—in the books they read, the political speeches they hear, and the advertisements that bombard them every day. In science, as in other fields, a questioning attitude toward assumptions is what drives progress. Some of the greatest scientific advances have been made by those who dared to doubt widespread assumptions: that the sun revolves around the earth, that illness can be cured by applying leeches to the skin, that madness is a sign of demonic possession.

Critical thinkers are willing to analyze and test not only other people's assumptions, but also their own (which is much harder). Researchers put their own assumptions to the test by stating a hypothesis in such a way that it can be *refuted*, or disproved by counterevidence. This principle, known as the

principle of falsifiability, does not mean that the hypothesis *will* be disproved, only that it *could be* if contrary evidence were to be discovered.

Another way of saying this is that a scientist must risk disconfirmation by predicting not only what will happen, but also what will *not* happen if the hypothesis is correct. In the misery-loves-company study, the hypothesis would be supported if most anxious people sought each other out, but disconfirmed if most anxious people went off alone to sulk and worry, or if anxiety had no effect on their behavior (see Figure 1.1). A willingness to risk disconfirmation forces scientists to take negative evidence seriously and to abandon mistaken assumptions. Any researcher who refuses to do this is not a true scientist.

The principle of falsifiability is often violated in everyday life because all of us are vulnerable to the **confirmation bias**: the tendency to look for and accept evidence that supports our pet theories and assumptions and to ignore or reject evidence that contradicts our beliefs. For example, once a police interrogator is convinced of a suspect's guilt, he or she tends to interpret anything the suspect says, even the person's maintenance of innocence, as confirming evidence that the suspect is guilty ("Of course he *says* he's innocent; he's a liar") (Leo, 2008). But what if the suspect *is* innocent? The principle of falsifiability compels scientists, and the rest of us, to resist the confirmation bias and to consider counterevidence.

5 Avoid Emotional Reasoning. Emotion has a place in critical thinking and in science, too. Passionate commitment to a view motivates people to think boldly, to defend unpopular ideas, and to seek evidence for creative new theories. But emotional conviction alone cannot settle arguments, and in fact it usually makes them worse. The fact that you *really, really* feel strongly that something is true—or want it to be—doesn't make it so.

All of us are apt to feel threatened and get defensive whenever our most cherished beliefs, or commitment to a course of action, are challenged by empirical evidence (Tavris & Aronson, 2007). At such times, it is especially important to separate the data from emotional reasoning. In the opening story in this chapter about the ruling that vaccines do not cause autism, one of the judges expressed sympathy and admiration for parents coping with their children's disorder, but added, "I must decide this case not on sentiment, but by analyzing the evidence." Another of the judges concluded, "Sadly, the petitioners in this litigation have been the victims of bad science conducted to support litigation rather than

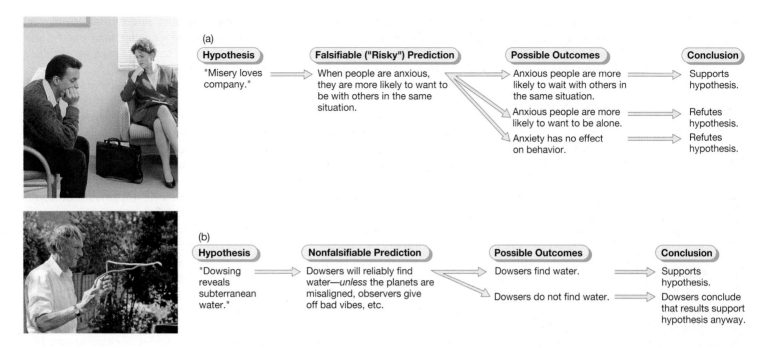

FIGURE 1.1
The Principle of Falsifiability
The scientific method requires researchers to expose their ideas to the possibility of counterevidence, as in row (a). In contrast, people claiming psychic powers, such as dowsers (who say they can find underground water with a "dowsing rod" that bends when water is present), typically interpret all possible outcomes as support for their assertions, as in row (b). Their claims are therefore untestable.

to advance medical and scientific understanding" of autism. (Later in this chapter, we will see how the parents might have mistakenly come to the conclusion that vaccines caused their children's autism.)

You probably already hold strong beliefs about child rearing, drugs, the causes of crime, racism, the origins of intelligence, gender differences, homosexuality, politics, and many other issues of concern to psychologists. As you read this book, you may find yourself quarreling with findings that you dislike. Disagreement is fine; it means that you are reading actively and are engaged with the material. All we ask is that you think about why you are disagreeing: Is it because the evidence is unpersuasive or because the results make you feel anxious or annoyed?

6 **Don't Oversimplify.** A critical thinker looks beyond the obvious, resists easy generalizations, and rejects either–or thinking. Is it better to feel you have control over what happens to you, or to accept with tranquility whatever life serves up? Either answer oversimplifies. As we will see in Chapter 13, control has many important benefits, but sometimes it's best to go with the flow.

One common form of oversimplification is *argument by anecdote*, generalizing from a personal experience or a few examples to everyone: One

crime committed by a paroled ex-convict means that parole should be abolished; one friend who hates his or her school means that everybody who goes there hates it; one friend who swears that seaweed cured her headaches means that seaweed is beneficial for everyone. Anecdotes are often the source of stereotyping, as well: One dishonest mother on public assistance means everyone on welfare is dishonest; one encounter with an unconventional Californian means they are all flaky. Critical and scientific thinkers want more evidence than one or two stories before drawing such sweeping conclusions.

7 **Consider Other Interpretations.** A critical thinker creatively formulates hypotheses that offer reasonable explanations of the topic at hand. In science, the goal is to arrive at a **theory**, an organized system of assumptions and principles that purports to explain a set of observations and how they are related. A scientific theory is not just someone's personal opinion, as in "It's only a theory" or "I have a theory about why he told that lie." It is true that some scientific theories are tentative, pending more research, but some, like the theories of gravity and evolution, are accepted by virtually all scientists. Theories that come to be accepted by the scientific community make as few assumptions as possible and account for many empirical findings.

theory An organized system of assumptions and principles that purports to explain a specified set of phenomena and their interrelationships.

Before settling on an explanation of some behavior, however, critical thinkers are careful not to shut out alternative possibilities. They generate as many interpretations of the evidence as they can before choosing the most likely one. Suppose a news magazine reports that people who are chronically depressed are more likely than nondepressed people to develop cancer. Before concluding that depression causes cancer, you would need to consider some other possibilities. Perhaps depressed people are more likely to smoke and to drink excessively, and these unhealthful habits increase their cancer risk. Or perhaps early, as-yet-undetected cancers produce biochemical changes that create the physical and emotional symptoms of depression. Alternative explanations such as these must be ruled out by further investigation before we can conclude that depression is a direct cause of cancer. (It's not, by the way.)

8 Tolerate Uncertainty. Ultimately, learning to think critically teaches us one of the hardest lessons of life: how to live with uncertainty. Sometimes there is little or no evidence available to examine. Sometimes the evidence permits only tentative conclusions. Sometimes the evidence seems strong enough to permit strong conclusions until, exasperatingly, new evidence throws our beliefs into disarray. Critical thinkers are willing to accept this state of uncertainty. They are not afraid to say, "We don't have answers yet" or "I'm not sure."

In science, tolerating uncertainty means that researchers must avoid drawing firm conclusions until other researchers have repeated, or *replicated*, their studies and verified their findings. Secrecy is a big no-no in science; you must be willing to tell others where you got your ideas and how you tested them so that others can challenge the findings if they think the findings are wrong. Replication is an essential part of the scientific process because sometimes what seems to be a major discovery turns out to be only a fluke.

The need to accept a certain amount of uncertainty does not mean that we must abandon all assumptions, beliefs, and convictions. That would be impossible, in any case: We all need values and principles to guide our actions. The problem is not that people hold convictions; it is that they so often refuse to give up their convictions when they prove to be outdated, dangerous, foolish, or simply wrong.

Critical thinking is a tool to guide us on a lifelong quest for understanding—a tool that we must keep sharpening. No one ever becomes a perfect critical thinker, entirely unaffected by emotional reasoning and wishful thinking. We are all less open-minded than we think; it is always easier to poke holes in another person's argument than to critically examine our own position. Yet we think the journey is well worth the mental effort, because the ability to think critically will help you in countless ways, from saving you money to improving your relationships.

As you read this book, keep in mind the eight guidelines we have described. Practice in critical thinking can help you bulk up your "thinking muscles" and understand psychological concepts better, which is why we have given you many opportunities to apply these guidelines to psychological theories and to the personal and social issues that affect us all. From time to time, a tab with a light bulb symbol (like the one shown here) will highlight a discussion where one or more of our critical-

> **Thinking Critically about...**

thinking guidelines are especially relevant. In Quick Quizzes, the light bulb will indicate questions that give you practice in applying the guidelines yourself. Keep in mind, however, that critical thinking is important throughout the book, not only where the light bulb appears. Finally, at the end of every chapter, a feature called "Taking Psychology with You" will help you apply critical thinking to a topic in the chapter and take its message home with you. ((•⎯**Listen**

((•⎯**Listen** to
**Science and
Pseudoscience** on
mypsychlab.com

Hypnosis has traditionally been considered a trance state in which people involuntarily do things they ordinarily could not or would not do. But might there be another interpretation of the surprising things that hypnotized people often do? (We will look at competing explanations in Chapter 5.)

 ✓●─┐**Study** and
Review on
mypsychlab.com

Quick Quiz

Bulk up your own thinking muscles by answering these questions.

1. Describe how the guidelines to critical thinking were violated in each of the following cases:

    a. For years, writer Norman Cousins told how he had cured himself of a rare, life-threatening disease through a combination of humor and vitamins. In a best-selling book, he recommended the same approach to others.

    b. Benjamin Rush, an eighteenth-century physician, believed that yellow fever should be treated by blood-letting. Many of his patients died, but Rush did not lose faith in his approach; he attributed each recovery to his treatment and each death to the severity of the disease (Stanovich, 2010).

2. Amelia and Harold are arguing about the death penalty. "Look, I just feel strongly that it's barbaric, ineffective, and wrong," says Harold. "You're nuts," says Amelia, "I believe in an eye for an eye, and besides, I'm absolutely sure it's a deterrent to further crime." Which lapses of critical thinking might Amelia and Harold be committing?

Answers:

1a. Cousins oversimplified, arguing by anecdote instead of examining evidence from controlled studies that included people who were not helped by humor and vitamins; and he may have been reasoning emotionally because of his own dramatic recovery. **1b.** Rush failed to analyze and test his assumptions; he violated the principle of falsifiability, interpreting a patient's survival as support for his hypothesis and explaining away each death by saying that the person had been too ill for the treatment to work. Thus, there was no possible counterevidence that could refute the theory (which, by the way, was dead wrong; the treatment was actually as dangerous as the disease). **2.** Harold and Amelia are reasoning emotionally ("I feel strongly about this, so I'm right and you're wrong"). They do not cite evidence that supports or contradicts their arguments. What do studies show about the link between the death penalty and crime? How often are innocent people executed? They have not examined their biases. And they may not be clearly defining the problem: What is the purpose of the death penalty? Is it to deter criminals, to satisfy the public desire for revenge, or to keep criminals from being paroled and returned to the streets?

 ## YOU are about to learn ...

● how participants are selected for psychological studies, and why it matters.

● the methods psychologists use to describe behavior.

● the advantages and disadvantages of each descriptive method.

Descriptive Studies: Establishing the Facts

Psychologists gather evidence to support their hypotheses by using different methods, depending on the kinds of questions they want to answer. These methods are not mutually exclusive, however. Just as a police detective may rely on DNA samples, fingerprints, and interviews of suspects to figure out "who done it," psychological sleuths often draw on different techniques at different stages of an ongoing investigation.

No matter what technique is used, one major challenge facing any researcher is to select the participants (sometimes called "subjects") for the study. Ideally, the researcher would prefer to get a **representative sample**, a group of randomly chosen participants that accurately represents the larger population that the researcher is interested in. Suppose you wanted to learn about drug use among college sophomores. Questioning or observing every sophomore in the country would obviously not be practical; instead, you would need to recruit a sample. You could use special selection procedures to ensure that this sample contained the same proportion of women, men, blacks, whites, poor people, rich people, Catholics, Jews, and so on as in the general population of college sophomores. Even then, a sample drawn just from your own school or town might not produce results applicable to the entire country, or even your state.

Plenty of studies are based on unrepresentative samples. The media had a field day when the American Medical Association reported, based on the replies of 664 women who were polled online, that binge drinking and unprotected sex were rampant among college women during spring break vacations. Yet that sample, it turned out, was hardly representative or randomly selected from the general population of college women: It

representative sample
A group of individuals, selected from a population for study, which matches that population on important characteristics such as age and sex.

descriptive methods Methods that yeild descriptions of behavior but not necessarily causal explanations.

case study A detailed description of a particular individual being studied or treated.

included only women who volunteered to answer questions, and only a fourth of them had ever taken a trip during spring break (Rosenthal, 2006).

A sample's size is less critical than its representativeness. A small but representative sample may yield extremely accurate results, whereas a study that fails to use proper sampling methods may yield questionable results, no matter how large the sample. In practice, psychologists must often settle for a sample of people who happen to be available, and more often than not, this means college students. Most of the time, that's fine; many psychological processes, such as basic perceptual or memory processes, are likely to be the same in students as in anyone else. But because college students differ in many ways from nonstudents, conclusions based on college students do not always generalize to the population at large, and they should be accepted with caution until the research is replicated with nonstudents.

We turn now to the specific methods used most commonly in psychological research. As you read about these methods, you may want to list their advantages and disadvantages to remember them better, and then check your list against the one in Table 1.3 on pages 27–28. We will begin with **descriptive methods**, which allow researchers to describe and predict behavior but not necessarily to choose one explanation over competing ones.

Case Studies

A **case study** (or *case history*) is a detailed description of a particular individual, based on careful observation or on formal psychological testing. It may include information about a person's childhood, dreams, fantasies, experiences, relationships, and hopes—anything that will provide insight into the person's behavior. Case studies are most commonly used by clinicians, but sometimes academic researchers use them as well, especially when they are just beginning to study a topic or when practical or ethical considerations prevent them from gathering information in other ways.

Suppose you want to know whether the first few years of life are critical for acquiring a first language. Can children who have missed out on hearing speech (or, in

the case of deaf children, seeing signs) catch up later? Obviously, psychologists cannot answer this question by isolating children and seeing what happens! So instead they have studied unusual cases of language deprivation.

One such case involved a 13-year-old girl who had been cruelly locked up in a small room since infancy. Her mother, a battered wife, barely cared for her, and no one in the family spoke a word to her. If she made the slightest sound, her severely disturbed father beat her with a large piece of wood. When she was finally rescued, Genie, as researchers called her, did not know how to chew or to stand erect, and her only sounds were high-pitched whimpers. Eventually, she was able to learn some rules of social conduct, and she began to understand short sentences and to use words to convey her needs, describe her moods, and even lie. But even after many years, Genie's grammar and pronunciation remained abnormal. She never learned to use pronouns correctly, ask questions, produce proper negative sentences, or use the little word endings that communicate tense, number, and possession (Curtiss, 1977, 1982; Rymer, 1993). This sad case, along with similar ones, suggests that a critical period exists for language development, with the likelihood of fully mastering a first language declining steadily after early childhood and falling off drastically at puberty (Pinker, 1994).

Case studies illustrate psychological principles in a way that abstract generalizations and cold statistics never can, and they produce a more detailed picture of an individual than other methods do. In biological research, cases of patients with brain damage have yielded important clues to how the brain is organized (see Chapter 4). But in most instances, case studies have serious drawbacks. Information is often missing or is hard to interpret; no one knows whether Genie was born with mental deficits. The observer who writes up the case may have biases that cause him or her to notice some facts and overlook others. The person who is the focus of the study may have selective or inaccurate memories, making conclusions unreliable. Most important, because that person may be unrepresentative of the group that the researcher is interested in, the case study has only limited usefulness for deriving general principles of behavior. For all these reasons, case studies are usually only sources, rather than tests, of hypotheses.

Be wary, then, of the compelling cases or sensationalized stories that some individuals or their psychiatrists promote to the media. Often these stories are only arguing by anecdote, and they are not a basis for drawing firm conclusions about anything.

This picture, drawn by Genie, a young girl who endured years of isolation and mistreatment, shows one of her favorite pastimes: listening to researcher Susan Curtiss playing the piano. Genie's drawings were used along with other case material to study her mental and social development.

Observational Studies

In **observational studies**, the researcher observes, measures, and records behavior while taking care to avoid intruding on the people (or animals) being observed. The purpose of *naturalistic observation* is to find out how people or other animals act in their normal social environments. Psychologists use naturalistic observation wherever people happen to be: at home, on playgrounds or streets, or in schoolrooms, offices, and bars. Observers must also take pains to avoid being obvious about what they are doing so that those who are being observed will behave naturally. Often, however, researchers prefer making their observations in a laboratory setting. In *laboratory observation*, they have more control. They can use cameras and recording devices, determine how many people will be observed at once, maintain a clear line of vision, and so forth.

Suppose that you wanted to know how infants of different ages respond when left with a stranger. The most efficient approach might be to have parents and their infants come to your laboratory, observe them playing together for a while through a one-way window, then have a stranger enter the room and, a few minutes later, have the parent leave. You could record signs of distress, interactions with the stranger, and other behavior, checking your observations against those of others to ensure accuracy. If you did this, you would find that very young infants carry on cheerfully with whatever they are doing when the parent leaves. However, by the age of about 8 months, children will often burst into tears or show other signs of what child psychologists call "separation anxiety" (see Chapter 3).

One shortcoming of laboratory observation is that the presence of researchers and special equipment may cause participants to behave differently than they would in their usual surroundings. Further, observational studies, like other descriptive studies, are more useful for describing behavior than for explaining it. If we observe infants protesting whenever a parent leaves the room, we cannot be sure why they are protesting. Is it because they have become

attached to their parents and want them nearby, or have they learned from experience that crying brings an adult with a cookie and a cuddle? Observational studies alone cannot answer such questions.

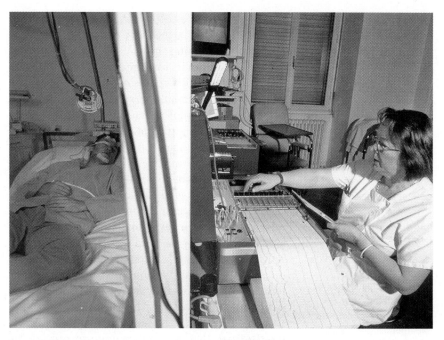

Psychologists using laboratory observation have gathered valuable information about brain and muscle activity during sleep.

Tests

Psychological tests, sometimes called *assessment instruments*, are procedures for measuring and evaluating personality traits, emotional states, aptitudes, interests, abilities, and values. Typically, tests require people to answer a series of written or oral questions. The answers may then be totaled to yield a single numerical score, or a set of scores. *Objective tests*, also called *inventories*, measure beliefs, feelings, or behaviors of which an individual is aware; *projective tests* are designed to tap unconscious feelings or motives (see Chapter 11).

At one time or another, you no doubt have taken a personality test, an achievement test, or a

observational study A study in which the researcher carefully and systematically observes and records behavior without interfering with the behavior; it may involve either naturalistic or laboratory observation.

psychological tests Procedures used to measure and evaluate personality traits, emotional states, aptitudes, interests, abilities, and values.

Get Involved! A Study of Personal Space

Try a little naturalistic observation of your own. Go to a public place where people seat themselves, such as a movie theater or a cafeteria with large tables. You might recruit some friends to help you; you can divide the area into sections and assign each observer one section to observe. As individuals and groups sit down, note how many seats they leave between themselves and the next person. On the average, how far do people tend to sit from strangers? Once you have your results, see how many possible explanations you can come up with.

standardize In test construction, to develop uniform procedures for giving and scoring a test.

norms In test construction, established standards of performance.

reliability In test construction, the consistency of test scores from one time and place to another.

validity The ability of a test to measure what it was designed to measure.

surveys Questionnaires and interviews that ask people directly about their experiences, attitudes, or opinions.

vocational-aptitude test. Hundreds of psychological tests are used in industry, education, the military, and the helping professions. Some are given to individuals, others to large groups. These measures help clarify differences among individuals, as well as differences in the reactions of the same person on different occasions or at different stages of life. Tests may be used to promote self-understanding, to evaluate treatments and programs, or, in scientific research, to draw generalizations about human behavior. Well-constructed psychological tests are a great improvement over simple self-evaluation because many people have a distorted view of their own abilities and traits. In the workplace, employees tend to overestimate their skills and CEOs are overconfident in their judgments; in school and on the job, people are often blissfully unaware of their own lack of competence (Dunning, Heath, & Suls, 2004).

One test of a good test is whether it is **standardized**, that is, whether uniform procedures exist for giving and scoring the test. It would hardly be fair to give some people detailed instructions and plenty of time and others only vague instructions and limited time. Those who administer the test must know exactly how to explain the tasks involved, how much time to allow, and what materials to use. Scoring is usually done by referring to **norms**, or established standards of performance. The usual procedure for developing norms is to give the test to a large group of people who resemble those for whom the test is intended. Norms determine which scores can be considered high, low, or average.

Test construction presents two central challenges. First, the test must have **reliability**, producing the same results from one time and place to the next. A vocational-interest test is not reliable if it tells Tom that he would make a wonderful engineer but a poor journalist, and then gives different results when Tom retakes the test a week later. Nor is it reliable if alternate forms of the test, intended to be comparable, yield different results. Second, the test must have **validity**, measuring what it is designed to measure. A creativity test is not valid if what it actually measures is verbal sophistication. The validity of a test is often measured by its ability to predict other, independent measures, or *criteria*, of the trait in question. The criterion for a scholastic aptitude test might be college grades; the criterion for a test of shyness might be behavior in social situations. Among psychologists, controversy exists about the validity of even some widely used tests, such as the Scholastic Assessment Test (SAT) and standardized IQ tests.

Many people attach a lot of importance to their test scores!

Criticisms and reevaluations of psychological tests keep psychological assessment honest and scientifically rigorous. In contrast, the pop-psych tests frequently found in magazines and newspapers and on the Internet usually have not been evaluated for either validity or reliability. These questionnaires often have inviting headlines such as "What Breed of Dog Do You Most Resemble?" or "What's Your Love Profile?" but they are merely lists of questions that someone thought sounded good.

Surveys

Psychological tests usually generate information about people indirectly. In contrast, **surveys** are questionnaires and interviews that gather information by asking people *directly* about their experiences, attitudes, or opinions about everything from consumer preferences to sexual preferences. Most of us are familiar with national opinion surveys, such as the Gallup and Roper polls, and the unscientific surveys that are forever popping up on the Internet.

Surveys produce bushels of data, but they are not easy to do well. Sampling is the first difficult problem. When a talk-radio host or TV personality invites people to post comments on their website about a political matter, the results are not likely to generalize to the population as a whole, even if thousands of people respond. Why? As a group, people who listen to Bill O'Reilly are more conservative than fans of Jon Stewart.

Popular polls and surveys (like the one about college women on spring break) also frequently

> **Thinking Critically about Opinion Polls and Surveys**

suffer from a **volunteer bias**: People who are willing to volunteer their opinions may differ from those who decline to take part. When you read about a survey, or any other kind of study, always ask who participated. A nonrepresentative sample does not necessarily mean that a survey is worthless or uninteresting, but it does mean that the results may not hold true for other groups.

Yet another problem with surveys, as with self-reports in general, is that people sometimes lie, especially when the survey is about a touchy or embarrassing topic ("I would never do that disgusting/dishonest/fattening thing!") or an illegal act, such as using banned drugs (Tourangeau & Yan, 2007). The likelihood of lying is reduced when respondents are guaranteed anonymity and allowed to respond in private. Researchers can also check for lying by asking the same question several times with different wording to see whether the answers are consistent. Technology can also help: Because many people feel more anonymous when they interact with a computer than when they fill out a paper-and-pencil questionnaire, computerized questionnaires can reduce lying (Turner et al., 1998).

When you hear about the results of a survey or opinion poll, you also need to consider which questions were (and were not) asked, and how the questions were phrased. These aspects of a survey's design may encourage responses in a particular direction, as political pollsters well know ("Do you favor raising your property tax to spend millions of dollars to repair your local schools?" is more likely to evoke a *no* than "Do you favor rebuilding schools that are decaying, lack heat, and are infested with rats?"). Many years ago, the famed sex researcher Alfred Kinsey made it his practice always to ask, "*How many times have you* (masturbated, had nonmarital sex, etc.)?" rather than "*Have you ever* (masturbated, had nonmarital sex, etc.)?" The first way of phrasing the question tended to elicit more truthful responses than the second because it removed the respondent's self-consciousness about having done any of those things. The second way of phrasing the question would have permitted embarrassed respondents to reply with a simple but dishonest "No."

As you can see, although surveys can be extremely informative, they must be conducted and interpreted carefully.

"Are you (a) contented, (b) happy, (c) very happy, (d) wildly happy, (e) deliriously happy?"

volunteer bias A shortcoming of findings derived from a sample of volunteers instead of a representative sample; the volunteers may differ from those who did not volunteer.

Quick Quiz

How would you describe your understanding of descriptive methods?

A. Which descriptive method would be most appropriate for studying each of the following topics? (All of them, by the way, have been investigated by psychologists.)

1. Ways in which the games of boys differ from those of girls

2. Changes in attitudes toward nuclear disarmament after a TV movie about nuclear holocaust

3. The math skills of children in the United States versus Japan

4. Physiological changes that occur when people watch violent movies

5. The development of a male infant who was reared as a female after his penis was accidentally burned off during a routine surgery

a. case study

b. naturalistic observation

c. laboratory observation

d. survey

e. test

B. Professor Flummox gives her new test of aptitude for studying psychology to her psychology students at the start of the year. At the end of the year, she finds that those who did well on the test averaged only a C in the course. The test lacks _____.

Answers:

1.b 2.d 3.e 4.c 5.a   B. validity

correlational study A descriptive study that looks for a consistent relationship between two phenomena.

correlation A measure of how strongly two variables are related to each other.

variables Characteristics of behavior or experience that can be measured or described by a numeric scale; variables are manipulated and assessed in scientific studies.

positive correlation An association between increases in one variable and increases in another, or between decreases in one and in the other.

negative correlation An association between increases in one variable and decreases in another.

 YOU are about to learn…

● what it means to say that two things, such as grades and TV watching, are "negatively" correlated.

● whether a positive correlation between TV watching and hyperactivity means that too much TV makes kids hyperactive.

Correlational Studies: Looking for Relationships

In descriptive research, psychologists often want to know whether two or more phenomena are related and, if so, how strongly. Are students' grade point averages related to the number of hours they spend watching TV shows, playing video games, and texting? To find out, a psychologist would do a **correlational study.**

Measuring Correlations

The word **correlation** is often used as a synonym for "relationship." Technically, however, a correlation is a numerical measure of the *strength* of the relationship between two things. The things may be events, scores, or anything else that can be recorded and tallied. In psychological studies, such things are called **variables** because they can vary in quantifiable ways. Height, weight, age, income, IQ scores, number of items recalled on a memory test, number of smiles in a given time period—anything that can be measured, rated, or scored can serve as a variable.

A **positive correlation** means that high values of one variable are associated with high values of the other, and that low values of one variable are associated with low values of the other:

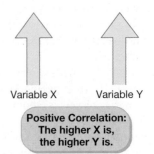

Variable X   Variable Y

Positive Correlation: The higher X is, the higher Y is.

Height and weight are positively correlated; so are IQ scores and school grades. Rarely is a correlation perfect, however. Some tall people weigh less than some short ones; some people with average IQs are superstars in the classroom, and some with high IQs get poor grades. Figure 1.2(a) shows a positive correlation between men's educational level and their annual income.

A **negative correlation** means that high values of one variable are associated with low values of the other:

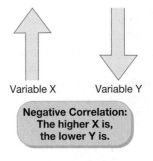

Variable X   Variable Y

Negative Correlation: The higher X is, the lower Y is.

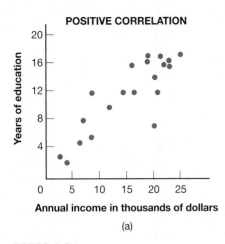

POSITIVE CORRELATION

Years of education (y-axis: 4, 8, 12, 16, 20)
Annual income in thousands of dollars (x-axis: 0, 5, 10, 15, 20, 25)

(a)

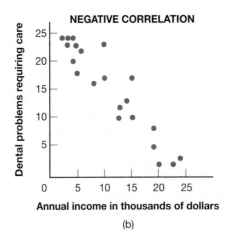

NEGATIVE CORRELATION

Dental problems requiring care (y-axis: 5, 10, 15, 20, 25)
Annual income in thousands of dollars (x-axis: 0, 5, 10, 15, 20, 25)

(b)

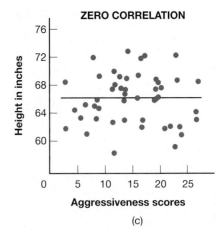

ZERO CORRELATION

Height in inches (y-axis: 60, 64, 68, 72, 76)
Aggressiveness scores (x-axis: 0, 5, 10, 15, 20, 25)

(c)

FIGURE 1.2
Correlations
Graph (a) shows a positive correlation: In general, income rises with education. Graph (b) shows a negative correlation: In general, the higher people's incomes are, the fewer dental problems they have. Graph (c) shows a zero correlation between height and aggressiveness.

Figure 1.2(b) shows a negative correlation between average income and the incidence of dental disease for groups of 100 families. In general, as you can see, the higher the income, the fewer the dental problems. In the automobile business, the age of a car is negatively correlated with its price: The older the car, the lower the price, except for antiques and models favored by collectors. How about hours spent watching TV and average grades? They too are negatively correlated: Lots of hours in front of the television are associated with lower grades (Potter, 1987; Ridley-Johnson, Cooper, & Chance, 1983). See whether you can think of other variables that are negatively correlated. Remember that a negative correlation means a relationship exists; the more of one thing, the less of another. If there is no relationship between two variables, as in Figure 1.2(c), we say that they are *uncorrelated*. Shoe size and IQ scores are uncorrelated.

The statistic used to express a correlation is called the **coefficient of correlation.** This number conveys both the size of the correlation and its direction. A perfect positive correlation has a coefficient of +1.00, and a perfect negative correlation has a coefficient of –1.00. Suppose you weighed ten people and listed them in order, from lightest to heaviest, then measured their heights and listed them in order, from shortest to tallest. If the names on the two lists were in exactly the same order, the correlation between weight and height would be +1.00. If the correlation between two variables is +.80, it means that the two are strongly related. If the correlation is –.80, the relationship is just as strong, but it is negative. When there is no association between two variables, the coefficient is zero or close to zero.

Cautions about Correlations

Correlational studies are common in psychology and often make the news. But beware; many supposed correlations reported in the media or on the Internet are based on rumor and anecdote. Some are based on coincidence, which is why they are called *illusory correlations*; they are nonexistent or meaningless. **Explore**

The alleged link between vaccines and autism is an illusory correlation, a result of the fact that most symptoms of childhood autism emerge at about the same time that children are vaccinated. Some thought the culprit was thimerosal, a preservative that was used in childhood vaccines until 1999, and is now contained in trace amounts in only a few. Yet there is no convincing evidence that thimerosal ever was involved in autism, and after it

was removed from most vaccines, the incidence of autism did not decline, as it would have if thimerosal were to blame. Moreover, major international studies have failed to find any causal connection whatsoever between vaccines and autism (Offit, 2008). As just one example, in a study of the more than 500,000 children born in Denmark between 1991 and 1998, the incidence of autism in vaccinated children was actually a bit *lower* than in unvaccinated children (Madsen et al., 2002). Tragically, rates of measles, a disease that can be lethal, are rising in children whose parents have refused to have them vaccinated.

Even when correlations are meaningful and strong, they can be hard to interpret because *a correlation does not establish causation*. It is easy to assume that if variable A predicts variable B, then A must be causing B, but that is not necessarily so. A positive correlation has been found between the number of hours that children watch television between ages 1 and 3 and their risk of hyperactivity (impulsivity, attention problems, difficulty concentrating) by age 7 (Christakis et al., 2004). Does this mean that watching TV *causes* hyperactivity? Maybe, but it is also possible that children with a disposition to become hyperactive are more attracted to television than those disposed to being calm. Or perhaps the harried parents of distractible children are more likely than other parents to rely on TV as a babysitter. Or it is possible that neither variable causes the other directly: Perhaps parents who allow their young kids to watch a lot of TV have attention problems themselves, and therefore create a home environment that fosters hyperactivity and inattentiveness. Likewise, that negative correlation between TV watching and grades might exist because heavy TV watchers have less time to study, or because they have some personality trait that causes an attraction to TV *and* an aversion to studying, or because they use TV as an escape when their grades are low . . . you get the idea.

The moral of the story: When two variables are associated, one variable may or may not be causing the other.

Explore
Correlations
Do Not Show
Causation on
mypsychlab.com

The number of hours toddlers spend watching TV is correlated with their risk of being hyperactive at age 7. Does that mean TV watching causes hyperactivity problems? What other explanations for this correlation are possible?

✓•─ **Study** and
Review on
mypsychlab.com

Quick Quiz

In your experience, are taking quizzes and getting good grades positively correlated?

1. Identify each of the following as a positive or negative correlation:

   a. The higher a male monkey's level of the hormone testosterone, the more aggressive he is likely to be.

   b. The older people are, the less frequently they tend to have sexual intercourse.

   c. The hotter the weather, the higher the rate of crimes against people, such as muggings.

2. Now see whether you can generate two or three possible explanations for each of the preceding findings.

Answers:

these correlations are not the only ones possible.)
outside; criminals may find it more comfortable to be out committing their crimes in warm weather than in cold. (Our explanations for
make people edgy and cause them to commit crimes; potential victims may be more plentiful in warm weather because more people go
may have less interest in sex than younger people, have less energy or more physical ailments, or lack partners. **c.** Hot temperatures may
tion; or a third factor, such as age or dominance, may influence aggressiveness and hormone production independently. **b.** Older people
1. a. positive **b.** negative **c.** positive   **2. a.** The hormone may cause aggressiveness; acting aggressively may stimulate hormone produc-

◆▶ **YOU** are about to learn...

- why psychologists rely so heavily on experiments.

- what control groups control for.

- who is "blind" in single- and double-blind experiments, and what they are not supposed to "see."

The Experiment: Hunting for Causes

experiment A controlled test of a hypothesis in which the researcher manipulates one variable to discover its effect on another.

informed consent The doctrine that human research subjects must participate voluntarily and must know enough about a study to make an intelligent decision about whether to participate.

independent variable A variable that an experimenter manipulates.

dependent variable A variable that an experimenter predicts will be affected by manipulations of the independent variable.

Researchers gain plenty of information from descriptive studies, but when they want to actually track down the causes of behavior, they rely heavily on the experimental method. An **experiment** allows them to *control*, or manipulate, the situation being studied. Instead of being passive recorders of what is going on, researchers actively do something that they believe will affect people's behavior and then observe what happens. These procedures allow experimenters to draw conclusions about cause and effect—about what causes what.

All psychological studies must conform to ethical guidelines, but such guidelines are especially important in experimental research. In colleges and universities, a review committee must approve all studies and be sure they conform to federal regulations. Volunteers in a study must consent to participate and know enough about the study to make an intelligent decision, a doctrine known as **informed consent**. Researchers must protect participants from physical and mental harm, and if any risk exists, must warn them and give them an opportunity to withdraw at any time.

Ethical guidelines also require the humane treatment of research animals, which are used in only a small minority of psychological studies but are crucial to progress in some fields, especially biological psychology and behavioral research. Because of increased concern about the rights and welfare of animals, the American Psychological Association's guidelines for using animals in research have been made more comprehensive, and federal regulations governing the housing and care of animals have been strengthened.

Experimental Variables

Imagine that you are a psychologist whose research interest is multitasking. Almost everyone multitasks these days, and you would like to know whether that's a good thing or a bad thing. Specifically, you would like to know whether or not using a handheld cell phone while driving is dangerous. Motor vehicle statistics show that talking on a cell phone while driving is associated with an increase in accidents, but maybe that's just for people who are risk takers or lousy drivers to begin with. To pin down cause and effect, you decide to do an experiment.

In a laboratory, you ask participants to "drive" using a computerized driving simulator equipped with an automatic transmission, steering wheel, gas pedal, and brake pedal. The object, you tell them, is to maximize the distance covered by driving on a busy highway while avoiding collisions with other cars. Some of the participants talk on the phone for 15 minutes to a research assistant in the next room about a topic that interests them; others just drive. You are going to compare how many collisions the two groups have. The basic design of this experiment is illustrated in Figure 1.3, which you may want to refer to as you read the next few pages.

The aspect of an experimental situation manipulated or varied by the researcher is known as the **independent variable**. The reaction of the subjects—the behavior that the researcher tries to predict—is the **dependent variable**. Every experiment has at least one independent and one dependent variable. In our example, the independent variable is cell phone use (use versus nonuse). The dependent variable is the number of collisions.

Ideally, everything in the experimental situation except the independent variable is held constant—that is, kept the same for all participants. You would not have some people use a stick shift and others an automatic, unless shift type were an independent variable. Similarly, you would not have some people go through the experiment alone and others perform in front of an audience. Holding everything but the independent variable constant ensures that whatever happens is due to the researcher's manipulation and nothing else. It allows you to rule out other interpretations.

Understandably, students often have trouble keeping independent and dependent variables straight. You might think of it this way: The dependent variable—the outcome of the study—*depends* on the independent variable. When psychologists set up an experiment, they think, "If I do X, the people in my study will do Y." The X represents the independent variable; the Y represents the dependent variable: ⊙►Simulate

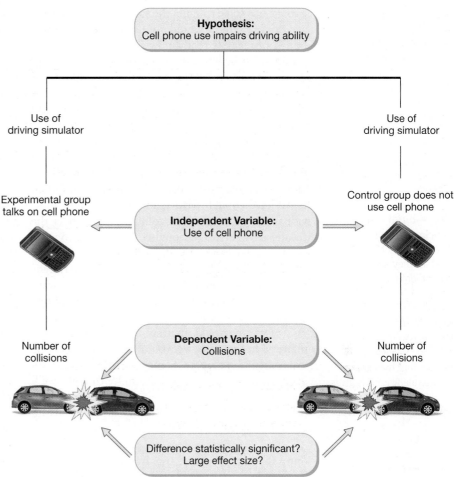

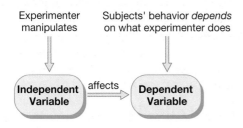

Most variables may be either independent or dependent, depending on what the experimenter wishes to find out. If you want to know whether eating chocolate makes people nervous, then the amount of chocolate eaten is the independent variable. If you want to know whether feeling nervous makes people eat chocolate, then the amount of chocolate eaten is the dependent variable.

Experimental and Control Conditions

Experiments usually require both an experimental condition and a comparison, or **control condition**. People in the control condition are treated exactly like those in the experimental condition, except that they are not exposed to the same treatment, or manipulation of the independent variable. Without a control condition, you cannot be sure that the behavior you are interested in would not have occurred anyway, even without your manipulation. In some studies, the same subjects can be used in both the control and the experimental condition; they are said to serve as their own controls. In other studies, people are assigned to either an *experimental group* or a *control group*.

In our cell phone study, we could have drivers serve as their own controls, but for this illustration, we will use two different groups. Participants who talk on the phone while driving make up the experimental group, and those who just drive along silently make up the control group. We want these

FIGURE 1.3
Do Cell Phone Use and Driving Mix?
The text describes this experimental design to test the hypothesis that talking on a cell phone while driving impairs driving skills and leads to accidents.

⊙►**Simulate Distinguishing Independent & Dependent Variables** on **mypsychlab.com**

control condition In an experiment, a comparison condition in which subjects are not exposed to the same treatment as are those in the experimental condition.

random assignment A procedure for assigning people to experimental and control groups in which each individual has the same probability as any other of being assigned to a given group.

placebo An inactive substance or fake treatment used as a control in an experiment.

single-blind study An experiment in which subjects do not know whether they are in an experimental or a control group.

experimenter effects Unintended changes in subjects' behavior due to cues that the experimenter inadvertently gives.

👁—⏹**Watch** the **Video** of **Konrad Lorenz** on **controlling an experiment** on **mypsychlab.com**

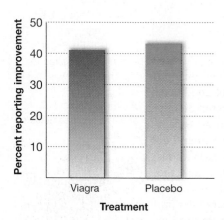

FIGURE 1.4

Does Viagra Work for Women?
Placebos are essential to determine whether people taking a new drug improve because of the drug or because of their expectations about it. In one study, 41 percent of women taking Viagra said their sex lives had improved. That sounds impressive, but 43 percent taking a placebo pill also said their sex lives had improved (Basson et al., 2002).

two groups to be roughly the same in terms of average driving skill. It would not do to start out with a bunch of reckless roadrunners in the experimental group and a bunch of tired tortoises in the control group. We also probably want the two groups to be similar in age, education, driving history, and other characteristics so that none of these variables will affect our results. One way to accomplish this is to use **random assignment** of people to one group or another—such as by randomly assigning them numbers and putting those with even numbers in one group and those with odd numbers in another. If we have enough participants in our study, individual characteristics that could possibly affect the results are likely to be roughly balanced in the two groups, so we can safely ignore them.

Sometimes researchers use several experimental or control groups. In our study, we might want to examine the effects of short versus long phone conversations, or conversations on different topics—say, work, personal matters, and *very* personal matters. In that case, we would have more than one experimental group to compare with the control group. In our hypothetical example, though, we'll just have one experimental group, and all participants in it will drive for 15 minutes while talking about a topic of their own choice.

This description does not cover all the procedures that experimenters use. In some kinds of studies, people in the control group get a **placebo**, a fake treatment or sugar pill that looks, tastes, or smells like the real treatment or medication but is phony. If the placebo produces the same result as the real thing, the reason must be the participants' expectations rather than the treatment itself. Placebos are critical in testing new drugs, because of the optimism that a potential cure often brings with it (see Chapter 12). Medical placebos usually take the form of pills or injections that contain no active ingredients. To see what placebos revealed in a study of Viagra for women's sexual problems, see Figure 1.4.

Control groups, by the way, are also crucial in many nonexperimental studies. Some psychotherapists have published books arguing that girls develop problems with self-esteem and confidence as soon as they hit adolescence. Unless the writers have also tested or surveyed a comparable group of teenage boys, however, there

is no way of knowing whether low self-esteem afflicts teenagers regardless of their sex or is more common among adolescent girls (it's not, as it turns out). If someone makes a claim about a new therapeutic method, asserts that women and men differ in some psychological way, or touts the benefits of a new pill, always ask: What did the control group show? 👁—⏹Watch

Experimenter Effects

Because expectations can influence the results of a study, participants should not know whether they are in an experimental or a control group. When this is so, as it usually is, the experiment is said to be a **single-blind study**. But participants are not the only ones who bring expectations to the laboratory; so do researchers. And researchers' expectations and hopes for a particular result may cause them to inadvertently influence the participants' responses through facial expressions, posture, tone of voice, or some other cue. Such **experimenter effects** can be powerful; even an experimenter's friendly smile can affect people's responses in a study (Rosenthal, 1994).

One solution to this problem is to do a **double-blind study**. In such a study, the person running the experiment, the one having actual contact with the participants, also does not know who is in which group until the data have been gathered. Double-blind procedures are standard in drug research. Different doses of a drug are coded in some way, and the person administering the drug is kept in the dark about the code's meaning until after the experiment. To run our cell phone study in a double-blind fashion, we could use a simulator that automatically records collisions and have the experimenter give instructions through an intercom so as not to know which group a participant was in until after the results were tallied.

Advantages and Limitations of Experiments

Because experiments allow conclusions about cause and effect, and because they permit researchers to distinguish real effects from placebo effects, they have long been the method of choice in psychology.

However, like all methods, the experiment has its limitations. Just as in other kinds of studies, the participants are not always representative of the larger population. Moreover, in an experiment, the researcher determines which questions are asked and which behaviors are recorded, and the participants try to do as they are told. In their desire to cooperate, advance scientific knowledge, or present themselves in a positive light, they may act in ways that they ordinarily would not (Kihlstrom, 1995).

Thus, experimental psychologists confront a dilemma: The more control they exercise over the situation, the more unlike real life it may be. For this reason, many psychologists have called for more **field research**, the study of behavior in natural contexts such as schools and the workplace. Have you ever wondered if women are more "talkative" than men, as the stereotype suggests? A field study of people in their everyday lives would be the best way to answer this question. Indeed, such a study has been done: The participants wore an unobtrusive recording device as they went about their normal lives, talking and chatting. The researchers found no gender differences at all (Mehl et al., 2007).

Every research method has strengths and weaknesses. Did you make a list of each method's advantages and disadvantages, as we suggested earlier? If so, compare it now with the one in Table 1.3.

Psychologists doing field research have studied diverse questions, such as whether men and women differ in how much they talk and how people in crowded places modify their gaze and body position to preserve a sense of privacy.

TABLE 1.3
Research Methods in Psychology: Their Advantages and Disadvantages

Method	Advantages	Disadvantages
Case study	Good source of hypotheses.	Vital information may be missing, making the case hard to interpret.
	Provides in-depth information on individuals.	The person's memories may be selective or inaccurate.
	Unusual cases can shed light on situations or problems that are unethical or impractical to study in other ways.	The individual may not be representative or typical.
Naturalistic observation	Allows description of behavior as it occurs in the natural environment.	Allows researcher little or no control of the situation.
	Often useful in first stages of a research program.	Observations may be biased.
		Does not allow firm conclusions about cause and effect.
Laboratory observation	Allows more control than naturalistic observation.	Allows researcher only limited control of the situation.
	Allows use of sophisticated equipment.	Observations may be biased.
		Does not allow firm conclusions about cause and effect.
		Behavior may differ from behavior in the natural environment.

Continued

double-blind study An experiment in which neither the participants nor the individuals running the study know which participants are in the control group and which are in the experimental group until after the results are tallied.

field research Descriptive or experimental research conducted in a natural setting outside the laboratory.

TABLE 1.3 *(Continued)*

Method	Advantages	Disadvantages
Test	Yields information on personality traits, emotional states, aptitudes, and abilities.	Difficult to construct tests that are reliable and valid.
Survey	Provides a large amount of information on large numbers of people.	If sample is nonrepresentative or biased, it may be impossible to generalize from the results. Responses may be inaccurate or untrue.
Correlational study	Shows whether two or more variables are related. Allows general predictions.	Does not permit identification of cause and effect.
Experiment	Allows researcher to control the situation. Permits researcher to identify cause and effect and to distinguish placebo effects from treatment effects.	Situation is artificial, and results may not generalize well to the real world. Sometimes difficult to avoid experimenter effects.

✓•─ **Study** and **Review** on **mypsychlab.com**

Quick Quiz

There are many advantages and no disadvantages of taking this quiz.

A. Name the independent and dependent variables in studies designed to answer the following questions:

   1. Whether sleeping after learning a poem improves memory for the poem.

   2. Whether the presence of other people affects a person's willingness to help someone in distress.

   3. Whether people get agitated from listening to heavy metal.

B. On a talk show, Dr. Blitznik announces a fabulous new program: Chocolate Immersion Therapy (CIT). "People who spend one day a week doing nothing but eating chocolate are soon cured of eating disorders, depression, drug abuse, and poor study habits," claims Dr. Blitznik. What should you find out about CIT before signing up?

Answers:

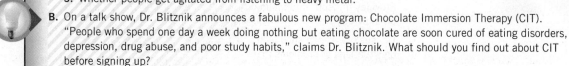

A. 1. Opportunity to sleep after learning is the independent variable; memory for the poem is the dependent variable. **2.** The presence of other people is the independent variable; willingness to help others is the dependent variable. **3.** Exposure to heavy metal music is the independent variable; agitation is the dependent variable. **B.** Some questions to ask: Is there research showing that people who go through CIT did better than those in a control group who did not have the therapy, or who had a different therapy, say, Broccoli Immersion Therapy? If so, how many people were studied, and how were they assigned to the therapy and nontherapy groups? Did the person running the experiment know who was and was not getting CIT? How long did the apparent cures last? Has the research been replicated?

 YOU are about to learn...

- why averages can be misleading.

- how to tell whether a finding is strong or trivial.

- why some findings are significant statistically yet unimportant in practical terms.

- how psychologists can combine results from many studies to better understand the problem.

Evaluating the Findings

If you are a psychologist who has just done an observational study, a survey, or an experiment, your work has only just begun. Once you have some results in hand, you must do three things with them: (1) describe them, (2) assess how reliable and meaningful they are, and (3) figure out how to explain them.

Why Psychologists Use Statistics

Let's say that 30 people in the cell phone experiment talked on the phone and 30 did not. We have recorded the number of collisions for each person on the driving simulator. Now we have 60 numbers. What can we do with them?

The first step is to summarize the data. The world does not want to hear how many collisions each person had. It wants to know what happened in the cell phone group as a whole, compared to what happened in the control group. To provide this information, we need numbers that sum up our data. Such numbers, known as **descriptive statistics**, are often depicted in graphs and charts.

A good way to summarize the data is to compute group averages. The most commonly used type of average is the **arithmetic mean.** (For two other types, see the Appendix.) The mean is calculated by adding up all the individual scores and dividing the result by the number of scores. We can compute a mean for the cell phone group by adding up the 30 collision scores and dividing the sum by 30. Then we can do the same for the control group. Now our 60 numbers have been boiled down to 2. For the sake of our example, let's assume that the cell phone group had an average of 10 collisions, whereas the control group's average was only 7.

We must be careful, however, about how we interpret these averages. It is possible that no one in our cell phone group actually had 10 collisions. Perhaps half the people in the group were motoring maniacs and had 15 collisions, whereas the others were more cautious and had only 5. Perhaps almost all of the participants had 9, 10, or 11 collisions. Perhaps the number of accidents ranged from 0 to 15. The mean does not tell us about such variability in the subjects' responses. For that, we need other descriptive statistics. For example, the **standard deviation** tells us how clustered or spread out the individual scores are around the mean; the more spread out they are, the less typical of everybody the mean is. (For details, see the Appendix.) Unfortunately, when research is reported in the news, you usually hear only about the mean. **Simulate**

At this point in our experiment, we have one group with an average of 10 collisions and another with an average of 7. Should we break out the champagne? Try to get on CNN? Call our mothers? Better hold off. Perhaps if one group had an average of 15 collisions and the other an average of 1, we could get excited. But rarely does a psychological study hit you between the eyes with a sensationally clear result. In most cases, there is some possibility that the difference between the two groups was due simply to chance. Perhaps the people in the cell phone group just happened to be a little more accident-prone, and their collisions had nothing to do with talking on the phone.

To find out how impressive the data are, psychologists use **inferential statistics**. These statistics do not merely describe or summarize the data; they permit researchers to draw inferences (conclusions based on evidence) about how meaningful the findings are. Like descriptive statistics, inferential statistics involve the application of mathematical formulas to the data. (Again, see the Appendix for details.)

Historically, the most commonly used inferential statistics have been **significance tests**, which tell researchers how likely a result was to have occurred by chance. In our cell phone experiment, a significance test will tell us how likely it is that the difference between the experimental group and the control group occurred by chance. It is not possible to rule out chance entirely, but if the likelihood that a result occurred by chance is extremely low, we say that the result is *statistically significant.*

By convention, psychologists consider a result to be significant if it would be expected to occur by chance 5 or fewer times in 100 repetitions of the study. Another way of saying this is that the result is significant at the .05 ("point oh five") level. If the difference could be expected to occur by chance in 6 out of 100 studies, we would have to say that the results failed to support the hypothesis—that the difference we obtained might well have occurred merely by chance—although we might still want to do further research to be sure. You can see that psychologists refuse to be impressed by just any old result.

By the way, many studies similar to our hypothetical one have confirmed the dangers of talking on a cell phone while driving. In one study, cell phone users, whether their phones were handheld

descriptive statistics Statistics that organize and summarize research data.

arithmetic mean An average that is calculated by adding up a set of quantities and dividing the sum by the total number of quantities in the set.

standard deviation A commonly used measure of variability that indicates the average difference between scores in a distribution and their mean.

inferential statistics Statistical procedures that allow researchers to draw inferences about how statistically meaningful a study's results are.

significance tests Statistical tests that assess how likely it is that a study's results occurred merely by chance.

Simulate Doing Simple Statistics on **mypsychlab.com**

Averages can be misleading if you don't know the extent to which events deviated from the statistical mean and how they were distributed.

or hands-free, were as impaired in their driving ability as intoxicated drivers were (Strayer, Drews, & Crouch, 2006). Because of such research, some states have made it illegal to drive while holding a cell phone to your ear. Others are considering making any cell phone use by a driver illegal. We will revisit this topic, and the general issue of multitasking, in Chapter 7.

✓•⟨**Study** and **Review** on **mypsychlab.com**

Quick Quiz

Don't try this quiz while you're driving—or doing other tasks!

Check your understanding of the descriptive–inferential distinction by mentally placing a check in the appropriate column for each phrase:

	Descriptive Statistics	Inferential Statistics
1. Summarize the data	_____	_____
2. Give likelihood of data occurring by chance	_____	_____
3. Include the mean	_____	_____
4. Give a measure of statistical significance	_____	_____
5. Tell you whether to call your mother about your results	_____	_____

Answers:

1. descriptive   2. inferential   3. descriptive   4. inferential   5. inferential

From the Laboratory to the Real World

The last step in any study is to figure out what the findings mean. Trying to understand behavior from uninterpreted findings is like trying to become fluent in Swedish by reading a Swedish–English dictionary. Just as you need the grammar of Swedish to tell you how the words fit together, psychologists need hypotheses and theories to explain how the facts that emerge from research fit together.

Choosing the Best Explanation   Sometimes it is hard to choose between competing explanations. Does cell phone use disrupt driving by impairing coordination, by increasing a driver's vulnerability to distraction, by interfering with the processing of information, by distorting the driver's perception of danger, or by some combination of these or other factors? Several explanations may fit the results equally well, which means that more research will be needed to determine the best one.

Sometimes the best interpretation of a finding does not emerge until a hypothesis has been tested in different ways. If the findings of studies using different methods converge, there is greater reason to be confident about them. On the other hand, if they conflict, researchers will know they must modify their hypotheses or do more research.

Here is an example. When psychologists compare the mental-test scores of young people and old people, they usually find that younger people consistently outscore older ones. In a **cross-sectional study**, different groups are compared at the same time:

Cross-Sectional Study
Different groups compared at one time:

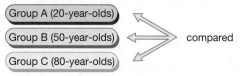

But other psychologists prefer to investigate mental abilities across the life span. In a **longitudinal study**, the same people are followed over a period of time and are reassessed at regular intervals:

Longitudinal Study
Same group compared at different times:

In contrast to cross-sectional studies, longitudinal studies find that as people age, they sometimes continue to perform as well as they ever did on many mental tests. A *general* decline in ability may

cross-sectional study A study in which individuals of different ages are compared at a given time.

longitudinal study A study in which individuals are followed and periodically reassessed over a period of time.

not occur until people reach their 70s or 80s (see Chapter 3). Why do results from the two types of studies conflict? Probably because cross-sectional studies measure generational differences. Younger generations tend to outperform older ones because they are better educated or are more familiar with the tests used. Without longitudinal studies, we might falsely conclude that all types of mental ability inevitably decline sharply with advancing age.

Judging the Result's Importance Sometimes psychologists agree on the reliability and meaning of a finding, but not on its ultimate relevance for theory or practical application. A result may be statistically significant at the "point oh-five level," yet may be small and of little consequence in everyday life because the independent variable does not explain most of the variation in people's behavior (Cumming et al., 2007; Erceg-Hurn & Mirosevich, 2008). Conversely, a result may not quite reach statistical significance yet be worth following up on. Many scholarly journals now encourage the use of statistical procedures that reveal the **effect size**—that is, how powerful the independent variable really is (how much of the variation in the data the variable accounts for). If the independent variable explains 5 percent of the variation, it's not very powerful, even if the result is statistically significant; if it explains 40 percent, it's pretty impressive.

> **Thinking Critically about "Significant" Research Findings**

One popular statistical technique, called **meta-analysis**, combines and analyzes data from many studies on a particular topic instead of assessing each study's results separately. Meta-analysis tells the researcher how much of the variation in scores across *all* the studies in the analysis can be explained by a particular variable. Suppose we did ten studies on everybody's favorite subject, gender differences. We might get contradictory results, or some results that were significant and others that were not. Meta-analysis can come to the rescue, providing us with a clearer picture.

For example, what is the reason for the gender gap in math achievement, which persists in some nations but not others? Is it largely due, as the stereotype holds, to a "natural" male superiority in math, or to gender differences in educational and professional opportunities to succeed in the sciences? A meta-analysis of studies across 69 nations, representing nearly 500,000 students ages 14 to 16, found that although boys have more positive attitudes toward math than girls, average effect sizes in actual mathematics achievement are very small. However, *national* effect sizes show considerable variability; that is, a male-female math gap is wider in some countries than others. The most powerful predictors of that cross-national variation were whether boys and girls were equally likely to be enrolled in school; the percentage of women in research jobs; and women's representation in their nation's government (Else-Quest, Hyde, & Linn, 2010).

Techniques such as meta-analysis are useful because rarely does one study prove anything, in psychology or any other field. That is why you should be suspicious of headlines that announce a sudden major scientific breakthrough based on a single study. Such breakthroughs do occur, but they are rare.

effect size The amount of variance among scores in a study accounted for by the independent variable; thus it is a measure of the strength or power of that variable.

meta-analysis A procedure for combining and analyzing data from many studies; it determines how much of the variance in scores across all studies can be explained by a particular variable.

Psychology in the News REVISITED

Now that you have finished this chapter, you are ready to explore more deeply what psychologists have learned about human behavior.

At the start of each of the remaining chapters, we will present a real news story, one that raises some fascinating psychological questions. Then, at the end of the chapter, we will revisit the story to show how the material you have learned can help you answer those questions. For now, if you are ready to share the excitement of studying human behavior; if you love mysteries and want to know not only who did it but also why they did it; if you are willing to reconsider what you think you think . . . then you are ready to read on.

Taking Psychology with You

What Psychology Can Do for You—and What it Can't

If you intend to become a psychologist or a mental health professional, you have an obvious reason for taking a course in psychology. But psychology can contribute to your life in many ways, even if you do not plan to work in the field. Here are a few things psychology can do for you:

Make you a more informed person. One purpose of education is to acquaint people with their cultural heritage and with human achievements in literature, the arts, and science. Because psychology plays a large role in contemporary society, being a well-informed person requires knowing something about psychological methods and findings.

Satisfy your curiosity about human nature. When the Greek philosopher Socrates admonished his students, "Know thyself," he was only telling them to do what most people want to do anyway. Psychology—along with the other social sciences, literature, history, and philosophy—can contribute to a better understanding of yourself and others.

Help you increase control over your life. Psychology cannot solve all your problems, but it does offer helpful techniques for handling your emotions, improving your memory, and eliminating unwanted habits. It can also foster an attitude of objectivity that is useful for analyzing your behavior and your relationships.

Help you on the job. A bachelor's degree in psychology is useful for getting a job in a helping profession, such as a welfare caseworker or a rehabilitation counselor. Anyone who works as a nurse, doctor, member of the clergy, police officer, or teacher can also put psychology to work on the job. So can waiters, flight attendants, bank tellers, salespeople, receptionists, and others whose jobs involve customer service. Finally, psychology can be useful to those whose jobs require them to predict people's behavior: labor negotiators, politicians, advertising copywriters, managers, product designers, buyers, market researchers, magicians....

Give you insights into political and social issues. Crime, drug abuse, discrimination, and war are not only social issues but also psychological ones. Psychological knowledge alone cannot solve the complex political, social, and ethical problems that plague every society, but it can help citizens make informed judgments about them. If you know how social and cultural practices affect rates of illegal drug use and abuse, this knowledge may affect your views about drug policies.

We are optimistic about psychology's role in the world, but we want to caution you that sometimes people expect things from psychology that it can't deliver. Psychology can't tell you the meaning of life. A philosophy about the purpose of life requires not only knowledge but also reflection and a willingness to learn from life's experiences. Nor does psychological understanding relieve people of responsibility for their actions. Knowing that your short temper is a result, in part, of your unhappy childhood does not give you a green light to yell at your family or mistreat your own kids. Most important, as we have repeatedly emphasized, psychology will not provide you with simple answers to complex questions.

Yet despite the complexity of behavior and the lack of simple answers to human problems, psychologists have made enormous progress in unraveling the secrets of the human brain, mind, and heart. The study of psychology will provide you with sound information, empirical findings, and the skills of critical thinking, all of which can help guide your thinking and your decisions. At the end of each chapter, starting with the next one, "Taking Psychology with You" will suggest ways to apply psychological findings to your own life—at school, on the job, or in your relationships.

"I still don't have all the answers, but I'm beginning to ask the right questions."

Summary   ((•—[**Listen** to an **audio file** of your chapter on **mypsychlab.com**

The Science of Psychology

● *Psychology* is the discipline concerned with behavior and mental processes and how they are affected by an organism's external and internal environment. Psychology's methods and reliance on *empirical evidence* distinguish it from pseudoscience and "psychobabble."

● Psychological findings sometimes confirm, but often contradict, common sense. An introductory psychology course can correct many misconceptions about human behavior. But a finding from research does not have to be surprising or counterintuitive to be scientifically important.

● Psychology's forerunners made some valid observations and had some useful insights, but without rigorous empirical methods, they also made serious errors in the description and explanation of behavior, as in the case of *phrenology*.

● The official founder of scientific psychology was Wilhelm Wundt, who established the first psychological laboratory in 1879, in Leipzig, Germany. Wundt emphasized the analysis of experience into basic elements, through *trained introspection*. A competing approach, *functionalism*, which was inspired in part by the evolutionary theories of Charles Darwin, emphasized the functions of behavior. One of its leading proponents was William James.

● Psychology as a method of psychotherapy was born in Vienna, with the work of Sigmund Freud and the establishment of *psychoanalysis*.

● Five points of view predominate today in psychology. The *biological perspective* emphasizes bodily events associated with actions, thoughts, and feelings, and also genetic contributions to behavior. Within this perspective, a popular new specialty, *evolutionary psychology*, emphasizes the purposes and functions of behavior, as functionalism did. The *learning perspective* emphasizes how the environment and a person's history affect behavior; within this perspective, *behaviorists* reject mentalistic explanations and *social–cognitive learning theorists* combine elements of behaviorism with the study of thoughts, values, and intentions. The *cognitive perspective* emphasizes mental processes in perception, problem solving, belief formation, and other human activities. The *sociocultural perspective* explores how social contexts and cultural rules affect an individual's beliefs and behavior. And the *psychodynamic perspective*, which originated with Freud's theory of psychoanalysis, emphasizes unconscious motives, conflicts, and desires; it differs greatly from the other approaches in its methods and standards of evidence.

● Each approach has made important contributions to psychology, but many, if not most, psychologists draw on more than one school of thought.

What Psychologists Do

● Psychologists do research and teach in colleges and universities, provide mental health services (*psychological practice*), and conduct research and apply findings in a wide variety of nonacademic settings. *Applied psychology* is concerned with the practical uses of psychological knowledge. *Basic psychology* is concerned with knowledge for its own sake.

● *Psychotherapist* is an unregulated term for anyone who does therapy, including people who have no credentials or training at all. Licensed therapists differ according to their training and approach. *Clinical psychologists* have a Ph.D., an Ed.D., or a Psy.D.; *psychiatrists* have an M.D.; *psychoanalysts* are trained in psychoanalytic institutes; and licensed clinical social workers, counselors with various specialties, and marriage, family, and child counselors may have a variety of postgraduate degrees. Many psychologists are concerned about an increase in poorly trained psychotherapists who lack credentials or a firm understanding of research methods and findings.

Critical and Scientific Thinking in Psychology

● One benefit of studying psychology is the development of *critical-thinking* skills and attitudes. Critical thinkers ask questions, define terms clearly, examine the evidence, analyze assumptions and biases, avoid emotional reasoning, avoid oversimplification, consider alternative interpretations, and tolerate uncertainty. These activities not only are useful in ordinary life but also are the basis of the scientific method. Scientists are required to state hypotheses and predictions precisely and formulate operational definitions ("define your terms"); to gather empirical evidence; to comply with the *principle of falsifiability* ("analyze assumptions") and resist the *confirmation bias*; to be cautious in settling on a theory ("consider other interpretations"); and to resist drawing firm conclusions until results are replicated ("tolerate uncertainty").

Descriptive Studies: Establishing the Facts

● Psychological scientists try whenever possible to use samples that are representative of the larger population they wish to describe. In practice, they must often rely on college students as subjects. Most of the time, that does not pose a problem, but some conclusions based on college student samples may not generalize to the larger population, and thus should be accepted with caution until the research is replicated with nonstudents.

● *Descriptive methods* allow psychologists to describe and predict behavior but not necessarily to choose one explanation over others. Such methods include case studies, observational studies, psychological tests, and surveys, as well as correlational methods.

● *Case studies* are detailed descriptions of individuals. They are often used by clinicians, and they can be valuable in exploring new research topics and addressing questions that would otherwise be difficult to study. But because information is often missing or hard to interpret, and because the person under study may not be representative of people in general, case studies are typically sources rather than tests of hypotheses.

● In *observational studies*, researchers systematically observe and record behavior without interfering in any way with the behavior. *Naturalistic observation* is used to find out how people behave in their natural environments. *Laboratory observation* allows more control and the use of special equipment; behavior in the laboratory, however, may differ from behavior in natural contexts.

● *Psychological tests* are used to measure and evaluate personality traits, emotional states, aptitudes, interests, abilities, and values. A good test is one that has been *standardized*, is scored using established *norms*, and has both *reliability* and *validity*. Critics have questioned the reliability and validity of even some widely used tests, such as the IQ test and the SAT.

● *Surveys* are questionnaires or interviews that ask people directly about their experiences, attitudes, and opinions. They are difficult to do well; sampling problems are often an issue, and the results can be affected by a *volunteer bias*. Findings can also be affected by biased questions and by the fact that respondents sometimes lie, misremember their experiences, or misinterpret the questions.

Correlational Studies: Looking for Relationships

● In descriptive research, studies that look for relationships between phenomena are known as *correlational*. A *correlation* is a measure of the strength of a positive or negative relationship between two variables, and is expressed by the *coefficient of correlation*. An *illusory correlation* may occur because of a coincidental link between two variables. A correlation does not necessarily demonstrate a causal relationship between the variables.

The Experiment: Hunting for Causes

● *Experiments* allow researchers to control the situation being studied, manipulate an *independent variable*, and assess the effects of the manipulation on a *dependent variable*. Because of the element of manipulation, ethical guidelines are especially important in experimental research. These guidelines govern studies with human beings, who must give *informed consent* before participating, and also with animals, which must be treated humanely.

● Experimental studies usually require a comparison or *control condition*, and often involve *random assignment* of subjects to experimental and control groups. In some studies, people in the control group receive a *placebo*. *Single-blind* and *double-blind* procedures can be used to prevent the expectations of the subjects or the experimenter from affecting the results. Because experiments allow conclusions about cause and effect, they have long been the method of choice in psychology. However, like laboratory observations, experiments create a special situation that may call forth behavior not typical in other environments. Many psychologists, therefore, have called for more *field research*.

Evaluating the Findings

● Psychologists use *descriptive statistics*, such as the *arithmetic mean* and *standard deviation*, to summarize data. They use *inferential statistics* to find out how impressive the data are. *Significance tests* tell researchers how likely it is that the results of a study occurred merely by chance. The results are said to be *statistically significant* if this likelihood is very low.

● Choosing among competing interpretations of a finding can be difficult, and care must be taken to avoid going beyond the facts. Sometimes the best interpretation does not emerge until a hypothesis has been tested in more than one way, such as by using both *cross-sectional* and *longitudinal methods*.

● Statistical significance does not always imply real-world importance because the amount of variation in the data accounted for by a particular variable—the *effect size*—may be small. Conversely, a result that does not quite reach significance may be potentially useful. Therefore, many psychologists are now turning to other statistical measures such as the technique of *meta-analysis*, which reveals how much of the variation in scores across many different studies can be explained by a particular variable.

Taking Psychology with You

● Psychology is useful in many ways—for your personal life, your professional life, and your understanding of the world. But critical thinkers realize that psychology cannot solve all of their problems or absolve them of responsibility for faults and misdeeds.

Key Terms

Use this list to check your understanding of terms and people in this chapter. If you have trouble with a term, you can find it on the page listed.

The Science of Psychology

Psychology is the discipline concerned with behavior and mental processes and how they are affected by an organism's physical state, mental state, and external environment. Unlike pseudoscientific approaches to behavior, it relies on **empirical** data.

The Birth of Modern Psychology

- Wilhelm Wundt founded the first psychology laboratory in Leipzig, Germany, in 1879, and emphasized the analysis of experience through trained introspection.
- American William James emphasized the adaptive nature of behavior, an approach known as **functionalism.**
- Sigmund Freud developed **psychoanalysis,** an early form of psychotherapy, in Vienna, Austria.

Today's Five Major Psychological Perspectives

- The **biological perspective** focuses on how bodily events interact with the external environment to affect behavior, feelings, and thoughts.
- The **learning perspective** emphasizes the environment's effect on behavior.
- The **cognitive perspective** emphasizes mental processes in reasoning, memory, perception, language, problem solving, and beliefs.
- The **sociocultural perspective** focuses on the influence of social and cultural forces on behavior.
- The **psychodynamic perspective** looks at unconscious dynamics, such as inner forces, conflicts, and instinctual energy.

What Psychologists Do

- Conduct research in **basic psychology**, to gain knowledge for its own sake; and **applied psychology**, to find practical uses for knowledge.
- Teach.
- Provide mental health services (psychological practice).
- Consult with business, governmental, and other groups to apply the findings of research.

- Psychotherapist is an unregulated term.
- Clinical psychologists have Ph.D., Ed.D., or Psy.D. degrees.
- Psychiatrists have M.D. degrees.
- Psychoanalysts have completed training in psychoanalytic institutes.

Critical and Scientific Thinking in Psychology

Critical thinking rests on eight basic guidelines:
- Ask questions.
- Define terms.
- Examine the evidence for a claim.
- Analyze assumptions (beliefs taken for granted) and biases (beliefs that prevent us from considering the evidence fairly).
  — **Principle of falsifiability**, the statement of a hypothesis in such a way that it can be disproved by counterevidence
  — **Confirmation bias**, the tendency to look for and accept evidence that supports our beliefs and ignore evidence that disconfirms them.
- Avoid emotional reasoning.
- Avoid oversimplification.
- Consider alternative explanations.
  — In science, the goal is to develop a **theory**, an organized system of assumptions and principles that explain a set of phenomena and their interrelationships.
- Tolerate uncertainty.
  — In science, resist drawing firm conclusions until others have *replicated* the study and gotten the same results.

Principle of falsifiablility

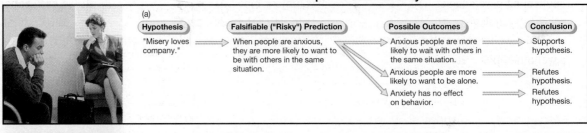

(a)

Hypothesis	Falsifiable ("Risky") Prediction	Possible Outcomes	Conclusion
"Misery loves company."	When people are anxious, they are more likely to want to be with others in the same situation.	Anxious people are more likely to wait with others in the same situation.	Supports hypothesis.
		Anxious people are more likely to want to be alone.	Refutes hypothesis.
		Anxiety has no effect on behavior.	Refutes hypothesis.

(b)

Hypothesis	Nonfalsifiable Prediction	Possible Outcomes	Conclusion
"Dowsing reveals subterranean water."	Dowsers will reliably find water—*unless* the planets are misaligned, observers give off bad vibes, etc.	Dowsers find water.	Supports hypothesis.
		Dowsers do not find water.	Dowsers conclude that results support hypothesis anyway.

Research Methods in Psychology

Representative Samples

A **representative sample** is a group of partici-pants that accurately represents the larger popu-lation that the researcher is interested in.

Descriptive Studies: Establishing the Facts

- **Case study:** a detailed description of a particular individual, based on observation or formal psy-chological testing.
- **Observational study:** careful observation, measurement, and recording of behavior without intruding on the subjects.
- **Psychological tests:** assessment instruments that measure and evaluate personality traits, emotional states, aptitudes, interest, abilities, and values.
- **Surveys:** questionnaires or interviews that ask people directly about their experiences, attitudes, or opinions.

Correlational Studies: Looking for Relationships

A **positive** or **negative correlation** is a measure of the strength of a relationship between two variables.

- A **Coefficient of correlation** summarizes the strength and direction of a relationship.
- A correlation does not establish cause and effect.

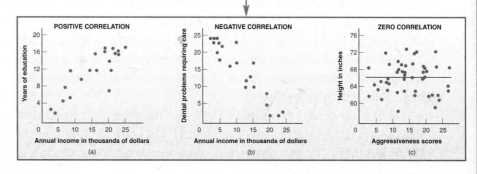

The Experiment: Hunting for Causes

- **Experiments** allow researchers to control all aspects of a situation except the **independent variable**, which is ma-nipulated to determine its effects on a **dependent variable**.

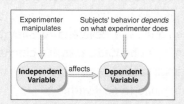

- Experiments usually require a **control condition** in which subjects are not exposed to the experimental condition.
- Participation in an experimental or control group is deter-mined by **random assignment.**
- Drug experiments typically include the use of a **placebo,** an inactive substance used as a control.

Experimenter Effects

The expectations of participants can influence a study's results. To counteract this problem, experimenters may conduct:

- A **single-blind study,** an experiment in which subjects do not know whether they are in an experimental or a control group.
- A **double-blind study,** an experiment in which neither the participants nor the experimenters know which par-ticipants are in the control group and which are in the experimental group until after the results are tallied.

Evaluating the Findings

- **Descriptive statistics** (including the **arithmetic mean** and **standard deviation**) organize and summarize data.
- **Inferential statistics** help to determine how meaningful the findings are.
- **Significance tests** measure the probability that the study's findings could have occurred by chance.
- Interpretation of findings may need to await studies using different methods. For example, **cross-sectional** studies compare subjects of different ages; **longitudinal** methods follow subjects over many years.

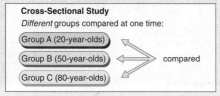

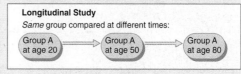

- Statistical procedures can reveal the **effect size**, how powerful the independent variable is.
- **Meta-analysis** combines and analyzes data from many studies to determine how much of the variance across all studies can be explained by a particular variable.

Michael Jackson Memorial Draws Thousands

LOS ANGELES, July 7, 2009. Thousands of friends, family, and fans gathered at the Staples Center today to pay tribute to Michael Jackson, the King of Pop. Jackson died of cardiac arrest at age 50, at his rented mansion on June 25. The organizer of the memorial gave away 17,500 free tickets to fans through an online lottery that drew over 1.2 million applicants in 24 hours and over a half billion hits on its web page.

At the ceremony, Jackson's 11-year-old daughter Paris tearfully told the crowd, "Ever since I was born, Daddy has been the best father you could ever imagine." Berry Gordy, founder of Motown Records, lauded him as "the greatest entertainer who ever lived."

Throughout his life, people have argued over who Michael Jackson really was. Many think of him simply as an enormously gifted entertainer who transformed the music video and created a unique choreographic style. Others remember him as a philanthropist who raised more than $300 million for dozens of charities and for his own Heal the World Foundation. On hearing of his death, one of his closest friends, Elizabeth Taylor, said they had shared "the purest, most giving love" and that she could not imagine life without him.

Yet Jackson was also the subject of many sensational reports and rumors that painted a different picture. His androgynous appearance, his change in skin color from dark brown to pale white, and the marked changes in his facial features inspired debate about his comfort with his gender and racial identities. (Jackson said the change in skin color was due to treatment for a skin condition and he admitted to only two rhinoplasties.)

The biggest controversy surrounding the star concerned allegations of child sexual abuse. A 13-year-old boy and the boy's father accused him of abuse, but Jackson's insurance company settled out of court and Jackson was never charged. Later, another boy made a similar accusation and Jackson was charged with seven counts of child molestation. He was eventually acquitted on all counts.

The many twists and turns of Jackson's life led some to refer to him as "Wacko Jacko," a term he despised. But at the memorial, the Reverend Al Sharpton got a standing ovation when he told Jackson's children, "Wasn't nothing strange about your Daddy. It was strange what your Daddy had to deal with."

Michael Jackson (in purple pants) as a child with the Jackson Five and as the superstar he became.

Theories of Personality

Who was the real Michael Jackson? Was he a "born performer," as his childhood stardom with the Jackson Five would suggest? How much of his life was shaped by childhood experiences with verbal and physical abuse? Was his personality characterized primarily by the sweetness and generosity that friends like Elizabeth Taylor saw, by neurotic patterns of coping with the celebrity that the world conferred on him, by his childlike attraction to children, or by other factors? Who was the real Michael Jackson? *Was* there a real one?

In this chapter, we will see how psychologists answer such questions—how they define and study personality. **Personality** refers to a distinctive pattern of behavior, mannerisms, thoughts, motives, and emotions that characterizes an individual over time and across different situations. This pattern consists of many distinctive **traits**, habitual ways of behaving, thinking, and feeling: shy, outgoing, friendly, hostile, gloomy, confident, and so on.

We will begin with the oldest theory of personality, the psychodynamic view, so that you will have a sense of how influential it was, why it still appeals to some, and why many of its ideas have become outdated. Next we will consider evidence for the newest theory, the genetic view. Few scientists think anymore that babies are tiny lumps of clay, shaped entirely by their experiences, or that parents alone determine whether their infant becomes an adventurer, a sourpuss, a worrywart, . . . or Michael Jackson. On the other hand, if only half of the human variation in personality traits is due to genetics, what is responsible for the other half?

To answer that question, we will then examine leading approaches to personality that are neither psychodynamic nor biological: the environmental approach, which emphasizes the role of social learning, situations, parents, and peers; the cultural approach, which emphasizes cultural influences on traits and behavior; and the humanist and existential approaches, which emphasize self-determination and people's own view of themselves. When we are done, we will return to the puzzle of Michael Jackson and the forces that may have contributed to his unique personality.

personality A distinctive and relatively stable pattern of behavior, thoughts, motives, and emotions that characterizes an individual.

trait A characteristic of an individual, describing a habitual way of behaving, thinking, or feeling.

psychoanalysis A theory of personality and a method of psychotherapy, originally formulated by Sigmund Freud, that emphasizes unconscious motives and conflicts.

psychodynamic theories Theories that explain behavior and personality in terms of unconscious energy dynamics within the individual.

id In psychoanalysis, the part of personality containing inherited psychic energy, particularly sexual and aggressive instincts.

Sigmund Freud (1856–1939)

YOU are about to learn...

- Freud's theory of the structure and development of personality.
- Carl Jung's theory of the collective unconscious and how it applies to Harry Potter's archenemy, Lord Voldemort.
- the nature of the "objects" in the object-relations approach to personality.
- why many psychologists reject most psychodynamic ideas.

Psychodynamic Theories of Personality

A man apologizes for "displacing" his frustrations at work onto his family. A woman suspects that she is "repressing" a childhood trauma. An alcoholic reveals that he is no longer "in denial" about his drinking. A teacher informs a divorcing couple that their 8-year-old child is "regressing" to immature behavior. All of this language about displacing, repressing, denying, and regressing can be traced to the first psychodynamic theory of personality, Sigmund Freud's theory of **psychoanalysis**.

Freud's theory is called "psychodynamic" because it emphasizes the movement of psychological energy within the person, in the form of attachments, conflicts, and motivations. (Freud did not use "dynamic" in today's sense, to mean "powerful" or "energetic." *Dynamics* is a term from physics that refers to the motion and balance of systems under the action of outside or internal forces.) Modern **psychodynamic theories** have changed a great deal since Freud's time, and they differ from one another; but they all share an emphasis on unconscious processes going on within the mind. They also share an assumption that adult personality and ongoing problems are formed primarily by experiences in early childhood. These experiences produce unconscious thoughts and feelings, which later lead to characteristic habits, conflicts, and often self-defeating behavior.

Freud and Psychoanalysis

To enter the world of Sigmund Freud is to enter a realm of unconscious motives, passions, guilty secrets, unspeakable yearnings, and conflicts between desire and duty. These unseen forces, Freud believed, have far more power over our personalities than our conscious intentions do. The unconscious reveals itself, said Freud, in art, dreams, jokes, apparent accidents, and slips of the tongue (which came to be called "Freudian slips"). According to Freud (1920/1960), the British member of Parliament who referred to the "honourable member from Hell" when he meant to say "from Hull" was revealing his actual, unconscious appraisal of his colleague.

The Structure of Personality In Freud's theory, personality consists of three major systems: the id, the ego, and the superego. Any action we take or problem we have results from the interaction and degree of balance among these systems (Freud, 1905, 1920/1960, 1923/1962).

The **id**, which is present at birth, is the reservoir of unconscious psychological energies and the motives to avoid pain and obtain pleasure. The id contains two competing instincts: the life, or sexual, instinct (fueled by psychic energy called the **libido**) and the death, or aggressive, instinct. As energy builds up in the id, tension results. The id may discharge this tension in the form of reflex actions, physical symptoms, or uncensored mental images and unbidden thoughts.

The **ego**, the second system to emerge, is a referee between the needs of instinct and the demands of society. It bows to the realities of life, putting a rein on the id's desire for sex and aggression until a suitable, socially appropriate outlet for them can be found. The ego, said Freud, is both conscious and unconscious, and it represents "reason and good sense."

The **superego**, the last system of personality to develop, is the voice of conscience, representing morality and parental authority. The superego judges the activities of the id, handing out good feelings of pride and satisfaction when you do something well and handing out miserable feelings of guilt and shame when you break the rules. The superego is partly conscious but largely unconscious.

According to Freud, the healthy personality must keep all three systems in balance. Someone

"VERY WELL I'LL INTRODUCE YOU. EGO MEET ID. NOW GET BACK TO WORK."

who is too controlled by the id is governed by impulse and selfish desires. Someone who is too controlled by the superego is rigid, moralistic, and bossy. Someone who has a weak ego is unable to balance personal needs and wishes with social duties and realistic limitations.

If a person feels anxious or threatened when the wishes of the id conflict with social rules, the ego has weapons at its command to relieve the tension. These unconscious strategies, called **defense mechanisms**, deny or distort reality, but they also protect us from conflict and anxiety. They become unhealthy only when they cause self-defeating behavior and emotional problems. Freud, his daughter Anna Freud, and later other analysts identified a number of defenses; here are five of the primary ones (A. Freud, 1967; Vaillant, 1992):

1 **Repression** occurs when a threatening idea, memory, or emotion is blocked from consciousness. A woman who had a frightening childhood experience that she cannot remember, for example, is said to be repressing her memory of it. Freud used the term *repression* to mean both unconscious expulsion of disturbing material from awareness and conscious suppression of such material. However, modern analysts tend to think of it only as an unconscious defense mechanism.

2 **Projection** occurs when a person's own unacceptable or threatening feelings are repressed and then attributed to someone else. A person who is embarrassed about having sexual feelings toward members of a different ethnic group, for example, may project this discomfort onto them, saying, "Those people are dirty-minded and oversexed."

3 **Displacement** occurs when people direct their emotions (especially anger) toward things, animals, or other people that are not the real object of their feelings. A boy who is forbidden to express anger toward his father may "take it out" on his toys or his younger sister. When displacement serves a higher cultural or socially useful purpose, as in the creation of art or inventions, it is called *sublimation*. Freud argued that society has a duty to help people sublimate their unacceptable impulses for the sake of civilization. Sexual passion, he observed, is often sublimated into the creation of art or literature.

4 **Regression** occurs when a person reverts to a previous phase of psychological development. An 8-year-old boy who is anxious about his parents' divorce may regress to earlier habits of thumb sucking or clinging. Adults may regress to immature behavior when they are under pressure—say, by having temper tantrums when they don't get their way.

5 **Denial** occurs when people refuse to admit that something unpleasant is happening, such as mistreatment by a partner; that they have a problem, such as drinking too much; or that they are feeling a forbidden emotion, such as anger. Denial protects a person's self-image and preserves the illusion of invulnerability: "It can't happen to me."

The Development of Personality Freud argued that personality develops in a series of **psychosexual stages**, in which sexual energy takes different forms as the child matures. Each new stage produces a certain amount of frustration, conflict, and anxiety. If these are not resolved properly, normal development may be interrupted, and the

libido (li-BEE-do) In psychoanalysis, the psychic energy that fuels the life or sexual instincts of the id.

ego In psychoanalysis, the part of personality that represents reason, good sense, and rational self-control.

superego In psychoanalysis, the part of personality that represents conscience, morality, and social standards.

defense mechanisms Methods used by the ego to prevent unconscious anxiety or threatening thoughts from entering consciousness.

psychosexual stages In Freud's theory, the idea that sexual energy takes different forms as the child matures; the stages are oral, anal, phallic (Oedipal), latency, and genital.

"I'm sorry, I'm not speaking to anyone tonight. My defense mechanisms seem to be out of order."

Oedipus complex In psychoanalysis, a conflict occurring in the phallic (Oedipal) stage, in which a child desires the parent of the other sex and views the same-sex parent as a rival.

child may remain *fixated*, or stuck, at the current stage. Some people, he thought, remain fixated at the *oral stage*, which occurs during the first year of life, when babies experience the world through their mouths. As adults, they will seek oral gratification in smoking, overeating, nail biting, or chewing on pencils; some may become clinging and dependent, like a nursing child. Others remain fixated at the *anal stage*, at ages 2 to 3, when toilet training and control of bodily wastes are the key issues. They may become "anal retentive," holding everything in, obsessive about neatness and cleanliness. Or they may become just the opposite, "anal expulsive"—messy and disorganized.

For Freud, however, the most crucial stage for the formation of personality was the *phallic (Oedipal) stage*, which lasts roughly from age 3 to age 5 or 6. During this stage, said Freud, the child unconsciously wishes to possess the parent of the other sex and to get rid of the parent of the same sex. Children often proudly announce, "I'm going to marry Daddy (or Mommy) when I grow up," and they reject the same-sex "rival." Freud labeled this phenomenon the **Oedipus complex**, after the Greek legend of King Oedipus, who unwittingly killed his father and married his mother.

Boys and girls, Freud believed, go through the Oedipal stage differently. Boys are discovering the pleasure and pride of having a penis, so when they see a naked girl for the first time, they are horrified. Their unconscious exclaims (in effect), "Her penis has been cut off! Who could have done such a thing to her? Why, it must have been her powerful father. And if he could do it to her, my father could do it to me!" This realization, said Freud, causes the boy to repress his desire for his mother and identify with his father. He accepts his father's authority and the father's standards of conscience and morality; the superego has emerged.

Freud admitted that he did not quite know what to make of girls, who, lacking a penis, could not go through the same steps. He speculated that a girl, upon

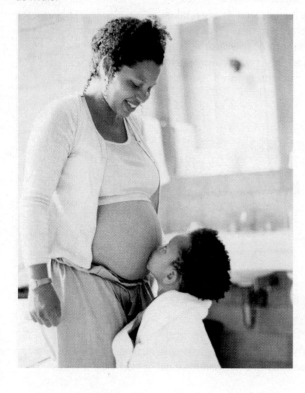

Freud believed that during the Oedipal stage, little boys fantasize about marrying their mothers and regard their fathers as rivals.

discovering male anatomy, would panic that she had only a puny clitoris instead of a stately penis. She would conclude that she already had lost her penis. As a result, Freud said, girls do not have the powerful motivating fear that boys do to give up their Oedipal feelings and develop a strong superego; they have only a lingering sense of "penis envy."

Freud believed that when the Oedipus complex is resolved, at about age 5 or 6, the child's personality is fundamentally formed. Unconscious conflicts with parents, unresolved fixations and guilt, and attitudes toward the same and the other sex will continue to replay themselves throughout life. The child settles into a supposedly nonsexual *latency* stage, in preparation for the *genital stage*, which begins at puberty and leads to adult sexuality.

In Freud's view, therefore, your adult personality is shaped by how you progressed through the early psychosexual stages, which defense mechanisms you developed to reduce anxiety, and whether your ego is strong enough to balance the conflict between the id (what you would like to do) and the superego (your conscience).

As you might imagine, Freud's ideas were not exactly received with yawns. Sexual feelings in 5-year-olds! Repressed longings in respectable adults! Unconscious meanings in dreams! Penis envy! This was strong stuff in the early years of the twentieth century, and before long, psychoanalysis had captured the public imagination in Europe and America. But it also produced a sharp rift with the emerging schools of empirical psychology.

This rift continues to divide scholars today. Many believe that the overall framework of Freud's theory is timeless and brilliant, even if some specific ideas have proved faulty (Westen, 1998). Others think that psychoanalytic theory is nonsense, with little empirical support, and that Freud was not the theoretical genius, impartial scientist, or even successful clinician that he claimed to be. On the contrary, Freud often bullied his patients into accepting his explanations of their symptoms and ignored all evidence disconfirming his ideas (McNally, 2003; Powell & Boer, 1995; Webster, 1995).

On the positive side, Freud welcomed women into the profession of psychoanalysis, wrote eloquently about the devastating results to women of society's suppression of their sexuality, and argued, ahead of his time, that homosexuality was neither a sin nor a perversion but a "variation of the sexual function" and "nothing to be ashamed of" (Freud, 1961). Freud was thus a mixture of intellectual vision and blindness, sensitivity and arrogance. His provocative ideas left a powerful legacy to psychology, one that others began to tinker with immediately.

✓—|Study and
Review on
mypsychlab.com

Quick Quiz

Have Freudian concepts registered in your unconscious? Which Freudian concepts do the following events suggest?

1. A 4-year-old girl wants to snuggle on Daddy's lap but refuses to kiss her mother. *oedi*
2. A celibate priest writes poetry about sexual passion. — *sublimation*
3. A man who is angry with his boss shouts at his kids for making noise. — *displacement*
4. A racist justifies segregation by saying that black men are only interested in sex with white women. *projection*
5. A 9-year-old boy who moves to a new city starts having tantrums. — *regression*

Answers:

1. Oedipus complex 2. sublimation 3. displacement 4. projection 5. regression

Other Psychodynamic Approaches

Some of Freud's followers stayed in the psychoanalytic tradition and modified Freud's theories from within. Women, as you might imagine, were not too pleased about "penis envy." Clara Thompson (1943/1973) and Karen Horney [HORN-eye] (1926/1973) argued that it was insulting and unscientific to claim that half the human race is dissatisfied with its anatomy. When women feel inferior to men, they said, we should look for explanations in the disadvantages that women live with and their second-class status. Other psychoanalysts broke away from Freud, or were actively rejected by him, and went off to start their own schools.

Jungian Theory Carl Jung (1875–1961) was originally one of Freud's closest friends and a member of his inner circle, but the friendship ended with a furious quarrel about the nature of the unconscious. In addition to the individual's own unconscious, said Jung (1967), all human beings share a vast **collective unconscious**, containing universal memories, symbols, images, and themes, which he called *archetypes*.

An archetype can be an image, such as the "magic circle," called a *mandala* in Eastern religions, which Jung thought symbolizes the unity of life and "the totality of the self." Or it can be a figure found in fairy tales, legends, and popular stories, such as the Hero, the nurturing Earth Mother, the Powerful Father, or the Wicked Witch. It can even be an aspect of the self. For example, the *shadow* archetype reflects the prehistoric fear of wild animals and represents the bestial, evil side of human nature. Scholars have found that some basic archetypes, such as the Hero and the Earth Mother, do appear in the stories and images of virtually every society

(Campbell, 1949/1968; Neher, 1996). Jungians would consider the Joker, Darth Vader, Dracula, the Dark Lord Sauron, and Harry Potter's tormentor Voldemort as expressions of the shadow archetype.

Although Jung shared with Freud a fascination with the darker aspects of the personality, he had more confidence in the positive, forward-moving strengths of the ego. He believed that people are motivated not only by past conflicts but also by their future goals and their desire to fulfill themselves. Jung was also among the first to identify extroversion/ introversion as a basic dimension of personality. Nonetheless, many of Jung's ideas were more suited to mysticism and philosophy than to empirical psychology, which may be why so many Jungian ideas later became popular with New Age movements.

The Object-Relations School Freud essentially regarded the baby as if it were an independent, greedy little organism ruled by its own instinctive desires; other people were relevant only insofar as they gratified the infant's drives or blocked them. But by the 1950s, increased awareness of the importance of human attachments led to a different view of infancy, put forward by the **object-relations school**, which Melanie Klein, D. W. Winnicott, and others developed in Great Britain. To object-relations theorists, the central problem in life is to find a balance between the need for independence and the need for others.

In *The Wizard of Oz*, the Wicked Witch of the West is a beloved example of the archetype of evil.

collective unconscious
In Jungian theory, the universal memories and experiences of humankind, represented in the symbols, stories, and images (archetypes) that occur across all cultures.

According to object-relations theory, a baby constructs unconscious representations of his or her parents that will influence the child's relations with others throughout life.

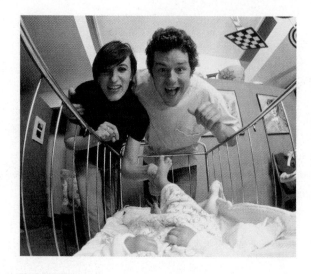

This balance requires constant adjustment to separations and losses: small ones that occur during quarrels, moderate ones such as leaving home for the first time, and major ones such as divorce or death. The way we react to these separations, according to object-relations analysts, is largely determined by our experiences in the first year or two of life. The baby will find parts of himself or herself that the mother appreciates and values, to get her recognition. If the baby's need for recognition goes unheeded, the baby's personality will be warped. The infant may develop what Winnicott called a "false self," because certain parts of the baby's "true self" remain undeveloped (Orbach, 2009).

The reason for the clunky word *object* in object-relations school, instead of the warmer word *human* or *parent*, is that the infant's attachment is not only to a real person (usually the mother) but also to the infant's evolving perception of her. The child creates a *mental representation* of the mother—someone who is kind or fierce, protective or rejecting. The child's representations of important adults, whether realistic or distorted, unconsciously affect personality throughout life, influencing whether the person relates to others with trust or suspicion, acceptance or criticism.

The object-relations school also departs from Freudian theory regarding the nature of male and female development (Sagan, 1988; Winnicott, 1957/1990). In the object-relations view, children of both sexes identify first with the mother. Girls, who are the same sex as the mother, do not need to separate from her; the mother treats a daughter as an extension of herself. But boys must break away from the mother to develop a masculine identity; the mother encourages a son to be independent and separate. Thus men, in this view, develop more

object-relations school
A psychodynamic approach that emphasizes the importance of the infant's first two years of life and the baby's formative relationships, especially with the mother.

rigid boundaries between themselves and other people than women do.

Evaluating Psychodynamic Theories

Although modern psychodynamic theorists differ in many ways, they share a general belief that to understand an individual's personality we must explore the unconscious dynamics of that person's mind. Many psychologists in other fields, however, regard most psychodynamic ideas as literary metaphors rather than as scientific explanations (Cioffi, 1998; Crews, 1998). They point out that most of the cornerstone assumptions in psychoanalytic theory, such as the notion that the mind "represses" traumatic experiences, have not been supported scientifically (McNally, 2003; Rofé, 2008; see Chapter 8). Object-relations analysts make all kinds of assumptions about what an infant feels and wants, but how do they know that a "true self" is being suppressed? Moreover, psychological scientists have shown that psychodynamic theories are guilty of three scientific failings:

> **Thinking Critically about Psychodynamic Ideas**

1 Violating the principle of falsifiability. As we saw in Chapter 1, a theory that is impossible to disconfirm in principle is not scientific. Many psychodynamic concepts about unconscious motivations are, in fact, impossible to confirm or disconfirm. Followers often accept an idea because it seems intuitively right or their experience seems to support it. Anyone who doubts the idea or offers disconfirming evidence is then accused of being defensive or in denial.

2 Drawing universal principles from the experiences of a few atypical patients. Freud and most of his followers generalized from a few individuals, often patients in therapy, to all human beings. Of course, sometimes case studies can generate valid insights about human behavior. The problem occurs when observers fail to confirm their observations by studying larger, more representative samples and including appropriate control groups. For example, some psychodynamically oriented therapists, believing in Freud's notion of a childhood latency stage, have assumed that if a child masturbates or enjoys sex play, the child has probably been sexually molested. But research finds that masturbation and sexual curiosity are not found just in abused children; these are normal and common childhood behaviors (Bancroft, 2006; Friedrich et al., 1998).

3 **Basing theories of personality development on the retrospective accounts of adults.** Most psychodynamic theorists have not observed random samples of children at different ages, as modern child psychologists do, to construct their theories of development. Instead they have worked backward, creating theories based on themes in adults' recollections of childhood. The analysis of memories can be an illuminating way to achieve insights about our lives; in fact, it is the only way we can think about our own lives! But, as we discuss in Chapter 8, memory is often inaccurate, influenced as much by what is going on in our lives now as by what happened in the past. That is why, if you are currently not getting along with your mother, you may remember all the times when she was hard on you and forget the counterexamples of her kindness.

Retrospective analysis has another problem: It creates an *illusion of causality* between events. People often assume that if A came before B, then A must have caused B. If your mother spent three months in the hospital when you were 5 years old and today you feel shy and insecure in college, an object-relations analyst might draw a connection between the two facts. But a lot of other things could be causing your shyness and insecurity, such as being away from home for the first time, at a large and impersonal college. When psychologists conduct longitudinal studies, following people from childhood to adulthood, they often get a very different picture of causality from the one that emerges by looking backward (see Chapter 3).

Despite these serious problems, some psychodynamic concepts have been empirically tested and validated. Researchers have identified unconscious processes in thought, memory, and behavior (Bargh & Morsella, 2008). They have found evidence for the major defense mechanisms, such as projection, denial, and displacement (Baumeister, Dale, & Sommer, 1998; Cramer, 2000; Marcus-Newhall et al., 2000). They have demonstrated the interaction of mind and body in the generation of stress-related physical problems. And they have confirmed the important psychodynamic idea that we are often unaware of the motives behind our own puzzling or self-defeating actions.

Some psychodynamic theories can be tested empirically, such as Freud's belief that playing or observing aggressive sports will channel aggressive energy into socially accepted forms. But empirical research finds just the opposite: Aggressive sports often *increase* the hostility and aggression of participants and observers, such as these soccer fans.

✓• **Study** and **Review** on **mypsychlab.com**

Quick Quiz

Are you feeling defensive about answering this quiz?

1. An 8-year-old boy is hitting classmates and disobeying his teacher. Which of the following explanations of his behavior might come from a Freudian, Jungian, or object-relations analyst?
   a. The boy is expressing his *shadow* archetype. — *Jung*
   b. The boy is expressing the aggressive energy of the id and has not developed enough ego control. — *Freud*
   c. The boy has had unusual difficulty separating from his mother and is compensating by behaving aggressively. — *object relation analyst*
2. What criticism of all three of the preceding explanations might a psychological scientist make?
3. In the 1950s and 1960s, many psychoanalysts, observing unhappy gay men who had sought therapy, concluded that homosexuality was a mental illness. What violation of the scientific method were they committing?

Answers:

1. a. Jung **b.** Freud **c.** object-relations analyst **2.** All three explanations are nonfalsifiable; that is, there is no way to disconfirm them or confirm them. They are just subjective interpretations. **3.** The analysts were drawing conclusions from patients in therapy and failing to test these conclusions with gay men who were not in therapy or with heterosexuals. When such research was done using appropriate control groups, it turned out that gay men were not more mentally disturbed or depressed than heterosexuals (Hooker, 1957).

YOU are about to learn...

- whether you can trust tests that tell you what "personality type" you are.

- how psychologists can tell which personality traits are more central or important than others.

- the five dimensions of personality that describe people the world over.

The Modern Study of Personality

People love to fit themselves and their friends into "types"; they have been doing it forever. Early Greek philosophers thought our personalities fell into four fundamental categories depending on mixes of body fluids. If you were an angry, irritable sort of person, you supposedly had an excess of choler, and even now the word *choleric* describes a hothead. If you were sluggish and unemotional, you supposedly had an excess of phlegm, making you a "phlegmatic" type.

The four basic personality types

Popular Personality Tests

That particular theory is long gone, but other unscientific tests of personality types still exist, aimed at predicting how people will do at work, whether they will get along with others, or whether they will succeed as leaders. One such test, the Myers-Briggs Type Indicator, is hugely popular in business, at motivational seminars, and with matchmaking services; at least 2.5 million Americans a year take it (Gladwell, 2004). The test assigns people to one of 16 different types, depending on how the individual scores on the dimensions of introverted or extroverted, logical or intuitive. Unfortunately, the Myers-Briggs test is not much more reliable than measuring body fluids; one study found that fewer than half of the respondents scored as the same type a mere five weeks later. And there is little evidence that knowledge of a person's type reliably predicts behavior on the job or in relationships (Barbuto, 1997; Paul, 2004; Pittenger, 1993). Equally useless are many of the tests that some businesses and government agencies require their employees to take, hoping to predict which "types" are apt to steal, take drugs, or be disloyal on the job (Ehrenreich, 2001).

Thinking Critically about Personality Tests

In contrast, many measures of personality traits *are* scientifically valid and useful in research. These **objective tests (inventories)** are standardized questionnaires requiring written responses, typically to multiple-choice or true–false items. They provide information about literally hundreds of different aspects of personality, including needs, values, interests, self-esteem, emotional problems, and typical ways of responding to situations. Using well-constructed inventories, psychologists have identified hundreds of traits, ranging from sensation seeking (the enjoyment of risk) to erotophobia (the fear of sex).

Core Personality Traits

Are some personality traits more important or central than others? Do some of them overlap or cluster together? For Gordon Allport, one of the most influential psychologists in the empirical study of personality, the answer to both questions was yes. Allport (1961) recognized that not all traits have equal weight and significance in people's lives. Most of us, he said, have five to ten *central traits* that reflect a characteristic way of behaving, dealing with others, and reacting to new situations. For instance, some people see the world as a hostile, dangerous place, whereas others see it as a place for fun and frolic. *Secondary traits*, in contrast, are more changeable aspects of personality, such as music preferences, habits, casual opinions, and the like.

Raymond B. Cattell (1973) advanced the study of this issue by applying a statistical method called **factor analysis**. Performing a factor analysis is like adding water to flour: It causes the material to clump up into little balls. When applied to traits, this procedure identifies clusters of correlated items that seem to be measuring some common, underlying factor. Today, hundreds of factor-analytic studies support the existence of a cluster of five central "robust factors," known informally as the *Big Five* (McCrae & Costa, 2008; McCrae et al., 2005; Paunonen, 2003; Roberts & Mroczek, 2008):

1 **Extroversion versus introversion** describes the extent to which people are outgoing or shy. It includes such traits as being sociable or reclusive, adventurous or cautious, socially dominant or more passive, eager to be in the limelight or inclined to stay in the shadows.

2 **Neuroticism (negative emotionality) versus emotional stability** describes the extent to which a person suffers from such traits as anxiety, an inability to control impulses, and a tendency to feel negative emotions such as anger, guilt, contempt, and resentment. Neurotic individuals are worriers, complainers, and defeatists, even when they have no major problems. They are always ready to see the sour side of life and none of its sweetness.

3 **Agreeableness versus antagonism** describes the extent to which people are good-natured or irritable, cooperative or abrasive, secure or suspicious and jealous. It reflects the tendency to have friendly relationships or hostile ones.

4 **Conscientiousness versus impulsiveness** describes the degree to which people are responsible or undependable, persevering or quick to give up, steadfast or fickle, tidy or careless, self-disciplined or impulsive.

5 **Openness to experience versus resistance to new experience** describes the extent to which people are curious, imaginative, questioning, and creative or conforming, unimaginative, predictable, and uncomfortable with novelty.

Culture can affect the prominence of these personality factors and how they are reflected in language (Toomela, 2003). Nonetheless, in spite of some semantic and cultural variations, the Big Five have emerged as distinct, central personality dimensions throughout the world, in countries as

Where do you think this man would score on extroversion?

diverse as Britain, Canada, the Czech Republic, China, Ethiopia, Turkey, the Netherlands, Japan, Spain, the Philippines, Germany, Portugal, Israel, Korea, Russia, and Australia (Digman & Shmelyov, 1996; Katigbak et al., 2002; McCrae et al., 2005; Somer & Goldberg, 1999). One monumental research venture gathered data from thousands of people across 50 cultures. In this massive project as in many smaller ones, the five personality factors emerged whether people were asked for self-reports or were assessed by others (McCrae et al., 2005; Terracciano & McCrae, 2006). ✳ Explore

Although the Big Five are quite stable over a lifetime, especially once a person hits 30, there are some exceptions. In later adulthood, people tend to become less extroverted and less open to new experiences (see Figure 2.1), and, with the right experiences, many young people eventually become more self-confident and emotionally stable (Roberts & Mroczek, 2008). There is also some good news for crabby neurotics, especially young ones. A survey of thousands of people in 10 countries, and a meta-analysis of 92 longitudinal studies, found that although young people, ages 16 to 21, are the most neurotic (emotionally negative) and the least agreeable and conscientious, people tend to become more agreeable and conscientious and less negative between ages 30 and 40 (Costa et al., 1999; Roberts, Walton, & Viechtbauer, 2006). Because these changes have been found in many different countries, they may reflect the universality of adult experiences, such as work and family responsibilities, or common maturational changes over the life span.

The Big Five do not provide a complete picture of personality, of course. Clinical psychologists note that important traits involved in mental disorders are missing, such as psychopathy (lack of remorse and empathy), self-absorption, and obsessiveness

✳ Explore the **Five Factor Model** on mypsychlab.com

factor analysis A statistical method for analyzing the intercorrelations among various measures or test scores; clusters of measures or scores that are highly correlated are assumed to measure the same underlying trait, ability, or attitude (factor).

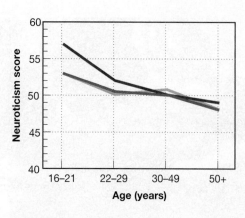
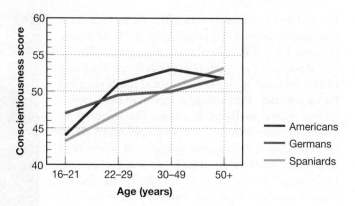

FIGURE 2.1

Consistency and Change in Personality over the Life Span

Although the Big Five traits are fairly stable, changes do occur over the life span. As you can see, neuroticism (negative emotionality) is highest among young adults and then declines, whereas conscientiousness is lowest among young adults and then steadily increases (Costa et al., 1999).

(Westen & Shedler, 1999). Personality researchers note that other important traits are missing, such as religiosity, dishonesty, humorousness, independence, and conventionality (Abrahamson, Baker, & Caspi, 2002; Paunonen & Ashton, 2001). But most researchers today agree that the Big Five do lie at the core of key personality variations among individuals, and not only human individuals, either.

Get Involved!   Rate your Traits

For each of the ten items that follow, write a number from 1 to 7 indicating the extent to which you see that trait as being characteristic of you, where 1 = "I *disagree* strongly that this trait describes me" to 7 = "I *agree* strongly that this trait describes me." Use the midpoint, 4, if you neither agree nor disagree that the trait describes you. (This self-test was designed by Samuel D. Gosling.)

1. ____   Extroverted, enthusiastic
2. ____   Critical, quarrelsome
3. ____   Dependable, self-disciplined
4. ____   Anxious, easily upset
5. ____   Open to new experiences, complex
6. ____   Reserved, quiet
7. ____   Sympathetic, warm
8. ____   Disorganized, careless
9. ____   Calm, emotionally stable
10. ____   Conventional, uncreative

To score yourself on the Big Five traits, use this key:

Extroversion:	High on question 1, low on question 6
Neuroticism:	High on question 4, low on question 9
Agreeableness:	High on question 7, low on question 2
Conscientiousness:	High on question 3, low on question 8
Openness:	High on question 5, low on question 10

Now ask a friend or relative to rate you on each of the ten items. How closely does that rating match your own? If there is a discrepancy, what might be the reason for it?

✓•⎯**Study** and
Review on
mypsychlab.com

Quick Quiz

Show that you have the trait of conscientiousness by taking this quiz.

1. What is the advantage of inventories over projective tests in measuring personality?
2. Raymond Cattell advanced the study of personality by (a) developing case-study analysis, (b) using factor analysis, (c) devising the Myers-Briggs Type Indicator.
3. Which of the following are *not* among the Big Five personality factors? (a) introversion, (b) agreeableness, (c) psychoticism, (d) openness to experience, (e) intelligence, (f) neuroticism, (g) conscientiousness.
4. Which one of the Big Five typically decreases by age 40? (a) agreeableness, (b) extroversion, (c) openness to experience, (d) neuroticism.

Answers:

1. In general, they have better reliability and validity.   2. b   3. c, e   4. d

YOU are about to learn...

• whether animals have "personalities" just as people do.

• the extent to which genes influence temperamental and personality differences among people.

• why people who have highly heritable personality traits are not necessarily stuck with them forever.

Genetic Influences on Personality

A mother we know was describing her two children: "My daughter has always been difficult, intense, and testy," she said, "but my son is the opposite, placid and good-natured. They came out of the womb that way." Was this mother right? Is it possible to be born touchy or good-natured? What aspects of personality might have an inherited component?

For centuries, efforts to understand why people differ from one another have swung from biological answers ("It's in their nature; they are born that way") to learning and environmental ones ("It's all a matter of nurture—how they are raised and the experiences they have"). The *nature–nurture* debate has been one of the longest-running either–or arguments in philosophy and psychology. Edward L. Thorndike (1903), one of the leading psychologists of the early 1900s, staked out the nature position by claiming that "in the actual race of life . . . the chief determining factor is heredity." But in stirring words that became famous, his contemporary, behaviorist John B. Watson (1925), insisted that experience could

write virtually any message on the blank slate of human nature:

> Give me a dozen healthy infants, well-formed, and my own specified world to bring them up in and I'll guarantee to take any one at random and train him to become any type of specialist I might select—doctor, lawyer, artist, merchant-chief and yes, even beggar-man and thief, regardless of his talents, penchants, tendencies, abilities, vocations, and race of his ancestors.

Today, almost all psychologists would say the nature–nurture debate is over. The answer is both. Biology and experience, genes and environment, are interacting influences, each shaping the other over time (Johnson et al., 2009). In this section and the next, we will examine the interlaced influences of nature and nurture on personality.

How can heredity affect personality? **Genes**, the basic units of heredity, are made up of elements of *DNA* (deoxyribonucleic acid). These elements form chemical codes for the synthesis of proteins. Proteins, in turn, affect virtually every aspect of the body, from its structure to the chemicals that keep it running. Genes can affect the behaviors we call "personality" through their effects on an infant's developing brain and nervous system. They can also affect the functioning of an adult's brain and nervous system, directly and also indirectly, by switching other genes on or off. Interestingly, 98.8 percent of our total DNA, called *noncoding DNA*, lies *outside* the genes. This DNA used to be called "junk DNA" as scientists believed it was not very important, but this belief is changing fast. Noncoding DNA may also affect the expression (activity) of

genes The functional units of heredity; they are composed of DNA and specify the structure of proteins.

temperaments
Physiological dispositions to respond to the environment in certain ways; they are present in infancy and are assumed to be innate.

key genes, and mutations in it may be associated with common diseases. This exciting line of research means that genes do not provide a static blueprint for development. Rather, our genetic heritage is more like a changing network of interlinked influences, including environmental ones, affecting us throughout life (Feinberg, 2008).

Researchers measure genetic contributions to personality in three ways: by studying personality traits in other species, by studying the temperaments of human infants and children, and by doing heritability studies of twins and adopted individuals. You will be hearing lots more about genetic discoveries in the coming years, so it is important to understand what they mean and don't mean.

Puppies and Personalities

In 1993, scientists published the first academic article that referred to personality in a nonhuman species. Can you guess what species it was? Dogs? Horses? No, it was the humble, squishy octopus! When the researchers dropped a crab into a tank of octopuses and had independent observers note what happened, some of the creatures would aggressively grab that dinner right away; others seemed more passive and waited for the crab to swim near them; and some waited and attacked the crab when no one was watching (Mather & Anderson, 1993). Apparently, you don't have to be a person to have a personality. You don't even have to be a primate.

In recent years, scientists have been drawing on research in physiology, genetics, ecology, and ethology (the study of animals in their natural habitats) to better understand the evolutionary and biological underpinnings of human personality traits. These investigators argue that just as it has been evolutionarily beneficial for human beings to vary

Family portraits of dogs, as of people, often reveal different personalities: Someone is bored, someone is cuddling up next to a pal, and someone is really grumpy about being there at all.

in their ways of responding to the world and those around them, so it has been for animals. It would be good for a species if some of its members were bold or impulsive enough to risk life and limb to confront a stranger or to experiment with a new food, and if other members were more cautious.

In an imaginative set of studies, Samuel D. Gosling and his colleagues (2003) recruited dog owners and their dogs in a local park. In their first study, the owners provided personality assessments of their dogs and filled out the same personality inventory for themselves. The owners then designated another person who knew them and their dogs, and who could judge the personalities of both. In a second study, the owners brought their dogs to an enclosed section of the park where three independent observers rated the dogs, so the researchers could compare the owners' judgments of their dogs' personalities with the observers' ratings. The dog owners, their friends, and the neutral observers all agreed strongly in their ratings of the dogs' personalities along four of the Big Five dimensions: extroversion, agreeableness, emotional reactivity (neuroticism), and openness to experience.

To date, Gosling and his colleagues have found evidence of most of the Big Five factors in 64 different species, including the squishy squid, bears, dogs, pigs, hyenas, goats, cats, and of course primates; all have distinctive, characteristic ways of behaving that make them different from their fellows (Weinstein, Capitanio, & Gosling, 2008). These findings point to the evolutionary importance of the Big Five and their biological basis. So when you hear your dog- or horse- or cat-crazy friend say, "Pluto is such a shy and nervous guy, whereas Pepper is outgoing and sociable," your friend is probably being a pretty accurate observer.

Heredity and Temperament

Let's turn now to human personalities. Even in the first weeks after birth, human babies differ in activity level, mood, responsiveness, heart rate, and attention span (Fox et al., 2005a). Some are irritable and cranky; others are placid and calm. Some will cuddle up in an adult's arms and snuggle; others squirm and fidget, as if they cannot stand being held. Some smile easily; others fuss and cry.

These differences appear even when you control for possible prenatal influences, such as the mother's nutrition, drug use, or problems with the pregnancy. The reason is that babies are born with genetically determined **temperaments**, dispositions to respond to the environment in certain ways (Clark & Watson, 2008). Temperaments include

Extreme shyness and fear of new situations tend to be biologically based, stable aspects of temperament, both in human beings and in monkeys. On the right, a timid infant rhesus monkey cowers behind a friend in the presence of an outgoing stranger.

reactivity (how excitable, arousable, or responsive a baby is), *soothability* (how easily the baby is calmed when upset), and positive and negative emotionality. Temperaments are quite stable over time and are the clay out of which later personality traits are molded (Clark & Watson, 2008; Else-Quest et al., 2006; Rothbart, Ahadi, & Evans, 2000).

For example, highly reactive infants, even at 4 months of age, are excitable, nervous, and fearful; they overreact to any little thing, even a colorful picture placed in front of them. As toddlers, they tend to be wary and fearful of new things—toys that make noise, odd-looking robots—even when their moms are right there with them. At 5 years, many of these children are still timid and uncomfortable in new situations and with new people (Hill-Soderlund & Braungart-Rieker, 2008). At 7 years, many still have symptoms of anxiety. They are afraid of being kidnapped, they need to sleep with the light on, and they are afraid of sleeping in an unfamiliar house, even if they have never experienced any sort of trauma.

In contrast, nonreactive infants take things easy. They lie there without fussing; they rarely cry; they babble happily. As toddlers, they are outgoing and curious about new toys and events. They continue to be easygoing and extroverted throughout childhood (Fox et al., 2005b; Kagan, 1997). Children at these two extremes differ physiologically too. During mildly stressful tasks, reactive children are more likely than nonreactive children to have increased heart rates, heightened brain activity, and high levels of stress hormones.

You can see how biologically based temperaments might form the basis of the later personality traits we call extroversion, agreeableness, or neuroticism.

Heredity and Traits

A third way to study genetic contributions to personality is to estimate the **heritability** of specific traits within groups of children or adults. This method is central to the field of **behavioral genetics**, which attempts to identify the genetic bases of individual differences in personality, behavior, and mental ability. Within any group, individuals will vary in shyness, cheerfulness, impulsiveness, or any other quality. Heritability gives us a statistical estimate of the *proportion of the total variation in a trait that is attributable to genetic variation within a group*. Because the heritability of a trait is expressed as a proportion (such as .60 or 60/100), the maximum value it can have is 1.0 (which would mean that 100 percent of the variation in the trait was due to genetic variation).

We know that heritability is a tough concept to understand at first, so here's an example. Suppose that your entire psychology class takes a test of shyness, and you compute an average shyness score for the group. Some students will have scores close to the average, whereas others will have scores that are much higher or lower than the average. Heritability gives you an estimate of the extent to which your class's variation in shyness is due to genetic differences among the students who took the test. Note that this estimate applies only to the group as a whole. It does not tell you anything about the impact of genetics on any *particular* individual's shyness or extroversion. You might be shy primarily because of your genes, but your friend might be shy because of an embarrassing experience she had in a school play at the age of 8.

One obvious example of a highly heritable trait is height: Within a group of equally well-nourished

heritability A statistical estimate of the proportion of the total variance in some trait that is attributable to genetic differences among individuals within a group.

behavioral genetics An interdisciplinary field of study concerned with the genetic bases of individual differences in behavior and personality.

"THERE'S ANOTHER HEREDITARY DISEASE THAT RUNS IN THE ROYAL FAMILY. YOUR GRANDFATHER WAS A STUBBORN FOOL, YOUR FATHER WAS A STUBBORN FOOL, AND YOU ARE A STUBBORN FOOL."

individuals, most of the variation among them will be accounted for by their genetic differences. In contrast, table manners have low heritability because most variation among individuals is accounted for by differences in upbringing. Even highly heritable traits, however, can be modified by the environment. Although height is about 90 percent heritable, malnourished children may not grow up to be as tall as they would have if given sufficient food. Conversely, if children eat an extremely nutritious diet, they may grow up to be taller than anyone thought they could. North and South Koreans share the same genetic background, yet they currently differ in average height by fully 6 inches (Schwekendiek, 2008).

Computing Heritability Scientists have no way to estimate the heritability of a trait or behavior directly, so they must infer it by studying people whose degree of genetic similarity is known. You might think that the simplest approach would be to compare blood relatives within families; everyone knows of families that are famous for some talent or personality trait. But the fact that a trait runs in a family doesn't tell us much, because close relatives usually share environments as well as genes. If Carlo's parents and siblings all love lasagna, that doesn't mean a taste for lasagna is heritable! The same applies if everyone in Carlo's family is shy, moody, or loves music.

A better approach is to study adopted children (e.g., Loehlin, Horn, & Willerman, 1996; Plomin & DeFries, 1985). Such children share half of their genes with each birth parent, but they grow up in a different environment, apart from their birth parents. On the other hand, they share an environment with their adoptive parents and siblings, but not their genes. Researchers can compare correlations between the children's traits and those of their biological and adoptive relatives and can then use the results to estimate heritability.

Another approach is to compare identical twins with fraternal twins. *Identical twins* develop when a fertilized egg divides into two parts that then become separate embryos. Because the twins come from the same fertilized egg, scientists have always assumed that they share all their genes. Some surprising recent work, however, suggests that duplicated or missing blocks of DNA can exist in one identical twin but not the other (Bruder et al., 2008). (Identical twins may also differ slightly at birth because of different prenatal experiences, such as differences in the blood supply to the two fetuses or other chance factors.) Nonetheless, identical twins are far more genetically alike than are other siblings.

In contrast, *fraternal twins* develop when a woman's ovaries release two eggs instead of one and each egg is fertilized by a different sperm. Fraternal twins are wombmates, but they are no more alike genetically than any other two siblings (that is, they share, on average, only half their genes), and they may be of different sexes.

Behavioral geneticists can estimate the heritability of a trait by comparing groups of same-sex fraternal twins with groups of identical twins. The assumption is that if identical twins are more alike than fraternal twins, then the increased similarity must be due to genetic influences. Perhaps, however, people do not treat identical and fraternal twins the same way. To avoid this problem, investigators have studied identical twins who were separated early in life and were reared apart. (Until relatively recently, adoption policies and attitudes toward births out of wedlock permitted such separations to occur.) In theory, separated identical twins share all their genes but not their environments. Any similarities between them should therefore be primarily genetic and should permit a direct estimate of heritability.

There is still another problem, though. Some psychologists argue that the range of environments in adoptive homes, including those of separated twins, is quite narrow, because most people who adopt children are screened to be sure they have a pretty secure income, are psychologically stable, and so forth. As a result, there is not much variation in adopted children's environments, and this fact spuriously inflates the variation due to heredity (Nisbett, 2009). When environments are similar, any differences among individuals appear to be heritable. As soon as environments differ, the proportion of genetic influence on individuals wanes (Johnson et al., 2009).

How Heritable Are Personality Traits?

Nonetheless, findings from adoption and twin studies—representing some 800,000 pairs of twins and more than 50 different study samples—have provided compelling support for a genetic contribution to personality (Johnson et al., 2009). Identical twins reared apart will often have unnerving similarities in gestures, mannerisms, and moods; indeed, their personalities often seem as similar as their physical features. If one twin tends to be optimistic, glum, or excitable, the other will probably be that way too (Braungert et al. , 1992; Plomin et al., 2001).

Behavioral-genetic findings have produced remarkably consistent results on the heritability of personality traits. For the Big Five and for many other traits, from aggressiveness to overall happiness, heritability ranges from .20 to .50 (Bouchard,

Separated at birth, the Mallifert twins meet accidentally.

© Tee and Charles Addams Foundation

1997a; Jang et al., 1998; Lykken & Tellegen, 1996; Waller et al., 1990; Weiss, Bates, & Luciano, 2008). This means that within a group of people, up to 50 percent of the variation in such traits is attributable to genetic differences among the individuals in the group. These findings have been replicated in many countries. ◉ Watch

◉ **Watch** the **Video** on **Twins Separated at Birth, Reunited** on **mypsychlab.com**

Identical twins Gerald Levey (left) and Mark Newman were separated at birth and raised in different cities. When they were reunited at age 31, they discovered some astounding similarities. Both were volunteer firefighters, wore mustaches, and were unmarried. Both liked to hunt, watch old John Wayne movies, and eat Chinese food. They drank the same brand of beer, held the can with the little finger curled around it, and crushed the can when it was empty. It's tempting to conclude that all of these similarities are due to heredity, but we should also consider other explanations: Some could result from shared environmental factors such as social class and upbringing and some could be due merely to chance. For any given set of twins, we can never know for sure.

Evaluating Genetic Theories

Psychologists hope that one intelligent use of behavioral-genetic findings will be to help people become more accepting of themselves and their children. Although we can all learn to make improvements and modifications to our personalities, most of us probably will never be able to transform our personalities completely because of our genetic dispositions and temperaments.

Yet we should not oversimplify by assuming that "It's all in our genes!" A genetic *predisposition* does not necessarily imply genetic *inevitability*. A person might have genes that predispose him or her to depression, but without certain environmental stresses or circumstances, the person will probably never become depressed. When people oversimplify, they mistakenly assume that personality problems that have a genetic component are permanent—say, that someone is "born to be bad" or to be a miserable grump forever. That belief can affect their behavior and actually make matters worse (Dweck, 2008). Oversimplification can also lead people to incorrectly assume that if a problem, such as depression

Thinking Critically about Genetic "Inevitability"

or shyness, has a genetic contribution, it will respond only to medication, so there is no point trying other interventions. We discuss what is wrong with this assumption in Chapter 12.

It seems that nearly every year brings another report about some gene that supposedly explains a human trait. A few years back, newspapers even announced the discovery of a "worry gene." Don't worry about it! Most human traits, even such seemingly straightforward ones as height and eye color, are influenced by more than one gene. Psychological traits are especially likely to depend on multiple genes, with each one accounting for just a small part of the variance among people. Conversely, any single gene is apt to influence many different behaviors. So at this point, all announcements of a "gene for this" or a "gene for that" should be viewed with extreme caution.

Robert Plomin (1989), a leading behavioral geneticist, once observed, "The wave of acceptance of genetic influence on behavior is growing into a tidal wave that threatens to engulf the second message of this research: These same data provide the best available evidence for the importance of environmental influences." Let us now see what some of those influences might be.

✔•—Study and Review on mypsychlab.com

Quick Quiz

We hope you have a few quiz-taking genes.

1. What three broad lines of research support the hypothesis that personality differences are due in part to genetic differences?

2. In behavioral-genetic studies, the heritability of personality traits, including the Big Five, is typically about (a) .50, (b) .90, (c) .10 to .20, (d) zero.

3. Researchers announce that their study of identical twins has revealed a high heritability for divorce (McGue & Lykken, 1992). Given that our prehistoric ancestors hadn't yet invented marriage, let alone divorce, what on earth could this finding mean?

Answers:

1. Research on animal personalities, human temperaments, and the heritability of traits 2. a 3. There obviously cannot be a "divorce gene," but perhaps personality factors with a heritable component, such as neuroticism and hostility, make it harder for a person to get along with a partner and thereby increase the likelihood of getting divorced (Rogge et al., 2006).

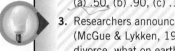

YOU are about to learn...

- how social-cognitive theory accounts for apparent changes in personality across situations.

- the extent to which parents can—and can't—influence their children's personalities.

- how your peers shape certain aspects of your personality and suppress others.

Environmental Influences on Personality

social-cognitive learning theory A major contemporary learning view of personality, which holds that personality traits result from a person's learning history and his or her expectations, beliefs, perceptions of events, and other cognitions.

The environment may be half of the influence on variations in personality, but what *is* the environment, exactly? In this section, we will consider the relative influence of three aspects of the environment: the particular situations you find yourself in, how your parents treat you, and who your peers are.

Situations and Social Learning

The very definition of a trait is that it is consistent across situations. But people often behave one way with their parents and a different way with their friends, one way at home and a different way in other situations. In behavioral learning terms, the reason for people's inconsistency is that different behaviors are rewarded, punished, or ignored in different contexts. (In Chapter 9, we will examine in greater depth the important principles of behavioral theory.) You are likely to be more extroverted in an audience of screaming, cheering *American Idol* fans than at home with relatives who would regard such noisy displays with alarm and condemnation. Because of such variations in behavior across situations, strict behaviorists think it does not even make sense to talk about personality. In their view, people don't have traits; they simply show certain behavior patterns in some situations and not others.

However, a major contemporary learning view, **social-cognitive learning theory**, holds that personality traits result, in part, from your learning history and your resulting expectations and beliefs. A child who studies hard and gets good grades, attention from teachers, admiration from friends, and praise from parents will come to expect that hard work in other situations will also pay off. That child will become, in terms of personality traits, "ambitious" and "industrious." A child who studies hard and gets poor grades, is ignored by teachers and parents, and is rejected by friends for being a grind will come to expect that working hard isn't worth it. That child will become (in the view of others) "unambitious" or "unmotivated."

Today, most personality researchers recognize that people can have a core set of stable traits *and* that their behavior can vary across situations (Fleeson, 2004). There is a continual interaction between your particular qualities and the situation you are in. Your temperaments, habits, and beliefs influence how you respond to others, whom you hang out with, and the situations you seek (Bandura, 2001; Cervone & Shoda, 1999; Mischel & Shoda, 1995). In turn, the situation influences your behavior and beliefs, rewarding some behaviors and extinguishing others. In social-cognitive learning theory, this process is called **reciprocal determinism**.

Is Susan Boyle, a plain woman who stunned the world with her great voice, a shy, modest introvert or a self-confident performer? Social-cognitive learning theory holds that genetic dispositions and personality traits, such as Boyle's remarkable skill as a singer, cause people to choose some situations over others. But situations, such as Boyle's appearance on "Britain's Got Talent," in turn influence which aspects of their personalities people express.

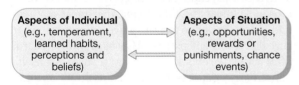

Aspects of Individual (e.g., temperament, learned habits, perceptions and beliefs)

Aspects of Situation (e.g., opportunities, rewards or punishments, chance events)

The two-way process of reciprocal determinism (as opposed to the one-way determinism of "genes determine everything" or "everything is learned") helps answer a question asked by everyone who has a sibling: What makes children who grow up in the same family so different, apart from their genes? The answer seems to be an assortment of experiences that affect each child differently, chance events that cannot be predicted, situations that children find themselves in, and peer groups that the children belong to (Harris, 2006; Plomin, Asbury, & Dunn, 2001; Rutter et al., 2001). Behavioral geneticists refer to these unique and chance experiences that are not shared with other family members as the **nonshared environment**: for example, being in Mrs. Miller's class in the fourth grade (which might inspire you to become a scientist), winning the lead in the school play (which might push you toward an

acting career), or being bullied at school (which might have caused you to see yourself as weak and powerless). All of these experiences work reciprocally with your own interpretation of them, your temperament, and your perceptions (did Mrs. Miller's class excite you or bore you?).

Keeping the concept of reciprocal determinism in mind, let us take a look at two of the most powerful environmental influences in people's lives: their parents and their friends.

Parental Influence—and Its Limits

If you check out parenting books online or in a bookstore, you will find that in spite of the zillion different kinds of advice they offer, they share one entrenched belief: Parental child-rearing practices are the strongest influence, maybe even the *sole* influence, on children's personality development. For many decades, few psychologists thought to question this assumption, and many still accept it. Yet the belief that personality is primarily determined by how parents treat their children has begun to crumble under the weight of three kinds of evidence (Harris, 2006, 2009):

Thinking Critically about the Influence of Parents

1 **The shared environment of the home has little if any influence on personality.** In behavioral-genetic research, the "shared environment" includes the family you grew up with and the

reciprocal determinism In social-cognitive theories, the two-way interaction between aspects of the environment and aspects of the individual in the shaping of personality traits.

nonshared environment Unique aspects of a person's environment and experience that are not shared with family members.

experiences and background you shared with your siblings and parents. If these had as powerful an influence as commonly assumed, then studies should find a strong correlation between the personality traits of adopted children and those of their adoptive parents. In fact, the correlation is weak to nonexistent, indicating that the influence of child-rearing practices and family life is small compared to the influence of genetics (Cohen, 1999; Plomin, Asbury, & Dunn, 2001).

2 Few parents have a single child-rearing style that is consistent over time and that they use with all their children. Developmental psychologists have tried for many years to identify the effects of specific child-rearing practices on children's personality traits. The problem is that parents are inconsistent from day to day and over the years. Their child-rearing practices vary, depending on their own stresses, moods, and marital satisfaction (Holden & Miller, 1999). As one child we know said to her exasperated mother, "Why are you so mean to me today, Mommy? I'm this naughty every day." Moreover, parents tend to adjust their methods of child rearing according to the temperament of the child; they are often more lenient with easygoing children and more punitive with difficult ones.

3 Even when parents try to be consistent in the way they treat their children, there may be little relation between what they do and how the children turn out. Some children of troubled and abusive parents are resilient and do not suffer lasting emotional damage, as we discuss in Chapter 3. Conversely, some children of the kindest and most nurturing parents succumb to drugs, mental illness, or gangs.

Of course, parents do influence their children in lots of ways that are unrelated to the child's personality. They contribute to their children's religious beliefs, intellectual and occupational interests, motivation to succeed, skills, values, and adherence to traditional or modern notions of masculinity and femininity (Beer, Arnold, & Loehlin, 1998; Krueger, Hicks, & McGue, 2001). Above all, what parents do profoundly affects the quality of

their relationship with their children—whether their children feel loved, secure, and valued or humiliated, frightened, and worthless (Harris, 2009).

Parents also have some influence even on traits in their children that are highly heritable. In one longitudinal study that followed children from age 3 to age 21, kids who were impulsive, uncontrollable, and aggressive at age 3 were far more likely than calmer children to grow up to be impulsive, unreliable, and antisocial and more likely to commit crimes (Caspi, 2000). Early temperament was a strong and consistent predictor of these later personality traits. But not *every* child came out the same way. What protected some of those at risk, and helped them move in a healthier direction, was having parents who made sure they stayed in school, supervised them closely, and gave them consistent discipline.

Nevertheless, it is clear that, in general, parents have less influence on a child's personality than many people think. Because of reciprocal determinism, the relationship runs in both directions, with parents and children continually influencing one another. Moreover, as soon as children leave home, starting in preschool, parental influence on children's behavior *outside* the home begins to wane. The nonshared environment—peers, chance events, and circumstances—takes over.

The Power of Peers

When two psychologists surveyed 275 freshmen at Cornell University, they found that most of them had secret lives and private selves that they never revealed to their parents (Garbarino & Bedard, 2001). On Facebook too, many teenagers unselfconsciously report having committed crimes, drinking, doing drugs, cheating in school, sexting, and having sex, all without their parents having a clue. (They assume, incorrectly, that what they reveal is "private" and read only by their friends.) This phenomenon of showing one facet of your personality to your parents and an entirely different one to your peers becomes especially apparent in adolescence.

Children, like adults, live in two environments: their homes and their world outside the home. At

Get Involved! Situation and Self

Are you a different person when you are alone, with your parents, hanging out with friends, in class, or at a party? If so, in what ways? Do you have a secret self that you do not show to your family? Consider the Big Five factors, or any other personality traits that are important to you, as you answer these questions.

home, children learn how their parents want them to behave and what they can get away with; as soon as they go to school, however, they conform to the dress, habits, language, and rules of their peers. Most adults can remember how terrible they felt when their classmates laughed at them for pronouncing a word "the wrong way" or doing something "stupid" (that is, not what the rest of the kids were doing), and many recall the pain of being excluded. To avoid the controlling forces of being laughed at or rejected, most children will do what they can to conform to the norms and rules of their immediate peer group (Harris, 2009). Children who were law-abiding in the fifth grade may start breaking the law in high school, if that is what it takes—or what they think it takes—to win the respect of their peers.

It has been difficult to tease apart the effects of parents and peers because parents usually try to arrange things so that their children's environments duplicate their own values and customs. To see which has the stronger influence on personality and behavior, therefore, we must look at situations in which the peer group's values clash with the parents' values. For example, when parents value academic achievement and their child's peers think that success in school is only for sellouts or geeks, whose view wins? The answer, typically, is peers (Arroyo & Zigler, 1995; Harris, 2009). Conversely, children whose parents gave them no encouragement or motivation to succeed may find themselves with peers who are working like mad to get into college, and start studying hard themselves.

Thus, peers play a tremendous role in shaping our personality traits and behavior, causing us to emphasize some attributes or abilities and downplay

Have you ever been in this situation, as the excluded student or the one doing the excluding? Being rejected by peers is one of the most painful experiences that adolescents report having.

others. Of course, as the theory of reciprocal determinism would predict, our temperaments and dispositions also cause us to select particular peer groups (if they are available) instead of others, and our temperaments influence how we behave within the group. But once we are among peers, most of us go along with them, molding facets of our personalities to the pressures of the group.

In sum, core personality traits may stem from genetic dispositions, but they are profoundly shaped by learning, peers, situations, experience, and, as we will see next, the largest environment of all: the culture.

✓• Study and Review on mypsychlab.com

Quick Quiz

Do your peers take these quizzes? Does the answer determine whether you will?

1. What three lines of evidence have challenged the belief that parents are the major influence on their children's personalities?

2. Which contributes most to the variation among siblings in their personality traits: (a) the unique experiences they have that are not shared with their families, (b) the family environment that all of them share, or (c) the way their parents treat them?

3. Eight-year-old Dwayne is pretty shy at home, where he is the middle of six children, but extroverted at school, where he is the leader of his friends. What might be the reason for his apparent personality change?

Answers:

1. The shared family environment has little if any influence on personality; few parents have a consistent child-rearing style; and even when parents try to be consistent in the way they treat their children, there may be little relation between what they do and how the children turn out. 2. a 3. Peer groups have a powerful influence on which personality traits are encouraged and expressed, and peers can even override the child's situation at home.

YOU are about to learn...

- how culture influences your personality, and even whether you think you have a stable one.

- why men in the South and West are more likely to get angry when insulted than other American men are.

- how to appreciate cultural influences on personality without stereotyping.

Cultural Influences on Personality

If you get an invitation to come to a party at 7 P.M., what time are you actually likely to get there? If someone gives you the finger or calls you a rude name, are you more likely to become furious or laugh it off? Most Western psychologists regard conscientiousness about time and quickness to anger as personality traits that result partly from genetic dispositions and partly from experience. But culture also has a profound effect on people's behavior, attitudes, and the traits they value or disdain. A **culture** is a program of shared rules that govern the behavior of members of a community or society, and a set of values and beliefs shared by most members of that community and passed from one generation to another. It provides countless rules that govern our actions and shape our beliefs (see Chapter 10). And it is just as powerful an influence on personality and behavior as any biological process.

Culture, Values, and Traits

Quick! Answer this question: Who are you?

Your answer will be influenced by your cultural background, and particularly by whether your culture emphasizes individualism or community

(Hofstede & Bond, 1988; Kanagawa, Cross, & Markus, 2001; Markus & Kitayama, 1991; Triandis, 1996, 2007). In **individualist cultures**, the independence of the individual often takes precedence over the needs of the group, and the self is often defined as a collection of personality traits ("I am outgoing, agreeable, and ambitious") or in occupational terms ("I am a psychologist"). In **collectivist cultures**, group harmony often takes precedence over the wishes of the individual, and the self is defined in the context of relationships and the community ("I am the son of a farmer, descended from three generations of storytellers on my mother's side and five generations of farmers on my father's side."). In one fascinating study that showed how embedded this dimension is in language and how it shapes our thinking, bicultural individuals born in China tended to answer "Who am I?" in terms of their own individual attributes when they were writing in English—but they described themselves in terms of their relations to others when they were writing in Chinese (Ross, Xun, & Wilson, 2002).

As Table 2.1 shows, individualist and collectivist ways of defining the self influence many aspects of life, including which personality traits we value, how and whether we express emotions, how much we value having relationships or maintaining freedom, and how freely we express angry or aggressive feelings (Forbes et al., 2009; Oyserman & Lee, 2008). Individualist and collectivist orientations affect us in countless subtle but powerful ways. For example, in one study, Chinese and American pairs had to play a communication game that required each partner to be able to take the other's perspective. Eye-gaze measures showed that the Chinese players were almost always able to look at the target from their partner's perspective, whereas the American players often completely failed at this task (Wu & Keysar, 2007).

culture A program of shared rules that govern the behavior of members of a community or society and a set of values, beliefs, and attitudes shared by most members of that community.

individualist cultures Cultures in which the self is regarded as autonomous, and individual goals and wishes are prized above duty and relations with others.

collectivist cultures Cultures in which the self is regarded as embedded in relationships, and harmony with one's group is prized above individual goals and wishes.

Individualistic Americans exercise by running, walking, bicycling, and skating, all in different directions and wearing different clothes. Collectivist Japanese employees at their hiring ceremony exercise in identical fashion.

TABLE 2.1

Some Average Differences between Individualist and Collectivist Cultures

Members of Individualist Cultures	Members of Collectivist Cultures
Define the self as autonomous, independent of groups.	Define the self as an interdependent part of groups.
Give priority to individual, personal goals.	Give priority to the needs and goals of the group.
Value independence, leadership, achievement, and self-fulfillment.	Value group harmony, duty, obligation, and security.
Give more weight to an individual's attitudes and preferences than to group norms as explanations of behavior.	Give more weight to group norms than to individual attitudes as explanations of behavior.
Attend to the benefits and costs of relationships; if costs exceed advantages, a person is likely to drop a relationship.	Attend to the needs of group members; if a relationship is beneficial to the group but costly to the individual, the individual is likely to stay in the relationship.

Source: Triandis, 1996.

Of course, members of both cultures understand the difference between their own view of things and that of another person's, but the collectivist-oriented Chinese pay closer attention to other people's nonverbal expressions, the better to monitor and modify their own responses. People in these two cultural traditions also tend to develop different cognitive styles: Westerners value analytic ways of thinking, such as focusing on the individual as a cause of an event; Asians value holistic ways of thinking, focusing on contexts and relationships (Varnum et al., 2010).

Because people from collectivist cultures are concerned with adjusting their own behavior depending on the social context, they tend to regard personality and the sense of self as being more flexible than people from individualist cultures do. In a study comparing Japanese and Americans, the Americans reported that their sense of self changes only 5 to 10 percent in different situations, whereas the Japanese said that 90 to 99 percent of their sense of self changes (de Rivera, 1989). For the group-oriented Japanese, it is important to enact *tachiba*, to perform your social roles correctly so that there will be harmony with others. Americans, in contrast, tend to value "being true to your self" and having a "core identity."

Culture and Traits When people fail to understand the influence of culture on behavior, they often attribute another person's mysterious or annoying actions to individual personality traits when they are really due to cultural norms. Take cleanliness. How often do you bathe? Once a day, once a week? Do you regard baths as healthy and invigorating or as a disgusting wallow in dirty

water? How often, and where, do you wash your hands—or feet? A person who would seem obsessively clean in one culture might seem an appalling slob in another (Fernea & Fernea, 1994).

Or consider helpfulness. Many years ago, in a classic cross-cultural study of children in Kenya, India, Mexico, the Philippines, Okinawa, the United States, and five other cultures, researchers measured how often children behaved altruistically (offering help, support, or unselfish suggestions) or egoistically (seeking help and attention or wanting to dominate others) (Whiting & Edwards, 1988; Whiting & Whiting, 1975). American children were the least altruistic on all measures and the most egoistic. The most altruistic children came from societies in which children are assigned many tasks, such as caring for younger children and gathering and preparing food. These children knew that their work made a genuine contribution to the well-being or economic survival of the family. In cultures that value individual achievement and self-advancement, altruism as a personality trait is not cultivated to the same extent.

Or consider tardiness. Individuals differ in whether

In many cultures, children are expected to contribute to the family's needs, by taking care of their younger siblings or doing important work for the family's income. These experiences encourage helpfulness rather than independence.

they try to be places "on time" or are always late, but cultural norms affect how individuals regard time in the first place. In northern Europe, Canada, the United States, and most other individualistic cultures, time is organized into linear segments in which people do one thing "at a time" (Hall, 1983; Hall & Hall, 1990; Leonard, 2008). The day is divided into appointments, schedules, and routines, and because time is a precious commodity, people don't like to "waste" time or "spend" too much time on any one activity (hence the popularity of multitasking). In such cultures, being on time is taken as a sign of conscientiousness or thoughtfulness and being late as a sign of indifference or intentional disrespect. Therefore, it is considered the height of rudeness (or high status) to keep someone waiting. But in Mexico, southern Europe, the Middle East, South America, and Africa, time is organized along parallel lines. People do many things at once, and the needs of friends and family supersede mere appointments; they think nothing of waiting for hours or days to see someone. The idea of having to be somewhere "on time," as if time were more important than a person, is unthinkable.

Culture and Violence: The Cultivation of Male Aggression

Many people think that men are more violent than women because men have higher levels of testosterone. But if that is so, then why, given that men everywhere have testosterone, do rates of male aggressiveness vary enormously across cultures and throughout history? Why are rates of violence higher in some regions of the United States than others?

To answer these questions, Richard Nisbett (1993) began by examining the historical record. He found that the American South, along with some western regions of the country originally settled by Southerners, have much higher rates of white homicide and other violence than the rest of the country has—but only particular kinds of violence: the use of fists or guns to protect a man's sense of honor, protect his property, or respond to perceived insults. Nisbett considered various explanations, such as poverty or racial tensions. But when he controlled for regional differences in poverty and the percentage of blacks in the population, by county, "Southernness" remained an independent predictor of homicide. Nisbett also ruled out a history of slavery as an explanation: Regions of the South that had the highest concentrations of slaves in the past have the lowest white homicide rates today.

Nisbett hypothesized that the higher rates of violence in the South derive from economic causes: The higher rates occur in cultures that were originally based on herding, in contrast to cultures based on agriculture. Why would this be so? People who depend economically on agriculture tend to develop and promote cooperative strategies for survival. But people who depend on their herds are extremely vulnerable; their livelihoods can be lost in an instant by the theft of their animals. To reduce the likelihood of theft, Nisbett theorized, herders learn to be hyperalert to any threatening act (real or perceived) and respond to it immediately with force. This would explain why cattle rustling and horse thievery were capital crimes in the Old West, and why Mediterranean and Middle Eastern herding cultures even today place a high value on male aggressiveness. And indeed, when Nisbett looked at

Many people assume that men can't help being violent because of their biology. Yet, on average, men in agricultural economies are far more cooperative and nonviolent than men in herding economies. Amish farmers have always had very low rates of violence, whereas in the Old West, the cattle-herding cowboy culture was a violent one. (Fortunately, the shoot-out here is a reenactment.)

agricultural practices *within* the South, he found that homicide rates were more than twice as high in the hills and dry plains areas (where herding occurs) as in farming regions.

The emphasis on aggressiveness and vigilance in herding communities, in turn, fosters a *culture of honor*, in which even small disputes and insults put a man's reputation for toughness on the line, requiring him to respond with violence to restore his status (Cohen, 1998). Although the herding economy has become much less important in the South and West, the legacy of its culture of honor remains. These regions have rates of honor-related homicides (such as murder to avenge a perceived insult to one's family) that are five times higher than in other regions of the country. High school students in culture-of-honor states are far more likely than students from other states to bring a weapon to school and to use that weapon: They have more than twice as many school shootings per capita than other states (Brown, Osterman, & Barnes, 2009). Cultures of honor also have higher rates of domestic violence. Both sexes in such cultures believe it is appropriate for a man to physically assault a woman if he believes she is threatening his honor and reputation by being unfaithful or by leaving him (Vandello & Cohen, 2008).

Nisbett and his colleagues also wanted to demonstrate how these external cultural norms literally get under the skin to affect physiology and personality. They brought 173 Northern and Southern male students into their lab and conducted three experiments to measure how these students would respond psychologically and physiologically to being insulted (Cohen et al., 1996). They explained that the experiment would assess the students' performance on various tasks and that the experimenter would be taking saliva samples to measure everyone's blood sugar levels throughout the procedure. Actually, the saliva samples were used to measure levels of cortisol, a hormone associated with high levels of stress, and testosterone, which is associated with dominance and aggression. At one point in the experiment, a confederate of the experimenter, who seemed to be another student participant, bumped into each man and called him an insulting name (a seven-letter word beginning with "a," if you want to know).

As you can see in Figure 2.2, northerners responded calmly to the insult; if anything, they thought it was funny. But many southerners were immediately inflamed and their levels of cortisol and testosterone shot up. They were more likely to feel that their masculinity had been threatened, and they were more likely to retaliate aggressively than northerners were. Southerners and northerners who were not insulted were alike on most measures,

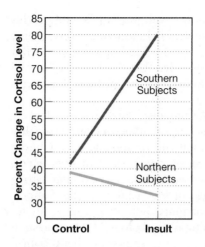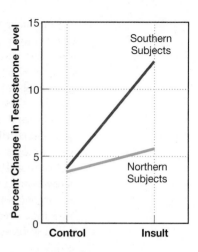

FIGURE 2.2

Aggression and Cultures of Honor

As these two graphs show, when young men from northern states were insulted in an experiment, they shrugged it off, thinking it was funny or unimportant. But for young Southern men, levels of the stress hormone cortisol and of testosterone shot up, and they were more likely to retaliate aggressively (Cohen et al., 1996).

with the exception that the southerners were actually more polite and deferential. It appears that they have more obliging manners than northerners—until they are insulted. Then, look out.

Being raised in a culture of honor, however, is only one cause of male aggression. Another cause has to do with the dangers that a culture faces. In cultures in which competition for resources is fierce and survival is difficult, men are "toughened up" and pushed to take risks, even with their lives (Gilmore, 1990). In contrast, among the Ifaluk, the Tahitians, and the people of Sudest Island near New Guinea, where resources are abundant and there are no serious hazards or enemies to worry about, men do not feel they have to prove themselves and they are not raised to be tough and aggressive (Lepowsky, 1994; Levy, 1984). When a society becomes more peaceful, so do its men.

Evaluating Cultural Approaches

A woman we know, originally from England, married a Lebanese man. They were happy together but had the usual number of marital misunderstandings and squabbles. After a few years, they visited his family home in Lebanon, where she had never been before. "I was stunned," she told us. "All the things I thought he did because of his *personality* turned out to be because he's *Lebanese!* Everyone there was just like him!"

Our friend's reaction illustrates both the contributions and the limitations of cultural studies of personality. She was right in recognizing that some of her husband's behavior was attributable to his culture; for example, his Lebanese notions of time were very different from her English notions. But she was wrong to infer that the Lebanese are all "just like him": Individuals are affected by their culture, but they vary within it.

Cultural psychologists face the problem of how to describe cultural influences on personality without oversimplifying or stereotyping (Church & Lonner, 1998). As one student of ours put it, "How come when we students speak of 'the' Japanese or 'the' blacks or 'the' whites or 'the' Latinos, it's called stereotyping, and when you do it, it's called 'cross-cultural psychology'?" This question shows excellent critical thinking! The study of culture does not rest on the assumption that all members of a culture behave the same way or have the same personality traits. As we have seen, people vary according to their temperaments, beliefs, and learning histories, and this variation occurs within every culture.

Moreover, culture itself may have regional variations within every society. America is an individualist culture overall, but the Deep South, with its history of strong regional identity, is more collectivist than the rugged, independent West (Vandello & Cohen, 1999). The collectivist Chinese and the Japanese both value group harmony, but the Chinese are more likely to also promote individual achievement, whereas the Japanese are more likely to strive for group consensus (Dien, 1999; Lu, 2008). And African Americans are more likely than white Americans to blend elements of American individualism and African collectivism. That difference may help explain why an individualist philosophy predicts grade point average for white students, but collectivist values are a better predictor for black students (Komarraju & Cokley, 2008). So it is important not to think of average cross-cultural differences, even in a dimension as influential as individualist-collectivist, as rigidly fixed (Oyserman & Lee, 2008). ◉ **Watch**

Finally, in spite of their differences, cultures have many human concerns and needs in common—for love, attachment, family, work, and religious or communal tradition. Nonetheless, cultural rules are what, *on average*, make Swedes different from Bedouins and Cambodians different from Italians. The traits that we value, our sense of self versus community, and our notions of the right way to behave—all key aspects of personality—begin with the culture in which we are raised.

◉ **Watch Cognition, Emotion, & Motivation Across Cultures: Shinobu Kitayama** on **mypsychlab.com**

Thinking Critically about Culture and Personality

✓ **Study** and **Review** on **mypsychlab.com**

Quick Quiz

At the moment, you live in a culture that values the importance of quizzes.

1. Cultures whose members regard the "self" as a collection of stable personality traits are (individualist/collectivist).

2. Which cultural practice tends to foster the traits of helpfulness and altruism? (a) Every family member "does his or her own thing," (b) parents insist that children obey, (c) children contribute to the family welfare, (d) parents remind children often about the importance of being helpful.

3. Why, according to one theory, do men in the American South and West respond more aggressively to perceived insults than other American men do?

Answers:

1. individualist 2. c 3. These men come from regions in which economies based on herding gave rise to cultures of honor, requiring males to be vigilant and aggressive toward potential threats.

YOU are about to learn...

- how humanist approaches to personality differ from psychodynamic and genetic ones.

- the contributions of Abraham Maslow, Carl Rogers, and Rollo May to understanding our inner lives.

- how psychological scientists evaluate humanist views.

The Inner Experience

A final way to look at personality starts from each person's own point of view, from the inside out. Biology may hand us temperamental dispositions that benefit or limit us, the environment may deal us some tough or fortunate experiences, our parents may treat us as we would or would not have wished. But the sum total of our personality is how we, individually, weave all of these elements together into a *life narrative*, the story that each of us develops to explain ourselves and make meaning of our experiences (Bruner, 1990; McAdams, 2008; McAdams & Pals, 2006; Sarbin, 1997).

Humanist Approaches

One such approach to personality comes from **humanist psychology**, which was launched as a movement in the early 1960s. The movement's chief leaders—Abraham Maslow (1908–1970), Carl Rogers (1902–1987), and Rollo May (1909–1994)—argued that it was time to replace psychoanalysis and behaviorism with a "third force" in psychology, one that would draw a fuller picture of human potential and personality. Psychologists who take a humanist approach to personality emphasize our uniquely human capacity to determine our own actions and futures.

Abraham Maslow The trouble with psychology, said Maslow (1970, 1971), was that it had ignored many of the positive aspects of life, such as joy, laughter, love, happiness, and *peak experiences*, rare moments of rapture caused by the attainment of excellence or the experience of beauty. The traits that Maslow thought most important to personality were not the Big Five, but rather the qualities of the *self-actualized person*, someone who strives for a life that is meaningful, challenging, and satisfying.

For Maslow, personality development could be viewed as a gradual progression toward self-actualization. Most psychologists, he argued, had a lopsided view of human nature, a result of their emphasis on studying emotional problems and negative traits such as neuroticism or insecurity. As Maslow (1971) wrote, "When you select out for careful study very fine and healthy people, strong people, creative people . . . then you get a very different view of mankind. You are asking how tall can people grow, what can a human being become?"

Carl Rogers As a clinician, Carl Rogers (1951, 1961) was interested not only in why some people cannot function well but also in what he called the "fully functioning individual." How you behave, he said, depends on your subjective reality, not on the external reality around you. Fully functioning people experience *congruence*, or harmony, between the image they project to others and their true feelings and wishes. They are trusting, warm, and open, rather than defensive or intolerant. Their beliefs about themselves are realistic.

To become fully functioning people, Rogers maintained, we all need **unconditional positive regard**, love and support for the people we are, without strings (conditions) attached. This doesn't mean that Winifred should be allowed to kick her brother when she is angry with him or that Wilbur may throw his dinner out the window because he doesn't like pot roast. In these cases, a parent can correct the child's behavior without withdrawing love from the child. The child can learn that the behavior, not the child, is what is bad. "House rules are 'no violence,' children," is a very different message from "You are horrible children for behaving so badly."

Unfortunately, Rogers observed, many children are raised with *conditional* positive regard: "I will love you if you behave well, and I won't love you if you behave badly." Adults often treat each other this way, too. People treated with conditional regard begin to suppress or deny feelings or actions that they believe are unacceptable to those they love. The result, said Rogers, is incongruence, a sense of being out of touch with your feelings, of not being true to your real self, which in turn produces low self-regard, defensiveness, and unhappiness. A person experiencing incongruence scores high on neuroticism, becoming bitter and negative.

Rollo May May shared with the humanists a belief in free will. But he also emphasized some of the inherently difficult and tragic aspects of the human condition, including loneliness, anxiety, and alienation. May brought to American psychology elements of the European philosophy of **existentialism**, which emphasizes such inevitable challenges of existence as the search for the meaning of life, the need to confront death, and the necessity of taking responsibility for our actions.

Free will, wrote May, carries a price in anxiety and despair, which is why so many people try to escape from freedom into narrow certainties and blame others for their misfortunes. For May, our personalities reflect the ways we cope with the struggles to find meaning in existence, to use our freedom wisely, and to face suffering and death bravely. May popularized the humanist idea that we can choose to make the best of ourselves by drawing on inner resources such as love and courage, but he added that we can never escape the harsh realities of life and loss.

You are never too old for self-actualization. Hulda Crooks, shown here at age 91 climbing Mount Fuji, took up mountain climbing at 54. "It's been a great inspiration for me," she said. "When I come down from the mountain I feel like I can battle in the valley again." She died at the age of 101.

humanist psychology A psychological approach that emphasizes personal growth, resilience, and the achievement of human potential.

unconditional positive regard To Carl Rogers, love or support given to another person with no conditions attached.

existentialism A philosophical approach that emphasizes the inevitable dilemmas and challenges of human existence.

IF YOU WERE AN ICEBERG...

THE PART EVERYONE GETS TO SEE

ALL THE GREAT ASPECTS OF YOUR PERSONALITY

S. Harris

Evaluating Humanist Approaches

As with psychodynamic theories, the major scientific criticism of humanist psychology is that many of its assumptions are untestable. Freud looked at humanity and saw destructive drives, selfishness, and lust. Maslow and Rogers looked at humanity and saw cooperation, selflessness, and love. May looked at humanity and saw fear of freedom, loneliness, and the struggle for meaning. These differences, say critics, may tell us more about the observers than about the observed.

Many humanist concepts, although intuitively appealing, are hard to define operationally (see Chapter 1). How can we know whether a person is self-fulfilled or self-actualized? How can we tell whether a woman's decision to quit her job and become a professional rodeo rider represents an "escape from freedom" or a freely made choice? And what exactly is unconditional positive regard? If it is defined as unquestioned support of a child's efforts at mastering a new skill, or as assurance that the child

Thinking Critically about Testing Humanist Ideas

is loved in spite of his or her mistakes, then it is clearly a good idea. But in the popular culture, it has often been interpreted as an unwillingness ever to say "no" to a child or to offer constructive criticism and set limits, which children need.

Despite such concerns, humanist psychologists have added balance to the study of personality. A contemporary specialty known as *positive psychology* follows in the footsteps of humanism by focusing on the qualities that enable people to be optimistic and resilient in times of stress (Gable & Haidt, 2005; Seligman & Csikszentmihaly, 2000). Influenced in part by the humanists, psychologists are studying many positive human traits, such as courage, altruism, the motivation to excel, and self-confidence. Developmental psychologists are studying ways to foster children's empathy and creativity. And social psychologists are studying the emotional and behavioral effects of the existential fear of death (Cohen et al., 2009; Pyszczynski, Rothschild, & Abdollahi, 2008).

The humanist and existential views of personality share one central message: We have the power to choose our own destinies, even when fate delivers us into tragedy. Across psychology, this message has fostered an appreciation of resilience in the face of adversity. ⊙▸ Simulate

Simulate the **experiment Multiple Selves** on **mypsychlab.com**

Study and **Review** on **mypsychlab.com**

Psychology in the News REVISITED

How are the dimensions of personality woven together in the case of Michael Jackson, whom his friends, fans, and critics viewed so differently? How might the approaches to personality described in this chapter help us to understand this fascinating man and his unusual life?

A psychodynamic theorist would emphasize Jackson's early years and unconscious motives in accounting for the entertainer's Peter Pan-like cultivation of friendships with children and his creation of a fantasy estate, Neverland Ranch. The eighth of ten siblings in a working-class family, Jackson had a troubled relationship with his father, Joe, who routinely abused him physically and emotionally during rehearsals. In 1993, in an interview with Oprah Winfrey, Michael said that he would sometimes even vomit when he saw his father. Was his creation of Neverland an unconscious effort to capture a childhood he himself never had? And what about Jackson's increasingly androgynous, indeed feminine, appearance and voice? Psychodynamic theorists would want to understand Jackson's psychosexual development; did he remain fixated at some childhood level, unable to assume adult sexuality?

Psychologists taking a biological view of personality would emphasize the genetic contributions to Jackson's unique talents and his extroversion—his desire to be in the limelight—which were apparent early on. In 1964, when he was only 6 years old, he joined his brothers' band, which became the Jackson 5. By age 8, he was doing lead vocals, and by the time he was 10, the band had signed a contract with Motown Records. Throughout his life, he cultivated publicity, sometimes leaking the sensational stories that circulated about him. He was famous for his flamboyant costumes and occasional sexual choreography, infamously grabbing or touching his crotch in the video for his album *Bad*.

Psychologists who take a learning or environmental perspective would examine situational influences on Jackson's personality, perhaps most powerfully his father's abusiveness. But they would find no inconsistency in the fact that Jackson was an extrovert when performing and, by many accounts, quite shy offstage:

All of us, they would note, display different parts of ourselves publicly depending on the circumstances and whom we are with. Social-cognitive learning theorists would especially emphasize the process of reciprocal determinism: Just as his musical career and blistering fame rewarded and encouraged certain traits and attitudes (such as self-promotion, extravagance, and flashiness), his own traits and attitudes would have attracted him to that world in the first place.

Cultural psychologists might observe that America encourages the kind of constant reinvention of oneself that Jackson was famous for. That culture often values image over reality, transience over permanence, and celebrity over obscurity. It promotes the belief that people can change their bodies, their personalities, and their emotional problems, and that medication or illegal drugs can cure anything that ails us. The culture of celebrity can, however, devour those who are its most successful beneficiaries. Jackson said that he had been able to cope with his worldwide celebrity because of a loving family, strong faith, and supportive friends and fans. But his apparent dependence on powerful prescription drugs, allegedly to help him sleep, and his cosmetic surgeries illuminate a darker corner of the American dream.

Finally, in the humanist view, all of us are free to write and rewrite our life stories and to choose the beliefs and values that guide our lives, and Michael Jackson was no exception. But humanists would also remind us that we do not know anything for sure about Jackson's inner, private self. The private man could have been quite different from his public persona.

Ultimately, we can only speculate about who the "real" Michael Jackson was. Nonetheless, all of us can use the insights of the theorists in this chapter to better understand ourselves and those we care about. Each of us is a mix of genetic influences, learned habits, the pressure of peers, new experiences, cultural norms, unconscious fears and conflicts, and our own private visions of possibility. This mix gives each of us the stamp of our personality, the qualities that make us feel uniquely . . . us.

Taking Psychology with You

How to Avoid the "Barnum Effect"

How well does the following paragraph describe you?

Some of your aspirations tend to be pretty unrealistic. At times you are extroverted, affable, and sociable, while at other times you are introverted, wary, and reserved. You pride yourself on being an independent thinker and do not accept others' opinions without satisfactory proof. You prefer a certain amount of change and variety, and you become dissatisfied when hemmed in by restrictions and limitations. At times you have serious doubts as to whether you have made the right decision or done the right thing.

When people believe that this description was written just for them, as the result of a personalized horoscope or handwriting analysis, they all say the same thing: "It describes me *exactly!*" Everyone thinks this description is accurate because it is vague enough to apply to almost everyone and it is flattering. Don't we all consider ourselves to be "independent thinkers"?

This is why many psychologists worry about the "Barnum effect" (Snyder & Shenkel, 1975). P. T. Barnum was the great circus showman who said, "There's a sucker born every minute." He knew that the formula for success was to "have a little something for everybody," which is just what unscientific personality profiles, horoscopes, and handwriting analysis (graphology) have in common. They have "a little something for everyone" and are therefore nonfalsifiable.

For example, graphologists claim that they can identify your personality traits from the form and distribution of your handwritten letters. Wide spacing between words means you feel isolated and lonely. If your lines drift upward, you are an "uplifting" optimist, and if your lines droop downward, you are a pessimist who feels you are being "dragged down." If you make large capital *I*'s, you have a large ego.

Graphologists are not the same as handwriting experts, who are trained to determine, say, whether a document is a forgery. Graphologists, like astrologers, usually know little or nothing about the scientific method, how to correct for their biases, or how to empirically test their claims. That is why the many different graphological approaches usually conflict. For example, according to one system, a certain way of crossing *t*'s reveals someone who is vicious and sadistic; according to another, it reveals a practical joker (Beyerstein, 1996).

Whenever graphology *has* been tested empirically, it has failed. A meta-analysis of 200 published studies found no validity or reliability to graphology in predicting work performance, aptitudes, or personality. No school of graphology fared better than any other, and no graphologist was able to perform better than untrained amateurs making guesses from the same writing samples (Dean, 1992; Klimoski, 1992).

If graphology were just an amusing game, no one would worry about it, but unfortunately it can have harmful consequences. Graphologists have been hired by companies to predict a person's leadership ability, attention to detail, willingness to be a good team player, and more. They pass judgment on people's honesty, generosity, and even supposed criminal tendencies. How would you feel if you were turned down for a job because some graphologist branded you a potential thief on the basis of your alleged "desire-for-possession hooks" on your *S*'s?

If you do not want to be a victim of the Barnum effect, research offers this advice to help you think critically about graphology and its many cousins:

Beware of all-purpose descriptions that could apply to anyone. Sometimes you doubt your decisions; who among us has not? Sometimes you feel outgoing and sometimes shy; who does not? Do you "have sexual secrets that you are afraid of confessing"? Just about everybody does.

Beware of your own selective perceptions. Most of us are so impressed when an astrologer, psychic, or graphologist gets something right that we overlook all the descriptions that are plain wrong. Be aware of the confirmation bias—the tendency to explain away all the descriptions that don't fit.

Resist flattery and emotional reasoning. This is a hard one! It is easy to reject a profile that describes you as selfish or stupid. Watch out for the ones that make you feel good by telling you how wonderful and smart you are, what a great leader you will be, or how modest you are about your exceptional abilities.

If you keep your ability to think critically with you, you won't end up paying hard cash for soft answers or taking a job you dislike because it fits your "personality type." In other words, you'll have proved Barnum wrong.

Summary ((•─|Listen to an **audio file** of your chapter on **mypsychlab.com**

• *Personality* refers to an individual's distinctive and relatively stable pattern of behavior, motives, thoughts, and emotions. Personality is made up of many different *traits*, characteristics that describe a person across situations.

Psychodynamic Theories of Personality

• Sigmund Freud was the founder of *psychoanalysis*, which was the first *psychodynamic* theory. Modern psychodynamic theories share an emphasis on unconscious processes and a belief in the formative role of childhood experiences and early unconscious conflicts.

• To Freud, the personality consists of the *id* (the source of sexual energy, which he called the *libido*, and the aggressive instinct); the *ego* (the source of reason); and the *superego* (the source of conscience). *Defense mechanisms* protect the ego from unconscious anxiety. They include, among others, repression, projection, displacement (one form of which is sublimation), regression, and denial.

• Freud believed that personality develops in a series of *psychosexual stages*, with the *phallic (Oedipal) stage* most crucial. During this stage, Freud believed, the *Oedipus complex* occurs, in which the child desires the parent of the other sex and feels rivalry with the same-sex parent. When the Oedipus complex is resolved, the child identifies with the same-sex parent, but females retain a lingering sense of inferiority and "penis envy"—a notion later contested by female psychoanalysts like Clara Thompson and Karen Horney.

• Carl Jung believed that people share a *collective unconscious* that contains universal memories and images, or *archetypes,* such as the *shadow* (evil) and the Earth Mother.

• The *object-relations school* emphasizes the importance of the first two years of life rather than the Oedipal phase; the infant's relationships to important figures, especially the mother, rather than sexual needs and drives; and the problem in male development of breaking away from the mother.

• Psychodynamic approaches have been criticized for violating the principle of falsifiability; for overgeneralizing from atypical patients to everyone; and for basing theories on the unreliable memories and retrospective accounts of adults, which can create an *illusion of causality*. However, some psychodynamic ideas have received empirical support, including the existence of nonconscious processes and defenses.

The Modern Study of Personality

• Most popular tests that divide personality into "types" are not valid or reliable. In research, psychologists typically rely on *objective tests (inventories)* to identify and study personality traits and disorders.

• Gordon Allport argued that people have a few *central traits* that are key to their personalities and a greater number of *secondary traits* that are less fundamental. Raymond Cattell used *factor analysis* to identify clusters of traits that he considered the basic components of personality. There is strong evidence, from studies around the world, for the *Big Five* dimensions of personality: extroversion versus introversion, neuroticism (negative emotionality) versus emotional stability, agreeableness versus antagonism, conscientiousness versus impulsiveness, and openness to experience versus resistance to new experience. Although these dimensions are quite stable over time and across circumstances, some of them do change over the life span, reflecting maturational development or common adult responsibilities.

Genetic Influences on Personality

• The nature–nurture debate is one of the oldest controversies in philosophy and psychology, but it is pretty much over. Today most psychologists recognize that *genes*, the basic units of heredity, account for about half of the variation in human traits, but the environment and experience account for the other half. Genes are made up of elements of *DNA* (deoxyribonucleic acid), but most of our total DNA, called *noncoding DNA*, lies outside the genes and may have greater influence than realized.

• One line of evidence for the biological origins of personality differences comes from studies of many other species, including octopuses, pigs, hyenas, bears, horses, dogs, and all primates, which reveal variation in many of the same characteristic traits that humans have.

• In human beings, individual differences in *temperaments*, such as reactivity, soothability, and positive or negative emotionality, appear to be inborn, emerging early in life and influencing subsequent personality development. Temperamental differences in extremely reactive and nonreactive children may be due to variations in the responsiveness of the sympathetic nervous system to change and novelty.

● *Behavioral-genetic* data from twin and adoption studies suggest that the *heritability* of many adult personality traits is about .50. Genetic influences create dispositions and set limits on the expression of specific traits. But even traits that are highly heritable are often modified throughout life by circumstances, chance, and learning.

Environmental Influences on Personality

● People often behave inconsistently in different circumstances when behaviors that are rewarded in one situation are punished or ignored in another. According to *social-cognitive learning theory*, personality results from the interaction of the environment and aspects of the individual, in a pattern of *reciprocal determinism*.

● Behavioral geneticists have found that an important influence on personality is the *nonshared environment*, the unique experiences that each child in a family has.

● Three lines of evidence challenge the popular assumption that parents have the greatest impact on their children's personalities and behavior: (1) Behavioral-genetic studies find that shared family environment has little if any influence on variations in personality; (2) few parents have a consistent child-rearing style over time and with all their children; and (3) even when parents try to be consistent, there may be little relation between what they do and how the children turn out. However, parents can modify their children's temperaments, prevent children at risk of delinquency and crime from choosing a path of antisocial behavior, influence many of their children's values and attitudes, and teach them to be kind and helpful. And, of course, parents profoundly affect the quality of their relationship with their children.

● One major environmental influence on personality comes from a person's peer groups, which can be more powerful than parents. Most children and teenagers behave differently with their parents than with their peers.

Cultural Influences on Personality

● Many qualities that Western psychologists treat as individual personality traits are heavily influenced by *culture*. People from *individualist cultures* define themselves in different terms than those from *collectivist cultures*, and they perceive their "selves" as more stable across situations. Cultures vary in their norms for many behaviors, such as cleanliness, notions of time, and expectations of helpfulness. Altruistic children tend to come from cultures in which their families assign them many tasks that contribute to the family's well-being or economic survival.

● Male aggression is not simply a result of male hormones; it is also influenced by the economic requirements of the culture a man grows up in, which in turn shape men's beliefs about when violence is necessary and men's predisposition to respond to perceived insults with violence. Herding economies foster male aggressiveness more than agricultural economies do. Men in *cultures of honor*, including certain regions of the American South and West, are more likely to become angry when they feel insulted and to behave aggressively to restore their sense of honor than are men from other cultures; when they are insulted, their levels of cortisol and testosterone rise quickly, whereas men from other cultures and regions of the United States generally do not show this reaction.

● Cultural theories of personality face the problem of describing broad cultural differences and their influences on personality without promoting stereotypes or overlooking universal human needs.

The Inner Experience

● *Humanist psychologists* focus on a person's subjective sense of self, the free will to change, and the *life narrative* each person creates. They emphasize human potential and the strengths of human nature, as in Abraham Maslow's concepts of *peak experiences* and *self-actualization*. Carl Rogers stressed the importance of *unconditional positive regard* in creating a fully functioning person. Rollo May brought *existentialism* into psychology, emphasizing some of the inherent challenges of human existence that result from having free will, such as the search for meaning in life.

● Some ideas from humanist psychology are subjective and difficult to measure, but others have fostered research in *positive psychology*, which emphasizes positive aspects of personality such as optimism, hope, and resilience under adversity. Other psychologists are studying the emotional and behavioral effects of the existential fear of death.

Psychology in the News, Revisited

● Genetic influences, life experiences and learned habits, cultural norms, unconscious fears and conflicts, and our private, inner sense of self all combine in complex ways to create our complex, distinctive personalities.

Taking Psychology with You

● Critical thinkers can learn to avoid the "Barnum effect"—being a sucker for fake inventories, horoscopes, handwriting analysis, and other pseudoscientific "tests" of personality.

Key Terms

personality 39

traits 39

Sigmund Freud 40

psychoanalysis 40

psychodynamic theories 40

id 40

libido 40

ego 40

superego 40

defense mechanisms 41

repression 41

projection 41

displacement and sublimation 41

regression 41

denial 41

psychosexual stages (oral, anal, phallic, latency, genital) 41

Oedipus complex 42

Clara Thompson and Karen Horney 43

Carl Jung 43

collective unconscious 43

archetypes 43

shadow 43

object-relations school 43

mental representations 44

illusion of causality 45

objective tests (inventories) 46

Gordon Allport 46

central and secondary traits 46, 47

Raymond Cattell 47

factor analysis 47

the Big Five personality factors 47

genes 50

temperaments 51

heritability 51

behavioral genetics 51

social-cognitive learning theory 54

reciprocal determinism 55

nonshared environment 55

culture 58

individualist cultures 58

collectivist cultures 58

culture of honor 61

life narratives 63

humanist psychology 63

Abraham Maslow 63

peak experiences 63

self-actualization 63

Carl Rogers 63

congruence 63

unconditional positive regard 63

Rollo May 63

existentialism 63

positive psychology 64

Personality is a distinctive pattern of behavior, mannerisms, thoughts, and emotions that characterizes an individual over time.
• **Traits:** habitual ways of behaving, thinking, and feeling.

Psychodynamic Theories of Personality

Psychodynamic theories emphasize unconscious processes, the role of childhood experiences, and unconscious conflicts.

Sigmund Freud

To Freud, personality consists of three systems, which ideally should be in balance.
• **Id**
• **Ego**
• **Superego**
Defense mechanisms, such as repression, denial, and projection, serve to protect the ego from conflict, but they can distort reality and cause self-defeating behavior.

Psychosexual stages of personality development:
• Oral
• Anal
• Phallic (Oedipal)
• Latency
• Genital

Carl Jung

Jung believed that all people share a **collective unconscious**, consisting of universal memories and **archetypes**—universal symbols, stories, or human characters representing good, evil, and other mythic qualities.

Object-Relations School

The **object-relations school** emphasizes the importance of the first two years of life and formative relationships, especially with the mother.

Evaluating Psychodynamic Theories

These theories are often guilty of three scientific flaws:
• They violate the principle of falsifiability.
• They draw universal principles from the experiences of a few atypical patients.
• They are based on retrospective accounts and fallible memories of patients.

Some psychodynamic concepts have been empirically supported:
• Unconscious processes
• Some defense mechanisms (e.g., denial)
• The mind-body link in creating symptoms of stress

The Modern Study of Personality

Measuring Personality Traits

Core Personality Traits

• Many popular personality tests, especially those designed to identify "types," lack reliability and validity.
• **Objective tests** (inventories) are standardized questionnaires about needs, values, interests, emotional problems, typical ways of responding to situations, and personality traits.

Clustering Traits

• Raymond B. Cattell used **factor analysis** to identify the core clusters of personality traits.
• Factor-analytic studies today support the existence of basic personality dimensions, known informally as the Big Five:
— Extroversion versus introversion
— Neuroticism versus emotional stability
— Agreeableness versus antagonism
— Conscientiousness versus impulsiveness
— Openness to experience versus resistance to new experience

The Big Five dimensions have been documented around the world, emerging whether people are asked for self-reports or are assessed by others. They are remarkably stable over a lifetime, although neuroticism tends to decrease and conscientiousness tends to increase in young adulthood.

Genetic Influences

Animal Personalities

Some researchers study the biological basis of personality by identifying traits in other species. They have found evidence for some of the Big Five in species as varied as octopuses, bears, and dogs.

Heredity and Temperament

Babies are born differing in certain key **temperaments**, such as reactivity and soothability, which may form the basis of later personality traits.

Heredity and Traits

- Some researchers investigate genetic contributions to personality by doing **heritability** studies of twins and adopted individuals.
- **Behavioral-genetic** data from these studies show that the heritability of most traits is between 20 and 50%.

Evaluating Genetic Theories

- A genetic predisposition does not imply genetic inevitability.
- Today, almost all psychologists who study personality regard biology and experience as interacting influences.

Environmental Influences

Social-cognitive learning theory:
- Holds that personality traits result in part from a person's learning history and resulting expectations and beliefs.
- Emphasizes **reciprocal determinism**, the two-way interaction between a person's qualities and the specific demands of the situation.
- Finds that the most influential experiences that shape personality are those in the **nonshared environment**, unique and chance events not shared with parents and siblings.

Parental Influence—and Its Limits

- Few parents have a single child-rearing style that is consistent over time and that they use with all their children.
- Even when parents try to be consistent, there may be little relation between what they do and how their children turn out.
- Parents do influence their children's interests, self-esteem, religious views, and other values, and can modify their children's genetic predispositions.

The Power of Peers

Peer groups' influence can be more powerful than parents' influence on a child's personality development.

Cultural Influences

A **culture** is a program of shared rules or values that govern the behavior of members of a community or society.
- In **individualist cultures**, the independence of the individual often takes precedence over the needs of the group.
- In **collectivist cultures**, group harmony often takes precedence over the wishes of the individual.

Culture and Traits

- When people fail to understand the influence of culture on behavior, they may misattribute a person's behavior to personality. For example, cultures differ in their rules governing notions of cleanliness, helpfulness, and timeliness.
- Male aggressiveness is often less a matter of testosterone or personality than of cultural norms, determined turn by a culture's economy and notions of male honor.

Evaluating Cultural Approaches

- Cultural psychologists face the problem of how to describe cultural influences on personality without stereotyping.
- Individuals are affected by their culture, but they vary within it.

The Inner Experience

Humanist psychology emphasizes a person's subjective sense of self.
- Abraham Maslow introduced the concepts of **peak experiences** and **self-actualization**.
- Carl Rogers stressed the importance of **unconditional positive regard**.
- Rollo May's inclusion of **existentialism** emphasized some of the inherent human challenges that result from free will.

Many humanist assumptions are untestable and hard to define operationally, but humanist ideas about positive human traits, such as courage and resilience, have added balance to the study of personality.

Age Record Broken as 70-Year-Old Gives Birth

MUZAFFARNAGER, INDIA, July 5, 2008. At age 70, Omkari Panwar has become the oldest women ever to give birth after delivering twins, a boy and a girl, by emergency cesarean section. The babies arrived a month early and weigh only two pounds each, but are healthy.

Ms. Panwar and her 77-year-old husband, Charan Singh Panwar, already have two adult daughters and five grandchildren, but they were determined to produce a male heir. To pay for in vitro fertilization, Charan, a retired farmer, sold his buffaloes, mortgaged his land, spent his savings, and took out a credit card loan. His family now relies on financial help from friends, but he says that he can die a happy man and proud father because he finally has a son.

Other women around the world have had babies when they were past the age of 60. In Los Angeles in 1997, Arceli Keh, 63, gave birth to a daughter with sperm donated by her husband. In India in 2003, a 65-year-old schoolteacher, Satyabhama Mahapatra, gave birth to her first child, a boy, after 50 years of marriage; she was impregnated with sperm from her husband and an egg from her 26-year-old niece. In Romania in 2005, a 66-year-old unmarried professor of literature, Adriana Iliescu, became pregnant through in vitro fertilization using sperm and an egg from anonymous donors. And in 2006, in Spain, Carmela Bousada, who had no husband or other children, gave birth to twins a week before her 67th birthday.

Across the globe, countries are wrestling with the complicated biological, ethical, and legal issues that late in vitro pregnancies create. In some European nations, legislation prohibits in vitro procedures after age 50. But opponents of such restrictions point out that no country prohibits older men from conceiving children, so there should likewise be no limits on women, as long as they are healthy enough to maintain a pregnancy.

Omkari Panwar, at 70, the world's oldest mother, and her husband Charan Singh Panwar, 77, hold their infant son and daughter, born a month early. The Panwars have two daughters and five grandchildren but wanted a male heir.

Development Over the Life Span

How do you react to the idea of a couple in their 70s having twins? Would it make any difference if the mother were "only" 65 years old, or 60? Would it make any difference if their motive were something other than a desire for a male heir? What if the parents had no other children? And do you feel the same about older fathers as you do about older mothers?

There were no headlines when James Doohan, who had played Scotty in the original *Star Trek* series and movies, became a father for the fourth time at the age of 80 (his second wife, Wende, was then age 43). Doohan died five years later of pneumonia and Alzheimer's disease. Was it loving and natural, or selfish and unethical, for James Doohan to father a child when he was 80? When Carmela Bousada's mother died at the age of 101, Bousada, at 66, decided it was "the right time" for her to have children.

Is there a right time to become a parent? For that matter, is there a right time to do anything in life—go to school, get married, retire . . . die? The universal human journey from birth to death was once far more predictable than it is today. Going to college, choosing a job, starting a family, and advancing up the ladder to retirement were all events that tended to happen in sequence. But because of demographic changes, an unpredictable economy, advances in reproductive technology, and many other forces, millions of people are now doing things out of order, if they do them at all. Today, going to college, having children, changing careers, or starting a family may occur in almost any decade of adulthood.

Developmental psychologists study physiological and cognitive changes across the life span and how these are affected by a person's genetic predispositions, culture, circumstances, and experiences. Some focus on children's mental and social development, including **socialization**, the process by which children learn the rules and behavior expected of them by society. Others specialize in the study of adolescents, adults, or the very old. In this chapter, we will explore some of their major findings, starting at the very beginning of human development, with the period before birth, and continuing through adulthood into old age. And at the end of the chapter, you will find out what has happened to some of those older mothers since they had their babies.

73

YOU are about to learn...

- the stages of prenatal development and some factors that can harm an embryo or fetus during pregnancy.
- how culture affects a baby's physical maturation.
- why contact comfort and attachment are so important for infants (and adults).
- the varieties of infant attachment.

From Conception through the First Year

A baby's development, before and after birth, is a marvel of *maturation*, the sequential unfolding of genetically influenced behavior and physical characteristics. In only 9 months of a mother's pregnancy, a cell grows from a dot this big (.) to a squalling bundle of energy who looks just like Aunt Sarah. In another 15 months, that bundle of energy grows into a babbling toddler who is curious about everything. No other time in human development brings so many changes so fast.

Prenatal Development

Prenatal development is divided into three stages: the germinal, the embryonic, and the fetal. The *germinal stage* begins at fertilization, when the male sperm unites with the female ovum (egg); the fertilized single-celled egg is called a *zygote*. The zygote soon begins to divide, and in 10 to 14 days, it has become a cluster of cells that attaches itself to the wall of the uterus. The outer portion of this cluster will form part of the placenta and umbilical cord, and the inner portion becomes the embryo. The placenta, connected to the embryo by the umbilical cord, serves as the growing embryo's link for food from the mother. It allows nutrients to enter and wastes to exit, and it screens out some, but not all, harmful substances.

Once implantation is completed, about two weeks after fertilization, the *embryonic stage* begins, lasting until the eighth week after conception, at which point the embryo is only 1½ inches long. During the fourth to eighth weeks, the hormone testosterone is secreted by the rudimentary testes in embryos that are genetically male; without this hormone, the embryo will develop to be anatomically female. After eight weeks, the *fetal stage* begins. The organism, now called a *fetus*, further develops the organs and systems that existed in rudimentary form in the embryonic stage. ✳ Explore

Although the womb is a fairly sturdy protector of the growing embryo or fetus, the prenatal environment—which is influenced by the mother's own health, allergies, and diet—can affect the course of development, for example, by predisposing an infant to later obesity or immune problems (Coe & Lubach, 2008). Most people don't realize it, but fathers play an important role in prenatal development, too. Fathers over 50 have three times the risk of conceiving a child who develops schizophrenia as do fathers under age 25 (Malaspina, 2001); teenage fathers have an increased risk that their babies will be born prematurely or have low birth weight; babies of men exposed to solvents and other chemicals in the workplace are more likely to be miscarried, be stillborn, or develop cancer later in life; and being an older father increases the probability that a child will be autistic or bipolar (Frans et al., 2008; Reichenberg et al., 2006; Saey, 2008).

During a woman's pregnancy, some harmful influences can cross the placental barrier (O'Rahilly & Müller, 2001). These influences include the following:

1 **German measles** (rubella), especially early in the pregnancy, can affect the fetus's eyes, ears, and heart. The most common consequence is deafness. Rubella is preventable if the mother has been vaccinated, which can be done up to three months before pregnancy.

2 **X-rays or other radiation and toxic substances** can cause fetal deformities and cognitive abnormalities that can last throughout life. Exposure

socialization The processes by which children learn the behaviors, attitudes, and expectations required of them by their society or culture.

✳ Explore
Embryonic Period on mypsychlab.com

Developmental psychologists study people across the life span. They would have a living laboratory with this six-generation family: Sara Knauss, age 118 (center); her daughter, age 95 (right), her grandson, age 73 (center), her great granddaughter, age 49 (standing with her dad), her great-great granddaughter, age 27 (on floor), and her great-great-great grandson, age 3.

to lead is associated with attention problems and lower IQ scores, as is exposure to mercury, found most commonly in contaminated fish (Newland & Rasmussen, 2003).

3 **Sexually transmitted diseases** can cause mental retardation, blindness, and other physical disorders. Genital herpes affects the fetus only if the mother has an outbreak at the time of delivery, which exposes the newborn to the virus as the baby passes through the birth canal. (This risk can be avoided by having a cesarean section.) HIV, the virus that causes AIDS, can also be transmitted to the fetus, especially if the mother has developed AIDS and has not been treated.

4 **Cigarette smoking** during pregnancy increases the likelihood of miscarriage, premature birth, an abnormal fetal heartbeat, and an underweight baby. The negative effects may last long after birth, showing up in increased rates of infant sickness, sudden infant death syndrome (SIDS), and, in later childhood, hyperactivity, learning difficulties, asthma, and even antisocial behavior (Button, Thapar, & McGuffin, 2005).

5 **Regular consumption of alcohol** can kill neurons throughout the fetus's developing brain and impair the child's later mental abilities, attention span, and academic achievement (Ikonomidou et al., 2000; Streissguth, 2001). Having more than two drinks a day significantly increases the risk of *fetal alcohol syndrome (FAS)*, which is associated with low birth weight, a smaller brain, facial deformities, lack of coordination, and mental retardation. Because alcohol can affect many different aspects of fetal brain development, most specialists recommend that a pregnant woman abstain from drinking alcohol.

6 **Drugs other than alcohol** can be harmful to the fetus, whether they are illicit ones such as cocaine and heroin, or commonly used legal substances such as antibiotics, antihistamines, tranquilizers, acne medication, and diet pills. Cocaine can cause subtle impairments in children's cognitive and language abilities and larger ones in the ability to manage impulses and frustrations (Lester, LaGasse, & Seifer, 1998; Stanwood & Levitt, 2001).

The lesson is clear. A pregnant woman does well to stop smoking and drinking alcohol, and to take no other drugs of any kind unless they are

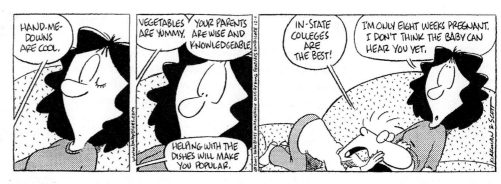

Many parents hope to have an influence on their offspring even before their babies are born.

medically necessary—and then to accept the fact that her child will never be properly grateful for all that sacrifice!

The Infant's World

Newborn babies could never survive on their own, but they are far from being passive and inert. Many abilities, tendencies, and characteristics are universal in human beings and are present at birth or develop very early, given certain experiences. Indeed, experience plays a crucial role in shaping the infant's mind, brain, and gene expression right from the get-go. Newborn infants who get little touching will grow more slowly and release less growth hormone than their amply cuddled peers, and throughout their lives, they have stronger reactions to stress and are more prone to depression and its cognitive deficits (Diamond & Amso, 2008; Field, 2009).

Physical and Perceptual Abilities
Newborns begin life with several *motor reflexes*, automatic behaviors that are necessary for survival. They will suck on anything suckable, such as a

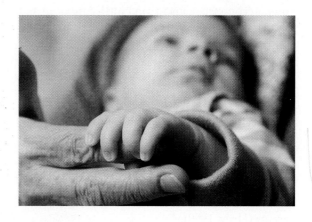

Infants are born with a grasping reflex; they will cling to any offered finger. And they need the comfort of touch, which their adult caregivers love to provide.

contact comfort In primates, the innate pleasure derived from close physical contact; it is the basis of the infant's first attachment.

separation anxiety The distress that most children develop, at about 6 to 8 months of age, when their primary caregivers temporarily leave them with strangers.

Watch the **Video Attachment in Infants** on mypsychlab.com

nipple or finger. They will grasp tightly a finger pressed on their tiny palms. They will turn their heads toward a touch on the cheek or corner of the mouth and search for something to suck on, a handy rooting reflex that allows them to find the breast or bottle. Many of these reflexes eventually disappear, but others—such as the knee-jerk, eye-blink, and sneeze reflexes—remain.

Babies are also equipped with a set of inborn perceptual abilities. They can see, hear, touch, smell, and taste (bananas and sugar water are in, rotten eggs are out). A newborn's visual focus range is only about 8 inches, the average distance between the baby and the face of the person holding the baby, but visual ability develops rapidly. Newborns can distinguish contrasts, shadows, and edges. And they can discriminate their mother or other primary caregiver on the basis of smell, sight, or sound almost immediately.

Culture and Maturation Although infants everywhere develop according to the same maturational sequence, many aspects of their development depend on cultural customs that govern how their parents hold, touch, feed, and talk to them (Rogoff, 2003). In the United States, Canada, and Germany and most other European countries, babies are expected to sleep for eight uninterrupted hours by the age of 4 or 5 months. This milestone is considered a sign of neurological maturity, although many babies wail when the parent puts them in the crib at night and leaves the room.

But among Mayan Indians, rural Italians, African villagers, Indian Rajput villagers, and urban Japanese, this nightly clash of wills rarely occurs because the infant sleeps with the mother for the first few years of life, waking and nursing about every four hours. These differences in babies' sleep arrangements reflect cultural and parental values. Mothers in these cultures believe it is important to sleep with the baby so that both will forge a close bond; in contrast, many urban North American and German parents believe it is important to foster the child's independence as soon as possible (Keller et al., 2005; Morelli et al., 1992).

Attachment

Emotional attachment is a universal capacity of all primates and is crucial for health and survival all through life. The mother is usually the first and primary object of attachment for an infant, but in many cultures (and other species), babies become just as attached to their fathers, siblings, and grandparents (Hrdy, 1999).

Interest in the importance of early attachment began with the work of British psychiatrist John Bowlby (1969, 1973), who observed the devastating effects on babies raised in orphanages without touches or cuddles, and on other children raised in conditions of severe deprivation or neglect. The babies were physically healthy but emotionally despairing, remote, and listless. By becoming attached to their caregivers, Bowlby said, children gain a secure base from which they can explore the environment and a haven of safety to return to when they are afraid. Ideally, infants will find a balance between feeling securely attached to the caregiver and feeling free to explore and learn in new environments.

Contact Comfort Attachment begins with physical touching and cuddling between infant and parent. **Contact comfort**, the pleasure of being touched and held, is not only crucial for newborns; it continues to be important throughout life, releasing a flood of pleasure-producing and stress-reducing endorphins (see Chapter 14). In hospital settings, even the mildest touch by a nurse or physician on the patient's arm or forehead is reassuring psychologically and lowers blood pressure.

Margaret and Harry Harlow first demonstrated the importance of contact comfort by raising infant rhesus monkeys with two kinds of artificial mothers (Harlow, 1958; Harlow & Harlow, 1966). One, which they called the "wire mother," was a forbidding construction of wires and warming lights, with a milk bottle connected to it. The other, the "cloth mother," was constructed of wire but covered in foam rubber and cuddly terry cloth (see Figure 3.1). At the time, many psychologists thought that babies become attached to their mothers simply because mothers provide food (Blum, 2002). But the Harlows' baby monkeys ran to the terry-cloth mother when they were frightened or startled, and snuggling up to it calmed them down. Human children also seek contact comfort when they are in an unfamiliar situation, are scared by a nightmare, or fall and hurt themselves. **Watch**

Separation and Security Once babies are emotionally attached to the mother or other caregiver, separation can be a wrenching experience. Between 6 and 8 months of age, babies become wary or fearful of strangers. They wail if they are put in an unfamiliar setting or are left with an unfamiliar person. And they show **separation anxiety** if the primary caregiver temporarily leaves them. This reaction usually continues until the middle of

FIGURE 3.1
The Comfort of Contact
Infants need cuddling as much as they need food. In Margaret and Harry Harlow's studies, infant rhesus monkeys were reared with a cuddly terry-cloth "mother" and with a bare-wire "mother" that provided milk (left). The infants would cling to the cuddly mother even when they were not being fed, and they would run to her for comfort when they were frightened.

the second year, but many children show signs of distress until they are about 3 years old (Hrdy, 1999). All children go through this phase, though cultural child-rearing practices influence how strongly the anxiety is felt and how long it lasts. In cultures where babies are raised with lots of adults and other children, separation anxiety is not as intense or as long-lasting as it can be in countries where babies form attachments primarily or exclusively with the mother (Rothbaum et al., 2000).

To study the nature of the attachment between mothers and babies, Mary Ainsworth (1973, 1979) devised an experimental method called the *Strange Situation*. A mother brings her baby into an unfamiliar room containing lots of toys. After a while, a stranger comes in and attempts to play with the child. The mother leaves the baby with the stranger. She then returns and plays with the child, and the stranger leaves. Finally, the mother leaves the baby alone for three minutes and returns. In each case, observers carefully note how the baby behaves with the mother, with the stranger, and when the baby is alone.

Ainsworth divided children into three categories on the basis of their reactions to the Strange Situation. Some babies are *securely attached*: They cry or protest if the parent leaves the room; they welcome her back and then play happily again; they are clearly more attached to the mother than to the stranger. Other babies are *insecurely attached*, and this insecurity can take two forms. The child may be *avoidant*, not caring if the mother leaves the room, making little effort to seek contact with her

on her return, and treating the stranger about the same as the mother. Or the child may be *anxious* or *ambivalent*, resisting contact with the mother at reunion but protesting loudly if she leaves. Anxious-ambivalent babies may cry to be picked up and then demand to be put down, or they may behave as if they are angry with the mother and resist her efforts to comfort them.

What Causes Insecure Attachment?
Ainsworth believed that the difference between secure, avoidant, and anxious-ambivalent attachment lies primarily in the way mothers treat their babies during the first year. Mothers who are sensitive and responsive to their babies' needs, she said, create securely attached infants; mothers who are uncomfortable with or insensitive to their babies create insecurely attached infants. To many, the implication was that babies needed exactly the right kind of mothering from the very start to become securely attached, and that putting a child in daycare would retard this important development—notions that have caused considerable insecurity among mothers!

Ainsworth's measure of attachment, however, did not take the baby's experience into account. Babies who become attached to many adults, because they live in large extended families or have spent a lot of time with adults in daycare, may seem to be avoidant in the Strange Situation because they don't panic when their mothers leave. But perhaps they have simply learned to be comfortable with strangers. Moreover, although there is a mod-

STYLES OF ATTACHMENT

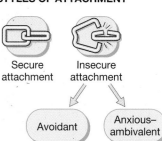

Secure attachment

Insecure attachment

Avoidant

Anxious–ambivalent

est correlation between a mother's sensitivity to her child and the security of her child's attachment, this doesn't tell us which causes what, or whether something else causes both sensitivity and secure attachment. Programs designed to help new mothers become less anxious and more attuned to their babies do help some moms become more sensitive, but these programs only modestly affect the child's degree of secure attachment (Bakermans-Kranenburg et al., 2008).

The emphasis on maternal sensitivity also overlooks the fact that most children, all over the world, form a secure attachment to their mothers in spite of wide variations in child-rearing practices (LeVine & Norman, 2008; Mercer, 2006). German babies are frequently left on their own for a few hours at a stretch by mothers who believe that even babies should become self-reliant. And among the Efe of Africa, babies spend about half their time away from their mothers in the care of older children and other adults (Tronick, Morelli, & Ivey, 1992). Yet German and Efe children are not insecure, and they develop as normally as children who spend more time with their mothers.

Likewise, time spent in daycare has no effect on the security of a child's attachment. In a longitudinal study of more than 1,000 children, researchers compared infants who were in child care 30 hours or more a week, from age 3 months to age 15 months, with children who spent fewer than 10 hours a week in child care. The two groups did not differ on any measure of attachment (NICHD Early Child Care Research Network, 2006). (The daycare group also did better than children at home on measures of social, language, and cognitive development, although some children in daycare were more aggressive and disobedient as well.)

What factors, then, do promote insecure attachment?

- *Abandonment and deprivation in the first year or two of life.* Institutionalized babies are more likely than adopted children to have later problems with attachment, whereas babies adopted before age 1 or 2 eventually become as securely attached as their nonadopted peers (Rutter et al., 2004; van den Dries et al., 2009).

- *Parenting that is abusive, neglectful, or erratic because the parent is chronically irresponsible or clinically depressed.* A South African research team observed 147 mothers with their 2-month-old infants and followed up when the babies were 18 months old. Many of the mothers who had suffered from postpartum depression became either too intrusive with their infants or too remote and insensitive. In turn, their babies were more likely to be insecurely attached at 18 months (Tomlinson, Cooper, & Murray, 2005).

- *The child's own genetically influenced temperament.* Babies who are fearful and prone to crying from birth are more likely to show insecure behavior in the Strange Situation, suggesting that their later insecure attachment may reflect a temperamental predisposition (Belsky et al., 1996; Gillath et al., 2008; Seifer et al., 1996).

- *Stressful circumstances in the child's family.* Infants and young children may temporarily shift from secure to insecure attachment, becoming clingy and fearful of being left alone, if their families are undergoing a period of stress, as during parental divorce or a parent's chronic illness (Belsky et al., 1996; Mercer, 2006).

The bottom line, however, is that infants are biologically disposed to become attached to their caregivers. Normal, healthy attachment will occur within a wide range of cultural, family, and individual variations in child-rearing customs. Although, sadly, things can go wrong in prenatal development and in the first year after birth, the plasticity of the brain and human resilience can often overcome early deprivation or even harm. We will return to the issue of resilience at the end of this chapter, and in "Taking Psychology with You," we will consider other information that might alleviate the anxieties many parents feel about whether they are doing the right thing.

"Please, Jason. Don't you want to grow up to be an autonomous person?"

Quick Quiz

Are you feeling secure, anxious, or avoidant about quizzes?

1. Name as many potentially harmful influences on fetal development as you can.

2. Melanie is playing happily on a jungle gym at her daycare center when she falls off and badly scrapes her knee. She runs to her caregiver for a consoling cuddle. Melanie seeks _____.

3. A baby left in the Strange Situation does not protest when his mother leaves the room, and he seems to ignore her when she returns. According to Ainsworth, what style of attachment does this behavior reflect?

4. In Item 3, what else besides the child's style of attachment could account for the child's reaction?

Answers:

1. German measles early in pregnancy; exposure to radiation or toxic substances such as lead or mercury; sexually transmitted diseases; the mother's use of cigarettes, alcohol, or other drugs 2. contact comfort 3. insecure (avoidant) 4. the child's own temperament and familiarity with being temporarily left alone

YOU are about to learn...

• what a language is—and what it allows us to do that other animals cannot.

• the importance of baby talk in the development of language.

• milestones in the development of language.

• innate and learned aspects of acquiring language.

Language Development

Try to read this sentence aloud:

Kamaunawezakusomamanenohayaweweni-
mtuwamaanasana.

Can you tell where one word begins and another ends? Unless you know Swahili, the syllables of this sentence will sound like gibberish.[1]

Well, to a baby learning its native tongue, *every* sentence must be gibberish at first. How, then, does an infant pick out discrete syllables and words from the jumble of sounds in the environment, much less figure out what the words mean? And how is it that in only a few years, children not only understand thousands of words but can also produce and understand an endless number of new word combinations? Is there something special about the human brain that allows a baby to discover how language works? Darwin (1874) thought so: Language, he wrote, is an instinctive ability unique to human beings.

[1]*Kama unaweza kusoma maneno haya, wewe ni mtu wa maana sana,* in Swahili, means "If you can read these words, you are a remarkable person."

To evaluate Darwin's claim, we must first appreciate that a **language** is not just any old communication system; it is a set of rules for combining elements that are inherently meaningless into utterances that convey meaning. The elements are usually sounds, but they can also be the gestures of American Sign Language (ASL) and other manual languages that deaf and hearing-impaired people use. Because of language, we can refer not only to the here and now but also to past and future events, and to things or people who are not present. Language, whether spoken or signed, allows human beings to express and comprehend an infinite number of novel utterances, created on the spot. This ability is critical; except for a few fixed phrases ("How are you?" "Get a life!"), most of the utterances we produce or hear over a lifetime are new.

Many psychologists today believe that an innate facility for language evolved in human beings because it was extraordinarily beneficial (Pinker, 1994). It permitted our prehistoric ancestors to convey precise information about time, space, and events (as in "Honey, are you going on the mammoth hunt today?") and allowed them to negotiate alliances that were necessary for survival ("If you share your nuts and berries with us, we'll share our mammoth with you"). Language may also have developed because it provides the human equivalent of the mutual grooming that other primates rely on to forge social bonds (Dunbar, 2004; Tomasello, 2008). Just as other primates will clean, stroke, and groom one another for hours as a sign of affection and connection, human friends will sit for hours and chat over coffee. The difference between chimpanzee and human forms of "stroking" is that language allows us to maintain cooperative social relations in ever-larger groups.

language A system that combines meaningless elements such as sounds or gestures to form structured utterances that convey meaning.

From Cooing to Communicating The acquisition of language may begin in the womb. Canadian psychologists tested newborn babies' preference for hearing English or Tagalog (a major language of the Philippines) by measuring the number of times the babies sucked on a rubber nipple while hearing each language alternating during a ten-minute span. Those whose mothers spoke only English during pregnancy showed a clear preference for English by sucking more during the minutes when English was spoken. Those whose bilingual mothers spoke both languages showed equal preference for both languages (Byers-Heinlein, Burns, & Werker, 2010).

Thus, infants are already responsive to the pitch, intensity, and sound of language, and they also react to the emotions and rhythms in voices. When most people speak to babies, their pitch is higher and more varied than usual and their intonation and emphasis on vowels are exaggerated. Adult use of baby talk, which researchers call *parentese*, has been documented all over the world. In fact, adult members of the Shuar, a nonliterate hunter-gatherer culture in South America, can accurately distinguish American mothers' infant-directed speech from their adult-directed speech just by tone (Bryant & Barrett, 2007). Parentese helps babies learn the melody and rhythm of their native language (Fernald & Mazzie, 1991).

In what has to have been one of the most adorable research projects ever, three investigators compared the way mothers spoke to their babies and to pets, which also tend to evoke baby talk. They found that mothers exaggerate vowel sounds for their babies but not for Puffy the poodle or Cuddles the cat, suggesting that parentese is, indeed, a way of helping infants acquire language (Burnham, Kitamura, & Vollmer-Conna, 2002).

By 4 to 6 months of age, babies can often recognize their own names and other words that are regularly spoken with emotion, such as "mommy" and "daddy." They also know many of the key consonant and vowel sounds of their native language and can distinguish such sounds from those of other languages (Kuhl et al., 1992). Then, over time, exposure to the baby's native language reduces the child's ability to perceive speech sounds that do not exist in their own. Thus, Japanese infants can hear the difference between the English sounds *la* and *ra*, but older Japanese

children cannot. Because this contrast does not exist in their language, they become insensitive to it.

Between 6 months and 1 year, infants become increasingly familiar with the sound structure of their native language. They are able to distinguish words from the flow of speech. They will listen longer to words that violate their expectations of what words should sound like and even to sentences that violate their expectations of how sentences should be structured (Jusczyk, 2002). They start to babble, making many ba-ba and goo-goo sounds, endlessly repeating sounds and syllables. At 7 months, they begin to remember words they have heard, but because they are also attending to the speaker's intonation, speaking rate, and volume, they can't always recognize the same word when different people speak it (Houston & Jusczyk, 2003). Then, by 10 months, they can suddenly do it—a remarkable leap forward in only three months. And at about 1 year of age, though the timing varies considerably, children take another giant step: They start to name things. They already have some concepts in their minds for familiar people and objects, and their first words represent these concepts ("mama," "doggie," "truck").

Also at the end of the first year, babies develop a repertoire of symbolic gestures. They gesture to refer to objects (e.g., sniffing to indicate "flower"), to request something (smacking the lips for "food"), to describe objects (raising the arms for "big"), and to reply to questions (opening the palms or shrugging the shoulders for "I don't know"). They clap in response to pictures of things they like. Children whose parents encourage them to use gestures acquire larger vocabularies, have better comprehension, are better listeners, and are less frustrated in their efforts to communicate than children who are not encouraged to use gestures (Goodwyn & Acredolo, 1998; Rowe & Goldin-Meadow, 2009). When babies begin to speak, they continue to gesture along with their words, just as adults often gesture when talking. These gestures are not a substitute for language but are deeply related to its development, as well as to the development of thinking and problem solving (Goldin-Meadow, Cook, & Mitchell, 2009).

One surprising discovery is that babies who are given infant "brain stimulation" videos to look at are actually *slower* at acquiring words than babies who do not watch videos. In a survey of 1,000 parents and their babies, researchers found that for every hour a day that 8- to 16-month-old babies watch one of these videos, they acquire six to eight fewer words than other children (Zimmermann,

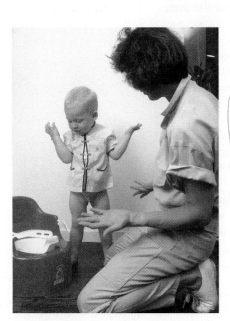

Symbolic gestures emerge early!

Christakis, & Meltzoff, 2007). Babies and children whose parents read to them, or even watch videos with them and talk about what they are all seeing, have larger vocabularies.

Between the ages of 18 months and 2 years, toddlers begin to produce words in two- or three-word combinations ("Mama here," "go 'way bug," "my toy"). The child's first combinations of words have been described as **telegraphic speech**. When people had to pay for every word in a telegram, they quickly learned to drop unnecessary articles (*a*, *an*, or *the*) and auxiliary verbs (*is* or *are*). Similarly, the two-word sentences of toddlers omit articles, word endings, auxiliary verbs, and other parts of speech, yet these sentences are remarkably accurate in conveying meaning. Children use two-word sentences to locate things ("there toy"), make demands ("more milk"), negate actions ("no want," "all gone milk"), describe events ("Bambi go," "hit ball"), describe objects ("pretty dress"), show possession ("Mama dress"), and ask questions ("where Daddy?"). Pretty good for a little kid, don't you think?

By the age of 6, the average child has a vocabulary of between 8,000 and 14,000 words, meaning that children acquire several new words a day between the ages of 2 and 6. (When did you last learn and use five new words in a day?) They absorb new words as they hear them, inferring their meaning from their knowledge of grammatical contexts and from the social contexts in which they hear the words used (Golinkoff & Hirsh-Pasek, 2006; Rice, 1990). (Table 3.1 summarizes the early stages of language development.) How on earth do children do all this?

The Innate Capacity for Language At one time, most psychologists assumed that children acquired language by imitating adults and paying attention when adults corrected their mistakes. Then along came linguist Noam Chomsky (1957, 1980), who argued that language was far too complex to be learned bit by bit, as one might learn a list of world capitals.

The task facing children, said Chomsky, is far more complicated than merely figuring out which sounds form words. They must also take the *surface structure* of a sentence—the way the sentence is actually spoken or signed—and apply grammatical rules (*syntax*) to infer an underlying *deep structure*, or how the sentence is to be understood. Although "Mary kissed John" and "John was kissed by Mary" have different surface structures, any 5-year-old knows that the two sentences have essentially the same deep structure, in which Mary is the actor and John gets the kiss.

Because no one actually teaches us grammar when we are toddlers, said Chomsky, the human brain must contain an innate mental module that allows young children to develop language if they are exposed to an adequate sampling of conversation. Children are born with a *universal grammar*—that is, their brains are sensitive to the core features common to all languages, such as nouns and verbs, subjects and objects, and negatives. These common features occur even in languages as seemingly different as Mohawk and English, or Okinawan and Bulgarian (Baker, 2001; Cinque, 1999; Pesetsky, 1999). In English, even 2-year-olds use syntax to help them acquire new verbs in context: They understand that "Jane blicked the baby!" involves two people, but the use of the same verb in "Jane blicked!" involves only Jane (Yuan & Fisher, 2009). ⦿ Watch

telegraphic speech A child's first word combinations, which omit (as a telegram did) unnecessary words.

⦿ Watch the **Video Bilingual Education** on **mypsychlab.com**

TABLE 3.1
The Early Development of Language

First few months	Babies cry and coo; they respond to emotions and rhythms in voices.
4–6 months	Babies begin to recognize key vowel and consonant sounds of their native language.
6 months–1 year	Infants' familiarity with the sound structure of their native language increases; they can distinguish words from the flow of speech.
End of first year	Infants start to name things based on familiar concepts and use symbolic gestures to communicate.
18–24 months	Children begin to speak in two- and three-word phrases (telegraphic speech) and understand verbs from the context in which they occur.
2–6 years	Children rapidly acquire new words, inferring their meaning from the grammatical and social contexts in which they hear them.

Over the years, researchers who study language have gathered much evidence to support the Chomskyan position:

1 **Children in different cultures go through similar stages of linguistic development.** For example, they will often form their first negatives simply by adding *no* or *not* at the beginning or end of a sentence ("No get dirty"). At a later stage, they will use double negatives ("He don't want no milk"; "Nobody don't like me"), even when their language does not allow such constructions (Klima & Bellugi, 1966; McNeill, 1966).

2 **Children combine words in ways that adults never would.** They reduce a parent's sentences ("Let's go to the store!") to their own two-word versions ("Go store!") and make many charming errors that an adult would not ("The alligator goed kerplunk," "Daddy taked me," "Hey, Horton heared a Who") (Ervin-Tripp, 1964; Marcus et al., 1992). Such errors, which psycholinguists call *overregularizations*, are not random; they show that the child has grasped a grammatical rule (add the *t* or *d* sound to make a verb past tense, as in *walked* and *hugged*) and is merely overgeneralizing it (*taked*, *goed*).

3 **Adults do not consistently correct their children's syntax, yet children learn to speak or sign correctly anyway.** Learning explanations of language acquisition assume that children are rewarded for saying the right words and are punished for making errors. But parents do not stop to correct every error in their children's speech, so long as they can understand what the child is trying to say (Brown, Cazden, & Bellugi, 1969). Indeed, parents often *reward* children for incorrect statements! The 2-year-old who says "Want milk!" is likely to get it; most parents would not wait for a more grammatical (or polite) request.

These deaf Nicaraguan children have invented their own grammatically complex sign language, one that is unrelated to Spanish or to any conventional gestural language.

4 **Children who are not exposed to adult language may invent a language of their own.** Deaf children who have never learned a standard language, either signed or spoken, have made up their own sign languages out of thin air. These languages often show similarities in sentence structure across cultures as varied as America, Taiwan, Spain, and Turkey (Goldin-Meadow, 2003). The most astounding case comes from Nicaragua, where a group of deaf children, attending special schools, created a homegrown but grammatically complex sign language that is unrelated to Spanish (Senghas, Kita, & Özyürek, 2004).

5 **Infants as young as 7 months can derive simple linguistic rules from a string of sounds.** If babies are repeatedly exposed to artificial sentences with an ABA pattern, such as "Ga ti ga" or "Li na li," until they get bored, they will then prefer new sentences with an ABB pattern (such as "Wo fe fe") over new sentences with an ABA pattern (such as "Wo fe wo"). (They indicate this preference by looking longer at a flashing light associated with the novel pattern than one associated with the familiar pattern.) Conversely, when the original sentences have an ABB structure, babies will prefer novel ones with an ABA structure. To many researchers, these responses suggest that babies can discriminate the different types of structures (Marcus et al., 1999). Astonishingly, this ability emerges even before they can understand or produce any words.

The Influence of Learning on Language Although there are commonalities in language acquisition around the world,

Even when parents try to correct their children's syntax, it usually doesn't work.

there are also some major differences that do not seem explainable by a universal grammar (Gopnik, Choi, & Bamberger, 1996). Many researchers therefore give experience at least as great a role in language development. They argue that instead of inferring grammatical rules because of an innate disposition to do so, children learn the *probability* that any given word or syllable will follow another, something infants as young as 8 months are able to do (Seidenberg, MacDonald, & Saffran, 2002). In this view, infants are more like statisticians than grammarians, and their "statistics" are based on experience (Gerken, Wilson, & Lewis, 2005; Lany & Gómez, 2008).

Using computers, some theorists have been able to design mathematical models of the brain that can acquire some aspects of language, such as regular and irregular past-tense verbs, without the help of a preexisting mental module or preprogrammed rules. These computer programs simply adjust the connections among hypothetical neurons in response to incoming data, such as repetitions of a word in its past-tense form. The success of these computer models, say their designers, suggests that children, too, may be able to acquire linguistic features without getting a head start from

inborn brain modules (Rodriguez, Wiles, & Elman, 1999).

Even theorists who emphasize an inborn grammatical capacity acknowledge that in any behavior as complex as language, nurture must also play a role. Although most children have the capacity to acquire language from mere exposure to it, parents do help things along. They may not go around correcting their children's speech all day, but they do recast and expand their children's clumsy or ungrammatical sentences ("Monkey climbing!" "Yes, the monkey is climbing the tree"). Children, in turn, often imitate those recasts and expansions, suggesting that they are learning from them (Bohannon & Symons, 1988).

Language development, therefore, depends on both biological readiness and social experience. Abused children who are not exposed to language during their early years (such as Genie, whom we mentioned in Chapter 1), rarely speak normally or catch up grammatically. Such sad evidence suggests a critical period in language development during the first few years of life or possibly the first decade. During these years, children need exposure to language and opportunities to practice their emerging linguistic skills in conversation with others.

✔—**Study** and **Review** on **mypsychlab.com**

Quick Quiz

Use your human capacity for language to answer these questions.

1. The central distinction between human language and other communication systems is that language (a) allows for the generation of an infinite number of new utterances, (b) is spoken, (c) is learned only after explicit training, (d) expresses meaning directly through surface structures.

2. In Chomsky's view, why are children able to acquire language as quickly and easily as they do?

3. What five findings support the existence of an innate universal grammar?

4. Those who reject Chomsky's ideas believe that instead of figuring out grammatical rules when acquiring language, children learn _____.

Answers:

1. a 2. An innate mental module permits young children to develop language if they are exposed to an adequate sampling of conversation. 3. Children everywhere go through similar stages of linguistic development; children combine words in ways that adults would not; adults do not consistently correct their children's syntax; groups of children not exposed to adult language may make up their own; and even infants only a few months old appear to distinguish different sentence structures. 4. the probability that any given word or syllable will follow another one.

 ## YOU are about to learn…

- Piaget's stages of cognitive development and their hallmarks.

- modern approaches to children's mental development.

Cognitive Development

Children do not think the way adults do. For most of the first year of life, if something is out of sight, it's out of mind: If you cover a baby's favorite rattle with a cloth, the baby thinks the rattle has vanished and stops looking for it. And a 4-year-old may protest that a

This child is not intentionally trying to drive his parents crazy. Like a good little scientist, he is trying to figure out cause and effect: "If I throw this dish, what will happen? Will there be a noise? Will mom come and give it back to me? How many times will she give it back to me?"

object permanence
The understanding, which develops throughout the first year, that an object continues to exist even when you cannot see it or touch it.

conservation The understanding that the physical properties of objects—such as the number of items in a cluster or the amount of liquid in a glass—can remain the same even when their form or appearance changes.

sibling has more fruit juice when it is only the shapes of the glasses that differ, not the amount of juice.

Yet children are smart in their own way. Like good little scientists, children are always testing their child-sized theories about how things work (Gopnik, 2009; Gopnik, Meltzoff, & Kuhl, 1999). When your toddler throws her spoon on the floor for the sixth time as you try to feed her, and you say, "That's enough! I will *not* pick up your spoon again!" the child will immediately test your claim. Are you serious? Are you angry? What will happen if she throws the spoon again? She is not doing this to drive you crazy. Rather, she is learning that her desires and yours can differ, and that sometimes those differences are important and sometimes they are not.

How and why does children's thinking change? In the 1920s, Swiss psychologist Jean Piaget [Zhan Pee-ah-ZHAY] (1896–1980) proposed that children's cognitive abilities unfold naturally, like the blooming of a flower, almost independent of what else is happening in their lives. Piaget's keen observations of children caused a revolution in thinking about how thinking develops. Piaget's great insight was that children's errors are as interesting as their correct responses. Children will say things that seem cute or wildly illogical to adults, but the strategies that children use to think and solve problems, said Piaget, are not random or meaningless. They reflect a predictable interaction between the child's maturational stage and the child's experience in the world. Although many of Piaget's specific conclusions have been rejected or modified over the years, his ideas inspired thousands of studies by investigators all over the world.

Piaget's Theory of Cognitive Stages
According to Piaget (1929/1960, 1984), as children develop, their minds constantly adapt to new situations and experiences. Sometimes they *assimilate* new information into their existing mental categories; thus a German shepherd and a terrier both fit the category *dogs*. At other times, however, children must change their mental categories to *accommodate* their new experiences; a cat does not belong to the category *dogs* and a new category is required, one for *cats*. Both processes are constantly interacting, Piaget said, as children go through four stages of cognitive development:

From birth to age 2, said Piaget, babies are in the *sensorimotor stage*. In this stage, the infant learns through concrete actions: looking, touching, putting things in the mouth, sucking, grasping. "Thinking" consists of coordinating sensory information with bodily movements. Gradually, these movements become more purposeful as the child explores the environment and learns that specific movements will produce specific results. Pulling a cloth away will reveal a hidden toy; letting go of a fuzzy toy duck will cause it to drop out of reach; banging on the table with a spoon will produce dinner (or Mom, taking away the spoon).

A major accomplishment at this stage, said Piaget, is **object permanence**, the understanding that something continues to exist even when you can't see it or touch it. In the first few months, infants will look intently at a little toy, but if you hide it behind a piece of paper, they will not look behind the paper or make an effort to get the toy. By about 6 months of age, however, infants begin to grasp the idea that the toy exists whether or not they can see it. If a baby of this age drops a toy from her playpen, she will look for it; she also will look under a cloth for a toy that is partially hidden. By 1 year of age, most babies have developed an awareness of the permanence of objects; even if a toy is covered by a cloth, it must be under there. This is when they love to play peekaboo. Object permanence, said Piaget, represents the beginning of the child's capacity to use mental imagery and symbols. The child becomes able to hold a concept in mind, to learn that the word *fly* represents an annoying, buzzing creature and that *Daddy* represents a friendly, playful one.

From about ages 2 to 7, the child's use of symbols and language accelerates. Piaget called this the *preoperational stage*, because he believed that children still lack the cognitive abilities necessary for understanding abstract principles and mental *operations*. An operation is a train of thought that can be run backward or forward. Multiplying 2 times 6 to get 12 is an operation; so is the reverse operation, dividing 12 by 6 to get 2. A preoperational child knows that Jessie is his sister, but he may not get the reverse operation, the idea that he is Jessie's brother. Piaget also believed (mistakenly, as we will see) that preoperational children cannot take another person's point of view because their thinking is *egocentric:* They see the world only from their own frame of reference and cannot imagine that others see things differently.

Further, said Piaget, preoperational children cannot grasp the concept of **conservation**, the

FIGURE 3.2
Piaget's Principle of Conservation
In a typical test for conservation of number (left), the number of blocks is the same in two sets, but those in one set are then spread out and the child must say whether one set has more blocks than another. Preoperational children think that the set that takes up more space has more blocks. In a test for conservation of quantity (right), the child is shown two short glasses with equal amounts of liquid. Then the contents of one glass are poured into a tall, narrower glass, and the child is asked whether one container now has more. Most preoperational children do not understand that pouring liquid from a short glass into a taller one leaves the amount of liquid unchanged. They judge only by the height of liquid in the glass.

notion that physical properties do not change when their form or appearance changes. Children at this age do not understand that an amount of liquid or a number of blocks remains the same even if you pour the liquid from one glass to another of a different size or if you stack the blocks (see Figure 3.2). If you pour liquid from a short, fat glass into a tall, narrow glass, preoperational children will say there is more liquid in the second glass. They attend to the appearance of the liquid (its height in the glass) to judge its quantity, and so they are misled.

From the ages of 7 to about 12, Piaget said, children increasingly become able to take other people's perspectives and they make fewer logical errors. Piaget called this the *concrete operations* stage because he thought children's mental abilities are tied to information that is concrete, that is, to actual experiences that have happened or concepts that have a tangible meaning to them. Children at

this stage make errors of reasoning when they are asked to think about abstract ideas such as "patriotism" or "future education." During these years, nonetheless, children's cognitive abilities expand rapidly. They come to understand the principles of conservation, reversibility, and cause and effect. They learn mental operations, such as addition, subtraction, multiplication, and division. They are able to categorize things (e.g., oaks as trees) and to order things serially from smallest to largest, lightest to darkest, and shortest to tallest.

Finally, said Piaget, beginning at about age 12 or 13 and continuing into adulthood, people become capable of abstract reasoning and enter the *formal operations* stage. They are able to reason about situations they have not experienced firsthand, and they can think about future possibilities. They are able to search systematically for answers to problems. They are able to draw logical conclusions from premises common to their culture and experience.

Get Involved! A Test of Conservation

If you know any young children, try one of Piaget's conservation experiments. A simple one is to make two rows of seven buttons or pennies, aligned identically. Ask the child whether one row has more. Now simply spread out the buttons in one of the rows, and ask the child again whether one row has more. If the child says, "Yes," ask which one and why. Try to do this experiment with a 3-year-old and a 7- or 8-year-old. You will probably see a big difference in their answers.

Current Views of Cognitive Development

Piaget was a brilliant observer of children, and his major point has been well supported: New reasoning abilities depend on the emergence of previous ones. You cannot learn algebra before you can count, and you cannot learn philosophy before you understand logic. But since Piaget's original work, the field of developmental psychology has undergone an explosion of imaginative research that has allowed investigators to get into the minds of even the youngest infants. The result has been a modification of Piaget's ideas, and some scientists go so far as to say that his ideas have been overturned. Here's why.

1 **Cognitive abilities develop in continuous, overlapping waves rather than discrete steps or stages.** If you observe children at different ages, as Piaget did, it will seem that they reason differently. But if you study the everyday learning of children at any given age, you will find that a child may use several different strategies to solve a problem, some more complex or accurate than others (Siegler, 2006). Learning occurs gradually, with retreats to former ways of thinking as well as advances to new ones. Children's reasoning ability also depends on the circumstances—who is asking them questions, the specific words used, and what they are reasoning about—and not just on the stage they are in. In short, cognitive development is *continuous*; new abilities do not simply pop up when a child turns a specific age (Courage & Howe, 2002).

2 **Preschoolers are not as egocentric as Piaget thought.** Most 3- and 4-year-olds *can* take another person's perspective (Flavell, 1999). When 4-year-olds play with 2-year-olds, they modify and simplify their speech so the younger children will understand (Shatz & Gelman, 1973). One preschooler we know showed her teacher a picture she had drawn of a cat and an unidentifiable blob. "The cat is lovely," said the teacher, "but what is this thing here?" "That has nothing to do with you," said the child. "That's what the *cat* is looking at."

By about ages 3 to 4, children also begin to understand that you cannot predict what a person will do just by observing a situation or knowing the facts. You also have to know what the person is feeling and thinking; the person might even be lying. They start asking why other people behave as they do ("Why is Johnny so mean?"). In short, they are developing a **theory of mind**, a system of beliefs about how their own and other people's minds work and how people are affected by their beliefs

and emotions. They start using verbs like *think* and *know*, and by age 4 they understand that what another person thinks might not match their own beliefs (Flavell, 1999; Wellman, Cross, & Watson, 2001). The ability to understand that people can have false beliefs is a milestone, because it means the child is beginning to question how we know things—the foundation for later higher-order thinking.

3 **Children, even infants, reveal cognitive abilities much earlier than Piaget believed possible.** Taking advantage of the fact that infants look longer at novel or surprising stimuli than at familiar ones, psychologists have designed delightfully innovative methods of testing what babies know. These methods reveal that babies may be born with mental modules or core knowledge systems for numbers, spatial relations, the properties of objects, and other features of the physical world (Izard et al., 2009; Spelke & Kinzler, 2007).

For example, at only 4 months of age, babies will look longer at a ball if it seems to roll through a solid barrier, leap between two platforms, or hang in midair than they do when the ball obeys the laws of physics. This suggests that the unusual event is surprising to them (see Figure 3.3). Infants as young as 2½ to 3½ months are aware that objects continue to exist even when masked by other

Possible event

Impossible event

FIGURE 3.3
Testing Infants' Knowledge
In this clever procedure, a baby watches as a box is pushed from left to right along a striped platform. The box is pushed until it reaches the end of the platform (a possible event) or until only a bit of it rests on the platform (an impossible event). Babies look longer at the impossible event, suggesting that it surprises them. Somehow they know that an object needs physical support and can't just float on air (Baillargeon, 1994).

theory of mind A system of beliefs about the way one's own mind and the minds of others work, and of how individuals are affected by their beliefs and feelings.

objects, a form of object permanence that Piaget never imagined possible in babies so young (Baillargeon, 2004). And, most devastating to Piaget's notion of infant egocentrism, even 5-month-old infants are able to perceive other people's actions as being intentional; they detect the difference between a person who is reaching for a toy with her hand rather than accidentally touching it with a stick (Woodward, 2009). Even 3-month-old infants can learn this!

4 **Cognitive development is influenced by a child's culture.** Culture—the world of tools, language, rituals, beliefs, games, and social institutions—shapes and structures children's cognitive development, fostering some abilities and not others (Tomasello, 2000). Nomadic hunters excel in spatial abilities, because spatial orientation is crucial for finding water holes and successful hunting routes. In contrast, children who live in settled agricultural communities, such as the Baoulé of the Ivory Coast, develop rapidly in the ability to quantify but much more slowly in spatial reasoning.

Experience and culture influence cognitive development. Children who work with clay, wood, and other materials, such as this young potter in India, tend to understand the concept of conservation sooner than children who have not had this kind of experience.

Despite these modifications, Piaget left an enduring legacy: the insight that children are not passive vessels into which education and experience are poured. Children actively interpret their worlds, using their developing abilities to assimilate new information and figure things out.

✔—**Study** and **Review** on **mypsychlab.com**

Quick Quiz

Please use language (and thought) to answer these questions.

1. "More cake!" and "Mommy come" are examples of _____ speech.
2. Understanding that two rows of six pennies are equal in number, even if one row is flat and the other is stacked up, is an example of _____.
3. Understanding that a toy exists even after Mom puts it in her purse is an example of _____.
4. A 5-year-old boy who tells his dad that "Sally said she saw a bunny but she was lying" has developed a _____.
5. List four findings from contemporary research on children's cognitive development that have expanded or modified Piaget's theory.

Answers:

1. telegraphic 2. conservation 3. object permanence 4. theory of mind 5. The changes from one stage to another occur in continuous, overlapping waves rather than distinct stages. Children are less egocentric than Piaget thought. Infants and young children reveal cognitive abilities much earlier than Piaget believed possible. And cognitive development is affected by cultural practices and experiences.

◆ **YOU** are about to learn...

• how moral feelings and behavior develop.

• why shouting "Because I say so!" does not get most children to behave well.

• the importance of a child's ability to delay gratification.

Moral Development

How do children learn to tell right from wrong, resist the temptation to behave selfishly, and obey the rules of social conduct? In the 1960s, Lawrence Kohlberg (1964), inspired by Piaget's work, argued that children's ability to understand right from

How do children internalize moral rules? How do they learn that cheating, stealing, and grabbing a younger sibling's toy are wrong?

power assertion A method of child rearing in which the parent uses punishment and authority to correct the child's misbehavior.

wrong evolved along with the rest of their cognitive abilities, progressing through three levels. In studies of how children reason about moral dilemmas, he found that very young children obey rules because they fear being punished if they disobey, and later because they think it is in their best interest to obey. At about age 10, their moral judgments shift to ones based on conformity and loyalty to others, and then to an understanding of the rule of law. In adulthood, a few individuals go on to develop a moral standard based on universal human rights: Martin Luther King, Jr. fought against laws supporting segregation, Mohandas Gandhi advocated nonviolent solutions to injustice in India, and Susan B. Anthony fought for women's right to vote.

Kohlberg was right that moral reasoning ability increases during the school years. Unfortunately, so do cheating, lying, cruelty, and the cognitive ability to rationalize these actions. As Thomas Lickona (1983) wryly summarized, "We can reach high levels of moral reasoning, and still behave like scoundrels." Accordingly, developmental psychologists today place greater emphasis on how children learn to regulate their own emotions and behavior (Mischel & Ayduk, 2004). Most children learn to inhibit their wishes to beat up their younger siblings, steal a classmate's toy, or scream at the top of their lungs if they don't get their way. The child's emerging ability to understand right from wrong, and to behave accordingly, depends on the emergence of conscience and moral emotions such as shame, guilt, and empathy (Kochanska et al., 2005).

As we saw in discussing criticisms of Piaget's theory, even very young children are capable of feeling empathy for others and taking another person's point of view. Children do not obey rules only because they are afraid of what will happen to them if they disobey, but also because they understand right from wrong. By age 5, they know it is wrong to hurt someone even if a teacher tells them to (Turiel, 2002). Therefore, many psychologists conclude that the capacity for understanding right from wrong, like that for language, is inborn. Jerome Kagan (1984) wrote, "Without this fundamental human capacity, which nineteenth-century observers called a *moral sense*, the child could not be

socialized." Evolutionary psychologists argue that this moral sense underlies the basic beliefs, judgments, and behavior that are considered moral almost everywhere, and that it originated in cooperative, altruistic strategies that permitted our forbears to resolve conflicts and get along (Krebs, 2008).

Can the moral sense and the desire to behave well with others be nurtured or extinguished by specific methods of child rearing? For decades, most developmental psychologists assumed that the answer was "Of course!" and they set about trying to pinpoint which parental techniques create well-behaved, kind, unselfish children. Then came a flood of behavioral-genetic studies that led to a very different assumption: The effects of the parents' methods depend—of course!—on the kind of child they have. Does the child heed discipline or become more resistant and hostile? Is the child easygoing or difficult?

Thinking Critically about Assumptions about Childrearing

Today, many researchers are seeking a middle ground by studying gene-environment interactions (Schmidt et al., 2009). One controversial hypothesis suggests that infants and toddlers who show high levels of distress and irritability are actually more responsive to, and influenced by, styles of parenting than easygoing babies are. When temperamentally difficult babies have impatient, rejecting, or coercive parents, they later tend to become aggressive and even more difficult and defiant. When they have patient, supportive, firm parents, they become better-natured and happier. In contrast, easygoing babies may not benefit as much from good parenting nor suffer as much from bad parenting because they are, well, easygoing (Belsky, Bakermans-Kranenburg, & van IJzendoorn, 2007; Belsky & Pluess, 2009a).

Keeping the complexity of this issue in mind, let's look at how parental discipline methods interact with a child's temperament in the development of conscience and moral behavior.

Getting Children to be Good When you did something wrong as a child, did the adults in your family spank you, shout at you, threaten you, or explain the error of your ways? One of the most common methods that parents use to enforce moral standards and good behavior is **power assertion**, which includes threats, physical punishment, depriving the child of privileges, and generally taking advantage of being bigger, stronger, and more

Power assertion is the use of physical force, threats, insults, or other kinds of power to get the child to obey ("Do it because I say so!" "Stop that right now!"). The child may obey, but only when the parent is present, while feeling resentful and waiting for the chance to misbehave again.

The parent who uses induction appeals to the child's good nature, empathy, love for the parent, and sense of responsibility to others and offers explanations of rules ("You're too grown up to behave like that"; "Fighting hurts your little brother"). The child tends to internalize reasons for good behavior.

powerful. Of course, a parent may have no alternative other than "Do it because I say so!" if the child is too young to understand a rule or impishly keeps trying to break it. Moreover, the culture and context in which the discipline occurs makes an enormous difference. Is the parent–child relationship fundamentally loving and trusting or one full of hostility and fighting? Does the child interpret the parents' actions as being fair and caring, or unfair and cruel?

But when power assertion consists of sheer parental bullying, cruel insults ("You are so stupid, I wish you'd never been born"), and frequent physical punishment, it is associated with greater aggressiveness in children and reduced empathy (Alink et al., 2009; Gershoff, 2002; Moore & Pepler, 2006). As we discuss in Chapter 9, physical punishment often backfires, especially when it is used inappropriately or harshly; it spirals out of control, causing the child to become angry and resentful. Moreover, harsh but ineffective discipline methods are often transmitted to the next generation: Aggressive parents teach their children that the way to discipline children is by behaving aggressively (Capaldi et al., 2003).

What is the alternative? In contrast to power assertion, a parent can use **induction**, appealing to the child's own abilities, empathy, helpful nature, affection for others, and sense of responsibility ("You made Doug cry; it's not nice to bite"; "You must never poke anyone's eyes because that could hurt them seriously"). Or the parent might appeal to the child's own helpful inclinations ("I know you're a person who likes to be nice to others") rather than citing external reasons to be good ("You'd better be nice or you won't get dessert").

Self-Control and Conscience One of the most important social-emotional skills that children need to acquire is *self-regulation*, the ability to suppress their initial wish to do something in favor of doing something else that is not as much fun. This ability predicts a child's ability to delay gratification now for a larger reward later, control negative emotions, pay attention to the task at hand, and do well in school, from kindergarten to college (Eigsti et al., 2006; Ponitz et al., 2009).

To explore the links between parental discipline, the child's self-regulation, and the emergence of conscience, two psychologists conducted a longitudinal study of 106 children at ages 22, 33, and 45 months (Kochanska & Knaack, 2003). When the children were 56 and 73 months old, the researchers measured the development of conscience by giving the children a series of charming tests disguised as games. Some of the games required the child to whisper instead of shout, walk instead of run, ignore the dominant image in a picture and find a more subtle one, and delay gratification by not reaching immediately for candy under a cup or by resisting the urge to open a bag to get out a toy. The researchers also observed what the mothers did when they were asked to get their child to clean up the play area or to prevent the child from playing with some appealing, easily accessible toys. Did the mother explain the reasons for her request to the child (induction) or did she issue strict orders (power assertion)? After interacting with her child, the mother left the room, and the child was free to

induction A method of child rearing in which the parent appeals to the child's own resources, abilities, sense of responsibility, and feelings for others in correcting the child's misbehavior.

Children's ability to regulate their impulses and delay gratification are important milestones in the development of conscience and moral behavior.

✔•—Study and Review on **mypsychlab.com**

obey or disobey. The researchers observed what the child did in her absence.

When the children were 56 months old, the researchers assessed the children's conscience in several moral realms, including being willing to apologize, feeling empathy, being concerned about others' wrongdoing, feeling guilty after doing something naughty or wrong, and being concerned about their parents' feelings. The researchers also measured the children's actual behavior, such as whether they cheated on the rules in playing a ball-tossing game. Then the researchers devised a composite conscience score for each child. Finally, when the

children were 73 months old, their mothers rated them on the frequency of antisocial problems such as being irritable and quick to fly off the handle, destroying their own or others' belongings, or fighting with other children.

The children who were most able to regulate their impulses early in life were the least likely to get in trouble later by fighting or destroying things, and the most likely to have a high conscience score at 56 months of age. Self-regulation was negatively correlated with the mother's use of power assertion, meaning that mothers who ordered their children to "behave" tended to have children who were impulsive and aggressive (see also Alink et al., 2009). But cause and effect worked in both directions: Some mothers relied on power assertion *because* their children were impulsive, defiant, and aggressive and would not listen to them. This pattern of findings teaches us to avoid oversimplification by concluding that "It's all in what the mother does" or that "It's all in the child's personality." Mothers and children, it seems, raise each other.

Quick Quiz

Exercise self-regulation by taking this quiz.

1. What is a major limitation of cognitive theories of moral reasoning in understanding how children develop a conscience?

2. Which method of disciplining a child who is hitting his younger brother is most likely to teach empathy? (a) induction, (b) indulgence, (c) power assertion, (d) spanking

3. What early ability predicts the development of conscience later on?

Answers:

1. Moral behavior is not necessarily related to the ability to reason morally. 2. a 3. self-regulation, the ability to control one's immediate impulses and wishes

 YOU are about to learn...

• why some people fail to identify themselves as either male or female.

• the biological explanation of why most little boys and girls are "sexist" in their choice of toys, at least for a while.

• when and how children learn that they are male or female.

• learning explanations of some typical sex differences in childhood behavior.

Gender Development

No parent ever excitedly calls a relative to exclaim, "It's a baby! It's a 7½-pound, black-haired baby!" The baby's sex is the first thing everyone notices and announces. How soon do children notice that boys and girls are different sexes and understand which sex they themselves are? How do children learn the rules of masculinity and femininity, the things that boys do that are different from what girls do? Why, as one friend of ours observed, do most preschool children act like the "gender police," insisting, say, that boys can't be nurses and girls can't be doctors? And why do some children come to feel they don't belong to the sex everyone else thinks they do?

Gender Identity

Let's start by clarifying some terms. **Gender identity** refers to a child's sense of being male or female, of belonging to one sex and not the other. **Gender typing** is the process of socializing children into their gender roles, and thus reflects society's ideas about which abilities, interests, traits, and behaviors are appropriately masculine or feminine. A person can have a strong gender identity and not be gender typed: A man may be confident in his maleness and not feel threatened by doing "unmasculine" things such as needlepointing a pillow; a woman may be confident in her femaleness and not feel threatened by doing "unfeminine" things such as serving in combat.

In the past, psychologists often reserved the term *sex* for the physiological or anatomical attributes of males and females, and *gender* for differences that are learned. Today, these two terms are often used interchangeably because, as we have noted repeatedly in this book, nature and nurture are inextricably linked.

The complexity of sex and gender development is especially apparent in the cases of people who do not fit the familiar categories of male and female. Every year, thousands of babies are born with **intersex conditions**, formerly known as hermaphroditism. In these conditions, chromosomal or hormonal anomalies cause the child to be born with ambiguous genitals, or genitals that conflict with the infant's chromosomes, and the child becomes "gender variant." A child who is genetically female might be born with an enlarged clitoris that looks like a penis. A child who is genetically male might be born with androgen insensitivity, a condition that causes the external genitals to appear female.

As adults, many intersexed individuals call themselves *transgender*, a term describing a broad category of people who do not fit comfortably into the usual categories of male and female, masculine and feminine. Some transgender people are comfortable living with the physical attributes of both sexes, considering themselves to be "gender queer" and even refusing to be referred to as he or she. Some feel uncomfortable in their sex of rearing and wish to be considered a member of the other sex. You have probably also heard the term *transsexual*, describing people who are not intersexed yet who feel that they are male in a female body or vice versa; their gender identity is at odds with their anatomical sex or appearance. Many transsexuals try to make a full transition to the other sex through surgery or hormones. Intersexed and transsexual people have been found in virtually all cultures throughout history (Denny, 1998; Roughgarden, 2004).

Influences on Gender Development

To understand the typical course of gender development, as well as the variations, developmental psychologists study the interacting influences of

gender identity The fundamental sense of being male or female; it is independent of whether the person conforms to the social and cultural rules of gender.

gender typing The process by which children learn the abilities, interests, and behaviors associated with being masculine or feminine in their culture.

intersex conditions Conditions in which chromosomal or hormonal anomalies cause a child to be born with ambiguous genitals, or genitals that conflict with the infant's chromosomes.

Throughout history and across cultures, there have been people who broke out of conventional gender categories. Some women have lived as men, as did the eighteenth-century pirates Ann Bonny and Mary Read (left). Some men have lived as women: The Muxes (pronounced moo-shays) of Oaxaca, Mexico, are men who consider themselves women, live as women, and are a socially accepted category. Carmelo López Bernal, age 13 (center), first appeared publicly as a female at the annual town-wide muxe celebration. Luke Woodward (right), who was born and raised female, came out as a male, and became active in a campus movement to make life better for fellow transgender students.

biology, cognition, and learning on gender identity and gender typing.

Biological Influences Starting in the preschool years, boys and girls congregate primarily with other children of their sex, and most prefer the toys and games of their own sex. They will play together if required to, but given their druthers, they usually choose to play with same-sex friends. The kind of play that young boys and girls enjoy also differs, on average. Little boys, like young males in all primate species, are more likely than females to go in for physical roughhousing, risk taking, and aggressive displays. These sex differences occur all over the world, almost regardless of whether adults encourage boys and girls to play together or separate them (Lytton & Romney, 1991; Maccoby, 1998, 2002). Many parents lament that although they try to give their children the same toys, it makes no difference; their sons want trucks and guns and their daughters want dolls.

Biological researchers believe that these play and toy preferences have a basis in prenatal hormones, particularly the presence or absence of prenatal androgens (masculinizing hormones). Girls who were exposed to higher-than-normal prenatal androgens in the womb are later more likely than nonexposed girls to prefer "boys' toys" such as cars and fire engines, and they are also more physically aggressive than other girls (Berenbaum & Bailey, 2003). A study of more than 200 healthy children in the general population also found a relationship between fetal testosterone and play styles. (Testosterone is produced in fetuses of both sexes, although it is higher on average in males.) The higher the levels of fetal testosterone, as measured in the amniotic fluid of the children's mothers during pregnancy, the higher the children's later scores on a measure of male-typical play (Auyeung et al., 2009). In studies of rhesus monkeys, who of course are not influenced by their parents' possible gender biases, male monkeys, like human boys, consistently and strongly prefer to play with wheeled toys rather than cuddly plush toys, whereas female monkeys, like human girls, are more varied in their toy preferences (Hassett, Siebert, & Wallen, 2008).

Do these findings have anything to do with gender identity, the core sense of being male or female? In the past, gender identity was believed to be almost entirely learned, a result of the child's socialization and learning. Then a widely publicized case study appeared to show that gender identity is hardwired in the brain. At the age of 7 months, a genetically and hormonally male child had lost his penis in a freak accident during a routine surgical procedure. When he was nearly 2 years old, his desperate parents, on the advice of a leading scientist in the field of gender identity, agreed to raise him as a girl, renaming him Brenda. But Brenda preferred boys' toys and by the age of 14, refused to keep living as a female. Her father told her the truth and, in relief, Brenda turned to a male identity (Diamond & Sigmundson, 1997). He changed his name to David, had reconstructive surgery to build a penis, and, in his 20s, got married. But the story did not end happily. After David's twin brother, who had schizophrenia, committed suicide, and after David lost his job and separated from his wife, he became deeply depressed. At the age of 38, David killed himself.

Unfortunately, dramatic case studies such as this one cannot really tell us whether gender identity is fixed in the brain prenatally. Perhaps David's experience was atypical. Perhaps there is a critical period after birth during which gender identity develops. (David's parents did not decide to raise him as a girl until he was nearly 2 years old.) A psychologist

Thinking Critically about Gender Identity

who reviewed hundreds of cases of children whose sex of rearing was discrepant with their anatomical or genetic sex found that the picture is enormously complex: A person's gender identity depends on the interactions of genes, prenatal hormones, anatomical structures, and experiences in life (Zucker, 1999). As a result, the outcome in any particular case is hard to predict.

Look familiar? In a scene typical of many nursery schools and homes, the boy builds a gun out of anything he can, and the girl dresses up in any pretty thing she can find. Whether or not such behavior is biologically based, the gender rigidity of the early years does not inevitably continue into adulthood unless cultural rules reinforce it.

Cognitive Influences Cognitive psychologists explain the mystery of children's gender segregation and toy and play preferences by studying children's changing cognitive abilities. Even before babies can speak, they recognize that there are two sexes. By the age of 9 months, most babies can discriminate male from female faces (Fagot & Leinbach, 1993), and they can match female faces with female voices (Poulin-Dubois et al., 1994). By the age of 18 to 20 months, most toddlers have a concept of gender labels; they can accurately identify the gender of people in picture books and begin correctly using the words *boy, girl,* and *man* (interestingly, *lady* and *woman* come later) (Zosuls et al., 2009).

Once children can label themselves and others consistently as being a boy or a girl, shortly before age 2, they change their behavior to conform to the category they belong to. Many begin to prefer same-sex playmates and sex-traditional toys without being explicitly taught to do so (Martin, Ruble, & Szkrybalo, 2002; Zosuls et al., 2009). They become more gender typed in their toy play, games, aggressiveness, and verbal skills than children who still cannot consistently label males and females. Most notably, girls stop behaving aggressively (Fagot, 1993). It is as if they go along behaving like boys until they know they are girls. At that moment, they seem to decide: "Girls don't do this; I'm a girl; I'd better not either."

It's great fun to watch 3- to 5-year-old children struggle to figure out what makes boys and girls different: "The ones with eyelashes are girls; boys don't have eyelashes," said one 4-year-old girl to her aunt in explaining her drawing. After dinner at an Italian restaurant, a 4-year-old boy told his parents that he'd got the answer: "Men eat pizza and women don't" (Bjorkland, 2000).

At about age 5, most children develop a stable gender identity, a sense of themselves as being male or female regardless of what they wear or how they behave. Only then do they understand that what boys and girls do does not necessarily indicate what sex they are: A girl remains a girl even if she can climb a tree (or eats a pizza!), and a boy remains a boy even if he has long hair. At this age, children consolidate their knowledge, with all of its mistakes and misconceptions, into a **gender schema**, a mental network of beliefs and expectations about what it means to be male or female and about what each sex is supposed to wear, do, feel, and think (Bem, 1993; Martin & Ruble, 2004). Gender schemas even include metaphors: After age 4, children of both sexes will usually say that rough, spiky, black, or mechanical things are male and that soft, pink, fuzzy, or

flowery things are female; that black bears are male and pink poodles are female (Leinbach, Hort, & Fagot, 1997). Gender schemas are most rigid between ages 5 and 7; at this age, it's really hard to dislodge a child's notion of what boys and girls can do (Martin, Ruble, & Szkrybalo, 2002). A little girl at this stage may tell you stoutly that "girls can't be doctors," even if her own mother is a doctor.

Many people retain inflexible gender schemas throughout their lives, feeling uncomfortable or angry with men or women who break out of traditional roles—let alone with transgendered individuals who don't fit either category or want to change the one they grew up with. However, with experience and cognitive sophistication, older children often become more flexible in their gender schemas, especially if they have friends of the other sex and if their families and cultures encourage such flexibility (Martin & Ruble, 2004). Children begin to modify their gender schemas, understanding that women can be engineers and men can be cooks.

Cultures and religions, too, differ in their schemas for the roles of women and men. In all Western, industrialized nations, it is taken for granted that women and men alike should be educated; indeed, laws mandate a minimum education for both sexes. But in cultures where female education is prohibited in the name of religious law, as in the parts of Afghanistan controlled by the Taliban, many girls who attend school receive death threats and some have had acid thrown on their faces. Gender schemas can be very powerful, and events that challenge their legitimacy can be enormously threatening.

gender schema A cognitive schema (mental network) of knowledge, beliefs, metaphors, and expectations about what it means to be male or female.

"Jason, I'd like to let you play, but soccer is a girls' game."

Get Involved! Gender and Generations

Gender norms have been changing rapidly, and one way to see this for yourself is to interview older members of your family. Ask at least one man and one woman these questions: (1) When you were growing up, was there anything your parents did not permit you to do because of your sex? (2) Is there any job you think is unsuitable for a man or a woman to do? (3) Did you ever experience discrimination because of your sex? Now consider how you would answer those questions. Do your answers agree with theirs? Why or why not?

Shocking images or nothing new? The idea of women serving in the military and men teaching preschoolers would once have startled most people and offended others. As women soldiers became common, they lost the power to shock, at least if they remained in service jobs. But the wars in Iraq and Afghanistan have again changed the gender rules, creating a generation of female soldiers who fight on the front lines with their male peers. In the photo on the left, Staff Sergeant Patricia Bradford and Specialist Jennifer Hoeppner are briefed before going out on patrol in Iraq in 2009.

Learning Influences A third influence on gender development is the environment, which is full of subtle and not-so-subtle messages about what girls and boys are supposed to do. Behavioral and social-cognitive learning theorists study how the process of gender socialization instills these messages in children. They find that gender socialization begins at the moment of birth. Parents tend to portray their newborn girls as more feminine and delicate than boys, and boys as stronger and more athletic than girls, although it is hard to know how athletic a newborn boy could be (Karraker, Vogel, & Lake, 1995). Many parents are careful to dress their baby in outfits they consider to be the correct color and pattern for his or her sex. Clothes don't matter to the infant, of course, but they are signals to adults about how to treat the child. Adults often respond to the same baby differently, depending on whether the child is dressed as a boy or a girl.

Parents, teachers, and other adults convey their beliefs and expectations about gender even when they are entirely unaware that they are doing so. For example, when parents believe that boys are naturally better at math or sports and that girls are naturally better at English, they unwittingly communicate those beliefs by how they respond to a child's success or failure. They may tell a son who did well in math, "You're a natural math whiz, Johnny!" But if a daughter gets good grades, they may say, "Wow, you really worked hard in math, Joanie, and it shows!" The implication is that girls have to try hard but boys have a natural gift. Messages like these are not lost on children. Both sexes tend to lose interest in activities that are supposedly not natural for them, even when they all start out with equal abilities (Dweck, 2006; Frome & Eccles, 1998).

In today's fast-moving world, society's messages to men and women keep shifting. As a result, gender development has become a lifelong

process, in which gender schemas, attitudes, and behavior evolve as people have new experiences and as society itself changes. Five-year-old children may behave like sexist piglets while they are trying to figure out what it means to be male or female. Their behavior is shaped by a combination of hormones, genetics, cognitive schemas, parental and social lessons, religious and cultural customs, and experiences. But their gender-typed behavior as 5-year-olds often has little to do with how they

will behave at 25 or 45. In fact, by early adulthood, men and women show virtually no average differences in cognitive abilities, personality traits, self-esteem, or psychological well-being (Hyde, 2007). Children can grow up in an extremely gender-typed family and yet, as adults, find themselves in careers or relationships they would never have imagined for themselves. If 5-year-olds are the gender police, many adults end up breaking the law.

✔● **Study** and **Review** on **mypsychlab.com**

Quick Quiz

Taking quizzes is appropriate behavior for all sexes and genders.

1. Three-year-old Paulo thinks that if he changed from wearing pants to wearing dresses he could become a girl. He still lacks a stable _____ .

2. *True or false:* All intersexed people are transsexual.

3. A biological psychologist would say that a 3-year-old boy's love of going "vroom, vroom" with his truck collection is probably a result of _____ .

4. Which statement about gender schemas is *false*? (a) They are present in early form by 1 year of age; (b) they are permanent conceptualizations of what it means to be masculine or feminine; (c) they eventually expand to include many meanings and associations to being male and female; (d) they probably reflect the status of women and men in society.

5. Herb hopes his 4-year-old daughter will become a doctor like him, but she refuses to play with the toy stethoscope he bought her and insists that she will be a princess when she grows up. What conclusions can Herb draw about his daughter's future career?

Answers:

1. gender identity 2. false 3. prenatal hormones, specifically androgen 4. b 5. Not many. His daughter's rigid gender-typed behavior is typical when children are acquiring gender schemas, but it does not necessarily predict much of anything about her adult interests or occupation.

◆ **YOU** are about to learn...

● the physiological changes of adolescence.

● the psychological issues of adolescence.

● findings on brain development in adolescence.

Adolescence

Adolescence refers to the period of development between **puberty**, the age at which a person becomes capable of sexual reproduction, and adulthood. In some cultures, the time span between puberty and adulthood is only a few months; a sexually mature boy or girl is expected to marry and assume adult tasks. In modern Western societies, however, teenagers are not considered emotionally mature enough to assume the full rights, responsibilities, and roles of adulthood.

The Physiology of Adolescence

Until puberty, boys and girls produce roughly the same levels of male hormones (androgens) and female hormones (estrogens). At puberty, however, the brain's pituitary gland begins to stimulate hormone production in the adrenal and reproductive glands. From then on, boys have a higher level of androgens than girls do, and girls have a higher level of estrogens than boys do.

The Onset of Puberty In boys, the reproductive glands are the testes (testicles), which produce sperm; in girls, the reproductive glands are the ovaries, which release eggs. During puberty, these organs mature and the individual becomes capable of reproduction. In girls, signs of sexual maturity are the development of breasts and **menarche**, the onset of menstruation. In boys, the

puberty The age at which a person becomes capable of sexual reproduction.

menarche [men-ARR-kee] The onset of menstruation during puberty.

To their embarrassment, children typically reach puberty at different times. These girls are all the same age, but they differ considerably in physical maturity.

Watch the Video **Adolescent Behavior** on mypsychlab.com

signs are the onset of nocturnal emissions and the growth of the testes, scrotum, and penis. Hormones are also responsible for the emergence of *secondary sex characteristics*, such as a deepened voice and facial and chest hair in boys and pubic hair in both sexes.

The onset of puberty depends on both biological and environmental factors. Menarche depends on a female's having a critical level of body fat, which is necessary to sustain a pregnancy and which triggers the hormonal changes associated with puberty. An increase in body fat among children in developed countries may help explain why the average age of puberty declined in Europe and North America until the mid-twentieth century. The average age of menarche now occurs at about 12 years and 6 months in white girls and a few months earlier in black girls.

Individuals vary enormously in the onset and length of puberty. Some girls go through menarche at 9 or 10 and some boys are still growing in height after age 19. Early-maturing boys generally have a more positive view of their bodies than late-maturing boys do, and their relatively greater size and strength give them a boost in sports and the prestige that being a good athlete brings young men. But they are also more likely to smoke, drink alcohol, use other drugs, and break the law than later-maturing boys (Cota-Robles, Neiss, & Rowe, 2002; Duncan et al., 1985). Some early-maturing girls have the prestige of being socially popular, but, partly because others in their peer group regard them as being sexually precocious, they are also more likely to fight with their parents, drop out of school, have a negative body image, and be angry or depressed. Early menarche itself does not cause these problems; rather, it tends to accentuate existing behavioral problems and family conflicts. Girls who go through puberty relatively late, in contrast, have a more difficult time at first, but by the end of adolescence, many are happier with their appearance and are more popular than their early-maturing classmates (Caspi & Moffitt, 1991; Stattin & Magnusson, 1990).

Brain Development   When people think of physical changes in adolescence, they usually think of hormones and maturing bodies. But the adolescent brain undergoes significant developmental changes, notably a major pruning of neural connections. This pruning occurs primarily in the prefrontal cortex, which is responsible for impulse control and planning, and the limbic system, which is involved in emotional processing (Spear, 2000). In Chapter 11, we will see that errors in the pruning process during adolescence may be involved in the onset of schizophrenia in vulnerable individuals.

Another change involves *myelinization*, which provides a fatty sheath of insulation for some cells (see Chapter 4). Myelinization strengthens the connections between the emotional limbic system and the reasoning prefrontal cortex. This process may continue through the late teens to the mid-20s, which would help explain why the strong emotions of the adolescent years often overwhelm rational decision making and cause some teenagers to behave more impulsively than adults (Steinberg, 2007). It would explain why adolescents are more vulnerable to peer pressure that encourages them to try risky, dumb, or dangerous things—why taunts of "I dare you!" and "You're chicken!" have more power over a 15-year-old than a 25-year-old. Even when teenagers know they are doing the wrong thing, many lack the reasoning ability to foresee the consequences of their actions down the line (Reyna & Farley, 2006).   Watch

In 2005, the U.S. Supreme Court banned the death penalty for juveniles as cruel and unusual punishment, partly on the basis of evidence showing that adolescents often get into trouble because of the neurological immaturity of their brains (Steinberg, 2007). Some researchers have even concluded that many teenagers who commit crimes should be considered "less guilty by reason of adolescence" (Steinberg & Scott, 2003). Do you agree?

The Psychology of Adolescence

The media love sensational stories about teenagers who are angry, violent, live in emotional turmoil, feel lonely, hate their parents, and are running wild sexually. Tyra Banks and Oprah Winfrey have warned parents about an alleged teenage "sex crisis," in which teens are having sex at ever-younger ages. Parents and prosecutors are alarmed about "sexting," the practice of emailing nude pictures to friends. (In ten states so far, this practice has led to 14- and 15-year-olds being arrested on charges of creating and distributing child pornography.) Some observers worry that teenagers have too little self-esteem, which is why they are forever getting in trouble; others worry that, thanks to the self-esteem movement, teenagers have too much self-esteem. One psychologist argues that today's young people have become so narcissistic that they deserve to be called "Generation Me" (Twenge et al., 2008).

How realistic is this portrait of adolescence? Not very. The rate of violent crimes committed by adolescents has been dropping steadily since 1993. Overall feelings of self-esteem do not suddenly plummet after the age of 13 for either sex (Gentile et al., 2009; Kling et al., 1999). How about overinflated self-esteem? One team of researchers examined large samples of high school seniors surveyed every year from 1976 to 2006 (nearly a half million students). In addition to looking at scores on the Narcissistic Personality Inventory, which measures a grandiose sense of importance and entitlement, they developed another measure of narcissism: unreasonable self-enhancement, the discrepancy between how good you actually are academically and how good you *think* you are. They found very little change in narcissism on either measure over the decades (Trzesniewski, Donnellan, & Robins, 2008). They also found little change over the decades in self-esteem, feelings of control, hopelessness, happiness, life satisfaction, the importance of religion, and many other qualities (Trzesniewski & Donnellan, 2010). All young people are more narcissistic than their elders, other investigators concluded, simply because adolescence and young adulthood are a developmental stage when people get to think about themselves and their futures, and those concerns are not particular to "Generation Me" (Roberts, Edmonds, & Grijalva, 2010).

Thinking Critically about Adolescent Psychology

What about sex? According to the National Youth Risk Behavior Survey, today's teenagers are actually more conservative than their parents were at their age. In 1991, 54.1 percent of all high school students had had sex; in 2007, fewer than half (47.8 percent) had ever had sex, and only a third were currently sexually active (Eaton et al., 2008). The number of sexual partners has also declined (Bogle, 2008). Only the rate of births to teenage girls has risen in the past few years, a result of declining contraceptive use.

Similarly, studies of representative samples of adolescents find that only a small minority is seriously troubled, angry, or unhappy. Most teenagers have supportive families, a sense of purpose and self-confidence, good friends, and the skill to cope with their problems. Nevertheless, three kinds of problems are more common during adolescence than during childhood or adulthood: conflict with parents, mood swings and depression, and, as we saw, higher rates of reckless, rule breaking, and risky behavior (Steinberg, 2007). Rule breaking often occurs because teenagers are developing their own standards and values, often by trying on the styles, actions, and attitudes of their peers, in contrast to those of their parents.

"So I blame you for everything—whose fault is that?"

Peers become especially important to adolescents because they represent the values and style of the generation that teenagers identify with, the generation that they will share experiences with as adults (Bukowski, 2001; Harris, 2009). Many people report that feeling rejected by their peers when they were teenagers was more devastating than punitive treatment by parents. According to a government-sponsored review of whether and how online technologies affect child safety, the most frequent dangers that teenagers face on the Internet are not pornography or even predatory adults, and definitely not sexting. "Bullying and harassment, most often by peers, are the most frequent threats that minors face, both online and offline," the report found (Berkman Center for Internet & Society, 2008).

Adolescents who are lonely, depressed, worried, or angry tend to express these concerns in ways characteristic of their sex. Boys are more likely than girls to externalize their emotional problems in acts of aggression and other antisocial behavior. Girls are more likely than boys to internalize their feelings and problems, by becoming withdrawn or developing eating disorders (Wicks-Nelson & Israel, 2003). Although, as we said, there are no gender differences in overall self-esteem, a gender gap in two specific *areas* of self-esteem emerges in adolescence, reflecting the externalizing/internalizing difference in habits of coping. Girls are more dissatisfied than boys with their bodies and general appearance; boys are more dissatisfied than girls with their social behavior at school and with friends (Gentile et al., 2009).

✓• ⌐**Study** and
      └**Review** on
         mypsychlab.com

Quick Quiz

If you are not in the midst of adolescent turmoil, try these questions.

1. What is the difference between *puberty* and *adolescence*?
2. Extreme turmoil and rebellion in adolescence are (a) nearly universal, (b) the exception rather than the rule, (c) rare.
3. *True or false*: Teenage boys have much higher self-esteem than teenage girls do.
4. What changes occur in the brain during adolescence?

Answers:

1. Puberty refers to the physiological process of sexual maturation; adolescence is a social category marking the years between puberty and adulthood.   2. b   3. false   4. pruning of neural connections, myelinization, and strengthening of connections between the limbic system and the prefrontal cortex

YOU are about to learn...

- Erik Erikson's theory of the stages of adult development.

- the typical attitudes and experiences of "emerging adulthood," the years from 18 to 25.

- some common midlife changes for women and men.

- which mental abilities decline in old age and which ones do not.

Adulthood

According to ancient Greek legend, the Sphinx was a monster—half lion, half woman—who terrorized passersby on the road to Thebes. The Sphinx would ask each traveler a question and then murder those who failed to answer correctly. (The Sphinx was a pretty tough grader.) The question was: What animal walks on four feet in the morning, two feet at noon, and three feet in the evening? Only one traveler, Oedipus, knew the solution to the riddle. The animal, he said, is man, who crawls on all fours as a baby, walks upright as an adult, and limps in old age with the aid of a staff.

The Sphinx was the first life span theorist. Since then, many philosophers, writers, and scientists have speculated on the course of adult development. Are the changes of adulthood predictable, like those of childhood? What are the major psychological issues of adult life? Is mental and physical deterioration in old age inevitable?

Stages and Ages

One of the first modern theorists to propose a life span approach to psychological development was psychoanalyst Erik H. Erikson (1902–1994).

Erikson (1950/1963, 1982) wrote that all individuals go through eight stages in their lives. Each stage is characterized by what he called a "crisis," a particular psychological challenge that ideally should be resolved before the individual moves on.

1 **Trust versus mistrust** is the challenge that occurs during the baby's first year, when the baby depends on others to provide food, comfort, cuddling, and warmth. If these needs are not met, the child may never develop the essential trust of others necessary to get along in the world.

2 **Autonomy (independence) versus shame and doubt** is the challenge that occurs when the child is a toddler. The young child is learning to be independent and must do so without feeling too ashamed or uncertain about his or her actions.

3 **Initiative versus guilt** is the challenge that occurs as the preschooler develops. The child is acquiring new physical and mental skills, setting goals, and enjoying newfound talents, but must also learn to control impulses. The danger lies in developing too strong a sense of guilt over his or her wishes and fantasies.

4 **Competence versus inferiority** is the challenge for school-age children, who are learning to make things, use tools, and acquire the skills for adult life. Children who fail these lessons of mastery and competence may come out of this stage feeling inadequate and inferior.

5 **Identity versus role confusion** is the great challenge of adolescence, when teenagers must decide who they are, what they are going to do, and what they hope to make of their lives. Erikson used the term *identity crisis* to describe what he considered to be the primary conflict of this stage. Those who resolve it will emerge with a strong identity, ready to plan for the future. Those who do not will sink into confusion, unable to make decisions.

6 **Intimacy versus isolation** is the challenge of young adulthood. Once you have decided who you are, said Erikson, you must share yourself with another and learn to make commitments. No matter how successful you are in your work, you are not complete until you are capable of intimacy.

7 **Generativity versus stagnation** is the challenge of the middle years. Now that you know who you are and have an intimate relationship, will you sink into complacency and selfishness, or will you experience generativity—creativity and renewal? Parenthood is the most common route to generativity, but people can be productive, creative, and nurturant in other ways, in their work or their relationships with the younger generation.

8 **Ego integrity versus despair** is the final challenge of old age. As they age, people strive to reach the ultimate goals of wisdom, spiritual tranquility, and acceptance of their lives. Just as the healthy child will not fear life, said Erikson, the healthy adult will not fear death.

Erikson recognized that cultural and economic factors affect people's progression through these stages. Some societies make the passages relatively easy. If you know you are going to be a farmer like your parents and you have no alternative, you are unlikely to have an adolescent identity crisis (unless you hate farming). If you have many choices, however, as adolescents in urban societies often do, the transition can become prolonged (Schwartz, 2004). Similarly, cultures that place a high premium on independence and individualism will make it difficult for many of their members to resolve Erikson's sixth crisis, that of intimacy versus isolation.

Erikson was also aware that the psychological themes and crises of life can occur out of order, although that was not his emphasis. As people's lives became less traditional and predictable, researchers discovered just how out of order they can be. Today, for instance, an identity crisis is no longer limited to the teen years. A man who has worked in one job for 20 years, and then is laid off at 45 and must find an entirely new career, may have an identity crisis too. Likewise, competence is not mastered once and for all in childhood. People learn new skills and lose old ones throughout their lives, and their sense of competence rises and falls accordingly. And people who are highly generative, in terms of being committed to helping their communities or the next generation, tend to do volunteer work or choose occupations that allow them to contribute to society throughout their lives (McAdams, 2006).

Stage theories, therefore, do not adequately describe how adults grow and change, or remain the same, across the life span. Yet Erikson was right to show that development does not stop at adolescence or young adulthood; it is an ongoing process. His ideas were important because he placed adult development in the context of family, work, and society, and he specified many of the timeless and universal concerns of adulthood: trust, competence, identity, generativity, and the ability to enjoy life and accept death (Dunkel & Sefcek, 2009).

The Transitions of Life

Some events tend to occur at particular times in life: going to school, learning to drive a car, having a baby, retiring from work. When nearly everyone your age goes through the same experience or enters a new role at the same time, adjusting to these transitions is relatively easy. Conversely, if you aren't doing these things and hardly anyone you know is doing them either, you will not feel out of step.

In modern societies, however, most people will face unanticipated transitions, events that happen without warning, such as being fired from a job because of downsizing. And many people have to deal with changes that they expect to happen that do not, such as not getting a job right out of college, not getting married at the age they expected, not

According to Erik Erikson, children must master the crisis of competence and older adults must resolve the challenge of generativity. This child and her grandmother are certainly helping each other with their life tasks. But are the needs for competence and generativity important at only one stage of life?

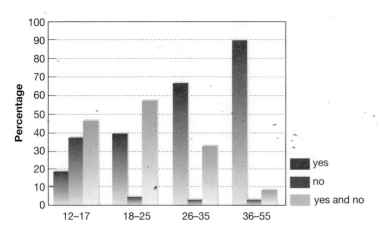

FIGURE 3.4

Are You an Adult Yet?

When people are asked, "Do you feel that you have reached adulthood?" the percentage that answers "yes" steadily increases over time. But as you can see, people between the ages of 18 and 25, emerging adults, are most likely to say "yes *and* no" (Arnett, 2004).

getting promoted, not being able to afford to retire, or realizing that they cannot have children (Schlossberg & Robinson, 1996). With this in mind, let's consider some of the major transitions of life.

Emerging Adulthood In industrialized nations, major demographic changes have postponed the timing of career decisions, marriage or cohabitation, and parenthood until a person's late 20s or even 30s, on the average. Many young people between the ages of 18 and 25 are in college and at least partly dependent financially on their parents. This phenomenon has created a phase of life that some call *emerging adulthood* (Arnett, 2004). When emerging adults are asked whether they feel they have reached adulthood, the majority answer "in some ways yes, in some ways no" (see Figure 3.4).

In certain respects, emerging adults have moved beyond adolescence into maturity, becoming more emotionally controlled, more confident, less dependent, and less angry and alienated (Roberts, Caspi, & Moffitt, 2001). But they are also the group most likely to live unstable lives and feel unrooted. Emerging adults move more often than people in other demographic groups do—back to their parents' homes and then out again, from one city to another, from living with roommates to living on their own. And their rates of risky behavior (such as binge drinking, having unprotected sex, and driving at high speeds or while drunk) are higher than those of any other age group, including adolescents (Arnett, 2004).

Of course, not all young people in this age group are alike. Some groups within the larger society, such as Mormons, promote early marriage and parenthood. And young people who are poor, who have dropped out of school, who had a child at 16, or who have few opportunities to get a good job will not have the income or leisure to explore many options. But the overall shift in all industrialized nations toward a global economy, increased education, and delayed career and family decisions means that emerging adulthood is likely to grow in importance as a distinct phase of prolonged exploration and freedom.

The Middle Years For most women and men, the midlife years between 35 and 65 are the prime of life (MacArthur Foundation, 1999; Mroczek & Sprio, 2005; Newton & Stewart, 2010). These years are typically a time of the greatest well-being, good health, productivity, and community involvement. They are also often a time of reflection and reassessment. People look back on what they have accomplished, take stock of what they regret not having done, and think about what they want to do

Doonesbury   BY GARRY TRUDEAU

with their remaining years. When crises occur, they are for reasons not related to aging but to specific life-changing events, such as illness or the loss of a job or partner (Wethington, 2000).

But doesn't menopause make most midlife women depressed, irritable, and irrational? **Menopause**, which usually occurs between ages 45 and 55, is the cessation of menstruation after the ovaries stop producing estrogen and progesterone. Menopause does produce physical symptoms in many women, notably hot flashes, as the vascular system adjusts to the decrease in estrogen. But only about 10 percent of all women have unusually severe physical symptoms.

The negative view of menopause as a syndrome that causes depression and other negative emotional reactions is based on women who have undergone early menopause following a hysterectomy (removal of the uterus) or who have had a lifetime history of depression. But these women are not typical. According to many surveys of thousands of healthy, randomly chosen women in the general population, most women view menopause with relief that they no longer have to worry about pregnancy or menstrual periods. The vast majority have only a few physical symptoms (which can be annoying and bothersome but are temporary), and most do not become depressed; only 3 percent even report regret at having reached menopause (McKinlay, McKinlay, & Brambilla, 1987). In one study of 1,000 postmenopausal women, fewer than half reported physical symptoms and only 5 percent of those complained of mood symptoms (Ness, Aronow, & Beck, 2006). Contrary to stereotype, women in their 40s and 50s often report being most satisfied with the Eriksonian issues of identity, intimacy, and generativity (Newton & Stewart, 2010).

Although women lose their fertility after menopause and men theoretically remain fertile throughout their lives, men have a biological clock too. Testosterone diminishes, although it never drops as sharply in men as estrogen does in women. The sperm count may also gradually drop, and the sperm that remain are more susceptible to genetic mutations that can increase the risk of some diseases in children conceived by older fathers, as we saw earlier (Wyrobek et al., 2006).

The physical changes of midlife do not by themselves predict how people will feel about aging or how they will respond to it (Schaie & Willis, 2002). People's views of aging are profoundly influenced by the culture they live in and by the promises of technology to prolong life and health—some realistic, some still science fiction. Is aging something natural and inevitable, to be accepted gracefully? Or is it a process to be fought tooth and nail, with every chemical, surgical, and genetic weapon we can lay our hands on? To what extent should society pay for life-extending interventions? These issues will be hotly debated in the years to come. **⊙▸ Simulate**

Old Age

When does old age start? Not long ago, you would have been considered old in your 60s. Today, the fastest-growing segment of the population in North America consists of people over the age of 85. There were 4 million Americans age 85 or older in 2000, and the Census Bureau projects that there may be as many as 31 million by 2050. Close to one million of them will be over the age of 100. How will these people do? *Gerontologists*, researchers who study aging and the old, have been providing some answers.

The first prediction is that the life phase of retirement will change significantly because of demographic changes affecting older people. When people expected to live only until their early 70s, retirement at 65 was associated with loss—a withdrawal from work and fulfilling activities, with not much to look forward to but illness and old age. Today, thanks to the enormous cohort of healthy baby boomers and a changed economy, retirement might last 20 or 30 years. Thus, it is no longer simply a life transition from working to not working. People in the phase of what some psychologists are calling "positive retirement" often find a new career, volunteer work, or new, engrossing activities (Halpern, 2008).

Still, various aspects of intelligence, memory, and other forms of mental functioning do decline

menopause The cessation of menstruation and of the production of ova; it is usually a gradual process lasting up to several years.

⊙▸ Simulate Aging and Change in Physical Appearance on **mypsychlab.com**

The two images of old age: More and more old people are living healthy, active, mentally stimulating lives. But with increasing longevity, many people are also falling victim to degenerative diseases such as Alzheimer's.

fluid intelligence The capacity for deductive reasoning and the ability to use new information to solve problems; it is relatively independent of education and tends to decline in old age.

crystallized intelligence Cognitive skills and specific knowledge of information acquired over a lifetime; it is heavily dependent on education and tends to remain stable over the lifetime.

⊙—Watch the Video **Successfully Aging—Thelma at 83** on **mypsychlab.com**

FIGURE 3.5 Changes in Mental Functioning over Time

As these graphs show, some intellectual abilities tend to dwindle with age, but numerical and verbal abilities remain relatively steady over the years.

significantly with age. Older adults score lower on tests of reasoning, spatial ability, and complex problem solving than do younger adults. The ability to produce and spell familiar words declines, a change that often causes great frustration and annoyance (Burke & Shafto, 2004). It takes older people longer to retrieve names, dates, and other information; in fact, the speed of cognitive processing in general slows down. However, older people vary considerably, with some declining significantly and others remaining sharp (Salthouse, 2006).

Fortunately, not all cognitive abilities worsen with age. **Fluid intelligence** is the capacity for deductive reasoning and the ability to use new information to solve problems. It reflects in part an inherited predisposition, and it parallels other biological capacities in its growth and later decline (Bosworth & Schaie, 1999; Li et al., 2004). **Crystallized intelligence** consists of knowledge and skills built up over a lifetime, the kind of intelligence that gives us the ability to do arithmetic, define words, or take political positions. It depends heavily on education and experience, and it tends to remain stable or even improve over the life span (see Figure 3.5). This is why physicians, lawyers, teachers, farmers, musicians, insurance agents, politicians, psychologists, and people in many other occupations can continue working well into old age (Halpern, 2008). ⊙—Watch

Many of the physical and mental losses that do occur in old age are genetically based and are seen in all societies, but others have to do with cultural, behavioral, and psychological factors (Park & Gutchess, 2006). Psychologists have made great strides in separating conditions once thought to be

an inevitable part of old age from those that are preventable or treatable:

- Apparent senility in the elderly is often caused by malnutrition, prescription medications, harmful combinations of medications, and even over-the-counter drugs (such as sleeping pills and antihistamines), all of which can be hazardous to old people.

> Thinking Critically about Mental Declines in Old Age

- Weakness, frailty, and even many of the diseases associated with old age are often caused by being inactive and sedentary (Booth & Neufer, 2005).

- Depression, passivity, and memory problems may result from the loss of meaningful activity, intellectual stimulation, goals to pursue, and control over events (Hess, 2005; Schaie & Zuo, 2001).

As these findings would predict, older people can profit from aerobic exercise and strength training, which maintain physical strength and flexibility, boost the brain's blood supply, promote the development of new cells, and can even suppress genetic predispositions for various infirmities. The result is improved cognitive functioning in skills such as planning, concentration, and scheduling (Colcombe & Kramer, 2003; Hertzog et al., 2008). Mental stimulation also fosters the growth of neural connections in the brain, even well into old age. Older adults can sometimes do as well on memory tests as people in their 20s, when given instruction and training. In one project, older people who had shown a decline in inductive reasoning and spatial ability over a 14-year

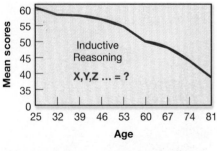

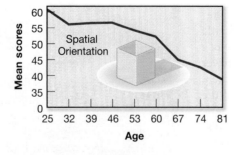

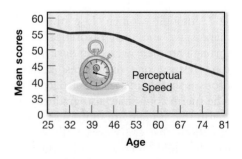

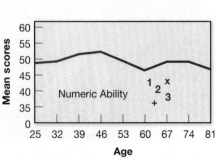

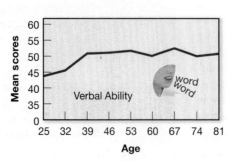

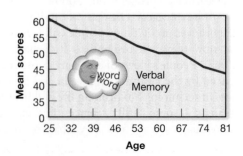

span were given five hours of training in these skills. This brief intervention produced significant improvements in two-thirds of the sample, and many people performed at or above the level of skill they had had 14 years earlier. More impressive, the effects were still apparent up to seven years later (Kramer & Willis, 2002). Cognitive enrichment cannot prevent most cases of serious cognitive decline and dementia, which are often strongly influenced or even caused directly by genes, but the declines may be delayed (Gatz, 2007; Hertzog et al., 2008).

Perhaps the best news is that as people get older, most become better able to regulate negative feelings and emphasize the positive. The frequency of intense negative emotions is highest among people aged 18 to 34, then drops sharply to age 65. After 65, it levels off, rising only slightly among old people facing crises of illness and bereavement

(Charles & Carstensen, 2004; Charles, Reynolds, & Gatz, 2001). Apparently, many people do grow wiser, or at least more tranquil, with age.

Some researchers who study aging are therefore optimistic. In their view, people who have challenging occupations and interests, who remain active mentally, who exercise regularly, and who adapt flexibly to change and loss are likely to maintain their cognitive abilities and well-being. "Use it or lose it," they say. Other researchers, however, are less upbeat. "When you've lost it, you can't use it," they reply. They are worried about the growing numbers of people living into their 90s and beyond, when rates of cognitive impairment and dementia rise dramatically. The challenge for society is to prepare for the many people who will be living into advanced old age, by helping as many as possible to keep using their brains instead of losing them.

✓• Study and Review on mypsychlab.com

Quick Quiz

People of any age can answer this quiz.

1. The key psychological issue during adolescence, said Erikson, is a(n) _____ crisis.

2. What new phase of life development has emerged because of demographic changes, and what years does it include?

3. Most women react to menopause by (a) feeling depressed, (b) regretting the loss of femininity, (c) going a little crazy, (d) feeling relieved or neutral.

4. Which of these statements about the decline of mental abilities in old age is *false*? (a) It can often be lessened with training programs; (b) it inevitably declines sharply; (c) it is sometimes a result of malnutrition, medication, or disease rather than aging; (d) it is slowed when people live in stimulating environments.

5. Suddenly, your 80-year-old grandmother has become confused and delusional. Before concluding that old age has made her senile, what other explanation should you rule out?

Answers:

1. identity 2. emerging adulthood, ages 18 to 25 3. d 4. b 5. You should be sure she is not malnourished and you should rule out the possibility that she is taking too many medications, including nonprescription drugs.

YOU are about to learn...

• why terrible childhood experiences do not inevitably affect a person forever.

• what makes most children resilient in the face of adversity.

The Wellsprings of Resilience

Most people take it for granted that the path from childhood to adolescence to adulthood is a fairly straight one. We think of the lasting attitudes, habits, and values our parents taught us. We continue to have deep attachments to our families, even when we are fighting with them. And many people carry with them the scars of emotional wounds they suffered as children. Children who have been beaten, neglected, or constantly subjected to verbal or physical abuse by their parents are more likely than other children to have emotional problems, become delinquent and violent, commit crimes, have low IQs, drop out of school, develop mental disorders such as depression, and develop chronic stress-related illnesses (Emery & Laumann-Billings, 1998; Margolin & Gordis, 2004; Repetti, Taylor, & Seeman, 2002).

And yet, when researchers began to question the entrenched assumption that early trauma always has long-lasting negative effects and considered the evidence for alternative views, they got quite a different picture. Most children, they found, are resilient, eventually overcoming even the effects of war, childhood illness, having abusive or alcoholic parents, early deprivation, or being sexually molested (Kaufman & Zigler, 1987; Nelson et al., 2007; Rathbun, DiVirgilio, & Waldfogel, 1958; Rind, Tromovitch, & Bauserman, 1998; Rutter et al., 2004; Werner, 1989; West & Prinz, 1987).

Thinking Critically about the Effects of Childhood Traumas

Psychologist Ann Masten (2001) observed that most people assume there is something special and rare about people who recover from adversity. But the great surprise of the research, she concluded, is how ordinary resilience is. Many of the children who outgrow early deprivation and trauma have easygoing temperaments or personality traits, such as self-efficacy and self-control, that help them roll with even severe punches. They have a secure attachment style, which helps them work through traumatic events in a way that heals their wounds and restores hope and emotional balance (Mikulincer, Shaver, & Horesh, 2006). If children lack secure attachments with their own parents, they may be rescued by love and attention from their siblings, peers, extended family members, or other caring adults. And some have experiences outside the family—in schools, places of worship, or other organizations—that give them a sense of competence, moral support, solace, religious faith, and self-esteem (Cowen et al., 1990; Garmezy, 1991).

Perhaps the most powerful reason for the resilience of so many children, and for the changes that all of us make throughout our lives, is that we are all constantly interpreting our experiences. We can decide to repeat the mistakes our parents made or break free of them. We can decide to remain prisoners of childhood or to strike out in new directions at age 20, 50, or 70. We can decide for ourselves whether we want to remain prisoners of childhood or to be liberated by the possibilities of adulthood.

Psychology in the News   REVISITED

Has our review of events across the life span helped you to clarify your thoughts about women and men who become parents in their 60s or 70s? As we have seen, the whole concept of natural, limited stages in the life cycle is changing. Having a child in one's 40s used to seem as weird and unnatural as having a baby in one's 60s, but now it is common. Will giving birth after 50 come to be seen the same way? After all, adolescence has stretched into "emerging adulthood." Retirement has extended into "positive retirement." Parenthood occurs ... virtually at any age? If we can live to 100, why not have a baby at 70?

Adriana Iliescu, who had her daughter at age 66, held a party on the child's first birthday, telling the press, "I can't describe how I feel when I hug her, when I kiss her. It's a special kind of feeling. And [raising her] is not as tough as I had expected." At this writing, Iliescu is alive and caring for her daughter. But when her child is 16, how will it be for her to have a mother who is 82? What if her mother becomes ill? Iliescu is unmarried and says she does not have much of an extended family or many friends. She admits she has no plans for the child if she should become ill and unable to care for her. In contrast, Arceli Keh, who was merely 63 when she had her baby, has a husband and extended family involved in the child's care.

What about the Indian couple in their 70s, whose story opened this chapter? Will they survive to see their twins even through childhood? Carmela Bousada's case is instructive. After being inseminated with an embryo from a donor egg and sperm, Bousada delivered twin boys a week before her 67th birthday. Because her mother died at the age of 101, and because she herself felt physically fit, she assumed she would live as long. But Bousada, who was single, died of cancer at age 69, when her twins were only 2 years old.

Some fertility experts and ethicists are extremely concerned about the medical, social, and psychological costs of pregnancy and raising a child so late in life. They worry that stories about old women giving birth raise women's expectations to unreasonable heights

Adriana Iliescu with Eliza Maria on the baby's first birthday.

and create false hopes that technology can easily overcome any biological limitations. For every successful pregnancy among older women, there are thousands of failures; and the older a woman is, the greater her chance of developing medical problems in pregnancy (such as gestational diabetes and high blood pressure). Moreover, we have seen that age brings a decline in some cognitive and physical abilities and an increasing chance of dementia.

So it seems legitimate to worry about whether elderly parents—of either sex—will have the mental resources and energy to guide their children through the many hurdles of childhood and adolescence. On the other hand, although it is true that women who choose to have children in their 60s and 70s are rare, millions of older people, required by unforeseen circumstances to rear their grandchildren, have risen to the challenge.

In the next decades, as the world changes in countless unpredictable ways, the territory of adulthood will continue to expand, providing new frontiers as well as fewer signposts and roadmaps to guide us. Increasingly, age will be what we make of it.

Taking Psychology with You

Bringing Up Baby

Every year or so another best-selling book arrives to tell parents they've been doing it all wrong. Countless books have advised parents to treat their children in very specific, if contradictory, ways: Pick them up, don't pick them up; respond when they cry, don't respond when they cry; let them sleep with you, never let them sleep with you; be affectionate, be stern; be highly sensitive to their every need so they will securely attach to you, don't overreact to their every mood or complaint or you will spoil them. A billion-dollar industry has emerged to calm (and inflame) parental worries, offering expensive strollers, toys, and "fetal education" and baby sign language programs—all to create the perfect child (Paul, 2008).

No need to panic. Critical thinkers can call upon two lines of evidence, described in this chapter, to protect themselves from the guilt-mongers and marketers. One is that babies and young children thrive under a wide variety of child-rearing methods. The second is that babies bring their own temperaments and other genetic predispositions to the matter of how best to raise them. Most respond readily to induction, but others require stricter discipline.

Well, then, how should you treat your children? Should you be strict or lenient, powerful or permissive? Should you require them to stop having tantrums, to clean up their rooms, to be polite? Should you say, "Oh, nothing I do will matter, anyway," or "If I don't get 100 percent compliance on every order, this kid is going to boot camp"? Child development research does suggest general principles that can help parents find that middle way and foster their children's confidence and helpfulness:

Set high expectations that are appropriate to the child's age and temperament, and teach the child how to meet them. Some parents make few demands on their children, either unintentionally or because they believe a parent should not impose standards. Others make many demands, such as requiring children to be polite, help with chores, control their anger, be thoughtful of others, and do well in school. The children of parents who make few demands tend to be aggressive, impulsive, and immature. The children of parents who have high but realistic expectations tend to be helpful and above average in competence and self-confidence (Damon, 1995).

Explain, explain, explain. Induction, telling a child why you have applied a rule, teaches a child to be responsible. Punitive methods ("Do it or I'll spank you") may result in compliance, but the child will tend to disobey as soon as you are out of sight. Explanations also teach children how to reason and understand. While setting standards for your children, you can also allow them to express disagreements and feelings. This does not mean you have to argue with a 4-year-old about the merits of table manners or permit antisocial and destructive behavior. Once you have explained a rule, you need to enforce it consistently.

Encourage empathy. Call the child's attention to the effects of his or her actions on others and appeal to the child's sense of fair play and desire to be good. As we saw, even very young children are capable of empathy. Vague orders, such as "Don't fight," are less effective than showing the child how fighting disrupts and hurts others.

Notice, approve of, and reward good behavior. Many parents punish the behavior they dislike, a form of attention that may be rewarding to the child. It is much more effective to praise the behavior you do want, which teaches the child what is expected.

Remember the critical-thinking guideline "don't oversimplify." The challenge is to avoid the twin fallacies of "It's all genetic" and "If I just do all the right things, whatever they are, my child will be intelligent, kind, and successful." Even with the best skills and intentions, you cannot control everything that happens to your child or remodel your child's temperamental dispositions. Besides, as children grow up, they are influenced by their peers and generation and by particular experiences that shape their interests and motivation. But you do have the power to make your children's lives miserable or secure. You also have the power to profoundly affect the *quality* of the relationship you will have with your child throughout life: one filled with conflict and resentment, or one that is close and loving.

Summary (⫶•⫶ Listen to an audio file of your chapter on mypsychlab.com

● *Developmental psychologists* study how people grow and change over the life span. Many study *socialization*, the process by which children learn the rules and behavior society expects of them.

From Conception through the First Year

● *Maturation* is the unfolding of genetically influenced behavior and characteristics. Prenatal development consists of the *germinal, embryonic*, and *fetal* stages. Harmful influences that can adversely affect the fetus's development include German measles, toxic substances, some sexually transmitted diseases, cigarettes, alcohol (which can cause *fetal alcohol syndrome* and cognitive deficits), illegal drugs, and even over-the-counter medications. Fathers affect prenatal development too; the sperm of teenage boys and men over 50 may have mutations that increase the risk of miscarriage, birth defects, and certain diseases in their offspring.

● Babies are born with *motor reflexes* and a number of perceptual abilities. Cultural practices affect the timing of physical milestones.

● Babies' innate need for *contact comfort* gives rise to emotional attachment to their caregivers, and by the age of 6 to 8 months, infants begin to feel *separation anxiety*. Studies of the *Strange Situation* have distinguished *secure* from *insecure* attachment; insecurity can take one of two forms, *avoidant* or *anxious-ambivalent* attachment.

● Styles of attachment are relatively unaffected by the normal range of child-rearing practices, and also by whether or not babies spend time in daycare. Insecure attachment is promoted by parents' rejection, mistreatment, or abandonment of their infants; by a mother's postpartum depression, which can affect her ability to care for the baby; by the child's own fearful, insecure temperament; or by stressful family situations.

Language Development

● Human beings are the only species that uses *language* to express and comprehend an infinite number of novel utterances, think about the past and future, and describe things or people who are not present. An innate capacity for language may have evolved in humans because it enhanced the chances of survival and the establishment of social bonds.

● Language acquisition may begin in the womb, as even newborns can distinguish the language their mother spoke during pregnancy from an unfamiliar language. Infants are responsive to the pitch, intensity, and sound of language, which may be why adults in many cultures speak to babies in *parentese*, using higher-pitched words and exaggerated intonation of vowels. At 4 to 6 months of age, babies can often recognize their own names and other words that are regularly spoken with emotion. Babies go through a babbling phase from age 6 months to 1 year, and at about 1 year, they start saying single words and using symbolic gestures, which continue to be important for language, thinking, and problem solving. At age 2, children speak in two- or three-word *telegraphic* sentences that convey a variety of messages.

● Noam Chomsky argued that the ability to take the *surface structure* of any utterance and apply rules of *syntax* to infer its underlying *deep structure* must depend on an innate faculty for language, a mental module that is sensitive to a *universal grammar* (features common to all languages). Many findings support this view: Children from different cultures go through similar stages of language development; children's language is full of *overregularizations* reflecting grammatical rules; adults do not consistently correct their children's syntax; groups of children who have never been exposed to adult language often invent their own; and young infants can derive linguistic rules from strings of sounds.

● Some scientists, on the other hand, have devised computer models of language acquisition that do not assume an innate capacity. Some argue that instead of inferring grammatical rules, children learn the statistical probability that any given word or syllable will follow another. Parental practices also aid a child's language acquisition. Biological readiness and experience interact in the development of language.

Cognitive Development

● Jean Piaget argued that cognitive development depends on an interaction between maturation and a child's experiences in the world. Children's thinking changes and adapts through *assimilation* and *accommodation*. Piaget proposed four stages of cognitive development: (1) *sensorimotor* (birth to age 2), during which the child learns *object permanence*; (2) *preoperational* (ages 2 to 7), during which language and symbolic thought develop, although the child remains *egocentric* in reasoning and has difficulty with some mental *operations*; (3) *concrete operations* (ages 7 to 12), during which the child comes to understand *conservation*, identity, and serial ordering; and (4) *formal operations* (age 12 to adulthood), during which abstract reasoning develops.

● Modern researchers have found that the changes from one stage to another are not as clear-cut as Piaget implied; development is more continuous and overlapping. More important, babies and young children have greater cognitive abilities than Piaget thought, perhaps because of the core knowledge they are born with. Young children are not always egocentric in their thinking. By the age of 4 or 5, they have developed a *theory of mind* to account for their own and other people's behavior. Cultural practices affect the pace and content of cognitive development.

Moral Development

● Lawrence Kohlberg proposed that as children mature cognitively, they go through three levels of moral reasoning. But people can reason morally without behaving morally. Developmental psychologists study how children learn to internalize standards of right and wrong and to behave accordingly. This ability depends on the emergence of conscience and the moral emotions of guilt, shame, and empathy, and on the ability of children to learn to regulate their impulses, wishes, and feelings.

● As a strategy for teaching children to behave, a parent's use of *power assertion* is associated with a child's aggressiveness and lack of empathy. *Induction* is associated with children who develop empathy, internalize moral standards, and can resist temptation. But all methods of discipline interact with the child's own temperament.

● The capacity of very young children for *self-regulation* is associated with the development of internalized moral standards and conscience. This ability is enhanced by mothers who use induction as a primary form of discipline. It also may reflect a personality trait, because it tends to emerge very early in life and to be consistent over time and across situations.

Gender Development

● Gender development includes the emerging awareness of *gender identity*, the understanding that people are biologically male or female regardless of what they do or wear, and *gender typing*, the process by which boys and girls learn what it means to be masculine or feminine in their culture. Some individuals are born with *intersex* physical conditions, living with the physical attributes of both sexes, and consider themselves to be *transgender*. *Transsexuals* feel that they are male in a female body or vice versa; their gender identity is at odds with their anatomical sex.

● Universally, young children tend to prefer same-sex toys and playing with other children of their own sex. Biological psychologists account for this phenomenon in terms of genes and prenatal androgens, which appear to be involved in gender-typed play. Cognitive psychologists study how children develop *gender schemas* for the categories "male" and "female," which in turn shape their gender-typed behavior. Gender schemas tend to be inflexible at first. Later they become more flexible as the child cognitively matures and assimilates new information, if the child's culture promotes flexible gender schemas. Learning theorists study the direct and subtle reinforcers and social messages that foster gender typing.

● Gender development changes over the life span, depending on people's experiences with work and family life and larger events in society and their culture.

Adolescence

● *Adolescence* begins with the physical changes of *puberty*. In girls, puberty is signaled by *menarche* and the development of breasts; in boys, it begins with the onset of nocturnal emissions and the development of the testes, scrotum, and penis. Hormones produce *secondary* sex characteristics, such as pubic hair in both sexes and a deeper voice in males.

● The adolescent brain undergoes a major pruning of neural connections, primarily in the prefrontal cortex and the limbic system, and *myelinization*, which improves the efficiency of neural transmission and strengthens the connections between these two brain areas. These neurological changes may not be complete until the early 20s, which would help explain why the strong emotions of the adolescent years sometimes overwhelm rational decision making and why teenagers often behave more impulsively than adults. This evidence may have implications for how teenagers who break the law should be treated.

● Most American adolescents do not go through extreme emotional turmoil, anger, or rebellion, and do not dislike their parents. They do not suffer from unusually low self-esteem or its opposite, extreme narcissism. However, conflict with parents, mood swings and depression, and reckless or rule-breaking behavior do increase in adolescence. The peer group becomes especially important, and peer bullying, online or offline, is often the source of teenagers' greatest unhappiness. Boys tend to externalize their emotional problems in acts of aggression and other antisocial behavior; girls tend to internalize their problems by becoming depressed or developing eating disorders.

Adulthood

● Erik Erikson proposed that life consists of eight stages, each with a unique psychological challenge, or crisis, that must be resolved, such as an *identity crisis* in adolescence. Erikson identified many of the essential concerns of adulthood and showed that development is a lifelong process. However, psychological issues or crises are not confined to particular chronological periods or stages.

● When most people in an age group go through the same event at about the same time, transitions are easier than when people feel out of step. In industrialized nations, major demographic changes have caused young adults to postpone the timing of career decisions, marriage or commitment to a partner, and parenthood. Many people between the ages of 18 and 25, especially if they are not financially independent, find themselves in a life phase often called *emerging adulthood*.

● The middle years are generally not a time of turmoil or crisis but the prime of most people's lives. In women, *menopause* begins in the late 40s or early 50s. Many women have temporary physical symptoms, but most do not regret the end of fertility or become depressed and irritable. In middle-aged men, hormone production slows down and sperm counts decline; fertility continues, but with increased risk of fetal abnormalities.

● *Gerontologists* have revised our ideas about old age, now that people are living longer and healthier lives and entering an extended phase of positive retirement. The speed of cognitive processing slows down, and *fluid intelligence* parallels other biological capacities in its eventual decline. *Crystallized intelligence*, in contrast, depends heavily on culture, education, and experience, and it tends to remain stable over the life span.

● Many supposedly inevitable results of aging, such as senility, depression, and physical frailty, are often avoidable. They may result from disease, medication, or poor nutrition, and also from lack of stimulation, control of one's environment, and physical strength and fitness. Exercise and mental stimulation promote the growth of synapses in the human brain, even well into old age, although some mental losses are inevitable.

The Wellsprings of Resilience

● Children who experience violence or neglect are at risk of many problems later in life, but most children are resilient and are able to overcome early adversity. Psychologists now study not only the sad consequences of neglect, poverty, and violence but also the reasons for resilience under adversity.

Taking Psychology with You

● Many child-rearing experts claim to have the one right way to make children smarter, nicer, and more successful. Research in child development can help people think critically about such claims and also offers some general guidelines: Set high but realistic expectations, explain the reasons for your rules, encourage empathy, and reward good behavior.

Key Terms

Developmental psychologists study people's growth and change over the life span. They begin with **socialization,** the process by which children learn the attitudes and behaviors expected of them by their society.

From Conception through the First Year

Stages of Prenatal Development

• Germinal
• Embryonic
• Fetal

Prenatal Influences

• Some diseases, including German measles and sexually transmitted diseases
• Cigarettes, drugs, alcohol (which can cause *fetal alcohol syndrome*)
• Exposure to X-rays or toxic chemicals

The Infant's World

• Babies are born with motor reflexes, including rooting, sucking, and grasping.
• Newborns also have some innate perceptual abilities.
• Cultural influences affect maturational milestones, such as an infant's sleeping through the night.

Attachment

Attachment begins with **contact comfort,** the reassuring pleasure of being touched and held by the parent or other caregiver.

Between 6 and 8 months of age, babies develop **separation anxiety** if their primary caregiver temporarily leaves them.

Styles of attachment are unaffected by normal child-rearing practices and whether a child goes to daycare. Insecure attachment is promoted by extreme deprivation in infancy; abusive or erratic parenting; stressful family changes; and the child's own fearful temperament.

Babies may be securely or insecurely attached. Insecure babies may, in turn, be avoidant or anxious-ambivalent.

Cognitive Development

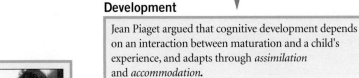

Language is a set of rules for combining elements that are inherently meaningless into utterances that convey meaning.

Language Development

• Acquiring language begins in the womb, as newborns recognize the language their mothers spoke during pregnancy.
• First few months: Babies coo and respond to rhythms and emotions in voices.
• 4 to 6 months: Babies begin to recognize key consonant and vowel sounds of their native language.
• 6 months to 1 year: Infants become able to distinguish words from the flow of speech.
• End of first year: Infants start to name things based on familiar concepts and use symbolic gestures to communicate.
• 18 to 24 months: Children begin to speak in two- and three-word phrases (**telegraphic speech**) and understand verbs from the context in which they occur.
• 2 to 6 years: Children rapidly acquire new words, inferring their meaning from the grammatical and social contexts in which they hear them.

Noam Chomsky argued that the human brain contains an innate mental module containing a *universal grammar,* which enables young children to acquire language readily. Children learn to take the surface structure of a sentence and apply grammatical rules (syntax) to infer an underlying deep structure, which contains the sentence's meaning.
Findings supporting Chomsky's view:
1. Children in different cultures go through similar stages of linguistic development.
2. Children combine words in ways that adults never would.
3. Adults do not consistently correct their children's syntax, yet children learn language correctly.
4. Children who are not exposed to adult language may invent a language of their own.
5. Infants as young as 7 months can derive simple linguistic rules from a string of sounds.
Findings contradicting Chomsky's view:
1. Computer programs, despite being incapable of inheriting an innate mental module, can acquire many linguistic features of language.
2. Adults do frequently correct the speech of children and model correct language usage.
3. Children not exposed to language at an early age rarely acquire completely normal speech.

Cognitive Development

Jean Piaget argued that cognitive development depends on an interaction between maturation and a child's experience, and adapts through *assimilation* and *accommodation.*

Piaget's four stages of cognitive development:
1. Sensorimotor (birth to age 2): child learns **object permanence**
2. Preoperational (ages 2 to 7): development of language and symbolic thought
3. Concrete operations (ages 7 to 12): understanding of **conservation**, identity, and serial ordering
4. Formal operations (age 12 to adulthood): development of abstract reasoning

Findings challenge many of Piaget's views:
1. Cognitive abilities develop in continuous, overlapping waves, rather than in discrete stages.
2. Preschoolers are not as **egocentric** as Piaget thought. As young as 3 to 4 years, children begin developing a **theory of mind**, a system of beliefs about how their own and other people's minds work.
3. Children, event infants, reveal cognitive abilities much earlier than Piaget believed possible.
4. Cognitive development is influenced by a child's culture.

Learning to be Good

Moral Development

Parental methods of discipline often have different consequences for children's moral behavior.
- **Power assertion** is associated with children who are aggressive and fail to internalize moral standards.
- **Induction** is associated with children who develop empathy and internalized moral standards and who can resist temptation.
- Young children's ability to regulate their impulses is associated with later internalized moral standards and conscience.

Gender Development

Gender identity: The cognitive understanding that a person is biologically male or female.
Gender typing: The process by which boys and girls learn what it means to be masculine or feminine.
Intersex conditions: Conditions in which children are born with ambiguous genitals, or genitals that conflict with their chromosomes; as adults, they may consider themselves **transgender**.

- **Biological psychologists** account for gender differences in behavior in terms of genes and prenatal hormones.
- **Cognitive psychologists** study how children develop **gender schemas** of "male" and "female" qualities, which shape their gender-typed behavior.
- **Learning theorists** study the direct and subtle reinforcers and social messages that foster gender typing.
- People's gender schemas, attitudes, and behavior evolve throughout their lives, with new experiences and societal changes.

Adolescence

Biological Changes

- Adolescence begins with the physical changes of **puberty**, including **menarche** in females and genital maturation in males.
- The brain goes through significant development as new connections among brain cells are added and others are pruned away.

Psychological Issues

- The stereotype of "adolescent turmoil"—rebellion and misery—is inaccurate for most teens. However, conflicts with parents, mood swings, and rule-breaking behavior do increase.
- The peer group becomes especially important.

Adulthood

Erik Erikson's Stages

- Trust versus mistrust
- Autonomy (independence) versus shame and doubt
- Initiative versus guilt
- Competence versus inferiority
- Identity versus role confusion
- Intimacy versus isolation
- Generativity versus stagnation
- Ego integrity versus despair

The Transitions of LIfe

- "Emerging adulthood" describes a life phase that occurs between 18 and 25, in which young adults accept some responsibilities of adulthood and delay others.
- The middle years are the prime of most people's lives. **Menopause** begins in women during their late 40s or early 50s, causing some physical symptoms but rarely the emotional distress portrayed in the media. In men, testosterone and sperm production decline.
- People's views of aging are influenced by the culture they live in and by the promises of technology—realistic and unrealistic—to prolong life and health.

Old Age

- Research in the field of **gerontology** shows that **fluid intelligence** parallels other biological capacities in its eventual decline, whereas **crystallized intelligence** tends to remain stable or even improve over the life span.
- Senility, depression, and physical frailty in old age are often the result of disease, medication, poor nutrition, and lack of stimulation and control of one's environment. Exercise and mental stimulation promote the growth of synapses in the human brain, even well into old age.

Traces of Consciousness Found in Some Patients Diagnosed as "Vegetative"

LIEGE, BELGIUM, February 4, 2010. A 29-year-old man thought to have been in a persistent vegetative state for five years following a car accident has shown signs of brain activity in response to questions from doctors. Most patients who are in a vegetative state can open and move their eyes and may make sounds and facial expressions, but they have no conscious awareness of themselves or their environment and cannot think or reason.

The man is one of 54 patients with severe brain damage, resulting in their being either in a vegetative or minimally conscious state, who are being studied by an international team of scientists in England and Belgium. Researchers prompted them to imagine themselves playing tennis or walking through the house they grew up in, as their brains were being scanned by functional magnetic resonance imaging (MRI). Five of the 54 were able to intentionally modulate their brain activity in response to these prompts, just as healthy people in a control group could. The researchers then instructed these five patients to respond to yes–no questions by using one type of mental imagery (either playing tennis or walking through the house) for "yes" and the other for "no." Only the man who had been injured in the car accident was able to do this successfully. He responded accurately to simple questions, such as whether his father's name was Paul (yes) or Alexander (no), and whether he had ever been to the United States. Yet, at a bedside evaluation by a skilled clinical team, he showed no consciousness or ability to communicate.

Experts continue to debate just what these findings mean for a patient's state of cognition and consciousness. In 2009, Rom Houben, another victim of a car crash who apparently was unconscious for 23 years, made headlines when neurological tests indicated that he too had some possible awareness, and a brain scan revealed nearly normal activity in his brain. Therapists provided Houben with a computer touch screen that seemed to allow him to communicate by spelling out words. But skeptics pointed out that all of Houben's messages were typed with the help of an aide who supported and guided his hand. Scientific research has discredited such "facilitated communication" and has found that the typed messages come from the facilitator, not the patient. After watching a video of Houben supposedly communicating as a facilitator guided his hand, bioethics expert Arthur Caplan commented, "That is Ouija board stuff."

Nonetheless, these studies suggest that, in rare cases, patients with brain injury may have a greater degree of consciousness than previously believed possible. "With further development," the researchers conclude, "this technique could be used by some patients to express their thoughts, control their environment, and increase their quality of life."

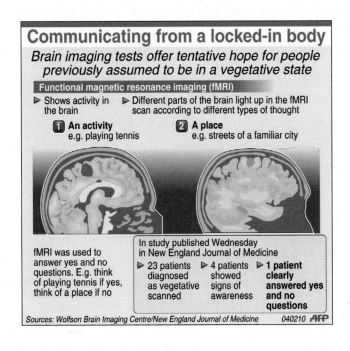

Communicating from a locked-in body

Brain imaging tests offer tentative hope for people previously assumed to be in a vegetative state

Functional magnetic resonance imaging (fMRI)

▶ Shows activity in the brain ▶ Different parts of the brain light up in the fMRI scan according to different types of thought

1 An activity e.g. playing tennis

2 A place e.g. streets of a familiar city

fMRI was used to answer yes and no questions. E.g. think of playing tennis if yes, think of a place if no

In study published Wednesday in New England Journal of Medicine
▶ 23 patients diagnosed as vegetative scanned ▶ 4 patients showed signs of awareness ▶ 1 patient clearly answered yes and no questions

Sources: Wolfson Brain Imaging Centre/New England Journal of Medicine   040210 AFP

Neurons, Hormones, and the Brain

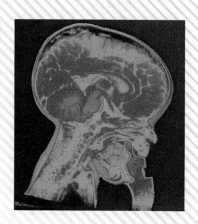

There is almost nothing that human beings fear more than having a conscious brain in a paralyzed head and body—with a brain that is alive and functioning yet with no way to communicate to the outside world. So it is no wonder that stories of people who seem to recover from comas or vegetative states after many years, or who show signs of brain activity when they were previously thought to be brain dead, are both exciting and terrifying.

Incidents of apparent consciousness in vegetative patients raise all sorts of difficult medical, psychological, and ethical issues. How can we know for sure whether a person has become incapable of higher mental function? Does brain-scan technology offer an answer, or merely a possible clue? Will rare cases of awareness give families false hope that their loved one is "really in there" when the person actually lacks all cognitive function? Should a patient's apparent responses to yes–no questions be used to draw conclusions about whether the person is in pain—or wants to live or die?

Cases of brain injury and disease vividly remind us that the 3-pound organ inside our skulls provides the bedrock for everything we do, feel, and think. *Neuropsychologists*, along with neuroscientists from other disciplines, study the brain and the rest of the nervous system in hopes of gaining a better understanding of normal behavior and of the outer reaches of what is possible for this organ. They are concerned with the biological foundations of consciousness, perception, memory, emotion, stress, and mental disorders—of everything, in fact, that human beings feel and do. In this chapter, we will examine the structure of the brain and the rest of the nervous system as background for our later discussions of these and other topics.

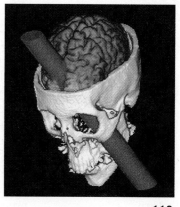

At this very moment, your own brain, assisted by other parts of your nervous system, is busily taking in these words. Whether you are excited, curious, or bored, your brain is registering some sort of emotional reaction. As you continue reading, your brain will (we hope) store away much of the information in this chapter. Later on, your brain may enable you to smell a flower, climb the stairs,

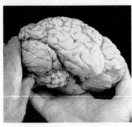

The study of this mysterious 3-pound organ raises many challenging questions. Why can a small glitch in the brain's circuits be devastating to some people, whereas others can function with major damage? How do experiences alter our brains? And where in this collection of cells and circuits are the mind and our sense of self to be found?

greet a friend, solve a problem, or chuckle at a joke. But the brain's most startling accomplishment is its knowledge that it is doing all these things. This self-awareness makes brain research different from the study of anything else in the universe. Scientists must use the cells, biochemistry, and circuitry of their own brains to understand the cells, biochemistry, and circuitry of brains in general.

William Shakespeare called the brain "the soul's frail dwelling house." Actually, this miraculous organ is more like the main room in a house filled with many alcoves and passageways—the "house" being the nervous system as a whole. Before we can understand the windows, walls, and furniture of this house, we need to become acquainted with the overall floor plan.

 YOU are about to learn...

- why you automatically pull your hand away from something hot, without thinking.

- the major parts of the nervous system and their primary functions.

The Nervous System: A Basic Blueprint

The function of a nervous system is to gather and process information, produce responses to stimuli, and coordinate the workings of different cells. Even the lowly jellyfish and the humble earthworm have the beginnings of such a system. In very simple organisms that do little more than move, eat, and eliminate wastes, the "system" may be no more than one or two nerve cells. In human beings, who do such complex things as dance, cook, and take psychology courses, the nervous system contains billions of cells. Scientists divide this intricate network into two main parts: the central nervous system and the peripheral (outlying) nervous system (see Figure 4.1).

The Central Nervous System

central nervous system (CNS) The portion of the nervous system consisting of the brain and spinal cord.

spinal cord A collection of neurons and supportive tissue running from the base of the brain down the center of the back, protected by a column of bones (the spinal column).

The **central nervous system (CNS)** receives, processes, interprets, and stores incoming sensory information—information about tastes, sounds, smells, color, pressure on the skin, the state of internal organs, and so forth. It also sends out messages destined for muscles, glands, and internal organs. The CNS is usually conceptualized as having two components: the brain, which we will consider in detail later, and the **spinal cord**, which is actually an extension of the brain. The spinal cord runs from the base of the brain down the center of the back, protected by a column of bones (the spinal column),

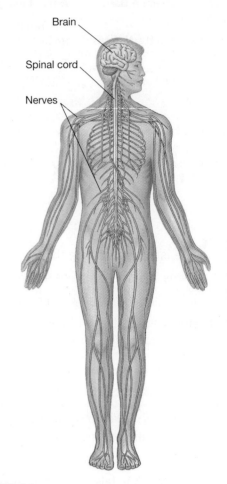

FIGURE 4.1
The Central and Peripheral Nervous Systems
The central nervous system includes the brain and the spinal cord. The peripheral nervous system consists of 43 pairs of nerves that transmit information to and from the central nervous system. Twelve pairs of cranial nerves in the head enter the brain directly; 31 pairs of spinal nerves enter the spinal cord at the spaces between the vertebrae.

and it acts as a bridge between the brain and the parts of the body below the neck.

The spinal cord produces some behaviors on its own without any help from the brain. These *spinal reflexes* are automatic, requiring no conscious effort. If you accidentally touch a hot iron, you will immediately pull your hand away, even before your brain has had a chance to register what has happened. Nerve impulses bring a message to the spinal cord (hot!), and the spinal cord immediately sends out a command via other nerve impulses, telling muscles in your arm to contract and to pull your hand away from the iron. (Reflexes above the neck, such as sneezing and blinking, involve the lower part of the brain rather than the spinal cord.)

The neural circuits underlying many spinal reflexes are linked to neural pathways that run up and down the spinal cord, to and from the brain.

Because of these connections, reflexes can sometimes be influenced by thoughts and emotions. An example is erection in men, a spinal reflex that can be inhibited by anxiety or distracting thoughts and initiated by erotic thoughts. Moreover, some reflexes can be brought under conscious control. If you concentrate, you may be able to keep your knee from jerking when it is tapped, as it normally would. Similarly, most men can learn to voluntarily delay ejaculation, another spinal reflex. (Yes, they can.)

The Peripheral Nervous System

The **peripheral nervous system (PNS)** handles the central nervous system's input and output. It contains all portions of the nervous system outside the brain and spinal cord, right down to the nerves in the tips of the fingers and toes. If your brain could not collect information about the world by means of a peripheral nervous system, it would be like a radio without a receiver. In the peripheral nervous system, *sensory nerves* carry messages from special receptors in the skin, muscles, and other internal and external sense organs to the spinal cord, which sends them along to the brain. These nerves put us in touch with both the outside world and the activities of our own bodies. *Motor nerves* carry orders from the central nervous system to muscles, glands, and internal organs. They enable us to move, and they cause glands to contract and to secrete substances, including chemical messengers called *hormones*.

Scientists further divide the peripheral nervous system into two parts: the somatic (bodily) nervous system and the autonomic (self-governing) nervous system. The **somatic nervous system**, sometimes called the *skeletal nervous system*, consists of nerves that are connected to sensory receptors—cells that enable you to sense the world—and also to the skeletal muscles that permit voluntary action. When you feel a bug on your arm, or when you turn off a light or write your name, your somatic system is active. The **autonomic nervous system** regulates the functioning of blood vessels, glands, and internal (visceral) organs such as the bladder, stomach, and heart. When you see someone you have a crush on and your heart pounds, your hands get sweaty, and your cheeks feel hot, you can blame your autonomic nervous system.

The autonomic nervous system is itself divided into two parts: the **sympathetic nervous system** and the **parasympathetic nervous system**. These two parts work together, but in opposing ways, to adjust the body to changing circumstances (see Figure 4.2).

peripheral nervous system (PNS) All portions of the nervous system outside the brain and spinal cord; it includes sensory and motor nerves.

somatic nervous system The subdivision of the peripheral nervous system that connects to sensory receptors and to skeletal muscles; sometimes called the *skeletal nervous system*.

autonomic nervous system The subdivision of the peripheral nervous system that regulates the internal organs and glands.

sympathetic nervous system The subdivision of the autonomic nervous system that mobilizes bodily resources and increases the output of energy during emotion and stress.

parasympathetic nervous system The subdivision of the autonomic nervous system that operates during relaxed states and that conserves energy.

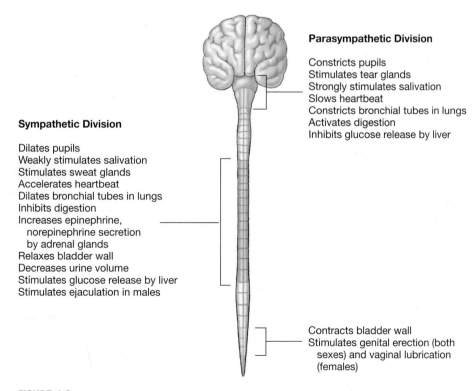

Sympathetic Division

Dilates pupils
Weakly stimulates salivation
Stimulates sweat glands
Accelerates heartbeat
Dilates bronchial tubes in lungs
Inhibits digestion
Increases epinephrine,
  norepinephrine secretion
  by adrenal glands
Relaxes bladder wall
Decreases urine volume
Stimulates glucose release by liver
Stimulates ejaculation in males

Parasympathetic Division

Constricts pupils
Stimulates tear glands
Strongly stimulates salivation
Slows heartbeat
Constricts bronchial tubes in lungs
Activates digestion
Inhibits glucose release by liver

Contracts bladder wall
Stimulates genital erection (both
  sexes) and vaginal lubrication
  (females)

FIGURE 4.2
The Autonomic Nervous System
In general, the sympathetic division of the autonomic nervous system prepares the body to expend energy and the parasympathetic division restores and conserves energy. Sympathetic nerve fibers exit from areas of the spinal cord (shown in red); parasympathetic fibers exit from the base of the brain and from spinal cord areas (shown in green).

Explore Autonomic Nervous System on mypsychlab.com

Study and **Review** on mypsychlab.com

The sympathetic system acts like the accelerator of a car, mobilizing the body for action and an output of energy. It makes you blush, sweat, and breathe more deeply, and it pushes up your heart rate and blood pressure. As we discuss in Chapter 13, when you are in a situation that requires you to fight, flee, or cope, the sympathetic nervous system whirls into action. The parasympathetic system is more like a brake: It does not stop the body, of course, but it does tend to slow things down and keep them running smoothly. It enables the body to conserve and store energy. In everyday life, the two systems work in harmony. If you have to jump out of the way of a speeding motorcyclist, sympathetic nerves increase your heart rate. Afterward, parasympathetic nerves slow it down again and keep its rhythm regular. ✸

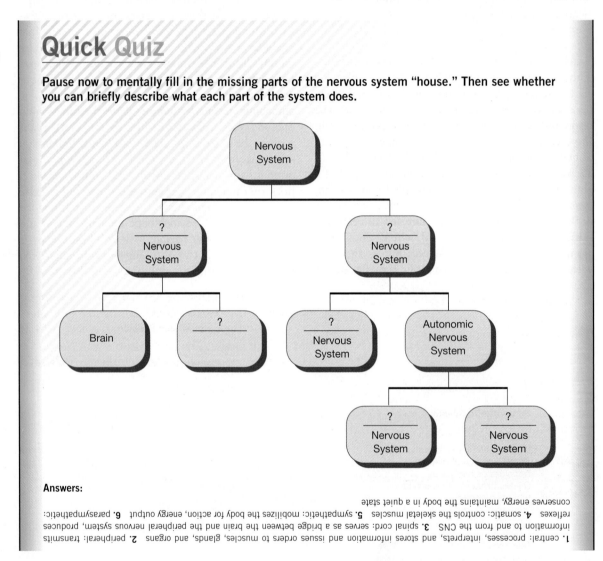

Quick Quiz

Pause now to mentally fill in the missing parts of the nervous system "house." Then see whether you can briefly describe what each part of the system does.

Answers:

1. central: processes, interprets, and stores information and issues orders to muscles, glands, and organs　2. peripheral: transmits information to and from the CNS　3. spinal cord: serves as a bridge between the brain and the peripheral nervous system, produces reflexes　4. somatic: controls the skeletal muscles　5. sympathetic: mobilizes the body for action, energy output　6. parasympathetic: conserves energy, maintains the body in a quiet state

 YOU are about to learn…

- which cells function as the nervous system's communication specialists, and how they "talk" to each other.
- the functions of glial cells, the most numerous cells in the brain.
- why researchers are excited about the discovery of stem cells in the brain.
- how learning and experience alter the brain's circuits.
- what happens when levels of neurotransmitters are too low or too high.
- which brain chemicals mimic the effects of morphine by dulling pain and promoting pleasure.
- which hormones are of special interest to psychologists, and why.

Communication in the Nervous System

The blueprint we just described provides only a general idea of the nervous system's structure. Now let's turn to the details.

The nervous system is made up in part of **neurons**, or *nerve cells.* They are the brain's communication specialists, transmitting information to, from, and within the central nervous system. Neurons are held in place by **glia**, or *glial cells* (from the Greek word for "glue"), which make up 90 percent of the brain's cells.

Glial cells are more than just glue, however. They provide the neurons with nutrients, insulate them, protect the brain from toxic agents, and remove cellular debris when neurons die. They also communicate chemically with each other and with neurons, and without them, neurons could not function effectively. One kind of glial cell appears to give neurons the go-ahead to form connections and to start "talking" to each other (Ullian, Christopherson, & Barres, 2004). And over time, glia help determine which neural connections get stronger or weaker, suggesting that they play a vital role in learning and memory (Fields, 2004).

It's neurons, however, that are considered the building blocks of the nervous system, though in structure they are more like snowflakes than blocks, exquisitely delicate and differing from one another greatly in size and shape (see Figure 4.3). In the giraffe, a neuron that runs from the spinal cord down the animal's hind leg may be 9 feet long! In the human brain, neurons are microscopic. No one is sure how many neurons the human brain contains, but a typical estimate is 100 billion, about the same number as there are stars in our galaxy, and some estimates go much higher.

The Structure of the Neuron

As you can see in Figure 4.4, a neuron has three main parts: *dendrites*, a *cell body*, and an *axon*. The **dendrites** look like the branches of a tree; indeed, the word *dendrite* means "little tree" in Greek. Dendrites act like antennas, receiving messages from as many as 10,000 other nerve cells and transmitting these messages toward the cell body. They also do some preliminary processing of those messages. The **cell body**, which is shaped roughly like a sphere or a pyramid, contains the biochemical machinery for keeping the neuron

FIGURE 4.3
Different Kinds of Neurons
Neurons vary in size and shape, depending on their location and function. More than 200 types of neurons have been identified in mammals. This photo shows neurons in the outer layers of the brain.

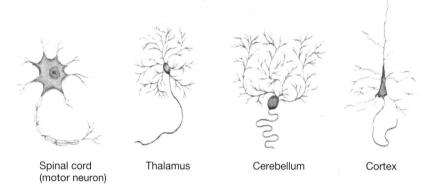

Spinal cord (motor neuron)   Thalamus   Cerebellum   Cortex

alive. It also plays the key role in determining whether the neuron should fire—transmit a message to other neurons—depending on inputs from other neurons. The **axon** (from the Greek for "axle") transmits messages away from the cell body

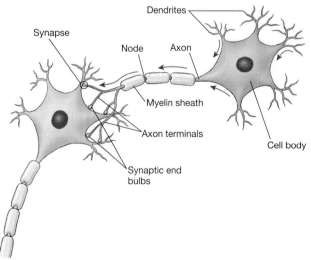

Dendrites
Synapse
Node   Axon
Myelin sheath
Axon terminals
Cell body
Synaptic end bulbs

FIGURE 4.4
The Structure of a Neuron
Incoming neural impulses are received by the dendrites of a neuron and are transmitted to the cell body. Outgoing signals pass along the axon to terminal branches.

neuron A cell that conducts electrochemical signals; the basic unit of the nervous system; also called a *nerve cell.*

glia [GLY-uh or GLEE-uh] Cells that support, nurture, and insulate neurons, remove debris when neurons die, enhance the formation and maintenance of neural connections, and modify neuronal functioning.

dendrites A neuron's branches that receive information from other neurons and transmit it toward the cell body.

cell body The part of the neuron that keeps it alive and determines whether it will fire.

axon A neuron's extending fiber that conducts impulses away from the cell body and transmits them to other neurons or to muscle or gland cells.

myelin sheath A fatty insulation that may surround the axon of a neuron.

nerves A bundle of nerve fibers (axons and sometimes dendrites) in the peripheral nervous system.

neurogenesis The production of new neurons from immature stem cells.

stem cells Immature cells that renew themselves and have the potential to develop into mature cells; given encouraging environments, stem cells from early embryos can develop into any cell type.

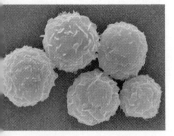

Tiny stem cells like these (magnified 1,200 times in this photo) have provoked both excitement and controversy.

to other neurons or to muscle or gland cells. Axons commonly divide at the end into branches called *axon terminals*. In adult human beings, axons vary from only four-thousandths of an inch to a few feet in length. Dendrites and axons give each neuron a double role: As one researcher put it, a neuron is first a catcher, then a batter (Gazzaniga, 1988).

Many axons, especially the larger ones, are insulated by a surrounding layer of fatty material called the **myelin sheath**, which in the central nervous system is made up of glial cells. Constrictions in this covering, called *nodes*, divide it into segments, which make it look a little like a string of link sausages (see Figure 4.4 again). One purpose of the myelin sheath is to prevent signals in adjacent cells from interfering with each other. Another, as we will see shortly, is to speed up the conduction of neural impulses. In individuals with multiple sclerosis, loss of myelin causes erratic nerve signals, leading to loss of sensation, weakness or paralysis, lack of coordination, or vision problems.

In the peripheral nervous system, the fibers of individual neurons (axons and sometimes dendrites) are collected together in bundles called **nerves**, rather like the lines in a telephone cable. The human body has 43 pairs of peripheral nerves; one nerve from each pair is on the left side of the body and the other is on the right. Most of these nerves enter or leave the spinal cord, but 12 pairs in the head, the *cranial nerves*, connect directly to the brain. In Chapter 6, we will discuss cranial nerves that are involved in the senses of smell, hearing, and vision.

Neurons in the News

For most of the twentieth century, scientists assumed that if neurons in the central nervous system were injured or damaged, they could never grow back (regenerate). But then the conventional wisdom got turned upside down. Animal studies showed that severed axons in the spinal cord *can* regrow if you treat them with particular nervous system chemicals (Schnell & Schwab, 1990). Researchers are hopeful that regenerated axons will eventually enable people with spinal cord injuries to use their limbs again.

In the past two decades, scientists have also had to rethink another entrenched assumption: that mammals produce no new CNS cells after infancy. In the early 1990s, Canadian neuroscientists, working with mice, immersed immature cells from the animals' brains in a growth-promoting protein and showed that these cells could give birth to new neu-

rons in a process called **neurogenesis**. Even more astonishing, the new neurons continued to divide and multiply (Reynolds & Weiss, 1992). Since then, scientists have discovered that the human brain and other body organs also contain such cells, which are now known as **stem cells**. Stem cells involved in learning and memory seem to divide and mature throughout adulthood. Animal studies find that physical exercise, effortful mental activity, and an enriched environment promote the production and survival of new cells, whereas aging and stress can inhibit their production and nicotine can kill them (Berger, Gage, & Vijayaraghavan, 1998; Kempermann, 2006; Shors, 2009).

Stem-cell research is one of the hottest areas in biology and neuroscience. But in the United States, federal funding for basic stem-cell research has faced strong resistance by antiabortion activists who are opposed to taking cells from embryos that are a few days old, which consist of just a few cells. (Fertility clinics store many such embryos because several test-tube fertilizations are created for every patient who hopes to become pregnant; eventually, the extra embryos are destroyed.) Embryonic stem (ES) cells are especially useful because they can differentiate into any type of cell, from neurons to kidney cells, whereas those from adults are more limited and are harder to keep alive. Scientists have also been able to reprogram cells from adult organs, most notably skin cells, to become stem cells (e.g., Takahashi et al., 2007; Yu et al., 2007). Like ES cells, these "induced pluripotent stem (iPS) cells" seem capable of giving rise to all types of cells, although it is still unclear whether they will prove to be equally versatile; in one comparison test, the embryonic stem cells made more than 1,000 times more of the desired cells than did the iPS cell lines (Feng et al., 2010). Some scientists have directly turned skin cells taken from the tails of mice into neurons without first turning the cells into iPS cells (Vierbuchen et al., 2010). The next step will be to see if the same can be done with human cells.

Advocacy groups hope that transplanted stem cells will eventually help people recover from diseases of the brain (such as Parkinson's) and from damage to the spinal cord and other parts of the body. Scientists have already had some success in animals. In one study, mice with recent spinal cord injuries regained much of their ability to walk normally after being injected with stem cells derived from human fetal brain tissue. Microscopic analysis showed that most of the cells had turned into either neurons or a particular type of glial cell (Cummings et al., 2005). In 2009, the FDA approved the first

In an area associated with learning and memory, immature stem cells give rise to new neurons, and physical and mental stimulation promotes the production and survival of these neurons. These mice have toys to play with, tunnels to explore, wheels to run on, and other mice to share their cage with. They will grow more cells than mice living alone in standard cages.

small U.S. trial with human patients with spinal cord injuries (Couzin, 2009).

A long road lies ahead, and many daunting technical hurdles remain to be overcome before stem-cell research yields practical benefits for human patients. Increasing the rate of neurogenesis may alleviate or improve some medical conditions but have negative or no effects on others (Scharfman & Hen, 2007). We live in exciting times. Each year brings more incredible findings about neurons, findings that only a short time ago would have seemed like science fiction.

How Neurons Communicate

Neurons do not directly touch each other, end to end. Instead, they are separated by a minuscule space called the *synaptic cleft*, where the axon terminal of one neuron nearly touches a dendrite or the cell body of another. The entire site—the axon terminal, the cleft, and the covering membrane of the receiving dendrite or cell body—is called a **synapse**. Because a neuron's axon may have hundreds or even thousands of terminals, a single neuron may have synaptic connections with a great many others. As a result, the number of communication links in the nervous system runs into the trillions or perhaps even the quadrillions.

Neurons speak to one another, or in some cases to muscles or glands, in an electrical and chemical language. When a nerve cell is stimulated, a change in electrical potential occurs between the inside and

the outside of the cell. The physics of this process involves the sudden, momentary inflow of positively charged sodium ions across the cell's membrane, followed by the outflow of positively charged potassium ions. The result is a brief change in electrical voltage, called an **action potential**, which produces an electric current, or impulse.

If an axon is unmyelinated, the action potential at each point in the axon gives rise to a new action potential at the next point; thus, the impulse travels down the axon somewhat as fire travels along the fuse of a firecracker. But in myelinated axons, the process is a little different. Conduction of a neural impulse beneath the sheath is impossible, in part because sodium and potassium ions cannot cross the cell's membrane except at the breaks (nodes) between the myelin's "sausages." Instead, the action potential "hops" from one node to the next. (More precisely, the action potential regenerates at each node.) This arrangement allows the impulse to travel faster than it could if the action potential had to be regenerated at every point along the axon. Nerve impulses travel more slowly in babies than in older children and adults, because when babies are born, the myelin sheaths on their axons are not yet fully developed.

When a neural impulse reaches the axon terminal's buttonlike tip, it must get its message across the synaptic cleft to another cell. At this point, *synaptic vesicles*, tiny sacs in the tip of the axon terminal, open and release a few thousand molecules of a chemical substance called a **neurotransmitter**. Like sailors carrying a message from one island to another, these molecules then diffuse across the synaptic cleft (see Figure 4.5 on the next page).

When they reach the other side, the neurotransmitter molecules bind briefly with *receptor sites*, special molecules in the membrane of the receiving neuron's dendrites (or sometimes cell body), fitting these sites much as a key fits a lock. Changes occur in the receiving neuron's membrane, and the ultimate effect is either *excitatory* (a voltage shift in a positive direction) or *inhibitory* (a voltage shift in a negative direction), depending on which receptor sites have been activated. If the effect is excitatory, the probability that the receiving neuron will fire increases; if it is inhibitory, the probability decreases. Inhibition in the nervous system is extremely important. Without it, we could not sleep or coordinate our movements. Excitation of the nervous system would be overwhelming, producing convulsions.

What any given neuron does at any given moment depends on the net effect of all the messages being received from other neurons. Only when the

synapse The site where transmission of a nerve impulse from one nerve cell to another occurs; it includes the axon terminal, the synaptic cleft, and receptor sites in the membrane of the receiving cell.

action potential A brief change in electrical voltage that occurs between the inside and the outside of an axon when a neuron is stimulated; it serves to produce an electrical impulse.

neurotransmitter A chemical substance that is released by a transmitting neuron at the synapse and that alters the activity of a receiving neuron.

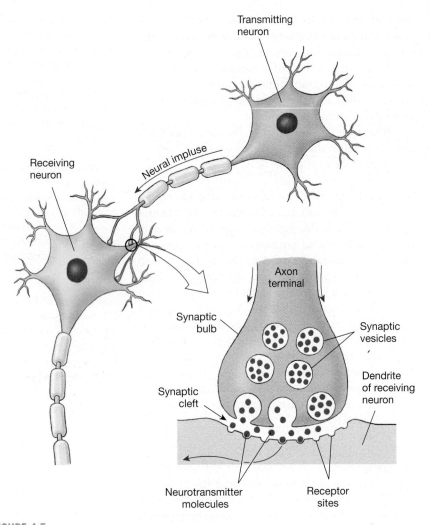

FIGURE 4.5

Neurotransmitter Crossing a Synapse

Neurotransmitter molecules are released into the synaptic cleft between two neurons from vesicles (chambers) in the transmitting neuron's axon terminal. The molecules then bind to receptor sites on the receiving neuron. As a result, the electrical state of the receiving neuron changes and the neuron becomes either more likely to fire an impulse or less so, depending on the type of neurotransmitter.

cell's voltage reaches a certain threshold will it fire. Thousands of messages, both excitatory and inhibitory, may be coming into the cell, and the receiving neuron must essentially average them. The message that reaches a final destination depends on the rate at which individual neurons are firing, how many are firing, what types of neurons are firing, where the neurons are located, and the degree of synchrony among different neurons. It does *not* depend on how strongly the individual neurons are firing, however, because a neuron always either fires or doesn't. Like the turning on of a light switch, the firing of a neuron is an all-or-none event.

plasticity The brain's ability to change and adapt in response to experience, by reorganizing or growing new neural connections.

The Plastic Brain

When we are born, most of our synapses have not yet formed, but new synapses proliferate at a great rate during infancy (see Figure 4.6). Axons and dendrites continue to grow, and tiny projections on dendrites, called *spines*, increase in size and number, producing more complex connections among the brain's nerve cells. Just as new learning and stimulating environments promote the production of new neurons, they also produce increases in synaptic complexity (Diamond, 1993; Greenough & Anderson, 1991; Greenough & Black, 1992; Rosenzweig, 1984). During childhood, unused synaptic connections are also pruned away as cells or their branches die and are not replaced, leaving behind a more efficient neural network. These changes may help explain why critical or sensitive periods for the development of some sensory and cognitive abilities occur early in life. During these periods, acquisition of these skills is amazingly rapid, but when the period ends, learning slows and may even become irreversible (Thomas & Johnson, 2008). (We discuss critical periods in language development in Chapter 3 and in visual development in Chapter 6.) Pruning and increases in synaptic density, however, are not confined to childhood. They have another important developmental phase in adolescence and may continue all through life. For the most part, the brain retains flexibility in adapting to new experiences, an adaptability neuroscientists call **plasticity**.

Plasticity is vividly demonstrated in cases of people with brain damage who have experienced

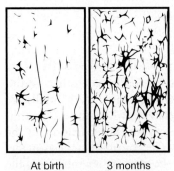

At birth   3 months

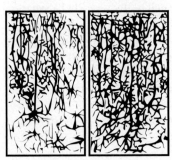

6 months   15 months

FIGURE 4.6

Getting Connected

Neurons in a newborn's brain are widely spaced, but they immediately begin to form new connections. These drawings show the marked increase in the number of connections from birth to age 15 months.

remarkable recoveries—such as individuals who cannot recall simple words after a stroke but are speaking normally within months, or who cannot move an arm after a head injury but regain full use of the limb after physical therapy. Their brains have apparently rewired themselves to adapt to the damage (Liepert et al., 2000).

When people who have been blind from birth or early childhood try to determine where a sound is coming from, what happens in the part of the brain that, in sighted people, processes visual information? In some blind people, might regions normally devoted to vision begin to process input from other senses instead? Using brain-scan technology, a team of researchers examined the brains of people as they localized sounds heard through speakers (Gougoux et al., 2005). Some participants were sighted and others had been blind from early in life. When the participants heard sounds through both ears, activity in the occipital cortex, an area associated with vision, decreased in the sighted people but *not* in the blind ones. When one ear was plugged, blind participants who did especially well at localizing sounds showed activation in two areas of the occipital cortex; neither sighted people nor blind people with ordinary ability showed such activation. The degree of activation in these regions was correlated with the blind people's accuracy on the task, suggesting that their brains had adapted to blindness by recruiting visual areas to take part in activities involving hearing—a dramatic example of plasticity.

Building on this research, the researchers wondered what would happen if sighted people were blindfolded for five days and had to adapt to their temporary inability to see. Before donning the blindfolds, the volunteers' brain scans showed that the visual areas in their brains were quiet during tasks requiring hearing or touch. By the fifth day, however, these areas were lighting up during the tasks. Then, after the blindfolds were removed, the visual centers once again quieted down (Pascual-Leone et al., 2005). The visual areas of the brain apparently possess the computational machinery necessary for processing nonvisual information, but this machinery remains dormant until circumstances require its activation (Amedi et al., 2005). When people have been blind for most of their lives, new connections may form, permitting lasting structural changes in the brain's wiring.

This research teaches us that the brain is a dynamic organ: Its circuits are continually being modified in response to information, challenges, and changes in the environment. As scientists come to understand this process better, they may be able to apply their knowledge by designing improved rehabilitation programs for people with sensory impairments, developmental disabilities, and brain injuries.

Chemical Messengers in the Nervous System

The nervous system "house" would remain forever dark and lifeless without chemical couriers such as the neurotransmitters. Let's look more closely now at these substances and at two other types of chemical messengers: endorphins and hormones.

Neurotransmitters: Versatile Couriers As we have seen, neurotransmitters make it possible for one neuron to excite or inhibit another. Neurotransmitters exist not only in the brain but also in the spinal cord, the peripheral nerves, and certain glands. Through their effects on specific nerve circuits, these substances can affect mood, memory, and well-being. The nature of the effect depends on the level of the neurotransmitter, its location, and the type of receptor it binds with. Here are a few of the better-understood neurotransmitters and some of their known or suspected effects:

- *Serotonin* affects neurons involved in sleep, appetite, sensory perception, temperature regulation, pain suppression, and mood.

- *Dopamine* affects neurons involved in voluntary movement, learning, memory, emotion, pleasure or reward, and, possibly, response to novelty.

- *Acetylcholine* affects neurons involved in muscle action, cognitive functioning, memory, and emotion.

- *Norepinephrine* affects neurons involved in increased heart rate and the slowing of intestinal activity during stress, and neurons involved in learning, memory, dreaming, waking from sleep, and emotion.

- *GABA (gamma-aminobutyric acid)* is the major inhibitory neurotransmitter in the brain.

- *Glutamate* is the major excitatory neurotransmitter in the brain; it is released by about 90 percent of the brain's neurons.

Harmful effects can occur when neurotransmitter levels are too high or too low. Abnormal GABA levels have been implicated in sleep and eating disorders and in convulsive disorders, including epilepsy. People with Alzheimer's disease lose brain cells responsible for producing acetylcholine and other neurotransmitters, and these deficits help account for their devastating memory problems. A loss of cells that produce dopamine is responsible for the tremors and rigidity of Parkinson's disease. In multiple sclerosis, immune cells overproduce

✳ Explore Neuronal Transmission on mypsychlab.com

✳ Explore

Former heavyweight champion Muhammad Ali and actor Michael J. Fox both have Parkinson's disease, which involves a loss of dopamine-producing cells. They have used their fame to draw public attention to the disorder.

glutamate, which damages or kills glial cells that normally make myelin.

We want to warn you, however, that pinning down the relationship between neurotransmitter abnormalities and behavioral or physical abnormalities is extremely tricky. Each neurotransmitter plays multiple roles, and the functions of different substances often overlap. Further, it is always possible that something about a disorder leads to abnormal neurotransmitter levels instead of the other way around. For example, although drugs that boost or decrease levels of particular neurotransmitters are sometimes effective in treating some mental disorders, such as depression, this fact does not necessarily mean that abnormal neurotransmitter levels *cause* the disorders. After all, aspirin can relieve a headache, but headaches are not caused by a lack of aspirin!

Many of us regularly ingest things that affect our own neurotransmitters. Even ordinary foods can influence the availability of neurotransmitters in the brain. Most recreational drugs produce their effects by blocking or enhancing the actions of neurotransmitters. So do some herbal remedies. St. John's wort, which is often taken for depression, prevents the cells that release serotonin from reabsorbing excess molecules that have remained in the synaptic cleft; as a result, serotonin levels rise. Many people do not realize that such remedies, because they affect the nervous system's biochemistry, can interact with other medications and can be harmful in high doses.

Endorphins: The Brain's Natural Opiates

Another intriguing group of chemical messengers is known collectively as *endogenous opioid peptides*, or more popularly as **endorphins**. Endorphins have effects similar to those of natural opiates; that is, they reduce pain and promote pleasure. They are also thought to play a role in appetite, sexual activity, blood pressure, mood, learning, and memory. Some endorphins function as neurotransmitters,

but most of them act primarily by limiting, prolonging, or altering the effects of neurotransmitters.

Endorphin levels seem to shoot up when an animal or a person is afraid or under stress. This is no accident; by making pain bearable in such situations, endorphins give a species an evolutionary advantage. When an organism is threatened, it needs to do something fast. Pain, however, can interfere with action: A mouse that pauses to lick a wounded paw may become a cat's dinner; a soldier who is overcome by an injury may never get off the battlefield. But, of course, the body's built-in system of counteracting pain is only partly successful, especially when painful stimulation is prolonged.

In Chapter 14, we will see that a link also exists between endorphins and human attachment. Research with animals suggests that, in infancy, contact with the mother stimulates the flow of endorphins, which strengthens the infant's bond with her. Some researchers now think that this endorphin rush also occurs in the early stages of passionate love between adults, accounting for the feeling of euphoria that "falling" for someone creates (Diamond, 2004).

Hormones: Long-Distance Messengers

Hormones, which make up the third class of chemical messengers, are produced primarily in **endocrine glands**. They are released directly into the bloodstream, which carries them to organs and cells that may be far from their point of origin. Hormones have dozens of jobs, from promoting bodily growth to aiding digestion to regulating metabolism. Neurotransmitters and hormones are not always chemically distinct; the two classifications are like social clubs that admit some of the same members. A particular chemical, such as norepinephrine, may belong to more than one classification, depending on where it is located and what function it is performing. Nature has been efficient, giving some substances more than one task.

endorphins [en-DOR-fins] Chemical substances in the nervous system that are similar in structure and action to opiates; they are involved in pain reduction, pleasure, and memory and are known technically as *endogenous opioid peptides*.

hormones Chemical substances, secreted by organs called *glands*, that affect the functioning of other organs.

endocrine glands Internal organs that produce hormones and release them into the bloodstream.

"PSST—ENDORPHINS. AND THEY'RE PERFECTLY LEGAL."

The following hormones, among others, are of particular interest to psychologists:

1 **Melatonin**, which is secreted by the *pineal gland* deep within the brain, helps to regulate daily biological rhythms and promotes sleep, as we discuss in Chapter 5.

2 **Oxytocin**, which is secreted by another small gland in the brain, the *pituitary gland*, enhances uterine contractions during childbirth and facilitates the ejection of milk during nursing. Psychologists are interested in this hormone because, along with another hormone called *vasopressin*, it also contributes to relationships in both sexes by promoting attachment and trust (see Chapter 14).

3 **Adrenal hormones**, which are produced by the *adrenal glands* (organs that are perched right above the kidneys), are involved in emotion and stress (see Chapter 13). These hormones also rise in response to other conditions, such as heat, cold, pain, injury, burns, and physical exercise, and in response to some drugs, such as caffeine and nicotine. The outer part of each adrenal gland produces *cortisol*, which increases blood-sugar levels and boosts energy. The inner part produces *epinephrine* (commonly known as adrenaline) and *norepinephrine*. When adrenal hormones are released in your body, activated by the sympathetic nervous system, they increase your arousal level and prepare you for action. Adrenal hormones also enhance memory, as we discuss in Chapter 8.

4 **Sex hormones**, which are secreted by tissue in the gonads (testes in men, ovaries in women) and also by the adrenal glands, include three main types, all occurring in both sexes but in differing amounts and proportions in males and females after puberty. *Androgens* (the most important of which is *testosterone*) are masculinizing hormones produced mainly in the testes but also in the ovaries and the adrenal glands. Androgens set in motion the physical changes males experience at puberty—notably a deepened voice and facial and chest hair—and cause pubic and underarm hair to develop in both sexes. Testosterone also influences sexual arousal in both sexes. *Estrogens* are feminizing hormones that bring on physical changes in females at puberty, such as breast development and the onset of menstruation, and that influence the course of the menstrual cycle. *Progesterone* contributes to the growth and maintenance of the uterine lining in preparation for a fertilized egg, among other functions. Estrogens and progesterone are produced mainly in the ovaries but also in the testes and the adrenal glands.

Researchers are studying the possible involvement of sex hormones in behavior not linked to sex or reproduction. The body's natural estrogen may contribute to learning and memory in both sexes by promoting the formation of synaptic connections in areas of the brain (Lee & McEwen, 2001; Maki & Resnick, 2000; Sherwin, 1998a). But the common belief that fluctuating levels of estrogen and progesterone make most women "emotional" before menstruation has not been supported by research, as we discuss in Chapter 5.

melatonin A hormone, secreted by the pineal gland, that is involved in the regulation of daily biological rhythms.

oxytocin A hormone, secreted by the pituitary gland, that stimulates uterine contractions during childbirth, facilitates the ejection of milk during nursing, and seems to promote, in both sexes, attachment and trust in relationships.

adrenal hormones Hormones that are produced by the adrenal glands and that are involved in emotion and stress.

sex hormones Hormones that regulate the development and functioning of reproductive organs and that stimulate the development of male and female sexual characteristics; they include androgens, estrogens, and progesterone.

✔•—**Study** and **Review** on **mypsychlab.com**

Quick Quiz

Get your glutamate going by taking this quiz.

A. Which word in parentheses better fits each of the following definitions?

1. Basic building blocks of the nervous system (*nerves, neurons*)
2. Cell parts that receive nerve impulses (*axons, dendrites*)
3. Site of communication between neurons (*synapse, myelin sheath*)
4. Opiatelike substance in the brain (*dopamine, endorphin*)
5. Chemicals that make it possible for neurons to communicate (*neurotransmitters, hormones*)
6. Hormone closely associated with emotional excitement (*epinephrine, estrogen*)

B. Imagine that you are depressed, and you hear about a treatment for depression that affects the levels of several neurotransmitters thought to be involved in the disorder. Based on what you have learned, what questions would you want to ask before deciding whether to try the treatment?

Answers:

A. 1. neurons **2.** dendrites **3.** synapse **4.** endorphin **5.** neurotransmitters **6.** epinephrine **B.** You might want to ask, among other things, about side effects (each neurotransmitter has several functions, all of which might be affected by the treatment); evidence that the treatment works; whether there is any reason to believe that your own neurotransmitter levels are abnormal; and whether there may be other reasons for your depression.

YOU are about to learn...

- why patterns of electrical activity in the brain are called "brain waves."

- how scanning techniques reveal changes in brain activity while people listen to music, solve math problems, or do other activities.

- the limitations of brain scans as a way of understanding the brain.

Mapping the Brain

electroencephalogram (EEG) A recording of neural activity detected by electrodes.

transcranial magnetic stimulation (TMS) A method of stimulating brain cells, using a powerful magnetic field produced by a wire coil placed on a person's head; it can be used by researchers to temporarily inactivate neural circuits and is also being used therapeutically.

We come now to the main room of the nervous system house: the brain. A disembodied brain stored in a formaldehyde-filled container is a putty-colored, wrinkled glob of tissue that looks a little like an oversized walnut. It takes an act of imagination to envision this modest-looking organ writing *Hamlet*, discovering radium, or inventing the paper clip.

In a living person, of course, the brain is encased in a thick protective vault of bone. How, then, can scientists study it? One approach is to study patients who have had a part of the brain damaged or removed because of disease or injury. Another, the *lesion method*, involves damaging or removing sections of brain in animals and then observing the effects.

Electrical and Magnetic Detection The brain can also be probed with devices called *electrodes*. Some electrodes are coin-shaped and are simply pasted or taped onto the scalp. They detect the electrical activity of millions of neurons in particular regions of the brain and are widely used in research and medical diagnosis. The electrodes are connected by wires to a machine that translates the electrical energy from the brain into wavy lines on a moving piece of paper or visual patterns on a screen. That is why electrical patterns in the brain are known as "brain waves." Different wave patterns are associated with sleep, relaxation, and mental concentration (see Chapter 5).

A brain-wave recording is called an **electroencephalogram (EEG)**. A standard EEG is useful but not very precise because it reflects the activities of many cells at once. "Listening" to the brain with an EEG machine is like standing outside a sports stadium: You know when something is happening, but you can't be sure what it is or who is doing it. Fortunately, computer technology can be combined with EEG technology to get a clearer picture of brain activity patterns associated with specific events and mental processes. The computer suppresses all the background noise, leaving only the pattern of electrical response to the event being studied.

For even more precise information, researchers use *needle electrodes*, very thin wires or hollow glass tubes that can be inserted into the brain, either directly in an exposed brain or through tiny holes in the skull. Only the skull and the membranes covering the brain need to be anesthetized; the brain itself, which processes all sensation and feeling, paradoxically feels nothing when touched. Therefore, a human patient or an animal can be awake and not feel pain during the procedure. Needle electrodes can be used both to record electrical activity from the brain and to stimulate the brain with weak electrical currents. Stimulating a given area often results in a specific sensation or movement. *Microelectrodes* are so fine that they can be inserted into single cells.

A newer method of stimulating the brain, **transcranial magnetic stimulation (TMS)**, delivers a large current through a wire coil placed on a person's head. The current produces a magnetic field about 40,000 times greater than the earth's natural magnetic field. This procedure causes neurons under the coil to fire. It can be used to produce motor responses (say, a twitch in the thumb or a knee jerk) and can also be used by researchers to briefly inactivate an area and observe the effects on behavior—functioning, in effect, as a virtual (and temporary) lesion method. The drawback is that when neurons fire, they cause many other neurons to become active too, so it is often hard to tell which neurons are critical for a particular task. TMS has also been used to treat depression (see Chapter 12), but there is little reliable evidence of its effectiveness so far.

Electrodes are used to produce an overall picture of electrical activity in different areas of the brain.

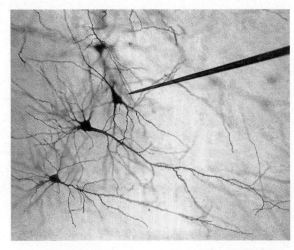

This microelectrode is being used to record the electrical impulses generated by a single cell in the brain of a monkey.

Scanning the Brain Since the mid-1970s, many other amazing doors to the brain have opened. The **PET scan (positron-emission tomography)** goes beyond anatomy to record biochemical changes in the brain as they are happening. One type of PET scan takes advantage of the fact that nerve cells convert glucose, the body's main fuel, into energy. A researcher can inject a person with a glucoselike substance that contains a harmless radioactive element. This substance accumulates in brain areas that are particularly active and are therefore consuming glucose rapidly. The substance emits radiation, which is detected by a scanning device, and the result is a computer-processed picture of biochemical activity on a display screen, with different colors indicating different activity levels. Other kinds of PET scans measure blood flow or oxygen consumption, which also reflect brain activity.

PET scans, which were originally designed to diagnose abnormalities, have produced evidence that some brain areas in people with emotional disorders are either unusually quiet or unusually active. But PET technology can also show which parts of the brain are active during ordinary activities and emotions. It lets researchers see which areas are busiest when a person hears a song, recalls a sad memory, works on a math problem, or shifts attention from one task to another. The PET scans in Figure 4.7a show what an average brain looks like when a person is doing various tasks.

Another technique, **MRI (magnetic resonance imaging)**, allows the exploration of inner space without injecting chemicals. Powerful magnetic fields and radio frequencies are used to produce vibrations in the nuclei of atoms making up body organs. The vibrations are then picked up as signals by special receivers. A computer analyzes the signals, taking into account their strength and duration, and converts them into a high-contrast picture of the organ (see Figure 4.7b). An ultrafast version of MRI, called *functional MRI* (fMRI), can capture brain changes many times a second as a person performs a task, such as reading a sentence or solving a puzzle. Today, thousands of facilities across the United States are using MRIs for research and assessment.

Other methods are becoming available with each passing year. Researchers are using fMRI scans, in particular, to correlate activity in specific brain areas with everything from racial attitudes to moral reasoning to spiritual meditation. Researchers in an applied field called "neuromarketing" are even using them to study which parts of the brain are activated while people watch TV commercials or political ads.

Controversies and Cautions Exciting though these developments and technologies are, we need to understand that technology cannot replace critical thinking (Wade, 2006). Because brain-scan images seem so "real" and scientific, many people fail to realize that these images can convey oversimplified and sometimes misleading impressions. By manipulating the color scales used in PET scans, researchers can either accentuate or minimize contrasts between two brains. Small contrasts can be made to look dramatic, larger ones to look insignificant. An individual's brain can even be made to

PET scan (positron-emission tomography) A method for analyzing biochemical activity in the brain, using injections of a glucoselike substance containing a radioactive element.

MRI (magnetic resonance imaging) A method for studying body and brain tissue, using magnetic fields and special radio receivers; *functional MRI* (fMRI) is a faster form often used in psychological research.

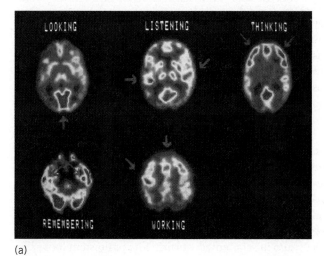

(a)

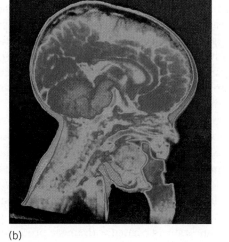

(b)

FIGURE 4.7

Scanning the Brain

In the PET scans on the left, arrows and the color red indicate areas of highest activity, and violet indicates areas of lowest activity, as a person does different things. On the right, an MRI shows a child's brain, along with the bottle he was drinking from while the image was obtained.

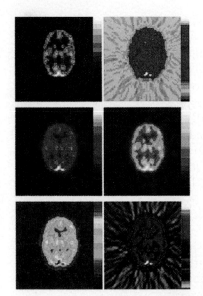

FIGURE 4.8
Coloring the Brain
By altering the colors used in a PET scan, researchers can create the appearance of dramatic brain differences. These scans are actually images of the same brain.

localization of function Specialization of particular brain areas for particular functions.

brain stem The part of the brain at the top of the spinal cord, consisting of the medulla and the pons.

pons A structure in the brain stem involved in, among other things, sleeping, waking, and dreaming.

medulla [muh-DUL-uh] A structure in the brain stem responsible for certain automatic functions, such as breathing and heart rate.

appear completely different depending on the colors used, as the photographs in Figure 4.8 show (Dumit, 2004).

Further, in fMRI studies, questionable statistical procedures have often produced highly inflated correlations between brain activity and measures of personality and emotion (Vul et al., 2009). Yet the press usually reports these findings uncritically, giving the impression that neuroscientists know more about the relationship between the brain and psychological processes than they really do.

There is a final reason for caution about these methods: As of yet, brain scans do not tell us precisely what is happening inside a person's head, either mentally or physiologically. They tell us *where* things happen, but not *why* or *how* they happen—how different circuits connect to produce behavior. Enthusiasm for technology has produced a mountain of findings, but it has also resulted in some unwarranted conclusions about "brain centers" or "critical circuits" for this or that behavior. If you know that one part of the brain is activated when you are thinking hot thoughts of your beloved, what exactly do you know about love? Does that part also light up when you are watching a hot love scene in a movie, looking at a luscious hot fudge sundae, or thinking about happily riding your horse Horace through the hills?

> **Thinking Critically about Brain Technology**

For these reasons, one neuroscientist has called the search for brain centers and circuits "the new phrenology" (Uttal, 2001). Another drew this analogy (cited in Wheeler, 1998): A researcher scans the brains of gum-chewing volunteers, finds out which parts of their brains are active, and concludes that she has found the brain's "gum-chewing center"!

Even if there were a gum-chewing center, yours might not be in the same place as someone else's. Each brain is unique for two reasons: First, a unique genetic package is present in each of us at birth; second, a lifetime of experiences and sensations is constantly altering the brain's biochemistry and neural networks. Thus, if you are a string musician, the area in your brain associated with music production is likely to be larger than that of nonmusicians; the earlier in life you started to play, the larger it becomes (Jancke, Schlaug, & Steinmetz, 1997). And if you are a cab driver, the area in your hippocampus responsible for visual representations of the

environment is likely to be larger than average (Maguire et al., 2000). Technological measurements often promote the incorrect view that all brains are alike—if we scan a few, we understand them all.

Nonetheless, scans do provide an exciting look at the brain at work and play, and we will be reporting many findings from PET scan and fMRI research throughout this book. The brain can no longer hide from researchers behind the fortress of the skull.

YOU are about to learn...

- the major parts of the brain and some of their major functions.
- why it is a good thing that the outer covering of the human brain is so wrinkled.
- how a bizarre nineteenth-century accident illuminated the role of the frontal lobes.

A Tour through the Brain

Most modern brain theories assume that different brain parts perform different (though greatly overlapping) tasks. This concept, known as **localization of function**, goes back at least to Joseph Gall (1758–1828), the Austrian anatomist who thought that personality traits were reflected in the development of specific areas of the brain. Gall's theory of phrenology was completely wrong-headed (so to speak), but his general notion of specialization in the brain had merit.

To learn about what the major brain structures do, let's take an imaginary stroll through the brain. Pretend that you have shrunk to a microscopic size and that you are wending your way through the "soul's frail dwelling house," starting at the lower part, just above the spine. Figure 4.9 shows the major structures we will encounter along our tour; you may want to refer to it as we proceed. But keep in mind that any activity—feeling an emotion, having a thought, performing a task—involves many different structures. Our description, therefore, is a simplification.

The Brain Stem

We begin at the base of the skull with the **brain stem**, which began to evolve some 500 million years ago in segmented worms. The brain stem looks like a stalk rising out of the spinal cord. Pathways to and from upper areas of the brain pass through its two main structures: the medulla and the pons. The **pons** is involved in (among other things) sleeping, waking, and dreaming. The **medulla** is responsible for bodily functions that do not have to be consciously willed, such as breathing and heart rate. Hanging has long been used as a method of execution because when it breaks the neck, nerve pathways from the medulla are severed, stopping respiration.

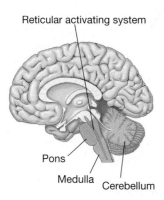

Extending upward from the core of the brain stem is the **reticular activating system (RAS)**. This dense network of neurons, which extends above the brain stem into the center of the brain and has connections with areas that are higher up, screens incoming information and arouses the higher centers when something happens that demands their attention. Without the RAS, we could not be alert or perhaps even conscious.

The Cerebellum

Standing atop the brain stem and looking toward the back part of the brain, we see a structure about the size of a small fist. It is the **cerebellum**, or "lesser brain," which contributes to a sense of balance and coordinates the muscles so that movement is smooth and precise. If your cerebellum were damaged, you would probably become exceedingly clumsy and uncoordinated. You might have trouble using a pencil, threading a needle, or even walking. In addition, this structure is involved in remembering simple skills and acquired reflexes. But the cerebellum, which was once considered just a motor center, is not as "lesser" as its name implies: It plays a part in such complex cognitive tasks as analyzing sensory information, solving problems, and understanding words.

The Thalamus

Deep in the brain's interior, roughly at its center, we can see the **thalamus**, the busy traffic officer of the brain. As sensory messages come into the brain, the thalamus directs them to higher areas: The sight of a sunset sends signals that the thalamus directs to a vision area, and the sound of an oboe

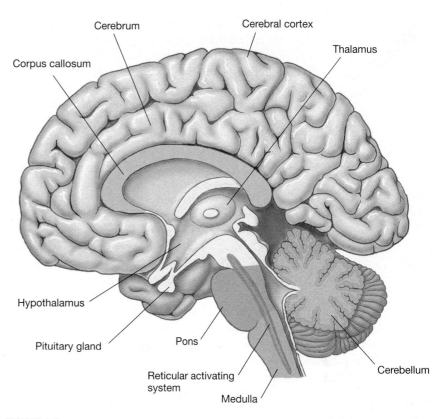

FIGURE 4.9
Major Structures of the Human Brain
This cross section depicts the brain as if it were split in half. The view is of the inside surface of the right half, and it shows the structures described in the text.

sends signals that the thalamus sends on to an auditory area. The only sense that completely bypasses the thalamus is the sense of smell, which has its own private switching station, the *olfactory bulb*. The olfactory bulb lies near areas involved in emotion. Perhaps that is why particular odors—the smell of fresh laundry, gardenias, a steak sizzling on the grill—often rekindle vivid memories.

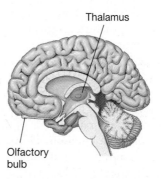

The Hypothalamus and the Pituitary Gland

Beneath the thalamus sits a structure called the **hypothalamus** (*hypo* means "under"). It is involved in

reticular activating system (RAS) A dense network of neurons found in the core of the brain stem; it arouses the cortex and screens incoming information.

cerebellum A brain structure that regulates movement and balance and is involved in some cognitive tasks.

thalamus A brain structure that relays sensory messages to the cerebral cortex.

hypothalamus A brain structure involved in emotions and drives vital to survival, such as fear, hunger, thirst, and reproduction; it regulates the autonomic nervous system.

drives associated with the survival of both the individual and the species—hunger, thirst, emotion, sex, and reproduction. It regulates body temperature by triggering sweating or shivering, and it controls the complex operations of the autonomic nervous system. It also contains the biological clock that controls the body's daily rhythms (see Chapter 5).

Hanging down from the hypothalamus, connected to it by a short stalk, is a cherry-sized endocrine gland called the **pituitary gland**, mentioned earlier in our discussion of hormones. The pituitary is often called the body's "master gland" because the hormones it secretes affect many other endocrine glands. The master, however, is really only a supervisor. The true boss is the hypothalamus, which sends chemicals to the pituitary that tell it when to "talk" to the other endocrine glands. The pituitary, in turn, sends hormonal messages out to these glands.

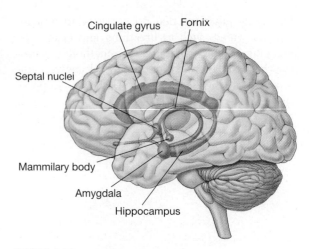

Cingulate gyrus   Fornix
Septal nuclei
Mammilary body
Amygdala
Hippocampus

FIGURE 4.10
The Limbic System
Structures of the limbic system play an important role in memory and emotion. The text describes two of these structures, the amygdala and the hippocampus. The hypothalamus is also often included as part of the limbic system.

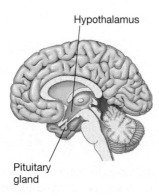

Hypothalamus

Pituitary
gland

The hypothalamus, along with the two structures we will come to next, has often been considered part of a loosely interconnected set of structures called the **limbic system**, shown in Figure 4.10. (*Limbic* comes from the Latin word for "border": These structures form a sort of border between the higher and lower parts of the brain.) Some anatomists also include parts of the thalamus in this system. Structures in this region are heavily involved in emotions that we share with other animals, such as rage and fear (MacLean, 1993). The usefulness of speaking of the limbic system as an integrated set of structures is now in dispute, because these structures also have other functions, and because parts of the brain outside of the limbic system are involved in emotion. However, the term *limbic system* is still in wide use among researchers, so we thought you should know it.

The Amygdala

The **amygdala** (from the ancient Greek word for "almond") is responsible for evaluating sensory information, quickly determining its emotional importance, and contributing to the initial decision to approach or withdraw from a person or situation (see Chapter 13). It instantly assesses danger or threat, and it plays an important role in mediating anxiety and depression; PET scans find that depressed and anxious patients show increased neural activity in this structure (Davidson et al., 1999; Drevets, 2000). In addition, the amygdala is involved in forming and retrieving emotional memories (see Chapter 8).

The Hippocampus

Another important area traditionally classified as limbic is the **hippocampus**, whose shape must have reminded someone of a sea horse, for in Latin, that is what its name means. This structure compares sensory information with what the brain has learned to expect about the world. When expectations are met, it tells the reticular activating system to cool it. There's no need for neural alarm bells to go off every time a car goes by, a bird chirps, or you feel your saliva trickling down the back of your throat!

The hippocampus has also been called the "gateway to memory." It enables us to form spatial memories so that we can accurately navigate through our environment. And, along with adjacent brain areas, it enables us to form new memories about facts and events—the kind of information you need to identify a flower, tell a story, or recall a vacation trip. The information is then stored in the cerebral cortex, which we will be discussing shortly. When you recall meeting someone yesterday,

pituitary gland A small endocrine gland at the base of the brain that releases many hormones and regulates other endocrine glands.

limbic system A group of brain areas involved in emotional reactions and motivated behavior.

amygdala [uh-MIG-dul-uh] A brain structure involved in the arousal and regulation of emotion and the initial emotional response to sensory information.

hippocampus A brain structure involved in the storage of new information in memory.

cerebrum [suh-REE-brum] The largest brain structure, consisting of the upper part of the brain; divided into two hemispheres, it is in charge of most sensory, motor, and cognitive processes. From the Latin for "brain."

various aspects of the memory—information about the person's greeting, tone of voice, appearance, and location—are probably stored in different locations in the cortex. But without the hippocampus, the information would never get to these destinations. As we discuss in Chapter 8, this structure is also involved in the retrieval of information during recall.

The Cerebrum

At this point in our tour, the largest part of the brain still looms above us. It is the cauliflower-like **cerebrum**, where the higher forms of thinking take place. The complexity of the human brain's circuitry far exceeds that of any computer in existence, and much of its most complicated wiring is packed into this structure. Compared to many other creatures, we humans may be ungainly, feeble, and thin-skinned, but our well-developed cerebrum enables us to overcome these limitations and creatively control our environment (and, some would say, to mess it up).

The cerebrum is divided into two separate halves, or **cerebral hemispheres**, connected by a large band of fibers called the **corpus callosum**. In general, the right hemisphere is in charge of the left side of the body and the left hemisphere is in charge of the right side of the body. The two hemispheres also have somewhat different tasks and talents, a phenomenon known as **lateralization**.

The Cerebral Cortex Working our way right up through the top of the brain, we find that the cerebrum is covered by several thin layers of densely packed cells known collectively as the **cerebral cortex**. Cell bodies in the cortex, as in many other parts of the brain, produce a grayish tissue, hence the term *gray matter*. In other parts of the brain (and in the rest of the nervous system), long, myelin-covered axons prevail, providing the brain's *white matter*. Although the cortex is only about 3 millimeters (1/8 inch) thick, it contains almost three-fourths of all the cells in the human brain. The cortex has many deep crevasses and wrinkles, which enable it to contain its billions of neurons without requiring us to have the heads of giants—heads that would be too big to permit us to be born. In other mammals, which have fewer neurons, the cortex is less crumpled; in rats, it is quite smooth.

Lobes of the Cortex In each cerebral hemisphere, deep fissures divide the cortex into four distinct regions, or lobes (see Figure 4.11):

- The **occipital lobes** (from the Latin for "in back of the head") are at the lower back part of the

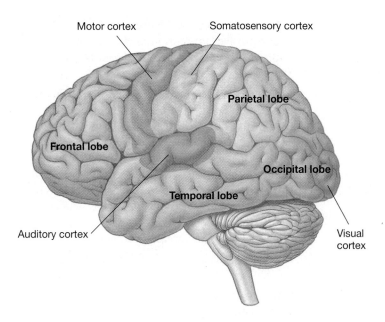

FIGURE 4.11
Lobes of the Cerebrum
Deep fissures divide the cortex of each cerebral hemisphere into four regions.

brain. Among other things, they contain the *visual cortex*, where visual signals are processed. Damage to the visual cortex can cause impaired visual recognition or blindness.

- The **parietal lobes** (from the Latin for "pertaining to walls") are at the top of the brain. They contain the *somatosensory cortex*, which receives information about pressure, pain, touch, and temperature from all over the body. The areas of the somatosensory cortex that receive signals from the hands and the face are disproportionately large because these body parts are particularly sensitive.

- The **temporal lobes** (from the Latin for "pertaining to the temples") are at the sides of the brain, just above the ears and behind the temples. They are involved in memory, perception, and emotion, and they contain the *auditory cortex*, which processes sounds. An area of the left temporal lobe known as *Wernicke's area* is involved in language comprehension.

- The **frontal lobes**, as their name indicates, are located toward the front of the brain, just under the skull in the area of the forehead. They contain the *motor cortex*, which issues orders to the 600 muscles of the body that produce voluntary movement. In the left frontal lobe, a region known as *Broca's area* handles speech production. During short-term memory tasks, areas in the frontal

cerebral hemispheres
The two halves of the cerebrum.

corpus callosum
[CORE-puhs cah-LOW-suhm] The bundle of nerve fibers connecting the two cerebral hemispheres.

lateralization Specialization of the two cerebral hemispheres for particular operations.

cerebral cortex A collection of several thin layers of cells covering the cerebrum; it is largely responsible for higher mental functions. *Cortex* is Latin for "bark" or "rind."

occipital [ahk-SIP-uh-tuhl] **lobes** Lobes at the lower back part of the brain's cerebral cortex; they contain areas that receive visual information.

parietal [puh-RYE-uh-tuhl] lobes Lobes at the top of the brain's cerebral cortex; they contain areas that receive information on pressure, pain, touch, and temperature.

temporal lobes Lobes at the sides of the brain's cerebral cortex; they contain areas involved in hearing, memory, perception, emotion, and (in the left lobe, typically) language comprehension.

frontal lobes Lobes at the front of the brain's cerebral cortex; they contain areas involved in short-term memory, higher-order thinking, initiative, social judgment, and (in the left lobe, typically) speech production.

lobes are especially active. The frontal lobes are also involved in emotion and in the ability to make plans, think creatively, and take initiative.

Because of their different functions, the lobes of the cerebral cortex tend to respond differently when stimulated. If a surgeon applied electrical current to your somatosensory cortex in the parietal lobes, you might feel a tingling in the skin or a sense of being gently touched. If your visual cortex in the occipital lobes were electrically stimulated, you might report a flash of light or swirls of color. And, eerily, many areas of your cortex, when stimulated, would produce no obvious response or sensation. These "silent" areas are sometimes called the *association cortex* because they are involved in higher mental processes.

The Prefrontal Cortex Psychologists are especially interested in the most forward part of the frontal lobes, the *prefrontal cortex*. This area barely exists in mice and rats and takes up only 3.5 percent of the cerebral cortex in cats and about 7 percent in dogs, but it accounts for approximately one-third of the entire cortex in human beings. It is the most recently evolved part of our brains, and is associated with such complex abilities as reasoning, decision making, and planning.

Scientists have long known that the frontal lobes, and the prefrontal cortex in particular, must also have something to do with personality. The first clue appeared in 1848, when a bizarre accident drove an inch-thick, 3½-foot-long iron rod clear through the head of a young railroad worker named Phineas Gage. As you can see in the photo, the rod (which is still on display at Harvard University, along with Gage's skull) entered beneath the left eye and exited through the top of the head, destroying much of the prefrontal cortex (H. Damasio et al., 1994). Miraculously, Gage survived this trauma and, by most accounts, he retained the ability to speak, think, and remember. But his friends complained that he was "no longer Gage." In a sort of Jekyll-and-Hyde transformation, he had changed from a mild-mannered, friendly, efficient worker into a foul-mouthed, ill-tempered, undependable lout who could not hold a steady job or stick to a plan. His employers had to let him go, and he was reduced to exhibiting himself as a circus attraction.

There is some controversy about the details of this sad incident, but many other cases of brain injury, whether from stroke or trauma, support the conclusion that most scientists draw from the Gage case: Parts of the frontal lobes are involved in social judgment, rational decision making, and the ability to set goals and to make and carry

 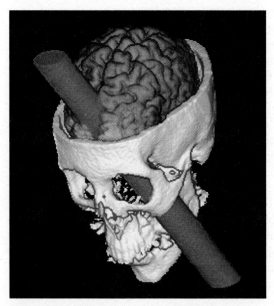

On the left is the only known photo of Phineas Gage, taken after his recovery from an accident in which an iron rod penetrated his skull, altering his behavior and personality dramatically. The exact location of the brain damage remained controversial for almost a century and a half, until Hanna and Antonio Damasio and their colleagues (1994) used measurements of Gage's skull and MRIs of normal brains to plot possible trajectories of the rod. The reconstruction on the right shows that the damage occurred in an area of the prefrontal cortex associated with emotional processing and rational decision making.

through plans. Like Gage, people with damage in these areas sometimes mismanage their finances, lose their jobs, and abandon their friends. Interestingly, the mental deficits that characterize damage to these areas are accompanied by a flattening out of emotion and feeling, which suggests that normal emotions are necessary for everyday reasoning and the ability to learn from mistakes (Damasio, 1994, 2003; Levenson & Miller, 2007).

The frontal lobes also govern the ability to do a series of tasks in the proper sequence and to stop doing them at the proper time. The pioneering Soviet psychologist Alexander Luria (1980) studied many cases in which damage to the frontal lobes disrupted these abilities. One man Luria observed kept trying to light a match after it was already lit. Another planed a piece of wood in the hospital carpentry shop until it was gone and then went on to plane the workbench!

✓—Study and Review on mypsychlab.com

Quick Quiz

Pause to see how your own brain is working by taking this quiz.
Match each description on the left with a term on the right.

1. Filters out irrelevant information
2. Known as the "gateway to memory"
3. Controls the autonomic nervous system; involved in drives associated with survival
4. Consists of two hemispheres
5. Wrinkled outer covering of the brain
6. Site of the motor cortex; associated with planning and taking initiative

a. reticular activating system
b. cerebrum
c. hippocampus
d. cerebral cortex
e. frontal lobes
f. hypothalamus

Answers:

1.a 2.c 3.f 4.b 5.d 6.e

YOU are about to learn...

• what would happen if the two cerebral hemispheres could not communicate with each other.

• why researchers often refer to the left hemisphere as "dominant."

• why "left-brainedness" and "right-brainedness" are exaggerations.

The Two Hemispheres of the Brain

We have seen that the cerebrum is divided into two hemispheres that control opposite sides of the body. Although similar in structure, these hemispheres have somewhat separate talents, or areas of specialization.

Split Brains: A House Divided

In a normal brain, the two hemispheres communicate with one another across the corpus callosum,

the bundle of fibers that connects them. Whatever happens in one side of the brain is instantly flashed to the other side. What would happen, though, if the two sides were cut off from one another?

In 1953, Ronald E. Myers and Roger W. Sperry took the first step toward answering this question by severing the corpus callosum in cats. They also cut parts of the nerves leading from the eyes to the brain. Normally, each eye transmits messages to both sides of the brain. (See Figure 4.12 on the next page.) After this procedure, a cat's left eye sent information only to the left hemisphere and its right eye sent information only to the right hemisphere.

At first, the cats did not seem to be affected much by this drastic operation. But Myers and Sperry showed that something profound had happened. They trained the cats to perform tasks with one eye blindfolded; a cat might have to push a panel with a square on it to get food but ignore a panel with a circle. Then the researchers switched the blindfold to the cat's other eye and tested the animal again. Now the cats behaved as if they had never learned the trick. Apparently, one side of the

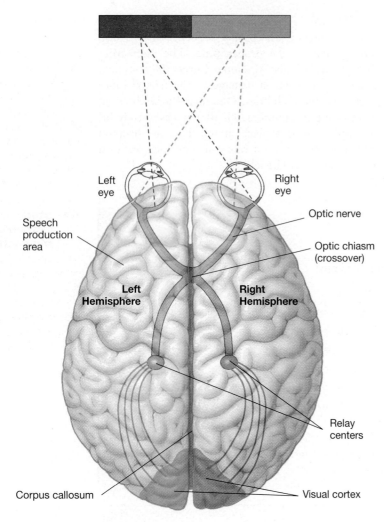

FIGURE 4.12
Visual Pathways

Each cerebral hemisphere receives information from the eyes about the opposite side of the visual field. Thus, if you stare directly at the corner of a room, everything to the left of the juncture is represented in your right hemisphere and vice versa. This is so because half the axons in each optic nerve cross over (at the optic chiasm) to the opposite side of the brain. Normally, each hemisphere immediately shares its information with the other one, but in split-brain patients, severing the corpus callosum prevents such communication.

brain did not know what the other side was doing; it was as if the animals had two minds in one body. Later studies confirmed this result with other species, including monkeys (Sperry, 1964).

In all of the animal studies, ordinary behavior, such as eating and walking, remained normal. In the early 1960s, a team of surgeons decided to try cutting the corpus callosum in patients with debilitating, uncontrollable epilepsy. In severe forms of this disease, disorganized electrical activity spreads

from an injured area to other parts of the brain. The surgeons reasoned that cutting the connection between the two halves of the brain might stop the spread of electrical activity from one side to the other. The surgery was done, of course, for the sake of the patients, who were desperate. But there was a bonus for scientists, who would be able to find out what each cerebral hemisphere can do when it is quite literally cut off from the other.

The results of this *split-brain surgery* generally proved successful. Seizures were reduced and sometimes disappeared completely. In their daily lives, split-brain patients did not seem much affected by the fact that the two hemispheres were incommunicado. Their personalities and intelligence remained intact; they could walk, talk, and lead normal lives. Apparently, connections in the undivided deeper parts of the brain kept body movements and other functions normal. But in a series of ingenious studies, Sperry and his colleagues (and later, other researchers) showed that perception and memory had been affected, just as they had been in the earlier animal research. Sperry won a Nobel Prize for his work.

It was already known that the two hemispheres are not mirror images of each other. In most people, language is largely handled by the left hemisphere; thus, a person who suffers brain damage because of a stroke—a blockage in or rupture of a blood vessel in the brain—is much more likely to have language problems if the damage is in the left side than if it is in the right. Sperry and his colleagues wanted to know how splitting the brain would affect language and other abilities.

To understand this research, you must know how nerves connect the eyes to the brain. (The human patients, unlike Myers and Sperry's cats, did not have these nerves cut.) If you look straight ahead at the *visual field* in front of you, everything in the left side of the scene goes to the right half of your brain, and everything in the right side of the scene goes to the left half of your brain. This is true for both eyes. (Refer again to Figure 4.12.)

The procedure was to present information only to one or the other side of the patients' brains. In one early study, the researchers took photographs of different faces, cut them in two, and pasted different halves together (Levy, Trevarthen, & Sperry, 1972). The reconstructed photographs were then presented on slides (see Figure 4.13). The patients were told to stare at a dot in the middle of the screen, so that half of the image fell to the left of this point and half to the right. Each image was flashed so quickly that they had no time to move their eyes. When the patients were asked to

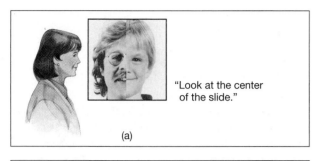

"Look at the center of the slide."

(a)

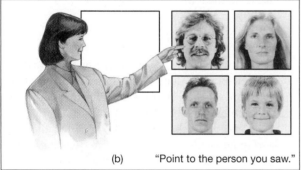

(b)   "Point to the person you saw."

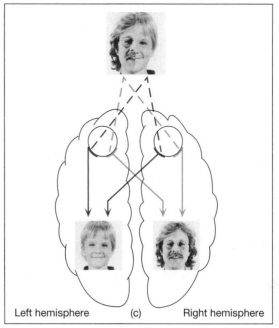

Left hemisphere   (c)   Right hemisphere

FIGURE 4.13
Divided View
Split-brain patients were shown composite photographs (a) and were then asked to pick out the face they had seen from a series of intact photographs (b). They said they had seen the face on the right side of the composite, yet they pointed with their left hands to the face that had been on the left. Because the two cerebral hemispheres could not communicate, the verbal left hemisphere was aware of only the right half of the picture, and the relatively mute right hemisphere was aware of only the left half (c).

say what they had seen, they named the person in the right part of the image (which would be the little boy in Figure 4.13). But when they were asked to point with their left hands to the face they had seen, they chose the person in the left side of the image (the mustached man in the figure). Further, they claimed they had noticed nothing unusual about the original photographs! Each side of the brain saw a different half-image and automatically filled in the missing part. Neither side knew what the other side had seen.

Why did the patients name one side of the picture but point to the other? Speech centers are usually in the left hemisphere. When patients responded with speech, it was the left side of the brain doing the talking. When patients pointed with the left hand, which is controlled by the right side of the brain, the right hemisphere was giving its version of what they had seen.

In another study, the researchers presented slides of ordinary objects and then suddenly flashed a slide of a nude woman. Both sides of the brain were amused, but because only the left side has speech, the two sides responded differently. When the picture was flashed to one woman's left hemisphere, she laughed and identified it as a nude. When it was flashed to her right hemisphere, she said nothing but began to chuckle. Asked what she was laughing at, she said, "I don't know … nothing … oh—that funny machine." The right hemisphere could not describe what it had seen, but it reacted emotionally just the same (Gazzaniga, 1967).

The Two Hemispheres: Allies or Opposites?

The split-brain operation is still being performed, and split-brain patients continue to be studied, but research on left–right differences has also been done with people whose brains are intact (Springer & Deutsch, 1998). Electrodes and brain scans have been used to measure activity in the left and right hemispheres while people perform different tasks. The results confirm that nearly all right-handed people and a majority of left-handers process language mainly in the left hemisphere. The left side is also more active during some logical, symbolic, and sequential tasks, such as solving math problems and understanding technical material. ⊙▸ **Simulate**

Because of its cognitive talents, many researchers refer to left-hemisphere *dominance*. They believe that the left hemisphere usually exerts control over the right hemisphere. Split-brain researcher Michael Gazzaniga (1983) once argued that without help from the left side, the right side's mental skills would probably be "vastly inferior to the cognitive skills of a chimpanzee." He and others also believe that a part of the left hemisphere is constantly trying to explain actions and emotions generated by brain parts whose workings are nonverbal and outside of awareness. As one neuropsychologist put it, the left hemisphere is the brain's spin doctor (Broks, 2004).

Other researchers, including Sperry (1982), have rushed to the right hemisphere's defense. The

⊙▸ **Simulate**
Split-Brain Experiments on **mypsychlab.com**

Get Involved! TAP, TAP, TAP

Have a right-handed friend tap on a paper with a pencil held in the right hand for one minute. Then have the person do the same with the left hand, using a fresh sheet of paper. Finally, repeat the procedure, having the person talk at the same time as tapping. For most people, talking will decrease the rate of tapping—but more for the right hand than for the left, probably because both activities involve the same hemisphere (the left one), and there is competition between them. Left-handed people vary more in terms of which hemisphere is dominant for language, so the results for them will be more varied.

Harley Schwadron/CartoonStock Ltd. CSL

right side, they point out, is no dummy. It is superior in problems requiring spatial–visual ability, the ability you use to read a map or follow a dress pattern, and it excels in facial recognition and the ability to read facial expressions. It is active during the creation and appreciation of art and music. It recognizes nonverbal sounds, such as a dog's barking. The right brain also has some language ability. Typically, it can read a word briefly flashed to it and

can understand an experimenter's instructions. In a few split-brain patients, right-brain language ability has been well developed, showing that individual variation exists in brain lateralization.

Some researchers have also credited the right hemisphere with having a cognitive style that is intuitive and holistic, in contrast to the left hemisphere's more rational and analytic mode. This idea has been oversold by books and programs that promise to make people more creative by making them more "right-brained." But the right hemisphere is not always a hero: It contains frontal lobe regions that process fear and sadness, emotions that often cause us to withdraw from others. Further, the differences between the two hemispheres are relative, not absolute—a matter of degree. In most activities, the two sides cooperate naturally, with each making a valuable contribution. Be cautious, then, about thinking of the two sides as two "minds." As Sperry (1982) himself noted long ago, "The left–right dichotomy . . . is an idea with which it is very easy to run wild."

Thinking Critically about Right Brain/ Left Brain Theories

Study and **Review** on mypsychlab.com

Quick Quiz

Use as many parts of your brain as necessary to answer these questions.

1. Bearing in mind that both sides of the brain are involved in most activities, identify which of the following is (are) more closely associated with the left hemisphere: (a) enjoying a musical recording, (b) wiggling the left big toe, (c) giving a speech in class, (d) balancing a checkbook, (e) recognizing a long-lost friend.

2. Thousands of people have taken courses and bought tapes that promise to develop the creativity and intuition of their right hemispheres. What characteristics of human thought might explain the eagerness of some people to glorify "right-brainedness" and disparage "left-brainedness" (or vice versa)?

Answers:

1. c, d 2. One possible answer: Human beings like to make sense of the world, and one easy way to do that is to divide humanity into opposing categories. This kind of either-or thinking can lead to the conclusion that fixing up one brain hemisphere (e.g., making "left-brained" types more "right-brained,") will make individuals happier and the world a better place. If only it were that simple!

YOU are about to learn...

- why some brain researchers think a unified "self" is only an illusion.

- findings and fallacies about sex differences in the brain.

Two Stubborn Issues in Brain Research

If you have mastered the definitions and descriptions in this chapter, you are prepared to follow news of advances in neuropsychology. Yet many questions remain about how the brain works, and we will end this chapter with two of them.

Where Is the Self?

When you say, "I am feeling unhappy," your amygdala, your serotonin receptors, your endorphins, and all sorts of other brain parts and processes are active, but who, exactly, is the "I" doing the feeling?

Thinking Critically about the Brain and the Self

When you say, "My mind is playing tricks on me," who is the "me" watching your mind play those tricks, and who is it that's being tricked? Isn't the self observing itself a little like a finger pointing at its own tip? Because the brain is the site of self-awareness, people even disagree about what language to use when referring to it. If we say that your brain stores events or registers emotions, we imply a separate "you" that is "using" that brain. But if we leave "you" out of the picture and just say the brain does these things, we risk ignoring the motives, personality traits, and social conditions that powerfully affect what people do—what *you* do.

Most religions resolve the problem by teaching that an immortal self or soul exists entirely apart from the mortal brain, a doctrine known as *dualism*. But modern brain scientists usually consider mind to be a matter of matter. They may have religious convictions about a soul or a spiritual response to the awesome complexity and interconnectedness of nature, but most assume that what we call "mind," "consciousness," "self-awareness," or "subjective experience" can be explained in physical terms as a product of the cerebral cortex.

Our conscious sense of a unified self may even be an illusion. Neurologist Richard Restak (1994) notes that many of our actions and choices occur without any direction by a central, conscious self. Cognitive scientist Daniel Dennett (1991) suggests

"THEN IT'S AGREED—YOU CAN'T HAVE A MIND WITHOUT A BRAIN, BUT YOU CAN HAVE A BRAIN WITHOUT A MIND."

that the brain or mind consists of independent brain parts that deal with different aspects of thought and perception, constantly conferring with each other and revising their versions of reality. And Michael Gazzaniga proposes that the brain is organized as a loose confederation of independent modules, or mental systems, all working in parallel, with most of these modules operating outside of conscious awareness. One verbal module, an "interpreter" (usually in the left hemisphere), is constantly explaining the actions, moods, and thoughts produced by the other modules (Gazzaniga, 1998; Roser & Gazzaniga, 2004). The result is the sense of a unified self.

The idea that the self is an illusion echoes the teachings of many Eastern spiritual traditions, such as Buddhism. Buddhism teaches that the self is not a unified, tangible thing but rather a collection of thoughts, perceptions, concepts, and feelings that shift and change from moment to moment. To Buddhists, the unity and the permanence of the self are a mirage. Such notions are contrary, of course, to what most people in the West, including psychologists, have always believed about their "selves."

Whether or not the self is an illusion, we all have a sense of self; otherwise, there would be no need for the words *I* and *me*. Yet even in these days of modern technology, and despite much debate among scientists and philosophers, the neural circuits responsible for our sense of self remain hazy. How is the inner life of the mind, our sense of subjective experience, linked to the physical processes of the brain? Some neuroscientists argue that specific groups of neurons form unique neuronal coalitions for seeing red, seeing our grandmother, or feeling joy (Koch, 2004). Others emphasize the transient synchronization of millions of neurons across wide areas of the brain, synchronization that changes from moment to moment (Greenfield & Collins, 2005). But in either case, how does that brain activity *cause* a person's joy on seeing her adored grandmother in a new red hat? We don't know. Nor do we understand why some patients with severe degeneration of the frontal lobes have unimpaired memories and language yet undergo a change in self comparable to Phineas Gage's transformation (Levenson & Miller, 2007). These patients can walk, talk, and function, and yet their families and friends don't know them; they are no longer "themselves."

Psychologists, neuroscientists, cognitive scientists, and philosophers all hope to learn more about how our brains and nervous systems give rise to the self. In the meantime, what do you think about the existence and location of your own "self" . . . and who, by the way, is doing the thinking?

Are There "His" and "Hers" Brains?

A second stubborn issue for brain scientists concerns sex differences in the brain. On this issue, either–or thinking is a great temptation. Because of the centuries of prejudice against women and a legacy of biased research on gender differences, some scientists and laypeople do not even want to consider the possibility that the brains of women and men might differ, on average, in some ways. Others go overboard in the opposite direction, convinced that most, if not all, differences between the sexes are in fact "all in the brain." Every year, more books arrive claiming that the "female brain" and the "male brain" are as unlike as tomatoes and artichokes. To evaluate this issue intelligently, we need to ask two separate questions: *Do the brains of males and females differ? And if so, what, if anything, do the differences have to do with men's and women's behavior, abilities, or ways of solving problems?*

Let's consider the first question. Many anatomical and biochemical sex differences have been found in animal brains, and advances in technology have revealed some intriguing differences in human brains as well. In a study of nine autopsied brains, researchers found that the women's brains had an average of 11 percent more cells in areas of the cortex associated with the processing of auditory information; in fact, all of the women had more of these cells than did any of the men (Witelson, Glazer, & Kigar, 1994). Brain scans show that parts of the frontal lobes and the limbic system are larger in women, relative to the overall size of their brains, whereas parts of the parietal cortex and the amygdala are larger in men (Goldstein et al., 2001; Gur et al., 2002). Women also have more cortical folds in the frontal and parietal lobes (Luders et al., 2004).

Researchers are also using brain scans to search for average sex differences in brain activity when people work on particular tasks. In one study, 19 men and 19 women were asked to say whether pairs of nonsense words rhymed, a task that required them to process and compare sounds. MRI scans showed that in both sexes an area at the front of the left hemisphere was activated. But in 11 of the women and none of the men, the corresponding area in the right hemisphere was also active (Shaywitz et al., 1995). In another MRI study, 10 men and 10 women listened to a John Grisham thriller being read aloud. Men and women alike showed activity in the left temporal lobe, but women also showed some activity in the right temporal lobe, as you can see in Figure 4.14 (Phillips et al., 2001). These findings, along with many others, provide evidence for a sex difference in lateralization: For some types of tasks, especially those involving language, men seem to rely more heavily on one side of the brain whereas women tend to use both sides.

Thus, the answer to our first question is that yes, average sex differences in the brain do exist. But we are still left with our second question: *What do the differences mean for the behavior or personality traits of men and women in ordinary life?* Some writers have been quick to assume that brain differ-

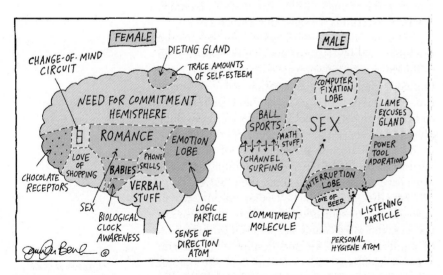

Cartoons like this one make most people laugh because men and women do differ, on average, in things like "love of shopping" and "power-tool adoration." But what does the research show about sex differences in the brain? And what do they mean for how people behave in real life?

ences explain, among other things, women's allegedly superior intuition, women's love of talking about feelings and men's love of talking about

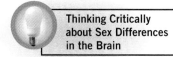

Thinking Critically about Sex Differences in the Brain

sports, women's greater verbal ability, men's edge in math ability, why women can't read maps, and why men won't ask for directions when they're lost. There are at least three problems with such conclusions:

1 Many supposed gender differences (in intuition, abilities, and so forth) are stereotypes, which are misleading because the overlap between the sexes is usually greater than the difference between them. As we saw in Chapter 1, even when gender differences are statistically significant, they are often quite small in practical terms. Some supposed differences, on closer inspection, even disappear. For instance, are women more talkative than men, as many pop-psych books about the sexes assert? To test this assumption, psychologists wired up a sample of men and women with voice recorders that tracked their conversations while they went about their daily lives. There was no significant gender difference in the number of words spoken: Both sexes used about 16,000 words per day on average, with large individual differences among the participants (Mehl et al., 2007). Likewise, the difference between boys and girls in math scores is shrinking and in some studies is approaching zero (Else-Quest, Hyde, & Linn, 2010).

2 A brain difference does not necessarily produce a difference in behavior or performance. In many studies, males and females have shown different patterns of brain activity while they are doing something or while an ability is being tested, but they have not differed in the behavior or ability in question—which, after all, is presumably the thing to be explained. In the rhyme-judgment task, both sexes did equally well, despite the differences in their MRIs. Another research team used MRI scans to examine the brains of men and women who had equivalent IQ scores. Women's brains had more white-matter areas related to intelligence, whereas men's brains had more gray-matter areas related to intelligence; there were some other differences as well (Haier et al., 2005). The researchers concluded that brains may be organized differently yet produce the same intellectual abilities.

3 Sex differences in the brain could be the result rather than the cause of behavioral differences. Culture and experience are constantly sculpting the circuitry of the brain, affecting the

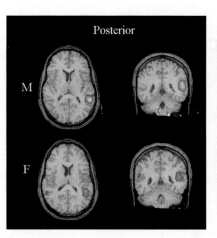
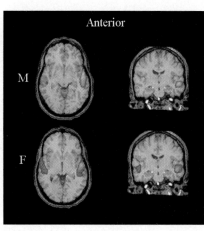

FIGURE 4.14
Gender and the Brain
When women and men listened to a John Grisham thriller read aloud, they showed activity in the left temporal lobe, but women also showed some activity in the right temporal lobe (Phillips et al., 2001). (Because of the orientation of these MRI images, the left hemisphere is seen on the right and vice versa.) Along with other evidence, these results suggest a sex difference in lateralization on tasks involving language.

way brains are organized and how they function. Women and men, of course, often have different experiences in childhood and throughout their lives. Thus, in commenting on the study that had people listen to a John Grisham novel, one of the researchers noted: "We don't know if the [sex difference we found] is because of the way we're raised, or if it's hard-wired in the brain" (quoted in Hotz, 2000).

In sum, the answer to our second question, whether anatomical differences are linked to behavior and abilities, is: It's uncertain. Animal studies have provided tantalizing clues, suggesting that sex differences in the brain influence reactions to acute or chronic stress, the likelihood of suffering depression and attention deficit/hyperactivity disorder, memory for emotional events, strategies for navigating around the environment, and other aspects of behavior (Cahill, 2005; Becker et al., 2008). But we simply do not yet know which of these findings are important for how human males and females manage their everyday lives—their work, their relationships, their families. It is good to keep an open mind about new findings on sex differences in the brain, but because the practical significance of these findings (if any) is not yet clear, it is also important not to oversimplify, as one popular book after another keeps doing. The topic of sex differences in the brain is a sexy one, and research in this area can easily be exaggerated and misused. ⊙ **Simulate**

⊙ **Simulate**
Physiological Bases of Behavioral Problems on **mypsychlab.com**

✓•─ **Study** and
Review on
mypsychlab.com

Quick Quiz

Men and women alike have brains that can answer these questions.

1. Many brain researchers and cognitive scientists believe that the self is not a unified "thing" but a collection of _____.

2. A new study reports that in a sample of 11 brains, 4 of the 6 women's brains but only 2 of the 5 men's brains had multiple chocolate receptors. (*Note:* We made this up; there's no such thing as a chocolate receptor!) The researchers conclude that their findings explain why so many women are addicted to chocolate. What concerns should a critical thinker have about this study?

Answers:

1. independent modules or mental systems   2. The sample size was very small; have the results been replicated? Were the sex differences more impressive than the similarities? Might eating chocolate affect chocolate receptors rather than the other way around? Most important, was the number of receptors actually related to the amount of chocolate eaten by the brains' owners in real life?

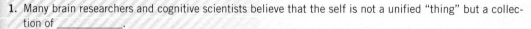

Psychology in the News REVISITED

Now that you know more about the workings of the brain, let's return to the opening story of the patients who were in vegetative or minimally conscious states but who appeared to have some brain function. Political and religious debates continue over the rights of incapacitated people, the meaning of "death by natural causes," and when life should end if a person has left no written instructions. We cannot resolve these debates here, but the information in this chapter, and an increased understanding of the brain, can help us to separate what we might wish to be true about a patient's mental abilities from what really is true.

Consider the tragic case of Terri Schiavo, whose parents and husband fought over the decision to terminate her life. She had been in a persistent vegetative state for 15 years, after a heart attack cut off oxygen to her brain. A few years before her death, a scan of Schiavo's brain showed widespread destruction of brain cells in the cerebral cortex and their replacement by fluid. Yet her parents were convinced that she could recognize them and respond to questions. To a loving and desperately hopeful family, these intermittent, rare reactions seemed like signs of recognition and mental functioning. What they failed to accept is that activity in the brain stem can produce *reflexive* responses such as facial expressions and eye movements, without any awareness or thought on the patient's part and without any connection to events in the environment.

Eventually, a judge gave Terri's husband permission to have her feeding tube removed, and she died peacefully soon thereafter.

What, then, about the man who responded to yes–no questions by imagining scenarios that produced

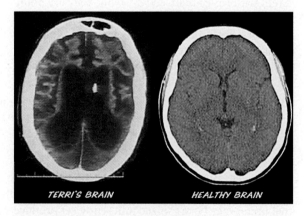

TERRI'S BRAIN   HEALTHY BRAIN

The scan on the left, which was made three years before Terri Schiavo's death, shows severe atrophy in her brain. The dark areas are massively enlarged ventricles filled with cerebral spinal fluid, which had by then replaced much of her cerebral cortex. On the right is a normal brain, showing typical small ventricles.

different patterns of activity in his brain? His brain responses suggest that he does have some awareness. His case holds out the tantalizing possibility that fMRI technology will eventually help doctors distinguish with greater certainty among conscious, minimally conscious, and persistent vegetative states (Monti et al., 2010).

Yet many challenges remain, and at present we must tolerate uncertainty about the implications of this research. Consciousness comes in many forms, including intense alertness, as when you are faced with danger or an exam; a loss of self-awareness, as when you are immersed in a good book or movie; and the floating state between sleep and wakefulness. Brain scans alone cannot necessarily reveal what form of consciousness, if any, someone with brain damage due to accident or disease is experiencing. Evidence of cortical activity is not evidence of an internal stream of conscious thought (Ropper, 2010). As we saw in this chapter, neural correlates of consciousness remain murky and, besides, a brain scan does not tell us exactly what a person is thinking or understands. As we also saw, the brain needs stimulation to survive. We do not yet know how years of what amounts to solitary confinement may affect a patient's brain.

The study of our most miraculous organ, the brain, can help us to better understand the effects of brain damage, and it inspires us to hope for the benefits that future discoveries will bring. But it also teaches us to be cautious and skeptical about the medical and ethical implications of dramatic findings that make the news. Heart-warming reports that Rom Houben, also described in our opening story, had communicated with his mother and his neurologist through "facilitated communication" flashed around the world before independent scientists demonstrated unmistakably that Houben's communications were coming from the facilitators, not Houben. When the researchers shielded the facilitator's eyes from the keyboard, for example, Houben began typing gibberish (Boudry, Termote, & Betz, 2010).

The study of the brain provides valuable insights into the abilities those of us with healthy brains take for granted every day. However, keep in mind that analyzing a human being in terms of physiology alone is like analyzing the Taj Mahal solely in terms of the materials that were used to build it. Even if we could monitor every cell and circuit of the brain, we would still need to understand the circumstances, thoughts, and cultural rules that affect whether we are gripped by hatred, consumed by grief, lifted by love, or transported by joy.

Taking Psychology with You

Cosmetic Neurology: Tinkering with the Brain

Should healthy people be permitted, even encouraged, to take "brain boosters" or "neuroenhancers"—drugs that will sharpen concentration and memory? What about a pill that could erase a traumatic memory? If having cosmetic surgery can change parts of your body that you don't like, what's wrong with allowing cosmetic neurology to tinker with parts of your brain that you don't like?

For centuries, people have been seeking ways to stimulate their brains to work more efficiently, with caffeine being an especially popular drug of choice. No one objects to research showing that diet and exercise can improve learning and memory. No one has a problem with the finding that omega-3s, found in some kinds of fish, may help protect

against age-related mental decline (Beydoun et al., 2007; van Gelder et al., 2007). But when it comes to medications that increase alertness or appear to enhance memory and other cognitive functions, it's another kettle of fish oil, so to speak.

What questions should critical thinkers ask, and what kind of evidence would be needed, to make wise decisions about using such medications? A new interdisciplinary specialty, *neuroethics,* has been formed to address the many legal, ethical, and scientific questions raised by brain research, including those raised by the development of neuroenhancing drugs (Gazzaniga, 2005).

Much of the buzz has focused on Provigil (modafinil), a drug approved for treating

narcolepsy and other sleep disorders, and Ritalin and Adderall, approved for attention deficit disorders. Many students, pilots, business people, and jet-lagged travelers are taking one or another of these drugs, either obtaining them illegally from friends or the Internet or getting their own prescriptions. Naturally, most of these users claim the drugs help them, and one review of the literature concluded that Provigil does improve memory and may have other cognitive benefits (Minzenberg & Carter, 2008).

Yet, as is unfortunately true of just about all medications, there is a down side that rarely makes news, especially with new drugs that promise easy fixes to old human problems and have not yet been tested over many years. Adderall, like all amphetamines, can cause nervousness, headaches, sleeplessness, allergic rashes, and loss of appetite, and, as the label says, it has "a high potential for abuse." Provigil, too, is habit-forming. Another memory-enhancing drug being studied targets a type of glutamate receptor in the brain. The drug apparently improves short-term memory nicely—at the price of detracting from long-term memories (Talbot, 2009).

Even when a drug is benign for most of its users, it may have some surprising and unexpected consequences. For example, cognitive psychologists have found that the better able people are to focus and concentrate on a task—the reason for taking stimulants in the first place—the less *creative* they often are. Creativity, after all, comes from being able to let our minds roam freely, at leisure. One neurologist therefore worries that the routine use of mind-enhancing drugs among students could create "a generation of very focussed accountants" (quoted in Talbot, 2009).

Some bioethicists and neuroscientists feel that cognitive enhancement is perfectly fine, because it is human nature for people to try to improve themselves and society will benefit when people learn faster and remember more. After all, we use eyeglasses to improve vision and hearing aids to improve hearing; why not use pills to improve our memories and other mental skills? One team of scientists has argued that improving brain function with pills is no more objectionable than eating right or getting a good night's sleep. They wrote, "In a world in which human workspans and life spans are increasing, cognitive enhancement tools . . . will be increasingly useful for improved quality of life and extended work productivity, as well as to stave off normal and pathological age-related cognitive declines" (Greely et al., 2008).

Other scientists and social critics, however, consider cosmetic neurology to be a form of cheating that will give those who can afford the drugs an unfair advantage and increase socioeconomic inequalities. They think the issue is no different from the (prohibited) use of performance-enhancing steroids in athletics. Yes, people wear glasses and hearing aids, but glasses and hearing aids do not have side effects or interact negatively with other treatments. Many neuroethicists also worry that ambitious parents will start giving these medications to their children to try to boost the child's academic performance, despite possible hazards for the child's developing brain. One reporter covering the pros and cons of neuroenhancers concluded, "All this may be leading to the kind of society I'm not sure I want to live in: a society where we're even more overworked and driven by technology than we already are, and where we have to take drugs to keep up" (Talbot, 2009).

How about using drugs not to enhance memory but to erase it, especially memories of sorrowful and traumatic events? By altering the biochemistry of the brain in mice or rats, or using a toxin to kill targeted cells, researchers have been able to wipe out the animals' memories of a learned shock, their ability to recall a learned fear, or their memory of an object previously seen, while leaving other memories intact (Cao et al., 2008; Han et al., 2009; Serrano et al., 2008). If these results eventually apply to human beings, what, again, are the implications?

Some victims of sexual or physical abuse, wartime atrocities, or a sudden horrifying disaster might welcome the chance to be rid of their disturbing memories. But could a "delete" button for the brain be used too often, changing the storehouse of memories that make us who we are? Could memory erasure be misused by unscrupulous governments to eliminate dissent, as George Orwell famously predicted it would in his great novel *1984*? Should we wish to erase memories that evoke embarrassment or guilt, emotions that are unpleasant yet enable us to develop and retain a sense of morality and learn from our mistakes? And would we come to regret the obliteration of a part of our lives that contributed to creating the person we are now? Such concerns may be the reason that most people, when asked if they would take a pill to eradicate a painful memory, respond loudly and clearly: No, thanks (Berkowitz et al., 2008).

In contrast, many people might say "Yes, please" to brain-enhancing drugs. But before they do, they will need to think critically—by separating anecdotes from data, real dangers from false alarms, and immediate benefits from long-term risks. What is to be gained from neuroenhancers, and what might be lost?

Summary

((•─[Listen to an **audio file** of your chapter on **mypsychlab.com**

● Neuropsychologists and other scientists study the brain because it is the bedrock of consciousness, perception, memory, and emotion.

The Nervous System: A Basic Blueprint

● The function of the nervous system is to gather and process information, produce responses to stimuli, and coordinate the workings of different cells. Scientists divide it into the *central nervous system* (CNS) and the *peripheral nervous system* (PNS). The CNS, which includes the brain and *spinal cord*, receives, processes, interprets, and stores information and sends out messages destined for muscles, glands, and organs. The PNS transmits information to and from the CNS by way of *sensory* and *motor nerves*.

● The peripheral nervous system consists of the *somatic nervous system*, which permits sensation and voluntary actions, and the *autonomic nervous system*, which regulates blood vessels, glands, and internal (visceral) organs. The autonomic system usually functions without conscious control. The autonomic nervous system is further divided into the *sympathetic nervous system*, which mobilizes the body for action, and the *parasympathetic nervous system*, which conserves energy.

Communication in the Nervous System

● Neurons are the basic units of the nervous system. They are held in place by *glial cells*, which nourish, insulate, and protect them, and enable them to function properly. Each neuron consists of *dendrites*, a *cell body*, and an *axon*. In the peripheral nervous system, axons (and sometimes dendrites) are collected together in bundles called *nerves*. Many axons are insulated by a *myelin sheath* that speeds up the conduction of neural impulses and prevents signals in adjacent cells from interfering with one another.

● Research has disproven two old assumptions: that neurons in the human central nervous system cannot be induced to regenerate and that no new neurons form after early infancy. In the laboratory, neurons have been induced to regenerate. And scientists have learned that *stem cells* in brain areas associated with learning and memory continue to divide and mature throughout adulthood, giving rise to new neurons. A stimulating environment seems to enhance this process of *neurogenesis*.

● Communication between two neurons occurs at the *synapse*. Many synapses have not yet formed at birth. During development, axons and dendrites continue to grow as a result of both physical maturation and experience with the world, and throughout life, new learning results in new synaptic connections in the brain. Thus, the brain's circuits are not fixed and immutable but are continually changing in response to information, challenges, and changes in the environment, a phenomenon known as *plasticity*. In some people who have been blind from an early age, brain regions usually devoted to vision are activated by sound, a dramatic example of plasticity.

● When a wave of electrical voltage *(action potential)* reaches the end of a transmitting axon, *neurotransmitter* molecules are released into the *synaptic cleft*. When these molecules bind to *receptor sites* on the receiving neuron, that neuron becomes either more likely to fire or less so. The message that reaches a final destination depends on how frequently particular neurons are firing, how many are firing, what types are firing, their degree of synchrony, and where they are located.

● Neurotransmitters play a critical role in mood, memory, and psychological well-being. Abnormal levels of neurotransmitters have been implicated in various emotional and physical disorders, such as Alzheimer's disease and Parkinson's disease.

● *Endorphins*, which act primarily by modifying the action of neurotransmitters, reduce pain and promote pleasure. Endorphin levels seem to shoot up when an animal or person is afraid or is under stress. Endorphins have also been linked to the pleasures of social contact.

● *Hormones*, produced mainly by the *endocrine glands*, affect and are affected by the nervous system. Psychologists are especially interested in *melatonin*, which promotes sleep and helps regulate bodily rhythms; *oxytocin* and *vasopressin*, which play a role in attachment and trust; *adrenal hormones* such as *epinephrine* and *norepinephrine*, which are involved in emotions and stress; and the *sex hormones*, which are involved in the physical changes of puberty, the menstrual cycle (*estrogens* and *progesterone*), sexual arousal (*testosterone*), and some nonreproductive functions—including, some researchers believe, mental functioning.

Mapping the Brain

● Researchers study the brain by observing patients with brain damage; by using the *lesion method* with animals; and by using such techniques as *electroencephalograms* (EEGs), *transcranial magnetic stimulation* (TMS), *positron emission tomography* (PET scans), *magnetic resonance imaging* (MRI), and *functional MRI* (fMRI).

● Brain scans reveal which parts of the brain are active during different tasks but do not tell us precisely what is happening, either physically or mentally, during the task. They do not reveal discrete "centers" for a particular function, and they must be interpreted cautiously.

A Tour through the Brain

● All modern brain theories assume *localization of function*, although a particular area may have several functions and many areas are likely to be involved in any particular activity.

● In the lower part of the brain, in the *brain stem*, the *medulla* controls automatic functions such as heartbeat and breathing, and the *pons* is involved in sleeping, waking, and dreaming. The *reticular activating system* (RAS) screens incoming information and is responsible for alertness. The *cerebellum* contributes to balance and muscle coordination, and may also play a role in some higher mental operations.

● The *thalamus* directs sensory messages to appropriate higher centers. The *hypothalamus* is involved in emotion and in drives associated with survival. It also controls the operations of the autonomic nervous system, and sends out chemicals that tell the *pituitary gland* when to "talk" to other endocrine glands. Along with other structures, the hypothalamus has traditionally been considered part of the *limbic system*, which is involved in emotions that we share with other animals. However, the usefulness of speaking of the limbic system as an integrated set of structures is now in dispute.

● The *amygdala* is responsible for evaluating sensory information and quickly determining its emotional importance, and for the initial decision to approach or withdraw from a person or situation. It is also involved in forming and retrieving emotional memories. The *hippocampus* has been called the "gateway to memory" because it plays a critical role in the formation of long-term memories for facts and events. It is also involved in other aspects of memory. Like the hypothalamus, these two structures have traditionally been classified as "limbic."

● Much of the brain's circuitry is packed into the *cerebrum*, which is divided into two *hemispheres* and is covered by thin layers of cells known collectively as the *cerebral cortex*. The *occipital, parietal, temporal,* and *frontal lobes* of the cortex have specialized (but partially overlapping) functions. The *association cortex* appears to be responsible for higher mental processes. The *frontal lobes,* particularly areas in the *prefrontal cortex,* are involved in social judgment, the making and carrying out of plans, and decision making.

The Two Hemispheres of the Brain

● Studies of *split-brain* patients, who have had the *corpus callosum* cut, show that the two cerebral hemispheres have somewhat different talents. In most people, language is processed mainly in the left hemisphere, which generally is specialized for logical, symbolic, and sequential tasks. The right hemisphere is associated with spatial–visual tasks, facial recognition, and the creation and appreciation of art and music. In most mental activities, however, the two hemispheres cooperate as partners, with each making a valuable contribution.

Two Stubborn Issues in Brain Research

● One of the oldest questions in the study of the brain is where the "self" resides. Many brain researchers and cognitive scientists believe that a unified self may be something of an illusion. Some argue that the brain operates as a collection of independent modules or mental systems, perhaps with one of them functioning as an "interpreter." But much remains to be learned about the relationship between the brain and the mind.

● Brain scans and other techniques have revealed some differences in the brains of males and females and in lateralization during tasks involving language (with females more likely to use both hemispheres). Controversy exists, however, about what such differences mean in real life. Speculation has often focused on behavioral or cognitive differences that are small and insignificant. Biological differences do not necessarily explain behavioral ones, and sex differences in experience could affect brain organization rather than the other way around.

Psychology in the News, Revisited

● Knowledge about the brain can help physicians assess the consequences of severe brain damage and improve their methods of diagnosing patients who are in persistent vegetative states, minimally conscious, or conscious. Consciousness itself comes in many different forms, and brain scans to date do not tell us exactly what a person is thinking or understands. The study of the brain can help us to better understand the effects of brain damage, and it also teaches us to be hopeful but cautious about the medical and ethical implications of dramatic findings that make the news.

Taking Psychology with You

● Scholars in the new field of *neuroethics* are addressing the implications of "cosmetic neurology," especially questions raised by the development of drugs that are "neuroenhancers."

Key Terms

Neuropsychologists study the brain and the rest of the nervous system to gain a better understanding of consciousness, perception, memory, emotion, stress, mental disorders, and self-identity.

The Nervous System: A Basic Blueprint

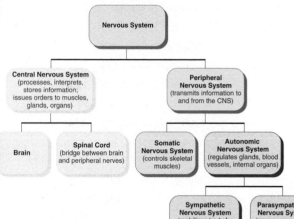

Communication in the Nervous System

- **Neurons:** basic units of the nervous system, composed of **dendrites**, a **cell body**, and an **axon**
- **Glial cells:** hold neurons in place as well as nourish, insulate, and protect them
- **Nerves:** bundles of axons and some dendrites in the peripheral nervous system
- **Myelin sheath:** speeds up the conduction of neural impulses and prevents adjacent cells from interfering with one another
- **Stem cells:** seem to give rise to new neurons throughout adulthood (**neurogenesis**)

How Neurons Communicate

Communication between neurons occurs at **synapses**, most of which develop after birth:
1. **Action potential** (changes in electrical voltage) produces a neutral impulse.
2. **Neurotransmitter** molecules are released into the synaptic cleft and bind to receptor sites on the receiving neuron.
3. Receiving neuron becomes more likely to fire or less likely to fire.

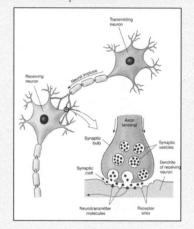

Mapping the Brain

Methods for studying the brain:
- Observing patients with brain damage; *lesion method*
- **Electroencephalogram (EEG):** brain-wave recording
- **Transcranial magnetic stimulation (TMS):** used as a "virtual" lesion method
- **Positron-emission tomography (PET scan):** method for analyzing biochemical activity in the brain
- **Magnetic resonance imaging (MRI):** method for studying body and brain tissue, using magnetic fields and special radio receivers

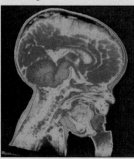

Chemical Messengers in the Nervous System

Neurotransmitters such as serotonin, dopamine, and acetylcholine play a critical role in mood, memory, and psychological well-being.
1. **Endorphins** modify the action of neurotransmitters to reduce pain and promote pleasure.
2. **Hormones,** chemical substances produced primarily by the **endocrine glands,** are released into the bloodstream and affect many organs and cells.
   - **Melatonin** promotes sleep.
   - **Oxytocin** plays a role in attachment and trust.
   - **Adrenal hormones,** such as *epinephrine* and *norepinephrine*, are involved in emotions, memory, and stress.
   - **Sex hormones** are involved in the physical changes of puberty; *estrogen* and *progesterone* are involved in the menstrual cycle, and *testosterone* is involved in sexual arousal.

The Plastic Brain

- Learning and stimulating environments increase the complexity of synaptic connections, whereas unused connections are pruned away.
- The flexibility of the brain to adapt is known as **plasticity**, and can account for many instances of skill recovery following brain damage.

A Tour through the Brain

All modern brain theories assume **localization of function**.

The **brain stem** is in the lower brain.
- The **medulla** controls automatic functions such as heartbeat and breathing.
- The **pons** is involved in sleeping, waking, and dreaming.
- The **reticular activating system (RAS)**, a dense network of neurons, screens incoming information and is responsible for alertness.

- The **cerebellum** contributes to balance and muscle coordination.
- The **thalamus** directs sensory messages.
- The **hypothalamus** is involved in emotion and drives vital to survival and controls operations of the autonomic nervous system. It controls the **pituitary gland,** or master gland.
- The **limbic system** is group of brain areas involved in emotional reactions and motivated behavior.
- The **amygdala** evaluates sensory information and determines its emotional importance and helps to make the initial decision to approach or withdraw from a situation.
- The **hippocampus** plays a critical role in long-term memory for facts and events.
- The **cerebrum** contains much of the brain's circuitry; it is divided into two **cerebral hemispheres**, connected by a band of fibers called the **corpus callosum.** The cerebrum is covered by thin layers of cells called the **cerebral cortex.**

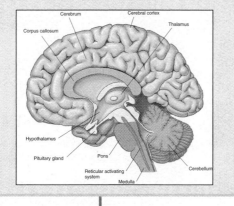

The Two Hemispheres of the Brain

Split Brains

- **Lateralization** is the specializing of each hemisphere.
- The left hemisphere is more active in processing language, logic, and symbolic–sequential tasks.
- The right hemisphere is associated with spatial-visual tasks, facial recognition, the creation and appreciation of art and music, and the processing of negative emotions.
- In most mental activities, the two sides cooperate.

Two Stubborn Issues in Brain Research

Where Is the Self?

The issue of where the "self" resides in the brain is unanswered, with some researchers viewing the brain as a collection of independent modules or mental systems, perhaps with one functioning as "interpreter." An area of the prefrontal cortex may bind together perceptions and memories that produce a sense of self.

Are There "His" and "Her" Brains?

Brain scans reveal some anatomical differences in male and female brains, and sex differences in lateralization during language tasks. However, the real-life significance of these and other findings remains unclear:
- Most supposed gender differences are stereotypes; the overlap between the sexes is greater than their differences.
- Small differences found in MRI studies are often unrelated to how men and women actually behave or score on a test.
- Brain differences could be a result of sex differences in behavior and experience, rather than a cause; experience constantly sculpts the brain.

Lobes of the Cortex

- The **occipital lobes** contain the visual cortex.
- The **parietal lobes** contain the somatosensory cortex, which receives information about pressure, pain, touch, and temperature.
- The **temporal lobes** involve memory, perception, and emotion.
- The **frontal lobes** are involved in social judgment, the making and carrying out of plans, and decision making. Also contains the motor cortex, which controls voluntary movement, and Broca's area, which handles speech production.
- The *association cortex* appears to be responsible for higher mental process.

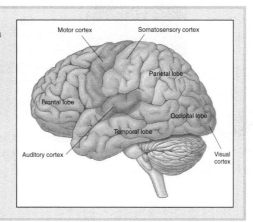

Measure to Legalize Marijuana Fails in California

LOS ANGELES, November 3, 2010. An initiative to make California the first state to legalize small amounts of marijuana for recreational use failed yesterday at the polls. The vote was 54 percent opposed to legalization versus 46 percent in favor.

The initiative, Proposition 19, would have allowed anyone 21 or older to possess up to an ounce of marijuana and to grow plants in an area up to 25 square feet, so long as the drug was for personal use. In addition, cities and counties would have been able to pass laws allowing the production and sale of marijuana and to tax profits on it. Most law enforcement groups, many clergy, the California League of Cities, and Mothers Against Drunk Driving opposed the measure. The California Young Democrats, the Republican Liberty Caucus, the California Council of Churches, some law enforcement officials, and several large labor unions supported it.

Despite the measure's defeat, Richard Lee, the wheelchair-bound medical-marijuana millionaire who largely bankrolled the measure, called the effort a "tremendous moral victory" because millions of Californians voted for it. Lee, who was paralyzed from the waist down after an accident in 1990, owns several medicinal- marijuana businesses in Oakland. He says that after his accident, marijuana helped control his severe back spasms. His successful dispensaries have contributed to the revival of part of downtown Oakland.

The use of pot for medical purposes has been legal in California since 1996, and in January, a new law will change possession of less than an ounce from a criminal misdemeanor to a civil infraction. But California law conflicts with federal law, and within the state, attitudes and policies often clash. Some cities permit pot clubs, some currently have moratoriums in effect until they can come up with regulations, and some prohibit them outright.

In San Diego, the District Attorney's office considers marijuana for any use to be illegal, yet a jury there recently acquitted a Navy veteran who was operating a medical-marijuana dispensary. In Los Angeles, the law caps the number of dispensaries at 70 and exempts another 100 that were in existence as of 2007, but now bans the more than 800 dispensaries established after that.

At a cannabis buyers cooperative in Oakland, California, customer Ken Estes chooses a marijuana muffin. Estes has been a quadriplegic for 22 years, due to a motorcycle accident.

5

Body Rhythms and Mental States

Californians, who years ago voted to permit the use of marijuana for medical reasons, still prefer to keep its recreational use illegal. Whether the drug is legal or illegal, however, many people will continue to use marijuana and others will continue to try to prohibit it.

Marijuana is just one of many drugs used throughout the world to alter *consciousness*, our awareness of ourselves and the environment. But consciousness also changes in predictable ways without any help from drugs. Each day, we all experience swings in mood, alertness, and efficiency. Each night, we all undergo a dramatic shift in consciousness when the ordinary rules of logic are suspended in the dream world of sleep. And performance and mood may be subject to much longer cycles as well, stretching over a month or even a season.

In this chapter, we will see that fluctuations in subjective experience are accompanied by ups and downs in brain activity and hormone levels, and that the mental and physical aspects of consciousness are as intertwined as sunshine and shadow. We will begin with a discussion of the body's natural rhythms, which ebb and flow over time. Next we will zoom in on one fascinating state of consciousness: dreaming. And then we will explore what psychologists have learned about two techniques used to alter consciousness deliberately: hypnosis and the use of recreational drugs. Our goal is to give you a better understanding of the human fascination with altered states of consciousness and why some people use drugs to achieve them.

Are all drugs equally dangerous? Should there be different policies for medical, recreational, and religious use? Are current drug laws realistic? We will return to these issues at the end of the chapter.

YOU are about to learn...

- how biological rhythms affect our physiology and performance.
- why you feel out of sync when you fly across time zones or change shifts at work.
- why some people get the winter blues.
- how culture and learning affect reports of PMS and estimates of its incidence.

Biological Rhythms: The Tides of Experience

Do an Internet search on "biorhythm charts," and you'll get hundreds of sites advertising them. Such charts supposedly foretell daily fluctuations in mood, alertness, and physical performance over your entire lifetime, solely on the basis of when you were born. They even warn you about days when you will be susceptible to accidents, errors, and illness. But you can save your money: Whenever researchers have taken the trouble to test such claims scientifically, they have found biorhythm charts to be utterly useless (Hines, 1998).

It *is* true, however, that the human body goes through dozens of ups and downs in physiological functioning over the course of a day, a week, a year, changes that are known as **biological rhythms**. A biological clock in our brains governs the waxing and waning of hormone levels, urine volume, blood pressure, and even the responsiveness of brain cells to stimulation. Biological rhythms are typically in tune with external time cues, such as changes in clock time, temperature, and daylight, but many rhythms continue to occur even in the absence of such cues; they are **endogenous**, or generated from within.

Circadian rhythms are biological rhythms that occur approximately every 24 hours. The best-known circadian rhythm is the sleep–wake cycle, but hundreds of others affect physiology and performance. For example, body temperature fluctuates about 1 degree centigrade each day, peaking, on average, in the late afternoon and hitting a low point, or trough, in the wee hours of the morning. Other rhythms occur less frequently than once a day—say, once a month, or once a season. In the animal world, seasonal rhythms are common. Birds migrate south in the fall, bears hibernate in the winter, and marine animals become active or inactive, depending on bimonthly changes in the tides. In human beings, the female menstrual cycle occurs every 28 days on average. And some rhythms occur more frequently than once a day, many of them on about a 90-minute cycle. These include physiological changes during sleep and (unless social customs intervene) stomach contractions, hormone levels, susceptibility to visual illusions, verbal and spatial performance, brain-wave responses during cognitive tasks, and daydreaming (Escera, Cilveti, & Grau, 1992; Klein & Armitage, 1979; Kripke, 1974; Lavie, 1976).

With a better understanding of our internal tempos, we may be able to design our days to take better advantage of our bodies' natural tempos.

Circadian Rhythms

Circadian rhythms exist in plants, animals, insects, and human beings. They reflect the adaptation of organisms to the many changes associated with the rotation of the earth on its axis, such as changes in light, air pressure, and temperature.

In most societies, clocks and other external time cues abound, and people's circadian rhythms become tied to them, following a strict 24-hour schedule. Therefore, to identify endogenous rhythms, scientists must isolate volunteers from sunlight, clocks, environmental sounds, and all other cues to time. Some hardy souls have spent weeks isolated in underground caves; usually, however, researchers have people live in specially designed rooms equipped with audio systems, comfortable furniture, and temperature controls.

When participants in these studies have been allowed to sleep, eat, and work whenever they wished, free of the tyranny of the timepiece, a few have lived a "day" that is much shorter or longer than 24 hours. If allowed to take daytime naps, however, most people soon settle into a day that averages about 24.3 hours (Moore, 1997). And when people are put on an artificial 28-hour day, in an environment free of all time cues, their body temperature and hormone levels follow a cycle that is very close to 24 hours—24.18 hours, to be precise (Czeisler et al., 1999). These rhythms are remarkably similar in length from one person to the next. For many people, alertness, like temperature, peaks in the late afternoon and falls to a low point in the very early morning (Lavie, 2001). ((•─ **Listen**

The Body's Clock Circadian rhythms are controlled by a biological clock, or overall coordinator, located in a tiny cluster of cells in the hypothalamus called the **suprachiasmatic nucleus (SCN)**. Neural pathways from special receptors in the back of the eye transmit information to the SCN and allow it

---

((•─ **Listen** to **Brain Time** on **mypsychlab.com**

biological rhythms Periodic, more or less regular fluctuations in a biological system; they may or may not have psychological implications.

endogenous Generated from within rather than by external cues.

circadian [sur-CAY-dee-un] rhythms Biological rhythms with a period (from peak to peak or trough to trough) of about 24 hours; from the Latin *circa*, "about," and *dies*, "a day."

suprachiasmatic [soo-pruh-kye-az-MAT-ick] nucleus (SCN) An area of the brain containing a biological clock that governs circadian rhythms.

Stefania Follini (left) spent four months in a New Mexico cave (above), 30 feet underground, as part of an Italian study on biological rhythms. Her only companions were a computer and two friendly mice. In the absence of clocks, natural light, or changes in temperature, she tended to stay awake for 20 to 25 hours and then sleep for 10. Because her days were longer than usual, when she emerged, she thought she had been in the cave for only two months.

to respond to changes in light and dark. The SCN then sends out messages that cause the brain and body to adapt to these changes. Other clocks also exist, scattered around the body, but for most circadian rhythms, the SCN is regarded as the master pacemaker.

The SCN regulates fluctuating levels of hormones and neurotransmitters, and they in turn provide feedback that affects the SCN's functioning. During the dark hours, one hormone regulated by the SCN, **melatonin**, is secreted by the pineal gland, deep within the brain. Melatonin induces sleep. When you go to bed in a darkened room, your melatonin level rises; when light fills your room in the morning, it falls. Melatonin, in turn, appears to help keep the biological clock in phase with the light–dark cycle (Haimov & Lavie, 1996; Lewy et al., 1992).

When the Clock Is Out of Sync Under normal conditions, the rhythms governed by the SCN are in phase with one another. Their peaks may occur at different times, but if you know when one rhythm peaks, you can predict fairly well when another will. It is a little like knowing the time in London if you know the time in New York. But when your normal routine changes, your circadian rhythms may be thrown out of phase. Such **internal desynchronization** often occurs when people take airplane flights across several time zones. Sleep and wake patterns usually adjust quickly, but temperature and hormone cycles can take several

melatonin A hormone secreted by the pineal gland; it is involved in the regulation of circadian rhythms.

internal desynchronization A state in which biological rhythms are not in phase with one another.

```
Regulates
         ────────▶
 SCN              Neurotransmitters,
         ◀────────    hormones
         Feedback   (e.g., melatonin)
```

Melatonin treatments have been used to regulate the disturbed sleep–wake cycles of blind people who lack light perception and whose melatonin production does not cycle normally (Sack & Lewy, 1997).

Travel can be exhausting, and jet lag makes it worse.

"IF WE EVER INTEND TO TAKE OVER THE WORLD, ONE THING WE'LL HAVE TO DO IS SYNCHRONIZE OUR BIOLOGICAL CLOCKS."

days to return to normal. The resulting jet lag affects energy level, mental skills, and motor coordination.

Internal desynchronization also occurs when workers must adjust to a new shift. Efficiency drops, the person feels tired and irritable, accidents become more likely, and sleep disturbances and digestive disorders may occur. For police officers, emergency room personnel, airline pilots, truck drivers, and operators of nuclear power plants, the consequences can be a matter of life and death. Night work itself is not necessarily a problem: With a schedule that always stays the same, even on weekends, people often adapt. However, many swing- and night-shift assignments are made on a rotating basis, so a worker's circadian rhythms never have a chance to resynchronize.

Some scientists hope eventually to help rotating-shift workers adjust more quickly by using melatonin, drugs, or other techniques to "reset the clock" (Revell & Eastman, 2005), but so far these techniques do not seem ready for prime time. A comprehensive government-sponsored review of melatonin research, which took the quality of the research into account, found little or no support for melatonin's effectiveness in treating shift-work desynchronization (or for ordinary insomnia and sleep disturbances associated with jet lag) (Buscemi et al., 2004). The best approach at present is to follow circadian principles by switching workers from one shift to another as infrequently as possible.

One reason that a simple cure for desynchronization has so far eluded scientists is that circadian rhythms are not perfectly regular in daily life. They can be affected by illness, stress, fatigue, excitement, exercise, drugs, mealtimes, and ordinary daily experiences. In research with mice, these rhythms have even been influenced by diet. Mice usually sleep during the day, but putting them on a high-fat diet altered the activity of genes involved in appetite and metabolism, and the mice began waking up and eating during the day (Kohsaka et al., 2007).

Further, circadian rhythms can differ greatly from individual to individual because of genetic differences. A variation in a single gene seems to be the reason that some people are early birds, bouncing out of bed at the crack of dawn, whereas others are night owls who do their best work late at night and can't be pried out of bed until noon (Archer et al., 2003). (Schools are not designed to accommodate night owls.) You may be able to learn about your own personal pulses through careful self-observation, and you may want to try putting that information to use when planning your daily schedule.

Moods and Long-Term Rhythms

According to Ecclesiastes, "To every thing there is a season, and a time for every purpose under heaven." Modern science agrees: Long-term cycles

Get Involved! Measuring Your Alertness Cycles

For at least three days, except when you are sleeping, keep an hourly record of your mental alertness level, using this five-point scale: 1 = extremely drowsy or mentally lethargic, 2 = somewhat drowsy or mentally lethargic, 3 = moderately alert, 4 = alert and efficient, 5 = extremely alert and efficient. Does your alertness level appear to follow a circadian rhythm, reaching a high point and a low point once every 24 hours? Or does it follow a shorter rhythm, rising and falling several times during the day? Are your cycles the same on weekends as during the week? Most important, how well does your schedule mesh with your natural fluctuations in alertness?

have been observed in everything from the threshold for tooth pain to conception rates. Folklore holds that our moods follow similar rhythms, particularly in response to seasonal changes and, in women, menstrual changes. But do they?

Does the Season Affect Moods?

Clinicians report that some people become depressed during particular seasons, typically winter, when periods of daylight are short. This pattern of depression has come to be known as **seasonal affective disorder (SAD)** (Rosenthal, 2006). During the winter months, patients with SAD report feelings of sadness, lethargy, drowsiness, and a craving for carbohydrates. To counteract the effects of sunless days, physicians and therapists often treat them with phototherapy, having them sit in front of bright fluorescent lights at specific times of the day, usually early in the morning. Some physicians also prescribe antidepressants.

Some therapists, generalizing from clinical cases of patients who report symptoms of SAD, believe the disorder may affect as much as 20 percent of the population, but this estimate is highly exaggerated. A national survey estimated the lifetime prevalence of major seasonal depression in the United States at only 0.4 percent, and the prevalence of major or minor seasonal depression at only 1 percent (Blazer, Kessler, & Swartz, 1998). Other estimates vary from about 1 to 9 percent, with the higher estimates usually associated with greater distance from the equator.

As for the effectiveness of light treatments, much of the research on this question has been flawed. A review of 173 light-treatment studies published between 1975 and 2003 found that only 20 studies—12 percent of the total—had used an acceptable design and suitable controls (Golden et al., 2005). But a meta-analysis of the data from those 20 studies did throw some light on the subject, so to speak. When people with SAD were exposed to either a brief period (e.g., 30 minutes) of bright light after waking or to light that slowly became brighter, simulating the dawn, their symptoms were in fact reduced. Light therapy even helped people with mild to moderate nonseasonal depression (see also Wirz-Justice et al., 2005).

Many researchers believe that the circadian rhythms of patients with SAD are out of sync—that, in essence, the individuals have a chronic form of jet lag (Lewy et al., 2006). Others argue that they must have some abnormality in the way they produce or respond to melatonin (Wehr et al., 2001). They may produce too much daytime melatonin in the winter, or their morning levels may not fall as

These young Norwegian women are receiving light therapy for seasonal affective disorder (SAD). This type of treatment has become popular and appears to be effective. But fewer people actually have SAD than is commonly thought, and the causes remain uncertain.

quickly as other people's. However, it is not clear why light therapy also appears to help some people with *non*seasonal depression. True cases of SAD may have a biological basis, but if so, the mechanism remains unclear. Keep in mind, too, that many people get the winter blues because they hate cold weather, are physically inactive, do not get outside much, or feel lonely during the winter holidays.

Does the Menstrual Cycle Affect Moods?

Controversy has persisted about another long-term rhythm, the female menstrual cycle, which occurs, on average, every 28 days. During the first half of this cycle, an increase in the hormone estrogen causes the lining of the uterus to thicken in preparation for a possible pregnancy. At mid-cycle, the ovaries release a mature egg, or ovum. Afterward, the ovarian sac that contained the egg begins to produce progesterone, which helps prepare the uterine lining to receive the egg. Then, if conception does not occur, estrogen and progesterone levels fall, the uterine lining sloughs off as the menstrual flow, and the cycle begins again. The interesting question for psychologists is whether these physical changes cause emotional or intellectual changes, as folklore and tradition would have us believe.

Most people are surprised to learn that it was not until the 1970s that a vague cluster of physical and emotional symptoms associated with the days preceding menstruation—including fatigue, headache, irritability, and depression—was packaged together and given a label: *premenstrual syndrome* ("PMS") (Parlee, 1994). Since then, most laypeople, doctors, and psychiatrists have assumed, uncritically, that many women "suffer" from PMS

seasonal affective disorder (SAD) A controversial disorder in which a person experiences depression during the winter and an improvement of mood in the spring.

Many women say they become more irritable or depressed premenstrually, and PMS remedies line the shelves of drugstores. But what does the evidence show about this so-called syndrome? How might attitudes and expectations affect reports of emotional symptoms? What happens when women report their daily moods and feelings to researchers without knowing that menstruation is being studied?

or from its supposedly more extreme and debilitating version, "premenstrual dysphoric disorder" (PMDD). What does the evidence actually show?

"PMS" symptoms have been reported most often in North America, western Europe, and Australia. In most tribal cultures, PMS has been virtually unknown; the concern has been with menstruation itself, which is often considered "unclean." In other cultures, women report physical symptoms but not emotional symptoms: For example, during the 1990s, research found that women in China reported fatigue, water retention, pain, and cold (American women rarely report cold), but not depression or irritability (Yu et al., 1996).

Many women do have physical symptoms associated with menstruation, including cramps, breast tenderness, and water retention, although women vary tremendously in this regard. And, of course, these physical symptoms can make some women feel grumpy or unhappy, just as pain can make men feel grumpy or unhappy. But emotional symptoms associated with menstruation—notably, irritability and depression—are pretty rare, which is why we put "PMS" in quotation marks. In reality, fewer than 5 percent of all women have such symptoms predictably over their cycles (Brooks-Gunn, 1986; Reid, 1991; Walker, 1994).

Then why do so many women think they have it? One possibility is that they tend to notice feelings of depression or irritability when these moods happen to occur premenstrually but overlook times when such moods are *absent* premenstrually. Or they may label symptoms that occur before a period as PMS ("I am irritable and cranky; I must be getting my period") and attribute the same symptoms

at other times of the month to a stressful day or a low grade on an English paper ("No wonder I'm irritable and cranky; I worked really hard on that paper and only got a C"). Some studies have encouraged biases in the reporting of premenstrual and menstrual symptoms by using questionnaires with gloomy titles such as "Menstrual Distress Questionnaire."

To get around these problems, some psychologists have polled women about their psychological and physical well-being without revealing the true purpose of the study (e.g., AuBuchon & Calhoun, 1985; Chrisler, 2000; Englander-Golden, Whitmore, & Dienstbier, 1978; Gallant et al., 1991; Hardie, 1997; Parlee, 1982; Rapkin, Chang, & Reading, 1988; Slade, 1984; Vila & Beech, 1980; Walker, 1994). Using double-blind procedures, they have had women report symptoms for a single day and have then gone back to see what phase of the menstrual cycle the women were in; or they have had women keep daily records over an extended period of time.

Some studies have also included a control group that is usually excluded from research on hormones and moods: men. In one such study, men and women filled out a symptom questionnaire that made no mention of menstruation (Callaghan et al., 2009). The proportion of men who met the criteria for PMDD, the more extreme version of "PMS," did not differ significantly from the proportion of women who did so!

In another study, researchers examined changes in the pleasantness, arousal level, and stability of moods over time by having 15 women on

"You've been charged with driving under the influence of testosterone."

For both sexes, the hormonal excuse rarely applies.

birth control pills, 12 normally cycling women, and 15 men rate their moods every day for 70 days (McFarlane, Martin, & Williams, 1988). None of the participants knew that the study had anything to do with menstruation; they thought it was a straightforward study of mood and health. After the 70 days were up, the women then recalled their average moods for each week and phase of their menstrual cycle. In their daily reports, normally cycling women reported more pleasant moods than the other participants during the menstrual phase and the follicular phase (when an egg is forming). But there were no differences at all during the premenstrual phase. In fact, women's moods fluctuated less over the menstrual cycle than over days of the week. Mondays, it seems, are tough for most of us. Moreover, women and men did not differ significantly in their emotional symptoms or the number of mood swings they reported at any time of the month, as you can see in Figure 5.1. In their retrospective reports, however, women *recalled* feeling more angry, irritable, and depressed in the premenstrual and menstrual phases than they had reported in their daily journals.

Other investigations have confirmed that most women do not have typical PMS symptoms even when they firmly believe that they do (Hardie, 1997; McFarlane & Williams, 1994). For example, women often say they cry more premenstrually than at other times, but an interesting Dutch study had women keep "crying diaries" and found no association at all between crying and phase of the menstrual cycle (van Tilburg, Becht, & Vingerhoets, 2003).

The key question in all this is whether premenstrual symptoms of any kind affect women's ability to work, think, study, do brain surgery, run for office, or run a business. In the laboratory, some researchers have found that women tend to be faster on tasks such as reciting words quickly or sorting objects manually before and after ovulation, when their estrogen is high (e.g., Saucier & Kimura, 1998). But empirical research has failed to establish any connection between phase of the menstrual cycle and work efficiency, problem solving, college exam scores, creativity, or any other behavior that matters in real life (Golub, 1992; Richardson, 1992). In a British study, female college students *said* that PMS interfered with their academic work, but the researchers could find no association between the number of symptoms reported by the students and their actual grades and test scores (Earl-Novell & Jessop, 2005). In the workplace, men and women report similar levels of stress, well-being, and ability to do the work required of

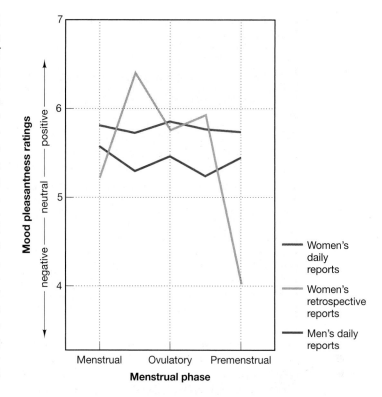

FIGURE 5.1
Mood Changes in Men and Women
In a study that challenged popular stereotypes about "PMS," college women and men recorded their moods daily for 70 days without knowing the purpose of the study. At the end of the study, the women thought their moods had been more negative premenstrually than during the rest of the month (green line), but their daily diaries showed otherwise (purple line). Both sexes experienced only moderate mood changes, and there were no significant differences between women and men at any time of the month (McFarlane, Martin, & Williams, 1988).

them—and it doesn't matter whether the women are premenstrual, menstrual, postmenstrual, or nonmenstrual (Hardie, 1997).

With the rise of globalization, the exporting of American media, and the influence of drug marketing worldwide, PMS symptoms are now increasing in cultures where previously there were no reports of them—from Mexico (Marvan et al., 1998) to Saudi Arabia (Rasheed & Al-Sowielem, 2003). The belief that PMS is universal, along with promotion of products to treat it, makes it more probable that women will interpret their premenstrual moods and symptoms as part of a syndrome that requires medicating.

In sum, the body only provides the clay for our symptoms and feelings. Learning and culture mold that clay by teaching us which symptoms are important or worrisome and which are not. Whether we are male or female, the impact of most of the changes associated with our biological rhythms depends on how we interpret and respond to them.

✔● **Study** and **Review** on **mypsychlab.com**

Quick Quiz

There are no hormonal excuses for avoiding this quiz.

1. The functioning of the biological clock governing circadian rhythms is affected by the hormone _____.

2. Jet lag occurs because of _____.

3. For most women, the days before menstruation are reliably associated with (a) depression, (b) irritability, (c) elation, (d) creativity, (e) none of these, (f) a and b.

4. A researcher tells male subjects that testosterone usually peaks in the morning and that it probably causes hostility. She then asks them to fill out a "HyperTestosterone Syndrome Hostility Survey" in the morning and again at night. Based on your knowledge of menstrual cycle findings, what do you think her study will reveal? How could she improve her study?

Answers:

1. melatonin 2. internal desynchronization 3. e 4. Because of the expectations that the men now have about testosterone, they may be biased to report more hostility in the morning. It would be better to keep them in the dark about the hypothesis and to measure their actual hormone levels at different points in the day, because individuals vary in their biological rhythms. Also, a control group of women could be added to see whether their hostility levels vary in the same way that men's do. Finally, the title on that questionnaire is pretty biased. A more neutral title, such as "Health and Mood Checklist," would be better.

◆ **YOU** are about to learn...

• the stages of sleep.

• what happens when we go too long without enough sleep.

• how sleep disorders disrupt normal sleep.

• the mental benefits of sleep.

The Rhythms of Sleep

Perhaps the most perplexing of all our biological rhythms is the one governing sleep and wakefulness. Sleep, after all, puts us at risk: Muscles that are usually ready to respond to danger relax, and senses grow dull. As the British psychologist Christopher Evans (1984) once noted, "The behavior patterns involved in sleep are glaringly, almost insanely, at odds with common sense." Then why is sleep such a profound necessity?

The Realms of Sleep

**Simulate Stages of Sleep** on **mypsychlab.com**

Let's start with some of the changes that occur in the brain during sleep. Until the early 1950s, little was known about these changes. Then a breakthrough occurred in the laboratory of physiologist Nathaniel Kleitman, who at the time was the only person in the world who had spent his entire career studying sleep. Kleitman had given one of his graduate students, Eugene Aserinsky, the tedious task of finding out whether the slow, rolling eye movements that characterize the onset of sleep continue throughout the night. To both men's surprise, eye movements

rapid eye movement (REM) sleep Sleep periods characterized by eye movement, loss of muscle tone, and vivid dreams.

did occur but they were rapid, not slow (Aserinsky & Kleitman, 1955). Using the electroencephalograph (EEG) to measure the brain's electrical activity (see Chapter 4), these researchers, along with another of Kleitman's students, William Dement, were able to correlate the rapid eye movements with changes in sleepers' brain-wave patterns (Dement, 1992). Adult volunteers were soon spending their nights sleeping in laboratories, while scientists measured changes in their brain activity, muscle tension, breathing, and other physiological responses.

As a result of this research, today we know that during sleep, periods of **rapid eye movement (REM)** alternate with periods of fewer eye movements, or *non-REM (NREM) sleep*, in a cycle that recurs every 90 minutes or so. The REM periods last from a few minutes to as long as an hour, averaging about 20 minutes in length. Whenever they begin, the pattern of electrical activity from the sleeper's brain changes to resemble that of alert wakefulness. Non-REM periods are themselves divided into distinct stages, each associated with a particular brain-wave pattern (see Figure 5.2). ◆ **Simulate**

When you first climb into bed, close your eyes, and relax, your brain emits bursts of *alpha waves*. On an EEG recording, alpha waves have a regular, slow rhythm and high amplitude (height). Gradually, these waves slow down even further, and you drift into the Land of Nod, passing through four stages, each deeper than the previous one:

Stage 1. Your brain waves become small and irregular, and you feel yourself drifting on the edge of consciousness, in a state of light sleep. If awakened, you may recall fantasies or a few visual images.

Stage 2. Your brain emits occasional short bursts of rapid, high-peaking waves called *sleep spindles*. Minor noises probably won't disturb you.

Stage 3. In addition to the waves that are characteristic of Stage 2, your brain occasionally emits *delta waves*, very slow waves with very high peaks. Your breathing and pulse have slowed down, your muscles are relaxed, and you are hard to waken.

Stage 4. Delta waves have now largely taken over, and you are in deep sleep. It will probably take vigorous shaking or a loud noise to awaken you. Oddly, though, if you walk in your sleep, this is when you are likely to do so. No one yet knows what causes sleepwalking, which occurs more often in children than adults, but it seems to involve unusual patterns of delta-wave activity (Bassetti et al., 2000).

This sequence of stages takes about 30 to 45 minutes. Then you move back up the ladder from Stage 4 to 3 to 2 to 1. At that point, about 70 to 90 minutes after the onset of sleep, something peculiar happens. Stage 1 does not turn into drowsy wakefulness, as one might expect. Instead, your brain begins to emit long bursts of very rapid, somewhat irregular waves. Your heart rate increases, your blood pressure rises, and your breathing gets faster and more irregular. Small twitches in your face and fingers may occur. In men, the penis may become somewhat erect as vascular tissue relaxes and blood fills the genital area faster than it exits. In women, the clitoris may enlarge and vaginal lubrication may increase. At the same time, most skeletal muscles go limp, preventing your aroused brain from producing physical movement. You have entered the realm of REM.

Because the brain is extremely active while the body is entirely inactive, REM sleep has also been called "paradoxical sleep." During these periods, vivid dreams are most likely to occur. People report dreams when they are awakened from non-REM sleep, too; in one study, dream reports occurred 82 percent of the time when sleepers were awakened during REM sleep, but they also occurred 51 percent of the time when people were awakened during non-REM sleep (Foulkes, 1962). Non-REM dreams, however, tend to be shorter, less vivid, and more realistic than REM dreams, except in the hour or so before a person wakes up in the morning.

Occasionally, as the sleeper wakes up, a curious phenomenon occurs. The person emerges from REM sleep before the muscle paralysis characteristic of that stage has entirely disappeared, and becomes aware of an inability to move. About 30 percent of

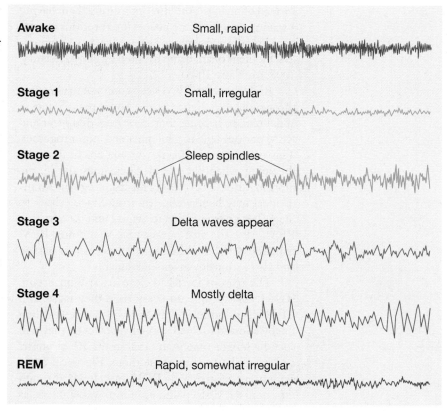

Awake	Small, rapid
Stage 1	Small, irregular
Stage 2	Sleep spindles
Stage 3	Delta waves appear
Stage 4	Mostly delta
REM	Rapid, somewhat irregular

FIGURE 5.2
Brain-Wave Patterns During Wakefulness and Sleep
Most types of brain waves are present throughout sleep, but different ones predominate at different stages.

the general population has experienced at least one such episode, and about 5 percent have had a "waking dream" in this state. Their eyes are open, but what they "see" are dreamlike hallucinations, most often shadowy figures. They may even "see" a ghost or space alien sitting on their bed or hovering in a hallway, a scary image that they would regard as perfectly normal it if were part of a midnight nightmare.

Thinking Critically about Waking Dream Images

Because cats sleep up to 80 percent of the time, it is easy to catch them in the various stages of slumber. A cat in non-REM sleep (left) remains upright, but during the REM phase (right), its muscles go limp and it flops onto its side.

Instead of saying, "Ah! How interesting! I am having a waking dream!" some people interpret this experience literally and come to believe they have been visited by aliens or are being haunted by ghosts (Clancy, 2005; McNally, 2003).

REM and non-REM sleep continue to alternate throughout the night. As the hours pass, Stages 3 and 4 tend to become shorter or even disappear and REM periods tend to get longer and closer together. This pattern may explain why you are likely to be dreaming when the alarm clock goes off in the morning. But the cycles are far from regular. An individual may bounce directly from Stage 4 back to Stage 2 or go from REM to Stage 2 and then back to REM. Also, the time between REM and non-REM is highly variable, differing from person to person and also within any given individual.

The reasons for REM sleep are still uncertain. If you wake people up every time they lapse into REM sleep, nothing dramatic will happen. When finally allowed to sleep normally, however, they will spend a longer time than usual in the REM phase, and it will be hard to rouse them. Electrical brain activity associated with REM may burst through into non-REM sleep and even into wakefulness, as if the person is making up for something he or she had been deprived of.

Some researchers have proposed that this "something" is connected with dreaming, but that idea has problems. For one thing, in rare cases, brain-damaged patients have lost the capacity to dream, yet they continue to show the normal sleep stages, including REM (Bischof & Bassetti, 2004). Moreover, although nearly all mammals experience REM sleep—the only known exceptions are the bottlenose dolphin and the porpoise—it seems unlikely that rats and anteaters have the cognitive abilities required to construct dreams. Moles, which can hardly move their eyes at all, nonetheless show EEG patterns associated with REM sleep. As William Domhoff, a prominent dream researcher, told us, "no one, but no one, has been able to come up with a convincing explanation for REM sleep."

Why We Sleep

A leading sleep scientist, Jerome Siegel (2009), observes that sleep falls along a continuum of states that range from one extreme, hibernation (bears, bats, and many rodents), to continuous activity for significant lengths of time (birds don't sleep while they are migrating, walruses may stop sleeping for days at a time, and whale mothers and their calves remain awake for several weeks after birth). The reason for this variation in sleep patterns, he

Whatever your age, sometimes the urge to sleep is irresistible, especially because in fast-paced modern societies, many people do not get as much sleep as they need. Late hours or inadequate sleep won't do anything for your grade point average. Daytime drowsiness can interfere with reaction time, concentration, and the ability to learn.

argues, has to do with which strategy is beneficial for the species. Lions sleep long and deeply, whereas their favorite prey, giraffes, have one of the lowest recorded sleep durations—giraffes had better not sleep deeply if they are going to survive!

Among species that do sleep, such as human beings, sleep increases efficiency, for example by decreasing muscle tone and brain and body metabolism during periods of inactivity. This process, says Siegel (2009), is "analogous to turning out the lights when you leave a room." Sleep provides a time-out period, so that the body can eliminate waste products from muscles, repair cells, conserve or replenish energy stores, strengthen the immune system, and recover abilities lost during the day. When we do not get enough sleep, our bodies operate abnormally. Although most people can still get along reasonably well after a day or two of sleeplessness, sleep deprivation that lasts for four days or longer becomes uncomfortable and soon becomes unbearable. (This is why forced sleeplessness is an especially cruel weapon of torturers.)

The Mental Consequences of Sleeplessness

Sleep is also necessary for normal mental functioning. Chronic sleep deprivation increases levels of the stress hormone cortisol, which may damage or impair brain cells that are necessary for learning and memory (Leproult, Copinschi et al., 1997). Also, new brain cells may either fail to develop or may mature abnormally (Guzman-Marin et al., 2005). Perhaps in part because of such damage, after the loss of even a single night's sleep, mental flexibility, attention, and creativity all suffer. After several days of staying awake, people may even begin to have hallucinations and delusions (Dement, 1978).

Of course, sleep deprivation rarely reaches that point, but people do frequently suffer from milder sleep problems. According to the National Sleep Foundation, about 10 percent of adults are plagued by difficulty in falling or staying asleep. The causes of their insomnia include worry and anxiety, psychological problems, physical problems such as arthritis, and irregular or overly demanding work and study schedules. In addition, many drugs interfere with the normal progression of sleep stages—not just the ones containing caffeine, but also alcohol and some tranquilizers. The result can be grogginess and lethargy the next day.

Another cause of daytime sleepiness is **sleep apnea**, a disorder in which breathing periodically stops for a few moments, causing the person to choke and gasp. Breathing may cease hundreds of

times a night, often without the person knowing it. Sleep apnea is seen most often in older males and overweight people but also occurs in others. It has several causes, from blockage of air passages to failure of the brain to control respiration correctly. Over time it can cause high blood pressure and irregular heartbeat; it may gradually erode a person's health, and is associated with a shortened life expectancy (Young et al., 2008).

With **narcolepsy**, an even more serious disorder that often develops in the teenage years, an individual is subject to irresistible and unpredictable daytime attacks of sleepiness lasting from 5 to 30 minutes. When the person lapses into sleep, he or she is likely to fall immediately into the REM stage. A quarter of a million people in the United States suffer from this condition, many, again, without knowing it. Narcolepsy seems to be caused by the degeneration of neurons in the hypothalamus, possibly due to an autoimmune malfunction or genetic abnormalities (Lin, Hungs, & Mignot, 2001; Mieda et al., 2004).

Other disorders also disrupt sleep, including some that cause odd or dangerous behavior. In **REM behavior disorder**, the muscle paralysis associated with REM sleep does not occur, and the sleeper (most often an older male) becomes physically active, often acting out a dream without any awareness of what he is doing (Schenck & Mahowald, 2002). If he is dreaming about football, he may try to "tackle" a piece of furniture; if he is dreaming about a kitten, he may try to pet it. Other people may consider this disorder amusing, but it is no joke. Sufferers may hurt themselves or others, and they have an increased risk of later developing Parkinson's disease and dementia (Postuma et al., 2008).

However, the most common cause of daytime sleepiness is the most obvious one—not getting enough sleep. Some people do fine on relatively few hours, but most adults need more than six hours and many adolescents need ten hours for optimal performance. The National Transportation Safety Board estimates that drowsiness is

sleep apnea A disorder in which breathing briefly stops during sleep, causing the person to choke and gasp and momentarily awaken.

narcolepsy A sleep disorder involving sudden and unpredictable daytime attacks of sleepiness or lapses into REM sleep.

REM behavior disorder A disorder in which the muscle paralysis that normally occurs during REM sleep is absent or incomplete, and the sleeper is able to act out his or her dreams.

"Judith is someone who needs her sleep."

consolidation The process by which a memory becomes durable and stable.

involved in 100,000 vehicle accidents a year, causing 1,500 road deaths and 71,000 injuries. Sleep deprivation also leads to accidents and errors in the workplace, a concern especially for first-year doctors doing their medical residency. In the United States, federal law limits work hours for airline pilots, truck drivers, and operators of nuclear plants, but medical residents still often work 24- to 30-hour shifts (Landrigan et al., 2008).

Don't doze off as we tell you this, but lack of sleep has also been linked to lower grades. Researchers had a group of elementary and middle school students go to sleep at their normal time for a week, earlier than usual for a week, and much later than usual for a week. Their teachers, who were blind to which condition a child was in during any given week, reported more academic and attention problems when the children stayed up late (Fallone et al., 2005). These results probably apply to high school and college students as well. ◉─⎡**Watch**

◉─⎡**Watch How to Get a Good Night's Sleep** on mypsychlab.com

The Mental Benefits of Sleep Just as sleepiness can interfere with good mental functioning, a good night's sleep can promote it, and not just because you are well rested. In a classic study conducted nearly a century ago, students who slept for eight hours after learning lists of nonsense syllables retained them better than students who went about

their usual business (Jenkins & Dallenbach, 1924). For years, researchers attributed this result to the lack of new information coming into the brain during sleep, information that could interfere with already-established memories. Today, however, many scientists believe that sleep plays a more active role by contributing to **consolidation**, in which synaptic changes associated with recently stored memories become durable and stable (Racsmány, Conway, & Demeter, 2010). One theory is that during sleep, the neural changes involved in a recent memory are reactivated, making those changes more permanent (Rasch et al., 2007).

Improvements in memory have been associated most closely with REM sleep and slow-wave sleep (Stages 3 and 4), and with memory for specific motor and perceptual skills. In one study, when people or animals learned a perceptual task and were allowed to get normal REM sleep, their memory for the task was better the next day, even when they had been awakened during non-REM periods. When they were deprived of REM sleep, however, their memories were impaired (Karni et al., 1994). But sleep also seems to strengthen other kinds of memories, including the recollection of events, locations, and facts (Rasch & Born, 2008). Emotional memories, especially, are improved with sleep. When people look at emotionally arousing scenes in the morning or evening and are then tested for their memory of the materials after 12 hours of daytime wakefulness or normal nighttime sleep, those tested after sleeping rather than wakefulness recall the emotional scenes more reliably than the neutral ones (Hu, Stylos-Allan, & Walker, 2006). They also do better at remembering negative emotional scenes than other participants do (Payne et al., 2008). (See Figure 5.3.)

If sleep enhances memory, perhaps it also enhances problem solving, which relies on information stored in memory. To find out, German researchers gave volunteers a math test that required them to use two mathematical rules to generate one string of numbers from another and to deduce the final digit in the new sequence as quickly as possible. The volunteers were not told about a hidden shortcut that would enable them to calculate the final digit almost immediately. One group was trained in the evening and then got to snooze for eight hours before returning to the problem. Another group was also trained in the evening but then stayed awake for eight hours before coming back to the problem. A third group was trained in the morning and stayed awake all day, as they normally would, before taking the test. Those people who got the nighttime sleep were nearly three times likelier

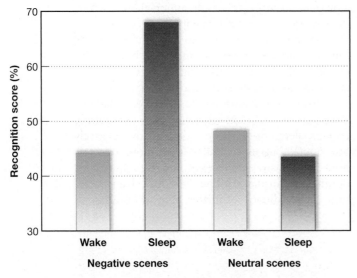

FIGURE 5.3

Sleep and Consolidation in Memory
When college students studied neutral scenes (e.g., an ordinary car) and emotionally negative scenes (e.g., a car totaled in an accident), sleep affected how well they later recognized the objects in the scenes. Students who studied the scenes in the evening and then got a night's sleep before being tested did better at recognizing emotional objects than did those who studied the scenes in the morning and were tested after 12 hours of daytime wakefulness (Payne et al., 2008).

to discover the hidden shortcut as those in the other two groups (Wagner et al., 2004).

Researchers are not unanimous on the role of sleep in learning; some studies have failed to find that sleep improves memory (Vertes & Siegel, 2005). In one study, researchers who believe that sleep promotes consolidation found, to their surprise, that depriving people of REM sleep actually *improved* memory for motor and perceptual skills involving finger tapping and mirror tracing (Rasch et al., 2009). Of course, not many of us have much occasion to use these particular skills!

Nonetheless, the evidence for the importance of sleep in human memory and problem solving is mounting (Cai et al., 2009). The underlying biology may involve the formation of new synaptic connections in the brain and also the weakening of connections that are no longer needed (Donlea, Ramanan, & Shaw, 2009; Gilestro, Tononi, & Cirelli, 2009). In other words, we sleep to remember, but we also sleep to forget, so that the brain will have space and energy for new learning. Remember that the next time you are tempted to pull an all-nighter. Even a quick nap may help your mental functioning and increase your ability to put together separately learned facts in new ways (Lau, Alger, & Fishbein, 2008; Mednick et al., 2002). Sleep on it.

✓●─Study and Review on mypsychlab.com

Quick Quiz

Now wake up and take this quiz.

A. Match each term with the appropriate phrase:

1. REM periods
2. alpha
3. Stage 4 sleep
4. Stage 1 sleep

a. delta waves and sleepwalking
b. irregular brain waves and light sleep
c. relaxed but awake
d. active brain but inactive muscles

B. Sleep is necessary for normal (a) physical and mental functioning, (b) mental functioning but not physical functioning, (c) physical functioning but not mental functioning.

C. *True or false:* Most people need more than six hours of sleep a night.

D. *True or false:* Only REM sleep has been associated with dreaming and memory consolidation.

Answers:

A.1 d 2 c 3 a 4 b   B. a   C. true   D. false

YOU are about to learn...

• Freud's theory that dreams are the "royal road to the unconscious."

• how dreams might be related to your current problems and concerns.

• how dreams might be related to ordinary daytime thoughts.

• how dreams could be caused by meaningless brain-stem signals.

Exploring the Dream World

For years, researchers believed that everyone dreams, and indeed most people who claim they never have dreams will report them if they are awakened during REM sleep. There are rare cases of people who apparently do not dream at all (Pagel, 2003; Solms, 1997). Most, but not all, of these individuals have suffered some brain injury.

In dreaming, the focus of attention is inward, though occasionally an external event, such as a wailing siren, can influence the dream's content. While a dream is in progress, it may be vivid or vague, terrifying or peaceful. It may also seem to make perfect sense—until you wake up and recall it as illogical, bizarre, and disjointed. Although most of us are unaware of our bodies or where we are while we are dreaming, some people say that they occasionally have **lucid dreams**, in which they know they are dreaming and feel as though they are conscious (LaBerge & Levitan, 1995). A few even claim that they can control the action in these dreams, much as a scriptwriter decides what will happen in a movie, although this ability is probably uncommon.

lucid dreams Dreams in which the dreamer is aware of dreaming.

Why do the images in dreams arise at all? Why doesn't the brain just rest, switching off all thoughts and images and launching us into a coma? Why, instead, do we spend our nights taking a chemistry exam, reliving an old love affair, flying through the air, or fleeing from dangerous strangers or animals in the fantasy world of our dreams? We will consider four leading explanations and then evaluate them. ◉—|Watch

|Watch **Lucid Dreaming** on mypsychlab.com

Dreams as Unconscious Wishes

One of the first psychological theorists to take dreams seriously was Sigmund Freud, the founder of psychoanalysis. After analyzing many of his patients' dreams and some of his own, Freud (1900/1953) concluded that our nighttime fantasies provide insight into desires, motives, and conflicts of which we are unaware. Because dreams allow us to express our unconscious wishes and desires, which are often sexual or violent in nature, they provide a "royal road to the unconscious."

According to Freud, every dream is meaningful, no matter how absurd the images might seem. But if a dream's message arouses anxiety, the rational part of the mind must disguise and distort it. Otherwise, the dream would intrude into consciousness and waken the dreamer. In dreams, therefore, one person is often disguised as another: A brother may be disguised as a father or may even be represented by several different characters. Similarly, thoughts and objects are translated into symbolic images. A penis may be disguised as a snake, umbrella, or dagger; a vagina as a tunnel or cave; and the human body as a house. Because reality is distorted in such ways, a dream resembles a psychosis, a severe mental disturbance; each night, we

must become temporarily delusional so that our anxiety will be kept at bay and our sleep will not be disrupted.

To understand a dream, said Freud, we must distinguish its *manifest content*, the aspects of it that we consciously experience during sleep and may remember upon wakening, from its *latent* (hidden) *content*, the unconscious wishes and thoughts being expressed symbolically. Freud warned against the simpleminded translation of symbols (the kind that today often turn up in magazines and pop-psych books promising to tell you exactly what your dreams mean). Each dream, said Freud, should be analyzed in the context of the dreamer's waking life, as well as the person's associations to the dream's contents. Not everything in a dream is symbolic. Sometimes, Freud cautioned, "A cigar is only a cigar."

Dreams as Efforts to Deal with Problems

Another explanation holds that dreams reflect the ongoing *conscious* preoccupations of waking life, such as concerns over relationships, work, sex, or health (Cartwright, 2010; Hall, 1953a, 1953b). In this *problem-focused approach* to dreaming, the symbols and metaphors in a dream do not disguise its true meaning; they convey it. Psychologist Gayle Delaney told of a woman who dreamed she was swimming underwater. The woman's 8-year-old son was on her back, his head above the water. Her husband was supposed to take a picture of them, but for some reason he wasn't doing it, and she was starting to feel as if she were going to drown. To Delaney, the message was obvious: The woman was "drowning" under the responsibilities of child care and her husband wasn't "getting the picture" (in Dolnick, 1990).

The problem-focused explanation of dreaming is supported by findings that dreams are more likely to contain material related to a person's current concerns—such as a breakup or exams—than chance would predict (Cartwright et al., 2006; Domhoff, 1996). Among college students, who are often worried about grades and tests, test-anxiety dreams are common: The dreamer is unprepared for or unable to finish an exam, or shows up for the wrong exam, or can't find the room where the exam is being given. (Sound familiar?) For their part, instructors sometimes dream that they have left their lecture notes at home, or that they are expected to give a lecture in a foreign language on a subject they know nothing about. Traumatic experiences can also affect people's dreams. In a cross-cultural study in which children kept dream diaries for a

CAST OF DREAM

THE MONSTER . . . . . . YOUR FATHER
KIND WOMAN . . . . . . YOUR MOTHER
POLICEMAN . . . . YOUR ANALYST
FIRST STRANGER . . . . YOUR BROTHER
SECOND STRANGER . . YOUR SISTER
LITTLE BOY . . . . . YOU

Dana Fradon

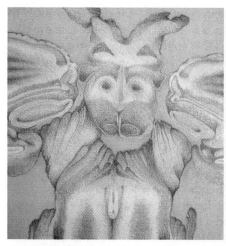
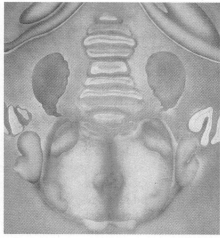
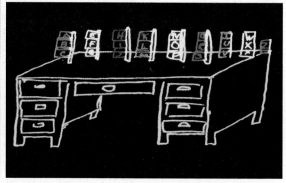

These drawings from dream journals show that the images in dreams can be either abstract or literal. In either case, the dream may reflect a person's concerns, problems, and interests. The two fanciful paintings (left and center) represent the dreams of a person who worked all day long with brain tissue, which the drawings rather resemble. The desk was sketched in 1939 by a scientist to illustrate his dream about a mechanical device for instantly retrieving quotations—a sort of early desktop computer!

week, Palestinian children living in neighborhoods under threat of violence reported more themes of persecution and violence than did Finnish or Palestinian children living in peaceful environments (Punamaeki & Joustie, 1998).

Some psychologists believe that dreams not only reflect our waking concerns but also provide us with an opportunity to resolve them (Cartwright, 2010). In people suffering from the grief of divorce, recovery is related to a particular pattern of dreaming: The first dream of the night often comes sooner than it ordinarily would, lasts longer, and is more emotional and story-like. Depressed people's dreams tend to become less negative and more positive as the night wears on, and this pattern, too, predicts recovery (Cartwright et al., 1998). The researchers concluded that getting through a crisis or a rough period in life takes "time, good friends, good genes, good luck, and a good dream system."

Dreams as Thinking

Like the problem-focused approach, the *cognitive approach* to dreaming emphasizes current concerns, but it makes no claims about problem solving during sleep. In this view, dreaming is simply a modification of the cognitive activity that goes on when we are awake. In dreams, we construct reasonable simulations of the real world, drawing on the same kinds of memories, knowledge, metaphors, and assumptions about the world that we do when we are not sleeping (Antrobus, 1991, 2000; Domhoff, 2003; Foulkes, 1999). Thus, the content of our dreams may include

thoughts, concepts, and scenarios that may or may not be related to our daily problems. We are most likely to dream about our families, friends, studies, jobs, or recreational interests—topics that also occupy our waking thoughts.

In the cognitive view, the brain is doing the same kind of work during dreams as it does when we are awake; indeed, parts of the cerebral cortex involved in perceptual and cognitive processing during the waking hours are highly active during dreaming. The difference is that when we are asleep we are cut off from sensory input and feedback from the world and from our bodily movements; the only input to the brain is its own output. That is why our dreaming thoughts tend to be more unfocused and diffuse than our waking ones—unless of course we're daydreaming!

This view predicts that if a person could be totally cut off from all external stimulation while awake, mental activity would be much like that during dreaming, with the same hallucinatory quality. In Chapter 6, we will see that this is, in fact, the case. The cognitive approach also predicts that as cognitive abilities and brain connections mature during childhood, dreams should change in nature, and they do. Toddlers may not dream at all in the sense that adults do. And although young children may experience visual images during sleep, their cognitive limitations keep them from creating true narratives until age 7 or 8 (Foulkes, 1999). Their dreams are infrequent and tend to be bland and static, often about everyday things ("I saw a dog; I was sitting"). But as they grow up, their dreams gradually become more and more intricate and story-like.

activation–synthesis theory The theory that dreaming results from the cortical synthesis and interpretation of neural signals triggered by activity in the lower part of the brain.

Dreams as Interpreted Brain Activity

A fourth approach to dreaming, the **activation–synthesis theory**, draws heavily on physiological research. According to this explanation, first proposed by psychiatrist J. Allan Hobson (1988, 1990), dreams are not "children of an idle brain," as Shakespeare called them. Rather, they are largely the result of neurons firing spontaneously in the pons (in the lower part of the brain) during REM sleep. These neurons control eye movement, gaze, balance, and posture, and they send messages to sensory and motor areas of the cortex responsible for visual processing and voluntary action during wakefulness.

According to the activation–synthesis theory, the signals originating in the pons have no psychological meaning in themselves. But the cortex tries to make sense of them by *synthesizing*, or integrating, them with existing knowledge and memories to produce some sort of coherent interpretation. This is just what the cortex does when signals come from sense organs during ordinary wakefulness. The idea that one part of the brain interprets what has gone on in other parts, whether you are awake or asleep, is consistent with many modern theories of how the brain works (see Chapter 4).

ACTIVATION–SYNTHESIS THEORY OF DREAMS

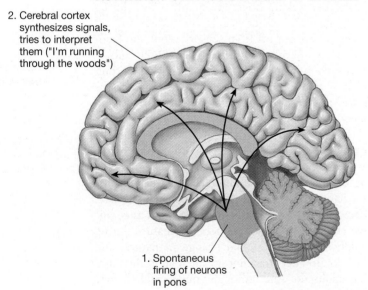

2. Cerebral cortex synthesizes signals, tries to interpret them ("I'm running through the woods")

1. Spontaneous firing of neurons in pons

When neurons fire in the part of the brain that handles balance, for instance, the cortex may generate a dream about falling. When signals occur that would ordinarily produce running, the cortex may manufacture a dream about being chased. Because the signals from the pons occur randomly, the cortex's interpretation—the dream—is likely to be incoherent and confusing. And because the cortical neurons that control the initial storage of new memories are turned off during sleep, we typically forget our dreams upon waking unless we write them down or immediately recount them to someone else.

Since Hobson's original formulation, he and his colleagues have added further details and modifications (Hobson, Pace-Schott, & Stickgold, 2000). The brain stem, they say, sets off responses in emotional and visual parts of the brain. At the same time, brain regions that handle logical thought and sensations from the external world shut down. These changes could account for the fact that dreams are often emotionally charged, hallucinatory, and illogical.

In this view, wishes do not cause dreams; brain mechanisms do. Dream content, says Hobson (2002), may be "as much dross as gold, as much cognitive trash as treasure, and as much informational noise as a signal of something." But that does not mean dreams are *always* meaningless. Hobson (1988) has argued that the brain "is so inexorably bent upon the quest for meaning that it attributes and even creates meaning when there is little or none to be found in the data it is asked to process." By studying these attributed meanings, you can learn about your unique perceptions, conflicts, and concerns—not by trying to dig below the surface of the dream, as Freud would, but by examining the surface itself. Or you can relax and enjoy the nightly entertainment that dreams provide.

Evaluating Dream Theories

How are we to evaluate these attempts to explain dreaming? All four approaches account for some of the evidence, but each one also has its drawbacks.

Most psychologists today accept Freud's notion that dreams are more than incoherent ramblings of the mind and that they can have psychological meaning. But most also consider the traditional psychoanalytic interpretations of dreams to be far-fetched. No reliable rules exist for interpreting the supposedly latent content of dreams, and there is no objective way to know whether a particular interpretation is correct. Nor is there any convincing empirical support for most of Freud's specific claims. Freudian interpretations are common in popular books and on the Internet, but they reflect the writers' imaginations, not your life.

Thinking Critically about Dream Theories

Get Involved! Keep a Dream Diary

It can be fun to record your dreams. Keep a notebook or a recorder by your bedside. As soon as you wake up in the morning (or if you awaken during the night while dreaming), record everything you can remember about your dreams, even short fragments. After you have collected several dreams, see which theory or theories discussed in this chapter seem to best explain them. Do your dreams contain any recurring themes? Do you think they provide any clues to your current problems, activities, or concerns? (By the way, if you are curious about other people's dreams, you can find lots of them online at www.dreambank.net.)

As for dreaming as a way of solving problems, it seems pretty clear that some dreams are related to current worries and concerns, but skeptics doubt that people can actually solve problems or resolve conflicts while sound asleep (Blagrove, 1996; Squier & Domhoff, 1998). Dreams, they say, merely give expression to our problems. The insights into those problems that people attribute to dreaming could be occurring after they wake up and have a chance to think about what is troubling them.

The activation–synthesis theory has also come in for criticism (Domhoff, 2003). Not all dreams are as disjointed or as bizarre as the theory predicts; in fact, many tell a coherent, if fanciful, story. Moreover, the activation–synthesis approach does not account well for dreaming that goes on outside of REM sleep. Some neuropsychologists emphasize different brain mechanisms involved in dreams, and many believe that dreams do reflect a person's goals and desires.

Finally, the cognitive approach to dreams is fairly new, so some of its claims remain to be tested against neurological and cognitive evidence. At present, however, it is a leading contender because it incorporates many elements of other theories and fits what we currently know about waking cognition and cognitive development.

Perhaps it will turn out that different kinds of dreams have different purposes and origins. We all know from experience that some of our dreams seem to be related to daily problems, some are vague and incoherent, and some are anxiety dreams that occur when we are worried or depressed. But whatever the source of the images in our sleeping brains may be, we need to be cautious about interpreting our own dreams or anyone else's. A study of people in India, South Korea, and the United States showed that individuals are biased and self-serving in their dream interpretations, accepting those that fit in with their preexisting beliefs or needs and rejecting those that do not. For example, they will give more weight to a dream in which God commands them to take a year off to travel the world than one in which God commands them to take a year off to work in a leper colony (Morewedge & Norton, 2009). Our biased interpretations may tell us more about ourselves than do our actual dreams. ✳ Explore

 **Explore** **Theories of Dreaming** on mypsychlab.com

✓ **Study** and **Review** on mypsychlab.com

Quick Quiz

See if you can dream up an answer to this question.

In his dreams, Andy is an infant crawling through a dark tunnel looking for something he has lost. Which theory of dreams would be most receptive to each of the following explanations?

1. Andy recently found a valuable watch he had misplaced.
2. While Andy was sleeping, neurons in his pons that would ordinarily stimulate parts of the brain involved in leg-muscle movements were active.
3. Andy has repressed an early sexual attraction to his mother; the tunnel symbolizes her vagina.
4. Andy has broken up with his lover and is working through the emotional loss.

Answers:

1. the cognitive approach (the dreamer is thinking about a recent experience) 2. the activation–synthesis theory 3. psychoanalytic theory 4. the problem-focused approach

YOU are about to learn...

- common misconceptions about what hypnosis can do.
- the legitimate uses of hypnosis in psychology and medicine.
- two ways of explaining what happens during hypnosis.

The Riddle of Hypnosis

For many years, stage hypnotists, "past-lives channelers," and some psychotherapists have been reporting that they can "age regress" hypnotized people to earlier years or even earlier centuries. Some therapists claim that hypnosis helps their patients accurately retrieve long-buried memories, and a few even claim that hypnosis has helped their patients recall alleged abductions by extraterrestrials. What are we to make of all this?

Hypnosis is a procedure in which a practitioner suggests changes in the sensations, perceptions, thoughts, feelings, or behavior of the subject (Kirsch & Lynn, 1995). The hypnotized person, in turn, tries to alter his or her cognitive processes in accordance with the hypnotist's suggestions (Nash & Nadon, 1997). Hypnotic suggestions typically involve performance of an action ("Your arm will slowly rise"), an inability to perform an act ("You will be unable to bend your arm"), or a distortion of normal perception or memory ("You will feel no pain," "You will forget being hypnotized until I give you a signal"). People usually report that their response to a suggestion feels involuntary, as if it happened without their willing it.

To induce hypnosis, the hypnotist typically suggests that the person being hypnotized feels relaxed, is getting sleepy, and feels the eyelids getting heavier and heavier. In a singsong or monotonous voice, the hypnotist assures the subject that he or she is sinking "deeper and deeper." Sometimes the hypnotist has the person concentrate on a color or a small object, or on a particular bodily sensation. People who have been hypnotized report that the focus of attention turns outward, toward the hypnotist's voice. They sometimes compare the experience to being totally absorbed in a good movie or favorite piece of music. The hypnotized person almost always remains fully aware of what is happening and remembers the experience later unless explicitly instructed to forget it. Even then, the memory can be restored by a prearranged signal.

Because hypnosis has been used for everything from parlor tricks and stage shows to medical and psychological treatments, it is important to understand just what this procedure can and cannot

hypnosis A procedure in which the practitioner suggests changes in a subject's sensations, perceptions, thoughts, feelings, or behavior.

achieve. We will begin with the major findings on hypnosis and then consider two leading explanations of hypnotic effects.

The Nature of Hypnosis

Thousands of controlled laboratory and clinical studies support the following conclusions about hypnosis (Kirsch & Lynn, 1995; Nash, 2001; Nash & Nadon, 1997):

1 **Hypnotic responsiveness depends more on the efforts and qualities of the person being hypnotized than on the skill of the hypnotist.** Some people are more responsive to hypnosis than others, but why they are is unknown. Surprisingly, hypnotic susceptibility is unrelated to general personality traits such as gullibility, trust, submissiveness, or conformity (Nash & Nadon, 1997). And it is only weakly related to the ability to become easily absorbed in activities and the world of imagination (Council, Kirsch, & Grant, 1996; Nash & Nadon, 1997).

2 **Hypnotized people cannot be forced to do things against their will.** Like drunkenness, hypnosis can be used to justify letting go of inhibitions ("I know this looks silly, but after all, I'm hypnotized"). Hypnotized individuals may even comply with a suggestion to do something that looks embarrassing or dangerous. But the individual is choosing to turn responsibility over to the hypnotist and to cooperate with the hypnotist's suggestions (Lynn, Rhue, & Weekes, 1990). There is no evidence that hypnotized people will do anything that actually violates their morals or constitutes a real danger to themselves or others.

3 **Feats performed under hypnosis can be performed by motivated people without hypnosis.** Hypnotized subjects sometimes perform what seem like extraordinary mental or physical feats, but most research finds that hypnosis does not actually enable people to do things that would otherwise be impossible. With proper motivation, support, and encouragement, the same people could do the same things even without being hypnotized (Chaves, 1989; Spanos, Stenstrom, & Johnson, 1988).

4 **Hypnosis does not increase the accuracy of memory.** In rare cases, hypnosis has been used successfully to jog the memories of crime victims, but usually the memories of hypnotized witnesses have been completely mistaken. Although hypnosis does sometimes boost the amount of information recalled, it also increases *errors*, perhaps because hypnotized people are more willing than others to

Is it hypnosis that enables the man stretched out between two chairs to hold the weight of the man standing on him, without flinching? This audience assumes so, but the only way to find out whether hypnosis produces unique abilities is to do research with control groups. It turns out that people can do the same thing even when they are not hypnotized.

guess, or because they mistake vividly imagined possibilities for actual memories (Dinges et al., 1992; Kihlstrom, 1994). Because pseudomemories and errors are so common in hypnotically induced recall, the American Psychological Association and the American Medical Association oppose the use of "hypnotically refreshed" testimony in courts of law.

5 Hypnosis does not produce a literal reexperiencing of long-ago events. Many people believe that hypnosis can be used to recover memories from as far back as birth. When one clinical psychologist who uses hypnosis in his own practice surveyed over 800 marriage and family therapists, he was dismayed to find that more than half agreed with this common belief (Yapko, 1994). However, it is just plain wrong. When people are regressed to an earlier age, their mental and moral performance remains adultlike (Nash, 1987). Their brain-wave patterns and reflexes do not become childish; they do not reason as children do or show child-sized IQs. They may use baby talk or report that they feel 4 years old again, but the reason is not that they are actually reliving the experience of being 4; they are just willing to play the role.

6 Hypnotic suggestions have been used effectively for many medical and psychological purposes. Although hypnosis is not of much use for finding out what happened in the past, it can be useful in the treatment of psychological and medical problems. Its greatest success is in pain management; some people experience dramatic relief of pain resulting from conditions as diverse as burns, cancer, and childbirth, and others have learned to cope better emotionally with chronic pain. Hypnotic suggestions have also been used in the treatment of stress, anxiety, obesity, asthma, irritable bowel syndrome, chemotherapy-induced nausea, and even skin disorders (Nash & Barnier, 2007; Patterson & Jensen, 2003).

Theories of Hypnosis

Over the years, people have proposed many explanations of what hypnosis is and how it produces its effects. Today, two competing theories predominate.

Dissociation Theories One leading approach was originally proposed by Ernest Hilgard (1977, 1986), who argued that hypnosis, like lucid dreaming and even simple distraction, involves **dissociation**, a split in consciousness in which one part of the mind operates independently of the rest of consciousness. In many hypnotized people, said Hilgard, although most of the mind is subject to hypnotic suggestion, one part is a *hidden observer*, watching but not participating. Unless given special instructions, the hypnotized part remains unaware of the observer.

In his research, Hilgard attempted to question the hidden observer directly. In one procedure, hypnotized volunteers had to submerge an arm in ice water for several seconds, an experience that is normally excruciating. They were told that they would feel no pain, but that the unsubmerged hand would be able to signal the level of any hidden pain by pressing a key. In this situation, many people said they felt little or no pain—yet at the same time, their free hand was busily pressing the key. After the session, these people continued to insist that they had been painfree unless the hypnotist asked the hidden observer to issue a separate report.

A related theory holds that during hypnosis, dissociation occurs between an executive-control system in the frontal lobes of the brain and other brain systems involved in thinking and acting (Woody & Bowers, 1994). The result is an altered state of consciousness similar to that found in patients with frontal lobe disorders. Because the dissociated systems are freed from control by the executive, they are more easily influenced by suggestions from the hypnotist. Like the

dissociation A split in consciousness in which one part of the mind operates independently of others.

activation–synthesis theory of dreaming, dissociation theories of hypnosis are consistent with modern brain theories, which hold that one part of the brain operates as a reporter and interpreter of activities carried out unconsciously by other brain parts (see Chapter 4).

DISSOCIATION THEORIES OF HYPNOSIS

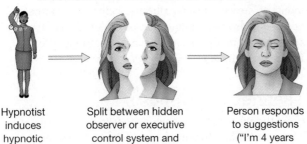

Hypnotist induces hypnotic state

Split between hidden observer or executive control system and rest of mind

Person responds to suggestions ("I'm 4 years old")

The Sociocognitive Approach The second major approach to hypnosis, the *sociocognitive explanation*, holds that the effects of hypnosis result from an interaction between the social influence of the hypnotist (the "socio" part) and the abilities, beliefs, and expectations of the subject (the "cognitive" part) (Kirsch, 1997; Sarbin, 1991; Spanos, 1991). The hypnotized person is basically playing a role. This role has analogies in ordinary life, where we willingly submit to the suggestions of parents, teachers, doctors, therapists, and television commercials. In this view, even the "hidden observer" is simply a reaction to the social demands of the situation and the suggestions of the hypnotist (Kirsch & Lynn, 1998).

SOCIOCOGNITIVE THEORIES OF HYPNOSIS

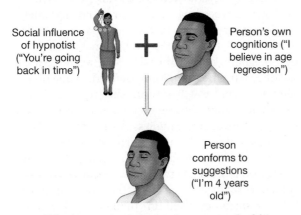

Social influence of hypnotist ("You're going back in time")

Person's own cognitions ("I believe in age regression")

Person conforms to suggestions ("I'm 4 years old")

The hypnotized person is not merely faking or playacting, however. A person who has been instructed to fool an observer by faking a hypnotic state will tend to overplay the role and will stop playing it as soon as the other person leaves the room. In contrast, hypnotized subjects continue to follow the hypnotic suggestions even when they think they are not being watched (Kirsch et al., 1989; Spanos et al., 1993). Like many social roles, the role of hypnotized person is so engrossing and involving that actions required by the role may occur without the person's conscious intent.

Sociocognitive views explain why some people under hypnosis have reported having memories of alien abductions (Clancy, 2005; Spanos, 1996). The individual goes to a therapist or hypnotist looking for an explanation of his or her loneliness, unhappiness, nightmares, puzzling symptoms (such as waking up in the middle of the night in a cold sweat), or the waking dreams we described earlier. If the therapist already believes in alien abduction, he or she may hypnotize the person and then shape the client's story by giving subtle and not-so-subtle cues about what the person should say.

The sociocognitive view can also explain apparent cases of past-life regression. In a fascinating program of research, Nicholas Spanos and his colleagues (1991) directed hypnotized Canadian university students to regress past their own births to previous lives. About a third of the students (who already believed in reincarnation) reported being able to do so. But when they were asked, while supposedly reliving a past life, to name the leader of their country, say whether the country was at peace or at war, or describe the money used in their community, the students could not do it. (One young man, who thought he was Julius Caesar, said the year was A.D. 50 and he was emperor of Rome. But Caesar died in 44 B.C. and was never crowned emperor, and,

"THE WITNESS HAS BARKED, MEOWED AND GIVEN US FIVE MINUTES OF BABY TALK. I'D SAY HYPNOSIS IS NOT THE ANSWER."

besides, dating years as A.D. or B.C. did not begin until several centuries later.) Not knowing anything about the language, dates, customs, and events of their "previous life" did

Thinking Critically about Hypnosis and "Past Lives"

not deter the students from constructing a story about it. They tried to fulfill the requirements of the role by weaving events, places, and people from their *present* lives into their accounts, and by picking up cues from the experimenter.

The researchers concluded that the act of "remembering" another self involves the construction of a fantasy that accords with the rememberer's own beliefs and also the beliefs of others—in this case, those of the authoritative hypnotist.  Watch

Further work may tell us whether or not there is something special about hypnosis. But whatever the outcome of this debate, all hypnosis researchers agree on certain things—for example, that hypnosis does not cause memories to become sharper or allow early experiences to be replayed with perfect accuracy. The study of hypnosis is teaching us much about human suggestibility, the power of imagination, and the way we perceive the present and remember the past.

Watch the **Video Hypnosis** on **mypsychlab.com**

✔ **Study** and **Review** on **mypsychlab.com**

Quick Quiz

We'd like to plant a suggestion in your mind: You'd be wise to take this quiz. . . .

A. True or false:

1. A hypnotized person is usually aware of what is going on and remembers the experience later.
2. Hypnosis gives us special powers that we do not ordinarily have.
3. Hypnosis reduces errors in memory.
4. Hypnotized people play no active part in controlling their behavior and thoughts.
5. According to Hilgard, hypnosis is a state of consciousness involving a "hidden observer."
6. Sociocognitive theorists view hypnosis as mere faking or conscious playacting.

B. Some people believe that hypnotic suggestions can bolster the immune system and help a person fight disease, but the findings have been mixed and many studies have been flawed (Miller & Cohen, 2001). One therapist dismissed these concerns by saying that a negative result just means that the hypnotist isn't skilled enough. As a critical thinker, can you spot what is wrong with his reasoning? (Think back to Chapter 1 and the way a scientific hypothesis must be stated.)

Answers:

A. 1. true **2.** false **3.** false **4.** false **5.** true **6.** false **B.** The therapist's argument violates the principle of falsifiability. If a result is positive, he counts it as evidence. But if a result is negative, he refuses to count it as counterevidence ("Maybe the hypnotist just wasn't good enough"). With this kind of reasoning, there is no way to tell whether the hypothesis is right or wrong.

YOU are about to learn...

- the major types of psychoactive drugs.
- how recreational drugs affect the brain.
- how people's prior drug experiences, individual characteristics, expectations, and mental sets influence their reactions to drugs.

Consciousness-Altering Drugs

In Jerusalem, hundreds of Hasidic men celebrate the completion of the annual reading of the holy Torah by dancing for hours in the streets. For them, dancing is not a diversion; it is a path to religious ecstasy. In South Dakota, several Lakota (Sioux) adults sit naked in the darkness and crushing heat of the sweat lodge; their goal is euphoria, the transcendence of pain, and connection with the Great Spirit of the Universe. In the Amazon jungle, a young man training to be a shaman, a religious leader, takes a whiff of hallucinogenic snuff made from the bark of the virola tree; his goal is to enter a trance and communicate with animals, spirits, and supernatural forces.

These three rituals, seemingly quite different, are all aimed at release from the confines of ordinary consciousness. Because cultures around the world have devised such practices, some writers believe they reflect a human need, one as basic as

All cultures have found ways to alter consciousness. The Maulavis of Turkey (left), the famous whirling dervishes, spin in an energetic but controlled manner to achieve religious rapture. People in many cultures meditate (center) as a way to quiet the mind and achieve spiritual enlightenment. And in some cultures, psychoactive drugs are used for religious or artistic inspiration, as in the case of the Huichol Indians of western Mexico, shown here harvesting hallucinogenic mushrooms.

the need for food and water (Siegel, 1989). William James (1902/1936), who was fascinated by alterations in consciousness, would have agreed. After inhaling nitrous oxide ("laughing gas"), he wrote, "Our normal waking consciousness, rational consciousness as we call it, is but one special type of consciousness, whilst all about it, parted from it by the filmiest of screens, there lie potential forms of consciousness entirely different." But it was not until the 1960s, as millions of people began to seek ways to deliberately produce *altered states of consciousness*, that researchers became interested in the psychology, as well as the physiology, of psychoactive drugs. The filmy screen described by James finally began to lift.

Classifying Drugs

A **psychoactive drug** is a substance that alters perception, mood, thinking, memory, or behavior by changing the body's biochemistry. Around the world and throughout history, the most common ones have been tobacco, alcohol, marijuana, mescaline, opium, cocaine, peyote—and, of course, tea and coffee. The reasons for taking psychoactive drugs have varied: to alter consciousness, as part of a religious ritual, for recreation, to decrease physical pain or discomfort, and for psychological escape.

In Western societies, a whole pharmacopeia of recreational drugs exists, and every few years seem to see the introduction of new ones, both natural and synthetic. Most of these drugs can be classified as *stimulants, depressants, opiates,* or *psychedelics,* depending on their effects on the central nervous system and their impact on behavior and mood (see Table 5.1 on page 170). Chapter 11 discusses addiction and

Chapter 12 covers drugs used in the treatment of mental and emotional disorders; here we describe only their physiological and psychological effects:

1 **Stimulants speed up activity in the central nervous system.** They include, among other drugs, nicotine, caffeine, cocaine, amphetamines ("uppers"), and methamphetamine ("meth"). In moderate amounts, stimulants produce feelings of excitement, confidence, and well-being or euphoria. In large amounts, they make a person anxious, jittery, and hyperalert. In very large doses, they may cause convulsions, heart failure, and death.

Amphetamines are synthetic drugs taken in pill form, injected, smoked, or inhaled. Methamphetamine is structurally similar to amphetamines and is used in the same ways; it comes in two forms, as a powder ("crank," "speed") or in a purer form, a crystalline solid ("glass," "ice"). Cocaine ("coke") is a natural drug, derived from the leaves of the coca plant. Rural workers in Bolivia and Peru chew coca leaf every day without apparent ill effects. In North America, the drug is usually inhaled, injected, or smoked in the highly refined form known as *crack*. These methods give the drug a more immediate, powerful, and dangerous effect than when coca leaf is chewed. Amphetamines, methamphetamine, and cocaine make users feel charged up but do not actually increase energy reserves. Fatigue, irritability, and depression may occur when the effects of these drugs wear off.

2 **Depressants slow down activity in the central nervous system.** They include alcohol, tranquilizers, barbiturates, and common chemicals that some people inhale ("huffing"). Depressants usually

psychoactive drugs Drugs capable of influencing perception, mood, cognition, or behavior.

stimulants Drugs that speed up activity in the central nervous system.

depressants Drugs that slow activity in the central nervous system.

make a person feel calm or drowsy, and they may reduce anxiety, guilt, tension, and inhibitions. In large amounts, they may produce insensitivity to pain and other sensations. Like stimulants, in very large doses they can cause irregular heartbeats, convulsions, and death.

People are often surprised to learn that alcohol is a central nervous system depressant. In small amounts, alcohol has some of the effects of a stimulant because it suppresses activity in parts of the brain that normally inhibit impulsive behavior, such as loud laughter and clowning around. In the long run, however, it slows down nervous system activity. Like barbiturates and opiates, alcohol can be used as an anesthetic; if you drink enough, you will eventually pass out. ☀️⟶Explore

Over time, alcohol damages the liver, heart, and brain. Extremely large amounts of alcohol can kill by inhibiting the nerve cells in brain areas that control breathing and heartbeat. Every so often, a news report announces the death of a college student who had large amounts of alcohol "funneled" into him as part of an initiation or drinking competition. On the other hand, *moderate* drinking—a daily drink or two of wine, beer, or liquor—is associated with a variety of health benefits, including antidiabetic effects and a reduced risk of heart attack and stroke (Brand-Miller et al., 2007; Mukamal et al., 2003; Reynolds et al., 2003).

3 **Opiates relieve pain.** They include opium, derived from the opium poppy; morphine, a derivative of opium; heroin, a derivative of morphine;

synthetic drugs such as methadone; and codeine and codone-based pain relievers such as oxycodone and hydrocodone. These drugs mimic the action of endorphins, and some have a powerful effect on the emotions. When injected, they may produce a rush, a sudden feeling of euphoria. They may also decrease anxiety and motivation. Opiates are highly addictive and when taken in large amounts, they can cause coma and death.

4 **Psychedelic drugs disrupt normal thought processes,** such as the perception of time and space. Sometimes they produce hallucinations, especially visual ones. Some psychedelics, such as lysergic acid diethylamide (LSD), are made in the laboratory. Others, such as mescaline (from the peyote cactus), *Salvia divinorum* (from an herb native to Mexico), and psilocybin (from a species of mushroom), are natural substances. Emotional reactions to psychedelics vary from person to person and from one time to another for any individual. A trip may be mildly pleasant or unpleasant, a mystical revelation or a nightmare. For decades, research on psychedelics languished because of a lack of funding, but a few clinical researchers are now exploring their potential usefulness in psychotherapy, the relief of psychological distress, and the treatment of anxiety disorders (Griffiths et al., 2008).

Some commonly used drugs fall outside these four classifications or combine elements of more than one category. One is *marijuana* ("pot," "grass," "weed"), which is smoked or, less commonly, eaten

opiates Drugs, derived from the opium poppy, that relieve pain and commonly produce euphoria.

psychedelic drugs Consciousness-altering drugs that produce hallucinations, change thought processes, or disrupt the normal perception of time and space.

☀️⟶Explore
Behavioral Effects Associated with Various Blood Alcohol Levels on mypsychlab.com

An LSD trip can be a ticket to agony or ecstasy. These drawings were done under the influence of the drug as part of a test conducted by the U.S. government in the late 1950s. Before the drug had taken effect, the artist drew the charcoal self-portrait on the left. Within a few hours after taking the first dose, he had become agitated and inarticulate and drew the "portrait" in the center. Three hours later, as the drug was wearing off ("I can feel my knees again"), he made the crayon drawing on the right, complaining that the "pencil" in his hand was hard to hold.

Table 5.1

Some Psychoactive Drugs and Their Effects

Class of Drug	Type	Common Effects	Some Results of Abuse/Addiction
Amphetamines Methamphetamine	Stimulants	Wakefulness, alertness, raised metabolism, elevated mood	Nervousness, headaches, loss of appetite, high blood pressure, delusions, psychosis, heart damage, convulsions, death
Cocaine	Stimulant	Euphoria, excitation, feelings of energy, suppressed appetite	Excitability, sleeplessness, sweating, paranoia, anxiety, panic, depression, heart damage, heart failure, injury to nose if sniffed
Tobacco (nicotine)	Stimulant	Varies from alertness to calmness, depending on mental set, setting, and prior arousal; decreases appetite for carbohydrates	*Nicotine:* heart disease, high blood pressure, impaired circulation, erectile problems in men, damage throughout the body due to lowering of a key enzyme; *Tar:* lung cancer, emphysema, mouth and throat cancer, many other health risks
Caffeine	Stimulant	Wakefulness, alertness, shortened reaction time	Restlessness, insomnia, muscle tension, heartbeat irregularities, high blood pressure
Alcohol (1–2 drinks)	Depressant	Depends on setting and mental set; tends to act like a stimulant because it reduces inhibitions and anxiety	
Alcohol (several/ many drinks)	Depressant	Slowed reaction time, tension, depression, reduced ability to store new memories or to retrieve old ones, poor coordination	Blackouts, cirrhosis of the liver, other organ damage, mental and neurological impairment, psychosis, death with very large amounts
Tranquilizers (e.g., Valium); barbiturates (e.g., phenobarbital)	Depressants	Reduced anxiety and tension, sedation	Increased dosage needed for effects; impaired motor and sensory functions, impaired permanent storage of new information, withdrawal symptoms; possibly convulsions, coma, death (especially when taken with other drugs)
Opium, heroin, morphine, codeine, codone-based pain relievers	Opiates	Euphoria, relief of pain	Loss of appetite, nausea, constipation, withdrawal symptoms, convulsions, coma, possibly death
LSD, psilocybin, mescaline, *Salvia divinorum*	Psychedelics	Depending on the drug: exhilaration, visions and hallucinations, insightful experiences	Psychosis, paranoia, panic reactions
Marijuana	Mild psychedelic (classification controversial)	Relaxation, euphoria, increased appetite, reduced ability to store new memories, other effects depending on mental set and setting	Throat and lung irritation, possible lung damage if smoked heavily

in foods such as brownies; it is the most widely used illicit drug in North America and Europe. Some researchers classify it as a psychedelic, but others feel that its chemical makeup and its psychological effects place it outside the major classifications. The main active ingredient in marijuana is tetrahydrocannabinol (THC), derived from the hemp plant, *Cannabis sativa*. In some respects, THC appears to be a mild stimulant, increasing heart rate and making tastes, sounds, and colors seem more intense. But users often report reactions ranging from mild euphoria to relaxation or even sleepiness.

Some researchers believe that very heavy smoking of marijuana (which is high in tar) may increase the risk of lung damage (Barsky et al., 1998; Zhu et al., 2000). In moderate doses, it can interfere with the transfer of information to long-term memory and impair coordination and reaction times, characteristics it shares with alcohol. In large doses, it can cause hallucinations and a sense of unreality. However, a meta-analysis found only a small impairment in memory and learning among long-term users versus nonusers, less than that typically found in users of alcohol and other drugs (Grant et al., 2003).

Marijuana also has some medical benefits. It reduces the nausea and vomiting that often accompany chemotherapy treatment for cancer and AIDS treatments; it reduces the physical tremors, loss of appetite, and other symptoms caused by multiple sclerosis; it helps reduce the frequency of seizures in some patients with epilepsy; and it alleviates the retinal swelling caused by glaucoma (Grinspoon & Bakalar, 1993; Zimmer & Morgan, 1997).

The Physiology of Drug Effects

Psychoactive drugs produce their effects primarily by acting on brain neurotransmitters, the chemical substances that carry messages from one nerve cell to another. A drug may increase or decrease the release of neurotransmitters at the synapse, prevent the reabsorption of excess neurotransmitter molecules by the cells that have released them, block the effects of a neurotransmitter on a receiving nerve cell, or bind to receptors that would ordinarily be triggered by a neurotransmitter (see Chapter 4). Figure 5.4 shows how one drug, cocaine, increases the amount of norepinephrine and dopamine in the brain by blocking the reabsorption of these substances.

These biochemical changes affect cognitive and emotional functioning, but users are often unable to gauge their own competence. In the case of alcohol, just a couple of drinks can affect perception, response time, coordination, and balance,

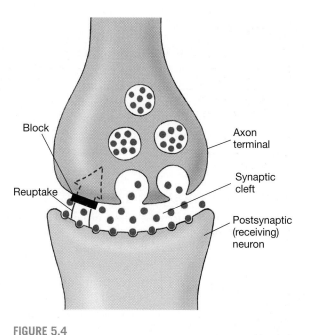

FIGURE 5.4
Cocaine's Effect on the Brain
Cocaine blocks the brain's reabsorption ("reuptake") of the neurotransmitters dopamine and norepinephrine, so levels of these substances rise. The result is overstimulation of brain circuits and a brief euphoric high. Then, when the drug wears off, a depletion of dopamine may cause the user to crash, becoming sleepy and depressed.

despite the drinker's own impression of unchanged or even improved performance. In fact, one research team reported that "Alcohol increases mind wandering while simultaneously reducing the likelihood of noticing one's mind wandering" (Sayette, Reichle, & Schooler, 2009). Liquor also affects memory, possibly by interfering with the work of serotonin. Information stored before a drinking session remains intact during the session but is retrieved more slowly (Haut et al., 1989). Consuming small amounts does not seem to affect *sober* mental performance, but even occasional heavy drinking impairs later abstract thought. In other words, a Saturday night binge is potentially more dangerous than a daily drink.

As for other recreational drugs, there is little evidence that *light* or *moderate* use can damage the human brain enough to affect cognitive functioning, but nearly all researchers agree that heavy or very frequent use is another matter (see Chapter 11). Heavy drug use may interfere with a person's social functioning because of its effects on the frontal lobes (Homer et al., 2008) and also may affect cognitive functioning. In one study, heavy users of methamphetamine had damage to dopamine cells and performed more poorly than other people on tests of memory, attention, and

tolerance Increased resistance to a drug's effects accompanying continued use.

withdrawal Physical and psychological symptoms that occur when someone addicted to a drug stops taking it.

movement, even though they had not used the drug for at least 11 months (Volkow et al., 2001).

The use of some psychoactive drugs, such as heroin and tranquilizers, can lead to **tolerance**: Over time, more and more of the drug is needed to get the same effect. When habitual heavy users stop taking a drug, they may suffer severe **withdrawal** symptoms, which may include nausea, abdominal cramps, sweating, muscle spasms, depression, and disturbed sleep.

The Psychology of Drug Effects

People often assume that the effects of a drug are automatic, the inevitable result of the drug's chemistry.

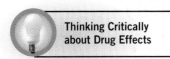
Thinking Critically about Drug Effects

But reactions to a psychoactive drug involve more than the drug's chemical properties. They also depend on a person's experience with the drug, individual characteristics, environmental setting, and mental set.

1 **Experience with the drug refers to the number of times a person has taken it.** Trying a drug—a cigarette, an alcoholic drink, a stimulant—for the first time is often a neutral or unpleasant experience. But reactions typically change once a person has used the drug for a while and has become familiar with the drug's effects.

2 **Individual characteristics include body weight, metabolism, initial state of emotional arousal, personality characteristics, and physical tolerance for the drug.** Women generally get drunker than men on the same amount of alcohol because women are smaller, on average, and their bodies metabolize alcohol differently (Fuchs et al., 1995). Similarly, many Asians have a genetically determined adverse reaction to even small amounts of alcohol, which can cause severe headaches, facial flushing, and diarrhea (Cloninger, 1990). For individuals, a drug may have one effect after a tiring day and a different one after a rousing quarrel, or the effect may vary with the time of day because of the body's circadian rhythms. And some differences among individuals in their responses to a drug may be due to their personality traits. When people who are prone to anger and irritability wear nicotine patches, dramatic bursts of activity occur in the brain while they are working on competitive or aggressive tasks. These changes do not occur, however, in more relaxed and cheerful people (Fallon et al., 2004).

3 **"Environmental setting" refers to the context in which a person takes the drug.** A person might have one glass of wine at home alone and feel sleepy but have three glasses of wine at a party and feel full of energy. Someone might feel happy and

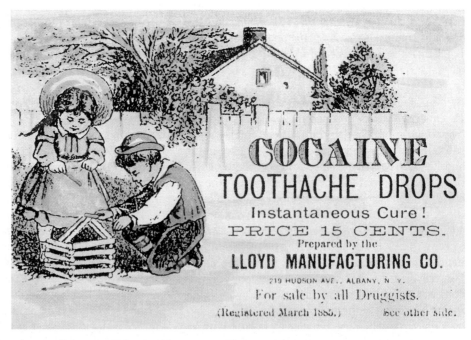

Attitudes about drugs vary with the times. Cigarette smoking was once promoted as healthy and glamorous, and though no doctor would pose in an ad like this one anymore, smoking is still portrayed glamorously in many current films. Before cocaine was banned in the United States in the 1920s, it was widely touted as a cure for everything from toothaches to timidity. It was used in teas, tonics, throat lozenges, and even soft drinks (including, briefly, Coca-Cola, which derived its name from the coca plant).

high drinking with good friends but fearful and nervous drinking with strangers. In an early study of reactions to alcohol, most of the drinkers became depressed, angry, confused, and unfriendly. Then it dawned on the researchers that anyone might become depressed, angry, confused, and unfriendly if asked to drink bourbon at 9:00 A.M. in a bleak hospital room, which was the setting for the experiment (Warren & Raynes, 1972).

4 **"Mental set" refers to a person's expectations about the drug's effects and reasons for taking it.** Some people drink to become more sociable, friendly, or seductive; some drink to try to reduce feelings of anxiety or depression; and some drink to have an excuse for abusiveness or violence. Addicts use drugs to escape from the real world; people living with chronic pain use the same drugs to function in the real world. As we will see again in Chapter 11, the motives for taking a drug greatly influence its effects.

Expectations can sometimes have a more powerful effect than the chemical properties of the drug itself. In several imaginative studies, researchers compared people who were drinking liquor (vodka and tonic) with those who *thought* they were drinking liquor but were actually getting only tonic and lime juice. (Vodka has a subtle taste, and most people could not tell the real and phony drinks apart.) The experimenters found a *"think–drink" effect:*

Men behaved more belligerently when they thought they were drinking vodka than when they thought they were drinking plain tonic water, regardless of the actual content of the drinks. And both sexes reported feeling sexually aroused when they thought they were drinking vodka, whether or not they actually received vodka (Abrams & Wilson, 1983; Marlatt & Rohsenow, 1980). Expectations and beliefs about drugs are, in turn, shaped by the culture in which you live. The belief that alcohol "releases" anger and aggression, for example, often justifies drunken acts of violence, but alcohol alone doesn't cause them; the link weakens when people believe they will be held responsible for their actions while drunk (Critchlow, 1983). In the nineteenth century, Americans regarded marijuana as a mild sedative. They did not expect it to give them a high, and it didn't; it put them to sleep. Today, motives for using marijuana have changed, and these changes have affected how people respond to it. We will discuss the cultural influences on responses to drugs in Chapter 11.

None of this means that alcohol and other drugs are merely placebos. Psychoactive drugs, as we have seen, have physiological effects, many of them extremely potent. By understanding the psychological factors involved in drug use, we can think more critically about the ongoing debate over which drugs, if any, should be legal.

✓● Study and Review on mypsychlab.com

Quick Quiz

There is no debate about whether you should take this quiz.

A. Name the following:

1. Three stimulants used illegally
2. Two drugs that interfere with the formation of new long-term memories
3. Three types of depressant drugs
4. A legal recreational drug that acts as a depressant on the central nervous system
5. Four factors that influence a person's reactions to a psychoactive drug

B. A bodybuilder who has been taking anabolic steroids says the drugs make him more aggressive. What are some other possible interpretations?

Answers:

A. 1. cocaine, amphetamines, and methamphetamine **2.** marijuana and alcohol **3.** barbiturates, tranquilizers, and alcohol **4.** alcohol **5.** prior experience with the drug; the person's physical, emotional, and personality traits; the person's mental set; and the environmental setting **B.** The bodybuilder's increased aggressiveness could be due to his expectations (a placebo effect); bodybuilding itself may increase aggressiveness; the culture of the bodybuilding gym may encourage aggressiveness; other influences in his life or other drugs he is taking may be making him more aggressive; or he may only think he is more aggressive, and his behavior may contradict his self-perceptions.

Psychology in the News REVISITED

L et us return now to the emotional debate raised by the news story at the beginning of this chapter, about whether marijuana should be legalized. What was your reaction to this story?

This chapter has reported on the universal human longing to experience altered states of consciousness. As we have seen, throughout history, human beings have sought ways to improve their moods and mental states when their biological rhythms temporarily ebb, and many have used drugs to seek spiritual enlightenment or seek connection with a divine power. And, of course, many people use them to relax, get high, or for medical reasons.

Because the consequences of drug *abuse* are so devastating to individuals and to society, people often have trouble thinking critically about drug laws and policies: Which drugs should be legal, which should be illegal, and which should be decriminalized (that is, not made legal, but not used as a reason for arresting and jailing their users)? What if an otherwise illegal drug has medicinal or religious uses? Native Americans are allowed to use peyote in religious rituals,

This alarmist poster from the 1930s seems funny and exaggerated today, but even in current debates over drug policy, emotional reasoning often takes precedence over logic and evidence. Should any drugs be decriminalized, or permitted for medical or religious use? Why or why not?

and in 2006, the U.S. Supreme Court ruled unanimously that a small church in New Mexico could use hoasca tea, which contains a prohibited narcotic, in its ceremonies.

At one extreme, some people cannot accept evidence that their favorite drug—be it coffee, tobacco, alcohol, or marijuana—might have harmful effects. At the other extreme, some cannot accept the evidence that their most hated drug—be it alcohol, morphine, marijuana, or the coca leaf—might not be dangerous in all forms or amounts and might even have some beneficial effects. Both sides often confuse potent drugs with others that have only subtle effects and confuse light or moderate use with heavy or excessive use.

Once a drug is declared illegal, many people assume it is deadly, even though some legal drugs are more dangerous than illegal ones. Addiction to prescription painkillers and sedatives used for recreational rather than medical purposes ("pharming") has risen dramatically among teenagers and adults. Nicotine, which of course is legal, is as addictive as heroin and cocaine, which are illegal. No one has ever died from smoking marijuana, but tobacco use contributes to between 400,000 and 500,000 deaths in the United States every year, 24 times the number of deaths from all illegal forms of drug use combined, and worldwide it is the largest single cause of preventable deaths (Brandt, 2007). Yet most people have a far more negative view of marijuana, heroin, and cocaine than of nicotine and prescription painkillers.

Emotions run especially high in the debate about marijuana. Heavy use has some physical risks, just as heavy use of any drug does. However, a review of studies done between 1975 and 2003 failed to find any compelling evidence that marijuana causes chronic mental or behavioral problems in teenagers or young adults. The researchers observed that cause and effect could just as well work in the other direction; that is, people with problems could be more likely to abuse the drug (Macleod et al., 2004). Because marijuana has medical benefits, Canada, Spain, Italy, Portugal, Israel, Austria, Finland, the Netherlands, and Belgium have either decriminalized it or made it legally available for patients who demonstrate a medical need for it. In the United States, voters in 14 states (as of 2010) have approved the medical use of marijuana; but in other states, possession of any amount of pot remains illegal, and punishment even for first offenses can be years in prison. In many states, a person who has been convicted of marijuana possession cannot later get food stamps or welfare, which even convicted rapists and murderers are entitled to.

There are, however, alternatives to the extreme positions of "eradicate all illegal drugs" versus "legalize them all." One is to develop programs to reduce or at least delay drug use by young teens, because multiple drug use before age 15 increases the risk of drug dependence, criminal activity, and other problems in adulthood (Odgers et al., 2008). Another approach would legalize narcotics for people who are in chronic

pain and marijuana for recreational and medicinal use, but would ban tobacco and most hard drugs. A third approach, instead of punishing or incarcerating people who use drugs, would regulate where drugs are used (never at work or when driving, for example), provide treatment for addicts, and educate people about the benefits and hazards of particular drugs.

Where, given the research findings, do you stand in this debate? Which illegal psychoactive drugs, if any, do you think should be legalized? Can we create mental sets and environmental settings that promote safe recreational use of some drugs, minimize the likelihood of drug abuse, and permit the medicinal use of beneficial drugs? What do you think?

Taking Psychology with You

How to Get a Good Night's Sleep

You hop into bed, turn out the lights, close your eyes, and wait for slumber. An hour later, you're still waiting. Finally you drop off, but at 3:00 A.M., to your chagrin, you're awake again. By the time the rooster crows, you have put in a hard day's night.

Insomnia affects most people at one time or another, and many people most of the time. No wonder that sleeping pills are a multimillion-dollar business. But many of these pills have side effects, such as making you feel a little foggy-headed the next day. Many hasten sleep only slightly, and lose their effectiveness over time. Some can actually make matters worse; barbiturates greatly suppress REM sleep, a result that eventually causes wakefulness, and they also suppress Stages 3 and 4, the deeper stages of sleep. Although pills can be helpful on a temporary basis, they do not get at stress and anxiety that may be at the root of your insomnia, and your insomnia is likely to return once you stop taking the pills. Sleep research suggests some alternatives:

Be sure you actually have a sleep problem. Many people only *think* they sleep poorly. They overestimate how long it takes them to doze off and underestimate how much sleep they are getting. When they are observed in the laboratory, they usually fall asleep in less than 30 minutes and are awake only for very short periods during the night (Bonnet, 1990;

Carskadon, Mitler, & Dement, 1974). The real test for diagnosing a sleep deficit is not how many hours you sleep—as we saw, people vary in how much they need—but how you feel during the day. Do you doze off without intending to? Do you feel drowsy in class or at meetings?

Get a correct diagnosis of the sleep problem. Do you suffer from sleep apnea? Do you have a physical disorder that is interfering with sleep? Do you live in a noisy place? Are you fighting your personal biological rhythms by going to bed too early or too late? Do you go to bed early one night and late another? It's better to go to bed at about the same time every night and get up at the same time every morning.

Avoid excessive use of alcohol or other drugs. Many drugs interfere with sleep, and so do coffee, tea, cola, "energy drinks," and chocolate, which all contain caffeine. Alcohol suppresses REM sleep; tranquilizers such as Valium and Librium reduce Stage 4 sleep.

Use relaxation techniques. Listening to soft music at bedtime slows down the heartbeat and breathing, thereby helping older people sleep better and longer (Lai & Good, 2005). Relaxation and meditation techniques help younger people as well.

Avoid lying awake for hours waiting for sleep. Your frustration will cause arousal that will keep you awake. If you can't sleep, get up and do something else, preferably something dull and relaxing, in another room. When you feel drowsy, try sleeping again.

When insomnia is related to anxiety and worry, it makes sense to get to the source of your problems, and that may mean a brief round of cognitive-behavior therapy (CBT), which teaches you how to change the negative thoughts that are keeping you awake. (We discuss this form of therapy in Chapter 12.) A placebo-controlled study that compared the effectiveness of a leading sleep pill and a six-week course of CBT found that both approaches helped alleviate chronic insomnia, but CBT worked better both in the short run and the long run (Jacobs at al., 2004). Other research, too, finds that CBT helps people fall asleep sooner and stay asleep longer than pills do (Morin, 2004).

Woody Allen once said, "The lamb and the lion shall lie down together, but the lamb will not be very sleepy." Like a lamb trying to sleep with a lion, you cannot expect to sleep well with stress hormones pouring through your bloodstream and worries crowding your mind. In an evolutionary sense, sleeplessness is an adaptive response to danger and threat. When your anxieties decrease, so may your sleepless nights.

Summary

Biological Rhythms: The Tides of Experience

● *Consciousness* is the awareness of oneself and the environment. Changing states of consciousness are often associated with *biological rhythms*—periodic fluctuations in physiological functioning. These rhythms are typically tied to external time cues, but many are also *endogenous,* generated from within even in the absence of such cues. *Circadian* fluctuations occur about once a day; other rhythms occur less frequently or more frequently than that.

● When people live in isolation from all time cues, they tend to live a day that is slightly longer than 24 hours. Circadian rhythms are governed by a biological clock in the *suprachiasmatic nucleus (SCN)* of the hypothalamus. The SCN regulates and, in turn, is affected by the hormone *melatonin,* which is responsive to changes in light and dark and which increases during the dark hours. When a person's normal routine changes, the person may experience *internal desynchronization*, in which the usual circadian rhythms are thrown out of phase with one another. The result may be fatigue, mental inefficiency, and an increased risk of accidents.

● Some people experience depression every winter in a pattern that has been labeled *seasonal affective disorder (SAD)*, but serious seasonal depression is rare. The causes of SAD are not yet clear but may involve biological rhythms that are out of phase and/or an abnormality in the secretion of melatonin, although there can also be other, nonbiological causes. Light treatments can be effective.

● Another long-term rhythm is the menstrual cycle, during which various hormones rise and fall. Wellcontrolled, double-blind studies on PMS do not support claims that emotional symptoms are reliably and universally tied to the menstrual cycle. Overall, women and men do not differ in the emotional symptoms they report or in the number of mood swings they experience over the course of a month.

● Expectations and learning affect how both sexes interpret bodily and emotional changes. Few people of either sex are likely to undergo dramatic monthly mood swings or personality changes because of hormones.

The Rhythms of Sleep

● During sleep, periods of *rapid eye movement (REM)* alternate with *non-REM sleep* in approximately a 90-minute rhythm. Non-REM sleep is divided into four stages on the basis of characteristic brain-wave patterns. During REM sleep, the brain is active, and there are other signs of arousal, yet most of the skeletal muscles are limp; vivid dreams are reported most often during REM sleep. Some people have had "waking dreams" when they emerge from REM sleep before the paralysis of that stage has subsided, and occasionally, people have interpreted the resulting hallucinations as real. The purposes of REM are still a mystery.

● Sleep is necessary not only for bodily restoration but also for normal mental functioning. Many people get less than the optimal amount of sleep. Some suffer from insomnia, *sleep apnea, narcolepsy,* or *REM behavior disorder*, but the most common reason for daytime sleepiness is probably a simple lack of sleep.

● Sleep may contribute to the *consolidation* of memories and subsequent insight and problem solving. These benefits have been associated most closely with REM sleep and slow-wave sleep.

Exploring the Dream World

● Dreams are sometimes recalled as illogical and disjointed. Some people say they have *lucid dreams* in which they know they are dreaming.

● The *psychoanalytic theory of dreams* holds that they allow us to express forbidden or unrealistic wishes and desires that have been forced into the unconscious part of the mind and disguised as symbolic images. The *problem-solving approach to dreams* holds that dreams express current concerns and may even help us solve current problems and work through emotional issues, especially during times of crisis. The *cognitive approach to dreams* holds that they are simply a modification of the cognitive activity that goes on when we are awake. The difference is that during sleep we are cut off from sensory input from the world and our bodily movements, so our thoughts tend to be more diffuse and unfocused. The *activation–synthesis theory of dreaming* holds that dreams occur when the cortex tries to make sense of, or interpret, spontaneous neural firing initiated in the pons. The resulting synthesis of these signals with existing knowledge and memories results in a dream.

● All of the current theories of dreams have some support, and all have weaknesses. Most psychologists today accept the notion that dreams are more than incoherent ramblings of the mind, but many psychologists quarrel with psychoanalytic interpretations. Some psychologists doubt that people can solve problems during sleep. The activation–synthesis theory does not seem to explain coherent, story-like dreams or non-REM dreams. The cognitive approach is now a leading contender, although some of its specific claims remain to be tested.

The Riddle of Hypnosis

● *Hypnosis* is a procedure in which the practitioner suggests changes in a subject's sensations, perceptions, thoughts, feelings, or behavior, and the subject tries to comply. Although hypnosis has been used successfully for many medical and psychological purposes, there are many misconceptions about what it can accomplish. It cannot force people to do things against their will, confer special abilities that are otherwise impossible, increase the accuracy of memory, or produce a literal reexperiencing of long-ago events.

● A leading explanation of hypnosis is that it involves *dissociation*, a split in consciousness. In one version of this approach, the split is between a part of consciousness that is hypnotized and a *hidden observer* that watches but does not participate. In another version, the split is between an executive-control system in the brain and other brain systems responsible for thinking and acting.

● Another leading approach, the *sociocognitive explanation*, regards hypnosis as a product of normal social and cognitive processes. In this view, hypnosis is a form of role-playing in which the hypnotized person uses active cognitive strategies, including imagination, to comply with the hypnotist's suggestions. The role is so engrossing that the person interprets it as real. Sociocognitive processes can account for the apparent age and past-life "regressions" of people under hypnosis and their reports of alien abductions.

Consciousness-Altering Drugs

● In all cultures, people have found ways to produce *altered states of consciousness*, often by using *psychoactive drugs*, which alter cognition and emotion by acting on neurotransmitters in the brain. Most psychoactive drugs are classified as *stimulants*, *depressants*, *opiates*, or *psychedelics*, depending on their central nervous system effects and their impact on behavior and mood. Some common drugs, such as marijuana, fall outside these categories.

● When used frequently and in large amounts, some psychoactive drugs can damage neurons in the brain and impair learning and memory. Their use may lead to *tolerance*, in which increasing dosages are needed for the same effect, and *withdrawal* symptoms if a person tries to quit. But some drugs, such as alcohol and marijuana, are also associated with health benefits when used in moderation.

● Reactions to a psychoactive drug are influenced not only by its chemical properties but also by the user's prior experience with the drug, individual characteristics, environmental setting, and *mental set*—the person's expectations and motives for taking the drug. Expectations can be even more powerful than the drug itself, as shown by the *"think–drink" effect*.

Psychology in the News, Revisited

● People often find it difficult to distinguish drug use from drug abuse, to differentiate between heavy use and light or moderate use, and to separate a drug's legality or illegality from its potential dangers and benefits.

Key Terms

Biological Rhythms: The Tides of Experience

Consciousness is the awareness of oneself and the environment.

Biological rhythms are periodic fluctuations in physiological functioning, synchronized to external cues or **endogenous** (generated from within).

Circadian Rhythms

Circadian rhythms occur about once a day.

Circadian rhythms are governed by a biological clock in the **suprachiasmatic nucleus (SCN)** in the hypothalamus.

SCN — Regulates → Neurotransmitters, hormones (e.g. melatonin) — Feedback → SCN

Melatonin, secreted by the pineal gland, helps keep the biological clock in phase with the light-dark cycle.

Internal desynchronization occurs when circadian rhythms are out of phase with one another.

Moods and Long-Term Rhythms

- In the treatment of **seasonal affective disorder (SAD)**, a placebo effect may play a role, but light treatments are somewhat effective.
- Well-controlled double-blind studies of "PMS" do not support claims that emotional symptoms are tied to the menstrual cycle in most women, or that the menstrual cycle affects the ability to work or study.
- Expectations and learning affect interpretations of bodily and emotional changes.

Why We Sleep

Across species, sleep falls along a continuum from hibernation to continuous activity for long lengths of time. In humans, sleep is necessary not only for bodily restoration but for normal mental functioning.

Mental Consequences of Sleeplessness

Sleep deprivation of even one night can result in reduced:
- Mental flexibility
- Attention
- Creativity

Longer periods of sleep deprivation can result in:
- Hallucinations
- Delusions

Sleep disorders include:
- **Sleep apnea**, in which breathing periodically stops for a few moments, causing the person to choke or gasp
- **Narcolepsy**, in which an individual is subject to irresistible and unpredictable daytime attacks of sleepiness or actual sleep, lasting from 5 to 30 minutes
- **REM behavior disorder**, in which muscle paralysis characteristic of REM sleep does not occur and people become physically active while asleep

The Rhythms of Sleep

Periods of **rapid eye movement (REM)** alternate with non-REM sleep in a 90-minute rhythm.
- The body is limp.
- The brain is active.
- Vivid dreams occur.

The reasons for REM sleep are still a matter of controversy.

Awake	Small, rapid
Stage 1	Small, irregular
Stage 2	Sleep spindles
Stage 3	Delta waves appear
Stage 4	Mostly delta
REM	Rapid, somewhat irregular

Mental Benefits of Sleep

Many scientists believe that sleep:
- Contributes to **consolidation** and retention of memories.
- Enhances problem-solving ability.

Exploring the Dream World

Dreams are a fascinating psychological mystery. They seem to be out of our control, although some people say they have **lucid dreams**, in which they control the action. There are four leading theories of dreams:

1. The psychoanalytic theory holds that dreams provide insight into unconscious motives, forbidden desires, and mental conflicts.
2. The problem-solving approach holds that dreams reflect the ongoing conscious concerns of waking life and may help us resolve them.
3. The cognitive approach holds that dreams are a modification of normal waking cognitive activity.
4. The **activation–synthesis theory** holds that dreams occur when the cortex tries to make sense of spontaneous neural firing initiated in the pons during REM sleep.

ACTIVATION–SYNTHESIS THEORY OF DREAMS

2. Cerebral cortex synthesizes signals, tries to interpret them ("I'm running through the woods")

1. Spontaneous firing of neurons in pons

The Riddle of Hypnosis

Hypnosis is a procedure in which the practitioner suggests changes in the sensations, perceptions, thoughts, feelings, or behavior of the subject.

- Hypnotic responsiveness depends more on the efforts and qualities of the person being hypnotized than on the skill of the hypnotist.
- Hypnotized people cannot be forced to do things against their will.
- Feats performed under hypnosis can be performed by motivated people without hypnosis.
- Hypnosis does not increase the accuracy of memory or produce a literal reexperiencing of long-ago events.
- Hypnotic suggestions have been used effectively for many medical and psychological purposes.

Theories of Hypnosis

1. The **dissociation** view is that hypnosis is a split in consciousness between a hypnotized part of the mind and a hidden observer or an executive control system.

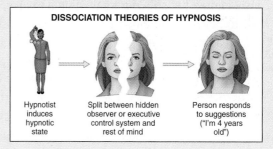

DISSOCIATION THEORIES OF HYPNOSIS

Hypnotist induces hypnotic state

Split between hidden observer or executive control system and rest of mind

Person responds to suggestions ("I'm 4 years old")

2. The **sociocognitive** view regards the hypnotized person as using cognitive strategies, such as imagination, to comply with the hypnotist's suggestions.

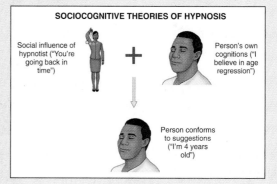

SOCIOCOGNITIVE THEORIES OF HYPNOSIS

Social influence of hypnotist ("You're going back in time")

Person's own cognitions ("I believe in age regression")

Person conforms to suggestions ("I'm 4 years old")

Consciousness-Altering Drugs

Psychoactive drugs alter perception, mood, thinking, memory, or behavior by changing the body's biochemistry.

Classifying Drugs

Drug classifications, based on their effects on the central nervous system, include:
- **Stimulants**
- **Depressants**
- **Opiates**
- **Psychedelics**

Marijuana may fall outside of these classifications.

The Physiology and Psychology of Drug Effects

The physiology of drug effects:
- The use of some psychoactive drugs can lead to **tolerance**: increased resistance to a drug's effects.
- When heavy users stop taking a drug, they may suffer severe **withdrawal symptoms**.

The psychology of drug effects may vary, depending on:
- A person's experience with the drug
- A person's physical condition
- The environmental setting
- The person's *mental set*, or expectations

Lindsey Vonn Defeats Pain to Win Olympic Gold

WHISTLER, BRITISH COLUMBIA, February 18, 2010. Lindsey Vonn today became the first U.S. woman to win the gold medal in the Olympic downhill race. "I was completely overwhelmed," Vonn said. "It was one of the best feelings I've ever had in my life. Everyone expected me to do it, but it's not as easy as just saying you can do it."

That's a huge understatement, since Vonn had seriously injured her shin during training a week earlier and had to have fluid drained from the deep bruise, which was bleeding internally. "When I tried my boot on, I was just standing there in the hotel room barely flexing forward, and it was excruciatingly painful. And I've got to try to ski downhill at 75, 80 miles an hour with a lot of forces pushed up against my shin," Vonn said at the time of the injury. "I don't know honestly if I'll be able to do it."

Vonn said she fought through pain the whole way down the bumpy, challenging course, on which several other skiers had crashed. When Vonn took off, she shaved every millisecond she could off her time by skiing tightly around the turns. "It wasn't an option to ski passively," Vonn said. "I had to really take it."

UFO Sighting Over St. Louis

CLEVELAND, OH, March 15, 2010. Thousands of Cleveland residents have been flocking to the Lake Erie riverfront to take pictures of mysterious lights in the night sky. For almost two weeks, the lights have been appearing at about 7:30 p.m., moving back and forth for a while and then disappearing.

"At first, I figured it was just a star," said medical technician Eugene Erlikh, 20. "But the way it would move, I've never seen anything like it." The local NASA facility said the lights have nothing to do with their work, and air-traffic controllers could not explain them either. UFO sightings are common in Ohio. More than 20 reports of mysterious lights or objects have been made in the past two years.

One of the earliest UFO accounts occurred in the late 1940s, when a rancher noticed some strange objects strewn about his property near Roswell, New Mexico. When the Air Force quickly blocked off and cleared the site, stories circulated that a spacecraft had crashed and that alien corpses had been recovered. Thousands of believers in UFOs still flock to the International UFO Museum in Roswell.

Are these alien spacecraft? Many people who viewed these odd objects in the skies above Santos, Brazil, were convinced they were seeing UFOs.

Sensation and Perception

How in the world does anyone win an Olympic gold medal while skiing in pain after an injury, and why do some people think they have seen UFOs that others dismiss as planes and planets in the night sky? And what in the world do these two stories have in common? The answer is that our sensations often deceive us. We think of pain, sights, tastes, and sounds as being obvious, "real," right there. "I saw it with my own eyes!" people exclaim, meaning "Don't argue with me," as they report seeing an image of Jesus on a garage door, Osama bin Laden's face in smoke billowing from the doomed World Trade Center, or Mother Theresa's face in a cinnamon bun. These illusions seem very real to the people who see them, and the reverse is also true: A real sensation, as of intense pain, can disappear under the stress of battle or the thrill of competition.

In this chapter, we will explore how our senses take in information from the environment and how our brains use this information to construct a model of the world. We will focus on two closely connected sets of processes that enable us to know what is happening both inside our bodies and in the world beyond our own skins. The first, **sensation**, is the detection of physical energy emitted or reflected by physical objects. The cells that do the detecting are located in the *sense organs*—the eyes, ears, tongue, nose, skin, and internal body tissues. Sensory processes produce an immediate awareness of sound, color, form, and other building blocks of consciousness. Without sensation, we would lose touch—literally—with reality.

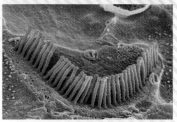

But to make sense of the world impinging on our senses, we also need **perception**, a set of mental operations that organizes sensory impulses into meaningful patterns. Our sense of vision produces a two-dimensional image on the back of the eye, but we perceive the world in three dimensions. Our sense of hearing brings us the sound of a C, an E, and a G played simultaneously on the piano, but we perceive a C-major chord. Sometimes, a single sensory image produces two alternating perceptions, and the result is an image that keeps changing, as illustrated by the two examples on the next page.

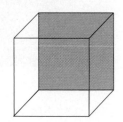

If you stare at the cube, the colored panel will alternate from being at the back to being at the front. The second drawing can also be perceived in two ways. Can you see the word?

sensation The detection of physical energy emitted or reflected by physical objects; it occurs when energy in the external environment or the body stimulates receptors in the sense organs.

perception The process by which the brain organizes and interprets sensory information.

sense receptors Specialized cells that convert physical energy in the environment or the body to electrical energy that can be transmitted as nerve impulses to the brain.

doctrine of specific nerve energies The principle that different sensory modalities exist because signals received by the sense organs stimulate different nerve pathways leading to different areas of the brain.

Sensation and perception are the foundation for learning, thinking, and acting. Findings on these processes can also be put to practical use, as in the design of industrial robots and in the training of astronauts, who must make crucial decisions based on what they sense and perceive. An understanding of sensation and perception also helps us think more critically about our own experiences, and encourages humility: Usually we are sure that what we sense and perceive must be true, yet sometimes we are just plain wrong. As you read this chapter, you will learn why people sometimes perceive things that are not there and, conversely, why they sometimes miss things that *are* there—why we can look without seeing, listen without hearing.

◆ YOU are about to learn...

- why we experience separate sensations even though they all rely on similar neural signals.
- what kind of code in the nervous system helps explain why a pinprick and a kiss feel different.
- how psychologists measure the sensitivity of our senses.
- the bias that influences whether or not you think you hear the phone ringing when you are in the shower.
- what happens when people are deprived of all external sensory stimulation.
- why we sometimes fail to see an object that we're looking straight at.

Our Sensational Senses

At some point, you probably learned that there are five senses: vision, hearing, taste, touch, and smell. Actually, there are more than five senses, though scientists disagree about the exact number. The skin, which is the organ of touch or pressure, also senses heat, cold, and pain, not to mention itching and tickling. The ear, which is the organ of hearing, also contains receptors that account for a sense of balance. The skeletal muscles contain receptors responsible for a sense of bodily movement.

All of our senses evolved to help us survive. Even pain, which causes so much human misery, is an indispensable part of our evolutionary heritage, for it alerts us to illness and injury. Some people are born with a rare condition that prevents them from feeling the usual hurts and aches of life, but you shouldn't envy them: They are susceptible to burns, bruises, and broken bones, and they often die at an early age because they can't take advantage of pain's warning signals.

The Riddle of Separate Sensations

Sensation begins with the **sense receptors**, cells located in the sense organs. The receptors for smell, pressure, pain, and temperature are extensions (dendrites) of sensory neurons (see Chapter 4). The receptors for vision, hearing, and taste are specialized cells separated from sensory neurons by synapses.

When the sense receptors detect an appropriate stimulus—light, mechanical pressure, or chemical molecules—they convert the energy of the stimulus into electrical impulses that travel along nerves to the brain. Sense receptors are like military scouts who scan the terrain for signs of activity. These scouts cannot make many decisions on their own; they must transmit what they learn to "field officers," sensory neurons in the nerves of the peripheral nervous system. The field officers in turn must report to generals at a command center, the cells of the brain. The generals are responsible for analyzing the reports, combining information brought in by different scouts, and deciding what it all means.

The sensory-neuron "field officers" all use the same form of communication, a neural impulse. It is as if they must all send their messages on a bongo drum and can only go "boom." How, then, are we able to experience so many different kinds of sensations? The answer is that the nervous system *encodes* the messages. One kind of code, which is *anatomical*, was first described in 1826 by the German physiologist Johannes Müller in his **doctrine of specific nerve energies**. According to this doctrine, different sensory modalities (such as vision and hearing) exist because signals received by the sense organs stimulate different nerve pathways leading to different areas of the brain. Signals from the eye cause impulses to travel along the optic nerve to the visual cortex. Signals from the ear cause impulses to travel along the auditory nerve to the auditory cortex. Light and sound waves produce different sensations because of these anatomical differences.

The doctrine of specific nerve energies implies that what we know about the world ultimately reduces to what we know about the state of our own nervous system: We see with the brain, not the eyes, and we hear with the brain, not the ears. It follows that if sound waves could stimulate nerves that end in the visual part of the brain, we would "see" sound. In fact, a similar sort of crossover does occur if you close your right eye and press lightly on the right side of the lid: You will see a flash of light seemingly coming from the left. The pressure produces an impulse that travels up the optic nerve to the visual area in the right side of the brain, where it is interpreted as coming from the left side of the visual field. By taking advantage of such crossover from one sense to another, researchers hope to enable blind people to see by teaching them to interpret impulses from other senses that are then routed to the visual areas of the brain. Canadian neuroscientists are developing a device that translates images from a camera into a pattern of electronic pulses that is sent to electrodes on the tongue, which in turn sends information about the pattern to visual areas of the brain that process images (Chabat et al., 2007; Ptito et al., 2005). Using this device, congenitally blind people have been able to make out shapes, and their visual areas, long quiet, have suddenly become active.

Sensory crossover also occurs in a rare condition called **synesthesia**, in which the stimulation of one sense also consistently evokes a sensation in another. A person with synesthesia may say that the color purple smells like a rose, the aroma of cinnamon feels like velvet, or the sound of a note on a clarinet tastes like cherries. Most synesthetes are born with the condition, but it can also result from damage to the brain. In one interesting case, a woman who had recovered from a stroke experienced sounds as a tingling sensation on the left side of her body (Ro et al., 2007). No one is sure yet about the neurological basis of synesthesia, but there are two leading theories. One attributes the condition to a lack of normal disinhibition in signals between different sensory areas of the brain

(e.g., Cohen Kadosh et al., 2009). The other attributes it to a greater number of neural connections between different sensory brain areas (e.g., Bargary & Mitchell, 2008; Rouw & Scholte, 2007).

Synesthesia, however, is an anomaly; for most of us, the senses remain separate. Anatomical encoding does not completely solve the riddle of why this is so, nor does it explain variations of experience *within* a particular sense—the sight of pink versus red, the sound of a piccolo versus the sound of a tuba, or the feel of a pinprick versus the feel of a kiss. An additional kind of code is therefore necessary. This second kind of code has been called *functional*. Functional codes rely on the fact that sensory receptors and neurons fire, or are inhibited from firing, only in the presence of specific sorts of stimuli. At any particular time, then, some cells in the nervous system are firing and some are not. Information about *which* cells are firing, *how many* cells are firing, the *rate* at which cells are firing, and the *patterning* of each cell's firing forms a functional code. You might think of such a code as the neurological equivalent of Morse code but much more complicated. Functional encoding may occur all along a sensory route, starting in the sense organs and ending in the brain.

Measuring the Senses

Just how sensitive are our senses? The answer comes from the field of *psychophysics*, which is concerned with how the physical properties of stimuli are related to our psychological experience of them. Drawing on principles from both physics and psychology, psychophysicists have studied how

synesthesia A condition in which stimulation of one sense also evokes another.

Different species sense the world differently. The flower on the left was photographed under normal light. The one on the right, photographed under ultraviolet light, is what a butterfly might see, because butterflies have ultraviolet receptors. The hundreds of tiny bright spots are sources of nectar.

absolute threshold
The smallest quantity of physical energy that can be reliably detected by an observer.

difference threshold
The smallest difference in stimulation that can be reliably detected by an observer when two stimuli are compared; also called *just noticeable difference (jnd)*.

the strength or intensity of a stimulus affects the strength of sensation in an observer.

Absolute Thresholds   One way to find out how sensitive the senses are is to show people a series of signals that vary in intensity and ask them to say which signals they can detect. The smallest amount of energy that a person can detect reliably is known as the **absolute threshold**. The word *absolute* is a bit misleading because people detect borderline signals on some occasions and miss them on others. Reliable detection is said to occur when a person can detect a signal 50 percent of the time.

If your absolute threshold for brightness were being measured, you might be asked to sit in a dark room and look at a wall or screen. You would then be shown flashes of light varying in brightness, one flash at a time. Your task would be to say whether you noticed a flash. Some flashes you would never see. Some you would always see. And sometimes you would miss seeing a flash, even though you had noticed one of equal brightness on other trials. Such errors seem to occur in part because of random firing of cells in the nervous system, which produces fluctuating background noise, something like the static in a radio transmission that is slightly out of range.

By studying absolute thresholds, psychologists have found that our senses are very sharp indeed. If you have normal sensory abilities, you can see a candle flame on a clear, dark night from 30 miles away. You can taste a teaspoon of sugar diluted in two gallons of water, smell a drop of perfume diffused through a three-room apartment, and feel the wing of a bee falling on your cheek from a height of only one centimeter (Galanter, 1962).

Despite these impressive skills, our senses are tuned in to only a narrow band of physical energies. We are visually sensitive to only a tiny fraction of the electromagnetic energy that surrounds us; we do not see radio waves, infrared waves, or microwaves (see Figure 6.1). Many other species can pick up signals that we cannot. Dogs can detect high-frequency sound waves that are beyond our range, as you know if you have ever called your pooch with a "silent" doggie whistle. Bees can see ultraviolet light, which merely gives human beings a sunburn.

Difference Thresholds   Psychologists also study sensory sensitivity by having people compare two stimuli—such as the weight of two blocks, the brightness of two lights, or the saltiness of two liquids—and judge whether they are the same or different. The smallest difference in stimulation that a person can detect reliably (again, half of the time) is called the **difference threshold** or *just noticeable difference (jnd)*. When you compare two stimuli, A and B, the difference threshold will depend on the intensity or size of A. The larger or more intense A is, the greater the change must be before you can detect a difference. If you are comparing the weights of two pebbles, you might be able to detect a difference of only a fraction of an ounce, but you would not be able to detect such a subtle difference if you were comparing two massive boulders.

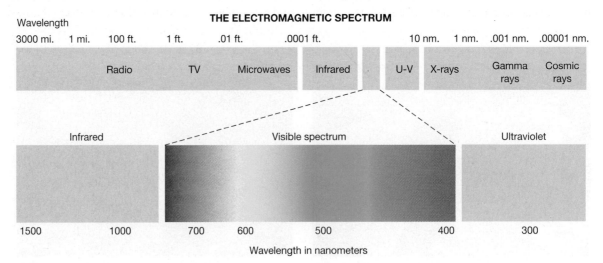

FIGURE 6.1
The Visible Spectrum of Electromagnetic Energy
Our visual system detects only a small fraction of the electromagnetic energy around us.

Signal-Detection Theory Despite their usefulness, the procedures we have described have a serious limitation. Measurements for any given individual may be affected by the person's general tendency, when uncertain, to respond, "Yes, I noticed a signal (or a difference)" or "No, I didn't notice anything." Some people are habitual yea-sayers, willing to gamble that the signal was there. Others are habitual naysayers, cautious and conservative. In addition, alertness, motives, and expectations can influence how a person responds on any given occasion. If you are in the shower and you are expecting an important call, you may think you heard the telephone ring when it did not. In laboratory studies, when observers want to impress the experimenter, they may lean toward a positive response.

Fortunately, these problems of *response bias* are not insurmountable. According to **signal-detection theory**, an observer's response in a detection task can be divided into a *sensory process*, which depends on the intensity of the stimulus, and a *decision process*, which is influenced by the observer's response bias. To separate these two components, a researcher may include some trials in which no stimulus is present and others in which a weak stimulus is present. Under these conditions, four kinds of responses are possible: The person (1) detects a signal that was present (a "hit"), (2) says the signal was there when it wasn't (a "false alarm"), (3) fails to detect the signal when it was present (a "miss"), or (4) correctly says that the signal was absent when it was absent (a "correct rejection").

Yea-sayers will have more hits than naysayers, but they will also have more false alarms because they are too quick to say, "Yup, it was there." Naysayers will have more correct rejections than yea-sayers, but they will also have more misses because they are too quick to say, "Nope, nothing was there." This information can be fed into a mathematical formula that yields separate estimates of a person's response bias and sensory capacity. The individual's true sensitivity to a signal of any particular intensity can then be predicted.

The original method of measuring thresholds assumed that a person's ability to detect a stimulus depended solely on the stimulus. Signal-detection theory assumes that there is no single threshold because at any given moment a person's sensitivity to a stimulus depends on a decision that he or she actively makes. Signal-detection methods have many real-world applications, from screening applicants for jobs that require keen hearing to training air-traffic controllers, whose decisions about the presence or absence of a blip on a radar screen may mean the difference between life and death.

signal-detection theory A psychophysical theory that divides the detection of a sensory signal into a sensory process and a decision process.

Get Involved! Now You See It, Now You Don't

Sensation depends on change and contrast in the environment. Hold your hand over one eye and stare at the dot in the middle of the circle on the right. You should have no trouble maintaining an image of the circle. However, if you do the same with the circle on the left, the image will fade. The gradual change from light to dark does not provide enough contrast to keep your visual receptors firing at a steady rate. The circle reappears only if you close and reopen your eye or shift your gaze to the X.

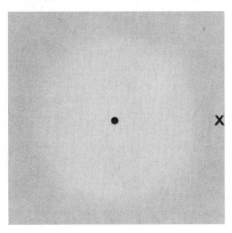
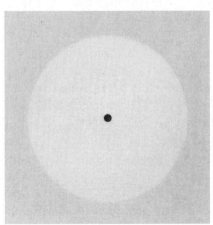

sensory adaptation
The reduction or disappearance of sensory responsiveness when stimulation is unchanging or repetitious.

sensory deprivation
The absence of normal levels of sensory stimulation.

⊙▸ **Simulate Methods of Constant Stimuli** on **mypsychlab.com**

Is sensory deprivation pleasant or unpleasant? The answer isn't "either–or"; it depends on the circumstances and how you interpret your situation. Being isolated against your will can be terrifying. But many people have found meditating alone, away from all sights and sounds—as this woman is doing in a "flotation tank"—to be calming and pleasant.

Sensory Adaptation

Variety, they say, is the spice of life. It is also the essence of sensation, for our senses are designed to respond to change and contrast in the environment. When a stimulus is unchanging or repetitious, sensation often fades or disappears. Receptors or nerve cells higher up in the sensory system get "tired" and fire less frequently. The resulting decline in sensory responsiveness is called **sensory adaptation**. Usually, such adaptation spares us from having to respond to unimportant information; most of the time you have no need to feel your watch sitting on your wrist. Sometimes, however, adaptation can be hazardous, as when you no longer smell a gas leak that you thought you noticed when you first entered the kitchen. ⊙▸ **Simulate**

We never completely adapt to extremely intense stimuli—a terrible toothache, the odor of ammonia, the heat of the desert sun. And we rarely adapt completely to visual stimuli, whether they are weak or intense. Eye movements, voluntary and involuntary, cause the location of an object's image on the back of the eye to keep changing, so visual receptors do not have a chance to "fatigue."

What would happen if our senses adapted to *most* incoming stimuli? Would we sense nothing, or would the brain substitute its own images for the sensory experiences no longer available by way of the sense organs? In early studies of **sensory deprivation**, researchers studied this question by isolating male volunteers from all patterned sight and sound. Vision was restricted by a translucent visor,

hearing by a U-shaped pillow and noise from an air conditioner and fan, and touch by cotton gloves and cardboard cuffs. The volunteers took brief breaks to eat and use the bathroom, but otherwise they lay in bed, doing nothing. The results were dramatic. Within a few hours, many of the men felt edgy. Some were so disoriented that they quit the study the first day. Those who stayed longer became confused, restless, and grouchy. Many reported bizarre visions, such as a squadron of squirrels or a procession of marching eyeglasses. It was as though they were having the kind of waking dreams described in Chapter 5. Few people were willing to remain in the study for more than two or three days (Heron, 1957).

But the notion that sensory deprivation is unpleasant or even dangerous turned out to be an oversimplification (Suedfeld, 1975). Later research, using better methods, showed that hallucinations are less frequent and less disorienting than had first been thought. Many people enjoy limited periods of deprivation, and some perceptual and intellectual abilities actually improve. Your response to sensory deprivation depends on your expectations and interpretations of what is happening. Reduced sensation can be scary if you are locked in a room for an indefinite period, but relaxing if you have retreated to that room voluntarily for a little time-out, perhaps at a luxury spa or a monastery.

Thinking Critically about Sensory Deprivation

Still, the human brain does require a minimum amount of sensory stimulation to function normally. This need may help explain why people who live alone often keep the radio or television on continuously, and why prolonged solitary confinement is used as a form of punishment or even torture.

Sensing without Perceiving

If too little stimulation can be bad for you, so can too much, because it can lead to fatigue and mental confusion. If you have ever felt exhausted, nervous, and headachy after a day crammed with activities, you know firsthand about sensory overload. When people find themselves in a state of overload, they often cope by blocking out unimportant sights and sounds and focusing only on those they find interesting or useful. When you become engrossed in a great conversation at a noisy party, you are likely to ignore other voices, the clink of ice cubes, and bursts of laughter across the room.

Hard though it is to believe, even a person in a gorilla suit may go unnoticed if people's attention is elsewhere.

Even when overload is not a problem, our capacity for **selective attention**—the ability to focus on some parts of the environment and block out others—protects us from being overwhelmed by the countless sensory signals that are constantly impinging on our sense receptors. Competing sensory messages all enter the nervous system, however, and get processed at varying levels of awareness; this is the reason that we are able to pick up anything important, such as our own name spoken by someone several yards away.

That's the good news. The bad news is that selective attention, by its very nature, causes us to miss much that is going on around us. As a result, our conscious awareness of the environment is much less complete than most people think. We may even fail to consciously register objects that we are looking straight at, a phenomenon known as **inattentional blindness**: We look, but we do not see (Mack, 2003). When people are shown a video of a ball-passing game and are asked to count up the passes, they may even miss something as seemingly obvious as a man in a gorilla suit walking slowly through the ball court, thumping his chest (Simons & Chabris, 1999).

Selective attention, then, is a mixed blessing. It protects us from overload and allows us to focus on what's important, but it also deprives us of sensory information that we may need. That could be disastrous if you are so focused on texting a friend that you walk right into a pothole or a street full of traffic.

selective attention The focusing of attention on selected aspects of the environment and the blocking out of others.

inattentional blindness Failure to consciously perceive something you are looking at because you are not attending to it.

✓● Study and Review on mypsychlab.com

Quick Quiz

If you are not on overload, try answering these questions.

1. Even on the clearest night, some stars cannot be seen by the naked eye because they are below the viewer's _____ threshold.

2. If you jump into a cold lake but moments later the water no longer seems so cold, sensory _____ has occurred.

3. You are immobilized in a hospital bed, with no roommate, TV, or cell phone. If you feel edgy and disoriented, you may be suffering the effects of _____.

4. During a break from your job in a restaurant, you are so caught up in a book that you fail to notice the clattering of dishes or orders being called out to the cook. This is an example of _____.

5. In real-life detection tasks, is it better to be a "naysayer" or a "yea-sayer"?

Answers:

1. absolute 2. adaptation 3. sensory deprivation 4. selective attention 5. Neither; it depends on the consequences of a "miss" or a "false alarm." Suppose that you are in the shower and you're not sure whether your phone is ringing in the other room. You might want to be a yea-sayer if you are expecting a call about a job interview, but a naysayer if you are not expecting any calls and don't want to get out dripping wet for nothing.

YOU are about to learn...

- how the physical characteristics of light waves correspond to the psychological dimensions of vision.

- the basics of how the eye works, and why the eye is not a camera.

- how we see colors, and why we can describe a color as bluish green but not as reddish green.

- how we know how far away things are.

- why we see objects as stable even though sensory stimulation from the object is constantly changing.

- why perceptual illusions are valuable to psychologists.

Vision

Vision is the most frequently studied of all the senses, and with good reason. More information about the external world comes to us through our eyes than through any other sense organ. Because we evolved to be most active in the daytime, we are equipped to take advantage of the sun's illumination. Animals that are active at night tend to rely more heavily on hearing.

What We See

The stimulus for vision is light; even cats, raccoons, and other creatures famous for their ability to get around in the dark need some light to see. Visible light comes from the sun and other stars and from lightbulbs, and it is also reflected off objects. Light travels in the form of waves, and the *physical* characteristics of these waves affect three *psychological* dimensions of our visual world: hue, brightness, and saturation.

1 Hue, the dimension of visual experience specified by color names, is related to the *wavelength* of light—that is, to the distance between the crests of a light wave. Shorter waves tend to be seen as violet and blue, longer ones as orange and red. The sun produces white light, which is a mixture of all the visible wavelengths. Sometimes, drops of moisture in the air act like a prism: They separate the sun's white light into the colors of the visible spectrum, and we are treated to a rainbow.

2 Brightness is the dimension of visual experience related to the amount, or *intensity*, of the light an object emits or reflects. Intensity corresponds to the amplitude (maximum height) of the wave. Generally speaking, the more light an object reflects, the brighter it appears. However, brightness is also affected by wavelength: Yellows appear brighter than reds and blues even when their physical intensities are equal.

3 Saturation (colorfulness) is the dimension of visual experience related to the *complexity* of light—that is, to how wide or narrow the range of wavelengths is. When light contains only a single wavelength, it is said to be pure, and the resulting color is completely saturated. At the other extreme is white light, which lacks any color and is completely unsaturated. In nature, pure light is extremely rare. We usually sense a mixture of wavelengths, and we see colors that are duller and paler than completely saturated ones.

Variations in hue

Variations in brightness

Variations in saturation

An Eye on the World

Light enters the visual system through the eye, a wonderfully complex and delicate structure. As you read this section, examine Figure 6.2. Notice that

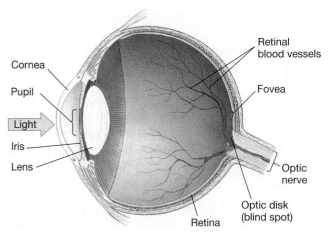

FIGURE 6.2
Major Structures of the Eye
Light passes through the pupil and lens and is focused on the retina at the back of the eye. The point of sharpest vision is at the fovea.

hue The dimension of visual experience specified by color names and related to the wavelength of light.

brightness Lightness or luminance; the dimension of visual experience related to the amount (intensity) of light emitted from or reflected by an object.

saturation Vividness or purity of color; the dimension of visual experience related to the complexity of light waves.

the front part of the eye is covered by the transparent *cornea*. The cornea protects the eye and bends incoming light rays toward a *lens* located behind it. A camera lens focuses incoming light by moving closer to or farther from the shutter opening. However, the lens of the eye works by subtly changing its shape, becoming more or less curved to focus light from objects that are close by or far away. The amount of light that gets into the eye is controlled by muscles in the *iris*, the part of the eye that gives it color. The iris surrounds the round opening, or *pupil*, of the eye. When you enter a dim room, the pupil widens, or dilates, to let more light in. When you emerge into bright sunlight, the pupil gets smaller, contracting to allow in less light.

The visual receptors are located in the back of the eye, or **retina**. (The retina also contains special cells that communicate information about light and dark to the brain area that regulates biological rhythms, as discussed in Chapter 5.) In a developing embryo, the retina forms from tissue that projects out from the brain, not from tissue destined to form other parts of the eye; thus, the retina is actually an extension of the brain. As Figure 6.3 shows, when the lens of the eye focuses light on the retina, the result is an upside-down image. Light from the top of the visual field stimulates light-sensitive receptor cells in the bottom part of the retina, and vice versa. The brain interprets this upside-down pattern of stimulation as something that is right side up.

About 120 to 125 million receptors in the retina are long and narrow, and are called **rods**. Another 7 or 8 million receptors are cone-shaped, and are called, appropriately, **cones**. The center of the retina, or *fovea*, where vision is sharpest, contains only

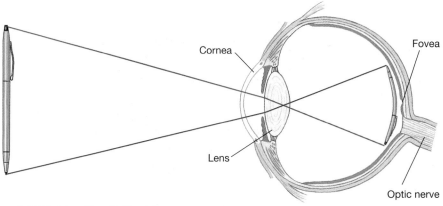

FIGURE 6.3 The Retinal Image
When we look at an object, the light pattern on the retina is upside down. René Descartes (1596–1650) was probably the first person to demonstrate this fact. He cut a piece from the back of an ox's eye and replaced the piece with paper. When he held the eye up to the light, he saw an upside-down image of the room on the paper!

cones, clustered densely together. From the center to the periphery, the ratio of rods to cones increases, and the outer edges contain virtually no cones.

Rods are more sensitive to light than cones are. They enable us to see in dim light and at night. (Cats see well in dim light in part because they have a high proportion of rods.) Because rods occupy the outer edges of the retina, they also handle peripheral (side) vision. But rods cannot distinguish different wavelengths of light so they are not sensitive to color, which is why it is often hard to distinguish colors clearly in dim light. The cones, on the other hand, are differentially sensitive to specific wavelengths of light and allow us to see colors. But they need much more light than rods do to respond, so they don't help us much when we are trying to find a seat in a darkened movie theater. (These differences are summarized in Table 6.1.) ✳ Explore

✳ Explore
Light and the Optic Nerve on mypsychlab.com

TABLE 6.1
Differences Between Rods and Cones

	Rods	Cones
How many?	120–125 million	7–8 million
Where most concentrated?	Periphery of retina	Center (fovea) of retina
How sensitive?	High sensitivity	Low sensitivity
Sensitive to color?	No	Yes

retina Neural tissue lining the back of the eyeball's interior, which contains the receptors for vision.

rods Visual receptors that respond to dim light.

cones Visual receptors involved in color vision.

dark adaptation A process by which visual receptors become maximally sensitive to dim light.

ganglion cells Neurons in the retina of the eye, which gather information from receptor cells (by way of intermediate bipolar cells); their axons make up the optic nerve.

feature-detector cells Cells in the visual cortex that are sensitive to specific features of the environment.

We have all noticed that it takes some time for our eyes to adjust fully to dim illumination. This process of **dark adaptation** involves chemical changes in the rods and cones. The cones adapt quickly, within 10 minutes or so, but they never become very sensitive to the dim illumination. The rods adapt more slowly, taking 20 minutes or longer, but are ultimately much more sensitive. After the first phase of adaptation, you can see better but not well; after the second phase, your vision is as good as it ever will get.

Rods and cones are connected by synapses to *bipolar cells*, which in turn communicate with neurons called **ganglion cells** (see Figure 6.4). The axons of the ganglion cells converge to form the *optic nerve*, which carries information out through the back of the eye and on to the brain. Where the optic nerve leaves the eye, at the *optic disk*, there are no rods or cones. The absence of receptors produces a blind spot in the field of vision. Normally, we are unaware of the blind spot because (1) the

image projected on the spot is hitting a different, "nonblind" spot in the other eye; (2) our eyes move so fast that we can pick up the complete image; and (3) the brain fills in the gap. You can find your blind spot by doing the Get Involved exercise on the facing page.

Why the Visual System Is Not a Camera

Although the eye is often compared with a camera, the visual system, unlike a camera, is not a passive recorder of the external world. Neurons in the visual system actively build up a picture of the world by detecting its meaningful features.

Ganglion cells and neurons in the thalamus of the brain respond to simple features in the environment, such as spots of light and dark. But in mammals, special **feature-detector cells** in the visual cortex respond to more complex features. This fact was first demonstrated by David Hubel and Torsten

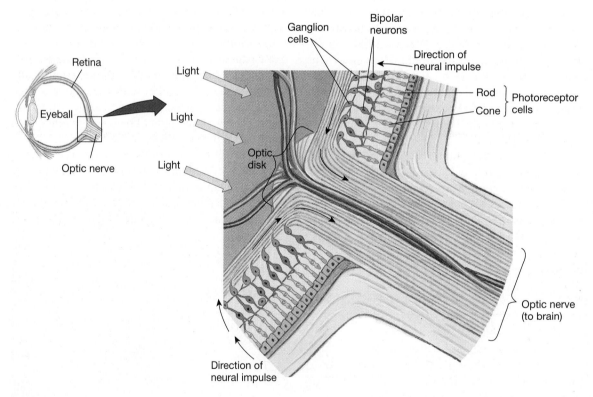

FIGURE 6.4
The Structures of the Retina
For clarity, all cells in this drawing are greatly exaggerated in size. To reach the receptors for vision (the rods and cones), light must pass through the ganglion and bipolar cells as well as the blood vessels that nourish them (not shown). Normally, we do not see the shadow cast by this network of cells and blood vessels because the shadow always falls on the same place on the retina, and such stabilized images are not sensed. But when an eye doctor shines a moving light into your eye, the treelike shadow of the blood vessels falls on different regions of the retina and you may see it—a rather eerie experience.

Get Involved! Find Your Blind Spot

A blind spot exists where the optic nerve leaves the back of your eye. Find the blind spot in your left eye by closing your right eye and looking at the magician. Then slowly move the book toward and away from yourself. The rabbit should disappear when the book is between 9 and 12 inches from your eye.

Wiesel (1962, 1968), who painstakingly recorded impulses from individual cells in the brains of cats and monkeys. In 1981, they were awarded a Nobel Prize for their work. Hubel and Wiesel found that different neurons were sensitive to different patterns projected on a screen in front of an animal's eyes. Most cells responded maximally to moving or stationary lines that were oriented in a particular direction and located in a particular part of the visual field. One type of cell might fire most rapidly in response to a horizontal line in the lower right part of the visual field, another to a diagonal line at a specific angle in the upper left part of the visual field. In the real world, such features make up the boundaries and edges of objects.

Since this pioneering work was done, scientists have found that other cells in the visual system have more complex specialties, such as bull's eyes and spirals. Some cells in the right temporal lobe even appear to respond maximally to *faces* (Kanwisher, 2000; Ó Scalaidhe, Wilson, & Goldman-Rakic, 1997; Young & Yamane, 1992). Some scientists have concluded that evolution has equipped us with an innate *face module* in the brain. The existence of such a module could help explain why infants prefer looking at faces instead of images that scramble the features of a face, and why a person with brain damage may continue to recognize faces even after losing the ability to recognize other objects.

A facility for deciphering faces makes evolutionary sense because it would have ensured our ancestors' ability to quickly distinguish friend from foe, or, in the case of infants, mothers from strangers. However, some psychologists and neuroscientists think that infants' apparent preference for faces is really a preference for curved lines, eye contact, or patterns that have more elements in the upper part (e.g., two eyes) than in the lower part (e.g., just a mouth) (Turati, 2004). Moreover, some of the brain cells that supposedly make up the face module respond to other things as well, depending on a person's experiences and interests. In one study, cells in the presumed face module fired when car buffs examined pictures of classic cars but not when they

Cases of brain damage support the idea that particular systems of brain cells are highly specialized for identifying important objects or visual patterns, such as faces. One man's injury left him unable to identify ordinary objects, which, he said, often looked like "blobs." Yet he had no trouble with faces, even when they were upside down or incomplete. When shown this painting, he could easily see the face but he could not see the vegetables comprising it (Moscovitch, Winocur, & Behrmann, 1997).

trichromatic theory A theory of color perception that proposes three mechanisms in the visual system, each sensitive to a certain range of wavelengths; their interaction is assumed to produce all the different experiences of hue.

opponent-process theory A theory of color perception that assumes that the visual system treats pairs of colors as opposing or antagonistic.

looked at pictures of exotic birds; the exact opposite was true for bird watchers (Gauthier et al., 2000). Cars, of course, do not have faces! In another study by the same researchers, cells in the "face module" fired after people were trained to distinguish among cute—but faceless—imaginary creatures called greebles (Gauthier et al., 1999).

Even if face and other specialized modules do exist, the brain cannot possibly contain a special area for every conceivable object. In general, the brain's job is to take fragmentary information about edges, angles, shapes, motion, brightness, texture, and patterns and figure out that a chair is a chair and the thing next to it is a dining room table. The perception of any given object probably depends on the activation of many cells in far-flung parts of the brain and on the overall pattern and rhythm of their activity

How We See Colors

For over 300 years, scientists have been trying to figure out why we see the world in living color. We now know that different processes explain different stages of color vision.

The Trichromatic Theory The **trichromatic theory** (also known as the *Young-Helmholtz theory*) applies to the first level of processing, which occurs in the retina of the eye. The retina contains three basic types of cones. One type responds maximally to blue, another to green, and a third to red. The thousands of colors we see result from the combined activity of these three types of cones.

Total color blindness is usually due to a genetic variation that causes cones of the retina to be absent or malfunctional. The visual world then consists of black, white, and shades of gray. Many species of animals are totally color-blind, but the condition is extremely rare in human beings. Most "color-blind" people are actually *color deficient*. Usually, the person is unable to distinguish red and green; the world is painted in shades of blue, yellow, brown, and gray. In rarer instances, a person may be blind to blue and yellow and may see only reds, greens, and grays. Color deficiency is found in about 8 percent of white men, 5 percent of Asian men, and 3 percent of black men and Native American men (Sekuler & Blake, 1994). Because of the way the condition is inherited, it is rare in women.

The Opponent-Process Theory The **opponent-process theory** applies to the second stage of color processing, which occurs in ganglion cells in the retina and in neurons in the thalamus and visual cortex of the brain. These cells, known as *opponent-process cells*, either respond to short wavelengths but are inhibited from firing by long wavelengths, or vice versa (DeValois & DeValois, 1975). Some opponent-process cells respond in opposite fashion to red and green, or to blue and yellow; that is, they fire in response to one and turn off in response to the other. (A third system responds in opposite fashion to white and black and thus yields information about brightness.) The net result is a color code that is passed along to the higher visual centers. Because this code treats red and green, and also blue and yellow, as antagonistic, we can describe a color as bluish green or yellowish green but not as reddish green or yellowish blue.

Get Involved! A Change of Heart

Opponent-process cells that switch on or off in response to green send an opposite message—"red"—when the green is removed, producing a negative afterimage. Stare at the black dot in the middle of this heart for at least 20 seconds. Then shift your gaze to a white piece of paper or a white wall. Do you get a "change of heart"? You should see an image of a red or pinkish heart with a blue border.

Opponent-process cells that are *inhibited* by a particular color produce a burst of firing when the color is removed, just as they would if the opposing color were present. Similarly, cells that *fire* in response to a color stop firing when the color is removed, just as they would if the opposing color were present. These facts explain why we are susceptible to *negative afterimages* when we stare at a particular hue—why we see, for instance, red after staring at green (do the Get Involved exercise to see for yourself). A sort of neural rebound effect occurs: The cells that switch on or off to signal the presence of "green" send the opposite signal ("red") when the green is removed and vice versa.

Constructing the Visual World

We do not actually see a retinal image; the mind must actively interpret the image and construct the world from the often-fragmentary data of the senses. In the brain, sensory signals that give rise to vision, hearing, taste, smell, and touch are combined from moment to moment to produce a unified model of the world. This is the process of *perception*.

Form Perception To make sense of the world, we must know where one thing ends and another begins. In vision, we must separate the teacher from the lectern; in hearing, we must separate the piano solo from the orchestral accompaniment; in taste, we must separate the marshmallow from the hot chocolate. This process of dividing up the world occurs so rapidly and effortlessly that we take it completely for granted, until we must make out objects in a heavy fog or words in the rapid-fire conversation of someone speaking a language we don't know.

The *Gestalt psychologists*, who belonged to a movement that began in Germany and was influential in the 1920s and 1930s, were among the first to study how people organize the world visually into meaningful units and patterns. In German, *Gestalt* means "form" or "configuration." The Gestalt psychologists' motto was "The whole is more than the sum of its parts." They observed that when we perceive something, properties emerge from the configuration as a whole that are not found in any particular component.

The Gestalt psychologists also noted that people always organize the visual field into *figure* and *ground*. The figure stands out from the rest of the environment (see Figure 6.5). Some things stand out as figure by virtue of their intensity or size; it is

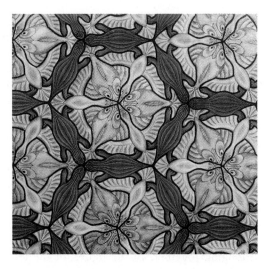

FIGURE 6.5
Figure and Ground
Which do you notice first in this drawing by M. C. Escher—the fish, geese, or salamanders? It will depend on whether you see the blue, red, or gold sections as figure or ground.

hard to ignore the bright glare of a flashlight at night or a tidal wave approaching your piece of beach. The lower part of a scene tends to be seen as figure, the upper part as background (Vecera, Vogel, & Woodman, 2002). Unique objects also stand out, such as a banana in a bowl of oranges, and so do moving objects in an otherwise still environment, such as a shooting star. Indeed, it is hard to ignore a sudden change of any kind in the environment because our brains are geared to respond to change and contrast. However, selective attention—the ability to concentrate on some stimuli and to filter out others—gives us some control over what we perceive as figure and ground, and sometimes it blinds us to things we would otherwise interpret as figure, as we saw earlier. 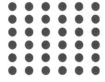 **Simulate**

Other **Gestalt principles** describe strategies used by the visual system to group sensory building blocks into perceptual units (Köhler, 1929; Wertheimer, 1923/1958). The Gestalt psychologists believed that these strategies were present from birth or emerged early in infancy as a result of maturation. Modern research, however, suggests that at least some of them depend on experience (Quinn & Bhatt, 2005). Here are a few well-known Gestalt principles:

1 Proximity. Things that are near each other tend to be grouped together. Thus you perceive the dots on the left as three groups of dots, not as twelve separate, unrelated ones. Similarly, you perceive the pattern on the right as vertical columns of dots, not as horizontal rows:

Simulate
Gestalt Laws of Perception on **mypsychlab.com**

Gestalt principles
Principles that describe the brain's organization of sensory information into meaningful units and patterns.

2 Closure. The brain tends to fill in gaps and thereby perceive complete forms. This is fortunate because we often need to decipher less-than-perfect images. The following figures are easily perceived as a triangle, a face, and the letter *e*, even though none of the figures is complete:

3 Similarity. Things that are alike in some way (as in color, shape, or size) tend to be perceived as belonging together. In the figure on the left, you see the circles as forming an *X*. In the one on the right, you see horizontal bars rather than vertical columns because the horizontally aligned stars are either all red or all outlined in red:

4 Continuity. Lines and patterns tend to be perceived as continuing in time or space. You perceive the figure on the left as a single line partially covered by an oval rather than as two separate lines touching an oval. In the figure on the right, you see two lines, one curved and one straight, instead of two curved and two straight lines, touching at one focal point:

Unfortunately, many consumer products are designed with little thought for Gestalt principles,

Monocular Cues to Depth

Most cues to depth do not depend on having two eyes. Some monocular (one-eyed) cues are shown here.

LIGHT AND SHADOW

Both of these attributes give objects the appearance of three dimensions.

INTERPOSITION

An object that partly blocks or obscures another one must be in front of the other one, and is therefore seen as closer.

MOTION PARALLAX

When an observer is moving, objects appear to move at different speeds and in different directions. The closer an object, the faster it seems to move; and close objects appear to move backward, whereas distant ones seem to move forward.

which is why it can be a major challenge to find the pause button on your DVD player's remote control or to change from AM to FM on your car radio (Bjork, 2000; Norman, 1988). Good design requires, among other things, that crucial distinctions be visually obvious.

Depth and Distance Perception Ordinarily we need to know not only *what* something is but also *where* it is. Touch gives us this information directly, but vision does not, so we must infer an object's location by estimating its distance or depth.

To perform this remarkable feat, we rely in part on **binocular cues**, cues that require the use of two eyes. One such cue is **convergence**, the turning of the eyes inward, which occurs when they focus on a nearby object. The closer the object, the greater the convergence, as you know if you have ever tried to cross your eyes by looking at your own nose. As the angle of convergence changes, the corresponding muscular changes provide information to the brain about distance.

The two eyes also receive slightly different retinal images of the same object. You can prove this by holding a finger about 12 inches in front of your face and looking at it with only one eye at a time. Its position will appear to shift when you change eyes. Now hold up two fingers, one closer to your nose than the other. Notice that the amount of space between the two fingers appears to change when you switch eyes. The slight difference in lateral (sideways) separation between two objects as seen by the left eye and the right eye is called **retinal disparity**. Because retinal disparity increases as the distance between two objects increases, the brain can use it to infer depth and calculate distance.

Binocular cues help us estimate distances up to about 50 feet. For objects farther away, we use only **monocular cues**, cues that do not depend on using both eyes. One such cue is *interposition*: When an

binocular cues Visual cues to depth or distance requiring two eyes.

convergence The turning inward of the eyes, which occurs when they focus on a nearby object.

retinal disparity The slight difference in lateral separation between two objects as seen by the left eye and the right eye.

monocular cues Visual cues to depth or distance, which can be used by one eye alone.

RELATIVE SIZE

The smaller an object's image on the retina, the farther away the object appears.

TEXTURE GRADIENTS

Distant parts of a uniform surface appear denser; that is, its elements seem spaced more closely together.

RELATIVE CLARITY

Because of particles in the air from dust, fog, or smog, distant objects tend to look hazier, duller, or less detailed.

LINEAR PERSPECTIVE

Parallel lines will appear to be converging in the distance; the greater the apparent convergence, the greater the perceived distance. Artists often exaggerate this cue to convey an impression of depth.

object is interposed between the viewer and a second object, partly blocking the view of the second object, the first object is perceived as being closer. Another monocular cue is *linear perspective*: When two lines known to be parallel appear to be coming together or converging (say, railroad tracks or a highway stretching for miles ahead of you), they imply the existence of depth. These and other monocular cues are illustrated on the previous pages.

The perception of distance is also influenced by some factors that have nothing to do with vision, such as your emotional state, a goal you are trying to reach, and the effort necessary to reach that goal (Proffitt, 2006). Suppose you are out walking and, tired and cranky, you see an appealing coffee shop up ahead. You are likely to think it is farther away if you are wearing a heavy backpack than if you are wearing a light one, because of the increased energy it would take you to get there.

Likewise, if you are asked to throw a ball into a basket, you will probably estimate the distance of that basket as farther when the ball is heavy than when it is light. If an object is just out of reach, you may think it is nearer when you can touch it with a baton than when you can't touch it, because touching it makes it seem closer to your "personal space." And if you are looking down from a balcony, you will probably overestimate the distance to the ground if you are afraid of heights but not if heights don't worry you.

Visual Constancies: When Seeing Is Believing Your perceptual world would be a confusing place without still another important perceptual skill. Lighting conditions, viewing angles, and the distances of stationary objects are all continually changing as we move about, yet we rarely confuse these changes with changes in the objects themselves. This ability to perceive objects as stable, or unchanging, even though the sensory patterns they produce are constantly shifting, is called **perceptual constancy**. The five kinds of constancies that have been most thoroughly studied are visual, and they are:

1 **Size constancy.** We see an object as having a constant size even when its retinal image becomes smaller or larger. A friend approaching on the street does not seem to be growing; a car pulling away from the curb does not seem to be shrinking. Size constancy depends in part on familiarity with objects; you know that people and cars and your dog Ruby

do not change size from moment to moment. It also depends on the apparent distance of an object. An object that is close produces a larger retinal image than the same object farther away, and the brain takes this into account. When you move your hand toward your face, your brain registers the fact that the hand is getting closer, and you correctly perceive its unchanging size despite the growing size of its retinal image. There is, then, an intimate relationship between perceived size and perceived distance.

2 **Shape constancy.** We continue to perceive an object as having a constant shape even though the shape of the retinal image produced by the object changes when our point of view changes. If you hold a Frisbee directly in front of your face, its image on the retina will be round. When you set the Frisbee on a table, its image becomes elliptical, yet you continue to see it as round.

3 **Location constancy.** We perceive stationary objects as remaining in the same place even though the retinal image moves about as we move our eyes, heads, and bodies. As you drive along the highway, telephone poles and trees fly by on your retina. But you know that these objects do not move on their own, and you also know that your

BIZARRO   By DAN PIRARO

When size constancy fails.

© 1999 Dan Piraro. Reprinted with special permission of King Features Syndicate.

perceptual constancy
The accurate perception of objects as stable or unchanged despite changes in the sensory patterns they produce.

body is moving, so you perceive the poles and trees as staying put.

4 Brightness constancy. We see objects as having a relatively constant brightness even though the amount of light they reflect changes as the overall level of illumination changes. Snow remains white even on a cloudy day and a black car remains black even on a sunny day. We are not fooled because the brain registers the total illumination in the scene and automatically adjusts for it.

5 Color constancy. We see an object as maintaining its hue despite the fact that the wavelength of light reaching our eyes from the object may change as the illumination changes. For example, outdoor light is "bluer" than indoor light, and objects outdoors therefore reflect more "blue" light than those indoors. Conversely, indoor light from incandescent lamps is rich in long wavelengths and is therefore "yellower." Yet an apple looks red whether you look at it in your kitchen or outside on the patio.

Part of the explanation involves sensory adaptation, which we discussed earlier. Outdoors, we quickly adapt to short-wavelength (bluish) light, and indoors, we adapt to long-wavelength light. As a result, our visual responses are similar in the two situations. Also, when computing the color of a particular object, the brain takes into account *all* the wavelengths in the visual field immediately around the object. If an apple is bathed in bluish light, so, usually, is everything else around it. The

increase in blue light reflected by the apple is canceled in the visual cortex by the increase in blue light reflected by the apple's surroundings, and so the apple continues to look red. Color constancy is further aided by our knowledge of the world. We know that apples are usually red and bananas are usually yellow, and the brain uses that knowledge to recalibrate the colors in those objects when the lighting changes (Mitterer & de Ruiter, 2008).

Visual Illusions: When Seeing Is Misleading Perceptual constancies allow us to make sense of the world. Occasionally, however, we can be fooled, and the result is a *perceptual illusion*. For psychologists, illusions are valuable because they are systematic errors that provide us with hints about the perceptual strategies of the mind.

Although illusions can occur in any sensory modality, visual illusions have been the best studied. Visual illusions sometimes occur when the strategies that normally lead to accurate perception are overextended to situations where they do not apply. Compare the lengths of the two vertical lines in Figure 6.6. You will probably perceive the line on the right as slightly longer than the one on the left, yet they are exactly the same. (Go ahead, measure them; everyone does.) This is the Müller-Lyer illusion, named after the German sociologist who first described it in 1889.

One explanation for the Müller-Lyer illusion is that the branches on the lines serve as perspective cues that normally suggest depth (Gregory, 1963). The line on the left is like the near edge of a

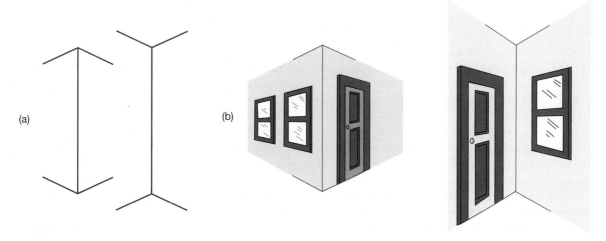

(a)   (b)

FIGURE 6.6
The Müller-Lyer Illusion
The two lines in (a) are exactly the same length. We are probably fooled into perceiving them as different because the brain interprets the one with the outward-facing branches as farther away, as if it were the far corner of a room, and the one with the inward-facing branches as closer, as if it were the near edge of a building (b).

 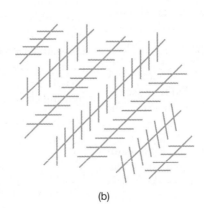 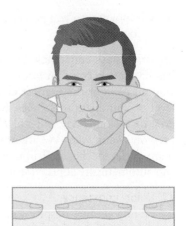

(a)   (b)   (c)

FIGURE 6.7
Fooling the Eye
Although perception is usually accurate, we can be fooled. In (a), the cats as drawn are exactly the same size; in (b), the diagonal lines are all parallel. To see the illusion depicted in (c), hold your index fingers 5 to 10 inches in front of your eyes as shown and then focus straight ahead. Do you see a floating "fingertip frankfurter"? Can you make it shrink or expand?

building; the one on the right is like the far corner of a room (see part b of the figure). Although the two lines produce retinal images of the same size, the one with the outward-facing branches suggests greater distance. We are fooled into perceiving it as longer because we automatically apply a rule about the relationship between size and distance that is normally useful: When two objects produce the same-sized retinal image and one is farther away, the farther one is larger. The problem, in this case, is that there is no actual difference in the distance of the two lines, so the rule is inappropriate.

Just as there are size, shape, location, brightness, and color constancies, so there are size, shape, location, brightness, and color *in*constancies, resulting in illusions. The perceived color of an object depends on the wavelengths reflected by its immediate surroundings, a fact well known to artists and interior designers. That is why you never see a good, strong red unless other objects in the surroundings reflect the blue and green part of the spectrum. When two objects that are the same color have different surroundings, you may mistakenly perceive them as different.

Some illusions are simply a matter of physics. Thus, a chopstick in a half-filled glass of water looks bent because water and air refract light differently. Other illusions occur due to misleading messages from the sense organs, as in sensory adaptation. Still others occur because the brain misinterprets sensory information, as in the Müller-Lyer illusion. Figure 6.7 shows some other startling illusions.

Perhaps the ultimate perceptual illusion occurred when Swedish researchers tricked people into feeling that they were swapping bodies with another person or even a mannequin (Petkova & Ehrsson, 2008). The participants wore virtual-reality goggles connected to a camera on the other person's (or mannequin's) head. This allowed them to see the world from the other body's point of view as an experimenter simultaneously stroked both bodies with a rod. Most people soon had the weird sensation that the other body was actually their own; they even cringed when the other body was poked or threatened. The researchers speculate that some day the body-swapping illusion could be helpful in marital counseling, allowing each partner to *literally* see things from the other's point of view, or in therapy with people who have distorted body images.

In everyday life, most illusions are harmless and entertaining. Occasionally, however, an illusion interferes with the performance of some task or skill, or may even cause an accident. For example, because large objects often appear to move more slowly than small ones, drivers sometimes underestimate the speed of onrushing trains at railroad crossings. They think they can beat the train, with tragic results.

**Study** and **Review** on **mypsychlab.com**

Quick Quiz

This quiz is no illusion.

1. How can two Gestalt principles help explain why you can make out the Big Dipper on a starry night?

2. *True or false*: Binocular cues help us locate objects that are very far away.

3. Hold one hand about 12 inches from your face and the other one about 6 inches away. (a) Which hand will cast the smaller retinal image? (b) Why don't you perceive that hand as smaller?

4. From an evolutionary point of view, people are most likely to have a mental module for recognition of (a) flowers, (b) bugs, (c) faces, (d) chocolate, (e) cars.

Answers:

1. *Proximity* of certain stars clustered together to form a pattern; *closure* allows you to "fill in the gaps" and see the contours of a "dipper."   **2.** false   **3. a.** The hand that is 12 inches away will cast a smaller retinal image. **b.** Your brain takes the differences in distance into account in estimating size; also, you know how large your hands are. The result is size constancy.   **4.** c

 YOU are about to learn...

- the basics of how we hear.
- why a note played on a flute sounds different from the same note played on an oboe.
- how we locate the source of a sound.

Hearing

Like vision, the sense of hearing, or *audition*, provides a vital link with the world around us. Because social relationships rely so heavily on conversations, people who lose their hearing sometimes come to feel socially isolated. That is why many people with hearing impairment feel strongly about teaching deaf children American Sign Language (ASL) or other gestural systems, which allow them to communicate with other signers.

What We Hear

The stimulus for sound is a wave of pressure created when an object vibrates (or, sometimes, when compressed air is released, as in a pipe organ). The vibration (or release of air) causes molecules in a transmitting substance to move together and apart. This movement produces variations in pressure that radiate in all directions. The transmitting substance is usually air, but sound waves can also travel through water and solids, as you know if you have ever put your ear to the wall to hear voices in the next room.

As with vision, *physical* characteristics of the stimulus—in this case, a sound wave—are related in a predictable way to *psychological* aspects of our experience:

1 Loudness is the psychological dimension of auditory experience related to the *intensity* of a wave's pressure. Intensity corresponds to the amplitude, or maximum height, of the wave. The more energy contained in the wave, the higher it is at its peak. Perceived loudness is also affected by how high or low a sound is. If low and high sounds produce waves with equal amplitudes, the low sound may seem quieter.

Sound intensity is measured in units called *decibels* (dB). A decibel is one-tenth of a *bel*, a unit named for Alexander Graham Bell, the inventor of the telephone. The average absolute threshold of hearing in human beings is zero decibels. Unlike inches on a rule, decibels are not equally distant; each 10 decibels denotes a tenfold increase in sound intensity. On the Internet, decibel estimates for various sounds vary a lot from site to site; this is because the intensity of a sound depends on things like how far away it is and the particular person or object producing the sound. The important thing to know is that a 60-decibel conversation is not twice as loud as a 30-decibel whisper; it is 1,000 times louder.

2 Pitch is the dimension of auditory experience related to the frequency of the sound wave and, to some extent, its intensity. *Frequency* refers to how rapidly the air (or other medium) vibrates—the number of times per second the wave cycles through a peak and a low point. One cycle per second is known as 1 *hertz* (Hz). The healthy ear of a young person normally detects frequencies in the

loudness The dimension of auditory experience related to the intensity of a pressure wave.

pitch The dimension of auditory experience related to the frequency of a pressure wave; the height or depth of a tone.

timbre The distinguishing quality of a sound; the dimension of auditory experience related to the complexity of the pressure wave.

organ of Corti [core-tee] A structure in the cochlea containing hair cells that serve as the receptors for hearing.

cochlea [KOCK-lee-uh] A snail-shaped, fluid-filled organ in the inner ear, containing the organ of Corti, where the receptors for hearing are located.

range of 16 Hz (the lowest note on a pipe organ) to 20,000 Hz (the scraping of a grasshopper's legs).

3 **Timbre** is the distinguishing quality of a sound. It is the dimension of auditory experience related to the *complexity* of the sound wave, the relative breadth of the range of frequencies that make up the wave. A pure tone consists of only one frequency, but pure tones in nature are extremely rare. Usually what we hear is a complex wave consisting of several subwaves with different frequencies. Timbre is what makes a note played on a flute, which produces relatively pure tones, sound different from the same note played on an oboe, which produces complex sounds.

When many sound-wave frequencies are present but are not in harmony, we hear noise. When all the frequencies of the sound spectrum occur, they produce a hissing sound called *white noise*. Just as white light includes all wavelengths of the visible light spectrum, so white noise includes all frequencies of the audible sound spectrum.

An Ear on the World

As Figure 6.8 shows, the ear has an outer, a middle, and an inner section. The soft, funnel-shaped outer ear is well designed to collect sound waves, but hearing would still be pretty good without it. The essential parts of the ear are hidden from view, inside the head.

A sound wave passes into the outer ear and through an inch-long canal to strike an oval-shaped membrane called the *eardrum*. The eardrum is so sensitive that it can respond to the movement of a single molecule! A sound wave causes it to vibrate with the same frequency and amplitude as the wave itself. This vibration is passed along to three tiny bones in the middle ear, the smallest bones in the human body. These bones, known informally as the hammer, the anvil, and the stirrup, move one after the other, which has the effect of intensifying the force of the vibration. The innermost bone, the stirrup, pushes on a membrane that opens into the inner ear.

The actual organ of hearing, the **organ of Corti**, is a chamber inside the **cochlea**, a snail-shaped

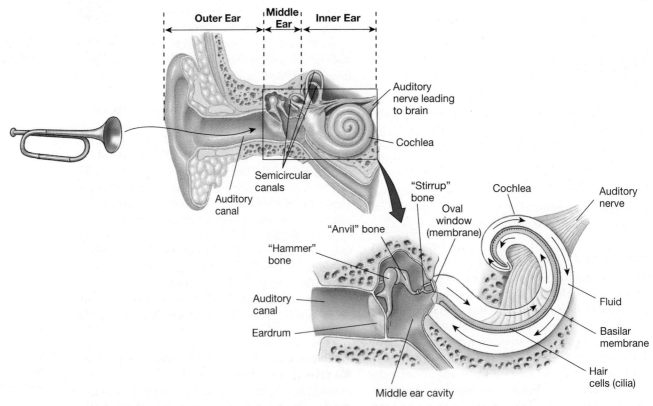

FIGURE 6.8
Major Structures of the Ear
Sound waves collected by the outer ear are channeled down the auditory canal, causing the eardrum to vibrate. These vibrations are then passed along to the tiny bones of the middle ear. Movement of these bones intensifies the force of the vibrations separating the middle and inner ear. The receptor cells for hearing (hair cells), located in the organ of Corti (not shown) within the snail-shaped cochlea, initiate nerve impulses that travel along the auditory nerve to the brain.

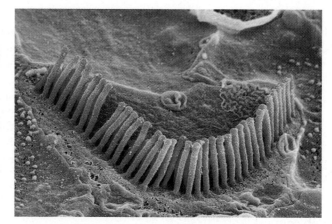

If prolonged, the 120-decibel music at a rock concert can damage or destroy the delicate hair cells of the inner ear and impair the hearing of fans standing close to the speakers. The microphotograph on the right shows minuscule bristles (cilia) projecting from a single hair cell.

structure within the inner ear. The organ of Corti plays the same role in hearing that the retina plays in vision. It contains the all-important receptor cells, which in this case look like bristles and are called *hair cells* and are topped by tiny bristles, or *cilia*. Brief exposure to extremely loud noises, like those from a gunshot or a jet airplane (140 dB), or sustained exposure to more moderate noises, like those from shop tools or truck traffic (90 dB), can damage these fragile cells. The cilia flop over like broken blades of grass, and if the damage affects a critical number, hearing loss occurs. In modern societies, with their rock concerts, deafening bars, leaf blowers, jackhammers, and MP3 players turned up to full blast, such damage is increasingly common, even among teenagers and young adults (Agrawal, Platz, & Niparko, 2008). Scientists are looking for ways to grow new, normally functioning hair cells (Izumikawa et al., 2005; Sage et al., 2005). But hair-cell damage is currently irreversible.

The hair cells of the cochlea are embedded in the rubbery *basilar membrane*, which stretches across the interior of the cochlea. When pressure reaches the cochlea, it causes wavelike motions in fluid within the cochlea's interior. These waves of fluid push on the basilar membrane, causing it to move in a wavelike fashion, too. Just above the hair cells is yet another membrane. As the hair cells rise and fall, their tips brush against it, and they bend. This causes the hair cells to initiate a signal that is passed along to the *auditory nerve*, which then carries the message to the brain. The particular pattern of hair-cell movement is affected by the manner in which the basilar membrane moves. This pattern determines which neurons fire and how rapidly they fire, and the resulting code in turn helps determine the sort of sound we hear. We discriminate high-pitched sounds largely on the basis of where activity occurs along the basilar membrane; activity at different sites leads to different neural codes. We discriminate low-pitched sounds largely on the basis of the frequency of the basilar membrane's vibration; again, different frequencies lead to different neural codes.

Could anyone ever imagine such a complex and odd arrangement of bristles, fluids, and snail shells if it did not already exist? ✻ Explore

Constructing the Auditory World

Just as we do not see a retinal image, so we do not hear a chorus of brushlike tufts bending and swaying in the dark recesses of the cochlea. Instead, we use our perceptual powers to organize patterns of sound and to construct a meaningful auditory world.

In class, your psychology instructor hopes you will perceive his or her voice as *figure* and distant cheers from the athletic field as *ground*. Whether these hopes are realized will depend, of course, on where you choose to direct your attention. Other Gestalt principles also seem to apply to hearing. The *proximity* of notes in a melody tells you which notes go together to form phrases; *continuity* helps you follow a melody on one violin when another violin is playing a different melody; *similarity* in timbre and pitch helps you pick out the soprano voices in a chorus and hear them as a unit; *closure* helps you understand a cell phone caller's words even when interference makes some of the individual sounds unintelligible.

Besides needing to organize sounds, we also need to know where they are coming from. We can

✻ Explore
**Structures
of the Ear** on
mypsychlab.com

estimate the *distance* of a sound's source by using loudness as a cue; we know that a train sounds louder when it is 20 yards away than when it is a mile off. To locate the *direction* a sound is coming from, we depend in part on the fact that we have two ears. A sound arriving from the right reaches the right ear a fraction of a second sooner than it reaches the left ear, and vice versa. The sound may also provide a bit more energy to the right ear (depending on its frequency) because it has to get around the head to reach the left ear. It is hard to localize sounds that are coming from directly in back of you or from directly above your head because such sounds reach both ears at the same time. When you turn or cock your head, you are actively trying to overcome this problem. Horses, dogs, rabbits, deer, and many other animals do not need to do this because, lucky creatures that they are, they can move their ears independently of their heads.

✔•─ **Study** and
Review on
mypsychlab.com

Quick Quiz

How well can you localize the answers to these questions?

1. Which psychological dimensions of hearing correspond to the intensity, frequency, and complexity of the sound wave?
2. Fred's voice is nasal and Ted's is gravelly. Which psychological dimension of hearing describes the difference?
3. An extremely loud or sustained noise can permanently damage the _____ of the ear.
4. During a lecture, a classmate draws your attention to a buzzing fluorescent light that you had not previously noticed. What will happen to your perception of figure and ground?

Answers:

1. loudness, pitch, timbre   2. timbre   3. hair cells (cilia)   4. The buzzing sound will become figure and the lecturer's voice will become ground, at least momentarily.

 YOU are about to learn...

- the basics of how we taste, smell, and feel.
- why saccharin and caffeine taste bitter to some people but not to others.
- why you have trouble tasting your food when you have a cold.
- why pain is complicated to understand and treat.
- how two senses inform us of the movement of our own bodies.

Other Senses

Psychologists have been particularly interested in vision and audition because of the importance of these senses to human survival. However, research on other senses is growing rapidly, as awareness of how they contribute to our lives increases and new ways are found to study them.

Taste: Savory Sensations

Taste, or *gustation*, occurs because chemicals stimulate thousands of receptors in the mouth. These receptors are located primarily on the tongue, but some are also found in the throat, inside the cheeks, and on the roof of the mouth. If you look at your tongue in a mirror, you will notice many tiny bumps; they are called **papillae** (from the Latin for "pimples"), and they come in several forms. In all but one of these forms, the sides of each papilla are lined with **taste buds**, which up close look a little like segmented oranges (see Figure 6.9). Because of genetic differences, human tongues can have as few as 500 or as many as 10,000 taste buds (Miller & Reedy, 1990).

The taste buds are commonly referred to, mistakenly, as the receptors for taste. The actual receptor cells are *inside* the buds, 15 to 50 to a bud. These cells send tiny fibers out through an opening in the bud; the receptor sites are on these fibers. New receptor cells replace old ones about every ten days. However, after age 40 or so, the total number of taste buds (and therefore receptors) declines. Interestingly, the center of the tongue contains no taste buds. However, as in the case of the eye's blind spot, you will not usually notice the lack of sensation because the brain fills in the gap.

There are four basic tastes that are part of our evolutionary heritage: *salty*, *sour*, *bitter*, and *sweet*, each produced by a different type of chemical.

papillae
[pa-PILL-ee] Knoblike elevations on the tongue, containing the taste buds. (Singular: *papilla*.)

taste buds Nests of taste-receptor cells.

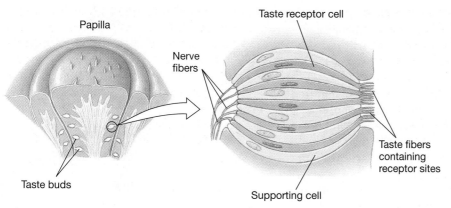

FIGURE 6.9
Taste Receptors
The illustration on the left shows taste buds lining the sides of a papilla on the tongue's surface. The illustration on the right shows an enlarged view of a single taste bud.

These hardwired taste receptors are tuned to molecules that alert us to good or dangerous tastes: Bitter tastes detect poison; sweet tastes attract us to eat biologically useful sugars; salty tastes enable us to identify sodium, a mineral crucial to survival; and sour tastes permit us to avoid acids in concentrations that might injure tissue (Bartoshuk, 2009). All of the basic tastes can be perceived at any spot on the tongue that has receptors, and differences among the areas are small. When you bite into an egg or a piece of bread or an orange, its unique flavor is composed of some combination of these tastes.

Some researchers believe that there is a fifth basic taste, *umami*, the taste of monosodium glutamate (MSG), which is supposed to detect protein. (Umami, which means "delicious" in Japanese, was identified by Japanese chemists in the early 1900s as a flavor enhancer.) However, findings from research on umami, which has largely been funded by the MSG industry, are debatable for two reasons: First, the umami taste is not perceptible in many foods containing protein. Second, umami lacks one of the most important properties of a basic taste: a hardwired response causing most people everywhere to react to it the same way. On the contrary, some individuals like umami, but others do not (Bartoshuk, 2009).

The evidence that umami is probably not a hardwired fifth taste has led to another fascinating discovery: Taste receptors are found throughout the gastrointestinal tract and may have different functions in different locations. Protein molecules are too large to be sensed by taste or smell; but when they are eaten, they are broken into their constituent amino acids, stimulating glutamate receptors in the gut, which in turn signal the brain that protein has been consumed, and creating a conditioned preference for the sensory properties of protein-rich foods such as bacon, roast beef, and cheese. Response to umami therefore occurs in the gut, not the mouth, and is a learned preference rather than a universal one (Bartoshuk, 2009).

Everyone knows that people live in different "taste worlds" (Bartoshuk, 1998). Some people love broccoli and others hate it. Some people can eat chili peppers that are burning hot and others cannot tolerate the mildest jalepeño. One reason for these differences is genetic. In the United States, about 25 percent of people are *supertasters* who find saccharin, caffeine, broccoli, and many other substances to be unpleasantly bitter. (Women, especially Asian women, are overrepresented in this group.) In contrast, "tasters" detect less bitterness in these foods, and "nontasters" detect none at all. Supertasters also perceive sweet tastes as sweeter and salty tastes as saltier than other people do, and they feel more "burn" from substances such as ginger, pepper, and hot chilies (Bartoshuk et al., 1998;

Get Involved! The Smell of Taste

Demonstrate for yourself that smell enhances the sense of taste. While holding your nose, take a bite of a slice of apple, and then do the same with a slice of raw potato. You may find that you can't taste much difference. If you think you do taste a difference, perhaps your expectations are influencing your response. Try the same thing, but close your eyes this time and have someone else feed you the slices. Can you still tell them apart? It's also fun to do this little test with flavored jelly beans. They are still apt to taste sweet, but you may be unable to identify the separate flavors.

Lucchina et al., 1998). Supertasters have more taste buds than other people. In addition, the papillae on their tongues are smaller, are more densely packed, and look different from those of nontasters (Reedy et al., 1993).

Other taste preferences are a matter of culture and learning. Many North Americans who enjoy raw food such as oysters, smoked salmon, and herring are nevertheless put off by other forms of raw seafood that are popular in Japan, such as sea urchin and octopus. And within a given culture, some people will greedily gobble up a dish that makes others turn green. Some of these learned taste preferences may begin in the womb or during breastfeeding. A baby whose mother drank carrot juice while pregnant or nursing is likely to be more enthusiastic about eating porridge mixed with carrot juice than porridge mixed with water, whereas babies without this exposure show no such preference (Mennella, Jagnow, & Beauchamp, 2001). The same findings turn up for many other flavors transmitted to an infant in breast milk, such as vanilla, cheese, mint, hot spices, and garlic.

The attractiveness of a food can also be affected by its color, temperature, and texture. As Goldilocks found out, a bowl of cold porridge is not nearly as delicious as one that is properly heated. And any peanut butter fan will tell you that chunky and smooth peanut butters just don't taste the same. Even more important for taste is a food's odor. Much of what we call "flavor" is really the smell of gases released by the foods we put in our mouths. Indeed, subtle flavors such as chocolate and vanilla would have little taste if we could not smell them (see Figure 6.10). Smell's influence on flavor explains why you have trouble tasting your food when you have a stuffy nose. Most people who have chronic trouble detecting tastes have a problem with smell, not taste.

Smell: The Sense of Scents

The great author and educator Helen Keller, who became blind and deaf as a toddler, once called smell "the fallen angel of the senses." Yet our sense of smell, or *olfaction*, although seemingly crude when compared to a bloodhound's, is actually quite good; the human nose can detect aromas that sophisticated machines fail to detect.

The receptors for smell are specialized neurons embedded in a tiny patch of mucous membrane in the upper part of the nasal passage, just beneath the eyes (see Figure 6.11). Millions of receptors in each nasal cavity respond to chemical molecules in the air. When you inhale, you pull these molecules into

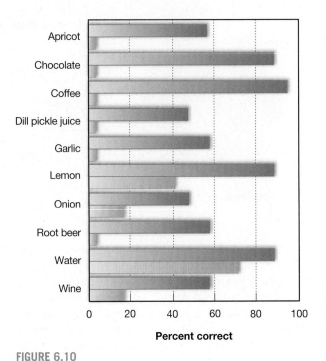

FIGURE 6.10
Taste Test
The turquoise bars show the percentages of people who could identify a substance dropped on the tongue when they were able to smell it. The green bars show the percentage that could identify the substance when they were prevented from smelling it (Mozell et al., 1969).

the nasal cavity, but they can also enter from the mouth, wafting up the throat like smoke up a chimney. These molecules trigger responses in the receptors that combine to yield the yeasty smell of freshly baked bread or the spicy smell of a curry. Signals from the receptors are carried to the brain's olfactory bulb by the *olfactory nerve*, which is made up of the receptors' axons. From the olfactory bulb, they travel to a higher region of the brain.

Figuring out the neural code for smell has been a real challenge. Of the 10,000 or so smells we detect (rotten, burned, musky, fruity, fishy, spicy, and so on), none seems to be more basic than any other. Moreover, roughly 1,000 kinds of receptors exist, each kind responding to a part of an odor molecule's structure (Axel, 1995; Buck & Axel, 1991). Distinct odors activate unique combinations of receptors, and signals from different types of receptors are combined in individual neurons in the brain.

Although smell is less vital for human survival than for the survival of other animals, it is still important. We sniff out danger by smelling smoke, rotten food, and gas leaks, so a deficit in the sense of smell is nothing to turn up your nose at. Such a loss can result from infection, disease, injury to the olfactory nerve, or smoking. A person who has

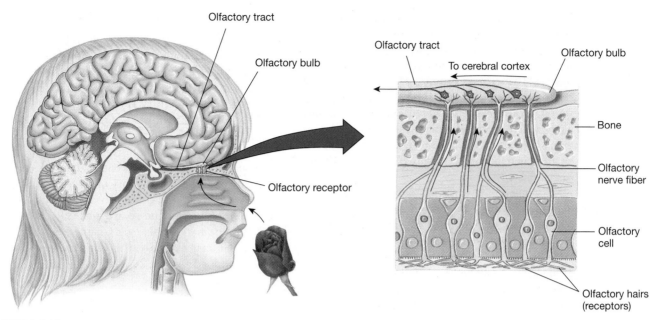

FIGURE 6.11
Receptors for Smell
Airborne chemical molecules (vapors) enter the nose and circulate through the nasal cavity, where the smell receptors are located. The receptors' axons make up the olfactory nerve, which carries signals to the brain. When you sniff, you draw more vapors into the nose and speed their circulation. Vapors can also reach the nasal cavity through the mouth by way of a passageway from the throat.

smoked two packs a day for ten years must abstain from cigarettes for ten more years before the sense of smell returns to normal (Frye, Schwartz, & Doty, 1990).

Odors, of course, have psychological effects on us, which is why we buy perfumes and sniff flowers. Perhaps because olfactory centers in the brain are linked to areas that process memories and emotions, specific smells often evoke vivid, emotionally colored memories (Herz & Cupchik, 1995; Vroon, 1997). The smell of hot chocolate may trigger fond memories of cozy winter mornings from your childhood; the smell of rubbing alcohol may remind you of an unpleasant trip to the hospital. Odors can also influence people's everyday behavior, which is why shopping malls and hotels often install aroma diffusers in hopes of putting you in a good mood.

Many dubious, unsupported claims have been made for the powers of particular aromas, but now some serious research is being done. For example, Dutch researchers have found that the citrus scent of an all-purpose cleaner,

unobtrusively left in a hidden bucket, can activate the mental concept *cleaning* and can even affect people's "cleaning behavior" (Holland, Hendriks, & Aarts, 2005). In one of their studies, participants wrote down five activities they were planning to do during the rest of the day. Those who had been exposed to the scent listed a cleaning activity more often than those who had not been exposed to it. In another study, participants did a task and then moved to another room, where they were invited to

Smell has not only evolutionary but also cultural significance. These pilgrims in Japan are purifying themselves with holy incense for good luck and health.

sit at a table and eat a crumbly biscuit as a hidden video camera recorded their hand movements. People who had been exposed to the cleaning scent while working on the initial task were much more likely to wipe away crumbs from the table than those who had not been exposed! Apparently, activation of the concept *cleaning* made them more likely to clean up after themselves. Later experiments found that clean scents even prime people to be more generous and trusting (Liljenquist, Zhong, & Galinsky, 2010).

After each of these studies, the researchers questioned the participants and found that none had been aware of the scent's influence. In fact, most were not even aware of having smelled the scent at all. Clearly, scent can have a nonconscious influence on what we think and do. This information should be helpful for anyone who has (or is!) a selfish or sloppy roommate. ⊙—Watch

⊙—Watch the Video **Aromatherapy** on **mypsychlab.com**

Senses of the Skin

The skin's usefulness is more than just skin deep. Besides protecting our innards, our two square yards of skin help us identify objects and establish intimacy with others. By providing a boundary between ourselves and everything else, the skin also gives us a sense of ourselves as distinct from the environment.

The basic skin senses include *touch* (or pressure), *warmth*, *cold*, and *pain*. Within these four types are variations such as itch, tickle, and painful burning. Although some spots on the skin are especially sensitive to the four basic skin sensations, scientists had difficulty finding distinct receptors and nerve fibers for these sensations, except in the case of pressure. But then Swedish researchers discovered a nerve fiber that seems responsible for the kind of itching caused by histamines (Schmelz et al., 1997). Another team has found that the same fibers that detect pain from a punch in the nose or a burn also seem to detect the kind of pathological itch that is unrelated to histamines and that can't be relieved by antihistamine medications (Johanek et al., 2008). Scientists have also identified a possible cold receptor (McKemy, Neuhausser, & Julius, 2002; Peier et al., 2002).

Perhaps specialized fibers will be discovered for other skin sensations as well. In the meantime, many aspects of touch remain baffling. Scientists still do not know why gently touching adjacent pressure spots in rapid succession produces tickle and why scratching relieves (or sometimes worsens) an itch. Decoding the messages of the skin senses will eventually tell us how we are able to distinguish sandpaper from velvet and glue from grease.

gate-control theory The theory that the experience of pain depends in part on whether pain impulses get past a neurological "gate" in the spinal cord and thus reach the brain.

The Mystery of Pain

Pain, which is both a skin sense and an internal sense, has come under special scrutiny. Pain differs from other senses in an important way: Even when the stimulus producing it is removed, the sensation may continue, sometimes for years. Understanding the physiology of pain has been an enormous challenge, because different types of pain (from, say, a thorn, a bruise, or a hot iron) involve different chemical changes and different changes in nerve-cell activity at the site of injury or disease, as well as in the spinal cord and brain. Several chemical substances are involved and so are glial cells, the cells that support nerve cells (see Chapter 4); they release inflammatory substances that can worsen the pain (Watkins & Maier, 2003).

The Physiology of Pain For many years, a leading explanation of pain has been the **gate-control theory**, which was first proposed by Canadian psychologist Ronald Melzack and British physiologist Patrick Wall (1965). According to this theory, pain impulses must get past a "gate" in the spinal cord. The gate is not an actual structure, but rather a pattern of neural activity that either blocks pain messages from the skin, muscles, and internal organs or lets those signals through. Normally, the gate is kept shut, either by impulses coming into the spinal cord from large fibers that respond to pressure and other kinds of stimulation or by signals coming down from the brain itself. But when body tissue is injured, the large fibers are damaged and smaller fibers open the gate, allowing pain messages to reach the brain unchecked. The gate-control theory correctly predicts that mild pressure, or other kinds of stimulation, can interfere with severe or protracted pain by closing the spinal gate. When we vigorously rub a banged elbow or apply ice packs, heat, or stimulating ointments to injuries, we are applying this principle.

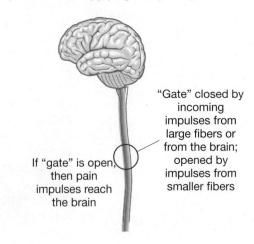

"Gate" closed by incoming impulses from large fibers or from the brain; opened by impulses from smaller fibers

If "gate" is open, then pain impulses reach the brain

In the gate theory, the brain not only responds to incoming signals from sensory nerves but is also capable of generating pain entirely on its own (Melzack, 1992, 1993). An extensive *matrix* (network) of neurons in the brain gives us a sense of our own bodies and body parts. When this matrix produces abnormal patterns of activity, the result is pain. The brain's ability to generate pain can help explain the many instances of severe, chronic pain that occur without any sign of injury or disease whatsoever.

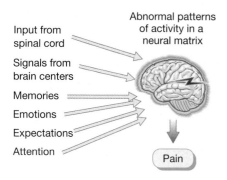

An extreme version of pain without injury occurs in **phantom pain**, in which a person continues to feel pain that seemingly comes from an arm or leg that has been amputated or a bodily organ that has been surgically removed. Phantom limb pain afflicts up to 90 percent of amputees. The person may feel the same aching, burning, or sharp pain from sores, calf cramps, throbbing toes, or even ingrown toenails that he or she endured before the surgery. Even when the spinal cord has been completely severed, amputees often continue to report phantom pain from areas below the break. There are no nerve impulses for the spinal-cord gate to block or let through, yet the pain can be constant and excruciating; some sufferers commit suicide.

A leading explanation of phantom pain is that the brain has reorganized itself: The area in the sensory cortex that formerly corresponded to the missing body part has been "invaded" by neurons from another area, often one corresponding to the face. Higher brain centers then interpret messages from those neurons as coming from the nonexistent body part (Cruz et al., 2005; Ramachandran & Blakeslee, 1998). Even though the missing limb can no longer send signals through touch and internal sensations, memories of these signals remain in the nervous system, including memories of pain, paralysis, and cramping that occurred prior to amputation. The result is an inaccurate "body map" in the brain and pain signals that cannot be shut off.

Vilayanur Ramachandran, the neurologist who first proposed this theory, has developed an extraordinarily simple but effective treatment for

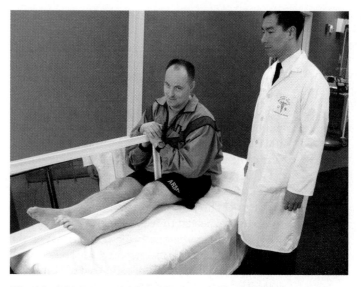

After his right leg was destroyed in an explosion while he was in Iraq, Army Sergeant Nicholas Paupore experienced excruciating phantom limb pain—as though the missing leg were constantly being shocked or stabbed. Even morphine didn't help. Then, as part of a clinical trial, he underwent a simple daily treatment. A mirror was placed at a strategic angle to reflect his intact leg, tricking his brain into registering two healthy legs that he could move freely. The pain subsided almost immediately. A year after therapy, he had only occasional, milder pain and needed no medication. In some patients, mirror therapy has eliminated phantom pain entirely.

phantom limb pain. Ramachandran wondered whether he could devise an illusion to trick the brain of an amputee with phantom arm pain into perceiving the missing limb as moving and pain-free. He placed a simple mirror upright and perpendicular to the sufferer's body, such that the amputee's intact arm was reflected in the mirror. From the amputee's perspective, the result was an illusion of two functioning arms. The amputee was then instructed to move both arms in synchrony while looking into the mirror. With this technique, which has now been used with many people, the brain is fooled into thinking its owner has two healthy arms, resynchronizes the signals—and phantom pain vanishes (Ramachandran & Altschuler, 2009). Neurologists have been testing this method with Iraq veterans, and are finding it to be more successful than control therapies in which patients just mentally visualize having two intact limbs (Anderson-Barnes et al., 2009; Chan et al., 2007).

The Psychology of Pain Whether pain arises normally or arises abnormally in the absence of tissue damage, psychological as well as physiological factors affect the severity of chronic pain and a person's reactions to it. When people dwell on their pain and talk about it constantly, or begin to define

phantom pain The experience of pain in a missing limb or other body part.

kinesthesis [KIN-es-THEE-sís] The sense of body position and movement of body parts; also called *kinesthesia*.

equilibrium The sense of balance.

themselves as a sick, suffering person, their pain typically intensifies (Pincus & Morley, 2001).

Expectations also exert a powerful influence. If you expect to feel pain, you may focus on it, producing a self-fulfilling prophecy. And if you expect *not* to feel pain, that expectation, too, can become self-fulfilling. In one study, ten healthy volunteers had heat applied to their lower legs (Koyama et al., 2005). The volunteers had been trained to expect jolts of heat of varying intensity depending on the delay between a tone and application of the heat; the longer the delay, the stronger the heat. Functional MRI showed that the stronger the pain the volunteers expected to feel, the greater the activity in certain brain regions prior to delivery of the pain, and most of these regions overlapped with those that responded to the actual pain. Moreover, when the researchers gave the signal for moderately painful heat and instead delivered the most painful heat, the subjects' self-reported pain fell by 28 percent, compared with when they expected the most painful heat and actually got it (see Figure 6.12). This decrease was equal to what they would have experienced had they received a shot of morphine!

Findings like these suggest a mechanism for how placebos reduce pain: When placebos affect expectations ("I'm going to get relief"), they also

affect the brain mechanism's underlying pain. Indeed, when volunteers in another study had an "analgesic cream" (actually a placebo) rubbed on their skin before getting a painful shock to the wrist, MRI scans showed decreased activity in the pain matrix, the pain-sensitive areas of their brains (Wager et al., 2004).

Placebos also promote the production of endorphins, the body's natural pain-relieving opiates. Researchers gave volunteers a slow, harmless injection of a pain-inducing solution in the jaw and had them rate their pain level (Zubieta et al., 2005). As the injection continued, the researchers told some of the participants (falsely) that a pain-relieving serum had been added and again asked all of the subjects to rank their discomfort. Throughout the procedure, PET scans tracked the activity of endorphins in the subjects' brains. Those who got the placebo produced endorphins in pain-control areas of the brain, which is just what would have happened had they taken a real pain killer.

As a result of such research, pain management programs now take psychological factors into account. Many are based on cognitive-behavior therapy, which teaches people living with chronic pain how to substitute adaptive thoughts for negative ones, and to use coping strategies such as distraction and imagery (see Chapter 12). These cognitive and behavioral strategies, in turn, affect pain-processing and pain-modifying circuits in the brain (Edwards et al., 2009). As scientists explore the puzzles of pain, they are beginning to see why it is that some people experience great pain when there is no apparent physiological reason for it, whereas others do not experience pain even when there is a physiological reason. Pain is not "just in people's heads," but it may be in their brains.

The Environment Within

We usually think of our senses as pipelines to the world around us, but two senses keep us informed about the movements of our own bodies. **Kinesthesis** tells us where our bodily parts are located and lets us know when they move. This information is provided by pain and pressure receptors located in the muscles, joints, and tendons. Without kinesthesis, you would have trouble with any voluntary movement. Think of how hard it is to walk when your leg has fallen asleep or how awkward it feels to chew when a dentist has numbed your jaw.

Equilibrium, or the sense of balance, gives us information about our bodies as a whole. Along with vision and touch, it lets us know whether we

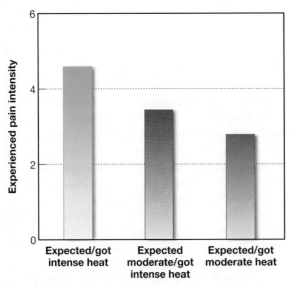

FIGURE 6.12

Expectations and Pain

When people expected moderate heat but got intense heat (purple bar), their self-reported pain was lower than it would have been had they expected the intense heat (green bar).

This break-dancer obviously has exceptional kinesthetic talents and equilibrium.

are standing upright or on our heads and tells us when we are falling or rotating. Equilibrium relies primarily on three **semicircular canals** in the inner ear (refer back to Figure 6.8 on page 200). These

thin tubes are filled with fluid that moves and presses on hairlike receptors whenever the head rotates. The receptors initiate messages that travel through a part of the auditory nerve that is not involved in hearing.

Normally, kinesthesis and equilibrium work together to give us a sense of our own physical reality, something we take utterly for granted but should not. Oliver Sacks (1985) told the heartbreaking story of Christina, a young British woman who suffered irreversible damage to her kinesthetic nerve fibers because of a mysterious inflammation. At first, Christina was as floppy as a rag doll; she could not sit up, walk, or stand. Then, slowly, she learned to do these things, relying on visual cues and sheer willpower. But her movements remained unnatural; she had to grasp a fork with painful force or she would drop it. More important, despite her remaining sensitivity to light touch on the skin, she said she could no longer experience herself as physically embodied: "It's like something's been scooped right out of me," she told Sacks, "right at the center."

With equilibrium, we come, as it were, to the end of our senses. Every single second, millions of sensory signals reach the brain, which combines and integrates them to produce a model of reality. How does it know how to do this? Are our perceptual abilities inborn, or must we learn them? We turn next to this issue.

semicircular canals Sense organs in the inner ear that contribute to equilibrium by responding to rotation of the head.

✓ **Study** and **Review** on mypsychlab.com

Quick Quiz

See if you can make sense of the following quiz items.

A. What explanation of each problem is most likely?

1. April always has trouble tasting foods, especially those with subtle flavors.

2. May, a rock musician, does not hear as well as she used to.

3. June has chronic shoulder pain, though the injury that initially caused it seems to have healed. (Hint: Think about the gate-control theory.)

B. After reading about the research on how scent affects "cleaning behavior," what further questions might you want to ask?

C. After seeing a new pain-relief ointment advertised on TV, you try it and find that it seems to work. What other explanation is possible for the decrease in your pain?

Answers:

A. 1. April may have an impaired sense of smell, possibly due to disease, illness, or cigarette smoking. **2.** Hearing impairment has many causes, but in May's case, we might suspect that prolonged exposure to loud music has damaged the hair cells of her cochlea. **3.** Nerve fibers that normally close the pain "gate" may have been damaged, or a matrix of cells in the brain may be producing abnormal activity. **B.** Some questions to ask: Do other scents also affect behavior, and if so, which ones? (We do not want to oversimplify by assuming that similar results would occur for all scents.) Are pleasant and unpleasant scents equally likely to affect behavior? Would the effects be even stronger if the participants were aware of the scent? Most important, will other research replicate these initial findings? **C.** The relief you feel may be due at least in part to a placebo effect, which has reduced activity in the pain matrix of your brain or has led to increased production of endorphins.

YOU are about to learn...

- whether babies see the world in the way adults do.

- what happens when people who are born blind or deaf have their sight or hearing restored.

- how psychological and cultural factors affect perception.

Perceptual Powers: Origins and Influences

What happens when babies first open their eyes? Do they see the same sights, hear the same sounds, and smell the same smells as an adult does? Or is an infant's world, as William James once suggested, only a "blooming, buzzing confusion," waiting to be organized by experience and learning? The truth lies somewhere between these two extremes.

Inborn Abilities

In human beings, most basic sensory abilities and many perceptual skills are inborn or develop very early. Infants can distinguish salty from sweet and can discriminate among odors. They can distinguish a human voice from other sounds. They will startle to a loud noise and turn their heads toward its source, showing that they perceive sound as being localized in space. Many visual skills, too, are present at birth or develop shortly afterward. Human infants can discriminate sizes and colors

very early, possibly even right away. They distinguish contrasts, shadows, and complex patterns after only a few weeks, and depth perception develops during the first few months.

Testing an infant's perception of depth requires considerable ingenuity. In a classic procedure, infants are placed on a device called a *visual cliff* (Gibson & Walk, 1960). The "cliff" is a pane of glass covering a shallow surface and a deep one (see Figure 6.13). Both surfaces are covered by a checkerboard pattern. The infant is placed on a board in the middle, and the child's mother tries to lure the baby across either the shallow side or the deep side. Babies only 6 months of age will crawl across the shallow side but will refuse to crawl out over the "cliff." Their hesitation shows that they have depth perception.

Even younger infants have been tested on the visual cliff, although they cannot yet crawl. At only 2 months of age, babies show a drop in heart rate when placed on the deep side but no change when they are placed on the shallow side. A slowed heart rate is usually a sign of increased attention. Thus, although these infants may not be frightened the way an older infant would be, it seems they can perceive the difference between the shallow and deep sides of the cliff (Banks & Salapatek, 1984).

Critical Periods

Although many perceptual abilities are inborn, experience also plays a vital role. If an infant misses

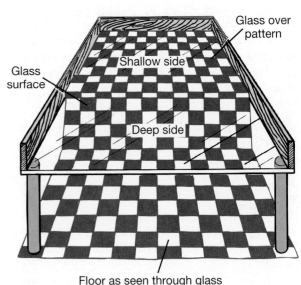

Glass over pattern

Shallow side

Glass surface

Deep side

Floor as seen through glass

FIGURE 6.13
A Cliff-Hanger
Infants as young as 6 months usually hesitate to crawl past the apparent edge of a visual cliff, which suggests that they are able to perceive depth.

out on important experiences during a crucial window of time called a *critical period* (sometimes called a *sensitive period*), perception will be impaired. Innate abilities may not survive because cells in the nervous system deteriorate, change, or fail to form appropriate neural pathways.

One way to study critical periods is to see what happens when the usual perceptual experiences of early life fail to take place. To do this, researchers have studied kittens and other animals whose sensory and perceptual systems are similar to our own. Like human infants, kittens are born with the visual ability to detect horizontal and vertical lines and other spatial orientations; at birth, kittens' brains are equipped with the same kinds of feature-detector cells that adult cats have. But if they are deprived of normal visual experience, these cells deteriorate or change and perception suffers (Crair, Gillespie, & Stryker, 1998; Hirsch & Spinelli, 1970).

In one famous study, kittens were exposed to either vertical or horizontal black and white stripes. Special collars kept them from seeing anything else, even their own bodies. After several months, the kittens exposed only to vertical stripes seemed blind to all horizontal contours; they bumped into horizontal obstacles, and they ran to play with a bar that an experimenter held vertically but not to a bar held horizontally. In contrast, those exposed only to horizontal stripes bumped into vertical obstacles and ran to play with horizontal bars but not vertical ones (Blakemore & Cooper, 1970).

What about human beings? Because of the brain's impressive plasticity (see Chapter 4), some people who were unable to see until middle childhood or even adulthood can regain enough perceptual ability to get along fine in daily life (Ostrovsky, Andalman, & Sinha, 2006). However, their perception is unlikely to fully recover. When adults who have been blind from infancy have their vision restored, most of them do not see well. Areas in the brain normally devoted to vision may have taken on different functions when these individuals were blind. As a result, their depth perception may be poor, causing them to trip constantly. They cannot always make sense of what they see; to identify objects, they may have to touch or smell them. They may have trouble recognizing faces and emotional expressions. They may even lack size constancy and may need to remind themselves that people walking away from them are not shrinking in size (Fine et al., 2003). Generally, the best recoveries occur when an infant's congenital blindness is corrected early, probably because a critical period for visual development occurs in infancy or early childhood.

Similar findings apply to hearing. When adults who were born deaf, or who lost their hearing before learning to speak, receive cochlear implants (devices that stimulate the auditory nerve and allow auditory signals to travel to the brain), they tend to find sounds confusing. They are unable to learn to speak normally, and sometimes they ask to have the implants removed. But cochlear implants are more successful in children and in adults who became deaf late in life (Rauschecker, 1999). Young children presumably have not yet passed through the critical period for processing sounds, and older adults have already had years of auditory experience.

In sum, our perceptual powers are both inborn and dependent on experience. Because neurological connections in infants' brains and sensory systems are not completely formed, their senses are far less acute than an adult's. It takes time and experience for their sensory abilities to fully develop. But an infant's world is clearly not the blooming, buzzing confusion that William James took it to be.

Psychological and Cultural Influences

The fact that some perceptual processes appear to be innate does not mean that all people perceive the world in the same way. A camera doesn't care what it "sees." A digital recorder doesn't ponder what it "hears." But because we human beings care about what we see, hear, taste, smell, and feel, psychological factors can influence what we perceive and how we perceive it. Here are a few of these factors:

1 Needs and motives. When we need something, have an interest in it, or want it, we are especially likely to perceive it. For example, hungry individuals are faster than others at seeing words related to hunger when the words are flashed briefly on a screen (Wispé & Drambarean, 1953). People also tend to perceive objects that they want—a water bottle if they are thirsty, money they can win in a game, a personality test with favorable results—as being physically closer to them than objects they don't want or need. The researchers call these motivated misperceptions "wishful seeing" (Balcetis & Dunning, 2010).

2 Beliefs. What we hold to be true about the world can affect our interpretation of ambiguous sensory signals. If you believe that extraterrestrials occasionally visit the earth and one evening you see a round object in the sky, you may think you are seeing a spaceship. (Impartial investigations of UFO sightings show that they are actually weather balloons, rocket launchings, swamp

People often see what they want to see. Diana Duyser, a cook at a Florida casino, took a bite out of a grilled cheese sandwich and believed she saw the image of the Virgin Mary in what remained of it. She preserved the sandwich in plastic for ten years and then decided to sell it. An online casino bought it on eBay for $28,000, even with a bite of it missing!

gas, military aircraft, or ordinary celestial bodies, such as planets and meteors.) Images that remind people of Jesus or Mary have been reported on walls, dishes, tortillas, and plates of spaghetti; the Arabic script for "Allah" has been reported on fish scales, chicken eggs, and beans. Such images cause great excitement among those who believe that divine messages can be found on everyday objects. However, inevitably mundane explanations prove to be the right ones. A purported image of Jesus on a garage door in California turned out to be caused by two streetlights that merged the shadows of a bush and a "For Sale" sign in the yard.

3 **Emotions.** Emotions can also influence our interpretation of sensory information, as when a small child afraid of the dark sees a ghost instead of a robe hanging on the bedroom door. Pain is particularly intensified by negative emotions such as anxiety and sadness. Interestingly, when people perceive their pain as resulting from another person's malicious intent (e.g., they think the other person intentionally stepped on their toe), they feel the hurt more than they would if they thought it was simply due to a clumsy accident (Gray & Wegner, 2008).

4 **Expectations.** Previous experiences often affect how we perceive the world (Lachman, 1996). The tendency to perceive what you expect is called a **perceptual set.** Perceptual sets can come in handy; they help us fill in words in sentences when we haven't really heard every one. But perceptaul sets can also cause misperceptions. In Center Harbor, Maine, local legend has it that veteran newscaster Walter Cronkite was sailing into port one day when he heard a small crowd on shore shouting

"Hello, Walter . . . Hello, Walter." Pleased, he waved and took a bow. Only when he ran aground did he realize what they had really been shouting: "Shallow water . . . shallow water!"

By the way, the previous paragraph has a misspelled word. Did you notice it? If not, probably it was because you expected all the words in this book to be spelled correctly.

Culture and Context Our needs, beliefs, emotions, and expectations are all affected, in turn, by the culture we live in. Different cultures give people practice with different environments. In a classic study done in the 1960s, researchers found that members of some African tribes were much less likely to be fooled by the Müller-Lyer illusion and other geometric illusions than were Westerners. In the West, the researchers observed, people live in a "carpentered" world, full of rectangular structures. Westerners are also used to interpreting two-dimensional photographs and perspective drawings as representations of a three-dimensional world. Therefore, they interpret the kinds of angles used in the Müller-Lyer illusion as right angles extended in space, a habit that increases susceptibility to the illusion. The rural Africans in the study, living in a less carpentered environment and in round huts, seemed more likely to take the lines in the figures literally, as two-dimensional, which could explain why they were less susceptible to the illusion (Segall, Campbell, & Herskovits, 1966; Segall et al., 1999).

Culture also affects perception by shaping our stereotypes, directing our attention, and telling us what to notice or ignore. Westerners tend to focus mostly on the figure when viewing a scene and

perceptual set A habitual way of perceiving, based on expectations.

much less on the ground. East Asians, in contrast, tend to pay attention to the overall context and the relationship between figure and ground. When Japanese and Americans were shown underwater scenes containing brightly colored fish that were larger and moving faster than other objects in the scene, they reported the same numbers of details about the fish, but the Japanese reported more details about everything else in the background (Masuda & Nisbett, 2001). If it doesn't move, most Americans don't see it.

As you can see . . . well, what you see partly depends on the culture you live in! When travelers visit another culture and are surprised to find that its members "see things differently," they may be literally correct.

✔●⎯Study and Review on mypsychlab.com

Quick Quiz

Direct your perceptual attention now to this quiz.

1. On the visual cliff, most 6-month-old babies (a) go right across because they cannot detect depth, (b) cross even though they are afraid, (c) will not cross because they can detect depth, (d) cry or get bored.

2. Newborns and infants (a) have few perceptual abilities, (b) need visual experiences during a critical period for vision to develop normally, (c) see as well as adults.

3. "Have a nice . . . " says Dewey, but then he gets distracted and doesn't finish the thought. Yet Clarence is sure he heard Dewey wish him a nice *day*. Why?

Answers:

1. c　2. b　3. perceptual set due to expectations

 YOU are about to learn...

• that perception is often unconscious.

• whether "subliminal perception" tapes will help you lose weight or reduce your stress.

Perception without Awareness

It would be impossible to be consciously aware of every single thing we see, hear, touch, or even smell in the course of a day; we rely on selective filters to focus our attention. Much of our perception occurs without our conscious awareness, yet may nonetheless influence our behavior.

Behavior can be affected even by stimuli that are so weak or brief that they are below a person's absolute threshold for detecting them—that is, *subliminal*. People sometimes correctly sense a change in a scene (say, in the color or location of an object) even though the change took place too quickly to be consciously recognized and identified (Rensink, 2004). And individuals who are subliminally exposed to a face will tend to prefer that face over one they did not "see" in this way (Bornstein, Leone, & Galley, 1987).

In many studies of nonconscious perception, researchers have used a method called **priming**, in which a person is exposed to information explicitly or subliminally and is later tested to see whether the information affects performance on another task. For example, when words flashed subliminally are

priming A method used to measure unconscious cognitive processes, in which a person is exposed to information and is later tested to see whether the information affects behavior or performance on another task or in another situation.

© Baby Blues Partnership. Reprinted with special permission of King Features Syndicate.

related to some personality trait, such as honesty, people are more likely later to judge someone they read about as having that trait. They have been "primed" to evaluate the person that way (Bargh, 1999).

Thus, people often know more than they know they know. In fact, nonconscious processing occurs not only in perception but also in memory, thinking, and decision making, as we discuss in Chapters 7 and 8. However, even in the laboratory, where researchers have considerable control, subliminal perception can be hard to demonstrate and replicate. The strongest evidence for its existence comes from studies using simple stimuli (faces or single words such as *bread*) rather than complex stimuli such as sentences ("Eat whole wheat bread, not white bread, if you know what's good for you!").

If subliminal priming can affect judgments and preferences in the laboratory, you may be wondering whether it can be used to manipulate people's attitudes and behavior in ordinary life. Subliminal persuasion techniques first became a hot topic back in the 1950s, when an advertising executive claimed to have increased popcorn and Coke sales at a theater by secretly flashing the words EAT POPCORN and DRINK COKE on the movie screen. The claim turned out to be a hoax, devised to save the man's struggling advertising company.

Ever since, scientists have been skeptical, but that has not deterred people who market subliminal tapes that promise to help you lose weight, stop smoking, relieve stress, boost your motivation, lower your cholesterol, or stop biting your nails, all without any effort on your part. Ah, if only those claims were true! But they are not. In study after study, placebo tapes—tapes that do not contain the

((•— **Listen** to **Subliminal Messages** on **mypsychlab.com**

messages that participants think they do—have been just as "effective" as subliminal tapes (Eich & Hyman, 1992; Merikle & Skanes, 1992; Moore, 1992, 1995). In one typical experiment, people listened to tapes labeled "memory" or "self-esteem," but some heard tapes that were incorrectly labeled.

Thinking Critically about Subliminal Persuasion

About half showed improvement in the area specified by the label *whether it was correct or not*. The improvement was due to expectations alone (Greenwald et al., 1991).

However, previous efforts at subliminal persuasion may have left out an important ingredient: the person's motivation. A team of researchers used subliminal messages—the words *thirst* and *dry*—to make subjects feel thirsty and prime them to drink. Later, when given a chance to drink, the primed participants did in fact drink more than control subjects did, but only if they had been moderately thirsty to begin with (Strahan, Spencer, & Zanna, 2002). ((•— **Listen**

Does this mean that advertisers can seduce us into buying soft drinks or voting for political candidates by slipping subliminal slogans and images into television and magazine ads? The priming research has renewed the debate. Yet given the many studies that have found no evidence of subliminal persuasion in real life and the subtlety of the effects that occur in the laboratory (e.g., you have to be somewhat thirsty already to be primed to want to drink), we think there's little cause for worry about subliminal manipulation. And if you want to improve yourself or your life, you'll have to do it the old-fashioned way: by working at it consciously.

✓•— **Study** and **Review** on **mypsychlab.com**

Quick Quiz

Please remain conscious while you answer this question.

A study appears to find evidence of "sleep learning"—the ability to perceive and retain material played on an audio recording while a person sleeps. What would you want to know about this research before deciding to record this chapter and play it by your bedside all night instead of studying it in the usual way?

Answers:

Was there a control group that listened to, say, a musical selection or white noise? How complicated was the material that was allegedly learned: a few key words, whole sentences, a whole lecture by Professor Arbuckle? Were the results large enough to have any practical applications? How did the researchers determine that the participants really were asleep? When brain-wave measures are used to verify that volunteers are actually sleeping, no "sleep learning" takes place.

Psychology in the news REVISITED

The great Greek philosopher Plato once said that "knowledge is nothing but perception." But simple perception is not always the best path to knowledge. As we have seen throughout this chapter, we do not passively register the world "out there"; we mentally construct it. If we are critical thinkers, therefore, we will be aware of how our beliefs, motivations, and assumptions shape our perceptions.

Sometimes those perceptions work to our advantage, as in the case of Lindsey Vonn, whose ability to ski in the Olympics trumped excruciating pain from an injury. The human capacity for selective attention, and our ability to focus on goals we are strongly motivated to achieve, can temporarily make people oblivious to pain they would otherwise feel, which is why we so often hear of athletes and dancers who are able to finish a performance despite sprained ankles, serious bruises, or even broken bones. Similarly, soldiers who are seriously wounded often deny being in much pain, even though they are alert and are not in shock. Their relief at being alive may offset the worry and fear that would otherwise make their pain worse, although the body's own pain-fighting mechanisms may also be involved.

At other times, our perceptions work to our disadvantage, as in the second story that opened this chapter, about people who report seeing spaceships. Some people, as we noted, are habitual yea-sayers who, because of their expectations, are quick to think they saw something that wasn't there. Others are fooled by the normal distortions of perception: When you are looking up at the sky, where there are few points of reference, it is difficult to judge how far away or how big an object is. And still others believe in UFOs and are longing to see one, and that wish can affect their perception of ambiguous objects.

Whenever impartial investigators have looked into UFO reports, they have found that what people actually saw were weather balloons, rocket launchings, swamp gas, military aircraft, or (in the vast majority of cases) ordinary celestial bodies, such as planets and meteors. The strange objects in the photo accompanying our news story, which look so much like flying saucers, are really lenticular (lens-shaped) clouds. And the "alien bodies" reported in Roswell were simply test dummies made of rubber, which the Air Force was dropping from high-altitude balloons before subjecting human beings to jumps from the same height. But even capable, intelligent people can be fooled. One astronomer who investigates UFO reports says, "I've been with Air Force pilots who thought they were seeing a UFO. But it was actually the moon. I've seen people look at Venus and say they could see portholes on a spaceship" (quoted in Ratcliffe, 2000).

None of this means that the only real world is the mundane one we see in everyday life. Because our sense organs evolved for particular purposes, our sensory windows on the world are partly shuttered. But we can use reason, ingenuity, and science to pry those shutters open. Ordinary perception tells us that the sun circles the earth, but the great astronomer Copernicus was able to figure out nearly five centuries ago that the opposite is true. Ordinary perception will never let us see ultraviolet and infrared rays directly, but we know they are there, and we can measure them. If science can enable us to overturn the everyday evidence of our senses, who knows what surprises science has in store for us?

Remember this amazing photo from Chapter 1? After reading this chapter, you should have a better idea of why "seeing" should not always be "believing."

Can Perception Be "Extrasensory"?

Eyes, ears, mouth, nose, skin: We rely on these organs for our experience of the external world. Some people, however, claim they can send and receive messages about the world without relying on the usual sensory channels, by using *extrasensory perception (ESP)*. Reported ESP experiences involve things like telepathy, the direct communication of messages from one mind to another without the usual sensory signals, and precognition, the perception of an event that has not yet happened. How should critical thinkers respond to such claims? What questions should they ask, and what kind of evidence should they look for?

Evidence or Coincidence? Much of the supposed evidence for extrasensory perception comes from anecdotal accounts. But people are not always reliable reporters of their own experiences. They often embellish and exaggerate, or they recall only part of what happened. They also tend to forget incidents that do not fit their beliefs, such as "premonitions" of events that fail to occur. Many ESP experiences could merely be unusual coincidences that are memorable because they are dramatic. What passes for telepathy or precognition could also be based on what a person knows or deduces through ordinary means. If Joanne's father has had two recent heart attacks, her premonition that her father will die shortly (followed, in fact, by her father's death) may not be so impressive.

The scientific way to establish a phenomenon is to produce it under controlled conditions. ESP has been studied extensively by researchers in the field of *parapsychology*, but studies have often been poorly designed, with inadequate precautions against fraud and improper statistical analysis. As a result, the history of research in this area has been one of initial enthusiasm because of apparently positive results (Bem & Honorton, 1994; Dalton et al., 1996), followed by disappointment when the results cannot be replicated (Milton & Wiseman, 1999, 2001). One researcher who tried for 30 years to establish the reality

of psychic phenomena finally gave up in defeat. "I found no psychic phenomena," she wrote, "only wishful thinking, self-deception, experimental error, and even an occasional fraud. I became a skeptic" (Blackmore, 2001).

The issue has not gone away, however. Many people *really, really* want to believe that ESP exists. James Randi, a famous magician who is dedicated to educating the public about psychic deception, has for years offered a million dollars to anyone who can demonstrate ESP or other paranormal powers in the presence of independent observers and under controlled conditions. Many have taken up the challenge; no one has succeeded. We think Randi's money is safe.

Lessons from a Magician. Despite the lack of evidence for ESP, many people say they believe in it. Perhaps you yourself have had an experience that seemed to involve ESP, or perhaps you have seen a convincing demonstration by someone else. Surely you can trust the evidence of your own eyes. Or can you? We will answer this question with a true story, one that contains an important lesson about why it's a good idea to think critically regarding ESP.

During the 1970s, Andrew Weil (now known for his efforts to promote alternative medicine) set out to investigate the claims of a self-proclaimed psychic named Uri Geller (Weil, 1974a, 1974b). Weil, who believed in telepathy, felt that ESP might be explained by principles of modern physics, and he was receptive to Geller's claims. When he met Geller at a private gathering, he was not disappointed. Geller correctly identified a cross and a Star of David sealed inside separate envelopes. He made a stopped watch start running and made a ring sag into an oval shape, apparently without touching them. He made keys

change shape. Weil came away a convert. What he had seen with his own eyes seemed impossible to deny . . . until he went to visit the Amazing Randi.

To Weil's astonishment, Randi was able to duplicate much of what Geller had done. He, too, could bend keys and guess the contents of sealed envelopes. But Randi's feats were tricks, and he was willing to show Weil exactly how they were done. Weil suddenly experienced "a sense of how strongly the mind can impose its own interpretations on perceptions; how it can see what it expects to see, but not see the unexpected."

Weil was dis-illusioned—literally. Even when he knew what to look for in a trick, he could not catch the Amazing Randi doing it. Weil learned that our sense impressions of reality are not the same as reality. Our eyes, our ears, and especially our brains can play tricks on us.

"What do you mean you didn't know that we were having a pop quiz today?"

Summary ((•─[**Listen** to an **audio file** of your chapter on **mypsychlab.com**

- *Sensation* is the detection and direct experience of physical energy as a result of environmental or internal events. *Perception* is the process by which sensory impulses are organized and interpreted.

Our Sensational Senses

- Sensation begins with the *sense receptors*, which convert the energy of a stimulus into electrical impulses that travel along nerves to the brain. Separate sensations can be accounted for by *anatomical codes* (as set forth by the *doctrine of specific nerve energies*) and *functional codes* in the nervous system. In *sensory substitution*, sensory crossover from one modality to another occurs, and in *synesthesia*, sensation in one modality consistently evokes a sensation in another, but these experiences are rare.

- Psychologists specializing in *psychophysics* have studied sensory sensitivity by measuring *absolute* and *difference thresholds*. *Signal-detection theory*, however, holds that responses in a detection task consist of both a sensory process and a decision process and will vary with the person's motivation, alertness, and expectations.

- Our senses are designed to respond to change and contrast in the environment. When stimulation is unchanging, *sensory adaptation* occurs. Too little stimulation can cause *sensory deprivation*. Too much stimulation can cause *sensory overload*. *Selective attention* prevents overload and allows us to focus on what is important, but it also deprives us of sensory information we may need, as in *inattentional blindness*.

Vision

- Vision is affected by the wavelength, intensity, and complexity of light, which produce the psychological dimensions of visual experience—*hue, brightness,* and *saturation*. The visual receptors, *rods* and *cones*, are located in the *retina* of the eye. They send signals (via other cells) to the *ganglion cells* and ultimately to the *optic nerve*, which carries visual information to the brain. Rods are responsible for vision in dim light; cones are responsible for color vision. *Dark adaptation* occurs in two stages.

- Specific aspects of the visual world, such as lines at various orientations, are detected by *feature-detector cells* in the visual areas of the brain. Some of these cells respond maximally to complex patterns. A debate is going on about the possible existence of specialized "face modules" in the brain. In general, however, the brain must take in fragmentary information about lines, angles, shapes, motion, brightness, texture, and other features of what we see and come up with a unified view of the world.

- The *trichromatic* and *opponent-process* theories of color vision apply to different stages of processing. In the first stage, three types of cones in the retina respond selectively to different wavelengths of light. In the second, *opponent-process cells* in the retina and the thalamus respond in opposite fashion to short and long wavelengths of light.

- Perception involves the active construction of a model of the world from moment to moment. The *Gestalt principles* (e.g., *figure and ground, proximity, closure, similarity,* and *continuity*) describe visual strategies used by the brain to perceive forms.

- We localize objects in visual space by using both *binocular* and *monocular* cues to depth. Binocular cues include *convergence* and *retinal disparity*. Monocular cues include, among others, *interposition* and *linear perspective*. *Perceptual constancies* allow us to perceive objects as stable despite changes in the sensory patterns they produce. *Perceptual illusions* occur when sensory cues are misleading or when we misinterpret cues.

Hearing

- Hearing (*audition*) is affected by the intensity, frequency, and complexity of pressure waves in the air or other transmitting substance, corresponding to the experience of *loudness, pitch,* and *timbre* of the sound. The receptors for hearing are *hair cells (cilia)* embedded in the *basilar membrane*, located in the *organ of Corti* in the interior of the *cochlea*. These receptors pass signals along to the *auditory nerve*. The sounds we hear are determined by patterns of hair-cell movement, which produce different neural codes. When we localize sounds, we use as cues subtle differences in how pressure waves reach each of our ears.

Other Senses

- Taste (*gustation*) is a chemical sense. Elevations on the tongue, called *papillae*, contain many *taste buds*, which in turn contain the taste receptors. The four hardwired basic tastes are salty, sour, bitter, and sweet, which evolved to ensure that humans would eat healthful, biochemically necessary food and avoid rancid or poisonous food. Some researchers believe that umami is a fifth basic taste, but the current evidence disputes this conclusion. Responses to a particular taste depend in part on genetic differences among individuals; some people are "supertasters." Taste preferences are also affected by culture and learning and by the texture, temperature, and smell of food.

- Smell (*olfaction*) is also a chemical sense. No basic odors have been identified, and up to a thousand different receptor types exist. But researchers have discovered that distinct odors activate unique combinations of receptor types, and they have identified some of those combinations. Odors also have psychological effects and can affect behavior even when people are unaware of their influence. Cultural and individual differences affect people's responses to particular odors.

- The skin senses include touch (pressure), warmth, cold, pain, and variations such as itch and tickle. Receptors for some types of itching and a possible receptor for cold have been discovered.

- Pain has proven to be physiologically complicated, involving the release of several different chemicals and changes in both neurons and *glial cells*. According to the *gate-control theory*, the experience of pain depends on whether neural impulses get past a "gate" in the spinal cord and reach the brain; in addition, a matrix of neurons in the brain can generate pain even in the absence of signals from sensory neurons. A leading theory of *phantom pain* holds that it occurs when the brain rewires itself after amputation of a limb or removal of a body organ. Expectations and placebos affect the subjective experience of pain through their effects on brain activity and endorphin production.

- *Kinesthesis* tells us where our body parts are located and *equilibrium* tells us the orientation of the body as a whole. Together, these two senses provide us with a feeling of physical embodiment.

Perceptual Powers: Origins and Influences

- Many fundamental perceptual skills are inborn or are acquired shortly after birth. By using the *visual cliff*, psychologists have learned that babies have depth perception by the age of 6 months and probably even earlier. However, without certain experiences during *critical periods* early in life, cells in the nervous system deteriorate, change, or fail to form appropriate neural pathways, and perception is impaired. This is why efforts to correct congenital blindness or deafness are most successful when they take place early in life.

- Psychological influences on perception include needs, beliefs, emotions, and expectations (which produce *perceptual sets*). Cultures give people practice with different kinds of experiences and influence what they attend to.

Perception without Awareness

- In the laboratory, studies using *priming* show that simple visual subliminal messages can influence behaviors and judgments, depending on a person's motivational state (e.g., thirst). However, there is no evidence that complex behaviors in everyday life can be altered by "subliminal-perception" tapes or similar products.

Psychology in the News, Revisited

- Human perception does not merely capture objective reality but also reflects our needs, biases, and beliefs. Our eyes and our ears (and especially our brains) can play tricks on us—causing us to "see" things that are not there and sometimes to overcome pain that is there.

Taking Psychology with You

- Years of research have failed to produce convincing evidence for extrasensory perception. What so-called psychics do is no different from what all good magicians do: capitalize on people's beliefs, expectations, wishful thinking, and, literally, mis-perceptions.

Key Terms

sensation 181

perception 181

sense receptors 182

anatomical codes 182

doctrine of specific nerve energies 182

synesthesia 183

functional codes 183

psychophysics 183

absolute threshold 184

difference threshold 184

signal-detection theory 185

sensory adaptation 186

sensory deprivation 186

selective attention 187

inattentional blindness 187

hue 188

brightness 188

saturation 188

retina 189

rods 189

cones 189

dark adaptation 190

ganglion cells 190

optic nerve 190

feature-detector cells 190

face module 191

trichromatic theory 192

opponent-process theory 192

negative afterimage 193

figure and ground 193

Gestalt principles 193

binocular cues 195

convergence 195

retinal disparity 195

monocular cues 195

perceptual constancy 196

perceptual illusion 197

audition 199

loudness 199

pitch 199

frequency (sound wave) 199

timbre 200

organ of Corti 200

cochlea 200

hair cells (cilia) 201

basilar membrane 201

auditory nerve 201

gustation 202

papillae 202

taste buds 202

supertasters 203

olfaction 204

gate-control theory
  of pain 206

phantom pain 207

kinesthesis 208

equilibrium 208

semicircular canals 209

critical period 211

perceptual set 212

subliminal perception 213

priming 213

extrasensory perception
  (ESP) 216

parapsychology 216

Sensation is the detection and direct experience of physical energy as a result of environmental or internal events.
Perception is the process by which sensory impulses are organized and interpreted.

The Senses

- Sensation begins with the **sense receptors,** which convert the energy of a stimulus into electrical impulses that travel along the nerves to the brain.
- Anatomical codes (as set forth by the **doctrine of specific nerve energies**) and functional codes in the nervous system account for separate sensations. In rare cases, however, sensory crossover results in **synesthesia.**

Measuring the Senses

- Psychologists specializing in psychophysics have studied sensory sensitivity by measuring **absolute** and **difference thresholds.**
- **Signal-detection theory** holds that responses in a detection task consist of both a sensory process and a decision process and vary with the person's motivation, alertness, and expectations.

Sensory Adaptation

- **Sensory adaptation** occurs when sensation is unchanging.
- **Sensory deprivation** occurs with too little stimulation.

Sensing without Perceiving

- We use **selective attention** to avoid sensory overload.
- **Inattentional blindness** is a failure to consciously perceive something you are looking at because you are not attending to it.

Hearing

The stimulus for hearing (*audition*) is a pressure wave or the release of compressed air.

What We Hear

- Intensity corresponds to the experience of **loudness.**
- Frequency corresponds to the experience of **pitch.**
- Complexity corresponds to the experience of **timbre.**

The receptors for hearing are hair cells (*cilia*) embedded in the basilar membrane of the **organ of Corti** in the interior of the **cochlea.**

Vision

The stimulus for vision is light, which travels in waves.

What We See

- Wavelength of light produces the experience of **hue.**
- Intensity of light produces the experience of **brightness.**
- Complexity of light produces the experience of **saturation.**

Visual Receptors

Visual receptors are located in the **retina** of the eye and send signals to the ganglion cells and ultimately to the *optic nerve*.
- **Rods** are responsible for vision in dim light.
- **Cones** are responsible for color vision.
- Rods and cones take time to adjust to dim illumination, a process known as **dark adaptation**.
- Information from rods and cones is processed and communicated by **ganglion cells**, the axons of which converge to form the *optic nerve*.
- **Feature-detector cells** in the visual areas of the brain detect specific aspects of the environment, such as line orientation.
- Some researchers believe that certain brain cells comprise a *face module*.

Color Vision

- The **trichromatic theory** accounts for the first level of color processing, which occurs in the retina, where three types of cones respond to different wavelengths of light.
- In the second level of color processing, **opponent-process** cells in the retina and thalamus respond in opposite fashion to short and long wavelengths of light.

Gestalt Principles

Gestalt principles—such as figure and ground, proximity, closure, similarity, and continuity—describe visual strategies used by the brain to perceive form, distance, and depth.

Depth and Distance Perception

- **Binocular cues** include **convergence** and **retinal disparity**.
- **Monocular cues** include light and shadow; interposition; motion parallax; relative size; texture gradients; relative clarity; and linear perspective.

Constancies and Illusions

- **Perceptual constancy** is the accurate perception of objects as stable despite changes in size, shape, location, brightness, and color.
- *Perceptual illusions* occur when sensory cues are misleading or we misinterpret them.

(b)

Other Senses

Taste

Taste (*gustation*) is a chemical sense.

- **Papillae** on the tongue contain **taste buds**, which contain taste receptors.
- The basic tastes are each produced by a different type of chemical: salty, sour, bitter, and sweet. A fifth taste, umami, is a conditioned preference that occurs in the gut, not the mouth, and is not hardwired.
- Genetic and cultural differences influence responses to a particular taste.

Smell

Smell (*olfaction*) is also a chemical sense.

- There are up to 1,000 different kinds of receptors.
- Distinct odors activate unique combinations of receptors.
- Cultural and individual differences affect people's responses to odors.

Senses of the Skin

Include *touch* (pressure), *warmth, cold,* and *pain* and variations such as itch and tickle.

Pain

Pain is both a skin sense and an internal sense.

The **gate-control theory** holds that the experience of pain depends on whether neural impulses get past a "gate" in the spinal cord and reach the brain.

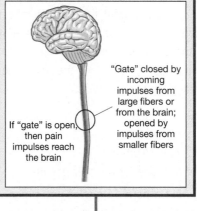

If "gate" is open, then pain impulses reach the brain

"Gate" closed by incoming impulses from large fibers or from the brain; opened by impulses from smaller fibers

In the gate theory, the brain can generate pain even in the absence of signals from sensory neurons, because an extensive *matrix* of neurons in the brain gives us a sense of our own bodies. When the matrix produces abnormal activity, the result is pain.

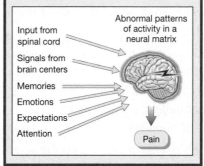

Input from spinal cord
Signals from brain centers
Memories
Emotions
Expectations
Attention

Abnormal patterns of activity in a neural matrix

Pain

A leading explanation of **phantom pain** is that the brain has reorganized itself, incorrectly interpreting messages from neurons as coming from a nonexistent body part.

The Environment Within

Kinesthesis tells us where our body parts are located. **Equilibrium** tells us the orientation of the body as a whole, and relies on three **semicircular canals** in the inner ear.

Perceptual Powers

Inborn Abilities

- *Visual cliff* experiments show that even at 6 months, babies have depth perception.
- Without certain experiences during *critical periods*, perception is impaired.

Psychological Influences on Perception

- Psychological influences on perception include needs, beliefs, emotions, and expectations (which produce **perceptual sets**).
- These influences are affected by culture.

Perception without Awareness

- In **priming**, a person is exposed to explicit or subliminal information and is later tested to see whether the information affects performance on another task. This method is often used to measure unconscious cognitive processes, including perception.
- When simple stimuli are used, subliminal priming can influence certain behaviors, judgments, and motivational states.
- However, no evidence of subliminal persuasion has been found with commercially marketed subliminal ads and tapes conveying complex messages.

Ig Nobel Prize Winners Announced

CAMBRIDGE, MA, October 2, 2009. The Nineteenth First Annual Ig Nobel ceremony was held last night in Harvard University's Sanders Theatre. The Ig Nobel Prizes are sponsored by the organization Improbable Research, whose goal is to honor achievements that "first make people laugh, then make them think."

Like the real Nobels, the Ig Nobels are awarded in diverse areas, ranging from public health to peace to biology. The sponsors explain that the prizes "are intended to celebrate the unusual, honor the imaginative—and spur people's interest in science, medicine, and technology." This year's winners include:

- *Public Health:* Elena Bodnar and her colleagues, for inventing a bra that in an emergency can quickly be transformed into a pair of protective face masks—one for the wearer and one for another person.

- *Veterinary Medicine:* Catherine Douglas and Peter Rowlinson of Britain's Newcastle University, for showing that cows that are given names produce more milk than cows without names.

- *Medicine:* Donald L. Unger, of Thousand Oaks, California, for investigating arthritis of the fingers by cracking the knuckles of his left hand (but not his right hand) every day for 50 years. Contrary to what his mother had warned him, knuckle cracking did not lead to arthritis.

- *Mathematics:* Gideon Gono, governor of Zimbabwe's Reserve Bank, for having his bank print bank notes ranging from one cent to one hundred trillion dollars, as a way of helping people learn to cope with a wide range of numbers.

- *Literature:* Ireland's police service, for writing and presenting more than 50 traffic tickets to the most frequent driving offender in the country, Prawo Jazdy. The Irish police, faced with a sudden influx of Polish immigrants, had failed to learn a little basic Polish—namely, that "prawo jazdy" is Polish for "driving license."

- *Biology:* Fumiaki Taguchia and four colleagues at Kitasato University, for showing that kitchen refuse can be reduced more than 90 percent by using bacteria extracted from the feces of giant pandas.

The Improbable Research organization depends on volunteers in many countries and an editorial board of some 50 eminent scientists, including several Nobel (and Ig Nobel) Prize winners. The group publishes a magazine, a newsletter, a newspaper column, books, and a daily blog. But it is best known for the Ig Nobel awards, which the British journal *Nature* calls "arguably the highlight of the scientific calendar."

Dr. Elena Bodnar, the Ig Nobel prizewinner in public health, demonstrates her patented "Emergency Bra" that can quickly be converted into a pair of gas masks—one for the brassiere wearer and one to be given to a needy bystander. Behind her, two colleagues are wearing the bras as protective face masks.

Thinking and Intelligence

The Ig Nobel awards may seem a little off the wall, but they reflect the human mind's love of wordplay, wit, parody, and imagination. Indeed, the mind is an amazing thing. Each day, in the course of ordinary living, we make decisions, draw inferences about other people's behavior, try to understand our motives, laugh at something that strikes us as funny, and organize and reorganize the contents of our mental world. Descartes' famous declaration "I think, therefore I am" could just as well have been reversed: "I am, therefore I think." Our powers of thought and intelligence have inspired humans to immodestly call ourselves *Homo sapiens*, Latin for wise or rational man.

Think for a moment about what thinking does for you. It frees you from the confines of the immediate present: You can think about a trip taken three years ago, a party next Saturday, or the War of 1812. It carries you beyond the boundaries of reality: You can imagine unicorns and utopias, Martians and magic. You can make plans far into the future and judge the probability of events, both good and bad. Because you think, you do not need to grope your way blindly through your problems but can apply knowledge and reasoning to solve them intelligently and creatively.

Yet just how "sapiens" are we, really? In Florida, a woman driving to see her boyfriend decided to shave her bikini line while her passenger, her remarkably tolerant ex-husband, held the steering wheel. They crashed. In Berlin, Germany, a radio station decided to find out how easily people could be manipulated on the Internet by posting an obviously fake video on YouTube, purportedly showing the recently deceased Michael Jackson emerging from a coroner's van—alive. In a single day, the video got 880,000 hits, and the rumor that Jackson was alive and well quickly spread around the globe. We could go on.

The human mind, which has managed to come up with poetry, penicillin, and panty hose, is a miraculous thing; but the human mind has also managed to come up with traffic jams, spam, and war. To better understand why the same species that figured out how to get to the moon is also capable of breathtaking bumbling here on earth, we will examine in this chapter how people reason, solve problems, and grow in intelligence, as well as some sources of their mental shortcomings.

223

> ◆ **YOU** are about to learn...
>
> - the basic elements of thought.
>
> - whether the language you speak affects the way you think.
>
> - how subconscious thinking, nonconscious thinking, and mindlessness help us—and can also cause trouble.

Thought: Using What We Know

Many cognitive psychologists liken the human mind to an information processor, analogous to a computer but far more complex. Information-processing approaches capture the fact that the brain does not passively record information but actively alters and organizes it. When we take action, we physically manipulate the environment; when we think, we *mentally* manipulate internal representations of objects, activities, and situations.

The Elements of Cognition

One type of mental representation is the **concept**, a mental category that groups objects, relations, activities, abstractions, or qualities having common properties. The instances of a concept are seen as roughly similar: *Golden retriever, cocker spaniel*, and *border collie* are instances of the concept *dog*; and *anger, joy*, and *sadness* are instances of the concept

concept A mental category that groups objects, relations, activities, abstractions, or qualities having common properties.

basic concepts Concepts that have a moderate number of instances and that are easier to acquire than those having few or many instances.

prototype An especially representative example of a concept.

emotion. Concepts simplify and summarize information about the world so that it is manageable and so that we can make decisions quickly and efficiently. You may never have seen a *basenji* or a *schnoodle*, but if you know that these are both instances of *dog*, you will know, roughly, how to respond (and perhaps be curious enough to learn that a schnoodle is a schnauzer-poodle mix).

Basic concepts have a moderate number of instances and are easier to acquire than those having either few or many instances (Rosch, 1973). The concept *apple* is more basic than *fruit*, which includes many more instances and is more abstract. It is also more basic than *McIntosh apple*, which is quite specific. Similarly, *book* is more basic than either *publication* or *novel*. Children seem to learn basic-level concepts earlier than others, and adults use them more often than others, because basic concepts convey an optimal amount of information in most situations.

The qualities associated with a concept do not necessarily all apply to every instance: Some apples are not red; some dogs do not bark; some birds do not fly. But all the instances of a concept do share a family resemblance. When we need to decide whether something belongs to a concept, we are likely to compare it to a **prototype**, a representative example of the concept (Rosch, 1973). For instance, which dog is doggier, a golden retriever or a Chihuahua? Which fruit is more fruitlike, an apple or a pineapple? Which activity is more representative of sports, football or weight lifting? Most people

Some instances of a concept are more representative or prototypical than others. TV heartthrob Chace Crawford clearly qualifies as a "bachelor," an unmarried man. In fact, in 2009, *People* put him on its cover as "Summer's Hottest Bachelor." But is the Pope a bachelor? What about Elton John, who celebrated a civil union ceremony in England with his longtime male partner?

within a culture can easily tell you which instances of a concept are most representative, or *prototypical*.

The words used to express concepts may influence or shape how we think about them. Many decades ago, Benjamin Lee Whorf (1956), an insurance inspector by profession and a linguist and anthropologist by inclination, proposed that language molds cognition and perception. His most famous example was that because English has only one word for snow and Eskimos (the Inuit) have many (for powdered snow, slushy snow, falling snow ...), the Inuit notice differences in snow that English speakers do not. He also argued that grammar—the way words are formed and arranged to convey tense and other concepts—affects how we think about the world.

Whorf's theory was popular for a while and then fell from favor; English speakers can see all those Inuit kinds of snow, after all, and they have plenty of adjectives to describe the different varieties. But Whorf's ideas are once again getting attention. Some researchers are finding that vocabulary and grammar do affect how we perceive the location of objects, think about time, attend to shapes and colors, and remember events (Boroditsky, 2003; Gentner & Goldin-Meadow, 2003). A language spoken by a group in Papua, New Guinea, refers to blue and green with one word, but distinct shades of green with two separate words. On perceptual discrimination tasks, New Guineans who speak this language handle green contrasts better than blue–green ones, whereas the reverse holds true for English speakers (Roberson, Davies, & Davidoff, 2000).

Here's another example: In many languages, speakers must specify whether an object is linguistically masculine or feminine. (In Spanish, *la cuenta*, the bill, is feminine but *el cuento*, the story, is masculine.) It seems that labeling a concept as masculine or feminine affects the attributes that native speakers ascribe to it. Thus, a German speaker will describe a key (masculine in German) as hard, heavy, jagged, serrated, and useful, whereas a Spanish speaker is more likely to describe a key (feminine in Spanish) as golden, intricate, little, lovely, and shiny. German speakers will describe a bridge (feminine in German) as beautiful, elegant, fragile, peaceful, and slender, whereas Spanish speakers are more likely to describe a bridge (masculine in Spanish) as big, dangerous, strong, sturdy, and towering (Boroditsky, Schmidt, & Phillips, 2003).

Concepts are the building blocks of thought, but they would be of limited use if we merely stacked them up mentally. We must also represent their relationships to one another. One way we accomplish this may be by storing and using **propositions**, units of meaning that are made up of concepts and that express a unitary idea. A proposition can express nearly any sort of knowledge ("Hortense raises border collies") or belief ("Border collies are smart"). Propositions, in turn, are linked together in complicated networks of knowledge, associations, beliefs, and expectations. These networks, which psychologists call **cognitive schemas**, serve as mental models of aspects of the world. People have schemas about cultures, occupations, animals, geographical locations, and many other features of the social and natural environment; gender schemas represent a person's beliefs and expectations about what it means to be male or female (see Chapter 3). ⊙▶ **Simulate**

Mental images—especially visual images, pictures in the mind's eye—are also important in thinking and in the construction of cognitive schemas. One method of studying them is to measure how long it takes people to rotate an image in their imaginations, scan from one point to another in an image, or read off some detail from an image. The results suggest that visual images are much like images on a computer screen: We can manipulate them, they occur in a mental space of a fixed size, and small ones contain less detail than larger ones (Kosslyn, 1980; Shepard & Metzler, 1971). Most people also report auditory images (for instance, a song, slogan, or poem you can hear in your "mind's ear"), and many report images in other sensory modalities as well—touch, taste, smell, or pain.

Here, then, is a visual summary of the elements of cognition:

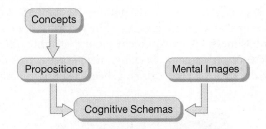

How Conscious Is Thought?

When we think about thinking, we usually have in mind those mental activities that are carried out in a deliberate way with a conscious goal in mind, such as solving a problem, drawing up plans, or making calculated decisions. However, not all mental processing is conscious.

Subconscious Thinking Some cognitive processes lie outside of awareness but can be brought into consciousness with a little effort when necessary. These **subconscious processes** allow us to handle more information and to perform more

proposition A unit of meaning that is made up of concepts and expresses a single idea.

cognitive schema An integrated mental network of knowledge, beliefs, and expectations concerning a particular topic or aspect of the world.

mental image A mental representation that mirrors or resembles the thing it represents; mental images occur in many and perhaps all sensory modalities.

subconscious processes Mental processes occurring outside of conscious awareness but accessible to consciousness when necessary.

⊙▶ **Simulate Schemas** at **mypsychlab.com**

nonconscious processes Mental processes occurring outside of and not available to conscious awareness.

implicit learning Learning that occurs when you acquire knowledge about something without being aware of how you did so and without being able to state exactly what it is you have learned.

complex tasks than if we depended entirely on conscious, deliberate thought. Many automatic routines are performed "without thinking," though they might once have required careful, conscious attention: knitting, typing, driving a car, or decoding the letters in a word to read it.

Because of the capacity for automatic processing, people can eat lunch while reading a book or drive a car while listening to music. In such cases, one of the tasks has become automatic and does not require much executive control from the brain's prefrontal cortex. But in daily life, multitasking is usually inefficient. In fact, far from saving time, toggling between two or more tasks increases the time required to complete them; stress goes up, errors increase, reaction times lengthen, and memory suffers (Lien, Ruthruff, & Johnston, 2006). This is *especially* true for people who consider themselves to be accomplished multitaskers and who are heavy users of electronic information. In a series of experiments designed to test the supposed skills of such multitaskers, their performance on each of the tasks was impaired by interference from the other tasks (Ophir, Nass, & Wagner, 2009). "The shocking discovery of this research," said one of the investigators, is that high multitaskers "are lousy at everything that's necessary for multitasking. They're suckers for irrelevancy. Everything distracts them."

Multitasking can even be hazardous to your health. Cell phone use greatly impairs a person's ability to drive, even when the phone is hands-free. The driver's attention is diverted far more by a phone conversation than by listening to music on the car radio (Strayer & Drews, 2007). Other distractions are equally dangerous; remember that driver shaving her bikini line? She is hardly alone in foolishness. A government study caught other drivers on camera checking their stocks, fussing with MP3 players, drinking beer, reading emails,

Some well-learned skills do not require much conscious thought and can be performed while doing other things, but multitasking can also get you into serious trouble. It's definitely not a good idea to talk on your cell phone, eat, and try to drive all at the same time.

applying makeup, flossing their teeth, and putting in contact lenses, all while hurtling down the highway at high speeds (Klauer et al., 2006). Of course, there's also texting: In 2008, a commuter train's engineer violated company policy by texting while on the job, and never saw an oncoming freight train. The resulting collision killed 25 people, including the engineer himself.

Even when multitasking doesn't put you at risk of an accident, it can be a bad idea. When you do two things at once, brain activity devoted to each task decreases. And while you are switching between tasks, your prefrontal cortex, which prioritizes tasks and enables higher-order thinking, becomes relatively inactive (Jiang, Saxe, & Kanwisher, 2004; Just et al., 2001). That's why we hope you are not trying to learn these facts while you're also watching TV and texting your friends.

Nonconscious Thinking Other kinds of thinking, **nonconscious processes**, remain outside of awareness. You undoubtedly have had the odd experience of having a solution to a problem pop into mind after you have given up trying to find one. With sudden insight, you see how to solve an equation, assemble a cabinet, or finish a puzzle without quite knowing how you managed to find the solution. Similarly, people will often say they rely on intuition—hunches and gut feelings—rather than conscious reasoning to make judgments and decisions.

Insight and intuition involve several stages of mental processing (Bowers et al., 1990; Kounios & Beeman, 2009). First, clues in the problem automatically activate memories or knowledge. You begin to see a pattern or structure in the problem, although you cannot yet say what it is; possible solutions percolate in your mind. This nonconscious processing guides you toward a hunch or a hypothesis. Eventually, your thinking becomes conscious, and you become aware of a probable solution. At this stage, you may feel that a sudden revelation has popped into your mind from nowhere ("Aha, now I see!"), but considerable nonconscious mental work has already occurred. Cognitive neuroscientists are now working on establishing links between changes in the brain and the steps involved in insightful problem solving (Kounios & Beeman, 2009; Sheth, Sandkühler, & Bhattacharya, 2009).

Sometimes people solve problems or learn new skills without experiencing the conscious stage at all. For example, some people discover the best strategy for winning a card game without ever being able to consciously identify what they are doing (Bechara et al., 1997). Psychologists call this phenomenon **implicit learning**: You learn a rule or an adaptive behavior, either with or without a conscious intention to do so, but you don't know how you learned it and you can't state, either to yourself or to others, exactly what it is you have learned (Frensch & Rünger, 2003; Lieberman, 2000). Many of our abilities, from speaking our native language properly to walking up a flight of stairs, are the result of implicit learning.

Mindlessness Even when our thinking is conscious, often we are not thinking very *hard*. We may act, speak, and make decisions out of habit, without stopping to analyze what we are doing or why we are doing it. This sort of *mindlessness*—mental inflexibility, inertia, and obliviousness to the present context—keeps people from recognizing when a change in a situation requires a change in behavior.

In a classic study of mindlessness, a researcher approached people as they were about to use a photocopier and made one of three requests: "Excuse me, may I use the Xerox machine?" "Excuse me, may I use the Xerox machine, because I have to make copies?" or "Excuse me, may I use the Xerox machine, because I'm in a rush?" Normally, people will let someone go before them only if the person has a legitimate reason, as in the third request. In this study, however, people also complied when the reason sounded like an authentic explanation but was actually meaningless ("because I have to make copies"). They heard the form of the request but they did not hear its content, and they mindlessly stepped aside (Langer, Blank, & Chanowitz, 1978).

Multitasking, mindlessness, and operating on automatic pilot have their place; life would be impossible if we had to think carefully about every little thing we do, see, or hear. But they can also

Advertisers sometimes count on mindlessness in consumers.

lead to errors and mishaps, ranging from the trivial (misplacing your keys) to the serious (walking into traffic because you're daydreaming). Cognitive psychologists have, therefore, devoted a great deal of study to mindful, conscious thought and the capacity to reason.

Quick Quiz

Stay mindful while taking this quiz.

1. Which concept is most basic: *furniture, chair,* or *high chair*?

2. Which example of the concept *chair* is prototypical: *high chair, rocking chair,* or *dining room chair*?

3. What two findings in the previous section support Whorf's theory that language affects perception and cognition?

4. In addition to concepts and images, _____, which express a unitary idea, have been suggested as a basic form of mental representation.

5. Peter's mental representation of Thanksgiving includes associations (e.g., to turkeys), attitudes ("It's a time to be with relatives"), and expectations ("I'm going to gain weight from all that food"). They are all part of his _____ for the holiday.

6. Zelda discovers that she has called her boyfriend's number instead of her mother's, as she intended. Her error can be attributed to _____.

Answers:

1. chair 2. A plain, straight-backed dining room chair will be prototypical for most people. 3. Color terms can affect how people respond to colors on visual discrimination tasks, and the linguistic gender of a word can affect people's descriptions of the concept it represents. 4. propositions 5. cognitive schema 6. mindlessness

YOU are about to learn...

- why algorithms and logic can't solve all of our problems.

- the difference between deductive and inductive reasoning.

- the importance of heuristics and dialectical reasoning in solving real-life problems.

- how cognitive development affects the ways in which people reason and justify their views.

Reasoning Rationally

Watch the **Video** on **Deductive Reasoning** at mypsychlab.com

Reasoning is purposeful mental activity that involves operating on information to reach conclusions. Unlike impulsive or nonconscious responding, reasoning requires us to draw specific inferences from observations, facts, or assumptions.

Formal Reasoning: Algorithms and Logic

In *formal reasoning problems*—the kind you might find, say, on an intelligence test or a college entrance exam—the information needed for drawing a conclusion or reaching a solution is specified clearly, and there is a single right (or best) answer. Established methods usually exist for solving the problem, and you usually know when it has been solved (Galotti, 1989).

In some formal problems and well-defined tasks, all you have to do is apply an **algorithm**, a set of procedures guaranteed to produce a solution even if you do not really know how it works. To solve a problem in long division, you apply a series of operations that you learned in elementary school. To make a cake, you apply an algorithm called a recipe. For other formal problems, the rules of formal logic are crucial tools to have in your mental toolbox. One such tool is **deductive reasoning**, in which a conclusion *necessarily* follows from a set of observations or propositions (*premises*):

reasoning The drawing of conclusions or inferences from observations, facts, or assumptions.

algorithm A problem-solving strategy guaranteed to produce a solution even if the user does not know how it works.

deductive reasoning A form of reasoning in which a conclusion follows necessarily from given premises; if the premises are true, the conclusion must be true.

inductive reasoning A form of reasoning in which the premises provide support for a conclusion, but it is still possible for the conclusion to be false.

heuristic A rule of thumb that suggests a course of action or guides problem solving but does not guarantee an optimal solution.

DEDUCTIVE REASONING

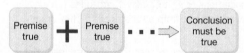

For example, if the premises "All human beings are mortal" and "I am a human being" are true, then the conclusion "I am mortal" must also be true. **Watch**

In contrast, in **inductive reasoning**, a conclusion *probably* follows from the given premises but could conceivably be false:

INDUCTIVE REASONING

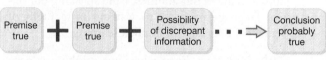

For example, if your premises are "I had a delicious meal at Joe's restaurant on Monday" and "I had a delicious meal again at Joe's on Tuesday," you might reasonably reach the conclusion that "Joe's restaurant consistently serves good food." But those meals could have been a fluke; maybe the regular cook, who is terrible, was on vacation and those great meals were made by a visiting chef.

Science depends heavily on inductive reasoning, because scientists make careful observations and then draw conclusions from those observations that they think are probably true. But in inductive reasoning, no matter how much supporting evidence you gather, it is always possible that new information will turn up to show you are wrong and that your previous conclusions were faulty and must therefore be revised or modified.

Informal Reasoning: Heuristics and Dialectical Thinking

Useful as they are, algorithms and logical reasoning cannot solve all, or even most, of life's problems. In *informal reasoning problems*, there is often no clearly correct solution. Many approaches, viewpoints, or possible solutions may compete, and you may have to decide which one is most reasonable. Further, the information at your disposal may be incomplete, or people may disagree on what the premises should be. Your position on the controversial issue of abortion will depend on your premises about when meaningful human life begins, what rights an embryo has, and what rights a woman has to control her own body. People on opposing sides of this issue even disagree on how the premises should be phrased, because they have different emotional reactions to terms such as "rights," "meaningful life," and "control her own body."

Formal and informal problems usually call for different approaches. Whereas formal problems can often be solved with an algorithm, informal problems often call for a **heuristic**, a rule of thumb that suggests a course of action without guaranteeing an optimal solution. Anyone who has ever played chess or a card game is familiar with heuristics (e.g., "Get rid of high cards first"). In these games, working out

Get Involved! Practice Your Dialectical Reasoning

Choose a controversial topic, such as whether marijuana should be legalized or the death penalty should be revoked. First list all the arguments you can to support your own position. Then list all the arguments you can on the other side of the issue. You do not have to agree with these arguments; just list them. Do you feel a mental block or emotional discomfort while doing this? Can you imagine how opponents of your position would answer your arguments? Having strong opinions is fine; you should have an informed opinion on matters of public interest. But does that opinion get in the way of even imagining a contrary point of view or of altering your view if the evidence warrants a change?

all the possible sequences of moves would be impossible. Heuristics are also useful to an investor trying to predict the stock market, a doctor trying to determine the best treatment for a patient, and a factory owner trying to boost production: All are faced with incomplete information on which to base a decision and may therefore resort to rules of thumb that have proven effective in the past.

In thinking about real-life problems, a person must also be able to use **dialectical reasoning**, the process of comparing and evaluating opposing points of view to resolve differences. Philosopher Richard Paul (1984) once described dialectical reasoning as movement "up and back between contradictory lines of reasoning, using each to critically cross-examine the other":

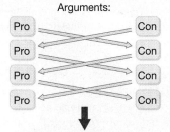

DIALECTAL REASONING

Arguments:

Most reasonable conclusion based on evidence and logic

Dialectical reasoning is what juries are supposed to do to arrive at a verdict: consider arguments for and against the defendant's guilt, point and counterpoint. It is also what voters are supposed to do when thinking about whether the government should raise or lower taxes, or about the best way to improve public education.

Reflective Judgment

Many adults clearly have trouble thinking dialectically; they take one position, and that's that. When do people develop the ability to think critically—to

question assumptions, evaluate and integrate evidence, consider alternative interpretations, and reach conclusions that can be defended as most reasonable?

To find out, Patricia King and Karen Kitchener (1994, 2002, 2004) provided adolescents and adults, representing a wide variety of backgrounds, with statements describing opposing viewpoints on various topics. Each person then had to answer these questions: What do you think about these statements? How did you come to hold that point of view? On what do you base your position? Can you ever know for sure that your position is correct? From the responses of thousands of participants, gathered over more than a quarter of a century, King and Kitchener have identified seven cognitive stages on the road to what they call *reflective judgment* (and what we have called critical thinking). At each stage, people make different assumptions about how things are known and use different ways of justifying or defending their beliefs.

dialectical reasoning
A process in which opposing facts or ideas are weighed and compared, with a view to determining the best solution or resolving differences.

Talk-radio shows do not exactly encourage reflective judgment!

In general, people in two *prereflective stages* tend to assume that a correct answer always exists and that it can be obtained directly through the senses ("I know what I've seen") or from authorities ("They said so on the news"; "That's what I was brought up to believe"). If authorities do not yet have the truth, prereflective thinkers tend to reach conclusions on the basis of what "feels right" at the moment. They do not distinguish between knowledge and belief or between belief and evidence, and they see no reason to justify a belief. One respondent at this stage, when asked about evolution, said: "Well, some people believe that we evolved from apes and that's the way they want to believe. But I would never believe that way and nobody could talk me out of the way I believe because I believe the way that it's told in the Bible."

During three *quasi-reflective stages*, people recognize that some things cannot be known with absolute certainty, and they realize that judgments should be supported by reasons, yet they pay attention only to evidence that fits what they already believe. They seem to think that because knowledge is uncertain, any judgment about the evidence is purely subjective. Quasi-reflective thinkers will defend a position by saying, "We all have a right to our own opinion," as if all opinions are created equal. One college student at this stage, when asked whether one opinion on the safety of food additives was right and others were wrong, answered: "No. I think it just depends on how you feel personally because people make their decisions based upon how they feel and what research they've seen. So what one person thinks is right, another person might think is wrong. If I feel that chemicals cause cancer and you feel that food is unsafe without it, your opinion might be right to you and my opinion is right to me."

In the last two stages, people become capable of reflective judgment. They understand that although some things can never be known with certainty, some judgments are more valid than others because of their coherence, their fit with the available evidence, and their usefulness. People at these *reflective stages* are willing to consider evidence from a variety of sources and to reason dialectically. This interview with a graduate student illustrates reflective thinking:

Interviewer: Can you ever say you know for sure that your point of view on chemical additives is correct?

Student: No, I don't think so [but] I think that we can usually be reasonably certain, given the information we have now, and considering our methodologies . . . it might be that the research wasn't conducted rigorously enough. In other words, we might have flaws in our data or sample, things like that.

Interviewer: How then would you identify the "better opinion"?

Student: One that takes as many factors as possible into consideration. I mean one that uses the higher percentage of the data that we have, and perhaps that uses the methodology that has been most reliable.

Interviewer: And how do you come to a conclusion about what the evidence suggests?

Student: I think you have to take a look at the different opinions and studies that are offered by different groups. Maybe some studies offered by the chemical industry, some studies by the government, some private studies. . . . You have to try to interpret people's motives and that makes it a more complex soup to try to strain out.

Most people show no evidence of reflective judgment until their middle or late twenties, if ever. However, when students get support for thinking reflectively and have opportunities to practice it in their courses, their thinking tends to become more complex, sophisticated, and well-grounded (Kitchener et al., 1993). You can see why, in this book, we emphasize thinking about and evaluating psychological findings, and not just memorizing them.

One reason that Auguste Rodin's *The Thinker* became world famous and has been much imitated is that it captures so perfectly the experience of thinking reflectively.

Study and
Review on
mypsychlab.com

Quick Quiz

Reflect on the answers to these questions.

1. Most of the holiday gifts Mervin bought this year cost more than they did last year, so he concludes that inflation is increasing. Is he using inductive, deductive, or dialectical reasoning?

2. Yvonne is arguing with Henrietta about whether real estate is a better investment than stocks. "You can't convince me," says Yvonne. "I just know I'm right." Yvonne needs training in _____ reasoning.

3. Seymour thinks the media have a liberal political bias, and Sophie thinks they are too conservative. "Well," says Seymour, "I have my truth and you have yours. It's purely subjective." Which of King and Kitchener's stages of thinking describes Seymour's statement?

Answers:

1. inductive 2. dialectical 3. quasi-reflective

 ## YOU are about to learn...

- how biases in reasoning impair the ability to think rationally and critically.

- why people worry more about vivid but rare disasters than about dangers that are far more likely.

- how the way a decision is framed affects the choices people make.

- why people often value fairness above rational self-interest.

- how the need to justify the expenditure of time, money, and effort affects how people think about a group they joined or a product they bought.

Barriers to Reasoning Rationally

Although most people have the capacity to think logically, reason dialectically, and make judgments reflectively, it is abundantly clear that they do not always do so. One obstacle is the need to be right;

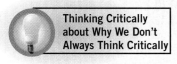
Thinking Critically about Why We Don't Always Think Critically

if your self-esteem depends on winning arguments, you will find it hard to listen with an open mind to competing views. Other obstacles include limited information and a lack of time to reflect carefully. But human thought processes are also tripped up by many predictable, systematic biases and errors. Psychologists have studied dozens of these cognitive pitfalls (Kahneman, 2003). Here we describe just a few.

Exaggerating the Improbable (and Minimizing the Probable)

One common bias is the inclination to exaggerate the probability of rare events. This bias helps to explain why so many people enter lotteries and buy disaster insurance, and why some irrational fears persist. As we discuss in Chapter 9, evolution has equipped us to fear natural dangers, such as snakes. However, in modern life, many of these dangers are no longer much of a threat; the risk of a renegade rattler sinking its fangs into you in Chicago or New York is pretty low! Yet the fear lingers on, so we overestimate the danger. Evolution has also given us brains that are terrific at responding to an immediate threat or to acts that provoke moral outrage even though they pose no threat to the survival of the species. Unfortunately, our brains were not designed to become alarmed by serious *future* threats that do not seem to pose much danger right now, such as global warming (Gilbert, 2006).

When judging probabilities, people are strongly influenced by the **affect heuristic**: the tendency to consult their emotions (affect) to judge the "goodness" or "badness" of a situation instead of judging probabilities objectively (Slovic & Peters, 2006; Slovic et al., 2002). Emotions can often help us make decisions by narrowing our options or by allowing us to act quickly in an ambiguous or dangerous situation. But emotions can also mislead us by preventing us from accurately assessing risk. One unusual field study looked at how people in France responded to the "mad cow" crisis that occurred a few years ago. (Mad cow disease affects the brain and can be contracted by eating meat from contaminated cows.) Whenever many newspaper articles reported the dangers of "mad cow disease," beef consumption fell

affect heuristic The tendency to consult one's emotions instead of estimating probabilities objectively.

Because of the affect and availability heuristics, many of us overestimate the chances of suffering a shark attack. Shark attacks are extremely rare, but they are terrifying and easy to visualize.

during the following month. But when news articles, reporting the same dangers, used the technical names of the disease—Creutzfeldt-Jakob disease, or bovine spongiform encephalopathy—beef consumption stayed the same (Sinaceur, Heath, & Cole, 2005). The more alarming labels caused people to reason emotionally and to overestimate the danger. (During the entire period of the supposed crisis, only six people in France were diagnosed with the disease.)

Our judgments about risks are also influenced by the **availability heuristic**, the tendency to judge the probability of an event by how easy it is to think of examples or instances of it (Tversky & Kahneman, 1973). The availability heuristic often works hand in hand with the affect heuristic. Catastrophes and shocking accidents evoke a strong emotional reaction in us, and thus stand out in our minds. They are more available mentally than other kinds of negative events. (An image of a "mad cow"—that sweet, placid creature running amok!—is highly available.) This is why people overestimate the frequency of deaths from tornadoes and underestimate the frequency of deaths from asthma, which occur more than 20 times as often but do not make headlines.

Avoiding Loss

In general, people try to avoid or minimize the risk of incurring losses when

availability heuristic
The tendency to judge the probability of a type of event by how easy it is to think of examples or instances.

framing effect The tendency for people's choices to be affected by how a choice is presented or framed, such as whether it is worded in terms of potential losses or gains.

they make decisions. That strategy is rational enough, but people's perceptions of risk are subject to the **framing effect**: the tendency for choices to differ, depending on how the choice is presented. When a choice is framed in terms of the risk of losing something, people will respond more cautiously than when the very same choice is framed in terms of gain. They will choose a ticket that has a 1 percent chance of winning a raffle but reject one that has a 99 percent chance of losing. Or they will rate a condom as effective when they are told it has a 95 percent success rate in protecting against the AIDS virus, but not when they are told it has a 5 percent failure rate—which of course is exactly the same thing (Linville, Fischer, & Fischhoff, 1992).

Suppose you had to choose between two health programs to combat a disease expected to kill 600 people. Which would you prefer: a program that will definitely save 200 people, or one with a one-third probability of saving all 600 people and a two-thirds probability of saving none? (Problem 1 in Figure 7.1

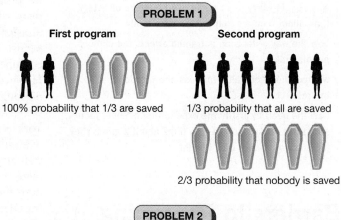

PROBLEM 1

First program — 100% probability that 1/3 are saved

Second program — 1/3 probability that all are saved / 2/3 probability that nobody is saved

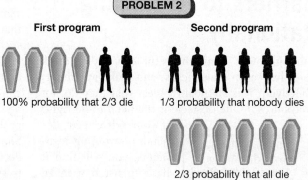

PROBLEM 2

First program — 100% probability that 2/3 die

Second program — 1/3 probability that nobody dies / 2/3 probability that all die

FIGURE 7.1
A Matter of Wording
The decisions we make often depend on how the alternatives are framed. When asked to choose between the two programs in Problem 1, which are described in terms of lives saved, most people choose the first program. When asked to choose between the programs in Problem 2, which are described in terms of lives lost, most people choose the second program. Yet the alternatives in the two problems are actually identical.

illustrates this choice.) When asked this question, most people, including physicians, say they would prefer the first program. In other words, they reject the riskier though potentially more rewarding solution in favor of a sure gain. However, people will take a risk if they see it as a way to *avoid loss*. Suppose now that you have to choose between a program in which 400 people will definitely die and a program in which there is a one-third probability of nobody dying and a two-thirds probability that all 600 will die. If you think about it, you will see that the alternatives are exactly the same as in the first problem; they are merely worded differently (see Problem 2 in Figure 7.1). Yet this time, most people choose the second solution. They reject risk when they think of the outcome in terms of lives saved, but they accept risk when they think of the outcome in terms of lives lost (Tversky & Kahneman, 1981).

Few of us will have to face a decision involving hundreds of lives, but we may have to choose between different medical treatments for ourselves or a relative. Our decision may be affected by whether the doctor frames the choice in terms of chances of surviving or chances of dying.

The Fairness Bias

Interestingly, in some circumstances we do not try to avoid loss altogether, because we are subject to a *fairness bias*. Imagine that you are playing a two-person game called the *Ultimatum Game*, in which your partner gets $20 and must decide how much to share with you. You can choose to accept your partner's offer, in which case you both get to keep your respective portions, or you can reject the offer, in which case neither of you gets a penny. How low an offer would you accept?

If you think about it, you'll see that it makes sense to accept any amount at all, no matter how paltry, because then at least you will get *something*. But that is not how people respond when playing the Ultimatum Game. If the offer is too low, they are likely to reject it. In industrial societies, offers of 50 percent are typical and offers below 20 or 30 percent are commonly rejected, even when the absolute sums are large. In other societies, the amounts offered and accepted may be higher or lower, but there is always some amount that people consider unfair and refuse to accept (Henrich et al., 2001). People may be competitive and love to win, but they are also powerfully motivated to cooperate and to see fairness prevail.

Using the Ultimatum Game and other laboratory games, scientists are exploring how a sense of fairness often takes precedence over rational self-interest when people make economic choices.

Their work, which belongs to a field called *behavioral economics*, verifies and extends the pioneering work of Nobel Prize winner Herbert Simon (1955), who first showed that economic decisions are not always rational. Psychologist Daniel Kahneman also won a Nobel for his work on the irrational processes of decision making, but because there is (as yet) no Nobel Prize in psychology, he won it in economics. This was a delicious irony, because many economists still have a difficult time accepting the evidence of human irrationality.

Why does a desire for fair play sometimes outweigh the desire for economic gain? Evolutionary theorists believe that cooperative tendencies and a desire for fairness and reciprocity evolved because they were beneficial to our forbears (Fehr & Fischbacher, 2003; Trivers, 2004).

The idea that the Golden Rule has a basis in biology has gained support from research with nonhuman primates. In one study, capuchin monkeys received a token that they could then exchange for a slice of cucumber. The monkeys regarded this exchange as a pretty good deal—until they saw a neighboring monkey exchanging tokens for an even better reward, a grape. At that point, they began to refuse to exchange their tokens, even though they were then left with no reward at all (Brosnan & de Waal, 2003). Sometimes they even threw the cucumber slice on the ground in apparent disgust!

Some behavioral economists are using MRI scans to examine brain activity when people play variations of the Ultimatum Game (Camerer, 2003; Sanfey et al., 2003). While a person is deciding whether to accept a low offer, two brain areas are active: a part of the prefrontal cortex linked to rational problem solving and an area that is associated with disgust and other unpleasant feelings. According to economist Colin Camerer, "Basically the brain toggles between 'Yes, money is good' and 'Ugh, this guy is treating me like crap'" (quoted in D'Antonio, 2004). Some people choose the money, and others go for respect. Which choice do you think you would make?

The Hindsight Bias

There is a reason for the observation that the vision of hindsight is 20/20. When people learn the outcome of an event or the answer to a question, they are often sure that they "knew it all along." They see the outcome that actually occurred as inevitable, and they overestimate their ability to have predicted what happened beforehand (Fischhoff, 1975; Hawkins & Hastie, 1990). This **hindsight bias** shows up all the time in evaluating relationships ("I always knew their marriage wouldn't

hindsight bias The tendency to overestimate one's ability to have predicted an event once the outcome is known; the "I knew it all along" phenomenon.

confirmation bias The tendency to look for or pay attention only to information that confirms one's own belief.

last"), medical judgments ("I could have told you that mole was cancerous"), and military opinions ("The generals should have known that the enemy would attack").

The hindsight bias can be adaptive. When we try to make sense of the past, we focus on explaining just one outcome, the one that actually occurred, because explaining outcomes that did not occur can be a waste of time. Then, in light of current knowledge, we reconstruct and misremember our previous judgment (Hoffrage, Hertwig, & Gigerenzer, 2000). But as Scott Hawkins and Reid Hastie (1990) wrote, "Hindsight biases represent the dark side of successful learning and judgment." They are the dark side because when we are sure that we knew something all along, we are also less willing to find out what we need to know to make accurate predictions in the future. In medical conferences, when doctors are told what the postmortem findings were for a patient who died, they tend to think the case was easier to diagnose than it actually was ("I would have known it was a brain tumor"), and so they learn less from the case than they should (Dawson et al., 1988).

Perhaps you feel that we are not telling you anything new because you have always known about the hindsight bias. If so, you may just have a hindsight bias about the hindsight bias!

The Confirmation Bias

When people want to make the most accurate judgment possible, they usually try to consider all of the relevant information. But as we saw in Chapter 1, when they are thinking about an issue they already feel strongly about, they often succumb to the **confirmation bias**, paying attention only to evidence that confirms their belief and finding fault with evidence or arguments that point in a different direction (Edwards & Smith, 1996; Nickerson, 1998). You rarely hear someone say, "Oh, thank you for explaining to me why my lifelong philosophy of child rearing (or politics, or investing) is wrong. I'm so grateful for the facts!" The person usually says, "Oh, buzz off, and take your cockamamie ideas with you."

Once you start looking for it, you will see the confirmation bias everywhere. Politicians brag about economic reports that confirm their party's position and dismiss counterevidence as biased or unimportant. Police officers who are convinced of a suspect's guilt take anything the suspect says or does as evidence that confirms it, including the suspect's claims of innocence (Davis, 2010). Many jury members, instead of weighing possible verdicts against the evidence, quickly construct a story about what happened at the start of the trial and then consider only the evidence that supports it (Kuhn, Weinstock, & Flaton, 1994). We bet you can see the confirmation bias in your own reactions to what you are learning in psychology. In thinking critically, most of us apply a double standard; we think most critically about results we dislike. That is why the scientific method can be so difficult: It forces us to consider evidence that disconfirms our beliefs.

Get Involved! Confirming the Confirmation Bias

Suppose someone deals out four cards, each with a letter on one side and a number on the other. You can see only one side of each card:

Your task is to find out whether the following rule is true: "If a card has a vowel on one side, then it has an even number on the other side." Which two cards do you need to turn over to find out?

The vast majority of people say they would turn over the E and the 6, but they are wrong. You do need to turn over the E (a vowel), because if the number on the other side is even, it confirms the rule, and if it is odd, the rule is false. However, the card with the 6 tells you nothing. The rule does *not* say that a card with an even number must always have a vowel on the other side. Therefore, it doesn't matter whether the 6 has a vowel or a consonant on the other side. The card you do need to turn over is the 7, because if it has a vowel on the other side, that fact disconfirms the rule.

People do poorly on this problem because they are biased to look for confirming evidence and to ignore the possibility of disconfirming evidence. Don't feel too bad if you missed it. Most judges, lawyers, and people with Ph.D.s do, too.

Mental Sets

Another barrier to rational thinking is the development of a **mental set**, a tendency to try to solve new problems by using the same heuristics, strategies, and rules that worked in the past on similar problems. Mental sets make human learning and problem solving efficient; because of them, we do not have to keep reinventing the wheel. But mental sets are not helpful when a problem calls for fresh insights and methods. They cause us to cling rigidly to the same old assumptions and approaches, blinding us to better or more rapid solutions.

One general mental set is the tendency to find patterns in events. This tendency is adaptive because it helps us understand and exert some control over what happens in our lives. But it also leads us to see meaningful patterns even when they do not exist. For example, many people with arthritis think that their symptoms follow a pattern dictated by the weather. They suffer more, they say, when the barometric pressure changes or when the weather is damp or humid. Yet when researchers followed 18 arthritis patients for 15 months, no association whatsoever emerged between weather conditions and the patients' self-reported pain levels, their ability to function in daily life, or a doctor's evaluation of their joint tenderness (Redelmeier & Tversky, 1996). Of course, because of the confirmation bias, the patients refused to believe the results.

The Need for Cognitive Consistency

Mental sets and the confirmation bias cause us to avoid evidence that contradicts our beliefs. But what happens when disconfirming evidence finally smacks us in the face, and we cannot ignore or discount it any longer? Consider the popularity of doomsday predictions, which have been made throughout history and continue to the present: "The world will end on (fill in the date)!" When these predictions fail, how come we never hear believers say, "Boy, what a fool I was"?

According to the theory of **cognitive dissonance**, people will resolve such conflicts in predictable, though not always obvious, ways (Festinger, 1957). *Dissonance*, the opposite of consistency (*consonance*), is a state of tension that occurs when you hold either two cognitions (beliefs, thoughts, attitudes) that are psychologically inconsistent with one another or a belief that is incongruent with your behavior. This tension is uncomfortable, so you will be motivated to reduce it. You may do this by rejecting or modifying one of those inconsistent beliefs, changing your behavior, denying the evidence, or rationalizing:

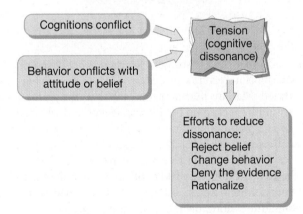

COGNITIVE DISSONANCE

Many years ago, in a famous field study, Leon Festinger and two associates explored people's reactions to failed prophecies by infiltrating a group of people who thought the world would end on

mental set A tendency to solve problems using procedures that worked before on similar problems.

cognitive dissonance A state of tension that occurs when a person holds two cognitions that are psychologically inconsistent, or when a person's belief is incongruent with his or her behavior.

Get Involved! Connect the Dots

Copy this figure, and try to connect the dots by using no more than four straight lines without lifting your pencil or pen. A line must pass through each point. Can you do it?

Most people have difficulty with this problem because they have a mental set to interpret the arrangement of dots as a square. They then assume that they can't extend a line beyond the apparent boundaries of the square. Now that you know this, you might try again if you haven't yet solved the puzzle. Some solutions are given at the end of this chapter.

December 21 (Festinger, Riecken, & Schachter, 1956). The group's leader, whom the researchers called Marian Keech, promised that the faithful would be picked up by a flying saucer and whisked to safety at midnight on December 20. Many of her followers quit their jobs and spent all their savings, waiting for the end to come. What would they do or say, Festinger and his colleagues wondered, to reduce the dissonance between "The world is still muddling along on the 21st" and "I predicted the end of the world and sold off all my worldly possessions"?

The researchers predicted that believers who had made no public commitment to the prophecy, who awaited the end of the world by themselves at home, would simply lose their faith. Those who had acted on their conviction by selling their property and waiting with Keech for the spaceship, however, would be in a state of dissonance. They would have to *increase* their religious belief to avoid the intolerable realization that they had behaved foolishly and others knew it. That is just what happened. At 4:45 a.m., long past the appointed hour of the saucer's arrival, the leader had a new vision. The world had been spared, she said, because of the impressive faith of her little band.

Cognitive-dissonance theory predicts that in more ordinary situations as well, people will resist or rationalize information that conflicts with their existing ideas, just as the people in the arthritis study did. Cigarette smokers are often in a state of

postdecision dissonance In the theory of cognitive dissonance, tension that occurs when you believe you may have made a bad decision.

dissonance, because smoking is dissonant with the fact that smoking causes illness. Smokers may try to reduce the dissonance by trying to quit, by rejecting evidence that smoking is bad, by persuading themselves that they will quit later on, by emphasizing the benefits of smoking ("A cigarette helps me relax"), or by deciding that they don't want a long life, anyhow ("It will be shorter but sweeter").

You are particularly likely to reduce dissonance under three conditions (Aronson, 2008):

1 When you need to justify a choice or decision that you freely made. All car dealers know about buyer's remorse: The second that people buy a car, they worry that they made the wrong decision or spent too much, a phenomenon called **postdecision dissonance.** You may try to resolve this dissonance by deciding that the car you chose (or the toaster, or house, or spouse) is really, truly the best in the world. *Before* people make a decision, they can be open-minded, seeking information on the pros and cons of the choice at hand. *After* they make that choice, however, the confirmation bias will kick in, so that they will now notice all the good things about their decision and overlook or ignore evidence that they might have been wrong.

2 When you need to justify behavior that conflicts with your view of yourself. If you consider yourself to be honest, cheating will put you in a state of dissonance. To avoid feeling like a hypocrite, you will try to reduce the dissonance by justifying your behavior ("Everyone else does it"; "It's just this once"; "I had to do it to get into med school and learn to save lives"). Or if you see yourself as a kind person and you harm someone, you may reduce your dissonance by blaming the person you have victimized ("She brought it on herself"; "It's his fault") (Tavris & Aronson, 2007).

3 When you need to justify the effort put into a decision or choice. The harder you work to reach a goal, or the more you suffer for it, the more you will try to convince yourself that you value the goal, even if the goal turns out to be not so great after all (Aronson & Mills, 1959). This explains why hazing, whether in social clubs, on athletic teams, or in the military, turns new recruits into loyal members (see Figure 7.2). You might think that people would hate the group that caused them pain and embarrassment. But the cognition "I went through a lot of awful stuff to join this group" is dissonant with the cognition "only to find I hate the group." Therefore, people must decide either that the hazing was not so bad or that they really like the

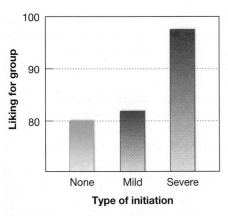

FIGURE 7.2
The Justification of Effort

The more effort you put into reaching a goal, the more highly you are likely to value it. As you can see in the graph on the left, after people listened to a boring group discussion, those who went through a severe initiation to join the group rated it most highly (Aronson & Mills, 1959). In the photo on the right, new cadets at the Virginia Military Institute are forced to crawl through mud until they are covered from head to toe. They will probably become devoted to the military.

group. This mental reevaluation is called the **justification of effort**, and it is one of the most popular methods of reducing dissonance.

Some people are secure enough to own up to their mistakes instead of justifying them, and individuals and cultures vary in the kinds of experiences that cause them to feel dissonance. For example, Americans are more likely to experience dissonance following a decision that makes them doubt their competence, whereas the Japanese feel more dissonance when a decision evokes worry about social approval or possible rejection (Kitayama et al., 2004). However, the need for cognitive consistency in those beliefs that are most central to our sense of self and our values is universal (Tavris & Aronson, 2007).

Overcoming Our Cognitive Biases

Our mental biases have survived because often they are helpful. The ability to reduce cognitive dissonance following a decision helps preserve our self-confidence and avoid sleepless nights second-guessing ourselves; having a sense of fairness keeps us from behaving like self-centered louts; having mental sets keeps us from having to reinvent solutions to problems we could otherwise solve quickly. But our mental biases can also get us into trouble.

The confirmation bias, the justification of effort, and postdecision dissonance reduction permit people to stay stuck with decisions that eventually prove to be self-defeating, harmful, or incorrect. Physicians may stick with outdated methods, district attorneys may overlook evidence that a criminal suspect might be innocent, and managers may refuse to consider better business practices.

To make matters worse, most people have a "bias blind spot": They acknowledge that *other* people have biases that distort reality, but they think that they themselves are free of bias and see the world as it really is (Pronin, Gilovich, & Ross, 2004; Ross, 2010). This blind spot is itself a bias! And it is a dangerous one, because it can prevent individuals, nations, ethnic groups, and religious groups from resolving conflicts with others. Each side thinks that its own proposals for ending a conflict, or its own analyses of political events, are reasonable and fair but the other side's are biased. Fortunately, once we understand a bias, we may, with some effort, be able to reduce or eliminate it, especially if we make an active, mindful effort to do so and take time to think carefully (Kida, 2006).

Some people, of course, seem to think more mindfully and rationally than others; we call them "intelligent." Just what is intelligence, and how can we measure and improve it? We take up these questions next.

justification of effort
The tendency of individuals to increase their liking for something that they have worked hard or suffered to attain; a common form of dissonance reduction.

✓•⧠**Study** and
Review on
mypsychlab.com

Quick Quiz

In hindsight, will you say this quiz was easy?

1. In 2001, an unknown person sent anthrax through the United States post office, causing the deaths of five people. Many people became afraid to open their mail, although the risk for any given individual was extremely small. What heuristics help to explain this reaction?

2. *True or false:* Research on the Ultimatum Game shows that people usually act out of rational self-interest.

3. Stu meets a young woman at the student cafeteria. They hit it off and eventually get married. Says Stu, "I knew when I woke up that morning that something special was about to happen." What cognitive bias is affecting his thinking, charmingly romantic though it is?

4. In a classic experiment on cognitive dissonance, students did some boring, repetitive tasks and then had to tell another student, who was waiting to participate in the study, that the work was interesting and fun (Festinger & Carlsmith, 1959). Half the students were offered $20 for telling this lie and the others only $1. Based on what you have learned about cognitive dissonance reduction, which students do you think decided later that the tasks had been fun after all? Why?

Answers:

1. the affect and availability heuristics   2. false   3. the hindsight bias   4. The students who got only $1 were more likely to say that the task had been fun. They were in a state of dissonance because "The task was as dull as dishwater" is dissonant with "I said I enjoyed it—and for a mere dollar, at that." Those who got $20 could rationalize that the large sum (which really was large in the 1950s) justified the lie.

 YOU are about to learn...

- both sides of the debate about whether a single thing called "intelligence" actually exists.

- how the original purpose of intelligence testing changed when IQ tests came to America.

- the difficulties of designing intelligence tests that are free of cultural influence.

Measuring Intelligence: The Psychometric Approach

Intelligent people disagree on just what intelligence is. Some equate it with the ability to reason abstractly, others with the ability to learn and profit from experience in daily life. Some emphasize the ability to think rationally, others the ability to act purposefully. These qualities are all probably part of what most people mean by **intelligence**, but theorists weigh them differently.

The traditional approach to intelligence, the **psychometric** approach, focuses on how well people perform on standardized aptitude tests, which are designed to measure the ability to acquire skills and knowledge. A typical intelligence test asks you to do several things: provide a specific bit of information, notice similarities between objects, solve arithmetic problems, define words, fill in the missing parts of incomplete pictures, arrange pictures in a logical order, arrange blocks to resemble a design, assemble puzzles, use a coding scheme, or judge what behavior would be appropriate in a given situation. A statistical method called **factor analysis** identifies clusters of correlated items on the test that seem to be measuring some common ability, or factor.

Most psychometric psychologists believe that a general ability, or **g factor**, underlies the various abilities and talents measured by intelligence tests (Gottfredson, 2002; Jensen, 1998; Lubinski, 2004; Spearman, 1927; Wechsler, 1955). They marshal a century of research to support their view (Lubinski, 2004). Tests of *g* do a good job of predicting not

A psychologist gives a student an intelligence test.

---

intelligence An inferred characteristic of an individual, usually defined as the ability to profit from experience, acquire knowledge, think abstractly, act purposefully, or adapt to changes in the environment.

psychometrics The measurement of mental abilities, traits, and processes.

factor analysis A statistical method for analyzing the intercorrelations among various measures or test scores; clusters of measures or scores that are highly correlated are assumed to measure the same underlying trait, ability, or aptitude (factor).

g factor A general intellectual ability assumed by many theorists to underlie specific mental abilities and talents.

only academic achievement but also the cognitive complexity of people's work, occupational success, and eminence in many fields (Kuncel, Hezlett, & Ones, 2004; Schmidt & Hunter, 2004; Simonton & Song, 2009).

However, others dispute the existence of a global quality called "intelligence," observing that a person can excel in some kinds of reasoning and problem solving yet do poorly in others (Gardner, 1983; Gould, 1994; Guilford, 1988). This disagreement over how to define intelligence has generated enormous debate among psychologists and has led some writers to argue, only half-jokingly, that intelligence is "whatever intelligence tests measure."

The Invention of IQ Tests

The first widely used intelligence test was devised in 1904, when the French Ministry of Education asked psychologist Alfred Binet (1857–1911) to find a way to identify children who were slow learners so they could be given remedial work. The ministry was reluctant to let teachers identify such children because the teachers might have prejudices about poor children, or might assume that shy or disruptive children were mentally impaired. The government wanted a more objective approach.

Binet's Brainstorm Wrestling with the problem, Binet had a great insight: In the classroom, the responses of "dull" children resembled those of ordinary children of younger ages. Bright children, on the other hand, responded like children of older ages. The thing to measure, then, was a child's **mental age (MA)**, or level of intellectual development relative to that of other children. Then instruction could be tailored to the child's capabilities.

The test devised by Binet and his colleague, Théodore Simon, measured memory, vocabulary, and perceptual discrimination. Items ranged from those that most young children could do easily to those that only older children could handle, as determined by the testing of large numbers of children. A scoring system developed later by others used a formula in which the child's mental age was divided by the child's chronological age to yield an **intelligence quotient**, or **IQ** (a quotient is the result of division). Thus a child of 8 who performed like the average 10-year-old would have a mental age of 10 and an IQ of 125 (10 divided by 8, times 100). All average children, regardless of age, would have an IQ of 100 because mental age and chronological age would be the same.

However, this method of figuring IQ had serious flaws. At one age, scores might cluster tightly around the average, whereas they might be more dispersed at another age. As a result, the score necessary to be in the top 10 or 20 or 30 percent of your age group varied, depending on your age. Also, the IQ formula did not make sense for adults; a 50-year-old who scores like a 30-year-old does not have low intelligence! Today, therefore, intelligence tests are scored differently. The average is usually set arbitrarily at 100, and tests are constructed so that about two-thirds of all people score between 85 and 115. Individual scores are computed from tables based on established norms. These scores are still informally referred to as IQs, and they still reflect how a person compares with other people, either children of a particular age or adults in general. At all ages, the distribution of scores approximates a normal bell-shaped curve, with scores near the average (mean) more common than high or low scores (see Figure 7.3).

The IQ Test Comes to America In the United States, Stanford psychologist Lewis Terman revised Binet's test and established norms for American children. His version, the *Stanford–Binet Intelligence Scale*, was first published in 1916, and has been updated several times since. The test asks a person to perform a variety of tasks, such as filling in missing words in sentences, answering questions requiring general knowledge, predicting how a folded paper will look when unfolded, measuring a quantity of

mental age (MA) A measure of mental development expressed in terms of the average mental ability at a given age.

intelligence quotient (IQ) A measure of intelligence originally computed by dividing a person's mental age by his or her chronological age and multiplying the result by 100; it is now derived from norms provided for standardized intelligence tests.

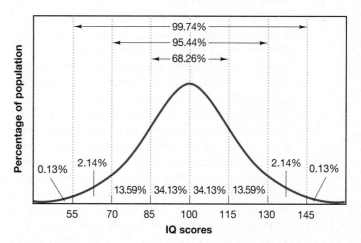

FIGURE 7.3
Expected Distribution of IQ Scores
In a large population, IQ scores tend to be distributed on a normal (bell-shaped) curve. On most tests, about 68 percent of all people will score between 85 and 115; about 95 percent will score between 70 and 130, and about 97.7 percent will score between 55 and 145. In any actual sample, however, the distribution will depart somewhat from the theoretical ideal.

Picture arrangement
(Arrange the panels to make a meaningful story)

Object assembly
(Put together a jigsaw puzzle)

Digit symbol
(Using the key at the top, fill in the appropriate symbol beneath each number)

Picture completion
(Supply the missing feature)

FIGURE 7.4
Performance Tasks on the Wechsler Tests
Nonverbal items such as these are particularly useful for measuring the abilities of those who have poor hearing, are not fluent in the tester's language, have limited education, or resist doing classroom-type problems. A large gap between a person's verbal score and performance on nonverbal tasks such as these sometimes indicates a specific learning problem (adapted from Cronbach, 1990).

water using two containers of different sizes, and distinguishing concepts that are similar but not exactly the same (such as *vigor* and *energy*). The older the test taker is, the more the test requires in the way of verbal comprehension and fluency, spatial ability, and reasoning.

Two decades later, David Wechsler designed another test expressly for adults, which became the *Wechsler Adult Intelligence Scale (WAIS)*; it was followed by the *Wechsler Intelligence Scale for Children (WISC)*. Although the Wechsler tests produced a general IQ score, they also provided specific scores for different kinds of ability. Verbal items tested vocabulary, arithmetic abilities, immediate memory span, ability to recognize similarities (e.g., "How are books and movies alike?"), and general knowledge and comprehension (e.g., "Who was Thomas Jefferson?" "Why do people who want a divorce have to go to court?"). Performance items tested nonverbal skills, such as the ability to re-create a block design within a specified time limit and to identify a part missing from a picture. The current versions of the Wechsler tests have more subtests and, in addition to an overall IQ score, they yield separate scores for verbal comprehension, perceptual reasoning, processing speed, and working memory (the ability to hold information in mind so

it can be used for a task). (See Figure 7.4 for some sample items.)

Binet had emphasized that his test merely *sampled* intelligence and did not measure everything covered by that term. A test score, he said, could be useful, along with other information, for predicting school performance, but it should not be confused with intelligence itself. The tests were designed to be given individually, so that the test giver could tell when a child was ill or nervous, had poor vision, or was unmotivated. The purpose was to identify children with learning problems, not to rank all children. But when intelligence testing was brought from France to the United States, its original purpose got lost at sea. In America, IQ tests became widely used not to bring slow learners up to the average, but to categorize people in school and in the armed services according to their presumed "natural ability." The testers overlooked the fact that in America, with its many ethnic groups, people did not all share the same background and experience (Gould, 1996). ◉—Watch

Culture and Intelligence Testing Intelligence tests developed between World War I and the 1960s favored city children over rural ones, middle-class children over poor ones, and white children over

◉—Watch the Video
Are Intelligence Tests Valid? on mypsychlab.com

nonwhite children. One item asked whether the Emperor Concerto was written by Beethoven, Mozart, Bach, Brahms, or Mahler. (The answer is Beethoven.) Critics complained that the tests did not measure the kinds of knowledge and skills that indicate intelligent behavior in a minority neighborhood or in the hills of Appalachia. They feared that because teachers thought IQ scores revealed the limits of a child's potential, low-scoring children would not get the educational attention or encouragement they needed.

Test makers responded by trying to construct tests that were unaffected by culture or that incorporated knowledge and skills common to many different cultures. But these efforts were disappointing. One reason was that cultures differ in the problem-solving strategies they emphasize (Serpell, 1994). In the West, white, middle-class children typically learn to classify things by category—to say that an apple and a peach are similar because they are both fruits, and that a saw and a rake are similar because they are both tools. But children who are not trained in middle-class ways of sorting things may classify objects according to their sensory qualities or functions; they may say that an apple and a peach are similar because they taste good. We think that's a charming and innovative answer, but it is one that test administrators have interpreted as less intelligent (Miller-Jones, 1989).

Testing experts also discovered that cultural values and experiences affect many things besides responses to specific test items. These include a person's general attitude toward exams, motivation, rapport with the test giver, competitiveness, comfort in solving problems independently rather than with others, and familiarity with the conventions for taking tests (Anastasi & Urbina, 1997; López, 1995; Sternberg, 2004).

Moreover, people's performance on IQ and other mental-ability tests depends in part on their own expectations about how they will do, and those expectations are affected by cultural stereotypes. Stereotypes that portray women, old people, poor people, or members of ethnic minorities as unintelligent, or "naturally" inferior to white men on some cognitive skill such as visual-spatial ability, can actually depress the performance of people in those groups (Campbell & Collaer, 2009). You might think that a woman would say, "So sexists think women are dumb at math? I'll show them!" or that an African American would say, "So racists believe that blacks aren't as smart as whites? Just give me that exam." But often that is not what happens.

On the contrary, such individuals commonly feel a burden of doubt about their abilities that Claude Steele (1992, 1997) has labeled **stereotype threat**. The threat occurs when people believe that if they do not do well, they will confirm the stereotypes about their group. Negative thoughts intrude and disrupt their concentration ("I hate this test," "I'm no good at math") (Cadinu et al., 2005). The resulting anxiety may then worsen their performance or kill their motivation to even try to do well.

stereotype threat A burden of doubt a person feels about his or her performance, due to negative stereotypes about his or her group's abilities.

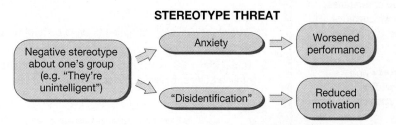

STEREOTYPE THREAT

More than 300 studies have shown that stereotype threat can affect the test performance of many African Americans, Latinos, low-income people, women, and elderly people, all of whom perform better when they are not feeling self-conscious about themselves as members of negatively stereotyped groups (e.g., J. Aronson, 2010; Brown & Josephs, 1999; Inzlicht & Ben-Zeev, 2000; Levy, 1996; Quinn & Spencer, 2001; Steele & Aronson, 1995). Anything that increases the salience of group stereotypes can increase stereotype threat and affect performance, including taking the test in a setting where you are the only member from your group, or being asked to state your race, ethnicity, or age before taking the test.

What can be done to reduce stereotype threat? One possibility is simply to tell people about it, which often inoculates them against its effects (Schmader, 2010). When students taking introductory statistics were given a difficult test, with no mention of stereotype threat, women did worse than men. But when students were informed about stereotype threat, the sex difference disappeared (Johns, Schmader, & Martens, 2005). (See how helpful psychology can be?) ((•─Listen

Although stereotype threat is thus an important contributing factor for group differences in test performance, it is not the only one (Sackett, Hardison, & Cullen, 2004). Sometimes, for any number of reasons, groups do differ, on average, in some skill or ability. And that fact points to a

Whether or not you feel "stereotype threat" depends on what category you are identifying with at the time. Asian women do worse on math tests when they see themselves as "women" (stereotype = poor at math) rather than as "Asians" (stereotype = good at math) (Shih, Pittinsky, & Ambady, 1999).

((•─Listen to **Stereotype Threat** on **mypsychlab.com**

triarchic [try-ARE-kick] theory of intelligence A theory of intelligence that emphasizes information-processing strategies, the ability to creatively transfer skills to new situations, and the practical application of intelligence.

metacognition The knowledge or awareness of one's own cognitive processes.

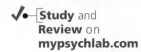

✔ **Study** and **Review** on **mypsychlab.com**

dilemma at the heart of intelligence and mental-ability testing. Intelligence and other mental-ability tests put some groups of people at a disadvantage, yet they also measure skills and knowledge useful in the classroom and on the job. How can psychologists and educators recognize and accept cultural differences and, at the same time, promote the mastery of the skills, knowledge, and attitudes that can help people succeed in school and in the larger society?

Quick Quiz

What's your Quiz Quotient (QQ)?

1. What was Binet's great insight?

2. *True or false:* IQ tests designed to avoid cultural bias have failed to eliminate average group differences in IQ scores.

3. Hilda, who is 68, is about to take an IQ test, but she is worried because she knows that older people are often assumed to have diminished mental abilities. Hilda is being affected by _____.

Answers:

1. Mental age does not necessarily correspond to chronological age.   **2.** true   **3.** stereotype threat

---

◆ **YOU** are about to learn...

- which kinds of intelligence are not measured by standard IQ tests.

- the meaning of "emotional intelligence" and why it might be as important as IQ.

- some reasons that Asian children perform much better in school than American students do.

✳ **Explore Sternberg's Triarchic Theory of Intelligence** on **mypsychlab.com**

Dissecting Intelligence: The Cognitive Approach

Critics of standard intelligence tests point out that such tests tell us little about *how* a person goes about answering questions and solving problems. Nor do the tests explain why people with low scores often behave intelligently in real life, making smart

 Thinking Critically about What It Means to be Smart

consumer decisions, winning at the racetrack, and making wise choices in their relationships instead of repeating the same dumb patterns. Some researchers, therefore, have rejected the psychometric approach in favor of a *cognitive approach*, which assumes that there are many kinds of intelligence and emphasizes the strategies people use when thinking about a problem and arriving at a solution.

The Triarchic Theory

One well-known cognitive theory is Robert Sternberg's **triarchic theory of intelligence** (1988) (*triarchic* means "three-part"). Sternberg (2004) defines intelligence as "the skills and knowledge needed for success in life, according to one's own definition of success, within one's sociocultural context." He distinguishes three aspects of intelligence: ✳ **Explore**

1 Componential intelligence refers to the information-processing strategies you draw on when you are thinking intelligently about a problem. These mental components include recognizing and defining the problem, selecting a strategy for solving it, mastering and carrying out the strategy, and evaluating the result.

Some of the operations in componential intelligence require not only analytic skills but also **metacognition**, the knowledge or awareness of your own cognitive processes and the ability to monitor and control those processes. Students who are weak in metacognition fail to notice when a passage in a textbook is difficult, and they do not always realize that they haven't understood what they've been reading. As a result, they spend too little time on difficult material and too much time on material they already know. They are overconfident about their comprehension and memory, and are surprised when they do poorly on exams (Dunlosky & Lipko, 2007). In contrast, students who are strong in metacognition check their comprehension by restating what they have read, testing themselves, backtracking when necessary, and questioning what they are reading. When time is limited, they first tackle fairly easy material (where the payoff will be great), and then move on to more difficult material; as a result, they learn better (Metcalfe, 2009).

It works in the other direction, too: The kind of intelligence that enhances academic performance can also help you develop metacognitive skills. Students with poor academic skills typically fail to realize how little they know; they think they're doing fine (Dunning, 2005). The very weaknesses that keep them from doing well on tests or in their courses also keep them from realizing their weaknesses. In one study, students in a psychology course estimated how well they had just done on an exam relative to other students. As you can see in Figure 7.5, those who had performed in the bottom quartile greatly overestimated their own performance (Dunning et al., 2003). In contrast, people with strong academic skills tend to be more realistic. Often they even underestimate slightly how their performance compares with the performance of others.

2 **Experiential or creative intelligence** refers to your creativity in transferring skills to new situations. People with experiential intelligence cope well with novelty and learn quickly to make new tasks automatic. Those who are lacking in this area perform well only under a narrow set of circumstances. Students may do well in school, where assignments have specific due dates and feedback is immediate, but be less successful after graduation if the job requires them to set their own deadlines and no one tells them how they are doing.

3 **Contextual or practical intelligence** refers to the practical application of intelligence, which requires you to take into account the different contexts in which you find yourself. If you are strong in contextual intelligence, you know when to adapt to

"You're wise, but you lack tree smarts."

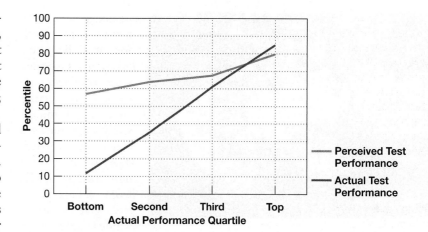

FIGURE 7.5
Ignorance Is Bliss
In school and in other settings, people who perform poorly often have poor metacognitive skills and therefore fail to recognize their own lack of competence. As you can see, the lower that students scored on an exam, the greater the gap between how they thought they had done and how they actually had done (Dunning et al., 2003).

the environment (you are in a dangerous neighborhood, so you become more vigilant). You know when to change environments (you had planned to be a teacher but discover that you dislike working with kids, so you switch to accounting). And you know when to fix the situation (your marriage is rocky, so you and your spouse go for counseling).

Contextual knowledge allows you to acquire **tacit knowledge**—practical, action-oriented strategies for achieving your goals that usually are not formally taught or even verbalized but must instead be inferred by observing others. Among college students, tacit knowledge about how to be a good student actually predicts academic success as well as entrance exams do (Sternberg et al., 2000).

Emotional Intelligence

One of the most important kinds of nonintellectual "smarts" may be **emotional intelligence**, the ability to identify your own and other people's emotions accurately, express your emotions clearly, and manage emotions in yourself and others (Mayer & Salovey, 1997; Salovey & Grewal, 2005). People with high emotional intelligence, popularly known as "EQ," use their emotions to motivate themselves, to spur creative thinking, and to deal empathically with others. People who are lacking in emotional intelligence are often unable to identify their own emotions; they may insist that they are not depressed when a relationship ends, but meanwhile they start drinking too much, become extremely

tacit knowledge
Strategies for success that are not explicitly taught but that instead must be inferred.

emotional intelligence
The ability to identify your own and other people's emotions accurately, express your emotions clearly, and regulate emotions in yourself and others.

People with emotional intelligence are skilled at reading nonverbal emotional cues. Which of these children do you think feels the most confident and relaxed, which one is shyest, and which feels most anxious? What cues are you using to answer?

irritable, and stop going out with friends. They may express emotions inappropriately, perhaps by acting violently or impulsively when they are angry or worried. They often misread nonverbal signals from others; they will give a long-winded account of all their problems even when the listener is obviously bored.

Some psychologists believe that emotional intelligence is not a special cognitive ability but a collection of ordinary personality traits, such as empathy and extroversion (Matthews, Zeidner, & Roberts, 2003). Wherever it comes from, it may have a biological basis. Neuroscientist Antonio Damasio (1994) has studied patients with prefrontal-lobe damage that makes them incapable of experiencing strong feelings. Although they score

in the normal range on conventional mental tests, these patients persistently make "dumb," irrational decisions in their lives because they cannot assign values to different options based on their own emotional reactions and cannot read emotional cues from others. As we discuss in Chapter 13, feeling and thinking are not as incompatible as many people assume; in fact, one often requires the other.

Broadening the notion of intelligence has been useful for several reasons. It has forced us to think more critically about what we mean by intelligence and to consider how different abilities help us function in our everyday lives. It has generated research on tests that provide ongoing feedback to the test taker so that the person can learn from the experience and improve performance. The cognitive approach has also led to a focus on teaching children strategies for improving their abilities in reading, writing, doing homework, and taking tests (Sternberg, 2004; Sternberg et al., 1995). Most important, new approaches to intelligence encourage us to overcome the mental set of assuming that the only kind of abilities necessary for a successful life are the kind captured by IQ tests.

Study and **Review** on **mypsychlab.com**

Quick Quiz

A good strategy for improving your own test performance is to take the quizzes in this book.

1. What goals do cognitive theories of intelligence have that psychometric theories do not?

2. Logan understands the material in his statistics class, but on tests he spends the entire period on the most difficult problems and never even gets to the problems he can solve easily. According to the triarchic theory of intelligence, which aspect of intelligence does he need to improve?

3. Tracy has an average IQ, but at work she is quickly promoted because she knows how to set priorities, communicate with management, and make others feel valued. Tracy has _____ knowledge about how to succeed on the job.

4. What is wrong with defining intelligence as "whatever intelligence tests measure"?

Answers:

1. to understand people's strategies for solving problems and use this information to improve mental performance 2. componential intelligence (specifically, metacognition) 3. tacit 4. This definition implies that a low score must be entirely the scorer's fault rather than the fault of the test. But the test taker may be intelligent in ways that the test fails to measure, and the test may be measuring traits other than intelligence.

YOU are about to learn...

- the extent to which intelligence may be heritable.
- a common error in the argument that one group is genetically smarter than another.
- how the environment nurtures or thwarts mental ability.

The Origins of Intelligence

"Intelligence," as we have seen, can mean many things. But however we define or measure it, clearly some people think and behave more intelligently than others. What accounts for these differences?

Genes and Individual Differences Behavioral geneticists approach this question by doing heritability studies, focusing mainly on the kind of intelligence measured by IQ tests. In Chapter 2, we saw that **heritability** is the proportion of the total variance in a trait within a group that is attributable to genetic variation within the group. This proportion can have a maximum value of 1.0, which means that the trait is completely heritable—although most traits, including height, are not perfectly heritable; genes interact constantly with the environment throughout our lives (Johnson et al., 2009). (You might review pages 51–53 to refresh your memory about heritability.)

Behavioral-genetic studies show that the kind of intelligence that produces high IQ scores is highly heritable. For children and adolescents, heritability estimates average around .40 or .50; that is, about half of the variance in IQ scores is explainable by genetic differences (Chipuer, Rovine, & Plomin, 1990; Devlin, Daniels, & Roeder, 1997; Plomin, 1989). For adults, most estimates are even higher—in the .60 to .80 range (Bouchard, 1995; McClearn et al., 1997; McGue et al., 1993). That is, the genetic contribution becomes relatively larger and the environmental one relatively smaller with age. This finding surprises many people who think of heritability as a fixed, permanent number. It is not, precisely because it depends on how varied the environment is for the group being studied.

Nonetheless, in studies of twins, the scores of identical twins are always much more highly correlated than those of fraternal twins. In fact, the scores of identical twins reared *apart* are more highly correlated than those of fraternal twins reared *together*, as you can see in Figure 7.6. In adoption studies, the scores of adopted children are more highly correlated with those of their birth parents than with those of their biologically unrelated adoptive parents; the higher the birth parents' scores, the higher the child's score is likely to be. As adopted children grow into adolescence, the correlation between their IQ scores and those of their biologically unrelated family members diminishes, and in adulthood, the correlation falls to *zero* (Bouchard, 1997b; Scarr, 1993; Scarr & Weinberg, 1994). Of course, adoption often has positive effects; as a group, adopted children score higher on IQ tests than do birth siblings who were not adopted, probably because adoptees grow up in a more enriched environment (van IJzendoorn et al., 2005).

How might genes affect intelligence? One possibility is by influencing the number of nerve cells in the brain or the number of connections among them, as reflected in the total volume of gray

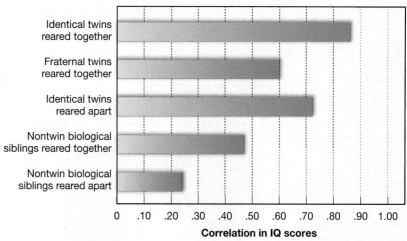

matter. Two brain-scan studies, conducted in Holland and Finland, have reported a moderately strong association between general intelligence and gray-matter volume. The amount of gray matter was strongly correlated in identical twins—over 80 percent, compared to only about 50 percent in fraternal twins—indicating that gray-matter volume is highly heritable (Posthuma et al., 2002; Thompson et al., 2001).

The Question of Group Differences If genes influence individual differences in intelligence, do they also help account for differences *between* groups, as many people assume? Because this question has enormous political and social importance, we are going to examine it closely.

Most of the focus has been on black–white differences in IQ, because African-American children score lower, on average, than do white children. (We are talking about *averages;* the distributions of scores for black children and white children overlap considerably.) A few psychologists have proposed a genetic explanation of this difference and conclude that there is little point in spending money on programs that try to raise the IQs of low-scoring children, of whatever race (Murray, 2008; Rushton & Jensen, 2005). Genetic explanations of group differences, however, have a fatal flaw, and we want to explain what it is. This flaw may seem pretty technical at first, but it is really not too difficult to understand, so stay with us.

Consider, first, not people but tomatoes. (Figure 7.7 will help you visualize the following "thought experiment.") Suppose you have a bag of tomato seeds that vary genetically; all things being equal, some will produce tomatoes that are puny

> **Thinking Critically about Group Differences in IQ**

FIGURE 7.6
Correlations in Siblings' IQ Scores
The IQ scores of identical twins are highly correlated, even when they are reared apart. The figures represented in this graph are based on average correlations across many studies (Bouchard & McGue, 1981).

heritability A statistical estimate of the proportion of the total variance in some trait that is attributable to genetic differences among individuals within a group.

**FIGURE 7.7
The Tomato Plant Experiment**
In the hypothetical experiment described in the text, even if the differences among plants within each pot were due entirely to genetics, the average differences between pots could be environmental. The same general principle applies to individual and group differences among human beings.

and tasteless, and some will produce tomatoes that are plump and delicious. Now you take a bunch of these seeds in your left hand and another bunch from the same bag in your right hand. Although one seed differs genetically from another, there is no *average* difference between the seeds in your left hand and those in your right. You plant the left hand's seeds in pot A, with some enriched soil that you have doctored with nitrogen and other nutrients, and you plant the right hand's seeds in pot B, with soil from which you have extracted nutrients. You sing to pot A and put it in the sun; you ignore pot B and leave it in a dark corner.

When the tomato plants grow, they will vary *within* each pot in terms of height, the number of tomatoes produced, and the size of the tomatoes, purely because of genetic differences. But there will also be an average difference between the plants in

pot A and those in pot B: The plants in pot A will be healthier and bear more tomatoes. This difference *between* pots is due entirely to the different soils and the care that has been given to them, even though the heritability of the *within*-pot differences is 100 percent (Lewontin, 1970, 2001).

The principle is the same for people as it is for tomatoes. Although intellectual differences *within* groups are at least partly genetic in origin, that does not mean differences *between* groups are genetic. Blacks and whites do not grow up, on the average, in the same "pots" (environments). Because of a long legacy of racial discrimination and de facto segregation, black children, as well as Latino and other minority children, often receive far fewer nutrients—literally, in terms of food, and figuratively, in terms of education, encouragement by society, and intellectual opportunities (Nisbett, 2009). And, as we have seen, negative stereotypes about ethnic groups may cause members of these groups to doubt their own abilities, become anxious and self-conscious, and perform more poorly on tests than they otherwise would.

Doing good research on the origins of group differences in IQ is extremely difficult in the United States, where racism has affected the lives of even many affluent, successful African Americans. However, the few studies that have overcome past methodological problems fail to support a genetic explanation. Children fathered by black and white American soldiers in Germany after World War II and reared in similar German communities by similar families did not differ significantly in IQ (Eyferth, 1961). Contrary to what a genetic theory would predict, degree of African ancestry (which can be roughly estimated from skin color, blood analysis, and genealogy) is not related to measured

The children of migrant workers (left) often spend long hours in backbreaking field work and may miss out on the educational opportunities and intellectual advantages available to middle-class children from the same culture (right).

intelligence (Scarr et al., 1977). And white and black infants do equally well on a test that measures their preference for novel stimuli, a predictor of later IQ scores (Fagan, 1992).

An intelligent reading of the research on intelligence, therefore, does not direct us to conclude that differences among cultural, ethnic, or national groups are permanent, genetically determined, or signs of any group's innate superiority (J. Aronson, 2010). On the contrary, the research suggests that we should make sure that all children grow up in the best possible soil, with room for the smartest and the slowest to find a place in the sun.

The Environment and Intelligence

By now you may be wondering what kinds of experiences hinder intellectual development and what kinds of environmental "nutrients" promote it. Here are some of the factors associated with reduced mental ability:

- *Poor prenatal care.* If a pregnant woman is malnourished, contracts infections, smokes, is exposed to secondhand smoke, or drinks alcohol regularly, her child is at risk of having learning disabilities and a lower IQ.

- *Malnutrition.* The average IQ gap between severely malnourished and well-nourished children can be as high as 20 points (Stoch & Smythe, 1963; Winick, Meyer, & Harris, 1975).

- *Exposure to toxins.* Lead, especially, can damage the brain and nervous system, even at fairly low levels, producing attention problems, lower IQ scores, and poorer school achievement (Hornung, Lanphear, & Dietrich, 2009; Needleman et al., 1996). Many children in the United States are exposed to dangerous levels of lead from dust, contaminated soil, lead paint, and old lead pipes, and the concentration of lead in black children's blood is 50 percent higher than in white children's (Lanphear et al., 2002).

- *Stressful family experiences.* Factors that predict reduced intellectual competence include, among others, having a father who does not live with the family, a mother with a history of mental illness, parents with limited work skills, and a history of stressful events, such as domestic violence, early in life (Sameroff et al., 1987). On average, each risk factor reduces a child's IQ score by 4 points. And when children live in severely disadvantaged neighborhoods, their IQs decline over time, even after they have moved to better

Extreme poverty, exposure to toxic materials, a neglected neighborhood, and stressful family circumstances can all have a negative impact on children's cognitive development and IQ.

areas; the drop is comparable to that seen when a child misses a year of school (Sampson, 2008).

In contrast, a healthy and stimulating environment can raise IQ scores, as several intervention studies with at-risk children have shown. In one longitudinal study called the Abecedarian Project, inner-city children who got lots of mental enrichment at home and in child care or school, starting in infancy, showed signficant IQ gains and had much better school achievement than did children in a control group (Campbell & Ramey, 1995). In another important study, of abandoned children living in Romanian orphanages, researchers randomly assigned some children to remain in the orphanages and others to move to good foster homes. By age 4, the fostered children scored dramatically higher on IQ tests that did those left behind. Children who moved before age 2 showed the largest gains, almost 15 points on average. A comparison group of children reared in their biological homes did even better, with average test scores 10 to 20 points higher than those of the foster children (Nelson et al., 2007). (Since this study was done, Romania has stopped institutionalizing abandoned children younger than 2 years unless the infants are seriously disabled.)

Perhaps the best evidence for the importance of environmental influences on intelligence is the fact that around the world, IQ scores have been climbing steadily for at least three generations (Flynn, 1987, 1999). (See Figure 7.8.) The fastest increase in a group's average IQ scores ever reported has occurred in Kenya, where IQ scores of rural 6- to 8-year-old children jumped about 11 points

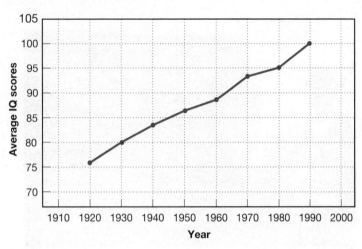

FIGURE 7.8
Climbing IQ Scores
Raw scores on IQ tests have been rising in developed countries for many decades at a rate much too steep to be accounted for by genetic changes. Because test norms are periodically readjusted to set the average score at 100, most people are unaware of the increase. On this graph, average scores are calibrated according to 1989 norms. As you can see, performance was much lower in 1918 than in 1989 (adapted from Horgan, 1995).

between 1984 and 1998 (Daley et al., 2003). Genes cannot possibly have changed enough to account for these findings, and most scientists attribute the increases to improvements in education, the growth in jobs requiring abstract thought, and better health.

We see, then, that although heredity may provide the range of a child's intellectual potential—a Homer Simpson can never become an Einstein—many other factors affect where in that range the child will fall.

Motivation, Hard Work, and Intellectual Success

Even with a high IQ, emotional intelligence, and practical know-how, you still might get nowhere at all. Talent, unlike cream, does not inevitably rise to the top; success also depends on drive and determination.

Consider a finding from one of the longest-running psychological studies ever conducted. In 1921, researchers began following more than 1,500 children with IQ scores in the top one percent of the distribution. These boys and girls were nicknamed Termites after Lewis Terman, who originally directed the research. The Termites started out bright, physically healthy, sociable, and well adjusted. As they entered adulthood, most became successful in the traditional ways of the times: men in careers and women as homemakers (Sears & Barbee, 1977; Terman & Oden, 1959). However, some gifted men

failed to live up to their early promise, dropping out of school or drifting into low-level work. When the researchers compared the 100 most successful men in the Terman study with the 100 least successful, they found that the successful men were ambitious, were socially active, had many interests, and had been encouraged by their parents. The least successful drifted casually through life. There was no average difference in IQ between the two groups.

Once you are motivated to succeed intellectually, you need self-discipline to reach your goals. In a longitudinal study of ethnically diverse eighth graders attending a magnet school, researchers assigned each student a self-discipline score based on the students' self-reports, parents' reports, teachers' reports, and questionnaires. They also had a behavioral measure of "delay of gratification," the students' ability to postpone getting an immediate reward now in favor of getting a bigger reward later (Duckworth & Seligman, 2005). Self-discipline accounted for more than twice as much of the variance in the students' final grades and achievement test scores as IQ did. As you can see in Figure 7.9, correlations between self-discipline and good grades were much stronger than those between IQ and grades.

Self-discipline and the motivation to work hard depend, in turn, on your attitudes about intelligence and achievement, which are strongly influenced by cultural values. For many years, Harold Stevenson and his colleagues studied attitudes toward achievement in Asia and the United States,

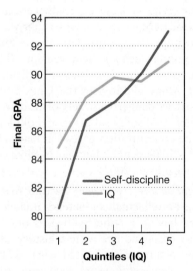

FIGURE 7.9
Grades, IQ, and Self-Discipline
When researchers divided eighth grade students into five groups (quintiles) based on their IQ scores and then followed them for a year to test their academic achievement, they found that self-discipline was a stronger predictor of success than IQ was (Duckworth & Seligman, 2005).

comparing large samples of grade school children, parents, and teachers in Minneapolis, Chicago, Sendai (Japan), Taipei (Taiwan), and Beijing (Stevenson, Chen, & Lee, 1993; Stevenson & Stigler, 1992). Their results have much to teach us about the cultivation of intellect.

In 1980, the Asian children far outperformed the American children on a broad battery of mathematical and reading tests. On computations, reading, and word problems, there was virtually no overlap between schools, with the lowest-scoring Beijing schools doing better than the highest-scoring Chicago schools. By 1990, the gulf between the Asian and American children had grown even greater. Only 4 percent of the Chinese children and 10 percent of the Japanese children had math scores as low as those of the *average* American child. These differences could not be accounted for by educational resources: The Chinese had worse facilities and larger classes than the Americans, and on average, the Chinese parents were poorer and less educated than the American parents. Nor did it have anything to do with intellectual abilities in general; the American children were just as knowledgeable and capable as the Asian children on tests of general information.

But the Asian and American children were worlds apart in their attitudes and efforts:

- *Beliefs about intelligence.* American parents, teachers, and children were far more likely than Asians to believe that mathematical ability is innate (see Figure 7.10). Americans tended to think that if you have this ability you don't have to work hard, and if you don't have it, there's no point in trying.

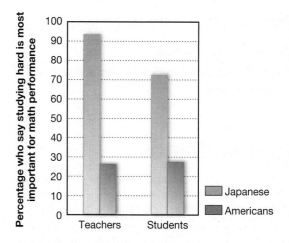

FIGURE 7.10
What's the Secret of Math Success?
Japanese schoolteachers and students are much more likely than their American counterparts to believe that the secret to doing well in math is working hard. Americans tend to think that you either have mathematical intelligence or you don't.

- *Standards.* American parents had far lower standards for their children's performance; they were satisfied with scores barely above average on a 100-point test. In contrast, Chinese and Japanese parents were happy only with very high scores.

- *Values.* American students did not value education as much as Asian students did, and they were more complacent about mediocre work. When asked what they would wish for if a wizard could give them anything they wanted, more than 60 percent of the Chinese fifth graders named something related to their education. Can you guess what the American children wanted? A majority said money or possessions.

When it comes to intellect, then, it's not just what you've got that counts, but what you do with it. Complacency, fatalism, low standards, and a desire for immediate gratification can prevent people from recognizing what they don't know and stifle their efforts to learn.

Quick Quiz

We hope you are not feeling complacent about your quiz performance.

1. On average, behavioral-genetic studies estimate the heritability of intelligence to be (a) about .90, (b) about .20, (c) low at all ages, (d) higher for adults than for children.

2. *True or false:* If a trait such as intelligence is highly heritable within a group, then differences between groups must also be due mainly to heredity.

3. The available evidence (does/does not) show that ethnic differences in average IQ scores are due to genetic differences.

4. Name four environmental factors associated with reduced mental ability.

5. According to a study of eighth graders, _____ is more strongly correlated with school performance than _____ is.

Answers:

1. d 2. false 3. does not 4. poor prenatal care, malnutrition, exposure to toxins, and stressful family circumstances 5. self-discipline; IQ

cognitive ethology The study of cognitive processes in nonhuman animals.

 YOU are about to learn...

- whether animals can think.
- whether some animal species can master aspects of human language.

Animal Minds

How smart is this otter?

A green heron swipes some bread from a picnicker's table and scatters the crumbs on a nearby stream. When a minnow rises to the bait, the heron strikes, swallowing its prey before you can say "dinner's ready." A sea otter, floating calmly on its back, bangs a mussel shell against a stone that is resting on its stomach. When the shell cracks apart, the otter devours the tasty morsel inside, tucks the stone under its flipper, and dives for another shell, which it *will* open in the same way. Incidents such as these and scores of others have convinced some biologists, psychologists, and ethologists that we are not the only animals with cognitive abilities—that "dumb beasts" are not so dumb after all. But how smart are they?

Animal Intelligence

In an early study of animal intelligence, Sultan, a talented chimpanzee studied by Wolfgang Köhler, was able to figure out how to reach a cluster of bananas by stacking some boxes and climbing on top of them.

In the 1920s, Wolfgang Köhler (1925) put chimpanzees in situations in which some tempting bananas were just out of reach and watched to see what the apes would do. Most did nothing, but a few turned out to be quite clever. If the bananas were outside the cage, the chimp might pull them

in with a stick. If they were hanging overhead, and there were boxes in the cage, the chimp might pile up the boxes and climb on top of them to reach the fruit. Often the solution came after the chimp had been sitting quietly for a while. It appeared as though the animal had been thinking about the problem and was struck by a sudden insight.

Learning theorists felt that this seemingly impressive behavior could be accounted for perfectly well by the standard principles of operant learning, without resorting to mental explanations (see Chapter 9). Because of their influence, for years any scientist who claimed that animals could think was likely to be ignored or laughed at. Today, however, the study of animal intelligence is booming, especially in the interdisciplinary field of **cognitive ethology**. (Ethology is the study of animal behavior, especially in natural environments.) Cognitive ethologists argue that some animals can anticipate future events, make plans, and coordinate their activities with those of their comrades (Griffin, 2001).

When we think about animal cognition, we must be careful, because even complex behavior that appears to be purposeful can be genetically prewired and automatic (Wynne, 2004). The assassin bug of South America catches termites by gluing nest material on its back as camouflage, but it is hard to imagine how the bug's tiny dab of brain tissue could enable it to plan this strategy consciously. Yet explanations of animal behavior that leave out any sort of consciousness at all and that attribute animals' actions entirely to instinct do not seem to account for some of the amazing things that animals can do.

Like the otter that uses a stone to crack mussel shells, many primates use objects in the natural environment as rudimentary tools, but the truly amazing thing is that their use of tools is learned rather than innate. Chimpanzee mothers occasionally show their young how to use stones to open hard nuts (Boesch, 1991). Orangutans in one Sumatran swamp have learned to use sticks as tools, held in their mouths, to pry insects from holes in tree trunks and to get seeds out of cracks in a bulb-like fruit, whereas nearby groups of orangutans use only brute force to get to the delicacies (van Schaik, 2006). Even some nonprimates may have the capacity to learn to use tools, although the evidence remains controversial among ethologists. Female bottlenose dolphins off the coast of Australia attach sea sponges to their beaks while hunting for food, which protects them from sharp coral and stinging stonefish, and they seem to have acquired this unusual skill from their mothers (Krützen et al., 2005). Is this yet another case of mothers telling their daughters what to wear?

In the laboratory, nonhuman primates have accomplished even more surprising things. For example, dozens of studies have found that chimpanzees have a rudimentary sense of number. In one study, chimpanzees compared two pairs of food wells containing chocolate chips. One pair might contain, say, five chips and three chips, the other four chips and three chips. Allowed to choose which pair they wanted, the chimps almost always chose the one with the higher combined total, showing some sort of summing ability (Rumbaugh, Savage-Rumbaugh, & Pate, 1988). Chimpanzees can even remember over a period of 20 minutes which of two containers holds more bananas (e.g., five versus eight, or six versus ten), after watching the bananas being placed one at a time into the containers. In fact, they do as well as young children on this task (Beran & Beran, 2004).

One of the most controversial questions about animal cognition is whether any animals besides human beings have a **theory of mind**: a system of beliefs about the way one's own mind and the minds of others work, and an understanding of how thoughts and feelings affect behavior. A theory of mind enables you to draw conclusions about the intentions, feelings, and beliefs of others; empathize with others ("What would I experience if I were in the other person's position?"); deceive others; recognize when someone else is lying; recognize yourself in a mirror; and know when others can or cannot see you. In human beings, a theory of mind starts to develop in the second year and is clearly present by about age 3

or 4 (see Chapter 3). Some researchers believe that the great apes (chimpanzees, gorillas, and orangutans), dolphins, and elephants have some abilities that reflect a theory of mind (de Waal, 2001a; Plotnik, de Waal, & Reiss, 2006; Suddendorf & Whiten, 2001). When looking in a mirror, these animals may try to find marks on their bodies that are not directly visible, suggesting self-recognition, or at least bodily awareness.

In addition, chimpanzees console other chimps who are in distress, use deceptive tactics when competing for food, and point to draw attention to objects, suggesting that they are able to grasp what is going on in another chimp's mind. In the wild, when one male African chimp makes an exaggerated scratching movement on part of its body during social grooming—say, on the forehead—a comrade will then groom the indicated spot, even if he was already grooming some other spot (Pika & Mitani, 2006). Chimps and even monkeys may also be capable of some metacognition. When they are tested on a new task, they will sometimes avoid difficult trials in which they are likely to be wrong. And they will press an icon on a touch screen to request a hint from their human observers when they are unsure of the correct response, even when seeking a hint means getting a lesser reward for a correct answer (Kornell, 2009). These findings suggest that the animals know what they know and don't know!

Dodger, a 2-year-old dolphin in Shark Bay, Australia, carries a sea sponge on her sensitive beak as protection against stinging creatures and sharp coral. Dolphin "sponge moms" apparently teach the behavior to their daughters.

theory of mind A system of beliefs about the way one's own mind and the minds of others work, and of how individuals are affected by their beliefs and feelings.

"It's always 'Sit,' 'Stay,' 'Heel'–never 'Think,' 'Innovate,' 'Be yourself.'"

Animals and Language

A primary ingredient of human cognition is *language*, the ability to combine elements that are themselves meaningless into an infinite number of utterances that convey meaning, and to express and comprehend an infinite number of novel utterances. Language is often regarded as the last bastion of human uniqueness, a result of evolutionary forces that produced our species (see Chapter 3). Do animals have anything comparable?

Animals do communicate, of course, using gestures, body postures, facial expressions, vocalizations, and odors. Some of these signals have highly specific meanings. Vervet monkeys have separate calls to warn each other about leopards versus eagles versus snakes (Cheney & Seyfarth, 1985). But vervets cannot combine these sounds to produce entirely novel utterances, as in "Look out, Harry, that eagle-eyed leopard is a real snake-in-the-grass."

Perhaps, however, some animals could acquire language if they got a little help from their human friends. Because the vocal tract of an ape does not permit speech, most researchers have used innovative approaches that rely on gestures or visual symbols. In one project, chimpanzees learned to use, as words, geometric plastic shapes arranged on a magnetic board (Premack & Premack, 1983). In another, they learned to punch symbols on a keyboard connected to a computer (Rumbaugh, 1977). In yet another, they learned hundreds of signs in American Sign Language (ASL) (Fouts & Rigby, 1977; Gardner & Gardner, 1969).

Animals in these studies learned to follow instructions, answer questions, and make requests. They even seemed to use their newfound skills to apologize for being disobedient, scold their trainers, and talk to themselves. Koko, a lowland gorilla, reportedly used signs to say that she felt happy or sad, to refer to past and future events, to mourn for her dead pet kitten, and to lie when she did something naughty (Patterson & Linden, 1981). Most important, the animals combined individual signs or symbols into longer utterances that they had never seen before.

Unfortunately, in their desire to talk to the animals and their affection for their primate friends, some early researchers overinterpreted the animals' communications, reading all sorts of meanings and intentions into a single sign or symbol, ignoring scrambled word order ("banana eat me"), and unwittingly giving nonverbal cues that might enable the apes to respond correctly.

But over the past few decades, as researchers have improved their techniques, they have discovered that with careful training, chimps can indeed acquire some aspects of language, including the ability to use symbols to refer to objects. Some have also used signs spontaneously to converse with one another, suggesting that they are not merely imitating or trying to get a reward (Van Cantfort & Rimpau, 1982). Bonobos (a type of ape) are especially adept at language. One bonobo named Kanzi has learned to understand English words, short sentences, and keyboard symbols without formal training (Savage-Rumbaugh & Lewin, 1994; Savage-Rumbaugh, Shanker, & Taylor, 1998). Kanzi responds correctly to commands such as "Put the key in the refrigerator" and "Go get the ball that is outdoors," even when he has never heard the words combined in that particular way before. He picked up language as children do, by observing others using it and through normal social interaction. He has also learned to manipulate keyboard symbols to request favorite foods or activities (games, TV, visits to friends) and to announce his intentions.

Research on animal language and comprehension of symbols is altering our understanding of animal cognition, and not only of primates. Dolphins have learned to respond to requests made in two artificial languages, one consisting of computer-generated whistles and another of hand and arm gestures (Herman, Kuczaj, & Holder, 1993; Herman & Morrel-Samuels, 1996). To interpret a request correctly, the dolphins had to take into account both the meaning of the individual symbols in a string of whistles or gestures and the order of the symbols (syntax). They had

Kanzi, a bonobo who answers questions and makes requests by punching symbols on a specially designed computer keyboard, also understands short English sentences. Kanzi is shown here with researcher Sue Savage-Rumbaugh.

to understand the difference between "To left Frisbee, right surfboard take" and "To right surfboard, left Frisbee take."

And some psychologists are calling border collies "the new chimps," ever since researchers in Germany reported that a border collie named Rico had a vocabulary of more than 200 words (Kaminski, Call, & Fisher, 2004). When Rico's owner asked him to retrieve an object from another room, Rico could pick the correct object 37 times out of 40. Even more impressive, Rico, like a human child, could learn a new word in just one trial, something chimpanzees cannot do. If given the name of a new object, he could usually infer that his owner wanted him to select that object from among more familiar ones and would often remember the new label weeks later. Similar results have since been reported for another border collie named Betsy (Morell, 2008).

Most amazingly, we now know that birds are not as birdbrained as once assumed. Irene Pepperberg (2000, 2002, 2008) has been working with African gray parrots since the late 1970s. Her favorite, named Alex, could count, classify, and compare objects by vocalizing English words. When he was shown up to six items and was asked how many there were, he responded with spoken (squawked?) English phrases, such as "two cork(s)" or "four key(s)." He even responded correctly to questions about items specified on two or three dimensions,

as in "How many blue key(s)?" or "What matter [material] is orange and three-cornered?" Alex also made requests ("Want pasta") and answered simple questions about objects ("What color [is this]?" "Which is bigger?"). When presented with a blue cork and a blue key and asked "What's the same?" he would correctly respond "color." He actually scored slightly better with new objects than with familiar ones, suggesting that he was not merely "parroting" a set of stock phrases. He could sum two small sets of objects, such as nuts or jelly beans, for amounts up to six (Pepperberg, 2006).

Alex was also able to say remarkably appropriate things in informal interactions. He would tell Pepperberg, "I love you," "I'm sorry," and, when she was feeling stressed out, "Calm down." One day, sitting on his perch as Pepperberg's accountant was working at a desk, Alex asked her: "Wanna nut?" "No," said the accountant. "Want some water?" "No," she said. "A banana?" "No." After making several other suggestions, Alex finally said, "What *do* you want?" (quoted in Talbot, 2008). To the sorrow of thousands of his admirers all over the world, Alex died in 2007. Pepperberg is continuing her work with other African grays. ◉─┤Watch

◉─┤Watch the Video
Birds and Language on
mypsychlab.com

Thinking about the Thinking of Animals

These results on animal language and cognition are impressive, but scientists are still divided over just what the animals in these studies are doing. Do they have true language? Are they thinking, in human terms? How intelligent are they? Are Kanzi, Rico, and Alex unusual, or are they typical of their species?

Thinking Critically about Animal Cognition

In their efforts to correct the centuries-old underestimation of animal cognition, are modern researchers now reading too much into their data and overestimating animals' abilities?

On one side are those who worry about *anthropomorphism*, the tendency to falsely attribute human qualities to nonhuman beings (Wynne, 2004). They like to tell the story of Clever Hans, a "wonder horse" at the turn of the century who was said to possess mathematical and other abilities (Spitz, 1997). Clever Hans would answer math problems by stamping his hoof the appropriate number of times. But a little careful experimentation by psychologist Oskar Pfungst (1911/1965) revealed that when Clever Hans was prevented from seeing his questioners, his powers left him. It seems that questioners were staring at the horse's feet and

Alex was a remarkably clever bird. His abilities have raised intriguing questions about the intelligence of animals and their capacity for specific aspects of language.

This old photo shows Clever Hans in action. His story has taught researchers to beware of anthropomorphism when they interpret findings on animal cognition.

✓•—**Study** and **Review** on **mypsychlab.com**

leaning forward expectantly after stating the problem, then lifting their eyes and relaxing as soon as he completed the right number of taps. Clever Hans was indeed clever, but not at math or other human skills. He was merely responding to nonverbal signals that people were inadvertently providing. (Perhaps he had a high EQ.)

On the other side are those who warn against *anthropodenial*—the tendency to think, mistakenly, that human beings have nothing in common with other animals, who are, after all, our evolutionary cousins (de Waal, 2001a; Fouts, 1997). The need to see our own species as unique, they say, may keep us from recognizing that other species, too, have cognitive abilities, even if not as sophisticated as our own. Those who take this position point out that most modern researchers have gone to great lengths to avoid the Clever Hans problem.

The outcome of this debate is bound to affect the way we view ourselves and our place among other species. Perhaps, as cognitive ethologist Marc Hauser (2000) has suggested, we can find a way to study animal minds and emotions without assuming sentimentally that they are just like our own. There is no disputing, however, that scientific discoveries are teaching us to have greater respect for the cognitive abilities of our animal relatives.

Quick Quiz

Your pet beagle may be incredibly smart, but she probably can't help you answer these questions.

1. Which of the following abilities have primates demonstrated, either in the natural environment or the laboratory? (a) the use of objects as simple tools; (b) the summing of quantities; (c) the use of symbols to make requests; (d) an understanding of short English sentences
2. Barnaby thinks his pet snake Curly is harboring angry thoughts about him because Curly has been standoffish and won't curl around his neck anymore. What error is Barnaby making?

Answers:

1. all of them   2. anthropomorphism

Psychology in the News REVISITED

Has reading this chapter given you an appreciation of what it takes, mentally speaking, to concoct the experiments that won the Ig Nobel prizes? Or, for that matter, to have the sense of humor to honor them? Some of the awards reflect great intelligence and creativity. Consider Catherine Douglas and Peter Rowlinson's research, which found that cows with names produce more milk than cows without names. That may seem to be a charming but trivial discovery, yet it shows that the quality of the human-animal relationship can affect not just an animal's behavior but even the animal's basic biology. Consider, too, the prize awarded to Donald Unger, who, as a boy, wondered whether his mother's stern warning to stop cracking his knuckles—"You'll get arthritis!"—would turn out to be true or false, and began a lifelong experiment using his own hands. Although his negative finding would need to be verified with more people and controlled procedures, it vividly demonstrates the first, most fundamental step in critical thinking: Ask questions and be willing to wonder.

So it is for good reason that we are used to thinking of ourselves as the smartest species around. Our cognitive abilities allow us to be funny, playful, smart, and creative. A great artist like Rodin can create "The Thinker," and then countless creative imitators will make their own versions of the Thinker in sand, metal, cartoons, ice, or, who knows, ice cream. Human beings can not only think critically, but also think critically about thinking critically—and understand the reasons that we often don't or can't.

Yet, as the studies in this chapter have shown, we also get ourselves into colossal muddles; we think we are better at many skills than we actually are; we have many cognitive biases that distort reality; and we often behave mindlessly. The Irish police who won an Ig Nobel Prize are, after all, an example of how mental sets can trap us. Their mental set—"the two main words on a driver's license are the driver's name"—caused them to overlook the possibility that "Prawo Jazdy" might not be the driver's name at all. And so they mindlessly kept issuing tickets to all those speeding Polish drivers, who no doubt were delighted with the officers' mistake.

As if our mental flaws in thinking and reasoning weren't bad enough, many people worry that machines are gaining on us in the mental abilities department—a frequent theme in science fiction. Enormous strides have been made in the field of *artificial intelligence* (AI), the use of computers to simulate human thinking. Avatars already are being designed to diagnose patients long distance, provide psychotherapy, handle grumpy but rambling customers, and be "virtual personal assistants." As speech recognition and other technologies of AI improve, ethicists are concerned about the potential for their manipulation and misuse. On a social level, will corporations shield themselves behind robot voices designed to chill out angry consumers? On a personal level, will computers and robots eventually be able to make crucial decisions for us on how to improve public education, choose a life partner, or manage a baseball team?

Computers are impressive, but keep in mind—your own complicated, remarkable, fallible mind!—that real intelligence is more than the capacity to perform computations with lightning speed. As we have seen, it involves the ability to deal with informal reasoning problems, reason dialectically and reflectively, devise mental shortcuts, read emotions, and acquire tacit knowledge. Robots and computers, of course, are not the least bit troubled by their lack of cleverness, inasmuch as they lack a mind to be troubled. As computer scientist David Gelernter (1997) put it, "How can an object that wants nothing, fears nothing, enjoys nothing, needs nothing, and cares about nothing have a mind?"

Because machines are mindless, they lack the one trait that distinguishes human beings not only from computers but also from other species: We try to understand our own misunderstandings (Gazzaniga, 2008). We want to know what we don't know; we are motivated to overcome our mental shortcomings. This uniquely human capacity for self-examination is probably the best reason to remain optimistic about our cognitive abilities.

Human beings worry that machines will outsmart us, but it's not likely.

Taking Psychology with You

Becoming More Creative

Throughout this book, we have been emphasizing the importance of asking questions, thinking of explanations other than just the most obvious ones, and examining assumptions and biases. All of these critical thinking guidelines involve creativity as much as they do reasoning.

Take a few moments to answer these items based on the Remote Associates Test, a test of the mental flexibility necessary for creativity. Your task is to come up with a fourth word that is associated with each item in a set of three words (Mednick, 1962). For example, an answer for the set *news–clip–wall* is *paper*. Got the idea? Now try these. (The answers are given at the end of this chapter.)

1. piggy—green—lash
2. surprise—political—favor
3. mark—shelf—telephone
4. stick—maker—tennis
5. cream—cottage—cloth

Creative thinking requires you to associate elements of a problem in new ways by finding unexpected connections among them. People who are uncreative rely on *convergent thinking*, following a particular set of steps that they think will converge on one correct solution. Then, once they have solved a problem, they tend to develop a mental set and approach future problems the same way. Creative people, in contrast, exercise *divergent thinking*; instead of stubbornly sticking to one tried-and-true path, they explore side alleys and generate several possible solutions. They come up with new hypotheses, imagine other interpretations, and look for connections that are not immediately obvious. For artists and novelists, of course, creativity is a job requirement, but it also takes creativity to invent a tool, put together a recipe from leftovers, find ways to distribute unsold food to the needy, decorate your room …

Creative people do not necessarily have high IQs. Personality characteristics seem more important, especially these three (Helson, Roberts, & Agronick, 1995; McCrae, 1987; Schank, 1988):

Nonconformity. Creative individuals are not overly concerned about what others think of them. They are willing to risk ridicule by proposing ideas that may initially appear foolish or off the mark. Geneticist Barbara McClintock's research was ignored or belittled by many for nearly 30 years. But she was sure she could show how genes move around and produce sudden changes in heredity. In 1983, when McClintock won the Nobel Prize, the judges called her work the second greatest genetic discovery of our time, after the discovery of the structure of DNA.

Curiosity. Creative people are open to new experiences; they notice when reality contradicts expectations, and they are curious about the reason. Wilhelm Roentgen, a German physicist, was studying cathode rays when he noticed a strange glow on one of his screens. Other people had seen the glow, but they ignored it because it didn't jibe with their understanding of cathode rays. Roentgen studied the glow, found it to be a new kind of radiation, and thus discovered X-rays.

Persistence. After that imaginary lightbulb goes on over your head, you still have to work hard to make the illumination last. Or, as Thomas Edison, who invented the real lightbulb, reportedly put it, "Genius is one percent inspiration and ninety-nine percent perspiration." No invention or work of art springs forth full-blown from a person's head. There are many false starts and painful revisions along the way.

If you are thinking critically (and creatively), you may wonder whether these personal qualities are enough. Do you recall the "Termites" who were the most successful? They were smart, but they also got plenty of encouragement for their efforts. Likewise, some individuals may be more creative than others, but there are also *circumstances* that foster creative accomplishment. Creativity flourishes when schools and employers encourage intrinsic motivation and not just extrinsic rewards such as gold stars and money (see Chapters 9 and 14). Intrinsic motives include a sense of accomplishment, intellectual fulfillment, the satisfaction of curiosity, and the sheer love of the activity. Creativity also increases when people have control over how to perform a task or solve a problem, are evaluated unobtrusively instead of being constantly observed and judged, and work independently (Amabile, 1983; Amabile & Khair, 2008). Organizations encourage creativity when they let people take risks, give them plenty of time to think about problems, and welcome innovation.

In sum, if you hope to become more creative, there are two things you can do. One is to cultivate qualities in yourself: your skills, curiosity, intrinsic motivation, and self-discipline. The other is to seek out the kinds of situations that will permit you to express your abilities and experiment with new ideas.

Summary

((•─ **Listen** to an **audio file** of your chapter on **mypsychlab.com**

Thought: Using What We Know

● Thinking is the mental manipulation of information. Our mental representations simplify and summarize information from the environment.

● A *concept* is a mental category that groups objects, relations, activities, abstractions, or qualities that share certain properties. *Basic concepts* have a moderate number of instances and are easier to acquire than concepts with few or many instances. *Prototypical* instances of a concept are more representative than others. The language we use to express concepts may influence how we perceive and think about the world.

● *Propositions* are made up of concepts and express a unitary idea. They may be linked together to form *cognitive schemas*, which serve as mental models of aspects of the world. *Mental images* also play a role in thinking.

● Not all mental processing is conscious. *Subconscious processes* lie outside of awareness but can be brought into consciousness when necessary. They allow us to perform two or more actions at once when one action is highly automatic. But multitasking is usually inefficient, introduces errors, and can even be dangerous, leading to accidents if done while driving. *Nonconscious processes* remain outside of awareness but nonetheless affect behavior; they are involved in insight and *implicit learning*. Conscious processing may be carried out in a *mindless* fashion if we overlook changes in context that call for a change in behavior.

Reasoning Rationally

● *Reasoning* is purposeful mental activity that involves drawing inferences and conclusions from observations, facts, or assumptions (premises). *Formal reasoning problems* can often be solved by applying an *algorithm* or by using logical processes, such as *deductive* and *inductive reasoning*. *Informal reasoning problems* often have no clearly correct solution. Disagreement may exist about basic premises, information may be incomplete, and many viewpoints may compete. Such problems often call for the application of *heuristics*, or may require *dialectical thinking* about opposing points of view.

● Studies of *reflective judgment* show that many people have trouble thinking dialectically. People in the *prereflective* stages do not distinguish between knowledge and belief or between belief and evidence. Those in the *quasi-reflective* stages think that because knowledge is sometimes uncertain, any judgment about the evidence is purely subjective. Those who think *reflectively* understand that although some things cannot be known with certainty, some judgments are more valid than others, depending on their coherence, fit with the evidence, and so on. Higher education moves people gradually closer to reflective judgment.

Barriers to Reasoning Rationally

● The ability to reason clearly and rationally is affected by many cognitive biases. People tend to exaggerate the likelihood of improbable events in part because of the *affect and availability heuristics*. They are swayed in their choices by the desire to *avoid loss* and by the *framing effect*, how the choice is presented. They forgo economic gain because of a *fairness bias*. They often overestimate their ability to have made accurate predictions (the *hindsight bias*), attend mostly to evidence that confirms what they want to believe (the *confirmation bias*), and are often mentally rigid, forming *mental sets* and seeing patterns where none exists.

● The theory of *cognitive dissonance* holds that people are motivated to reduce the tension that exists when two cognitions, or a cognition and a behavior, conflict. They can reduce dissonance by rejecting or changing a belief, changing their behavior, or rationalizing. Dissonance is most uncomfortable, and people are most likely to try to reduce it after a decision has been made (*postdecision dissonance*), when their actions violate their concept of themselves as honest and kind, and when they have put hard work into an activity (the *justification of effort*).

Measuring Intelligence: The Psychometric Approach

● *Intelligence* is hard to define. The *psychometric approach* focuses on how well people perform on standardized aptitude tests. Most psychometric psychologists believe that a general ability, a *g factor*, underlies this performance. Others, however, argue that a person can do well in some kinds of reasoning or problem solving but not others.

● The *intelligence quotient*, or *IQ*, represents how well a person has done on an intelligence test compared to other people. Alfred Binet designed the first widely used intelligence test to identify children who could benefit from remedial work. But in the United States, people assumed that intelligence tests revealed natural ability and used the tests to categorize people in school and in the armed services.

● IQ tests have been criticized for being biased in favor of white, middle-class people. However, efforts to construct tests that are free of cultural influence have been disappointing. Culture affects nearly everything to do with taking a test, from attitudes to problem-solving strategies. Negative stereotypes about a person's ethnicity, gender, or age may cause the person to feel *stereotype threat*, which can lead to anxiety that interferes with test performance.

Dissecting Intelligence: The Cognitive Approach

● In contrast to the psychometric approach, *cognitive approaches* to intelligence emphasize several kinds of intelligence and the strategies people use to solve problems. Sternberg's *triarchic theory of intelligence* proposes three aspects of intelligence: *componential* (including *metacognition*), *experiential* or *creative*, and *contextual* or *practical*. Contextual intelligence allows you to acquire *tacit knowledge*, practical strategies that are important for success but are not explicitly taught.

● Another important kind of intelligence, *emotional intelligence*, is the ability to identify your own and other people's emotions accurately, express emotions clearly, and regulate emotions in yourself and others.

The Origins of Intelligence

● Heritability estimates for intelligence (as measured by IQ tests) average about .40 to .50 for children and adolescents, and .60 to .80 for adults. Identical twins are more similar in IQ test performance than fraternal twins, and adopted children's scores correlate more highly with those of their biological parents than with those of their nonbiological relatives. These results do not mean that genes determine intelligence; the remaining variance in IQ scores must be due largely to environmental influences.

● Genes might contribute to intelligence by influencing the number of nerve cells in the brain or the number of connections among them, as reflected by the total volume of gray matter. The total volume of gray matter is highly heritable and is correlated with general intelligence.

● It is a mistake to draw conclusions about *group* differences from heritability estimates based on differences *within* a group. The available evidence fails to support genetic explanations of black–white differences in performance on IQ tests.

● Environmental factors such as poor prenatal care, malnutrition, exposure to toxins, and stressful family circumstances are associated with lower performance on intelligence tests. Conversely, a healthy and stimulating environment can improve performance. IQ scores have been rising in many countries for several generations, most likely because of improved education, better health, and the increase in jobs requiring abstract thought.

● Intellectual achievement also depends on motivation, hard work, and self-discipline. Cross-cultural work shows that beliefs about the origins of mental abilities, parental standards, and attitudes toward education can also help account for differences in academic performance.

Animal Minds

● Some researchers, especially those in *cognitive ethology*, argue that nonhuman animals have greater cognitive abilities than has previously been thought. Some animals can use objects as simple tools. Chimpanzees have shown evidence of a simple understanding of number. Some researchers believe that the great apes, and possibly other animals, have aspects of a *theory of mind*, an understanding of how their own minds and the minds of others work. In some apes and monkeys, these aspects may include some metacognition.

● In projects using visual symbol systems or American Sign Language (ASL), primates have acquired linguistic skills. Some animals, even nonprimates such as dolphins and African gray parrots, seem able to use simple grammatical ordering rules to convey or comprehend meaning. However, scientists are divided about how to interpret the findings on animal cognition, with some worrying about *anthropomorphism* and others about *anthropodenial*.

Psychology in the News, Revisited

● Our cognitive abilities allow us to be funny, playful, smart, and creative, yet we also are blinded by cognitive biases that distort reality and allow us to behave mindlessly. Although enormous strides have been made in the field of *artificial intelligence*, human intelligence is more than the capacity to perform computations with lightning speed. We remain the only creatures that try to understand our own minds and misunderstandings.

Taking Psychology with You

● Creativity is part of critical thinking. Creative people rely on *divergent* rather than *convergent* thinking when solving problems. They tend to be nonconformist, curious, and persistent, but circumstances can also foster (or suppress) creative accomplishment.

Key Terms

Answers to the creativity test on page 256: back, party, book, match, cheese

Some solutions to the nine-dot problem in the Get Involved exercise on page 235 (from Adams, 1986):

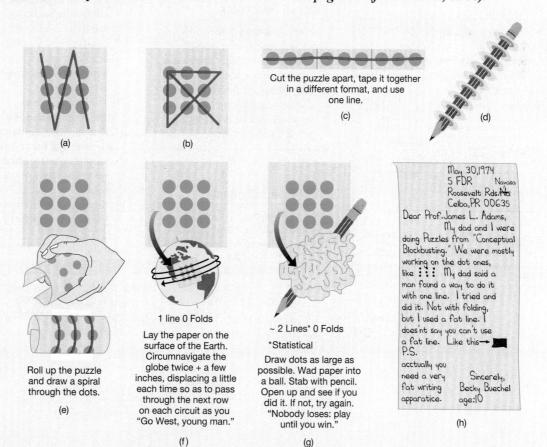

(a)

(b)

Cut the puzzle apart, tape it together in a different format, and use one line.
(c)

(d)

Roll up the puzzle and draw a spiral through the dots.
(e)

1 line 0 Folds
Lay the paper on the surface of the Earth. Circumnavigate the globe twice + a few inches, displacing a little each time so as to pass through the next row on each circuit as you "Go West, young man."
(f)

~ 2 Lines* 0 Folds
*Statistical
Draw dots as large as possible. Wad paper into a ball. Stab with pencil. Open up and see if you did it. If not, try again. "Nobody loses: play until you win."
(g)

May 30, 1974
5 FDR   Navasa
Roosevelt Rds. Na
Ceiba, PR 00635
Dear Prof. James L. Adams,
My dad and I were doing Puzzles from "Conceptual Blockbusting." We were mostly working on the dot ones, like ⋮⋮⋮ My dad said a man found a way to do it with one line. I tried and did it. Not with folding, but I used a fat line. I does'nt say you can't use a fat line. Like this→ ◤
P.S.
acctually you need a very fat writing apparatice.
Sincerely,
Becky Buechel
age:10
(h)

Thought

The Elements of Cognition

- *Thinking* is the mental manipulation of information.
- A **concept** is a mental category that groups objects, relations, activities, abstractions, or qualities that share certain properties.
- **Prototypical** instances of a concept are more representative than others.
  - **Basic concepts** have a moderate number of instances and are easier to acquire than those having few or many instances.
- The words and grammatical rules used to express concepts may influence how we think about them.
- **Propositions** are made up of concepts and express a unitary idea. They may be linked together to form **cognitive schemas**, which serve as mental models of aspects of the world.
- **Mental images** also play a role in thinking.

How Conscious Is Thought?

- **Subconscious processes** lie outside of awareness but can be brought into consciousness when necessary.
- Because of the capacity for automatic processing, many people think they are good multitaskers, but in reality *multitasking* increases stress, errors, and reaction times, while impairing memory and attention.
- **Nonconscious processes** remain outside of awareness but are involved in what we call "intuition" and in **implicit learning.**
- *Mindlessness* keeps people from recognizing the need for a change in behavior.

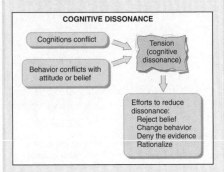

Reasoning Rationally

Reasoning

Reasoning is purposeful mental activity that involves drawing inferences and conclusions from observations or propositions.

Formal Reasoning

Formal reasoning problems can often be solved by:
- Applying an **algorithm**, a set of procedures guaranteed to produce each solution
- Using logical processes
- Using **deductive reasoning**

- Using **inductive reasoning**

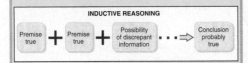

Informal Reasoning

Informal reasoning problems often have no clearly correct solution.
- **Heuristics** are rules of thumb that suggest a course of action without guaranteeing an optimal solution.
- **Dialectical reasoning** is a process of comparing and evaluating opposing points of view.

Reflective Judgment

Reflective judgment is the ability to evaluate and integrate evidence, consider alternative interpretations, and reach a defensible conclusion.

Barriers to Reasoning Rationally

Many cognitive biases are obstacles to rational thinking:
1. Exaggerating the probability of improbable events, in part because of the **affect** and **availability heuristics.**
2. Avoidance of loss, which makes people susceptible to the **framing effect**; in general, people are more cautious when a choice is framed in terms of loss rather than gain.
3. The *fairness bias*
4. The **hindsight bias**
5. The **confirmation bias**
6. Formation of **mental sets**
7. Avoidance of **cognitive dissonance**: people are motivated to reduce the tension created when two cognitions or a cognition and a behavior conflict. They reduce **postdecision dissonance** in various ways, including the **justification of effort.**

Intelligence

Intelligence is an inferred characteristic, usually defined as the ability to profit from experience, acquire knowledge, think abstractly, act purposefully, or adapt to change.

Measuring Intelligence

The **psychometric** approach to intelligence focuses on performance on standardized aptitude tests.

- The use of **factor analysis** can help identify clusters of correlated items on a test that measure some common ability, such as a **g factor** in intelligence.
- Alfred Binet came up with the idea of measuring a person's **mental age**, or level of intellectual development relative to that of others.
- The **intelligence quotient (IQ)** represents a person's score on a particular test, compared to others' scores.
- Efforts to create intelligence tests unaffected by culture have been disappointing.
- **Stereotype threat** can affect the test performance of women and minority groups.

Dissecting Intelligence

Cognitive approaches emphasize problem-solving strategies and several kinds of intelligence, rather than a g factor.

The **triarchic theory of intelligence** proposes three aspects of intelligence:
- Componential (includes **metacognition**)
- Experiential or creative
- Contextual or practical (which allows one to acquire **tacit knowledge**)

Other theories propose multiple domains of intelligence. A leading one emphasizes **emotional intelligence.**

The Origins of Intelligence

Behavioral-genetic studies show the **heritability** of intelligence (as measured by IQ tests) to be high.

The Question of Group Differences

- Genetic explanations of black–white differences in IQ inappropriately use heritability estimates based mainly on white samples.
- Environmental influences on intelligence include:
  — Poor prenatal care
  — Malnutrition
  — Exposure to toxins
  — Stressful family circumstances

Motivation, Hard Work, and Intellectual Success

- Intellectual performance is strongly influenced by motivation and self-discipline.
- These in turn are affected by cultural (parental) expectations, attitudes toward education, and beliefs about the origins of mental abilities.

Animal Minds

Animal Intelligence

Cognitive ethologists study animal intelligence, cognition, and behavior in natural environments:
- Some animals can use rudimentary tools.
- Chimpanzees can learn to use numerals and symbols.
- Whether or not animals possess a **theory of mind** is the subject of much debate. Some theorists argue that the great apes, and even some other animals, have some understanding of their own minds and those of others.

Animals and Language

In several studies, primates and other animals have acquired some aspects of human language.

In thinking about animal cognition, we must avoid both *anthropomorphism* and *anthropodenial*.

Wrongly Convicted Man and His Accuser Tell Their Story

NEW YORK, NY, January 5, 2010. St. Martin's Press has announced the release of the paperback edition of *Picking Cotton,* a remarkable true story of what novelist John Grisham calls an "account of violence, rage, redemption, and, ultimately, forgiveness."

The story began in 1987, in Burlington, North Carolina, with the rape of a young white college student named Jennifer Thompson. During her ordeal, Thompson swore to herself that she would never forget the face of her rapist, a man who climbed through the window of her apartment and assaulted her brutally. During the attack, she made an effort to memorize every detail of his face, looking for scars, tattoos, or other identifying marks. When the police asked her if she could identify the assailant from a book of mug shots, she picked one that she was sure was correct, and later she identified the same man in a lineup.

Based on her convincing eyewitness testimony, a 22-year-old black man named Ronald Cotton was sentenced to prison for two life terms. Cotton's lawyer appealed the decision, and by the time of the appeals hearing, evidence had come to light suggesting that the real rapist might have been a man who looked very like Cotton, an imprisoned criminal named Bobby Poole. Another trial was held. Jennifer Thompson looked at both men face to face, and once again said that Ronald Cotton was the one who raped her.

Eleven years later, DNA evidence completely exonerated Cotton and just as unequivocally convicted Poole, who confessed to the crime. Thompson was shocked and devastated. "The man I was so sure I had never seen in my life was the man who was inches from my throat, who raped me, who hurt me, who took my spirit away, who robbed me of my soul," she wrote. "And the man I had identified so emphatically on so many occasions was absolutely innocent."

Jennifer Thompson decided to meet Cotton and apologize to him personally. Remarkably, both were able to put this tragedy behind them, overcome the racial barrier that divided them, and write a book, which they have subtitled "Our memoir of injustice and redemption."

Nevertheless, Thompson says, she still lives "with constant anguish that my profound mistake cost him so dearly. I cannot begin to imagine what would have happened had my mistaken identification occurred in a capital case."

Ronald Cotton (left) was convicted of rape solely on the basis of Jennifer Thompson's eyewitness testimony. The real rapist, Bobby Peale (right), was eventually identified by DNA tests.

Memory

Many criminals are sent to prison on the basis of accurate testimony by eyewitnesses. But, in the absence of corroborating evidence, should a witness's confidence in his or her memory be sufficient for establishing guilt? Much is at stake in our efforts to answer this question: getting justice for crime victims and also avoiding the false conviction of defendants who are innocent.

Memory refers to the capacity to retain and retrieve information, and also to the structures that account for this capacity. Human beings are capable of astonishing feats of memory. Most of us can easily remember the tune of our national anthem, how to use an ATM, the most embarrassing experience we ever had, and hundreds of thousands of other bits of information. Memory confers competence; without it, we would be as helpless as newborns, unable to carry out even the most trivial daily tasks. Memory also endows us with a sense of identity; each of us is the sum of our recollections. Individuals and cultures alike rely on a remembered history for a sense of coherence and meaning; memory gives us our past and guides our future.

And yet our memories can be distorted, embellished, and even completely false. Have you ever had a conversation with a sibling, parent, or friend about a memory of a shared experience, only to realize you completely differ on what "really" happened? ("I was there and remember that evening perfectly!" one of you says. "You think you were *there*?" the other says in astonishment. "You weren't even in the same city! You didn't even *know* about that evening for three months!")

This chapter will raise some fascinating but troubling questions about memory: When should we trust our memories, and when should we be cautious about doing so? We all forget things that did happen; do we also "remember" things that never happened? Are memory malfunctions the exception to the rule or commonplace? And if memory is not always reliable, how can any of us hope to know the story of our own lives? How can we hope to understand the past?

YOU are about to learn...

- why memory does not work like a camera—and how it does work.
- why errors can creep into our memories of even surprising or shocking events.
- why having strong feelings about a memory does not mean that the memory is accurate.

Reconstructing the Past

Imagine what life would be like if you could never form any new memories. That tragedy occurs in older people who are suffering from dementia and sometimes in younger people who have brain injuries or diseases. The case of one man, Henry Molaison, whom researchers called H. M. until his death in 2008 at age 82, is probably the most intensely studied in the annals of medicine (Corkin, 1984; Corkin et al., 1997; Hilts, 1995; Milner, 1970; Ogden & Corkin, 1991). In 1953, when H. M. was 27, surgeons removed most of his hippocampus, along with part of the amygdala. The operation was a last-ditch effort to relieve H. M.'s severe and life-threatening epilepsy, which was causing unrelenting, uncontrollable seizures. The operation did achieve its goal: Afterward, the young man's seizures were milder and could be managed with medication. His memory, however, had been affected profoundly. Although he continued to recall most events that had occurred before the

If this little birthday boy, sitting somewhat overwhelmed in front of his cake among his happy relatives, remembers his birthday party later in life, his construction will include details picked up from this photograph, videos, and stories. He will probably be unable to distinguish an actual memory from information he got elsewhere.

operation, he could no longer remember new experiences for much longer than 15 minutes. Facts, songs, stories, and faces all vanished like water down the drain. He would read the same magazine over and over without realizing it. He could not recall the day of the week, the year, or even his last meal.

H. M. loved to do crossword puzzles and play bingo, skills acquired before the operation. But although he remained cheerful, he knew he had memory problems. He would occasionally recall an unusually emotional event, such as the assassination of someone named Kennedy, and he sometimes remembered that both of his parents were dead. But according to Suzanne Corkin, who studied H. M. extensively, these "islands of remembering" were the exceptions in a vast sea of forgetfulness. This good-natured man could not recognize a photograph of his own face, and he never remembered the scientists who studied him for decades; he was stuck in a time warp from the past.

The Manufacture of Memory

In ancient times, philosophers compared memory to a soft wax tablet that would preserve anything that chanced to make an imprint on it. Then, with the advent of the printing press, they began to think of memory as a gigantic library, storing specific events and facts for later retrieval. Today, many people compare memory to a digital recorder or video camera, automatically recording every moment of their lives.

Popular and appealing though this belief about memory is, it is utterly wrong. Not everything that happens to us or impinges on our senses is tucked away for later use. Memory is selective. If it were not, our minds would be cluttered with mental junk: the temperature at noon on Thursday, the price of turnips two years ago, a phone number needed only once. Moreover, recovering a memory is not at all like replaying a video of an event. It is more like watching a few unconnected frames and then figuring out what the rest of the scene must have been like.

One of the first scientists to make this point was the British psychologist Sir Frederic Bartlett (1932). Bartlett asked people to read lengthy, unfamiliar stories from other cultures and then tell the stories back to him. As the volunteers tried to recall the stories, they made interesting errors: They often eliminated or changed details that did not make sense to them, and they added other details to make the story coherent, sometimes even adding a moral. Memory, Bartlett concluded, must therefore be largely a *reconstructive* process. We may reproduce some kinds of simple information by rote, said Bartlett, but when we remember complex information, we typically alter it in ways that help us make sense of the material, based on what we already know or think we know. Since Bartlett's time, hundreds of studies have found this to be true for everything from stories to conversations to personal experiences.

In reconstructing their memories, people often draw on many sources. Suppose that someone asks you to describe one of your early birthday parties. You may have some direct recollection of the event, but you may also incorporate information from family stories, photographs, or home videos, and even from accounts of other people's birthdays and reenactments of birthdays on television. You take all these bits and pieces and build one integrated account. Later, you may not be able to distinguish your actual memory from information you got elsewhere. This phenomenon is known as **source misattribution**, or sometimes *source confusion* (Johnson, Hashtroudi, & Lindsay, 1993; Mitchell & Johnson, 2009).

Of course, some shocking or tragic events—such as earthquakes, accidents, a mass killing, an assassination—do hold a special place in memory, especially when we have experienced them personally. So do some unusual, exhilaratingly happy events, such as learning that you just won a lottery. Years ago, Roger Brown and James Kulik (1977) labeled these vivid recollections of emotional events *flashbulb memories* because that term captures the surprise, illumination, and seemingly photographic detail that characterize them.

Some flashbulb memories have lasted for years, even decades. In a Danish study, older people who had lived through the Nazi occupation of their country in World War II often had an accurate memory of verifiable wartime events, such as the time of day that the radio had announced liberation and what the weather had been like at the time (Berntsen & Thomsen, 2005). Yet even flashbulb memories are not always complete or accurate. People typically remember the *gist* of a startling, emotional event they experienced or witnessed, such as the destruction of the World Trade Centers in New York in 2001. But when researchers question them about their memories over time, errors creep into the details, and after a few years, some people even forget the gist (Neisser & Harsch, 1992; Talarico & Rubin, 2003).

Even with flashbulb memories, then, facts tend to get mixed with a little fiction. Remembering is an active process, one that involves not only

Do you remember where you were when you learned that Michael Jackson had died? Many of his fans probably have a "flashbulb" memory of hearing about his sudden death on June 25, 2009. But even flashbulb memories are not always complete or accurate, and distortions often creep in over time.

dredging up stored information but also putting two and two together to reconstruct the past. Sometimes, unfortunately, we put two and two together and get five.

The Conditions of Confabulation

Because memory is reconstructive, it is subject to **confabulation**—confusing an event that happened to someone else with one that happened to you, or coming to believe that you remember something that never really happened. Such confabulations are especially likely under the following circumstances

source misattribution The inability to distinguish an actual memory of an event from information you learned about the event elsewhere.

confabulation Confusion of an event that happened to someone else with one that happened to you, or a belief that you remember something when it never actually happened.

NEVER FORGETS

SOMETIMES FORGETS

ALWAYS FORGETS

In the 1980s, Whitley Strieber published the best seller *Communion*, in which he claimed to have had encounters with some sort of nonhuman beings, possibly aliens from outer space. An art director designed this striking cover. Ever since, many people have assumed that this is what an extraterrestrial must look like, and some have imported the image into their own confabulated memories of alien abduction.

⊙►⌐**Simulate**
**Creating False
Memories** on
mypsychlab.com

✓►⌐**Study** and
Review on
mypsychlab.com

(Garry et al., 1996; Hyman & Pentland, 1996; Mitchell & Johnson, 2009):

1 You have thought, heard, or told others about the imagined event many times. Suppose that at family gatherings you keep hearing about the time that Uncle Sam scared everyone at a New Year's party by pounding a hammer into the wall with such force that the wall collapsed. The story is so colorful that you can practically see Uncle Sam in your mind's eye. The more you think about this event, the more likely you are to believe that you were actually there, even if you were sound asleep in another house. This process has been called *imagination inflation*, because your own active imagination inflates your belief that the event really occurred (Garry & Polaschek, 2000). Even merely explaining how a hypothetical childhood experience *could* have happened inflates people's confidence that it really did. Explaining an event makes it seem more familiar and thus real (Sharman, Manning, & Garry, 2005).

2 The image of the event contains lots of details that make it feel real. Ordinarily, we can distinguish an imagined event from a real one by the amount of detail we recall; real events tend to produce more details. But the longer you think about an imagined event, the more details you are likely to add—what Sam was wearing, the fact that he'd had too much to drink, the crumbling plaster, people standing around in party hats—and these details may in turn persuade you that the event really happened and that you have a direct memory of it.

3 The event is easy to imagine. If imagining an event takes little effort (as does visualizing a man pounding a wall with a hammer), then we tend to think that our memory is real. In contrast, when we must make an effort to form an image of an experience—for example, of being in a place we have never seen or doing something that is utterly foreign to us—our cognitive efforts serve as a cue that the event did not really take place, or that we were not there when it did.

As a result of confabulation, you may end up with a memory that feels emotionally, vividly real to you and yet is completely false. Inaccuracies in memory can occur when you first form a memory (perhaps because your attention is divided or you are distracted) or when you later retrieve the memory (when you might confuse associated thoughts, wishes, and imagined ideas with what really happened) (Mitchell & Johnson, 2009). This means that your feelings about an event, no matter how strong they are, do not guarantee that the event really happened.

Consider again our Sam story, which happens to be true. A woman we know believed for years that she had been present as an 11-year-old child when her uncle destroyed the wall. Because the story was so vivid and upsetting to her, she felt angry at him for what she thought was his mean and violent behavior, and she assumed that she must have been angry at the time as well. Then, as an adult, she learned that she was not at the party at all but had merely heard about it repeatedly over the years. Moreover, Sam had not pounded the wall in anger, but as a joke, to inform the assembled guests that he and his wife were about to remodel their home. Nevertheless, our friend's family has had a hard time convincing her that her "memory" of this event is entirely wrong, and they are not sure she believes them yet.

As the Sam story illustrates, and as laboratory research verifies, false memories can be as stable over time as true ones (Roediger & McDermott, 1995). There's just no getting around it: Memory is reconstructive. ⊙►⌐**Simulate**

Quick Quiz

Can you reconstruct what you have read so far to answer these questions?

1. Memory is like (a) a wax tablet, (b) a giant file cabinet, (c) a video camera, (d) none of these.

2. *True or false:* Because they are so vivid, flashbulb memories remain perfectly accurate over time.

3. Which of the following confabulated "memories" might a person be most inclined to accept as having really happened to them, and why? (a) getting lost in a shopping center at the age of 5, (b) taking a class in astrophysics, (c) visiting a monastery in Tibet as a child, (d) being bullied by another kid in the fourth grade.

Answers:

1. d 2. false 3. a and d, because they are common events that are easy to imagine and that contain a lot of vivid details. It would be harder to induce someone to believe that he or she had studied astrophysics or visited Tibet because these are rare events that take an effort to imagine.

YOU are about to learn...

- how memories of an event can be affected by the way someone is questioned about it.

- why children's memories and testimony about sexual abuse cannot always be trusted.

Memory and the Power of Suggestion

The reconstructive nature of memory helps the mind work efficiently. Instead of cramming our brains with infinite details, we can store the essentials of an experience and then use our knowledge of the world to figure out the specifics when we need them. But precisely because memory is reconstructive, it is also vulnerable to suggestion—to ideas implanted in our minds after the event, which then become associated with it. This fact raises thorny problems in legal cases that involve eyewitness testimony or people's memories of what happened, when, and to whom.

The Eyewitness on Trial

Without the accounts of eyewitnesses, many guilty people would go free. But, as Jennifer Thompson learned to her sorrow, eyewitness testimony is not always reliable. Lineups and photo arrays don't necessarily help, because witnesses may simply identify the person who looks most like the perpetrator of the crime (Wells & Olson, 2003). As a result, some convictions based on eyewitness testimony, like that of Ronald Cotton, turn out to be tragic mistakes.

Eyewitnesses are especially likely to make mistaken identifications when the suspect's ethnicity differs from their own. Because of unfamiliarity with other ethnic groups, the eyewitness may focus solely on the ethnicity of the person they see committing a crime ("He's black"; "She's white"; "He's an Arab") and ignore the distinctive features that would later make identification more accurate (Levin, 2000; Meissner & Brigham, 2001).

In a program of research spanning nearly four decades, Elizabeth Loftus and her colleagues have shown that memories are also influenced by the way in which questions are put to the eyewitness and by suggestive comments made during an interrogation or interview. In one classic study, the researchers showed how even subtle changes in the wording of questions can lead a witness to give different answers. Participants first viewed short films depicting car collisions. Afterward, the researchers

On TV crime shows, witnesses often identify a criminal from a lineup or a group of photos. But these methods can mislead witnesses, who may wrongly identify a person because he or she resembles the actual culprit more closely than the other people do. Thanks to psychological research, many law enforcement agencies are now using better methods, such as having witnesses look at photos of suspects one at a time without being able to go back to an earlier one.

asked some of them, "About how fast were the cars going when they hit each other?" Other viewers were asked the same question, but with the verb changed to *smashed, collided, bumped,* or *contacted.* Estimates of how fast the cars were going varied, depending on which word was used. *Smashed* produced the highest average speed estimates (40.8 mph), followed by *collided* (39.3 mph), *bumped* (38.1 mph), *hit* (34.0 mph), and *contacted* (31.8 mph) (Loftus & Palmer, 1974).

In a similar study, the researchers asked some participants, "Did you see *a* broken headlight?" but asked others "Did you see *the* broken headlight?" (Loftus & Zanni, 1975). The question with *the* presupposes a broken headlight and merely asks whether the witness saw it, whereas the question with *a* makes no such presupposition. People who received questions with *the* were far more likely to report having seen something that had not really appeared in the film than were those who received questions with *a.* If a tiny word like *the* can lead people to "remember" what they never saw, you can imagine how the leading questions of police detectives and lawyers might influence a witness's recall.

Misleading information from sources other than the interviewer also can alter what witnesses report. Consider what happened when students were shown the face of a young man who had straight hair, then heard a description of the face supposedly written by another witness—a description that wrongly said the man had light, curly hair

A

B

FIGURE 8.1
The Influence of Misleading Information
In a study described in the text, students saw the face of a young man with straight hair and then had to reconstruct it from memory. On the left is one student's reconstruction in the absence of misleading information about the man's hair. On the right is another person's reconstruction of the same face after exposure to misleading information that mentioned curly hair (Loftus & Greene, 1980).

(see Figure 8.1). When the students reconstructed the face using a kit of facial features, a third of their reconstructions contained the misleading detail, whereas only 5 percent contained it when curly hair was not mentioned (Loftus & Greene, 1980).

Leading questions, suggestive comments, and misleading information affect people's memories not only for events they have witnessed but also for their own experiences. Researchers have successfully used these techniques to induce people to believe they are recalling complicated events from early in life that never actually happened, such as getting lost in a shopping mall, being hospitalized for a high fever, being harassed by a bully, getting in trouble for playing a prank on a first grade teacher, or spilling punch all over the mother of the bride at a wedding (Hyman & Pentland, 1996; Lindsay et al., 2004; Loftus & Pickrell, 1995; Mazzoni et al., 1999). When people were shown a phony Disneyland ad featuring Bugs Bunny, about 16 percent later recalled having met a Bugs character at Disneyland (Braun, Ellis, & Loftus, 2002). In later studies, the percentages were even higher. Some people even claimed to remember shaking hands with the character, hugging him, or seeing him in a parade. But these memories were impossible, because Bugs Bunny is a Warner Brothers

creation and would definitely be rabbit non grata at Disneyland!

Children's Testimony

The power of suggestion can affect anyone, but many people are especially concerned about its impact on children who are being questioned regarding possible sexual abuse. How can adults find out whether a young child has been sexually molested without influencing or tainting what the child says? The answer is crucial. Throughout the 1980s and 1990s, accusations of child abuse in daycare centers across the United States skyrocketed. After being interviewed by therapists and police investigators, children were claiming that their teachers had molested them in the most terrible ways: hanging them in trees, raping them, and even forcing them to eat feces. Although in no case had parents actually seen the daycare teachers treating the children badly, although none of the children had complained to their parents, and although none of the parents had noticed any symptoms or problems in their children, most of the accused teachers were sentenced to many years in prison.

Thinking Critically about Children's Testimony

Thanks largely to research by psychological scientists, the hysteria eventually subsided and people were able to assess more clearly what had gone wrong in the interviewing of the children in these cases. Today we know that although most children *do* recollect accurately much of what they have observed or experienced, many children will say that something happened when it did not. Like adults, they can be influenced by leading questions and suggestions from the person interviewing them (Ceci & Bruck, 1995). The question, therefore, is not "Can children's memories be trusted?" but "Under what conditions are children apt to be suggestible and to report that something happened to them when in fact it did not?"

The answer, from many experimental studies, is that a child is more likely to give a false report when the interviewer strongly believes that the child has been molested and then uses suggestive techniques to get the child to reveal molestation (Bruck, 2003). Interviewers who are biased in this way seek only confirming evidence and ignore discrepant evidence and other explanations for a child's behavior. They reject a child's denial of having been molested and assume the child is "in denial." They use techniques that encourage imagination inflation ("Let's pretend it happened!") and that blur reality and fantasy in the child's mind. They pressure or encourage the child to describe terrible events, badger the child with repeated questions, tell the child that "everyone else" said the events happened, or use bribes and threats (Poole & Lamb, 1998).

A team of researchers analyzed the actual transcripts of interrogations of children in the first highly publicized sexual abuse case, the McMartin preschool case (which ended in a hung jury). Then they applied the same suggestive techniques in an experiment with preschool children (Garven et al., 1998). A young man visited children at their preschool, read them a story, and handed out treats. The man did nothing aggressive, inappropriate, or surprising. A week later, an experimenter questioned the children individually about the man's visit. She asked children in one group leading questions ("Did he bump the teacher? Did he throw a crayon at a kid who was talking?" "Did he tell you a secret and tell you not to tell?"). She asked a second group the same questions but also applied influence techniques used by interrogators in the McMartin and other daycare cases, such as telling the children what "other kids" had supposedly said, expressing disappointment if answers were negative, and praising the children for making allegations.

In the first group, children said "Yes, it happened" to about 17 percent of the false allegations about the man's visit. And in the second group, they said "yes" to the false allegations suggested to them a whopping 58 percent of the time. As you can see in Figure 8.2, the 3-year-olds in this group, on average, said "yes" to over 80 percent of the false allegations, and the 4- to 6-year-olds said "yes" to over half of the allegations. Note that the interviews in this study lasted only 5 to 10 minutes, whereas in actual investigations, interviewers often question children repeatedly over many weeks or months.

Many people believe that children cannot be induced to make up experiences that are truly traumatic, but psychologists have shown that this assumption, too, is wrong. When schoolchildren were asked for their recollections of an actual sniper incident at their school, many of those who had been absent from school that day reported memories of hearing shots, seeing someone lying on the ground, and other details they could not possibly have experienced directly. Apparently, they had been influenced by the accounts of the children who had been there (Pynoos & Nader, 1989).

Of course, some children, especially those who lack language skills and self-control, are more

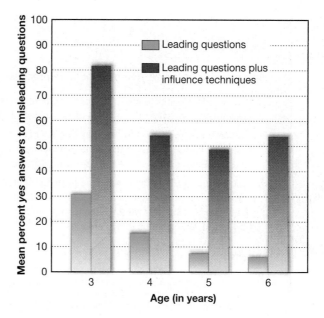

FIGURE 8.2

Social Pressure and Children's False Allegations

When researchers asked 3-year-olds leading questions about events that had not occurred—such as whether a previous visitor to their classroom had committed aggressive acts—nearly 30 percent said that yes, he had. This percentage declined among older children. But when the researchers used influence techniques taken from actual child-abuse investigations, most of the children of all ages agreed with the false allegation (Garven et al., 1998).

vulnerable to influence techniques than others. But all children can be misled under certain conditions. Rumor and hearsay play a big role in promoting false beliefs and memories in children, just as they do in adults (Principe et al., 2006).

As a result of such findings, psychologists have been able to develop ways of interviewing children that reduce the chances of false reporting. If the interviewer says, "Tell me the reason you came to talk to me today," and nothing more, most actual victims will disclose what happened to them (Bruck, 2003). The interviewer must not assume that the child was molested, must avoid leading or suggestive questions, and must understand that children do not speak the way adults do. Young children often drift from topic to topic, and their words may not be the words adults use (Poole & Lamb, 1998). One little girl being interviewed thought her "private parts" were her elbows!

In sum, children, like adults, can be accurate in what they report and, also like adults, they can distort, forget, fantasize, and be misled. Their memory processes are only human.

✓● Study and
Review on
mypsychlab.com

Quick Quiz

Now see how accurate your own memory processes are.

1. *True or false*: Mistaken identifications are more likely when a suspect's ethnicity differs from that of the eyewitness, even when the witness feels convinced that he or she is accurate.

2. Research suggests that the best way to encourage truthful testimony by children is to (a) reassure them that their friends have had the same experience, (b) reward them for saying that something happened, (c) scold them if you believe they are lying, (d) avoid leading questions.

3. Some time ago, hundreds of people in psychotherapy began claiming that they could recall long-buried memories of having taken part in satanic rituals involving animal and human torture and sacrifice. Yet local detectives and the FBI were unable to confirm any of these reports. Based on what you have learned so far, how might you explain such "memories"?

Answers:

1. true 2. d 3. Therapists who uncritically assumed that satanic cults were widespread may have asked leading questions and otherwise influenced their patients. Patients who were susceptible to their therapists' interpretations may then have confabulated and "remembered" experiences that did not happen, borrowing details from fictionalized accounts or from other troubling experiences in their lives. The result was source misattribution and the patients' mistaken conviction that their memories were real.

YOU are about to learn...

- why multiple-choice test items are generally easier than short-answer or essay questions.

- whether you can know something without knowing that you know it.

- why the computer is often used as a metaphor for the mind.

In Pursuit of Memory

Now that we have seen how memory *doesn't* work—namely, like an infallible recording of everything that happens to you—we turn to studies of how it *does* work.

Measuring Memory

Conscious, intentional recollection of an event or an item of information is called **explicit memory**. It is usually measured using one of two methods. The first method tests for **recall**, the ability to retrieve and reproduce information encountered earlier. Essay and fill-in-the-blank exams require recall. The second method tests for **recognition**, the ability to identify information you have previously observed, read, or heard about. The information is given to you, and all you have to do is say whether it is old or new, or perhaps correct or incorrect, or pick it out of a set of alternatives. The task, in other words, is to compare the information you are given with the information stored in your memory.

True–false and multiple-choice tests call for recognition.

Recognition tests can be tricky, especially when false items closely resemble correct ones. Under most circumstances, however, recognition is easier than recall. Recognition for visual images is particularly impressive. If you show people 2,500 slides of faces and places, and later you ask them to identify which ones they saw out of a larger set, they will be able to identify more than 90 percent of the original slides accurately (Haber, 1970).

The superiority of recognition over recall was once demonstrated in a study of people's memories of their high school classmates (Bahrick, Bahrick, & Wittlinger, 1975). The participants, ages 17 to 74, first wrote down the names of as many classmates as they could remember. Recall was poor; even when prompted with yearbook pictures, the youngest people failed to name almost a third of their classmates, and the oldest failed to name most of them. Recognition, however, was far better. When asked to look at a series of cards, each of which contained a set of five photographs, and asked to say which picture in each set showed a former classmate, recent graduates were right 90 percent of the time—and so were people who had graduated 35 years earlier. The ability to recognize names was nearly as impressive.

Sometimes, information encountered in the past affects our thoughts and actions even though we do not consciously or intentionally remember it, a phenomenon known as **implicit memory**

explicit memory Conscious, intentional recollection of an event or of an item of information.

recall The ability to retrieve and reproduce from memory previously encountered material.

recognition The ability to identify previously encountered material.

implicit memory Unconscious retention in memory, as evidenced by the effect of a previous experience or previously encountered information on current thoughts or actions.

(Schacter, Chiu, & Ochsner, 1993). To get at this subtle sort of memory, researchers must rely on indirect methods instead of the direct ones used to measure explicit memory. One common method, **priming**, which we introduced in Chapter 6 in our discussion of subliminal perception, asks you to read or listen to some information and then tests you later to see whether the information affects your performance on another type of task.

Suppose that you had to read a list of words, some of which began with the letters *def* (such as *define, defend,* or *deform*). Later you might be asked to complete word stems (such as *def-*) with the first word that came to mind. Even if you could not recognize or recall the original words very well, you would be more likely to complete the word fragments with words from the list than you would be if you had not seen the list. In this procedure, the original words "prime" responses on the word-completion task (that is, make them more available), showing that people can retain more knowledge about the past than they realize. They know more than they know that they know (Richardson-Klavehn & Bjork, 1988; Roediger, 1990). And they know it for a very long time. One study primed people with black-and-white picture fragments (rather than word fragments) for only 1 to 3 seconds, asking them to name the object the fragments were part of. When they were tested *17 years later,* they were again shown the same fragments and a set they had never seen. Their identification rate for the formerly primed objects was significantly higher, even when people couldn't remember having been in the original study (Mitchell, 2006).

Another way to measure implicit memory, the **relearning method,** or *savings method,* was devised by Hermann Ebbinghaus (1885/1913) in the nineteenth century. The relearning method requires you to relearn information or a task that you

PRIMING

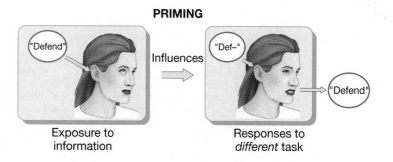

Exposure to information   Responses to *different* task

learned earlier. If you master it more quickly the second time around, you must be remembering something from the first experience.

Models of Memory

Although people usually refer to memory as a single faculty, as in "I must be losing my memory" or "He has a memory like an elephant's," the term *memory* actually covers a complex collection of abilities and processes. If a video camera is not an accurate metaphor for capturing these diverse components of memory, what metaphor would be better?

Many cognitive psychologists liken the mind to an information processor, along the lines of a computer, though more complex. They have constructed *information-processing models* of cognitive processes, liberally borrowing computer-programming terms such as *input, output, accessing,* and *information retrieval.* When you type something on your computer's keyboard, a software program encodes the information into an electronic language, stores it on a hard drive, and retrieves it when you need to use it. Similarly, in information-processing models of memory, we *encode* information (convert it to a form that the brain can process and use), *store* the information (retain it over time), and *retrieve* the information (recover it for use). In storage, the information may be represented as

priming A method for measuring implicit memory in which a person reads or listens to information and is later tested to see whether the information affects performance on another type of task.

relearning method A method for measuring retention that compares the time required to relearn material with the time used in the initial learning of the material.

Get Involved! Recalling Rudolph's Friends

You can try this test of recall if you are familiar with the poem that begins "'Twas the Night Before Christmas" or the song "Rudolph the Red-Nosed Reindeer." Rudolph had eight reindeer friends; name as many of them as you can. After you have done your best, turn to the Get Involved exercise on the next page for a recognition test on the same information.

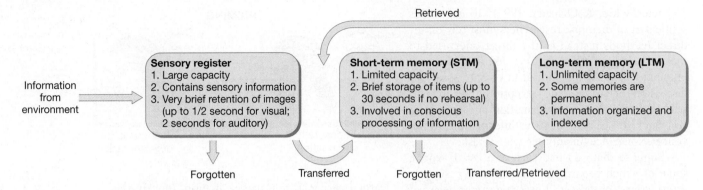

Retrieved

Information from environment →

Sensory register
1. Large capacity
2. Contains sensory information
3. Very brief retention of images (up to 1/2 second for visual; 2 seconds for auditory)

Short-term memory (STM)
1. Limited capacity
2. Brief storage of items (up to 30 seconds if no rehearsal)
3. Involved in conscious processing of information

Long-term memory (LTM)
1. Unlimited capacity
2. Some memories are permanent
3. Information organized and indexed

Forgotten   **Transferred**   **Forgotten**   **Transferred/Retrieved**

FIGURE 8.3
Three Memory Systems
In the three-box model, information that does not transfer out of the sensory register or short-term memory is assumed to be forgotten forever. Once in long-term memory, information can be retrieved for use in analyzing incoming sensory information or performing mental operations in short-term memory.

parallel distributed processing (PDP) model A model of memory in which knowledge is represented as connections among thousands of interacting processing units, distributed in a vast network, and all operating in parallel.

concepts, propositions, images, or *cognitive schemas*, mental networks of knowledge, beliefs, and expectations concerning particular topics or aspects of the world. (If you can't retrieve these terms, see Chapter 7.)

In most information-processing models, storage takes place in three interacting memory systems. A *sensory register* retains incoming sensory information for a second or two, until it can be processed further. *Short-term memory (STM)* holds a limited amount of information for a brief period of time, perhaps up to 30 seconds or so, unless a conscious effort is made to keep it there longer. *Long-term memory (LTM)* accounts for longer storage, from a few minutes to decades (Atkinson & Shiffrin, 1968, 1971). Information can pass from the sensory register to short-term memory and in either direction between short-term and long-term memory, as illustrated in Figure 8.3.

This model, which is known informally as the "three-box model," has dominated research on memory since the late 1960s. The problem is that the human brain does not operate like your average computer. Most computers process instructions and data sequentially, one item after another, and so the three-box model has emphasized sequential operations. In contrast, the brain performs many operations simultaneously, in parallel. It recognizes patterns all at once rather than as a sequence of information bits, and it perceives new information, produces speech, and searches memory all at the same time. It can do these things because millions of neurons are active at once, and each neuron communicates with thousands of others, which in turn communicate with millions more.

Because of these differences between human beings and machines, some cognitive scientists prefer a **parallel distributed processing (PDP)** or *connectionist* model. Instead of representing information as flowing from one system to another, a PDP model represents the contents of memory as connections among a huge number of interacting processing units, distributed in a vast network and all operating in parallel, just like the neurons of the brain (McClelland, 1994; Rumelhart, McClelland, & the PDP Research Group, 1986). As information enters the system, the ability of these units to excite or inhibit each other is constantly adjusted to reflect new knowledge.

In this chapter, we emphasize the three-box model, but keep in mind that the computer metaphor that inspired it could one day be as outdated as the metaphor of memory as a camera.

Get Involved!   Recognizing Rudolph's Friends

If you took the recall test in the Get Involved exercise on the previous page, now try a recognition test. From the following list, see whether you can identify the correct names of Rudolph the Red-Nosed Reindeer's eight reindeer friends. The answers are at the end of this chapter, but no fair peeking!

Blitzen	Dander	Dancer	Masher
Cupid	Dasher	Prancer	Comet
Kumquat	Donner	Flasher	Pixie
Bouncer	Blintzes	Trixie	Vixen

Which was easier, recall or recognition? Can you speculate on the reason?

✔●—[Study and **Review** on **mypsychlab.com**

Quick Quiz

How well have you encoded and stored what you just learned?

1. Alberta solved a crossword puzzle a few days ago. She no longer recalls the words in the puzzle, but while playing a game of Scrabble, she unconsciously tends to form words that were in the puzzle, showing that she has _____ memories of some of the words.

2. The three basic memory processes are _____, storage, and _____.

3. Do the preceding two questions ask for recall, recognition, or relearning? (And what about *this* question?)

4. One objection to traditional information-processing theories of memory is that, unlike most computers, the brain performs many independent operations _____.

Answers:

1. implicit 2. encoding, retrieval 3. The first two questions both measure recall; the third question measures recognition. 4. simultaneously, or in parallel

 ## YOU are about to learn...

- how the three "boxes" in the three-box model of memory operate.

- why short-term memory is like a leaky bucket.

- why a word can feel like it's "on the tip of your tongue" and what errors you are likely to make when you finally recall it.

- the difference between "knowing how" and "knowing that."

The Three-Box Model of Memory

The information model of three separate memory systems—sensory, short-term, and long-term—remains a leading approach because it offers a convenient way to organize the major findings on memory, does a good job of accounting for these findings, and is consistent with the biological facts about memory. Let us now peer into each of the "boxes."

The Sensory Register: Fleeting Impressions

In the three-box model, all incoming sensory information must make a brief stop in the **sensory register**, the entryway of memory. The sensory register includes a number of separate memory subsystems, as many as there are senses. Visual images remain in a visual subsystem for a maximum of a half second. Auditory images remain in an auditory subsystem for a slightly longer time, by most estimates up to two seconds or so.

The sensory register acts as a holding bin, retaining information in a highly accurate form until we can select items for attention from the stream of stimuli bombarding our senses. It gives us a brief time to decide whether information is extraneous or important; not everything detected by our senses warrants our attention. And the identification of a stimulus on the basis of information already contained in long-term memory occurs during the transfer of information from the sensory register to short-term memory.

Information that does not quickly go on to short-term memory vanishes forever, like a message written in disappearing ink. That is why people who see an array of twelve letters for just a fraction of a second can only report four or five of them; by the time they answer, their sensory memories are already fading (Sperling, 1960). The fleeting nature of incoming sensations is actually beneficial; it prevents multiple sensory images—"double exposures"—that might interfere with the accurate perception and encoding of information.

Short-Term Memory: Memory's Scratch Pad

Like the sensory register, **short-term memory (STM)** retains information only temporarily—for up to about 30 seconds by many estimates, although some researchers think that the maximum interval may extend to a few minutes for some tasks. In short-term memory, the material is no longer an exact sensory image but is an encoding of one, such as a word or a phrase. This material either transfers into long-term memory or decays and is lost forever.

sensory register A memory system that momentarily preserves extremely accurate images of sensory information.

short-term memory (STM) In the three-box model of memory, a limited-capacity memory system involved in the retention of information for brief periods; it is also used to hold information retrieved from long-term memory for temporary use.

In a dark room or closet, swing a flashlight rapidly in a circle. You will see an unbroken circle of light instead of a series of separate points. The reason: The successive images remain briefly in the sensory register.

Individuals with brain injury, such as H. M., demonstrate the importance of transferring new information from short-term memory into long-term memory. H. M. was able to store information on a short-term basis; he could hold a conversation and his behavior appeared normal when you first met him. Yet, for the most part, he could not retain explicit information about new facts and events for longer than a few minutes. His terrible memory deficits involved a problem in transferring explicit memories from short-term storage into long-term storage. With a great deal of repetition and drill, patients like H. M. can learn some new visual information, retain it in long-term memory, and recall it normally (McKee & Squire, 1992). But usually information does not get into long-term memory in the first place.

The Leaky Bucket People such as H. M. fall at the extreme end on a continuum of forgetfulness, but even those of us with normal memories know from personal experience how frustratingly brief short-term retention can be. We look up a telephone number, are distracted for a moment, and find that the number has vanished from our minds. We meet someone at a meeting and two minutes later find ourselves groping unsuccessfully for the person's name. Is it any wonder that short-term memory has been called a "leaky bucket"?

According to most memory models, if the bucket did not leak it would quickly overflow, because at any given moment, short-term memory can hold only so many items. Years ago, George Miller (1956) estimated its capacity to be "the magical number 7 plus or minus 2." Five-digit zip codes and 7-digit telephone numbers fall conveniently in this range; 16-digit credit card numbers do not. Some researchers have questioned whether Miller's magical number is so magical after all; estimates of STM's capacity have ranged from 2 items to 20, with one

estimate putting the "magical number" at 4 (Cowan, 2010; Cowan et al., 2008). Everyone agrees, however, that the number of items that short-term memory can handle at any one time is small.

If this is so, then how do we remember the beginning of a spoken sentence until the speaker reaches the end? After all, most sentences are longer than just a few words. According to most information-processing models of memory, we overcome this problem by grouping small bits of information into larger units, or **chunks**. The real capacity of STM, it turns out, is not a few bits of information but a few chunks (Cowan & Chen, 2009). A chunk may be a word, a phrase, a sentence, or even a visual image, and it depends on previous experience. For most Americans, the acronym *FBI* is one chunk, not three, and the date *1492* is one chunk, not four. In contrast, the number *9214* is four chunks and *IBF* is three, unless your address is

If you do not play chess, you probably will not be able to recall the positions of these chess pieces after looking away from the board for a while. But experienced chess players can remember the position of every piece after glancing only briefly at the board. They are able to "chunk" the pieces into a few standard configurations instead of trying to memorize where each piece is located.

chunk A meaningful unit of information; it may be composed of smaller units.

9214 or your initials are IBF. To take a visual example: If you are unfamiliar with football and look at a field full of players, you probably won't be able to remember their positions when you look away. But if you are a fan of the game, you may see a single chunk of information—say, a wishbone formation— and be able to retain it. ⊙➤ **Simulate**

But even chunking cannot keep short-term memory from eventually filling up. Information that is needed for longer periods must therefore be transferred to long-term memory. Items that are particularly meaningful or that have an emotional impact may transfer quickly. Items that require more processing will be displaced with new information, and will thus be lost, unless we do something to keep it in STM for a while, as we will discuss shortly.

Working Memory In the original three-box model, short-term memory functioned basically as a buffer for holding and rehearsing information until it could be transferred to long-term memory. Since then, many psychologists have concluded that a more complex model is needed, one in which STM also functions more actively as a **working memory** that is intimately involved in thought and intelligence (Baddeley, 1992, 2007; Engle, 2002). In this view, besides retaining new information for brief periods while we are learning it, working memory holds and operates on information that has been retrieved from long-term memory for temporary use, including verbal and visual information. It provides the mental equivalent of a scratch pad while we solve particular problems and carry out particular tasks. And it includes active "executive" processes that control the manipulation of information and interpret it appropriately depending on the task at hand. When you do an arithmetic problem, your working memory contains the numbers and the instructions for doing the necessary operations, and it also carries out those operations and retains the intermediate results from each step.

To accomplish a complex cognitive task, working memory also draws on processes that control attention and enable us to avoid distraction so that information will remain accessible and easily retrieved (Unsworth & Engle, 2007). People who do well on tests of working memory tend to do well in reading comprehension, following directions, taking notes, playing bridge, learning new words, and many other real-life tasks. When they are engrossed in challenging activities that require their concentration and effort, they stay on task longer, and their minds are less likely to wander (Kane et al., 2007).

Long-Term Memory: Final Destination

The third box in the three-box model of memory is **long-term memory (LTM)**. The capacity of long-term memory seems to have no practical limits. The vast amount of information stored there enables us to learn, get around in the environment, and build a sense of identity and a personal history.

Organization in Long-Term Memory Because long-term memory contains so much information, it must be organized in some way, so that we can find the particular items we are looking for. One way to organize words is by the *semantic categories* to which they belong. *Chair*, for example, belongs to the category *furniture*. In a study done many years ago, people had to memorize 60 words that came from four semantic categories: animals, vegetables, names, and professions. The words were presented in random order, but when people were allowed to recall the items in any order they wished, they tended to recall them in clusters corresponding to the four categories (Bousfield, 1953). This finding has been replicated many times.

Evidence on the storage of information by semantic category also comes from cases of people with brain damage. In one such case, a patient called M. D. appeared to have made a complete recovery after suffering several strokes, with one odd exception: He had trouble remembering the names of fruits and vegetables. M. D. could easily name a picture of an abacus or a sphinx, but he drew a blank when he saw a picture of an orange or a carrot. He could sort pictures of animals, vehicles, and other objects into their appropriate categories, but he did poorly with pictures of fruits and vegetables. On the other hand, when M. D. was *given* the names of fruits and vegetables, he immediately pointed to the corresponding pictures (Hart, Berndt, & Caramazza, 1985). Apparently, M. D. still had information about fruits and vegetables, but his brain lesion prevented him from using their names to get to the information when he needed it, unless someone else provided the names. This evidence suggests that information in memory about a particular concept (such as *orange*) is linked in some way to information about the concept's semantic category (such as *fruit*).

Indeed, many models of long-term memory represent its contents as a vast network of interrelated concepts and propositions (Anderson, 1990; Collins & Loftus, 1975). In these models, a small part of a conceptual network for *animals* might look something like the one in Figure 8.4 on the next page. The way people use these networks, however,

⊙➤ **Simulate Digit Span** on **mypsychlab.com**

working memory In many models of memory, a cognitively complex form of short-term memory that involves the active mental processes that control retrieval of information from long-term memory and interpret that information appropriately for a given task.

long-term memory (LTM) In the three-box model of memory, the memory system involved in the long-term storage of information.

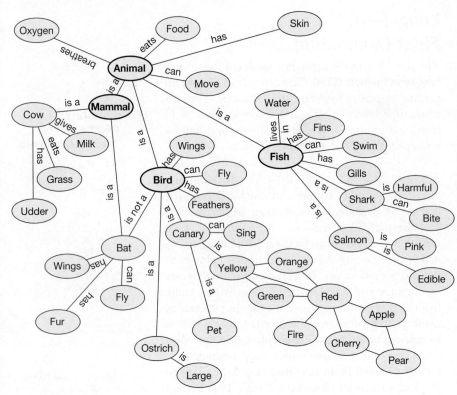

FIGURE 8.4
Part of a Conceptual Grid in Long-Term Memory
Many models of memory represent the contents of long-term semantic memory as an immense network or grid of concepts and the relationships among them. This illustration shows part of a hypothetical grid for *animals.*

procedural memories
Memories for the performance of actions or skills ("knowing how").

declarative memories
Memories of facts, rules, concepts, and events ("knowing that"); they include semantic and episodic memories.

semantic memories
Memories of general knowledge, including facts, rules, concepts, and propositions.

depends on experience and education. In rural Liberia, the more schooling children have, the more likely they are to use semantic categories in recalling lists of objects (Cole & Scribner, 1974). This makes sense, because in school, children must memorize a lot of information in a short time, and semantic grouping can help. Unschooled children, having less need to memorize lists, do not cluster items and do not remember them as well. But this does not mean that unschooled children have poor memories. When the task is one that is meaningful to them, such as recalling objects that were in a story or a village scene, they remember extremely well (Mistry & Rogoff, 1994).

We organize information in long-term memory not only by semantic groupings but also in terms of the way words sound or look. Have you ever tried to recall some word that was on the "tip of your tongue"? Nearly everyone experiences such *tip-of-the-tongue (TOT) states,* especially when trying to recall the names of acquaintances or famous people, the names of objects and places, or the titles of movies or books (Burke et al., 1991). TOT states are even reported by users of sign language, who call them tip-of-the-finger states (Thompson, Emmorey, & Gollan, 2005). When a word is on the tip of the tongue, people tend to come up with words that are similar in meaning to the right one—or similar in the starting letter, the prefix or suffix, or number of syllables—before they finally recall it (R. Brown & McNeill, 1966). For the

name *Kevin* they might say, "Wait . . . it starts with a K and has two syllables . . . Kenny? Kerran? . . ."

Information in long-term memory may also be organized by its familiarity, relevance, or association with other information. The method used in any given instance probably depends on the nature of the memory; you would no doubt store information about the major cities of Europe differently from information about your first romantic kiss. To understand the organization of long-term memory, then, we must know what kinds of information can be stored there.

The Contents of Long-Term Memory Most theories of memory distinguish skills or habits ("knowing how") from abstract or representational knowledge ("knowing that"). **Procedural memories** are memories of knowing how to do something—comb your hair, use a pencil, solve a jigsaw puzzle, knit a sweater, or swim. Many researchers consider procedural memories to be implicit, because once skills and habits are learned well, they do not require much conscious processing. **Declarative memories** involve knowing that something is true, as in knowing that Ottawa is the capital of Canada; they are usually assumed to be explicit.

Declarative memories come in two varieties: semantic memories and episodic memories (Tulving, 1985). **Semantic memories** are internal representations of the world, independent of any

Culture affects the encoding, storage, and retrieval of information in long-term memory. Navajo healers, who use stylized, symbolic sand paintings in their rituals, must commit to memory dozens of intricate visual designs because no exact copies are made and the painting is destroyed after each ceremony.

particular context. They include facts, rules, concepts, and other items of general knowledge. On the basis of your semantic memory of the concept *cat*, you can describe a cat as a small, furry mammal that typically spends its time eating, sleeping, prowling, and staring into space, even though a cat may not be present when you give this description, and you probably won't know how or when you first learned it. **Episodic memories** are internal representations of personally experienced events. When you remember how your cat once surprised you in the middle of the night by pouncing on you as you slept, you are retrieving an episodic memory. Figure 8.5 summarizes these kinds of memories.

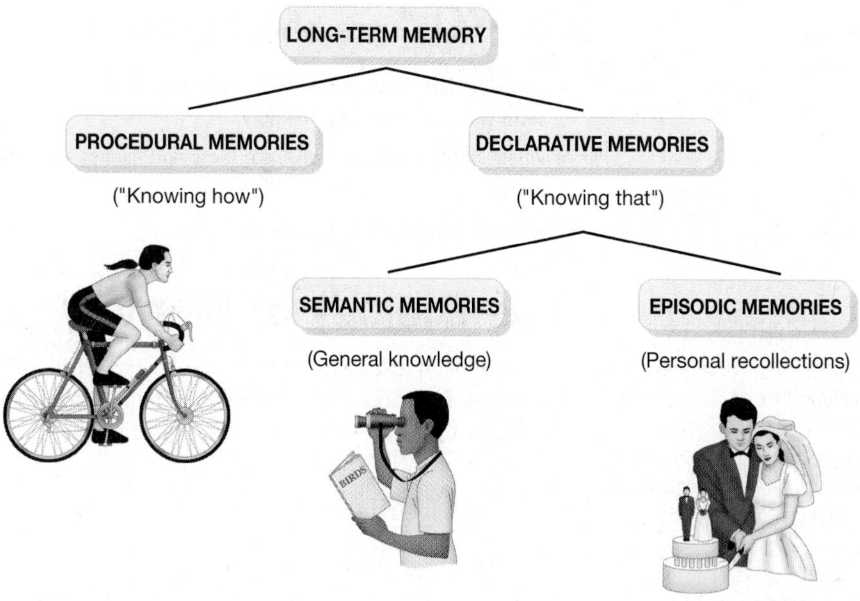

From Short-Term to Long-Term Memory: A Puzzle The three-box model of memory is often invoked to explain an interesting phenomenon called the **serial-position effect**. If you are shown a list of items and are then asked immediately to recall them, your retention of any particular item will depend on its position in the list (Bhatarah, Ward, & Tan, 2008; Johnson & Miles, 2009). Recall will be best for items at the beginning of the list (the *primacy effect*) and at the end of the list (the *recency effect*). A serial-position effect occurs when you are introduced to a lot of people at a party and find you can recall the names of the first few people you met and the last few, but almost no one in between.

According to the three-box model, the first few items on a list are remembered well because short-term memory is relatively empty when they enter, so these items do not have to compete with others to make it into long-term memory. They get thoroughly processed, so they remain memorable. The last few items are remembered for a different reason: At the time of recall, they are still sitting in short-term memory. The items in the middle of a list are not so well retained because by the time they get into short-term memory, it is already crowded. As a result, many of these items drop out of short-term memory before they can be stored in long-term memory. The problem with this explanation is that the recency effect sometimes occurs even after a considerable delay, when the items at the end of a list can no longer be in short-term memory (Davelaar et al., 2004). The serial-position curve, therefore, remains something of a puzzle.

FIGURE 8.5
Types of Long-Term Memories
This diagram summarizes the distinctions among long-term memories. Can you come up with other examples of each memory type?

LONG-TERM MEMORY

PROCEDURAL MEMORIES ("Knowing how")

DECLARATIVE MEMORIES ("Knowing that")

SEMANTIC MEMORIES (General knowledge)

EPISODIC MEMORIES (Personal recollections)

episodic memories
Memories of personally experienced events and the contexts in which they occurred.

serial-position effect
The tendency for recall of the first and last items on a list to surpass recall of items in the middle of the list.

Quick Quiz

Find out whether the findings just discussed have transferred from your short-term memory to your long-term memory.

1. The _____ holds images for a fraction of a second.
2. For most people, the abbreviation *USA* consists of _____ informational chunk(s).
3. Suppose you must memorize a long list of words that includes *desk, pig, gold, dog, chair, silver, table, rooster, bed, copper,* and *horse.* If you can recall the words in any order you wish, how are you likely to group these items in recall? Why?
4. When you go ice skating (assuming you know how), are you relying on procedural, semantic, or episodic memory? How about when you recall the months of the year? Or when you remember falling while learning to ice skate on an icy January day?
5. If a child is trying to memorize the alphabet, which sequence should present the greatest difficulty: *abcdefg, klmnopq,* or *tuvwxyz*? Why?

Answers:

1. sensory register 2. one 3. *Desk, chair, table,* and *bed* will probably form one cluster; *pig, dog, rooster,* and *horse* a second; and *gold, silver,* and *copper* a third. Concepts tend to be organized in long-term memory in terms of semantic categories, such as *furniture, animals,* and *metals.* 4. procedural; semantic; episodic 5. *klmnopq,* because of the serial-position effect.

YOU are about to learn...

- changes that occur in the brain when you store a short-term versus a long-term memory.

- where in the brain memories for facts and events are stored.

- which hormones can improve memory.

The Biology of Memory

long-term potentiation A long-lasting increase in the strength of synaptic responsiveness, thought to be a biological mechanism of long-term memory.

consolidation The process by which a long-term memory becomes durable and stable.

We have been discussing memory solely in terms of information processing, but what is happening in the brain while all of that processing is going on?

Changes in Neurons and Synapses

Forming a memory involves chemical and structural changes at the level of synapses, and these changes differ for short-term memory and long-term memory.

In short-term memory, changes within neurons *temporarily* alter their ability to release neurotransmitters, the chemicals that carry messages from one cell to another (Kandel, 2001). In contrast, long-term memory involves *lasting* structural changes in the brain. To mimic what they think may happen during the formation of a long-term memory, researchers apply brief, high-frequency electrical stimulation to groups of neurons in the brains of animals or to brain cells in a laboratory culture. In various areas, especially the hippocampus, this stimulation causes neurons at some synapses to become more responsive to transmitting neurons, making certain synaptic pathways more excitable (Bliss & Collingridge, 1993; Whitlock et al., 2006). The result of these changes, known as **long-term potentiation**, is like increasing the diameter of a funnel's neck to permit more flow through the funnel. During long-term potentiation, dendrites also grow and branch out, and some types of synapses increase in number (Greenough, 1984). At the same time, some neurons become less responsive than they were previously (Bolshakov & Siegelbaum, 1994).

Most of these changes take time, which probably explains why long-term memories remain vulnerable to disruption for a while after they are stored, and why a blow to the head may disrupt new memories even though old ones are unaffected. Just as concrete takes time to set, the neural and synaptic changes in the brain that underlie long-term memory take a while to develop fully. Memories therefore undergo a period of **consolidation**, or stabilization, before they solidify. Consolidation can continue for weeks in animals and for several years in human beings. The process is usually gradual, because rapid changes would constantly disrupt the brain's existing schemas, which have been built up on the basis of past knowledge and experience (Squire, 2007).

Locating Memories

Scientists have used microelectrodes, brain-scan technology, and other techniques to identify the brain structures responsible for the formation and storage of specific types of memories. The amygdala is involved in the formation, consolidation, and retrieval of memories of fearful and other emotional events (Buchanan, 2007; see Chapter 13). Areas in the frontal lobes of the brain are especially active during short-term and working memory tasks (Goldman-Rakic, 1996; Mitchell & Johnson, 2009). The prefrontal cortex and areas adjacent to the hippocampus in the temporal lobe are also important for the efficient encoding of pictures and words.

But it is the hippocampus that has the starring role in many aspects of memory. It is critical to the formation of long-term declarative memories ("knowing that"); as we have seen in the case of H. M., damage to this structure can cause amnesia for new facts and events. And studies of rats and human beings suggest that the hippocampus is also critical in recalling past experiences (Pastalkova et al., 2008).

NICE TRY, BUT "MID-TERM MEMORY LOSS" ISN'T RECOGNIZED BY THE MEDICAL COMMUNITY!

Unfortunately, the most likely reason for midterm memory loss is not studying enough—or in the right way.

A team of researchers has identified how neurons in the hippocampus may become involved in specific memories. They implanted electrodes into the brains of 13 people about to undergo surgery for severe epilepsy. (This is standard procedure because it enables doctors to pinpoint the location of the brain activity causing the seizures.) As the patients were being prepped, they watched a series of 5- to 10-second film clips of popular shows such as *Seinfeld* or *The Simpsons*, or of animals and landmarks. The researchers recorded which neurons in the hippocampus were firing as the patients watched; for each patient, particular neurons might become highly active during particular videos and respond only weakly to others. After a few minutes, the patients were asked to recall what they had seen. They remembered almost all of the clips, and as they recalled each one, the very neurons that had been active when they first saw it were reignited (Gelbard-Sagiv et al., 2008). Other evidence also supports the idea that the brain regions involved in *encoding* an episode are partially reactivated when the person later *remembers* it (Danker & Anderson, 2010).

The formation and retention of procedural memories (memory for skills and habits) seem to involve other brain structures and pathways. In work with rabbits, Richard Thompson (1983, 1986) showed that one kind of procedural memory—a simple, classically conditioned response to a stimulus, such as an eye blink in response to a tone—depends on activity in the cerebellum. Human patients with damage in the cerebellum are incapable of this type of conditioning (Daum & Schugens, 1996).

The formation of declarative and procedural memories in different brain areas could explain a curious finding about patients like H. M. Despite their inability to form new declarative memories, with sufficient practice such patients can acquire new procedural memories that enable them to solve a puzzle, read mirror-reversed words, or play tennis—even though they do not recall the training sessions in which they learned these skills. Apparently, the parts of the brain involved in acquiring new procedural memories have remained intact. Patients such as H. M. also retain some implicit memory for verbal material, as measured by priming tasks. Some psychologists conclude that there must therefore be separate systems in the brain for implicit and explicit tasks. As Figure 8.6 shows, this view has been bolstered by brain scans, which reveal differences in the location of brain activity when ordinary people perform explicit versus implicit memory tasks (Reber, Stark, & Squire, 1998; Squire et al., 1992).

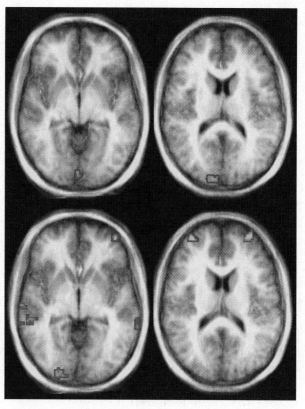

FIGURE 8.6
Brain Activity in Explicit and Implicit Memory
As these composite functional MRI scans show, patterns of brain activity differ depending on the type of memory task involved. When people had an explicit memory for dot patterns they had seen earlier, areas in the visual cortex, temporal lobes, and frontal lobes (indicated by orange in the lower photos) were more active. When people's implicit memories were activated, areas in the visual cortex (blue in the upper photos) were relatively inactive (Reber, Stark, & Squire, 1998).

The brain circuits that take part in the *formation* and *retrieval* of long-term memories, however, are not the same as those involved in long-term *storage* of those memories. Although the hippocampus is vital for formation and retrieval, the ultimate destinations of declarative memories seem to lie in parts of the cerebral cortex (Maviel et al., 2004). In fact, memories may be stored in the same cortical areas that were involved in the original perception of the information: When people remember pictures, visual parts of the brain become active. And when people remember sounds, auditory areas become active, just as they did when the information was first perceived (Nyberg et al., 2000; Thompson & Kosslyn, 2000).

The typical "memory" is a complex cluster of information. When you recall meeting a man yesterday, you remember his greeting, his tone of voice, how he looked, and where he was. These different pieces of information are probably processed separately and stored at different locations that are distributed across wide areas of the brain, with all the sites participating in the representation of the event or concept as a whole. The hippocampus may somehow bind together the diverse aspects of a memory at the time it is formed, so that even though these aspects are stored in different cortical sites, the memory can later be retrieved as one coherent entity (Squire & Zola-Morgan, 1991).

Hormones, Emotion, and Memory

Have you ever smelled fresh cookies and recalled a tender scene from your childhood? Do you have a vivid memory of seeing a particularly horrifying horror movie? Emotional memories such as these are often especially intense, and the explanation resides partly in our hormones.

Hormones released by the adrenal glands during stress and emotional arousal, including epinephrine (adrenaline) and norepinephrine, can enhance memory, probably by influencing the effects of neurotransmitters in the brain. If you give people a drug that prevents their adrenal glands from producing these hormones, they will remember less about emotional stories they heard than a control group will (Cahill et al., 1994). Conversely, if you give animals norepinephrine right after learning, their memories will improve. The link between emotional arousal and memory makes evolutionary sense: Arousal tells the brain that an event or piece of information is important enough to encode and store for future use.

However, extreme arousal is not necessarily a good thing. When animals or people are given very high doses of stress hormones, their memories for learned tasks sometimes suffer instead of improving; a moderate dose may be optimal (Andreano & Cahill, 2006). Two psychologists demonstrated the perils of high stress and anxiety in a real-life setting: the Horror Labyrinth of the London Dungeon (Valentine & Mesout, 2009). The labyrinth is a maze of disorienting mirrored walls set in Gothic vaults. As visitors walk through it, they hear strange noises and screams, and alarming things suddenly appear, including a "scary person"—an actor dressed in a dark robe, wearing makeup to appear scarred and bleeding. Volunteers wore a wireless heart-rate monitor as they walked through the labyrinth so that their stress and anxiety levels could be recorded. The higher their stress and anxiety, the less able they were to accurately describe the "scary person" later, and the fewer correct identifications they made of him in a lineup. Such effects on memory do not matter much at an amusement attraction. But they can have serious consequences when crime victims, police officers, and soldiers must recall details of a highly stressful experience, such as a shoot-out or the identity of an enemy interrogator (Morgan et al., 2007).

We have given you just a few small nibbles from the smorgasbord of findings now available about the biology of memory. Neuroscientists hope that someday they will be able to describe the entire stream of events in the brain that occur from the moment you say to yourself "I must remember this" to the moment you actually do remember . . . or find that you can't.

Study and **Review** on **mypsychlab.com**

Quick Quiz

We hope your memory circuits will link up to help you answer this quiz.

1. Is long-term potentiation associated with (a) increased responsiveness of certain receiving neurons to transmitting neurons, (b) a decrease in receptors on certain receiving neurons, or (c) reaching your true potential?

2. The cerebellum has been associated with _____ memories; the hippocampus has been associated with _____ memories.

3. *True or false:* Hormone research suggests that if you want to remember well, you should be as relaxed as possible while learning.

Answers:

1. a   2. procedural, declarative   3. false

YOU are about to learn...

- how memory can be improved, and why rote methods are not the best strategy.

- why memory tricks, although fun, are not always useful.

How We Remember

Once we understand the basics of how memory works, we can use that knowledge to encode and store information so that it sticks in our minds and will be there when we need it. What are the best strategies to use?

Effective Encoding

Our memories, as we have seen, are not exact replicas of experience. When you hear a lecture you may hang on every word (we hope you do), but you do not memorize those words verbatim. You extract the main points and encode them.

To remember information well, you have to encode it accurately in the first place. With some kinds of information, accurate encoding takes place automatically, without effort. Think about where you usually sit in your psychology class. When were you last there? You can probably provide this information easily, even though you never made a deliberate effort to encode it. But many kinds of information require *effortful encoding:* the plot of a novel, the procedures for assembling a cabinet, the arguments for and against a proposed law. To retain such information, you might have to select the main points, label concepts, or associate the information with personal experiences or with material you already know. Experienced students know that most of the information in a college course requires effortful encoding, otherwise known as studying. The mind does not gobble up information automatically; you must make the material digestible.

Rehearsal

An important technique for keeping information in short-term memory and increasing the chances of long-term retention is *rehearsal*, the review or practice of material while you are learning it. When people are prevented from rehearsing, the contents of their short-term memories quickly fade (Peterson & Peterson, 1959). You are taking advantage of rehearsal when you look up a phone number and then repeat it over and over to keep it in short-term memory until you no longer need it. And when you can't remember a phone number because you have always used speed dial to call it, you are learning what happens when you *don't* rehearse!

Short-term memory holds many kinds of information, including visual information and abstract meanings. But most people, or at least most hearing people, seem to favor speech for encoding and rehearsing the contents of short-term memory. The speech may be spoken aloud or to oneself. When people make errors on short-term memory tests that use letters or words, they often confuse items that sound the same or similar, such as *d* and *t*, or *bear* and *bare*. These errors suggest that they have been rehearsing verbally.

Encoding classroom material for later recall usually requires deliberate effort. Which of these students do you think will remember best?

Some strategies for rehearsing are more effective than others. **Maintenance rehearsal** involves merely the rote repetition of the material. This kind of rehearsal is fine for keeping information in STM, but it will not always lead to long-term retention. A better strategy if you want to remember for the long haul is **elaborative rehearsal**, also called *elaboration of encoding* (Cermak & Craik, 1979; Craik & Tulving, 1975). Elaboration involves associating new items of information with material that has already been stored or with other new facts. It can also involve analyzing the physical, sensory, or semantic features of an item.

maintenance rehearsal
Rote repetition of material in order to maintain its availability in memory.

elaborative rehearsal
Association of new information with already stored knowledge and analysis of the new information to make it memorable.

When actors learn a script, they do not rely on maintenance rehearsal alone. They also use elaborative rehearsal and deep processing, analyzing the meaning of their lines and associating their lines with imagined information about the character they are playing.

deep processing In the encoding of information, the processing of meaning rather than simply the physical or sensory features of a stimulus.

Suppose that you are studying the hypothalamus, first discussed in Chapter 4. Simply memorizing the definition of the hypothalamus is unlikely to help much. But if you can elaborate the concept of the hypothalamus, you are more likely to remember it. Knowing that *hypo* means "under" tells you its location, under the thalamus. Knowing that it is part of the limbic system should clue you that it is involved in survival drives and emotion. Many students try to pare down what they are learning to the bare essentials, but in fact, knowing more details about something makes it more memorable; that is what elaboration means.

A related strategy for prolonging retention is **deep processing**, or the processing of meaning (Craik & Lockhart, 1972). If you process only the physical or sensory features of a stimulus, such as how the word *hypothalamus* is spelled and how it sounds, your processing will be shallow even if it is elaborated. If you recognize patterns and assign labels to objects or events ("The *hypo*thalamus is *below* the thalamus"), your processing will be somewhat deeper. If you fully analyze the meaning of what you are trying to remember (perhaps by encoding the functions and importance of the hypothalamus), your processing will be deeper yet. *Shallow processing* is sometimes useful; when you memorize a poem, you will want to pay attention to (and elaborately encode) the sounds of the words and the patterns of rhythm in the poem and not just the poem's meaning. Usually, though, deep processing is more effective. That is why, if you try to memorize information that has little or no meaning for you, the information may not stick. ✳Explore

✳ Explore **Maintaining Long-Term Memory** on mypsychlab.com

Read, Recite, Review

One of the reasons elaborate encoding and deep processing are so useful is that they force you to be an active rather than a passive learner. Many students believe that the best way to study for an exam is to read and reread a textbook passage until they think that they've "got it." This passive strategy feels intuitively right, but it is actually much less effective than actively rehearsing and recalling the material. In the *read-recite-review* strategy, you read the passage, close the book, hide your notes, write down (or say out loud) everything you can recall, and then review what you've read to see if you understood and remember the information. In a series of experiments, researchers compared this strategy with simply rereading and taking notes. Participants took free recall tests on the material, answered multiple-choice questions, and took short-answer tests right after studying and again a

week later. The active read-recite-review strategy was the hands-down winner (McDaniel, Howard, & Einstein, 2009).

Retrieval Practice

Most students define "learning" as the ability to retrieve the correct answer to a question from memory. But then what? Once retrieved, say for an exam, does it stay put or vanish quickly like steam on a bathroom mirror? Cognitive psychologists have found that *retrieval practice* is necessary if a memory is going to undergo consolidation and therefore remain available for a long time—even after your course is over. In a series of experiments in which students learned words in foreign languages, once a student had learned the word, it was (a) repeatedly studied but dropped from further testing, (b) repeatedly tested but dropped from further studying, or (c) dropped from studying and testing. To the surprise of the students themselves, who were completely unable to predict how they would do on the tests, studying after learning had no effect on their subsequent ability to recall the foreign words. But repeated testing (that is, practice in repeatedly retrieving the words from memory) had a large, significant benefit (Karpicke & Roediger, 2008). So when your professors and your textbook authors want to keep quizzing you, why, it's only for your own good . . .

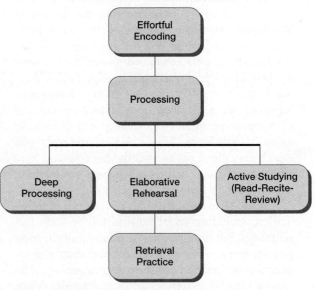

HOW TO REMEMBER BETTER

Effortful Encoding

Processing

Deep Processing | Elaborative Rehearsal | Active Studying (Read-Recite-Review)

Retrieval Practice

Mnemonics

In addition to using elaborative rehearsal, deep processing, strategies such as read-recite-review, and retrieval practice, people who want to give their powers

"YOU SIMPLY ASSOCIATE EACH NUMBER WITH A WORD, SUCH AS 'TABLE' AND 3,476,029."

of memory a boost sometimes use **mnemonics** [neh-MON-iks], formal strategies and tricks for encoding, storing, and retaining information. (Mnemosyne,

pronounced neh-MOZ-eh-nee, was the ancient Greek goddess of memory. Can you remember her?) Some mnemonics take the form of easily memorized rhymes (e.g., "Thirty days hath September/April, June, and November . . ."). Others use formulas (e.g., "**E**very **g**ood **b**oy **d**oes **f**ine" for remembering which notes are on the lines of the treble clef in musical notation). Still others use visual images or word associations. The best mnemonics force you to encode material actively and thoroughly. They may also reduce the amount of information by chunking it, which is why many companies use words for their phone numbers instead of unmemorable numbers.

Some stage performers with amazing recall rely on far more complicated mnemonics. But for ordinary memory tasks, such as remembering a grocery list, why use a fancy mnemonic when you can write down what you need to buy? The fastest route to a good memory is to follow the principles suggested by the findings in this section and in "Taking Psychology with You."

mnemonics Strategies and tricks for improving memory, such as the use of a verse or a formula.

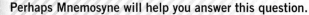

Quick Quiz

Perhaps Mnemosyne will help you answer this question.

Camille is furious with her history professor. "I read the chapter three times, but I still failed the exam," she fumes. "The test must have been unfair." What's wrong with Camille's reasoning, and what are some other possible explanations for her poor performance, based on principles of critical thinking and what you have learned so far about memory?

Answer:

Camille is reasoning emotionally and is not examining the assumptions underlying her explanation. Perhaps she relied on automatic rather than effortful encoding, used maintenance instead of elaborative rehearsal, and used shallow instead of deep processing when she studied. Perhaps she didn't try to actively retrieve and recall the material while studying. She may also have tried to encode everything instead of being selective.

✓—**Study** and **Review** on mypsychlab.com

YOU are about to learn...

- the problem with remembering everything.
- the major reasons we forget even when we'd rather not.
- why most researchers are skeptical about claims of repressed and recovered memories.

Why We Forget

Have you ever, in the heat of some deliriously happy moment, said to yourself, "I'll never forget this, never, *never*, NEVER"? Do you find that you can more clearly remember saying those words than the deliriously happy moment itself? Sometimes you

encode an event, you rehearse it, you analyze its meaning, you tuck it away in long-term storage, and still you forget it. Is it any wonder that most of us have wished, at one time or another, for a "photographic memory"?

Actually, having a perfect memory is not the blessing that you might suppose. The Russian psychologist Alexander Luria (1968) once told of a journalist, S., who could reproduce giant grids of numbers both forward and backward, even after the passage of 15 years. But you should not envy him, for he had a serious problem: He could not forget even when he wanted to. Along with the diamonds of experience, he kept dredging up the pebbles. Images he had formed to aid his memory kept creeping into consciousness, distracting him and interfering with his ability to concentrate. At times he even had trouble holding a conversation because the other person's words would set off a jumble of associations. Eventually, S. took to supporting himself by traveling from place to place, demonstrating his abilities for audiences.

Two modern people with extraordinary memories, Brad Williams and Jill Price, have offered to have their abilities studied by scientists. When given any date going back for decades, they are able

to say instantly what they were doing, what day of the week it was, and whether anything of great importance happened on that date. Mention November 7, 1991, to Williams, and he says (correctly), "Let's see; that would be around when Magic Johnson announced he had HIV. Yes, a Thursday. There was a big snowstorm here the week before." Neither Williams nor Price uses mnemonics or can say where their accurate memories come from. Although Williams and his family regard his abilities as a source of amusement, Price describes her nonstop recollections as a mixed blessing (Parker, Cahill, & McGaugh, 2006). The phenomenon of constant, uncontrollable recall, she has written, is "totally exhausting. Some have called it a gift, but I call it a burden. I run my entire life through my head every day and it drives me crazy!!!"

Paradoxically, then, forgetting is adaptive: We need to forget some things if we wish to remember efficiently. Piling up facts without distinguishing the important from the trivial is just confusing. Nonetheless, most of us forget more than we want to and would like to know why.

In the early days of psychology, in an effort to measure pure memory loss independent of personal experience, Hermann Ebbinghaus (1885/1913) memorized long lists of nonsense syllables, such as *bok*, *waf*, or *ged*, and then tested his retention over a period of several weeks. Most of his forgetting occurred soon after the initial learning and then leveled off (see Figure 8.7a). Ebbinghaus's method of studying memory was adopted by

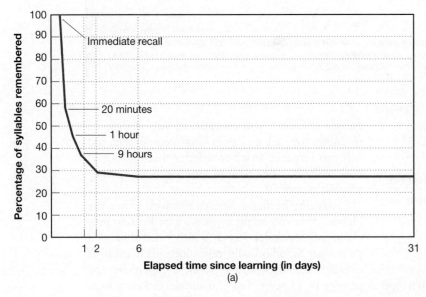

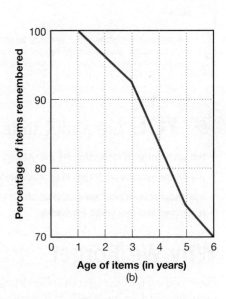

FIGURE 8.7 **Two Kinds of Forgetting Curves**
Hermann Ebbinghaus, who tested his own memory for nonsense syllables, found that his forgetting was rapid at first and then tapered off (a). In contrast, when Marigold Linton tested her own memory for personal events over a period of several years, her retention was excellent at first, but then it fell off at a gradual but steady rate (b).

generations of psychologists, but it did not tell them much about the kinds of memories that people care about most.

A century later, Marigold Linton decided to find out how people forget real events rather than nonsense syllables. Like Ebbinghaus, she used herself as a subject, but she charted the curve of forgetting over years rather than days. Every day for 12 years, she recorded on a 4- × 6-inch card two or more things that had happened to her that day. Eventually, she accumulated a catalogue of thousands of discrete events, both trivial ("I have dinner at the Canton Kitchen: delicious lobster dish") and significant ("I land at Orly Airport in Paris"). Once a month, she took a random sampling of all the cards accumulated to that point, noted whether she could remember the events on them, and tried to date the events. Linton (1978) expected the kind of rapid forgetting that Ebbinghaus reported. Instead, as you can see in Figure 8.7b, she found that long-term forgetting was slower and proceeded at a more constant pace, as details gradually dropped out of her memories.

Of course, some memories, especially those that mark important transitions, are more memorable than others. But why did Marigold Linton, like the rest of us, forget so many details? Psychologists have proposed five mechanisms to account for forgetting: decay, replacement of old memories by new ones, interference, cue-dependent forgetting, and repression.

Decay

One commonsense view, the **decay theory**, holds that memories simply fade with time if they are not accessed now and then. We have already seen that decay occurs in sensory memory and that it occurs in short-term memory as well unless we keep rehearsing the material. However, the mere passage of time does not account so well for forgetting in long-term memory. People commonly forget things that happened only yesterday while remembering events from many years ago. Indeed, some memories, both procedural and declarative, can last a lifetime. If you learned to swim as a child, you will still know how to swim at age 30, even if you have not been in a pool or lake for 22 years. We are also happy to report that some school lessons have great staying power. In one study, people did well on a Spanish test some 50 years after taking Spanish in high school, even though most had hardly used Spanish at all in the intervening years (Bahrick, 1984). Decay alone cannot entirely explain lapses in long-term memory.

Motor skills, which are stored as procedural memories, can last a lifetime; they never decay.

Replacement

Another theory holds that new information entering memory can wipe out old information, just as rerecording on an audiotape or videotape will obliterate the original material. In a study supporting this view, researchers showed people slides of a traffic accident and used leading questions to get them to think that they had seen a stop sign when they had really seen a yield sign, or vice versa (see Figure 8.8). People in a control group who were not misled in this way were able to identify the sign they had actually seen. Later, all the participants were told the purpose of the study and were asked to guess whether they had been misled. Almost all of those who had been misled continued to insist that they had *really, truly* seen the sign whose existence had been planted in their minds (Loftus, Miller, & Burns, 1978). The researchers interpreted this finding to mean that the subjects had not just been trying to please them and that people's original perceptions had in fact been erased by the misleading information.

Interference

A third theory holds that forgetting occurs because similar items of information interfere with one another in either storage or retrieval; the

decay theory The theory that information in memory eventually disappears if it is not accessed; it applies better to short-term than to long-term memory.

FIGURE 8.8
The Stop Sign Study
When people who saw a car with a yield sign (left) were later asked if they had seen "the stop sign" (a misleading question), many said they had. Similarly, when those shown a stop sign were asked if they had seen "the yield sign," many said yes. These false memories persisted even after the participants were told about the misleading questions, suggesting that misleading information had erased their original mental representations of the signs (Loftus, Miller, & Burns, 1978).

information may get into memory and stay there, but it becomes confused with other information. Such interference, which occurs in both short- and long-term memory, is especially common when you have to recall isolated facts such as names, addresses, passwords, and area codes.

Suppose you are at a party and you meet someone named Julie. A little later you meet someone named Judy. You go on to talk to other people, and after an hour, you again bump into Julie, but you call her Judy by mistake. The second name has interfered with the first. This type of interference, in which new information interferes with the ability to remember old information, is called **retroactive interference**:

Retroactive interference is illustrated by the story of the professor of ichthyology (the study of fish) who complained that whenever he learned the name of a new student, he forgot the name of a fish. With replacement, the new memory erases the old and makes it irretrievable; but in retroactive interference, the loss of the old memory is sometimes temporary. With a little concentration, that professor could probably recall his new students and his old fish.

Because new information is constantly entering memory, we are all vulnerable to the effects of retroactive interference, or at least most of us are. H. M. was an exception; his memories of childhood and adolescence were unusually detailed, clear, and unchanging. H. M. could remember actors who were famous when he was a child, the films they were in, and who their costars had been. He also knew the names of friends from the second grade. Presumably, these early declarative memories were not subject to interference from memories acquired after the operation, for the simple reason that H. M. had not acquired any new memories.

Interference also works in the opposite direction. Old information (such as the foreign language you learned in high school) may interfere with the ability to remember current information (such as the new language you are trying to learn now). This type of interference is called **proactive interference**:

Over a period of weeks, months, and years, proactive interference may cause more forgetting than retroactive interference does, because we have stored up so much information that can potentially interfere with anything new.

Cue-Dependent Forgetting

Often, when we need to remember, we rely on *retrieval cues*, items of information that can help us find the specific information we're looking for. If you are trying to remember the last name of an actor you saw in an old film, it might help to know the person's first name or a movie the actor starred in.

When we lack retrieval cues, we may feel as if we are lost in the mind's library. In long-term memory,

retroactive interference Forgetting that occurs when recently learned material interferes with the ability to remember similar material stored previously.

proactive interference Forgetting that occurs when previously stored material interferes with the ability to remember similar, more recently learned material.

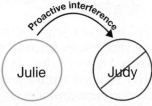

Retroactive interference
Julie — Learned first
Judy — Learned second

Proactive interference
Julie — Learned first
Judy — Learned second

FORGETFULNESS—
The seven warning signs:

1.

this type of memory failure, called **cue-dependent forgetting**, may be the most common type of all. Willem Wagenaar (1986), who, like Marigold Linton, recorded critical details about events in his life, found that he had forgotten 20 percent of those details within a year; after five years, he had forgotten 60 percent. Yet when he gathered cues from witnesses about 10 events that he thought he had forgotten, he was able to recall something about all 10, which suggests that some of his forgetting was cue dependent.

Cues that were present when you learned a new fact or had an experience are apt to be especially useful later as retrieval aids. That may explain why remembering is often easier when you are in the same physical environment as you were when an event occurred: Cues in the present context match those from the past. Ordinarily, this overlap helps us remember the past more accurately. But it may also help account for the eerie phenomenon of *déjà vu*, the fleeting sense of having been in *exactly* the same situation that you are in now (*déjà vu* means "already seen" in French). Some element in the present situation, familiar from some other context that you cannot identify—even a dream, a novel, or a movie—may make the entire situation seem so familiar that it feels like it happened before (Brown, 2004). In other words, déjà vu may be a kind of mistaken recognition memory. Similar feelings of familiarity can actually be produced in the laboratory. When something about newly presented words, shapes, or photographs resembles elements of stimuli seen previously,

people report that the new words, shapes, or photographs are familiar even though they can't recall the original ones (Cleary, 2008).

In everyday forgetting, your mental or physical state may act as a retrieval cue, evoking a **state-dependent memory**. If you were afraid or angry at the time of an event, you may remember that event best when you are once again in the same emotional state (Lang et al., 2001). Your memories can also be biased by whether or not your current mood is consistent with the emotional nature of the material you are trying to remember, a phenomenon known as **mood-congruent memory** (Bower & Forgas, 2000; Buchanan, 2007; Fiedler et al., 2001). You are more likely to remember happy events, and forget or ignore unhappy ones, when you are feeling happy than when you are feeling sad. Likewise, you are apt to remember unhappy events better and remember more of them when you are feeling unhappy, which in turn creates a vicious cycle. The more unhappy memories you recall, the more depressed you feel, and the more depressed you feel, the more unhappy memories you recall . . . so you stay stuck in your depression and make it even worse (Joormann & Gotlib, 2007; Wenzel, 2005).

The Repression Controversy

A final theory of forgetting is concerned with **amnesia**, the loss of memory for important personal information. Amnesia most commonly results from organic conditions such as brain disease or head injury, and is usually temporary. In *psychogenic amnesia*, however, the causes of forgetting are psychological, such as a need to escape feelings of embarrassment, guilt, shame, disappointment, or emotional shock. Psychogenic amnesia begins immediately after the precipitating event, involves massive memory loss including loss of personal identity, and usually ends suddenly, after just a few weeks. Despite its frequent portrayal in films and novels, it is quite rare in real life (McNally, 2003).

Psychologists generally accept the notion of psychogenic amnesia. *Traumatic amnesia*, however, is far more controversial. Traumatic amnesia allegedly involves the burying of specific traumatic events for a long period of time, often for many years. When the memory returns, it is supposedly immune to the usual processes of distortion and confabulation, and is recalled with perfect accuracy. The notion of traumatic amnesia originated with the psychoanalytic theory of Sigmund Freud, who argued that the mind defends itself from unwelcome and upsetting memories through the mechanism of **repression**, the involuntary pushing of threatening or upsetting information into the unconscious (see Chapter 2).

cue-dependent forgetting The inability to retrieve information stored in memory because of insufficient cues for recall.

state-dependent memory The tendency to remember something when the rememberer is in the same physical or mental state as during the original learning or experience.

mood-congruent memory The tendency to remember experiences that are consistent with one's current mood and overlook or forget experiences that are not.

amnesia The partial or complete loss of memory for important personal information.

repression In psychoanalytic theory, the selective, involuntary pushing of threatening or upsetting information into the unconscious.

Most memory researchers reject the argument that a special unconscious mechanism called "repression" is necessary to explain either psychogenic or traumatic amnesia (Rofé, 2008). Richard McNally (2003) reviewed the experimental and clinical evidence and concluded, "The notion that the mind protects itself by repressing or dissociating memories of trauma, rendering them inaccessible to awareness, is a piece of psychiatric folklore devoid of convincing empirical support." The problem for most people who have suffered disturbing experiences is not that they cannot remember, but rather that they cannot forget: The memories keep intruding. There is no case on record of anyone who has repressed the memory of being in a concentration camp, being in combat, or being the victim of an earthquake or a terrorist attack, although details of even these horrible experiences are subject to distortion and fading over time, as are all memories.

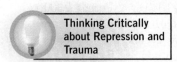

Thinking Critically about Repression and Trauma

Further, repression is hard to distinguish from normal forgetting. People who seem to forget disturbing experiences could be intentionally keeping themselves from retrieving their painful memories by distracting themselves whenever a memory is reactivated. Or they may be focusing consciously on positive memories instead. Perhaps, understandably, they are not rehearsing unhappy memories, so those memories fade with time. Perhaps they are simply avoiding the retrieval cues that would evoke the memories. But a reluctance to think about an upsetting experience is not the same as an *inability* to remember it (McNally, 2003).

The debate over traumatic amnesia and repression erupted into the public arena in the 1990s, when claims of recovered memories of sexual abuse began to appear. Many women and some men came to believe, during psychotherapy, that they could recall long-buried memories of having been sexually victimized in bizarre ways for many years, usually by their fathers. For therapists who accepted the notion of repression, such claims were entirely believable (Brown, Scheflin, & Whitfield, 1999; Herman, 1992). However, most researchers today believe that almost all of these memories were false, having been evoked by therapists who were unaware of the research we described earlier on the power of suggestion and the dangers of confabulation (Lindsay & Read, 1994; McHugh, 2008; McNally, 2003; Schacter, 2001). By asking leading questions, and by encouraging clients to construct vivid images of abuse, revisit those images frequently, and focus on emotional aspects of the images, such therapists unwittingly set up the very conditions that encourage confabulation and false memories.

Since the 1990s, accusations have steadily declined, yet the concept of repression lingers on. Many of its original proponents have turned to the term "dissociation" to account for memory failures in traumatized individuals (see Chapter 11), the idea being that upsetting memories are split off (dissociated) from everyday consciousness. But a review of the research has found no good evidence that early trauma causes such dissociation (Giesbrecht et al., 2008).

Of course, it is obviously possible for someone to forget a single unhappy or deeply unpleasant experience and not recall it for years, just as going back to your elementary school might trigger a memory of the time that you did something embarrassing in front of your whole class. How then should we respond to an individual's claim to have recovered memories of years of traumatic experiences that were previously repressed? How can we distinguish true memories from false ones?

Clearly, a person's recollections are likely to be trustworthy if there is corroborating evidence available, such as medical records, police or school reports, or the accounts of other people who had been present at the time. In the absence of supporting evidence, we may have to tolerate uncertainty, because a person might have a detailed, emotionally rich "memory" that feels completely real but that has been unintentionally confabulated (Bernstein & Loftus, 2009). In such cases, it is important to consider the content of the recovered memory and how it was recovered.

Thus, given what we know about memory, we should be skeptical if people say that they have memories from the first year or two of life; as we will see in the next section, this is not possible, physiologically or cognitively. We should be skeptical if, over time, those memories become more and more implausible; for instance, a person says that sexual abuse continued day and night for 15 years without ever being remembered and without anyone else in the household ever noticing anything amiss. We should also be skeptical if a person suddenly recovers a traumatic memory as a result of therapy or after hearing about supposed cases of recovered memory in the news or reading about one in a best-selling autobiography. And we should hear alarm bells go off if a therapist used suggestive techniques, such as hypnosis, dream analysis, "age regression," guided imagery, and leading questions, to "recover" the memories (see Chapter 12). These techniques are all known to increase confabulation.

✔● Study and
Review on
mypsychlab.com

Quick Quiz

If you have not repressed what you just read, try these questions.

1. Wilma has loved the novels of Tom Robbins for years. Recently, she developed a crush on the actor Tim Robbins, but every time she tries to recall his name, she calls him "Tom." Why?

2. When a man at his 20th high school reunion sees his old friends, he recalls incidents he thought were long forgotten. Why?

3. What mechanisms other than repression could account for a person's psychogenic amnesia?

Answers:

1. proactive interference. 2. The sight of his friends provides retrieval cues for the incidents. 3. The person could be intentionally avoiding the memory by using distraction or focusing on positive experiences; failure to rehearse the memory may be causing it to fade; or the person may be avoiding retrieval cues that would evoke the memory.

YOU are about to learn...

• why the first few years of life are a mental blank.

• why human beings have been called the storytelling animal.

Autobiographical Memories

For most of us, our memories about our own experiences are by far the most fascinating. We analyze them to learn more about who we are. We modify and embellish them to impress others. And we use them to entertain ("Did I ever tell you about the time . . . ?").

Childhood Amnesia: The Missing Years

A curious aspect of autobiographical memory is that most adults cannot recall any events from earlier than the third or fourth year of life. A few people apparently can vaguely recall momentous experiences that occurred when they were as young as 2 years old, such as the birth of a sibling, but not earlier ones (Fivush & Nelson, 2004; Usher & Neisser, 1993). As adults, we cannot remember being fed in infancy, taking our first steps, or uttering our first halting sentences. We are victims of **childhood amnesia** (sometimes called *infantile amnesia*).

There is something disturbing about childhood amnesia—so disturbing that some people adamantly deny it, claiming to remember events from the second or even the first year of life. But like other false memories, these are merely reconstructions based on photographs, family stories, and imagination. The "remembered" event may not even have taken place. Swiss psychologist Jean Piaget (1952) once reported a memory of nearly being kidnapped at the age of 2.

Piaget remembered sitting in his pram, watching his nurse as she bravely defended him from the kidnapper. He remembered the scratches she received on her face. He remembered a police officer with a short cloak and white baton who finally chased the kidnapper away. But when Piaget was 15, his nurse wrote to his parents confessing that she had made up the entire story. Piaget noted, "I therefore must have heard, as a child, the account of this story . . . and projected it into the past in the form of a visual memory, which was a memory of a memory, but false."

> **Thinking Critically about "Memories" from Infancy**

Of course, we all retain procedural memories from the toddler stage, when we first learned to use a fork, drink from a cup, and pull a wagon. We also retain semantic memories acquired early in life: the rules of counting, the names of people and things, knowledge about objects in the world, words and meanings. Moreover, toddlers who are only 1 to 2 years old often reveal nonverbally that they remember past experiences (for example, by imitating something they saw earlier); and some 4-year-olds can remember experiences that occurred before age (Bauer, 2002; McDonough & Mandler, 1994; Tustin & Hayne, 2006). What young children do not do well is encode and retain their early episodic memories—memories of particular events—and carry them into later childhood or adulthood. They can't start doing this consistently until about age 4 ½ (Fivush & Nelson, 2004).

Freud thought that childhood amnesia was a special case of repression, but memory researchers today think that repression has nothing to do with it, and they point to better explanations:

1 Brain development. Parts of the brain involved in the formation or storage of events, and other areas involved in working memory and decision

childhood (infantile) amnesia The inability to remember events and experiences that occurred during the first two or three years of life.

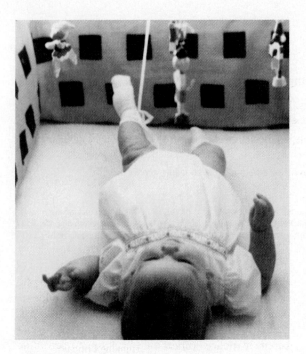

Psychologists have devised ingenious methods to measure memory in infants. This infant, whose leg is attached by a string to a colorful mobile, will learn within minutes to make the mobile move by kicking it. She may still remember the trick a week later, an example of procedural memory (Rovee-Collier, 1993). However, when she is older, she will not remember the experience itself. Like the rest of us, she will fall victim to childhood amnesia.

making, are not well developed until a few years after birth, especially the prefrontal cortex (McKee & Squire, 1993; Newcombe et al., 2000). In addition, the brains of infants and toddlers are busily attending to all the new experiences of life, but this very fact makes it difficult for them to focus on just one event and shut out everything else that's going on—the kind of focus necessary for encoding and remembering (Gopnik, 2009).

2 **Cognitive development.** Before you can carry memories about yourself with you into adulthood, you have to have a self to remember. The emergence of a self-concept usually does not take place before age 2 (Howe, Courage, & Peterson, 1994). In addition, the cognitive schemas that preschoolers use are very different from those that older children and adults use. Only after acquiring language and starting school do children form schemas that contain the information and cues necessary for recalling earlier experiences (Howe, 2000). Young children's limited vocabularies and language skills also prevent them from narrating some aspects of an experience to themselves or others. Later, after their linguistic abilities have matured, they still cannot use those abilities to recall earlier, preverbal memories, because the earlier memories were not encoded linguistically (Simcock & Hayne, 2002).

3 **Social development.** Preschoolers have not yet mastered the social conventions for reporting events, nor have they learned what is important to others. They focus on the routine aspects of an experience rather than the distinctive ones that will provide retrieval cues later, and they encode their experiences far less elaborately than adults do. Instead,

they tend to rely on adults' questions to provide retrieval cues ("Where did we go for breakfast?" "Who did you go trick or treating with?"). This dependency on adults may prevent them from building up a stable core of remembered material that will be available when they are older (Fivush & Hamond, 1991).

Nonetheless, our first memories, even when they aren't accurate, may provide useful insights into our personalities, current concerns, ambitions, and attitudes toward life. What are *your* first memories—or, at least, what do you think they are? What might they tell you about yourself?

Memory and Narrative: The Stories of Our Lives

The communications researcher George Gerbner once observed that human beings are unique because we are the only animal that tells stories—and lives by the stories we tell. This view of human beings as the "storytelling animal" has had a huge impact in cognitive psychology. The *narratives* we compose to simplify and make sense of our lives have a profound influence on our plans, memories, love affairs, hatreds, ambitions, and dreams.

Thus we say, "I have no academic motivation because I flunked the third grade." We say, "Let me tell you the story of how we fell in love." We say, "When you hear what happened, you'll understand why I felt entitled to take such coldhearted revenge." These stories are not necessarily fictions; rather, they are attempts to organize and give meaning to the events of our lives. But because these narratives rely heavily on memory, and because memories are reconstructed and are constantly shifting in response to current needs, beliefs, and experiences, our autobiographies are also, to some degree, works of interpretation and imagination. Adult memories thus reveal as much about the present as they do about the past.

When you construct a narrative about an incident in your life, you have many choices about how to do it. Your story depends on who the audience is; you are apt to put in, leave out, understate, and embellish different things depending on whether you are telling about an event in your life to a therapist, your boss, or friends on Facebook. Your story is also influenced by your purpose in relating it: Is it to convey facts, entertain, or elicit sympathy? As a result of these influences, distortions are apt to creep in, even when you think you are being accurate. And once those distortions have become embedded in your story, they are likely to become part of your memory of the events themselves (Marsh & Tversky, 2004). ✳ Explore

✳ Explore
Constructing & Reconstructing Our Pasts on mypsychlab.com

Your culture also affects how you encode and tell your story. American college students live in a culture that emphasizes individuality, personal feelings, and self-expression. Their earliest childhood memories reflect that fact: They tend to report lengthy, emotionally elaborate memories of events, memories that focus on—who else?—themselves. In contrast, Chinese students, who live in a culture that emphasizes group harmony, social roles, and personal humility, tend to report early memories of family or neighborhood activities, conflicts with friends or relatives that were resolved, and emotionally neutral events (Wang, 2008).

Once you have formulated a story's central theme ("My father never liked us"; "My partner was always so competitive with me"), that theme may then serve as a cognitive schema that guides what you remember and what you forget (Mather, Shafir, & Johnson, 2000). For example, teenagers who have strong and secure attachments to their mothers remember previous quarrels with their moms as being less intense and conflicted than they reported at the time, whereas teenagers who have more ambivalent and insecure attachments remember such quarrels as being worse than they were (Feeney & Cassidy, 2003).

"And here I am at two years of age. Remember? Mom? Pop? No? Or how about this one. My first day of school. Anyone?"

A story's theme may also influence our judgments of events and people in the present. If you have a fight with your lover, the central theme in your story about the fight might be negative ("He was a jerk") or neutral ("It was a mutual misunderstanding"). This theme may bias you to blame or forgive your partner long after you have forgotten what the conflict was all about or who said what (McGregor & Holmes, 1999). You can see that the spin you give a story is critical, so be careful about the stories you tell!

✓• Study and Review on mypsychlab.com

Quick Quiz

You can't blame childhood amnesia if you have forgotten the answers to these questions.

1. A friend of yours claims to remember her birth, her first tooth, and her first birthday party. She is most likely to be (a) lying, (b) confabulating, (c) repressing, (d) revealing wishful thinking, (e) accurately remembering.

2. Give three explanations for childhood amnesia (be specific).

3. Why are the themes in our life stories so important?

Answers:

1. b 2. d 2. the immaturity of certain brain structures, making it difficult for very young children to focus attention, encode, and remember; cognitive factors such as immature cognitive schemas, lack of linguistic skills, and lack of a self-concept; lack of knowledge of social conventions for encoding and reporting events 3. They guide what we remember and forget about our personal pasts, and affect our judgments of events and people.

Psychology in the News REVISITED

Psychological research is having a significant impact on people's ability to think critically about memory. Most notably, awareness of the fallibility of memory is growing among police, interrogators, prosecutors, and judges. The case of Ronald Cotton, described at the start of this chapter, is far from unique. When psychological scientists examined 40 cases in which wrongful conviction had been established beyond a doubt, they found that 90 percent of those cases had involved a false identification by one or more eyewitnesses (Wells et al., 1998). Of course, not all eyewitness testimony is erroneous. But the potential for errors in identification shows how important it is to gather evidence carefully, ensure adequate legal representation for defendants, conduct police interviews using proper procedures, reduce pressure on witnesses, and obtain a DNA analysis whenever possible.

Inspired by the Innocence Project at the Cardozo School of Law in New York City, grassroots organizations of lawyers and students have been successfully challenging questionable convictions. Since the early 1990s, these efforts have led to the exoneration of more than 250 innocent people, some of whom had been condemned to death. One man in Illinois, who had been on death row for 16 years, was just hours from execution when a group of Northwestern University journalism students produced evidence that another man had committed the crime.

How would you feel if your testimony resulted in the conviction of an innocent person? Would you, like Jennifer Thompson, be able to admit your mistake, or would you, as most people do, cling more stubbornly than ever to the accuracy of your memory? Thompson learned from personal experience what you have learned from this chapter: Eyewitnesses can and do make mistakes, ethnic differences can increase these mistakes, even memories for shocking or traumatic experiences are vulnerable to distortion and influence by others, and our confidence in our memories is not a reliable guide to their accuracy. To this day, Thompson and Cotton have made it their personal goal to educate the public and the criminal justice system, so that the

After Ronald Cotton was exonerated of the rape of Jennifer Thompson, the two became friends. Thompson says she has lived with constant anguish because of her mistaken identification.

mistake she made will be less likely to be repeated by others (Thompson-Cannino, Cotton, & Torneo, 2009).

By now, if you have been reading this chapter actively, you should be able to recall the many factors that can trip you up when you call upon your memory: confabulation, source misattribution, poor encoding and rehearsal strategies, interference, inadequate retrieval cues, suggestibility, and biases. By now, therefore, you should not be surprised that memory can be as fickle as it can be accurate. As cognitive psychologists have shown repeatedly, we are not merely actors in our personal life dramas; we also write the scripts.

Taking Psychology with You

How to Remember What You Study

Someday, a "memory pill" may be available to perk up our memories. For the time being, however, those of us who hope to improve our memories must rely on mental strategies. Some simple mnemonics can be useful, but complicated ones are often more bother than they're worth. A better approach is to remember and practice the principles in this chapter:

Pay attention! It seems obvious, but often we fail to remember because we never encoded the information in the first place. For example, which of these is the real Lincoln penny?

Most Americans have trouble recognizing the real penny because they have never

attended to the details of a penny's design (Nickerson & Adams, 1979). We are not advising you to do so, unless you happen to be a coin collector or a counterfeiting expert. Just keep in mind that when you do have something to remember, such as the material in this book, you will do better if you encode it well. (The real penny, by the way, is the left one in the bottom row.)

Add meaning. The more meaningful the material, the more likely it is to link up with information already in long-term memory. Meaningfulness also reduces the number of chunks of information you have to learn. Common ways of adding meaning include making up a story about the material, thinking of examples, and forming visual images. (Some people find that the odder the image, the better.) If your license plate happens to be 236MPL, you might think of 236 maples. If you are trying to remember the concept of procedural memory from this chapter, you might make the concept meaningful by thinking of an example from your own life, such as your ability to ride a mountain bike, and then imagine a *P* superimposed on an image of yourself on your bike.

Take your time. Leisurely learning, spread out over several sessions, usually produces better results than harried cramming (although *reviewing* material just before a test can be helpful). In terms of hours spent, "distributed" (spaced) learning sessions are more efficient than "massed" ones; in other words,

three separate one-hour study sessions may result in more retention than one session of three hours.

Take time out. If possible, minimize interference by using study breaks for rest or recreation. A good night's sleep or an afternoon nap reduce such interference and improve the chances that a new memory will be consolidated.

Overlearn. You can't remember something you never learned well in the first place. Overlearning—studying information even after you think you know it—is one of the best ways to ensure that you'll remember it.

Read, recite, review. Test yourself frequently, rehearse thoroughly, and review periodically to see how you are doing. Don't just evaluate your learning immediately after reading the

material, though; because the information is still in short-term memory, you are likely to feel a false sense of confidence about your ability to recall it later. If you delay making a judgment for at least a few minutes, your evaluation will probably be more accurate (Nelson & Dunlosky, 1991).

Most of all, you will find that active learning produces more comprehension and better retention than does passive reading or listening. Even then, you should not expect to remember everything you read or hear. Nor should you want to. Piling up facts without distinguishing the important from the trivial is just confusing. Popular books and tapes that promise to give you a perfect or photographic memory, or instant recall of everything you learn, fly in the face of what psychologists know about how the mind operates. Our advice: Forget them.

Summary   (•—Listen to an **audio file** of your chapter on **mypsychlab.com**

Reconstructing the Past

● Unlike a tape recorder or video camera, human memory is highly selective and is *reconstructive*: People add, delete, and change elements in ways that help them make sense of information and events. They often experience *source misattribution*, the inability to distinguish information stored during an event from information added later. Even vivid *flashbulb memories* tend to become less accurate or complete over time.

● Because memory is reconstructive, it is subject to *confabulation*, the confusion of imagined events with actual ones. Confabulation is especially likely when people have thought, heard, or told others about the imagined event many times and thus experience *imagination inflation*, the image of the event contains many details, or the event is easy to imagine. Confabulated memories can feel vividly real yet be false.

Memory and the Power of Suggestion

● The reconstructive nature of memory makes memory vulnerable to suggestion. Eyewitness testimony is especially vulnerable to error when the suspect's ethnicity differs from that of the witness, when leading questions

are put to witnesses, or when the witnesses are given misleading information.

● Like adults, children often remember the essential aspects of an event accurately. However, like adults, they can also be suggestible, especially when responding to biased interviewing by adults—when they are asked questions that blur the line between fantasy and reality, are asked leading questions, are told what "other kids" had supposedly said, and are praised for making false allegations.

In Pursuit of Memory

● The ability to remember depends in part on the type of performance called for. In tests of *explicit memory* (conscious recollection), *recognition* is usually better than *recall*. In tests of *implicit memory,* which is measured by indirect methods such as *priming* and the *relearning method*, past experiences may affect current thoughts or actions even when these experiences are not consciously remembered.

● In *information-processing models*, memory involves the *encoding, storage*, and *retrieval* of information. In the *three-box model*, there are three interacting systems: the sensory register, short-term memory, and long-term memory. Some cognitive scientists prefer a *parallel distributed processing (PDP)* or *connectionist* model, which represents knowledge as connections among numerous interacting processing units, distributed in a vast network and all operating in parallel. But the three-box model continues to offer a convenient way to organize the major findings on memory.

The Three-Box Model of Memory

● In the three-box model, incoming sensory information makes a brief stop in the *sensory register,* which momentarily retains it in the form of sensory images.

● *Short-term memory (STM)* retains new information for up to 30 seconds by most estimates (unless rehearsal takes place). The capacity of STM is extremely limited but can be extended if information is organized into larger units by *chunking.* Early models of STM portrayed it mainly as a storage and rehearsal buffer, but many models now envision it also as a *working memory,* which includes the mental processes that control the retrieval of information from long-term memory and that interpret that information appropriately depending on the task being performed. Working memory permits us to control attention, resist distraction, and therefore maintain information in an active, accessible state.

● *Long-term memory (LTM)* contains an enormous amount of information that must be organized to make it manageable. Words (or the concepts they represent) are often organized by semantic categories. Many models of LTM represent its contents as a network of interrelated concepts. The way people use these networks depends on experience and education. Research on *tip-of-the-tongue (TOT) states* shows that words are also indexed in terms of sound and form.

● *Procedural memories* ("knowing how") are memories for how to perform specific actions; *declarative memories* ("knowing that") are memories for abstract or representational knowledge. Declarative memories include *semantic memories* (general knowledge) and *episodic memories* (memories for personally experienced events).

● The three-box model is often invoked to explain the *serial-position effect* in memory, but although it can explain the *primacy effect,* it cannot explain why a *recency effect* sometimes occurs after a considerable delay.

The Biology of Memory

● Short-term memory involves temporary changes within neurons that alter their ability to release neurotransmitters, whereas long-term memory involves lasting structural changes in neurons and synapses. *Long-term potentiation,* an increase in the strength of synaptic responsiveness, seems to be an important mechanism of long-term memory. Neural changes associated with long-term potentiation take time to develop, which helps explain why long-term memories require a period of *consolidation.*

● The amygdala is involved in the formation, consolidation, and retrieval of emotional memories. Areas of the frontal lobes are especially active during short-term and working memory tasks. The prefrontal cortex and parts of the temporal lobes are involved in the efficient encoding of words and pictures. The hippocampus plays a critical role in the formation and retrieval of long-term declarative memories. Other areas, such as the cerebellum, are crucial for the formation of procedural memories. Studies of patients with amnesia suggest that different brain systems are active during explicit and implicit memory tasks. The various components of a memory are probably stored at different sites, with all of these sites participating in the representation of the event as a whole.

● Hormones released by the adrenal glands during stress or emotional arousal, including epinephrine and norepinephrine, enhance memory. But very high hormone levels can interfere with the retention of information; a moderate level is optimal for learning new tasks.

How We Remember

● To remember material well, we must encode it accurately in the first place. Some kinds of information, such as material in a college course, require *effortful,* as opposed to *automatic,* encoding. Rehearsal of information keeps it in short-term memory and increases the chances of long-term retention. *Elaborative rehearsal* is more likely to result in transfer to long-term memory than is *maintenance rehearsal,* and *deep processing* is usually a more effective retention strategy than *shallow processing.* The *read-recite-review* strategy encourages active learning and produces better results than simply reading and rereading material. *Retrieval practice* is necessary if a memory is going to be consolidated, and therefore last and be available for a long time. *Mnemonics* can enhance retention by promoting elaborative encoding and chunking the material to be recalled.

Why We Forget

● Forgetting can occur for several reasons. Information in sensory and short-term memory appears to *decay* if it does not receive further processing. New information may erase and replace old information in long-term memory. *Proactive* and *retroactive interference* may take place. *Cue-dependent forgetting* may occur when *retrieval cues* are inadequate. The most effective retrieval cues are those that were present at the time of the initial experience. A person's mental or physical state may also act as a retrieval cue, evoking a *state-dependent memory.* We tend to remember best those events that are congruent with our current mood (*mood-congruent memory*).

• *Amnesia*, the forgetting of personal information, usually occurs because of disease or injury to the brain. *Psychogenic amnesia*, which involves a loss of personal identity and has psychological causes, is rare. *Traumatic amnesia*, which allegedly involves the forgetting of specific traumatic events for long periods of time, is highly controversial, as is *repression*, the psychodynamic explanation of traumatic amnesia. Because these concepts lack good empirical support, psychological scientists are skeptical about their validity and about the accuracy of "recovered memories." Critics argue that many therapists, unaware of the power of suggestion and the dangers of confabulation, have encouraged false memories of victimization.

Autobiographical Memories

• Most people cannot recall any events from earlier than the third or fourth year of life. The reasons for such *childhood amnesia* include the immaturity of certain brain structures, making it difficult for very young children to focus attention, encode, and remember; cognitive factors such as immature cognitive schemas, lack of linguistic skills, and lack of a self-concept; and lack of knowledge of social conventions for encoding and reporting events.

• A person's *narrative* "life story" organizes the events of his or her life and gives them meaning.

Psychology in the News, Revisited

• Across the country, as DNA evidence has exonerated many people who were falsely convicted of rape, murder, and other crimes, people are becoming more aware of the limitations of eyewitness testimony and the fallibility of memory.

Taking Psychology with You

• The best techniques for improving memory are to pay attention, add meaning, take your time instead of cramming, take time out, overlearn, practice "read-recite-review," and learn actively rather than passively. Remember this advice!

Key Terms

Answers to the Get Involved exercises on pages 271 and 272
Rudolph's eight friends were Dasher, Dancer, Prancer, Vixen, Comet, Cupid, Donner ("Donder" in some versions), and Blitzen.

Memory refers to the capacity to retain and retrieve information, and also to the structures that account for this capacity.

Reconstructing the Past

The Manufacture of Memory

- Human memory is *reconstructive*: People add, delete, and change elements.
- **Source misattribution** is the inability to distinguish information stored during an event from information added later.
- Even *flashbulb memories*, though emotionally powerful and vivid, are often embellished or change over time.

The Conditions of Confabulation

Confabulation is the confusion of imagined events with real ones, or confusing an event that happened to someone else with one that happened to you. Such confabulations are especially likely under certain circumstances:
- One has thought, heard, or told others about the imagined event many times.
- The image of the event contains lots of details that make it feel real.
- The event is easy to imagine.

Memory and the Power of Suggestion

The Eyewitness on Trial

Eyewitness testimony is especially vulnerable to error when:
- The suspect's ethnicity differs from the witness's.
- Leading questions are put to the witness.
- Witnesses are exposed to misleading information.

Children's Testimony

Children can be suggestible when:
- Interviewers use leading questions or suggestive techniques, or pressure the child to give particular answers.
- Children are affected by rumor and hearsay.

In Pursuit of Memory

Measuring Memory

- In tests of **explicit memory**, or conscious recollection, **recognition** is usually better than **recall.**
- In tests of **implicit memory,** which is measured by indirect methods such as **priming** and the **relearning method,** past experiences may affect current thoughts or actions.

Models of Memory

- In *information-processing models*, memory involves encoding, storage, and retrieval.
- **Parallel distributed processing (PDP):** knowledge is represented as connections among thousands of interacting processing units, all operating in parallel.

The Three-Box Model of Memory

Sensory Register

Incoming information stops in the **sensory register**, which momentarily retains it in the form of sensory images.

Three Memory Systems

Information from environment

Retrieved

Sensory register
1. Large capacity
2. Contains sensory information
3. Very brief retention of images (up to 1/2 second for visual; 2 seconds for auditory)

Short-term memory (STM)
1. Limited capacity
2. Brief storage of items (up to 30 seconds if no rehearsal)
3. Involved in conscious processing of information

Long-term memory (LTM)
1. Unlimited capacity
2. Some memories are permanent
3. Information organized and indexed

Forgotten   Transferred   Forgotten   Transferred/Retrieved

Short-Term Memory (STM)

Short-term memory (STM) retains information for up to 30 seconds, although estimates extend to a few minutes for certain tasks.
- **Chunking** extends the capacity of STM.
- **Working memory** consists of STM, the mental processes that control the retrieval of information from long-term memory, and executive processes that control attention and the manipulation and interpretation of information required for a task.

Long-Term Memory (LTM)

Information in **long-term memory (LTM)** is organized as a network of interrelated concepts and includes:
- **Procedural memories**
- **Declarative memories**
  — Semantic
  — Episodic
- The **serial-position effect** is the tendency for strongest recall of the first and last items on a list.

How We Remember

- Rehearsal of information keeps it in STM longer and increases the chances of retention.
- **Elaborative rehearsal** is more likely to result in transfer to LTM than is **maintenance rehearsal.**
- **Deep processing** is usually more effective than shallow processing.
- The *read-recite-review strategy* and *retrieval practice* are more effective than passively reading the material.
- **Mnemonics** are strategies or tricks for improving memory.

The Biology of Memory

Changes in Neurons and Synapses

- In short-term memory, neurons temporarily change in their ability to release neurotransmitters.
- In long-term memory, dendrites grow and branch out, certain synapses increase in number, and some synaptic pathways become more excitable. These neuronal changes are known as **long-term potentiation.** These changes require some time for completion, during which memories undergo **consolidation.**

Locating Memories

- The amygdala is involved in the formation, consolidation, and retrieval of fearful and other emotional memories.
- The frontal lobes are involved in short-term and working memory.
- The hippocampus is critical to the formation of long-term declarative memories.
- The cerebellum helps form and retain certain procedural memories.
- The ultimate destinations of declarative memories seem to lie in parts of the cerebral cortex.

Hormones, Emotion, and Memory

- Hormones released by the adrenal glands can enhance memory.
- Extreme arousal, however, often impairs memory.

Why We Forget

- **Decay theory** holds that memory eventually disappears if it is not accessed; applies best to sensory and short-term memory.
- Another theory emphasizes the replacement of old information by new information.
- A third theory emphasizes **proactive** and **retroactive interference** in storage or retrieval.
- **Cue-dependent forgetting** may be the most common type of forgetting; it occurs because of inadequate retrieval cues. When one's physical or mental state acts as a retrieval cue, **state-dependent memory** may result. Similarly, when one's mood is consistent with the emotional nature of the material one is trying to remember, **mood-congruent memory** may result.

The Repression Controversy

- **Amnesia** usually occurs as a result of brain disease or head injury, and is usually temporary.
- *Psychogenic amnesia* has psychological causes and involves a loss of personal identity.
- *Traumatic amnesia,* which allegedly involves the burying of specific traumatic events for long periods of time, is highly controversial, as is **repression,** the psychodynamic explanation of traumatic amnesia.
- Critics argue that many therapists, unaware of the power of suggestion and the dangers of confabulation, have encouraged false memories of victimization.

Autobiographical Memories

Childhood Amnesia

Childhood amnesia may be due to:
- Immaturity of brain parts involved in memory.
- Cognitive factors, such as lack of a self-concept and limited language skills necessary for forming cognitive schemas useful for later recall.
- Social factors, such as a lack of mastery of social conventions for reporting events to others.

Memory and Narrative

- A person's *narrative* (life story) organizes remembered life events and gives them meaning.
- Adult memories can reveal as much about the present as they do about the past.

LONG-TERM MEMORY

PROCEDURAL MEMORIES
("Knowing how")

DECLARATIVE MEMORIES
("Knowing that")

SEMANTIC MEMORIES
(General knowledge)

EPISODIC MEMORIES
(Personal recollections)

First Grader Suspended Over Camping Utensil

NEWARK, DE, October 12, 2009. Zachary Christie was so excited about joining the Cub Scouts and going on campouts that he brought his favorite camping utensil to school to use at lunch. The utensil is handy because it can serve as a knife, fork, and spoon. But school officials have decided that the 6-year-old boy violated their zero-tolerance policy on weapons—which would include the "knife" part of the multipurpose utensil—and have suspended him. He now faces 45 days in the district's reform school. "It just seems unfair," Zachary said, while practicing writing his lowercase letters at home.

In response to shooting incidents in schools, many districts have adopted zero-tolerance policies on the possession of weapons on school grounds. In Zachary's case, officials felt they had no choice but to suspend him because the district bans knives regardless of the possessor's intent, age, or character.

"Zachary wears a suit and tie some days to school by his own choice because he takes school so seriously," said Debbie Christie, Zachary's mother. "He is not some sort of threat to his classmates." But George Evans, president of the school district's board, defended the decision. "There is no parent who wants to get a phone call where they hear that their child no longer has two good seeing eyes because there was a scuffle and someone pulls out a knife," he commented.

Critics argue that zero-tolerance policies like the one that landed Zachary in hot water have led to increased suspensions and expulsions, which results in kids spending time in places like the street, where their behavior only gets worse. Inflexible policies can also lead to heavy punishment for minor infractions. Last year, a third grader in Delaware was expelled for a year because her grandmother had sent a birthday cake to school along with a knife to cut it.

Zero-tolerance policies initially gave authorities more leeway in punishing students, but critics charged that they were being applied in a discriminatory manner against African-American children, who were more likely than white children to be suspended or expelled for committing the same offenses. As a result, many school districts have removed discretion in the application of the policies.

Zachary himself is reluctant to go back to school. "I just think the other kids may tease me for being in trouble," he said, and added, "but I think the rules are what is wrong, not me."

Zachary Christie with the camping utensil that got him in trouble.

Learning and Conditioning

re zero-tolerance policies justified? Should children who commit minor infractions be punished as severely as those who commit serious ones? If not, how should school administrators treat children who are disruptive or violent? Should schools expel them or are there alternatives? In the home, how should parents correct their children's misbehavior? Is "a good spanking" the best recourse for parents, or should there be "zero tolerance" for parents who use any kind of corporal punishment?

The debate over how to discipline children has been with us for a long time. It is part of a larger issue: How can we change unwanted, self-defeating, or dangerous behavior? Many people want to fix their own bad habits, of course, and they are forever trying to improve or fix other people's behavior as well. We imprison criminals, spank children, shout at spouses, and give the finger to a driver who cuts us off. On the positive side, we give children gold stars for good work, give parents bumper stickers that praise their children's successes, give bonuses to employees, and give out trophies for top performance. Do any of these efforts get the results we hope for? Well, yes and no. Once you understand the laws of **learning**, you will realize that behavior, whether it's your own or other people's, *can* change for the better. And you will also understand why often it does not.

Research on learning has been heavily influenced by **behaviorism**, the school of psychology that accounts for behavior in terms of observable acts and events, without reference to mental entities such as "mind" or "will" (see Chapter 1). Behaviorists focus on **conditioning**, which involves associations between environmental stimuli and responses. They have shown that two types of conditioning, *classical conditioning* and *operant conditioning*, can explain a great deal of behavior both in animals and in people. But other approaches, including *social-cognitive learning theories*, hold that omitting mental processes from explanations of human learning is like omitting passion from descriptions of sex:

learning A relatively permanent change in behavior (or behavioral potential) due to experience.

behaviorism An approach to psychology that emphasizes the study of observable behavior and the role of the environment as a determinant of behavior.

conditioning A basic kind of learning that involves associations between environmental stimuli and the organism's responses.

unconditioned stimulus (US) The classical-conditioning term for a stimulus that elicits a reflexive response in the absence of learning.

You may explain the form, but you miss its essence. To social-cognitive theorists, learning includes not only changes in behavior but also changes in thoughts, expectations, and knowledge, which in turn influence behavior in a reciprocal, or two-way, process.

As you read about the principles of conditioning and learning in this chapter, ask yourself what they can teach us about the use of punishment to control undesirable behavior. What happens when punishment is used inappropriately? What is the best way to modify other people's behavior—and our own?

YOU are about to learn...

- how classical conditioning explains why a dog might salivate when it sees a lightbulb or hears a buzzer.
- four important features of classical conditioning.
- what is actually learned in classical conditioning.

Classical Conditioning

At the turn of the twentieth century, the great Russian physiologist Ivan Pavlov (1849–1936) was studying salivation in dogs as part of a research program on digestion. One of his procedures was to make a surgical opening in a dog's cheek and insert a tube that conducted saliva away from the animal's salivary gland so that the saliva could be measured. To stimulate the reflexive flow of saliva, Pavlov placed meat powder or other food in the dog's mouth (see Figure 9.1).

Pavlov was a truly dedicated scientific observer. Many years later, as he lay dying, he even dictated his sensations for posterity! And he instilled in his students and assistants the same passion for detail. During his salivation studies, one of the assistants

noticed something that most people would have overlooked or dismissed as trivial. After a dog had been brought to the laboratory a few times, it would start to salivate *before* the food was placed in its mouth. The sight or smell of the food, the dish in which the food was kept, and even the sight of the person who delivered the food were enough to start the dog's mouth watering. These new salivary responses clearly were not inborn, so they must have been acquired through experience.

At first, Pavlov treated the dog's drooling as just an annoying secretion. But he quickly realized that his assistant had stumbled onto an important phenomenon, one that Pavlov came to believe was the basis of most learning in human beings and other animals (Pavlov, 1927). He called that phenomenon a "conditional" reflex because it depended on environmental conditions. Later, an error in the translation of his writings transformed "conditional" into "conditioned," the word most commonly used today.

Pavlov soon dropped what he had been doing and turned to the study of conditioned reflexes, to which he devoted the last three decades of his life. Why were his dogs salivating to things other than food?

New Reflexes from Old

Pavlov initially speculated about what his dogs might be thinking and feeling when they drooled before getting their food. Was the doggy equivalent of "Oh boy, this means chow time" going through their minds? He soon decided, however, that such speculation was pointless. Instead, he focused on analyzing the environment in which the conditioned reflex arose.

The original salivary reflex, according to Pavlov, consisted of an **unconditioned stimulus (US)**,

FIGURE 9.1
Pavlov's Method
The photo shows Ivan Pavlov (in the white beard), flanked by his students and a canine subject. The drawing depicts an apparatus similar to the one he used; saliva from a dog's cheek flowed down a tube and was measured by the movement of a needle on a revolving drum.

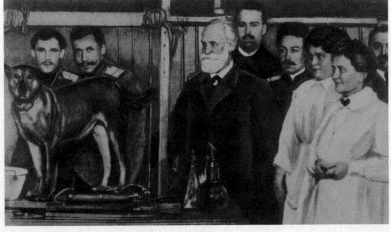

A

B

food in the dog's mouth, and an **unconditioned response (UR)**, salivation. By an unconditioned stimulus, Pavlov meant an event or thing that elicits a response automatically or reflexively. By an unconditioned response, he meant the response that is automatically produced:

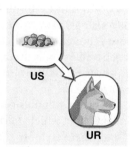

Learning occurs, said Pavlov, when a neutral stimulus (one that does not yet produce a particular response, such as salivation) is regularly paired with an unconditioned stimulus:

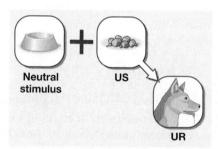

The neutral stimulus then becomes a **conditioned stimulus (CS)**, which elicits a learned or **conditioned response (CR)** that is usually similar or related to the original, unlearned one. In Pavlov's laboratory, the sight of the food dish, which had not previously elicited salivation, became a CS for salivation:

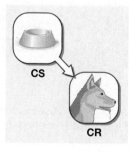

The procedure by which a neutral stimulus becomes a conditioned stimulus eventually became known as **classical conditioning**, and is sometimes also called *Pavlovian* or *respondent* conditioning. Pavlov and his students went on to show that all sorts of things can become conditioned stimuli for salivation if they are paired with food: the ticking of a metronome, the musical tone of a bell, the vibrating sound of a buzzer, a touch on the leg, even a pinprick or an electric shock. And since Pavlov's day, many automatic, involuntary responses besides salivation have been classically conditioned, including heartbeat, stomach secretions, blood pressure, reflexive movements, blinking, and muscle contractions. In the laboratory, the optimal interval between the presentation of the neutral stimulus and the presentation of the US is often quite short, sometimes less than a second.

Principles of Classical Conditioning

Classical conditioning occurs in all species, from one-celled amoebas to *Homo sapiens*. Let us look more closely at some important features of this process: extinction, higher-order conditioning, and stimulus generalization and discrimination.

Extinction Conditioned responses do not necessarily last forever. If, after conditioning, the conditioned stimulus is repeatedly presented without the unconditioned stimulus, the conditioned response eventually disappears and **extinction** is said to have occurred (see Figure 9.2 on the next page). Suppose that you train your dog Milo to salivate to the sound of a bell, but then you ring the bell every five minutes and do *not* follow it with food. Milo will salivate less and less to the bell and will soon stop salivating altogether; salivation will have been extinguished. Extinction is not the same as unlearning or forgetting, however. If you come back the next day and ring the bell, Milo may salivate again for a few trials, although the response will probably be weaker. The reappearance of the response, called **spontaneous recovery**, explains why completely eliminating a conditioned response often requires more than one extinction session.

Higher-Order Conditioning Sometimes a neutral stimulus can become a conditioned stimulus by being paired with an already-established CS, a procedure known as **higher-order conditioning**. Say Milo has learned to salivate to the sight of his food dish. Now you flash a bright light before presenting

unconditioned response (UR) The classical-conditioning term for a reflexive response elicited by a stimulus in the absence of learning.

conditioned stimulus (CS) The classical-conditioning term for an initially neutral stimulus that comes to elicit a conditioned response after being associated with an unconditioned stimulus.

conditioned response (CR) The classical-conditioning term for a response that is elicited by a conditioned stimulus; it occurs after the conditioned stimulus is associated with an unconditioned stimulus.

classical conditioning The process by which a previously neutral stimulus acquires the capacity to elicit a response through association with a stimulus that already elicits a similar or related response. Also called *Pavlovian* or *respondent* conditioning.

extinction The weakening and eventual disappearance of a learned response; in classical conditioning, it occurs when the conditioned stimulus is no longer paired with the unconditioned stimulus.

spontaneous recovery The reappearance of a learned response after its apparent extinction.

higher-order conditioning In classical conditioning, a procedure in which a neutral stimulus becomes a conditioned stimulus through association with an already established conditioned stimulus.

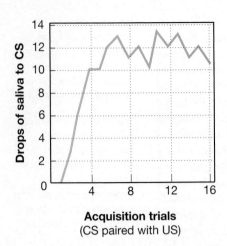

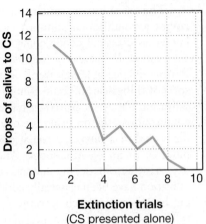

Acquisition trials
(CS paired with US)

Extinction trials
(CS presented alone)

FIGURE 9.2
Acquisition and Extinction of a Salivary Response
A neutral stimulus that is consistently followed by an unconditioned stimulus for salivation will become a conditioned stimulus for salivation (left). But when this conditioned stimulus is then repeatedly presented without the unconditioned stimulus, the conditioned salivary response will weaken and eventually disappear (right); it has been extinguished.

stimulus generalization After conditioning, the tendency to respond to a stimulus that resembles one involved in the original conditioning; in classical conditioning, it occurs when a stimulus that resembles the CS elicits the CR.

stimulus discrimination The tendency to respond differently to two or more similar stimuli; in classical conditioning, it occurs when a stimulus similar to the CS fails to evoke the CR.

the dish. With repeated pairings of the light and the dish, Milo may learn to salivate to the light. The procedure for higher-order conditioning is illustrated in Figure 9.3.

Higher-order conditioning may explain why some words trigger emotional responses in us—why they can inflame us to anger or evoke warm, sentimental feelings. When words are paired with objects or other words that already elicit some emotional response, they too may come to elicit that response (Staats & Staats, 1957). A child may learn a positive response to the word *birthday* because of its association with gifts and attention. Conversely, the child may learn a negative response to ethnic or national labels if the labels are paired with words that the child has already learned are disagreeable, such as *dumb* or *dirty*. Higher-order

conditioning, in other words, may contribute to the formation of prejudices.

Stimulus Generalization and Discrimination After a stimulus becomes a conditioned stimulus for some response, other, similar stimuli may produce a similar reaction—a phenomenon known as **stimulus generalization**. If you condition your patient pooch Milo to salivate to middle C on the piano, Milo may also salivate to D, which is one tone above C, even though you did not pair D with food. Stimulus generalization is described nicely by an old English proverb: "He who hath been bitten by a snake fears a rope."

The mirror image of stimulus generalization is **stimulus discrimination**, in which *different* responses are made to stimuli that resemble the conditioned stimulus in some way. Suppose that you have conditioned Milo to salivate to middle C on the piano by repeatedly pairing the sound with food. Now you play middle C on a guitar, *without* following it by food (but you continue to follow C on the piano by food). Eventually, Milo will learn to salivate to a C on the piano and not to salivate to the same note on the guitar; that is, he will discriminate between the two sounds. If you keep at this long enough, you could train Milo to be a pretty discriminating drooler!

What Is Actually Learned in Classical Conditioning?

For classical conditioning to be most effective, the stimulus to be conditioned should *precede* the unconditioned stimulus rather than follow it or occur simultaneously with it. This makes sense because, in classical conditioning, the conditioned stimulus becomes a *signal* for the unconditioned stimulus. Classical conditioning is in fact an evolutionary

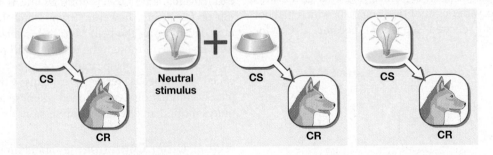

FIGURE 9.3
Higher-Order Conditioning
In this illustration of higher-order conditioning, the food dish is a previously conditioned stimulus for salivation (left). When the light, a neutral stimulus, is paired with the dish (center), the light also becomes a conditioned stimulus for salivation (right).

Get Involved! Conditioning an Eye-Blink Response

Try out your behavioral skills by conditioning an eye-blink response in a willing friend, using classical-conditioning procedures. You will need a drinking straw and something to make a ringing sound; a spoon tapped on a water glass works well. Tell your friend that you are going to use the straw to blow air in his or her eye, but do not say why. Immediately before each puff of air, make the ringing sound. Repeat this procedure ten times. Then make the ringing sound but *don't* puff. Your friend will probably blink anyway, and may continue to do so for one or two more repetitions of the sound before the response extinguishes. Can you identify the US, the UR, the CS, and the CR in this exercise?

adaptation, one that enables the organism to anticipate and prepare for a biologically important event that is about to happen. In Pavlov's studies, for instance, a bell, buzzer, or other stimulus was a signal that meat was coming, and the dog's salivation was preparation for digesting food. Today, therefore, many psychologists contend that what an animal or person actually learns in classical conditioning is not merely an association between two paired stimuli that occur close together in time, but rather *information* conveyed by one stimulus about another: "If a tone sounds, food is likely to follow."

This view is supported by the research of Robert Rescorla (1988), who showed, in a series of imaginative studies, that the mere pairing of an unconditioned stimulus and a neutral stimulus is not enough to produce learning. To become a conditioned stimulus, the neutral stimulus must reliably signal, or *predict*, the unconditioned stimulus. If food occurs just as often *without* a preceding tone as with it, the tone is unlikely to become a conditioned stimulus for salivation, because the tone does not provide any information about the probability of

getting food. Think of it this way: If every phone call you got brought bad news that made your heart race, your heart might soon start pounding every time the phone rang—a conditioned response. Ordinarily, though, upsetting calls occur randomly among a far greater number of routine ones. The ringtone may sometimes be paired with a racing heart, but it doesn't always signal disaster, so no conditioned heart-rate response occurs.

Rescorla concluded that "Pavlovian conditioning is not a stupid process by which the organism willy-nilly forms associations between any two stimuli that happen to co-occur. Rather, the organism is better seen as an information seeker using logical and perceptual relations among events, along with its own preconceptions, to form a sophisticated representation of its world." Not all learning theorists agree; an orthodox behaviorist would say that it is silly to talk about the preconceptions of a rat. The important point, however, is that concepts such as "information seeking," "preconceptions," and "representations of the world" open the door to a more cognitive view of classical conditioning. ✳ Explore

✳ Explore
Three Stages of Classical Conditioning on
mypsychlab.com

Study and **Review** on mypsychlab.com

Quick Quiz

Classical-conditioning terms can be hard to learn, so be sure to take this quiz before going on.

A. Name the unconditioned stimulus, unconditioned response, conditioned stimulus, and conditioned response in these two situations.

1. Five-year-old Samantha is watching a storm from her window. A huge bolt of lightning is followed by a tremendous thunderclap, and Samantha jumps at the noise. This happens several more times. There is a brief lull and then another lightning bolt. Samantha jumps in response to the bolt.

2. Gregory's mouth waters whenever he eats anything with lemon in it. One day, while reading an ad that shows a big glass of lemonade, Gregory finds that his mouth has started to water.

B. In the view of many learning theorists, pairing a neutral and unconditioned stimulus is not enough to produce classical conditioning; the neutral stimulus must _____ the unconditioned stimulus.

Answers:

A. 1. US = the thunderclap; UR = jumping elicited by the noise; CS = the sight of the lightning; CR = jumping elicited by the lightning. 2. US = the taste of lemon; UR = salivation elicited by the taste of lemon; CS = the picture of a glass of lemonade; CR = salivation elicited by the picture. B. signal or predict

YOU are about to learn...

- why advertisers often include pleasant music and gorgeous scenery in ads for their products.

- how classical conditioning might explain your irrational fear of heights or mice.

- how you might be conditioned to like certain tastes and odors and be turned off by others.

- how sitting in a doctor's office can make you feel sick and placebos can make you feel better.

- how technology is helping researchers study the biological basis of classical conditioning.

Classical Conditioning in Real Life

If a dog can learn to salivate to the ringing of a bell, so can you. In fact, you probably have learned to salivate to the sound of a lunch bell, the phrase *hot fudge sundae*, and "mouth-watering" pictures of food. But classical conditioning affects us every day in many other ways.

One of the first psychologists to recognize the real-life implications of Pavlovian theory was John B. Watson, who founded American behaviorism and enthusiastically promoted Pavlov's ideas. Watson believed that the whole rich array of human emotion and behavior could be accounted for by conditioning principles. He even suggested that we learn to love another person when that person is paired with stroking and cuddling. Watson was wrong about love, which is a lot more complicated than he thought (see Chapter 14). But he was right about the power of classical conditioning to affect our emotions, preferences, and tastes.

Learning to Like

Classical conditioning plays a big role in our emotional responses to objects, people, symbols, events, and places. It can explain why sentimental feelings sweep over us when we see a school mascot, a national flag, or the logo of the Olympic games. These objects have been associated in the past with positive feelings.

Many advertising techniques take advantage of classical conditioning's role in emotional responses. When you see ads, notice how many of them pair a product with music the advertiser

Why do most people fear snakes, and why do some even develop a snake phobia?

thinks you'll like, with good-looking people, with idyllic scenery, or with celebrities you admire or think are funny. In classical-conditioning terms, the music, attractive person, or celebrity is an unconditioned stimulus for internal responses associated with pleasure, and the advertiser hopes that the product in the ad will become a conditioned stimulus, evoking similar responses in you.

Learning to Fear

Positive emotions are not the only ones that can be classically conditioned; so can dislikes and fears. A person can learn to fear just about anything if it is paired with something that elicits pain, surprise, or embarrassment. Human beings, however, are biologically primed to acquire some kinds of fears more readily than others. It is far easier to establish a conditioned fear of spiders, snakes, and heights than of butterflies, flowers, and toasters. The former can be dangerous to your health, so in the process of evolution, human beings acquired a tendency to learn quickly to be wary of them and to retain this fear (LoBue & DeLoache, 2008; Öhman & Mineka, 2001). Some theorists believe that evolution has also instilled in humans a readiness to learn to fear unfamiliar members of ethnic groups other than their own, and that this tendency too resists extinction and may contribute to the emotional underpinnings of prejudice (Navarrete et al., 2009; Olsson et al., 2005).

The Birth of a Phobia When fear of an object or situation becomes irrational and interferes with normal activities, it qualifies as a *phobia* (see Chapter 11). To demonstrate how a phobia might be learned, John Watson and Rosalie Rayner (1920/2000) deliberately established a rat phobia in an 11-month-old boy named Albert. Their goal was to demonstrate how an inborn reaction of fear could transfer to a wide range of stimuli; today we call this stimulus generalization. They also wanted to demonstrate that adult emotional responses, such as specific fears, could originate in early childhood. The research procedures that Watson and Rayner used had some flaws, and for ethical reasons, no psychologist today would attempt to do such a thing to a child. Nevertheless, the study's main conclusion, that fears can be conditioned, is still well accepted.

"Little Albert" was a placid child who rarely cried. (Watson and Rayner deliberately chose such a child because they thought their demonstration would do him relatively little harm.) When Watson and Rayner gave Albert a live, furry rat to play with,

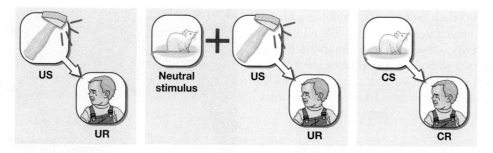

FIGURE 9.4
The Creation of a Fear
In the Little Albert study, noise from a hammer striking a steel bar was an unconditioned
stimulus for fear (left). When a white rat, a neutral stimulus, was paired with the noise (center),
the rat then became a conditioned stimulus for fear (right).

he showed no fear; in fact, he was delighted. The same was true when they showed him a variety of other objects, including a rabbit and some cotton wool. However, like most children, Albert was innately afraid of loud noises. When the researchers made a loud noise behind his head by striking a steel bar with a hammer, he would jump and fall sideways onto the mattress where he was sitting. The noise made by the hammer was an unconditioned stimulus for the unconditioned response of fear.

Having established that Albert liked rats, Watson and Rayner set about teaching him to fear them. Again they offered him a rat, but this time, as he reached for it, one of the researchers struck the steel bar. Startled, Albert fell onto the mattress. A week later, the researchers repeated this procedure several times. Albert began to whimper and tremble. Finally, they held out the rat to him without making the noise. Albert fell over, cried, and crawled away so quickly that he almost reached the edge of the table he was sitting on before an adult caught him; the rat had become a conditioned

stimulus for fear (see Figure 9.4). Tests done a few days later showed that Albert's fear had generalized to other hairy or furry objects, including a white rabbit, cotton wool, a Santa Claus mask, and even John Watson's hair. ✳ Explore

Unfortunately, Watson and Rayner lost access to Little Albert, so we do not know how long the child's fears lasted. Further, because the study ended early, Watson and Rayner had no opportunity to reverse the conditioning. However, Watson and Mary Cover Jones did reverse another child's conditioned fear—one that was, as Watson put it, "home-grown" rather than psychologist-induced (Jones, 1924). A 3-year-old named Peter was deathly afraid of rabbits. Watson and Jones eliminated his fear with a method called **counterconditioning**, in which a conditioned stimulus is paired with some other stimulus that elicits a response incompatible with the unwanted response (see Figure 9.5).

At first, the researchers kept the rabbit some distance from Peter, so that his fear would remain at a low level. Otherwise, Peter might have learned to fear milk and crackers! Then gradually, over

counterconditioning
In classical conditioning, the process of pairing a conditioned stimulus with a stimulus that elicits a response that is incompatible with an unwanted conditioned response.

✳ Explore
Classical Conditioning of Little Albert on mypsychlab.com

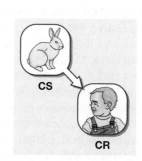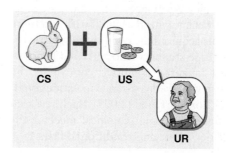

FIGURE 9.5
The Counterconditioning of a Fear
Three-year-old Peter had acquired a conditioned response of fear of rabbits. To countercondition this fear, the researchers paired a rabbit (the CS) with a snack of milk and crackers (a US), which produced pleasant feelings that were incompatible with the conditioned response of fear. Eventually, Peter felt as comfortable with the rabbit as with the crackers.

several days, they brought the rabbit closer and closer. Eventually Peter learned to like rabbits and Peter was even able to sit with the rabbit in his lap, playing with it with one hand while he ate with the other. A variation of this procedure, called *systematic desensitization*, was later devised for treating phobias in adults (see Chapter 12).

Biology and Conditioned Fears Researchers today are exploring the biological basis of fear conditioning and fear extinction. The acquisition of a conditioned fear appears to involve a receptor in the amygdala for the neurotransmitter glutamate. Giving rats a drug that blocks this receptor prevents extinction of a conditioned fear, whereas giving a drug that enhances the receptor's activity speeds up extinction (Walker et al., 2002). Inspired by these results, researchers set out to learn whether the receptor-enhancing drug (which is safe in humans) could help people with a phobic fear of heights (Davis et al., 2005). Using a double-blind procedure, they gave the drug to 15 such people and a placebo to 15 others. The participants then underwent two therapy sessions in which they donned virtual reality goggles and "rode" a glass elevator to progressively higher floors in a virtual hotel—an incredibly scary thing to do if you're terrified of heights! They could also "walk" out on a bridge and look down on a fountain in the hotel lobby. During each session, and again at one-week and three-month follow-up sessions, the participants rated their discomfort at each "floor." Combining the therapy with the drug reduced symptoms far more than combining it with the placebo. Further, in their everyday lives, people who got the drug were less likely than the control subjects to avoid heights.

Genetic differences might explain why some people are more likely than others to become anxious and fearful. In a study done in Sweden, researchers conditioned university students to startle in response to pictures of faces. Only those students who had a particular gene associated with reactivity in the amygdala acquired the conditioned startle response. And those students who carried a gene associated with impaired cognitive control in the prefrontal cortex showed resistance to extinction of the response (Lonsdorf et al., 2009). Such research helps us to understand the biological mechanisms that underlie our innate and conditioned fears.

Accounting for Taste

Classical conditioning can also explain learned reactions to many foods and odors. In the laboratory, researchers have taught animals to dislike foods or

Whether we say "yuck" or "yum" to a food may depend on a past experience involving classical conditioning.

odors by pairing them with drugs that cause nausea or other unpleasant symptoms. One research team trained slugs to associate the smell of carrots, which slugs normally like, with a bitter-tasting chemical they detest. Soon the slugs were avoiding the smell of carrots. The researchers then demonstrated higher-order conditioning by pairing the smell of carrots with the smell of potato. Sure enough, the slugs began to avoid the smell of potato as well (Sahley, Rudy, & Gelperin, 1981).

Many people have learned to dislike a food after eating it and then falling ill, even when the two events were unrelated. The food, previously a neutral stimulus, becomes a conditioned stimulus for nausea or other symptoms produced by the illness. Psychologist Martin Seligman once told how he himself was conditioned to hate béarnaise sauce. One night, shortly after he and his wife ate a delicious filet mignon with béarnaise sauce, he came down with the flu. Naturally, he felt wretched. His misery had nothing to do with the béarnaise sauce, of course, yet the next time he tried it, he found to his annoyance that he disliked the taste (Seligman & Hager, 1972).

Notice that, unlike conditioning in the laboratory, Seligman's aversion to the sauce occurred after only one pairing of the sauce with illness and with a considerable delay between the conditioned and unconditioned stimuli. Moreover, Seligman's wife did not become a conditioned stimulus for nausea, and neither did his dinner plate or the waiter, even though they also had been paired with illness. Why? In earlier work with rats, John Garcia and Robert Koelling (1966) had provided the answer: the existence of a greater biological readiness to associate sickness with taste than with sights or sounds. Like the tendency to acquire certain fears, this biological tendency probably evolved because it enhanced survival. Eating bad food, after all, is more likely to be followed by illness than are sights or sounds.

Psychologists have taken advantage of this phenomenon to develop humane ways of discouraging predators from preying on livestock, using conditioned taste aversions instead of traps and poisons. In one classic study, researchers laced sheep meat with a nausea-inducing chemical. Coyotes and wolves fell for the bait, and as a result they developed a conditioned aversion to sheep (Gustavson et al., 1974). Similar techniques have been used to deter raccoons from killing chickens, and ravens and crows from eating crane eggs (Garcia & Gustavson, 1997).

Reacting to Medical Treatments

Because of classical conditioning, medical treatments can create unexpected misery, because reactions to treatment may generalize to stimuli that are entirely unrelated to the treatment itself. A particular problem for cancer patients is that the nausea and vomiting resulting from chemotherapy often generalize to the place where the therapy takes place, the waiting room, the sound of a nurse's voice, or the smell of rubbing alcohol. The drug treatment is an unconditioned stimulus for nausea and vomiting, and through association, the other previously neutral stimuli become conditioned stimuli for these responses. Even *mental images* of the sights and smells of the clinic can become conditioned stimuli for nausea (Dadds et al., 1997; Redd et al., 1993).

Some cancer patients also acquire a classically conditioned anxiety response to anything associated with their chemotherapy. In one study, patients who drank lemon-lime Kool-Aid before their therapy sessions developed an anxiety response to the drink—an example of higher-order conditioning. They continued to feel anxious even when the drink was offered in their homes rather than at the clinic (Jacobsen et al., 1995).

Conversely, patients may have *reduced* pain and anxiety when they receive *placebos*, pills and injections that have no active ingredients or treatments that have no direct physical effect on the problem. Placebos can be amazingly powerful, especially when they take the form of an injection, a large pill, or a pill with a brand name (Benedetti & Levi-Montalcini, 2001). Why do they work? Biological psychologists have shown that placebos can actually

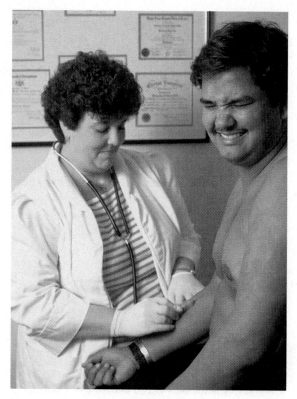

The anxiety that many people feel about having blood drawn can generalize to the nurse, the room, the sight of needles . . . .

affect the brain in much the same way as real treatments do (see Chapter 6). Cognitive psychologists emphasize the role of expectations of getting better, which may reduce anxiety and thus boost the immune system, or simply encourage people to cope better with their symptoms. But behaviorists argue that the doctor's white coat, the doctor's office, and pills or injections all become conditioned stimuli for relief from symptoms because these stimuli have been associated in the past with *real* drugs (Ader, 2000). The real drugs are the unconditioned stimuli, and the relief they bring is the unconditioned response. Placebos acquire the ability to elicit similar reactions, thereby becoming conditioned stimuli.

The expectancy explanation of placebo effects and the classical-conditioning explanation are not mutually exclusive (Kirsch, 2004; Stewart-Williams & Podd, 2004). As we saw earlier, many researchers now accept the view that classical conditioning itself involves the expectation that the conditioned stimulus will be followed by the unconditioned stimulus. Thus, at least some classically conditioned placebo effects may involve the patient's expectations. In fact, the patient's previous conditioning history may be what created those expectations to begin with.

Study and
Review on
mypsychlab.com

Quick Quiz

We hope you have not acquired a classically conditioned fear of quizzes.

A. See whether you can supply the correct term to describe the outcome in each of these situations.

1. After a child learns to fear spiders, he also responds with fear to ants, beetles, and other crawling bugs.

2. A toddler is afraid of the bath, so her father puts just a little water in the tub and gives the child a lollipop to suck on while she is being washed. Soon the little girl loses her fear of the bath.

3. A factory worker's mouth waters whenever a noontime bell signals the beginning of his lunch break. One day, the bell goes haywire and rings every half hour. By the end of the day, the worker has stopped salivating to the bell.

B. A boy who gets weekly allergy shots starts to feel anxious as soon as he enters the doctor's waiting room. What is the behavioral explanation?

Answers:

A. 1. stimulus generalization 2. counterconditioning 3. extinction B. The sight and smells of the waiting room have become a conditioned stimulus for the anxiety and discomfort provoked by the shots.

◆ YOU are about to learn...

• how the consequences of your actions affect your future behavior.

• what praising a child and quitting your nagging have in common.

Operant Conditioning

At the end of the nineteenth century, in the first known scientific study of anger, G. Stanley Hall (1899) asked people to describe angry episodes they had experienced or observed. One person told of a 3-year-old girl who broke out in seemingly uncontrollable sobs when she was kept home from a ride. In the middle of her outburst, the child suddenly stopped and asked her nanny in a perfectly calm voice if her father was in. Told no, and realizing that he was not around to put a stop to her tantrum, she immediately resumed her sobbing.

Children, of course, cry for many valid reasons—pain, discomfort, fear, illness, fatigue—and these cries deserve an adult's sympathy and attention. The child in Hall's study, however, was crying because she had learned from prior experience that an outburst of sobbing would pay off by bringing her attention and possibly the ride she wanted. Her tantrum illustrates one of the most basic laws of learning: *Behavior becomes more likely or less likely depending on its consequences.*

This principle is at the heart of **operant conditioning** (also called *instrumental conditioning*), the second type of conditioning studied by behaviorists.

In classical conditioning, it does not matter whether an animal's or person's behavior has consequences. In Pavlov's procedure, the dog learned an association between two events that were not under its control (e.g., a tone and the delivery of food), and the animal got food whether or not it salivated. But in operant conditioning, the organism's response (such as the little girl's sobbing) *operates* or produces effects on the environment. These effects, in turn, influence whether the response will occur again.

Classical conditioning and operant conditioning also tend to differ in the types of responses they

the neighborhood. Jerry Van Amerongen

STAY OUT

© 1989 Cowles Syndicate, Inc.   10-21

An instantaneous learning experience.

operant conditioning The process by which a response becomes more likely to occur or less so, depending on its consequences.

involve. In classical conditioning, the response is typically reflexive, an automatic reaction to something happening in the environment, such as the sight of food or the sound of a bell. Generally, responses in operant conditioning are complex and are not reflexive—for instance, riding a bicycle, writing a letter, climbing a mountain, . . . or throwing a tantrum.

The Birth of Radical Behaviorism

Operant conditioning has been studied since the start of the twentieth century, although it was not called that until later. Edward Thorndike (1898), then a young doctoral candidate, set the stage by observing cats as they tried to escape from a complex "puzzle box" to reach a scrap of fish located just outside the box. At first, the cat would scratch, bite, or swat at parts of the box in an unorganized way. Then, after a few minutes, it would chance on the successful response (loosening a bolt, pulling a string, or hitting a button) and rush out to get the reward. Placed in the box again, the cat now took a little less time to escape, and after several trials, the animal immediately made the correct response. According to Thorndike, this response had been "stamped in" by the satisfying result of getting the food. In contrast, annoying or unsatisfying results "stamped out" behavior. Behavior, said Thorndike, is controlled by its consequences.

This general principle was elaborated and extended to more complex forms of behavior by B. F. (Burrhus Frederic) Skinner (1904–1990). Skinner called his approach "radical behaviorism" to distinguish it from the behaviorism of John Watson, who emphasized classical conditioning. Skinner argued that to understand behavior we should focus on the external causes of an action and the action's consequences. He avoided terms that Thorndike used, such as "satisfying" and "annoying," which reflect assumptions about what an organism feels and wants. To explain behavior, he said, we should look outside the individual, not inside.

The Consequences of Behavior

In Skinner's analysis, which has inspired an immense body of research, a response ("operant") can be influenced by two types of consequences:

1 **Reinforcement strengthens the response or makes it more likely to recur.** When your dog begs for food at the table, and you give her the lamb chop off your plate, her begging is likely to increase:

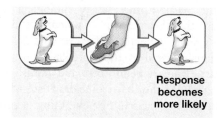

Response becomes more likely

Reinforcers are roughly equivalent to rewards, and many psychologists use *reward* and *reinforcer* as approximate synonyms. However, strict behaviorists avoid the word *reward* because it implies that something has been earned that results in happiness or satisfaction. To a behaviorist, a stimulus is a reinforcer if it strengthens the preceding behavior, whether or not the organism experiences pleasure or a positive emotion. Conversely, no matter how pleasurable a reward is, it is not a reinforcer if it does not increase the likelihood of a response. It's great to get a paycheck, but if you get paid regardless of the effort you put into your work, the money will not reinforce "hard-work behavior."

2 **Punishment weakens the response or makes it less likely to recur.** Any aversive (unpleasant) stimulus or event may be a *punisher*. If your dog begs for a lamb chop off your plate, and you lightly swat her nose and shout "No," her begging is likely to decrease—as long as you don't feel guilty and then give her the lamb chop anyway:

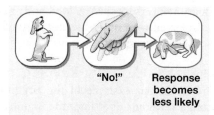

"No!" Response becomes less likely

Parents, employers, and governments resort to reinforcers and punishers all the time—to get kids to behave well, employees to work hard, and constituents to pay taxes—but they do not always use them effectively. Often, they wait too long to deliver the reinforcer or punisher. In general, the sooner a consequence follows a response, the greater its effect; you are likely to respond more reliably when you do not have to wait ages for a grade, a smile, or a compliment. When there is a delay, other responses occur in the interval, and the connection between the desired or undesired response and the consequence may not be made.

reinforcement The process by which a stimulus or event strengthens or increases the probability of the response that it follows.

punishment The process by which a stimulus or event weakens or reduces the probability of the response that it follows.

primary reinforcer A stimulus that is inherently reinforcing, typically satisfying a physiological need; an example is food.

primary punisher A stimulus that is inherently punishing; an example is electric shock.

secondary reinforcer A stimulus that has acquired reinforcing properties through association with other reinforcers.

secondary punisher A stimulus that has acquired punishing properties through association with other punishers.

positive reinforcement A reinforcement procedure in which a response is followed by the presentation of, or increase in intensity of, a reinforcing stimulus; as a result, the response becomes stronger or more likely to occur.

negative reinforcement A reinforcement procedure in which a response is followed by the removal, delay, or decrease in intensity of an unpleasant stimulus; as a result, the response becomes stronger or more likely to occur.

Primary and Secondary Reinforcers and Punishers

Food, water, light stroking of the skin, and a comfortable air temperature are naturally reinforcing because they satisfy biological needs. They are therefore known as **primary reinforcers.** Similarly, pain and extreme heat or cold are inherently punishing and are therefore known as **primary punishers.** Primary reinforcers and punishers can be powerful, but they have some drawbacks, both in real life and in research. For one thing, a primary reinforcer may be ineffective if an animal or person is not in a deprived state; a glass of water is not much of a reward if you just drank three glasses. Also, for obvious ethical reasons, psychologists cannot go around using primary punishers (say, by hitting the people in their study) or taking away primary reinforcers (say, by starving their volunteers).

Fortunately, behavior can be controlled just as effectively by **secondary reinforcers** and **secondary punishers,** which are learned. Money, praise, applause, good grades, awards, and gold stars are common secondary reinforcers. Criticism, demerits, scolding, fines, and bad grades are common secondary punishers. Most behaviorists believe that secondary reinforcers and punishers acquire their ability to influence behavior by being paired with primary reinforcers and punishers. (If that reminds you of classical conditioning, reinforce your excellent thinking with a pat on the head! Indeed, secondary reinforcers and punishers are often called *conditioned* reinforcers and punishers.) As a secondary reinforcer, money has considerable power over most people's behavior because it can be exchanged for primary reinforcers such as food and shelter. It is also associated with other secondary reinforcers, such as praise and respect.

Positive and Negative Reinforcers and Punishers

In our example of the begging dog, something pleasant (getting the lamb chop) followed the dog's begging response, so the response increased. Similarly, if you get a good grade after studying, your efforts to study are likely to continue or increase. This kind of process, in which a pleasant consequence makes a response more likely, is known as **positive reinforcement.** But there is another type of reinforcement, **negative reinforcement,** which involves the *removal* of something *unpleasant.* Negative reinforcement occurs when you *escape* from something aversive or *avoid* it by preventing it from ever occurring. For example, if someone nags you to study but stops nagging when you comply, your studying is likely to increase because you will then avoid the nagging:

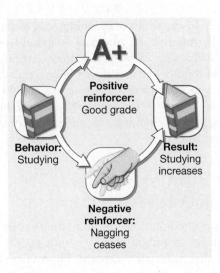

Likewise, negative reinforcement occurs when taking a pill eliminates your pain or when you take a certain route across campus to avoid a rude person.

The positive–negative distinction can also be applied to punishment: Something unpleasant may occur following some behavior (positive punishment), or something *pleasant* may be *removed* (negative punishment). For example, if your friends tease you for being an egghead (positive punishment) or if studying makes you lose time with your friends (negative punishment), you may stop studying:

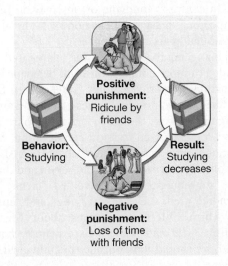

The distinction between positive and negative reinforcement and punishment has been a source of confusion for generations of students, turning many strong minds to mush. You will master these terms more quickly if you understand that "positive" and "negative" have nothing to do with "good" or "bad." They refer to whether something is given or taken away. In the case of reinforcement, think of a positive reinforcer as something that is added or obtained (imagine a plus sign) and a negative reinforcer as avoidance of, or escape from, something unpleasant (imagine a minus sign). *In either case, a response becomes more likely.* Do you recall what happened when Little Albert learned to fear rats through a process of classical conditioning? After he acquired this fear, crawling away was negatively reinforced by escape from the now-fearsome rodent. The negative reinforcement that results from escaping or avoiding something unpleasant explains why so many fears are long-lasting. When you avoid a feared object or situation, you also cut off all opportunities to extinguish your fear.

Understandably, people often confuse negative reinforcement with positive punishment, because both involve an unpleasant stimulus. With punishment, you are subjected to the unpleasant stimulus;

with negative reinforcement, you escape from it or avoid it. To keep these terms straight, remember that punishment, whether positive or negative, *decreases* the likelihood of a response; and reinforcement, whether positive or negative, *increases* it. In real life, punishment and negative reinforcement often go hand in hand. If you use a chain collar to teach your dog to heel, a brief tug on the collar punishes the act of walking; release of the collar negatively reinforces the act of standing by your side.

You can positively reinforce your studying of this material by taking a short break. As you master the material, a decrease in your anxiety will negatively reinforce studying. But we hope you won't punish your efforts by telling yourself "I'll never get it" or "It's too hard"! ((•─Listen

((•─Listen to the **Podcast** on **Punishment and Reinforcement** on **mypsychlab.com**

✓•─**Study** and **Review** on **mypsychlab.com**

Quick Quiz

What kind of consequence will follow if you can't answer these questions?

1. A child nags her father for a cookie; he keeps refusing. Finally, unable to stand the nagging any longer, he hands over the cookie. For him, the ending of the child's pleading is a _____. For the child, the cookie is a _____.

2. An able-bodied driver is careful not to park in a handicapped space anymore after paying a large fine for doing so. The loss of money is a _____.

3. Identify which of the following are commonly used as secondary reinforcers: quarters spilling from a slot machine, a winner's blue ribbon, a piece of candy, an A on an exam, frequent-flyer miles.

4. During late afternoon "happy hours," bars and restaurants sell drinks at a reduced price and appetizers are often free. What undesirable behavior may be rewarded by this practice?

Answers:

1. negative reinforcer; positive reinforcer. 2. punisher—or more precisely, a negative punisher (because something desirable was taken away) 3. All but the candy are secondary reinforcers. 4. One possible answer: The reduced prices, free appetizers, and cheerful atmosphere all reinforce heavy alcohol consumption just before rush hour, thus possibly contributing to binge drinking and drunk driving.

◆ **YOU** are about to learn...

- four important features of operant conditioning.
- why it's not always a good idea to reinforce a response every time it occurs.
- how operant principles help explain superstitious behavior.
- what it means to "shape" behavior.
- some biological limits on operant conditioning.

Principles of Operant Conditioning

Thousands of operant conditioning studies have been done, many using animals. A favorite experimental tool is the *Skinner box,* a chamber equipped with a device that delivers a reinforcer, usually food, when an animal makes a desired response, or a punisher, such as a brief shock, when the animal makes an undesired response (see Figure 9.6). In modern versions, a computer records responses and charts the rate of responding and cumulative responses across time.

Early in his career, Skinner (1938) used the Skinner box for a classic demonstration of operant conditioning. A rat that had previously learned to eat from the pellet-releasing device was placed in the box. The animal proceeded to scurry about the box, sniffing here and there, and randomly touching parts of the floor and walls. Quite by accident, it happened to press a lever mounted on one wall, and immediately a pellet of tasty rat food fell into the food dish. The rat continued its movements and again happened to press the bar, causing another

The Skinner Box
When a rat in a Skinner box presses a bar, a food pellet or drop of water is automatically released. The photo shows Skinner at work on one of the boxes.

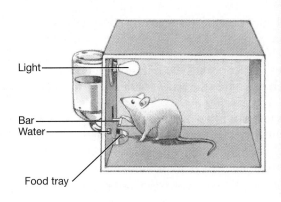

Light

Bar
Water

Food tray

extinction The weakening and eventual disappearance of a learned response; in operant conditioning, it occurs when a response is no longer followed by a reinforcer.

stimulus generalization In operant conditioning, the tendency for a response that has been reinforced (or punished) in the presence of one stimulus to occur (or be suppressed) in the presence of other similar stimuli.

stimulus discrimination In operant conditioning, the tendency of a response to occur in the presence of one stimulus but not in the presence of other, similar stimuli that differ from it on some dimension.

discriminative stimulus A stimulus that signals when a particular response is likely to be followed by a certain type of consequence.

continuous reinforcement A reinforcement schedule in which a particular response is always reinforced.

pellet to fall into the dish. With additional repetitions of bar pressing followed by food, the animal began to behave less randomly and to press the bar more consistently. Eventually, Skinner had the rat pressing the bar as fast as it could.

Extinction In operant conditioning, as in classical, **extinction** is a procedure that causes a previously learned response to stop. In operant conditioning, extinction takes place when the reinforcer that maintained the response is withheld or is no longer available. At first, there may be a spurt of responding, but then the responses gradually taper off and eventually cease. Suppose you put a coin in a vending machine and get nothing back. You may throw in another coin, or perhaps even two, but then you will probably stop trying. The next day, you may put in yet another coin, an example of *spontaneous recovery*. Eventually, however, you will give up on that machine. Your response will have been extinguished.

Stimulus Generalization and Discrimination In operant conditioning, as in classical, **stimulus generalization** may occur. That is, responses may generalize to stimuli that were not present during the original learning situation but resemble the original stimuli in some way; a pigeon that has been trained to peck at a picture of a circle may also peck at a slightly oval figure. But if you wanted to train the bird to discriminate between the two shapes, you would present both the circle and the oval, giving reinforcers whenever the bird pecked at the circle and withholding reinforcers when it pecked at the oval. Eventually, **stimulus discrimination** would occur. Pigeons, in fact, have

learned to make some extraordinary discriminations. They even learned to discriminate between two paintings by different artists, such as Vincent Van Gogh and Marc Chagall (Watanabe, 2001). And then, when presented with a new pair of paintings by those same two artists, they were able to tell the difference between them!

Sometimes an animal or person learns to respond to a stimulus only when some other stimulus, called a **discriminative stimulus**, is present. The discriminative stimulus signals whether a response, if made, will pay off. In a Skinner box containing a pigeon, a light may serve as a discriminative stimulus for pecking at a circle. When the light is on, pecking brings a reward; when it is off, pecking is futile. Human behavior is controlled by many discriminative stimuli, both verbal ("Store hours are 9 to 5") and nonverbal (traffic lights, doorbells, the ring of your cell phone, other people's facial expressions). Learning to respond correctly when such stimuli are present allows us to get through the day efficiently and to get along with others.

Learning on Schedule When a response is first acquired, learning is usually most rapid if the response is reinforced each time it occurs; this procedure is called **continuous reinforcement**. However, once a response has become reliable, it will be more resistant to extinction if it is rewarded on an **intermittent (partial) schedule of reinforcement**, which involves reinforcing only some responses, not all of them. Skinner (1956) happened on this fact when he ran short of food pellets for his rats and was forced to deliver reinforcers less often. (Not all scientific discoveries are planned!) On intermittent schedules, a reinforcer is delivered only after a certain number of responses occur or after a certain amount of time has passed since a response was last reinforced; these patterns affect the rate, form, and timing of behavior. (The details are beyond the scope of this book.)

Intermittent reinforcement helps explain why people often get attached to "lucky" hats, charms, and rituals. A batter pulls his earlobe, gets a home

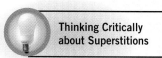
Thinking Critically about Superstitions

run, and from then on always pulls his earlobe before each pitch. A student takes an exam with a purple pen and gets an A, and from then on will not take an exam without a purple pen. Such rituals persist because sometimes they are followed purely coincidentally by a reinforcer—a home run, a good grade—and so they become resistant to extinction.

Skinner (1948/1976) once demonstrated this phenomenon by creating eight "superstitious" pigeons in his laboratory. He rigged the pigeons' cages so that food was delivered every 15 seconds, even if the birds didn't lift a feather. Pigeons are often in motion, so when the food came, each animal was likely to be doing something. That something was then reinforced by delivery of the food. The behavior, of course, was reinforced entirely by chance, but it still became more likely to occur and thus to be reinforced again. Within a short time, six of the pigeons were practicing some sort of consistent ritual: turning in counterclockwise circles, bobbing their heads up and down, or swinging their heads to and fro. None of these activities had the least effect on the delivery of the reinforcer; the birds were behaving "superstitiously," as if they thought their movements were responsible for bringing the food.

Now listen up, because here comes one of the most useful things to know about operant conditioning: If you want a response to persist after it has been learned, you should reinforce it *intermittently*, not continuously. If you are giving Harry, your hamster, a treat every time he pushes a ball with his nose, and then you suddenly stop the reinforcement, Harry will soon stop pushing that ball. Because the change in reinforcement is large, from continuous to none at all, Harry will easily discern the change. But if you have been reinforcing Harry's behavior only every so often, the change will not be so dramatic, and your hungry hamster will keep responding for quite a while. Pigeons, rats, and people on intermittent schedules of reinforcement have responded in the laboratory thousands of times without reinforcement before throwing in the towel, especially when the timing of the reinforcer varies. Animals will sometimes

"Maybe you're right, maybe it won't ward off evil spirits, but maybe it will, and these days who wants to take a chance?"

work so hard for an unpredictable, infrequent bit of food that the energy they expend is greater than that gained from the reward; theoretically, they could actually work themselves to death.

It follows that if you want to get rid of a response, whether it's your own or someone else's, you should be careful *not* to reinforce it intermittently. If you are going to extinguish undesirable behavior by ignoring it—a child's tantrums, a friend's midnight phone calls, a parent's unwanted advice—you must be absolutely consistent in withholding reinforcement (your attention). Otherwise, the other person will learn that if he or she keeps up the screaming, calling, or advice giving long enough, it will eventually be rewarded. One of the most common errors people make is to reward intermittently the very responses that they would like to eliminate.

Shaping   For a response to be reinforced, it must first occur. But suppose you want to train Harry the hamster to pick up a marble, a child to use a knife and fork properly, or a friend to play terrific tennis. Such behaviors, and most others in everyday life, have almost no probability of appearing spontaneously. You could grow old and gray waiting for them to occur so that you could reinforce them. The operant solution is a procedure called **shaping**.

In shaping, you start by reinforcing a tendency in the right direction, and then you gradually require responses that are more and more similar to the final desired response. The responses that you reinforce on the way to the final one are called **successive approximations**. In the case of Harry and the marble, you might deliver a food pellet if the hamster merely turned toward the marble. Once this response was established, you might then reward the hamster for taking a step toward the marble. After that, you could reward him for approaching the marble, then for touching the marble, then for putting both paws on the marble,

intermittent (partial) schedule of reinforcement A reinforcement schedule in which a particular response is sometimes but not always reinforced.

shaping An operant-conditioning procedure in which successive approximations of a desired response are reinforced.

successive approximations In the operant-conditioning procedure of shaping, behaviors that are ordered in terms of increasing similarity or closeness to the desired response.

Simulate Shaping on **mypsychlab.com**

Behavioral techniques such as shaping have many useful applications. Monkeys have been trained to assist their paralyzed owners by opening doors, helping with feeding, and turning the pages of books. Miniature guide horses help blind people navigate city streets and subways. Note the horse's cool protective sneakers!

instinctive drift During operant learning, the tendency for an organism to revert to instinctive behavior.

and finally for holding it. With the achievement of each approximation, the next one would become more likely, making it available for reinforcement.

Using shaping and other techniques, Skinner was able to train pigeons to play Ping-Pong with their beaks and to "bowl" in a miniature alley, complete with a wooden ball and tiny bowling pins. (Skinner had a great sense of humor.) Animal trainers routinely use shaping to teach animals to act as the "eyes" of the blind and to act as the "limbs" of people with spinal cord injuries; these talented companions learn to turn on light switches, open refrigerator doors, and reach for boxes on shelves.

Biological Limits on Learning All principles of operant conditioning, like those of classical conditioning, are limited by an animal's genetic dispositions and physical characteristics; if you try to teach a fish to dance the samba, you're going to get pretty frustrated (and wear out the fish). Operant conditioning procedures always work best when they capitalize on inborn tendencies.

"Why? You cross the road because it's in the script—that's why!"

Years ago, two psychologists who became animal trainers, Keller and Marian Breland (1961), learned what happens when you ignore biological constraints on learning. They found that their animals were having trouble learning tasks that should have been easy. One animal, a pig, was supposed to drop large wooden coins in a box. Instead, the animal would drop the coin, push at it with its snout, throw it in the air, and push at it some more. This odd behavior actually delayed delivery of the reinforcer (food, which is *very* reinforcing to a pig), so it was hard to explain in terms of operant principles. The Brelands finally realized that the pig's rooting instinct—using its snout to uncover and dig up edible roots—was keeping it from learning the task. They called such a reversion to instinctive behavior **instinctive drift**.

In human beings, too, operant learning is affected by genetics, biology, and the evolutionary history of our species. As we saw in Chapter 3, human children are biologically disposed to learn language without much effort, and even young infants appear to have a rudimentary understanding of number (Izard et al., 2009). Further, temperaments and other inborn dispositions may affect how a person responds to reinforcers and punishments. It will be easier to shape belly-dancing behavior if a person is temperamentally disposed to be outgoing and extroverted than if the person is by nature shy.

Skinner: The Man and the Myth

Because of his groundbreaking work on operant conditioning, B. F. Skinner is one of the best known of American psychologists. He is also one of the most misunderstood. Many people (even some psychologists) think that Skinner denied the existence of human consciousness and the value of studying it. In reality, Skinner (1972, 1990) maintained that

Get Involved! Shape Up!

Would you like to improve your study habits? Start exercising? Learn to play a musical instrument? Here are a few guidelines for shaping your own behavior: (1) Set goals that are achievable and specific. "I am going to jog ten minutes and increase the time by five minutes each day" will be far more effective than the vague goal to "get in shape." (2) Track your progress on a graph or in a diary; evidence of progress serves as a secondary reinforcer. (3) Avoid punishing yourself with self-defeating thoughts such as "I'll never be a good student" or "I'm a food addict." (4) Reinforce small improvements (successive approximations) instead of expecting perfection. By the way, a reinforcer does not have to be a thing; it can be something you like to do, like watching a movie. Above all, be patient. New habits are not built in a day.

private internal events—what we call perceptions, emotions, and thoughts—are as real as any others, and we can study them by examining our own sensory responses, the verbal reports of others, and the conditions under which such events occur. But he insisted that thoughts and feelings cannot *explain* behavior. These components of consciousness, he said, are themselves simply behaviors that occur because of reinforcement and punishment.

Skinner aroused strong passions in both his supporters and his detractors. Perhaps the issue that most provoked and angered people was his insistence that free will is an illusion. In contrast to humanist and some religious doctrines that human beings have the power to shape their own destinies, his philosophy promoted the *determinist view* that our actions are determined by our environments and our genetic heritage.

Because Skinner thought the environment should be manipulated to alter behavior, some critics have portrayed him as cold-blooded. One famous controversy regarding Skinner occurred when he invented an enclosed living space, the Air Crib, for his younger daughter Deborah when she was an infant. This "baby box," as it came to be known, had

temperature and humidity controls to eliminate the usual discomforts that babies suffer: heat, cold, wetness, and confinement by blankets and clothing. Skinner believed that to reduce a baby's cries of discomfort and make infant care easier for the parents, you should fix the environment. But people imagined, incorrectly, that the Skinners were leaving their child in the baby box all the time without cuddling and holding her, and rumors circulated for years (and still do from time to time) that she had sued her father, gone insane, or killed herself. Actually, both of Skinner's daughters were cuddled and doted on, loved their parents deeply, and turned out to be successful, perfectly well adjusted adults.

Skinner, who was a kind and mild-mannered man, felt that it would be unethical *not* to try to improve human behavior by applying behavioral principles. And he practiced what he preached, proposing many ways to improve society and reduce human suffering. At the height of public criticism of Skinner's supposedly cold and inhumane approach to understanding behavior, the American Humanist Association recognized his efforts on behalf of humanity by honoring him with its Humanist of the Year Award. ◉─┤Watch

◉─┤**Watch B. F. Skinner Biography** on mypsychlab.com

✓─┤**Study** and **Review** on mypsychlab.com

Quick Quiz

We hope you won't think we're cold or inhumane if we advise you to take this quiz.

In each of the following situations, choose the best alternative and give your reason for choosing it.

1. You want your 2-year-old to ask for water with a word instead of a grunt. Should you give him water when he says "wa-wa" or wait until his pronunciation improves?

2. Your roommate keeps interrupting your studying even though you have asked her to stop. Should you ignore her completely or occasionally respond for the sake of good manners?

3. Your father, who rarely calls you, has finally left a voice-mail message. Should you reply quickly, or wait a while so he will know how it feels to be ignored?

Answers:

1. You should reinforce "wa-wa," an approximation of *water,* because complex behaviors need to be shaped. 2. From a behavioral view, you should ignore her completely because intermittent reinforcement (attention) could cause her interruptions to persist. 3. If you want to encourage communication, you should reply quickly because immediate reinforcement is more effective than delayed reinforcement.

YOU are about to learn...

- how the use of operant principles through behavior modification is being applied to many real-world problems.

- when punishment works in real life and why it often does not.

- some effective alternatives to punishment.

- how reinforcement can be misused.

- why paying children for good grades sometimes backfires.

Operant Conditioning in Real Life

Operant principles can clear up many mysteries about why people behave as they do. They can also explain why people have trouble changing when they want to, in spite of all the motivational seminars they attend or resolutions they make. If life remains full of the same old reinforcers, punishers, and discriminative stimuli (a grumpy boss, an unresponsive roommate, a refrigerator stocked with high-fat goodies), any new responses that have been acquired may fail to generalize.

To help people change unwanted, dangerous, or self-defeating habits, behaviorists have carried operant principles out of the laboratory and into the wider world of the classroom, athletic field, prison, mental hospital, nursing home, rehabilitation ward, child care center, factory, and office. The use of operant techniques in such real-world settings is called **behavior modification** (also known as *applied behavior analysis*).

Behavior modification has had some enormous successes (Kazdin, 2001; Martin & Pear, 2007). Behaviorists have taught parents how to toilet train their children in only a few sessions. They have trained disturbed and intellectually impaired adults to communicate, dress themselves, mingle socially with others, and earn a living. They have taught brain-damaged patients to control inappropriate behavior, focus their attention, and improve their language abilities. They have helped autistic children improve their social and language skills. And they have helped ordinary folk get rid of unwanted habits, such as smoking and nail biting, or acquire desired ones, such as practicing the piano or studying.

Yet when nonpsychologists try to apply the principles of conditioning to commonplace problems without thoroughly understanding those principles, their efforts sometimes miss the mark, as we are about to see.

behavior modification The application of operant conditioning techniques to teach new responses or to reduce or eliminate maladaptive or problematic behavior; also called *applied behavior analysis*.

The Pros and Cons of Punishment

In a novel called *Walden Two* (1948/1976), Skinner imagined a utopia in which reinforcers were used so wisely that undesirable behavior was rare. Unfortunately, we do not live in a utopia; bad habits and antisocial acts abound.

Punishment might seem to be an obvious solution. Almost all Western countries have banned the physical punishment of schoolchildren by principals and teachers, but many American states still permit it for disruptiveness, vandalism, and other misbehavior. The United States is also far more likely than any other developed country to jail its citizens for nonviolent crimes such as drug use, and to enact the ultimate punishment—the death penalty—for violent crimes. And, of course, in their relationships, people punish one another frequently by yelling, scolding, and sulking. Does all this punishment work?

When Punishment Works   Sometimes punishment is unquestionably effective. For example, punishment can deter some young criminals from repeating their offenses. A study of the criminal records of all Danish men born between 1944 and 1947 (nearly 29,000 men) examined repeat arrests (recidivism) through age 26 (Brennan & Mednick, 1994). After any given arrest, punishment reduced rates of subsequent arrests for both minor and serious crimes, though recidivism still remained fairly high. Contrary to the researchers' expectations, however, the severity of punishment made no difference: Fines and probation were about as effective as jail time. What mattered most was the *consistency* of the punishment. This is understandable in behavioral terms: When lawbreakers sometimes get away with their crimes, their behavior is intermittently reinforced and therefore becomes resistant to extinction.

Unfortunately, that is often the situation in the United States. Young offenders are punished less consistently than in Denmark, in part because prosecutors, juries, and judges do not want to condemn them to mandatory prison terms. This helps to explain why harsh sentencing laws and simplistic efforts to crack down on wrongdoers often fail or even backfire. Because many things influence crime rates—the proportion of young versus older people in the population, poverty levels, drug policies, discriminatory arrest patterns—the relationship

> **Thinking Critically about Punishment**

between incarceration rates and crime rates in the United States varies considerably from state to state (King, Maurer, & Young, 2005). But international surveys find that, overall, the United States has a high rate of violent crime compared to many other industrialized countries, in spite of its extremely high incarceration rates.

When Punishment Fails   What about punishment that occurs every day in families, schools, and workplaces? Laboratory and field studies find that it, too, often fails, for several reasons:

1 **People often administer punishment inappropriately or mindlessly.** They swing in a blind rage or shout things they don't mean, use harsh methods with toddlers, apply punishment so broadly that it covers all sorts of irrelevant behaviors, or misunderstand the proper application of punishment. One student told us his parents used to punish their children before leaving them alone for the evening because of all the naughty things they were *going* to do. Naturally, the children did not bother to behave like angels.

2 **The recipient of harsh or frequent punishment often responds with anxiety, fear, or rage.** Through a process of classical conditioning, these emotional side effects may then generalize to the entire situation in which the punishment occurs—the place, the person delivering the punishment, and the circumstances. These negative emotional reactions can create more problems than the punishment solves. A teenager who has been severely punished may strike back or run away. A spouse who is constantly insulted, belittled, and criticized will feel bitter and resentful and is likely to retaliate with small acts of hostility. And extreme punishment—physical abuse—is a risk factor, especially in children, for the development of depression, low self-esteem, violent behavior, and many other problems (Gershoff, 2002; Widom, DuMont, & Czaja, 2007).

3 **The effectiveness of punishment is often temporary, depending heavily on the presence of the punishing person or circumstances.** All of us can probably remember some transgressions of childhood that we never dared commit when our parents were around but that we promptly resumed as soon as they were gone and reinforcers were once again available. All we learned was not to get caught.

4 **Most misbehavior is hard to punish immediately.** Punishment, like reward, works best if it quickly follows a response. But outside the laboratory,

As we all know, people often do things they're not supposed to. Have you ever wondered why so many people ignore warnings and threats of punishment?

rapid punishment is often hard to achieve, and during the delay, the behavior may be reinforced many times. If you punish your dog when you get home for getting into the doggie biscuits and eating them all up, the punishment will not do any good because you are too late: Your pet's misbehavior has already been reinforced by all those delicious treats.

5 **Punishment conveys little information.** It may tell the recipient what *not* to do, but it does not communicate what the person (or animal) *should* do. Spanking a toddler for messing in her pants will not teach her to use the potty chair, and scolding a student for learning slowly will not teach him to learn more quickly.

6 **An action intended to punish may instead be reinforcing because it brings attention.** Indeed, in some cases, angry attention may be just what the offender is after. If a mother yells at a child who is throwing a tantrum, the very act of yelling may give him what he wants: a reaction from her. In the schoolroom, teachers who scold children in front of other students, thus putting them in the limelight, may unwittingly reward the very misbehavior they are trying to eliminate.

Because of these drawbacks, most psychologists believe that punishment, especially when it's severe, is a poor way to eliminate unwanted behavior. In special cases, as when mentally disabled children are in immediate danger of seriously injuring themselves or a school bully is about to beat up a classmate, temporary physical restraint may be necessary. But even then, alternatives are often available. School programs have successfully reduced school violence by teaching kids problem-solving skills, emotional control, and conflict resolution, and by rewarding good behavior (Hahn et al., 2008; Wilson & Lipsey, 2007). And in some cases, the

Many harried parents habitually resort to physical punishment without being aware of its many negative consequences. Based on your reading of this chapter, what alternatives does this parent have?

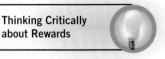

best way to discourage a behavior—a child's nagging for a cookie before dinner, a roommate's interruptions when you're studying—is to extinguish it by ignoring it.

Of course, ignoring a behavior requires patience and is not always feasible. A dog owner who ignores Fido's backyard barking may soon hear "barking" of another sort from the neighbors. A parent whose child is a video-game addict cannot ignore the behavior because playing video games is rewarding to the child. One solution: Combine extinction of undesirable acts with reinforcement of alternative ones. The parent of a video-game addict might ignore the child's pleas for "just one more game" and at the same time praise the child for doing something else that is incompatible with video-game playing, such as reading or playing basketball.

Finally, when punishment must be applied, these guidelines should be kept in mind: (1) It should not involve physical abuse; instead, parents can use time-outs and loss of privileges (negative punishers); (2) it should be consistent; (3) it should be accompanied by information about the kind of behavior that would be appropriate; and (4) it should be followed, whenever possible, by the reinforcement of desirable behavior.

The Problems with Reward

So far, we have been praising the virtues of praise and other reinforcers. But like punishers, rewards do not always work as expected. Let's look at two complications that arise when people try to use them.

Misuse of Rewards   Suppose you are a fourth grade teacher, and a student has just turned in a paper full of grammatical and punctuation errors. This child has little self-confidence and is easily discouraged. What should you do? Many people think you should give the paper a high mark anyway, to bolster the child's self-esteem. Teachers everywhere are handing out lavish praise, happy-face stickers, and high grades in hopes that students' performance will improve as they learn to "feel good about themselves." Scientifically speaking, however, there are two things wrong with this approach. First, study after study finds that high self-esteem does not improve academic performance (Baumeister et al.,

2003). Second, genuine self-esteem emerges from effort, persistence, and the gradual acquisition of skills. It is nurtured by a teacher's honest appreciation of the content of a student's work combined with constructive feedback on how to correct mistakes or fix weaknesses (Damon, 1995).

One obvious result of the misuse of rewards in schools has been grade inflation at all levels of education. In many colleges and universities, Cs, which once meant average or satisfactory, are nearly extinct. One study found that a third of college students expected Bs just for showing up to class, and 40 percent felt they were entitled to a B merely for doing the required reading (Greenberger et al., 2008). We have talked to students who feel that hard work should even be enough for an A. If you yourself have benefited from grade inflation, you may feel it's a good thing—but remember that critical thinking requires us to separate feelings from facts! The problem is that rewards, including grades, serve as effective reinforcers only when they are tied to the behavior one is trying to increase, not when they are dispensed indiscriminately. Getting a good grade for "showing-up-in-class behavior" reinforces going to class, but not necessarily for learning much once you are there. Would you want to be treated by a doctor, represented by a lawyer, or have your taxes done by an accountant who got through school just by showing up for class?

Why Rewards Can Backfire   Most of our examples of operant conditioning have involved **extrinsic reinforcers**, which come from an outside source and are not inherently related to the activity being reinforced. Money, praise, gold stars, applause, hugs, and thumbs-up signs are all extrinsic reinforcers. But people (and probably some other animals as well) also work for **intrinsic reinforcers**, such as enjoyment of the task and the satisfaction of accomplishment. As psychologists have applied operant conditioning in real-world settings, they have found that extrinsic reinforcement sometimes becomes too much of a good thing: If you focus on it exclusively, it can kill the pleasure of doing something for its own sake.

Consider what happened in a classic study of how praise affects children's intrinsic motivation (Lepper, Greene, & Nisbett, 1973). Researchers gave nursery school children the chance to draw with felt-tipped pens during free play and recorded how long each child spontaneously played with the pens. The children clearly enjoyed this activity. Then the researchers told some of the children that

extrinsic reinforcers
Reinforcers that are not inherently related to the activity being reinforced.

intrinsic reinforcers
Reinforcers that are inherently related to the activity being reinforced.

if they would draw with felt-tipped pens they would get a "Good Player Award," complete with gold seal and red ribbon. After drawing for six minutes, each child got the award as promised. Other children did not expect an award and were not given one. A week later, the researchers again observed the children's free play. Those children who had expected and received an award spent much less time with the pens than they had before the start of the experiment. In contrast, children who had neither expected nor received an award continued to show as much interest in playing with the pens as they had initially, as you can see in Figure 9.7. Similar results have occurred in other studies when children have been offered a reward for doing something they already enjoy.

Why should extrinsic rewards undermine the pleasure of doing something for its own sake? The researchers who did the felt-tipped pen study suggested that when we are paid for an activity, we interpret it as work. We see our actions as the result of external factors instead of our own interests, skills, and efforts. It is as if we say to ourselves, "Since I'm being paid, it must be something I wouldn't do if I didn't have to." Then, when the reward is withdrawn, we refuse to "work" any longer. Another possibility is that we tend to regard extrinsic rewards as controlling, so they make us feel pressured and reduce our sense of autonomy and choice ("I guess I have to do what I'm told to do, but *only* what I'm told to do") (Deci et al., 1999). A third, more

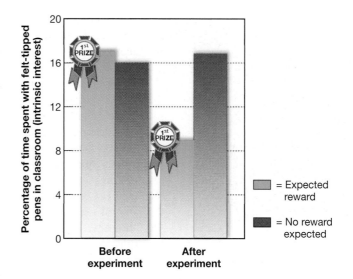

FIGURE 9.7
Turning Play into Work
Extrinsic rewards can sometimes reduce the intrinsic pleasure of an activity. When preschoolers were promised a prize for drawing with felt-tipped pens, the behavior temporarily increased. But after they got their prizes, they spent less time with the pens than they had before the study began.

behavioral explanation is that extrinsic reinforcement sometimes raises the rate of responding above some optimal, enjoyable level, such as by causing the children in the felt-tipped-pen study to play with the pens longer than they would have on their

Get Involved! What's Reinforcing Your Behavior?

For each activity that you do, indicate whether the reinforcers controlling your behavior are primarily extrinsic or intrinsic.

Activity	Reinforcers mostly extrinsic	Reinforcers mostly intrinsic	Reinforcers about equally extrinsic and intrinsic
Studying	_____	_____	_____
Housework	_____	_____	_____
Worship	_____	_____	_____
Grooming	_____	_____	_____
Job	_____	_____	_____
Dating	_____	_____	_____
Attending class	_____	_____	_____
Reading unrelated to school	_____	_____	_____
Sports	_____	_____	_____
Cooking	_____	_____	_____

Is there an area of your life in which you would like intrinsic reinforcement to play a larger role? What can you do to make that happen?

"That is the correct answer, Billy, but I'm afraid you don't win anything for it."

own. Then the activity really does become work.

Findings on extrinsic versus intrinsic reinforcements have wide-ranging implications. Economists have shown that financial rewards can undermine ethical and moral norms like honesty, hard work, and fairness toward others, and can decrease people's willingness to contribute to the common good (e.g., by paying taxes and giving to charity). In other words, an emphasis solely on money encourages selfishness (Bowles, 2008).

We must be careful, however, not to oversimplify this issue. The effects of extrinsic rewards depend on many factors, including a person's initial motivation, the context in which rewards are achieved, and in the case of praise, the sincerity of the praiser (Henderlong & Lepper, 2002). If you get praise, money, a high grade, or a trophy for doing a task *well*, for achieving a certain level of performance, or for improving your performance rather than for just doing the task, your intrinsic motivation is not likely to decline. In fact, it may increase (Cameron, Banko, & Pierce, 2001; Pierce et al., 2003). Such rewards are apt to make you feel competent rather than controlled. And if you have always been crazy about reading or about playing the banjo, you will keep reading or playing even when you do not happen to be getting a grade or applause for doing so. In such cases, you will probably attribute your continued involvement in the activity to your own intrinsic interests and motivation rather than to the reward.

So what is the take-home message about extrinsic rewards? First, they are often useful or necessary: Few people would trudge off to work every morning if they never got paid; and in the classroom, teachers may need to offer incentives to unmotivated students. But extrinsic rewards should be used carefully and should not be overdone, so that intrinsic pleasure in an activity can blossom. Educators, employers, and policy makers can avoid the trap of either–or thinking by recognizing that most people do their best when they get tangible rewards for real achievement *and* when they have interesting, challenging, and varied kinds of work to do.

Quick Quiz

Is the art of mastering quizzes intrinsically reinforcing yet?

A. According to behavioral principles, what is happening here?

1. An adolescent whose parents have hit him for minor transgressions since he was small runs away from home.

2. A young woman whose parents paid her to clean her room while she was growing up is a slob when she moves to her own apartment.

3. Two parents scold their young daughter every time they catch her sucking her thumb. The thumb sucking continues anyway.

B. In cities across America, public school systems are rewarding students for perfect attendance by giving them money, shopping sprees, laptops, and video games. What are the pros and cons of such practices?

Answers:

A. 1. The physical punishment was painful, and through a process of classical conditioning, the situation in which it occurred also became unpleasant. Because escape from an unpleasant stimulus is negatively reinforcing, the boy ran away. **2.** Extrinsic reinforcers are no longer available, and room-cleaning behavior has been extinguished. Also, extrinsic rewards may have displaced the intrinsic satisfaction of having a tidy room. **3.** Punishment has failed, possibly because it rewards thumb sucking with attention or because thumb sucking still brings the child pleasure whenever the parents are not around. **B.** The rewards may improve attendance (they have in some schools), and students who attend more regularly may become more interested in their studies and do better in school. But extrinsic rewards can also decrease intrinsic motivation, and when they are withdrawn (e.g., when the student goes to another school or to college), attendance may plummet ("If there's no reward, why should I attend?"). Further, students may come to expect bigger and bigger rewards, upping the ante. In some schools, especially those that have deemphasized penalties for *poor* attendance, the rewards have backfired and attendance has actually fallen.

YOU are about to learn...

- how you can learn something without any obvious reinforcement.

- why two people can learn different lessons from exactly the same experience.

- how we often learn not by doing but by watching.

Learning and the Mind

For half a century, most American learning theories held that learning could be explained by specifying the behavioral ABCs: *antecedents* (events preceding behavior), *behaviors*, and *consequences*. Behaviorists liked to compare the mind to an engineer's hypothetical "black box," a device whose workings must be inferred because they cannot be observed directly. To them, the box contained irrelevant wiring; it was enough to know that pushing a button on the box would produce a predictable response. But even as early as the 1930s, a few behaviorists could not resist peeking into that black box.

Latent Learning

Behaviorist Edward Tolman (1938) committed virtual heresy at the time by noting that his rats, when pausing at turning points in a maze, seemed to be *deciding* which way to go. Moreover, the animals sometimes seemed to be learning even without any reinforcement. What, he wondered, was going on in their little rat brains that might account for this puzzle?

In a classic experiment, Tolman and C. H. Honzik (1930) placed three groups of rats in mazes and observed their behavior daily for more than two weeks. The rats in Group 1 always found food at the end of the maze and quickly learned to find it without going down blind alleys. The rats in Group 2 never found food and, as you would expect, they followed no particular route. Group 3 was the interesting group. These rats found no food for ten days and seemed to wander aimlessly, but on the eleventh day they received food, and then they quickly learned to run to the end of the maze. By the following day, they were doing as well as Group 1, which had been rewarded from the beginning (see Figure 9.8).

Group 3 had demonstrated **latent learning**, learning that is not immediately expressed in performance. A great deal of human learning also remains latent until circumstances allow or require it to be expressed. A driver gets out of a traffic jam

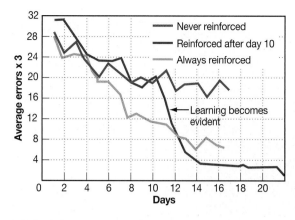

FIGURE 9.8

Latent Learning

In a classic experiment, rats that always found food in a maze made fewer and fewer errors in reaching the food (green curve). In contrast, rats that received no food showed little improvement (blue curve). But rats that got no food for ten days and then found food on the eleventh day showed rapid improvement from then on (red curve). This result suggests that learning involves cognitive changes that can occur in the absence of reinforcement and that may not be acted on until a reinforcer becomes available (Tolman & Honzik, 1930).

and finds her way to Fourth and Kumquat Streets using a route she has never used before (without GPS!). A little boy observes a parent setting the table or tightening a screw but does not act on this learning for years; then he finds he knows how to do these things.

Latent learning raises questions about what, exactly, is learned during operant learning. In the Tolman and Honzik study, the rats that did not get any food until the eleventh day seemed to have acquired a mental representation of the maze. They had been learning the whole time; they simply had no reason to act on that learning until they began to find food. Similarly, the driver taking a new route can do so because she already knows how the city is laid out. What seems to be acquired in latent learning, therefore, is not a specific response, but *knowledge* about responses and their consequences. We learn how the world is organized, which paths lead to which places, and which actions can produce which payoffs. This knowledge permits us to be creative and flexible in reaching our goals.

Social-Cognitive Learning Theories

During the 1960s and 1970s, many learning theorists concluded that human behavior could not be understood without taking into account the human

latent learning A form of learning that is not immediately expressed in an overt response; it occurs without obvious reinforcement.

Social-cognitive theorists emphasize the influence of thoughts and perceptions on behavior (at least in humans).

social-cognitive theories Theories that emphasize how behavior is learned and maintained through observation and imitation of others, positive consequences, and cognitive processes such as plans, expectations, and beliefs.

observational learning A process in which an individual learns new responses by observing the behavior of another (a model) rather than through direct experience; sometimes called *vicarious conditioning*.

capacity for higher-level cognitive processes. They agreed with behaviorists that human beings, along with the rat and the rabbit, are subject to the laws of operant and classical conditioning. But they added that human beings, unlike the rat or the rabbit, are full of attitudes, beliefs, and expectations that affect the way they acquire information, make decisions, reason, and solve problems. This view became very influential.

We will use the term **social-cognitive theories** for all theories that combine behavioral principles with cognitive ones to explain behavior (Bandura, 1986; Mischel, 1973; Mischel & Shoda, 1995). These theories share an emphasis on the importance of beliefs, perceptions, and observations of other peoples' behavior in determining what we learn, what we do at any given moment, and the personality traits we develop (see Chapter 2). To a social-cognitive theorist, differences in beliefs and perceptions help explain why two people who live through the same event may come away with entirely different lessons from it (Bandura, 2001). All siblings know this. One sibling may regard being grounded by their father as evidence of his all-around meanness, whereas another may see the same behavior as evidence of his care and concern for his children. For these siblings, being grounded is likely to affect their behavior very differently.

Learning by Observing Late one night, a friend living in a rural area was awakened by a loud clattering noise. A raccoon had knocked over a "raccoon-proof" garbage can and seemed to be demonstrating to an assembly of other raccoons how to open it: If you jump up and down on the can's side, the lid will pop off. According to our friend, the observing raccoons learned from this episode how to open stubborn garbage cans, and the observing humans learned how smart raccoons can be. In short, they all benefited from **observational learning**: learning by watching what others do and what happens to them for doing it.

The behavior learned by the raccoons through observation was an operant one, but observational learning also plays an important role in the acquisition of automatic, reflexive responses, such as fears and phobias (Mineka & Zinbarg, 2006; Olsson & Phelps, 2004). Thus, in addition to learning to be frightened of rats directly through classical conditioning, as Little Albert did, you might also learn to fear rats by observing the emotional expressions of other people when they see or touch one. The perception of someone else's reaction serves as an unconditioned stimulus for your own fear, and the learning that results may be as strong as it would be if you had had a direct encounter with the rat yourself. Children often learn to fear things in this way, for example, by observing a parent's fearful reaction whenever a dog approaches. Adults can acquire fears even by watching suspenseful movies. After seeing the classic horror film *Psycho*, in which a character is knifed to death in a shower, some viewers became nervous about taking a shower. Similarly, after seeing *Jaws*, with its horrific scenes of shark attacks and its gripping music, some people became afraid to swim in the ocean.

Like father, like daughter. Observational learning starts early.

Behaviorists refer to observational learning as *vicarious conditioning*, and believe it can be explained in stimulus–response terms. But social-cognitive theorists believe that observational learning in human beings cannot be fully understood without taking into account the thought processes of the learner (Meltzoff & Gopnik, 1993). They emphasize the knowledge that results when a person sees a *model*—another person—behaving in certain ways and experiencing the consequences (Bandura, 1977).

None of us would last long without observational learning. Learning would be both inefficient and dangerous. We would have to learn to avoid oncoming cars by walking into traffic and suffering the consequences, or learn to swim by jumping into a deep pool and flailing around. Parents and teachers would be busy 24 hours a day shaping children's behavior. Bosses would have to stand over their employees' desks, rewarding every little link in the complex behavioral chains we call typing, report writing, and accounting. But observational learning has its dark side as well. People often imitate antisocial or unethical actions (they observe a friend cheating and decide they can get away with it too) or self-defeating and harmful ones (they watch a film star smoking and take up the habit in an effort to look just as cool).

Many years ago, Albert Bandura and his colleagues showed just how important observational learning is for children who are learning the rules of social behavior (Bandura, Ross, & Ross, 1963). The researchers had nursery school children watch a short film of two men, Rocky and Johnny, playing with toys. (Apparently the children did not think this behavior was the least bit odd.) In the film, Johnny refuses to share his toys, and Rocky responds by clobbering him. Rocky's aggressive actions are rewarded because he winds up with all the toys. Poor Johnny sits dejectedly in the corner, while Rocky marches off with a sack full of loot and a hobbyhorse under his arm.

After viewing the film, each child was left alone for 20 minutes in a playroom full of toys, including some of the items shown in the film. Watching through a one-way mirror, the researchers found that the children were much more aggressive in their play than a control group that had not seen the film. Some children imitated Rocky almost exactly. At the end of the session, one little girl even asked the experimenter for a sack! ✱⎡Explore

Of course, people imitate positive activities that they observe, too. Matt Groening, the creator of the cartoon show *The Simpsons*, decided it would be funny if the Simpsons' 8-year-old daughter Lisa played the baritone sax. Sure enough, little girls across the country began imitating her. Cynthia Sikes, a saxophone teacher in New York, told *The New York Times*, "When the show started, I got an influx of girls coming up to me saying, 'I want to play the saxophone because Lisa Simpson plays the saxophone.'"

Findings on latent learning, observational learning, and the role of cognition in learning can help us evaluate arguments in the passionate debate about the effects of media violence. Children and teenagers in America and many other countries see countless acts of violence on television, in films, and in video games. Does all this mayhem of blood and guts affect them? Do you think it has affected *you*? In "Taking Psychology with You," we offer evidence that bears on these questions, and suggest ways of resolving them without oversimplifying the issues.

✱⎡Explore
Bandura's Study on Observational Learning on mypsychlab.com

✓•⎡**Study** and **Review** on **mypsychlab.com**

Quick Quiz

Does your perception of quizzes make you eager to answer them?

1. A friend asks you to meet her at a new restaurant across town. You have never been to this specific address, but you find your way there anyway because you have experienced _____ learning.

2. To a social-cognitive theorist, the fact that we can learn without being reinforced for any obvious responses shows that we do not learn specific responses but rather _____.

3. After watching her teenage sister put on lipstick, a little girl takes a lipstick and applies it to her own lips. She has acquired this behavior through a process of _____.

Answers:

1. latent 2. knowledge about responses and their consequences 3. observational learning

Psychology in the News

First Grader Suspended Over Camping Utensil

Zachary Christie with the camping utensil that got him in trouble.

H ow can the behavioral and social-cognitive learning principles covered in this chapter help us think about our opening story, in which Zachary Christie was expelled for carrying a camping utensil to school?

As we've seen, findings on learning do not rule out all use of punishment when children misbehave. Certainly, when children or teenagers bring weapons to school, authorities cannot simply ignore the behavior in hopes of extinguishing it; they have an obligation to protect the other students. But when severe penalties are imposed inappropriately for minor infractions, as in Zachary's case, punishment can make the recipient feel betrayed and angry at the injustice of it. As Zachary said, "It just seems unfair." Social-cognitive theorists remind us that human beings, including children, bring their minds to their experiences, and if they perceive a punishment for breaking a rule as being undeserved or overly harsh, they may continue to break that rule as an act of defiance. Undeserved severe punishment may also bring attention from peers, with the same result—defiance and persistence.

Fortunately, in Zachary's case, school district officials realized the inappropriateness of their rigid zero-tolerance policy, and reversed themselves the very next day. Recognizing the importance of taking age into account, the school board voted to reduce the punishment for kindergartners and first graders to a suspension ranging from three to five days, and 6-year-old Zachary got a reprieve. Zachary's mother thanked the board, but noted that it was only the first step toward making necessary changes in the district's code of conduct.

What about punishment of children at home? Some psychologists believe that occasional, moderate punishment, even spanking, has no long-term detrimental outcomes for most middle-class children, so long as it occurs in an otherwise loving context or as a last resort (Baumrind, Larzelere, & Cowan, 2002). But, as we saw, punishment does not teach the child *good* behavior, and has all the drawbacks listed in this chapter. And when parents insult, humiliate, or ridicule a child, the results are often devastating. Humiliation and shame can last for years.

What, then, should parents and teachers do when a child's behavior is seriously disruptive or dangerous? First, from a learning perspective, other punishments (time-outs, loss of privileges, and so forth) are preferable to physical punishment, as long as the adult is consistent (no intermittent reinforcement of bad behavior!), applies the punishment as soon as possible after the behavior occurs, and, most important, remembers to reinforce successive approximations toward desirable behavior. It is also important to know *why* a child is misbehaving: Is the child angry, worried, or frightened? Parents and teachers can help children identify their feelings while teaching them how to control their emotions and find nonaggressive, constructive ways to resolve conflicts. In this way, they can learn that they are being punished not for feeling bad, but for acting inappropriately or harming others: "It is all right to be upset but not to hit or bite."

Finally, a learning theorist would emphasize the role of the environment in causing or maintaining a child's misbehavior. Is the child bored? Does the child have trouble keeping still in the controlled environment of a classroom? From a learning perspective, it may be more effective to change the child's environment than the child, for example by instituting more breaks for physical activities.

Skinner himself never wavered in his determination to apply learning principles to fashion better, healthier environments for everyone. In 1990, just a week before his death, ailing and frail, he addressed an overflow crowd at the annual meeting of the American Psychological Association, making the case one last time for the approach he was convinced could create a better society. When you see the world as the learning theorist views it, Skinner was saying, you see the folly of human behavior, but you also see the possibility of improving it.

Does Media Violence Make You Violent?

In a $5 billion lawsuit against video-game manufacturers, the families of victims shot by two fellow students at a high school claimed that the tragedy would never have happened had the killers not played video games that were full of violence and bloodshed. When another gunman went on a murderous rampage at a university, several commentators immediately assumed that video games must have spurred him to kill. How should we evaluate such claims? Does violence depicted in films, on TV, and in video games lead to violent crime?

Psychologists are strongly divided in their answers to this question. As one group of researchers concluded, "Research on violent television and films, video games, and music reveals unequivocal evidence that media violence increases the likelihood of aggressive and violent behavior," both in the short term and long term (Anderson et al., 2003). Their meta-analyses find that the greater the exposure to violence in movies and on television, the stronger the likelihood of a person's behaving aggressively, and this correlation holds for both sexes and across cultures, from Japan to England (Anderson et al., 2010). Video games that directly reward violence, as by awarding points or moving the player to the next level after a "kill," increase feelings of hostility, aggressive thinking, and aggressive behavior (Carnagey & Anderson, 2005). Moreover, when grade school children cut back on time spent watching TV or playing violent video games, the children's aggressiveness declines (Robinson et al., 2001).

Violent media may also desensitize people to the pain or distress of others. In a field study, people who had just seen a violent movie took longer to come to the aid of a woman struggling to pick up her crutches than did people who had seen a nonviolent movie or people still waiting to see one of the two movies (Bushman & Anderson, 2009).

However, an opposing group of psychologists believes that the effects of video games have been exaggerated and sensationalized (Ferguson & Kilburn, 2010). The correlation between playing violent video games and behaving aggressively is, they maintain, too small to worry about (Ferguson, 2007; Sherry, 2001). Other factors that are correlated with violent criminality are far more powerful; they include genetic influences (.75), perceptions of criminal opportunity (.58), owning a gun (.35), poverty (.25), and childhood physical abuse (.22). In these researchers' calculations, watching violent video games has the lowest correlation, only .04 (Ferguson, 2009; Ferguson & Kilburn, 2010). Besides, they observe, rates of teenage violence *declined* significantly throughout the 1990s, a period in which the number of violent video games was *increasing* astronomically.

In the social-cognitive view, both conclusions about the relationship of media violence to violent behavior have merit. Repeated acts of aggression in the media *do* model behavior and responses to conflict that a few people may imitate, just as media ads influence what many people buy and what many people think the ideal male or female body should look like. However, children and teens watch many different programs and movies and have many models to observe besides those they see in the media, including parents and peers. For every teenager who is obsessed with playing *Resident Evil* and who entertains grim fantasies of blowing up the world, hundreds more think the game is just plain fun and then go off to do their homework.

Moreover, perceptions and interpretations of events, personality dispositions such as aggressiveness and sociability, and the social context in which the violence is viewed can all affect how a person responds (Feshbach & Tangney, 2008). One person may learn from seeing people being blown away in a film that violence is cool and masculine; another may decide that the violent images are ugly and stupid; a third may conclude that they don't mean anything at all, that they are just part of the story.

What should be done, if anything, about media violence? Even if only a small percentage of viewers learn to be aggressive from observing all that violence, the social consequences can be serious, because the total audiences for TV, movies, and video games are immense. But censorship, which some people think is the answer, brings its own set of problems, quite apart from constitutional issues of free speech: Should we ban *Hamlet*? Bloody graphic comics? Funny martial arts films? Special-effects action films where the bad guys get blown to bits? Films that truthfully depict the realities of war, murder, and torture?

Consider, too, that it's not just video games and other visual media that can increase aggression. In two studies, students read a violent passage from the Bible, with two sentences inserted in which God sanctions the violence. Later, in what they thought was a different study, they played a competitive reaction-time game with a partner. In the game, they were more willing to blast their competitor with a loud noise than were students who had been told the violent passage was from an ancient scroll or students who had read a passage that did not mention God (Bushman et al., 2007). Participants who believed in God were most affected by the passage in which God condones the violence, but many nonbelievers were affected too. Although the general message of the scriptures is one of peace and reconciliation, the Bible is also full of violence, some of it sanctioned by God. Yet few people would be willing to ban the Bible or censure its violent parts.

As you can see, determining a fair and equitable policy regarding media violence will not be easy. It will demand good evidence—and good thinking.

Does playing violent video games make children and teenagers more aggressive? The answer is more complicated than "yes" or "no."

Summary ((•—[**Listen** to an **audio file** of your chapter on **mypsychlab.com**

● Research on *learning* has been heavily influenced by *behaviorism*, which accounts for behavior in terms of observable events without reference to mental entities such as "mind" or "will." Behaviorists have focused on two types of *conditioning*: classical and operant.

Classical Conditioning

● *Classical conditioning* was first studied by Russian physiologist Ivan Pavlov. In this type of learning, when a neutral stimulus is paired with an *unconditioned stimulus* (*US*) that elicits some reflexive *unconditioned response* (*UR*), the neutral stimulus comes to elicit a similar or related response. The neutral stimulus then becomes a *conditioned stimulus* (*CS*), and the response it elicits is a *conditioned response* (*CR*). Nearly any kind of involuntary response can become a CR.

● In *extinction*, the conditioned stimulus is repeatedly presented without the unconditioned stimulus, and the conditioned response eventually disappears, although later it may reappear (*spontaneous recovery*). In *higher-order conditioning*, a neutral stimulus becomes a conditioned stimulus by being paired with an already-established conditioned stimulus. In *stimulus generalization*, after a stimulus becomes a conditioned stimulus for some response, other similar stimuli may produce the same reaction. In *stimulus discrimination*, different responses are made to stimuli that resemble the conditioned stimulus in some way.

● Many theorists believe that what an animal or person learns in classical conditioning is not just an association between the unconditioned and conditioned stimulus, but also information conveyed by one stimulus about another. Indeed, classical conditioning appears to be an evolutionary adaptation that allows an organism to prepare for a biologically important event. Considerable evidence exists to show that a neutral stimulus does not become a CS unless it reliably signals or predicts the US.

Classical Conditioning in Real Life

● Classical conditioning helps account for positive emotional responses to particular objects and events, fears and phobias, reactions to particular foods and odors, and reactions to medical treatments and placebos. John Watson showed how fears may be learned and then may be unlearned through a process of *counterconditioning*. Because of evolutionary adaptations, human beings (and many other species) are biologically primed to acquire some classically conditioned responses easily, such as conditioned taste aversions and certain fears.

Operant Conditioning

● In *operant conditioning*, behavior becomes more likely to occur or less so depending on its conse-

quences. Responses in operant conditioning are generally not reflexive and are more complex than in classical conditioning. Research in this area is closely associated with B. F. Skinner, who called his approach "radical behaviorism."

● In the Skinnerian analysis, *reinforcement* strengthens or increases the probability of a response, and *punishment* weakens or decreases the probability of a response. Immediate consequences usually have a greater effect on a response than do delayed consequences.

● Reinforcers are called *primary* when they are naturally reinforcing because they satisfy a biological need. They are called *secondary* when they have acquired their ability to strengthen a response through association with other reinforcers. A similar distinction is made for punishers.

● Reinforcement and punishment may be either positive or negative, depending on whether the consequence involves a stimulus that is presented or one that is removed or avoided. In *positive reinforcement*, something pleasant follows a response; in *negative reinforcement*, something unpleasant is removed. In *positive punishment*, something unpleasant follows the response; in *negative punishment*, something pleasant is removed.

● Using the Skinner box and similar devices, behaviorists have shown that *extinction, stimulus generalization*, and *stimulus discrimination* occur in operant conditioning as well as in classical conditioning. A *discriminative stimulus* signals that a response is likely to be followed by a certain type of consequence.

● *Continuous reinforcement* leads to the most rapid learning. However, *intermittent* (*partial*) *reinforcement* makes a response resistant to extinction (and, therefore, helps account for the persistence of superstitious rituals). One of the most common errors people make is to reward intermittently the responses they would like to eliminate.

● *Shaping* is used to train behaviors with a low probability of occurring spontaneously. Reinforcers are given for *successive approximations* to the desired response until the desired response is achieved.

● Biology places limits on what an animal or person can learn through operant conditioning or how easily a behavior is learned. Animals may have trouble learning a task because of *instinctive drift*.

Operant Conditioning in Real Life

● *Behavior modification*, the application of operant conditioning principles, has been used successfully in many settings, but when used inappropriately or incorrectly, reinforcement and punishment both have their pitfalls.

● Punishment, when used properly, can discourage undesirable behavior, including criminal behavior. But it is frequently misused and can have unintended consequences. It is often administered inappropriately because of the emotion of the moment; it may produce rage and fear; its effects are often only temporary; it is hard to administer immediately; it conveys little information about the kind of behavior that is desired; and it may provide attention that is rewarding. Extinction of undesirable behavior, combined with reinforcement of desired behavior, is generally preferable to the use of punishment.

● Reinforcers can also be misused. Rewards that are given out indiscriminately, as in efforts to raise children's self-esteem, do not reinforce desirable behavior. And an exclusive reliance on *extrinsic reinforcement* can sometimes undermine the power of *intrinsic reinforcement*. But money and praise do not usually interfere with intrinsic pleasure when a person is rewarded for succeeding or making progress rather than for merely participating in an activity, or when a person is already highly interested in the activity.

Learning and the Mind

● Even during behaviorism's heyday, some researchers were probing the "black box" of the mind. In the 1930s, Edward Tolman studied *latent learning*, in which no obvious reinforcer is present during learning and a response is not expressed until later on, when reinforcement does become available. What appears to be acquired in latent learning is not a specific response but rather knowledge about responses and their consequences.

● The 1960s and 1970s saw the increased influence of *social-cognitive theories* of learning, which focus on *observational learning* and the role played by beliefs, interpretations of events, and other cognitions in determining behavior. Social-cognitive theorists argue that, in both observational learning and latent learning, what is acquired is knowledge rather than a specific response. Perceptions, personality traits, and the social context all influence how people respond to what they see and the different lessons they take from any experience.

Psychology in the News, Revisited

● Behavioral and social-cognitive learning theories help us understand when punishment might be constructive and appropriate, and also when it backfires, causing resentment and other undesirable results. The learning perspective also offers good alternatives to physical punishment, and helps us appreciate the role of the environment in promoting "bad" behavior. Learning techniques can be enormously helpful for individuals and institutions, so long as they are applied wisely and carefully.

Taking Psychology with You

● Because people differ in their perceptions and beliefs, some people become more aggressive after exposure to violent images in the media, but most people do not.

Key Terms

learning **299**

behaviorism **299**

conditioning **299**

unconditioned stimulus (US) **300**

unconditioned response (UR) **301**

conditioned stimulus (CS) **301**

conditioned response (CR) **301**

classical conditioning **301**

extinction (in classical conditioning) **301**

spontaneous recovery **301**

higher-order conditioning **301**

stimulus generalization (in classical conditioning) **302**

stimulus discrimination (in classical conditioning) **302**

phobia **304**

counterconditioning **305**

operant conditioning **308**

reinforcement/ reinforcers **309**

punishment/punishers **309**

primary reinforcers and punishers **310**

secondary reinforcers and punishers **310**

positive and negative reinforcement and punishment **310**

Skinner box **311**

extinction (in operant conditioning) **312**

stimulus generalization (in operant conditioning) **312**

stimulus discrimination (in operant conditioning) **312**

discriminative stimulus **312**

continuous reinforcement **312**

intermittent (partial) reinforcement **312**

shaping **313**

successive approximations **313**

instinctive drift **314**

determinist view **315**

behavior modification (applied behavior analysis) **316**

extrinsic reinforcers **318**

intrinsic reinforcers **318**

behavioral ABCs **321**

latent learning **321**

social-cognitive theories **322**

observational (vicarious) learning **322**

CONCEPT MAP

- **Learning** is any relatively permanent change in behavior resulting from experience.
- **Behaviorism** explains learning as the result of observable acts and events without reference to mental entities, such as "mind" or "will."
- **Conditioning** involves associations between environmental stimuli and responses.

Classical Conditioning

New Reflexes from Old

Classical conditioning is the process by which a previously neutral stimulus acquires the capacity to elicit a response through association with a stimulus that already elicits a similar or related response (first studied by Ivan Pavlov).

- **Unconditioned stimulus (US):** stimulus that elicits a reflexive response in the absence of learning

- **Unconditioned response (UR):** reflexive response elicited by a stimulus in the absence of learning
- **Conditioned stimulus (CS):** initially neutral stimulus that comes to elicit a conditioned response after being associated with an unconditioned stimulus
- **Conditioned response (CR):** response that is elicited by a conditioned stimulus

Principles of Classical Conditioning

- **Extinction:** gradual disappearance of CR after CS is repeatedly presented without US.
- **Counterconditioning:** gradual disappearance of a CR produced by pairing a CS with another stimulus that elicits an incompatible response.
- **Higher-order conditioning:** a neutral stimulus becomes a CS after being associated with another CS.

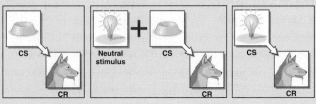

- **Stimulus generalization:** a CR occurs upon presentation of a stimulus similar to the CS.
- **Stimulus discrimination:** stimuli similar to the CS produce different responses.

What is Learned in Classical Conditioning?
- Many psychologists argue that classical conditioning involves information conveyed by one stimulus about another, that the CS becomes a signal for the US.
- Classical conditioning appears to be an evolutionary adaptation that allows an organism to prepare for a biologically important event.

Classical Conditioning in Real Life

Classical conditioning plays an important role in:
- Positive emotional responses to particular objects and events
- Learned fears and phobias (as demonstrated in the Little Albert study)

- Acquired tastes: likes and dislikes for particular foods and odors
- Unpleasant reactions to stimuli associated with medical treatments and reduced pain or anxiety in response to placebos

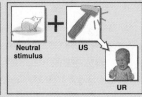

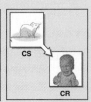

The Consequences of Behavior

- **Reinforcement** strengthens a response or makes it more likely to recur.

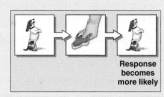

- **Punishment** weakens a response or makes it less likely to recur.

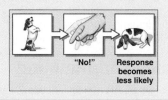

Primary and Secondary Reinforcers and Punishers

- A **primary reinforcer** strengthens responses because it satisfies a biological need.
- A **secondary reinforcer** strengthens a response because of its association with another reinforcer.
- A **primary punisher** is a stimulus that produces discomfort.
- A **secondary punisher** is a stimulus that has acquired punishing properties through association with a another reinforcer.

Positive and Negative Reinforcers and Punishers

- **Positive reinforcement:** response is followed by the presentation of, or increase in intensity of, a reinforcing stimulus.
- **Negative reinforcement:** response is followed by the removal, delay, or decrease in intensity of an unpleasant stimulus.
- In *positive punishment*, something unpleasant follows the response; in *negative punishment*, something pleasant is removed.

Operant Conditioning

Operant conditioning is the process by which a response becomes more likely or less likely to occur, depending on its consequences; associated with the work of B. F. Skinner.

Principles of Operant Conditioning

- **Extinction:** occurs when the behavior is no longer followed by the consequence that reinforced it.
- **Stimulus generalization:** responses occur to stimuli that resemble those present during original learning.
- **Stimulus discrimination:** responses occur in the presence of one stimulus but not to stimuli that resemble the ones originally present but differ from them on some dimension.

- Schedules of reinforcement:
  — **Continuous reinforcement** leads to fastest learning.
  — **Intermittent (partial) schedule of reinforcement** makes a response resistant to extinction.
- **Shaping:** used to train behaviors through reinforcement of **successive approximations** until the desired behavior occurs.
- **Instinctive drift:** the tendency for an organism to revert to instinctive behavior.

Operant Conditioning in Real Life

Behavior modification (also known as *applied behavior analysis*): the application of conditioning techniques to teach new responses or eliminate behavior problems.

The Pros and Cons of Punishment

Punishment can effectively discourage undesirable behavior. However, as a method of correcting behavior, it often fails, for these reasons:
- It is often administered inappropriately or mindlessly.
- Recipients often respond with anxiety, fear, or anger.
- Effectiveness is only temporary, depending on presence of punishing person.
- Because most misbehavior is hard to punish immediately, punishment is often too delayed to be effective.
- Punishment does not convey what the person or animal *should* do that is correct or appropriate.
- Punishment sometimes inadvertently rewards the unwanted behavior because it brings attention.

The Problems with Reward

- Rewards are often misused by being given indiscriminately, unrelated to desired behavior.
- Exclusive reliance on **extrinsic reinforcement** can sometimes undermine the power of **intrinsic reinforcement**, such as enjoyment of the task. However, the effects of extrinsic reinforcers depend on many factors, such as a person's initial motivation, the context, and whether improvement at a task is reinforced.

Learning and the Mind

Latent Learning

- **Latent learning** is not immediately expressed in performance.
- It can occur without obvious reinforcers.
- It involves acquiring knowledge about responses and their consequences, which permits flexibility in reaching goals.

Social-Cognitive Learning Theories

- **Social-cognitive theories** focus on **observational learning** and the role played by beliefs, interpretations of events, and other cognitions.

- Social-cognitive theorists argue that because people differ in their perceptions and beliefs, they may learn different lessons from the same situations, as in the case of media violence.

Notorious Symbol of Abu Ghraib Scandal Released From Prison

"She was following orders," says sister.

KEYSER, WV, March 25, 2007. Lynndie R. England, the U.S. Army reservist who became one of the most notorious faces of the Iraqi prisoner abuse scandal in 2003 after photos of her posing with naked prisoners were leaked to the international media, has been released from a military prison after serving half of her three-year sentence. She is now back home in Mineral County on parole. After pleading guilty in 2005, England was convicted of conspiracy, maltreating Iraqi detainees, and committing an indecent act. When her parole is over, she will receive a dishonorable discharge from the Army.

The photos of Private England, taken at Abu Ghraib prison near Baghdad, shocked the world when they were released. One infamous photo showed her holding a leash around the neck of a naked detainee; others showed her grinning or giving a thumbs-up over a pile of naked prisoners or pointing to the Iraqis' genitals.

Other soldiers were also involved in the scandal. Photos and videos showed them forcing detainees to simulate fellatio on each other, wear women's underwear on their heads, pile naked on top of one another to form a pyramid, or stand for hours attached to electrodes that the prisoners believed could cause them to be electrocuted at any moment. The photos set off worldwide outrage against the American military and prompted investigations by Congress and the Pentagon.

Throughout her court-martial, England maintained that she posed in the photos only at the direction of her superiors and because she was influenced by an older fellow soldier, Specialist Charles A. Graner, with whom she was having an affair and who later became the father of her child. Graner was sentenced to ten years in prison and was dismissed from the military.

In addition to England and Graner, five other soldiers were charged in the abuses committed at Abu Ghraib prison. All seven soldiers who took part in these incidents defended themselves by saying they were simply following orders. Their families told reporters that the soldiers were kind people who would never voluntarily harm another human being.

"Certain people in the Army told her to do what she did. She was following orders," said Lynndie England's sister, who called England "a kind-hearted, dependable person." Asked if she ever physically abused a detainee, Private England told investigators, "Yes, I stepped on some of them, push them or pull them, but nothing extreme."

This photograph of Private Lynndie England keeping an Iraqi prisoner on a leash at Abu Ghraib prison shocked the world.

10

Behavior in Social and Cultural Context

Why did the soldiers at Abu Ghraib prison treat the detainees so cruelly? Is Lynndie England a "caring person" who was "simply following orders"? Was she mentally disturbed or cognitively impaired? Was she under the influence of a sadistic boyfriend? Did she and her fellow soldiers behave as they did not because they were unusually brutal or heartless individuals but because of conditions at the prison where they were ordered to work as guards? Were they "bad apples" in an otherwise good barrel, or was the barrel itself rotten? Is the answer to be found in some combination of these explanations?

In 1961, Adolf Eichmann, who had been a high-ranking officer of the Nazi elite, was sentenced to death for his part in the deportation and killing of millions of Jews during World War II. But he insisted that he was not anti-Semitic. Shortly before his execution, Eichmann said, "I am not the monster I am made out to be. I am the victim of a fallacy" (R. Brown, 1986). The fallacy to which Eichmann referred was the widespread belief that a person who does monstrous deeds must be a monster. There does seem to be so much evil and cruelty in the world, and yet so much kindness, sacrifice, and heroism, too. How can we even begin to explain either side of human nature?

The fields of *social psychology* and *cultural psychology* approach this question by examining the powerful influence of the social and cultural environment on the actions of individuals and groups. In this chapter, we will focus on the foundations of social psychology, basic principles that can help us understand why people who are not "crazy" or "monstrous" nonetheless do unspeakably evil things, and, conversely, why some otherwise ordinary people may reach heights of heroism when the occasion demands. We will look at the influence of roles and attitudes, how people's behavior is affected by the groups and situations they are in, and the conditions under which people conform or dissent. Finally, we will consider some of the social and cultural reasons for prejudice and conflict between groups.

YOU are about to learn...

- how social roles and cultural norms regulate behavior without our being aware of it.

- the power of roles and situations to make people behave in ways they never would have predicted for themselves.

- how people can be entrapped into violating their moral principles.

Roles and Rules

"We are all fragile creatures entwined in a cobweb of social constraints," social psychologist Stanley Milgram once said. The constraints he referred to are social **norms**, rules about how we are supposed to act, enforced by threats of punishment if we violate them and promises of reward if we follow them. Norms are the conventions of everyday life that make interactions with other people predictable and orderly; like a cobweb, they are often as invisible as they are strong. Every society has norms for just about everything in human experience: for conducting courtships, for raising children, for making decisions, for behavior in public places. Some norms are enshrined in law, such as "A person may not beat up another person, except in self-defense." Some are unspoken cultural understandings, such as "A man may beat up another man who insults his masculinity." And some are tiny, unspoken regulations that people learn to follow unconsciously, such as "You may not sing at the top of your lungs on a public bus."

When people observe that "everyone else" seems to be violating a social norm, they are more likely to do so too—and this is the mechanism by which entire neighborhoods can deteriorate. In six natural field experiments conducted in the Netherlands, researchers found that passersby were more likely to litter, to park illegally, and even to steal a five-euro bill from a mailbox if the sidewalks were dirty and unswept, if graffiti marked the walls, or if strangers were setting off illegal fireworks (Keizer, Linderberg, & Steg, 2008). Conversely, people's behavior will become more constructive if they think that's the norm. When hotels put notices in guest bathrooms that "the majority of guests in this room reuse their towels" (in contrast to simply requesting the guest to do the same because it's good for the environment), more than half agree to participate in the reuse program (Goldstein, Cialdini, & Griskevicius, 2008).

In every society, people also fill a variety of social **roles**, positions that are regulated by norms about how people in those positions should behave.

Many roles in modern life require us to give up our individuality. If one of these members of the British Coldstream Guards suddenly broke into a dance, his career would be brief—and the dazzling effect of the parade would be ruined. But when does adherence to a role go too far?

Gender roles define the proper behavior for a man and a woman. Occupational roles determine the correct behavior for a manager and an employee, a professor and a student. Family roles set tasks for parent and child. Certain aspects of every role must be carried out or there will be penalties—emotional, financial, or professional. As a student, for instance, you know just what you have to do to pass your psychology course (or you should by now!). How do you know what a role requirement is? You know when you violate it, intentionally or unintentionally, because you will probably feel awfully uncomfortable, or other people will try to make you feel that way.

The requirements of a social role are in turn shaped by the culture you live in. **Culture** can be defined as a program of shared rules that govern the behavior of people in a community or society, and a set of values, beliefs, and customs shared by most members of that community and passed from one generation to another (Lonner, 1995). You learn most of your culture's rules and values the way you learn your culture's language: without thinking about it.

norms (social) Rules that regulate social life, including explicit laws and implicit cultural conventions.

role A given social position that is governed by a set of norms for proper behavior.

culture A program of shared rules that govern the behavior of members of a community or society, and a set of values, beliefs, and customs shared by most members of that community.

Get Involved! Dare To Be Different

Either alone or with a friend, try a mild form of norm violation (nothing alarming, obscene, dangerous, or offensive). You might stand backward in line at the grocery store or cafeteria; sit right next to a stranger in the library or at a movie, even when other seats are available; sing or hum loudly for a couple of minutes in a public place; or stand "too close" to a friend in conversation. Notice the reactions of onlookers, as well as your own feelings, while you violate this norm. If you do this exercise with someone else, one of you can be the "violator" and the other can write down the responses of others; then switch places. Was it easy to do this exercise? Why or why not?

Arabs stand much closer in conversation than Westerners do. Most Westerners would feel "crowded" standing so close, even when talking to a close friend. How does it feel when you violate the norm for conversational distance that *your* culture dictates?

For example, cultures differ in their rules for *conversational distance*: how close people normally stand to one another when they are speaking (Hall, 1959, 1976). In general, Arabs like to stand close enough to feel your breath, touch your arm, and see your eyes—a distance that makes most white Americans, Canadians, and northern Europeans uneasy, unless they are talking intimately with a lover. The English and the Swedes stand farthest apart when they converse; southern Europeans stand closer; and Latin Americans and Arabs stand the closest (Keating, 1994; Sommer, 1969).

If you are talking to someone who has different cultural rules for distance from yours, you are likely to feel very uncomfortable without knowing why. You may feel that the person is crowding you or being strangely cool and distant. A student from Lebanon told us how relieved he was to understand how cultures differ in their rules for conversational distance. "When Anglo students moved away from me, I thought they were prejudiced," he said. "Now I see why I was more comfortable talking with Latino students. They like to stand close, too."

Naturally, people bring their own personalities and interests to the roles they play. Just as two actors will play the same part differently although they are reading from the same script, you will have your own reading of how to play the role of student, friend, parent, or employer. Nonetheless, the requirements of a social role are strong, so strong that

they may even cause you to behave in ways that shatter your fundamental sense of the kind of person you are. We turn now to two classic studies that illuminate the power of social roles in our lives.

The Obedience Study

In the early 1960s, Stanley Milgram (1963, 1974) designed a study that would become world-famous. Milgram wanted to know how many people would obey an authority figure when directly ordered to violate their ethical standards. Participants in the study thought they were part of an experiment on the effects of punishment on learning. Each was assigned, apparently at random, to the role of "teacher." Another person, introduced as a fellow volunteer, was the "learner." Whenever the learner, seated in an adjoining room, made an error in reciting a list of word pairs he was supposed to have memorized, the teacher had to give him an electric shock by depressing a lever on a machine (see Figure 10.1). With each error, the voltage (marked from 0 to 450) was to be increased by another 15 volts. The shock levels on the machine were labeled from SLIGHT SHOCK to DANGER—SEVERE SHOCK and, finally, ominously, XXX. In reality, the learners were confederates of Milgram and did not receive any shocks, but none of the teachers ever realized this during the study. The actor-victims played their parts convincingly: As the study

FIGURE 10.1

The Milgram Obedience Experiment

On the left is Milgram's original shock machine; in 1963, it looked pretty ominous. On the right, the "learner" is being strapped into his chair by the experimenter and the "teacher."

(left) Archives of the History of American Psychology–The University of Akron (right) Copyright 1965 by Stanley Milgram. From the film OBEDIENCE, distributed by Penn State Media Sales.

continued, they shouted in pain and pleaded to be released, all according to a prearranged script.

Before doing this study, Milgram asked a number of psychiatrists, students, and middle-class adults how many people they thought would "go all the way" to XXX on orders from the researcher. The psychiatrists predicted that most people would refuse to go beyond 150 volts, when the learner first demanded to be freed, and that only one person in a thousand, someone who was disturbed and sadistic, would administer the highest voltage. The nonprofessionals agreed with this prediction, and all of them said that they personally would disobey early in the procedure.

That is not, however, the way the results turned out. Every single person administered some shock to the learner, and about two-thirds of the participants, of all ages and from all walks of life, obeyed to the fullest extent. Many protested to the experimenter, but they backed down when he calmly asserted, "The experiment requires that you continue." They obeyed no matter how much the victim shouted for them to stop and no matter how painful the shocks seemed to be. They obeyed even when they themselves were anguished about the pain they believed they were causing. As Milgram (1974) noted, participants would "sweat, tremble, stutter, bite their lips, groan, and dig their fingernails into their flesh"—but still they obeyed.

Watch the **Video** **Milgram Obedience Study Today** on mypsychlab.com

Over the decades, more than 3,000 people of many different ethnicities have gone through replications of the Milgram study. Most of them, men and women equally, inflicted what they thought were dangerous amounts of shock to another person. Researchers in other countries have also found high percentages of obedience, ranging to more than 90 percent in Spain and the Netherlands (Meeus & Raaijmakers, 1995; Smith & Bond, 1994).

Milgram and his team subsequently set up several variations of the study to determine the circumstances under which people might disobey the experimenter. They found that virtually nothing the victim did or said changed the likelihood of compliance, even when the victim said he had a heart condition, screamed in agony, or stopped responding entirely, as if he had collapsed. However, people *were* more likely to disobey under certain conditions:

In Milgram's study, when the "teacher" had to administer shock directly to the learner, most subjects refused, but this one continued to obey.

- *When the experimenter left the room*, many people subverted authority by giving low levels of shock but reporting that they had followed orders.

- *When the victim was right there in the room*, and the teacher had to administer the shock directly to the victim's body, many people refused to go on.

- *When two experimenters issued conflicting demands*, with one telling participants to continue and another saying to stop at once, no one kept inflicting shock.

- *When the person ordering them to continue was an ordinary man*, apparently another volunteer instead of the authoritative experimenter, many participants disobeyed.

- *When the participant worked with peers who refused to go further*, he or she often gained the courage to disobey.

Obedience, Milgram concluded, was more a function of the *situation* than of the personalities of the participants. "The key to [their] behavior," Milgram (1974) summarized, "lies not in pent-up anger or aggression but in the nature of their relationship to authority. They have given themselves to the authority; they see themselves as instruments for the execution of his wishes; once so defined, they are unable to break free." **Watch**

The Milgram study has had numerous critics. Some consider it unethical because people were kept in the dark about what was really happening until the session was over (of course, telling them in advance would have invalidated the study) and because many suffered emotional pain (Milgram countered that they would not have felt pain if they had simply disobeyed instructions). The original study could never be repeated in the U.S. today because of these ethical concerns. However, a "softer" version of the experiment has been done, in which "teachers" were asked to administer shocks only up to 150 volts, when they first heard the learner protest. That amount of shock was a critical choice point in Milgram's study: Nearly 80 percent of those who went past 150 ended up going all the way to the end (Packer, 2008).

In the replication, the experimenter rejected anyone who already knew about the original Milgram study and anyone a clinician judged to be emotionally vulnerable. Even so, he found that obedience rates were only slightly lower than Milgram's. Once again, gender, education, age, and ethnicity had no effect on the likelihood of obeying (Burger, 2009). In another, rather eerie cyberversion replication of Milgram's study, participants had to shock a virtual woman on a computer screen. Even though they knew she wasn't real, their heart rates increased and they reported feeling bad about delivering the "shocks." Yet they kept doing it (Slater et al., 2006). And in 2010 in France, 80 participants in "The Game of Death," a fake game show modeled on the Milgram experiment, were instructed to deliver increasingly powerful shocks to a man until he appeared to die. All but 16 of the players gave the maximum jolt.

Some psychologists have questioned Milgram's conclusion that personality traits are virtually irrelevant to whether or not people obey an authority. Certain traits, they note, especially hostility, narcissism, and rigidity, do increase obedience and a willingness to inflict pain on others (Blass, 2000; Twenge, 2009). Others have objected to the parallel Milgram drew between the behavior of the study's participants and the brutality of the Nazis and others who have committed acts of barbarism in the name of duty (Darley, 1995). The people in Milgram's study typically obeyed only when the experimenter was hovering right there, and many of them felt enormous discomfort and conflict. In contrast, most Nazis acted without direct supervision by authorities, without external pressure, and without feelings of anguish.

Nevertheless, no one disputes that Milgram's compelling study has had a tremendous influence on public awareness of the dangers of uncritical obedience. As John Darley (1995) observed, "Milgram shows us the beginning of a path by means of which ordinary people, in the grip of social forces, become the origins of atrocities in the real world."

The Prison Study

Another famous demonstration of the power of roles is known as the Stanford prison study. Its designers, Philip Zimbardo and Craig Haney, wanted to know what would happen if ordinary college students were randomly assigned to the roles of prisoners and guards (Haney, Banks, & Zimbardo, 1973). And so they set up a serious-looking "prison" in the basement of a Stanford building, complete with individual cells, different uniforms for prisoners and guards, and nightsticks for the guards. The students agreed to live there for two weeks.

Within a short time, most of the prisoners became distressed and helpless. They developed emotional symptoms and physical ailments. Some became apathetic; others became rebellious. One panicked and broke down. The guards, however, began to enjoy their new power. Some tried to be nice, helping the prisoners and doing little favors for them. Some were "tough but fair," holding

Prisoners and guards quickly learn their respective roles, which often have more influence on their behavior than their personalities do.

strictly to "the rules." But about a third became punitive and harsh, even when the prisoners were not resisting in any way. One guard became unusually sadistic, smacking his nightstick into his palm as he vowed to "get" the prisoners and instructing two of them to simulate sexual acts (they refused). The researchers, who had not expected such a speedy and alarming transformation of ordinary students, ended this study after only six days.

Generations of students and the general public have seen emotionally charged clips from videos of the study made at the time. To the researchers, the results demonstrated how roles affect behavior: The guards' aggression, they said, was entirely a result of wearing a guard's uniform and having the power conferred by a guard's authority (Haney & Zimbardo, 1998). Some social psychologists, however, have argued that the prison study is really another example of obedience to authority and of how willingly some people obey instructions—in this case, from Zimbardo himself (Haslam & Reicher, 2003). Consider the briefing that Zimbardo provided to the guards at the beginning of the study:

> You can create in the prisoners feelings of boredom, a sense of fear to some degree, you can create a notion of arbitrariness that their life is totally controlled by us, by the system, you, me, and they'll have no privacy... We're going to take away their individuality in various ways. In general what all this leads to is a sense of powerlessness. That is, in this situation we'll have all the power and they'll have none (The Stanford Prison Study video, quoted in Haslam & Reicher, 2003).

These are pretty powerful suggestions to the guards about how they would be permitted to behave, and they convey Zimbardo's personal encouragement ("*we'll* have all the power"), so perhaps it is not surprising that some took Zimbardo at his word and behaved quite brutally. The one sadistic guard later said he was just trying to play the role of the "worst S.O.B. guard" he'd seen in the movies. Even the investigators themselves noted at the time that the data were "subject to possible errors due to selective sampling. The video and audio recordings tended to be focussed upon the more interesting, dramatic events which occurred" (Haney, Banks, & Zimbardo, 1973).

Despite these flaws, the Stanford prison study remains a useful cautionary tale. In real prisons, guards do have the kind of power that was given to these students, and they too may be given instructions that encourage them to treat prisoners harshly. Thus the prison study provides a good example of how the social situation affects behavior, causing some people to behave in ways that seem out of character. ◉⌐**Watch**

◉⌐**Watch** the **Video The Power of the Situation: Zimbardo** on **mypsychlab.com**

Why People Obey

Of course, obedience to authority or to the norms of a situation is not always harmful or bad. A certain amount of routine compliance with rules is necessary in any group, and obedience to authority has many benefits for individuals and society. A nation could not operate if all its citizens ignored traffic signals, cheated on their taxes, dumped garbage wherever they chose, or assaulted each other. A business organization could not function if its members came to work only when they felt like it. But obedience also has a darker aspect. Throughout history, the plea "I was only following orders" has been offered to excuse actions carried out on behalf of orders that were foolish, destructive, or criminal. The writer C. P. Snow once observed that "more hideous crimes have been committed in the name of obedience than in the name of rebellion."

Most people follow orders because of the obvious consequences of disobedience: They can be suspended from school, fired from their jobs, or arrested. But they may also obey because they hope to gain advantages or promotions from the authority, or because they expect to learn from the authority's greater knowledge or experience. They obey because they respect the authority's legitimacy. And most of all, they obey because they do not want to rock the boat, appear to doubt the experts, or be rude, fearing that they will be

entrapment A gradual process in which individuals escalate their commitment to a course of action to justify their investment of time, money, or effort.

disliked or rejected for doing so (Collins & Brief, 1995).

But what about all those obedient people in Milgram's study who felt they were doing wrong and who wished they were free, but who could not untangle themselves from the "cobweb of social constraints"? How do people become morally disengaged from the consequences of their actions?

One answer is **entrapment**, a process in which individuals escalate their commitment to a course of action in order to justify their investment in it (Brockner & Rubin, 1985). The first stages of entrapment pose no difficult choices. But as people take a step, or make a decision to continue, they will justify that action, which makes them feel that it is the right one and that they haven't done anything foolish or unethical (Tavris & Aronson, 2007). Each step thus leads to another. Before long, the person has become committed to a course of action that is increasingly self-defeating, cruel, or foolhardy. Thus, in Milgram's study, once participants had given a 15-volt shock, they committed themselves to the experiment. The next level was "only" 30 volts. Because each increment was small, before they knew it most people were administering what they believed were dangerously strong shocks. At that point, it was difficult to justify and explain a sudden decision to quit, especially after reaching 150 volts, the point at which the "learner" made his first verbal protests.

Whichever decision a person makes, to obey an authority or protest, he or she will feel an urgency to justify the choice made (Tavris & Aronson, 2007). Those who obey frequently justify their behavior by handing over responsibility to the

Slot machines rely on the principle of entrapment, which is why casinos make millions and most players don't. A person vows to spend only a few dollars but, after losing them, says, "Well, maybe another couple of tries" or "I've spent so much, now I really have to win something to get back what I've lost."

authority, thereby absolving themselves of accountability for their own actions (Kelman & Hamilton, 1989; Modigliani & Rochat, 1995). In Milgram's study, many who administered the highest levels of shock adopted the attitude "It's his problem; I'm just following orders." In contrast, individuals who refused to give high levels of shock took responsibility for their actions. "One of the things I think is very cowardly," said a 32-year-old engineer, "is to try to shove the responsibility onto someone else. See, if I now turned around and said, 'It's your fault . . . it's not mine,' I would call that cowardly" (Milgram, 1974).

A chilling study of entrapment was conducted with 25 men who had served in the Greek military police during the authoritarian regime that ended in 1974 (Haritos-Fatouros, 1988). A psychologist interviewed the men, identifying the steps used in training them to torture prisoners in the hope of gaining information. First, the men were ordered to stand guard outside the interrogation and torture cells. Then they stood guard inside the detention rooms, where they observed the torture of prisoners. Then they "helped" beat up prisoners. Once they had obediently followed these orders and became actively involved, the torturers found their actions easier to carry out. Similar procedures have been used to train military and police interrogators to torture political opponents and criminal suspects.

Investigative journalists and social scientists have documented the use of torture all over the world, although torture is expressly forbidden under international law (Huggins, Haritos-Fatouros, & Zimbardo, 2003). In Chicago in the 1980s, at the height of black-white community tensions, an investigation following the torture of a black man arrested for murder led to the exposure

of at least 62 other cases in which police detectives had severely beaten, burned, or applied electric shock to black suspects or criminals for information or revenge. In England during the conflict between the British and Northern Ireland, British officers took Irish prisoners suspected of being terrorists and put them in hoods, dehydrated them, and beat them nearly to death (Conroy, 2000). And, as noted in our opening story, members of the American military tortured Arab detainees held in "extraordinary rendition" centers and Abu Ghraib prison (Mayer, 2009).

From their standpoint, torturers justify their actions because they see themselves as good guys who are just doing their jobs, especially in wartime. And perhaps they are, but such a justification overlooks entrapment. This prisoner might be a terrorist, but what if this other one is completely innocent? Before long, the torturer has shifted his reasoning from "If this person is guilty, he deserves to be tortured" to "If I am torturing this person, he must be guilty." And so the abuse escalates (Tavris & Aronson, 2007).

This is a difficult concept for people who divide the world into "good guys" versus "bad guys" and cannot imagine that good guys might do brutal things; if the good guys are doing it, by definition it's all right to do. Yet in everyday life, as in the Milgram study, people often set out on a path that is morally ambiguous, only to find that they have traveled a long way toward violating their own principles. From Greece's torturers to members of the American military, from Milgram's well-meaning volunteers to all of us in our everyday lives, people face the difficult task of drawing a line beyond which they will not go. For many, the demands of the role and the social pressures of the situation defeat the inner voice of conscience.

✓●─ **Study** and **Review** on mypsychlab.com

Quick Quiz

Step into your role of student to answer these questions.

1. About what proportion of the people in Milgram's obedience study administered the highest level of shock? (a) two-thirds, (b) one-half, (c) one-third, (d) one-tenth

2. Which of the following actions by the "learner" reduced the likelihood of being shocked by the "teacher" in Milgram's study? (a) protesting noisily, (b) screaming in pain, (c) complaining of having a heart ailment, (d) nothing he did made a difference

3. A friend of yours, who is moving, asks you to bring over a few boxes. As long as you are there anyway, he asks you to fill them with books. Before you know it, you have packed up his kitchen, living room, and bedroom. What social-psychological process is at work here?

Answers:

1. a 2. d 3. entrapment

YOU are about to learn...

- two general ways that people explain their own or other people's behavior—and why it matters.

- three self-serving biases in how people think about themselves and the world.

- why most people will believe outright lies and nonsensical statements if they are repeated often enough.

- whether certain fundamental political and religious attitudes have a genetic component.

Social Influences on Beliefs and Behavior

Explore
Fundamental
Attribution
Error on
mypsychlab.com

Social psychologists are interested not only in what people do in social situations, but also in what is going on in their heads while they are doing it. Researchers in the area of **social cognition** examine how people's perceptions of themselves and others affect their relationships and also how the social environment influences their perceptions, beliefs, and values. Current approaches draw on evolutionary theory, neuroimaging studies, surveys, and experiments to identify universal themes in how human beings perceive and feel about one another. In this section, we will consider two important topics in social cognition: attributions and attitudes. **Explore**

Explore Social
Psychology:
How Others
Affect Us on
mypsychlab.com

Attributions

People read detective stories to find out *who* did the dirty deed, but in real life, we also want to know *why* people do bad things. Was it because of a terrible childhood, a mental illness, possession by a demon, or what? According to **attribution theory**, the explanations we make of our behavior and the behavior of others generally fall into two categories. When we make a *situational attribution*, we are identifying the cause of an action as something in the situation or environment: "Joe stole the money because his family is starving." When we make a *dispositional attribution*, we are identifying the cause of an action as something in the person, such as a trait or a motive: "Joe stole the money because he is a born thief."

When people are trying to explain someone else's behavior, they tend to overestimate personality traits and underestimate the influence of the situation (Forgas, 1998; Nisbett & Ross, 1980). In terms of attribution theory, they tend to ignore situational attributions in favor of dispositional ones. This tendency has been called the **fundamental attribution**

social cognition An area in social psychology concerned with social influences on thought, memory, perception, and beliefs.

attribution theory The theory that people are motivated to explain their own and other people's behavior by attributing causes of that behavior to a situation or a disposition.

fundamental attribution error The tendency, in explaining other people's behavior, to overestimate personality factors and underestimate the influence of the situation.

error (Jones, 1990). Were the hundreds of people who obeyed Milgram's experimenters sadistic by nature? Were the student guards in the prison study cruel and the prisoners cowardly by temperament? Were the individuals who pocketed the money from a mailbox on a dirty street "born thieves"? Those who think so are committing the fundamental attribution error. The impulse to explain other people's behavior in terms of their personalities is so strong that we do it even when we know that the other person was *required* to behave in a certain way (Yzerbyt et al., 2001). **Explore**

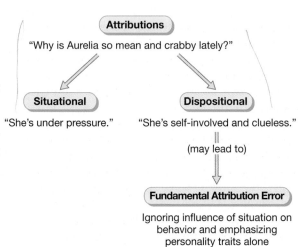

The fundamental attribution error is especially prevalent in Western nations, where middle-class people tend to believe that individuals are responsible for their own actions and dislike the idea that the situation has much influence over them. They think that *they* would have refused the experimenter's cruel orders and *they* would have treated fellow-students-temporarily-called-prisoners fairly. In contrast, in countries such as India, where everyone is embedded in caste and family networks, and in Japan, China, Korea, and Hong Kong, where people are more group oriented than in the West, people are more likely to be aware of situational constraints on behavior, including their own behavior (Balcetis, Dunning, & Miller, 2008; Choi et al., 2003). Thus, if someone is behaving oddly, makes a mistake, or commits an ethical lapse, a person from India or China, unlike a Westerner, is more likely to make a situational attribution of the person's behavior ("He's under pressure") than a dispositional one ("He's incompetent").

A primary reason for the fundamental attribution error is that people rely on different sources of information to judge their own behavior and that of others. We know what we ourselves are thinking and feeling, but we can't always know the same of others. Thus, we assess our own actions by introspecting about our feelings and intentions, but when we observe the actions of others, we have only their behavior to guide our interpretations (Pronin, 2008; Pronin, Gilovich, & Ross, 2004). This basic asymmetry in social perception is further widened by self-serving biases, habits of thinking that make us feel good about ourselves, even (perhaps especially) when we shouldn't. We discuss other cognitive biases in Chapter 7, but here are three that are especially relevant to the attributions (and misattributions) that people often make:

1 **The bias to choose the most flattering and forgiving attributions of our own lapses.** When it comes to explaining their own behavior, people tend to choose attributions that are favorable to them, taking credit for their good actions (a dispositional attribution) but letting the situation account for their failures, embarrassing mistakes, or harmful actions (Mezulis et al., 2004). For instance, most North Americans, when angry, will say, "I am furious for good reason; this situation is intolerable." They are less likely to say, "I am furious because I am an ill-tempered grinch." On the other hand, if they do something admirable, such as donating to charity, they are likely to attribute their motives to a personal disposition ("I'm so generous") instead of the situation ("That guy on the phone pressured me into it").

2 **The bias that we are better, smarter, and kinder than others.** This bias has been called the "holier-than-thou" effect: the tendency of most people to be overly optimistic about their own abilities, competence, and good qualities such as generosity and compassion (Balcetis, Dunning, & Miller, 2008; Dunning et al., 2003). They overestimate their willingness to "do the right thing" in a moral dilemma, give to a charity, cooperate with a stranger in trouble, and so on. But when they are actually in a situation that calls for generosity, compassion, or ethical action, they often fail to live up to their own self-image because the demands of the situation have a stronger influence. The holier-than-thou effect is actually greatest among people who *literally* strive to be "holier than thou" and "humbler than thee" (Rowatt et al., 2002). In two studies conducted at fundamentalist Christian colleges, the greater the students' intrinsic religiousness and fundamentalism, the greater was their tendency to rate themselves as being more adherent to biblical commandments than other people—and more humble than other people, too!

"When I was making money, I made the most money, and now that I'm spiritual I'm the most spiritual."

© Barbara Smaller/Conde Nast Publications/www.cartoonbank.com

3 **The bias to believe that the world is fair.** According to the **just-world hypothesis**, attributions are also affected by the need to believe that justice usually prevails, that good people are rewarded and bad guys punished (Lerner, 1980). When this belief is thrown into doubt—especially when bad things happen to "good people" who are just like us—we are motivated to restore it (Aguiar et al., 2008). Unfortunately, one common way of restoring the belief in a just world is to call upon a dispositional attribution called *blaming the victim:* Maybe that person wasn't so good after all; he or she must have done something to deserve what happened or to provoke it. Blaming the victim is virtually universal when people are ordered to harm others or find themselves entrapped into harming others (Bandura, 1999). In the Milgram study, some "teachers" made comments such as, "[The learner] was so stupid and stubborn he deserved to get shocked" (Milgram, 1974).

It may be good for our self-esteem to feel that we are kinder, more competent, and more moral than other people, and that we are not influenced by external circumstances (except when they excuse our mistakes). But these flattering delusions can distort communication, impede the resolution of conflicts, and lead to serious misunderstandings.

Of course, sometimes dispositional (personality) attributions do explain a person's behavior. The point to remember is that the attributions you make can have huge consequences. Happy couples usually attribute their partners' occasional lapses to

just-world hypothesis
The notion that many people need to believe that the world is fair and that justice is served, that bad people are punished and good people rewarded.

something in the situation ("Poor guy is under a lot of stress") and their partners' loving actions to something about them ("He has the sweetest nature"). But unhappy couples do just the reverse. They attribute lapses to their partners' personalities ("He is totally selfish") and good behavior to the situation ("Yeah, he gave me a present, but only because his mother told him to") (Karney & Bradbury, 2000). You can see why the attributions you make about your partner, your parents, and your friends will affect how you get along with them—and how long you will put up with their failings.

✓●─[**Study** and **Review** on **mypsychlab.com**]

Quick Quiz

To what do you attribute your success in answering these questions?

1. What kind of attribution is being made in each case, situational or dispositional? (a) A man says, "My wife has sure become a grouchy person." (b) The same man says, "I'm grouchy because I had a bad day at the office." (c) A woman reads about high unemployment in poor communities and says, "Well, if those people weren't so lazy, they would find work."

2. What principles of attribution theory are suggested by the items in the preceding question?

Answers:

1. a. dispositional b. situational c. dispositional   2. Item *a* illustrates the fundamental attribution error; *b*, the bias to choose a flattering or forgiving explanation of our own lapses; and *c*, blaming the victim, possibly because of the just-world hypothesis.

Attitudes

People hold attitudes about all sorts of things—politics, food, children, movies, sports heroes, you name it. An *attitude* is a belief about people, groups, ideas, or activities. Some attitudes are *explicit*: We are aware of them, they shape our conscious decisions and actions, and they can be measured on self-report questionnaires. Others are *implicit*: We are unaware of them, they may influence our behavior in ways we do not recognize, and they are measured in indirect ways (Stanley, Phelps, & Banaji, 2008).

Some of your attitudes change when you have new experiences, and on occasion they change because you rationally decide you were wrong about something. But attitudes also change because of the psychological need for consistency and the mind's normal biases in processing information. In Chapter 7, we discuss **cognitive dissonance**, the uncomfortable feeling that occurs when two attitudes, or an attitude and behavior, are in conflict (are dissonant). To resolve this dissonance, most people will change one of their attitudes. Thus, if a politician or celebrity you admire does something stupid, immoral, or illegal, you can restore consistency either by lowering your opinion of the person or by deciding that the person's behavior wasn't so stupid or immoral after all. Usually, and unfortunately for critical thinking, people restore cognitive consistency by dismissing evidence that might otherwise throw their fundamental beliefs into question (Aronson, 2008).

cognitive dissonance
A state of tension that occurs when a person simultaneously holds two cognitions that are psychologically inconsistent or when a person's belief is incongruent with his or her behavior.

Shifting Opinions and Bedrock Beliefs

All around you, every day, advertisers, politicians, and friends are trying to influence your attitudes. One weapon they use is the drip, drip, drip of a repeated idea. Repeated exposure even to a nonsense syllable such as *zug* is enough to make a person feel more positive toward it (Zajonc, 1968). The

In spite of Barack Obama's lifelong affiliation as a Christian, some of his opponents spread the big lie that he is a Muslim. After this lie was repeated countless times on the Internet, many people fell for it.

familiarity effect, the tendency to hold positive attitudes toward familiar people or things, has been demonstrated across cultures, across species, and across states of awareness, from alert to preoccupied. It works even for stimuli you aren't aware of seeing (Monahan, Murphy, & Zajonc, 2000). A related phenomenon is the **validity effect**, the tendency to believe that something is true simply because it has been repeated many times. Repeat something often enough, even the basest lie, and eventually the public will believe it. Hitler's propaganda minister, Joseph Goebbels, called this technique the "Big Lie."

In a series of experiments, Hal Arkes and his associates demonstrated how the validity effect operates (Arkes, 1993; Arkes, Boehm, & Xu, 1991). In a typical study, people read a list of statements, such as "Mercury has a higher boiling point than copper" or "Over 400 Hollywood films were produced in 1948." They had to rate each statement for its validity, on a scale of 1 (definitely false) to 7 (definitely true). A week or two later, they again rated the validity of some of these statements and also rated others that they had not seen previously. The result: Mere repetition increased the perception that the familiar statements were true. The same effect also occurred for other kinds of statements, including unverifiable opinions (e.g., "At least 75 percent of all politicians are basically dishonest"), opinions that subjects initially felt were true, and even opinions they initially felt were false. "Note that no attempt has been made to persuade," said Arkes (1993). "No supporting arguments are offered. We just have subjects rate the statements. Mere repetition seems to increase rated validity. This is scary."

On most everyday topics, such as movies, sports, and the boiling point of mercury, people's attitudes range from casual to committed. If your best friend is neutral about baseball whereas you are an insanely devoted fan, your friendship will probably survive. But when the subject is one involving beliefs that give meaning and purpose to a person's life—most notably, politics and religion—it's another ball game, so to speak. Wars have been fought, and are being fought as you read this, over people's most passionate convictions. Perhaps the attitude that causes the most controversy and bitterness around the world is the one toward religious diversity: accepting or intolerant. Some people of all religions accept a world of differing religious views and practices; they believe that church and state should be separate. But for many fundamentalists (in any religion), religion and politics are inseparable; they believe that one religion should prevail (Jost et al., 2003). You can see, then, why these irreconcilable attitudes cause continuing conflict, and

When people hold attitudes that are central to their religious and political philosophies, they often fail to realize that the other side feels just as strongly.

sometimes are used to justify terrorism and war. Why are people so different in these views?

Do Genes Influence Attitudes? Do you support or disapprove of the death penalty, bans on assault weapons, tolerant immigration policies? Are you worried about global warming or do you think its dangers have been exaggerated? Do you prefer Rush Limbaugh or Jon Stewart? Where did your attitudes on these issues and people come from?

Many attitudes result from learning and experience, of course. But research from behavioral genetics has found that some core attitudes stem from personality traits that are heritable. That is, the variation among people in these attitudes is due in part to their genetic differences (see Chapter 2). Two such traits are "openness to experience" and "conscientiousness." We would expect people who are open to new experiences to hold positive attitudes toward novelty and change in general. We would expect people who prefer the familiar and conventional, and who are conscientious about order and obligations, to be drawn to conservative politics and religious denominations.

And that is what research finds. In one study of Protestant groups, fundamentalist Christians scored much lower than liberal Christians on the dimension of openness to experience (Streyffeler & McNally, 1998). Conversely, conservatives score

familiarity effect The tendency of people to feel more positive toward a person, item, product, or other stimulus the more familiar they are with it.

validity effect The tendency of people to believe that a statement is true or valid simply because it has been repeated many times.

higher than liberals on conscientiousness (Jost, 2006). These personality traits underlie a host of specific attitudes. A study at the University of Texas found that liberal students were more likely than conservatives to have favorable attitudes toward atheists, poetry, Asian food, jazz, street people, tattoos, foreign films, erotica, big cities, recreational drugs, and foreign travel—all examples of "openness to experience" rather than preference for the familiar (Jost, Nosek, & Gosling, 2008).

Religious *affiliation*—whether a person is a Methodist, Muslim, Catholic, Jew, Hindu, and so on—is not heritable. Most people choose a religious group because of their parents, ethnicity, culture, and social class, and many Americans switch their religious affiliation at least once in their lives. But *religiosity*—a person's depth of religious feeling and adherence to a religion's rules—does have a genetic component. When religiosity combines with conservatism and authoritarianism (an unquestioning trust in authority), the result is a deeply ingrained acceptance of tradition and dislike of those who question it (Olson et al., 2001; Saucier, 2000).

Likewise, political affiliation is not heritable; it is largely related to your upbringing and to the friends you make in early adulthood, the key years for deciding which party you want to join. But political conservatism has high heritability: .65 in men and .45 in women (Bouchard, 2004). Various political positions on emotionally hot topics that are associated with conservative or liberal views are also partly heritable. A team of researchers investigated this possibility by drawing on two large samples of more than 8,000 sets of twins who had been surveyed about their personality traits, religious beliefs, and political attitudes (Alford, Funk, & Hibbing, 2005). The researchers compared the opinions of fraternal twins (who share, on average, 50 percent of their genes) with those of identical twins (who share 100 percent of their genes). They calculated how often the identical twins agreed on each issue, subtracted the rate at which fraternal twins agreed, and ended up with a rough measure of heritability.

As you can see in Figure 10.2, the attitudes showing the highest heritability were those toward school prayer and property taxes; attitudes showing the lowest influence of genes included those toward nuclear power, divorce, modern art, and abortion.

As a result of such evidence, some psychological scientists maintain that ideological belief systems may have evolved in human societies to be organized along a left-right dimension, consisting of two core sets of attitudes: (1) whether a person advocates social change or supports the system as it is, and (2) whether a person thinks inequality is a result of human policies and can be overcome, or is inevitable and should be accepted as part of the natural order (Graham, Haidt, & Nosek, 2009). Liberals tend to prefer the values of progress, rebelliousness, chaos, flexibility, feminism, and equality, whereas conservatives tend to prefer tradition, conformity, order, stability, traditional values, and hierarchy.

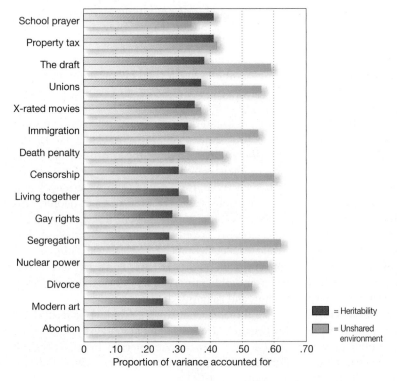

FIGURE 10.2
The Genetics of Belief
A study of thousands of identical and fraternal twins identified the approximate genetic contribution to the variation in attitudes about diverse topics. Heritability was greatest for school prayer and property tax, and lowest for divorce, modern art, and abortion. But notice that, in almost all cases, a person's unique life experiences (the nonshared environment) were far more influential than genes, especially on attitudes toward topics as unrelated as the draft, censorship, and segregation (Alford, Funk, & Hibbing, 2005).

Evolutionary psychologists point out that both sets of attitudes would have had adaptive benefits over the centuries: Conservatism would have promoted stability, tradition, and order, whereas liberalism would have promoted flexibility and change (Graham, Haidt, & Nosek, 2009).

These findings are provocative, but it is important not to oversimplify them—say, by incorrectly assuming that everyone's political opinions are hardwired and unaffected by events. In fact, the factor that accounts for even more of the variation in political attitudes than heritability is individual life experiences, or what behavioral geneticists call the *nonshared environment* (Alford, Funk, & Hibbing, 2005; see Chapter 2). What experiences have you had, because of your family, gender, ethnicity, social class, or unique history, that have shaped your own political views?

> **Thinking Critically about the Genetics of Belief**

Persuasion or "Brainwashing"? The Case of Suicide Bombers

Let's now see how the social-psychological factors discussed thus far might help explain the tragic and disturbing phenomenon of suicide bombers. In many countries, young men and women have wired themselves with explosives and blown up soldiers, civilians, and children, sacrificing their own lives in the process. Although people on two sides of a war dispute the definition of terrorism—one side's "terrorist" is the other side's "freedom fighter"—most social scientists define *terrorism* as politically motivated violence specifically designed to instill feelings of terror and helplessness in a population (Moghaddam, 2005). Are these perpetrators mentally ill? Have they been "brainwashed"?

A researcher who surveyed all known female suicide attacks throughout the world since 1981 (including Afghanistan, Israel, Iraq, India, Lebanon, Pakistan, Russia, Somalia, Sri Lanka, and Turkey) found that "the main motives and circumstances that drive female suicide attackers are quite similar to those that drive men"—loyalty to their country or religion, anger at being occupied by a foreign military, and revenge for loved ones killed by the enemy (O'Rourke, 2008). But most of their peers might feel just as patriotic and angry, without being moved to blow up random passersby and babies. Why does a small minority go that far?

"Brainwashing" implies that a person has had a sudden change of mind without being aware of what is happening; it sounds mysterious and strange. On the contrary, studies of terrorist cells have found that the methods used to create a terrorist suicide bomber are neither mysterious nor unusual (Bloom, 2005; Moghaddam, 2005). Some people may be more emotionally vulnerable than others to these methods, but most of the people who become terrorists are not easily distinguishable from the general population. Indeed, research on contemporary suicide bombers in the Middle East—including Mohamed Atta, who led the 9/11 attack on the World Trade Center—shows that they usually have no psychopathology and are often quite educated and affluent (Krueger, 2007; Sageman, 2008; Silke, 2003). And far from being seen as crazy loners, most suicide bombers are celebrated and honored by their families and communities for their "martyrdom" (Bloom, 2005). The methods of indoctrination include these elements:

- *The person is subjected to entrapment.* Just as ordinary people do not become torturers overnight, they do not become terrorists overnight either; the process proceeds step by step. At first, the new recruit to the cause agrees only to do small things, but gradually the demands increase to spend more time, more money, more sacrifice. Like other revolutionaries, people who become suicide bombers are idealistic and angry about injustices, real and perceived. But some ultimately take extreme measures because, over time, they have become entrapped in closed groups led by strong or charismatic leaders (Moghaddam, 2005).

- *The person's problems, personal and political, are explained by one simple attribution,* which is repeatedly emphasized: "It's all the fault of those bad people; we have to eliminate them."

These members of the Aum Shinrikyo ("Supreme Truth") sect in Japan, wearing masks of their leader's face, took the uniformity of cult identity to an extreme. The group's founder instructed his devotees to place nerve gas in a Japanese subway, which killed ten people and sickened thousands of other passengers. One former member said of the sect, "Their strategy is to wear you down and take control of your mind. They promise you heaven, but they make you live in hell."

The group fans the "emotional fuel" that feeds suicide bombers' motivation: their grievances, their perceived humiliation at the hands of those "bad people," their feelings of impotence and meaninglessness (Kruglanski et al., 2009).

- *The person is offered a new identity and is promised salvation.* The recruit is told that he or she is part of the chosen, the elite, or the saved. In 1095, Pope Urban II launched a holy war against Muslims, assuring his forces that killing a Muslim was an act of Christian penance. Anyone killed in battle, the Pope promised, would bypass thousands of years of torture in purgatory and go directly to heaven. This is what young Muslim terrorists are promised today for killing Western "infidels."

- *The person's access to disconfirming (dissonant) information is severely controlled.* As soon as a person is a committed believer, the leader limits the person's choices, denigrates critical thinking, and suppresses private doubts. Recruits may be physically

isolated from the outside world and thus from antidotes to the leader's ideas. They are separated from their families, are indoctrinated and trained for 18 months or more, and eventually become emotionally bonded to the group and the leader (Atran, 2003).

These methods are similar to those that have been used to entice Americans into religious and other sects (Ofshe & Watters, 1994; Singer, 2003). In the 1970s, the cult leader Jim Jones told members of his "People's Temple" that the time had come to die, and 913 people dutifully lined up to drink Kool-Aid mixed with cyanide; many gave it to their children. In the 1990s, David Koresh, leader of the Branch Davidian cult in Waco, Texas, led his followers to a fiery death in a shootout with the FBI. In these groups, as in the case of terrorist cells, most recruits started out as ordinary people. Yet, after being subjected to the influence techniques we have described, they ended up doing things that they once would have found unimaginable.

Study and
Review on
mypsychlab.com

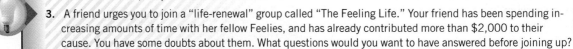

Quick Quiz

Now, how can we persuade you to take this quiz without brainwashing you?

1. Candidate Carson spends $3 million to make sure his name is seen and heard frequently and to repeat unverified charges that his opponent is a thief. What psychological processes is he relying on to win?

2. Which of the following has a significant heritable component? (a) religious affiliation, (b) political affiliation, (c) attitudes that favor stability and order versus those favoring equality and change, (d) attitudes toward modern art, (e) political conservatism

3. A friend urges you to join a "life-renewal" group called "The Feeling Life." Your friend has been spending increasing amounts of time with her fellow Feelies, and has already contributed more than $2,000 to their cause. You have some doubts about them. What questions would you want to have answered before joining up?

Answers:

1. The familiarity effect and the validity effect. 2. c, e 3. A few things to consider: Is there an autocratic leader who suppresses dissent and criticism, while rationalizing this practice as a benefit for members—for example, by saying to potential skeptics, "Doubt and disbelief are signs that your feeling side is being repressed"? Have long-standing members given up their friends, families, interests, and ambitions for this group? Does the leader offer simple but unrealistic promises to repair your life and all your troubles? Are members required to make sacrifices by donating large amounts of time and money?

YOU are about to learn...

- why people in groups often go along with the majority even when the majority is dead wrong.

- how "groupthink" can lead to bad decisions.

- how crowds can create "bystander apathy" and unpredictable violence.

- the conditions that increase the likelihood that some people will dissent, take risks to help others, or blow the whistle on wrongdoers.

Individuals in Groups

The need to belong may be the most powerful of all human motivations (Baumeister et al., 2007). Human beings are so powerfully connected to one another, and so dependent upon human companionship, that most people feel and remember the *social* pain of being rejected, humiliated, or excluded more intensely than actual *physical* pain they have endured (Chen et al., 2008; Williams, 2009). The need for social connection also explains why sending a prisoner to solitary confinement is internationally considered a form of torture: Its psychological consequences are even more devastating than physical abuse (Gawande, 2009).

Accordingly, the most powerful weapon that groups have to ensure their members' cooperation, and to weed out unproductive or disruptive members, is ostracism—rejection or permanent banishment. Social rejection impedes the ability to empathize, think critically, and solve problems. It can lead to mental disorders, eating disorders, and attempted suicide. No wonder that when people are rejected by a group they care about, some try to mend the rift, change their behavior to get back in the group's good graces, or respond with rage and violence (Baumeister et al., 2007).

Of course, we all belong to many different groups, which vary in their importance to us. But the point to underscore is that as soon as we join a bunch of other people, we act differently than we would on our own. This change occurs regardless of whether the group has convened to solve problems and make decisions, has gathered to have a party, consists of anonymous bystanders or members of an Internet chat room, or is a crowd of spectators or celebrants.

Conformity

The first thing that people in groups do is conform, taking action or adopting attitudes as a result of real or imagined group pressure. Suppose that you are required to appear at a psychology laboratory for an experiment on perception. You join seven other students seated in a room. You are shown a 10-inch line and asked which of three other lines is identical to it. The correct answer, line A, is obvious, so you are amused when the first person in the group chooses line B. "Bad eyesight," you say to yourself. "He's off by 2 whole inches!" The second person also chooses line B. "What a dope," you think. But by the time the fifth person has chosen line B, you are beginning to doubt yourself. The sixth and seventh students also choose line B, and now you are worried about *your* eyesight. The experimenter looks at you. "Your turn," he says. Do you follow the evidence of your own eyes or the collective judgment of the group?

Test line   A   B   C

This was the design for a series of famous studies of conformity conducted by Solomon Asch (1952, 1965). The seven "nearsighted" students were actually Asch's confederates. Asch wanted to know what people would do when a group unanimously contradicted an obvious fact. He found that when people made the line comparisons on their own, they were almost always accurate. But in the group, only 20 percent of the students remained completely independent on every trial, and often they apologized for not agreeing with the others. One-third conformed to the group's incorrect decision more than half the time, and the rest conformed at least some of the time. Whether or not they conformed, the students often felt uncertain of their decision. As one participant later said, "I felt disturbed, puzzled, separated, like an outcast from the rest." Asch's experiment has been replicated

Get Involved! Can You Disconnect?

To see for yourself how social you are, try this simple experiment: Turn off your cell phone and laptop for a full 24 hours. *Off!* You may use your laptop to take notes in class, but that's all. No email, IMs, Twitter, Facebook, RSS, YouTube, or anything else on the Web. Keep track of your feelings on a (written!) notepad as time passes. Are you feeling anxious? Nervous? How long can you remain "cut off" before you start to feel isolated from your friends and family?

Sometimes people like to conform to feel part of the group . . . and sometimes they like to assert their individuality.

many times and in many countries (Bond & Smith, 1996).

Like obedience, conformity has positive aspects. Society runs more smoothly when people know how to behave in a given situation and when they share the same attitudes and manners. Conformity in dress, preferences, and ideas confers a sense of being in sync with friends and colleagues. Moreover, people often intuitively understand that sometimes the group knows more than they do. In fact, a reliance on group judgment begins in very early childhood, suggesting its adaptive function for the species. In two experiments with 3- and 4-year-old children, researchers found that when children were given a choice between relying on information provided by a three-adult majority or a single adult about the name of an unfamiliar object, they sided with the majority (Corriveau, Fusaro, & Harris, 2009).

But also like obedience, conformity has negative consequences, notably its power to suppress critical thinking and creativity. In a group, many people will deny their private beliefs, agree with silly notions, and even repudiate their own values.

Groupthink

Close, friendly groups usually work well together. But they face the problem of getting the best ideas and efforts from their members while avoiding an extreme form of conformity called **groupthink**, the tendency to think alike and suppress dissent. According to Irving Janis (1982, 1989), groupthink occurs when a group's need for total agreement overwhelms its

groupthink The tendency for all members of a group to think alike for the sake of harmony and to suppress disagreement.

need to make the wisest decision. The symptoms of groupthink include the following:

- *An illusion of invulnerability.* The group believes it can do no wrong and is 100 percent correct in its decisions.
- *Self-censorship.* Dissenters decide to keep quiet rather than make trouble, offend their friends, or risk being ridiculed.
- *Pressure on dissenters to conform.* The leader teases or humiliates dissenters or otherwise pressures them to go along.
- *An illusion of unanimity.* By discouraging dissent and failing to consider alternative courses of action, leaders and group members create an illusion of consensus; they may even explicitly order suspected dissenters to keep quiet.

Throughout history, groupthink has led to disastrous decisions in military and civilian life. In 1961, President John F. Kennedy and his advisers approved a CIA plan to invade Cuba at the Bay of Pigs and try

to overthrow the government of Fidel Castro; the invasion was a humiliating defeat. In the mid-1960s, President Lyndon Johnson and his cabinet escalated the war in Vietnam in spite of obvious signs that further bombing and increased troops were not bringing the war to an end. In 1986, NASA officials insulated themselves from the dissenting objections of engineers who warned them that the space shuttle *Challenger* was unsafe; NASA launched it anyway, and it exploded shortly after takeoff. And when President George W. Bush launched an invasion of Iraq, claiming the country had weapons of mass destruction and was allied with al Qaeda, he and his team ignored dissenters and evidence from intelligence agencies that neither claim was true (Mayer, 2009). The agencies themselves later accused the Bush administration of "groupthink."

Fortunately, groupthink can be minimized if the leader rewards the expression of doubt and dissent, protects and encourages minority views, asks group members to generate as many alternative solutions to a problem as they can think of, and has everyone try to think of the risks and disadvantages of the preferred decision. Resistance to groupthink can also be fostered by creating a group identity that encourages members to think of themselves as open-minded problem solvers rather than invulnerable know-it-alls (Turner, Pratkanis, & Samuels, 2003). Leaders who encourage group members to identify strongly with the collective enterprise are also more likely to hear dissenting opinions, because members will be less willing to support a decision they regard as harmful to the group's goal (Packer, 2009).

Not all leaders want to run their groups this way, of course. For many people in positions of power, from presidents to company executives to movie moguls, the temptation is great to surround themselves with others who agree with what they want to do, and to demote or fire those who disagree on the grounds that they are being "disloyal." Perhaps a key quality of great leaders is that they are able to rise above this temptation.

The Wisdom and Madness of Crowds

On the TV show "Who Wants to be a Millionaire?", contestants are given the chance to ask the audience how it would answer a question. This gimmick comes straight from a phenomenon known as the "wisdom of crowds": the fact that a crowd's judgment is often more accurate than that of its individual members (Surowiecki, 2004; Vul & Pashler, 2008). Just as neurons interconnect in networks that create thoughts and actions beyond the scope of any individual neuron, so a crowd creates a social network whose behavior is more than individual members may intend or even be aware of (Goldstone, Roberts, & Gureckis, 2008). But crowds can create havoc, too. They can spread gossip, rumors, misinformation, and panic as fast as the flu. They can turn from joyful and peaceful to violent and destructive in a flash.

Diffusion of Responsibility Suppose you were in trouble on a city street or in another public place—say, being mugged or having a sudden appendicitis attack. Do you think you would be more likely to get help if (a) one other person was passing by, (b) several other people were in the area, or (c) dozens of people were in the area? Most people would choose the third answer, but that is not how human beings operate. On the contrary, the more people there are around you, the *less* likely it is that one of them will come to your aid. Why? **⊙▶ Simulate**

The answer has to do with a group process called the **diffusion of responsibility**, in which responsibility for an outcome is diffused, or spread, among many people, reducing each individual's personal sense of accountability. One result is *bystander apathy:* In crowds, when someone is in trouble, individuals often fail to take action or call for help because they assume that someone else will do so (Darley & Latané, 1968).

When the "crowd" consists of online observers, it's even easier to pass the buck. Abraham Biggs Jr., age 19, had been posting to an online discussion board for two years. One day he announced his intention to commit suicide with an overdose of drugs, adding a link to a live video feed from his bedroom. None of the watchers called the police for more than ten hours, and Biggs died. In contrast, people are more likely to come to a stranger's aid if they are the only ones around to help, because responsibility cannot be diffused.

Deindividuation The most extreme instances of the diffusion of responsibility occur in large, anonymous mobs or crowds. The crowds may consist of cheerful sports spectators or angry rioters. Either way, people often lose awareness of their individuality and seem to hand themselves over to the mood and actions of the crowd, a state called **deindividuation** (Festinger, Pepitone, & Newcomb, 1952). You are more likely to feel deindividuated in a large city, where no one recognizes you, than in a small town, where it is hard to hide. (You are also more likely to feel deindividuated in large classes, where you might—mistakenly—think you are

⊙▶ Simulate Helping a Stranger on **mypsychlab.com**

diffusion of responsibility In groups, the tendency of members to avoid taking action because they assume that others will.

deindividuation In groups or crowds, the loss of awareness of one's own individuality.

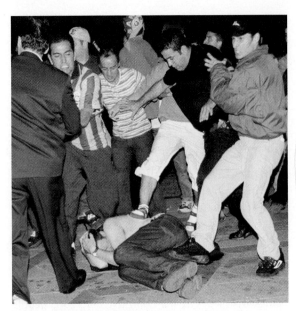

People in crowds, feeling anonymous, may do destructive things they would never do on their own. These soccer hooligans are kicking a fan of the opposition team during a night of violence.

Deindividuation has long been considered a prime reason for mob violence. According to this explanation, because deindividuated people in crowds "forget themselves" and do not feel accountable for their actions, they are more likely to violate social norms and laws than they would be on their own: breaking store windows, looting, getting into fights, or rioting at a sports event. But deindividuation does not always make people more combative. Sometimes it makes them more friendly; think of all the chatty, anonymous people on buses and planes who reveal things to their seatmates they would never tell anyone they knew.

What really seems to be happening when people are in large crowds or anonymous situations is not that they become mindless or uninhibited. Rather, they become more likely to conform to the norms of the *specific situation* (Postmes & Spears, 1998). College students who go on wild sprees during spring break may be violating the local laws and norms of Palm Springs or Key West not because their aggressiveness has been released but because they are conforming to the "Let's party!" norms of their fellow students. Crowd norms can also foster helpfulness, as they often do in the aftermath of disasters, when strangers come out to help victims and rescue workers, leaving food, clothes, and tributes.

invisible to the teacher, than in small ones.) Sometimes organizations actively promote the deindividuation of their members as a way of enhancing conformity and allegiance to the group. This is an important function of uniforms or masks, which eliminate each member's distinctive identity.

✓●─ **Study** and **Review** on mypsychlab.com

Quick Quiz

On your own, take responsibility for identifying which phenomenon is illustrated in each of the following situations.

1. The president's closest advisers are afraid to disagree with his views on energy policy.
2. You are at a costume party wearing a silly gorilla suit. When you see a chance to play a practical joke on the host, you do it.
3. Walking down a busy street, you see that fire has broken out in a store window. "Someone must already have called the fire department," you say.

Answers:

1. groupthink   2. deindividuation   3. bystander apathy brought on by diffusion of responsibility

Altruism and Dissent

We have seen how roles, norms, and pressures to obey authority and conform to one's group can cause people to behave in ways they might not otherwise. Yet throughout history men and women have disobeyed orders they believed to be wrong and have gone against prevailing cultural beliefs; their actions have sometimes changed the course of

history. In 1955, in Montgomery, Alabama, a shy, quiet woman named Rosa Parks refused to give up her bus seat to a white passenger, and she was arrested for breaking the law. Her protest sparked a 381-day bus boycott and helped launch the modern civil rights movement.

When people think of heroes, they usually think of men rescuing a child, risking gunfire to bring a fellow soldier to safety, standing up to a bully, or landing an injured plane safely. This is the kind of heroism traditionally associated with men, who on average have greater physical strength than women. But when people are asked to name heroes they personally know, they name women and men equally (Rankin & Eagly, 2008). The reason is that many acts of selfless risk taking do not require physical strength. During the Holocaust, women in France, Poland, and the Netherlands were as likely as men to risk their lives to save Jews. Women are more likely than men to donate an organ such as a kidney to save another person's life, and women are more likely to volunteer to serve in dangerous postings around the world in the Peace Corps (Becker & Eagly, 2004).

Sadly, the costs of dissent, courage, and honesty are often high; remember that most groups do not welcome nonconformity and disagreement. Most whistle-blowers, far from being rewarded for their bravery, are punished for it. Three women were named *Time* magazine's Persons of the Year for their courage in exposing wrongdoing in their organizations—Enron, WorldCom, and the FBI—yet all paid a steep professional price for doing so. Studies of whistle-blowers find that half to two-thirds lose their jobs and have to leave their professions entirely. Many lose their homes and families (Alford, 2001). The two soldiers who first exposed the abuses going on at Abu Ghraib were shunned by many of their peers and received death threats; one was threatened with a court-martial.

Nonconformity, protest, and *altruism*, the willingness to take selfless or dangerous action on behalf of others, are in part a matter of personal convictions and conscience. However, just as there are situational reasons for obedience and conformity, so there are external influences on a person's decision to state an unpopular opinion, choose conscience over conformity, or help a stranger in trouble. Here are some of the situational factors that can overcome bystander apathy and increase the likelihood of helping others or behaving courageously:

1 **You perceive the need for intervention or help.** It may seem obvious, but before you can take independent action, you must realize that such action is necessary. Sometimes people willfully blind themselves to wrongdoing to justify their own inaction ("I'm just minding my business"; "I have no idea what they're doing over there at that concentration camp"). But blindness to the need for action also occurs when a situation imposes too many demands on people's attention, as it often does for residents of densely populated cities.

2 **Cultural norms encourage you to take action.** Would you spontaneously tell a passerby that he or she had dropped a pen? Offer to help a person with an injured leg who had dropped an armful of magazines? Assist a blind person across the street? An international field study investigated strangers' helpfulness to one another with those three non-emergency acts of kindness, in 23 American cities and 22 cities in other countries. Cultural norms for helping were more important than population density in predicting levels of helpfulness: Pedestrians in busy Copenhagen and Vienna were kinder to strangers than were passersby in busy New York City. Large differences in helping rates emerged, ranging from 93 percent in Rio de Janeiro, Brazil, to 40 percent in Kuala Lampur, Malaysia (Levine, 2003; Levine, Norenzayan, & Philbrick, 2001). People in Brazil and other Latin American cultures value *simpatía*, a cultural ideal of harmony and helping others (Holloway, Waldrip, & Ickes, 2009).

We tend to think of "heroes" as men who are physically brave, like the rescuers who searched for survivors in the rubble of the 2010 earthquake in Haiti. But heroism comes in many forms, such as blowing the whistle on your employer's cover-up of wrongdoing or negligence. FBI special agent Coleen Rowley was fired for testifying to the Senate that the FBI had blocked the investigation of a man involved in planning the terrorist attacks on the World Trade Centers.

3 You have an ally. In Asch's conformity experiment, the presence of one other person who gave the correct answer was enough to overcome agreement with the majority. In Milgram's experiment, the presence of someone who disobeyed the experimenter's instruction to shock the learner sharply increased the number of people who also disobeyed. One dissenting member of a group may be viewed as a troublemaker, but two or three are a coalition. An ally reassures a person of the rightness of the protest, and their combined efforts may eventually persuade the majority (Wood et al., 1994).

4 You become entrapped. Does this sound familiar by now? Once having taken the initial step of getting involved, most people will increase their commitment. In one study, nearly 9,000 federal employees were asked whether they had observed wrongdoing at work, whether they had told anyone about it, and what happened if they had told. Nearly half of the sample had observed some serious cases of wrongdoing, such as stealing federal funds, accepting bribes, or creating a situation that was dangerous to public safety. Of that half, 72 percent had done nothing at all, but the other 28 percent reported the problem to their immediate supervisors. Once they had taken that step, a majority of the whistle-blowers eventually took the matter to higher authorities (Graham, 1986).

As you can see, certain social and cultural factors make altruism, disobedience, and dissent more likely to occur, just as other external factors suppress them.

✓● **Study** and
Review on
mypsychlab.com

Quick Quiz

We hope you won't disobey our order to answer this question.

Imagine that you are chief executive officer of a new electric-car company. You want your employees to feel free to offer their suggestions and criticisms to improve productivity and satisfaction. You also want them to inform managers if they find any evidence that the cars are unsafe, even if that means delaying production. What concepts from this chapter could you use in setting company policy?

Answers:

Some possibilities: You could encourage, or even require, dissenting views; avoid deindividuation by rewarding innovative suggestions and implementing the best ones; stimulate employees' commitment to the task (building a car that will solve the world's pollution problem); and establish a written policy to protect whistle-blowers. What else can you think of?

---

social identity The part of a person's self-concept that is based on his or her identification with a nation, religious or political group, occupation, or other social affiliation.

ethnic identity A person's identification with a racial or ethnic group.

acculturation The process by which members of minority groups come to identify with and feel part of the mainstream culture.

◆ YOU are about to learn...

• how people in a multicultural society balance ethnic identity and acculturation.

• what causes ethnocentric, us–them thinking and how to decrease it.

• how stereotypes benefit us and how they distort reality.

Us versus Them: Group Identity

Each of us develops a personal identity that is based on our particular traits and unique life history. But we also develop **social identities** based on the groups we belong to, including our national, religious, political, and occupational groups (Brewer & Gardner, 1996; Tajfel & Turner, 1986).

Ethnic Identity

In multicultural societies such as the United States and Canada, different social identities often collide. In particular, people often face the dilemma of balancing an **ethnic identity**, a close identification with a religious or ethnic group, and **acculturation**, identification with the dominant culture (Berry, 2006; Phinney, 1996). The hallmarks of having an ethnic identity are that you identify with the group, feel proud to be a member, feel emotionally attached to the group, and behave in ways that conform to the group's rules, values, and norms. Interestingly, many Americans these days do not want to be pigeonholed into only one ethnic category. Millions list themselves in the national census as having various combinations of identities, such as Blaxican (African American and Mexican), Negripino (African American and Filipino), Hafu (half Japanese, half something else), and Chino-Latino (Chinese and Hispanic).

Monica Almeida/The New York Times

Ethnic identities are changing these days, as bicultural North Americans blend aspects of mainstream culture with their own traditions. Many people still like to celebrate the traditions of their ethnic heritage, as illustrated in these photos of Japanese-American college students reviving *taiko*, traditional Japanese drumming, Ukrainian-American teens wearing national dress, and African-American children lighting Kwanzaa candles.

Nevertheless, any observer of the world today knows that acculturation is not always easy and seamless. Many immigrants arrive in their host country with every intention of becoming part of the mainstream culture. If they encounter discrimination or setbacks, however, they may realize that acculturation is harder than they anticipated and that their original ethnic identity offers greater solace; this is why new immigrants often report poorer mental and physical health in response to the stresses of trying to acculturate than their children do (Schwartz et al., 2010). In any case, a person's degree of acculturation may change throughout life in response to experiences and societal events. At any given moment in their lives, people pick and choose among the values, food, traditions, and customs of the mainstream culture, while also keeping aspects of their heritage that are important to their self-identity.

Ethnocentrism

Social identities give us a sense of place and position in the world. Without them, most of us would feel like loose marbles rolling around in an unconnected universe. It feels good to be part of an "us." But does that mean that we must automatically feel superior to "them"?

Ethnocentrism is the belief that your own culture, nation, or religion is superior to all others. Ethnocentrism is universal, probably because it aids survival by increasing people's attachment to their own group and their willingness to work on its behalf. It is even embedded in some languages: The Chinese word for China means "the center of the world" (consigning the other five billion people to the suburbs?) and the Navajo, the Kiowa, and the Inuit call themselves simply "The People."

Ethnocentrism rests on a fundamental social identity: us. As soon as people have created a category called "us," however, they invariably perceive everybody else as "not-us." This in-group solidarity can be manufactured in a minute in the laboratory, as Henri Tajfel and his colleagues (1971) demonstrated in an experiment with British schoolboys. Tajfel showed the boys slides with varying numbers of dots on them and asked the boys to guess how many dots

ethnocentrism The belief that one's own ethnic group, nation, or religion is superior to all others.

there were. The boys were arbitrarily told that they were "overestimators" or "underestimators" and were then asked to work on another task. In this phase, they had a chance to give points to other boys identified as overestimators or underestimators. Although each boy worked alone in his cubicle, almost every single one assigned far more points to boys he thought were like him, an overestimator or an underestimator. As the boys emerged from their rooms, they were asked, "Which were you?" The answers received either cheers or boos from the others.

Us–them social identities are strengthened when two groups compete with each other. Years ago, Muzafer Sherif and his colleagues used a natural setting, a Boy Scout camp called Robbers Cave, to demonstrate the effects of competition on hostility and conflict between groups (Sherif, 1958; Sherif et al., 1961). Sherif randomly assigned 11- and 12-year-old boys to two groups, the Eagles and the Rattlers. To build a sense of in-group identity and team spirit, he had each group work together on projects such as making a rope bridge and building a diving board. Sherif then put the Eagles and Rattlers in competition for prizes. During fierce games of football, baseball, and tug-of-war, the boys whipped up a competitive fever that soon spilled off the playing fields. They began to raid each other's cabins, call each other names, and start fistfights. No one dared to have a friend from the rival group. Before long, the Eagles and the Rattlers were as hostile toward each other as any two gangs fighting for turf. Their hostility continued even when they were just sitting around together watching movies.

Then Sherif decided to try to undo the hostility he had created and make peace between the Eagles and Rattlers. He and his associates set up a series of predicaments in which both groups needed to work together to reach a desired goal, such as pooling their resources to get a movie they all wanted to see or pulling a staff truck up a hill on a camping trip. This policy of *interdependence in reaching mutual goals* was highly successful in reducing the boys' "ethnocentrism," competitiveness, and hostility; the boys eventually made friends with their former enemies (see Figure 10.3). Interdependence has a similar effect in adult groups (Gaertner et al., 1990). The reason, it seems, is that cooperation causes people to think of themselves as members of one big group instead of two opposed groups, us and them.

Stereotypes

Think of all the ways your friends and family members differ: Jeff is stodgy, Ruth is bossy, Farah is outgoing. But if you have never met a person from

stereotype A summary impression of a group, in which a person believes that all members of the group share a common trait or traits (positive, negative, or neutral).

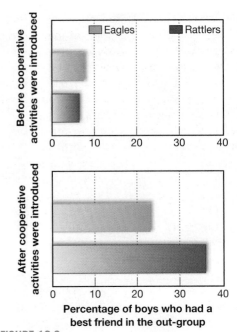

FIGURE 10.3

The Experiment at Robbers Cave
In this study, competitive games fostered hostility between the Rattlers and the Eagles. Few boys had a best friend from the other group (upper graph). But after the teams had to cooperate to solve various problems, the percentage who made friends across "enemy lines" shot up (lower graph) (Sherif et al., 1961).

Turkey or Tibet, you are likely to stereotype Turks and Tibetans. A **stereotype** is a summary impression of a group of people in which all members of the group are viewed as sharing a common trait or traits. There are stereotypes of people who drive Hummers or Hondas, of engineering students and art students, of feminists and fraternity men.

Stereotypes aren't necessarily bad and they are sometimes very accurate (Jussim et al., 2009). They are, as some psychologists have called them, useful tools in the mental toolbox—energy-saving devices that allow us to make efficient decisions (Macrae & Bodenhausen, 2000). They help us quickly process new information and retrieve memories. They allow us to organize experience, make sense of differences among individuals and groups, and predict how people will behave. In fact, the brain automatically registers and encodes the basic categories of gender, ethnicity, and age, suggesting that there is a neurological basis for the cognitive efficiency of stereotyping (Ito & Urland, 2003).

However, although stereotypes may reflect real differences among people, they also distort that reality in three ways (Judd et al., 1995). First, *they exaggerate differences between groups*, making the stereotyped group seem odd, unfamiliar, or dangerous, not like "us." Second, *they produce selective perception*; people tend to see only the evidence that fits the stereotype and reject any perceptions that do not fit. Third, *they underestimate differences within the stereotyped group*, creating the impression that all members of that group are the same.

When people like a group, their stereotype of the group's behavior tends to be positive. When they dislike a group, their stereotype *of the same behavior* tends to be negative. A person who is careful with money, after all, can be seen as "thrifty" or "stingy"; someone who values family life might be "family-loving" or "clannish" (Peabody, 1985). Cultural values affect how people evaluate the actions of another group and whether a stereotype becomes positive or negative. Chinese students in Hong Kong, where communalism and respect for elders are valued, think that a student who comes late to class or argues with a parent about grades is being selfish and disrespectful of adults. But Australian students, who value individualism, think that the same behavior is perfectly appropriate (Forgas & Bond, 1985). You can see how the Chinese might form negative stereotypes of "disrespectful" Australians, and how the Australians

What is this woman's occupation? Among non-Muslims in the West, the assumption is that Muslim women who wear the full-length black *niqab* must be repressed sexually as well as politically. But the answer shatters the stereotype. Wedad Lootah, a Muslim living in Dubai, United Arab Emirates, is a marriage counselor and sexual activist, author of a best-selling Arabic book, *Top Secret: Sexual Guidance for Married Couples.*

might form negative stereotypes of the "spineless" Chinese. And it is a small step from negative stereotypes to prejudice.

Quick Quiz

Do you have a positive or a negative stereotype of quizzes?

1. Frank, an African-American college student, has to decide between living in a dorm with mostly white students who share his interest in science, or living in a dorm with other black students who are studying the history and contributions of African culture. The first choice values _____ whereas the second values_____.
2. John knows and likes the Chicano minority in his town, but he privately believes that Anglo culture is superior to all others. His belief is evidence of his _____.
3. What strategy does the Robbers Cave study suggest for reducing us–them thinking and hostility between groups?
4. What are three ways in which stereotypes can distort reality?

Answers:

1. acculturation, ethnic identity 2. ethnocentrism 3. interdependence in reaching mutual goals 4. They exaggerate differences between groups; they produce selective perception; and they underestimate differences *within* the stereotyped group.

 YOU are about to learn...

• four causes and functions of prejudice.

• four indirect ways of measuring prejudice.

• four conditions necessary for reducing prejudice and conflict.

Group Conflict and Prejudice

A **prejudice** consists of a negative stereotype and a strong, unreasonable dislike or hatred of a group. A central feature of a prejudice is that it remains

prejudice A strong, unreasonable dislike or hatred of a group, based on a negative stereotype.

immune to evidence. In his classic book *The Nature of Prejudice*, Gordon Allport (1954/1979) described the responses characteristic of a prejudiced person when confronted with evidence contradicting his or her beliefs:

Mr. X: The trouble with Jews is that they only take care of their own group.

Mr. Y: But the record of the Community Chest campaign shows that they give more generously, in proportion to their numbers, to the general charities of the community, than do non-Jews.

Mr. X: That shows they are always trying to buy favor and intrude into Christian affairs. They think of nothing but money; that is why there are so many Jewish bankers.

Mr. Y: But a recent study shows that the percentage of Jews in the banking business is negligible, far smaller than the percentage of non-Jews.

Mr. X: That's just it; they don't go in for respectable business; they are only in the movie business or run night clubs.

Notice that Mr. X doesn't even try to respond to Mr. Y's evidence; he just moves along to another reason for his dislike of Jews. That is the slippery nature of prejudice in general and toward Jews in particular. Indeed, many of the stereotypes underlying anti-Semitism are mutually contradictory and constantly shift across generations and nations. Jews were attacked for being Communists in Nazi Germany and Argentina, and for being greedy capitalists in the Communist Soviet Union. They have been criticized for being too secular and also for being too mystical, for being weak and also for being powerful enough to dominate the world. Although anti-Semitism declined in the 50 years after World War II, it has been on the rise again in the United States, Europe, the Middle East, and around the world (Cohen et al., 2009).

The Origins of Prejudice

Prejudice provides the fuel for ethnocentrism. Its specific targets change, but it persists everywhere in some form because it has so many sources and functions: psychological, social, economic, and cultural:

1 Psychological causes. Prejudice often serves to ward off feelings of doubt, fear, and insecurity. Around the world, people puff up their low self-esteem or self-worth by disliking or hating groups they see as inferior (Islam & Hewstone, 1993; Stephan et al., 1994). Prejudice also allows people to use the target group as a scapegoat ("Those people

are the source of all my troubles"), to displace anger and cope with feelings of powerlessness. Immediately after 9/11, some white Americans took out their anger on fellow Americans who happened to be Arab, Sikh, Pakistani, Hindu, or Afghan. Two men in Chicago beat up an Arab-American taxi driver, yelling, "This is what you get, you mass murderer!"

Prejudice may also help people defend against the existential terror of death (Cohen et al., 2009; Pyszczynski, Rothschild, & Abdollahi, 2008). People in every culture hold political or religious worldviews that provide them with a sense of meaning, purpose, and hope of immortality (either through an afterlife or through a connection to something greater than themselves). If that worldview helps alleviate the fear of their own mortality, they will be deeply threatened by the mere existence of others who reject their way of seeing things. Many people manage that threat by denigrating opposing groups, attempting to convert them, or even trying to exterminate them (Greenberg, Solomon, & Arndt, 2008).

2 Social causes. Not all prejudices, however, have deep-seated psychological roots. Some are acquired through pressure to conform to the views of friends, relatives, or associates; if you don't agree with a group's prejudices toward another group, you may be gently or abruptly asked to leave the group. Some are passed along mindlessly from one generation to another, as when parents communicate to their children, "We don't associate with people like that."

3 Economic causes. Prejudice makes official forms of discrimination seem legitimate, by justifying the majority group's dominance, status, or greater wealth. Wherever a majority group systematically discriminates against a minority to preserve its power—whites, blacks, Muslims, Hindus, Japanese, Christians, Jews, you name it—they will claim that their actions are legitimate because the minority is so obviously inferior and incompetent (Islam & Hewstone, 1993; Jost, Nosek, & Gosling, 2008; Morton et al., 2009; Sidanius, Pratto, & Bobo, 1996).

You can see how prejudice rises and falls with changing economic conditions by observing what happens when two groups are in direct competition for jobs, or when people are worried about their incomes: Prejudice between them increases. Consider how white attitudes toward Chinese immigrants in the United States fluctuated during the nineteenth century, as reflected in newspapers of the time (Aronson, 2008). When the Chinese were working in the gold mines and potentially taking jobs from white laborers, the white-run newspapers described them as depraved, vicious, and bloodthirsty. Just a decade later, when the Chinese began working on the transcontinental railroad, doing difficult and dangerous jobs that few white men wanted, prejudice against them declined. Whites described them as hardworking, industrious, and law-abiding. Then, after the railroad was finished and the Chinese had to compete with Civil War veterans for scarce jobs, white attitudes changed again. Whites now thought the Chinese were "criminal," "crafty," "conniving," and "stupid." (The newspapers did not report the attitudes of the Chinese.) Today's Chinese are Mexican, particularly the migrant workers whose labor is needed in America but who are perceived as costing Americans their jobs.

The oldest prejudice in the world may be sexism, and it, too, serves to legitimize existing sex roles and inequities in power. In research with 15,000 men and women in 19 nations, psychologists found that *hostile sexism*, which reflects active dislike of women, is different from *benevolent sexism*, which puts women on a pedestal. The latter type of sexism is affectionate but patronizing, conveying the attitude that women are so good, kind, and moral that they should stay at home, away from the rough-and-tumble (and power and income) of public life (Glick et al., 2000; Glick, 2006). Because benevolent sexism lacks a tone of hostility to women, it doesn't seem like a prejudice to many people, and many women find it alluring to think they are better than men. But both forms of sexism, whether someone thinks women are too good for equality or not good enough, legitimize discrimination against women (Christopher & Wojda, 2008).

Perhaps you are thinking: "Hey, what about men? There are plenty of prejudices against men, too—that they are sexual predators, emotionally heartless, domineering, and arrogant." In fact, according to a 16-nation study of attitudes toward men, many people do believe that men are aggressive and predatory, and overall just not as warm and wonderful as women (Glick et al., 2004). This attitude seems hostile to men, the researchers found,

In times of war, most people fall victim to emotional reasoning, thinking of the enemy as being less than human, often as vermin, dogs, or pigs. After 9/11, anti-American demonstrators in Jakarta portrayed former president George W. Bush as a rabid dog, while an American cartoonist lumped the Taliban, Iraq, and Iran into a "barrel of vermin."

but it also reflects and supports gender inequality by characterizing men as being designed for leadership and dominance.

4 Cultural and national causes. Finally, prejudice bonds people to their own ethnic or national group and its ways; by disliking "them," we feel closer to our own group. That feeling, in turn, justifies whatever we do to "them" to preserve our customs and national policies. In fact, although many people assume that prejudice causes war, the reverse is far more often the case: War causes prejudice. When two nations declare war, when one country decides to invade another, or when a weak leader displaces the country's economic problems onto a minority scapegoat, the citizenry's prejudice against that enemy or scapegoat will be inflamed. Of course, sometimes anger at an enemy is justified, but war usually turns legitimate anger into blind prejudice: Those people are not only the enemy; they are less than human and deserve to be exterminated (Keen, 1986; Staub, 1999). That is why enemies are so often described as vermin, rats, mad dogs, heathens, baby killers, or monsters—anything but human beings like us.

Get Involved! Probing Your Prejudices

Are you prejudiced? Is there any group of people you dislike because of their gender, ethnicity, sexual orientation, nationality, religion, physical appearance, or political views? Write down your deepest thoughts and feelings about this group. Take as long as you want, and do not censor yourself or say what you think you ought to say. Now reread what you have written. Which of the sources of prejudice discussed in the text might be contributing to your views? Do you feel that your attitudes toward the group are legitimate, or are you uncomfortable about having them?

Defining and Measuring Prejudice

With the historic election in 2008 of Barack Obama as the nation's first African-American president, many people became hopeful that the worst forms of racism in America were ending. Certainly, on surveys in the United States and Canada, overt prejudice of all kinds has been declining sharply. The numbers of people who admit to believing that blacks are inferior to whites, women inferior to men, and gays inferior to straights have been steadily dropping in the last 65 years (Weaver, 2008).

Yet, as Gordon Allport (1954/1979) observed so long ago, "defeated intellectually, prejudice lingers emotionally." Discriminatory behavior may be outlawed, but deep-seated negative feelings and bigotry may nonetheless persist in subtle ways (Dovidio & Gaertner, 2008). And, as we just saw, such feelings may lie dormant during good times, only to be easily aroused during bad times or when people feel threatened socially or economically. By the end of 2009, anti-black hate crimes had risen 8 percent over the previous two years (Blow, 2009).

That is why prejudice is like a weasel—hard to grasp and hold on to. One problem is that not all prejudiced people are prejudiced in the same way or to the same extent. Suppose that Raymond wishes to be

> **Thinking Critically about Defining Prejudice**

The Many Targets of Prejudice

Prejudice has a long and universal history. Why do new prejudices keep emerging, others fade away, and some old ones persist?

Some prejudices rise and fall with events. When France refused to support America's decision to go to war with Iraq in 2003, anti-French anger erupted (as the scrawled sign telling the French to go back to France, where they were anyway, indicates). Anti-Japanese feelings in the United States ran high in the 1920s and again in the 1990s as a result of economic competition between the two countries, and Irish immigrants in the nineteenth and early twentieth centuries also endured extensive discrimination. Today, prejudices against the French, Japanese, and Irish have faded. In contrast, some hatreds, notably homophobia and anti-Semitism, reflect people's deeper anxieties and are therefore more persistent.

tolerant and open-minded, but he grew up in a small homogeneous community and feels uncomfortable with members of other cultural and religious groups. Should we put Raymond in the same category as Rupert, an outspoken bigot who actively detests all ethnic groups other than his own? Do good intentions count? What if Raymond knows nothing about Muslims and mindlessly blurts out a remark that reveals his ignorance? Is that prejudice or thoughtlessness? And what about people who say they are not prejudiced but then make sexist or racist remarks when they are drunk or angered?

Some social psychologists, while welcoming the evidence that *explicit*, conscious prejudices have declined, have used ingenious measures to see whether *implicit*, unconscious negative feelings between groups have also diminished. They maintain that implicit attitudes, being automatic and unintentional, reflect lingering negative feelings that keep prejudice alive below the surface (Dovidio, 2009). They have developed several ways of measuring these feelings (Olson, 2009):

1 Measures of social distance. *Social distance* is a possible behavioral expression of prejudice, a reluctance to get "too close" to another group. Does a straight man stand farther away from a gay man than from another heterosexual? Does a nondisabled woman move away from a woman in

Today, it is Muslim Americans and Mexican Americans who are often the target of prejudice—the former, because of the fear of terrorism; the latter, because of the fear of economic competition.

a wheelchair? How close will a person let "those people" into his or her social life: work with them, live near them...marry them? A review of decades of representative surveys of the American population found that although overt prejudice among Hispanics, whites, blacks, Jews, and Asians has dropped, most people *within* each ethnic group are still strongly opposed to virtually all of the other ethnic groups living in their neighborhoods or marrying into their families (Weaver, 2008). But does this fact reflect prejudice or merely a comfort with and preference for one's own ethnicity?

2 **Measures of what people do when they are stressed or angry.** Many people are willing to control their negative feelings under normal conditions, but as soon as they are angry, drunk, or frustrated or get a jolt to their self-esteem, their unexpressed prejudice often reveals itself.

In one of the first experiments to demonstrate this phenomenon, white students were asked to administer shock to black or white confederates of the experimenter in what the students believed was a study of biofeedback. In the experimental condition, participants overheard the biofeedback "victim" (who actually received no shock) saying derogatory things about them. In the control condition, participants overheard no such nasty remarks. Then all the participants had another opportunity to shock the victims; their degree of aggression was defined as the amount of shock they administered. At first, white students showed *less* aggression toward blacks than toward whites. But as soon as the white students were angered by overhearing derogatory remarks about themselves, they showed *more* aggression toward blacks than toward whites (Rogers & Prentice-Dunn, 1981). The same pattern appears in studies of how English-speaking Canadians behave toward French-speaking Canadians (Meindl & Lerner, 1985), straights toward gays, non-Jewish students toward Jews (Fein & Spencer, 1997), and men toward women (Maass et al., 2003).

3 **Measures of brain activity.** Another method relies on fMRI and PET scans to determine which parts of the brain are involved in forming stereotypes, holding prejudiced beliefs, and feeling disgust, anger, or anxiety about another ethnic group (Cacioppo et al., 2003; Harris & Fiske, 2006; Stanley, Phelps, & Banaji, 2008). In one study, when African Americans and whites saw pictures of each other, activity in the amygdala (the brain structure associated with fear and other negative emotions) was elevated. But it was not elevated when people saw pictures of members of their own group (Hart et al., 2000).

However, the fact that parts of the brain are activated under some conditions does not mean a person is prejudiced. In a similar experiment, when white participants were registering the faces as individuals or as part of a simple visual test rather than as members of the category "blacks," there was no increased activation in the amygdala. The brain may be designed to register differences, it appears, but any negative associations with those differences depend on context and learning (Wheeler & Fiske, 2005).

4 **Measures of implicit attitudes.** A final, controversial method of assessing prejudice is the *Implicit Association Test (IAT)*, which measures the speed of people's positive and negative associations to a target group (Greenwald, McGhee, & Schwartz, 1998; Greenwald et al., 2009). Its proponents have argued that if white students take longer to respond to black faces associated with positive words (e.g., *triumph, honest*) than to black faces associated with negative words (e.g., *devil, failure*), it must mean that white students have an unconscious, implicit prejudice toward blacks, one that can affect behavior in various ways. More than three million people have taken the test online, and it has also been given to students, business managers, and many other groups to identify their alleged prejudices toward blacks, Asians, women, old people, and other categories (Nosek, Greenwald, & Banaji, 2007).

We say "alleged" prejudices because other social psychologists believe that whatever the test measures, it is not a stable prejudice; they point out that test–retest reliability is low, and scores on the IAT predict a person's actual discriminatory behavior only minimally (Blanton et al., 2009; De Houwer et al., 2009). Two researchers got an IAT effect by matching target faces with nonsense words and neutral words that had no evaluative connotations at all. They concluded that the IAT does not measure emotional evaluations of the target but rather the *salience* of the word associated with it—how much it stands out. (Negative words attract more attention in general.) When the researchers corrected for these factors, the presumed unconscious prejudice faded away (Rothermund & Wentura, 2004).

Moreover, as we saw earlier, people find familiar names, products, and even nonsense syllables to be more pleasant than unfamiliar ones. Some investigators argue that the IAT may simply be measuring, say, white subjects' unfamiliarity with African

Americans and the greater salience of white faces to them, rather than a true prejudice (Kinoshita & Peek-O'Leary, 2005). Nonetheless, it's clear that people often have unconscious dislikes of, and discomforts with, members of other groups—prejudices they may be unwilling to admit even to themselves.

As you can see, defining and measuring prejudice are not easy tasks, and it's important not to oversimplify. To understand prejudice, we must distinguish explicit attitudes from unconscious ones, active hostility from simple discomfort, what people say from what they feel, and what people feel from how they actually behave.

Reducing Conflict and Prejudice

The findings that emerge from the study of prejudice show us that efforts to reduce prejudice by appealing to moral or intellectual arguments are not enough. They must also touch people's deeper insecurities, fears, or negative associations with a group. Of course, given the many sources and functions of prejudice, no one method will work in all circumstances or for all prejudices. But just as social psychologists investigate the situations that increase prejudice and animosity between groups, they have also examined the situations that might reduce them. Here are four (Dovidio, Gaertner, & Validzic, 1998; Pettigrew & Tropp, 2006): **((•─Listen**

1 Both sides must have many opportunities to work and socialize together, formally and informally. According to the *contact hypothesis*, prejudice declines when people have the chance to get used to another group's rules, food, customs, and attitudes, thereby discovering their shared interests and shared humanity and learning that "those people" aren't, in fact, "all alike." The contact hypothesis has been supported by many studies in the laboratory and in the real world: studies of newly integrated housing projects in the American South during the 1950s and 1960s; young people's attitudes toward the elderly; healthy people's attitudes toward the mentally ill; nondisabled children's attitudes toward the disabled; and straight people's prejudices toward gay men and lesbians (Herek & Capitanio, 1996; Pettigrew & Tropp, 2006; Wilner, Walkley, & Cook, 1955).

Multiethnic college campuses are living laboratories for testing the contact hypothesis. White students who have roommates, friends, and romantic relationships across ethnic lines tend to become less prejudiced and find commonalities (Van Laar,

Levin, & Sidanius, 2008). Cross-group friendships benefit minorities and reduce their prejudices, too. Minority students who join ethnic student organizations tend to develop, over time, not only an even stronger ethnic identity, but also an increased sense of ethnic victimization. Just like white students who live in white fraternities and sororities, they often come to feel they have less in common with other ethnic groups (Sidanius et al., 2004). But a longitudinal study of black and Latino students at a predominantly white university found that friendships with whites increased their feelings of belonging and reduced their feelings of dissatisfaction with the school (Mendoza-Denton & Page-Gould, 2008). (See Figure 10.4.)

2 Both sides must have equal legal status, economic opportunities, and power. This requirement is the spur behind efforts to change laws that permit discrimination. Integration of public facilities in the American South would never have occurred if civil rights advocates had waited for segregationists to have a change of heart. Women

((•─Listen to **Prejudice** on **mypsychlab.com**

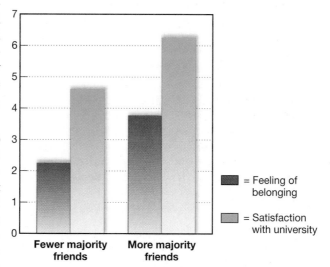

FIGURE 10.4

The Impact of Cross-Ethnic Friendships on Minority Students' Well-Being
Cross-ethnic friendships benefit both parties. In a longitudinal study of minority black students at a predominantly white university, many black students at first felt left out of school life and thus dissatisfied with their educational experience. But the more white friends they made, the higher their sense of belonging (purple bar) and satisfaction with the university (green bar). This finding was particularly significant for minority students who had initially been the most sensitive to rejection and who had felt the most anxious and insecure about being in a largely white school. The study was later replicated with minority Latino students (Mendoza-Denton & Page-Gould, 2008).

would never have gotten the right to vote, attend college, or do "men's work" (law, medicine, bartending...) without persistent challenges to the laws that barred them from having these rights. But changing the law is not enough if two groups remain in competition for jobs or if one group retains power and dominance over the other.

3 **Authorities and community institutions must provide moral, legal, and economic support for both sides.** Society must establish norms of equality and support them in the actions of its officials—teachers, employers, the judicial system, government officials, and the police. Where segregation is official government policy or an unofficial but established practice, conflict and prejudice not only will continue but also will seem normal and justified.

4 **Both sides must cooperate, working together for a common goal.** Although contact reduces prejudice, it is also true that prejudice reduces contact. And when groups don't like each other, forced contact just makes each side resentful and even more prejudiced, as a longitudinal field survey of students in Germany, Belgium, and England found (Binder et al., 2009). At many multiethnic American high schools, ethnic groups form cliques and gangs, fighting one another and defending their own ways.

To reduce the intergroup tension and competition that exist in many schools, Elliot Aronson and his colleagues developed the "jigsaw" method of building cooperation. Students from different ethnic groups work together on a task that is broken up like a jigsaw puzzle; each person needs to coop-

When classrooms are structured so that students of different ethnic groups must cooperate in order to do well on a lesson, prejudice decreases.

erate with the others to put the assignment together. Students in such classes, from elementary school through college, tend to do better, like their classmates better, and become less stereotyped and prejudiced in their thinking than students in traditional classrooms (Aronson, 2000; Slavin & Cooper, 1999). Cooperation and interdependence often reduce us–them thinking and prejudice by creating an encompassing social identity—the Eagles and Rattlers solution.

Each of these four approaches to creating greater harmony between groups is important, but none is sufficient on its own. Perhaps one reason that group conflicts and prejudice are so persistent is that all four conditions for reducing them are rarely met at the same time.

✓● **Study** and **Review** on **mypsychlab.com**

Quick Quiz

Try to overcome your prejudice against quizzes by taking this one.

1. What are four ways of measuring implicit or unconscious prejudice?
2. What are four important conditions required for reducing prejudice and conflict between groups?
3. Surveys find that African Americans, Asian Americans, and Latinos often hold prejudices about other minorities. What are some reasons that people who have themselves been victims of stereotyping and prejudice would hold the same attitudes toward others?

Answers:

1. Measures of social distance; of how aggressively people behave toward a target person when they are angry or stressed; of physiological changes in the brain; and of unconscious negative associations to socialize formally and informally; both sides must have equal status and power; have the moral, legal, and economic support of authorities; and cooperate for a common goal. 3. Their own ethnocentrism; low self-esteem; feelings of threat; conformity with relatives and friends who share their prejudices; parental lessons; and economic competition for jobs and resources.

Psychology in the News REVISITED

After reading this chapter, why do you think the guards at Abu Ghraib abused and humiliated their prisoners? As we have seen, it is not enough to offer a dispositional (personality) attribution, saying that the soldiers were bad or sadistic individuals.

Social psychologists would explain the behavior of Lynndie England and her fellow soldiers by considering the roles they were assigned, which gave them unlimited control over the detainees. They would also emphasize the group norms among the soldiers. The fact that the guards willingly posed for pictures—in many, they are smiling proudly—indicates that they were showing off for their friends and that they believed their behavior was appropriate. In all likelihood, they were able to justify their behavior by blaming the victims, saying that the detainees (who had not yet been found guilty of any crime) deserved whatever harsh treatment they got.

As for the soldiers' defense that they were "only following orders," this did not appear to be the case. There *should* have been orders from higher-ups, or at least clear rules for the treatment of detainees. But

Pentagon investigations concluded that no one authorized or encouraged the soldiers' abusive treatment of prisoners. The detention center was chaotic and poorly run, and rules on treatment of detainees were so vague and changed so frequently that even higher-ranking soldiers did not know the difference between abuse and acceptable interrogation techniques. In the midst of this chaos, the soldiers made up their own rules and group norms, and once they were in place, most went along with their peers.

The bright spot in this bleak picture is that not every soldier at Abu Ghraib humiliated and tortured the detainees. Some refused to participate. Some informed their commanding officers. Some, like Joe Darby, eventually blew the whistle publicly, at great personal cost. These individuals did not mindlessly pass along responsibility for their actions to their senior officers—or, in Lynndie England's case, to her then-boyfriend Charles Graner.

Throughout this chapter, we have seen that "human nature" contains the potential for unspeakable acts of cruelty and inspiring acts of goodness. Most people

The most difficult lesson of social psychology is that ordinary people can do monstrous things. Mohamed Atta (left) was described by his friends as being "full of idealism" and a "humanist" who was searching for justice; on September 11, 2001, Atta led the 19 hijackers who attacked the World Trade Center and the Pentagon, killing almost 3,000 people. In Rwanda in 1994, when the Hutu shot or hacked to death nearly one million Tutsi, a rival tribe, hundreds of Tutsi took refuge in a Benedictine convent. Instead of protecting them, the mother superior, Sister Gertrude, and another nun, Sister Maria Kisito, reported the refugees to the Hutu militia, who massacred the trapped victims. At their subsequent trial in Brussels, the two Hutu nuns were sentenced to 15- and 12-year prison terms for crimes against humanity.

Thinking Critically about "Evil" Cultures

believe that some cultures and individuals are inherently good or evil; if we can just get rid of those few evil ones, everything will be fine. But from the standpoint of social and cultural psychology, all human beings, like all cultures, contain the potential for both.

In this respect, virtually no country has bloodless hands. The Nazis, of course, systematically exterminated millions of Jews, Gypsies, homosexuals, disabled people, and anyone else not of the "pure" Aryan "race." But Americans and Canadians slaughtered native peoples in North America, Turks slaughtered Armenians, the Khmer Rouge slaughtered millions of fellow Cambodians, the Spanish conquistadors slaughtered native peoples in Mexico and South America, Idi Amin waged a reign of terror against his own people in Uganda, the Japanese slaughtered Koreans and Chinese, Iraqis slaughtered Kurds, despotic political regimes in Argentina and Chile killed thousands of dissidents and rebels, the Hutu in Rwanda murdered thousands of Tutsi, and in the former Yugoslavia, Bosnian Serbs massacred thousands of Bosnian Muslims in the name of "ethnic cleansing."

It is easy to conclude that outbreaks of violence like these are a result of inner aggressive drives, the sheer evilness of the enemy, or "age-old tribal hatreds." But in the social–psychological view, they result from the all-too-normal processes we have discussed in this chapter, including ethnocentrism, obedience to authority, conformity, groupthink, deindividuation, stereotyping, and prejudice. These processes are especially likely to be activated when a government feels weakened and vulnerable. By generating an outside enemy, rulers create us–them thinking as a means of imposing order and cohesion among their citizens and to create a scapegoat for the country's economic problems (Smith, 1998; Staub, 1996). The good news is that when circumstances within a nation change, societies can also change from being warlike to being peaceful. Sweden was once one of the most warlike nations on earth, but today they are among the most pacifistic and egalitarian.

The philosopher Hannah Arendt covered the trial of Adolf Eichmann, a Nazi officer who supervised the deportation and death of millions of Jews. Arendt (1963) used the phrase *the banality of evil* to describe how it was possible for Eichmann and other ordinary people in Nazi Germany to commit the atrocities they did. (*Banal* means "commonplace" or "unoriginal.") The compelling evidence for the banality of evil is, perhaps, the hardest lesson in psychology. The research discussed in this chapter suggests that aggression, ethnocentrism, and prejudice will always be with us, as long as differences exist among groups. But it can also help us formulate realistic yet nonviolent ways of living in a diverse world. By identifying the conditions that create the banality of evil, perhaps we can create situations that foster the "banality of virtue"—everyday acts of kindness, selflessness, and generosity.

Taking Psychology with You

Dealing with Cultural Differences

A French salesman worked for a company that was bought by Americans. When the new American manager ordered him to step up his sales within the next three months, the employee quit in a huff, taking his customers with him. Why? In France, it takes years to develop customers; in family-owned businesses, relationships with customers may span generations. The American manager wanted instant results, as Americans often do, but the French salesman knew this was impossible and quit. The American view was, "He wasn't up to the job; he's lazy and disloyal, so he stole my customers." The French view was, "There is no point in explaining anything to a person who is so stupid as to think you can acquire loyal customers in three months" (Hall & Hall, 1987).

Both men were committing the fundamental attribution error: assuming that the other person's behavior was due to personality rather than the situation, in this case a situation governed by cultural rules. Many corporations now realize that such rules are not trivial and that success in a global economy depends on understanding them. But you don't have to go to another country to encounter cultural differences; they are right here at home.

If you find yourself getting angry over something a person from another culture is doing or not doing, use the skills of critical thinking to find out whether your expectations and perceptions of that person's behavior are appropriate. Take the time to examine your assumptions and biases, consider other explanations of the other person's actions, and avoid emotional reasoning. For example, people who shake hands as a gesture of friendship and courtesy are likely to feel insulted if a person from a non-hand-shaking culture refuses to do the same, unless they have asked themselves the question, "Does everyone have the custom of shaking hands the way I do?"

Similarly, people from Middle Eastern and Latin American cultures are used to bargaining for what they buy; Americans and northern Europeans are used to having a fixed price. People who do not know how to bargain, therefore, are likely to find bargaining an exercise in frustration because they will not know whether they got taken or got a great deal. In contrast, people from bargaining cultures will feel just as exasperated if a seller offers a flat price. "Where's the fun in this?" they'll say. "The whole human transaction of shopping is gone!"

Learning another culture's rule or custom is hard enough, but it is much more difficult to comprehend cultural differences that are deeply embedded in its language. For instance, in Iran, the social principle of *taarof* describes the practice of deliberate insincerity, such as giving false praise and making promises you have no intention of keeping. Iranians know that they are supposed to tell you what you want to hear to avoid conflict or to offer hope for a compromise. To Iranians, these practices are a part of good manners; they are not offended by them. But Americans and members of other English-speaking cultures are used to "straight talking," to saying directly and succinctly what they want. Therefore they find *taarof* hard to learn, let alone to practice. As an Iranian social scientist told the *New York Times* (August 6, 2006), "Speech has a different function than it does in the West"—in the West, "yes" generally means yes; in Iran, "yes" can mean yes, but it often means maybe or no. "This creates a rich, poetic linguistic culture," he said. "It creates a multidimensional culture where people are adept at picking up on nuances. On the other hand, it makes for bad political discourse. In political discourse people don't know what to trust."

You can see why critical thinking can help people avoid the tendency to stereotype and to see cultural differences in communication solely in hostile, negative ways. "Why are the Iranians lying to me?" an American might ask. The answer is that they are not "lying" in Iranian terms; they are speaking in a way that is completely natural for them, according to their cultural rules for communication.

To learn the unspoken rules of a culture, you must look, listen, and observe. What is the pace of life like? Do people regard brash individuality and loud speech as admirable or embarrassing? When customers enter a shop, do they greet and chat with the shopkeeper or ignore the person as they browse? Are people expected to be direct in their speech or evasive? Sociocultural research enhances critical thinking by teaching us to appreciate the many cultural rules that govern people's behavior, values, attitudes, and ways of doing business. Before you write off someone from a culture different from your own as being rude, foolish, stubborn, or devious, consider other interpretations of that person's behavior— just as you would want that person to consider other, more forgiving, interpretations of yours.

Summary   ((•—[Listen to an **audio file** of your chapter on **mypsychlab.com**

● *Social psychologists* study how social roles, attitudes, relationships, and groups influence individuals; *cultural psychologists* study the influence of culture on human behavior. Many cultural rules, such as those governing correct *conversational distance,* are unspoken but nonetheless powerful.

Roles and Rules

● The environment influences people in countless subtle ways; observing that others have broken rules or laws increases the likelihood that a passerby will do the same. Two classic studies illustrate the power of *norms* and *roles* to affect individual actions. In Milgram's obedience study, most people in the role of "teacher" inflicted what they thought was extreme shock on another person because of the authority of the experimenter. In the Stanford prison study, college students tended to behave in accordance with the role of "prisoner" or "guard" that they had been assigned.

● Obedience to authority contributes to the smooth running of society, but obedience can also lead to actions that are deadly, foolish, or illegal. People obey orders because they can be punished if they do not, out of respect for authority, and to gain advantages. Even when they would rather not obey, they may do so because they have been *entrapped,* justifying each step and decision they make, and handing over responsibility for any harmful actions they commit to the authority.

Social Influences on Beliefs and Behavior

● Researchers in the area of *social cognition* study how people's perceptions affect their relationships and how the social environment affects their beliefs and perceptions. According to *attribution theory*, people are motivated to search for causes to which they can attribute their own and other people's behavior. Their attributions may be *situational* or *dispositional*. The *fundamental attribution error* occurs when people overestimate personality traits as a cause of behavior and underestimate the influence of the situation. A primary reason for the fundamental attribution error is that people rely on introspection to judge their own behavior but only have observation to judge the behavior of others.

● Attributions are further influenced by three *self-serving biases*: the bias to choose the most flattering and forgiving explanations of our own behavior; the bias that we are better, smarter, and kinder than others; and the bias that the world is fair (the *just-world hypothesis*).

● People hold many *attitudes* about people, things, and ideas. Attitudes may be *explicit* (conscious) or *implicit* (unconscious). Attitudes may change through experience, conscious decision, or as an effort to reduce *cognitive dissonance*. One powerful way to influence attitudes is by taking advantage of the *familiarity effect* and the *validity effect:* Simply exposing people repeatedly to a name or product makes them like it more, and repeating a statement over and over again makes it seem more believable.

● Many attitudes are acquired through learning and social influence, but some are associated with personality traits that have a genetic component. Religious and political affiliations are not heritable, but religiosity and certain political attitudes do have relatively high heritability. Ideological belief systems may have evolved to be organized along a left-right dimension, consisting of two central sets of attitudes: whether a person advocates or opposes social change, and whether a person thinks inequality is a result of human policies and can be overcome or is inevitable and should be accepted as part of the natural order. Attitudes are also profoundly affected by the *nonshared environment*, an individual's unique life experiences.

● Suicide bombers and terrorists have not been "brainwashed" and are not psychopaths. Most have been entrapped into taking increasingly violent actions against real and perceived enemies; encouraged to attribute all problems to that one enemy; offered a new identity and salvation; and cut off from access to dissonant information. These methods have been used to create religious and other cults as well.

Individuals in Groups

● The need to belong is so powerful that the pain of social rejection and exclusion is greater and more memorable than physical pain, which is why groups use the weapon of ostracism or rejection to enforce conformity.

● In groups, individuals often behave differently than they would on their own. Conformity permits the smooth running of society and allows people to feel in harmony with others like them. But as the Asch experiment showed, most people will conform to the judgments of others even when the others are plain wrong.

● Close-knit groups are vulnerable to *groupthink*, the tendency of group members to think alike, censor themselves, actively suppress disagreement, and feel that their decisions are invulnerable. Groupthink often produces faulty decisions because group members fail to seek disconfirming evidence for their ideas. However, groups can be structured to counteract groupthink.

● Sometimes a group's collective judgment is better than that of its individual members—the "wisdom of crowds." But crowds can also spread panic, rumor, and misinformation. *Diffusion of responsibility* in a group can lead to inaction on the part of individuals, as in *bystander apathy*. The diffusion of responsibility is likely to occur under conditions that promote *deindividuation*, the loss of awareness of one's individuality. Deindividuation increases when people feel anonymous, as in a large group or crowd or when they are wearing masks or uniforms. In some situations, crowd norms lead deindividuated people to behave aggressively, but in others, crowd norms foster helpfulness.

● The willingness to speak up for an unpopular opinion, blow the whistle on illegal practices, or help a stranger in trouble and perform other acts of *altruism* is partly a matter of personal belief and conscience. But several situational factors are also important: The person perceives that help is needed; cultural norms support taking action; the person has an ally; and the person becomes entrapped in a commitment to help or dissent.

Us Versus Them: Group Identity

● People develop *social identities* based on their ethnicity, nationality, religion, occupation, and other social memberships. In culturally diverse societies, many people face the problem of balancing their *ethnic identity* with *acculturation* into the larger society.

● *Ethnocentrism*, the belief that one's own ethnic group or religion is superior to all others, promotes "us–them" thinking. One effective strategy for reducing us–them thinking and hostility between groups is *interdependence,* having both sides work together to reach a common goal.

● *Stereotypes* help people rapidly process new information, organize experience, and predict how others will behave. But they distort reality by exaggerating differences between groups, underestimating the differences within groups, and producing selective perception.

Group Conflict and Prejudice

● A *prejudice* is an unreasonable negative feeling toward a category of people. Psychologically, prejudice wards off feelings of anxiety and doubt, bolsters self-esteem when a person feels threatened (by providing a scapegoat), and may alleviate the fear of death. Prejudice also has social causes: People acquire prejudices mindlessly, through conformity and parental lessons. Prejudice serves the cultural and national purpose of bonding people to their social groups and nations, and in extreme cases justifying war. Finally, prejudice also serves to justify a majority group's economic interests and dominance. Thus, although *hostile sexism* is different from *benevolent sexism*, both legitimize gender discrimination. During times of economic insecurity and competition for jobs, prejudice rises.

● Psychologists disagree on whether racism and other prejudices are declining or have merely taken new forms. Some are trying to measure prejudice indirectly, by measuring *social distance;* seeing whether people are more likely to behave aggressively toward a target when they are stressed or angry; observing changes in the brain; or assessing unconscious positive or negative associations with a group, as with the *Implicit Association Test* (IAT). However, the IAT has many critics who claim it is not capturing true prejudice.

● Efforts to reduce prejudice need to target both the explicit and implicit attitudes that people have. Four conditions help to reduce two groups' mutual prejudices and conflicts: Both sides must have opportunities to work and socialize together informally and formally (the *contact hypothesis*); both sides must have equal legal status, economic standing, and power; both sides must have the legal, moral, and economic support of authorities and cultural institutions; and both sides must work together for a common goal.

Psychology in the News, Revisited

● Although many people believe that only bad or evil people do bad deeds, the principles of social and cultural psychology show that under certain conditions, good people often can be induced to do bad things too. Everyone is influenced to one degree or another by the social processes of obedience, entrapment, conformity, persuasion, bystander apathy, groupthink, deindividuation, ethnocentrism, stereotyping, and prejudice.

Taking Psychology with You

● Sociocultural research enhances critical thinking by identifying the cultural rules that govern people's behavior, values, communication, and ways of doing business. Understanding these rules can help people examine their assumptions about people in other cultures, and avoid the tendency to jump to conclusions and reason emotionally about group differences.

Key Terms

- Social psychologists study how social roles, attitudes, relationships, and groups influence individuals.
- Cultural psychologists study the influence of culture on human behavior.

Roles and Rules

- **Norms**: rules that regulate social life, including explicit laws and implicit cultural conventions
- **Roles**: social positions that are regulated by norms about how people in those positions should behave
- Social roles are shaped by **culture**, a set of shared rules and values of a community or society.

Two Classic Studies

- In Milgram's obedience study, most people inflicted what they thought was extreme shock on another person because of the experimenter's authority.
- In Zimbardo's prison study, students quickly took on the role of "prisoner" or "guard."

Why People Obey

Several factors cause people to obey, including:
1. Unpleasant consequences for disobedience and benefits of obedience
2. Respect for the authority
3. Wanting to be polite or liked
4. **Entrapment**: increasing commitment to a course of action to justify one's investment in it
5. Allocating responsibility to the authority

Social Influences on Beliefs and Behavior

Social cognition: how people's perceptions of themselves and others affect their relationships and how the social environment influences thoughts, beliefs, and values.

Attributions

Attribution theory holds that people explain their own and other people's behavior by attributing its causes to a *situation* or *disposition*.
- The **fundamental attribution error** is the tendency to ignore situational factors in favor of dispositional ones.

Attributions

"Why is Aurelia so mean and crabby lately?"

Situational

"She's under pressure."

Dispositional

"She's self-involved and clueless."

(may lead to)

Fundamental Attribution Error

Ignoring influence of situation on behavior and emphasizing personality traits alone

Three cognitive biases contribute to the fundamental attribution error:
- The bias to choose forgiving and flattering attributions for our own lapses
- The bias that we are better, smarter, and kinder than other people
- The bias to believe that the world is fair (the **just-world hypothesis**)

Attitudes

- Attitudes may be *implicit* (unconscious) or *explicit* (conscious).
- They may be altered because of the need to reduce **cognitive dissonance**.

Shifting Opinions vs. Bedrock Beliefs

- Efforts to get people to change their attitudes often rely on the **familiarity effect** and the **validity effect**.
- Some attitudes are highly heritable (e.g., religiosity and certain political views) and thus are resistant to change, but many are influenced by the nonshared environment.

Persuasion or "Brainwashing"

The example of suicide bombers illustrates common social-psychological factors involved in the making of a terrorist:
- The person is subjected to entrapment.
- The person's problems are explained by a simple attribution ("It's the fault of those bad people").
- The person is offered a new identity and salvation.
- The person's access to disconfirming information is severely controlled.

CONCEPT MAP

Individuals in Groups

Conformity

The Asch experiment shows that most people will conform to others' judgments, even when others are obviously wrong.

Groupthink

Groupthink, an extreme form of conformity, leads to faulty decisions because group members are vulnerable to:
• An illusion of invulnerability
• Self-censorship
• Pressure on dissenters to conform
• An illusion of unanimity

The Anonymous Crowd

When people are part of large, anonymous groups, two processes may occur:
1. **Diffusion of responsibility**, the spreading out of responsibility among many people. It can lead to *bystander apathy*.
2. **Deindividuation**, the loss of awareness of one's own individuality:
— Increases as group gets larger
— Increases when group members wear masks or uniforms
— May increase helpfulness as well as destructiveness, depending on social norms

Altruism and Dissent

Situational factors can influence altruism and dissent, including:
• Perceiving that help is needed
• Norms that encourage action
• Having an ally
• Becoming entrapped in a commitment to help or dissent

Us Versus Them: Group Identity

Social identities are based on a person's identification with a nation, religion, political group, or other important affiliations.

Ethnic Identity

People often face the dilemma of balancing an **ethnic identity**, a close identification with a religious or ethnic group, and **acculturation**, identification with the dominant culture.

Ethnocentrism

Ethnocentrism, the belief that one's own ethnic group or nation is superior to all others, can create "us–them" thinking and hostile competition.

Stereotypes

Stereotypes can be efficient cognitive summaries of other groups, but they distort reality by:
• Exaggerating differences between groups
• Producing selective perception
• Underestimating the differences within other groups

Group Conflict and Prejudice

A **prejudice** consists of a negative stereotype and a persistent, unreasonable negative feeling toward a category of people.

The Origins of Prejudice

1. Psychological causes: Prejudice wards off feelings of anxiety and doubt, simplifies complex problems, boosts self-esteem.
2. Social causes: Prejudice bonds people to their social group and nation.
3. Economic causes: Prejudice justifies a majority group's economic interests and legitimizes war.
4. Cultural and national: Prejudice bonds people to their own group and fosters the dehumanization of other groups.

Defining and Measuring Prejudice

• Prejudice is a challenge to define and measure; for example, "hostile sexism" is different from "benevolent sexism," though both legitimize gender discrimination.
• Psychologists disagree on whether racism and other prejudices are declining or have merely taken new forms.
• Some researchers are trying to measure prejudice indirectly:
— By studying *social distance*, a measure of people's reluctance to get close to another group
— By seeing whether people are more likely to behave aggressively toward a target when they are stressed or insulted
— By observing changes in the brain
— By assessing unconscious positive or negative associations with a group, as with the *Implicit Association Test* (IAT). However, the IAT has critics who claim it is not capturing true prejudice.

Reducing Conflict and Prejudice

Social psychologists have examined the conditions that decrease prejudice and animosity between groups:
1. Both sides must have opportunities to work and socialize together (the *contact hypothesis*).
2. Both sides must have equal legal status, economic standing, and power.
3. Both sides must have the moral, legal, and economic support of authorities and cultural institutions.
4. Both sides must work toward a common goal.

Celebrity Scandals Revive Sex-Addiction Debate

TUCSON, AZ, March 31, 2010. Motorcycle mogul Jesse James, Sandra Bullock's estranged husband, has reportedly checked himself into an Arizona rehab facility, the Sierra Tucson treatment center. News recently emerged that James has had several extramarital flings, including an 11-month affair with a reputed stripper, Michelle "Bombshell" McGee. The Tucson facility specializes in treating addictions, and because James is not known to have abused drugs or alcohol, speculation has centered on whether he is being treated for a sexual addiction. His representative told *People* magazine only that James had entered rehab "to deal with personal issues," adding that "he realized that this time was crucial to help himself, help his family, and help save his marriage."

A similar scandal erupted earlier this year with the revelation that champion golfer Tiger Woods had had more than a dozen extramarital affairs. Woods promptly checked himself into the Pine Grove clinic in Mississippi for rehabilitation. The details were not made public, but among the courses offered at the clinic are "shame reduction" and "setting sexual boundaries."

These and other high-profile cases of sexual infidelity have provoked controversy about whether people who have serial sexual affairs have a sexual "addiction." Palo Alto sex therapist Marty Klein thinks sex addiction is a bogus term that trivializes the meaning of true addiction, which is a physiological reliance on a substance like drugs or alcohol. "I don't see sex addicts," Klein says. "I see people who use sex in destructive ways." If an addiction is defined as any behavior that someone repeats despite the risk of serious consequences, almost any sexual affair might qualify, and so might visiting a prostitute or viewing pornography. Because the diagnosis is so vague, many mental health professionals and laypeople alike think it is mostly an excuse for cheating. As comic Jimmy Kimmel said, "'I'm addicted to sex' is the new, grown-up version of 'the dog ate my homework.'"

Some psychotherapists, however, consider sexual addiction to be a true disorder that involves an escalating preoccupation with sexual activity to cover up past pain or trauma. Therapists may prescribe a 12-step program, group therapy, and sometimes medication to help "addicts" regulate their cravings. A more neutral term, "hypersexual disorder," is expected to appear in a revision of the *Diagnostic and Statistical Manual of Mental Disorders* in 2013.

Jesse James, whose wife Sandra Bullock left him after learning he had had several affairs, checked into a rehab facility specializing in addictions, saying he wanted help with his problems.

Psychological Disorders

Do Jesse James and Tiger Woods have a sexual addiction, a mental disorder comparable to alcohol or drug addiction? Or are they simply guys who believe that because they are rich, famous, and successful, they are entitled to all the sex they can get? How broadly should we define the term *addiction*? Should it include compulsive Internet use, shopping more than your budget can afford, or eating too much chocolate?

And how about college student Matthew Small, who had a 4.0 average until he began to immerse himself in the virtual World of Warcraft? He spent at least six hours a day collecting armor, swords, and other cyber-gear for his character. His close friends drifted away, and his grades slipped. One day he realized he had logged more than 1,000 hours playing the game in one semester and decided it was time to turn in his armor.

You don't have to be a psychologist to recognize the most extreme forms of abnormal behavior. When people think of mental illness, they usually think of people with delusions, people who behave in bizarre ways, or people who commit random murders and other heartless crimes. But most psychological problems are far less dramatic than the public's impression of them and far more common. Some people go through episodes of complete inability to function, yet get along fine between those episodes. Some people function adequately every day, yet suffer constant melancholy, always feeling below par. And some people cannot control their worries or tempers.

In this chapter, you will learn about the many psychological problems that cause people unhappiness and anguish, as well as about the severe disorders that really do make people unable to control their behavior. But be forewarned: One of the most common worries that people have is "Am I normal?" It is normal to fear being abnormal, especially when you are reading about psychological problems! But it is also normal to have problems. All of us on occasion have difficulties that seem too much to handle, and it is often unclear precisely when "normal" problems shade into "abnormal" ones.

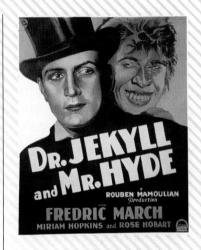

YOU are about to learn...

- why insanity is not the same thing as having a mental disorder.
- how mental disorders differ from normal problems.
- why the standard professional guide to the diagnosis of mental disorders is controversial.
- why popular "projective" tests like the Rorschach inkblot test are not reliable.

Defining and Diagnosing Mental Disorders

Many people confuse unusual behavior—behavior that deviates from the norm—with mental disorder, but the two are not the same. A person may behave in ways that are statistically rare (collecting ceramic pigs, being a genius at math, committing murder) without having a mental illness. Conversely, some mental disorders, such as depression and anxiety, are extremely common. People also confuse mental disorder and insanity. In the law, the definition of *insanity* rests primarily on whether a person is aware of the consequences of his or her actions and can control his or her behavior. But *insanity* is a legal term only; a person may have a mental illness and yet be considered sane by the court.

If frequency of the problem is not a guide, and if insanity reflects only one extreme kind of mental illness, how then should we define a "mental disorder"? Diagnosing mental problems is not as straightforward as diagnosing medical problems such as diabetes or appendicitis. One leading definition, which takes genetic and social factors into account, is that a mental disorder is a "harmful dysfunction." That is, it involves behavior or an emotional state that is (1) *harmful* to oneself or others, and (2) *dysfunctional* because it is not performing its evolutionary function (Wakefield, 1992, 2006). For example, evolution has prepared us to feel afraid when we are in danger, so that we can escape; dysfunction occurs when this normal alarm mechanism fails to turn off after the danger is past. But if the dysfunction is not troubling to the individual or harmful to society, it is not a "mental disorder." We have a friend who lives happily with her cat phobia. She just avoids cats.

This definition rules out behavior that simply departs from current social or cultural notions of what is healthy or normal: A student might think that getting tattooed all over his body is totally cool, but if his parents disagree, they don't get to accuse him of having a mental disorder! On the other hand, the definition does include the behavior of people who think they are perfectly fine yet who cause enormous harm to themselves or others, such as a child who is unable to control the desire to set fires, a compulsive gambler who loses the family's savings, or people who hear voices telling them to stalk a celebrity day and night. ⊙▶ **Simulate**

The main criticism of defining mental disorder as "harmful dysfunction" is that it is often unclear

⊙▶ **Simulate Psychological Disorders** on **mypsychlab.com**

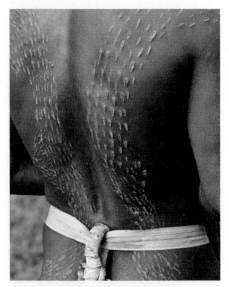  

What is a mental disorder? In Papua New Guinea, all young men to go through an initiation rite in which small, deep cuts are made on their backs to create permanent scars that signify a crocodile's scales (left). This common cultural practice would not be defined as a disorder. In contrast, most people would agree that a woman who mutilates herself for the sole purpose of inflicting injury and pain, as the patient on the right has done, has a mental disorder. But what about the scars on the arm of the 23-year-old woman from upstate New York (middle), who had them made by a "body artist"? She also has scars on her leg and her stomach, along with 29 piercings. Does she have a mental disorder?

what the evolutionary function or underlying pathology of a particular harmful behavior or emotional state might be. In this chapter, therefore, we define **mental disorder** as any condition that causes a person to suffer, is self-destructive, seriously impairs a person's ability to work or get along with others, or endangers others or the community. Mental disorders, like physical ailments, can range from mild to severe. By this definition, the great majority of people will have some mental health problem in the course of their lives.

Dilemmas of Diagnosis

Even armed with a general definition of mental disorder, psychologists have found that classifying mental disorders into distinct categories is not an easy job. In this section, we will see why this is so.

Classifying Disorders: The DSM The standard reference manual used to diagnose mental disorders is the *Diagnostic and Statistical Manual of Mental Disorders* (DSM), published by the American Psychiatric Association (1994, 2000). The DSM's primary aim is *descriptive*: to provide clear diagnostic categories, so that clinicians and researchers can agree on which disorders they are talking about and then can study and treat these disorders. Its diverse diagnostic categories include attention deficit disorders, disorders due to brain damage from disease or drugs, eating disorders, problems with sexual identity or behavior, impulse-control disorders (such as violent rages and pathological gambling or stealing), personality disorders, and "problems in living," along with other major disorders we will be discussing in this chapter.

The DSM lists the symptoms of each disorder and, wherever possible, gives information about the typical age of onset, predisposing factors, course of the disorder, prevalence of the disorder, sex ratio of those affected, and cultural issues that might affect diagnosis. In making a diagnosis, clinicians are encouraged to take into account many factors, such as the client's personality traits, medical conditions, stresses at work and at home, and the duration and severity of the problem. ✳ Explore

The DSM has had an extraordinary impact worldwide. Virtually all textbooks in psychiatry and psychology base their discussions of mental disorders on the DSM. With each new edition of the manual, the number of mental disorders has grown (see Figure 11.1). The first edition, published in 1952, was only 86 pages long and contained about 100 diagnoses. The DSM-IV, published in 1994 and slightly revised in 2000, is 900 pages long and

contains nearly 400 diagnoses of mental disorder. The DSM-V, due out in 2013, will contain even more diagnoses.

What is the reason for this explosion of mental disorders? Supporters of the new categories answer that it is important to distinguish disorders in a precise way so that clinicians can treat them properly. Critics point to an economic reason: Insurance companies require clinicians to assign their clients an appropriate DSM code number for whatever the client's problem is, which puts pressure on compilers of the manual to add more diagnoses so that physicians and psychologists will be compensated (Zur & Nordmarken, 2008).

Because of the DSM's powerful influence, it is important to be aware of its limitations and some of the inherent problems in the effort to classify and label mental disorders:

Thinking Critically about Diagnosing Disorders

1 The danger of overdiagnosis. If you give a small boy a hammer, the old saying goes, it will turn out that everything he runs into needs pounding. Likewise, say critics, if you give mental health professionals a diagnostic label, it will turn out that everyone they run into has the symptoms of the new disorder.

Consider attention deficit/hyperactivity disorder (ADHD), a diagnosis given to children and adults who are impulsive, messy, restless, and easily frustrated and who have trouble concentrating. Since ADHD was added to the DSM, the number of cases has skyrocketed in America, where it is diagnosed at least ten times as often as it is in Europe. Critics fear that parents, teachers, and mental health professionals are overdiagnosing this condition, especially in boys, who make up 80 to 90 percent of all cases of ADHD. The critics argue that normal boyish behavior—being rambunctious, refusing to nap, being playful, not listening to teachers in school—has been turned into a psychological problem (Cummings & O'Donohue, 2008; Panksepp, 1998). A longitudinal study of more than a hundred 4- to 6-year-olds found that the number of children who met the criteria for ADHD declined as the children got older (Lahey et al., 2005). Those who truly had the disorder remained highly impulsive and unable to concentrate, but others simply matured.

Likewise, the fastest-growing diagnosis given to young children is bipolar disorder, once thought to occur only in adolescents and adults; the number of diagnoses rose from 20,000 to 800,000 in just

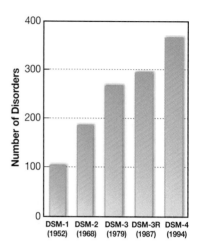

FIGURE 11.1
The Rising Number of Disorders in the DSM
Mental disorders in the DSM have increased nearly fourfold since the first edition (Houts, 2002).

✳ Explore **Axes of the DSM** on **mypsychlab.com**

mental disorder Any behavior or emotional state that causes an individual great suffering, is self-destructive, seriously impairs the person's ability to work or get along with others, or endangers others or the community.

one year (Moreno et al., 2007). Many experts think that only about 20 percent of the children currently diagnosed as bipolar meet the strict criteria for the disorder (Leibenluft & Rich, 2008). Partly for this reason, one of the groups working on the forthcoming DSM-V wants to add a new diagnosis: "temper dysregulation disorder with dysphoria (TDD)," which would apply to children who have "severe recurrent temper outbursts in response to common stressors"—about one-third of those now given a label of bipolar.

2 **The power of diagnostic labels.** Being given a diagnosis reassures people who are seeking an explanation for their emotional symptoms or those of their children ("Whew! So *that's* what it is!"). But once a person has been given a diagnosis, other people begin to see that person primarily in terms of the label; it sticks like lint. For example, when a rebellious, disobedient teenager is diagnosed as having "oppositional defiant disorder," or a child is labeled as having TDD, people tend to regard them as having a permanent, official condition. They then overlook other possible explanations for the person's actions: Maybe the teenager is "defiant" because he has been mistreated or his parents don't listen to him, and maybe a child has "recurrent temper outbursts" because his parents are not setting limits. And once a child is labeled, observers tend to ignore changes in his or her behavior—the times when the teenager is not being defiant or the situations in which a child gets along fine without having tantrums.

3 **The confusion of serious mental disorders with normal problems.** The DSM is not called "The Diagnostic and Statistical Manual of Mental Disorders and a Whole Bunch of Everyday Problems." Yet each edition of the DSM has added more everyday problems, including "disorder of written expression" (having trouble writing clearly), "mathematics disorder" (not doing well in math), "religious or spiritual problem," and "caffeine-induced sleep disorder" (which at least is easy to cure; just switch to decaf). Some critics fear that by lumping together normal difficulties with true mental illnesses, such as schizophrenia and major depression, the DSM implies that everyday problems are comparable to serious mental disorders (Houts, 2002). Revisers of the current DSM are debating whether to include "binge eating" and "shopping addiction," behaviors that can certainly be troublesome in their extreme form, but which many (if not most) people experience on occasion.

4 **The illusion of objectivity.** Finally, some psychologists argue that the whole enterprise of

the DSM is a vain attempt to impose a veneer of science on an inherently subjective process (Houts, 2002; Kutchins & Kirk, 1997; Tiefer, 2004). Many decisions about what to include as a disorder, say these critics, are based not on empirical evidence but on group consensus. The problem is that group consensus often reflects prevailing attitudes and prejudices rather than objective evidence. It is easy to see how prejudice operated in the past. In the early years of the nineteenth century, a physician named Samuel Cartwright argued that many slaves were suffering from *drapetomania*, an urge to escape from slavery (Kutchins & Kirk, 1997; Landrine, 1988). (He made up the word from *drapetes*, the Latin word for "runaway slave," and *mania*, meaning "mad" or "crazy.") Thus, doctors could assure slave owners that a mental illness, not the intolerable condition of slavery, made slaves seek freedom. This diagnosis was very convenient for slave owners. Today, of course, we know that "drapetomania" was foolish and cruel.

Over the years, psychiatrists have quite properly rejected many other "disorders" that reflected cultural prejudices, such as lack of vaginal orgasm, childhood masturbation disorder, and homosexuality (Wakefield, 1992). But critics argue that some DSM disorders are still affected by contemporary

Harriet Tubman (on the left) poses with some of the people she helped to escape from slavery on her "underground railroad." Slaveholders welcomed the idea that Tubman and others who insisted on their freedom had a mental disorder called "drapetomania."

prejudices and values, such as decisions about how much sex is "too much" or "too little." Emotional problems allegedly associated with menstruation remain in the DSM, but behavioral problems associated with testosterone have never even been considered for inclusion. In short, critics maintain, many diagnoses still stem from cultural biases about what constitutes normal or appropriate behavior.

Advantages of the DSM Defenders of the DSM agree that the boundaries between "normal problems" and "mental disorders" are fuzzy and often difficult to determine, because most psychological symptoms fall along a continuum from mild to severe (Helzer et al., 2008). But they believe that

when the manual is used correctly and diagnoses are made with valid objective tests, the DSM improves the reliability of diagnosis (Beutler & Malik, 2002; Widiger & Clark, 2000). This is important, they maintain, because the DSM's categories help clinicians distinguish among disorders that share certain symptoms (such as anxiety, irritability, or delusions) and thereby select the most appropriate treatment.

Moreover, in response to criticism about cultural influences on mental disorders and their diagnoses, the DSM-IV included a list of **culture-bound syndromes**, sets of symptoms specific to the culture in which they occur (see Table 11.1). Thus, in Japan, where people are extremely sensitive to

culture-bound syndromes Symptoms or mental disorders that are specific to particular cultural contexts and practices.

TABLE 11.1

From Amok to Zar: Some Culture-Bound Syndromes

Problem Name	Where Recognized	Description
Amok	Malaysia; similar patterns elsewhere	Brooding followed by a violent outburst; often precipitated by a slight or insult; seems to be prevalent only among men
Ataque de nervios	Latin America and Mediterranean	An episode of uncontrollable shouting, crying, trembling, heat in chest rising to the head, verbal or physical aggression
Brain fag	West Africa	"Brain tiredness," a mental and physical reaction to the challenges of schooling
Ghost sickness	Native American tribes	Preoccupation with death and the dead, with bad dreams, fainting, appetite loss, fear, hallucinations, etc.
Pibloktoq	Arctic and subarctic Inuit communities	Episodes of extreme excitement of up to 30 minutes, during which the individual behaves irrationally or violently
Qi-gong psychotic reaction	China	A short episode of mental symptoms after engaging in the Chinese folk practice of qi-gong, or "exercise of vital energy"
Taijin kyofusho	Japan	An intense fear that the body, its parts, or its functions displease, embarrass, or are offensive to others
Zar	North Africa and Middle East	Belief in possession by a spirit, causing shouting, laughing, head banging, weeping, withdrawal, etc.

Source: DSM-IV.

matters of social harmony and concerned about not offending other people, *taijin kyofusho* is a disorder in which a person feels intensely frightened and irrationally embarrassed that his or her body parts or functions are disgusting to others. Latinos may experience an *ataque de nervios*, an episode of uncontrollable screaming, crying, and agitation, and Malaysian men may run *amok* in a violent, even murderous outburst. Students everywhere may have special sympathy for sufferers of the West African syndrome of *brain fag*, mental exhaustion due to excessive studying.

By comparing mental and emotional symptoms across different times and places, researchers can distinguish universal disorders from those that are culture-bound. Bulimia nervosa, involving cycles of binge eating and vomiting to maintain weight, is a culture-bound syndrome that occurs primarily in the United States and is unknown in most other parts of the world; yet anorexia has been found throughout history and across cultures (Keel & Klump, 2003). Likewise, from the Inuit of Alaska to the Pacific Islanders to the Yoruba of Nigeria, some individuals have schizophrenic delusions, are severely depressed, have anxiety disorders, or cannot control their aggressive behavior (Butcher, Lim, & Nezami, 1998; Kleinman, 1988).

Dilemmas of Measurement

Clinical psychologists and psychiatrists usually arrive at a diagnosis by interviewing a patient and observing the person's behavior when he or she arrives at the office, hospital, or clinic. But many also use psychological tests to help them decide on a diagnosis. Such tests are also commonly used in schools (e.g., to determine whether a child has a learning disorder) and in court settings (e.g., to try to determine which parent should have custody in a divorce case, whether a child has been sexually abused, or whether a defendant is mentally competent).

Projective Tests **Projective tests** consist of ambiguous pictures, sentences, or stories that the test taker interprets or completes. A child or adult may be asked to draw a person, a house, or some other object, or to finish a sentence (such as "My father..." or "Women are..."). The psychodynamic assumption behind all projective tests is that the person's unconscious thoughts and feelings will be "projected" onto the test and revealed in the person's responses. (See Chapter 2 for a discussion of psychodynamic theories.)

Projective tests can help clinicians establish rapport with their clients and can encourage clients

projective tests
Psychological tests used to infer a person's motives, conflicts, and unconscious dynamics on the basis of the person's interpretations of ambiguous stimuli.

to open up about anxieties and conflicts they might be ashamed to discuss. But the evidence is overwhelming that these tests lack reliability and validity, which makes them inappropriate for their most common uses—assessing personality traits or diagnosing mental disorders. They lack reliability because different clinicians often interpret the same person's scores differently, perhaps projecting their own beliefs and assumptions when they decide what a specific response means. The tests have low validity because they fail to measure what they are supposed to measure (Hunsley, Lee, & Wood, 2003). One reason is that responses to a projective test are significantly affected by sleepiness, hunger, medication, worry, verbal ability, the clinician's instructions, the clinician's personality (friendly and warm, or cool and remote?), and other events occurring that day.

One of the most popular projective tests is the *Rorschach inkblot test*, which was devised by the Swiss psychiatrist Hermann Rorschach in 1921. It consists of ten cards with symmetrical abstract patterns, originally formed by spilling ink on paper and folding the paper in half. The test taker reports what he or she sees in the inkblots, and the clinician interprets the answers according to the symbolic meanings emphasized by psychodynamic theories. Although the Rorschach is widely used among clinicians, efforts to confirm its reliability and validity have repeatedly failed. The Rorschach does not reliably diagnose depression, posttraumatic stress reactions, personality disorders, or serious mental disorders. Claims of the Rorschach's success often come from testimonials at workshops where clinicians are taught how to use the test, which is hardly an impartial way of assessing it (Wood et al., 2003).

A Rorschach inkblot. What do you see in it?

Many psychotherapists use projective tests with young children to help them express feelings they cannot reveal verbally. But during the 1980s, some therapists began using projective methods for another purpose: to determine whether a child had been sexually abused. They claimed they could identify a child who had been abused by observing how the child played with "anatomically detailed" dolls (dolls with realistic genitals), and that is how many of them testified in hundreds of court cases (Ceci & Bruck, 1995).

Unfortunately, these therapists had not tested their beliefs by using a fundamental scientific procedure: comparison with a control group (see Chapter 1). They had not asked, "How do *nonabused* children play with these dolls?" When psychological scientists conducted controlled research to answer this question, they found that large percentages of nonabused children are also fascinated with the doll's genitals. They will poke at them, grab them, pound sticks into a female doll's vagina, and do other things that alarm adults! The crucial conclusion was that you cannot reliably diagnose sexual abuse on the basis of children's doll play (Bruck et al., 1995; Hunsley, Lee, & Wood, 2003; Koocher et al., 1995). You can see how someone who does not understand the problems with projective tests might make inferences about a child's behavior that are dangerously wrong.

Another situation in which projective tests are used widely but often inappropriately is in child custody assessments. Understandably, when faced with divorcing partners who are bitterly quarreling, calling each other names, and accusing each other of being a terrible parent, the courts long for an objective way to determine which one is better suited to have custody. But when a panel of psychological scientists impartially examined the leading psychological assessment measures, most of which are projective tests, they found that "these measures assess ill-defined constructs, and they do so poorly, leaving no scientific justification for their use in child custody evaluations" (Emery, Otto, & O'Donohue, 2005).

Objective Tests Many clinicians use **objective tests (inventories)**, standardized questionnaires that ask about the test taker's behavior and feelings. Inventories are generally more reliable and valid than either projective methods or subjective clinical judgments (Dawes, 1994; Meyer et al., 2001). The leading objective test of major depression is the Beck Depression Inventory, and the most widely used diagnostic assessment for personality and emotional disorders is the *Minnesota Multiphasic*

For years, many therapists used anatomically detailed dolls as a projective test to determine whether a child had been sexually abused. But the empirical evidence, including studies of nonabused children in a control group, shows that this practice is simply not valid. It can lead to false allegations because it often misidentifies nonabused children who are merely fascinated with the doll's genitals.

Personality Inventory (MMPI). The MMPI is organized into ten categories, or *scales*, covering such problems as depression, paranoia, schizophrenia, and introversion. Four additional *validity scales* indicate whether a test taker is likely to be lying, defensive, or evasive while answering the items.

Inventories are only as good as their questions and how knowledgeably they are interpreted. Some test items on the MMPI fail to consider differences among cultural, regional, and socioeconomic groups. For example, Mexican, Puerto Rican, and Argentine respondents score differently from non–Hispanic Americans, on average, on the Masculinity–Femininity Scale. This difference does not reflect emotional problems but traditional Latino attitudes toward sex roles (Cabiya et al., 2000). Also, the MMPI sometimes labels a person's responses as evidence of mental disorder when they are a result of understandable stresses, such as during divorce or other legal disputes, when participants are upset and angry (Guthrie & Mobley, 1994; Leib, 2008). However, testing experts continue to improve the reliability and validity of the MMPI in clinical assessment by restructuring the clinical scales to reflect current research on mental disorders and personality traits (Butcher & Perry, 2008; Sellbom, Ben-Porath, & Bagby, 2008).

We turn now to a closer examination of some of the disorders described in the DSM. Of course, we cannot cover all of them in one chapter, so we have singled out several that illustrate the range of psychological problems that afflict humanity, from the common to the very rare.

objective tests (inventories) Standardized objective questionnaires requiring written responses; they typically include scales on which people are asked to rate themselves.

✓• Study and
Review on
mypsychlab.com

Quick Quiz

Your mental health will be enhanced if you can answer these questions.

1. The primary purpose of the DSM is to (a) provide descriptive criteria for diagnosing mental disorders, (b) help psychologists assess normal as well as abnormal behavior, (c) describe the causes of common disorders, (d) keep the number of diagnostic categories of mental disorders to a minimum.

2. List four criticisms of the DSM.

3. Which of the following disorders is a culture-bound syndrome? (a) anorexia nervosa, (b) major depression, (c) bulimia, (d) schizophrenia, (e) panic attacks

4. What is the advantage of inventories, compared with clinical judgments and projective tests, in diagnosing mental disorders?

Answers:

1. a 2. It can foster overdiagnosis; it overlooks the power of diagnostic labels on the perceptions of others; it often confuses serious mental disorders with everyday problems in living; and it produces an illusion of objectivity. 3. c 4. Inventories have better reliability and validity.

YOU are about to learn...

- the difference between ordinary anxiety and an anxiety disorder.

- why the most disabling of all phobias is known as the "fear of fear."

- why some people recover quickly after a trauma whereas others develop posttraumatic stress disorder.

Anxiety Disorders

Anyone who is waiting for important news or living in an unpredictable situation quite sensibly feels *anxiety*, a general state of apprehension or psychological tension. And anyone who is in a dangerous and unfamiliar situation, such as making a first parachute jump or facing a peevish python, quite sensibly feels flat-out fear. In the short run, these emotions are adaptive because they energize us to cope with danger. They ensure that we don't make that first jump without knowing how to operate the parachute, and that we get away from that snake as fast as we can.

But sometimes fear and anxiety become detached from any actual danger, or these feelings continue even when danger and uncertainty are past. The result may be *chronic anxiety*, marked by long-lasting feelings of apprehension and doom; *panic attacks*, short-lived but intense feelings of anxiety; *phobias*, excessive fears of specific things or situations; or *obsessive-compulsive disorder*, in which repeated thoughts and rituals are used to ward off anxiety. ((•⁻ Listen

((•⁻ Listen to
Anxiety
Disorders on
mypsychlab.com

generalized anxiety disorder A continuous state of anxiety marked by feelings of worry and dread, apprehension, difficulties in concentration, and signs of motor tension.

Anxiety and Panic

The chief characteristic of **generalized anxiety disorder** is excessive, uncontrollable anxiety or worry—a feeling of foreboding and dread—that occurs on a majority of days during a six-month period and that is not brought on by physical causes such as disease, drugs, or drinking too much coffee.

Some people suffer from generalized anxiety disorder without having lived through any specific anxiety-producing event. They may have a genetic predisposition to experience its symptoms—sweaty palms, a racing heart, shortness of breath—when they are in unfamiliar or uncontrollable situations. Genes may also be involved in causing abnormalities in the amygdala, the core structure for the acquisition of fear (see Chapter 13), and in the prefrontal cortex, which is associated with the ability to realize when danger has passed (Lonsdorf et al., 2009). But anxiety disorders may also stem from experience: Some chronically anxious people have a history, starting in childhood, of being unable to control or predict their environments (Barlow, 2000; Mineka & Zinbarg, 2006). Whatever the origin of generalized anxiety disorder, its sufferers have mental biases in the way they attend to and process threatening information. They perceive everything as an opportunity for disaster, a cognitive habit that fuels their worries and keeps their anxiety bubbling along (Mitte, 2008).

Posttraumatic Stress Disorder Stress symptoms, including insomnia and agitation, are entirely normal in the immediate aftermath of any crisis or trauma, such as war, rape, torture, natural disasters, sudden bereavement, or terrorist attacks. But if the symptoms persist for one month or longer and begin to impair a person's functioning, the sufferer may have **posttraumatic stress disorder (PTSD)**. Symptoms of PTSD include reliving the trauma in recurrent, intrusive thoughts; a sense of detachment from others and a loss of interest in familiar activities; and increased physiological arousal, reflected in insomnia, irritability, and impaired concentration.

Most people who live through a traumatic experience eventually recover without developing PTSD (Bonanno et al., 2006). A national survey of Americans found that about 60 percent had experienced a traumatic event, but only 8 percent of the men and 20 percent of the women later developed PTSD (Kessler et al., 1995). Why, then, if most people recover from a traumatic experience, do others continue to have PTSD symptoms for years, sometimes for decades?

One answer, again, involves a genetic predisposition. Behavioral–genetic studies of twins in the general population and of combat veterans have found that PTSD symptoms have a heritable component (Stein et al., 2002). But PTSD has also been linked to certain personality and mental characteristics. A prospective study that followed children from their early years to about age 17 found that people who develop PTSD after a traumatic experience often have a prior history of psychological problems, such as anxiety and impulsive aggression. And they seem to lack the social, psychological, and neurological resources to avoid having preventable traumatic experiences in the first place or to cope with unavoidable ones (Breslau, Lucia, & Alvarado, 2006). PTSD sufferers, like others with anxiety disorders, are also more likely to have self-defeating, anxiety-producing ways of thinking that *preceded* the traumatic event. They tend to "catastrophize" about every little thing that goes wrong, to believe they are inadequate, and to feel that no one can be trusted (Bryant & Guthrie, 2005; Ozer et al., 2003).

Interestingly, in many PTSD sufferers, the hippocampus is smaller than average (McNally, 2003). The hippocampus is crucially involved in autobiographical memory. An abnormally small one may figure in the difficulty of some trauma survivors to react to their memories as events from their past, which may be why they keep reliving them in the present. An MRI study of identical twins, only one of whom in each pair had been in combat in Vietnam, showed that two things were necessary for a vet to develop chronic PTSD: serving in combat *and* having a smaller hippocampus than normal. Twins who had smaller hippocampi

This grief-stricken soldier has just learned that the body bag on the flight with him contains the remains of a close friend who was killed in action. Understandably, many soldiers suffer posttraumatic stress symptoms. But why do most eventually recover, whereas others have PTSD for many years?

but no military service did not develop PTSD, and neither did the twins who *did* experience combat but who had normal-sized hippocampi (Gilbertson et al., 2002).

In sum, many cases of long-lasting PTSD seem to be a result of impaired cognitive and neurological functioning that existed before the trauma took place, making it more likely that the trauma will trigger persistent, long-lasting symptoms.

Panic Disorder Another kind of anxiety disorder is **panic disorder**, in which a person has recurring attacks of intense fear or panic, often with feelings of impending doom or death. Panic attacks may last from a few minutes to (more rarely) several hours. Symptoms include trembling and shaking, dizziness, chest pain or discomfort, rapid heart rate, feelings of unreality, hot and cold flashes, sweating, and—as a result of all these scary physical reactions—a fear of dying, going crazy, or losing control. Many sufferers fear they are having a heart attack.

Although panic attacks seem to come out of nowhere, they in fact usually occur in the aftermath of stress, prolonged emotion, specific worries, or frightening experiences (McNally, 1998). A friend of ours was on a plane that was a target of a bomb threat while airborne at 33,000 feet. He coped beautifully at the time, but two weeks later, seemingly out of nowhere, he had a panic attack. Such delayed attacks after life-threatening scares are common. The essential difference between people

posttraumatic stress disorder (PTSD) An anxiety disorder in which a person who has experienced a traumatic or life-threatening event has symptoms such as psychic numbing, reliving of the trauma, and increased physiological arousal.

panic disorder An anxiety disorder in which a person experiences recurring panic attacks, periods of intense fear, and feelings of impending doom or death, accompanied by physiological symptoms such as rapid heart rate and dizziness.

Get Involved! What Scares You?

Everyone fears something. Stop for a moment to think about what you fear most. Is it heights? Snakes? Speaking in public? Ask yourself these questions: (1) How long have you feared this thing or situation? (2) How would you respond if you could not avoid this thing or situation? (3) How much would you be willing to rearrange your life to avoid this feared thing or situation? After considering these questions, would you regard your fear as a full-blown phobia or merely a normal source of apprehension?

who develop panic disorder and those who do not lies in how they *interpret* their bodily reactions (Barlow, 2000). Healthy people who have occasional panic attacks see them correctly as a result of a passing crisis or period of stress, comparable to another person's migraines. But people who develop panic disorder regard the attack as a sign of illness or impending death, and they begin to live their lives in restrictive ways, trying to avoid future attacks.

Fears and Phobias

Are you afraid of bugs, snakes, or dogs? Are you vaguely uncomfortable or so afraid that you can't stand to be around one? A **phobia** is an exaggerated fear of a specific situation, activity, or thing. Some common phobias—such as fear of snakes, insects, heights (acrophobia), thunder (brontophobia), or being trapped in enclosed spaces (claustrophobia)—may have evolved to be easily acquired in human beings because these fears reflected real dangers for the species (see Chapter 9). Some phobias, such as a fear of the color purple (porphyrophobia), dirt and germs (mysophobia), or the number 13 (triskaidekaphobia), may reflect idiosyncratic experiences, personality traits, or cultural traditions. Whatever its source, a phobia is truly frightening and often incapacitating for its sufferer. It is not just a tendency to say "ugh" at tarantulas or skip the snake display at the zoo.

People who have a *social phobia* become extremely anxious in situations in which they will be observed by others—eating in a restaurant, speaking in public, having to perform for an audience. They worry that they will do or say something that will be excruciatingly embarrassing and that other people will laugh at them or reject them. These phobias are more severe forms of the occasional shyness and social anxiety that everyone experiences. For people with a social phobia, the mere thought of being in a new situation with unfamiliar people is scary enough to cause sweating, trembling, nausea, and an overwhelming feeling of

phobia An exaggerated, unrealistic fear of a specific situation, activity, or object.

agoraphobia A set of phobias, often set off by a panic attack, involving the basic fear of being away from a safe place or person.

obsessive-compulsive disorder (OCD) An anxiety disorder in which a person feels trapped in repetitive, persistent thoughts (*obsessions*) and repetitive, ritualized behaviors (*compulsions*) designed to reduce anxiety.

inadequacy. So they don't go, increasing their isolation and imagined fears.

By far the most disabling fear disorder is **agoraphobia**. In ancient Greece, the *agora* was the social, political, business, and religious center of town, the public meeting place away from home. The fundamental fear in agoraphobia is of being trapped in a crowded public place, where escape might be difficult or where help might be unavailable if the person has a panic attack. Individuals with agoraphobia report many specific fears—of being in a crowded movie theater, driving in traffic or tunnels, or going to parties—but the underlying fear is of being away from a safe place, usually home, or a safe person, usually a parent or partner.

Agoraphobia typically begins with a panic attack that seems to have no cause. The attack is so unexpected and scary that the agoraphobic-to-be begins to avoid situations that he or she thinks may provoke another one. A woman we know had a panic attack while driving on a freeway. This was a perfectly normal posttraumatic response to the suicide of her husband a few weeks earlier. But thereafter she avoided freeways, as if the freeway, and not the suicide, had caused the attack. Because so many of the actions associated with agoraphobia arise as a mistaken effort to avoid a panic attack, psychologists regard agoraphobia as a "fear of fear" rather than simply a fear of places.

Obsessions and Compulsions

Obsessive-compulsive disorder (OCD) is characterized by recurrent, persistent, unwished-for thoughts or images (*obsessions*) and by repetitive, ritualized behaviors that the person feels must be carried out to avoid disaster (*compulsions*). Of course, many people have trivial compulsions and practice superstitious rituals. Baseball players are famous for them; one won't change his socks and another insists on eating chicken every day while he is on a hitting streak. Obsessions and compulsions become a disorder when they become uncontrollable and interfere with a person's life.

People who have obsessive thoughts often find them frightening or repugnant: thoughts of killing a child, of becoming contaminated by a handshake, or of having unknowingly hurt someone in a traffic accident. Obsessive thoughts take many forms, but they are alike in reflecting impaired ways of reasoning and processing information.

People who suffer from compulsions likewise feel they have no control over them. The most common compulsions are hand washing, counting, touching, and checking. A woman *must* check the furnace, lights, locks, and oven three times before she can sleep; a man *must* run up and down the stairs 60 times in 40 minutes or else start over from the beginning. OCD sufferers usually realize that their behavior is senseless, and they are often tormented by their rituals. But if they try to resist the compulsion, they feel mounting anxiety that is relieved only by giving in to it.

In many people with OCD, abnormalities in an area of the prefrontal cortex create a kind of cognitive rigidity, an inability to let go of intrusive thoughts, and behavioral rigidity, an inability to alter compulsive behavior after getting negative feedback (Chamberlain et al., 2008; Clarke et al., 2004). Normally, once danger has passed or a person realizes that there is no cause for fear, the brain's alarm signal turns off. In people with OCD, however, false alarms keep clanging and the emotional networks keep sending out mistaken fear messages (Schwartz et al., 1996). The sufferer feels in a constant state of danger and tries repeatedly to reduce the resulting anxiety.

OCD is not a single, unified disorder (Taylor, McKay, & Abramowitz, 2005). One subtype afflicts pathological hoarders who fill their homes with

Extreme hoarding is a form of obsessive-compulsive disorder. The person who lived here was unable to throw away any papers or magazines without feeling tremendous anxiety.

newspapers, bags of old clothing, used tissue boxes—all kinds of junk. They are tormented by fears of throwing out something they will need later. A PET-scan study that compared obsessive hoarders with other people with obsessive symptoms found that hoarders had less activity in parts of the brain involved in decision making, problem solving, spatial orientation, and memory (Saxena et al., 2004). Perhaps these deficits explain why hoarders keep things and why they often keep their papers and junk in the living room, kitchen, or even on the bed. Their inability to decide what to throw away creates a constant worry, and their difficulty in remembering where things are makes them feel the need to have them in sight.

✔— **Study** and **Review** on mypsychlab.com

Quick Quiz

We hope you don't feel anxious about matching each term on the left with its description on the right.

1. social phobia
2. generalized anxiety disorder
3. posttraumatic stress disorder
4. agoraphobia
5. compulsion
6. obsession

a. need to perform a ritual
b. fear of fear; of being trapped with no way of escape
c. continuing sense of doom
d. repeated, unwanted thoughts
e. fear of meeting new people
f. anxiety following severe shock

Answers:

1.e 2.c 3.f 4.b 5.a 6.d

YOU are about to learn...

- the difference between major depression and the blues.
- four contributing factors in depression.
- how some people can think themselves into depression.

Mood Disorders

In the DSM, *mood disorders* include disturbances in emotion ranging from extreme depression to extreme mania. Of course, most people feel sad and joyful from time to time, and, at some time in their lives, will know the grief that follows the loss of someone they love. These feelings, however, are a far cry from the clinical disorders described by the DSM.

Depression

Major depression involves emotional, behavioral, cognitive, and physical changes severe enough to disrupt a person's ordinary functioning and lasting at least two weeks. Some episodes can last as long as 20 weeks, subside, and later recur. People with major depression feel despairing and worthless. They feel unable to get up and do things; it takes an enormous effort even to get dressed. They may overeat or stop eating, have difficulty falling asleep or sleeping through the night, have trouble concentrating, and feel tired all the time. They lose interest in activities that usually give them satisfaction and pleasure.

The DSM's definition excludes people whose depression is caused by bereavement, and whose acute but understandable feelings of grief eventually subside within a few months. But as a community survey of more than 8,000 people found, the symptoms of major depression that would constitute a mental disorder are often indistinguishable from symptoms of extreme sorrow following the loss of a job and social status in one's community, a disastrous financial investment, or the end of an important relationship (Wakefield et al., 2007).

Major depression occurs at least twice as often among women as among men, all over the world. However, because women are more likely than men to talk about their feelings and more likely to seek help, depression in males is probably underdiagnosed. Men who are depressed often try to mask their feelings by withdrawing, abusing alcohol or other drugs, driving recklessly, or behaving violently (Canetto, 1992; Kessler et al., 1995). As Susan Nolen-Hoeksema, a leading depression researcher, put it, "Women think and men drink."

major depression A mood disorder involving disturbances in emotion (excessive sadness), behavior (loss of interest in one's usual activities), cognition (thoughts of hopelessness), and body function (fatigue and loss of appetite).

bipolar disorder A mood disorder in which episodes of both depression and mania (excessive euphoria) occur.

vulnerability-stress models Approaches that emphasize how individual vulnerabilities interact with external stresses or circumstances to produce mental disorders.

Bipolar Disorder

At the opposite pole from depression is *mania*, an abnormally high state of exhilaration. Mania is not the normal joy of being in love or winning the Pulitzer Prize. Instead of feeling fatigued and listless, the manic person is excessively wired and often irritable when thwarted. Instead of feeling hopeless and powerless, the person feels powerful and is full of plans; but these plans are usually based on delusional ideas, such as thinking that he or she has invented something that will solve the world's energy problems. People in a state of mania often get into terrible trouble by going on extravagant spending sprees or making rash decisions.

When people experience at least one episode of mania alternating with episodes of depression, they are said to have **bipolar disorder** (formerly called *manic-depressive disorder*). The great humorist Mark Twain had bipolar disorder, which he described as "periodical and sudden changes of mood... from deep melancholy to half-insane tempests and cyclones." Other writers, artists, musicians, and scientists have also suffered from this disorder (Jamison, 1992). During the highs, many of these creative people produce their best work, but the price of the lows is disastrous relationships, bankruptcy, and sometimes suicide. As noted earlier, bipolar disorder, once thought to emerge only in adulthood, is now being widely diagnosed among young children and adolescents, although the symptoms and mood swings often look different from those in adults, and the diagnosis in children remains controversial (Holden, 2008).

Origins of Depression

One of the great mysteries of depression is that most people who undergo a "depressing" experience do not become clinically depressed, and many people who are clinically depressed have not had "depressing" experiences (Monroe & Reid, 2009). Most researchers thus emphasize a **vulnerability-stress model:** A person's vulnerabilities (in genetic predispositions, personality traits, or habits of thinking) interact with stressful events (such as violence, death of a loved one, or losing a job) to produce most cases of major depression. Let's consider the evidence for the major contributing factors:

1 **Genetic predispositions.** Major depression is a moderately heritable disorder, so genes must be involved in some cases. But so far the search for specific genes has been unsuccessful. One focus of investigation has been the genes that regulate serotonin, a neurotransmitter involved in mood. An

Even people who are rich, successful, and adored by millions can suffer from major depression. The suicide of Nirvana's lead singer, Kurt Cobain, shocked and saddened his many fans.

early theory held that depression results from abnormally low levels of this neurotransmitter. However, many years of research have failed to support the notion that depression results from a simple neurotransmitter deficiency. Depleting animals of serotonin does not induce depression, nor does increasing brain serotonin necessarily alleviate it. The fact that some antidepressants raise serotonin levels (see Chapter 12) does not mean that low serotonin levels caused the depression—a common but mistaken inference (Lacasse & Leo, 2005).

In 2003, in a study of 847 New Zealanders who had been followed from birth to age 26, researchers reported that those who had a short form of a serotonin receptor gene called 5-HTT were much more likely to become severely depressed in the aftermath of major stressful events such as the loss of a job or a death in the family, compared to people with a long form of this gene. In fact, those with the long form were much less likely than others to become clinically depressed even after suffering emotional blows (Caspi et al., 2003). These findings

seemed to show unmistakably the interaction of genes and experience in causing depression in genetically vulnerable people and preventing depression in others. But these conclusions turned out to be premature. A subsequent meta-analysis of 14 studies that had investigated possible links among the 5-HTT gene, life stresses, and depression came up with nothing (Risch et al., 2009). The 5-HTT gene, whether alone or in interaction with life stresses, was not associated with an elevated risk of depression in either sex.

Nonetheless, the New Zealand study has stimulated a wave of research into gene-environment interactions in depression. Most researchers are confident that specific genes involved in some cases of depression will eventually be identified.

2 Violence, childhood physical abuse, and parental neglect. One of the most powerful environmental factors associated with clinical depression is repeated experience with violence. Inner-city adolescents of both sexes who are exposed to high rates of violence in their families or communities report higher levels of depression and more attempts to commit suicide than those who are not subjected to constant violence (Mazza & Reynolds, 1999). And domestic violence takes a particular toll on women. A longitudinal study, which followed men and women from ages 18 to 26, compared those in physically abusive relationships with those in nonabusive ones. Although depressed women were more likely to enter abusive relationships to begin with, involvement in a violent relationship independently increased their rates of depression and anxiety—but, interestingly, not men's (Ehrensaft, Moffitt, & Caspi, 2006).

Maltreatment in childhood, independent of all other childhood and adult risk factors, is associated with a particularly high risk of adult depressive episodes lasting a year or more (Brown & Harris, 2008; Widom, DuMont, & Czaja, 2007). A mechanism that might explain this increased risk is that prolonged stress in childhood and adolescence puts the body's responses to stress in overdrive, so that it overproduces the stress hormone cortisol (Gotlib et al., 2008). Depressed people tend to have high levels of cortisol, which can affect the hippocampus and amygdala, causing mood and memory abnormalities.

3 Losses of important relationships. A third line of investigation emphasizes the loss of important relationships in setting off depression in vulnerable individuals. When an infant is separated from a primary attachment figure, as in the Harlow studies of rhesus monkeys (see Chapter 3), the result is not only despair and passivity, but also harm to the immune system, which can later lead to depressive illness (Hennessy, Schiml-Webb, & Deak, 2009). Many depressed people have a history of separations, losses, rejections, and impaired, insecure attachments (Hammen, 2009; Nolan, Flynn, & Garber, 2003; Weissman, Markowitz, & Klerman, 2000). As we noted earlier, however, people with a history of happy and secure attachments may also fall into prolonged depression because of the loss of a beloved lifelong partner (Wakefield et al., 2007).

4 **Cognitive habits.** Finally, depression involves specific, negative ways of thinking about one's situation (Beck, 2005). Depressed people typically believe that their situation is *permanent* ("Nothing good will ever happen to me") and *uncontrollable* ("I'm depressed because I'm ugly and horrible and I can't do anything about it"). Expecting nothing to get better, they do nothing to improve their lives and therefore remain unhappy (Abramson, Metalsky, & Alloy, 1989; Chorpita & Barlow, 1998). When depressed and nondepressed people are put into a sad mood and given a choice between looking at sad faces or happy faces, depressed people choose the sad faces—a metaphor for how they process the world in general, attending to everything that confirms the gloominess of life rather than any of its joys (Joormann & Gotlib, 2007). And when asked to recall happier times, nondepressed people cheer up. But depressed people feel even worse, as if the happy memory makes them feel that they will never be happy again (Joormann, Siemer, & Gotlib, 2007).

The cognitive biases associated with depression are not just correlates of the disorder. Longitudinal studies show that they play a causal role, interacting with severe life stresses to generate further depressive episodes (Monroe et al., 2007). Depressed people tend to *ruminate*—brooding about everything that is wrong in their lives, persuading themselves that no one cares about them, and dwelling on reasons to feel hopeless. They have trouble preventing these gloomy thoughts from entering and remaining in their working memory, which keeps them stewing in negative thoughts and unhappy past events (Joormann, 2010). In contrast, nondepressed people who undergo stressful events are usually able to distract themselves, look outward, and seek solutions. Beginning in adolescence, women are much more likely than men to develop a ruminating, introspective style, which contributes both to longer-lasting depressions in women and to the sex difference in reported rates.

The findings about rumination are pretty interesting, because just about all of us know what it

Women are far more likely than men to ruminate and brood when they are sad, a habit that can easily turn into depression.

feels like to think that everything is hopeless, to brood over hurt feelings, to rehearse real and imagined insults ("Who does she think she is, anyway?"), and to wallow in our anxieties ("I'm never going to do well in this course—I can't possibly keep up"). When we think of examples like these, we can see why rumination might keep us stuck in an anxious, angry, or gloomy frame of mind. And, in fact, rumination predicts not only depression but also impaired thinking and problem solving, anxiety and worry, eating disorders, and drug abuse (Nolen-Hoeksema, Wisco, & Lyubomirsky, 2008; Zalta & Chambless, 2008).

The factors we have described—genetics, violence, loss of important people, and cognitive habits and biases—combine in different ways to produce any given case of depression. That is why the same sad event, such as flunking a course, being dumped by a lover, or losing a job, can affect two people entirely differently: One rolls with the punch and another is knocked flat.

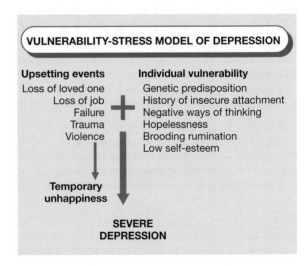

VULNERABILITY-STRESS MODEL OF DEPRESSION

Upsetting events	**Individual vulnerability**
Loss of loved one	Genetic predisposition
Loss of job	History of insecure attachment
Failure	Negative ways of thinking
Trauma	Hopelessness
Violence	Brooding rumination
	Low self-esteem

Temporary unhappiness

SEVERE DEPRESSION

Quick Quiz

Don't let another quiz make you vulnerable to depression!

1. Biological researchers find that depressed people have unusually high levels of the stress hormone
   _____.

2. What are four main contributing factors in depression?

3. Depressed people tend to believe that the reasons for their unhappiness are (a) controllable, (b) temporary, (c) out of their hands, (d) caused by the situation.

4. A news headline announces that a gene has been identified as the cause of depression. Does this mean that everyone with the gene will become depressed? How should critical thinkers interpret this research?

Answers:

1. cortisol 2. genetic factors; exposure to violence and childhood experiences of parental neglect and physical abuse; a history of insecure attachments and losses of close relationships; cognitive habits of negative thinking and rumination 3. c 4. No, it means that people with the gene are more likely to become depressed when they undergo severely stressful experiences. Critical thinkers would want to make sure the research is replicated, and they would realize that not all cases of depression are necessarily influenced by genetics.

YOU are about to learn...

• what a charming but heartless tycoon and a remorseless killer have in common.

• why some people are incapable of feeling guilt or pangs of conscience.

Antisocial/Psychopathic Personality Disorder

Personality disorders involve maladaptive traits that cause great distress or an inability to get along with others. One of the most researched types is **borderline personality disorder**, characterizing people who have a history of intense but unstable relationships in which they alternate between idealizing the partner and then devaluing the partner. They frantically try to avoid real or imagined abandonment by others, even if the "abandonment" is only a friend's brief vacation. They are self-destructive and impulsive, suffer chronic feelings of emptiness, and often mutilate themselves or threaten to commit suicide. And they are emotionally volatile, careening from anger to euphoria to anxiety. ("Borderline" comes from the original definition of the disorder, as one that fell between being neurotic and being psychotic.)

The DSM-IV also contains several other kinds of personality disorders. The DSM-V will revise the current set of diagnoses significantly, but it will retain one that has fascinated the public for centuries: a disorder describing people who lack all human connection to anyone else, people who can cheat, con, and kill without flinching.

Decades ago, in his influential book *The Mask of Sanity*, Hervey Cleckley (1976) popularized and standardized the term *psychopath* to describe a person who lacks conscience. A key characteristic of **psychopathy**, said Cleckley, is an inability to feel normal emotions. Psychopaths are incapable not only of remorse but also of fear of punishment and of shame, guilt, and empathy for those they have hurt. Because they lack emotional connections to others, they often behave cruelly and irresponsibly, as much for the thrill as for personal gain, and with no thought of the long-term consequences of their actions. If caught in a lie or a crime, psychopaths may seem sincerely sorry and promise to make amends, but it is all an act. Some psychopaths are violent and sadistic, able to kill a pet, a child, or a random adult without a twinge of regret, but others are charming and manipulative, able to direct their energies into con games or career advancement, abusing other people emotionally or economically rather than physically (Skeem et al., 2003; Skeem & Cooke, 2010). One researcher calls corporate psychopaths "snakes in suits" (Babiak & Hare, 2007).

Psychopaths are believed to exist in all cultures and throughout history, although they are more prevalent in individualistic Western societies. Even a close-knit culture such as the Yupik in Canada has a word for them—*kunlangeta* (Seabrook, 2008). An anthropologist once asked a member of the tribe what the group would do with a *kunlangeta*, and he said, "Somebody would have pushed him off the ice

borderline personality disorder A disorder characterized by intense but unstable relationships, impulsiveness, self-mutilating behavior, feelings of emptiness, and a fear of abandonment by others.

psychopathy A personality disorder characterized by a lack of remorse, empathy, anxiety, and other social emotions; the use of deceit and manipulation; and impulsive thrill seeking.

antisocial personality disorder (APD) A personality disorder characterized by a lifelong pattern of irresponsible, antisocial behavior such as lawbreaking, violence, and other impulsive, reckless acts; likely to be combined with *psychopathy* in the DSM-V.

when nobody else was looking." Psychopaths are feared and detested everywhere.

The DSM-IV replaced the term *psychopathy* with **antisocial personality disorder (APD)**, which applies to people who show "a pervasive pattern of disregard for, and violation of, the rights of others." People with APD repeatedly break the law; they are impulsive and seek quick thrills; they show reckless disregard for their own safety or that of others; they often get into physical fights or assault others; and they are irresponsible, failing to hold jobs or meet obligations (Widiger et al., 1996). As you can see, this definition covers a grab-bag set of behaviors. It does not specify what the underlying mental disorder might be, and it could apply both to teenagers who fall in with a bad crowd for a few years and to disturbed individuals who have been aggressive since early childhood. The latter become what one researcher calls "lifetime persistent offenders": Rule breaking and irresponsibility start in early childhood and take different forms at different ages: "biting and hitting at age 4, shoplifting and truancy at age 10, selling drugs and stealing cars at age 16, robbery and rape at age 22, and fraud and child abuse at age 30" (Moffitt, 1993, 2005).

The DSM-IV made the change in labeling to emphasize the behavioral signs of antisocial personality disorder. It put "lack of remorse," the prime feature of psychopathy, far down on the list of criteria for APD and did not make it essential for the diagnosis. But to many clinicians, the defining essence of psychopaths is their heartlessness and lack of conscience; they may not behave violently or commit criminal acts at all (Skeem & Cooke, 2010). People who commit violent crimes may be reckless and irresponsible, these clinicians point out, yet

differ greatly in their motivations for behaving this way and in their capacity for empathy, remorse, guilt, and loyalty. It does not appear that the DSM-V is likely to resolve the question of whether and how psychopathy and antisocial personality disorder overlap; it is likely to have a combined diagnosis called *antisocial/psychopathic personality disorder*.

Despite the definitional problems, researchers have identified a number of factors that are involved in the central features of psychopathy and of being a "lifetime persistent offender":

1 Abnormalities in the central nervous system. Something certainly seems to be amiss in the emotional wiring of psychopaths, the wiring that allows all primates, not just human beings, to feel connected to others of their kind. The psychopath's inability to feel emotional arousal suggests some aberration in the central nervous system (Hare, 1965, 1996; Lykken, 1995; Raine et al., 2000). Indeed, most psychopaths do not respond physiologically to the threat of punishment the way other people do, which may be why they can behave fearlessly in situations that would scare others to death.

Normally, when a person is anticipating danger, pain, or punishment, the electrical conductance of the skin changes, a classically conditioned response that indicates anxiety or fear. But psychopaths are slow to develop such responses, which suggests that they are unable to feel the anxiety necessary for learning that their actions will have unpleasant consequences (see Figure 11.2). Their lack of empathy for others also seems to have a physiological basis. When psychopaths are shown pictures of people crying and in distress, their skin conductance barely shifts, in contrast to that of

Some psychopaths are sadistic and violent. Gary L. Ridgway (left), the deadliest convicted serial killer in U.S. history, strangled 48 women, placing their bodies in "clusters" around the country. He did this because, he said coolly, he wanted to keep track of them. But others are confident men who use charm and elaborate scams to deceive and defraud. Christopher Rocancourt (right, with model Naomi Campbell) conned celebrities and others out of millions of dollars by adopting false identities, including movie producer, Brazilian race car driver, Russian prince, son of Sophia Loren, and financier. He was caught in Canada and spent a year in a correctional center— hosting media interviews and writing his autobiography.

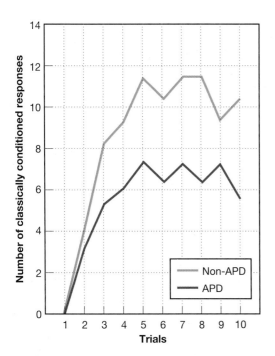

FIGURE 11.2
Emotions and Antisocial Personality Disorder

In several experiments, people with antisocial personality disorder (APD) were slow to develop classically conditioned responses to anticipated danger, pain, or shock—responses that indicate normal anxiety. This deficit may be related to the ability of psychopaths to behave in destructive ways without remorse or regard for the consequences (Hare, 1965, 1993).

nonpsychopaths, whose skin conductance shoots up (Blair et al., 1997). This emotional flatness may help distinguish psychopaths and violent career criminals from other aggressive individuals and lawbreakers who eventually give up their lives of crime (Lorber, 2004).

2 **Impaired frontal lobe functioning.** Psychopaths and violent career criminals often do not do as well as other individuals on neuropsychological tests of frontal lobe functioning, and they have less gray matter in the frontal lobes than other people do (Dinn & Harris, 2000; Raine, 2008). As we saw in Chapter 4, the frontal lobes are responsible for planning and impulse control, and impairments in this area can lead to an inability to control responses to frustration and provocation, to regulate emotions, and to understand the long-term consequences of indulging in immediate gratifications (Luengo et al., 1994; van Goozen et al., 2007). One PET-scan study found that cold-blooded, predatory murderers had less brain activity in the frontal lobe than did men who murdered in the heat of passion or a control group of criminals who had not murdered anybody (Raine et al., 1998).

Frontal lobe damage can be inherited or result from disease, accident, or physical abuse (Milner & McCanne, 1991). An analysis of two young adults whose prefrontal cortex was damaged in infancy—one was run over by a car when she was 15 months old and the other had a brain tumor removed—showed that both grew up to be compulsive liars, thieves, and heartless rule breakers. They could not hold jobs, make plans, distinguish right from wrong, or feel empathy (Anderson et al., 1999).

3 **Genetic influences.** Several genes seem to be involved in a range of disorders that involve frontal lobe causes of impulsivity—not only APD but also alcoholism, drug dependence, and childhood conduct disorder (Dick, 2007; Fowles & Dindo, 2009). In a longitudinal study of boys who had been physically abused in childhood, those who had a variation in a crucial gene later had far more arrests for violent crimes than did abused boys who had a normal gene (Caspi et al., 2002). Although only 12 percent of the abused boys had this variant, they accounted for nearly half of all later convictions for violent crimes.

4 **Environmental events.** Genes, however, are not destiny. In the study we just described, boys who had the genetic variant but whose parents treated them lovingly did not grow up to be violent. Genes may affect the brain, in turn predisposing a child to heartlessness or violent behavior, but many environmental influences can disrupt that pathway and alter the ways that genes express themselves. Poor nutrition in the first three years of life has been linked with antisocial behavior up through adolescence; so has early separation from the mother; and so has brain damage caused by parental cruelty (Raine, 2008).

Keep in mind that some children may have no genetic predisposition to psychopathy or APD, but years of living in violent worlds may blunt their ability to empathize with the suffering of others and may teach them that violence is a survival strategy. A culture that rewards ruthless behavior in work and politics will generate many "snakes in suits," and a culture that rewards the slaughter of innocents for purposes of political or religious genocide will generate many cases of "antisocial personality disorder." And genetics will not be the reason.

As you can see, the diverse causes of psychopathy and lifelong APD involve an individual's genetic predispositions, biological impairments, experiences in the world, and the culture the person lives in.

✓• Study and
Review on
mypsychlab.com

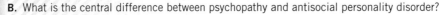
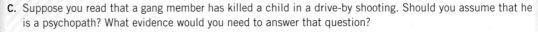

Quick Quiz

There is no such thing as test-avoidance personality disorder, so take this quiz.

A. Can you diagnose each of the following disorders?

1. Ann can barely get out of bed in the morning. She feels that life is hopeless and despairs of ever feeling good about herself.

2. Brad constantly feels a sense of impending doom; for days, he has been extremely worried about everything and can't relax.

3. Connie is emotionally dependent on others and panics or becomes angry when she thinks her friends have left her, even for vacation. She cuts herself and frequently threatens to commit suicide if she doesn't get what she wants.

4. Damon is the most charming of con artists; he can rob a widow of her life's savings without a moment's remorse.

B. What is the central difference between psychopathy and antisocial personality disorder?

C. Suppose you read that a gang member has killed a child in a drive-by shooting. Should you assume that he is a psychopath? What evidence would you need to answer that question?

Answers:

A. 1. major depression **2.** generalized anxiety disorder **3.** borderline personality disorder **4.** psychopathy **B.** Psychopathy is characterized by lack of remorse, guilt, and empathy, whereas antisocial personality disorder is characterized by a history of reckless rule breaking, aggression, and irresponsibility. **C.** The gang member might or might not be a psychopath or even have antisocial personality disorder. He might have killed the child to conform to the norms of his fellow gang members, yet privately feel terrible remorse. You would need to know whether he has a behavioral history of violence and rule breaking, starting in childhood, and whether he is able to feel empathy and connection to anyone, such as his gang and family.

Robert Downey, Jr., went to prison numerous times for abusing cocaine, heroin, and Valium. He told a judge, "It's like I have a loaded gun in my mouth and my finger's on the trigger, and I like the taste of the gunmetal." Downey's addictions nearly destroyed his acting career.

◆ YOU are about to learn...

• how genes might contribute to alcoholism.

• why alcoholism is more common in some cultures than others.

• why policies of abstinence from alcohol do not reduce problem drinking.

• why narcotics are not usually addictive when people take them for pain.

Drug Abuse and Addiction

Most people who use drugs (legal, illegal, or prescription) use them in moderation; but some people depend too much on them, and others abuse drugs even at the cost of their own health. The DSM-IV defines *substance abuse* as "a maladaptive pattern of substance use leading to clinically significant impairment or distress." Symptoms of such impairment include failure to hold a job, care for children, or complete schoolwork; use of the drug in hazardous situations (e.g., while driving a car or operating machinery); and frequent conflicts with others about use of the drug or as a result of using the drug.

In Chapter 5, we described the major psychoactive drugs and their effects. In this section, focusing primarily on the example of alcoholism, we will consider the two dominant approaches to understanding addiction and drug abuse—the biological model and the learning model—and then see how they might be reconciled.

Biology and Addiction

The *biological model* holds that addiction, whether to alcohol or any other drug, is due primarily to a person's neurology and genetic predisposition. The clearest example of the biology of addiction is nicotine. Although smoking rates have declined over the past fifty years, nicotine addiction remains one of the most serious health problems in the United States and worldwide. Unlike other addictions, it can begin quickly, within a month after the first cigarette—and for some teenagers, after only one cigarette—because nicotine almost immediately changes neuron receptors in the brain that react chemically to the drug (DiFranza, 2008). Genes produce variation in these nicotine receptors, which is one reason that some people are especially vulnerable to becoming addicted to cigarettes and have tremendous withdrawal symptoms when they try to give them up, whereas other people, even if they have been heavy smokers, can quit cold turkey (Bierut et al., 2008).

For alcoholism, the picture is more complicated. Genes are involved in some kinds of alcoholism but not all. There is a heritable component in the kind of alcoholism that begins in early adolescence and is linked to impulsivity, antisocial behavior, and criminality (Dick, 2007; Dick et al., 2008; Schuckit et al., 2007), but not in the kind of alcoholism that begins in adulthood and is unrelated to other disorders. (Robert Downey, Jr., shown on page 386, said he had been addicted to drugs since the age of 7.)

Genes also affect alcohol sensitivity: how quickly people respond to alcohol, whether they tolerate it, and how much they need to drink before feeling high (Hu et al., 2008). In an ongoing longitudinal study of 450 young men, those who at age 20 had to drink more than others to feel any reaction were at increased risk of becoming alcoholic within the decade. This was true regardless of their initial drinking habits or family history of alcoholism (Schuckit, 1998).

In contrast, people who have a high sensitivity to alcohol are less likely to drink to excess, and this may partly account for ethnic differences in alcoholism rates. One genetic factor causes low activity of an enzyme that is important in the metabolism of alcohol. People who lack this enzyme respond to alcohol with unpleasant symptoms, such as flushing and nausea. This genetic protection is common among Asians but rare among Europeans, which may be one reason that rates of alcoholism are much lower in Asian than in Caucasian populations; the Asian sensitivity to alcohol discourages them from drinking a lot (Heath et al., 2003). Not all Asians are the same in this regard, however. Korean-American college students have higher rates of alcohol-use disorders and family histories of alcoholism than do Chinese-American students (Duranceaux et al., 2008), and Native Americans have the same genetic protection that Asians do, yet they have much higher rates of alcoholism.

The usual way of looking at biological factors and addiction is to assume that the first causes the second. However, there is strong evidence that the relationship also works the other way: *Addictions can result from the abuse of drugs* (Crombag & Robinson, 2004). Many people become addicted not because their brains have led them to abuse drugs, but because the abuse of drugs has changed their brains. As you can see in Figure 11.3, heavy use of cocaine reduces the number of receptors for dopamine (Volkow et al., 2001); this is also true for alcohol and other drugs. Heavy drinking alters brain function, reduces the level of painkilling endorphins, produces nerve damage, and shrinks

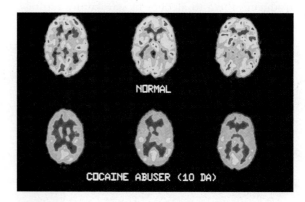

FIGURE 11.3
The Addicted Brain
PET studies show that the brains of cocaine addicts have fewer receptors for dopamine, a neurotransmitter involved in pleasurable sensations. (The more yellow and red in the brain image, the more receptors.) The brains of people addicted to methamphetamine, alcohol, and even food show a similar dopamine deficiency (Volkow et al., 2001).

the cerebral cortex. These changes can then create addiction, a craving for more of the drug. Rather than drinking alcohol for occasional pleasure, a person begins to drink as a relief from stressors and stays intoxicated for longer and longer times. At this point, long-term changes in the brain occur, and the person becomes alcoholic, drinking not for pleasure at all but simply to appease the craving (Heilig, 2008).

Thus, drug abuse, which begins as a voluntary action, can turn into drug addiction, a compulsive behavior that the addict finds almost impossible to control.

Learning, Culture, and Addiction

The *learning model* examines the role of the environment, learning, and culture in encouraging or discouraging drug abuse and addiction. Four major findings underscore the importance of understanding these factors:

1 Addiction patterns vary according to cultural practices. Alcoholism is much more likely to occur in societies that forbid children to drink but condone drunkenness in adults (as in Ireland) than in societies that teach children how to drink responsibly and moderately but condemn adult drunkenness (as in Italy, Greece, and France). In cultures with low rates of alcoholism (except for those committed to a religious rule that forbids use of all psychoactive drugs), adults demonstrate correct drinking habits to their children, gradually introducing them to alcohol in safe family settings.

Alcohol is not used as a rite of passage into adulthood. Abstainers are not sneered at, and drunkenness is not considered charming, comical, or manly; it is considered stupid and obnoxious (Peele & Brodsky, 1991; Vaillant, 1983).

The cultural environment may be especially crucial for the development of alcoholism among young people with a genetic vulnerability to alcohol (Schuckit et al., 2008). In one such group of 401 American Indian youths, those who later developed drinking problems lived in a community in which heavy drinking was encouraged and modeled by their parents and peers. But those who felt a cultural and spiritual pride in being Native American, and who were strongly attached to their religious traditions, were less likely to develop drinking problems, even when their parents and peers were encouraging them to drink (Yu & Stiffman, 2007).

Addiction rates can rise or fall rapidly as a culture changes. In colonial America, the average person drank two to three times the amount of liquor consumed today, yet alcoholism was not a serious problem. Drinking was a universally accepted social activity; families drank and ate together. Alcohol was believed to produce pleasant feelings and relaxation, and Puritan ministers endorsed its use (Critchlow, 1986). Then, between 1790 and 1830, when the American frontier was expanding, drinking came to symbolize masculine independence and toughness. The saloon became the place for drinking away from home. As people stopped drinking in moderation with their families, alcoholism rates shot up, as the learning model would predict.

Substance abuse and addiction problems also increase when people move from their culture of

When children learn the rules of social drinking with their families, as at this Jewish family's Passover seder (left), alcoholism rates are much lower than in cultures in which drinking occurs mainly in bars or in privacy. Likewise, when marijuana is used as part of a religious tradition, as it is by members of the Rastafarian church in Jamaica, use of the "wisdom weed" does not lead to addiction or harder drugs.

origin into another that has different drinking rules (Westermeyer, 1995). In most Latino cultures, women tend to drink rarely, if at all; they have few drinking problems until they move into an Anglo environment, when their rates of alcoholism rise (Canino, 1994). Likewise, when norms within a culture change, so may drinking habits and addiction rates. The cultural norm for American college women was once low to moderate drinking; today, college women are more likely to abuse alcohol than they ever used to. One reason is that the culture of many American college campuses encourages drinking games, binge drinking (having at least four to five drinks in a two-hour session), and getting drunk, especially among members of fraternities and sororities (Courtney & Polich, 2009). When everyone around you is downing shots one after another or playing beer pong, it's hard to say, "Gee, I'd really rather just have one drink" (or none).

2 **Policies of total abstinence tend to increase rates of addiction rather than reduce them.** In the United States, the temperance movement of the early twentieth century held that drinking inevitably leads to drunkenness, and drunkenness to crime. The solution it won for the Prohibition years (1920–1933) was national abstinence. But this victory backfired: Again in accordance with the learning model, Prohibition reduced rates of drinking overall, but it *increased* rates of alcoholism among those who did drink. Because people were denied the opportunity to learn to drink moderately, they drank excessively when given the chance (McCord, 1989). And, of course, when a substance is forbidden, it becomes more attractive to some people. Most schools in America have zero-tolerance policies regarding marijuana and alcohol, but large numbers of students have tried them or use them regularly. In fact, rates of binge drinking have increased the most among underage students, who are legally forbidden to drink until age 21.

3 **Not all addicts have withdrawal symptoms when they stop taking a drug.** When heavy users of a drug stop taking it, they often suffer such unpleasant symptoms as nausea, abdominal cramps, depression, and sleep problems, depending on the drug. But these symptoms are far from universal. During the Vietnam War, nearly 30 percent of American soldiers were taking heroin in doses far stronger than those available on the streets of U.S. cities. These men believed themselves to be addicted, and experts predicted a drug-withdrawal disaster among the returning veterans. It never materialized; over 90 percent of the men simply gave

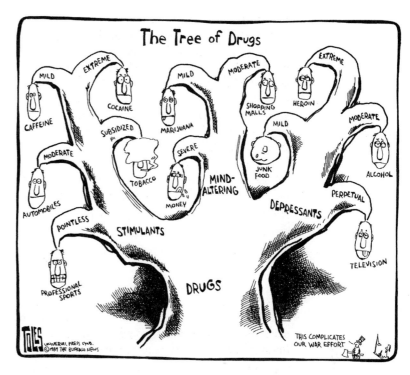

This cartoon, by poking fun at the things people do to make themselves feel better, reminds us that a person can become dependent on many things besides alcohol or other drugs.

up the drug, without significant withdrawal pain, when they came home to new circumstances (Robins, Davis, & Goodwin, 1974). Similarly, the majority of people who are dependent on cigarettes, tranquilizers, or painkillers are able to stop taking these drugs without outside help and without severe withdrawal symptoms (Prochaska, Norcross, & DiClemente, 1994). Many people find this information startling, even unbelievable. That is because people who can quit without help aren't entering programs to help them quit, so they are invisible to the general public and to the medical and therapeutic world. But they have been identified in random-sample community surveys.

One reason that many people are able to quit abusing drugs is that the environment in which a drug is used (the setting) and a person's expectations (mental set) have a powerful influence on the drug's *physiological* effects as well as its psychological ones (see Chapter 5). You might think a lethal dose of, say, amphetamines would be the same wherever the drug was taken. But studies of mice have found that the lethal dose varies depending on the mice's environment—whether they are in a large or small test cage, or whether they are alone or with other mice. Similarly, the physiological response of human addicts to certain drugs also changes, depending on whether the addicts are in a "druggy" environment, such as a crack house, or an unfamiliar one (Crombag & Robinson, 2004; Siegel, 2005). This is the primary reason that addicts need to change environments if they are going to kick their habits. It's

Get Involved! Test Your Motives for Drinking

If you drink, why do you do so? Check all of the motives that apply to you:

_____ to relax	_____ to cope with depression
_____ to escape from worries	_____ to get drunk and lose control
_____ to enhance a good meal	_____ to rebel against authority
_____ to conform to peers	_____ to relieve boredom
_____ to express anger	_____ to have sex
_____ to be sociable	_____ other (specify)

Do your reasons promote abuse or responsible use? How do you respond physically to alcohol? What have you learned about drinking from your family, your friends, and cultural messages? What do your answers tell you about your own vulnerability to addiction?

not just to get away from a peer group that might be encouraging them, but also to literally change and rewire their brain's response to the drug.

4 **Addiction does not depend on properties of the drug alone but also on the reasons for taking it.** For decades, doctors were afraid to treat people with chronic pain by giving them narcotics, fearing they would become addicts. As a result of this belief, millions of people were condemned to live with chronic suffering from back pain, arthritis, nerve disorders, and other conditions. But today we know that the vast majority of pain sufferers use morphine and other opiates not, as addicts do, to escape from the world but rather to function in the world, and they do not become addicted (Portenoy, 1994; Raja, 2008).

Similarly, in the case of alcohol, people who drink simply to be sociable or to relax when they have had a rough day are unlikely to become addicted. *Problem* drinking occurs when people drink to disguise or suppress their anxiety or depression, when they drink alone to drown their sorrows and forget their worries, or when they want an excuse to abandon inhibitions (Cooper et al., 1995; Mohr et al., 2001). College students who feel alienated and uninvolved with their studies are more likely than their happier peers to go out drinking with the conscious intention of getting drunk (Flacks & Thomas, 1998).

After five years in and out of rehab and facing more prison time, Robert Downey, Jr., got serious about getting help and was able to overcome his addictions.

Debating the Causes of Addiction

The biological and learning models both contribute to our understanding of drug use and addiction. Yet, among many researchers and public health professionals, these views are quite polarized, especially when it comes to thinking about treatment. The result is either–or thinking on a national scale: Either complete abstinence is the solution, or it is the problem.

Those who advocate the biological model say that alcoholics and problem drinkers must abstain completely, and that young people should not be permitted to drink, even at home with their parents, until they are 21. Those who champion the learning model argue that most problem drinkers can learn to drink moderately if they learn to drink

Thinking Critically about Theories of Addiction

safely and sensibly, acquire better ways of coping with stress, avoid situations that evoke conditioned responses to using drugs, and avoid friends who pressure them to drink excessively. Besides, they ask, how are young people going to learn to drink moderately if they don't first do so at home or in other safe environments? (Denning, Little, & Glickman, 2004; Rosenberg, 1993).

How can we assess these two positions critically? Because alcoholism and problem drinking occur for many reasons, neither model offers the only solution. On the one hand, many people who have been drinking heavily for years may not be able to learn to drink moderately, because, as we saw earlier, physiological changes in their brains and bodies may have turned them from alcohol abusers into addicts. On the other hand, total-abstinence groups like Alcoholics Anonymous (AA) are ineffective for many people. According to its own surveys and those done independently, one-third to one-half of all people who join AA drop out. Many of these dropouts benefit from programs such as Harm Reduction, which teach people how to drink moderately and keep their drinking under control (Witkiewitz & Marlatt, 2006).

So instead of asking, "Can problem drinkers learn to drink moderately?" perhaps we should ask, "What are the factors that make it more or less likely that someone can learn to control problem drinking?" Problem drinkers who are most likely to become moderate drinkers have a history of less severe dependence on the drug. They lead more stable lives and have jobs and families. In contrast, those who are at greater risk of alcoholism (or other drug abuse) have these risk factors: (1) They have a genetic vulnerability to the drug or have been using it long enough for it to have damaged or changed their brains; (2) they believe that they have no control over their drinking or other drug use; (3) they live in a culture or a peer group that promotes and rewards binge drinking or discourages moderate drug use; and (4) they have come to rely on the drug as a way of avoiding problems, suppressing anger or fear, or coping with stress.

Quick Quiz

If you are addicted to passing exams, answer these questions.

1. What is the most reasonable conclusion about the role of genes in alcoholism? (a) Without a key gene, a person cannot become alcoholic; (b) the presence of a key gene will almost always cause a person to become alcoholic; (c) genes may increase a person's vulnerability to some kinds of alcoholism.

2. Which cultural practice is associated with *low* rates of alcoholism? (a) a gradual introduction to drinking in family settings, (b) infrequent binge drinking, (c) drinking as a rite of passage into adulthood, (d) policies of prohibition

3. In a national survey, 52 percent of American college students said they drink to get drunk and 42 percent said they usually binge when drinking. To reduce this problem, many schools have instituted zero-tolerance programs. According to the research described in this section, are these programs likely to work? Why or why not?

Answers:

1. c 2. a 3. They are not likely to be successful because zero-tolerance programs do not address the reasons that students binge, do not affect the student culture that fosters binge drinking, and do not teach students how to drink moderately.

✔—**Study** and
Review on
mypsychlab.com

 YOU are about to learn...

- why most clinicians and researchers are skeptical about multiple personality disorder.

- why the number of "multiple personality" cases jumped from a handful to many thousands.

Dissociative Identity Disorder

One of the most controversial diagnoses ever to arise in psychiatry and psychology is **dissociative identity disorder**, formerly and still popularly called *multiple personality disorder* (MPD). This label describes the apparent emergence, within one person, of two or more distinct identities, each with its own name, memories, and personality traits. Cases of multiple personality portrayed on TV, in books, and in films such as *The Three Faces of Eve* and *Sybil* have captivated the public for years, and they still do. In 2009, Showtime came up with "The United States of Tara," in which a woman with a *very* tolerant husband and two teenagers keeps breaking into one of her three identities—a sex-and-shopping-mad teenage girl, a gun-loving redneck male, and a 1950s-style homemaker.

Some psychiatrists take MPD seriously, believing that it originates in childhood as a means of coping with sexual abuse or other traumatic experiences (Gleaves, 1996). In their view, the trauma produces a mental "splitting" (*dissociation*):

dissociative identity disorder A controversial disorder marked by the apparent appearance within one person of two or more distinct personalities, each with its own name and traits; formerly known as *multiple personality disorder (MPD).*

In the earliest cases, multiple personalities came only in pairs. In the 1886 story of *Dr. Jekyll and Mr. Hyde*, the kindly Dr. Jekyll turned into the murderous Mr. Hyde. At the height of the MPD epidemic in the 1990s, people were claiming to have dozens of alters, including demons, aliens, and animals.

One personality emerges to handle everyday experiences, and another personality (called an "alter") to cope with the bad ones. During the 1980s and 1990s, clinicians who believed a client had multiple personalities often used suggestive techniques to "bring out the alters," such as hypnosis, drugs, and even outright coercion (McHugh, 2008; Rieber, 2006; Spanos, 1996). Psychiatrist Richard Kluft (1987) wrote that efforts to determine the presence of MPD—that is, to get the person to reveal a dissociated personality—may require "between 2 1/2 and 4 hours of continuous interviewing. Interviewees must be prevented from taking breaks to regain composure. . . . In one recent case of singular difficulty, the first sign of dissociation was noted in the 6th hour, and a definitive spontaneous switching of personalities occurred in the 8th hour."

Mercy! After eight hours of "continuous interviewing" without a single break, how many of us wouldn't do what the interviewer wanted? Clinicians who conducted such interrogations argued that they were merely *permitting* other personalities to reveal themselves, but their skeptical critics countered that they were actively *creating* other personalities through suggestion and sometimes even intimidation with vulnerable clients who had other psychological problems (Lilienfeld & Lohr, 2003). Researchers have shown that "dissociative amnesia," the mechanism that supposedly causes traumatized children to repress their ordeal and develop several identities as a result, lacks historical and empirical support (see Chapter 8). Truly traumatic experiences are remembered all too long and all too well (McNally, 2003; Pope et al., 2006).

So what is MPD? The evidence suggests that it is a homegrown culture-bound syndrome. Only a handful of MPD cases had ever been diagnosed anywhere in the world before 1980; yet by the mid-1990s, tens of thousands of cases had been reported, mostly in the United States and Canada. MPD became a lucrative business, benefiting hospitals that opened MPD clinics, therapists who had

a new disorder to treat, and psychiatrists and patients who wrote best-selling books. Then, in the 1990s, as a result of numerous malpractice cases across the country, courts ruled, on the basis of the testimony of scientific experts in psychiatry and psychology, that MPD was being generated by the clinicians who believed in it. The MPD clinics in hospitals closed, psychiatrists became more wary, and the number of cases dropped sharply almost overnight.

No one disputes that some troubled, highly imaginative individuals can produce many different "personalities" when asked. But the *sociocognitive explanation* of MPD holds that this phenomenon is simply an extreme form of the ability we all have to present different aspects of our personalities to others (Lilienfeld et al., 1999). The disorder may seem very real to clinicians and their patients who believe in it, but in the sociocognitive view, it results from pressure and suggestion by clinicians, interacting with acceptance by vulnerable patients who find MPD a plausible explanation for their problems. The

Thinking Critically about "Multiple Personality Disorder"

diagnosis of MPD allows some people to account for past sexual or criminal behavior that they now regret or find intolerably embarrassing; they can claim their "other personality did it." In turn, therapists who believe in MPD reward such patients with attention and praise for revealing more and more personalities—and a culture-bound syndrome is born (Hacking, 1995; Piper & Merskey, 2004).

The rise and fall of MPD provide an important lesson in critical thinking, because unskeptical media coverage of sensational cases, along with all of those movies and TV shows, have played a major role in fostering the rise of MPD diagnoses. When Canadian psychiatrist Harold Merskey (1992) reviewed the published cases of MPD, he was unable to find a single one in which a patient had not been influenced by the therapist's suggestions or reports about the disorder in the media. Even the famous case of "Sybil," a huge hit as a book, film, and television special, was a hoax. Sybil never had a traumatic childhood of sexual abuse, she did not have multiple personality disorder, and her symptoms were largely generated by her psychiatrist (Borch-Jacobsen, 2009; Rieber, 2006). ✴⟦Explore

The story of MPD teaches us to think critically about new diagnoses and previously rare disorders that suddenly catch fire in popular culture: to consider other explanations, to examine assumptions and biases, and to demand good evidence.

✴⟦Explore
Dissociative identity Disorder on mypsychlab.com

✓• Study and
Review on
mypsychlab.com

Quick Quiz

Any one of your personalities may answer this question.

A woman named Donna Walker was arrested for trying to convince an Indiana couple that she was their long-missing daughter. She claimed that her "bad girl" personality (Allison) was responsible for this deception and also for her long history of perpetrating hoaxes on police, friends, and the media. Her "good girl" personality (Donna), she said, was a victim of childhood sexual abuse who spent years working as an FBI informant. The FBI verified that Walker had worked for them, although some of her reports were fabricated. One agent said that Walker has as many as seven personalities who come and go. As a critical thinker, what questions would you want to ask about Walker and her multiple-personality defense?

Answer:

Some possible questions to ask: Is there corroborating evidence for Walker's claims? (She said she was sexually abused from ages 4 to 13 by a family member and then by the minister of her church, and that she was sent to a psychiatric hospital at age 13; these claims could be checked.) How much of the rest of her life story can be independently corroborated? Did Walker only claim to have other personalities when she was in a jam with the law or was there evidence of MPD throughout her life? Could she have another mental disorder, such as psychopathy or major depression?

YOU are about to learn...

- the difference between schizophrenia and a "split personality."
- the five key signs of schizophrenia.
- whether schizophrenia is partly heritable.
- why schizophrenia might begin in the womb yet not emerge until adolescence.

Schizophrenia

In 1911, the Swiss psychiatrist Eugen Bleuler coined the term **schizophrenia** to describe cases in which the personality loses its unity. Contrary to popular belief, people with schizophrenia do not have a "split" or "multiple" personality. Rather, schizophrenia is a fragmented condition in which words are split from meaning, actions from motives, perceptions from reality. It is an example of a **psychosis**, a mental condition that involves distorted perceptions of reality and an inability to function in most aspects of life.

Symptoms of Schizophrenia

Schizophrenia is the cancer of mental illness: elusive, complex, varied in form, unpredictable to treat. The disorder involves the following symptoms:

1 Bizarre delusions. Some people with schizophrenia have delusions of identity, believing that they are Moses, Jesus, or another famous person. Some have paranoid delusions, taking innocent events—a stranger's cough, a helicopter overhead—as evidence that everyone is plotting against them. They may insist that their thoughts have been inserted into their heads by someone controlling them or are being broadcast on television. Some believe that everyday objects or animals are really something else, perhaps extraterrestrials in disguise. Some have delusional beliefs; Margaret Mary Ray believed with all her heart that talk-show host David Letterman was in love with her. Caught up in this delusion, she stalked Letterman day and night for a decade, writing him letters and repeatedly breaking into his house.

2 Hallucinations. People with schizophrenia suffer from false sensory experiences that feel intensely real, such as feeling insects crawling on their bodies or seeing snakes coming through walls. But by far the most common hallucination is hearing voices; it is virtually a hallmark of the disease. Some sufferers are so tormented by these voices that they commit suicide to escape them. One man said he heard as many as 50 voices cursing him, urging him to steal other people's brain cells, or ordering him to kill himself. Once he picked up a ringing telephone and heard them screaming, "You're guilty!" over and over. They yelled "as loud as humans with megaphones," he told a reporter. "It was utter despair. I felt scared. They were always around" (Goode, 2003).

3 Disorganized, incoherent speech. People with schizophrenia often speak in an illogical jumble of ideas and symbols, linked by meaningless rhyming words or by remote associations called "word salads." A patient of Bleuler's wrote, "Olive oil is an Arabian liquor-sauce which the Afghans, Moors and Moslems use in ostrich farming. The Indian plantain tree is the whiskey of the Parsees

schizophrenia A psychotic disorder marked by delusions, hallucinations, disorganized and incoherent speech, inappropriate behavior, and cognitive impairments.

psychosis An extreme mental disturbance involving distorted perceptions and irrational behavior; it may have psychological or organic causes. (Plural: *psychoses*.)

and Arabs. Barley, rice and sugar cane called artichoke, grow remarkably well in India. The Brahmins live as castes in Baluchistan. The Circassians occupy Manchuria and China. China is the Eldorado of the Pawnees" (Bleuler, 1911/1950).

4 **Grossly disorganized and inappropriate behavior.** Such behavior may range from childlike silliness to unpredictable and violent agitation. The person may wear three overcoats and gloves on a hot day, start collecting garbage, or hoard scraps of food.

Bryan Charnley painted 17 self-portraits, with comments reflecting his battle with schizophrenia. He painted the one above in March 1991, when his mind was clear. In June, he committed suicide.

5 **Impaired cognitive abilities.** People with schizophrenia do much worse than healthy people in almost every cognitive domain, especially verbal learning and recall of words and stories, language, perception, working memory, selective attention, and problem solving (Dominguez et al., 2009; Uhlhaas & Silverstein, 2005). Their speech is often impoverished; they make only brief, empty replies in conversation, because of diminished thought rather than an unwillingness to speak. Many of these cognitive impairments emerge in vulnerable children long before an actual schizophrenic breakdown occurs, and they last after the patient's psychotic symptoms subside as a result of medication (Heinrichs, 2005).

Other symptoms may appear months or years before hallucinations or delusions do, and they often persist even when more dramatic symptoms are in remission. Many people with schizophrenia lose the motivation and ability to take care of themselves and interact with others; they may stop working or bathing, and become isolated and withdrawn. They seem emotionally flat; their facial expressions are unresponsive and they make poor eye contact. Some completely withdraw into a private world, sitting for hours without moving, a condition called *catatonic stupor.* (Catatonic states can also produce frenzied, purposeless behavior that goes on for hours.)

The cognitive and social deficits in schizophrenia may emerge early, in late childhood or early adolescence (Tarbox & Pogue-Geile, 2008), but the first full-blown psychotic episode typically occurs in late adolescence or early adulthood. In some individuals, the breakdown occurs suddenly; in others, it is more gradual, a slow change in personality. The more breakdowns and relapses the individual has had, the poorer the chances for recovery. Yet, contrary to stereotype, over 40 percent of the people with schizophrenia *do* have one or more periods of recovery (lasting one year or longer) and go on to hold good jobs and have successful relationships,

April 20: "[I am feeling] paranoid. The person upstairs was reading my mind and speaking back to me to keep me in a sort of ego crucifixion.... I felt this was because I was discharging very strong vibrations."

May 6: "I had no tongue, no real tongue, and could only flatter.... The nail in the mouth expresses this. The people around me cannot understand how I was so stupid and cannot forgive me.... Thus I am a target. The nails in my eyes express that I cannot see whereas other people seem to have extra sensory perception and I am blind in this respect."

May 18: "My mind seemed to be thought broadcasting [and] it was beyond my will to do anything about it. I summed this up by painting my brain as an enormous mouth.... The trouble seemed to stem from a broken heart so I painted a great mass of gore there.... I feel I am giving off strong personality vibrations, hence the wavy lines emanating from my head."

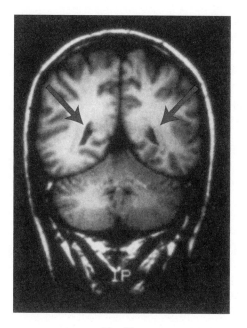
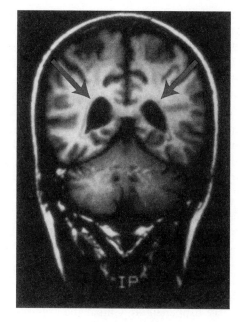

Healthy

Schizophrenic

FIGURE 11.4
Schizophrenia and the Brain
People with schizophrenia are more likely to have enlarged ventricles (spaces) in the brain than healthy people are. These MRI scans of 28-year-old male identical twins show the difference in the size of ventricles between the healthy twin (left) and the one with schizophrenia (right).

especially if they have strong family support and community programs (Harding, 2005; Hopper et al., 2007; Jobe & Harrow, 2010). What kind of mysterious disease could produce such a variety of symptoms and outcomes? ⊙▸ **Simulate**

Origins of Schizophrenia

Schizophrenia is clearly a brain disease. It involves reduced volumes of gray matter in the prefrontal cortex and temporal lobes; abnormalities in the hippocampus; and abnormalities in neurotransmitters, neural activity, and disrupted communication between neurons in areas involving cognitive functioning, such as memory, decision making, and emotion processing (Karlsgodt, Sun, & Cannon, 2010). Most individuals with schizophrenia also show enlargement of the *ventricles*, spaces in the brain that are filled with cerebrospinal fluid (see Figure 11.4) (Heinrichs, 2005). They are also more likely than healthy individuals to have abnormalities in the thalamus, the traffic-control center that filters sensations and focuses attention (Andreasen et al., 1994; Gur et al., 1998). Many have deficiencies in the auditory cortex and Broca's and Wernicke's areas, all involved in speech perception and processing; these might explain the nightmare of voice hallucinations.

Currently, researchers have identified three contributing factors to this disorder:

1 Genetic predispositions. Schizophrenia is highly heritable. A person has a much greater risk of developing the disorder if an identical twin

develops it, even if the twins are reared apart. Children with one schizophrenic parent have a lifetime risk of 7 to 12 percent, and children with two schizophrenic parents have a lifetime risk of 27 to 46 percent, compared to a risk in the general population of only about 1 percent (Gottesman, 1991; Gottesman et al., 2010; Heinrichs, 2005). (See Figure 11.5.) Researchers all over the world are trying to identify the genes that might be involved in specific symptoms, such as hallucinations, sensitivity to sounds,

⊙▸ **Simulate** with **Schizophrenia Overview** on **mypsychlab.com**

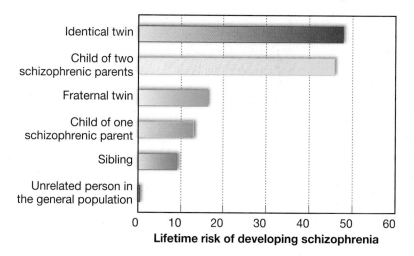

FIGURE 11.5
Genetic Vulnerability to Schizophrenia
This graph, based on combined data from 40 European twin and adoption studies conducted over seven decades, shows that the closer the genetic relationship to a person with schizophrenia, the higher the risk of developing the disorder (based on Gottesman, 1991; see also Gottesman et al., 2010).

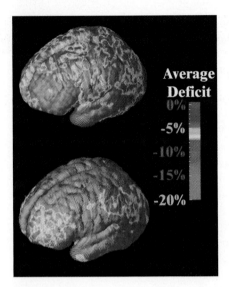

FIGURE 11.6
The Adolescent Brain and Schizophrenia
These dramatic images highlight areas of brain-tissue loss in adolescents with schizophrenia, over a five-year span. The areas of greatest tissue loss (regions that control memory, hearing, motor functions, and attention) are shown in red and magenta. A healthy brain (top) looks almost entirely blue (Thompson et al., 2001).

cognitive impairments, and social withdrawal (Desbonnet, Waddington, & O'Tuathaigh, 2009; Tomppo et al., 2009). However, efforts to find the critical genes in schizophrenia have been difficult because several appear to be involved, and those are linked not only to schizophrenia but also to bipolar disorder, depression, other mental disorders, and even dyslexia (Walker & Tessner, 2008).

2 Prenatal problems or birth complications. Damage to the fetal brain significantly increases the likelihood of schizophrenia later in life. Such damage may occur if the mother suffers from malnutrition; schizophrenia rates rise during times of famine, as happened in China and elsewhere (St. Clair et al., 2005). Damage may also occur if the mother gets the flu virus during the first four months of prenatal development, which triples the risk of schizophrenia (Brown et al., 2004; Mednick, Huttunen, & Machón, 1994). It may occur if there are complications during birth that injure the baby's brain or deprive it of oxygen (Cannon et al., 2000). Other nongenetic prenatal factors that increase the child's risk of schizophrenia, especially if they combine with each other, include maternal diabetes and emotional stress, older paternal age, birth during winter months, and low birth weight (King, St-Hilaire, & Heidkamp, 2010).

3 Biological events during adolescence. In adolescence, the brain undergoes a natural pruning away of synapses. Normally, this pruning helps make the brain more efficient in handling the new challenges of adulthood. But it appears that schizophrenic brains aggressively prune away too many synapses, which may explain why the first full-blown schizophrenic episode typically occurs in adolescence or early adulthood. Healthy teenagers lose about 1 percent of the brain's gray matter between ages 13 and 18. But as you can see in Figure 11.6, in a study that tracked the loss of gray matter in the brain over five years, adolescents with schizophrenia showed much more extensive and rapid tissue loss, primarily in the sensory and motor regions (Thompson et al., 2001). "We were stunned to see a spreading wave of tissue loss that began in a small region of the brain," said Paul Thompson, who headed the study. "It moved across the brain like a forest fire, destroying more tissue as the disease progressed."

Thus the developmental pathway of schizophrenia is something of a relay. It starts with genetic predispositions, which may combine with prenatal risk factors or birth complications that affect brain development. The resulting vulnerability then awaits the next stage, synaptic pruning within the brain during adolescence (Walker & Tessner, 2008). Then, according to the vulnerability-stress model of schizophrenia, these biological changes usually interact with an environmental stressor to trigger the disease. This model explains why one identical twin may develop schizophrenia but not the other: Both may have a genetic susceptibility, but only one may have been exposed to other risk factors in the womb, birth complications, or stressful life events. These factors may combine in different ways as well, explaining why some schizophrenics recover and others do not.

✓• **Study** and **Review** on **mypsychlab.com**

Quick Quiz

The following quiz is not a hallucination.

1. What are the five major kinds of symptoms in schizophrenia?
2. What are the three likely stages in the "relay" that produces schizophrenia?

Answers:

1. delusions, hallucinations, disorganized speech, inappropriate behavior, and impaired cognitive abilities 2. genetic predispositions, prenatal risk factors or birth complications, and excessive pruning of synapses in the brain during adolescence

Psychology in the News REVISITED

We have come to the end of a long walk along the spectrum of psychological problems: from those that cause temporary difficulty, such as occasional anxiety or "caffeine-induced sleep disorder," to others that are severely disabling, such as major depression and schizophrenia. Where on this spectrum would you place "sex addiction," the popular label for the behavior of the many men (and some women) whose sexual behavior has gotten them in trouble?

One of the great questions generated by all diagnoses of mental disorder concerns personal responsibility. In law and in everyday life, many people reach for a psychological reason to exonerate themselves of responsibility for their actions. Romance writer Janet Dailey was once caught having plagiarized whole passages from another writer's work, and in self-defense she said she was suffering from "a psychological problem that I never even suspected I had." We wonder if it was in the DSM! But would it matter if it were? What "psychological problem" would absolve a person of responsibility for cheating?

Similarly, many people nowadays claim they are "addicted" to some behavior, whether it is having sex, shopping, or eating chocolate, as an excuse for some habit that is unethical, self-defeating, or fattening. Is their behavior really an addiction in the same way that drug addiction is? As we saw in the opening story, psychologists disagree on the answer. The DSM-V's proposed new diagnosis of "hypersexual behavior" would apply to people who repeatedly engage in sexual fantasies and behaviors in response to stress, anxiety, or depression; who lack concern for the physical or emotional harm they cause themselves or others; and who claim they are unable to break their craving for sexual activity. But others believe that *any* behavior can fit this description and that most everyday "addictions" are not mental disorders; they are simply a person's self-justifying way of getting off the hook. Indeed, having many sexual affairs is often considered perfectly normal behavior for rich, powerful celebrities and politicians. It only seems to become a "disorder" when their partner finds out.

Now consider the tragic story of Andrea Yates, a Texas woman who killed her five young children. Yates had suffered from clinical depression and psychotic episodes for years, and had tried to kill herself twice. Her father, two brothers, and a sister had also suffered from mental illness. Yates was overwhelmed by raising and homeschooling all of her children by herself, with no help from her reportedly domineering husband, who permitted her two hours a week of personal time. Although she suffered a postpartum psychotic episode after the birth of their fourth child and a clinical psychologist warned against her having another baby, her husband refused to consider birth control, although not for religious reasons. Yates was convicted of murder and sentenced to life in prison; the jury rejected her claim that she was so psychotic that she thought she was saving the souls of her children by killing them. Four years later, on appeal, another jury found her not guilty by reason of insanity and she was sent to a mental institution.

Does Andrea Yates deserve our condemnation for her horrible acts of murder or our pity? Before you answer, you might keep this interesting evidence in mind: Many people feel angrier and less sympathetic toward people whose mental illnesses conform to gender stereotypes, such as men who are alcoholic and women who are depressed. They are more sympathetic to people whose illnesses do not conform to the stereotype—alcoholic women and depressed men (Wirth & Bodenhausen, 2009). Apparently, many people think that gender-typical mental disorders are less likely to be "real."

When thinking about the relationship of mental disorder to personal responsibility, therefore, we face a dilemma, one that requires us to tolerate uncertainty. The law recognizes, rightly, that people who are mentally incompetent, delusional, or disturbed should not be judged by the same standards as mentally healthy individuals. At the same time, society has an obligation to protect its citizens from harm and to reject easy excuses for violations of the law. To balance these two positions, we need to find ways to ensure first, that people who commit crimes or behave reprehensibly face the consequences of their behavior, and second, that people who are suffering from psychological problems have the compassionate support of society in their search for help. After all, psychological problems of one kind or another are challenges that all of us will face at some time in our lives.

Taking Psychology with You

When a Friend Is Suicidal

Suicide can be frightening to those who find themselves fantasizing about it, and it is devastating to the family and friends of those who go through with it. In the United States, suicide is the third leading cause of death among people ages 10 to 24, after accidents and homicides. Every year, more than 1,000 college students commit suicide, and thousands more make an unsuccessful attempt. The group at highest risk of suicide is American Indian men, and the group at lowest risk is African-American women (Goldston et al., 2008).

Women are more likely than men to attempt suicide, primarily as a cry for help, whereas men are four times more likely than women to succeed. Moreover, men's efforts to commit suicide are not always obvious: Some men provoke confrontations with the police, hoping to be shot; some intentionally kill themselves in car accidents; and men are more likely than women to destroy themselves with drugs.

Because of the many widespread myths about suicide, it is important to become informed and know what to do in a crisis:

Take all suicide threats seriously. Some people assume they can't do anything when a friend talks about committing suicide. "He'll just do it at another place, another time," they think. In fact, most suicides occur during an acute crisis. Once the person gets through the crisis, the desire to die fades. Others believe that if a friend is talking about committing suicide, he or she won't really do it. This belief also is false. Few people commit suicide without signaling their intentions. Most are ambivalent: "I want to kill myself, but I don't want to be dead—at least not forever." Most suicidal people want relief from the terrible pain of feeling that nobody cares and that life is not worth living. Getting these thoughts and fears out in the open is crucial.

Know the danger signs. One team of psychologists who specialize in the study of suicide looked up the "warning signs of suicide" that can be found on the Internet. The search turned up more than 75 supposed indicators, many of them vague or questionable, such as "perfectionism," "loss of security," "neurotransmitters," and "loss of religious faith." In fact, only a few core factors are crucial in predicting a person's risk of trying to commit suicide: The person feels hopeless, feels alienated and profoundly disconnected from other people, and believes that he or she is a burden to loved ones (Joiner, 2005; Mandrusiak et al., 2006; van Orden et al., 2006).

Get involved: Ask questions and get help. If you believe a friend is suicidal, do not be afraid to ask, "Are you thinking of suicide?" This question does not "put the idea" in anyone's mind. If your friend is contemplating the action, he or she will probably be relieved to talk about it, which in turn will reduce feelings of isolation and despair. Don't try to talk your friend out of it by debating whether suicide is right or wrong, and don't put on phony cheerfulness. If your friend's words scare you, say so. By allowing your friend to unburden his or her grief, you help the person get through the immediate crisis.

Do not leave your friend alone. If necessary, get the person to a clinic or a hospital emergency room, or call a local suicide hotline. Don't worry about doing the wrong thing. In an emergency, the worst thing you can do is nothing at all.

If you are the one who is contemplating suicide, remember that you are not alone and that help is a phone call or an email away. You can call the national hotline number, 1-800-273-TALK, or your school's counseling services. For more information, the Centers for Disease Control and Prevention have a website that provides facts about suicide (www.cdc.gov/safeusa/suicide.htm). Many students fear to get help because they think no one will understand, or they fear they will be made fun of by their friends, or they believe they cannot be helped. Wrong, wrong, wrong.

In her book *Night Falls Fast: Understanding Suicide,* Kay Jamison (1999), a psychologist who suffers from bipolar disorder, explored this difficult subject from the standpoint both of a mental health professional and of a person who has been there. In describing the aftermath of her own suicide attempt, she wrote: "I do know... that I should have been dead but was not—and that I was fortunate enough to be given another chance at life, which many others were not."

Summary

((•—[Listen to an **audio file** of your chapter on **mypsychlab.com**

Defining and Diagnosing Mental Disorders

● When defining *mental disorder*, mental health professionals emphasize the emotional suffering caused by the behavior, whether the behavior is harmful to others or society, and its degree of "harmful dysfunction."

● *The Diagnostic and Statistical Manual of Mental Disorders* (DSM) is designed to provide objective criteria and categories for diagnosing mental disorder. Critics argue that the diagnosis of mental disorders, unlike those of medical diseases, is inherently a subjective process that can never be entirely objective. They believe the DSM fosters overdiagnosis; overlooks the power of being given a diagnostic label; confuses serious mental disorders with everyday problems in living; and creates an illusion of objectivity.

● Supporters of the DSM believe that when the DSM criteria are used correctly and when empirically validated objective tests are used, reliability in diagnosis improves. The DSM now lists many *culture-bound syndromes* in addition to universal disorders such as depression, panic attacks, anorexia, and schizophrenia.

● In diagnosing psychological disorders, clinicians often use *projective tests* such as the Rorschach inkblot test or, with children, the use of anatomically detailed dolls. These methods have low reliability and validity, creating problems when they are used in the legal arena, as in custody disputes, or in diagnosing disorders. In general, *objective tests (inventories)*, such as the *MMPI*, are more reliable and valid than projective ones.

Anxiety Disorders

● *Generalized anxiety disorder* involves continuous, chronic anxiety and worry. When anxiety results from exposure to uncontrollable or unpredictable danger, it can lead to *posttraumatic stress disorder (PTSD)*, which involves mentally reliving the trauma, emotional detachment, and increased physiological arousal.

● Most people who live through a traumatic experience eventually recover, but a minority develop PTSD. The reasons for their increased vulnerability to traumatic events include genetic vulnerability; a history of psychological problems; a lack of social and cognitive resources; and having a smaller hippocampus than normal.

● *Panic disorder* involves sudden, intense attacks of profound fear. Panic attacks are common in the aftermath of stress or frightening experiences; those who go on to develop a disorder tend to interpret the attacks as a sign of impending disaster.

● *Phobias* are unrealistic fears of specific situations, activities, or things. Common *social phobias* include fears of speaking in public, eating in a restaurant, or having to perform for an audience. *Agoraphobia*, the fear of being away from a safe place or person, is the most disabling phobia—a "fear of fear." It often begins with a panic attack, which the person tries to avoid in the future by staying close to "safe" places or people.

● *Obsessive-compulsive disorder (OCD)* involves recurrent, unwished-for thoughts or images (obsessions) and repetitive, ritualized behaviors (compulsions) that a person feels unable to control. Some people with OCD have abnormalities in an area of the prefrontal cortex, which may contribute to their cognitive and behavioral rigidity. Parts of the brain involved in fear and responses to threat are also more active than normal in people with OCD; the "alarm mechanism," once activated, does not turn off when danger is past. One kind of OCD creates pathological hoarding and may involve deficiencies in other parts of the brain.

Mood Disorders

● Symptoms of *major depression* include distorted thinking patterns, feelings of worthlessness and despair, physical ailments such as fatigue and loss of appetite, and loss of interest in once-pleasurable activities. In severe cases, the feelings of worthlessness or "being a burden" to others can lead to suicide attempts, most of which are not repeated once the acute phase passes. Women are twice as likely as men to suffer from major depression, but depression in men may be underdiagnosed. In *bipolar disorder*, a person experiences episodes of both depression and *mania* (excessive euphoria). It is equally common in both sexes.

● *Vulnerability-stress models* of depression look at interactions between individual vulnerabilities and stressful experiences. The theory that depleted serotonin, perhaps caused by a genetic variant, causes depression has not been supported, but because depression is moderately heritable, the search for specific genes continues. For some vulnerable individuals, repeated losses of important relationships can set off episodes of major depression. Experiences with parental neglect and violence, especially in childhood, increase the risk of developing major depression in adulthood. Cognitive habits also play an important role: believing that the origin of one's unhappiness is permanent and uncontrollable; feeling hopeless and pessimistic; and brooding or *ruminating* about one's problems.

Antisocial/Psychopathic Personality Disorder

● Personality disorders are characterized by maladaptive traits that cause distress or an inability to get along with others. One, *borderline personality disorder*, is characterized by impulsiveness, self-mutilating behavior, feelings of emptiness, and a fear of abandonment by others.

● The term *psychopath* describes people who lack conscience and empathy; they do not feel remorse, shame, guilt, or anxiety over wrongdoing, and they can con others with ease. *Antisocial personality disorder (APD)* applies to people with a pattern of aggressive, reckless, impulsive, and often criminal behavior. The DSM-V is likely to combine these overlapping disorders under one label, *antisocial/psychopathic personality disorder*. Abnormalities in the central nervous system and prefrontal cortex are associated with lack of emotional responsiveness and with impulsivity. A genetic predisposition also plays a role in these disorders, but it usually must interact with stressful or violent environments to be expressed.

Drug Abuse and Addiction

● Signs of *substance abuse* include impaired ability to work or get along with others, use of the drug in hazardous situations, recurrent arrests for drug use, and conflicts with others caused by drug use.

● According to the *biological model* of addiction, some people have a genetic vulnerability to the kind of alcoholism that begins in early adolescence and is linked to impulsivity, antisocial behavior, and criminality. Genes also affect sensitivity to alcohol, which varies across ethnic groups as well as among individuals. But heavy drug abuse also changes the brain in ways that make addiction more likely.

● Advocates of the *learning model* of addiction point out that addiction patterns vary according to cultural practices and values; that policies of total abstinence tend to increase addiction rates and abuse because people who want to drink fail to learn how to drink in moderation; that many people can stop taking drugs without experiencing withdrawal symptoms; and that drug abuse depends on the reasons for taking a drug.

● The biological and learning models are polarized on many issues, notably that of abstinence versus moderation. People who are most likely to abuse alcohol and other drugs have a genetic vulnerability or prolonged drug use has damaged their brains; they believe that they have no control over the drug; their culture or peer group promotes drug abuse; and they rely on the drug to cope with problems.

Dissociative Identity Disorder

● In *dissociative identity disorder* (formerly called *multiple personality disorder*, or *MPD*), two or more distinct personalities and identities appear to split off (*dissociate*) within one person. Some clinicians think the disorder is legitimate and originates in childhood trauma. But most clinicians hold a *sociocognitive* explanation—that MPD is an extreme form of the ability to present different aspects of our personalities to others. In this view, the disorder emerges from pressure and suggestion by clinicians who believe in its prevalence, interacting with vulnerable patients who find MPD a plausible explanation for their problems, thereby creating a culture-bound syndrome. Media coverage of sensational alleged cases of MPD greatly contributed to the rise in the number of cases after 1980.

Schizophrenia

● *Schizophrenia* is a psychotic disorder involving delusions, hallucinations, disorganized speech (called "word salads"), inappropriate behavior, and severe cognitive impairments. Other symptoms, such as loss of motivation to take care of oneself and emotional flatness, may appear before a psychotic episode and persist even when the more dramatic symptoms are in remission. Some people with schizophrenia fall into a *catatonic stupor*. Contrary to stereotype, however, many people with schizophrenia recover.

● Schizophrenia is a brain disease that involves certain structural brain abnormalities, such as reduced gray matter, abnormalities in the hippocampus, and enlarged ventricles, as well as abnormalities in neurotransmitters and neuronal connections. In the "relay" that produces the disorder, genetic predispositions interact with prenatal problems (such as the mother's malnutrition or a prenatal viral infection) or birth complications, and excessive pruning of synapses during adolescence.

Psychology in the News, Revisited

● The diagnosis of mental disorder raises important questions for personal responsibility in the law and everyday life. When people claim to have a mental disorder, psychologists and others struggle to decide whether the claim is an excuse for illegal, unethical, or destructive behavior, or whether these individuals truly have a disorder that reduces their ability to control their behavior.

Key Terms

mental disorder   371

Diagnostic and Statistical Manual of Mental Disorders (DSM)   371

culture-bound syndromes   373

projective tests   374

Rorschach inkblot test   374

objective tests (inventories)   375

Minnesota Multiphasic Personality Inventory (MMPI)   375

generalized anxiety disorder   376

posttraumatic stress disorder (PTSD)   377

panic disorder (panic attack)   377

phobia   378

social phobia   378

agoraphobia   378

obsessive-compulsive disorder (OCD)   378

mood disorder   380

major depression   380

mania   380

bipolar disorder   380

vulnerability-stress model of depression   380

borderline personality disorder   383

psychopathy   383

antisocial personality disorder (APD)   384

substance abuse   386

biological model of addiction   387

learning model of addiction   388

dissociative identity disorder (multiple personality disorder, MPD)   391

dissociation   391

sociocognitive explanation of MPD   392

schizophrenia   393

psychosis   393

"word salad"   393

catatonic stupor   394

Defining and Diagnosing Mental Disorders

It is very difficult to define **mental disorder**, but most mental health professionals agree that it is any condition that causes a person to suffer, is self-destructive, seriously impairs a person's ability to work or get along with others, or endangers others or the community.

Dilemmas of Diagnosis

The Diagnostic and Statistical Manual of Mental Disorders (DSM) is designed to provide criteria and categories for diagnosing mental disorders.

Problems with the DSM include:
- Dangers of overdiagnosis
- The influence of diagnostic labels themselves
- The confusion of serious mental disorders with everyday problems
- The illusion of objectivity and universality

Advantages of the DSM include:
- Efforts to improve reliability in diagnosis
- Identification of many universal disorders, as well as **culture-bound syndromes**

Measuring Disorders

Projective tests, such as the *Rorschach inkblot test,* have low reliability and validity.

Objective tests (inventories), such as the *Minnesota Multiphasic Personality Inventory (MMPI),* have high reliability and validity.

Mood Disorders

- **Major depression** involves prolonged grief, hopelessness, and loss of energy, appetite, and interest in activities.
- **Bipolar disorder** involves episodes of both depression and mania (excessive euphoria).

Origins of Depression

Vulnerability-stress models of depression look at interactions between individual vulnerabilities and stressful experiences.

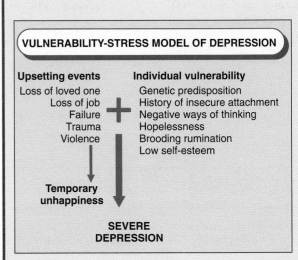

VULNERABILITY-STRESS MODEL OF DEPRESSION

Upsetting events
Loss of loved one
Loss of job
Failure
Trauma
Violence

Individual vulnerability
Genetic predisposition
History of insecure attachment
Negative ways of thinking
Hopelessness
Brooding rumination
Low self-esteem

Temporary unhappiness

SEVERE DEPRESSION

Four main factors may contribute to major depression:
1. Genetic factors that may protect against depression or create a predisposition toward it
2. Experiences with violence, childhood physical abuse, and parental neglect
3. Losses of important relationships
4. Cognitive habits, such as believing that unhappiness is permanent and uncontrollable, ruminating about problems, and feeling hopeless

Anxiety Disorders

- **Generalized anxiety disorder** involves continuous chronic anxiety.
- **Posttraumatic stress disorder** involves reliving the trauma in recurrent, intrusive thoughts; a sense of detachment; and increased physiological arousal.
- **Panic disorder** involves sudden, intense attacks of profound fear.
- **Phobias** are unrealistic fears of specific situations, activities, or things, or, in the case of **agoraphobia**, being away from a safe place.
- **Obsessive-compulsive disorder (OCD)** involves recurrent, unwished-for thoughts or images (*obsessions*) and repetitive, ritualized behaviors (*compulsions*).

Personality disorders are characterized by rigid, self-destructive traits that cause distress or an inability to get along with others, such as with **borderline personality disorder**.

Antisocial/Psychopathic Personality Disorder

- **Psychopathy** is an inability to feel normal social and moral emotions. Psychopaths are incapable of remorse, shame, guilt, and empathy, and lack the ability to fear punishment.
- **Antisocial personality disorder** describes people who repeatedly break the law, are impulsive and violent, and show reckless disregard for their own safety or that of others.
- Debate continues about the extent to which these two disorders overlap. However, certain factors are involved in the central features of psychopathy and of being a lifelong violent offender:
  — Abnormalities in the CNS
  — Impaired frontal-lobe functioning
  — Genetic influences
  — Environmental events

Dissociative Identity Disorder

Dissociative identity disorder, formerly called multiple personality disorder (MPD), involves two or more identities that appear to split off within one person.
- Some clinicians believe MPD is common and originates in childhood trauma; others believe that most cases result from suggestion by clinicians themselves.
- Media coverage has contributed to the rise in MPD diagnoses.
- The sociocognitive explanation of MPD holds that it is simply an extreme form of the ability we all have to present different aspects of our personalities to others.

Schizophrenia

Schizophrenia is a fragmented condition in which words are split from meaning, actions are split from motives, and perceptions are split from reality. It is a form of **psychosis**, a mental condition that involves distortions of reality and inhibits one's ability to function in everyday life.

Symptoms of schizophrenia:
- Bizarre delusions
- Hallucinations, sometimes visual but usually auditory
- Disorganized, incoherent speech ("word salads")
- Disorganized and inappropriate behavior
- Impaired cognitive abilities

Causes of Schizophrenia

Schizophrenia involves abnormalities in the brain, including a decrease in the volume of the temporal lobe or hippocampus, reduced numbers of neurons in the prefrontal cortex, and enlargement of the *ventricles,* spaces in the brain that are filled with cerebrospinal fluid.

Causes of this disease include:
1. Genetic predispositions
2. Prenatal problems or birth complications
3. Adolescent abnormalities in brain development

Drug Abuse and Addiction

Substance Abuse

Signs of substance abuse:
- Impaired ability to work or get along with others
- Use of the drug in hazardous situations
- Conflicts with others caused by drug use

Learning, Culture, and Addiction

The *biological model* holds that some people are genetically predisposed to addiction, or develop addictions as a result of the biological changes in the brain caused by heavy drug abuse.

The *learning model* holds that most kinds of addiction stem from conditions that encourage or discourage drug abuse. Evidence:
1. Addiction patterns vary according to culture.
2. Abuse increases under policies of total abstinence, because people do not learn to drink moderately.
3. Many people stop taking drugs without withdrawal symptoms.
4. Drug abuse depends on the reasons for taking the drug.

Use of Dogs for Vets with PTSD Is Growing

GULFPORT, FL, June 7, 2010. Many soldiers returning from duty in Afghanistan and Iraq suffer from severe medical and emotional problems. Lt. Col. Kathryn Champion was one of them. She had served 27 years in the Army, but after a particularly horrific tour of duty in Iraq, during which five soldiers under her command died, she began to suffer the symptoms of posttraumatic stress disorder. When she returned home, she fell into deep depression: A virus she contracted in Iraq was killing her optic nerves, causing her to go blind; her Army career was finished.

Then Champion found an organization that matched her with a guide dog, a golden retriever mix named Angel. Just two weeks after their training together ended, Angel began helping Champion with her psychological problems. Champion was terrified of flying and of having a panic attack in public, but whenever her heart started racing, she would reach down and touch

Kathryn Champion, who suffered from posttraumatic stress disorder and anxiety attacks after returning from duty in Iraq, with her dog Angel.

her dog. She was able to fly across country to visit her son before his deployment to Afghanistan.

Within weeks, Champion started going out again, since crowds were not bothering her as they had. She and Angel have traveled to the Grand Canyon and even to a "Space Camp" in Alabama.

Across the country, various organizations have begun providing service dogs to help soldiers recover from PTSD. Their efforts are part of a nationwide trend of animal-assisted therapy, also known as pet therapy, designed to help people with various psychological problems. Pet therapy is prominent in many hospitals, as volunteers and "certified therapy dogs" offer comfort and companionship to patients. When humans touch and play with dogs, horses, and other social animals, said Dr. Matt Zimmerman, Counseling and Psychological Services psychologist at the University of Virginia, it lowers their blood pressure and makes them less anxious. He added that animal-assisted therapy should generally be used with other forms of psychological treatment or medication.

Zimmerman says there are specific benefits of pet therapy for children with autism. "The animal serves as [a] reinforcement tool for appropriate social behavior," Zimmerman said. "If the child is being gentle and kind to the pet, then [it] stays. If the child is hitting or pulling on the animal, the pet leaves." When it comes to other disorders, however, the effectiveness of the treatment tends to depend more upon the individual in question, he said.

Kathryn Champion has started raising money to provide dogs for other veterans in trouble. She is once again engaged in life. As a spokeswoman for the program that provided her with the dog said, "Angel has been her ticket back in."

Approaches to Treatment and Therapy

Have you ever survived a traumatic event—war, assault, violence in your family or neighborhood, the unexpected death of a loved one, or a natural disaster such as an earthquake or hurricane? Have you ever had to move away from the country or ethnic group you grew up in, to find yourself lonely and struggling in a new world? How about the pressures of being in college; do they ever make you feel depressed, worried, or perhaps panicky?

If so, what kind of therapy might help you? For most of the emotional problems that all of us suffer on occasion, the two greatest healers are time and the support of friends—including pet friends. For some people, though, time and friends are not enough, and they continue to be troubled by normal life difficulties, such as family quarrels or fear of public speaking, or by one of the disorders described in the previous chapter: depression, generalized anxiety disorder, phobias, or schizophrenia. What kind of therapy might help them?

In this chapter, we will evaluate two major approaches: (1) *Biological treatments,* primarily provided by psychiatrists or other physicians, include medications or intervention in brain function. So many people today are taking medications routinely, for emotional disorders and normal problems alike, that few consumers stop to question whether medication is always the right treatment, especially in the long run, or whether nonmedical treatments might work as well. We will assess which biological treatments are effective and for which conditions, which ones are not, and when drugs can be dangerous. (2) *Psychotherapy* covers an array of psychological interventions, and we will consider the major approaches: psychodynamic therapies, cognitive and behavior therapies, humanist therapies, and family or couples therapy. We will assess which kinds of psychotherapy work best for which problems, which ones are not helpful, and which ones might even be harmful.

YOU are about to learn...

- the types of medications used to treat psychological disorders.
- six important cautions about medications for emotional problems.
- ways of electrically stimulating the brain—and whether they work.

Biological Treatments for Mental Disorders

For hundreds of years, people have tried to identify the origins of mental illness, attributing the causes at various times to evil spirits, pressure in the skull, disease, or bad environments. Today, biological explanations and treatments are dominant, partly because of evidence that some disorders have a genetic component or involve a biochemical or neurological abnormality (see Chapter 11), and partly because physicians and pharmaceutical companies are promoting biomedical solutions, often uncritically (Angell, 2004).

The Question of Drugs

The most commonly used biological treatment is medication that alters the production of or response to neurotransmitters in the brain. Because drugs are so widely advertised and prescribed these days, both for severe disorders such as schizophrenia and for more common problems such as anxiety and depression, consumers need to understand what these drugs are, how they can best be used, and their limitations.

Drugs Commonly Prescribed for Mental Disorders The main classes of drugs used in the treatment of mental and emotional disorders are the following:

1 **Antipsychotic drugs**, also called *neuroleptics*—older ones such as Thorazine and Haldol and second-generation ones such as Clozaril, Risperdal, Zyprexa, and Seroquel—are used primarily in the treatment of schizophrenia and other psychoses. However, antipsychotic drugs are increasingly being prescribed "off label" for people with nonpsychotic disorders, such as major depression, bipolar disorder, autism, attention deficit disorder, and dementia.

Because many psychoses are thought to be caused by an excess of the neurotransmitter dopamine, most antipsychotic drugs are designed to block or reduce the sensitivity of brain receptors that respond to dopamine. Some also increase levels of serotonin, a neurotransmitter that inhibits dopamine activity. Antipsychotic drugs can reduce agitation, delusions, and hallucinations, and they can shorten schizophrenic episodes. But they offer little relief from other symptoms of schizophrenia, such as jumbled thoughts, difficulty concentrating, apathy, emotional flatness, or inability to interact with others.

Antipsychotics often cause troubling effects, especially muscle rigidity, hand tremors, and other involuntary muscle movements that can develop into a neurological disorder. In addition, Zyprexa, Risperdal, and other antipsychotics, which manufacturers have been targeting for children and the elderly, often carry unacceptable risks for these very groups. The immediate side effect is extreme weight gain, anywhere from 24 to 100 extra pounds a year, which has led to the development of thousands of cases of diabetes. Other risks include strokes and death from sudden heart failure (Masand, 2000; Ray et al., 2009; Wallace-Wells, 2009).

Although the newer drugs now comprise 90 percent of the market for antipsychotics, a large federally funded study found that they are not significantly safer or more effective than the older, less expensive medications for schizophrenia—the only disorder for which they were originally approved (Lieberman et al., 2005; Swartz et al., 2007). And although antipsychotics are sometimes used to treat impulsive aggressiveness associated with attention deficit disorder, dementia, and mental retardation, they are ineffective for these disorders. One study followed 86 people, ages 18 to 65, who were given Risperdal, Haldol, or a placebo to treat their aggressive outbursts (Tyrer et al., 2008). The placebo group improved the most.

2 **Antidepressant drugs** are used primarily in the treatment of depression, anxiety, phobias, and obsessive-compulsive disorder. *Monoamine oxidase inhibitors* (MAOIs), such as Nardil, elevate the levels of norepinephrine and serotonin in the brain by blocking or inhibiting an enzyme that deactivates these neurotransmitters. *Tricyclic antidepressants*, such as Elavil and Tofranil, boost norepinephrine and serotonin levels by preventing the normal reabsorption, or "reuptake," of these substances by the cells that have released them. *Selective serotonin reuptake inhibitors* (SSRIs), such as Prozac, Zoloft, Lexapro, Paxil, and Celexa, work on the same principle as the tricyclics but specifically target serotonin. Cymbalta and Remeron target both

antipsychotic drugs Drugs used primarily in the treatment of schizophrenia and other psychotic disorders; they are often used off label and inappropriately for other disorders such as dementia and impulsive aggressiveness.

antidepressant drugs Drugs used primarily in the treatment of mood disorders, especially depression and anxiety.

These photos show the effects of antipsychotic drugs on the symptoms of a young man with schizophrenia. In the top photo, he was unmedicated; in the bottom photo, he had taken medication. However, these drugs do not help all people with psychotic disorders.

activity of the neurotransmitter gamma-aminobutyric acid (GABA). Tranquilizers may temporarily help individuals who are having an acute anxiety attack, but they are not considered the treatment of choice over a long period of time. Symptoms almost always return if the medication is stopped, and a significant percentage of people who take tranquilizers overuse them and develop problems with withdrawal and tolerance (that is, they need larger and larger doses to get the same effect). *Beta-blockers,* a class of drugs primarily used to manage heart irregularities and hypertension, are sometimes prescribed to relieve acute anxiety—for example, caused by stage fright or athletic competition—which they do by slowing the heart rate and lowering blood pressure. But beta-blockers are not approved for anxiety disorders.

4 A special category of drug, a salt called **lithium carbonate**, often helps people who suffer from bipolar disorder. It may produce its effects by moderating levels of norepinephrine or by protecting brain cells from being overstimulated by another neurotransmitter, glutamate. Lithium must be given in exactly the right dose, and bloodstream levels of the drug must be carefully monitored, because too little will not help and too much is toxic; in some people, lithium produces short-term side effects (tremors) and long-term problems (kidney damage). Other drugs commonly prescribed for people with bipolar disorder include Depakote and Tegretol.

tranquilizers Drugs commonly but often inappropriately prescribed for patients who complain of unhappiness, anxiety, or worry.

lithium carbonate A drug frequently given to people suffering from bipolar disorder.

serotonin and norepinephrine. Wellbutrin is chemically unrelated to the other antidepressants but is often prescribed for depression and sometimes as an aid to quitting smoking.

Antidepressants are nonaddictive and about equally effective, but they all tend to produce some unpleasant physical reactions, including dry mouth, headaches, constipation, nausea, restlessness, gastrointestinal problems, weight gain, and, in as many as one-third of all patients, decreased sexual desire and blocked or delayed orgasm (Hollon, Thase, & Markowitz, 2002). The specific side effects may vary with the particular drug. MAOIs interact with certain foods (such as cheese) and have the most risks, such as elevating blood pressure in some individuals to dangerously high levels, so they are prescribed least often.

3 **Antianxiety drugs (tranquilizers),** such as Valium, Xanax, Ativan, and Klonopin, increase the

"Before Prozac, she loathed company."

TABLE 12.1

Drugs Commonly Used in the Treatment of Psychological Disorders

	Antipsychotics (Neuroleptics)	Antidepressants	Antianxiety Drugs	Lithium Carbonate
Examples	Thorazine	Prozac (SSRI)	Valium	
	Haldol	Nardil (MAOI)	Xanax	
	Clozaril	Elavil (tricyclic)	Klonapin	
	Risperdal	Paxil (SSRI)	Beta-blockers	
	Seroquel	Wellbutrin (other)		
		Cymbalta (other)		
		Remeron (other)		
Primarily used for	Schizophrenia	Depression	Mood disorders	Bipolar disorder
	Other psychoses	Anxiety disorders	Panic disorder	
	Impulsive anger	Panic disorder	Acute anxiety (e.g., stage fright)	
	Bipolar disorder	Obsessive-compulsive disorder		

※ **Explore**
Drugs Commonly Used to Treat Psychiatric Disorders on mypsychlab.com

For a review of these drugs and their uses, see Table 12.1. ※ Explore

Some Cautions about Drug Treatments

Without question, drugs have rescued some people from emotional despair and helped countless others live with chronic problems such as obsessive-compulsive disorder and panic attacks. They have enabled severely depressed or mentally disturbed people to be released from hospitals, to function in the world, and to respond to psychotherapy. Yet many psychiatrists and drug companies are trumpeting the benefits of medication without informing the public of its limitations.

Most people are unaware of how a *publication bias*—the tendency for journals to publish positive findings rather than negative or ambiguous ones—affects what we know. Independent researchers reviewed unpublished data submitted to the U.S. Food and Drug Administration (FDA) on 12 popular antidepressants. Of the 74 studies they examined, 38 reported positive results, and all but one of those was later published. Of the remaining studies with negative or mixed results, only 14 were published—and most of them were given a positive spin (Turner et al., 2008).

Even more worrisome for the prospects of impartial research, the majority of researchers who are studying the effectiveness of medication have financial ties to the pharmaceutical industry, in the form of lucrative consulting fees, funding for their

placebo effect The apparent success of a medication or treatment due to the patient's expectations or hopes rather than to the drug or treatment itself.

clinical trials, stock investments, and patents. Studies that are independently funded often do not get the positive results that industry-funded drug trials do (Healy, 2002; Krimsky, 2003). In this section, therefore, we want to give you an idea of what you are not hearing from the drug companies.

Thinking Critically about Drug Treatments

1 The placebo effect. New drugs often promise quick and effective cures. But the **placebo effect** ensures that many people will respond positively to a new drug just because of the enthusiasm surrounding it and because of their own expectations that the drug will make them feel better. After a while, when placebo effects decline, many drugs turn out to be neither as effective as promised nor as widely applicable. This has happened repeatedly with each new generation of tranquilizer and each new "miracle" antipsychotic drug and antidepressant (Healy, 2004; Moncrieff, 2001).

In fact, some investigators maintain that much of the effectiveness of antidepressants, especially for people who are only mildly depressed, is due to a placebo effect (Khan et al., 2003). Overall, only about half of all depressed patients respond positively to any given antidepressant medication, and of those, only about 40 percent are actually responding to the specific biological effects of the drug (Hollon, Thase, & Markowitz, 2002). In a meta-analysis of more than 5,000 patients in

47 clinical trials, investigators found that the placebo effect was "exceptionally large," accounting for more than 80 percent of the alleviation of symptoms. The drugs were most effective for patients with severe depression (Kirsch et al., 2008). Research in neuroscience suggests how placebos might be working: The psychological expectation of improvement actually produces some of the same brain changes that medication does (Benedetti et al., 2005).

2 High relapse and dropout rates. A person may have short-term success with antipsychotic or antidepressant drugs. However, in part because of these drugs' unpleasant side effects, anywhere from one-half to two-thirds of people stop taking them. When they do, they are likely to relapse, especially if they have not learned how to cope with their disorders (Hollon, Thase, & Maskowitz, 2002).

3 Disregard for effective, possibly better non-medical treatments. The popularity of drugs has been fueled by pressure from insurance companies, which prefer to pay for one patient visit for a prescription rather than ten visits for psychotherapy, and by drug company marketing and advertising. In 1997, the FDA permitted pharmaceutical companies to advertise directly to the public, a practice still forbidden in Canada and Europe; sales of new drugs skyrocketed as consumers began to request them. Ads promise wonderful results for emotional and behavioral problems, yet nonmedical treatments may work just as well or better. For example, two psychologists examined data on more than 168,000 children with attention deficit disorder who had been referred for treatment to a behavioral-care facility. More than 60 percent of the boys and 23 percent of the girls were on Ritalin or another drug. But after six sessions of behavior therapy for the children and ten sessions for the parent, only 11 percent of the boys and 2 percent of the girls remained on medication (Cummings & Wiggins, 2001).

4 Dosage problems. One challenge in prescribing drugs is to find the right dose—enough but not too much. The same dose of a drug may be metabolized differently in men and women, old people and young people, and different ethnic groups. When psychiatrist Keh-Ming Lin moved from Taiwan to the United States, he was amazed to learn that the dosage of antipsychotic drugs given to American patients with schizophrenia was often ten times higher than the dose for Chinese patients. In subsequent studies, Lin and his colleagues confirmed that Asian patients require significantly lower doses of the

medication for optimal treatment (Lin, Poland, & Chien, 1990). Similarly, African Americans suffering from depression or bipolar disorder seem to need lower dosages of tricyclic antidepressants and lithium than other ethnic groups do (Strickland et al., 1991, 1995). Groups may differ in the dosages they can tolerate because of variations in metabolic rates, amount of body fat, the number or type of drug receptors in the brain, or cultural practices such as smoking and eating certain foods.

5 Unknown risks over time and in combination. The effects of taking antidepressants indefinitely are still unknown, especially for vulnerable groups such as children, pregnant women, the elderly, or the generation of young adults who have been taking them since childhood or adolescence, when the brain is still developing. After British drug authorities reported that nine unpublished studies of Paxil found that it tripled the risk of suicidal thoughts and suicide attempts in adolescents who were taking the drug compared to those given a placebo (Harris, 2003), the FDA now warns against prescribing SSRIs to anyone under 18.

The reason we don't know about long-term effects until a drug has been on the market for years is that new drugs are initially tested clinically on only a few hundred people for just a few weeks or months, even when the drug is one that a person might take indefinitely (Angell, 2004). Nonetheless, many psychiatrists, understandably frustrated

"I think the dosage needs adjusting. I'm not nearly as happy as the people in the ads."

by the failure of existing antipsychotics and antidepressants to help all of their patients, are prescribing "cocktails" of medications—this one for anxiety, plus this one for depression, plus another to manage the side effects. They report anecdotal success in some cases, but to date, there has been virtually no research on the benefits and risks of these combination approaches.

6 **Untested off-label uses.** Most consumers do not realize that once the FDA approves a drug, doctors are permitted to prescribe it for other conditions and to populations other than those on which it was originally tested. As already noted, antipsychotics such as Risperdal are being used for nonpsychotic disorders. Likewise, antidepressants are being marketed for "social phobias"; Prozac, when its patent expired, was renamed Sarafem and marketed to women for "premenstrual dysphoric disorder"; Ritalin, widely given to school-aged children, is being prescribed for 2- and 3-year-olds.

The overprescription of drugs for mood disorders also occurs because of a common but mistaken assumption: If a disorder appears to have biological origins or involve biochemical abnormalities, then biological treatments must be most appropriate. In fact, however, changing your behavior and thoughts through psychotherapy or other new experiences can also change the way your brain functions. In PET-scan studies of people with obsessive-compulsive disorder, among those who were taking the SSRI Prozac, the metabolism of glucose in a critical part of the brain decreased, suggesting that the drug was having a beneficial effect by calming that area. Yet exactly the *same* brain changes occurred in patients who were getting cognitive-behavior therapy (described later in this chapter) and no medication (Baxter et al., 1992; Schwartz et al., 1996) (see Figure 12.1).

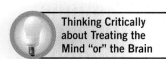

In coming years, you will be hearing about "promising medications" for such common psychological problems as memory loss, eating disorders, and smoking (Miller, 2008). Every major pharmaceutical company is working on one or more of these, and you are likely to hear enthusiastic researchers claiming, "We'll have it within five years!" But we hope you will resist the impulse to jump on any new-drug bandwagon. Critical thinkers must weigh the benefits and limitations of medication for psychological problems and wait for the data on safety and effectiveness.

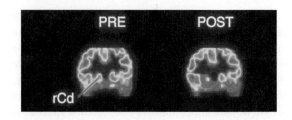

FIGURE 12.1
Psychotherapy and the Brain
These PET scans show the brain of a person with obsessive-compulsive disorder before and after behavior therapy. Before therapy, the glucose metabolic rates in the right caudate nucleus (rCd) were elevated. After therapy, this area calmed down, becoming less active, just as it did with medication (Schwartz et al., 1996).

Direct Brain Intervention

For most of human history, a person suffering from mental illness often got an extreme form of help. A well-meaning tribal healer or doctor would try to release the "psychic pressures" believed to be causing the symptoms by drilling holes in the victim's skull. It didn't work!

The most famous modern effort to cure mental illness by intervening directly in the brain was invented in 1935, when a Portuguese neurologist, António Egas Moniz, drilled two holes into the skull of a mental patient and used an instrument to crush nerve fibers running from the prefrontal lobes to other areas. This operation, called a *prefrontal lobotomy*, was supposed to reduce the patient's emotional symptoms without impairing intellectual ability. The procedure—which, incredibly, was never assessed or validated scientifically—was performed on more than 40,000 people in the United States. Tragically, lobotomies left many patients apathetic, withdrawn, and unable to care for themselves (Valenstein, 1986). Yet Moniz won a Nobel Prize for his work.

A different approach to altering brain function has been to stimulate the brain electrically. The oldest method is **electroconvulsive therapy (ECT)**, or "shock therapy," which is used for the treatment of severe depression, although no one knows how or why it works. An electrode is placed on one side of the head and a brief current is turned on. The current triggers a seizure that typically lasts one minute, causing the body to convulse. In the past, there were many horror stories about the misuse of ECT and its dire effects on memory. Today, however, patients are given muscle relaxants and anesthesia, so they sleep through the procedure and their convulsions are minimized. The World Psychiatric Association has endorsed ECT as safe and effective, especially for people with crippling depression and suicidal impulses and for those who have not responded to other treatments (Shorter & Healy, 2008). Still, the mood-improving effect of ECT is usually short-lived, and the depression almost always returns within a few weeks or months (Hollon, Thase, & Markowitz, 2002). ECT is ineffective with other disorders, such as schizophrenia or alcoholism, although it is occasionally misused for these conditions.

A different method of electrically stimulating the brains of individuals suffering from severe depression, still largely experimental, is *transcranial magnetic stimulation (TMS)*, which involves the use of a pulsing magnetic coil held to a person's skull over the left prefrontal cortex, an area of the brain that is less active in people with depression. Like ECT, the benefits of TMS, when they occur, are short-lived. At present, its benefits seem to depend more on *who* is doing it than on *what* is being done, suggesting the placebo effect is at work rather than the technology itself. Until controlled studies are done, we need to tolerate some uncertainty about whether TMS will prove to be effective.

Another, riskier approach is *deep brain stimulation (DBS)*, which was originally approved for patients with Parkinson's disease and epilepsy, and now is being used for at least a dozen mental disorders, although no one knows how or why it might be helpful. DBS requires surgery to implant electrodes

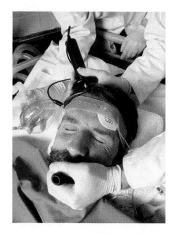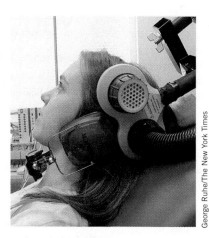

A man receives ECT (left); right, a researcher demonstrates transcranial magnetic stimulation (TMS).

George Ruhe/The New York Times

into the brain and to embed a small box, like a pacemaker, under the collarbone. But it also is still experimental and claims of its success are based only on patients' self-reports, so the powerful placebo effect of surgery cannot be ruled out (Lozano et al., 2008). The company that developed this $25,000-per-patient device has hired psychiatrists to lobby for it, mounted a vigorous marketing campaign to get it approved, and funded virtually all of the so-far unsuccessful efforts to show that it works (Barglow, 2008).

✓•—**Study** and **Review** on mypsychlab.com

Quick Quiz

No amount of electric shock will stimulate test-taking ability.

A. Match these treatments with the problems for which they are typically used.

1. antipsychotic drugs	**a.** suicidal depression
2. antidepressant drugs	**b.** bipolar disorder
3. lithium carbonate	**c.** schizophrenia
4. electroconvulsive therapy	**d.** depression and anxiety
	e. obsessive-compulsive disorder

B. What are six cautions about taking medications for psychological disorders?

C. In 2006, a news story reported that scientists had high hopes for new pills that would help people quit smoking, lose weight, and kick addictions to alcohol and cocaine. The pills supposedly worked by blocking pleasure centers in the brain that make people feel good when they smoke, overeat, or drink liquor. Based on what you have read in this section, what might you expect to have read in a follow-up story two years later? Why?

Answers:

A. 1. c 2. d 3. b 4. a **B.** Placebo effects are common; dropout and relapse rates are high; the availability of medication may prevent people from trying a possibly better nonmedical solution first; appropriate dosages can be difficult to determine and can vary by sex, age, and ethnicity; some drugs have unknown or long-term risks; and some drugs are prescribed off label for conditions for which they were never tested. **C.** You might expect to read that there were unexpected side effects of the new pills or their lack of effectiveness. One subsequent news story on this particular line of research concluded: "Now it seems the drugs may block pleasure too well, possibly raising the risk of depression and suicide." Indeed, a pill from one major drug company to help people quit smoking has been linked to dozens of reports of suicides and suicide attempts, and two obesity pills have been tied to higher rates of suicide and depression. Early reports of drugs in the testing pipeline usually promise exciting results, but many of these drugs do not pan out.

psychoanalysis A theory of personality and a method of psychotherapy, developed by Sigmund Freud, that emphasizes the exploration of unconscious motives and conflicts; modern psychodynamic therapies share this emphasis but differ from Freudian analysis in various ways.

transference In psychodynamic therapies, a critical process in which the client transfers unconscious emotions or reactions, such as emotional feelings about his or her parents, onto the therapist.

Psychodynamic therapists emphasize the clinical importance of transference, the process by which the client transfers emotional feelings toward other important people in his or her life (usually the parents) onto the therapist. They know that "love's arrow" isn't really intended for them!

 YOU are about to learn...

- the major approaches to psychotherapy.

- how behavior therapists can help you change bad habits, and how cognitive therapists can help you get rid of self-defeating thoughts.

- why humanist and existential therapists focus on the "here and now" instead of the "why and how."

- the benefits of treating a whole family instead of only one of its members.

Major Schools of Psychotherapy

All good psychotherapists want to help clients think about their lives in new ways and find solutions to the problems that plague them. In this section, we will consider the major schools of psychotherapy. To illustrate the philosophy and methods of each one, we will focus on a fictional fellow named Murray. Murray is a smart guy whose problem is all too familiar to many students: He procrastinates. He just can't seem to settle down and write his term papers. He keeps getting incompletes, and before long the incompletes turn to Fs. Why does Murray procrastinate, manufacturing his own misery? What kind of therapy might help him?

Psychodynamic Therapy

Sigmund Freud was the father of the "talking cure," as one of his patients called it. In his method of **psychoanalysis**, which required patients to come for treatment several days a week, often for years, pa-

tients talked not about their immediate problems but about their dreams and their memories of childhood. Freud believed that intensive analysis of these dreams and memories would give patients insight into the unconscious reasons for their symptoms. With insight and emotional release, he believed, the person's symptoms would disappear.

Today, Freud's psychoanalytic method has evolved into many different forms of *psychodynamic therapy*, which share the goal of exploring the unconscious dynamics of personality, such as defenses and conflicts. Its practitioners refer to them as "depth" therapies because the purpose is to delve into the deep, unconscious processes believed to be the source of the patient's problems, rather than to concentrate on "superficial" symptoms and conscious beliefs. Modern psychodynamic therapies share certain features, including the discussion of past experience, identification of recurring themes and patterns in the client's life, exploration of fantasies, and a focus on the client's contradictory emotions and feelings (Shedler, 2010).

In addition, a major element of most psychodynamic therapies is **transference**, the client's transfer (displacement) of emotional elements of his or her inner life—usually feelings about the client's parents—outward onto the analyst. Have you ever found yourself responding to a new acquaintance with unusually quick affection or dislike, and later realized it was because the person reminded you of a relative whom you loved or loathed? That experience is similar to transference. In therapy, a woman might transfer her love for her father to the analyst, believing that she has fallen in love with the analyst. A man who is unconsciously angry at his mother for rejecting him might become furious with his analyst for going on vacation. Through analysis of transference in the therapy setting, psychodynamic therapists believe that clients can see their emotional conflicts in action and work through them (Schafer, 1992; Westen, 1998). Experimental studies have found that transference is not limited to psychotherapy; mental representations of significant others are stored in memory and are often activated in new encounters (Andersen & Berk, 1998; Andersen & Chen, 2002).

A psychodynamic therapist might help our friend Murray gain the insight that he procrastinates as an unconscious way of expressing anger toward his parents. He might realize that he is angry because they insist he study for a career he dislikes.

Behavior and Cognitive Therapy

Clinical psychologists who practice behavior therapy would get right to the problem: What are the reinforcers in Murray's environment that are maintaining his behavior? "Mur," they would say, "forget about insight. You have lousy study habits." Clinicians who practice cognitive therapy would focus on helping Murray understand how his beliefs about studying, writing papers, and success are woefully unrealistic. Often these two approaches are combined.

Behavioral Techniques **Behavior therapy** is based on principles of classical and operant conditioning that are discussed in Chapter 9. (You may want to review those principles before going on.) Here are some of these methods (Martin & Pear, 2007):

1 Exposure. The most widely used behavioral approach for treating fears and panic is **graduated exposure**. When people are afraid of some situation, object, or upsetting memory, they usually do everything they can to avoid confronting or thinking of it. Naturally, this only makes the fear worse. Exposure treatments, either in the client's imagination or in actual situations, are aimed at reversing this tendency. In graduated exposure, the client controls the degree of confrontation with the source of the fear: Someone who is trying to avoid thinking of a traumatic event might be asked to imagine the event over and over, until it no longer evokes the same degree of panic. A more dramatic form of exposure is **flooding**, in which the therapist takes the client directly into the feared situation and remains there until the client's panic and anxiety decline. Thus a person suffering from agoraphobia might be taken into a department store or a subway, an action that would normally be terrifying to contemplate.

2 Systematic desensitization. Systematic desensitization is an older behavioral method, a step-by-step process of breaking down a client's conditioned associations with a feared object or experience (Wolpe, 1958). It is based on the classical-conditioning procedure of *counterconditioning*, in which a stimulus (such as a dog) for an unwanted response (such as fear) is paired with some other stimulus or situation that elicits a response incompatible with the undesirable one (see Chapter 9). In this case, the incompatible response is usually relaxation. The client learns to relax deeply while imagining or looking at a sequence of feared stimuli, arranged in a hierarchy from the least frightening to the most frightening. The hierarchy itself is provided by the client. The sequence for a person who is terrified of spiders might be to read the classic children's story *Charlotte's Web*, then look at

THERE. SEE? IT'S JUST STITCHED ANIMAL HIDE... HERE. TOUCH IT. CARESS IT. CLUTCH IT TO YOUR BOSOM.

Batters overcoming *bonkinogginophobia*, a fear of the ball.

pictures of small, cute spiders, then look at pictures of tarantulas, then move on to observing a real spider, and so on. At each step, the person must become relaxed before going on. Eventually, the fear responses are extinguished.

Some behavior therapists have developed virtual reality (VR) programs to desensitize clients to various phobias, notably of flying, heights, spiders, and public speaking, and to help clients reduce anxiety (Gregg & Tarrier, 2007). Others are experimenting with VR to treat combat veterans who are suffering from intractable posttraumatic stress symptoms. In Virtual Iraq, vets get a combination of exposure and desensitization. They wear a helmet with video goggles and earphones to hear the sounds of war, and then play a modified version of the VR game *Full Spectrum Warrior*, adapted to the Iraq experience (Halpern, 2008).

3 Behavioral self-monitoring. Before you can change your behavior, it helps to identify the reinforcers that are supporting your unwanted habits: attention from others, temporary relief from tension or unhappiness, or tangible rewards such as money or a good meal. One way to do this is to keep a record of the behavior that you would like to change. Would you like to cut back on eating sweets? You may not be aware of how much you are eating throughout the day to relieve tension, boost

behavior therapy A form of therapy that applies principles of classical and operant conditioning to help people change self-defeating or problematic behaviors.

graduated exposure In behavior therapy, a method in which a person suffering from a phobia or panic attacks is gradually taken into the feared situation or exposed to a traumatic memory until the anxiety subsides.

flooding In behavior therapy, a form of exposure treatment in which the client is taken directly into a feared situation until his or her panic subsides.

systematic desensitization In behavior therapy, a step-by-step process of desensitizing a client to a feared object or experience; it is based on the classical-conditioning procedure of counterconditioning.

behavioral self-monitoring In behavior therapy, a method of keeping careful data on the frequency and consequences of the behavior to be changed.

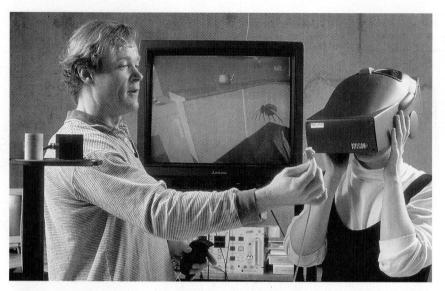

In this virtual reality version of systematic desensitization, people with spider phobias are gradually exposed to computerized but extremely lifelike images of spiders in a realistic, three-dimensional environment (Wiederhold & Wiederhold, 2000).

your energy, or just to be sociable when you are hanging out; a behavioral record will show how much and when you eat. A mother might complain that her child "always" has temper tantrums; a behavioral record will show when, where, and with whom those tantrums occur. Once the unwanted behavior is identified, along with the reinforcers that have been maintaining it, a treatment program can be designed to change it. You might find other ways to reduce stress besides eating, and make sure that you are nowhere near junk food in the late afternoon, when your energy is low. The mother can learn to respond to her child's tantrum not with her attention (or a cookie to buy silence) but with a time-out: banishing the child to a corner where no positive reinforcers are available.

4 Skills training. It is not enough to tell someone "Don't be shy" if the person does not know how to make small talk with others, or "Don't yell!" if the person does not know how to express feelings calmly. Therefore, some behavior therapists use

operant-conditioning techniques, modeling, and role-playing to teach the skills a client might lack. A shy person might learn how to converse in social settings by focusing on other people rather than on his or her own insecurity. Skills-training programs have been designed for all kinds of behavioral problems: to teach parents how to discipline their children, impulsive adults how to manage anger, autistic children how to behave appropriately, and people with schizophrenia how to hold a job. These skills are also being taught in virtual worlds, such as *Second Life*. After face-to-face sessions with a therapist, the client creates an avatar to explore a virtual environment and experiment with new behaviors; the therapist can be monitoring the client's psychological and even physiological reactions at the same time.

A behaviorist would treat Murray's procrastination in several ways. Monitoring his own behavior with a diary would let Murray know exactly how he spends his time, and how much time he should realistically allot to a project. Instead of having a vague, impossibly huge goal, such as "I'm going to reorganize my life," Murray would establish specific small goals, such as reading the two books necessary for an English paper and writing one page of an assignment. If Murray does not know how to write clearly, however, even writing one page might feel overwhelming; he might also need some skills training, such as a basic composition class. Most important, the therapist would change the reinforcers that are maintaining Murray's "procrastination behavior"—perhaps the immediate gratification of partying with friends—and replace them with reinforcers for getting the work done.

Cognitive Techniques Gloomy thoughts can generate an array of negative emotions and self-defeating behavior (see Chapter 11). The underlying

skills training In behavior therapy, an effort to teach the client skills that he or she may lack, as well as new constructive behaviors to replace self-defeating ones.

Get Involved! Cure Your Fears

In Chapter 11, a Get Involved exercise asked you to identify your greatest fear. Now see whether systematic desensitization procedures will help you conquer it. Write down a list of situations that evoke your fear, starting with one that produces little anxiety (e.g., seeing a photo of a tiny spider) and ending with the most frightening one possible (e.g., looking at live tarantulas at a pet store). Then find a quiet room where you will have no distractions or interruptions, sit in a comfortable reclining chair, and relax all the muscles of your body. Breathe slowly and deeply. Imagine the first, easiest scene, remaining as relaxed as possible. Do this until you can confront the image without becoming the least bit anxious. When that happens, go on to the next scene in your hierarchy. Do not try this all at once; space out your sessions over time. Does it work?

premise of **cognitive therapy** is that constructive thinking can do the opposite, reducing or dispelling anger, fear, and depression. Cognitive therapists help clients identify the beliefs and expectations that might be unnecessarily prolonging their unhappiness, conflicts, and other problems (Persons, Davidson, & Tompkins, 2001). They ask clients to examine the evidence for their beliefs that everyone is mean and selfish, that ambition is hopeless, or that love is doomed. Clients learn to consider other explanations for the behavior of people who annoy them: Was my father's strict discipline an attempt to control me, as I have always believed? What if he was really trying to protect and care for me? By requiring people to identify their assumptions and biases, examine the evidence, and consider other interpretations, cognitive therapy, as you can see, teaches critical thinking.

Aaron Beck (1976, 2005) pioneered in the application of cognitive therapy for depression, which often arises from specific pessimistic thoughts that the sources of your misery are permanent and that nothing good will ever happen to you again. For Beck, these beliefs are not "irrational"; rather, they are unproductive or based on misinformation. A therapist using Beck's approach would ask you to test your beliefs against the evidence. If you say, "But I *know* no one likes me," the therapist might say, "Oh, yes? How do you know? Do you really not have a single friend? Has anyone in the past year been nice to you?"

Another school of cognitive therapy is Albert Ellis's **rational emotive behavior therapy (REBT)** (Ellis, 1993; Ellis & Blau, 1998). In this approach, the therapist uses rational arguments to directly challenge a client's unrealistic beliefs or expectations. Ellis pointed out that people who are emotionally upset often *overgeneralize:* They decide

that one annoying act by someone means that person is bad in every way, or that a normal mistake they made is evidence that they are rotten to the core. Many people also *catastrophize,* transforming a small problem into disaster: "I failed this test, and now I'll flunk out of school, and no one will ever like me, and even my cat will hate me, and I'll never get a job." Many people drive themselves crazy with notions of what they "must" do. The therapist challenges these thoughts directly, showing the client why they are irrational and misguided.

A cognitive therapist might treat Murray's procrastination by having Murray write down his thoughts about work, read the thoughts as if someone else had said them, and then write a rational response to each one. This technique would encourage Murray to examine the validity of his assumptions and beliefs. Many procrastinators are perfectionists; if they cannot do something perfectly, they will not do it at all. Unable to accept their limitations, they set impossible standards and catastrophize:

Negative Thought	Rational Response
If I don't get an A+ on this paper, my life will be ruined.	My life will be a lot worse if I keep getting incompletes. It's better to get a B or even a C than to do nothing.
My professor is going to think I'm an idiot when he reads this. I'll feel humiliated by his criticism.	He hasn't accused me of being an idiot yet. If he makes some criticisms, I can learn from them and do better next time.

Traditional behavioral and cognitive therapists debated whether it is most helpful to work on changing clients' thoughts or changing their behavior. But today most of them believe that thoughts

Cognitive therapists encourage clients to emphasize the positive (the early sunny signs of spring) rather than the negative (the lingering icy clutch of winter). Poet Michael Casey described the first daffodil that bravely rises through the snow as "a gleam of laughter in a sullen face."

⊙—⌐**Watch Cognitive Behavioral Therapy** on **mypsychlab.com**

cognitive therapy A form of therapy designed to identify and change irrational, unproductive ways of thinking and, hence, to reduce negative emotions and their self-defeating consequences.

rational emotive behavior therapy (REBT) A form of cognitive therapy devised by Albert Ellis, designed to challenge the client's unrealistic or irrational thoughts.

Get Involved! Mind over Mood ⊙—⌐Watch

See whether cognitive-therapy techniques can help you control your moods. Think of a time recently when you felt a particularly strong emotion, such as depression, anger, or anxiety. On a piece of paper, record (1) the situation—who was there, what happened, and when; (2) the intensity of your feeling at the time, from weak to strong; and (3) the thoughts that were going through your mind (e.g., "She never cares about what I want to do"; "He's going to leave me").

Now examine your thoughts. What is the worst thing that could happen if those thoughts are true? Are your thoughts accurate or are you "mind reading" another person's intentions and motives? Is there another way to think about this situation or the other person's behavior? If you practice this exercise repeatedly, you may learn how your thoughts affect your moods, and find out that you have more control over your feelings than you realized (Greenberger & Padesky, 1995).

and behavior influence each other, which is why *cognitive-behavior therapy* (CBT) is more common than either cognitive or behavior therapy alone.

Mindfulness and Acceptance

Some CBT practitioners, inspired by Eastern philosophies such as Buddhism, have begun to question the goal of changing a client's self-defeating thoughts. They argue that it is difficult if not impossible to get rid of unwanted thoughts and feelings, especially when people have been rehearsing them for years. They therefore propose a form of CBT based on "mindfulness" and "acceptance": Clients learn to explicitly identify and accept whatever negative thoughts and feelings arise, without trying to eradicate them or letting them derail healthy behavior (Hayes, Follette, & Linehan, 2004). Instead of trying to persuade a client who is afraid of making public speeches that her fear is irrational, these therapists would encourage her to accept the anxious thoughts and feelings without judging them, or herself, harshly. Then she can focus on coping techniques and ways of giving speeches *despite* her anxiety.

Humanist and Existential Therapy

Humanist therapy, like its parent philosophy humanism, starts from the assumption that human nature is basically good and that people behave badly or develop problems when they have been warped by self-imposed limits. Humanist therapists, therefore, want to know how clients subjectively see their own situations and how they construe the world around them. They explore what is going on "here and now," not past issues of "why and how."

In **client-centered (nondirective) therapy**, developed by Carl Rogers, the therapist's role is to listen to the client's needs in an accepting, nonjudgmental way and to offer what Rogers called *unconditional positive regard*. Whatever the client's specific complaint is, the goal is to build the client's self-esteem and self-acceptance and help the client find a more productive way of seeing his or her problems. A Rogerian might assume that Murray's procrastination masks his low self-regard and that Murray is out of touch with his real feelings and wishes. Perhaps he is not passing his courses because he is trying to please his parents by majoring in pre-law when he would secretly rather become an artist. Rogers (1951, 1961) believed that effective therapists must be warm and genuine. For Rogerians, *empathy*, the therapist's ability to understand what the client says and identify the client's feelings, is

Humanist therapists emphasize the importance of warmth, concern, and listening empathically to what the client says.

the crucial ingredient of successful therapy: "I understand how frustrated you must be feeling, Murray, because no matter how hard you try, you don't succeed." The client, according to humanist therapists, will eventually internalize the therapist's support and become more self-accepting.

Existential therapy helps clients face the great questions of existence, such as death, freedom, loneliness, and meaninglessness. Existential therapists, like humanist therapists, believe that our lives are not inevitably determined by our pasts or our circumstances; we have the power and free will to choose our own destinies. As Irvin Yalom (1989) explained, "The crucial first step in therapy is the patient's assumption of responsibility for his or her life predicament. As long as one believes that one's problems are caused by some force or agency outside oneself, there is no leverage in therapy."

Yalom argues that the goal of therapy is to help clients cope with the inescapable realities of life and death and the struggle for meaning. However grim our experiences may be, he believes, "they contain the seeds of wisdom and redemption." Perhaps the most remarkable example of a man able to find seeds of wisdom in a barren landscape was Victor Frankl (1905–1997), who developed a form of existential therapy after surviving a Nazi concentration camp. In that pit of horror, Frankl (1955) observed, some people maintained their sanity because they were able to find meaning in the experience, shattering though it was.

Some observers believe that, ultimately, all therapies are existential. In different ways, therapy helps people determine what is important to them, what values guide them, and what changes they will have the courage to make. A humanist or existential therapist might help Murray think about the

humanist therapy A form of psychotherapy based on the philosophy of humanism, which emphasizes the client's free will to change rather than past conflicts.

client-centered (nondirective) therapy A humanist approach, devised by Carl Rogers, which emphasizes the therapist's empathy with the client and the use of unconditional positive regard.

existential therapy A form of therapy designed to help clients explore the meaning of existence and face the great questions of life, such as death, freedom, alienation, and loneliness.

significance of his procrastination, what his ultimate goals in life are, and how he might find the strength to reach them.

Family and Couples Therapy

Murray's situation is getting worse. His father has begun to call him Tomorrow Man, which upsets his mother, and his younger brother, the math major, has been calculating how much tuition money Murray's incompletes are costing. His older sister, Isabel, the biochemist who never had an incomplete in her life, now proposes that all of them go to a family therapist. "Murray's not the only one in this family with complaints," she says.

Family therapists would maintain that Murray's problem developed in the context of his family, that it is sustained by the dynamics of his family, and that any change he makes will affect all members of his family (Nichols & Schwartz, 2008). One of the most famous early family therapists, Salvador Minuchin (1984), compared the family to a kaleidoscope, a changing pattern of mosaics in which the pattern is larger than any one piece. In this view, efforts to isolate and treat one member of the family without the others are doomed. Only if all family members reveal their differing perceptions of each other can mistakes and misperceptions be identified. A teenager may see his mother as crabby and nagging when actually she is tired and worried. A parent may see a child as rebellious when in fact the child is lonely and desperate for attention.

Family members are usually unaware of how they influence one another. By observing the entire family, the family therapist hopes to discover tensions and imbalances in power and communication. For example, a child may have a chronic illness or a psychological problem that affects the workings of the whole family. One parent may become overinvolved with the troubled child while the other parent retreats, and each may start blaming the other. The child, in turn, may cling to the illness or disorder as a way of expressing anger, keeping the parents together, getting the parents' attention, or asserting control.

Even when it is not possible to treat the whole family, some therapists will treat individuals in a **family-systems perspective**, which recognizes that people's behavior in a family is as interconnected as that of two dancers (Bowen, 1978; Cox & Paley, 2003). Clients learn that if they change in any way, even for the better, their families may protest noisily or may send subtle messages that read, "Change back!" Why? Because when one family member changes, each of the others must change too. As the saying goes, it takes two to tango, and if one dancer

stops, so must the other. But most people do not like change. They are comfortable with old patterns and habits, even those that cause them trouble. They want to keep dancing the same old dance, even if their feet hurt.

When a couple is arguing frequently about issues that never seem to get resolved, they may be helped by going to *couples therapy*, which is designed to help couples manage the inevitable conflicts that occur in all relationships (Christensen & Jacobson, 2000). Couples therapists generally insist on seeing both partners, so that they will hear both sides of the story. They cut through the blaming and attacking ("She never listens to me!" "He never does anything!"), and instead focus on helping the couple resolve their differences, get over hurt and blame, and make specific behavioral changes to reduce anger and conflict. Many couples therapists, like some cognitive therapists, are moving away from the "fix all the differences" approach. Instead, they are helping couples learn to accept and live with qualities in both partners that aren't going to change much (Hayes, 2004). A wife can stop trying to turn her calm, steady husband into a spontaneous adventurer ("After all, that's what I originally loved about him; he's as steady as a rock"), and a husband can stop trying to make his shy wife more assertive ("I have always loved her remarkable serenity").

Family and couples therapists may use psychodynamic, behavioral, cognitive, or humanist approaches in their work; they share only a focus on the family or the couple. In Murray's case, a family therapist would observe how Murray's procrastination fits his family dynamics. Perhaps it allows Murray to get his father's attention and his mother's sympathy. Perhaps it keeps Murray from facing his greatest fear: If he finishes his work, it will not measure

family-systems perspective An approach to doing therapy with individuals or families by identifying how each family member forms part of a larger interacting system.

"I've been a cow all my life, honey. Don't ask me to change now."

◉—Watch
Family
Therapist on
mypsychlab.com

up to his father's impossibly high standards. The therapist will not only help Murray change his work habits, but will also help his family deal with a changed Murray.   ◉—Watch

Psychotherapy in Practice The kinds of psychotherapy that we have discussed are all quite different in theory, and so are their techniques (see Table 12.2). Yet in practice, many psychotherapists take an *integrative approach*, drawing on methods and ideas from various schools and avoiding strong allegiances to any one theory. This flexibility enables them to treat clients with whatever methods are most appropriate and effective. One Internet-based survey of more than 2,400 psychotherapists found that two-thirds said they practice cognitive-behavioral therapy—*and* that the single most influential therapist they followed was Carl Rogers *and* that they often incorporate ideas of mindfulness and acceptance (Cook, Biyanova, & Coyne, 2009).

All successful therapies, regardless of their approach, share a key element: They are able to motivate the client into wanting to change, and they replace a client's pessimistic or unrealistic life narrative with one that is more hopeful or attainable (Howard, 1991; Schafer, 1992).

TABLE 12.2

The Major Schools of Therapy Compared

	Primary Goal	Methods
Psychodynamic	Insight into unconscious motives and feelings that prolong symptoms	Probing unconscious motives and fantasies, exploring childhood experiences, identifying recurring themes in client's life; exploration of issues and emotions raised by transference
Cognitive-Behavioral		
Behavioral	Modification of self-defeating behaviors	Graduated exposure (flooding), systematic desensitization, behavioral records, skills training
Cognitive	Modification of irrational or unvalidated beliefs	Prompting the client to test beliefs against evidence; exposing the faulty reasoning in catastrophizing and mind reading; sometimes helping the client accept and live with unpleasant thoughts and feelings
Humanist and Existential		
Humanist	Insight; self-acceptance and self-fulfillment; new, optimistic perceptions of oneself and the world	Providing a nonjudgmental setting in which to discuss issues; use of empathy and unconditional positive regard by the therapist
Existential	Finding meaning in life and accepting inevitable losses	Varies with the therapist; philosophic discussions about the meaning of life, the client's goals, finding the courage to survive suffering and loss
Family and Couples		
Family	Modification of family patterns	May use any of the preceding methods to change family patterns that perpetuate problems and conflicts
Couples	Resolution of conflicts, breaking out of destructive habits	May use any of the preceding methods to help the couple communicate better, resolve conflicts, or accept differences

✔—⌐Study and
Review on
mypsychlab.com

Quick Quiz

Don't be a procrastinator like our friend Murray; take this quiz now.
Match each method or concept with the therapy associated with it.

1. transference
2. systematic desensitization
3. facing the fear of death
4. reappraisal of thoughts
5. unconditional positive regard
6. exposure to feared situation
7. avoidance of "catastrophizing"
8. assessment of family patterns

a. cognitive therapy
b. psychodynamic therapy
c. humanist therapy
d. behavior therapy
e. family therapy
f. existential therapy

Answers:

1.b 2.d 3.f 4.a 5.c 6.d 7.a 8.e

YOU are about to learn...

- the meaning of the "scientist–practitioner gap" and why it has been widening.
- which form of psychotherapy is most likely to help if you are anxious or depressed.
- why psychotherapy can sometimes be harmful.

Evaluating Psychotherapy

Poor Murray! He is getting a little baffled by all these therapies. He wants to make a choice soon; no sense in procrastinating about that, too! Is there any scientific evidence, he wonders, that might help him decide which therapy or therapist will be best for him?

Psychotherapy is, first and foremost, a relationship. Its success depends on the bond the therapist and client establish between them, called the **therapeutic alliance**. When both parties respect and understand one another and agree on the goals of treatment, the client is more likely to improve, regardless of the specific techniques the therapist uses (Klein et al., 2003).

Culture and the Therapeutic Alliance

Many therapists and clients work well together in spite of coming from different backgrounds. But sometimes cultural differences cause misunderstandings that result from ignorance or prejudice (Comas-Díaz, 2006; Sue et al., 2007). A lifetime of experience with racism and a general cultural distrust may keep some African Americans from

revealing feelings that they believe a white therapist would not understand or accept (Whaley & Davis, 2007). Misunderstandings and prejudice may be one reason Asian-American, Latino, and African-American clients are more likely to stay in therapy when their therapists' ethnicity matches their own. When there is a cultural match, clients and psychotherapists are more likely to share perceptions of what the client's problem is, agree on the best way of coping, and have the same expectations about what therapy can accomplish (Hwang, 2006; Zone et al., 2005).

Understanding a culture's particular traditions can also help clinicians design more effective interventions for individual and community problems. In the Pacific Northwest, where substance abuse among Native Americans and Alaska Natives has widespread and devastating effects, successful approaches combine bicultural life-skills training with community involvement, which plays an essential role in native life (Hawkins, Cummins, & Marlatt, 2004).

In establishing a bond with clients, therapists must distinguish normal cultural patterns from individual psychological problems. An Irish-American family therapist, Monica McGoldrick (2005), described some problems that are typical of Irish-American families. These problems arise from Irish history and religious beliefs. "In general, the therapist cannot expect the family to turn into a physically affectionate, emotionally intimate group, or to enjoy being in therapy very much," she observed. "The notion of Original Sin—that you are guilty before you are born—leaves them with a heavy sense of burden. Someone not sensitized to these issues may see this as pathological. It is not. But it is also not likely to change and the therapist should help the family

therapeutic alliance
The bond of confidence and mutual understanding established between therapist and client, which allows them to work together to solve the client's problems.

tolerate this inner guilt rather than try to get rid of it." (Did you notice the link between her observation and acceptance-based forms of cognitive therapy?)

More and more psychotherapists are becoming "sensitized to the issues" caused by cultural differences (Arredondo et al., 2005; Sue et al., 2007). In Latin American cultures, *susto*, or "loss of the soul," is a common response to extreme grief or fright; the person believes that his or her soul has departed along with that of the deceased relative. A psychotherapist unfamiliar with this culturally determined response might conclude that the sufferer was delusional or psychotic. Latino clients are also more likely than Anglos to value harmony in their relationships, which often translates into an unwillingness to express negative emotions or confront family members or friends directly, so therapists need to help such clients find ways to communicate better within that cultural context (Arredondo & Perez, 2003). Latino clinicians, being aware of the stigma associated with psychotherapy in their culture, are also developing ways to help their clients overcome ambivalence about seeking psychological help (Añez et al., 2008).

Being aware of cultural differences, however, does not mean that the therapist should stereotype clients. After all, some Latinos do have psychoses and some Irish do not carry burdens of guilt! It does mean that therapists must ensure that their clients find them to be trustworthy and effective; and it means that clients must be aware of their own prejudices too.

The Scientist–Practitioner Gap

Now suppose that Murray has found a nice psychotherapist who seems pretty smart and friendly. Is a good alliance enough? How important is the *kind* of therapy that an individual practices?

These questions have generated a huge debate among clinical practitioners and psychological scientists. Many psychotherapists believe that trying to evaluate psychotherapy using standard empirical methods is an exercise in futility: Numbers and graphs, they say, cannot possibly capture the complex exchange that takes place between a therapist and a client. What "works" in psychotherapy is usually not a good technique but a good *relationship*. Psychotherapy, they maintain, is an art that you acquire from clinical experience; it is not a science. That's why almost any method will help most people (Wampold, 2001). Other clinicians argue that efforts to measure the effectiveness of psychotherapy oversimplify the process, because, among other reasons, many patients have an assortment of emotional problems and need therapy for a longer time than research can reasonably allow (Westen, Novotny, & Thompson-Brenner, 2004).

For their part, psychological scientists agree that therapy is often a complex process. But that is no reason, they argue, that it cannot be scientifically investigated, just like any other complex psychological process such as the development of language or personality (Crits-Christoph, Wilson, & Hollon, 2005; Kazdin, 2008). Moreover, they are concerned

"Cuento" (story) therapy is a popular form of therapy among Latino psychotherapists, building as it does on a cultural tradition of storytelling and folk heroes (Comas-Díaz, 2006). For example, most Puerto Rican children know the tales of Juan Bobo (left), a foolish child ("bobo") who is always getting into trouble. The therapists on the right have adapted these stories for Puerto Rican children who are coping with problems and ethical conflicts in America. The children and their mothers watch a videotape of the folktale, discuss it together, and role-play its major themes, such as controlling aggression and understanding right from wrong. This method has been more successful than traditional therapies in reducing the children's transitional anxieties and improving their attention spans and achievement motivation (Costantino & Malgady, 1996).

that when therapists fail to keep up with empirical findings in the field, their clients may suffer. It is crucial, scientists say, for therapists to be aware of research findings on the most beneficial methods for particular problems, on ineffective or potentially harmful techniques, and on topics relevant to their practice, such as memory, hypnosis, and child development (Lilienfeld, Lynn, & Lohr, 2003).

Over the years, the breach between scientists and therapists has widened, creating what is commonly called the *scientist–practitioner gap*. One reason for the growing split has been the rise of professional schools that are not connected to academic psychology departments and that train students solely to do therapy. Graduates of these schools sometimes know little about research methods or even about research assessing different therapy techniques.

The scientist–practitioner gap has also widened because of the proliferation of unvalidated therapies in a crowded market. Some repackage established techniques under a new name. Consider Eye Movement Desensitization and Reprocessing (EMDR), which was built on the tried-and-true behavioral techniques of desensitization and exposure for treating anxiety (Lohr, Tolin, & Lilienfeld, 1998). EMDR's founder, Francine Shapiro (1995), added eye-movement exercises: Clients move their eyes from side to side, following the therapist's moving finger, while concentrating on the memory to be desensitized. Shapiro's (1994) explanation for why such eye movements work is that "the system may become unbalanced due to a trauma or through stress engendered during a developmental window, but once appropriately catalyzed and maintained in a dynamic state by EMDR, it transmutes information to a state of therapeutically appropriate resolution." (If you do not understand that, don't worry; we don't either.) Practitioners of EMDR have claimed success in treating everything from post-traumatic stress disorder and panic attacks to eating disorders and sexual dysfunction. Yet there is no evidence from controlled studies that it is any better than standard exposure treatments or that the supposedly essential eye movements are anything other than a sciency-sounding gimmick (Goldstein et al., 2000; Lohr et al., 1999; Taylor et al., 2003).

A blue-ribbon panel of clinical scientists, convened to assess the problem of the scientist–practitioner gap for the journal *Psychological Science in the Public Interest*, reported that the current state of clinical psychology is comparable to that of medicine in the early 1900s, when physicians typically valued personal experience over scientific research. The authors concluded that a new accreditation

system is necessary, one "that demands high quality science training as a central feature of doctoral training in clinical psychology" (Baker, McFall, & Shoham, 2008). The Academy of Psychological Clinical Science, an alliance of 49 clinical science graduate programs and nine clinical science internships, has begun a concerted effort to institute just such a system (Bootzin, 2009).

Problems in Assessing Therapy Because there are so many therapies all claiming to be successful, and because of economic pressures on insurers and rising health costs, clinical psychologists are increasingly being called on to provide empirical assessments of therapy. Why can't you just ask people if the therapy helped them? The answer is that no matter what kind of therapy is involved, clients are motivated to tell you it worked. "Dr. Blitznik is a genius!" they will exclaim. "I would *never* have taken that job (or moved to Cincinnati, or found my true love) if it hadn't been for Dr. Blitznik!" Every kind of therapy ever devised produces enthusiastic testimonials from people who feel it saved their lives.

 Thinking Critically about Research on Psychotherapy

The first problem with testimonials is that none of us can be our own control group. How do people know they wouldn't have taken the job, moved to Cincinnati, or found true love anyway—maybe even sooner, if Dr. Blitznik had not kept them in treatment? Second, Dr. Blitznik's success could be due to the placebo effect: The client's anticipation of success and the buzz about Dr. B.'s fabulous new method might be the active ingredients, rather than Dr. B.'s therapy itself. Third, notice that you never hear testimonials from the people who dropped out, who weren't helped, or who actually got worse. So researchers cannot be satisfied with testimonials, no matter how glowing. They know that thanks to the *justification of effort* effect (see Chapter 7), people who have put time, money, and effort into something will tell you it was worth it. No one wants to say, "Yeah, I saw Dr. Blitznik for five years, and boy, was it ever a waste of time."

To guard against these problems, some clinical researchers conduct **randomized controlled trials**, in which people with a given problem or disorder are randomly assigned to one or more treatment groups or to a control group. Sometimes the results of randomized controlled trials have been very surprising, as in the case of a form of therapy called critical incident stress debriefing (CISD). In the aftermath of any disaster, therapists often arrive on the scene to treat survivors for symptoms of

randomized controlled trials Research designed to determine the effectiveness of a new medication or form of therapy, in which people with a given problem or disorder are randomly assigned to one or more treatment groups or to a control group.

A man comforts his father after a devastating earthquake that left thousands homeless. There is a widespread belief that most survivors of any disaster will need the help of therapists to avoid developing posttraumatic stress disorder. What do randomized controlled studies show?

Simulate Ineffective Therapies on **mypsychlab.com**

trauma. In CISD, survivors gather in a group for "debriefing," which generally lasts from one to three hours. Participants are expected to disclose their emotions about the traumatic experience, and the group leader warns members about traumatic symptoms that might develop.

Yet randomized controlled studies with people who have been through terrible experiences—including burns, accidents, miscarriages, violent crimes, and combat—find that posttraumatic interventions can actually *delay* recovery in some people (van Emmerik et al., 2002; McNally, Bryant, & Ehlers, 2003). In one study, victims of serious car accidents were followed for three years; some had received the CISD intervention and some had not. As you can see in Figure 12.2, almost everyone had recovered in only four months and remained fine after three years. The researchers then divided the survivors into two groups: those who had had a highly emotional reaction to the accident at the outset ("high scorers"), and those who had not. For the latter group, the in-

tervention made no difference; they improved quickly.

Now, however, look at what happened to the people who had been the most traumatized by the accident: If they did *not* get CISD, they were fine in four months, too, like everyone else. But for those who *did* get the intervention, CISD actually blocked improvement, and they had higher stress symptoms than all the others in the study even after three years. The researchers concluded that "psychological debriefing is ineffective and has adverse long-term effects. It is not an appropriate treatment for trauma victims" (Mayou, Ehlers, & Hobbs, 2000). The World Health Organization, which deals with survivors of trauma around the world, has officially endorsed this conclusion (van Ommeren, Saxena, & Saraceno, 2005). **Simulate**

You can see, then, why the scientific assessment of psychotherapeutic claims and methods is so important.

When Therapy Helps

We turn now to the evidence showing the benefits of psychotherapy and which therapies work best in general, and for which disorders in particular (e.g., Chambless et al., 1998; Chambless & Ollendick, 2001). For many problems and most emotional disorders, cognitive and behavior therapies have emerged as the method of choice:

- *Depression.* Cognitive therapy's greatest success has been in the treatment of mood disorders, especially depression (Beck, 2005), and people in cognitive therapy are less likely than those on drugs to relapse when the treatment is over. The lessons learned in cognitive therapy last a long time after treatment, according to follow-ups done from 15 months to many years later (Hayes et al., 2004; Hollon, Thase, & Markowitz, 2002; Seligman et al., 1999).

- *Suicide attempts.* In a randomized controlled study of 120 adults who had attempted suicide and had been sent to an emergency room, those who were given ten sessions of cognitive therapy, in comparison to those who were simply given referrals for help, were only about half as likely to attempt suicide again in the next 18 months. They also scored significantly lower on tests of depressive mood and hopelessness (Brown et al., 2005).

- *Anxiety disorders.* Exposure techniques are more effective than any other treatment for posttraumatic stress disorder, agoraphobia, and specific phobias such as fear of dogs or flying. Cognitive-behavior therapy is often more effective than

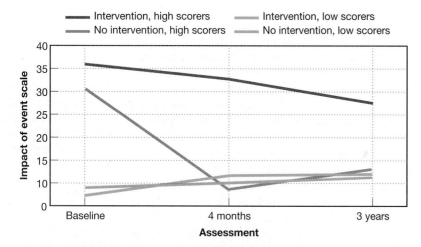

FIGURE 12.2

Do Posttraumatic Interventions Help or Harm?

In this study, victims of serious car accidents were assessed at the time of the event, four months later, and three years later. Half received a form of posttraumatic intervention called critical incident stress debriefing (CISD); half received no treatment. As you can see, almost everyone had recovered within four months, but one group had higher stress symptoms than everyone else even after three years: The people who were the most emotionally distressed right after the accident *and* who received CISD. The therapy actually impeded their recovery (Mayou et al., 2000).

medication for panic disorder, generalized anxiety disorder, and obsessive-compulsive disorder (Barlow, 2004; Dalgleish, 2004; Mitte, 2005).

• *Anger and impulsive violence.* Cognitive therapy is often successful in reducing chronic anger, abusiveness, and hostility, and it also teaches people how to express anger more calmly and constructively (Deffenbacher et al., 2003).

• *Health problems.* Cognitive and behavior therapies are highly successful in helping people cope with pain, chronic fatigue syndrome, headaches, and irritable bowel syndrome; quit smoking or overcome other addictions; recover from eating disorders such as bulimia and binge eating; overcome insomnia and improve their sleeping patterns; and manage other health problems (Butler et al., 1991; Crits-Christoph, Wilson, & Hollon, 2005; Skinner et al., 1990; Stepanski & Perlis, 2000; Wilson & Fairburn, 1993).

• *Child and adolescent behavior problems.* Behavior therapy is the most effective treatment for behavior problems that range from bed-wetting to impulsive anger, and even for problems that have biological origins, such as autism. A meta-analysis of more than 100 studies of children and adolescents found that behavioral treatments worked better than others regardless of the child's age, the therapist's experience, or the specific problem (Weisz et al., 1995).

• *Relapses.* Cognitive-behavioral approaches have also been highly effective in reducing the rate of relapse among people with problems such as substance abuse, depression, sexual offending, and even schizophrenia (Hayes et al., 2004; Witkiewitz & Marlatt, 2004).

However, no single type of therapy can help everyone. In spite of their many successes, behavior and cognitive therapies have had failures, especially with people who are unmotivated to carry out a behavioral or cognitive program. Also, cognitive-behavior therapies are designed for specific, identifiable problems, but sometimes people seek therapy for less clearly defined reasons, such as wishing to introspect about their feelings or explore moral issues.

Special Problems and Populations There is also no simple rule for how long therapy needs to last. Sometimes a single session of treatment is enough to bring improvement, if it is based on sound psychotherapeutic principles. A therapy called *motivational interviewing*, which focuses on increasing a client's motivation to overcome problems such as drinking, smoking, and binge eating,

has been shown to be effective in as few as one or two sessions (Burke et al., 2003; Cassin et al., 2008; Miller & Rollnick, 2002). The therapist, essentially, puts the client into a state of cognitive dissonance (see Chapter 7): "I want to be healthy and I see myself as a smart, competent person, but here I am doing something stupid and self-defeating. Do I want to feel better or not?"—and then offers the client a cognitive and behavioral strategy of improvement (Wagner & Ingersoll, 2008). Complex mental problems and personality disorders, however, are particularly difficult to treat and may respond better to long-term psychodynamic therapy than to short-term therapies (Leichsenring & Rabung, 2008; Shedler, 2010).

Further, some problems require combined approaches. Young adults with bipolar disorder or schizophrenia are best helped by combining medication with family intervention therapies that teach parents behavioral skills for dealing with their troubled children, and that educate the family about how to cope with the illness constructively (Chambless et al., 1998; Goldstein & Miklowitz, 1995; Miklowitz, 2007).

An important community intervention called *multisystemic therapy* (MST) has been highly successful in reducing teenage violence, criminal activity, drug abuse, and school problems in troubled inner-city communities. Its practitioners combine family-systems techniques with behavioral methods, but apply them in the context of forming "neighborhood partnerships" with local leaders, residents, parents, and teachers (Henggeler et al., 1998; Swenson et al., 2005). The premise of multisystemic therapy is that because aggressiveness and drug abuse are often reinforced or caused by the adolescent's family, classroom, peers, and local culture, you can't successfully treat the adolescent without also treating his or her environment. Indeed, MST has been shown to be more effective than other methods on their own (Schaeffer & Borduin, 2005).

Cognitive-behavior therapy can help people who are grumpy, bashful, and even a little dopey—as well as people who have more serious problems.

THE SEVEN DWARFS AFTER THERAPY

When Therapy Harms

In a tragic case that made news around the world, two social workers were convicted of recklessly causing the death of 10-year-old Candace Newmaker during a session of "rebirthing" therapy, which is supposed to help adopted children form attachments to their adoptive parents by "reliving" birth. Candace was wrapped in a blanket that supposedly simulated the womb and covered with large pillows. The therapists then pressed in on the pillows to simulate contractions and told the girl to push her way out of the blanket over her head. Candace repeatedly said that she could not breathe and felt she was going to die. Instead of unwrapping her, the therapists said, "You've got to push hard if you want to be born—or do you want to stay in there and die?" Candace lost consciousness and was rushed to a local hospital, where she died the next day.

Candace's tragic story is rare, but every treatment, including aspirin, carries some risks, and that includes psychotherapy. In a small percentage of cases, a person's symptoms may actually worsen as a result of the therapy, new symptoms may be created, the client may become too dependent on the therapist, or the client's outside relationships may deteriorate (Dimidjian & Hollon, 2010; Lilienfeld, 2007). The risks to clients increase when any of the following occurs:

Thinking Critically about the Risks of Psychotherapy

1 **The use of empirically unsupported, potentially dangerous techniques.** Rebirthing therapy was born (so to speak) in the 1970s, when its founder claimed that, while taking a bath, he had reexperienced his own traumatic birth. But the basic assumptions of this method—that people can recover from trauma, insecure attachment, or other psychological problems by "reliving" their emergence from the womb—are contradicted by the vast research on infancy, attachment, memory, and post-traumatic stress disorder and its treatment.

Rebirthing is one of a variety of practices, collectively referred to as "attachment therapy" (AT), that are based on the use of harsh tactics that allegedly will help children bond with their parents. These techniques include withholding food, isolating the children for extended periods, humiliating them, pressing great weights upon them, and requiring them to exercise to exhaustion (Mercer, Sarner, & Rosa, 2003). However, as we discuss in Chapter 9, abusive punishments are ineffective in treating behavior problems and often backfire, making the child angry, resentful, and withdrawn. They are hardly a way to help an adopted or emotionally troubled child feel more attached to his or her parents. And, tragically, more than 75 children and teenagers have died as a result of being in one form or another of AT.

Table 12.3 lists a number of therapies that have been shown, through randomized controlled trials or meta-analysis, to have a significant risk of harming clients.

2 **Inappropriate or coercive influence that creates new symptoms.** In a healthy therapeutic alliance, therapist and client come to agree on an explanation for the client's problems. Of course, the therapist will influence this explanation, according to his or her training and philosophy. Some therapists,

---

TABLE 12.3
Potentially Harmful Therapies

Intervention	Potential harm
Critical incident stress debriefing	Heightened risk of PTSD
Scared Straight interventions	Worsening of conduct problems
Facilitated communication	False allegations of sexual and child abuse
Attachment therapies	Death and serious injury to children
Recovered-memory techniques (e.g., dream analysis)	Induction of false memories of trauma, family breakups
"Multiple personality disorder"-oriented therapy	Induction of "multiple" personalities
Grief counseling for people with normal bereavement reactions	Increased depressive symptoms
Expressive-experiential therapies	Worsening and prolonging painful emotions
Boot-camp interventions for conduct disorder	Worsening of aggression and conduct problems
DARE (drug abuse and resistance education)	Increased use of alcohol and other drugs

Source: Lilienfeld (2007).

however, so zealously believe in the prevalence of certain disorders that they actually induce the client to produce the symptoms they are looking for (McHugh, 2008; Mazzoni, Loftus, & Kirsch, 2001; McNally, 2003; Watters & Ofshe, 1999). Therapist influence, and sometimes downright coercion, is a likely reason for the huge numbers of people who were diagnosed with multiple personality disorder in the 1980s and 1990s (see Chapter 11) and for an epidemic of alleged memories of sexual abuse during this period (see Chapter 8).

3 **Prejudice or cultural ignorance on the part of the therapist.** Some therapists may be prejudiced against some clients because of the client's gender, culture, religion, or sexual orientation. They may be unaware of their prejudices, yet express them in nonverbal ways that make the client feel ignored, disrespected, and devalued (Sue et al., 2007). A therapist may also try to induce a client to conform to the therapist's standards and values, even if they are not appropriate for the client or in the client's best interest.

For example, for many years, gay men and lesbians who entered therapy were told that homosexuality was a mental illness that could be cured. Some of the so-called treatments were harsh, such as electric shock for "inappropriate" arousal.

Although these methods were discredited decades ago (Davison, 1976), other "reparative" therapies (whose practitioners claim they can turn gay men and lesbians into heterosexuals) still surface from time to time. But there is no reliable empirical evidence supporting these claims, and both the American Psychological Association and the American Psychiatric Association oppose reparative therapies on ethical and scientific grounds.

4 **Sexual intimacies or other unethical behavior on the part of the therapist.** The ethical guidelines of both APAs prohibit therapists from having any sexual intimacies with their clients or violating other professional boundaries. Occasionally, some therapists behave like cult leaders, persuading their clients that their mental health depends on staying in therapy and severing their connections to their "toxic" families (Watters & Ofshe, 1999). Such psychotherapy cults are created by the therapist's use of techniques that foster the client's isolation, prevent the client from terminating therapy, and reduce the client's ability to think critically (see Chapter 10).

To avoid these risks and benefit from what effective psychotherapy has to offer, people looking for the right therapy must become educated consumers, willing to use the critical-thinking skills we have emphasized throughout this book.

✓• **Study** and **Review** on **mypsychlab.com**

Quick Quiz

Find out whether you are an educated consumer of quizzes.

1. Which of the following is the most important predictor of successful therapy? (a) how long it lasts, (b) the insight it provides the client, (c) the bond between therapist and client, (d) whether the therapist and client are matched according to gender

2. In general, which type of psychotherapy is most effective for anxiety and depression?

3. What are four possible sources of harm in psychotherapy?

4. Ferdie is spending too much time playing softball and not enough time studying, so he signs up for "sportaholic therapy" (ST). The therapist tells him the cure for his "addiction" is to quit softball cold turkey and tap his temples three times whenever he feels the urge to play. After a few months, Ferdie announces that ST isn't helping and he's going to stop coming. The therapist gives him testimonials of clients who swear by ST, adding that Ferdie's doubts are actually a sign that the therapy is working. What is the major scientific flaw in this argument? (Bonus: What kind of therapy might help Ferdie manage his time better?)

Answers:

1. c 2. cognitive-behavior 3. the use of empirically unsupported techniques, inappropriate or coercive influence, the therapist's prejudice or biased treatment, and unethical behavior 4. The therapist has violated the principle of falsifiability (see Chapter 1). If Ferdie is helped by the treatment, that shows it works; if he is not helped, that still shows it works, so Ferdie is simply denying its benefits. Also, Ferdie is not hearing testimonials from people who have dropped out of ST and were not helped by it. (Bonus: A good behavioral time-management program might help, so Ferdie can play softball and get other things done, too.)

Psychology in the News REVISITED

Now that we have reviewed the major kinds of psychotherapy, along with their successes and risks, let's return to the issues raised by the example of "pet therapy" in our opening story. Lt. Col. Kathryn Champion's success with her dog Angel, who helped her out of depression, anxiety, and even PTSD, turns out to be not just a charming anecdote. In a study of nearly 200 people with serious mental illnesses, those with pets were recovering more quickly than those without pets, and the reasons were not simply that pets provide companionship (Wisdom, Saedi, & Green, 2009). They also provide empathy, foster connections with other people, reduce their owners' blood pressure, and often make troubled individuals feel more in control of their lives, as was the case with Kathryn Champion.

Most dog owners would say, "Sure, we knew that!" But research *is* nonetheless important to verify whether pet therapy is effective, and for whom, and why. Many other therapies have been started on the basis of someone's intuitive idea that "Sure, this will work," only to have the therapy's basic premise turn out to be wrong, as in the case of post-crisis interventions, or to be horribly dangerous, as is the case with rebirthing and attachment therapies. Even when pet therapy is helpful, people suffering from serious emotional disorders may also need person-to-person psychotherapy and possibly medication.

How can consumers of psychological services distinguish between techniques that are beneficial and techniques that are useless or potentially harmful? We will offer some suggestions in "Taking Psychology with You," but for now, the research in this chapter suggests three general guidelines:

- **Make sure you are dealing with a reputable individual with appropriate credentials and training**. As we saw in Chapter 1, to become a licensed psychologist, a person must have an advanced degree and a period of supervised training. However, the word *psychotherapist* is unregulated; anyone can set up any kind of program and call it "therapy." In the United States and Canada, people can get credentialed as "experts" in various techniques and therapies simply by attending a weekend seminar or a training program lasting a week or two.

- **Ask whether the therapist practices one of the empirically supported methods described in this chapter,** and whether the basic assumptions of the therapist are likewise validated by empirical research.

- **Be realistic about what you expect of psychotherapy**. In the hands of an empathic and knowledgeable practitioner, psychotherapy can help you make decisions and clarify your values and goals. It can teach you new skills and new ways of thinking. It can help you get along better with your family and break out of destructive family patterns. It can get you through bad times when no one seems to care or to understand what you are feeling. It can teach you how to manage depression, anxiety, and anger.

However, despite its many benefits, psychotherapy cannot transform you into someone you're not. It cannot turn an introvert into an extrovert. It cannot cure an emotional disorder overnight. It cannot provide a life without problems. And it is not intended to substitute for experience—for work that is satisfying, relationships that are sustaining, activities that are enjoyable. As Socrates knew, the unexamined life is not worth living. But as we would add, the unlived life is not worth examining.

Taking Psychology with You

Becoming a Smart Consumer of Psychological Treatments

If you have a persistent problem that you do not know how to solve, one that causes you considerable unhappiness and that has lasted six months or more, it may be time to look for help. To take the lessons of this chapter with you, you might want to consider these suggestions:

Take all ads and Internet promotions for prescription drugs with a large grain of salt: Be skeptical! Remember that ads are not about educating you; they are about selling you a product. "New" is not necessarily better; many "me too" drugs simply tinker with a blockbuster drug's formula in the smallest way, and are then legally (if not medically) entitled to claim it is "new and improved." Consult your pharmacist or the FDA's website, and check out any drug you are about to take. Go to reliable sources that are not funded by the pharmaceutical industry, such as the Public Citizen's Health Research Group's consumer guide, *Worst Pills, Best Pills*.

Make an informed decision when you choose a therapist. To find a reputable individual with appropriate credentials and training, your school counseling center is a good place to start. You might also seek out a university psychology clinic, where you can get therapy with a graduate student in training; these students are closely supervised and the fees will be lower.

Choose a therapy or treatment most likely to help you. As we have seen, not all therapies are equally effective for all problems. You should not spend four years in psychodynamic therapy for panic attacks, which can generally be helped in a few sessions of cognitive-behavior therapy. Likewise, if you have a specific emotional problem, such as depression, anger, or anxiety, or if you are coping with chronic health problems, look for a cognitive or behavior therapist. However, if you mostly want to discuss your life with a wise and empathic counselor, the kind of therapy may not matter so much.

Consider a self-help group. Not all psychological problems require the aid of a professional. In the United States, an estimated 7 to 15 million adults belong to self-help groups (online and in person) for every possible problem—for alcoholics and relatives of alcoholics; people suffering from depression, anorexia, or schizophrenia; women with breast cancer; parents of murdered children; rape victims; relatives of Alzheimer's patients; and people with just about any other concern you can think of. Self-help groups can be reassuring and supportive in ways that family, friends, and psychotherapists sometimes may not be. For example, people with disabilities face unique challenges that involve coping not only with physical problems but also with the condescension and prejudice of many nondisabled people (Linton, 1998).

Nonetheless, keep your critical-thinking skills with you: Self-help groups are not regulated by law or by professional standards, and they vary widely in their philosophies and methods. Some are accepting and tolerant, offering support and spiritual guidance. Others are confrontational and coercive, and members who disagree with the premises of the group may be made to feel deviant, crazy, or "in denial."

Choose self-help books that are scientifically based and promote realistic goals. There is a self-help book available for every problem, from how to toilet train your children to how to find happiness. Critical thinkers can learn how to distinguish good ones from useless ones. To begin with, good self-help books do not promise the impossible. This rules out any that promise massive wealth, perfect love, or high self-esteem in 30 days. (Sorry!) Next, good self-help books are based on evidence and controlled studies. This rules out books that are based on the author's pseudoscientific theories, armchair observations, or personal adventures. People who have survived difficulties can tell inspirational stories, of course, but an author's own experience and vague advice to, say, "find love in your heart" or "take charge of your life" won't go far.

In contrast, when self-help books propose a specific, step-by-step empirically supported program for readers to follow, they can actually be as effective as treatment administered by a therapist, *if* readers follow through with the program (Rosen, Glasgow, & Moore, 2003). One such book is *Changing for Good* (Prochaska, Norcross, & DiClemente, 1994), which describes the ingredients of effective change that apply to people in and out of therapy.

It takes knowledge and critical thinking to know how to tell good therapies from phony ones, and the phony from the fraudulent. As long as people yearn for a magic bullet to cure their problems, quick-fix solutions will find a ready audience.

Summary

((•—[Listen to an **audio file** of your chapter on **mypsychlab.com**

Biological Treatments for Mental Disorders

● Biological treatments for mental disorders are in the ascendance because of research findings on the genetic and biological causes of some disorders and because of economic and social factors. The medications most commonly prescribed for mental disorders include *antipsychotic drugs*, used in treating schizophrenia and other psychotic disorders and, often inappropriately, in treating dementia and aggression disorders; *antidepressants*, used in treating depression, anxiety disorders, and obsessive-compulsive disorder; *tranquilizers*, often prescribed for emotional problems; and *lithium carbonate*, a salt used to treat bipolar disorder.

● Drawbacks of drug treatment include the *placebo effect*; high dropout and relapse rates among people who take medications without also learning how to cope with their problems; the difficulty of finding the correct dose for each individual, compounded by the fact that a person's ethnicity, sex, and age can influence a drug's effectiveness; and the long-term risks of medication and of possible drug interactions when several are being taken.

● The fact that a disorder appears to have biological origins or involve biochemical abnormalities does not mean that biological treatments are the only appropriate ones; psychotherapy can change brain patterns just as medication can.

● Medication can be helpful and can even save lives, but in an age in which commercial interests are heavily invested in promoting drugs for psychological problems, the public is largely unaware of drugs' limitations and potential risks.

● When drugs and psychotherapy have failed to help seriously disturbed people, some psychiatrists have intervened directly in the brain. *Prefrontal lobotomy* never had any scientific validation yet was performed on thousands of people. *Electroconvulsive therapy* (ECT), in which a brief current is sent through the brain, has been used successfully to treat suicidal depression, although its benefits rarely last. *Transcranial magnetic stimulation* (TMS), in which a magnetic coil is applied over the left prefrontal cortex, is being studied as a way of treating severe depression. *Deep brain stimulation* requires the surgical implantation of electrodes and a stimulation device, and has not been empirically validated for the treatment of depression or other emotional disorders.

Major Schools of Psychotherapy

● *Psychodynamic ("depth") therapies* stemmed from Freudian *psychoanalysis*. These therapies explore unconscious dynamics and emotions, childhood experiences, and fantasies, and focus on the process of *transference* to break through the patient's defenses.

● *Behavior therapists* draw on classical and operant principles of learning. Behavior therapists use such methods as *graduated exposure*, and sometimes immediate exposure, called *flooding*; *systematic desensitization*, based on *counterconditioning*; *behavioral self-monitoring*; and *skills training*. Some are applying these methods with virtual reality techniques.

● *Cognitive therapists* aim to change the irrational thoughts involved in negative emotions and self-defeating actions. Aaron Beck's cognitive therapy and Albert Ellis's *rational emotive behavior therapy* (REBT) are two leading approaches. *Cognitive-behavior therapy* (CBT) is now the most common approach. Some cognitive-behavioral therapists now teach clients to pay mindful attention to their negative emotions and "irrational" thoughts and learn to accept them, acting in spite of these feelings rather than constantly fighting to eradicate them.

● *Humanist therapy* holds that human nature is essentially good and attempts to help people feel better about themselves by focusing on here-and-now issues and on their capacity for change. Carl Rogers's *client-centered (nondirective) therapy* emphasizes the importance of the therapist's empathy and ability to provide *unconditional positive regard*. *Existential therapy* helps people cope with the dilemmas of existence, such as the meaning of life and the fear of death.

● *Family therapists* hold the view that individual problems develop in the context of the whole family network. In this *family-systems perspective*, any one person's behavior in the family affects everyone else. In *couples therapy*, a therapist usually sees both partners in a relationship to help them resolve ongoing quarrels and disputes or to help them accept and live with qualities that are unlikely to change.

● In practice, most therapists are *integrative*, drawing on many methods and ideas. They aim to replace a client's pessimistic or unrealistic life story with one that is more hopeful and attainable.

Evaluating Psychotherapy

● Successful therapy requires a *therapeutic alliance* between the therapist and the client, so that they understand each other and can work together. Good therapists are generally empathic and constructive. When therapist and client are of different ethnicities or cultures, the therapist must be able to distinguish normal cultural patterns from signs of mental illness, and both parties must be aware of potential prejudice and misunderstandings.

● A *scientist–practitioner gap* has developed because of the different assumptions that researchers and many clinicians hold regarding the value of empirical research for doing psychotherapy and for assessing its effectiveness. The gap has led to a proliferation of scientifically unsupported psychotherapies.

● In assessing the effectiveness of psychotherapy, researchers need to control for the placebo effect and the *justification of effort* effect. They rely on *randomized controlled trials* to determine which therapies are empirically supported. Such trials have shown that postcrisis debriefing programs are usually ineffective at best and can even slow recovery for some survivors.

● Some psychotherapies are better than others for specific problems. Behavior therapy and cognitive-behavior therapy are often the most effective for depression, anxiety disorders, anger problems, certain health problems (such as pain, insomnia, and eating disorders), and child and adolescent behavior problems. Family-systems therapies, especially when combined with behavioral techniques as in *multisystemic therapy*, are especially helpful for children with behavior problems, young adults with schizophrenia, and aggressive adolescents.

● The length of time needed for successful therapy depends on the problem and the individual. Some methods, such as *motivational interviewing*, have been able to change a client's willingness to begin a program of change in only a session or two; long-term psychodynamic therapy can be helpful for people with severe disorders and personality problems. Some problems and individuals respond best to combined therapeutic approaches.

● In some cases, therapy is harmful. A therapist may use empirically unsupported and potentially harmful techniques; inadvertently create new disorders in the client through undue influence or suggestion; hold a prejudice about the client's gender, ethnicity, religion, or sexual orientation; or behave unethically, for example by permitting a sexual relationship with the client.

Psychology in the News, Revisited

● Animal-assisted therapies are being studied empirically to assess their benefits and limitations, just as all psychotherapies should be. People who are seeking psychotherapy should make sure their psychotherapist is well trained and uses empirically validated methods, and they should have realistic expectations of what psychotherapy can do for them.

Key Terms

antipsychotic drugs (neuroleptics) **406**

antidepressant drugs **406**

monoamine oxidase inhibitors (MAOIs) **406**

tricyclic antidepressants **406**

selective serotonin reuptake inhibitors (SSRIs) **406**

tranquilizers **407**

beta-blockers **407**

lithium carbonate **407**

publication bias **408**

placebo effect **408**

prefrontal lobotomy **410**

electroconvulsive therapy (ECT) **410**

transcranial magnetic stimulation (TMS) **411**

deep brain stimulation (DBS) **411**

psychoanalysis **412**

psychodynamic ("depth") therapies **412**

transference **412**

behavior therapy **413**

graduated exposure **413**

flooding **413**

systematic desensitization **413**

counterconditioning **413**

behavioral self-monitoring **413**

skills training **414**

cognitive therapy **415**

Aaron Beck **415**

Albert Ellis **415**

rational emotive behavior therapy (REBT) **415**

cognitive-behavior therapy (CBT) **416**

humanist therapy **416**

client-centered (nondirective) therapy **416**

Carl Rogers **416**

unconditional positive regard **416**

existential therapy **416**

family therapy **417**

family-systems perspective **417**

couples therapy **417**

integrative approach to psychotherapy **418**

therapeutic alliance **419**

scientist–practitioner gap **421**

justification of effort **421**

randomized controlled trials **421**

motivational interviewing **423**

multisystemic therapy **423**

Biological Treatments for Mental Disorders

Drugs

Drugs commonly prescribed for mental disorders include:
- **Antipsychotics**, used in treating schizophrenia and other psychotic disorders
- **Antidepressants**, used in treating depression, anxiety disorders, and obsessive-compulsive disorder
- **Tranquilizers**, often prescribed for emotional problems
- **Lithium carbonate**, a salt used to treat bipolar disorder

Cautions about Drug Treatments

Drawbacks of drug treatment include:
- The placebo effect
- High dropout and relapse rates
- Disregard for effective nonmedical treatments
- The difficulty of finding the correct dose
- Unknown long-term risks
- Untested off-label uses

Direct Brain Intervention

- **Electroconvulsive therapy (ECT)**, in which a brief current is sent through the brain, has been used successfully to treat suicidal depression, but its effects are short-lived and the depression almost always returns. ECT is ineffective for other disorders.
- *Transcranial magnetic stimulation*, in which a pulsing magnetic coil is held over the left prefrontal cortex, is being used with depression but its effectiveness is still uncertain.

Major Schools of Psychotherapy

Psychodynamic Therapy

Psychodynamic therapies, including Freudian **psychoanalysis** and its modern variations, explore the unconscious through techniques such as **transference**.

Humanist and Existential Therapy

Humanist therapy focuses on the capacity for self-fulfillment and self-actualization.
- Carl Rogers's **client-centered therapy** emphasizes the therapist's role in providing *unconditional positive regard* for the client.

Existential therapy helps people cope with philosophical issues such as the meaning of life.

Behavior and Cognitive Therapy

Behavior therapy applies principles of classical and operant conditioning to help change problematic behaviors. Uses such methods as:
- **Graduated exposure** and **flooding**
- **Systematic desensitization**
- **Behavioral self-monitoring**
- **Skills training**

Cognitive therapy is designed to identify irrational, unproductive ways of thinking to reduce negative emotions and their behavioral consequences. In practice, it is often combined with behavioral methods and thus called *cognitive-behavior therapy* (CBT).
- One leading approach is Albert Ellis's **rational emotive behavior therapy**.
- A current CBT approach is based on mindfulness and acceptance; clients learn to recognize and accept unwanted, unpleasant thoughts and feelings without trying to eliminate them.

Family and Couples Therapies

- Family therapies tend to share a **family-systems perspective,** understanding that one person's behavior affects the whole family.
- Couples therapy is designed to help couples understand and resolve the inevitable conflicts that occur in all relationships.

Evaluating Psychotherapy

The Scientist–Practitioner Gap

A *scientist–practitioner gap* has developed, leading to a proliferation of scientifically un-supported therapies, such as critical incident stress debriefing.

Evaluations of psychotherapy must control for:
• The placebo effect
• Justification of effort
Scientific assessments of therapy rely on **randomized controlled trials**.

• The success of psychotherapy depends on the bond between the therapist and client, called the **therapeutic alliance**.
• Therapists and clients must be alert to cultural differences be-tween them that might cause misunderstandings.

When Therapy Helps

Cognitive-behavior therapy (CBT) is most effective for:
• Depression
• Suicide atttempts
• Anxiety disorders
• Anger problems
• Health problems
• Child and adolescent behavior problems
• Preventing relapse

Combined methods may be necessary to help particular individuals or difficult problems, such as *multisystemic therapy* for troubled, violent adolescents and combined medication and family therapy for people who are bipolar or have schizophrenia.

When Therapy Harms

Psychotherapy can be risky for clients if the therapist:
1. Uses empirically unsupported and potentially harmful techniques
2. Inadvertently creates disorders or new symptoms through suggestion
3. Is prejudiced against a client
4. Is unethical

TABLE 12.2
The Major Schools of Therapy Compared

	Primary Goal	Methods
Psychodynamic	Insight into unconscious motives and feelings that prolong symptoms	Probing unconscious motives and fantasies, exploring childhood experiences, identifying recurring themes in client's life; exploration of issues and emotions raised by transference
Cognitive-Behavioral		
Behavioral	Modification of self-defeating behaviors	Graduated exposure (flooding), systematic desensitization, behav-ioral records, skills training
Cognitive	Modification of irrational or unvalidated beliefs	Prompting the client to test be-liefs against evidence; exposing the faulty reasoning in catastro-phizing and mind reading; some-times helping the client accept and live with unpleasant thoughts and feelings
Humanist and Existential		
Humanist	Insight; self-acceptance and self-fulfillment; new, optimistic perceptions of oneself and the world	Providing a nonjudgmental setting in which to discuss issues; use of empathy and unconditional positive regard by the therapist
Existential	Finding meaning in life and accepting inevitable losses	Varies with the therapist; philo-sophic discussions about the meaning of life, the client's goals, finding the courage to survive suffering and loss
Family and Couples		
Family	Modification of family patterns	May use any of the preceding methods to change family patterns that perpetuate problems and conflicts
Couples	Resolution of conflicts, breaking out of destructive habits	May use any of the preceding methods to help the couple com-municate better, resolve conflicts, or accept differences

Man Crashes Plane Into Austin, Texas, I.R.S. Office

AUSTIN, TX, February 18, 2010. A software engineer who was angry with the Internal Revenue Service launched a suicide attack on the agency Thursday by crashing his small plane into a seven-story office building housing nearly 200 IRS employees, setting off a raging fire that sent workers fleeing for their lives. In addition to the attacker, two employees died in the blaze and two others were seriously burned.

The pilot has been identified as Andrew Joseph (Joe) Stack III, 53, of Austin, who posted a furious, six-page antigovernment farewell note on the Web before getting into his plane for his suicidal flight. Stack cited run-ins with the IRS and ranted about taxes, government bailouts, and corporate America's "thugs and plunderers." "I have had all I can stand," he wrote. "Well, Mr. Big Brother I.R.S. man, let's try something different, take my pound of flesh and sleep well."

Officials almost immediately ruled out the possibility that Stack was connected to terrorist groups. Friends described him as an easygoing man, a talented amateur musician, a husband with marital troubles, and a citizen with a grudge against the tax authorities. Although he was only 53, they said, he felt pushed "over the brink" because financial setbacks had required him to postpone his retirement dreams.

Stack also set fire to his house, which was about six miles from the crash site, before embarking on the suicide flight. His wife and her young daughter had escaped the night before.

Stack married Sheryl Housh about three years ago. He never spoke of his troubles with the IRS to her family, who thought he seemed fine when they gathered at Christmas. But recently his wife complained to her mother and stepfather, Jack Cook, of an increasingly frightening anger in her husband, which she said was causing terrible problems in the marriage. Worried about her husband's rage, Sheryl Stack took her 12-year-old daughter to a hotel to get away from her husband. They returned on Thursday morning to find their house ablaze and all of their belongings destroyed. Officials said the house fire was deliberately set, with Stack as the primary suspect.

"This is a shock to me that he would do something like this," Cook said. "But you get your anger up, you do it."

Fire inspectors assess the damage to the office building destroyed by a man who was angry at the IRS and upset about recent financial setbacks. Two workers died in the blaze.

Emotion, Stress, and Health

Almost everyone can understand Joe Stack's feelings of frustration, unhappiness, and anger, if not about their specific target. Fortunately, most people do not act on them the way Stack did. Why do some people give in to their emotions, whereas others are able to keep rage and other unpleasant feelings from turning into violent or self-destructive actions? Why are some people able to cope with the stresses of life—financial worries, broken expectations, marital conflicts, job loss—whereas others are completely overwhelmed and give up?

People often curse their emotions, wishing to be freed from anger, jealousy, shame, guilt, and grief. Yet imagine a life without emotions. You would be unmoved by the magic of music. You would never care about losing someone you love, not only because you would not know sadness but also because you would not know love. You would never laugh because nothing would strike you as funny. And you would be a social isolate because you would not be able to know what other people were feeling.

People often wish for a life without stress, too. Yet try to imagine a life without any stress whatsoever. You would live like a clam. You might have no difficulties, but nothing would surprise, delight, or challenge you either. You would never change, discover new frontiers, or be required to master skills you never imagined possible.

In this chapter, we will examine the physiology and psychology of emotions and stress. Prolonged negative emotions like anger can certainly be stressful, and stress can certainly produce negative emotions. Both of these processes, however, are shaped by how we interpret the events that happen to us, by the demands of the situation we are in, and by the rules of our culture.

YOU are about to learn...

- which facial expressions of emotion most people recognize the world over.
- which parts of the brain are involved with different aspects of emotion.
- how mirror neurons generate empathy, mood contagion, and synchrony.
- which two hormones provide the energy and excitement of emotion.
- how thoughts create emotions—and why an infant can't feel shame or guilt.

The Nature of Emotion

Emotions evolved to help people meet the challenges of life: They bind people together, motivate them to achieve their goals, and help them make decisions and plans (Nesse & Ellsworth, 2009). When you are faced with a decision between two appealing and justifiable career alternatives, your sense of which one "feels right" emotionally may help you make the better choice. Disgust, which no one enjoys feeling, evolved as a useful mechanism that protects infants and adults from eating tainted or poisonous food (Oaten, Stevenson, & Case, 2009).

Even embarrassment and blushing, so painful to an individual, serve important functions: appeasing others when you feel you have made a fool of yourself, broken a moral rule, or violated a social norm (Dijk, de Jong, & Peters, 2009; Keltner & Anderson, 2000). And the positive emotions of joy, love, laughter, and playfulness do not appear to be simply "selfish" feelings of pleasure; their adaptive function may be to help increase mental flexibility and resilience, build bonds with others, stimulate creativity, and reduce stress (Baas, De Dreu, & Nijstad, 2008; Kok, Catalino, & Frederickson, 2008).

In defining **emotion**, psychologists focus on three major components: *physiological* changes in the face, brain, and body; *cognitive* processes such as interpretations of events; and *cultural* influences that shape the experience and expression of emotion. If we compare human emotions to a tree, the biological capacity for emotion is the trunk and root system; thoughts and explanations create the many branches; and culture is the gardener that shapes the tree and prunes it, cutting off some limbs and cultivating others. Let's begin with the trunk.

Emotion and the Body

Research on the physiological aspects of emotion suggests that people everywhere are born with certain basic or **primary emotions**, which typically include fear, anger, sadness, joy, surprise, disgust, and contempt (Izard, 2007). These emotions have distinctive physiological patterns and corresponding facial expressions, and the situations that evoke them are the same all over the world: Everywhere, sadness follows perception of loss, fear follows perception of threat and bodily harm, anger follows perception of insult or injustice, and so forth (Scherer, 1997). In contrast, **secondary emotions** include all the variations and blends of emotion that vary from one culture to another or that depend on cognitive complexity.

Neuroscientists and other researchers are studying the biological aspects of emotions: facial expressions, brain regions and circuits, and the autonomic nervous system.

The Face of Emotion The most obvious place to look for emotion is on the face, where emotions are often visibly expressed. In 1872, Charles Darwin argued that human facial expressions—the smile, the frown, the grimace, the glare—are as innate as the wing flutter of a frightened bird, the purr of a contented cat, and the snarl of a threatened wolf. Such expressions evolved, he said, because they allowed our forebears to tell at a glance the difference between a friendly stranger and a hostile one.

Modern psychologists have supported Darwin's ideas about the evolutionary functions of emotion (Hess & Thibault, 2009). In particular, Paul Ekman and his colleagues have gathered abundant evidence for the universality of seven basic facial expressions of emotion, which correspond to the list of emotions usually identified as primary: anger, happiness, fear, surprise, disgust, sadness, and contempt (Ekman, 2003; Ekman et al., 1987). In every culture they have studied—in Brazil, Chile, Estonia, Germany, Greece, Hong Kong, Italy, Japan, New Guinea, Scotland, Sumatra, Turkey, and the United States—a large majority of people recognize the emotional expressions portrayed by those in other cultures (see Figure 13.1). Even most members of isolated tribes who have never watched a movie or read *People* magazine, such as the Foré of New Guinea or the Minangkabau of West Sumatra, can recognize the emotions expressed in pictures of people who are entirely foreign to them, and we can recognize theirs.

Lately, some researchers have argued that pride is also a basic human emotion; its adaptive function is to motivate people to achieve and excel, and thereby to increase their attractiveness to others and to their groups (Williams & DeSteno,

---

emotion A state of arousal involving facial and bodily changes, brain activation, cognitive appraisals, subjective feelings, and tendencies toward action.

primary emotions Emotions that are considered to be universal and biologically based.

secondary emotions Emotions that are specific to certain cultures.

FIGURE 13.1
Some Universal Expressions
Can you tell what feelings are being conveyed here? Most people around the world can readily identify expressions of surprise, disgust, happiness, sadness, anger, fear, and contempt, no matter what the age, culture, sex, or historical era of the person conveying the emotion. Some researchers think that pride might also be a universal emotion. Can you find the face of pride in this group?

2009). Children as young as 4 years old, and people from an isolated culture in Africa, can reliably identify facial and bodily expressions of pride. Blind people who have just won an athletic competition will spontaneously throw their arms in the air in a V-for-victory symbol of triumph, though they have never seen anyone do it (Tracy & Robins, 2007, 2008). ◉ Watch

Ekman and his associates developed a special coding system to analyze and identify each of the nearly 80 muscles of the face and the combinations of muscles associated with each emotion (Ekman, 2003). They learned that people generally use different groups of muscles when they are trying to convey a false emotion than when the expression is authentic. Thus, when people try to pretend that they feel sad, only 15 percent manage to get the eyebrows, eyelids, and forehead wrinkle exactly the

way that true grief is expressed spontaneously. Authentic smiles last only two seconds; false smiles may last ten seconds or more (Ekman, Friesen, & O'Sullivan, 1988).

The Functions of Facial Expressions
Interestingly, facial expressions not only reflect our internal feelings; they also *influence* them. In the process of **facial feedback**, the facial muscles send messages to the brain about the basic emotion being expressed: A smile tells us that we're happy, a frown that we're angry or perplexed (Izard, 1990). When people are told to smile and look pleased or happy, their positive feelings increase; when they are told to look angry, displeased, or disgusted, positive feelings decrease (Kleinke, Peterson, & Rutledge, 1998). If you put on an "angry" face, your heart rate will rise faster than if you put on a

◉ **Watch** the **Video Show Your Pride** on mypsychlab.com

facial feedback The process by which the facial muscles send messages to the brain about the basic emotion being expressed.

GREAT MOMS IN HISTORY.

IT WON'T KILL YOU TO SMILE A LITTLE, MONA!

Great moms have always understood the importance of facial feedback.

Simulate Recognizing Facial Expressions of Emotions on **mypsychlab.com**

"happy" face (Levenson, Ekman, & Friesen, 1990). The next time you are feeling sad or afraid, try purposely smiling, even if no one is around. Keep smiling. Does facial feedback work for you?

As Darwin suggested, facial expressions also probably evolved to help us communicate our emotional states to others and provoke a response from them—"Come help me!" "Get away!" (Fridlund, 1994). This signaling function begins in infancy. A baby's expressions of misery, angry frustration, or disgust are apparent to most parents, who respond by soothing an uncomfortable baby, feeding a grumpy one, or removing unappealing food from a disgusted one (Izard, 1994b; Stenberg & Campos, 1990). And an infant's smile of joy usually melts the heart of the weariest parent, provoking a happy cuddle. Babies seem primed to respond to adults' expressions, too. Newborns will suck longer on a pacifier if it produces a happy face than if it produces a face with a neutral or negative expression (Walker-Andrews, 1997). (If you become a parent, remember this.)

Starting at the end of their first year, babies begin to alter their own behavior in reaction to their parents' facial expressions of emotion, and this ability, too, has survival value. Do you recall the "visual cliff" studies described in Chapter 6? These studies were originally designed to test for depth perception, which emerges early in infancy. But in one experiment, 1-year-old babies were put on a more ambiguous visual cliff that did not drop off sharply and thus did not automatically evoke fear, as the original cliff did. In this case, the babies' behavior depended on their mothers' expressions: 74 percent crossed the cliff when their mothers put on a happy, reassuring expression, but not a single infant crossed when the mother showed an expression of fear (Sorce et al., 1985). If you have ever watched a toddler take a tumble and then look at his or her parent before deciding whether to cry or to forget it, you will understand the influence of parental facial expressions. And you can see why they have had such survival value for babies: An infant needs to be able to read the parent's facial signals of alarm or safety because young children do not yet have the experience necessary for judging danger.

However, there are cultural and social limits to the universal readability of facial expressions. For one thing, people are better at identifying emotions expressed by others in their own ethnic, national, or regional group than they are at recognizing the emotions of foreigners (Elfenbein & Ambady, 2003). Second, within a culture, facial expressions can have different meanings depending on the situation; a smile can mean "I'm happy!" or "I don't want to make you angry while I tell you this." Likewise, people will interpret identical facial expressions—even of "basic" emotions such as disgust, sadness, and anger—in very different ways, depending on what else they are observing in the social context (Barrett & Kensinger, 2010). Thus, almost everyone recognizes the facial expression of disgust, if that's all they see. But when they see a picture of the same disgusted expression on a man with his arm raised as if to strike, they will say the expression is anger (Aviezer et al., 2008). **Simulate**

Finally, of course, facial expressions are only part of the emotional picture. People can feel sad, anxious, or angry without letting it show—and, conversely, they can use facial expressions to lie about their feelings. In Shakespeare's play *Henry VI*, the villain who will become the evil King Richard III says:

Why, I can smile, and murder while I smile;
And cry content to that which grieves my heart;
And wet my cheeks with artificial tears,
And frame my face to all occasions.

Emotion and the Brain Various parts of the brain are involved in the different components of emotional experience: recognizing another person's emotion, feeling a specific emotion, expressing an emotion, and acting on an emotion. For example, people who have a stroke that affects brain areas involved in disgust are often unable to feel disgusted. One young man with stroke damage in these regions had little or no emotional response to images and ideas that would be disgusting to most people, such as feces-shaped chocolate (Calder et al., 2000). Are you making a disgusted expression as you read that? He couldn't.

Most emotions motivate a response of some sort: to embrace or approach the person who instills joy in you, attack a person who makes you angry, withdraw from a food that disgusts you, or flee from a person or situation that frightens you. The prefrontal regions of the brain are involved in these impulses to approach or withdraw. Regions of the *right* prefrontal region are specialized for the impulse to withdraw or escape (as in disgust and fear). Regions of the *left* prefrontal cortex are specialized for the motivation to approach others (as in happiness, a positive emotion, and anger, a negative one) (Carver & Harmon-Jones, 2009; Harmon-Jones, Peterson, & Harris, 2009). People who have greater-than-average activation of the left areas, compared with the right, have more positive feelings, a quicker ability to recover from negative emotions, and a greater ability to suppress negative emotions (Urry et al., 2004). People with damage to this area often lose the capacity for joy.

Parts of the prefrontal cortex are also involved in the *regulation* of emotion, helping us modify and control our feelings, keeping us on an even keel, and allowing us to respond appropriately to others (Jackson et al., 2003). When disease or head injury destroys cells in those areas of the frontal lobes, a person may become unable to respond to the emotions of others, understand why they and others feel as they do, and adjust their own emotional responses appropriately: A loving mother becomes indifferent to her child's injury; a businessman does embarrassing things and doesn't notice the reaction of others (Levenson & Miller, 2007).

The *amygdala*, a small structure in the brain's limbic system, plays a key role in emotion, especially anger and fear. The amygdala is responsible for evaluating sensory information, determining its emotional importance, and making the initial decision to approach or withdraw from a person or situation (LeDoux, 1996). The amygdala instantly assesses danger or threat, which is a good thing, because otherwise you could be standing in the street asking, "Is it wise to cross now, while that very large truck is coming toward me?" The amygdala's initial response may then be overridden by a more accurate appraisal from the cortex.

This is why you jump with fear when you suddenly feel a hand on your back in a dark alley, and why your fear evaporates when the cortex registers that the hand belongs to a friend whose lousy idea of humor is to scare you in a dark alley. If either the amygdala or critical areas of the cortex are damaged, abnormalities result in the ability to process fear. People with damage in the amygdala often have difficulty recognizing fear in others, and people with damage in the cortex may have difficulty "turning off" their own fear responses.

Mirror, Mirror, in the Brain: Neurons for Imitation and Empathy Some years ago, a team of Italian neuroscientists made an accidental, astonishing discovery. They had implanted wires in the brains of macaque monkeys, in regions involved in planning and carrying out movement. Every time a monkey moved and grasped an object, the cells fired and the monitor registered the brain activity. Then one day, a graduate student heard the monitor go off when the monkey was simply observing him eating an ice cream cone.

The neuroscientists looked more closely, and found that certain neurons in the monkeys' brains were firing not only when the monkeys were picking up peanuts and eating them but also when the monkeys were merely observing their human caretakers doing exactly the same thing (Ferrari, Rozzi, & Fogassi, 2005). Moreover, these neurons responded only to very specific actions: A neuron that fired when a monkey grasped a peanut would also

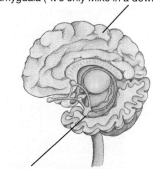

2. The cerebral cortex generates a more complete picture; it can override signals sent by the amygdala ("It's only Mike in a down coat").

1. The amygdala scrutinizes information for its emotional importance ("It's a bear! Be afraid! Run!").

Get Involved! Turn On Your Right Hemisphere

These faces have expressions of happiness on one side and sadness on the other. Look at the nose of each face; which face looks happier? Which face looks sadder?

You are likely to see face *b* as the happier one and face *a* as the sadder one. The likely reason is that in most people the left side of a picture is processed by the right side of the brain, where recognition of emotional expression primarily occurs (Oatley & Jenkins, 1996).

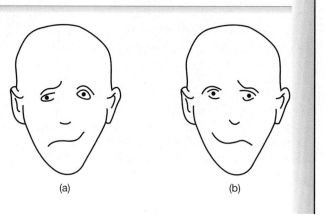

(a)　　　(b)

Mirror neurons are clearly at work in this conversation.

mirror neurons Brain cells that fire when a person or animal observes others carrying out an action; they are involved in empathy, imitation, and reading emotions.

fire when the scientist grasped a peanut but not when the scientist grasped something else. The scientists called these cells **mirror neurons**.

In human beings, mirror neurons enable us to identify with what others are feeling, understand other people's intentions, and imitate their actions and gestures (Iacoboni, 2008; Fogassi & Ferrari, 2007; Molnar-Szakacs et al., 2005). When you see another person in pain, one reason you feel a jolt of empathy is that mirror neurons involved in pain are firing. When you watch a spider crawl up someone's leg, one reason you have a creepy sensation is that your mirror neurons are firing—the same ones that would fire if the spider were crawling up your own leg. And when you see another

person's facial expression, your own facial muscles will often subtly mimic it, activating a similar emotional state (Dimberg, Thunberg, & Elmehed, 2000).

Mirror neurons thus appear to be the underlying mechanism for human empathy, nonverbal rapport, and *mood contagion*, the spreading of an emotion from one person to another. Have you ever been in a cheerful mood, had lunch with a depressed friend, and come away feeling vaguely depressed yourself? Have you ever stopped to have a chat with a friend who was nervous about an upcoming exam and ended up feeling edgy yourself? That's mood contagion at work.

When two people feel rapport with one another's *positive* emotions, nonverbal signals, and posture, however, the more synchronized their gestures become, the more cooperatively they will behave with each other, and the more cheerful they will feel (Wiltermuth & Heath, 2009). This phenomenon may be the reason that synchronized human activities—marches, bands, dancing—are socially and emotionally beneficial. And it means that our friends and neighbors may have more power over our moods than we realize. In a prospective study that followed nearly 5,000 people for 20 years, people who were in a "happy network"—whose partners, siblings, and neighbors living within a mile became happier over time—were more likely to become happier themselves (Fowler & Christakis, 2008). Conversely, those who had lonely friends were more likely to become more lonely themselves over time (Cacioppo, Fowler, & Christakis, 2009).

Talk about "mirror neurons"! These volunteers, videotaped in a study of conversational synchrony, are obviously in sync with each other, even though they have just met. The degree to which two people's gestures and expressions are synchronized affects the rapport they feel with one another. Such synchrony can also create a contagion of moods (Grahe & Bernieri, 1999).

The Energy of Emotion Once the brain areas associated with emotion are activated, the next stage of the emotional relay is the release of hormones to enable you to respond quickly. When you are under stress or feeling an intense emotion, the sympathetic division of the autonomic nervous system spurs the adrenal glands to send out *epinephrine* and *norepinephrine* (see Chapter 4). These chemical messengers produce arousal and alertness. The pupils dilate, widening to allow in more light; the heart beats faster; blood pressure increases; breathing speeds up; and blood sugar rises. These changes provide the body with the energy needed to take action, whether you are happy and want to get close to someone you love, or are scared and want to escape a person who is frightening you (Löw et al., 2008).

Epinephrine in particular provides the energy of an emotion, that familiar tingle of excitement. At high levels, it can create the sensation of being "seized" or "flooded" by an emotion that is out of your control. In a sense, you are out of control, because you cannot consciously alter your heart rate and blood pressure. However, you can learn to control your actions when you are under the sway of an emotion, even intense anger, as we discuss in "Taking Psychology with You." As arousal subsides, anger may pale into annoyance, ecstasy into contentment, fear into suspicion, past emotional whirlwinds into calm breezes.

Although epinephrine and norepinephrine are released during many emotional states, emotions also differ from one another physiologically: Fear, disgust, anger, sadness, surprise, and happiness are associated with different patterns of brain activity and autonomic nervous system activity, as measured by heart rate, electrical conductivity of the skin, and finger temperature (Damasio et al., 2000; Levenson, 1992). These distinctive patterns may explain why people all over the world use similar terms to describe the primary emotions, saying they feel "hot and bothered" when they are angry or "cold and clammy" when they are afraid. These metaphors capture what is going on in their bodies.

In sum, the physiology of emotion involves characteristic facial expressions; activity in specific parts of the brain, notably the amygdala, specialized parts of the prefrontal cortex, and mirror neurons; and sympathetic nervous system activity that prepares the body for action.

Biology and Deception: Can Lies Be Detected in the Brain and Body? For centuries, people have tried to determine when a person is lying by detecting physiological responses that cannot be controlled consciously. This is the idea behind the *polygraph machine* (lie detector), which is based on the assumption that a lie generates emotional arousal. A person who is guilty and fearful of being found out will therefore have increased activity in the autonomic nervous system while responding to incriminating questions: a faster heart rate, increased respiration rate, and increased electrical conductance of the skin.

Thinking Critically about "Lie Detectors"

Law-enforcement officers are still enthusiastic about the polygraph, but most psychological scientists regard polygraph tests as invalid because no physiological patterns of autonomic arousal are specific to lying (Leo, 2008; Lykken, 1998). Machines cannot tell whether you are feeling guilty, angry, nervous, amused, or revved up from an exciting day. Innocent people may be tense and nervous about the whole procedure. They may react to the word *bank*, not because they robbed a bank but because they recently bounced a check; in either case, the machine will record a lie. The reverse mistake is also common: People who are motivated to escape detection can often beat the machine by tensing muscles or thinking about an exciting experience during neutral questions.

The polygraph will correctly catch many liars and guilty people. The main problem is that it also falsely identifies many innocent people as having lied (Saxe, 1994). (See Figure 13.2.) For this reason,

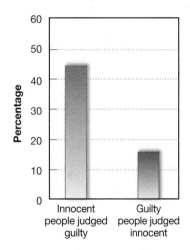

FIGURE 13.2
Misjudging the Innocent
This graph shows the average percentages across three studies of incorrect classifications by lie detectors. Nearly half of the innocent people were classified as guilty, and a significant number of guilty people were classified as innocent. The suspect's guilt or innocence had been independently confirmed by other means, such as confessions of other suspects (Iacono & Lykken, 1997).

"WE CAN'T DETERMINE IF YOU'RE TELLING THE TRUTH, BUT YOU SHOULD HAVE A DOCTOR CHECK YOUR PRESSURE."

about half of the states in the United States have ruled that polygraph results are inadmissible in court. But some government agencies and most police departments continue to use them, not for their accuracy but because they hope to scare people into telling the truth and induce suspects to confess—by telling them that they failed the test (Leo, 2008).

Because of the unreliability of the polygraph, researchers are trying to find other ways of measuring physiological signs of lying. The Computer Voice Stress Analyzer is based on the assumption that the human voice contains telltale signals that betray a speaker's emotional state and intent to deceive. Its promoters claim high degrees of accuracy, but research has yielded negative or inconclusive findings (Leo, 2008). Like the polygraph, the voice analyzer detects physiological changes that may indicate fear, anger, or other signs of stress rather than lying.

The hottest new effort at lie detection is brain imaging. Some researchers are trying to find "brain fingerprints" by using fMRIs of brain activity to see whether they can infer whether a person possesses guilty knowledge of a crime and is lying about it. Two companies are already advertising that they can predict with better than 90 percent certainty if someone is telling the truth (Stix, 2008). Don't buy it. Areas of the brain that light up on an MRI when people are allegedly lying are also those involved with many other cognitive functions, including memory, self-awareness, and self-monitoring (Greely & Illes, 2007). And because of the normal variability among people in their autonomic and brain reactivity, innocent but highly reactive people are still likely to be mislabeled guilty by these tests (Stix, 2008).

To date, efforts to find physiological markers of lying have produced unreliable results because they rest on a faulty assumption: that there are inevitable, universally identifiable biological signs that reveal with high accuracy when a person is lying. We're telling the truth!

Study and **Review** on **mypsychlab.com**

Quick Quiz

We hope that a little surge of hormonal energy will help you answer these questions.

1. Three-year-old Olivia sees her dad dressed as a gorilla and runs away in fear. What brain structure is probably involved in her emotional reaction?

2. Ana Maria is watching an old Laurel and Hardy film, which makes her chuckle and want to see more funny movies. Which side of her prefrontal cortex is likely to be most active?

3. Ana Maria is in a surly, grumpy mood but her friends make her come with them to a hilarious Laurel and Hardy film. She can't help laughing, and soon she finds that her grumpy mood is gone. What physiological mechanism might be the reason?

4. Casey is watching *Horrible Hatchet Homicides in the Haunted House*. What cells in his brain are making him wince when the hero is being attacked?

5. Casey is watching *Horrible Hatchet Homicides in the Haunted House II*. What hormones are causing his heart to pound and his palms to sweat when the murderer is stalking an unsuspecting victim?

Answers:

1. the amygdala 2. the left 3. facial feedback: smiling and laughing communicate to her brain that she is happy 4. mirror neurons 5. epinephrine and norepinephrine

Emotion and the Mind

Two friends of ours returned from a mountain-climbing trip to Nepal. One said, "I was ecstatic! The crystal-clear skies, the millions of stars, the friendly people, the majestic mountains, the harmony of the universe!" The other said, "I was miserable! The bedbugs and fleas, the lack of toilets, the yak-butter tea, the awful food, the unforgiving mountains!" Same trip, two different emotional reactions to it. Why?

In the first century A.D., the Stoic philosophers suggested an answer: People do not become angry or sad or ecstatic because of actual events, but because of their explanations of those events. Modern psychologists have verified the Stoics' ideas experimentally. They have found that emotions are often created or influenced by beliefs, perceptions of the situation, expectations, and *attributions*—the explanations that people make of their own and other people's behavior (see Chapter 10) (Fairholme et al., 2009; Lindquist & Barrett, 2008). Human beings, after all, are the only species that can say, "The more I thought about it, the madder I got." In fact, we often do think ourselves into an emotional state, and sometimes we can think ourselves out of it. ◉─│Watch

Psychologists have studied the role of cognitions in all kinds of emotions, from joy to sadness. Imagine that you get an A on your psychology midterm; how will you feel? Or perhaps you get a D on that midterm; how will you feel then? Most people assume that success brings happiness and failure brings unhappiness, but the emotions you feel will depend more on how you explain your grade than on what you actually get. Do you attribute your grade to your own efforts or to the teacher, fate, or luck? In a series of experiments, students who believed they did well because of their own efforts tended to feel proud, competent, and satisfied. Those who believed they did well because of a lucky fluke tended to feel gratitude, surprise, or guilt ("I don't deserve this"). Those who believed their failures were their own fault tended to feel regretful, guilty, or resigned. And those who blamed others tended to feel angry (Weiner, 1986).

Here is a more surprising example of how thoughts affect emotions. Of two Olympic finalists, one who wins a second-place silver medal and one who wins a third-place bronze medal, who will feel happier? Won't it be the silver medalist? Nope. In a study of athletes' reactions to placing second and third in the 1992 Olympics and the 1994 Empire State Games, the bronze medalists were happier than the silver medalists (Medvec, Madey, & Gilovich, 1995). Apparently, the athletes were comparing their performance to what might have been. The second-place winners, comparing themselves to the gold medalists, were unhappy that they didn't get the gold. But the third-place winners, comparing themselves to those who did worse than they, were happy that they earned a medal at all!

Cognitions and physiology are inextricably linked in the experience of emotion. Thoughts affect emotions, and emotional states influence thoughts (Fairholme et al., 2009). Blaming others for your woes can make you feel angry, but once you are angry you may be more inclined to think the worst of other people's motives. The

Most people assume that second-place winners feel happier about their performance than third-place winners do. Yet when psychologists questioned this assumption, they found that the opposite is true. Certainly, Olympic fencing bronze medalist Jean-Michel Henry of France (left) looks happier than silver medalist Pavel Kolobkov of the Unified Team (right). (Eric Strecki, center, won the gold for France.)

complicated mix of emotions that people feel when they have "disappointing wins" (outcomes that were not as good as they had expected) or "relieving losses" (bad outcomes that could have been worse) shows how powerfully thoughts affect emotional responses.

Some emotions require only minimal, simple cognitions or are primitive feelings that occur beneath awareness (Ruys & Stapel, 2008). A conditioned sentimental response to a patriotic symbol or a warm, fuzzy feeling toward a familiar souvenir involves simple, nonconscious reactions (Izard, 1994a; Murphy, Monahan, & Zajonc, 1995). An infant's primitive emotions do not have much mental sophistication: "Hey, I'm mad because no one is feeding me!" As a child's cerebral cortex matures, however, cognitions become more complex, as do emotions: "Hey, I'm mad because this situation is entirely unfair!" Some emotions depend completely on the maturation of higher cognitive capacities. Shame and guilt, for example, do not occur until a child is 2 or 3 years old. These *self*-conscious emotions require the emergence of a sense of self and the ability to perceive that you have behaved badly or let down another person (Baumeister, Stillwell, & Heatherton, 1994; Tangney et al., 1996).

◉─│Watch the **Video Emotion Regulation: James Coan** on **mypsychlab.com**

Children need to be old enough to have a sense of self before they can feel the moral emotions of shame, guilt, or remorse.

Today, almost all theories of emotion hold that attributions, beliefs, and the meanings people give to events are essential to the creation of most emotions. But where do these attributions, beliefs, and meanings come from? When people decide that it is shameful for a man to dance on a table with a lampshade on his head, or for a woman to walk down a street with her arms and legs uncovered, where do their ideas about shame originate? If you are a person who loudly curses others when you are angry, where did you learn that cursing is acceptable? To answer these questions, we turn to the third major aspect of emotional experience: the role of culture.

Study and
Review on
mypsychlab.com

Quick Quiz

How are your thoughts affecting your feelings about this quiz?

1. Dara and Dinah get Bs on their psychology midterm, but Dara is ecstatic and proud, and Dinah is furious. What expectations and attributions are probably affecting their emotional reactions?

2. At a party, you see a stranger flirting with your date. You are flooded with jealousy. What cognitions might be causing this emotion? *Be specific.* What alternative thoughts might reduce your jealous feelings?

Answers:

1. Dara was probably expecting a lower grade and is attributing her B to her own efforts; Dinah was probably expecting a higher grade and is attributing her B to the instructor's unfairness, bad luck, or other external reasons. 2. Possible thoughts causing jealousy are "My date finds other people more attractive," "That person is trying to steal my date," or "My date's behavior is humiliating me." But you could be thinking, "It's a compliment to me that other people find my date attractive" or "It pleases me that my date is getting such deserved attention."

YOU are about to learn...

- why people from different cultures disagree on what makes them angry, jealous, or disgusted.

- why psychologists debate whether there are primary and secondary emotions.

- how cultural rules affect the way people display or suppress their emotions.

- why people often do "emotion work" to convey emotions they do not feel.

- whether women are really more "emotional" than men.

Emotion and Culture

A young wife leaves her house one morning to draw water from the local well as her husband watches from the porch. On her way back from the well, a male stranger stops her and asks for some water. She gives him a cupful and then invites him home to dinner. He accepts. The husband, wife, and guest have a pleasant meal together. In a gesture of hospitality, the husband invites the guest to spend the night with his wife. The guest accepts. In the morning, the husband leaves early to bring home breakfast. When he returns, he finds his wife again in bed with the visitor.

At what point in this story will the husband feel angry? The answer depends on his culture (Hupka, 1981, 1991). A North American husband would feel rather angry at a wife who had an extramarital affair, and a wife would feel rather angry at being offered to a guest as if she were a lamb chop. But a Pawnee husband of the nineteenth century would be enraged at any man who dared ask his wife for water. An Ammassalik Inuit husband finds it perfectly honorable to offer his wife to a stranger, but only once; he would be angry to find his wife and the guest having a second encounter. And a century ago, a Toda husband in India would not be angry at all because the Todas allowed both husband and wife to take lovers. Both spouses might feel angry though if one of them had a *sneaky* affair, without announcing it publicly.

In most cultures, people feel angry in response to insult and the violation of social rules, but as this story shows, they often disagree about what an insult is or what the correct rule should be. In this section, we will explore how culture influences the emotions we feel and the ways in which we express them.

How Culture Shapes Emotions

Are some emotions specific to particular cultures and not found elsewhere? What does it mean that some languages have words for subtle emotional states that other languages lack? The Germans have *schadenfreude*, a feeling of joy at another's misfortune. The Japanese speak of *hagaii*, helpless anguish tinged with frustration. And Tahitians have *mehameha*, a trembling sensation that Tahitians feel when ordinary categories of perception are suspended—at twilight, in the brush, watching fires glow without heat (Levy, 1984). Do these interesting linguistic differences mean that Germans are more likely than others to actually feel *schadenfreude*, the Japanese to feel *hagaii*, and the Tahitians to feel *mehameha*? Or are they just more willing to give these subtle emotions a single name?

Many psychologists would say that all human beings are capable of feeling the primary, hardwired emotions, the ones that have distinctive physiological hallmarks in the brain, face, and nervous system. But individuals might indeed differ in their abilities to experience secondary emotions, including variations such as *schadenfreude*, *hagaii*, or *mehameha*.

The difference between primary emotions and more complex cultural variations is reflected in language all over the world. In Chapter 7, we noted that a *prototype* is a typical representative of a class of things. People everywhere consider the primary emotions to be prototypical examples of the concept *emotion*: Most people will say that *anger* and *sadness* are more representative of an emotion than *irritability* and *nostalgia* are. Prototypical emotions are reflected in the emotion words that young children learn first: *happy, sad, mad,* and *scared.* As children develop, they begin to draw emotional distinctions that are less prototypical and more specific to their language and culture, such as *ecstatic, depressed, hostile,* or *anxious* (Hupka, Lenton, & Hutchison, 1999; Shaver, Wu, & Schwartz, 1992). In this way, they come to experience the nuances of emotional feeling that their cultures emphasize.

Anger is considered a primary emotion in Western societies. But in some cultures, such as the Inuit, anger is not tolerated because it threatens the community's need for closeness. Inuit mothers like this one often calmly ignore an angry baby, conveying the message that complaining is not welcome. What emotions might be primary to the Inuit?

Other psychologists, however, don't think much of the primary–secondary distinction because, for them, there is *no* aspect of any emotion that is not influenced by culture or context or that even clearly separates one emotion from another (Barrett, 2006; Elfenbein & Ambady, 2003). Anger may be universal, but the way it is experienced will vary from culture to culture—whether it feels good or bad, useful or destructive. Culture even affects which emotions are defined as basic or primary. Anger is regarded as a primary emotion by Western psychologists, but in Asian cultures shame and loss of face are more central emotions (Kitayama & Markus, 1994). And on the Micronesian atoll of Ifaluk, everyone would say that *fago* is the most fundamental emotion. *Fago,* translated as "compassion/love/sadness," reflects the sad feeling one has when a loved one is absent or in need, and the pleasurable sense of compassion in being able to care and help (Lutz, 1988).

> Thinking Critically about "Basic" Emotions

Everyone agrees, however, that cultures determine much of what people feel emotional *about.* For example, disgust is universal, but the content of what produces disgust changes as an infant matures, and it varies across cultures (Rozin, Lowery, & Ebert, 1994). People in some cultures learn to become disgusted by bugs (which other people find beautiful or tasty), unfamiliar sexual practices, dirt, death, "contamination" by a handshake with a stranger, or particular foods (e.g., meat, if they are vegetarian; pork, if they are Muslims or Orthodox Jews).

Communicating Emotions

Suppose that someone who was dear to you died. Would you cry, and if so, would you do it alone or in public? Your answer will depend in part on your

Around the world, the cultural rules for expressing emotions differ. The display rule for a formal Japanese wedding portrait is "no direct expressions of emotion," but not every member of this family has learned that rule yet.

display rules Social and cultural rules that regulate when, how, and where a person may express (or suppress) emotions.

emotion work Expression of an emotion, often because of a role requirement, that a person does not really feel.

culture's **display rules** for emotion (Ekman et al., 1987; Gross, 1998). In some cultures, grief is expressed by weeping; in others, by tearless resignation; and in still others by dance, drink, and song. Once you feel an emotion, how you express it is rarely a matter of "I say what I feel." You may be obliged to disguise what you feel. You may wish you could feel what you say.

Even the smile, which seems a straightforward signal of friendliness, has many meanings and uses that are not universal. Americans smile more frequently than Germans, not because Americans are inherently friendlier but because they differ in their notions of when a smile is appropriate. After a German–American business meeting, the Americans often complain that the Germans were cold and aloof, and the Germans often complain that the Americans were excessively cheerful, hiding their real feelings under the mask of a smile (Hall & Hall, 1990). The Japanese smile even more than Americans do, to disguise embarrassment, anger, or other negative emotions whose public display is considered rude and incorrect.

Display rules also govern *body language*, nonverbal signals of body movement, posture, gesture, and gaze (Birdwhistell, 1970). Many aspects of body language are specific to particular languages and cultures, which makes even the simplest gesture subject to misunderstanding and offense. The

sign of the University of Texas football team, the Longhorns, is to extend the index finger and the pinkie. In Italy and other parts of Europe, it means you're saying a man's wife has been unfaithful to him—a serious insult.

Display rules tell us not only what to do when we are feeling an emotion, but also how and when to show an emotion we do not feel. Most people are expected to demonstrate sadness at funerals, happiness at weddings, and affection toward relatives. What if we don't actually feel sad, happy, or affectionate? Acting out an emotion we do not really feel because we believe it is socially appropriate is called **emotion work**. It is part of our efforts to regulate our emotions when we are with others (Gross, 1998). Sometimes emotion work is a job requirement. Flight attendants, waiters, and customer-service representatives must put on a happy face to convey cheerfulness, even if they are privately angry about a rude or drunken customer. Bill collectors must put on a stern face to convey threat, even if they feel sorry for the person they are collecting money from (Hochschild, 2003).

Gender and Emotion

"Women are too emotional," men often complain. "Men are too uptight," women often reply. This is a familiar gender stereotype. But what does "too emotional" mean? We need to define our terms and examine our assumptions. And we need to consider the larger culture in which men and women live, which shapes the rules and norms that govern how the sexes are supposed to behave.

> **Thinking Critically about Gender Stereotypes and Emotion**

Although women are more likely than men to suffer from clinical depression (see Chapter 11), there is little evidence that one sex feels any of the everyday emotions more often than the other, whether the emotion is anger, worry, embarrassment, anxiety, jealousy, love, or grief (Archer, 2004; Deffenbacher et al., 2003; Fischer et al., 1993; Harris, 2003; Kring & Gordon, 1998; Shields, 2005). The major difference between the sexes has less to do with whether they feel emotions than with how and when their emotions are expressed, and how they are perceived by others.

Consider anger. In Western cultures, both sexes unconsciously associate "angry" with male and "happy" with female. When researchers showed students a series of computer-generated, fairly sex-neutral faces with a range of expressions morphing from angry to happy, the students consistently rated the angry faces as being masculine and the happy faces as feminine (Becker et al., 2007). This stereotyped link between gender and emotion may explain why a man who expresses anger in a professional context is considered "high status," but a professional woman who does exactly the same thing loses status. She is considered to be an angry person, someone "out of control" (Brescoll & Uhlmann, 2008). Powerful women thus often face a dilemma: express anger when a subordinate or adversary has done something illegal or incompetent (and risk being thought "overemotional") or behave calmly (and risk being seen as "cold and unemotional").

Conversely, women who don't smile when others expect them to are often disliked, even if they are actually smiling as often as men would. This may be why North American women, on average, smile more than men do, gaze at their listeners more, have more emotionally expressive faces, use more expressive hand and body movements, and touch others more (DePaulo, 1992; Kring & Gordon, 1998). Women smile more than men to pacify others, convey deference to someone of higher status, or smooth over conflicts (Hess, Adams, & Kleck, 2005; Shields, 2005).

Women also talk about their emotions more than men do. They are far more likely to cry and to acknowledge emotions that reveal vulnerability and weakness, such as "hurt feelings," fear, sadness, loneliness, shame, and guilt (Grossman & Wood, 1993; Timmers, Fischer, & Manstead, 1998). In contrast, most North American men express only one emotion more freely than women: anger toward strangers, especially other men. Otherwise, men are expected to control and mask negative feelings. When they are worried or afraid, they are more likely than women to use vague terms, saying that they feel moody, frustrated, or on edge (Fehr et al., 1999).

However, the influence of a particular situation often overrides gender rules (LaFrance, Hecht, & Paluck, 2003). You won't find many gender differences in emotional expressiveness at a football game or the World Series! Another important situational constraint on emotional expression is the status of the participants (Snodgrass, 1992). A man is as likely as a woman to control his temper when the target of anger is someone with higher status or power; few people will readily sound off at a professor, police officer, or employer. And the sexes do similar emotion work when the situation or job requires it. A male flight attendant has to smile with passengers as much as a female attendant does, and a female FBI agent has to be as emotionally strong and controlled as a male agent does.

Even where gender differences exist, they are not universal. Italian, French, Spanish, and Middle Eastern men and women can have entire conversations using highly expressive hand gestures and facial expressions. In contrast, in Asian cultures, both sexes are taught to control emotional expression (Matsumoto, 1996; Mesquita & Frijda, 1992). Israeli and Italian men are more likely than women to mask feelings of sadness, but British, Spanish, Swiss, and German men are *less* likely than their female counterparts to inhibit this emotion (Wallbott, Ricci-Bitti, & Bänninger-Huber, 1986).

In sum, the answer to "Which sex is more emotional?" is: sometimes men, sometimes women, and sometimes neither, depending on the circumstances and their culture.

Both sexes feel emotionally attached to friends, but often they express their affections differently. From childhood on, girls tend to prefer "face-to-face" friendships based on shared feelings; boys tend to prefer "side-by-side" friendships based on shared activities.

Study and
Review on
mypsychlab.com

Quick Quiz

Please do not display anger if you miss a question.

1. In Western theories of emotion, anger would be called a _____ emotion, whereas *fago* would be called a _____ emotion.

2. Maureen is working in a fast-food restaurant and is becoming irritated with a customer who isn't ordering fast enough. She is supposed to be pleasant to all customers, but instead she snaps, "Hey, whaddaya want to order, slowpoke?" To keep her job and her temper, Maureen needs practice in _____.

3. In a class discussion, a student says something that embarrasses a student from another culture. The second student smiles to disguise his discomfort; the first student, thinking he is not being taken seriously, gets angry. This misunderstanding reflects the students' different _____ for the expression of embarrassment and anger.

4. *True or false:* Throughout the world, women are more emotionally expressive than men.

Answers:

1. primary, secondary   2. emotion work   3. display rules   4. false

◆◆ **YOU** are about to learn...

- how your body responds to physical, emotional, and environmental stressors.

- why being "stressed out" increases the risk of illness in some people but not others.

- how psychological factors affect the immune system.

- when having a sense of control over events is beneficial and when it is not.

The Nature of Stress

The emotion "tree," as we have seen, can take many shapes, depending on physiology, cognitive processes, and cultural rules. These same three factors can help us understand those difficult situations in which negative emotions become chronically stressful, and in which chronic stress can create negative emotions.

When people say they are under stress, they mean all sorts of things: having recurring conflicts with a parent, feeling frustrated about their lives, fighting with a partner, feeling overwhelmed with caring for a sick child or keeping up with work obligations, or having just lost a job. Are these stressors linked to illness—to migraines, stomachaches, flu, or more life-threatening diseases such as cancer? And do they affect everyone in the same way?

Stress and the Body

The modern era of stress research began in 1956, when physician Hans Selye published *The Stress of*

general adaptation syndrome According to Hans Selye, a series of physiological reactions to stress occurring in three phases: alarm, resistance, and exhaustion.

Life. Environmental stressors such as heat, cold, toxins, and danger, Selye wrote, disrupt the body's equilibrium. The body then mobilizes its resources to fight off these stressors and restore normal functioning. Selye described the body's response to stressors of all kinds as a **general adaptation syndrome**, a set of physiological reactions that occur in three phases:

1 **The alarm phase,** in which the body mobilizes the sympathetic nervous system to meet the immediate threat. The threat could be anything from taking a test you haven't studied for to running from a rabid dog. As we saw earlier, the release of adrenal hormones, epinephrine and norepinephrine, occurs with any intense emotion. It boosts energy, tenses muscles, reduces sensitivity to pain, shuts down digestion (so that blood will flow more efficiently to the brain, muscles, and skin), and increases blood pressure. Decades before Selye, psychologist Walter Cannon (1929) described these changes as the "fight or flight" response, a phrase still in use.

Stress hormones elevated → Blood flow increases / Heart rate speeds up / Digestion slows / Muscles tense

2 **The resistance phase,** in which your body attempts to resist or cope with a stressor that cannot be avoided. During this phase, the physiological responses of the alarm phase continue, but these very responses make the body more vulnerable to other stressors. That is why, when your body has mobilized to deal with a heat wave or pain from a broken leg, you may find you are more easily annoyed by minor frustrations. In most cases, the body will eventually adapt to the stressor and return to normal.

3 **The exhaustion phase**, in which persistent stress depletes the body of energy, thereby increasing vulnerability to physical problems and illness. The same reactions that allow the body to respond effectively in the alarm and resistance phases are unhealthy as long-range responses. Tense muscles can cause headache and neck pain. Increased blood pressure can become chronic hypertension. If normal digestive processes are interrupted or shut down for too long, digestive disorders may result.

Selye did not believe that people should aim for a stress-free life. Some stress, he said, is positive and productive, even if it also requires the body to produce short-term energy: competing in an athletic event, falling in love, working hard on a project you enjoy. And some negative stress is simply unavoidable; it's called life!

Current Approaches One of Selye's most important observations was that the very biological changes that are adaptive in the short run, because they permit the body to respond quickly to danger, can become hazardous in the long run (McEwen, 1998, 2007). Modern researchers are learning exactly how this happens.

When you are under stress, your brain's hypothalamus sends messages to the endocrine glands along two major pathways. One, as Selye observed, activates the sympathetic division of the autonomic nervous system for "fight or flight," producing the release of epinephrine and norepinephrine from

Most people think stress is something "out there" that just happens to them. However, there is another way of looking at stress: as something in you, something that depends on your thoughts and emotions. Do you see your work as an endless set of assignments you will never complete or as challenging tasks to master? The answer will affect how stressed you are.

the inner part (medulla) of the adrenal glands. In addition, the hypothalamus initiates activity along the **HPA axis** (HPA stands for hypothalamus–pituitary–adrenal cortex): The hypothalamus releases chemical messengers that communicate with the pituitary gland, which in turn sends messages to the outer part (cortex) of the adrenal glands. The adrenal cortex secretes *cortisol* and other hormones that elevate blood sugar and protect the body's tissues from inflammation in case of injury.

One result of HPA axis activation is increased energy, which is crucial for short-term responses to stress (Kemeny, 2003). But if cortisol and other stress hormones stay high too long, they can lead to hypertension, immune disorders, other physical ailments, and possibly emotional problems. Elevated

HPA (hypothalamus–pituitary–adrenal cortex) axis A system activated to energize the body to respond to stressors. The hypothalamus sends chemical messengers to the pituitary, which in turn prompts the adrenal cortex to produce cortisol and other hormones.

Alas, the same stress hormones that help in the short run can have unwanted long-term consequences.

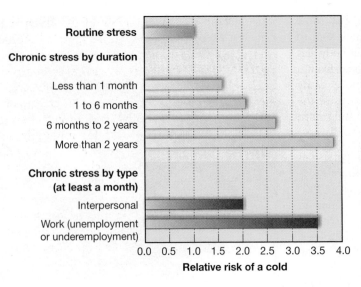

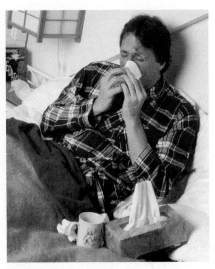

FIGURE 13.3

Stress and the Common Cold

Chronic stress lasting a month or more boosts the risk of catching a cold. The risk is increased among people undergoing problems with their friends or loved ones; it is highest among people who are out of work (Based on data from Cohen et al., 1998).

levels of cortisol also motivate animals (and presumably humans, too) to seek out rich comfort foods and store the extra calories as abdominal fat.

An understanding of the cumulative effects of external sources of stress may partly explain why people at the lower rungs of the socioeconomic ladder have worse health and higher mortality rates for almost every disease and medical condition than do those at the top (Adler & Snibbe, 2003). In addition to their lack of access to good medical care and frequent reliance on diets that lead to obesity and diabetes, low-income people often live with continuous environmental stressors—higher crime rates, discrimination, fewer community services, rundown housing, and greater exposure to hazards such as chemical contamination (Gallo & Matthews, 2003). These conditions affect urban blacks disproportionately and may help account for their higher incidence of hypertension (high blood pressure), which can lead to kidney disease, strokes, and heart attacks (Clark et al., 1999).

Children are particularly vulnerable to the stressors associated with poverty: The more years they are exposed to family disruption, chaos, and instability, the higher their cortisol levels and the greater the snowballing negative effect on their physical health, mental health, and cognitive abilities (such as memory) in adolescence and adulthood (Chen, Cohen, & Miller, 2010; Evans & Kim, 2007; Evans & Schamberg, 2009).

Because work is central in most people's lives, the effects of persistent unemployment can threaten health for people at all income levels, even

psychoneuroimmunology (PNI) The study of the relationships among psychology, the nervous and endocrine systems, and the immune system.

increasing their vulnerability to the common cold. In one study, heroic volunteers were given either ordinary nose drops or nose drops containing a cold virus, and then were quarantined for five days. The people most likely to get a cold's miserable symptoms were those who had been underemployed or unemployed for at least a month. As you can see in Figure 13.3, the longer the work problems lasted, the greater the likelihood of illness (Cohen et al., 1998).

Nonetheless, the physiological changes caused by stress do not occur to the same extent in everyone. People's responses to stress vary according to their learning history, gender, preexisting medical conditions, and genetic predisposition for high blood pressure, heart disease, obesity, diabetes, or other health problems (Belsky & Pluess, 2009b; McEwen, 2000, 2007; Røysamb et al., 2003). This is why some people respond to the same stressor with much greater increases in blood pressure, heart rate, and hormone levels than other individuals do, and their physical changes take longer to return to normal. These hyperresponsive individuals may be the ones most at risk for eventual illness.

The Immune System: PNI Researchers in the growing field of *health psychology* (and its medical relative, behavioral medicine) investigate all aspects of how mind and body affect each other to preserve wellness or cause illness. Some have formed an interdisciplinary specialty with the cumbersome name **psychoneuroimmunology**, or **PNI** for short. The "psycho" part stands for psychological

The immune system consists of fighter cells that look more fantastical than any alien creature Hollywood could design. This one is about to engulf and destroy a cigarette-shaped parasite that causes a tropical disease.

processes such as emotions and perceptions; "neuro" for the nervous and endocrine systems; and "immunology" for the immune system, which enables the body to fight disease and infection.

PNI researchers are especially interested in the white blood cells of the immune system, which are designed to recognize foreign or harmful substances (*antigens*), such as flu viruses and bacteria, and then destroy or deactivate them. The immune system deploys different kinds of white blood cells as weapons, depending on the nature of the enemy. Natural killer cells are important in tumor detection and rejection, and are involved in protection against the spread of cancer cells and viruses. Helper T cells enhance and regulate the immune response; they are the primary target of the HIV virus that causes AIDS. Chemicals produced by the immune cells are sent to the brain, and the brain in turn sends chemical signals to stimulate or restrain the immune system. Anything that disrupts this communication loop, whether drugs, surgery, or chronic stress, can weaken or suppress the immune system (Segerstrom & Miller, 2004).

Some PNI researchers have gotten right down to the level of cell damage to see how stress can lead to illness, aging, and even premature death. At the end of every chromosome is a protein complex called a *telomere* that, in essence, tells the cell how long it has to live. Every time a cell divides, en-

zymes whittle away a tiny piece of the telomere; when it is reduced to almost nothing, the cell stops dividing and dies. Chronic stress, especially if it begins in childhood, appears to shorten the telomeres (Epel, 2009). One team of researchers compared two groups of healthy women between the ages of 20 and 50: 19 who had healthy children and 39 who were primary caregivers of a child chronically ill with a serious disease, such as cerebral palsy. Of course, the mothers of the sick children felt that they were under stress, but they also had significantly greater cell damage than did the mothers of healthy children. In fact, the cells of the highly stressed women looked like those of women at least ten years older, and their telomeres were much shorter (Epel et al., 2004). ⊙► Simulate

⊙► **Simulate Stress and Health** on **mypsychlab.com**

Stress and the Mind

Before you try to persuade your instructors that the stress of constant studying is bad for your health, consider this mystery: The large majority of individuals who are living with stressors, even serious ones such as loss of a job or the death of a loved one, do not get sick (Bonanno, 2004; Taylor, Repetti, & Seeman, 1997). What protects them?

Optimism and Pessimism When something bad happens to you, what is your first reaction? Do you tell yourself that you will somehow come through it okay, or do you gloomily mutter, "More proof that if something can go wrong for me, it will"? In a fundamental way, optimism—the general expectation that things will go well in spite of occasional setbacks—makes life possible. If people are in a jam but believe things will get better

CartoonStock Ltd. CSL

locus of control A general expectation about whether the results of your actions are under your own control (internal locus) or beyond your control (external locus).

eventually, they will keep striving to make that prediction come true. Even despondent fans of the Chicago Cubs, who have not won the World Series in living memory, maintain a lunatic optimism that "there's always next year."

In general, optimism is better for your health and well-being than pessimism is (Carver & Scheier, 2002; Geers, Wellman, & Lassiter, 2009). This does not mean that an optimistic outlook will always prolong the life of a person who already has a serious illness: A team of Australian researchers who followed 179 patients with lung cancer over a period of eight years found that optimism made no difference in who lived or in how long they lived (Schofield et al., 2004). But optimism does seem to produce good health and even improved immune function in people without life-threatening illnesses, whereas the "catastrophizing" style of pessimists is associated with untimely death (Maruta et al., 2000; Peterson et al., 1998; Segerstrom & Sephton, 2010).

One reason is that optimists simply take better care of themselves. They do not deny their problems or avoid facing bad news; rather, they regard the problems and bad news as difficulties they can overcome. They are more likely than pessimists to be active problem solvers, get support from friends, and seek information that can help them (Brissette, Scheier, & Carver, 2002; Chang, 1998; Geers, Wellman, & Lassiter, 2009). They keep their senses of humor, plan for the future, and reinterpret the situation in a positive light. Pessimists, in contrast, often do self-destructive things: They drink too much, smoke, fail to wear seat belts, drive too fast, and refuse to take medication for illness (Peterson et al., 1998).

Pessimists naturally accuse optimists of being unrealistic, and often that is true. Yet health and well-being often depend on having some "positive illusions" about yourself, your abilities, and your circumstances (Taylor et al., 2000a). Can pessimists be cured of their gloomy outlook? Optimists think so! One way is by teaching pessimists to follow the oldest advice in the world: to count their blessings instead of their burdens. Even among people with serious illnesses, such as a neuromuscular disease, a focus on the positive aspects of life increases well-being and reduces the number of physical symptoms they report (Emmons & McCullough, 2003).

A Sense of Control Optimism is related to another important cognitive ingredient in health, **locus of control**, which refers to your general expectation about whether you can control the things that happen to you (Rotter, 1990). People who have an *internal locus of control* ("internals") tend to believe that they are responsible for what happens to them. Those who have an *external locus of control* ("externals") tend to believe that their lives are controlled by luck, fate, or other people. Having an internal locus of control is associated with good health, academic achievement, political activism, and emotional well-being (Lang & Heckhausen, 2001; Strickland, 1989).

Most people can tolerate all kinds of stressors if they feel able to predict or control them. Take crowding. Mice get really nasty when they're crowded, but many people love crowds, voluntarily getting squashed in New York's Times Square on New Year's Eve or at a rock concert. Human beings show signs of stress not when they are actually

Who has more stress: corporate managers in highly competitive jobs or assembly-line workers in routine and predictable jobs? People who are bossed suffer more from job stress than their bosses do, especially if the employees cannot control many aspects of their work (Karasek & Theorell, 1990).

crowded but when they *feel* crowded (Evans, Lepore, & Allen, 2000). Cortisol is also elevated when people feel that they are being judged negatively by others or have no control over the task at hand (Dickerson & Kemeny, 2004; Miller, Chen, & Zhou, 2007). People who have the greatest control over their work pace and activities, such as executives and managers, have fewer illnesses and stress symptoms than do employees who have little control, who feel trapped doing repetitive tasks, and who have a low chance of promotion (Karasek & Theorell, 1990). The greatest threat to health and well-being occurs when people feel caught in a situation they cannot escape, one that goes on without a foreseeable end.

Feeling in control affects the immune system, which may be why it helps to speed up recovery from surgery and some diseases (E. Skinner, 1996). People who have an internal locus of control are better able than externals to resist infection by cold viruses and even the health-impairing effects of poverty and discrimination (Cohen, Tyrrell, & Smith, 1993; Krieger & Sidney, 1996; Lachman & Weaver, 1998). As with optimism, feeling in control also makes people more likely to take action to improve their health when necessary. In a group of patients recovering from heart attacks, those who believed the heart attack occurred because they smoked, didn't exercise, or had a stressful job were more likely to change their bad habits and recover quickly. In contrast, those who thought their illness was due to bad luck or fate—factors outside their control—were less likely to generate plans for recovery and more likely to resume their old unhealthy habits (Affleck et al., 1987; Ewart, 1995).

Overall, a sense of control is a good thing, but critical thinkers might want to ask: Control over what? It is surely not beneficial for people to believe they can control absolutely every aspect of

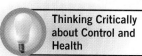

Thinking Critically about Control and Health

their lives; some things, such as death, taxes, or being a random victim of a crime, are out of anyone's control. Health and well-being are not enhanced by self-blame ("Whatever goes wrong with my health is my fault") or the belief that all disease can be prevented by doing the right thing ("If I take vitamins and hold the right positive attitude, I'll never get sick").

Culture and Control Eastern and Western cultures tend to hold different attitudes toward the ability and desirability of controlling one's own life. In general, Western cultures celebrate **primary**

control, in which people try to influence events by trying to exert direct control over them: If you are in a bad situation, you change it, fix it, or fight it. The Eastern approach emphasizes **secondary control**, in which people try to accommodate to a bad situation by changing their own aspirations or desires: If you have a problem, you live with it or act in spite of it (Rothbaum, Weisz, & Snyder, 1982).

A Japanese psychologist once offered some examples of Japanese proverbs that teach the benefits of yielding to the inevitable (Azuma, 1984): *To lose is to win* (giving in, to protect the harmony of a relationship, demonstrates the superior trait of generosity); *willow trees do not get broken by piled-up snow* (no matter how many problems pile up in your life, flexibility will help you survive them); and *the true tolerance is to tolerate the intolerable* (some "intolerable" situations are facts of life that no amount of protest will change). You can imagine how long "To lose is to win" would survive on an American football field, or how long most Americans would be prepared to tolerate the intolerable! Yet an important part of coping, for any of us, is learning to accept limited resources, irrevocable losses, and circumstances over which we have little or no direct influence—all aspects of secondary control (E. Skinner, 2007).

People who are ill or under stress can reap the benefits of both Western and Eastern forms of control by avoiding either–or thinking: taking responsibility for future actions while not blaming themselves unduly for past ones. Among college freshmen who are doing poorly in their classes, future success depends on maintaining enough primary control to keep working hard and learning to study better, *and* on the ability to come to terms with the fact that success is not going to drop into their laps without effort (Hall et al., 2006). Among women who are recovering from sexual assault or coping with cancer, adjustment is related to a woman's belief that she is not to blame for being raped or for getting sick but that she *is* in charge of taking care of herself from now on (Frazier, 2003; Taylor, Lichtman, & Wood, 1984). "I felt that I had lost control of my body somehow," said one cancer survivor, "and the way for me to get back some control was to find out as much as I could." This way of thinking allows people to avoid guilt and self-blame while retaining a belief that they can take steps to get better.

Many problems require us to decide what we can change and to accept what we cannot; perhaps the secret of healthy control lies in knowing the difference.

primary control An effort to modify reality by changing other people, the situation, or events; a "fighting back" philosophy.

secondary control An effort to accept reality by changing your own attitudes, goals, or emotions; a "learn to live with it" philosophy.

✓●─┤**Study** and
    Review on
    mypsychlab.com

Quick Quiz

We hope these questions are not sources of stress for you.

1. Steve is unexpectedly called on in class to discuss a question. He hasn't the faintest idea of the answer, and he feels his heart pound and his palms sweat. According to Selye, Steve is in the _____ phase of his stress response.

2. Maria has worked as a file clerk for 17 years in a job that is closely supervised and boring. Her boss must make many rapid-fire decisions every day and is always complaining of the pressures of responsibility. Which of them probably has the more stressful job? (a) Maria, (b) the boss, (c) both equally, (d) neither job is stressful (*Bonus:* Why?)

3. Anika usually takes credit for doing well on her work assignments and blames her failures on lack of effort. Benecia attributes her successes to luck and blames her failures on the fact that she is an indecisive Gemini. Anika has an _____ locus of control whereas Benecia has an _____ locus.

4. Adapting to the reality that you have a chronic medical condition is an example of (primary/secondary) control; joining a protest to make a local company clean up its hazardous wastes is an example of (primary/secondary) control.

5. On television, a self-described health expert explains that "no one gets sick if they don't want to be sick," because we can all control our bodies. As a critical thinker, how should you assess this claim?

Answers:

1. alarm **2.** a, because Maria has less control than her boss does over every aspect of her work **3.** internal; external **4.** secondary; primary **5.** First, you would want to define your terms: What does "control" mean, and what kind of control is the supposed expert referring to? People can control some things, such as how much they exercise and whether they smoke, and they can control some aspects of treatment once they become ill, but they cannot control everything that happens to them. Second, you would examine the assumption that control is always a good thing; the belief that we have total control over our lives could lead to depression and unwarranted self-blame when illness strikes.

◆ YOU are about to learn...

• which emotion may be most hazardous to your heart.

• whether chronic depression leads to physical illness.

• why confession is often as healthy for the body as it is for the soul.

Stress and Emotion

Perhaps you have heard people say things such as "She was so depressed, it's no wonder she got sick" or "He's always so angry, he's going to give himself a heart attack one day." Are negative emotions, especially anger and depression, hazardous to your health?

First, we can eliminate the popular belief that there is a "cancer-prone" personality. (This notion was initially promoted by the tobacco industry to draw attention away from smoking as a leading cause of cancer.) Research has thoroughly discredited this belief; studies of thousands of people around the world, from Japan to Finland, have found no link between personality traits and risk of cancer (Nakaya et al., 2003).

Second, we need to separate the effects of negative emotions on healthy people from the effects of such emotions on people who are ill. Once a person is already sick, negative emotions such as anxiety and helplessness can affect the speed of recovery (Kiecolt-Glaser et al., 1998). People who become depressed after a heart attack are significantly more likely to die from cardiac causes in the succeeding year, even controlling for severity of the disease and other risk factors (Frasure-Smith et al., 1999). But can anger and depression be causes of illness on their own?

Hostility and Depression: Do They Hurt?

One of the first modern efforts to link emotions and illness occurred in the 1970s, with research on the "Type A" personality, a set of qualities thought to be associated with heart disease: ambitiousness, impatience, anger, working hard, and having high standards for oneself. Later work ruled out all of these factors except one: The toxic ingredient in the Type A personality turned out to be hostility (Myrtek, 2007).

By "hostility" we do not mean the irritability or anger that everyone feels on occasion, but *cynical* or *antagonistic hostility*, which characterizes people who are mistrustful of others and always ready to provoke mean, furious arguments. In a classic study of male physicians who had been interviewed as medical students 25 years earlier, those who were chronically angry and resentful were five times as likely as nonhostile men to get heart disease, even when other risk factors such as smoking and a poor diet were taken into account (Ewart & Kolodner, 1994; Williams, Barefoot, & Shekelle, 1985) (see Figure 13.4). These findings have been replicated in other large-scale studies, with African Americans and whites, and with women as well as men (Krantz et al., 2006; Williams et al., 2000). Proneness to anger is a significant risk factor all on its own for impairments of the immune system, elevated blood pressure, heart disease, and even a slower healing of wounds (Chida & Hamer, 2008; Gouin et al., 2008; Suinn, 2001).

Clinical depression, too, is linked to at least a doubled risk of later heart attack and cardiovascular disease (Frasure-Smith & Lespérance, 2005; Schulz et al., 2000). But what accounts for that link? One prospective study of more than 1,000 men found that the answer was exercise: The depressed men who had further episodes were less physically active than men who exercised regularly (Whooley et al., 2008). But another large prospective study found no differences in physical activity between depressed and nondepressed older adults. Instead, they found that depressed people were more likely to accumulate fat in the belly and midriff (perhaps because of the elevated cortisol that often occurs with depression), where it is more likely to increase the risk of diabetes and cardiovascular disease (Vogelzangs et al., 2008). Either way, you can see that the reason depression might lead to heart disease over time is not depression itself, but more likely the lethargy and overeating that depression can produce in some of its sufferers.

For some time, researchers thought that depression might also lead to cancer, but now it looks as though cancer can cause depression, and not just because the diagnosis is "depressing." Cancerous tumors, as well as the immune system that is fighting them, produce high levels of a chemical that can cause the emotional and behavioral symptoms of depression. A study of rats, which after all are not aware of having cancer, found that the animals would float passively in water instead of swimming for safety, and show other signs of anxiety and apathy (Pyter et al., 2009).

Positive Emotions: Do They Help?

Just as negative emotions can be unhealthful, positive emotions seem to be healthful (Fredrickson et al., 2003). Consider the findings from a study of 180 Catholic nuns. Researchers examined autobiographies composed by the nuns when the women were about 22 years old, to see whether the quality of their writing predicted the onset of Alzheimer's disease later in life. (It did.) When other researchers scored the writings for their emotional content, they found a strong association between the frequency of positive emotions described—such

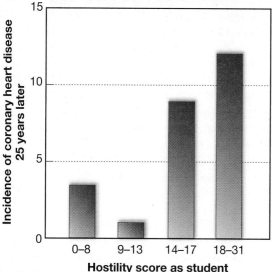

FIGURE 13.4

Hostility and Heart Disease

Anger is more hazardous to health than a heavy workload. Men who had the highest hostility scores as young medical students were the most likely to have coronary heart disease 25 years later (Williams, Barefoot, & Shekelle, 1985).

Hostility is hazardous, but humor is healthful!

✳ Explore
Happy Brains on
mypsychlab.com

as happiness, love, hope, gratitude, contentment, amusement—and longevity six decades later (Danner, Snowdon, & Friesen, 2001). The nuns whose life stories contained the most words describing positive emotions lived, on average, nine years longer than nuns who reported the fewest positive feelings. These differences in longevity could not have been due to the stress of poverty, raising children, or particular experiences. The women all had the same experiences and standard of living, at least after they entered the convent.

Psychologists are trying to find out just what it is about feeling happy, cheerful, and hopeful that could protect a person from getting sick. Of course, perhaps the cheerfulness of the long-lived nuns simply reflected an easygoing temperament or other genetic influences that promote long life. But positive emotions could also be physically beneficial because they soften or counteract the high arousal caused by negative emotions or chronic stressors. They may dispose people to think more creatively about their opportunities and choices and to take action to achieve their goals (Kok, Catalino, & Frederickson, 2008). People who express positive feelings are also more likely to attract friends and supporters than are people who are always bitter and brooding, and, as we will see, social support contributes to good health (Pressman & Cohen, 2005).

If you don't feel bouncy and happy all the time, don't worry; everyone feels grumpy, irritable, and unhappy on occasion. But according to one study in which college students kept a daily diary of their positive and negative emotions for 28 days, the students who had the greatest emotional well-being

Everyone has secrets and private moments of sad reflection, but when you feel sad or fearful for too long, keeping your feelings to yourself may increase your stress.

had a ratio of positive to negative emotions of at least 3 to 1 (Fredrickson & Losada, 2005). You might want to keep track of your own positive-to-negative emotion ratio for the next month to see where yours falls, and whether it seems related to any colds, flu, or other physical symptoms you might be having. Are positive emotions more typical of your emotional life than negative ones, or is it the other way around?   ✳ Explore

Emotional Inhibition and Expression

Well, then, if positive emotions are beneficial and negative emotions are risky, you might assume that the safest thing to do when you feel angry, depressed, or worried is to try to suppress those feelings. But anyone who has tried to banish an unwelcome thought, a bitter memory, or pangs of longing for an ex-lover knows how hard it can be to do this. When you are trying to avoid a thought, you are in fact processing the thought more frequently; you are rehearsing it. That is why, when you are obsessed with someone you were once romantically involved with, trying not to think of the person actually prolongs your emotional responsiveness to him or her (Wegner & Gold, 1995).

The continued inhibition of thoughts and emotions actually requires physical effort that can be stressful to the body. People who are able to express matters of great emotional importance to them show elevated levels of disease-fighting white blood cells, whereas people who suppress such feelings tend to have decreased levels (Petrie, Booth, & Pennebaker, 1998). There is also a social cost to suppressing important feelings. In a longitudinal study that followed first-year college students as they adjusted to being in a new environment, those who expressed their worries and fears openly with other students ended up with better relationships and greater satisfaction, compared to those those who said they preferred to keep their emotions to themselves (Srivastava et al., 2009).

The Benefits of Confession Given the findings on the harmful effects of feeling negative emotions and also the difficulty and costs of suppressing them, what is a person supposed to do with them? One way to reduce the wear and tear of negative emotions comes from research on the benefits of confession: divulging (even if only to yourself) private thoughts and feelings that make you ashamed, worried, or sad (Pennebaker, 2002). Freshmen who wrote about their "deepest thoughts and feelings" in a private journal reported greater short-term

Get Involved! True Confessions

To see whether the research on confession will benefit you, take a moment to wrote down your deepest thoughts and feelings about being in college, your past, a secret, your future . . . anything you have never told anyone. Do this again tomorrow and then again for a few days in a row. Note your feelings after writing. Are you upset, troubled, sad, or relieved? Does your account change over time? Research suggests that if you do this exercise now, you may have fewer colds, headaches, and trips to the doctor over the next few months (Pennebaker, Colder, & Sharp, 1990).

homesickness and anxiety, compared to students who wrote about trivial topics. But by the end of the school year, they had had fewer bouts of flu and fewer visits to the infirmary than the control group did (Pennebaker, Colder, & Sharp, 1990).

This method is especially powerful when people write about traumatic experiences. When a group of college students was asked to write about a personal, traumatic experience for 20 minutes a day for four days, many told stories of sexual coercion, physical beatings, humiliation, or parental abandonment. Yet most had never discussed these experiences with anyone. The researchers collected data on the students' physical symptoms, white blood cell counts, emotions, and visits to the health center. On every measure, the students who wrote about traumatic experiences were better off than those who wrote only about neutral topics (Pennebaker, Kiecolt-Glaser, & Glaser, 1988). Expressing and working through memories of traumatic events head on are more beneficial than trying to suppress intrusive, troubling thoughts (Dalgleish, Hauer, & Kuyken, 2008).

The benefits of this method occur primarily when the revelation produces insight and understanding, thereby ending the stressful repetition of obsessive thoughts and unresolved feelings (Kennedy-Moore & Watson, 2001; Lepore, Ragan, & Jones, 2000). One young woman, who had been molested at the age of 9 by a boy a year older, at first wrote about her feelings of embarrassment and guilt. By the third day, she was writing about how angry she felt at the boy. By the last day, she had begun to see the whole event differently; he was a child too, after all. When the study was over, she said, "Before, when I thought about it, I'd lie to myself. . . . Now, I don't feel like I even have to think about it because I got it off my chest. I finally admitted that it happened."

The Benefits of Letting Grievances Go

Another way of letting go of negative emotions is to give up the thoughts that produce them and adopt a perspective that might lead to forgiveness. When people rehearse their grievances and hold on to their grudges, their blood pressure, heart rate, and skin conductance rise. Forgiving thoughts (as in the preceding example, "He was a child too") reduce these signs of physiological arousal and restore feelings of control (Witvliet, Ludwig, & Vander Laan, 2001). (See Figure 13.5.) Forgiveness, like confession when it works, helps people see events in a new light. It promotes empathy, the ability to see the situation from another person's perspective. It strengthens and repairs relationships (Karremans et al., 2003).

Forgiveness does *not* mean that the offended person denies, ignores, or excuses the offense, which might be serious. It does mean that the victim is able, finally, to come to terms with the injustice and let go of obsessive feelings of hurt, rage, and vengefulness. As the Chinese proverb says, "He who pursues revenge should dig two graves."

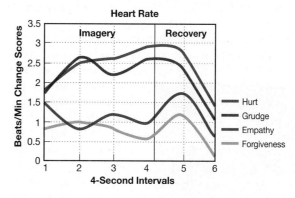

FIGURE 13.5

Heartfelt Forgiveness

Participants in this study were asked to think of someone who they felt had offended or hurt them. Then they were asked to imagine unforgiving reactions (rehearsing the hurt and harboring a grudge) and forgiving reactions (feeling empathy, forgiving). People's heart rates increased much more sharply, and took longer to return to normal, when their thoughts were unforgiving.

Quick Quiz

We'll never forgive you if you skip this quiz.

1. Which aspect of Type A behavior is most hazardous to the heart? (a) working hard, (b) being in a hurry, (c) cynical hostility, (d) irritability in traffic, (e) general grumpiness

2. Amber has many worries about being in college, but she is afraid to tell anyone. What might be the healthiest solution for her? (a) trying not to think about her feelings, (b) writing down her feelings and then rereading and rethinking what she wrote, (c) talking frequently to anyone who will listen, (d) tweeting her friends about her moods

3. We are giving away an answer to #2, but why might answer *d* not be helpful to Amber?

Answers:

1. c 2. b 3. Sending tweets, or posting her feelings on her Facebook page, might make Amber momentarily feel good, but she probably won't retrieve those messages later to reread and rethink about what she wrote; and rethinking her story is the important element.

◆ **YOU** are about to learn...

- ways of calming the body when you are feeling stressed.

- the difference between emotion-focused and problem-focused coping.

- how to reduce stress by rethinking and reappraising your problems.

- the importance and limitations of social support.

Coping with Stress

We have noted that most people who are under stress, even those living in difficult situations, do not become ill. In addition to feeling optimistic and in control, and not wallowing around in negative emotions, how do they manage to cope?

The most immediate way to deal with the physiological tension of stress and negative emotions is to take time out and reduce the body's physical arousal. Many people, from infants to the old, respond beneficially to the soothing touch of massage (Moyer, Rounds, & Hannum, 2004). Another successful method is the ancient Buddhist practice of *mindfulness meditation*, which fosters emotional tranquility. The goal is to learn to accept feelings of anger, sadness, or anxiety without judging them or trying to get rid of them (a form of secondary control) (Davidson et al., 2003). A third effective buffer between stressors and illness is exercise. People who are physically fit have fewer health problems than people who are less fit even when they are under the same pressures. They also show lower physiological arousal to stressors (Vita et al., 1998). These activities, along with any others that calm your body and focus your mind—including prayer, music, dancing, or baking bread—are all good for health. But if your house has burned down or you need a serious operation, other coping strategies will be necessary.

✳─[Explore

Solving the Problem

Years ago, at the age of 23, a friend of ours named Simi Linton was struck by tragedy. Linton, her new husband, and her best friend were in a horrific car accident. When she awoke in a hospital room, with only a vague memory of the crash, she learned that her husband and friend had been killed and that she herself had permanent spinal injury and would never walk again.

How in the world does anyone recover from such a devastating event? Some people advise survivors of disaster or tragedy to "get it out of your system" or to "get in touch with your feelings." But survivors know they feel miserable. What should they *do*? This question gets to the heart of the difference between *emotion-focused* and *problem-focused coping* (Lazarus, 2000; Lazarus & Folkman, 1984). Emotion-focused coping concentrates on the emotions the problem has caused, whether anger, anxiety, or grief. For a period of time after any tragedy or disaster, it is normal to give in to these emotions

These exuberant performers know all about coping—and thriving.

and feel overwhelmed by them. In this stage, people often need to talk constantly about the event, which helps them come to terms with it, make sense of it, and decide what to do about it (Lepore, Ragan, & Jones, 2000).

Eventually, most people become ready to concentrate on solving the problem itself. The specific steps in problem-focused coping depend on the nature of the problem: whether it is a pressing but one-time decision; a continuing difficulty, such as living with a disability; or an anticipated event, such as having an operation. Once the problem is identified, the coper can learn as much as possible about it from professionals, friends, books, and others in the same predicament (Clarke & Evans, 1998). Becoming informed increases the feeling of control and can speed recovery (Doering et al., 2000).

As for Simi Linton, she learned how to do just about everything in her wheelchair (including dancing!), and she went back to school. She got a Ph.D. in psychology, remarried, and became a highly respected teacher, counselor, writer, and activist committed to improving conditions and opportunities for people with disabilities (Linton, 2006).

Rethinking the Problem

Some problems cannot be solved; these are the unavoidable facts of life, such as an inability to have children, losing your job, or developing a chronic illness. Now what? Health psychologists have identified three effective cognitive coping methods:

1 **Reappraising the situation.** Although you may not be able to get rid of a stressor, you can choose to think about it differently, a process called *reappraisal*. Reappraisal can turn anger into sympathy, worry into determination, and feelings of loss into feelings of opportunity. Maybe that job you lost was dismal but you were too afraid to quit and look for another; now you can. Reappraisal improves well-being, softens negative emotions, and even lowers cortisol and other stress responses (Denson, Spanovic, & Miller, 2009; Gross & John, 2003; Moskowitz et al., 2009).

2 **Learning from the experience.** Some people emerge from adversity with newfound or newly acquired skills, having been forced to learn something they had not known before—say, how to cope with the medical system or how to manage a deceased parent's estate. Others discover sources of courage and strength they did not know they had. Those who draw lessons from the inescapable tragedies of life, and find meaning in them, thrive

as a result of adversity instead of simply surviving it (Davis, Nolen-Hoeksema, & Larson, 1998; Folkman & Moskowitz, 2000).

3 **Making social comparisons.** In a difficult situation, successful copers often compare themselves to others who they feel are less fortunate. Even if they have fatal diseases, they find someone who is worse off (Taylor & Lobel, 1989; Wood, Michela, & Giordano, 2000). One AIDS patient said in an interview, "I made a list of all the other diseases I would rather not have than AIDS. Lou Gehrig's disease, being in a wheelchair; rheumatoid arthritis, when you are in knots and in terrible pain." Sometimes successful copers also compare themselves to those who are doing better than they are (Collins, 1996). They might say, "She and I have the same kinds of problems; how come she's doing so much better in school than I am? What does she know that I don't?" Such comparisons provide a person with information about ways of coping, managing an illness, or improving a stressful situation (Suls, Martin, & Wheeler, 2002).

Drawing on Social Support

A final way to deal with negative emotions and stress is to reach out to others. Your health depends not only on what is going on in your body and mind but also on what is going on in your relationships: what you take from them, and what you give to them. When social groups provide individuals with a sense of meaning, purpose, and belonging, they produce positive psychological benefits for their members' health and well-being (Haslam et al., 2009).

When Friends Help You Cope . . . Think of all the ways in which family members, friends, neighbors, and co-workers can help you. They can offer concern and affection. They can help you evaluate problems and plan a course of action. They can offer resources and services such as lending you money or a car, or taking notes in class for you when you are sick. Most of all, they are sources of attachment and connection, which everyone needs throughout life.

Friends can even improve your health. As we saw, work-related stress and unemployment increase a person's vulnerability to the common cold, but having a lot of friends and social contacts helps to reduce that risk (Cohen et al., 2003). Social support is especially important for people who have stressful jobs that require high cardiovascular responsiveness day after day, such as firefighters.

Friends can be our greatest source of warmth, support, and fun . . .

Having social support helps the heart rate and stress hormones return to normal more quickly after a stressful episode (Roy, Steptoe, & Kirschbaum, 1998).

People who live in a network of close connections actually live longer than those who do not. In studies that followed thousands of adults for ten years, people who had many friends, connections, or memberships in church and other groups lived longer on average than those who had few. The importance of having social networks was unrelated to physical health at the time the studies began, to socioeconomic status, and to risk factors like smoking (House, Landis, & Umberson, 2003).

When social support comes from a loving partner, its benefits for the immune system can be quite powerful. In one study of 16 couples, the wives had to lie in an MRI machine, periodically receiving a mild but stressful electric shock on their ankle (Coan, Schaefer, & Davidson, 2006). During the procedure, some women received a touch on the hand from a stranger; others held hands with their husbands. The women's brain images showed activation in the hypothalamus and other regions involved with pain, physical arousal, and negative emotions. Yet, as you can see in Figure 13.6, the moment the women felt a husband's reassuring hand, their brain activation subsided in all the regions that had been revved up to cope with threat and fear. Holding hands with a stranger, while comforting, did not produce as great a decrease in brain activation as did a husband's touch.

When a touch is affectionate and welcome, it can actually elevate some "therapeutic" hormones, especially *oxytocin*, the hormone that induces relaxation and is associated with mothering and attachment. In fact, human bodies may be designed not only for a "fight or flight" response to stress and challenge, but also a "tend and befriend" response—being friendly and conciliatory, seeking out a friend or loved one, taking care of others (Taylor, 2006; Taylor et al., 2000b). Animal studies find that early nurturing by parents or other adults who "tend and befriend" the young can affect the sensitivity of the HPA axis, making the infants more resilient to later chronic stressors. Such findings may help explain why children who lack such nurturing become physically more vulnerable to illness (Young & Francis, 2008). Oxytocin might even be the key link between hugging and lower blood pressure, in men as well as women (Grewen et al., 2005).

However, once again it is important not to oversimplify, for instance by concluding that people can defeat any illness if they just have the right amount and kind of social support. Some years ago, a psychiatrist claimed, on the basis of a preliminary study, that women with advanced breast cancer lived longer if they joined support groups, but the study has been discredited and was never replicated (Coyne et al., 2009). Therapy does not prolong survival, although it often is emotionally and socially beneficial to individual members.

Moreover, not all cultural groups define "social support" the same way or benefit from the same kind. Asians and Asian Americans are more reluctant than white Americans to ask for help explicitly from friends, colleagues, and family and to disclose feelings of distress. Being particularly attuned to the harmony of their relationships, many Asians are concerned about the potentially negative and embarrassing effects of self-disclosure or of seeking help. As a result, they often feel more stressed and have elevated stress hormones when they are required to ask for help or reveal their private feelings (Kim, Sherman, & Taylor, 2008). But Asians do not differ from Anglos in their reliance on, and need for, *implicit* social support—the knowledge that someone will be there to help if they need it.

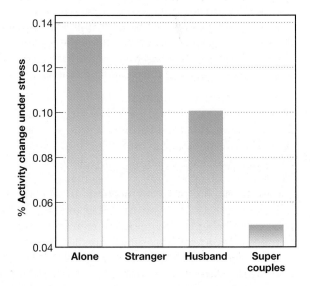

FIGURE 13.6
Hugs and Health
Women had to lie in an MRI machine while receiving mild but stressful shocks on their ankle. Those who showed the highest activation of the hypothalamus and other regions of the brain involved in stress and anxiety went through the test alone. A stranger's calming touch reduced activation somewhat and a husband's touch reduced it even more. The women in "super couples," who felt the closest to their husbands (right bar), showed the lowest signs of stress (Coan, Schaefer, & Davidson, 2006).

. . . And Coping with Friends Needless to say, sometimes other people aren't helpful. Sometimes they themselves are the source of unhappiness, stress, and anger.

In close relationships, the same person who is a source of support can also become a source of stress, especially if the two parties are arguing all the time. Being in an unhappy, bitter, uncommunicative relationship can significantly impair health. It makes the partners depressed and angry, affects their health habits, elevates stress hormones, and also directly influences their cardiovascular, endocrine, and immune systems (Kiecolt-Glaser & Newton, 2001). Married couples who argue in a hostile fashion—criticizing, interrupting, or insulting the other person, and becoming angry and defensive—show significant elevations of cortisol and poorer immune function afterward. In fact, any wounds or blisters a hostile couple has actually heal more slowly than they do in couples who do not argue in a hostile way (Kiecolt-Glaser et al., 2005). Couples who argue in a positive fashion—trying to find common ground, compromising, listening to each other's concerns, and using humor to defuse tension—do not show these impairments. As one student of ours observed, "This study gives new meaning to the accusation 'You make me sick!'"

In addition to being sources of conflict, friends and relatives may be unsupportive in times of trouble simply out of ignorance or awkwardness. They may abandon you or say something stupid and hurtful. Sometimes they actively block your efforts to change bad health habits such as binge drinking or smoking by

. . . and also sources of exasperation, anger, and misery.

making fun of you or pressuring you to conform to what "everyone" does. And sometimes, because they have never been in the same situation and do not know what to do to help, they offer the wrong kind of support. They may try to cheer you up, saying, "Everything will be fine," rather than let you talk about your fears or find solutions, or they may try to press you to join a support group "for your own good," even if you regard disclosing your feelings in groups as culturally or personally inappropriate for you.

Finally, we should not forget the benefits of giving support, rather than always being on the receiving end. Julius Segal (1986), a psychologist who worked with Holocaust survivors, hostages, refugees, and other survivors of catastrophe, wrote that a key element in their recovery was compassion for others: "healing through helping." Why? The ability to look outside yourself is related to all of the successful coping mechanisms we have discussed. It encourages you to solve problems instead of blaming others or just venting your emotions, helps you reappraise the situation by seeing it from another person's perspective, fosters forgiveness, and allows you to gain perspective on your own problems (Brown et al., 2003). Healing through helping thus helps everyone to accept difficult situations that are facts of life.

✓● Study and Review on mypsychlab.com

Quick Quiz

Can you cope with these questions?

1. You accidentally broke your glasses. Which response is an example of cognitive reappraisal? (a) "I am such a stupid, clumsy idiot!" (b) "I never do anything right." (c) "What a shame, but I've been wanting new frames anyway." (d) "I'll forget about it in aerobics class."

2. Finding out what your legal and financial resources are when you have been victimized by a crime is an example of (a) problem-focused coping, (b) emotion-focused coping, (c) distraction, (d) reappraisal.

3. "This class drives me crazy, but I'm better off than my friends who aren't in college" is an example of (a) distraction, (b) social comparison, (c) denial, (d) empathy.

4. What hormone is elevated when happy couples hug one another?

5. Your roommate has turned your room into a garbage dump, filled with rotten leftover food and unwashed clothes. Assuming that you don't like living with rotting food and dirty clothes, what coping strategies described in this section might help you?

Answers:

1. c 2. a 3. b 4. oxytocin 5. You might solve the problem by finding a compromise (e.g., cleaning the room together). You could reappraise the seriousness of the problem ("I only have to live with this person until the end of the term") or compare your roommate to others who are worse ("At least mine is generous and friendly"). And you might mobilize some social support, perhaps by offering your friends a pizza if they help you clean up.

Psychology in the News REVISITED

Psychology in the News

Man Crashes Plane Into Austin, Texas, I.R.S. Office

Joe Stack, whose story opened this chapter, burned down his house, with callous disregard for his wife and young stepdaughter, and then killed himself and two IRS employees. In the rant he posted on the Internet, he wrote: "Violence not only is the answer, it is the only answer." Really? What did it accomplish?

As we saw in this chapter, when we are feeling extreme emotions or when major stressors require the body to cope with threat, fear, or danger, the body whirls into action to give us the energy to respond. Just about everyone has had the unpleasant experience of a racing heart, sweaty palms, and other emotional symptoms when we feel betrayed, anxious, or angry. But does that mean we have no control over our emotions, especially those caused by extremely stressful experiences?

As we also saw, biology does not give us the whole picture. It is equally important to understand the role of perceptions, beliefs, and expectations in generating emotions and stress. Joe Stack blamed the IRS for his financial losses, and his rage resulted from his perception that he was an undeserving victim. But what if he had been able to interpret his problems differently? What if he had been able to evaluate, calmly and perhaps with the help of a financial planner or psychotherapist, the reasons he was in trouble, and perhaps had come to understand and accept his own responsibility for his misfortunes? What beliefs made him feel entitled to retire at a relatively young age, when millions of others work hard their whole lives, through hard times as well as boom times?

The findings on the stressful nature of bitter marital relationships may also be relevant to Stack's life. His cruel act of burning down their house certainly suggests he was blaming his wife for his misery as much as he blamed the government. But marital disputes involve two people, and it's rare that one partner is 100 percent to blame. What if he had been able to understand his own role in creating his unhappiness in his marriage?

This chapter also examined the importance of having a sense of control over events, noting the helplessness and panic that can ensue when people lose their feelings of control. Westerners, particularly, tend to have a philosophy of fighting back against unwelcome events rather than of accepting disappointments and losses. Stack would appear to have been an extreme example of this stance toward the world: feeling helpless and unable to control his life, he did not know what else to do other than end it in a blaze of fury.

Yet we saw that there are better ways of coping than by murdering your partner or employees of the institution that you think is causing your stress and anger. Stack could surely have found a way to improve his marriage and his financial situation without committing murder and suicide. These include rethinking the problem, learning from it, comparing oneself to others less fortunate, helping others, and finding a good support group. ("Taking Psychology with You" offers suggestions for handling anger.)

In the final analysis, successful coping does not mean eliminating all sources of stress or all difficult emotions. It does not mean constant happiness or a life without pain and frustration. The healthy person faces problems, deals with them, and gets beyond them, but the problems are necessary if the person is to acquire coping skills that endure. To wish for a life without stress, or a life without emotion, would be like wishing for a life without friends. The result might be calm, but it would be joyless. Daily hassles, chronic problems, and occasional tragedies are inescapable. How we handle them is the test of our humanity.

The ultimate example of rethinking your problems.

The Dilemma of Anger: "Let It Out" or "Bottle It Up"?

What do you do when you feel angry? Do you tend to brood and sulk, collecting your righteous complaints like acorns for the winter, or do you erupt, hurling your wrath upon anyone or anything at hand? Do you discuss your feelings when you have calmed down? Does "letting anger out" get rid of it for you, or does it only make it more intense? The answers are crucial for how you get along with your family, neighbors, employers, and strangers.

Critical thinkers can learn to think carefully about how and when to express anger, and make a calm decision on how to proceed. Chronic feelings of anger and an inability to control anger can be as emotionally devastating and unhealthy as chronic problems with depression or anxiety. Yet in contrast to much pop-psych advice, research shows that expressing anger does not always get it "out of your system"; often people feel worse, physically and mentally, after an angry confrontation. When people brood and ruminate about their anger, talk to others incessantly about how angry they are, or ventilate their feelings in hostile acts, their blood pressure shoots up, they often feel angrier, and they behave even *more* aggressively later than if they had just let their feelings of anger subside (Bushman et al., 2005; Tavris, 1989). Conversely, when people learn to control their tempers and express anger constructively, they usually feel better, not worse; calmer, not angrier.

When people are feeling angry, they have a choice of doing any number of things, some of which will be more beneficial than others. Some people sulk, expecting everyone else to read their minds, which is hardly a way to communicate clearly. Many post impulsive comments on blogs that have annoyed them or send nasty texts on the spur of the moment. Some scream abuses at their friends or family, or strike out physically. If a particular action soothes their feelings or gets the desired response from others, they are likely to acquire a habit. Soon that habit feels "natural," as if it could never be changed. Some habits are better than others, though! Baking bread or going for a jog is fine, whereas many people justify their violent tempers by saying, "I couldn't help myself." But they can. If you

have acquired an abusive or aggressive habit, the research in this chapter offers practical suggestions for learning constructive ways of managing anger:

Don't sound off in the heat of anger; let bodily arousal cool down. Whether your arousal comes from background stresses such as heat, crowds, or loud noise or from conflict with another person, take time to relax. Time allows you to decide whether you are really angry or just tired and tense. This is the reason for the sage old advice to count to 10, count to 100, or sleep on it. Other cooling-off strategies include taking a time-out in the middle of an argument, meditating or relaxing, and calming yourself with a distracting activity.

Don't take it personally. If you feel that you have been insulted, check your perception for its accuracy. Could there be another reason for the behavior you find offensive? People who are quick to feel anger tend to interpret other people's actions as intentional offenses. People who are slow to anger tend to give others the benefit of the doubt, and they are not as focused on their own injured pride. Empathy ("Poor guy, he's feeling rotten") is usually incompatible with anger, so practice seeing the situation from the other person's perspective.

Beware of road rage—yours and the other person's. Driving increases everyone's level of physiological arousal, but not everyone becomes a hotheaded driver. Some drivers make themselves angry by having vengeful and retaliatory thoughts about other drivers (who have the nerve to change lanes or want to park! Who dare to drive at the speed limit in a school zone!).Hotheaded drivers take more risks while driving (rapidly switching lanes in their impatience), behave more aggressively (swearing, giving other drivers the finger or cursing them), and have more accidents (Deffenbacher et al., 2003).

If you decide that expressing anger is appropriate, be sure you use the right verbal and nonverbal language to make yourself understood. Because cultures (and families) have different display rules, be sure the recipient of your

anger understands what you are feeling and what complaint you are trying to convey—and whether or not the person thinks your anger is *appropriate*. For example, a study compared the use of anger by Asian-American and Anglo-American negotiators. Expressing anger was effective for the Anglo teams—it got more concessions from the other side—but was much less effective for the Asian negotiators (Adam, Shirako, & Maddux, 2010).

Think carefully about how to express anger so that you will get the results you want. What do you want your anger to accomplish? Do you just want to make the other person feel bad, or do you want the other person to understand your concerns and make amends? Shouting "You moron! How *could* you be so stupid!" might accomplish the former goal, but it's not likely to get the person to apologize, let alone to change his or her behavior. If your goal is to improve a bad situation or achieve justice, learning how to express anger so the other person will listen is essential.

Of course, if you just want to blow off steam, go right ahead; but you risk becoming a hothead.

Would anyone in the group like to respond to the way Frank is dealing with his anger?

BIZARRO (NEW) © DAN PIRARO. KING FEATURES SYNDICATE.

Summary ((•─[Listen to an audio file of your chapter on **mypsychlab.com**

The Nature of Emotion

• Although negative emotions are often painful, emotions evolved to bind people together, motivate them to achieve their goals, and help them make decisions and plans. The experience of *emotion* involves physiological changes in the face, brain, and autonomic nervous system; cognitive processes; and cultural norms and regulations. *Primary emotions* are thought to be universal, whereas *secondary emotions* are specific to cultures.

• Some basic facial expressions—anger, fear, sadness, happiness, disgust, surprise, contempt, and possibly pride—are widely recognized across cultures. They foster communication with others, signal our intentions to others, enhance infant survival, and, as studies of *facial feedback* show, help us to identify our own emotional states. An accurate reading of others' facial expressions increases among members of the same ethnicity, and depends on the social context. Also, because people can and do disguise their emotions, their expressions do not always communicate accurately.

• Many aspects of emotion are associated with specific parts of the brain. The *amygdala* is responsible for initially evaluating the emotional importance of incoming sensory information and is especially involved in fear. The *cerebral cortex* provides the cognitive ability to override this initial appraisal. Emotions generally involve the motivation to approach or withdraw; regions of the *left* prefrontal cortex appear to be specialized for the motivation to approach others (as with happiness and anger), whereas regions of the *right* prefrontal region are specialized for withdrawal or escape (as with disgust and fear).

• *Mirror neurons* throughout the brain are activated when people observe others. These neurons are involved in empathy, imitation, synchrony, understanding another person's intentions, and *mood contagion.*

• During the experience of any emotion, *epinephrine* and *norepinephrine* produce a state of physiological arousal to prepare the body for an output of energy. Different emotions are also associated with different patterns of autonomic nervous system activity.

• The most popular method of "lie detection" is the *polygraph machine,* but it has low reliability and validity because there are no patterns of autonomic nervous system activity specific to lying; it has a high rate of labeling innocent people as guilty. Other methods, such as voice analyzers or brain scans, have similar drawbacks.

• Cognitive approaches to emotion emphasize the perceptions and *attributions* that are involved in different emotions. Thoughts and emotions operate reciprocally, each influencing the other. Some emotions involve simple, nonconscious reactions; others, such as shame and guilt, require complex cognitive capacities.

Emotion and Culture

• Many psychologists believe that all human beings share the ability to experience primary emotions, whereas secondary emotions may be culture-specific—a view supported by research on emotion *prototypes.* But others believe that culture affects every aspect of emotional experience, including which emotions are considered basic and what people feel emotional about.

• Culture strongly influences the *display rules,* including nonverbal *body language,* that regulate how and whether people express their emotions. *Emotion work* is the effort a person makes to display an emotion he or she does not feel but feels obliged to convey.

• Women and men are equally likely to feel all emotions, although gender rules shape differences in emotional expression. North American women on average are more expressive than men, except for anger at strangers. But both sexes are less expressive to a person of higher status than they, both sexes will do the emotion work their job requires, and some situations foster expressiveness in everybody. Gender differences vary across cultures.

The Nature of Stress

• The relationship between emotions and stress is both physiological and psychological. Chronic negative emotions can become chronically stressful, and chronic stress can create negative emotions.

• Hans Selye argued that environmental stressors such as heat, pain, and danger produce a *general adaptation syndrome,* in which the body responds in three stages: *alarm, resistance,* and *exhaustion.* If a stressor persists, it may overwhelm the body's ability to cope, and illness may result. Modern research has added to Selye's work. When a person is under stress or in danger, the hypothalamus sends messages to the endocrine glands along two major pathways. One activates the sympathetic division of the autonomic nervous system, releasing adrenal hormones from the inner part of the adrenal glands. In the other, the hypothalamus initiates activity along the *HPA axis.* Chemical messengers travel from the hypothalamus to the pituitary, and in turn to the outer part (cortex) of the adrenal glands. The adrenal cortex secretes *cortisol* and other hormones that increase energy. Excess levels of cortisol can become harmful if they persist over time.

● When the stressors of poverty and unemployment become chronic, they can increase people's stress levels and increase their chances of illness. Responses to stress differ across individuals, depending on the type of stressor and the individual's own genetic predispositions.

● *Health psychologists* and researchers in the interdisciplinary field of *psychoneuroimmunology* (PNI) are studying the interaction among psychological factors, the nervous and endocrine systems, and the immune system (particularly the white blood cells that destroy harmful foreign bodies, called *antigens*). Chronic stress can even shorten *telomeres*, a protein that determines cell life.

● Psychological factors affect people's responses to stress. Feeling optimistic rather than pessimistic and having an *internal locus of control* improve immune function and also increase a person's ability to tolerate pain, live with ongoing problems, and recover from illness. Cultures differ in the kind of control they emphasize and value: *primary control*, trying to change a stressful situation, or *secondary control*, learning to accept and accommodate to a stressful situation.

Stress and Emotion

● Researchers have sought links between emotions, stress, and illness. There is no "cancer-prone personality," but chronic anger, especially in the form of *cynical* or *antagonistic* hostility, is a strong risk factor in heart disease. Major depression also increases the risk of later heart disease. Positive emotions appear related to well-being, better health, and longevity.

● People who consciously suppress their emotions are at greater risk of illness than people who acknowledge and cope with negative emotions. The effort to suppress worries, secrets, and memories of upsetting experiences can become stressful to the body. Two ways of letting go of negative emotions include confession and forgiveness. The goal is to achieve insight and understanding, and let go of grudges.

Coping with Stress

● The first step in coping with stress and negative emotions is to reduce their physical effects, such as through relaxation, *mindfulness meditation*, and exercise. The second is to focus on solving the problem (*problem-focused coping*) rather than on venting the emotions caused by the problem (*emotion-focused coping*). A third approach is to rethink the problem, which involves *reappraisal*, learning from the experience, and comparing oneself to others.

● *Social support* is essential in maintaining physical health and emotional well-being; it even prolongs life and speeds recovery from illness. A touch or a hug from a supportive partner calms the alarm circuits of the brain and raises levels of *oxytocin*, which may result in reduced heart rate and blood pressure. However, friends and family can also be sources of stress. In close relationships, couples who fight in a hostile and negative way show impaired immune function. Giving support to others is also associated with health and hastens recovery from traumatic experiences.

Psychology in the News, Revisited

● We may not always be able to control the physiological arousal produced by stress or intense emotions, but we generally are able to decide how to behave when we are upset. Coping with stress does not mean trying to live without pain or problems. It means learning how to live with them.

Key Terms

The Nature of Emotion

Emotion involves physiological changes in the face, brain, and autonomic nervous system; cognitive interpretations of events; and tendencies toward action, all influenced by cultural norms.

Emotion and the Body

- **Primary emotions** are biologically based and thought to be universal.
- **Secondary emotions** include all the variations and blends of emotion that vary from one culture to another.

Some facial expressions are recognized across cultures and thus seem to reflect a key set of primary emotions: anger, fear, sadness, happiness, disgust, surprise, contempt, and possibly pride.

Functions of facial expressions include:
- Identifying our own emotions through **facial feedback**
- Communicating emotion
- Allowing us to lie about our true feelings

Brain areas associated with emotion:
- The amygdala evaluates incoming emotion, especially anger and fear.

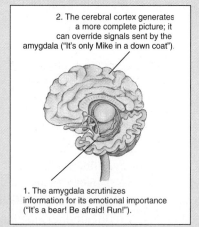

2. The cerebral cortex generates a more complete picture; it can override signals sent by the amygdala ("It's only Mike in a down coat").

1. The amygdala scrutinizes information for its emotional importance ("It's a bear! Be afraid! Run!").

- The left prefrontal cortex specializes in approach motivation and positive emotions; the right prefrontal cortex specializes in escape and negative emotions.
- **Mirror neurons** are brain cells that are activated when an animal or person observes others doing a specific task; they are involved in empathy, imitation, nonverbal rapport, and mood contagion.

During experience of any emotion, two hormones produce a state of arousal: epinephrine and norepinephrine.

Emotion and the Mind

People's perceptions, beliefs, and interpretations of events generate different emotions.
- Some emotions are cognitively primitive.
- As the cortex matures, cognitions become more complex, permitting the emergence of more complex and self-conscious emotions such as shame and guilt.

Biology and Deception

- The polygraph machine is assumed to detect lies, but it is actually a measure of emotional arousal.
- Polygraphs often correctly identify liars and guilty people, but their main problem is their high rate of falsely accusing innocent people of lying.
- No current technology exists that can directly and reliably determine whether someone is telling a falsehood.

Emotion and Culture

- Most psychologists believe that all human beings share the ability to experience primary emotions.
- Some psychologists believe that culture affects every aspect of emotional experience.

Communicating Emotions

- **Display rules** regulate how and whether people show emotion.
- *Body language* communicates emotions nonverbally.
- **Emotion work** is the effort to display an emotion a person does not feel because it is socially appropriate or required.

Gender and Emotion

- The sexes do not differ in how often they feel the range of everyday emotions.
- North American women are more verbally and nonverbally expressive than men.
- Men are more likely to express anger at strangers.

Situations can override gender rules:
- Both sexes are less expressive to a person of higher status.
- Both sexes do "emotion work" associated with their jobs.
- Some situations foster emotion in everybody.
- Gender differences vary across cultures.

The Nature of Stress

Stress and the Body

Hans Selye argued that environmental stressors produce a **general adaptation syndrome**, physiological reactions that occur in three phases:
1. Alarm
2. Resistance
3. Exhaustion

Stress hormones elevated

- Blood flow increases
- Heart rate speeds up
- Digestion slows
- Muscles tense

The Immune System: PNI

Researchers interested in **psychoneuroimmunology** study how psychological factors and physical changes, such as different levels of immune system functioning, interact with one another to protect health or increase the risk of illness.

Physical Changes

When a person is under stress, the hypothalamus sends messages to the endocrine glands along two major pathways to:
1. Activate the sympathetic nervous system for "fight or flight"
2. Initiate activity along the **HPA axis** to release chemical messengers that spur production of *cortisol* and other hormones to release energy

Chronic stressors that affect the immune system and increase the risk of illness include:
- Unemployment and work-related problems
- Poverty, powerlessness, and low status

Psychological Factors

Two psychological factors that can increase a person's ability to tolerate pain, live with ongoing problems, and recover from illness:
- Being optimistic
- Having an internal **locus of control**

Health and well-being may depend on a combination of:
- **Primary control,** trying to change the stressful situation
- **Secondary control,** learning to accept and to accommodate to the stressful situation

Stress and Emotion

Emotional factors that increase the risk of heart disease and other illness:
- Cynical or antagonistic hostility
- Chronic depression
- Prolonged inhibition of negative emotions

Two ways of letting go of negative emotions:
1. Confession: revealing private thoughts and feelings
2. Forgiveness: coming to terms with the injustice

Heartfelt Forgiveness

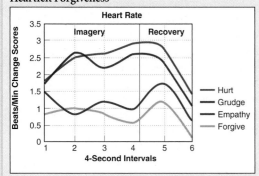

Coping with Stress

1. Reducing the physical effects of negative emotions and stress, such as through massage, meditation, relaxation, and exercise
2. Relying on problem-focused coping rather than emotion-focused coping
3. Rethinking the problem:
   - Reappraising the situation
   - Learning from the experience
   - Comparing yourself to others
4. Drawing on social support or giving it to others can speed recovery from illness, although the wrong kind of social support can be detrimental.

Psychology in the News

Ohio Girl, 14, Wins National Spelling Bee with "Stromuhr"

WASHINGTON, DC, June 4, 2010. Anamika Veeramani, 14, from North Royalton, Ohio, has won the 2010 Scripps National Spelling Bee by correctly spelling the medical term *stromuhr*. Indian Americans have won the trophy eight times in the past 12 years. Anamika's father, Alagaiya Veeramani, said he had no idea why Indian Americans do so well at the competition, but perhaps it has to do with a hard-work ethic, emphasis on education, and love of language. "This has been her dream for a very, very long time. It's been a family dream, too," he added, noting that his daughter studied as many as 16 hours on some days. Anamika hopes to attend Harvard University and become a cardiovascular surgeon.

Anamika Veeramani with her trophy.

New Website Features Love Story of Tortoise and Hippo

NEW YORK, March 1, 2010. A giant 130-year-old tortoise and a baby hippo who became fast friends after a devastating 2004 tsunami in the Indian Ocean now have their own website so that fans can check on how they are doing. Mzee, the tortoise, bonded with Owen, the hippo, after Owen was washed out to sea, rescued by Kenyan villagers, and taken to a wildlife park where Mzee lived. Owen was frightened and aggressive at first, but Mzee soon calmed him down. The hippo and the tortoise played, ate, and slept together, and used sounds, nods, and gentle shoves to communicate. Alas, this love story was not to last; since 2007, Owen has been living with Cleo, a female hippo. But people throughout the world continue to be inspired by the unlikely attachment between the tortoise and the hippo, perhaps reasoning that if two such different species can get along, so might human beings.

Owen and Mzee in happier days.

Soda Tax Signed into Law

DENVER, February 25, 2010. Colorado Governor Bill Ritter has signed a bill removing a 3 percent sales tax exemption for candy and soda. The state senate narrowly passed the bill recently after days of debate. More than 30 states now have either passed a soda tax or have removed an existing sales tax exemption in hopes of bringing in much-needed revenue and possibly reducing obesity as well.

Celebrity Designer Sentenced for Sexual Assault, Rape

LOS ANGELES, CA, August 31, 2009. Fashion designer Anand Jon Alexander has been sentenced to serve 59 years to life in prison after his conviction for sexually assaulting six women and raping another. The victims, some of them aspiring models who testified that they were lured to his Beverly Hills apartment by promises of jobs, ranged in age from 14 to 21. Anand Jon, as he was known professionally, graduated from Parsons, the prestigious art and design college of The New School in New York. He appeared on the TV show *America's Next Top Model* and was profiled by *Newsweek* as an emerging star in the fashion industry.

The Major Motives of Life:
Food, Love, Sex, and Work

What motivates people like Anamika Veeramani to pursue their dreams, even as young children, when so many others either give up or have no dream to pursue? How does the attachment between Mzee and Owen differ from love and friendship among humans? Why in the world would successful, wealthy men like Anand Jon Alexander resort to sexual coercion and rape? Will taxing sugary or fatty foods help to curb people's appetite for them and halt the epidemic of obesity?

The word *motivation*, like the word *emotion*, comes from the Latin root meaning "to move," and the psychology of motivation is indeed the study of what moves us, why we do what we do. To psychologists, **motivation** refers to a process within a person or animal that causes that organism to move toward a goal or away from an unpleasant situation. The motive may be to satisfy a psychological goal, say, by getting a great job or avoiding loss of the one you have; it may be to satisfy a biological need, say, by eating a sandwich to reduce hunger; or it may be to fulfill a personal ambition, say, by performing in a Broadway musical or being the youngest person to sail around the world.

For many decades, the study of motivation was dominated by a focus on biological *drives*, such as those to acquire food and water, to have sex, to seek novelty, and to avoid cold and pain. But drive theories do not account for the full complexity of human motivation, because people are conscious creatures who think and plan ahead, set goals for themselves, and plot strategies to reach those goals. People may have a drive to eat, for instance, but that doesn't tell us why some individuals will go on hunger strikes to protest injustice.

In this chapter, we will examine four central areas of human motivation: food, love, sex, and achievement. We will see how happiness and well-being are affected by the kinds of goals we set for ourselves, and by whether we are spurred to reach them because of **intrinsic motivation**, the desire to do something for its own sake and the pleasure it brings, or **extrinsic motivation**, the desire to do something for external rewards.

467

motivation An inferred process within a person or animal that causes movement either toward a goal or away from an unpleasant situation.

intrinsic motivation The pursuit of an activity for its own sake.

extrinsic motivation The pursuit of an activity for external rewards, such as money or fame.

set point The genetically influenced weight range for an individual; it is maintained by biological mechanisms that regulate food intake, fat reserves, and metabolism.

 YOU are about to learn...

- the biological mechanisms that make it difficult for obese people to lose weight and keep it off.

- how notions of the ideal male and female body change over time and across cultures.

- why people all over the world are getting fatter.

- the major forms of eating disorders, and why they are increasing among both sexes.

The Hungry Animal: Motives to Eat

Some people are skinny; others are plump. Some are shaped like string beans; others look more like pears. Some can eat anything they want without gaining an ounce; others struggle unsuccessfully their whole lives to shed pounds. Some hate being fat; others think that fat is fine. How much do genes, psychology, and environment affect our motivation to eat or not to eat?

The Biology of Weight

At one time, most psychologists thought that being overweight was a sign of emotional disturbance. If you were fat, it was because you hated your mother, feared intimacy, or were trying to fill an emotional hole in your psyche by loading up on rich desserts. The evidence for psychological theories of overweight, however, came mainly from self-reports and from flawed studies that lacked control groups or objective measures of how much people were actually eating. When researchers did controlled studies, they learned that fat people, on average, are no more and no less emotionally disturbed than average-weight people. Even more surprising, they found that heaviness is not always caused by overeating (Stunkard, 1980). Many heavy people do eat large quantities of food, but so do some thin people. In one early experiment, in

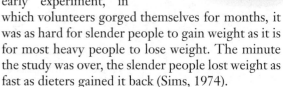
Thinking Critically about "Overeating" and Weight

which volunteers gorged themselves for months, it was as hard for slender people to gain weight as it is for most heavy people to lose weight. The minute the study was over, the slender people lost weight as fast as dieters gained it back (Sims, 1974).

Genetic Influences on Weight and Body Shape The explanation that emerged from such findings was that a biological mechanism keeps your body weight at a genetically influenced **set point**, the weight you stay at—plus or minus 10 percent—when you are not trying to gain or lose (Lissner et al., 1991). Set-point theory generated much research on how the body regulates appetite, eating, and weight. Everyone has a genetically programmed *basal metabolism rate*, the rate at which the body burns calories for energy, and a fixed number

Body weight and shape are strongly affected by genetic factors. Set-point theory helps explain why the Pimas of the American Southwest gain weight easily but lose it slowly, whereas the Bororo nomads of Nigeria can eat a lot of food yet remain slender.

of fat cells, which store fat for energy and can change in size. Obese people have about twice the number of fat cells as do adults of normal weight, and their fat cells are bigger (Spalding et al., 2008). When people lose weight, they don't lose the fat cells; the cells just get thinner, and easily plump up again.

A complex interaction of metabolism, fat cells, and hormones keeps people at the weight their bodies are designed to be, much in the way that a thermostat keeps a house at a constant temperature. When a heavy person diets, the body's metabolism slows down to conserve energy and fat reserves (Ravussin et al., 1988). When a thin person overeats, metabolism speeds up, burning energy. In one study, in which 16 slender volunteers ate 1,000 extra calories every day for eight weeks, their metabolisms sped up to burn the excess calories. They were like hummingbirds, in constant movement: fidgeting, pacing, changing their positions frequently while seated, and so on (Levine, Eberhardt, & Jensen, 1999).

What sets the set point? Genes, to start with. Pairs of adult identical twins who grow up in different families are just as similar in body weight and shape as twins raised together. And when identical twins gain weight, they gain it in the same place: Some pairs store extra pounds around their waists, others on their hips and thighs (Bouchard et al., 1990; Comuzzie & Allison, 1998). Genes also determine how much "brown fat" a person has in addition to the usual white fat. Brown fat is an energy-burning type of fat that seems important in regulating body weight and blood sugar. It is lacking in obese people, and may be one reason that people who have excess fat can't burn all the calories they consume (Cypess et al., 2009).

When there is a mutation in the genes that regulate normal eating and weight control, the result may be obesity. One gene, called *obese*, or *ob* for short, causes fat cells to secrete a protein, which researchers have named *leptin* (from the Greek *leptos*, "slender"). Leptin travels through the blood to the brain's hypothalamus, which is involved in the regulation of appetite. When leptin levels are normal, people eat just enough to maintain their weight. When a mutation of the *ob* gene causes leptin levels to be too low, however, the hypothalamus thinks the body lacks fat reserves and signals the individual to overeat. Injecting leptin into leptin-deficient mice reduces the animals' appetites, speeds up their metabolisms, and makes them more active; as a result, the animals shed weight. For this reason, researchers initially thought that leptin might be the answer to dieters' prayers: Take leptin, lose weight!

For a minority of obese people who have a congenital leptin deficiency, that is true (Farooqi et al., 2007). Alas, for most of them, and for people who are merely overweight, taking leptin does not produce much weight loss (Comuzzie & Allison, 1998).

Studies of mice suggest that leptin plays its most crucial role early in life, by altering the brain chemistry that influences how much an animal or a person later eats. More specifically, leptin helps regulate body weight by strengthening neural circuits in the hypothalamus that reduce appetite and by weakening circuits that stimulate it (Elmquist & Flier, 2004). During a critical period in infancy, leptin influences the formation of those neural connections, and the set point is, well, set (Bouret, Draper, & Simerly, 2004). Some researchers speculate that because of this early neural plasticity, overfeeding infants while the hypothalamus is developing may later produce childhood obesity.

Numerous other genes and body chemicals are linked to appetite, metabolism, and being overweight or obese (Farooqi & O'Rahilly, 2004; Frayling et al., 2007; Herbert et al., 2006; Stice et al., 2008). You have receptors in your nose and mouth that keep urging you to eat more ("The food is right there! It's good! Eat!"), receptors in your gut telling you to quit ("You've had enough already!"), and leptin and other chemicals telling you that you have stored enough fat or not enough. One hormone makes you hungry and eager to eat more, and another turns off your appetite after a meal, making you eat less.

As if all this weren't enough, your brain will get high on sugary foods even if your tongue can't taste them or enjoy their texture. Sweets increase pleasure-inducing dopamine levels in the brain, making you crave more rich food (de Araujo et al., 2008). (Forget about trying to fool your brain with artificial sweeteners; they just make you want the real thing.) Some obese individuals may have underactive reward circuitry, which leads them to overeat to boost their dopamine levels (Stice et al., 2008). When heavy people lament that they are "addicted" to food, they may be right. ✳ Explore

The complexity of the mechanisms governing appetite and weight explains why appetite-suppressing drugs and diets inevitably fail in the long run: They target only one of the many factors that

Both of these mice have a mutation in the *ob* gene, which usually makes mice chubby, like the one on the left. But when leptin is injected daily, the mice eat less and burn more calories, becoming slim, like his friendly pal. Unfortunately, leptin injections have not had the same results in most human beings.

✳ Explore
The Effects of the Hypothalamus on Eating Behavior on mypsychlab.com

Obesity is a global problem. Children around the world are eating too much food and too much fast food.

conspire to keep you the weight you are.

The Overweight Debate

More than half of all American adults, and at least 25 percent of all children and teenagers, are now overweight or obese. Increases in obesity rates have occurred in both sexes, all social classes, and all age groups, and in many other countries (Popkin, 2009). The United Nations, accustomed to dealing with problems of starvation and malnutrition, has announced that "obesity is the dominant unmet global health issue," especially in the United States, Mexico, Egypt, North Africa, Canada, Great Britain, Japan, and Australia, and even coastal China and Southeast Asia. Many health researchers are worried about this trend because obesity is considered a leading risk factor in diabetes, high blood pressure, heart disease, stroke, cancer, infertility, sleep apnea, and many other disorders. If genes and all the chemical factors and fat cells they regulate are so strongly implicated in weight and body shape, why are so many people, all over the world, getting fatter?

Environmental Influences on Weight

The leading culprits causing the worldwide rise in weight have to do with five sweeping changes in the environment (Critser, 2002; Popkin, 2009; Taubes, 2008):

1 **The increased abundance of fast food and processed foods** that are inexpensive, readily available, and high in sugar, starch, fat, and carbohydrates (Taubes, 2008). Human beings are genetically predisposed to gain weight when rich food is abundant because, in our species' evolutionary past, starvation was often a real possibility. Therefore, a tendency to store calories in the form of fat provided a definite survival advantage. Unfortunately, evolution did not produce a comparable mechanism to prevent people who do not have hummingbird metabolisms from gaining weight when food is easily available, tasty, rich, varied, and cheap.

That, of course, is precisely the situation today, surrounded as we are by three-quarter-pound burgers, fries, chips, tacos, candy bars, pizzas, and sodas.

One research team documented the direct effects of the proximity of fast-food outlets on obesity. They followed thousands of ninth-grade schoolchildren, before and after a new fast-food restaurant opened near their schools. The children whose schools were within a block of a burger or pizza outlet were more likely to become obese in the next year than students whose schools were a quarter of a mile or more away (Currie et al., 2010). Proximity to fast food seems to be a major cause of the "freshman 15" as well. In a study at two different American universities, one in the Midwest and the other in the East, more than 70 percent of all freshmen gained significant amounts of weight in their first year (Lloyd-Richardson et al., 2009).

2 **The widespread consumption of high-sugar, high-calorie soft drinks.** Throughout most of human history, the proportion of calories consumed in beverages (milk, wine, fruit juice, and the like) was very low, and thus the human body did not evolve a mechanism that would compensate for fluid intake by lowering food intake. Then, 50 years ago, soft drinks, which are loaded with sugar and calories, began spreading across the globe. Putting sweeteners into drinks has led to a weight gain of up to 14 pounds per person in those who drink two to three sodas a day (Popkin, 2009).

3 **The sharp decline in exercise and other expenditures of energy** because of remote controls, a preference for sedentary activities such as watching videos and television, sitting at a computer or working on a laptop all day, and the speed and convenience of driving rather than walking or biking.

4 **The increased portion sizes of food and drink.** Servings of food and drink have become supersized, double or triple what they were only one generation ago. Even babies and toddlers up to 2 years of age are being fed as much as 30 percent more calories than they need (Fox et al., 2004). In France, people eat rich food but much less of it than Americans do. Their notion of what a proper portion is—for yogurt, soda, a salad, a sandwich, anything—is way lower than in the United States (Rozin et al., 2003).

5 **The abundance of highly varied foods.** When diets are predictable and routine, people habituate to what they are eating and eat less of it. That is why all diets that restrict people to eating only a

Get Involved! What's Controlling How Much You Eat?

Many people believe that what they eat and how much they eat is regulated by how hungry they feel. But the motivation to eat is complicated. Here are some invisible external influences on your eating habits (Wansink, 2006):

- **Package size**: People eat more from a large container (say, of popcorn) than a small one.
- **Plate size**: People eat more when they serve themselves on large plates rather than small ones.
- **Cues of how much has been eaten**: People eat more from a buffet when waiters quickly replace their dirty dishes, thereby eliminating telltale signs of how much food has already been consumed.
- **Kitchen and table layouts**: People eat more when food and snacks are displayed prominently, are varied, and are easily accessible.
- **Distraction**: People eat more when they are being distracted by friends and the environment.

   The next time you are out with friends, note how much everyone is eating (including yourself), and notice whether any of the above influences are at work. If you are trying to lose weight, how can you alter your own environment to correct for these influences?

few kinds of foods are successful at first. As soon as food becomes more varied, however, people eat more and gain more weight (Remick, Polivy, & Pliner, 2009).

Cultural Influences on Weight and the Ideal Body

Eating habits and activity levels, in turn, are shaped by a culture's customs and standards of what the ideal body should look like: fat or thin, muscular or soft. In many places around the world, especially where famine and crop failures are common, fat is taken as a sign of health, affluence in men, and sexual desirability in women (Stearns, 1997). Among the Calabari of Nigeria, brides are put in special fattening huts where they do nothing but eat, so as to become fat enough to please their husbands.

   Cultural influences on obesity can also be observed among white farm families. Farmers originally ate large amounts of food for *intrinsic* reasons: When you do hard, labor-intensive work, you need a lot of calories. But today, many farm families eat for *extrinsic* motives: to be sociable and conform to family tradition. In the farm belt states of the American Midwest, people are expected to eat huge, hearty meals and plenty of sweet desserts. If you don't join in, you are being antisocial, insulting your hosts and rejecting your kin (Angier, 2000).

   Ironically, although people of all ethnicities and social classes have been getting fatter, the cultural ideal for women and men in the United States,

Canada, and Europe has been getting thinner. The plump, curvy female body, with ample hips and breasts, was fashionable in eras that celebrated women's role as mothers, such as after World War II, when women were encouraged to give up their wartime jobs and have many children (Stearns, 1997). Today's big-breasted but otherwise skinny female ideal may reflect today's norm: Women are supposed to be both professionally competent *and* maternal. For men too, the ideal body has changed. When most heavily muscled men were laborers and farmers, being physically strong and muscular was considered unattractive, a sign of being working class. Today, having a strong, muscular body is a sign of affluence rather than poverty. It means a man has the money and the time to join a gym and work out (Bordo, 2000).

   You can see why many people, especially women, find themselves caught in a battle between their biology and their culture. Evolution has designed women to store fat, which is necessary for the onset of menstruation, for pregnancy and nursing, and, after menopause, for the production of estrogen. In cultures that think women should be very thin, therefore, many women become obsessed with weight and are continually dieting, forever fighting their bodies' need for a little healthy roundness.

The Body as Battleground: Eating Disorders

Some people lose the battle between the body they have and the body they want, developing serious

Should a woman be voluptuous and curvy or slim as a reed? Should a man be thin and smooth or strong and buff? What explains cultural changes in attitudes toward the ideal body? During the 1950s, actresses like Jayne Mansfield embodied the postwar ideal: soft, curvy, buxom, and "womanly." Today, when women are expected to work and have families, the ideal is to be thin *and* have prominent breasts, like actress Salma Hayek. Men, too, have been caught up in body-image changes. In the 1960s, the ideal was the soft and scrawny hippie; today's ideal man looks like actor Hugh Jackman, tough and muscular.

bulimia nervosa An eating disorder characterized by episodes of excessive eating (bingeing) followed by forced vomiting or use of laxatives (purging).

anorexia nervosa An eating disorder characterized by fear of being fat, a distorted body image, radically reduced consumption of food, and emaciation.

eating disorders that reflect an irrational terror of being fat. In **bulimia nervosa**, the person binges (eats vast quantities of rich food, sometimes everything that is in the kitchen) and then purges by inducing vomiting or abusing laxatives. In **anorexia nervosa**, the person eats hardly anything and therefore becomes dangerously thin; people with anorexia typically have severely distorted body images, thinking they are fat even when they are emaciated. Anorexia has the highest mortality rate of all mental disorders; many of its sufferers die of heart or kidney failure or complications of osteoporosis. Their weakened bones simply collapse.

Bulimia and anorexia are the most well-known eating disorders, and occur most often among young white women. But more than 40 percent of all cases of eating disorders occur among men, the elderly, ethnic minority groups, young children, and athletes, and do not fit the diagnostic criteria for bulimia or anorexia (Thomas, Vartanian, & Brownell, 2009). People with *binge-eating disorder* binge without purging; others chew whatever food they want but spit it out without swallowing; others are normal weight but take no joy in eating because they worry obsessively about gaining a pound; some develop phobias about eating certain kinds of food. All of these disorders involve an unhealthy attitude toward food, weight, and the body.

Genes play a role in the development of anorexia nervosa, which has been found across cultures and throughout history (Striegel-Moore & Bulik, 2007). But most disorders are generated by psychological factors, including depression and anxiety, low self-esteem, perfectionism, and a distorted body image (Presnell, Bearman, & Stice, 2004; Sherry & Hall, 2009). Cultural factors can also generate dissatisfaction with one's body. As we note in Chapter 11, bulimia is rare to nonexistent in non-Western cultures and has only become a significant problem in Western cultures with the rise of the thin ideal for women (Keel & Klump, 2003). A meta-analysis of experimental and correlational studies found that women's exposure to the media ideal of impossibly thin women fosters the belief that "thin is beautiful" and increases the risk of disordered eating among women of all ethnicities who buy into it (Grabe & Hyde, 2006; Grabe, Ward, & Hyde, 2008). American culture is also rife with "body snarking," the relentlessly critical and snide appraisals of other people's bodies that get posted on blogs, YouTube, Facebook, and Twitter, and are constant topics for entertainment magazines and talk shows.

Eating disorders and body image distortions among boys and men are increasing too, though they take different forms. Just as anorexic women see their gaunt bodies as being too fat, some men have the delusion that their muscular bodies are too puny, so they abuse steroids and exercise or pump iron compulsively (Thompson & Cafri, 2007). Men

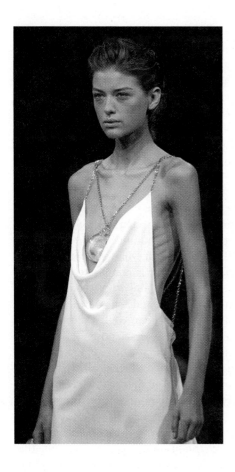

What is the difference between being slender and being too thin? Does the fashion model on the left look good to you or does she look emaciated? Likewise, what is the difference between being "pleasantly plump" and being fat? Nikki Blonsky, the exuberant star of the movie *Hairspray,* is overweight but physically fit. Does she look good to you or does she look too heavy?

in cultures that do not think the heavily muscled male body is desirable or attractive, as in Taiwan and Kenya, have fewer body image disorders than American men do (Campbell, Pope, & Filiault, 2005; Yang, Gray, & Pope, 2005). ⊙ Watch

In sum, within a given environment, genetic predispositions for a certain body weight and metabolism interact with psychological needs, cultural norms, and individual habits to shape, in this case quite literally, who we are.

⊙ **Watch** the **Video Eating Disorders** on **mypsychlab.com**

✓ **Study** and **Review** on **mypsychlab.com**

Quick Quiz

Is all this information about eating making you hungry for knowledge?

1. *True or false*: Most fat people are heavy because their emotional problems cause them to overeat.

2. What theory seems to explain why thin people rarely become fat and fat people have so much trouble losing weight?

3. Which hormone helps regulate appetite by telling the hypothalamus that the body has stored enough fat?

4. What are five major environmental reasons for the rising number of overweight people?

5. Bill, who is thin, reads in the newspaper that genes set the range of body weight and shape. "Oh, good," he exclaims, "now I can eat all the junk food I want; I was born to be skinny." What's wrong with Bill's conclusion?

Answers:

1. false 2. set-point theory 3. leptin 4. increased consumption of fast, high-calorie foods; increased consumption of sweetened sodas and other drinks; a decline in exercise; increased sizes of food and drink portions; increased variety of food 5. Bill is right to recognize that there may be limits to how heavy he can become, but he is oversimplifying and jumping to conclusions. Many people who have a set point for leanness will gain considerable weight on rich food and sugary drinks, especially if they don't exercise. Also, junk food is unhealthy for reasons that have nothing to do with becoming overweight.

YOU are about to learn...

- how biology affects attachment and love.
- some key psychological influences on whom and how you love.
- the three basic styles of attachment and how they affect relationships.
- how economic concerns influence love and marriage.

The Social Animal: Motives to Love

In 1875, a teenager named Annie Oakley defeated Frank Butler, the star of the Buffalo Bill Wild West Show, in a sharpshooting competition. "The next day I came back to see the little girl who had beaten me," wrote Butler many years later, "and it was not long until we married." He became her manager, and for the next 50 years, they traveled together across Europe and America, where her skills with a gun made her the toast of both continents. They remained devoted until their deaths in 1926 (Kreps, 1990).

What kept Annie Oakley and Frank Butler in love for 50 years, when so many other romantic passions die in five years, five weeks, or five hours? What *is* love, anyway—the crazy, heart-palpitating feeling of longing for another person, or the steady, stable feeling of deep and abiding attachment?

The Biology of Love

Psychologists who study love (a tough job, but someone has to do it) distinguish *passionate (romantic) love*, characterized by a whirlwind of intense emotions and sexual passion, from *companionate love*, characterized by affection and trust. Passionate love is the stuff of crushes, infatuations, "love at first sight," and the early stage of love affairs. It may burn out completely or evolve into companionate love. Passionate love is known in all cultures and has a long and passionate history. Wars and duels have been fought because of it, people have committed suicide because of it, great love affairs have begun, and been torn apart, because of it. Yet, although the experience of romantic love is universal, many cultures have not regarded it as the proper basis for anything serious, such as marriage (Hatfield & Rapson, 2008).

In this era of fMRIs and biotechnical advances, it was inevitable that researchers would seek to explain passionate love by rummaging around in the brain. And if you think that what scientists are finding about diet and weight is complicated, their efforts to tease apart the links between romantic passion, sexual yearning, and long-term love make the problem of obesity seem, well, a piece of cake. There are olfactory cues in a potential partner's scent that can turn you on (or off). There are physical cues in a potential partner's voice and body shape, and even in how similar his or her face is to yours. There is the dopamine jolt of reward, from the same dopamine that makes anticipation of a fabulous meal or an addictive drug so pleasurable, and there are the arousal and excitement that adrenaline provides (Aron et al., 2005; Cozolino, 2006). And then there are key hormones that turn that first phase of exhilaration into the longer-lasting phase of attachment and bonding.

The neurological origins of passionate love may begin in infancy, in the baby's attachment to the mother. In the view of evolutionary psychologists, maternal and romantic love, the deepest of human attachments, share a common evolutionary purpose—preserving the species—and so they share common neural mechanisms, the ones that make attachment and pair-bonding feel good. And, in fact, certain key neurotransmitters and hormones

Adult romantic love, with its exchange of loving gazes and depth of passionate attachment, may have its origins in the biology of the baby–mother bond.

that are involved in pleasure and reward are activated in the mother–baby pair-bond and again later in the pair-bond of adult lovers (Bartels & Zeki, 2004; Diamond, 2004).

Two of the most important hormones for social bonding are *vasopressin* and *oxytocin*, which influence feelings and expressions of love, caring, and trust between mothers and babies, between friends, and between lovers (Walum et al., 2008; Taylor et al., 2000b). In one study, volunteers who inhaled oxytocin in a nasal spray were later more likely than control subjects to trust one another in various risky interactions (Kosfeld et al., 2005). In another study, couples given oxytocin increased their nonverbal expressions of love for one another—gazing, smiling, and fondling—compared to couples given a placebo (Gonzaga et al., 2006). Conversely, when prairie voles, a monogamous species, are given a drug that blocks oxytocin, they continue to mate, but they don't get attached to their partners (Ross et al., 2009).

Studies of animals also find that the feelings and actions characteristic of attachment are mediated by the pleasure–reward circuits in the brain, stimulated by the release of *endorphins*, the brain's natural opiates (see Chapter 4). When baby mice and other animals are separated from their mothers, they cry out in distress, and the mother's touch (or lick) releases endorphins that soothe the infant. But when puppies, guinea pigs, and chicks are injected with low doses of either morphine or endorphins, the animals show much less distress than usual when separated from their mothers; the chemicals seem to be a biological replacement for mom (Panksepp et al., 1980). These findings suggest that endorphin-stimulated euphoria may be a child's initial motive for seeking affection and cuddling—that, in effect, a child attached to a parent is a child addicted to love. The addictive quality of adult passionate love, including the physical and emotional distress that lovers feel when they are apart, may involve the same biochemistry (Diamond, 2004).

Using fMRI, neuroscientists have found other neurological similarities between infant–mother love and adult romantic love. Certain parts of the brain light up when people look at images of their sweethearts, in contrast to other parts that are activated when they see pictures of friends or furniture. And these are the same areas that are activated when mothers see images of their own children as opposed to pictures of other children (Bartels & Zeki, 2004).

Clearly, then, the bonds of attachment are biologically based. Yet, as always, it is important to avoid the oversimplified conclusion that "love is all in our hormones" or "love occurs in this corner of the brain but not that one." Human love affairs involve many other factors that affect whom we choose, how we get along with that person, and whether we stay with a partner over the years.

The Psychology of Love

Many romantics believe that only one true love awaits them. Considering that there are 6.8 billion people on the planet, the odds of finding said person are a bit daunting. What if you're in Omaha or Winnipeg and your true love is in Dubrovnik or Kankakee? You could wander for years and never cross paths.

Fortunately, evolution has made it possible to form deep and lasting attachments without traveling the world. In fact, the first major predictor of whom we love is plain *proximity*: We choose our friends and lovers from the set of people who live close by, or who study or work near us. The people who are nearest to you are most likely to be dearest to you, too. The second major predictor is *similarity*—in looks, attitudes, beliefs, values, personality, and interests (Berscheid & Reis, 1998). Although it is commonly believed that opposites attract, the fact is that we tend to choose friends and loved ones who are most like us. Many students use Facebook to find romantic prospects who share their love of poker and vampire movies, their religious beliefs, or anything else they care about. ◉—|Watch

The Internet has made matching possible on all kinds of dimensions. There are nearly 1,000 dating websites in the U.S., matching couples by age, political attitudes, religion or secularism, sexual orientation, pet ownership, and many other criteria.

◉—|**Watch** the **Video Dating and Finding a Mate - Ralf 33** on **mypsychlab.com**

Internet services capitalize on the fact that like attracts like. "What type turns you on?" asks this ad. Usually, the type that is similar to you!

Some prominent matchmaking sites administer questionnaires and personality inventories, claiming to use scientific principles to pair up potential soul mates (Sprecher et al., 2008). These efforts vary in effectiveness. Can you think why? One reason is that many people think they know exactly what they "must have" in a partner, and then they meet someone who has few of those qualities but a whole bunch of others that suddenly become "essential." Another reason, though, is that the premises of some of these sciency-sounding matchmaking sites may be faulty, especially those based on un-validated "biological matches" and anecdotal testimonials (King, Austin-Oden, & Lohr, 2009). Yet one underlying premise of most Internet matching sites is basically correct: Like attracts like.

"My preference is for someone who's afraid of closeness, like me."

The Attachment Theory of Love Once you find someone to love, *how* do you love? According to Phillip Shaver and Cindy Hazan (1993), adults, just like babies, can be *secure, anxious,* or *avoidant* in their attachments (see Chapter 3). Securely attached lovers are rarely jealous or worried about being abandoned. They are more compassionate and helpful than insecurely attached people and are quicker to understand and forgive their partners if the partner does something thoughtless or annoying (Mikulincer et al., 2005; Mikulincer & Shaver, 2007). Anxious lovers are always agitated about their relationships; they want to be close but worry that their partners will leave them. Other people often describe them as clingy, which may be why they are more likely than secure lovers to suffer from unrequited love. Avoidant people distrust and avoid intimate attachments.

Where do these differences come from? According to the *attachment theory of love,* people's attachment styles as adults derive in large part from how their parents cared for them (Dinero et al., 2008; Mikulincer & Shaver, 2007). Children form internal "working models" of relationships: Can I trust others? Am I worthy of being loved? Will my parents leave me? If a child's parents are cold and rejecting and provide little or no emotional and physical comfort, the child learns to expect other relationships to be the same. When children form secure attachments to trusted parents, they become more trusting of others, expecting to form other secure attachments with friends and lovers in adulthood (Feeney & Cassidy, 2003).

Indeed, when asked to tell about their parents, securely attached adults report having had warm, close relationships. Although they recognize their parents' flaws, they describe their parents as having

been more loving and kind than insecurely attached people do. Anxious people feel more ambivalence toward their parents, especially their mothers, and also describe their parents ambivalently, as having been both harsh and kind. And people with an avoidant attachment style describe their parents in almost entirely negative terms. These individuals are most likely to report having had cold, rejecting parents, extended periods of separation from their mothers, or childhood environments that prevented them from forging close ties with others (Hazan & Shaver, 1994; Klohnen & Bera, 1998).

Keep in mind, though, that a child's own temperament and genetic predispositions could also help account for the consistency of attachment styles from childhood to adulthood, as well as for the working models of relationships that are formed during childhood (Gillath et al., 2008). A child who is temperamentally fearful or difficult, or whose reward circuits do not function normally, may reject even the kindest parent's efforts to console and cuddle (see Chapter 3). That child may therefore come to feel anxious or ambivalent in his or her adult relationships.

Interestingly, some leading attachment researchers believe that insecure attachment may be as evolutionarily beneficial as secure attachment. Social groups containing people with different attachment patterns may have been more likely to survive, because insecurely attached individuals, not having partners inducing them to remain cozily at home, might have been more likely to behave independently in ways that could benefit the group, as well as to take risks and face dangers in the environment that were threatening the group's safety (Ein-Dor et al., 2010).

The Ingredients of Love When people are asked to define the key ingredients of love, most agree that love is a mix of passion, intimacy, and commitment (Lemieux & Hale, 2000). Intimacy is based on deep knowledge of the other person, which accumulates gradually, but passion is based on emotion, which is generated by novelty and change. That is why passion is usually highest at the beginning of a relationship, when two people begin to disclose things about themselves to each other, and lowest when knowledge of the other person's beliefs and habits is at its maximum, when it seems that there is nothing left to learn about the beloved.

Nonetheless, according to an analysis of a large number of adult couples and a meta-analysis of 25 studies of couples in long- and short-term relationships, romantic love can persist for many years and is strongly associated with a couple's happiness. What diminishes among these happy couples is that part of romantic love we might call *obsessiveness*, constant thinking and worrying about the loved one and the relationship (Acevedo & Aron, 2009).

Biological factors such as the brain's opiate system may contribute to early passion, as we noted, but most psychologists believe that the ability to sustain a long and intimate love relationship has more to do with a couple's attitudes, values, and balance of power than with genes or hormones. One of the most important psychological predictors of satisfaction in long-term relationships is the perception, by both partners, that the relationship is fair, rewarding, and balanced. Partners who feel over-benefited (getting more than they are giving) tend to feel guilty; those who feel under-benefited (not getting what they feel they deserve) tend to feel resentful and angry (Pillemer, Hatfield, & Sprecher, 2008). A couple may tootle along comfortably until a stressful event—such as the arrival of children, serious illness, unemployment, or retirement—evokes simmering displeasure over issues of "what's fair."

Another key psychological factor in couples' ability to sustain love is the nature of their primary motivation to maintain the relationship: Is it positive (to enjoy affection and intimacy) or negative (to avoid feeling insecure and lonely)? Couples motivated by the former goal tend to report more satisfaction with their partners (Gable & Poore, 2008). We will see that this difference in motivation—positive or negative—affects happiness and satisfaction in many different domains of life.

The critical-thinking guideline "define your terms" may never be more important than in matters of love. The way we define love deeply affects our satisfaction with relationships and whether or not our relationships last. If you believe that the only real love is the kind defined by obsession and sexual passion, then you may decide you are out of love when the initial phase of attraction fades, as it eventually must—and you will be repeatedly disappointed. Robert Solomon (1994) argued that "We conceive of [love] falsely. . . . We expect an explosion at the beginning powerful enough to fuel love through all of its ups and downs instead of viewing love as a process over which we have control, a process that tends to increase with time rather than wane."

Some psychologists themselves have made this mistake. They have tended to define "falling in love" as a romantic thunderbolt: You are standing there, minding your own business, when Perfect Person strolls by and you are smitten at first sight; you "fall"; your brain lights up. However, people fall in love in different ways: Some couples do so gradually, over time, after "falling in friendship" first; couples in arranged marriages may come to love each other long after the wedding (Aron et al., 2008). All the fMRIs in the world can't capture that.

> **Thinking Critically about Defining Love**

Passionate love starts relationships, but companionate love keeps them going.

JUMP START reprinted by permission of United Feature Syndicate, Inc.

Gender, Culture, and Love

Which sex is more romantic? Which sex truly understands true love? Which sex falls in love but won't commit? Pop-psych books are full of answers, along with advice for dealing with all those love-challenged fools who love you and leave you. But all stereotypes oversimplify. Neither sex loves more than the other in terms of love at first sight, passionate love, or companionate love over the long haul (Dion & Dion, 1993; Hatfield & Rapson, 1996/2005). Men and women are equally likely to suffer the heart-crushing torments of unrequited love. They are equally likely to be securely or insecurely attached (Feeney & Cassidy, 2003). Both sexes suffer mightily when a love relationship ends, assuming they did not want it to.

However, women and men do differ, on average, in how they *express* the fundamental motives for love and intimacy. Males in many cultures learn early that revelations of emotion can be construed as evidence of vulnerability and weakness, which are considered unmasculine (see Chapter 13). Thus, men in such cultures often develop ways of revealing love that are based on actions rather than words: doing things for the partner, supporting the family financially, or just sharing the same activity, such as watching TV or a football game together (Shields, 2002).

These gender differences reflect gender roles, which are in turn shaped by social, economic, and cultural forces. For many years, Western men were more romantic than women in their choice of partner, and women in turn were far more pragmatic than men. One reason was that a woman did not just marry a man; she married a standard of living. Therefore, she could not afford to marry someone unsuitable or waste her time in a relationship that was not going anywhere, even if she loved the guy. She married, in short, for extrinsic reasons rather than intrinsic ones. In the 1960s, two-thirds of a sample of college men said they would not marry someone they did not love, but only one-fourth of the women ruled out the possibility (Kephart, 1967).

As women entered the workforce and as two incomes became necessary in most families, the gender difference in romantic love faded, and so did economic motivations to marry, all over the world. Nowadays, in every developed nation, people marry for intrinsic motives, for the pleasure of being with the partner they chose. Only tiny numbers of women and men would consider marrying someone they did not love, even if the person had all the right qualities. Pragmatic (extrinsic) reasons for marriage, with romantic love being a remote luxury, persist only in countries where the extended family still controls female sexuality and the financial terms of marriage (Hatfield & Rapson, 1996/2005). Yet even in these countries, such as India and Pakistan, the tight rules governing marriage choices are loosening. So are the rules forbidding divorce, even in extremely traditional nations such as Japan, China, and South Korea.

As you can see, our motivations to love may start with biology and the workings of the brain, but they are shaped and directed by our early experiences with parents, the culture we live in, the historical era that shapes us, and something as utterly unromantic as economic dependency or self-sufficiency.

Economic and social changes are transforming gender roles in all developed nations. But marriage for financial security is still the only option for many women from impoverished nations—like this bride, whose husband chose her from a mail-order catalog.

Study and **Review** on **mypsychlab.com**

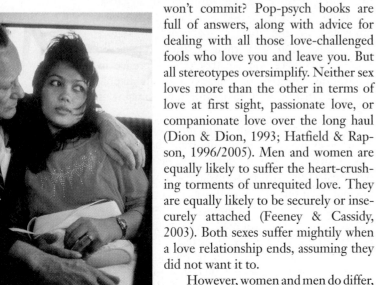

Quick Quiz

Are you passionately committed to quizzes yet?

1. How are adult passionate love and infant–mother love biologically similar?

2. The two major predictors of whom we love are _____ and _____.

3. Tiffany is wildly in love with Timothy, and he with her, but she can't stop worrying about his fidelity and doubting his love. She wants to be with him constantly, but she pushes him away whenever she feels jealous, which is often. According to the attachment theory of love, which style of attachment does Tiffany have?

4. *True or false:* Until recently, men in Western societies were more likely than women to marry for love.

Answers:

1. Both involve the release of neurotransmitters, vasopressin and oxytocin, and endorphins that make attachment literally feel good, by activating the pleasure–reward circuits in the brain. 2. proximity and similarity 3. anxious 4. true

YOU are about to learn...

- which part of the anatomy is the "sexiest sex organ."
- why pleasure is only one of many motives for having sex.
- how culture affects sexual practices.
- the puzzling origins of sexual orientation.

The Erotic Animal: Motives for Sex

Most people believe that sex is a biological drive, merely a matter of doing what comes naturally. "What's there to discuss about sexual motivation?" they say. "Isn't it all inborn, inevitable, and inherently pleasurable?"

It is certainly true that in most other species, sexual behavior is genetically programmed. Without instruction, a male stickleback fish knows exactly what to do with a female stickleback, and a whooping crane knows when to whoop. But as sex researcher and therapist Leonore Tiefer (2004) has observed, "sex is not a natural act" for human beings. Sex, she says, is more like dancing than digestion, something you learn and can be motivated to improve rather than a simple physiological process. For one thing, the activities that one culture considers "natural"—such as mouth-to-mouth kissing or oral sex—are often considered unnatural in another culture or historical time. Second, people have to learn from experience and culture what they are supposed to do with their sexual desires and how they are expected to behave. And third, people's motivations for sexual activity are by no means always and only for intrinsic pleasure. Human sexuality is influenced by a blend of biological, psychological, and cultural factors.

Desire and sensuality are lifelong pleasures.

The Biology of Desire

Physiological research has dispelled a lot of nonsense about sexuality, such as the once-common notions that men must have intercourse once they are aroused or they will get "blue balls"; that "good" women don't have orgasms at all; or that mature women should have the "right kind" of orgasm (Ehrenreich, 1978).

The first modern attack on these beliefs came from Alfred Kinsey and his associates (1948, 1953) in their pioneering books on male and female sexuality. Kinsey's team surveyed thousands of Americans about their sexual attitudes and behavior, and they also reviewed the existing research on sexual physiology. In *Sexual Behavior in the Human Female*, they observed that "males would be better prepared to understand females, and females to understand males, if they realized that they are alike in their basic anatomy and physiology." For example, the penis and the clitoris develop from the same embryonic tissues; they differ in size, of course, but not in sensitivity. At that time, many people believed that women were not as sexually motivated as men and that women cared more about affection than sexual satisfaction, notions soundly refuted by Kinsey's interviews.

The idea that men and women are sexually similar in any way, let alone that women were sexual at all, was extremely shocking in 1953, and Kinsey was attacked not only for his findings, but also for even daring to ask people (especially female people) about their sexual lives. The national hysteria that accompanied the Kinsey Reports seems hard to believe today. Yet it is still difficult for social scientists to conduct serious, methodologically sound research on the development of human sexuality. As John Bancroft, the current head of the Kinsey Institute, has observed, because many American adults need to believe that young children have no sexual feelings, they interpret any evidence of normal sexual expression in childhood (such as masturbation or "playing doctor") as a symptom of sexual abuse. And because many adults are uncomfortable about sexual activity among teenagers, they try to restrict or eliminate it by prohibiting sex education and promoting abstinence; then they reject research showing that such prohibitions either have no effect at all or actually increase the behavior they consider taboo (Bancroft, 2006; Levine, 2003; Santelli et al., 2006). Some conservative organizations also try to block research on sexual behavior they believe the Bible disapproves of, such as masturbation, homosexuality, and any form of sexual behavior outside of marriage.

The "Kinsey Report" on women, officially titled *Sexual Behavior in the Human Female*, was not exactly greeted with praise and acceptance, let alone clear thinking. Some critics were so emotionally upset by the book's message (that many women were enjoying sex and had had premarital sex) that they chose to attack the messenger.

Following Kinsey, the next wave of sex research began in the 1960s, with the laboratory research of physician William Masters and his associate Virginia Johnson (1966). Masters and Johnson's research helped to sweep away cobwebs of superstition and ignorance about how the body works. In studies of physiological changes during sexual arousal and orgasm, they confirmed that male and female orgasms are indeed remarkably similar and that all orgasms are physiologically the same, regardless of the source of stimulation. Masters and Johnson concluded that the sexes differ in just one major way: Women's capacity for sexual response "infinitely surpasses that of men," they said, because women, unlike most men, are able to have repeated orgasms (until, presumably, exhaustion or a ringing doorbell makes them stop).

If you have ever taken a sex-ed class, you may have had to memorize Masters and Johnson's description of the "four stages of the sexual response cycle": desire, arousal (excitement), orgasm, resolution. Unfortunately, the impulse to oversimplify—treating these four stages as if they were akin to the invariable cycles of a washing machine—led to a mistaken inference of universality. It later turned out that not everyone has an orgasm even following great excitement, and that in many women, desire *follows* arousal (Laan & Both, 2008). Masters and Johnson's research was limited by the selection of a sample consisting only of men and women who were easily orgasmic, and they did not investigate

how people's physiological responses might vary according to their age, experience, and culture (Tiefer, 2004). Sex researchers have since learned much more about individual variation in sexual physiology. People vary not only in their propensity for sexual excitation and responsiveness, but also in their ability to inhibit and control that excitement (Bancroft et al., 2009). That is, some people are all accelerator and no brakes, and others are slow to accelerate but quick to brake.

Hormones and Sexual Response One biological factor that promotes sexual desire in both sexes is the hormone testosterone, an androgen (masculinizing hormone). This fact has created a market for the legal and illegal use of androgens. The assumption is that if the goal is to reduce sexual desire, as in sex offenders, testosterone should be lowered, say through chemical castration; if the goal is to increase sexual desire in women and men who complain of low libido, testosterone should be increased, like adding fuel to your gas tank. Yet these efforts often fail to produce the expected results (Berlin, 2003; Anderson, 2005). Why?

One reason is that in primates, unlike other mammals, sexual motivation requires more than hormones; it is also affected by social experience and context (Wallen, 2001). That is why desire can persist in sex offenders who have lost testosterone, and why desire might remain low in people who have been given testosterone. Indeed, artificially administered testosterone does not do much more than a placebo to increase sexual satisfaction in healthy people, nor does a drop in testosterone invariably cause a loss of sexual motivation or enjoyment. In studies of women who had had their uteruses or ovaries surgically removed or who were going through menopause, use of a testosterone patch increased their sexual activity to only one more time a month over the placebo group (Buster et al., 2005).

There are also three significant medical problems with the use of testosterone to enhance sexual desire: (1) There is no consensus on the difference between normally low and abnormally deficient levels. (2) It is easy to misdiagnose the symptoms of androgen deficiency (low libido, fatigue, lack of well-being) because those are also symptoms of depression and relationship problems. (3) The side effects of androgen can range from unpleasant to harmful (International Consensus Conference, 2002), and side effects are unlikely to increase desire.

Sex and the "Sex Drive" The question of whether men and women are alike or different in some underlying, biologically based sex drive

"It's a guy thing."

continues to provoke lively debate. Although women on average are certainly as capable as men of sexual pleasure, men do have higher rates of almost every kind of sexual behavior, including masturbation, erotic fantasies and pornography use, and casual sex (Oliver & Hyde, 1993; Petersen & Hyde, 2010; Peplau, 2003). These sex differences occur even when men are forbidden by cultural or religious rules to engage in sex at all; Catholic priests have more of these sexual experiences than Catholic nuns

do (Baumeister, Catanese, & Vohs, 2001). Men are also more likely than women to admit to having sex because "I was slumming" or "The opportunity presented itself" (Meston & Buss, 2007).

Biological psychologists argue that these differences occur universally because the hormones and brain circuits involved in sexual behavior differ for men and women. They maintain that, for men, the wiring for sex overlaps with that for dominance and aggression, which is why sex and aggression are more likely to be linked in men than women. For women, the circuits and hormones governing sexuality and nurturance seem to overlap, which is why sex and love are more likely to be linked in women than in men (Diamond, 2008).

Other psychologists, however, believe that most gender differences in sexual behavior reflect women's and men's different roles and experiences in life and have little or nothing to do with biologically based drives or brain circuits (Eagly & Wood, 1999; Tiefer, 2008). A middle view is that men's sexual behavior is more biologically influenced than is women's, whereas women's sexual desires and responsiveness are more affected by circumstances, the specific relationship, and cultural norms (Baumeister, 2000).

Evolution and Sexual Strategies Evolutionary psychologists believe that differences between women and men in sex drive and courtship and mating practices evolved in response to species' survival needs (Buss, 1994). In this view, it was evolutionarily adaptive for males to compete with other males for access to young and fertile females,

This Kenyan man has 40 wives and 349 children. He is unusual even in his own culture, but around the world, it is more common for men than women to have multiple sexual partners. Evolutionary psychologists think the reason is that men have evolved to sow as many wild oats are they can, whereas women have evolved to be happy with just a few grains.

and to try to win and then inseminate as many females as possible. The more females a male mates with, the more genes he can pass along. The human record in this regard was achieved by a man who fathered 899 children (Daly & Wilson, 1983). What else he did with his time is unknown.

Females, according to many evolutionary psychologists, need to shop for the best genetic deal, as it were, because they can conceive and bear only a limited number of offspring. Having such a large biological investment in each pregnancy, females must choose partners more carefully than males do. Besides, mating with a lot of different males would produce no more offspring than staying with just one. So females try to attach themselves to dominant males who have resources and status and are likely to have superior genes.

The result of these two opposite sexual strategies, in this view, is that males generally want sex more often than females do; males are often fickle and promiscuous, whereas females are usually devoted and faithful; males are drawn to sexual novelty and even rape, whereas females want stability and security; males are relatively undiscriminating in their choice of sexual partners, whereas females are cautious and choosy; and males are competitive and concerned about dominance, whereas females are less so.

In human beings, some of these sex differences do appear to be universal or at least very common. In one massive project, 50 scientists studied 10,000 people in 37 cultures located on six continents and five islands (Buss, 1994; Schmitt, 2003). Around the world, they found, men are more violent than women and more socially dominant. They are more interested in the youth and beauty of their sexual partners, presumably because youth is associated with fertility. According to their responses on questionnaires, they are more sexually jealous and possessive, presumably because if a man's mate had sex with other men, he could never be 100 percent sure that her children were genetically his. They are more promiscuous than women, presumably so that their sperm will be distributed as widely as possible. Women are more sexually cautious than men; they tend to emphasize the financial resources or prospects of a potential mate, his status, and his willingness to commit to a relationship (Bailey et al., 1994; Buss, 2000; Buunk et al., 1996; Daly & Wilson, 1983; Mealey, 2000).

Ah, father love! Evolutionary approaches to sex assume that males across species have only a minimal investment in caring for offspring. But there are many exceptions, including these male snow monkeys and lions, who are doting dads.

Evolution, Culture, and Sex Evolutionary views of sex differences have become enormously popular. Many academics and laypeople are persuaded that there are indeed evolutionary advantages for males of sowing their seeds far and wide and evolutionary advantages for females of finding a man with a good paycheck. But critics, including some prominent evolutionary theorists, have challenged this conclusion on conceptual and methodological grounds.

Thinking Critically about Evolutionary Theories of Sex

1 Stereotypes versus actual behavior. The behavior of humans and other animals often fails to conform to the stereotyped images of sexually promiscuous males and coy, choosy females (Barash & Lipton, 2001; Birkhead, 2001; Fausto-Sterling, 1997; Hrdy, 1994; Roughgarden, 2004). In many species of birds, fish, and mammals, including human beings, females are sexually ardent and often have many male partners. They have sex when they are not ovulating and even when they are already pregnant. And in many species, from penguins to primates, males do not just mate and run. They stick around, feeding the infants, carrying them on their backs, and protecting them against predators (Hrdy, 1988; Snowdon, 1997).

In human beings, national and ethnic groups that value greater equality between the sexes have smaller gender differences in sexual behavior than do cultures that promote gender inequality. In America today, differences in sexual behaviors and attitudes are not as large as the evolutionary stereotype suggests: Men and women have become more alike than different (Petersen & Hyde, 2010).

2 Cultural variation. Human sexual behavior is amazingly varied and changeable across time and place. Cultures range from those in which women have many children to those in which they have very few, from those in which men are intimately involved in child rearing to those in which they take no part at all, from those in which women may have many lovers to those in which women may be killed for having sex outside of marriage. In many places, the chastity of a potential mate is much more important to men than to women, but in other places, it is important to both sexes—or to neither one. (See Figure 14.1.) In some places, just as evolutionary theory predicts, a relatively few men—those with the greatest wealth and power—have a far greater number of offspring than other men do; but in many societies, including some polygamous ones, powerful men do not have more children than men who are poor or who are low in status (Brown, Laland, & Mulder, 2009).

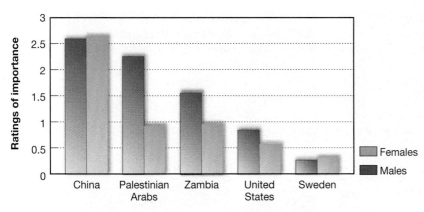

FIGURE 14.1
Attitudes toward Chastity
In many places, men care more about a partner's chastity than women do, as evolutionary psychologists would predict. But culture has a powerful impact on these attitudes, as this graph shows. Notice that in China, both sexes prefer a partner who has not yet had intercourse, whereas in Sweden, chastity is a nonissue (in Buss, 1995).

People's attitudes and sexual practices can change rapidly within a culture, too. In America, young people's sexual attitudes and behavior changed dramatically between 1943 and 1999, with the largest changes occurring among girls and young women. Approval of premarital sex leapt from 12 percent to 73 percent among young women, and from 40 percent to 79 percent among young men (Wells & Twenge, 2005). Behavior changed accordingly.

3 **What people say versus what they do.** Evolutionary psychologists have tended to rely on data from questionnaires and interviews, but people's responses can be a poor guide to their actual choices and actions. When people are asked to rank the traits they most value in a sexual partner or someone they'd like to go out with, sex differences appear, just as evolutionary theory would predict: People *say* they want a partner who is rich or beautiful (or both) (Kenrick et al., 2001). But the factors that predict whom people *actually* choose for mating and dating tell another story. As we saw in discussing love, most people choose partners based on their similarity and proximity. That's why people who are plain, pudgy, smart, foolish, rich, poor, gorgeous, or goofy all usually manage to find partners much like them.

This finding makes good evolutionary sense, because our prehistoric ancestors, unlike undergraduates filling out questionnaires about their ideal mates, did not have 5,000 fellow students to choose from. They lived in small bands, and if they were lucky they might get to choose between Urp and Ork, and that's about it. They could not hold out for some beauty or hunk down the road, even if there had been roads back then (Hazan & Diamond, 2000).

All of this evidence argues against a universal, genetically determined sexual strategy. What evolution *has* bestowed on us, however, is an amazingly flexible brain. Biology influences sexual

behavior but it is only one influence among many, as we shall see next.

The Psychology of Desire

Psychologists are fond of observing that the sexiest sex organ is the brain, where perceptions begin. People's values, fantasies, and beliefs profoundly affect their sexual desire and behavior. That is why a touch on the knee by an exciting new date feels terrifically sexy, but the same touch by a creepy stranger on a bus feels disgusting. It is why a worried thought can kill sexual arousal in a second, and why a fantasy can be more erotic than reality.

The Many Motives for Sex To most people, the primary motives for sex are pretty obvious: to enjoy the pleasure of it, to express love and intimacy, or to make babies. But there are other motives too, not all of them so positive, including money or perks, duty or feelings of obligation, rebellion, power over the partner, and submission to the partner to avoid anger or rejection.

One survey of nearly 2,000 people yielded 237 motives for having sex, and nearly every one of them was rated as the most important motive for someone. Most men and women listed the same top ten, including attraction to the partner, love, fun, and physical pleasure. But some said, "I wanted to feel closer to God," "I was drunk," "to get rid of a headache" (that was #173), "to help me fall asleep," "to make my partner feel powerful," "to return a favor," "because someone dared me"; or to hurt an enemy or a rival ("I wanted to make him pay so I slept with his girlfriend"; "I wanted someone else to suffer from herpes as I do"). Men were more likely than women to say they use sex to gain status, enhance their reputation (e.g., because the partner was normally "out of my league"), or get things (such as a promotion) (Meston & Buss, 2007).

The many motivations for sex range from sex for profit to sex for fun.

Across the many studies of motives for sex, there appear to be several major categories (Cooper, Shapiro, & Powers, 1998; Meston & Buss, 2007):

- *Pleasure*: the satisfaction and physical pleasure of sex

- *Intimacy*: emotional closeness with the partner, spiritual transcendence

- *Insecurity*: reassurance that you are attractive or desirable

- *Partner approval*: the desire to please or appease the partner; the desire to avoid the partner's anger or rejection

- *Peer approval*: the wish to impress friends, be part of the group, and conform to what everyone else seems to be doing

- *Attaining a goal*: to get status, money, revenge, or "even the score"

People's motives for having sex affect many aspects of their sexual behavior, including whether they engage in sex in the first place, whether they enjoy it, whether they have unprotected or otherwise risky sex, and whether they have few or many partners (Browning et al., 2000; Impett & Tolman, 2006). Extrinsic motives, such as having sex to gain approval from others or get some tangible benefit, are most strongly associated with risky sexual behavior, including having many partners, not using birth control, and pressuring a partner into sex (Hamby & Koss, 2003).

Unfortunately, significant numbers of women and men are having sex for extrinsic rather than intrinsic motives. In a study in which college students in dating relationships kept a daily diary of their sexual experiences, half of the women and a fourth of the men reported consenting on occasion to unwanted sexual activity (O'Sullivan & Allgeier, 1998). Men typically did so because of peer pressure, inexperience, a desire for popularity, or a fear of seeming homosexual or unmasculine. Women typically did so because they did not want to lose the relationship; because they felt obligated once the partner had spent time and money on them; because the partner made them feel guilty; or because they wanted to satisfy the partner and avoid conflict (Impett, Gable, & Peplau, 2005).

When one partner is feeling insecure about the relationship, he or she is also more likely to consent to unwanted sex. In a study of 125 college women, one-half to two-thirds of the Asian-American, white, and Latina women had consented to having sex when they didn't really want to, and all of the African-American women said they had. Do you remember the attachment theory of love discussed earlier? Anxiously attached women were the most willing to consent to unwanted sex, especially if they feared their partners were less committed than they were. They reported that they often had sex out of feelings of obligation and to prevent the partner from leaving. Securely attached women also occasionally had unwanted sex, but their reasons were different: to gain sexual experience, to satisfy their curiosity, or to actively please their partners and further the intimacy between them (Impett, Gable, & Peplau, 2005).

Sexual Coercion and Rape One of the most persistent differences in the sexual experiences of women and men has to do with their perceptions of, and experiences with, sexual coercion. In a nationally representative survey of more than 3,000 Americans ages 18 to 59, nearly one-fourth of the women said that a man, usually a husband or boyfriend, had forced them to do something sexually that they did not want to do (Laumann et al., 1994). But only about 3 percent of the men said they had ever forced a woman into a sexual act. Obviously, what many women regard as coercion is not always seen as coercive by men (Hamby & Koss, 2003). On the other hand, about half of all women who report a sexual assault that meets the legal definition of rape—being forced to engage in sexual acts against their will—do not label it as rape (McMullin & White, 2006). College women tend to define rape as being forced into intercourse by an acquaintance or stranger, or as having been molested as a child. They are least likely to call their experience rape if they were sexually assaulted by a boyfriend, were drunk or otherwise drugged, or were forced to have oral or digital sex (Kahn, 2004).

What causes some men to rape? Sociobiologists often answer by analogy with other animals: Because males of some species, such as ducks and scorpion flies, force themselves on females, human rape must have the same evolutionary origins and reproductive purposes: for the male to fertilize as many females as possible (Thornhill & Palmer, 2000). But among human beings, rape is often committed by high-status men, including sports heroes and other celebrities, who could easily find consenting sexual partners. All too frequently its victims are children or the elderly, who do not reproduce, or, in wartime, civilian women who are then murdered by the soldiers who raped them. And sadistic rapists also injure or kill their victims, hardly a way to perpetuate their genes. The human motives for rape thus appear to be primarily psychological:

- *Narcissism and hostility toward women.* Sexually aggressive males often are narcissistic, are unable to empathize with women, and feel entitled to have sexual relations with whatever woman they choose. They misperceive women's behavior in social situations, equate feelings of power with sexuality, and accuse women of provoking them (Bushman et al., 2003; Malamuth et al., 1995; Zurbriggen, 2000). One interesting study compared men who had forcibly raped a woman with men who used manipulative techniques to have sex and with men who had had consensual sex only. The rapists were more likely to have grown up in violent households, were more ac-

cepting of male violence, and were less likely to endorse love as a motive for sex than were men in the manipulation and consent groups (Lyden, White, & Kadlec, 2007).

- *A desire to dominate, humiliate, or punish the victim.* This motive is apparent among soldiers who rape captive women during war and then often kill them (Olujic, 1998). Similarly, reports of the systematic rapes of female cadets at the U.S. Air Force Academy suggest that the rapists' motives were to humiliate the women and get women to leave the Academy. Aggressive motives also occur in the rape of men by other men, usually by anal penetration (King & Woollett, 1997). This form of rape typically occurs in youth gangs, where the intention is to humiliate rival gang members, and in prison, where again the motive is to conquer and degrade the victim.

- *Sadism.* A minority of rapists are violent criminals who get pleasure out of inflicting pain on their victims and who often murder them in planned, grotesque ways (Turvey, 2008).

You can see that the answer to the question "Why do people have sex?" is not at all obvious. It is not a simple matter of "doing what's natural." In addition to the intrinsic motives of intimacy, pleasure, procreation, and love, extrinsic motives include intimidation, dominance, insecurity, appeasing the partner, approval from peers, and the wish to prove oneself a real man or a desirable woman.

The Culture of Desire

Think about kissing. Westerners like to think about kissing, and to do it, too. But if you think kissing is natural, try to remember your first serious kiss and all you had to learn about noses, breathing, and the position of teeth and tongue. The sexual kiss is so complicated that some cultures have never gotten around to it. They think that kissing another person's mouth—the very place that food enters!—is disgusting (Tiefer, 2004). Others have elevated the sexual kiss to high art; why do you suppose one version is called French kissing?

As the kiss illustrates, having the physical equipment to perform a sexual act is not all there is

Kissing is a learned skill—one that some people start practicing earlier than others.

sexual scripts Sets of implicit rules that specify proper sexual behavior for a person in a given situation, varying with the person's gender, age, religion, social status, and peer group.

to sexual motivation. People have to learn what is supposed to turn them on (or off), which parts of the body and what activities are erotic (or repulsive), and even how to have pleasurable sexual relations. In some cultures, oral sex is regarded as a bizarre sexual deviation; in others, it is considered not only normal but also supremely desirable. In many cultures, men believe that women who have experienced sexual pleasure of any kind will become unfaithful, so sexual relations are limited to quick intercourse; in other cultures, men's satisfaction and pride depend on knowing the woman is sexually satisfied too. In some cultures, sex itself is seen as something joyful and beautiful, a skill to be cultivated as one might cultivate the skill of gourmet cooking. In others, it is considered ugly and dirty, something to be gotten through as rapidly as possible.

Sexual Scripts How do cultures transmit their rules and requirements about sex to their members? During childhood and adolescence, people learn their culture's *gender roles*, collections of rules that determine the proper attitudes and behavior for men and women (see Chapter 10). Like any actor in a play, a person following a gender role relies on a **sexual script** that provides instructions on how to behave in sexual situations (Gagnon & Simon, 1973; Laumann & Gagnon, 1995). If you are a teenage girl, are you supposed to be sexually adventurous and assertive or sexually modest and passive? What if you are a teenage boy? What if you are an older woman or man? The answers differ from culture to culture, as members act in accordance with the sexual scripts for their gender, age, religion, social status, and peer group.

In many parts of the world, boys acquire their attitudes about sex in a competitive atmosphere where the goal is to impress other males, and they talk and joke with their friends about masturbation and other sexual experiences. Although their traditional sexual scripts are encouraging them to value physical sex, traditional scripts are teaching girls to value relationships and make themselves attractive, putting their own sexual pleasures and preferences secondary to their partner's. Needless to say, modern scripts for both sexes are changing. What do you think are the sexual scripts that describe appropriate behavior for *your* gender, religion, ethnicity, sexual orientation, social class, and age? Do they differ from those of your friends, male and female?

The answer is important, because scripts can be powerful determinants of behavior. For example, because African-American women now account for more than half of reported AIDS cases among women in the United States, researchers have sought to understand how sexual scripts might be reducing their likelihood of practicing safe sex. In interviews with 14 black women ages 22 to 39, researchers found that the women's behavior was governed by scripts fostering these beliefs: *Men control relationships; women sustain relationships; male infidelity is normal; men control sexual activity; women want to use condoms, but men control condom use* (Bowleg, Lucas, & Tschann, 2004). As one woman summarized, "The ball was always in his court." These scripts, the researchers noted, are rooted in African-American history and the recurring scarcity of men available for long-term commitments. The scripts originated to preserve the stability of the family, but today they encourage some women to maintain sexual relationships at the expense of their own needs and safety.

These teenagers are following the sexual scripts for their gender and culture—the boys, by ogling and making sexual remarks about girls to impress their peers, and the girls, by preening and wearing makeup to look good for boys.

When gender roles change because of social and economic shifts in society, so do sexual scripts. Thus, whenever women have needed marriage to ensure their social and financial security, they have regarded sex as a bargaining chip, an asset to be rationed rather than an activity to be enjoyed for its own sake (Hatfield & Rapson, 1996/2005). A woman with no economic resources of her own cannot afford to casually seek sexual pleasure if that means risking an unwanted pregnancy, the security of marriage, her reputation in society, her physical safety, or, in some cultures, her very life. When women become self-supporting and able to control their own fertility, however, they are more likely to want sex for pleasure rather than as a means to another goal.

The Riddle of Sexual Orientation

Why is it that most people become heterosexual, some homosexual, and others bisexual? Many psychological explanations for homosexuality have been proposed over the years, but none of them has been supported. Homosexuality is not a result of having a smothering mother, an absent father, or emotional problems. It is not caused by seduction by an older adult (Rind, Tromovich, & Bauserman, 1998). It is not caused by parental practices or role models. Most gay men recall that they rejected the typical boy role and boys' toys and games from an early age, in spite of enormous pressures from their parents and peers to conform to the traditional male role (Bailey & Zucker, 1995). Conversely, the overwhelming majority of children of gay parents do not become gay, as a learning explanation would predict, although they are more likely than the children of straight parents to be open-minded about homosexuality and gender roles (Bailey et al., 1995; Patterson, 2006).

Many researchers, therefore, have turned to biological explanations of sexual orientation. One line of supporting evidence is that homosexual behavior—including courtship displays, sexual activity, and rearing of young by two males or two females—has been documented in some 450 species, including bottlenose dolphins, penguins, albatrosses, and primates (Bagemihl, 1999). Sexual orientation also seems to be moderately heritable, particularly in men (Bailey, Dunne, & Martin, 2000; Rahman & Wilson, 2003). But the large majority of gay men and lesbians do not have a close gay relative, and their siblings, including twins, are overwhelmingly likely to be heterosexual (Peplau et al., 2000).

Prenatal exposure to androgens might affect brain organization and partner preference (McFadden, 2008; Rahman & Wilson, 2003).

Female babies accidentally exposed in the womb to masculinizing hormones are more likely than other girls to become bisexual or lesbian and to prefer typical boys' toys and activities (Collaer & Hines, 1995). However, most androgenized girls do not become lesbians, and most lesbians were not exposed in the womb to atypical prenatal hormones (Peplau et al., 2000).

Other prenatal events might predispose a child toward a same-sex orientation. More than a dozen studies have found that the probability of a man's becoming gay rises significantly according to the number of older brothers he has—gay or not—when these brothers are born of the same mother. (The percentage of males who become exclusively homosexual is nonetheless very low.) A study of 944 homosexual and heterosexual men suggests that this "brother effect" has nothing to do with family environment, but rather with conditions within the womb before birth (Bogaert, 2006). The only factor that predicted sexual orientation was having older biological brothers; growing up with older stepbrothers or adoptive brothers (or sisters) had no

Nicole Bengiveno/The New York Times

The assumption that homosexuality is rare or "unnatural" is contradicted by the ample evidence of same-sex sexual activity in more than 450 nonhuman species. These young male penguins, Squawk and Milou, entwine their necks, kiss, call to each other, have sex, and firmly reject females. Another male pair in the same zoo, Silo and Roy, seemed so desperate to incubate an egg together that they put a rock in their nest and sat on it. Their human keeper was so touched that he gave them a fertile egg to hatch. Silo and Roy sat on it for the necessary 34 days until their chick, Tango, was born, and then they raised Tango beautifully. "They did a great job," said the zookeeper.

influence at all. The increased chance of homosexuality occurred even when men had older brothers born to the same mother but raised in a different home. No one yet has any idea, however, what prenatal influence might account for these results.

Several other intriguing biological findings are also associated with sexual orientation. A team of Swedish scientists exposed people to two odors: a testosterone derivative found in men's sweat and an estrogen-like compound found in women's urine. It appears that when a hormone is from the sex you are *not* turned on by, the olfactory system registers it, but the hypothalamus, which regulates sexual arousal and response, does not. Thus, the brain activity of homosexual women in response to the odors was similar to that of heterosexual men, and the brain activity of gay men was similar to that of heterosexual women (Berglund, Lindström, & Savic, 2006; Savic, Berglund, & Lindström, 2005). But the researchers wisely noted that their study could not answer questions of cause and effect. "We can't say whether the differences are because of pre-existing differences in their brains, or if past sexual experiences have conditioned their brains to respond differently," said one.

The basic problem with trying to find a single origin of sexual orientation is that sexual identity and behavior take different forms, and they don't correlate strongly (Savin-Williams, 2006). Some people are heterosexual in behavior but have homosexual fantasies and even define themselves as gay or lesbian. Some men, such as prisoners, are homosexual in behavior because they lack opportunities for heterosexual sex, but they do not define themselves as gay and prefer women as sexual partners. In some cultures, teenage boys go through a homosexual phase that they do not define as homosexual and that does not affect their future relations

with women (Herdt, 1984). Similarly, in Lesotho, in South Africa, women have intimate relations with other women, including passionate kissing and oral sex, but they do not define these acts as sexual, as they do when a man is the partner (Kendall, 1999). Some gay men are feminine in interests and manner, but many are not; some lesbians are masculine in interests and manner, but most are not (Singh et al., 1999).

Moreover, although some lesbians have an exclusively same-sex orientation their whole lives, the majority have more fluid sexual orientations. A researcher interviewed 100 lesbian and bisexual women over a ten-year span, and found that only one-third reported consistent attraction only to other women; two-thirds also felt attracted to men. For many of these women, love was truly blind as far as gender was concerned; their sexual behavior depended on whether they loved the partner, not what sex he or she was (Diamond, 2008). Similarly, when men and women watch erotic films, men are more influenced than women are by the sex of the people having sex, whereas women are more influenced than men are by the context in which the sex occurs. Thus, most straight men are turned off by watching gay male couples coupling, most gay men are turned off by watching heterosexual couples, and most straight and lesbian women are turned on by watching anyone of either sex, as long as the context is erotic (Rupp & Wallen, 2008).

Biological factors cannot account for this diversity of sexual responses, cultural customs, or experience among gay men and lesbians. At present, therefore, we must tolerate uncertainty about the origins of sexual orientation. Perhaps the origins will turn out to differ, on average, for males and females, and also differ among individuals, whatever their primary orientation.

Phyllis Lyon and Del Martin (left) lived together for 56 years. In 2008, two months after they were finally legally allowed to marry, Del Martin died. Tom Howard (right) is shown with the three children he is raising with his partner. Howard left his job as a professor to be a stay-at-home dad. Why does the issue of legalizing gay and lesbian marriage evoke so much emotion and controversy?

Stephanie Diani/The New York Times

✓●─Study and
Review on
mypsychlab.com

Quick Quiz

Were you motivated to learn about sexual motivation?

1. Biological research finds that (a) homosexual behavior is found in hundreds of animal species, (b) male and female sexual responses are physiologically very different, (c) all women can have multiple orgasms, (d) women have a stronger sex drive than men do.

2. Research on the motives of rapists finds that rape is usually a result of (a) thwarted sexual desire, (b) hostility or a need for peer approval, (c) crossed signals, (d) female provocation.

3. Under what conditions are women most likely to use sex as a "bargaining chip"? (a) when they are employed and thus have their own money to bargain with, (b) when they don't know how to play poker, (c) when they are using birth control, (d) when they are financially dependent

4. *True or false:* Exclusively psychological theories of the origins of homosexuality have never been supported.

Answers:

1. a   2. b   3. d   4. true

 YOU are about to learn...

- the three kinds of goals most likely to improve the motivation to succeed.

- the important difference between mastery goals and performance goals.

- how the *desire* to achieve is affected by the *opportunity* to achieve.

- which aspects of a job are more important than money in increasing satisfaction with work.

The Competent Animal: Motives to Achieve

Almost every adult works. Students work at studying. Homemakers work, often more hours than salaried employees, at running a household. Artists, poets, and actors work, even if they are paid erratically (or not at all). Most people are motivated to work in order to meet the needs for food and shelter. Yet survival does not explain why some people want to do their work well and others want just to get it done. And it does not explain why some people work to make a living and then put their passion for achievement into unpaid activities, such as learning to become an accomplished trail rider or traveling to Madagascar to catch sight of a rare bird.

Psychologists, particularly those in the field of *industrial/organizational psychology*, have measured the psychological qualities that spur achievement and success and also the environmental conditions that influence productivity and satisfaction.

The Effects of Motivation on Work

In the early 1950s, David McClelland and his associates (1953) speculated that some people have an inner drive to achieve that motivates them as much as hunger motivates people to eat. To measure the strength of this motive, McClelland used a variation of the **Thematic Apperception Test (TAT)**, which requires the test taker to make up a story about a set of ambiguous pictures, such as a young man sitting at a desk. The strength of the achievement motive, said McClelland (1961), is captured in the fantasies the test taker reveals. High achievers tell stories of challenge and success; lower achievers tell stories of idyllic vacations at the beach. ✳─Explore

The TAT has modest empirical support for measuring achievement motivation, but it does not have strong test–retest reliability, meaning that people's responses are easily influenced by what is going on at that moment in their lives (Lilienfeld, Wood, & Garb, 2000). Some people might tell stories of

✳●─Explore
**Theories of
Motivation
and Job
Performance** on
mypsychlab.com

"Finish it? Why would I want to finish it?"

Thematic Apperception Test (TAT)
A projective test that asks respondents to interpret a series of drawings showing scenes of people; usually scored for unconscious motives, such as the need for achievement, power, or affiliation.

approach goals
Goals framed in terms of desired outcomes or experiences, such as learning to scuba dive.

avoidance goals Goals framed in terms of avoiding unpleasant experiences, such as trying not to look foolish in public.

achieving against all odds, not because they are determined to do so themselves, but because they are idly daydreaming about dazzling the world on *American Idol*. But the method launched investigations into the question of why some people seem determined to make it no matter what, and others drift along.

The Importance of Goals Today the predominant approach to understanding achievement motivation emphasizes goals rather than inner drives: What you accomplish depends on the goals you set for yourself and the reasons you pursue them (Dweck & Grant, 2008). Not just any old goals will promote achievement, though. A goal is most likely to improve your motivation and performance when three conditions are met (Locke & Latham, 2002, 2006):

- *The goal is specific.* Defining a goal vaguely, such as "doing your best," is as ineffective as having no goal at all. You need to be specific about what you

are going to do and when you are going to do it: "I will write four pages of this paper today."

- *The goal is challenging but achievable.* You are apt to work hardest for tough but realistic goals. The highest, most difficult goals produce the highest levels of motivation and performance, unless, of course, you choose impossible goals that you can never attain.

- *The goal is framed in terms of getting what you want rather than avoiding what you do not want.* **Approach goals** are positive experiences that you seek directly, such as getting a better grade or learning to scuba dive. **Avoidance goals** involve the effort to avoid unpleasant experiences, such as trying not to make a fool of yourself at parties or trying to avoid being dependent.

All of the motives discussed in this chapter are affected by approach versus avoidance goals.

The Many Motives of Accomplishment

IMMORTALITY

William Faulkner (1897–1962)
Novelist

"Really the writer doesn't want success . . . He wants to leave a scratch on that wall [of oblivion]—Kilroy was here—that somebody a hundred or a thousand years later will see."

JUSTICE

Martin Luther King, Jr. (1929–1968)
Civil rights activist

"I have a dream . . . that my four little children will one day live in a nation where they will not be judged by the color of their skin but the content of their character."

KNOWLEDGE

Helen Keller (1880–1968)
Blind/deaf author and lecturer

"Knowledge is happiness, because to have knowledge—broad, deep knowledge—is to know true ends from false, and lofty things from low."

AUTONOMY

Georgia O'Keeffe (1887–1986)
Artist

"[I] found myself saying to myself—I can't live where I want to, go where I want to, do what I want to . . . I decided I was a very stupid fool not to at least paint as I wanted to."

People who frame their goals in specific, achievable approach terms (e.g., "I'm going to lose weight by jogging three times a week") feel better about themselves, feel more competent, are more optimistic, and are less depressed than people who frame the same goals in avoidance terms (e.g., "I'm going to lose weight by cutting out rich foods") (Coats, Janoff-Bulman, & Alpert, 1996; Updegraff, Gable, & Taylor, 2004). Similarly, people who have sex for approach motives—to enjoy their own physical pleasure, to promote a partner's happiness, or to seek intimacy—tend to have happier and less conflicted relationships than those who have sex to *avoid* a partner's loss of interest or quarrels with the partner (Impett & Tolman, 2006). Can you guess why approach goals produce better results than avoidance goals? Approach goals allow you to focus on what you can actively do to accomplish them and on the intrinsic pleasure of the activity.

Avoidance goals make you focus on what you have to give up.

In the case of work, defining your goals will move you along the road to success, but what happens when you hit a pothole? Some people give up when a goal becomes difficult or they are faced with a setback, whereas others become even more determined to succeed. The crucial difference between them is *why* they are working for that goal: to show off in front of others or learn the task for the satisfaction of it?

People who are motivated by **performance goals** are concerned primarily with being judged favorably and avoiding criticism. Those who are motivated by **mastery (learning) goals** are concerned with increasing their competence and skills and finding intrinsic pleasure in what they are learning (Grant & Dweck, 2003; Senko, Durik, & Harackiewicz, 2008). When people who are motivated by performance goals do

performance goals Goals framed in terms of performing well in front of others, being judged favorably, and avoiding criticism.

mastery (learning) goals Goals framed in terms of increasing one's competence and skills.

DUTY

Eleanor Roosevelt (1884–1962)
Humanitarian, lecturer, stateswoman

"As for accomplishments, I just did what I had to do as things came along."

GREED

Ivan Boesky (b. 1937)
Financier, convicted of insider trading violations

"Greed is all right . . . I think greed is healthy. You can be greedy and still feel good about yourself."

POWER

Henry Kissinger (b. 1923)
Former Secretary of State

"Power is the ultimate aphrodisiac."

EXCELLENCE

Florence Griffith Joyner (1959–1998)
Olympic gold medalist

"When you've been second best for so long, you can either accept it, or try to become the best. I made the decision to try and be the best."

Get Involved! (Re)framing Your Goals

As the text discusses, people sometimes frame their goals in vague, unrealistic, or negative ways. Think of two goals you would like to accomplish. You might consider goals related to studying more efficiently, improving communication with a family member, solving problems in a relationship, or becoming more physically fit. Now phrase each of your two goals in a way that makes it (1) specific, (2) challenging but achievable, and (3) something to be approached rather than avoided. How can framing your goals in this way improve your motivation to reach them?

poorly, they will often decide the fault is theirs and stop trying to improve. Because their goal is to demonstrate their abilities, they set themselves up for grief when they temporarily fail, as all of us must if we are to learn anything new. In contrast, people who are motivated to master new skills will generally regard failure and criticism as sources of useful information that will help them improve. They know that learning takes time.

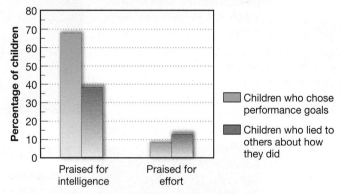

FIGURE 14.2
Mastery and Motivation
Children praised for "being smart" rather than for "working hard" tend to lose the pleasure of learning and focus on how well they are doing. Nearly 70 percent of fifth graders who were praised for intelligence (green bars) later chose performance goals rather than learning goals, compared to fewer than 10 percent of the children who were praised for their efforts (Mueller & Dweck, 1998). Notice also (purple bars) that the children praised for intelligence were much more likely to lie to others about how well they had done—since their goal was showing off, not learning.

Why do some children choose performance goals and others choose mastery goals? In a study of 128 fifth graders, the children worked independently on sets of puzzle problems (Mueller & Dweck, 1998). The experimenter scored their results, told them all they had done well, and gave them one of two additional types of feedback: She praised some of them for their ability ("You must be smart at these problems!") and others for their effort ("You must have worked hard at these problems!"). The children then worked on a more difficult set of problems, but this time the experimenter told them they had done a lot worse. Finally, the children described which goals they preferred to work for: performance (e.g., doing "problems that aren't too hard, so I don't get many wrong") or mastery (e.g., doing "problems that I'll learn a lot from, even if I won't look so smart").

The children praised for being smart rather than for working hard tended to lose the pleasure of learning and focused instead on how well they were doing. After these children failed the second set of problems, they tended to give up on subsequent ones, enjoyed them less, and actually performed less well than children who had been praised for their efforts. As you can see in Figure 14.2, nearly 70 percent of fifth graders who were praised for their intelligence later chose performance goals rather than learning goals, compared to fewer than 10 percent of children who were praised for their efforts. When children realize that all effort is subject to improvement, however, they realize that they can always try again. That is the key to mastery. As one learning-oriented child said to the experimenters, "Mistakes are our friends" (Dweck & Sorich, 1999).

Mastery goals are powerful intrinsic motivators at all levels of education and throughout life. Students who are in college primarily to master new areas of knowledge choose more challenging projects, persist in the face of difficulty, use deeper and more elaborate study strategies, are less likely than other students to cheat, and enjoy learning more than do students who are there only to get a degree and a meal ticket (Elliot & McGregor, 2001; Grant & Dweck, 2003). As usual, though, we should avoid oversimplifying: World class athletes, musicians, and others who strive to excel in their fields blend performance and mastery goals.

Expectations and Self-Efficacy How hard you work for something also depends on your expectations. If you are fairly certain of success, you will work harder to reach your goal than if you are fairly certain of failure.

A classic experiment showed how quickly experience affects these expectations. Young women were asked to solve 15 anagram puzzles. Before working on each one, they had to estimate their chances of solving it. Half of the women started off with very easy anagrams, but half began with insoluble ones. Sure enough, those who started with the easy ones increased their estimates of success on later ones. Those who began with the impossible ones decided they would all be impossible. These expectations, in turn, affected the young women's ability to actually solve the last 10 anagrams, which were the same for everyone. The higher the expectation of success, the more anagrams the women solved (Feather, 1966). Once acquired, therefore, expectations can create a **self-fulfilling prophecy** (Merton, 1948): Your expectations make you behave in ways that make the expectation come true. You expect to succeed, so you work hard—and succeed. Or you expect to fail, so you don't do much work—and do poorly.

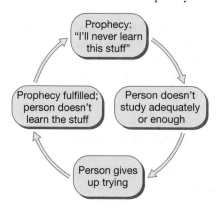

Your expectations are further influenced by your level of confidence in yourself and your abilities (Dweck & Grant, 2008; Judge, 2009). No one is born with a feeling of confidence, or **self-efficacy**. You acquire it through experience in mastering new skills (by making mistakes!), overcoming obstacles, and learning from occasional failures. Self-efficacy also comes from having successful role models who teach you that your ambitions are possible and from having people around to give you constructive feedback and encouragement (Bandura, 2006).

People who have a strong sense of self-efficacy are quick to cope with problems rather than stewing and brooding about them. Studies in North Amer-

ica, Europe, and Russia find that self-efficacy has a positive effect on just about every aspect of people's lives: how well they do on a task, the grades they earn, how persistently they pursue their goals, the kind of career choices they make, their ability to solve complex problems, their motivation to work for political and social goals, their health habits, and even their chances of recovery from heart attack (Bandura et al., 2001; Maddux, 1995; Stajkovic & Luthans, 1998).

The Effects of Work on Motivation

Imagine that you live in a town that has one famous company, Boopsie's Biscuits & Buns. Everyone in the town is grateful for the 3B company and goes to work there with high hopes. Soon, however, an odd thing starts happening to many employees. They complain of fatigue and irritability. They are taking lots of sick leave. Productivity declines.

> **Thinking Critically about Work Motivation**

What's going on at Boopsie's Biscuits & Buns? Is everybody suffering from sheer laziness? Most observers would answer that something is wrong with those employees. But what if something is wrong with Boopsie's? Psychologists want to know how the work we do, and the conditions under which we do it, nurture or crush our motivation to succeed.

One simple but powerful external factor that affects many people's motivation to work in a particular field is the proportion of men and women in that occupation (Kanter, 2006). When occupations are segregated by gender, many people form gender stereotypes about the requirements of such careers: Female jobs require kindness and nurturance; male jobs require strength and smarts. These stereotypes, in turn, stifle many people's aspirations to enter a nontraditional career and also create self-fulfilling prejudices in employers (Agars, 2004; Cejka & Eagly, 1999).

Thus, when law, veterinary medicine, and bartending were almost entirely male professions, and nursing, teaching, and child care were almost entirely female, few women aspired to enter the "male" professions and few men aspired to enter the "female" ones. As job segregation began breaking down, however, people's career motivations changed. Today, it is common to see a female lawyer, vet, or bartender and a male nurse or preschool teacher. And although women are still a minority in engineering, math, and science, their numbers have been rising: In 1970, women earned only 0.6 percent of the doctorates in engineering,

self-fulfilling prophecy An expectation that comes true because of the tendency of the person holding it to act in ways that bring it about.

self-efficacy A person's belief that he or she is capable of producing desired results, such as mastering new skills and reaching goals.

7.6 percent of those in mathematics, and 16.3 percent of those in biological sciences. Thirty years later, the percentages had jumped to 17.3 percent, 29 percent, and 44.3 percent, respectively (Cox & Alm, 2005). As these numbers have increased, the old view that women are not "naturally" suited to engineering, math, and science has been fading.

Working Conditions Once in a profession, though, what motivates people to do well or lose their motivation altogether? To begin with, achievement depends on having the *opportunity* to achieve. When someone does not do well at work, others are apt to say it is the individual's own fault because he or she lacks the internal drive to make it. But what the person may really lack is a fair chance to make it, and this is especially true for those who have been subjected to systematic discrimination (Sabattini & Crosby, 2009). Once they have entered a career, people may become more motivated to advance up the ladder or less so, depending on how many rungs they are permitted to climb. Women used to be rare in politics, but it's not news today that they are governors, senators, congresswomen, or presidential candidates.

Several other aspects of the work environment are likely to increase work motivation and satisfaction and reduce the chances of emotional burnout (Bond et al., 2004; Maslach et al., 2001; Rhoades & Eisenberger, 2002):

- The work feels meaningful and important to employees.
- Employees have control over many aspects of their work, such as setting their own hours and making decisions.
- Tasks are varied rather than repetitive.
- Employees have supportive relationships with their superiors and co-workers.
- Employees receive useful feedback about their work, so they know what they have accomplished and what they need to do to improve.
- The company offers opportunities for its employees to learn and advance.

Companies that foster these conditions tend to have more productive and satisfied employees. Workers tend to become more creative in their thinking and feel better about themselves and their work than they do if they feel stuck in routine jobs that give them no control or flexibility over their daily tasks.

Conversely, when people are put in situations that frustrate their desire and ability to succeed, they become dissatisfied, their desire to succeed declines, and they may drop out. Although the

Like employees, students can have poor working conditions that affect their motivation. They may have to study in crowded quarters or may have siblings who interrupt and distract them.

rising number of women entering the sciences is heartening news, many are not staying. A study of nearly 2,500 women and men in science, engineering, and technology found that although women made up 41 percent of the entry-level jobs, more than half of them had left their specific jobs by age 35, and a fourth had abandoned science altogether. The women who lost their motivation to work in these fields reported feeling isolated (many said they were the only woman in their work group), and two-thirds said they had been sexually harassed (Hewlitt, Luce, & Servon, 2008). Other reasons included being paid less than men for the same work and having working conditions that did not allow them to handle their family obligations. Mothers are still more likely than fathers to reduce their work hours, modify their work schedules, and report feeling distracted on the job because of child care concerns (Sabattini & Crosby, 2009).

As you can see, work motivation and satisfaction depend on the right fit between qualities of the individual and conditions of the work.

✓●─Study and
Review on
mypsychlab.com

Quick Quiz

Work on your understanding of work motivation.

1. Horatio wants to earn a black belt in karate. Which way(s) of thinking about this goal are most likely to help him reach it? (a) "I should do the best I can," (b) "I should be sure not to lose many matches," (c) "I will set specific goals that are tough but attainable," (d) "I will set specific goals that I know I can reach easily," (e) "I will strive to achieve key milestones on the way to my goal."

2. Ramón and Ramona are learning to ski. Every time she falls, Ramona says, "This is the most humiliating experience I've ever had! Everyone is watching me behave like a clumsy dolt!" When Ramón falls, he says, "&*!!@$@! I'll show these dratted skis who's boss!" Why is Ramona more likely than Ramón to give up? (a) She *is* a clumsy dolt, (b) she is less competent at skiing, (c) she is focused on learning, (d) she is focused on performance

3. Which of these factors significantly increase work motivation? (a) specific goals, (b) regular pay, (c) feedback, (d) general goals, (e) being told what to do, (f) being able to make decisions, (g) the chance of promotion, (h) having routine, predictable work

4. An employer is annoyed by the behavior of an employee and is thinking of firing her. Her work is competent, but she rarely arrives on time, doesn't seem as motivated as others to do well, and has begun to take an unusual number of sick days. The boss has decided she is lazy and unmotivated. What guidelines of critical thinking is the boss overlooking, and what information should the boss consider before taking this step?

Answers:

1. c, e   2. d   3. a, c, f, g   4. The boss is jumping to the conclusion that his employee has low work motivation. This may be true, but because her work is competent, the boss should consider other explanations and examine the evidence. Perhaps the work conditions are unsatisfactory: There may be few opportunities for promotion; she may have been getting no feedback that lets her know she is doing well or that could help her improve; perhaps the company does not provide child care, so she is arriving late because she has child care obligations. What other possible explanations come to mind?

YOU are about to learn …

● why people are poor at predicting what will make them happy or miserable.

● why money can't buy happiness—and what does.

● three basic kinds of motivational conflicts.

Motives, Values, and the Pursuit of Happiness

When you think about setting goals for yourself, here is a crucial psychological finding to keep in mind: People are really bad at predicting what will make them happy and what will make them miserable, and at estimating how long either of those feelings will last (Wilson & Gilbert, 2005).

For example, college students were asked how happy or unhappy they imagined they would feel after being randomly assigned to live in a dorm they thought was "desirable" or "undesirable" (Dunn, Wilson, & Gilbert, 2003). The students predicted that their dorm assignments would have a huge impact on their overall level of happiness and that

being assigned to an undesirable dorm would essentially wreck their satisfaction for the whole year. But one year later, everyone had nearly identical levels of happiness no matter where they were living, as you can see in Figure 14.3 on the next page.

Perhaps the undesirable dorms turned out to be unexpectedly pleasant, with cool people living in them? No. The students had focused on the wrong factors when imagining their future feelings of happiness in the houses; they had placed far more importance on what the house looked like and on its location than on its inhabitants. But it's people who make a place fun or unpleasant to live in, and all of the houses had likable people in them. Because the students could not foresee this, or how much they would like their new roommates, they mispredicted their future happiness.

These findings have been replicated in many different contexts: The good is rarely as good as we imagine it will be, and the bad is rarely as terrible. The reason is that people adjust quickly to happy changes—new relationships, a promotion, even winning the lottery—and fail to anticipate that they will manage bad experiences just as quickly. They will make sense of unexpected events, cope with

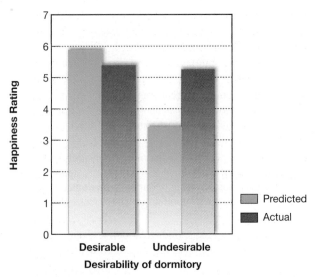

FIGURE 14.3
The Misprediction of Emotion
In a longitudinal study, college students about to be randomly assigned to a dorm had to predict how happy or unhappy they would feel about being assigned to a house they had ranked as "desirable" or "undesirable" (green bars). Most students thought that they would be much less happy in an "undesirable" dorm, but in fact, one year later, there was no difference between the two groups (purple bars) (Dunn, Wilson, & Gilbert, 2003).

tragedies, and make excuses for loved ones who hurt them. Yet people make many decisions based on how they imagine they will feel in the future. You might spend more money than you can afford on a car or sound system because you think that *this* is what will make you truly happy.

What, then, *does* make people happy? In all the domains of human motivation that we have examined, a key conclusion emerges: People who are motivated by the intrinsic satisfaction of an activity are happier and more satisfied than those motivated solely by extrinsic rewards (Deci & Ryan, 1985; Kasser & Ryan, 2001).

In American culture, many people are more motivated to make money than to find activities they enjoy. They imagine that greater wealth will bring greater happiness, yet once they are at a level that provides basic comfort and security, more isn't necessarily better. They adjust quickly to the greater wealth and then think they need even more of it to be happier (Gilbert, 2006a). In addition, regardless of whether they live in America (an affluent nation) or Russia (a struggling nation), people who are primarily motivated to get rich have poorer psychological adjustment and lower well-being than do people whose primary values are self-acceptance, affiliation with others, or wanting

to make the world a better place (Ryan et al., 1999). This is especially true when the reasons for striving for money are, again, extrinsic (e.g., you do it to impress others and show off your possessions) rather than intrinsic (e.g., you do it so you can afford to do the volunteer work you love) (Carver & Baird, 1998; Srivastava, Locke, & Bartol, 2001). Having positive, intrinsically enjoyable *experiences* makes most people happier than having *things*: Doing, in other words, is more satisfying than buying (Headey, 2008; Van Boven & Gilovich, 2003). **⊙►Simulate**

Whichever values and goals you choose, if they are in conflict, the discrepancy can produce emotional stress and unhappiness. Two motives conflict when the satisfaction of one leads to the inability to act on the other—when, that is, you want to eat your cake and have it, too. There are three kinds of motivational conflicts (Lewin, 1948):

1 **Approach–approach conflicts** occur when you are equally attracted to two or more possible activities or goals: You would like to be a veterinarian *and* a rock singer; you would like to go out Tuesday night with friends *and* study like mad for an exam Wednesday.

2 **Avoidance–avoidance conflicts** require you to choose between the lesser of two evils because you dislike both alternatives. Novice parachute

THE FAR SIDE **By GARY LARSON**

"C'mon, c'mon—it's either one or the other."

A classic avoidance–avoidance conflict.

jumpers, for example, must choose between the fear of jumping and the fear of losing face if they don't jump.

3 **Approach–avoidance conflicts** occur when a single activity or goal has both a positive and a negative aspect. In culturally diverse nations, differing cultural values produce many approach–avoidance conflicts, as students have told us. A Chicano student says he wants to become a lawyer, but his parents, valuing family closeness, worry that if he goes to graduate school, he will become independent and feel superior to his working-class family. A black student from a poor neighborhood, in college on scholarship, is torn between wanting to leave his background behind him forever and returning to help his home community. And a white student wants to be a marine biologist, but her friends tell her that only nerdy guys and dweebs go into science.

Conflicts like these are inevitable, part of the price and pleasure of living. But if conflicts remain unresolved, they can take an emotional toll. In students, high levels of conflict and ambivalence about goals and values are associated with anxiety, depression, headaches and other physical symptoms, and more visits to the health center (Emmons & King, 1988). Students who strive for goals that are consistent with the qualities they value are healthier and have a greater sense of meaning and purpose in life than do those who are pursuing goals discrepant with their core values (Sheldon & Houser-Marko, 2001).

Years ago, humanist psychologist Abraham Maslow (1970) envisioned people's motives as forming a pyramid. At the bottom level were basic survival needs for food, sleep, and water; at the next level were security needs, for shelter and safety; at the third level were social needs, for belonging and affection; at the fourth level were esteem needs, for self-respect and the respect of others; and at the top, when all other needs had been met, were those for self-actualization and self-transcendence.

Maslow's theory became immensely popular, and motivational speakers still often refer to it, using colorful pictures of the pyramid. But the theory, which was based mostly on Maslow's observations of people he personally decided were self-actualized, has had little empirical support (Sheldon et al., 2001; Smither, 1998). The main reason, as we have seen in this chapter, is that people have *simultaneous* needs for comfort and safety and for love, intimacy, and competence. Higher needs may even supersede lower ones. History is full of examples of people who would rather die of torture or starvation than sacrifice their convictions, or who would rather explore, risk, or create new art than be safe and secure at home.

Quick Quiz

Do you wish to approach or avoid this quiz?

1. Max has applied for a junior year abroad, but couldn't get into his first choice, a drama school in London. He is feeling so miserable about the rejection that he is thinking of staying home. "Why should I go to a second-rate school somewhere else?" he reasons. What is the matter with his reasoning?

2. A Pakistani student says she desperately wants an education and a career as a pharmacist, but she also does not want to be disobedient to her parents, who have arranged a marriage for her back home. Which kind of conflict does she have?

3. Letitia just got her law degree. She wants to take a job in environmental law, but a corporate firm specializing in real estate contracts has offered her a job with an enormous salary. Why should she think carefully and critically in making a decision?

Answers:

1. Max assumes that how he feels now is how he will feel in the future. He can't imagine the more likely scenario, that he will find things to like about any program he enters. 2. approach–avoidance 3. She should think critically because taking a job primarily for its extrinsic benefits might suppress her intrinsic satisfaction in the work. Also, people who are motivated solely to acquire money often have poorer psychological adjustment and lower well-being than people who are motivated by work they enjoy. Of course, money provides material benefits, but psychological needs such as autonomy, competence, self-esteem, and connection to others are also important.

Psychology in the News REVISITED

Understanding the biological, psychological, and cultural influences on motivation can help us understand the stories that opened this chapter and others that make the news every day.

For critical thinkers, the news item about soda taxes raises many questions. Since the late 1970s, the cost of soda has fallen more than any other food or beverage group; the cost of fresh fruits and vegetables has risen the most. Carbonated sodas have no nutritional value at all but they are cheap, and the typical American consumes almost three times as many calories from these drinks today as in the 1970s. As we saw, that increase in consumption of sugary, high-calorie drinks has contributed to the worldwide rise in obesity, so a sales tax on those drinks may seem like a good idea. (Certainly it raises revenues for cash-strapped states.) But a tax of just a few cents per can or bottle may not reduce consumption much, if at all. A larger tax may be needed, comparable to the tax on cigarettes, which has been effective in reducing the number of smokers. Moreover, if the tax causes people to switch to untaxed diet sodas, sugar consumption could actually increase, because, as we noted, artificial sweeteners make people crave more sugar. Finally, this chapter showed that the increase in obesity has many causes, including sedentary lifestyles, a wide variety of available foods, an increase in inexpensive fast foods and processed foods, and large portion sizes.

The saga of Mzee and Owen tempts us to conclude that nonhuman animals share with us the capacity for love, or at least for passionate, devoted friendship. No doubt many animals have that capacity, as any dog lover can tell you! Certainly our species shares with many other animals the biological bases of bonding, such as the hormones oxytocin and vasopressin. But human love takes different forms, and whether it fades away or lasts for years depends on social, economic, and cognitive factors such as a couple's attitudes, values, and perception of their relationship as being fair or unfair. Thus, Mzee and Owen's touching friendship illustrates that human attachments are both similar to and different from those of other animals.

The news item about the rape conviction of Anand Jon Alexander reflects some of the unpleasant motivations that some people bring to their sexual encounters. As we saw, the causes of rape and sexual assault have less to do with physical pleasure than with contempt for women, narcissism, insecurity, sadism, or a need to prove masculinity. In Alexander's case, prosecutors accused him of acting out sadistic fantasies during the assaults. Whatever his motivations might have been, convictions of successful men like Anand Jon Alexander, who could easily attract consensual partners, show that rape is not simply about sexual gratification or an evolutionary desire to reproduce.

Finally, and on a happier note, the story of Anamika Veeramani, the spelling bee champion, demonstrates the importance of having self-efficacy, setting challenging but achievable goals, and persisting in the pursuit of your dreams. Anamika may have been driven in part by performance goals, but we'll bet that she also found intrinsic pleasure in learning to spell as many difficult words as she could. Spelling bees are intensely competitive and are not for the faint of heart; they require young entrants to risk failure, and public failure at that. We're pretty confident that she will achieve her next dream, of becoming a cardiovascular surgeon.

Abraham Maslow may have been wrong about a universal hierarchy of motives, but perhaps each of us develops our own hierarchy as we grow from childhood to old age. For some people, the needs for love, security, or safety will dominate. For others, the need for achievement or power will rule. Some of us will wrestle with conflicting motives; for others, one consuming ambition will hold sway over all others. The motives and goals that inspire us, and the choices we make in their pursuit, are what give our lives passion, color, and meaning. Choose wisely.

Taking Psychology with You

How to Attain Your Goals

What are your values? What would you most like to achieve and accomplish in your life? Is the answer love, wealth, security, passion, freedom, fame, the desire to improve the world, being the best in a sport or other skill? Something else? What are your short-term goals: Would you like to improve your love life? Get better grades? Enjoy school more? Lose weight? Become a better tennis player?

There is a whole world of motivational speakers, books, and tapes that offer inspiration, enthusiasm, and a few magic steps to change your life, but we hope that by now you will apply critical thinking to their promises. Enthusiastic inspiration is fine as far as it goes, but it usually doesn't transfer into helping you make real-life changes. What does help? Think about some of the lessons of motivational research that you have learned in this chapter:

Seek activities that are intrinsically pleasurable. If you really, really want to study Swahili or Italian, even though these languages are not in your pre-law requirements, try to find a way to do it. As the great writer Ray Bradbury said at age 89, the secret to living to a grand old age is to "do what you love and love what you do." If you are not enjoying your major or your job, consider finding a career that would be more intrinsically pleasurable, or at least make sure you have other projects and activities that you do enjoy for their own sake.

Focus on learning goals, not only on performance goals. In general, you will be better able to cope with setbacks if your goal is to learn rather than to show others how good you are. Regard failure as a chance to learn rather than as a sign of incompetence.

Assess your working conditions. Everyone has working conditions. Whether you are a student, a self-employed writer, or a homemaker, if your motivation and well-being are starting to wilt, check out your environment. Are you getting support from others? Do you have opportunities to develop ideas and vary your routine, or are you expected to do the same thing day after day? Are there barriers that might limit your advancement in your chosen field?

Take steps to resolve motivational conflicts. Are you torn between competing goals? For instance, are you unhappily stuck between the goal of achieving independence and a desire to be cared for by your parents? The reconciliation of conflicts like these is important for your well-being.

For almost everyone, psychological well-being depends on finding activities and choosing goals that are intrinsically satisfying and on developing the self-efficacy to achieve them. That is why it is important to think critically about the goals you have chosen for yourself: Are they what *you* want to do or what someone else wants you to do? Do they reflect your values? If you are unhappy with your body, your relationships, or your work, why? Think about it.

Summary

((•─ **Listen** to an **audio file** of your chapter on **mypsychlab.com**

● *Motivation* refers to a process within a person or animal that causes that organism to move toward a goal—to satisfy a biological need or achieve an ambition—or away from an unpleasant situation. A few primary drives are based on physiological needs, but all human motives are affected by psychological, social, and cultural factors. Motivation may be *intrinsic*, for the inherent pleasure of an activity, or *extrinsic*, for external rewards.

The Hungry Animal: Motives to Eat

● Overweight and obesity are not simply a result of failed willpower, emotional disturbance, or overeating. Hunger, weight, and eating are regulated by a set of bodily mechanisms, such as *basal metabolism rate* and number of fat cells, that keep people close to their genetically influenced *set point*. Genes influence body shape, distribution of fat, number of fat cells and amount of brown fat, and whether the body will convert excess calories into fat. Genes may also account for certain types of obesity; the *ob* gene regulates *leptin*, which enables the hypothalamus to regulate appetite and metabolism.

● Genetics alone cannot explain why rates of overweight and obesity are rising all over the world among all social classes, ethnicities, and ages. The environmental reasons are (1) the increased abundance of inexpensive fast food and processed food, because humans have a genetic disposition to gain weight when rich food is plentiful; (2) the increased consumption of sugared high-calorie sodas; (3) the rise of sedentary life styles; (4) increased portion sizes; and (5) the availability of highly varied foods.

● When genetic predispositions clash with cultural standards, physical and mental problems can result. In cultures that foster overeating and regard overweight as a sign of attractiveness and health, obesity is acceptable. In cultures that foster unrealistically thin bodies, eating disorders increase, especially *bulimia nervosa*, *binge-eating disorder*, and *anorexia nervosa*, and also unhealthy attitudes toward food and weight. Bulimia and anorexia are more common in women than in men, but rates of body image problems and eating disorders among men are increasing.

The Social Animal: Motives to Love

● All human beings have a need for attachment and love. Psychologists distinguish *passionate ("romantic") love* from *companionate love*. Biologically oriented researchers believe that the neurological origins of passionate love begin in the baby's attachment to the mother. Various brain chemicals and hormones, including *vasopressin* and *oxytocin*, are associated with bonding and trust; endorphins and dopamine create the rushes of pleasure and reward associated with romantic passion.

● Two strong predictors of whom people will love are *proximity* and *similarity*. Once in love, people form different kinds of attachments. *Attachment theory* views adult love relationships, like those of infants, as being secure, avoidant, or anxious. People's attachment styles tend to be stable from childhood to adulthood and affect their close relationships.

● Men and women are equally likely to feel love and need attachment, but they differ, on average, in how they express feelings of love and how they define intimacy. A couple's attitudes, values, and perception that the relationship is fair and balanced are better predictors of long-term love than are genes or hormones. As women have entered the workforce in large numbers and pragmatic (extrinsic) reasons for marriage have faded, the two sexes have become more alike in endorsing intrinsic motives such as love and affection as a requirement for marriage.

The Erotic Animal: Motives for Sex

● Human sexuality is not simply a matter of "doing what comes naturally," because what is "natural" for one person or culture may not be so natural for others. The Kinsey surveys of male and female sexuality and the laboratory research of Masters and Johnson showed that physiologically, there is no right kind of orgasm for women to have, and that both sexes are capable of sexual arousal and response. However, there is enormous individual variation in sexual excitement, response, and inhibition.

● The hormone testosterone promotes sexual desire in both sexes, although hormones do not cause sexual behavior in a simple, direct way.

● Some researchers believe that men have a stronger sex drive than women do, because men have higher rates of almost every kind of sexual behavior. Others believe that gender differences in sexual motivation and behavior are a result of differences in roles, cultural norms, and opportunity. A compromise view is that male sexuality is more biologically influenced than is women's, whereas female sexuality is more governed by circumstances, relationships, and cultural norms.

● Evolutionary psychologists argue that males and females have evolved different sexual and courtship strategies in response to survival problems faced in the distant past. In this view, it has been adaptive for males to be promiscuous, to be attracted to young partners, and to want sexual novelty, and for females to be monogamous, to be choosy about partners, and to prefer security to novelty.

● Critics argue that evolutionary explanations of infidelity and monogamy are based on simplistic stereotypes of gender differences; that the remarkable variation in human sexual customs across and within cultures argues against a universal, genetically determined sexual strategy; and that evolutionary argument rely too heavily on answers to questionnaires, which often do not reflect real-life choices. Our ancestors probably did not have a wide range of partners to choose from; what may have evolved is mate selection based on similarity and proximity.

● Men and women have sex to satisfy many different psychological motives, including pleasure, intimacy, security, the partner's approval, peer approval, or to attain a specific goal. Extrinsic motives for sex, such as the need for approval, are associated with riskier sexual behavior than intrinsic motives are. Both sexes may agree to intercourse for nonsexual motives, including revenge, perks, power, to prove oneself, or to preserve the relationship. People's motives for consenting to unwanted sex vary, depending on their feelings of security and commitment in the relationship.

● What many women regard as rape or coercion is not always seen as such by men. Men who rape do so for diverse reasons, including narcissism and hostility toward women; a desire to dominate, humiliate, or punish the victim; and sometimes sadism.

● Cultures differ widely in determining which parts of the body people learn are erotic, which sexual acts are considered erotic or repulsive, and whether sex itself is good or bad. Cultures transmit these ideas through *gender roles* and *sexual scripts*, which specify appropriate behavior during courtship and sex, depending on a person's gender, age, ethnicity, religion, social class, and sexual orientation.

● As in the case of love, gender differences and similarities in sexuality are strongly affected by cultural and economic factors. When gender roles have become more alike, so does the sexual behavior of men and women, with more women wanting sex for pleasure rather than as a bargaining chip.

• Traditional psychological explanations for homosexuality have not been supported. Genetic and hormonal factors seem to be involved, although the evidence is stronger for gay men than for lesbians. The more older biological brothers a man has, the greater his likelihood of becoming homosexual, suggesting that prenatal events might be involved. In spite of the evidence of a biological contribution to sexual orientation, there is great variation in the expression of homosexuality around the world. Women's sexual orientation seems more fluid than men's.

The Competent Animal: Motives to Achieve

• The study of achievement motivation began with research using the *Thematic Apperception Test (TAT)*. The TAT has empirical problems, but it launched the study of the factors that motivate achievement.

• People achieve more when they have specific, focused goals; when they set high but achievable goals for themselves; and when they have *approach goals* (seeking a positive outcome) rather than *avoidance goals* (avoiding an unpleasant outcome). The motivation to achieve also depends on whether people set *mastery (learning) goals*, in which the focus is on learning the task well, or *performance goals*, in which the focus is on performing well for others. Mastery goals lead to persistence in the face of failures and setbacks; performance goals often lead to giving up after failure. People's expectations can create *self-fulfilling prophecies* of success or failure. These expectations stem from one's level of *self-efficacy*.

• Work motivation also depends on conditions of the job itself. One factor that strongly influences men's and women's choices of work is the gender ratio of people in an occupation. When jobs are highly gender segregated, people often stereotype the abilities of the women and men working in those fields. Working conditions that promote motivation and satisfaction are those that provide workers with a sense of meaningfulness, control, variation in tasks, supportive relationships, feedback, and opportunities for advancement. Jobs that lack these conditions, or that fail to allow employees to balance the demands of their families with those of work, are more likely to have high dropout rates.

Motives, Values, and the Pursuit of Happiness

• People are not good at predicting what will make them happy and what will make them miserable, and at estimating how long those feelings will last, so they often choose goals that do not bring them long-term satisfaction. Well-being increases when people enjoy the intrinsic satisfaction of an activity. Having intrinsically enjoyable experiences makes most people happier than having riches and possessions.

• In an *approach–approach conflict*, a person is equally attracted to two goals. In an *avoidance–avoidance conflict*, a person is equally repelled by two goals. An *approach–avoidance conflict* is the most difficult to resolve because the person is both attracted to and repelled by the same goal. Prolonged conflict can lead to physical symptoms and reduced well-being.

• Abraham Maslow believed that human motives could be ranked in a pyramid, from basic biological needs for survival to higher psychological needs for self-actualization. This popular theory has not been supported empirically. Rather, psychological well-being depends on finding activities and choosing goals that are intrinsically satisfying and on developing the self-efficacy to achieve them.

Taking Psychology with You

• Motivational research suggests that people are happiest and most fulfilled when they seek intrinsically pleasurable activities, focus on learning, improve their working conditions, resolve conflicts, and choose the goals that reflect their most important values.

Key Terms

Motivation refers to an inferred process within a person or animal that causes that organism to move toward a goal or away from an unpleasant situation.
• **Intrinsic motivation** is for the inherent pleasure of an activity.
• **Extrinsic motivation** is for external reward, such as money or fame.

The Hungry Animal: Motives to Eat

The Biology of Weight

Hunger, weight, and eating are governed by a genetically influenced **set point,** which regulates food intake, fat reserves, and basal metabolism rate. Genes also influence:
• Body shape
• Extent of weight gain
• Percentage and distribution of body fat
• Certain types of obesity
— The obese (ob) gene causes fat cells to secrete *leptin*, which helps the hypo-thalamus to regulate appetite.
— Other genes and chemicals are involved in appetite, metabolism, and weight gain.

Environmental Influences on Weight

The primary environmental causes of the worldwide epidemic of overweight and obesity are:
• Prevalence of fast food, processed food, and high-calorie soft drinks
• Decline in exercise and expenditures of energy
• Larger portions of food and drink
• Abundance of highly varied foods

Cultural Influences on Weight

• Eating habits are influenced by cultural standards of the ideal body—e.g., fat, thin, soft, muscular.
• These standards vary across cultures and may change within a culture (e.g., as gender roles change).
• When people believe that their bodies do not match the cultural ideal, eating disorders such as **bulimia** and **anorexia nervosa** may increase.
• Eating disorders are more common in women than in men, although body image disorders among men are increasing.

The Erotic Animal: Motives for Sex

The Biology of Desire

• Testosterone influences sexual desire in both sexes but does not "cause" sexual behavior.
• The Kinsey surveys of male and female sexuality and the lab research of Masters and Johnson showed that:
— There is much individual variability in sexual physiology.
— Both sexes are capable of sexual arousal and response.
Sex and the "sex drive":
• On average, men have a higher frequency of many sexual behaviors than women do.
• Some researchers believe the reason for this difference is that men have a stronger sex drive.
• Others believe the difference is a result of differences in roles and cultural norms.

Evolution and Sex

Evolutionary psychologists argue that men and women have evolved different sexual strategies and behavior in response to survival problems faced in the distant past.

In this view, it has been adaptive for males to:
• Be promiscuous
• Be attracted to young partners
• Want sexual novelty

Also in this view, females have evolved to:
• Be monogamous
• Be choosy about partners
• Prefer security to novelty

Critics counter that:
• The assumption that males are promiscuous and fe-males are choosy is a stereotype; in many species, males care for their young and females have multiple partners.
• Human sexual behavior is too varied to favor a single evolutionary explanation.
• Human sexual behavior changes with cultural changes.
• What people say is their ideal partner is not neces-sarily whom they choose.

The Psychology of Desire

Psychological approaches to sexual motivation emphasize the influences of values, beliefs, expecta-tions, and fantasies. The many mo-tives for having sex include:
• Pleasure
• Intimacy
• Insecurity
• Partner approval
• Peer approval
• Attaining a goal
Extrinsic motives for sex (e.g., for peer approval or fear of losing the relationship) are associated with risky sexual behavior and consenting to unwanted sex.

The Riddle of Sexual Orientation

• Homosexuality is not a result of psychologi-cal factors or of having gay parents.
• Same-sex behavior has been documented in more than 450 species.
• There is some evidence for prenatal and ge-netic contributions to homosexuality, but to date biological explanations cannot account for the sexual orientation of most gay men and lesbians.

The Culture of Desire

Cultures differ in determining:
• Which body parts are considered erotic
• Which sexual acts are considered erotic
• Whether sex itself is good or bad
Cultures transmit sexual norms through:
• Gender roles
• Sexual scripts

Sexual Coercion and Rape

Women and men differ in their views of rape and sexual coercion. Motives for rape include:
• Narcissism
• Hostility
• Desire to dominate, humiliate, or punish the victim
• Sadism

The Social Animal: Motives to Love

The Biology of Love

Biological origins of passionate love may begin in infancy, when the mother–infant bond releases neurotransmitters and hormones involved in pleasure and reward:
• Vasopressin and oxytocin
• Endorphins

The Psychology of Love

The two major predictors of whom people will love are:
• Proximity: The people nearest are most likely dearest
• Similarity: Like attracts like

Attachment Theory of Love

Attachment theory views adults' love relationships, like those of infants, as:
• Secure
• Avoidant
• Anxious-ambivalent

Gender, Culture, and Love

• In Western societies, the sexes do not differ in their feelings of love but in how they express those feelings:
— Women often express love in words.
— Men often express love in actions.
• Gender differences in love reflect economic and social forces, such as whether a person can afford to marry for love.

The Competent Animal: Motives to Achieve

The Effects of Motivation on Work

The need for achievement was first studied using the **Thematic Apperception Test (TAT).**

Expectations and Self-Efficacy

• Expectations of success or failure can create a **self-fulfilling prophecy.**
• Expectations of success stem in part from feelings of **self-efficacy.**

The Importance of Goals

People achieve more and feel better about themselves when goals are:
• Specific rather than vaguely defined
• Challenging but achieveable
• Framed as **approach goals** rather than as **avoidance goals**
Most people develop higher intrinsic pleasure in learning when they are motivated by:
• **Mastery (learning) goals,** learning the task well, rather than by **performance goals,** showing off for others.
• Top performers, however, such as world-class athletes and musicians, are motivated by both kinds of goals.

The Effects of Work on Motivation

Working conditions increase employees' satisfaction and motivation, especially when employees:
• Feel their work is meaningful
• Have control over many aspects of their work
• Have varied tasks
• Have supportive relationships
• Get useful feedback
• Have opportunities to learn and advance

Motives, Values, and the Pursuit of Happiness

Motivational Conflicts

• **Approach-approach conflict:** A person is equally attracted to two goals.
• **Avoidance-avoidance conflict:** A person is equally repelled by two goals.
• **Approach-avoidance conflict:** A person is both attracted to, and repelled by, the same goal.

Psychological Needs

• In setting goals, most people are not very good at predicting what will make them happy or miserable.
• People who are motivated by the intrinsic satisfaction of an activity are happier and more satisfied than those motivated solely by extrinsic rewards.
• Abraham Maslow believed that human motives could be ranked in a hierarchy of needs, from basic safety to personal transcendence, but this theory has had little empirical support.

Statistical Methods

Nineteenth-century English statesman Benjamin Disraeli reportedly once named three forms of dishonesty: "lies, damned lies, and statistics." It is certainly true that people can lie with the help of statistics. It happens all the time: Advertisers, politicians, and others with some claim to make either use numbers inappropriately or ignore certain critical ones. People also use numbers to convey a false impression of certainty and objectivity when the true state of affairs is uncertainty or ignorance. But it is people, not statistics, that lie. When statistics are used correctly, they neither confuse nor mislead. On the contrary, they expose unwarranted conclusions, promote clarity and precision, and protect us from our own biases and blind spots.

If statistics are useful anywhere, it is in the study of human behavior. If human beings were all alike, and psychologists could specify all the influences on behavior, there would be no need for statistics. Any time we measure human behavior, however, we are going to wind up with different observations or scores for different individuals. Statistics can help us spot trends amid the diversity.

This appendix will introduce you to some basic statistical calculations used in psychology. Reading the appendix will not make you a statistician, but it will acquaint you with some ways of organizing and assessing research data. If you suffer from a "number phobia," relax: You do not need to know much math to understand this material. However, you should have read Chapter 1, which discussed the rationale for using statistics and described various research methods. You may want to review the basic terms and concepts covered in that chapter. Be sure that you can define *hypothesis, sample, correlation, independent variable, dependent variable, random assignment, experimental group, control group, descriptive statistics, inferential statistics, test of statistical significance,* and *effect size.* (Correlation coefficients, which are described in Chapter 1, will not be covered here.)

To read the tables in this appendix, you will also need to know the following symbols:

N = the total number of observations or scores in a set
X = an observation or score
Σ = the Greek capital letter sigma, read as "the sum of"
$\sqrt{}$ = the square root of

(*Note:* Boldfaced terms in this appendix are defined in the glossary at the end of the book.)

Organizing Data

Before we can discuss statistics, we need some numbers. Imagine that you are a psychologist and that you are interested in that most pleasing of human qualities, a sense of humor. You suspect that a well-developed funny bone can protect people from the negative emotional effects of stress. You already know that in the months following a stressful event, people who score high on sense-of-humor tests tend to feel less tense and moody than more sober-sided individuals do. You realize, though, that this correlational evidence does not prove cause and effect. Perhaps people with a healthy sense of humor have other traits, such as flexibility or creativity, that act as the true stress buffers. To find out whether humor itself really softens the impact of stress, you do an experiment.

First, you randomly assign subjects to two groups, an experimental group and a control group. To keep our calculations simple, let's assume there are only 15 people per group. Each person individually views a silent film that most North Americans find fairly stressful, one showing Australian aboriginal boys undergoing a puberty rite involving genital mutilation. Subjects in the experimental group are instructed to make up a humorous monologue while watching the film. Those in the control group are told to make up a straightforward narrative. After the film, each person answers a mood questionnaire that measures current feelings of tension, depression, aggressiveness, and anxiety. A person's overall score on the questionnaire can range from 1 (no mood disturbance) to 7 (strong mood disturbance). This procedure provides you with 15 "mood disturbance" scores for each group. Have people who tried to be humorous reported less disturbance than those who did not?

Constructing a Frequency Distribution

Your first step might be to organize and condense the "raw data" (the obtained scores) by constructing a **frequency distribution** for each group. A frequency distribution shows how often each possible score actually occurred. To construct one, you first order all the possible scores from highest to lowest. (Our mood disturbance scores will be ordered from 7 to 1.) Then you tally how often each score was actually obtained. Table A.1 gives some hypothetical raw data for the two groups, and Table A.2 shows the two frequency distributions based on these data. From these distributions, you can see that the two groups differed. In the experimental group, the extreme scores of 7 and 1 did not occur at all,

TABLE A.1
Some Hypothetical Raw Data

These scores are for the hypothetical humor-and-stress study described in the text.

Experimental group
4,5,4,4,3,6,5,2,4,3,5,4,4,3,4

Control group
6,4,7,6,6,4,6,7,7,5,5,5,7,6,6

and the most common score was the middle one, 4. In the control group, a score of 7 occurred four times, the most common score was 6, and no one obtained a score lower than 4.

Because our mood scores have only seven possible values, our frequency distributions are quite manageable. Suppose, though, that your questionnaire had yielded scores that could range from 1 to 50. A frequency distribution with 50 entries would be cumbersome and might not reveal trends in the data clearly. A solution would be to construct a *grouped frequency distribution* by grouping adjacent scores into equal-sized *classes* or *intervals*. Each interval could cover, say, five scores (1–5, 6–10, 11–15, and so forth). Then you could tally the frequencies within each *interval*. This procedure would reduce the number of entries in each distribution from 50 to only 10, making the overall results much easier to grasp. However, information would be lost. For example, there would be no way of knowing how many people had a score of 43 versus 44.

Graphing the Data

As everyone knows, a picture is worth a thousand words. The most common statistical picture is a **graph**, a drawing that depicts numerical relationships. Graphs appear at several points in this book, and are routinely used by psychologists to convey their findings to others. From graphs, we can get a general impression of what the data are like, note the relative frequencies of different scores, and see which score was most frequent.

In a graph constructed from a frequency distribution, the possible score values are shown along a horizontal line (the *x-axis* of the graph) and frequencies along a vertical line (the *y-axis*), or vice versa. To construct a **histogram**, or **bar graph**, from our mood scores, we draw rectangles (bars) above each score, indicating the number of times it occurred by the rectangle's height (see Figure A.1).

A slightly different kind of "picture" is provided by a **frequency polygon**, or **line graph**. In a frequency polygon, the frequency of each score is indicated by a dot placed directly over the score on the horizontal axis, at the appropriate height on the vertical axis. The dots for the various scores are then joined together by straight lines, as in Figure A.2. When necessary, an "extra" score, with a frequency of zero, can be added at each end of the horizontal axis, so that the polygon will rest on this axis instead of floating above it.

A word of caution about graphs: They may either exaggerate or mask differences in the data, depending on which units are used on the vertical axis. The two graphs in Figure A.3, although they look quite different, actually depict the same data. Always read the units on the axes of a

TABLE A.2
Two Frequency Distributions

The scores are from Table A.1.

Experimental Group			Control Group		
Mood Disturbance Score	Tally	Frequency	Mood Disturbance Score	Tally	Frequency
7		0	7	////	4
6	/	1	6	ЦНТ /	6
5	///	3	5	///	3
4	ЦНТ //	7	4	//	2
3	///	3	3		0
2	/	1	2		0
1		0	1		0
		N = 15			N = 15

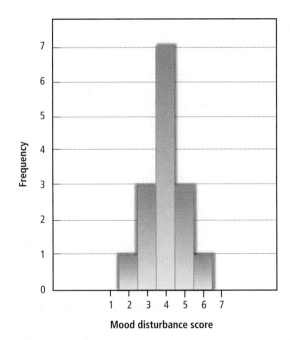

FIGURE A.1

A Histogram

This graph depicts the distribution of mood disturbance scores shown on the left side of Table A.2.

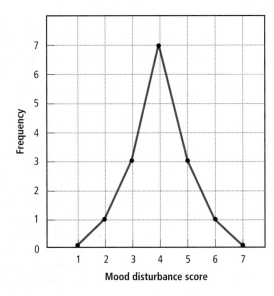

FIGURE A.2

Frequency Polygon

This graph depicts the same data as Figure A.1.

graph; otherwise, the shape of a histogram or frequency polygon may be misleading.

Describing Data

Having organized your data, you are now ready to summarize and describe them. As you will recall from Chapter 1,

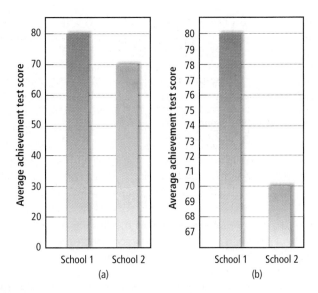

FIGURE A.3

Same Data, Different Impressions

These two graphs depict the same data, but have different units on the vertical axis.

procedures for doing so are known as **descriptive statistics**. In the following discussion, the word *score* will stand for any numerical observation.

Measuring Central Tendency

Your first step in describing your data might be to compute a **measure of central tendency** for each group. Measures of central tendency characterize an entire set of data in terms of a single representative number.

The Mean The most popular measure of central tendency is the arithmetic mean, usually called simply the **mean**. It is often expressed by the symbol *M*. Most people are thinking of the mean when they say "average." We run across means all the time: in grade point averages, temperature averages, and batting averages. The mean is valuable to psychologists because it takes all the data into account and it can be used in further statistical analyses. To compute the mean, you simply add up a set of scores and divide the total by the number of scores in the set. Recall that in mathematical notation, Σ means "the sum of," X stands for the individual scores, and N represents the total number of scores in a set. Thus, the formula for calculating the mean is:

$$M = \frac{\Sigma X}{N}$$

Table A.3 shows how to compute the mean for our experimental group. Test your ability to perform this calculation by computing the mean for the control group yourself. (You can find the answer, along with other control group statistics, on page A-7.) Later, we will describe how a psychologist would compare the two means statistically to see if there is a significant difference between them.

The Median Despite its usefulness, sometimes the mean can be misleading. Suppose you piled some children on a seesaw in such a way that it was perfectly balanced, and then a 200-pound adult came and sat on one end. The center of gravity would quickly shift toward the adult. In the same way, one extremely high score can dramatically raise the mean (and one extremely low score can dramatically lower it). In real life, this can be a serious problem. For example, in the calculation of a town's mean income, one millionaire would offset hundreds of poor people. The mean income would be a misleading indication of the town's actual wealth.

When extreme scores occur, a more representative measure of central tendency is the **median**, or midpoint in a set of scores or observations ordered from highest to lowest. In any set of scores, the same *number* of scores falls above the median as below it. The median is not affected by extreme scores. If you were calculating the median income of that same town, the one millionaire would offset only one poor person.

When the number of scores in the set is odd, calculating the median is a simple matter of counting in from the ends to the middle. However, if the number of scores is even, there will be two middle scores. The simplest solution is to find the mean of those two scores and use that number as the median. (When the data are from a grouped frequency distribution, a more complicated procedure is required, one beyond the scope of this appendix.) In our experimental group, the median score is 4 (see Table A.3 again). What is it for the control group?

The Mode A third measure of central tendency is the **mode**, the score that occurs most often. In our experimental group, the modal score is 4. In our control group, it is 6. In some distributions, all scores occur with equal frequency, and there is no mode. In others, two or more scores "tie" for the distinction of being most frequent. Modes are used less often than other measures of central tendency. They do not tell us anything about the other scores in the distribution; they often are not very "central"; and they tend to fluctuate from one random sample of a population to another more than either the median or the mean.

Measuring Variability

A measure of central tendency may or may not be highly representative of other scores in a distribution. To understand our results, we also need a **measure of variability** that will tell us whether our scores are clustered closely around the mean or widely scattered.

The Range The simplest measure of variability is the **range**, which is found by subtracting the lowest score from the highest one. For our hypothetical set of mood disturbance scores, the range in the experimental group is 4 and in the control group it is 3. Unfortunately, simplicity is not always a virtue. The range gives us some information about variability but ignores all scores other than the highest and lowest ones.

The Standard Deviation A more sophisticated measure of variability is the **standard deviation (SD)**. This statistic takes every score in the distribution into account. Loosely speaking, it gives us an idea of how much, on the average, scores in a distribution differ from the mean. If the scores were all the same, the standard deviation would be zero. The higher the standard deviation, the more variability there is among scores.

To compute the standard deviation, we must find out how much each individual score deviates from the mean. To do so, we simply subtract the mean from each score. This gives us a set of *deviation scores*. Deviation scores for numbers above the mean will be positive, those for numbers below the mean will be negative, and the positive scores will exactly balance the negative ones. In other words, the sum of the deviation scores will be zero. That is a problem, because the next step in our calculation is to add. The solution is to *square* all the deviation scores (that is, to multiply each score by itself). This step gets rid of negative values. Then we can compute the average of the squared deviation scores by adding them up and dividing the sum by the number of scores (N). Finally, we take the square root of the result, which takes us from squared units of measurement back to the same units that were used originally (in this case, mood disturbance levels).

TABLE A.3

Calculating a Mean and a Median

The scores are from the left side of Table A.1.

Mean (M)

$$M = \frac{4 + 5 + 4 + 4 + 3 + 6 + 5 + 2 + 4 + 3 + 5 + 4 + 4 + 3 + 4}{15}$$

$$= \frac{60}{15}$$

$$= 4$$

Median

Scores, in order: 2, 3, 3, 3, 4, 4, 4, 4, 4, 4, 4, 5, 5, 5, 6

↑

Median

The calculations just described are expressed by the following formula:

$$SD = \sqrt{\frac{\Sigma(X - M)^2}{N}}$$

Table A.4 shows the calculations for computing the standard deviation for our experimental group. Try your hand at computing the standard deviation for the control group.

Remember, a large standard deviation signifies that scores are widely scattered, and that therefore the mean is not terribly typical of the entire population. A small standard deviation tells us that most scores are clustered near the mean, and that therefore the mean is representative. Suppose two classes took a psychology exam, and both classes had the same mean score, 75 out of a possible 100. From the means alone, you might conclude that the classes were similar in performance. But if Class A had a standard deviation of 3 and Class B had a standard deviation of 9, you would know that there was much more variability in performance in Class B. This information could be useful to an instructor in planning lectures and making assignments.

Transforming Scores

Sometimes researchers do not wish to work directly with raw scores. They may prefer numbers that are more manageable, such as when the raw scores are tiny fractions. Or they may want to work with scores that reveal where a person stands relative to others. In such cases, raw scores can be transformed into other kinds of scores.

Percentile Scores One common transformation converts each raw score to a **percentile score** (also called a *centile rank*). A percentile score gives the percentage of people who scored at or below a given raw score. Suppose you learn that you have scored 37 on a psychology exam. In the absence of any other information, you may not know whether to celebrate or cry. But if you are told that 37 is equivalent to a percentile score of 90, you know that you can be pretty proud of yourself; you have scored as well as, or higher than, 90 percent of those who have taken the test. On the other hand, if you are told that 37 is equivalent to a percentile score of 50, you have scored only at the median—only as well as, or higher than, half of the other students. The highest possible percentile rank is 99, or more precisely, 99.99, because you can never do better than 100 percent of a group when you are a member of the group. (Can you say what the lowest possible percentile score is? The answer is on page A-7.) Standardized tests such as those described in previous chapters often come with tables that allow for the easy conversion of any raw score to the appropriate percentile score, based on data from a larger number of people who have already taken the test.

Percentile scores are easy to understand and easy to calculate. However, they also have a drawback: They merely rank people and do not tell us how far apart people are in terms of raw scores. Suppose you scored in the 50th percentile on an exam, June scored in the 45th, Tricia scored in the 20th, and Sean scored in the 15th. The difference between you and June may seem identical to that between Tricia and Sean (five percentiles). But in terms of raw scores, you and June are probably more alike than Tricia and Sean, because exam scores usually cluster closely together around the midpoint of the distribution and are farther apart at the extremes. Because percentile scores do not preserve the spatial relationships in the original distribution of scores, they are inappropriate for computing many kinds of statistics. For example, they cannot be used to calculate means.

TABLE A.4
Calculating a Standard Deviation

Scores (X)	Deviation scores (X – M)	Squared deviation scores (X – M)²
6	2	4
5	1	1
5	1	1
5	1	1
4	0	0
4	0	0
4	0	0
4	0	0
4	0	0
4	0	0
4	0	0
3	–1	1
3	–1	1
3	–1	1
2	–2	4
	0	14

$$SD = \sqrt{\frac{\Sigma(X - M)^2}{N}} = \sqrt{\frac{14}{15}} = \sqrt{.93} = .97$$

Note: When data from a sample are used to estimate the standard deviation of the population from which the sample was drawn, division is by $N - 1$ instead of N, for reasons that will not concern us here.

Z-scores Another common transformation of raw scores is to **z-scores**, or **standard scores**. A z-score tells you how far a given raw score is above or below the mean, using the standard deviation as the unit of measurement. To compute a z-score, you subtract the mean of the distribution from the raw score and divide by the standard deviation:

$$z = \frac{X - M}{SD}$$

Unlike percentile scores, z-scores preserve the relative spacing of the original raw scores. The mean itself always corresponds to a z-score of zero, because it cannot deviate from itself. All scores above the mean have positive z-scores and all scores below the mean have negative ones. When the raw scores form a certain pattern called a *normal distribution* (to be described shortly), a z-score tells you how high or low the corresponding raw score was, relative to the other scores. If your exam score of 37 is equivalent to a z-score of +1.0, you have scored 1 standard deviation above the mean. Assuming a roughly normal distribution, that's pretty good, because only about 16 percent of all scores fall at or above 1 standard deviation above the mean. But if your 37 is equivalent to a z-score of –1.0, you have scored 1 standard deviation below the mean—a poor score.

Z-scores are sometimes used to compare people's performance on different tests or measures. Say that Elsa earns a score of 64 on her first psychology test and Manuel, who is taking psychology from a different instructor, earns a 62 on his first test. In Elsa's class, the mean score is 50 and the standard deviation is 7, so Elsa's z-score is (64 – 50)/7 = 2.0. In Manuel's class, the mean is also 50, but the standard deviation is 6. Therefore, his z-score is also 2.0 [(62 – 50)/6]. Compared to their respective classmates, Elsa and Manuel did equally well. But be careful: This does not imply that they are equally able students. Perhaps Elsa's instructor has a reputation for giving easy tests and Manuel's for giving hard ones, so Manuel's instructor has attracted a more industrious group of students. In that case, Manuel faces stiffer competition than Elsa does, and even though he and Elsa have the same z-score, Manuel's performance may be more impressive.

You can see that comparing z-scores from different people or different tests must be done with caution. Standardized tests, such as IQ tests and various personality tests, use z-scores derived from a large sample of people assumed to be representative of the general population taking the tests. When two tests are standardized for similar populations, it is safe to compare z-scores on them. But z-scores derived from special samples, such as students in different psychology classes, may not be comparable.

Curves

In addition to knowing how spread out our scores are, we need to know the pattern of their distribution. At this

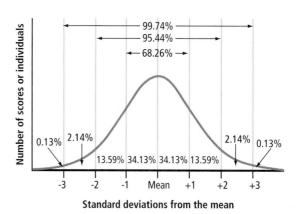

FIGURE A.4
A Normal Curve
When standard deviations (or z-scores) are used along the horizontal axis of a normal curve, certain fixed percentages of scores fall between the mean and any given point. As you can see, most scores fall in the middle range (between +1 and −1 standard deviations from the mean).

point, we come to a rather curious phenomenon. When researchers make a very large number of observations, many of the physical and psychological variables they study have a distribution that approximates a pattern called a **normal distribution**. (We say "approximates" because a perfect normal distribution is a theoretical construct and is not actually found in nature.) Plotted in a frequency polygon, a normal distribution has a symmetrical, bell-shaped form known as a **normal curve** (see Figure A.4).

A normal curve has several interesting and convenient properties. The right side is the exact mirror image of the left. The mean, median, and mode all have the same value and are at the exact center of the curve, at the top of the "bell." Most observations or scores cluster around the center of the curve, with far fewer out at the ends, or "tails" of the curve. Most important, as Figure A.4 shows, when standard deviations (or z-scores) are used on the horizontal axis of the curve, the percentage of scores falling between the mean and any given point on the horizontal axis is always the same. For example, 68.26 percent of the scores will fall between plus and minus 1 standard deviation from the mean; 95.44 percent of the scores will fall between plus and minus 2 standard deviations from the mean; and 99.74 percent of the scores will fall between plus and minus 3 standard deviations from the mean. These percentages hold for any normal curve, no matter what the size of the standard deviation. Tables are available, showing the percentages of scores in a normal distribution that lie between the mean and various points (as expressed by z-scores).

The normal curve makes life easier for psychologists when they want to compare individuals on some trait or performance. For example, because IQ scores from a population form a roughly normal curve, the mean and standard

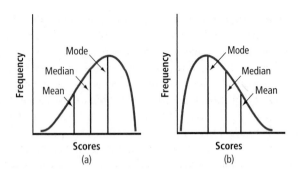

FIGURE A.5

Skewed Curves

Curve (a) is skewed negatively, to the left. Curve (b) is skewed positively, to the right. The direction of a curve's skew is determined by the position of the long tail, not by the position of the bulge. In a skewed curve, the mean, median, and mode fall at different points.

deviation of a test are all the information you need if you want to know how many people score above or below a particular score. On a test with a mean of 100 and a standard deviation of 15, about 68.26 percent of the population scores between 85 and 115—1 standard deviation below and 1 standard deviation above the mean.

Not all types of observations, however, are distributed normally. Some curves are lopsided, or *skewed*, with scores clustering at one end or the other of the horizontal axis (see Figure A.5). When the tail of the curve is longer on the right than on the left, the curve is said to be positively, or right, skewed. When the opposite is true, the curve is said to be negatively, or left, skewed. In experiments, reaction times typically form a right-skewed distribution. For example, if people must press a button whenever they hear some signal, most will react quite quickly; but a few will take an unusually long time, causing the right tail of the curve to be stretched out.

Knowing the shape of a distribution can be extremely valuable. Paleontologist Stephen Jay Gould (1985) once told how such information helped him cope with the news that he had a rare and serious form of cancer. Being a researcher, he immediately headed for the library to learn all he could about the disease. The first thing he found was that it was incurable, with a median mortality of only eight months after discovery. Most people might have assumed that a "median mortality of eight months" means "I will probably be dead in eight months." But Gould realized that although half of all patients died within eight months, the other half survived longer than that. Because his disease had been diagnosed in its early stages, he was getting top-notch medical treatment, and he had a strong will to live, Gould figured he could reasonably expect to be in the half of the distribution that survived beyond eight months. Even more cheering, the distribution of deaths from the disease was right-skewed: The cases to the left of the

median of eight months could only extend to zero months, but those to the right could stretch out for years. Gould saw no reason why he should not expect to be in the tip of that right-hand tail.

For Stephen Jay Gould, statistics, properly interpreted, were "profoundly nurturant and life-giving." They offered him hope and inspired him to fight his disease. The initial diagnosis was made in 1982. Gould remained professionally active for 20 more years. When he died in 2002, it was from an unrelated type of cancer.

Answers to Questions in this Appendix:

Control group statistics:

$$\text{Mean} = \frac{\Sigma X}{N} = \frac{87}{15} = 5.8$$

$$\text{Median} = 6$$

$$\text{Standard Deviation} = \sqrt{\frac{\Sigma(X - M)^2}{N}} = \sqrt{\frac{14.4}{15}}$$

$$= \sqrt{.96} = .98$$

Lowest possible percentile score: 1 (or, more precisely, .01).

Drawing Inferences

Once data are organized and summarized, the next step is to ask whether they differ from what might have been expected purely by chance (see Chapter 1). A researcher needs to know whether it is safe to infer that the results from a particular sample of people are valid for the entire population from which the sample was drawn. **Inferential statistics** provide this information. They are used in both experimental and correlational studies.

The Null versus the Alternative Hypothesis

In an experiment, scientists must assess the possibility that their experimental manipulations will have no effect on the subjects' behavior. The statement expressing this possibility is called the **null hypothesis**. In our stress-and-humor study, the null hypothesis states that making up a funny commentary will not relieve stress any more than making up a straightforward narrative will. In other words, it predicts that the difference between the means of the two groups will not deviate significantly from zero. Any obtained difference will be due solely to chance fluctuations. In contrast, the **alternative hypothesis** (also called the *experimental* or *research hypothesis*) states that on average, the experimental group will have lower mood disturbance scores than the control group.

The null hypothesis and the alternative hypothesis cannot both be true. Our goal is to reject the null hypothesis. If our results turn out to be consistent with the null hypothesis, we will not be able to do so. If the data are inconsistent with the null hypothesis, we will be able to reject it with some degree of confidence. Unless we study the entire population, though, we will never be able to say that the alternative hypothesis has been proven. No matter how impressive our results are, there will always be some degree of uncertainty about the inferences we draw from them. Because we cannot prove the alternative hypothesis, we must be satisfied with showing that the null hypothesis is unreasonable.

Students are often surprised to learn that in traditional hypothesis testing it is the null hypothesis, not the alternative hypothesis, that is tested. After all, it is the alternative hypothesis that is actually of interest. But this procedure does make sense. The null hypothesis can be stated precisely and tested directly. In the case of our fictitious study, the null hypothesis predicts that the difference between the two means will be zero. The alternative hypothesis does not permit a precise prediction because we don't know how much the two means might differ (if, in fact, they do differ). Therefore, it cannot be tested directly.

Testing Hypotheses

Many computations are available for testing the null hypothesis. The choice depends on the design of the study, the size of the sample, and other factors. We will not cover any specific tests here. Our purpose is simply to introduce you to the kind of reasoning that underlies hypothesis testing. With that in mind, let us return once again to our data. For each of our two groups, we have calculated a mean and a standard deviation. Now we want to compare the two sets of data to see if they differ enough for us to reject the null hypothesis. We wish to be reasonably certain that our observed differences did not occur entirely by chance.

What does it mean to be "reasonably certain"? How different from zero must our result be to be taken seriously? Imagine, for a moment, that we had infinite resources and could somehow repeat our experiment, each time using a new pair of groups, until we had run the entire population through the study. It can be shown mathematically that if only chance were operating, our various experimental results would form a normal distribution. This theoretical distribution is called "the sampling distribution of the difference between means," but because that is quite a mouthful, we will simply call it the *sampling distribution* for short. If the null hypothesis were true, the mean of the sampling distribution would be zero. That is, on average, we would find no difference between the two groups. Often, however, because of chance influences or *random error*, we would get a result that deviated to one degree or another from zero. On rare occasions, the result would deviate a great deal from zero.

We cannot test the entire population, though. All we have are data from a single sample. We would like to know whether the difference between means that we actually obtained would be close to the mean of the theoretical sampling distribution (if we could test the entire population) or far away from it, out in one of the tails of the curve. Was our result highly likely to occur on the basis of chance alone or highly unlikely?

Before we can answer that question, we must have some precise way to measure distance from the mean of the sampling distribution. We must know exactly how far from the mean our obtained result must be to be considered "far away." If only we knew the standard deviation of the sampling distribution, we could use it as our unit of measurement. We don't know it, but fortunately, we can use the standard deviation of our *sample* to estimate it. (We will not go into the reasons that this is so.)

Now we are in business. We can look at the mean difference between our two groups and figure out how far it is (in terms of standard deviations) from the mean of the sampling distribution. As mentioned earlier, one of the convenient things about a normal distribution is that a certain fixed percentage of all observations falls between the mean of the distribution and any given point above or below the mean. These percentages are available from tables. Therefore, if we know the distance of our obtained result from the mean of the theoretical sampling distribution, we automatically know how likely our result is to have occurred strictly by chance.

To give a specific example, if it turns out that our obtained result is 2 standard deviations above the mean of the theoretical sampling distribution, we know that the probability of its having occurred by chance is less than 2.3 percent. If our result is 3 standard deviations above the mean of the sampling distribution, the probability of its having occurred by chance is less than .13 percent—less than 1 in 800. In either case, we might well suspect that our result did not occur entirely by chance after all. We would call the result **statistically significant**. (Psychologists usually consider any highly unlikely result to be of interest, no matter which direction it takes. In other words, the result may be in either tail of the sampling distribution.)

To summarize: Statistical significance means that if only chance were operating, our result would be highly improbable, so we are fairly safe in concluding that more than chance was operating—namely, the influence of our independent variable. We can reject the null hypothesis and open the champagne. As we noted in Chapter 1, psychologists usually accept a finding as statistically significant if the likelihood of its occurring by chance is 5 percent or less (see Figure A.6). This cutoff point gives them a reasonable chance of confirming reliable results as well as reasonable protection against accepting unreliable ones.

Some cautions are in order, however. Conventional tests of statistical significance have drawn serious criticisms in recent years. Statistically significant results are not

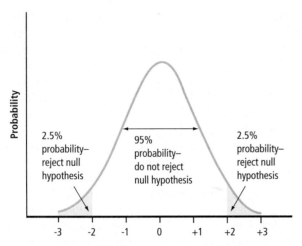

FIGURE A.6
Statistical Significance
This curve represents the theoretical sampling distribution discussed in the text. The curve is what we would expect by chance if we did our hypothetical stress-and-humor study many times, testing the entire population. If we used the conventional significance level of .05, we would regard our obtained result as significant only if the probability of getting a result that far from zero by chance (in either direction) totaled 5 percent or less. As shown, the result must fall far out in one of the tails of the sampling distribution. Otherwise, we cannot reject the null hypothesis.

always psychologically interesting or important. Further, statistical significance is related to the size of the sample. A large sample increases the likelihood of reliable results. But there is a trade-off: The larger the sample, the more probable it is that a small result having no practical importance will reach statistical significance. On the other hand, with the sample sizes typically used in psychological research, there is a good chance of falsely concluding that an experimental effect has not occurred when one actually has. For these reasons, it is always useful to know how much of the total variability in scores was accounted for by the independent variable (the **effect size**). (The computations are not discussed here.) If only 3 percent of the variance was accounted for, then 97 percent was due either to chance factors or to systematic influences of which the researcher was unaware. Because so many factors affect human behavior, the amount of variability accounted for by a single psychological variable is often modest. But sometimes the effect size is considerable even when the results don't quite reach significance.

Oh, by the way, the study of humor's effect on stress and health turns out to be pretty complicated. The results depend on how you define "sense of humor," how you do the study, and what aspects of humor you are investigating. Researchers have learned that humor probably doesn't help people live longer or hasten recovery from injury or illness. But it is certainly more emotionally beneficial than moping around. So, when gravity gets you down, try a little levity.

Summary

- When used correctly, statistics expose unwarranted conclusions, promote precision, and help researchers spot trends amid diversity.

- Often, the first step in data analysis is to organize and condense data in a *frequency distribution*, a tally showing how often each possible score (or interval of scores) occurred. Such information can also be depicted in a *histogram* (bar graph) or a *frequency polygon* (line graph).

- Descriptive statistics summarize and describe the data. *Central tendency* is measured by the *mean, median,* or, less frequently, the *mode.* Because a measure of central tendency may or may not be highly representative of other scores in a distribution, it is also important to analyze variability. A large *standard deviation* means that scores are widely scattered about the mean; a small one means that most scores are clustered near the mean.

- Raw scores can be transformed into other kinds of scores. *Percentile scores* indicate the percentage of people who scored at or below a given raw score. *Z-scores* (*standard scores*) indicate how far a given raw score is above or below the mean of the distribution.

- Many variables have a distribution approximating a *normal distribution,* depicted as a *normal curve.* The normal curve has a convenient property: When standard deviations are used as the units on the horizontal axis, the percentage of scores falling between any two points on the horizontal axis is always the same. Not all types of observations are distributed normally, however. Some distributions are *skewed* to the left or right.

- Inferential statistics can be used to test the *null hypothesis* and to tell researchers whether a result differed significantly from what might have been expected purely by chance. Basically, hypothesis testing involves estimating where the obtained result would have fallen in a theoretical *sampling distribution* based on studies of the entire population in question. If the result would have been far out in one of the tails of the distribution, it is considered statistically significant. A statistically significant result may or may not be psychologically interesting or important, so many researchers prefer to compute the *effect size.*

Key Terms

Glossary

absolute threshold The smallest quantity of physical energy that can be reliably detected by an observer.

acculturation The process by which members of minority groups come to identify with and feel part of the mainstream culture.

action potential A brief change in electrical voltage that occurs between the inside and the outside of an axon when a neuron is stimulated; it serves to produce an electrical impulse.

activation–synthesis theory The theory that dreaming results from the cortical synthesis and interpretation of neural signals triggered by activity in the lower part of the brain.

adrenal hormones Hormones that are produced by the adrenal glands and that are involved in emotion and stress.

affect heuristic The tendency to consult one's emotions instead of estimating probabilities objectively.

agoraphobia A set of phobias, often set off by a panic attack, involving the basic fear of being away from a safe place or person.

algorithm A problem-solving strategy guaranteed to produce a solution even if the user does not know how it works.

alternative hypothesis An assertion that the independent variable in a study will have a certain predictable effect on the dependent variable; also called an experimental or research hypothesis.

amnesia The partial or complete loss of memory for important personal information.

amygdala [uh-MIG-dul-uh] A brain structure involved in the arousal and regulation of emotion and the initial emotional response to sensory information.

anorexia nervosa An eating disorder characterized by fear of being fat, a distorted body image, radically reduced consumption of food, and emaciation.

antidepressant drugs Drugs used primarily in the treatment of mood disorders, especially depression and anxiety.

antipsychotic drugs Drugs used primarily in the treatment of schizophrenia and other psychotic disorders.

antisocial personality disorder (APD) A personality disorder characterized by a lifelong pattern of irresponsible, antisocial behavior such as lawbreaking, violence, and other impulsive, reckless acts; likely to be combined with *psychopathy* in the DSM-V.

applied psychology The study of psychological issues that have direct practical significance; also, the application of psychological findings.

approach goals Goals framed in terms of desired outcomes or experiences, such as learning to scuba dive.

archetypes [AR-ki-types] Universal, symbolic images that appear in myths, art, stories, and dreams; to Jungians, they reflect the collective unconscious.

arithmetic mean An average that is calculated by adding up a set of quantities and dividing the sum by the total number of quantities in the set.

attribution theory The theory that people are motivated to explain their own and other people's behavior by attributing causes of that behavior to a situation or a disposition.

autonomic nervous system The subdivision of the peripheral nervous system that regulates the internal organs and glands.

availability heuristic The tendency to judge the probability of a type of event by how easy it is to think of examples or instances.

avoidance goals Goals framed in terms of avoiding unpleasant experiences, such as trying not to look foolish in public.

axon A neuron's extending fiber that conducts impulses away from the cell body and transmits them to other neurons or to muscle or gland cells.

basic concepts Concepts that have a moderate number of instances and that are easier to acquire than those having few or many instances.

basic psychology The study of psychological issues in order to seek knowledge for its own sake rather than for its practical application.

behavior modification The application of conditioning techniques to teach new responses or to reduce or eliminate maladaptive or problematic behavior; also called *applied behavior analysis*.

behavior therapy A form of therapy that applies principles of classical and operant conditioning to help people change self-defeating or problematic behaviors.

behavioral genetics An interdisciplinary field of study concerned with the genetic bases of individual differences in behavior and personality.

behavioral self-monitoring In behavior therapy, a method of keeping careful data on the frequency and consequences of the behavior to be changed.

behaviorism An approach to psychology that emphasizes the study of observable behavior and the role of the environment as a determinant of behavior.

binocular cues Visual cues to depth or distance requiring two eyes.

biological perspective A psychological approach that emphasizes bodily events and changes associated with actions, feelings, and thoughts.

biological rhythm A periodic, more or less regular fluctuation in a biological system; it may or may not have psychological implications.

bipolar disorder A mood disorder in which episodes of both depression and mania (excessive euphoria) occur.

borderline personality disorder A disorder characterized by intense but unstable relationships, impulsiveness, self-mutilating behavior, feelings of emptiness, and a fear of abandonment by others.

brain stem The part of the brain at the top of the spinal cord, consisting of the medulla and the pons.

brightness Lightness or luminance; the dimension of visual experience related to the amount (intensity) of light emitted from or reflected by an object.

bulimia nervosa An eating disorder characterized by episodes of excessive eating (bingeing) followed by forced vomiting or use of laxatives (purging).

case study A detailed description of a particular individual being studied or treated.

cell body The part of the neuron that keeps it alive and determines whether it will fire.

central nervous system (CNS) The portion of the nervous system consisting of the brain and spinal cord.

cerebellum A brain structure that regulates movement and balance and that is involved in some cognitive tasks.

cerebral cortex A collection of several thin layers of cells covering the cerebrum; it is largely responsible for higher mental functions. *Cortex* is Latin for "bark" or "rind."

cerebral hemispheres The two halves of the cerebrum.

cerebrum [suh-REE-brum] The largest brain structure, consisting of the upper part of the brain; divided into two hemispheres, it is in charge of most sensory, motor, and cognitive processes. From the Latin for "brain."

childhood (infantile) amnesia The inability to remember events and experiences that occurred during the first two or three years of life.

chunk A meaningful unit of information; it may be composed of smaller units.

circadian [sur-CAY-dee-un] rhythm A biological rhythm with a period (from peak to peak or trough to trough) of about 24 hours; from the Latin *circa*, "about," and *dies*, "a day."

classical conditioning The process by which a previously neutral stimulus acquires the capacity to elicit a response through association with a stimulus that already elicits a similar or related response. Also called *Pavlovian* or *respondent* conditioning.

client-centered (nondirective) therapy A humanist approach to therapy devised by Carl Rogers, which emphasizes the therapist's empathy with the client and the use of unconditional positive regard.

cochlea [KOCK-lee-uh] A snail-shaped, fluid-filled organ in the inner ear, containing the organ of Corti, where the receptors for hearing are located.

coefficient of correlation A measure of correlation that ranges in value from -1.00 to $+1.00$.

cognitive dissonance A state of tension that occurs when a person simultaneously holds two cognitions that are psychologically inconsistent or when a person's belief is incongruent with his or her behavior.

cognitive ethology The study of cognitive processes in nonhuman animals.

cognitive perspective A psychological approach that emphasizes mental processes in perception, memory, language, problem solving, and other areas of behavior.

cognitive schema An integrated mental network of knowledge, beliefs, and expectations concerning a particular topic or aspect of the world.

cognitive therapy A form of therapy designed to identify and change irrational, unproductive ways of thinking and, hence, to reduce negative emotions and their self-defeating consequences.

collective unconscious In Jungian theory, the universal memories and experiences of humankind, represented in the symbols, stories, and images (archetypes) that occur across all cultures.

collectivist cultures Cultures in which the self is regarded as embedded in relationships, and harmony with one's group is prized above individual goals and wishes.

concept A mental category that groups objects, relations, activities, abstractions, or qualities having common properties.

conditioned response (CR) The classical-conditioning term for a response that is elicited by a conditioned stimulus; it occurs after the conditioned stimulus is associated with an unconditioned stimulus.

conditioned stimulus (CS) The classical-conditioning term for an initially neutral stimulus that comes to elicit a conditioned response after being associated with an unconditioned stimulus.

conditioning A basic kind of learning that involves associations between environmental stimuli and the organism's responses.

cones Visual receptors involved in color vision.

confabulation Confusion of an event that happened to someone else with one that happened to you, or a belief that you remember something when it never actually happened.

confirmation bias The tendency to look for or pay attention only to information that confirms one's own belief, and ignore, trivialize, or forget information that disconfirms that belief.

conservation The understanding that the physical properties of objects—such as the number of items in a cluster or the amount of liquid in a glass—can remain the same even when their form or appearance changes.

consolidation The process by which a long-term memory becomes durable and stable.

contact comfort In primates, the innate pleasure derived from close physical contact; it is the basis of an infant's first attachment.

continuous reinforcement A reinforcement schedule in which a particular response is always reinforced.

control condition In an experiment, a comparison condition in which subjects are not exposed to the same treatment as are those in the experimental condition.

convergence The turning inward of the eyes, which occurs when they focus on a nearby object.

corpus callosum [CORE-pus ca-LOW-suhm] The bundle of nerve fibers connecting the two cerebral hemispheres.

correlation A measure of how strongly two variables are related to each other.

correlational study A descriptive study that looks for a consistent relationship between two phenomena.

counterconditioning In classical conditioning, the process of pairing a conditioned stimulus with a stimulus that elicits a response that is incompatible with an unwanted conditioned response.

critical thinking The ability and willingness to assess claims and make objective judgments on the basis of well-supported reasons and evidence rather than emotion or anecdote.

cross-sectional study A study in which individuals of different ages are compared at a given time.

crystallized intelligence Cognitive skills and specific knowledge of information acquired over a lifetime; it is heavily dependent on education and tends to remain stable over the lifetime.

cue-dependent forgetting The inability to retrieve information stored in memory because of insufficient cues for recall.

culture A program of shared rules that govern the behavior of members of a community or society and a set of values, beliefs, and customs shared by most members of that community.

culture-bound syndromes Symptoms or mental disorders that are specific to particular cultural contexts and practices.

dark adaptation A process by which visual receptors become maximally sensitive to dim light.

decay theory The theory that information in memory eventually disappears if it is not accessed; it applies more to short-term than to long-term memory.

declarative memories Memories of facts, rules, concepts, and events ("knowing that"); they include semantic and episodic memories.

deductive reasoning A form of reasoning in which a conclusion follows necessarily from certain premises; if the premises are true, the conclusion must be true.

deep processing In the encoding of information, the processing of meaning rather than simply the physical or sensory features of a stimulus.

defense mechanisms Methods used by the ego to prevent unconscious anxiety or threatening thoughts from entering consciousness.

deindividuation In groups or crowds, the loss of awareness of one's own individuality.

dendrites A neuron's branches that receive information from other neurons and transmit it toward the cell body.

dependent variable A variable that an experimenter predicts will be affected by manipulations of the independent variable.

depressants Drugs that slow activity in the central nervous system.

descriptive methods Methods that yield descriptions of behavior but not necessarily causal explanations.

descriptive statistics Statistics that organize and summarize research data.

dialectical reasoning A process in which opposing facts or ideas are weighed and compared, with a view to determining the best solution or to resolving differences.

difference threshold The smallest difference in stimulation that can be reliably detected by an observer when two stimuli are compared; also called *just noticeable difference* (*jnd*).

diffusion of responsibility In groups, the tendency of members to avoid taking action because they assume that others will.

discriminative stimulus A stimulus that signals when a particular response is likely to be followed by a certain type of consequence.

display rules Social and cultural rules that regulate when, how, and where a person may express (or suppress) emotions.

dissociation A split in consciousness in which one part of the mind operates independently of others.

dissociative identity disorder A controversial disorder marked by the apparent appearance within one person of two or more distinct personalities, each with its own name and traits; formerly known as *multiple personality disorder* (*MPD*).

doctrine of specific nerve energies The principle that different sensory modalities exist because signals received by the sense organs stimulate different nerve pathways leading to different areas of the brain.

double-blind study An experiment in which neither the participants nor the individuals running the study know which participants are in the control group and which are in the experimental group until after the results are tallied.

effect size The amount of variance among scores in a study accounted for by the independent variable; thus it is a measure of the strength or power of that variable.

ego In psychoanalysis, the part of personality that represents reason, good sense, and rational self-control.

elaborative rehearsal Association of new information with already stored knowledge and analysis of the new information to make it memorable.

electroconvulsive therapy (ECT) A procedure used in cases of prolonged and severe major depression, in which a brief brain seizure is induced.

electroencephalogram (EEG) A recording of neural activity detected by electrodes.

emotion A state of arousal involving facial and bodily changes, brain activation, cognitive appraisals, subjective feelings, and tendencies toward action.

emotion work Expression of an emotion, often because of a role requirement, that a person does not really feel.

emotional intelligence The ability to identify your own and other people's emotions accurately, express your emotions clearly, and regulate emotions in yourself and others.

empirical Relying on or derived from observation, experimentation, or measurement.

endocrine glands Internal organs that produce hormones and release them into the bloodstream.

endogenous Generated from within rather than by external cues.

endorphins [en-DOR-fins] Chemical substances in the nervous system that are similar in structure and action to opiates; they are involved in pain reduction, pleasure, and memory and are known technically as *endogenous opioid peptides*.

entrapment A gradual process in which individuals escalate their commitment to a course of action to justify their investment of time, money, or effort.

episodic memories Memories of personally experienced events and the contexts in which they occurred.

equilibrium The sense of balance.

ethnic identity A person's identification with a religious or ethnic group.

ethnocentrism The belief that one's own ethnic group, nation, or religion is superior to all others.

evolutionary psychology A field of psychology emphasizing evolutionary mechanisms that may help explain human commonalities in cognition, development, emotion, social practices, and other areas of behavior.

existential therapy A form of therapy designed to help clients explore the meaning of existence and face the great questions of life, such as death, freedom, alienation, and loneliness.

existentialism A philosophical approach that emphasizes the inevitable dilemmas and challenges of human existence.

experiment A controlled test of a hypothesis in which the researcher manipulates one variable to discover its effect on another.

experimenter effects Unintended changes in subjects' behavior due to cues that the experimenter inadvertently gives.

explicit memory Conscious, intentional recollection of an event or of an item of information.

extinction The weakening and eventual disappearance of a learned response. In classical conditioning, it occurs when the conditioned stimulus is no longer paired with the unconditioned stimulus; in operant conditioning, it occurs when a response is no longer followed by a reinforcer.

extrinsic motivation The desire to do something for the sake of external rewards, such as money or fame.

extrinsic reinforcers Reinforcers that are not inherently related to the activity being reinforced, such as money, prizes, and praise.

facial feedback The process by which the facial muscles send messages to the brain about the basic emotion being expressed.

factor analysis A statistical method for analyzing the intercorrelations among various measures or test scores; clusters of measures or scores that are highly correlated are assumed to measure the same underlying trait, ability, or aptitude (factor).

familiarity effect The tendency of people to feel more positive toward a person, item, product, or other stimulus the more familiar they are with it.

family-systems perspective An approach to doing therapy with individuals or families by identifying how each family member forms part of a larger interacting system.

feature-detector cells Cells in the visual cortex that are sensitive to specific features of the environment.

field research Descriptive or experimental research conducted in a natural setting outside the laboratory.

flooding In behavior therapy, a form of exposure treatment in which the client is taken directly into the feared situation until his or her panic subsides.

fluid intelligence The capacity for deductive reasoning and the ability to use new information to solve problems; it is relatively independent of education and tends to decline in old age.

framing effect The tendency for people's choices to be affected by how a choice is presented or framed; for example, whether it is worded in terms of potential losses or gains.

frequency distribution A summary of how frequently each score in a set occurred.

frequency polygon (line graph) A graph showing a set of points obtained by plotting score values against score frequencies; adjacent points are joined by straight lines.

frontal lobes Lobes at the front of the brain's cerebral cortex; they contain areas involved in short-term memory, higher-order thinking, initiative, social judgment, and (in the left lobe, typically) speech production.

functionalism An early psychological approach that emphasized the function or purpose of behavior and consciousness.

fundamental attribution error The tendency, in explaining other people's behavior, to overestimate personality factors and underestimate the influence of the situation.

g factor A general ability assumed by many theorists to underlie specific mental abilities and talents.

ganglion cells Neurons in the retina of the eye, which gather information from receptor cells (by way of intermediate bipolar cells); their axons make up the optic nerve.

gate-control theory The theory that the experience of pain depends in part on whether pain impulses get past a neurological "gate" in the spinal cord and thus reach the brain.

gender identity The fundamental sense of being male or female; it is independent of whether the person conforms to the social and cultural rules of gender.

gender schema A cognitive schema (mental network) of knowledge, beliefs, metaphors, and expectations about what it means to be male or female.

gender typing The process by which children learn the abilities, interests, and behaviors associated with being masculine or feminine in their culture.

general adaptation syndrome According to Hans Selye, a series of physiological reactions to stressors occuring in three phases: alarm, resistance, and exhaustion.

generalized anxiety disorder A continuous state of anxiety marked by feelings of worry and dread, apprehension, difficulties in concentration, and signs of motor tension.

genes The functional units of heredity; they are composed of DNA and specify the structure of proteins.

Gestalt principles Principles that describe the brain's organization of sensory information into meaningful units and patterns.

glia [GLY-uh or GLEE-uh] Cells that support, nurture, and insulate neurons, remove debris when neurons die, enhance the formation and maintenance of neural connections, and modify neuronal functioning.

graduated exposure In behavior therapy, a method in which a person suffering from an anxiety disorder, such as a phobia or panic attacks, is gradually confronted with the feared object or situation until the anxiety subsides.

graph A drawing that depicts numerical relationships.

groupthink In close-knit groups, the tendency for all members to think alike for the sake of harmony and to suppress disagreement.

heritability A statistical estimate of the proportion of the total variance in some trait that is attributable to genetic differences among individuals within a group.

heuristic A rule of thumb that suggests a course of action or guides problem solving but does not guarantee an optimal solution.

higher-order conditioning In classical conditioning, a procedure in which a neutral stimulus becomes a conditioned stimulus through association with an already established conditioned stimulus.

hindsight bias The tendency to overestimate one's ability to have predicted an event once the outcome is known; the "I knew it all along" phenomenon.

hippocampus A brain structure involved in the storage of new information in memory.

histogram (bar graph) A graph in which the heights (or lengths) of bars are proportional to the frequencies of individual scores or classes of scores in a distribution.

hormones Chemical substances, secreted by organs called glands, that affect the functioning of other organs.

HPA (hypothalamus–pituitary–adrenal cortex) axis A system activated to energize the body to respond to stressors. The hypothalamus sends chemical messengers to the pituitary, which in turn prompts the adrenal cortex to produce cortisol and other hormones.

hue The dimension of visual experience specified by color names and related to the wavelength of light.

humanist psychology A psychological approach that emphasizes free will, personal growth, resilience, and the achievement of human potential.

humanist therapy A form of psychotherapy based on the philosophy of humanism, which emphasizes the client's free will to change rather than past conflicts.

hypnosis A procedure in which the practitioner suggests changes in a subject's sensations, perceptions, thoughts, feelings, or behavior.

hypothalamus A brain structure involved in emotions and drives vital to survival, such as fear, hunger, thirst, and reproduction; it regulates the autonomic nervous system.

hypothesis A statement that attempts to predict or to account for a set of phenomena; scientific hypotheses specify relationships among events or variables and are empirically tested.

id In psychoanalysis, the part of personality containing inherited psychic energy, particularly sexual and aggressive instincts.

implicit learning Learning that occurs when you acquire knowledge about something without being aware of how you did so and without being able to state exactly what it is you have learned.

implicit memory Unconscious retention in memory, as evidenced by the effect of a previous experience or previously encountered information on current thoughts or actions.

inattentional blindness Failure to consciously perceive something you are looking at because you are not attending to it.

independent variable A variable that an experimenter manipulates.

individualist cultures Cultures in which the self is regarded as autonomous, and individual goals and wishes are prized above duty and relations with others.

induction A method of child rearing in which the parent appeals to the child's own resources, abilities, sense of responsibility, and feelings for others in correcting the child's misbehavior.

inductive reasoning A form of reasoning in which the premises provide support for a conclusion, but it is still possible for the conclusion to be false.

inferential statistics Statistical procedures that allow researchers to draw inferences about how statistically meaningful a study's results are.

informed consent The doctrine that human research subjects must participate voluntarily and must know enough about a study to make an intelligent decision about whether to participate.

instinctive drift During operant learning, the tendency for an organism to revert to instinctive behavior.

intelligence An inferred characteristic of an individual, usually defined as the ability to profit from experience, acquire knowledge, think abstractly, act purposefully, or adapt to changes in the environment.

intelligence quotient (IQ) A measure of intelligence now derived from norms provided for standardized intelligence tests.

intermittent (partial) schedule of reinforcement A reinforcement schedule in which a particular response is sometimes but not always reinforced.

internal desynchronization A state in which biological rhythms are not in phase (synchronized) with one another.

intersex conditions Conditions, occurring in about one of every 2,000 births, in which chromosomal or hormonal anomalies cause a child to be born with ambiguous genitals, or genitals that conflict with the infant's chromosomes.

intrinsic motivation The desire to do something for its own sake and for the internal pleasure it provides.

intrinsic reinforcers Reinforcers that are inherently related to the activity being reinforced, such as enjoyment of the task and the satisfaction of accomplishment.

justification of effort The tendency of individuals to increase their liking for something that they have worked hard or suffered to attain; a common form of dissonance reduction.

just-world hypothesis The notion that many people need to believe that the world is fair and that justice is served, that bad people are punished and good people rewarded.

kinesthesis [KIN-es-THEE-sis] The sense of body position and movement of body parts; also called *kinesthesia*.

language A system that combines meaningless elements such as sounds or gestures to form structured utterances that convey meaning.

latent learning A form of learning that is not immediately expressed in an overt response; it occurs without obvious reinforcement.

lateralization Specialization of the two cerebral hemispheres for particular operations.

learning A relatively permanent change in behavior (or behavioral potential) due to experience.

learning perspective A psychological approach that emphasizes how the environment and experience affect a person's or animal's actions; it includes behaviorism and social-cognitive learning theories.

libido (li-BEE-do) In psychoanalysis, the psychic energy that fuels the life or sexual instincts of the id.

limbic system A group of brain areas involved in emotional reactions and motivated behavior.

lithium carbonate A drug frequently given to people suffering from bipolar disorder.

localization of function Specialization of particular brain areas for particular functions.

locus of control A general expectation about whether the results of your actions are under your own control (internal locus) or beyond your control (external locus).

longitudinal study A study in which individuals are followed and periodically reassessed over a period of time.

long-term memory (LTM) In the three-box model of memory, the memory system involved in the long-term storage of information.

long-term potentiation A long-lasting increase in the strength of synaptic responsiveness, thought to be a biological mechanism of long-term memory.

loudness The dimension of auditory experience related to the intensity of a pressure wave.

lucid dreams Dreams in which the dreamer is aware of dreaming.

maintenance rehearsal Rote repetition of material to maintain its availability in memory.

major depression A mood disorder involving disturbances in emotion (excessive sadness), behavior (loss of interest in one's usual activities), cognition (thoughts of hopelessness), and body function (fatigue and loss of appetite).

mastery (learning) goals Goals framed in terms of increasing one's competence and skills.

mean See arithmetic mean.

measure of central tendency A number intended to characterize an entire set of data.

measure of variability A number that indicates how dispersed scores are around the mean of the distribution.

median A measure of central tendency; the value at the midpoint of a distribution of scores when the scores are ordered from highest to lowest.

medulla [muh-DUL-uh] A structure in the brain stem responsible for certain automatic functions, such as breathing and heart rate.

melatonin A hormone, secreted by the pineal gland, that is involved in the regulation of daily biological (circadian) rhythms.

menarche [men-ARR-kee] The onset of menstruation during puberty.

menopause The cessation of menstruation and of the production of ova; it is usually a gradual process lasting up to several years.

mental age (MA) A measure of mental development expressed in terms of the average mental ability at a given age.

mental disorder Any behavior or emotional state that causes an individual great suffering, is self-destructive, seriously impairs the person's ability to work or get along with others, or endangers others or the community.

mental image A mental representation that mirrors or resembles the thing it represents; mental images can occur in many and perhaps all sensory modalities.

mental set A tendency to solve problems using procedures that worked before on similar problems.

meta-analysis A procedure for combining and analyzing data from many studies; it determines how much of the variance in scores across all studies can be explained by a particular variable.

metacognition The knowledge or awareness of one's own cognitive processes.

mirror neurons Brain cells that fire when a person or animal observes others carrying out an action; they are involved in empathy, imitation, and reading emotions.

mnemonics [neh-MON-iks] Strategies and tricks for improving memory, such as the use of a verse or a formula.

mode A measure of central tendency; the most frequently occurring score in a distribution.

monocular cues Visual cues to depth or distance that can be used by one eye alone.

mood-congruent memory The tendency to remember experiences that are consistent with one's current mood and overlook or forget experiences that are not.

motivation An inferred process within a person or animal that causes movement either toward a goal or away from an unpleasant situation.

MRI (magnetic resonance imaging) A method for studying body and brain tissue, using magnetic fields and special radio receivers; *functional MRI* (fMRI) is a faster form often used in psychological research.

myelin sheath A fatty insulation that may surround the axon of a neuron.

narcolepsy A sleep disorder involving sudden and unpredictable daytime attacks of sleepiness or lapses into REM sleep.

negative correlation An association between increases in one variable and decreases in another.

negative reinforcement A reinforcement procedure in which a response is followed by the removal, delay, or decrease in intensity of an unpleasant stimulus; as a result, the response becomes stronger or more likely to occur.

nerves A bundle of nerve fibers (axons and sometimes dendrites) in the peripheral nervous system.

neurogenesis The production of new neurons from immature stem cells.

neurons Cells that conduct electrochemical signals; the basic unit of the nervous system; also called *nerve cells*.

neurotransmitter A chemical substance that is released by a transmitting neuron at the synapse and that alters the activity of a receiving neuron.

nonconscious processes Mental processes occurring outside of and not available to conscious awareness.

nonshared environment Unique aspects of a person's environment and experience that are not shared with family members.

normal curve A symmetrical, bell-shaped frequency polygon representing a normal distribution.

normal distribution A theoretical frequency distribution having certain special characteristics. For example, the distribution is symmetrical; the mean, mode, and median all have the same value; and the farther a score is from the mean, the less the likelihood of obtaining it.

norms In test construction, established standards of performance.

norms (social) Rules that regulate social life, including explicit laws and implicit cultural conventions.

null hypothesis An assertion that the independent variable in a study will have no effect on the dependent variable.

object permanence The understanding, which develops throughout the first year, that an object continues to exist even when you cannot see it or touch it.

objective tests (inventories) Standardized objective questionnaires requiring written responses; they typically include scales on which people are asked to rate themselves.

object-relations school A psychodynamic approach that emphasizes the importance of the infant's first two years of life and the baby's formative relationships, especially with the mother.

observational learning A process in which an individual learns new responses by observing the behavior of another (a model) rather than through direct experience; sometimes called *vicarious conditioning.*

observational study A study in which the researcher carefully and systematically observes and records behavior without interfering with the behavior; it may involve either naturalistic or laboratory observation.

obsessive-compulsive disorder (OCD) An anxiety disorder in which a person feels trapped in repetitive, persistent thoughts (*obsessions*) and repetitive, ritualized behaviors (*compulsions*) designed to reduce anxiety.

occipital [ahk-SIP-uh-tuhl] lobes Lobes at the lower back part of the brain's cerebral cortex; they contain areas that receive visual information.

Oedipus complex In psychoanalysis, a conflict occurring in the phallic (Oedipal) stage, in which a child desires the parent of the other sex and views the same-sex parent as a rival.

operant conditioning The process by which a response becomes more likely to occur or less so, depending on its consequences.

operational definition A precise definition of a term in a hypothesis, which specifies the operations for observing and measuring the process or phenomenon being defined.

opiates Drugs, derived from the opium poppy, that relieve pain and commonly produce euphoria.

opponent-process theory A theory of color perception that assumes that the visual system treats pairs of colors as opposing or antagonistic.

organ of Corti [CORE-tee] A structure in the cochlea containing hair cells that serve as the receptors for hearing.

oxytocin A hormone, secreted by the pituitary gland, that stimulates uterine contractions during childbirth, facilitates the ejection of milk during nursing, and seems to promote, in both sexes, attachment and trust in relationships.

panic disorder An anxiety disorder in which a person experiences recurring panic attacks, periods of intense fear, and feelings of impending doom or death, accompanied by physiological symptoms such as rapid heart rate and dizziness.

papillae [pa-PILL-ee] Knoblike elevations on the tongue, containing the taste buds. (Singular: *papilla.*)

parallel distributed processing (PDP) A model of memory in which knowledge is represented as connections among thousands of interacting processing units, distributed in a vast network, and all operating in parallel. Also called a *connectionist model.*

parasympathetic nervous system The subdivision of the autonomic nervous system that operates during relaxed states and that conserves energy.

parietal [puh-RYE-uh-tuhl] lobes Lobes at the top of the brain's cerebral cortex; they contain areas that receive information on pressure, pain, touch, and temperature.

percentile score A score that indicates the percentage of people who scored at or below a given raw score; also called *centile rank.*

perception The process by which the brain organizes and interprets sensory information.

perceptual constancy The accurate perception of objects as stable or unchanged despite changes in the sensory patterns they produce.

perceptual set A habitual way of perceiving, based on expectations.

performance goals Goals framed in terms of performing well in front of others, being judged favorably, and avoiding criticism.

peripheral nervous system (PNS) All portions of the nervous system outside the brain and spinal cord; it includes sensory and motor nerves.

personality A distinctive and relatively stable pattern of behavior, thoughts, motives, and emotions that characterizes an individual.

PET scan (positron-emission tomography) A method for analyzing biochemical activity in the brain, using injections of a glucoselike substance containing a radioactive element.

phantom pain The experience of pain in a missing limb or other body part.

phobia An exaggerated, unrealistic fear of a specific situation, activity, or object.

phrenology The now discredited theory that different brain areas account for specific character and personality traits, which can be "read" from bumps on the skull.

pitch The dimension of auditory experience related to the frequency of a pressure wave; it is related to the height or depth of a tone.

pituitary gland A small endocrine gland at the base of the brain that releases many hormones and regulates other endocrine glands.

placebo An inactive substance or fake treatment used as a control in an experiment.

placebo effect The apparent success of a medication or treatment due to the patient's expectations or hopes rather than to the drug or treatment itself.

plasticity The brain's ability to change and adapt in response to experience, for example, by reorganizing or growing new neural connections.

pons A structure in the brain stem involved in, among other things, sleeping, waking, and dreaming.

positive correlation An association between increases in one variable and increases in another or between decreases in one and in the other.

positive reinforcement A reinforcement procedure in which a response is followed by the presentation of, or increase in intensity of, a reinforcing stimulus; as a result, the response becomes stronger or more likely to occur.

postdecision dissonance In the theory of cognitive dissonance, tension that occurs when you believe you may have made a bad decision.

posttraumatic stress disorder (PTSD) An anxiety disorder in which a person who has experienced a traumatic or life-threatening event has symptoms such as psychic numbing, reliving of the trauma, and increased physiological arousal.

power assertion A method of child rearing in which the parent uses punishment and authority to correct the child's misbehavior.

prejudice A strong, unreasonable dislike or hatred of a group, based on a negative stereotype.

primary control An effort to modify reality by changing other people, the situation, or events; a "fighting back" philosophy.

primary emotions Emotions that are considered to be universal and biologically based.

primary punisher A stimulus that is inherently punishing; an example is electric shock.

primary reinforcer A stimulus that is inherently reinforcing, typically satisfying a physiological need; an example is food.

priming A method for measuring implicit memory in which a person reads or listens to information and is later tested to see whether the information affects performance on another type of task.

principle of falsifiability The principle that a scientific theory must make predictions that are specific enough to expose the theory to the possibility of disconfirmation.

proactive interference Forgetting that occurs when previously stored material interferes with the ability to remember similar, more recently learned material.

procedural memories Memories for the performance of actions or skills ("knowing how").

projective tests Psychological tests used to infer a person's motives, conflicts, and unconscious dynamics on the basis of the person's interpretations of ambiguous stimuli.

proposition A unit of meaning that is made up of concepts and expresses a single idea.

prototype An especially representative example of a concept.

psychedelic drugs Consciousness-altering drugs that produce hallucinations, change thought processes, or disrupt the normal perception of time and space.

psychoactive drugs Drugs capable of influencing perception, mood, cognition, or behavior.

psychoanalysis A theory of personality and a method of psychotherapy, originally formulated by Sigmund Freud, that emphasizes the importance of unconscious motives and conflicts.

psychodynamic perspective A psychological approach that emphasizes unconscious dynamics within the individual, such as inner forces, conflicts, or the movement of instinctual energy.

psychodynamic theories Theories that explain behavior and personality in terms of unconscious dynamics, or movements of energy, within the individual.

psychodynamic therapies Psychotherapies that share the goal of exploring the unconscious dynamics of personality, although they differ from Freudian analysis in various ways.

psychological tests Procedures used to measure and evaluate personality traits, emotional states, aptitudes, interests, abilities, and values.

psychology The discipline concerned with behavior and mental processes and how they are affected by an organism's physical state, mental state, and external environment; often represented by Ψ, the Greek letter psi (usually pronounced "sy").

psychometrics The measurement of mental abilities, traits, and processes.

psychoneuroimmunology (PNI) The study of the relationships among psychology, the nervous and endocrine systems, and the immune system.

psychopathy A personality disorder characterized by a lack of remorse, empathy, anxiety, and other social emotions; the use of deceit and manipulation; and impulsive thrill seeking.

psychosexual stages In Freud's theory, the idea that sexual energy takes different forms as the child matures; the stages are oral, anal, phallic (Oedipal), latency, and genital.

psychosis An extreme mental disturbance involving distorted perceptions and irrational behavior; it may have psychological or organic causes. (Plural: *psychoses*.)

puberty The age at which a person becomes capable of sexual reproduction.

punishment The process by which a stimulus or event weakens or reduces the probability of the response that it follows.

random assignment A procedure for assigning people to experimental and control groups in which each individual has the same probability as any other of being assigned to a given group.

randomized controlled trials Research designed to determine the effectiveness of a new medication or form of therapy, in which people with a given problem or disorder are randomly assigned to one or more treatment groups or to a control group.

range A measure of the spread of scores, calculated by subtracting the lowest score from the highest score.

rapid eye movement (REM) sleep Sleep periods characterized by eye movement, loss of muscle tone, and vivid dreams.

rational emotive behavior therapy A form of cognitive therapy devised by Albert Ellis, designed to challenge the client's unrealistic or irrational thoughts.

reasoning The drawing of conclusions or inferences from observations, facts, or assumptions.

recall The ability to retrieve and reproduce from memory previously encountered material.

reciprocal determinism In social-cognitive theories, the two-way interaction between aspects of the environment and aspects of the individual in the shaping of personality traits.

recognition The ability to identify previously encountered material.

reinforcement The process by which a stimulus or event strengthens or increases the probability of the response that it follows.

relearning method A method for measuring retention that compares the time required to relearn material with the time used in the initial learning of the material.

reliability In test construction, the consistency of test scores from one time and place to another.

REM behavior disorder A disorder in which the muscle paralysis that normally occurs during REM sleep is absent or incomplete, and the sleeper is able to act out his or her dreams.

representative sample A group of individuals, selected from a population for study, which matches that population on important characteristics such as age and sex.

repression In psychoanalytic theory, the selective, involuntary pushing of threatening or upsetting information into the unconscious.

reticular activating system (RAS) A dense network of neurons in the core of the brain stem; it arouses the cortex and screens incoming information.

retina Neural tissue lining the back of the eyeball's interior, which contains the receptors for vision.

retinal disparity The slight difference in lateral separation between two objects as seen by the left eye and the right eye.

retroactive interference Forgetting that occurs when recently learned material interferes with the ability to remember similar material stored previously.

rods Visual receptors that respond to dim light.

role A given social position that is governed by a set of norms for proper behavior.

saturation Vividness or purity of color; the dimension of visual experience related to the complexity of light waves.

schizophrenia A psychotic disorder marked by delusions, hallucinations, disorganized and incoherent speech, inappropriate behavior, and cognitive impairments.

seasonal affective disorder (SAD) A controversial disorder in which a person experiences depression during the winter and an improvement of mood in the spring.

secondary control An effort to accept reality by changing your own attitudes, goals, or emotions; a "learn to live with it" philosophy.

secondary emotions Emotions that are specific to certain cultures.

secondary punisher A stimulus that has acquired punishing properties through association with other punishers.

secondary reinforcer A stimulus that has acquired reinforcing properties through association with other reinforcers.

selective attention The focusing of attention on selected aspects of the environment and the blocking out of others.

self-efficacy A person's belief that he or she is capable of producing desired results, such as mastering new skills and reaching goals.

self-fulfilling prophecy An expectation that is fulfilled because of the tendency of the person holding it to act in ways that bring it about.

semantic memories Memories of general knowledge, including facts, rules, concepts, and propositions.

semicircular canals Sense organs in the inner ear that contribute to equilibrium by responding to rotation of the head.

sensation The detection of physical energy emitted or reflected by physical objects.

sense receptors Specialized cells that convert physical energy in the environment or the body to electrical energy that can be transmitted as nerve impulses to the brain.

sensory adaptation The reduction or disappearance of sensory responsiveness that occurs when stimulation is unchanging or repetitious.

sensory deprivation The absence of normal levels of sensory stimulation.

sensory register A memory system that momentarily preserves extremely accurate sensory information before the information fades or moves into short-term memory.

separation anxiety The distress that most children develop, at about 6 to 8 months of age, when their primary caregivers temporarily leave them with others.

serial-position effect The tendency for recall of the first and last items on a list to surpass recall of items in the middle of the list.

set point The genetically influenced weight range for an individual, maintained by biological mechanisms that regulate food intake, fat reserves, and metabolism.

sex hormones Hormones that regulate the development and functioning of reproductive organs and that stimulate the development of male and female sexual characteristics; they include androgens, estrogens, and progesterone.

sexual scripts Sets of implicit rules that specify proper sexual behavior for a person in a given situation, varying with the person's gender, age, religion, social status, and peer group.

shaping An operant-conditioning procedure in which successive approximations of a desired response are reinforced.

short-term memory (STM) In the three-box model of memory, a limited-capacity memory system involved in the retention of information for brief periods; it is also used to hold information retrieved from long-term memory for temporary use.

signal-detection theory A psychophysical theory that divides the detection of a sensory signal into a sensory process and a decision process.

significance tests Statistical tests that assess how likely it is that a study's results occurred merely by chance.

single-blind study An experiment in which subjects do not know whether they are in an experimental or a control group.

skills training In behavior therapy, an effort to teach the client skills that he or she may lack, as well as new constructive behaviors to replace self-defeating ones.

sleep apnea A disorder in which breathing briefly stops during sleep, causing the person to choke and gasp and momentarily awaken.

social cognition An area in social psychology concerned with social influences on thought, memory, perception, and beliefs.

social identity The part of a person's self-concept that is based on his or her identification with a nation, religious or political group, or other social affiliation.

social-cognitive learning theory A major contemporary learning view of personality, which holds that personality traits result from a person's learning history and his or her expectations, beliefs, perceptions of events, and other cognitions.

social-cognitive theories Theories that emphasize how behavior is learned and maintained through observation and imitation of others, positive consequences, and cognitive processes such as plans, expectations, and beliefs.

socialization The process by which children learn the behaviors, attitudes, and expectations required of them by their society or culture.

sociocultural perspective A psychological approach that emphasizes social and cultural influences on behavior.

somatic nervous system The subdivision of the peripheral nervous system that connects to sensory receptors and to skeletal muscles; sometimes called the *skeletal nervous system*.

source misattribution The inability to distinguish an actual memory of an event from information you learned about the event elsewhere.

spinal cord A collection of neurons and supportive tissue running from the base of the brain down the center of the back, protected by a column of bones (the spinal column).

spinal reflexes Automatic behaviors produced by the spinal cord without brain involvement.

spontaneous recovery The reappearance of a learned response after its apparent extinction.

standard deviation A commonly used measure of variability that indicates the average difference between scores in a distribution and their mean; more precisely, the square root of the average squared deviation from the mean.

standardize In test construction, to develop uniform procedures for giving and scoring a test.

state-dependent memory The tendency to remember something when the remember is in the same physical or mental state as during the original learning or experience.

statistically significant A term used to refer to a result that is extremely unlikely to have occurred by chance.

stem cells Immature cells that renew themselves and have the potential to develop into mature cells; given encouraging environments, stem cells from early embryos can develop into any cell type.

stereotype A summary impression of a group, in which a person believes that all members of the group share a common trait or traits (positive, negative, or neutral).

stereotype threat A burden of doubt a person feels about his or her performance, due to negative stereotypes about his or her group's abilities.

stimulants Drugs that speed up activity in the central nervous system.

stimulus discrimination The tendency to respond differently to two or more similar stimuli. In classical conditioning, it occurs when a stimulus that resembles the conditioned stimulus fails to evoke the conditioned response. In operant conditioning, it occurs when an organism learns to make a response in the presence of one stimulus but not in the presence of other, similar stimuli that differ from it on some dimension.

stimulus generalization After conditioning, the tendency to respond to a stimulus that resembles one involved in the original conditioning. In classical conditioning, it occurs when a stimulus that resembles the conditioned stimulus elicits the conditioned response. In operant conditioning, it occurs when a response that has been reinforced (or punished) in the presence of one stimulus occurs (or is suppressed) in the presence of other, similar stimuli.

subconscious processes Mental processes occurring outside of conscious awareness but accessible to consciousness when necessary.

successive approximations In the operant-conditioning procedure of shaping, behaviors that are ordered in terms of increasing similarity or closeness to the desired response.

superego In psychoanalysis, the part of personality that represents conscience, morality, and social standards.

suprachiasmatic [soo-pruh-kie-az-MAT-ick] nucleus (SCN) An area of the brain containing a biological clock that governs circadian rhythms.

surveys Questionnaires and interviews that ask people directly about their experiences, attitudes, or opinions.

sympathetic nervous system The subdivision of the autonomic nervous system that mobilizes bodily resources and increases the output of energy during emotion and stress.

synapse The site where transmission of a nerve impulse from one nerve cell to another occurs; it includes the axon terminal, the synaptic cleft, and receptor sites in the membrane of the receiving cell.

synesthesia A condition in which stimulation of one sense also evokes another.

systematic desensitization In behavior therapy, a step-by-step process of desensitizing a client to a feared object or experience; it is based on the classical-conditioning procedure of counterconditioning.

tacit knowledge Strategies for success that are not explicitly taught but that instead must be inferred.

taste buds Nests of taste-receptor cells.

telegraphic speech A child's first word combinations, which omit (as a telegram did) unnecessary words.

temperaments Physiological dispositions to respond to the environment in certain ways; they are present in infancy and are assumed to be innate.

temporal lobes Lobes at the sides of the brain's cerebral cortex; they contain areas involved in hearing, memory, perception, emotion, and (in the left lobe, typically) language comprehension.

thalamus A brain structure that relays sensory messages to the cerebral cortex.

Thematic Apperception Test (TAT) A projective test that asks respondents to interpret a series of drawings showing scenes of people; usually scored for unconscious traits and motives, such as the need for achievement, power, or affiliation.

theory An organized system of assumptions and principles that purports to explain a specified set of phenomena and their interrelationships.

theory of mind A system of beliefs about the way one's own mind and the minds of others work, and of how individuals are affected by their beliefs and feelings.

therapeutic alliance The bond of confidence and mutual understanding established between therapist and client, which allows them to work together to solve the client's problems.

timbre The distinguishing quality of a sound; the dimension of auditory experience related to the complexity of the pressure wave.

tolerance Increased resistance to a drug's effects accompanying continued use.

trait A characteristic of an individual, describing a habitual way of behaving, thinking, or feeling.

tranquilizers Drugs commonly but often inappropriately prescribed for patients who complain of unhappiness, anxiety, or worry.

transcranial magnetic stimulation (TMS) A method of stimulating brain cells, using a powerful magnetic field produced by a wire coil placed on a person's head; it can be used by researchers to temporarily inactivate neural circuits and is also being used therapeutically.

transference In psychodynamic therapies, a critical process in which the client transfers unconscious emotions or reactions, such as emotional feelings about his or her parents, onto the therapist.

triarchic [try-ARE-kick] theory of intelligence A theory of intelligence that emphasizes information-processing strategies, the ability to creatively transfer skills to new situations, and the practical application of intelligence.

trichromatic theory A theory of color perception that proposes three mechanisms in the visual system, each sensitive to a certain range of wavelengths; their interaction is assumed to produce all the different experiences of hue.

unconditional positive regard To Carl Rogers, love or support given to another person with no conditions attached.

unconditioned response (UR) The classical-conditioning term for a reflexive response elicited by a stimulus in the absence of learning.

unconditioned stimulus (US) The classical-conditioning term for a stimulus that elicits a reflexive response in the absence of learning.

validity The ability of a test to measure what it was designed to measure.

validity effect The tendency of people to believe that a statement is true or valid simply because it has been repeated many times.

variables Characteristics of behavior or experience that can be measured or described by a numeric scale; variables are manipulated and assessed in scientific studies.

volunteer bias A shortcoming of findings derived from a sample of volunteers instead of a representative sample; the volunteers may differ from those who did not volunteer.

vulnerability-stress models Approaches that emphasize how individual vulnerabilities (e.g., in genes or personality traits) interact with external stresses or circumstances to produce mental disorders.

withdrawal Physical and psychological symptoms that occur when someone addicted to a drug stops taking it.

working memory Short-term memory plus the mental processes that control retrieval of information from long-term memory and interpret that information appropriately for a given task.

z-score (standard score) A number that indicates how far a given raw score is above or below the mean, using the standard deviation of the distribution as the unit of measurement.

References

Abrahamson, Amy C.; Baker, Laura A.; & Caspi, Avshalom (2002). Rebellious teens? Genetic and environmental influences on the social attitudes of adolescents. *Journal of Personality and Social Psychology, 83,* 1392–1408.

Abrams, David B., & Wilson, G. Terence (1983). Alcohol, sexual arousal, and self-control. *Journal of Personality and Social Psychology, 45,* 188–198.

Abramson, Lyn Y.; Metalsky, Gerald I.; & Alloy, Lauren B. (1989). Hopelessness depression: A theory-based subtype of depression. *Psychological Review, 96,* 358–372.

Acevedo, Bianca P., & Aron, Arthur (2009). Does a long-term relationship kill romantic love? *Review of General Psychology, 13,* 59–65.

Adam, Hajo; Shirako, Aiwa; & Maddux, William W. (2010). Cultural variance in the interpersonal effects of anger in negotiations. *Psychological Science, 21,* 882–889.

Adams, James L. (1986). *Conceptual blockbusting: A guide to better ideas* (3rd ed.). Boston: Addison-Wesley.

Ader, Robert (2000). True or false: The placebo effect as seen in drug studies is definitive proof that the mind can bring about clinically relevant changes in the body: The placebo effect: If it's all in your head, does that mean you only think you feel better? *Advances in Mind-Body Medicine, 16,* 7–11.

Adler, Nancy E., & Snibbe, Alana C. (2003). The role of psychosocial processes in explaining the gradient between socioeconomic status and health. *Current Directions in Psychological Science, 12,* 119–123.

Affleck, Glenn; Tennen, Howard; Croog, Sydney; & Levine, Sol (1987). Causal attribution, perceived control, and recovery from a heart attack. *Journal of Social and Clinical Psychology, 5,* 339–355.

Agars, Mark D. (2004). Reconsidering the impact of gender stereotypes on the advancement of women in organizations. *Psychology of Women Quarterly, 28,* 103–111.

Agrawal, Yuri; Platz, Elizabeth A.; & Niparko, John K. (2008). Prevalence of hearing loss and differences by demographic characteristics among US adults. *Archives of Internal Medicine, 168,* 1522–1530.

Aguiar, Patrícia; Vala, Jorge; Correia, Isabel; & Pereira, Cícero (2008). Justice in our world and in that of others: Belief in a just world and reactions to victims. *Social Justice Research, 21,* 50–68.

Ainsworth, Mary D. S. (1973). The development of infant–mother attachment. In B. M. Caldwell & H. N. Ricciuti (Eds.), *Review of child development research* (Vol. 3). Chicago: University of Chicago Press.

Ainsworth, Mary D. S. (1979). Infant–mother attachment. *American Psychologist, 34,* 932–937.

Alford, C. Fred (2001). *Whistleblowers: Broken lives and organizations.* Ithaca, NY: Cornell University Press.

Alford, John R.; Funk, Carolyn L.; & Hibbing, John R. (2005). Are political orientations genetically transmitted? *American Political Science Review, 99,* 153–167.

Alink, Lenneke R. A.; Mesman, Judi; van Zeijl, Jantien; et al. (2009). Maternal sensitivity moderates the relation between negative discipline and aggression in early childhood. *Social Development, 18,* 99–120.

Allport, Gordon W. (1954/1979). *The nature of prejudice.* Reading, MA: Addison-Wesley.

Allport, Gordon W. (1961). *Pattern and growth in personality.* New York: Holt, Rinehart and Winston.

Amabile, Teresa M. (1983). *The social psychology of creativity.* New York: Springer-Verlag.

Amabile, Teresa M., & Khaire, Mukti (2008). Creativity and the role of the leader. *Harvard Business Review. 86,* online.

Amedi, Amir; Merabet, Lotfi; Bermpohl, Felix; & Pascual-Leone, Alvaro (2005). The occipital cortex in the blind: Lessons about plasticity and vision. *Current Directions in Psychological Science, 14,* 306–311.

American Psychiatric Association (1994). *The diagnostic and statistical manual of mental disorders* (4th ed.). Washington, DC: American Psychiatric Association.

American Psychiatric Association (2000). *The diagnostic and statistical manual of mental disorders, IV-TR.* Washington, DC: American Psychiatric Association.

Anastasi, Anne, & Urbina, Susan (1997). *Psychological testing* (7th ed.). Upper Saddle River, NJ: Prentice Hall.

Andersen, Susan M., & Berk, Michele S. (1998). Transference in everyday experience: Implications of experimental research for relevant clinical phenomena. *Review of General Psychology, 2,* 81–120.

Andersen, Susan M., & Chen, Serena (2002). The relational self: An interpersonal social-cognitive theory. *Psychological Review, 109,* 619–645.

Anderson, Amanda (2005). *The way we argue now: A study in the cultures of theory.* Princeton, NJ: Princeton University Press.

Anderson, Cameron; Keltner, Dacher; & John, Oliver P. (2003). Emotional convergence between people over time. *Journal of Personality and Social Psychology, 84,* 1054–1068.

Anderson, Craig A.; Shibuya, Akiko; Ihori, Nobuko; et al. (2010). Violent video game effects on aggression, empathy, and prosocial behavior in Eastern and Western countries: A meta-analytic review. *Psychological Bulletin, 136,* 151–173.

Anderson, John R. (1990). *The adaptive nature of thought.* Hillsdale, NJ: Erlbaum.

Anderson, S. W.; Bechara, A.; Damasio, H.; Tranel, D.; & Damasio, A. R. (1999). Impairment of social and moral behavior related to early damage in human prefrontal cortex. *Nature Neuroscience, 2,* 1032–1037.

Anderson-Barnes, Victoria C.; McAuliffe, Caitlin; Swanberg, Kelly M.; & Tsao, Jack W. (2009, October). Phantom limb pain: A phenomenon of proprioceptive memory? *Medical Hypotheses, 73,* 555–558.

Andreano, Joseph M., & Cahill, Larry (2006). Glucocorticoid release and memory consolidation in men and women. *Psychological Science, 17,* 466–470.

Andreasen, Nancy C.; Arndt, Stephan; Swayze, Victor, II; et al. (1994). Thalamic abnormalities in schizophrenia visualized through magnetic resonance image averaging. *Science, 266,* 294–298.

Añez, Luis M.; Silva, Michelle A.; Paris Jr., Manuel; Bedregal, Luis E. (2008). Engaging Latinos through the integration of cultural values and motivational interviewing principles. *Professional Psychology: Research and Practice, 39,* 153–159.

Angell, Marcia (2004). *The truth about the drug companies: How they deceive us and what to do about it.* New York: Random House.

Angier, Natalie (2000, November 7). Who is fat? It depends on culture. *The New York Times,* Science Times, D1–2.

Antrobus, John (1991). Dreaming: Cognitive processes during cortical activation and high afferent thresholds. *Psychological Review, 98,* 96–121.

Antrobus, John (2000). How does the dreaming brain explain the dreaming mind? *Behavioral and Brain Sciences, 23,* 904–907.

Archer, John (2004). Sex differences in aggression in real-world settings: A meta-analytic review. *Review of General Psychology, 8,* 291–322

Archer, Simon N.; Robilliard, Donna L.; Skene, Debra J.; et al. (2003). A length polymorphism in the circadian clock gene Per3 is linked to delayed sleep phase syndrome and extreme diurnal preference. *Sleep, 26,* 413–415.

Arendt, Hannah (1963). *Eichmann in Jerusalem: A report on the banality of evil.* New York: Viking.

Arkes, Hal R. (1993). Some practical judgment and decision-making research. In N. J. Castellan, Jr., et al. (Eds.), *Individual and group decision making: Current issues.* Hillsdale, NJ: Erlbaum.

Arkes, Hal R.; Boehm, Lawrence E.; & Xu, Gang (1991). The determinants of judged validity. *Journal of Experimental Social Psychology, 27,* 576–605.

Arnett, Jeffrey J. (2004). Emerging adulthood: The winding road from the late teens through the twenties. New York: Oxford University Press.

Aron, Arthur; Fisher, Helen; Mashek, Debra J.; et al. (2005). Reward, motivation, and emotion systems associated with early-stage intense romantic love. *Journal of Neurophysiology, 94,* 327–337.

Aron, Arthur; Fisher, Helen E.; Strong, Greg; et al. (2008). Falling in love. In S. Sprecher, A. Wenzel, & J. Harvey (Eds.), *Handbook of relationship initiation.* New York: Pychology Press.

Aronson, Elliot (2000). *Nobody left to hate.* New York: Freeman.

Aronson, Elliot (2008). *The social animal* (10th ed.). New York: Worth.

Aronson, Elliot, & Mills, Judson (1959). The effect of severity of initiation on liking for a group. *Journal of Abnormal and Social Psychology, 59,* 177–181.

Aronson, Joshua (2010). Jigsaw and the nurture of human intelligence. In M. H. Gonzales, C. Tavris, & J. Aronson (Eds.), *The scientist and the humanist: A festschrift in honor of Elliot Aronson.* New York: Psychology Press.

Arredondo, Patricia, & Perez, Patricia (2003). Counseling paradigms and Latina/o Americans. In F. Harper & J. McFadden (Eds.), *Culture and counseling: New approaches.* Boston: Allyn & Bacon.

Arredondo, Patricia; Rosen, Daniel C.; Rice, Tiffany; Perez, Patricia; & Tovar-Gamero, Zoila G. (2005). Multicultural counseling: A 10-year content analysis of the *Journal of Counseling & Development. Journal of Counseling and Development, 83,* 155–161.

Arroyo, Carmen G., & Zigler, Edward (1995). Racial identity, academic achievement, and the psychological well-being of economically disadvantaged adolescents. *Journal of Personality and Social Psychology, 69,* 903–914.

Asch, Solomon E. (1952). *Social psychology.* Englewood Cliffs, NJ: Prentice-Hall.

Asch, Solomon E. (1965). Effects of group pressure upon the modification and distortion of judgments. In H. Proshansky & B. Seidenberg (Eds.), *Basic studies in social psychology.* New York: Holt, Rinehart and Winston.

Aserinsky, Eugene, & Kleitman, Nathaniel (1955). Two types of ocular motility occurring in sleep. *Journal of Applied Physiology, 8,* 1–10.

Atkinson, Richard C., & Shiffrin, Richard M. (1968). Human memory: A proposed system and its control processes. In K. W. Spence & J. T. Spence (Eds.), *The psychology of learning and motivation: Vol. 2. Advances in research and theory.* New York: Academic Press.

Atran, Scott (2003, March 7). Geneis of suicide terrorism. *Science, 299,* 1534–1539.

AuBuchon, Peter G., & Calhoun, Karen S. (1985). Menstrual cycle symptomatology: The role of social expectancy and experimental demand characteristics. *Psychosomatic Medicine, 47,* 35–45.

Auyeung, Bonnie; Baron-Cohen, Simon; Ashwin, Emma; et al. (2009). Fetal testosterone predicts sexually differentiated childhood behavior in girls and in boys. *Psychological Science, 20,* 144–148.

Aviezer, Hillel; Hassin, Ran R.; Ryan, Jennifer; et al. (2008). Angry, disgusted, or afraid? Studies on the malleability of emotion perception. *Psychological Science, 19,* 724–732.

Axel, Richard (1995, October). The molecular logic of smell. *Scientific American,* 154–159.

Azuma, Hiroshi (1984). Secondary control as a heterogeneous category. *American Psychologist, 39,* 970–971.

Baas, Matthijs; De Dreu, Carsten K. W.; & Nijstad, Bernard A. (2008). A meta-analysis of 25 years of mood-creativity research: Hedonic tone, activation, or regulatory focus? *Psychological Bulletin, 134,* 779–806.

Babiak, Paul, & Hare, Robert (2007). *Snakes in suits.* New York: Collins Business.

Baddeley, Alan D. (1992). Working memory. *Science, 255,* 556–559.

Baddeley, Alan D. (2007). *Working memory, thought, and action.* New York: Oxford.

Bagemihl, Bruce (1999). *Biological exuberance: Animal homosexuality and natural diversity.* New York: St. Martin's Press.

Bahrick, Harry P. (1984). Semantic memory content in permastore: Fifty years of memory for Spanish learned in school. *Journal of Experimental Psychology: General, 113,* 1–29.

Bahrick, Harry P.; Bahrick, Phyllis O.; & Wittlinger, Roy P. (1975). Fifty years of memory for names and faces: A cross-sectional approach. *Journal of Experimental Psychology: General, 104,* 54–75.

Bailey, J. Michael; Bobrow, David; Wolfe, Marilyn; & Mikach, Sarah (1995). Sexual orientation of adult sons of gay fathers. *Developmental Psychology, 31,* 124–129.

Bailey, J. Michael; Dunne, Michael P.; & Martin, Nicholas G. (2000). Genetic and environmental influences on sexual orientation and its correlates in an Australian twin sample. *Journal of Personality and Social Psychology, 78,* 524–536.

Bailey, J. Michael; Gaulin, Steven; Agyei, Yvonne; & Gladue, Brian A. (1994). Effects of gender and sexual orientation on evolutionarily relevant aspects of human mating psychology. *Journal of Personality and Social Psychology, 66,* 1081–1093.

Bailey, J. Michael, & Zucker, Kenneth J. (1995). Childhood sex-typed behavior and sexual orientation: A conceptual analysis and quantitative review. *Developmental Psychology, 31,* 43–55.

Baillargeon, Renée (1994). How do infants learn about the physical world? *Current Directions in Psychological Science, 5,* 133–140.

Baillargeon, Renée (2004). Infants' physical world. *Current Directions in Psychological Science, 13,* 89–94.

Baker, Mark C. (2001). *The atoms of language: The mind's hidden rules of grammar.* New York: Basic Books.

Baker, Timothy B.; McFall, Richard M.; & Shoham, Varda (2008). Current status and future prospects of clinical psychology: Toward a scientifically principled approach to mental and behavioral health care. *Psychological Science in the Public Interest, 9,* entire issue.

Bakermans-Kranenburg, Marian J.; Breddels-van Baardewijk, Philomeen; Juffer, Femmie; et al. (2008). Insecure mothers with temperamentally reactive infants: A chance for intervention. In F. Juffer, M. J. Bakermans-Kranenburg, & M. H. van IJzendoorn (Eds.), *Promoting positive parenting: An attachment-based intervention.* New York: Taylor & Francis.

Balcetis, Emily, & Dunning, David (2010). Wishful seeing: More desired objects are seen as closer. *Psychological Science, 21,* 147–152.

Balcetis, Emily; Dunning, David; & Miller, Richard L. (2008). Do collectivists know themselves better than individualists? Cross-cultural studies of the holier than thou phenomenon. *Journal of Personality and Social Psychology, 95,* 1252–1267.

Bancroft, John (2006). Normal sexual development. In H. E. Barbaree & W. L. Marshall (Eds.), *The juvenile sex offender* (2nd ed.). New York: Guilford.

Bancroft, John; Graham, Cynthia A.; Janssen, Erick; Sanders, Stephanie A. (2009). The dual control model: Current status and future directions. *Journal of Sex Research, 46,* 121–142.

Bandura, Albert (1977). *Social learning theory.* Englewood Cliffs, NJ: Prentice-Hall.

Bandura, Albert (1986). *Social foundations of thought and action: A social cognitive theory.* Englewood Cliffs, NJ: Prentice-Hall.

Bandura, Albert (1999). Moral disengagement in the perpetration of inhumanities. *Personality and Social Psychology Review, 3,* 193–209.

Bandura, Albert (2001). Social cognitive theory: An agentic perspective. *Annual Review of Psychology, 52,* 1–26. Palo Alto, CA: Annual Reviews.

Bandura, Albert (2006). Toward a psychology of human agency. *Perspectives on Psychological Science, 1,* 164–180.

Bandura, Albert; Caprara, Gian Vittorio; Barbaranelli, Claudio; Pastorelli, Concetta; & Regalia, Camillo (2001). Sociocognitive self-regulatory mechanisms governing transgressive behavior. *Journal of Personality and Social Psychology, 80,* 125–135.

Bandura, Albert; Ross, Dorothea; & Ross, Sheila A. (1963). Vicarious reinforcement and imitative learning. *Journal of Abnormal and Social Psychology, 67,* 601–607.

Banks, Martin S. (with Philip Salapatek) (1984). Infant visual perception. In P. Mussen (Series Ed.), M. M. Haith & J. J. Campos (Vol. Eds.), *Handbook of child psychology: Vol. II. Infancy and developmental psychobiology* (4th ed.). New York: Wiley.

Barash, David P., & Lipton, Judith Eve (2001). *The myth of monogamy: Fidelity and infidelity in animals and people.* New York: W. H. Freeman.

Barbuto, J. E. (1997). A critique of the Myers-Briggs Type Indicator and its operationalization of Carl Jung's psychological types. *Psychological Reports, 80,* 611–625.

Bargary, Gary, & Mitchell, Kevin J. (2008). Synaesthesia and cortical connectivity. *Trends in Neurosciences, 31,* 335–342.

Bargh, John A. (1999, January 29). The most powerful manipulative messages are hiding in plain sight. *The Chronicle of Higher Education,* B6.

Bargh, John A., & Morsella, Ezequiel (2008). The unconscious mind. *Perspectives on Psychological Science, 3,* 73–79.

Barglow, Peter (2008, September/October). Corporate self interest and vague nerve stimulation for depression. *Skeptical Inquirer,* 35–40.

Barlow, David H. (2000). Unraveling the mysteries of anxiety and its disorders from the perspective of emotion theory. *American Psychologist, 55,* 1247–1263.

Barlow, David H. (2004). Psychological treatments. *American Psychologist, 59,* 869–878.

Barrett, Lisa F. (2006). Are emotions natural kinds? *Perspectives on Psychological Science, 1,* 28–58.

Barrett, Lisa F., & Kensinger, Elizabeth A. (2010). Context is routinely encoded during emotion perception. *Psychological Science, 21,* 595–599.

Barsky, S. H.; Roth, M. D.; Kleerup, E. C.; Simmons, M.; & Tashkin, D. P. (1998). Histopathologic and molecular alterations in bronchial epithelium in habitual smokers of marijuana, cocaine, and/or tobacco. *Journal of the National Cancer Institute, 90,* 1198–1205.

Bartels, Andreas, & Zeki, Semir (2004). The neural correlates of material and romantic love. *NeuroImage, 21,* 1155–1166.

Bartlett, Frederic C. (1932). *Remembering.* Cambridge, England: Cambridge University Press.

Bartoshuk, Linda M. (1998). Born to burn: Genetic variation in taste. Paper presented at the annual meeting of the American Psychological Association, San Francisco.

Bartoshuk, Linda M. (2009). Taste. In J. M. Wolfe, K. R. Kluender, D. M. Levi, et al., *Sensation and perception* (2nd ed.). Sunderland, MA: Sinauer Associates.

Bartoshuk, Linda M.; Duffy, V. B.; Lucchina, L. A.; et al. (1998). PROP (6-n-propylthiouracil) supertasters and the saltiness of NaCl. *Annals of the New York Academy of Sciences, 855,* 793–796.

Bassetti, C.; Vella, S.; Donati, F.; et al. (2000). SPECT during sleepwalking. *Lancet, 356,* 484–485.

Bauer, Patricia (2002). Long-term recall memory: Behavioral and neurodevelopmental changes in the first 2 years of life. *Current Directions in Psychological Science, 11,* 137–141.

Baumeister, Roy F. (2000). Gender differences in erotic plasticity: The female sex drive as socially flexible and responsive. *Psychological Bulletin, 126,* 347–374.

Baumeister, Roy F.; Brewer, Lauren E.; Tice, Dianne M.; & Twenge, Jean M. (2007). The need to belong: Understanding the interpersonal and inner effects of social exclusion. *Social and Personality Psychology Compass, 1,* 506–520.

Baumeister, Roy F.; Campbell, Jennifer D.; Krueger, Joachim I.; & Vohs, Kathleen D. (2003). Does high self-esteem cause better performance, interpersonal success, happiness, or healthier lifestyles? *Psychological Science in the Public Interest, 4*(1)[whole issue].

Baumeister, Roy F.; Catanese, Kathleen R.; & Vohs, Kathleen D. (2001). Is there a gender difference in strength of sex drive? Theoretical views, conceptual distinctions, and a review of relevant evidence. *Personality and Social Psychology Review, 5,* 242–273.

Baumeister, Roy F.; Dale, Karen; & Sommer, Kristin L. (1998). Freudian defense mechanisms and empirical findings in modern social psychology: Reaction formation, projection, displacement, undoing, isolation, sublimation, and denial. *Journal of Personality, 66,* 1081–1124.

Baumeister, Roy F.; Stillwell, Arlene M.; & Heatherton, Todd F. (1994). Guilt: An interpersonal approach. *Psychological Bulletin, 115,* 243–267.

Baumrind, Diana; Larzelere, Robert E.; & Cowan, Philip (2002). Ordinary physical punishment—Is it harmful? Commentary on Gershoff's Review. *Psychological Bulletin, 128,* in press.

Baxter, Lewis R.; Schwartz, Jeffrey M.; Bergman, Kenneth S.; et al. (1992). Caudate glucose metabolic rate changes with both drug and behavior therapy for obsessive-compulsive disorder. *Archives of General Psychiatry, 49,* 681–689.

Bechara, Antoine; Dermas, Hanna; Tranel, Daniel; & Damasio, Antonio R. (1997). Deciding advantageously before knowing the advantageous strategy. *Science, 275,* 1293–1294.

Beck, Aaron T. (1976). *Cognitive therapy and the emotional disorders.* New York: International Universities Press.

Beck, Aaron T. (2005). The current state of cognitive therapy: A 40-year retrospective. *Archives of General Psychiatry, 62,* 953–959.

Becker, D. Vaughn; Kenrick, Douglas T.; Neuberg, Steven L.; et al. (2007). The confounded nature of angry men and happy women. *Journal of Personality and Social Psychology, 92,* 179–190.

Becker, Jill B.; Berkley, Karen J.; Geary, Nori; et al. (Eds.) (2008). *Sex differences in the brain: From genes to behavior.* New York: Oxford University Press.

Becker, Selwyn W., & Eagly, Alice H. (2004). The heroism of women and men. *American Psychologist, 59,* 163–178.

Beer, Jeremy M.; Arnold, Richard D.; & Loehlin, John C. (1998). Genetic and environmental influences on MMPI factor scales: Joint model fitting to twin and adoption data. *Journal of Personality and Social Psychology, 74,* 818–827.

Belsky, Jay; Bakermans-Kranenburg, Marian J.; & van IJzendoorn, Marinus H. (2007). For better *and* for worse: Differential susceptibility to environmental influences. *Current Directions in Psychological Science, 16,* 300–304.

Belsky, Jay; Campbell, Susan B.; Cohn, Jeffrey F.; & Moore, Ginger (1996). Instability of infant-parent attachment security. *Developmental Psychology, 32,* 921–924.

Belsky, Jay, & Pluess, Michael (2009). The nature (and nurture?) of plasticity in early human development. *Perspectives on Psychological Science, 4,* 345–351.

Belsky, Jay, & Pluess, Michael (2009). Beyond diathesis stress: Differential susceptibility to environmental influences. *Psychological Bulletin, 135,* 885–908.

Bem, Daryl J., & Honorton, Charles (1994). Does psi exist? Replicable evidence for an anomalous process of information transfer. *Psychological Bulletin, 115,* 4–18.

Bem, Sandra L. (1993). *The lenses of gender.* New Haven, CT: Yale University Press.

Benedetti, Fabrizio, & Levi-Montalcini, Rita (2001). Opioid and non-opioid mechanisms of placebo analgesia. Paper presented at the annual meeting of the American Psychological Society, Toronto.

Benedetti, Fabrizio; Mayberg, Helen S.; Wager, Tor D.; et al. (2005, November 9). Neurobiological mechanisms of the placebo effect. *The Journal of Neuroscience, 45,* 10390–10402.

Benjamin, Ludy T., Jr. (1998). Why Gorgeous George, and not Wilhelm Wundt, was the founder of psychology: A history of popular psychology in America. Invited address presented at the National Institute on the Teaching of Psychology, St. Petersburg Beach.

Benjamin, Ludy T., Jr. (2003). Why can't psychology get a stamp? *Journal of Applied Psychoanalytic Studies, 5,* 443–454.

Beran, Michael J., & Beran, Mary M. (2004). Chimpanzees remember the results of one-by-one addition of food items to sets over extended time periods. *Psychological Science, 15,* 94–99.

Berenbaum, Sheri A., & Bailey, J. Michael (2003). Effects on gender identity of prenatal androgens and genital appearance: Evidence from girls with congenital adrenal hyperplasia. *Journal of Clinical Endocrinology and Metabolism, 88,* 1102–1106.

Berger, F.; Gage, F. H.; & Vijayaraghavan, S. (1998). Nicotinic receptor-induced apoptotic cell death of hippocampal progenitor cells. *Journal of Neuroscience, 18,* 6871–6881.

Berglund, Hans; Lindström, Per; & Savic, Ivanka (2006). Brain response to putative pheromones in lesbian women. *Proceedings of the National Academy of Sciences, 103,* 8269–8274.

Berkman Center for Internet & Society (2008, December 31). Enhancing child safety and online technologies: Final report of the Internet Safety Task Force. Final report available at http://cyber.law.harvard.edu/sites/cyber.law.harvard.edu/files/ISTTF_Final_Report.pdf.

Berkowitz, Shari R.; Nelson, Kally J.; Newman, Eryn, J.; et al. (2008). Attitudes toward cosmetic neurology: An international perspective. Poster presented at the meeting of the Association for Psychological Science, Chicago, Illinois, May.

Berlin, Fred S. (2003). Sex offender treatment and legislation. *Journal of the American Academy of Psychiatry and the Law, 31,* 510–513.

Bernstein, Daniel M., & Loftus, Elizabeth F. (2009). How to tell if a particular memory is true or false. *Perspectives on Psychlogical Science, 4,* 370–374.

Berntsen, Dorthe, & Thomsen, Dorthe K. (2005). Personal memories for remote historical events: Accuracy and clarity of flashbulb memories related to World War II. *Journal of Experimental Psychology: General, 134,* 242–257.

Berry, John W. (2006). Contexts of acculturation. In D. L. Sam & J. W. Berry (Eds.), *Cambridge handbook of acculturation psychology.* New York: Cambridge University Press.

Berscheid, Ellen, & Reis, Harry T. (1998). Attraction and close relationships. In D. T. Gilbert, S. T. Fiske, & G. Lindzey (Eds.), *The handbook of social psychology, Vol. 2* (4th ed.). New York: McGraw-Hill.

Beutler, Larry E., & Malik, Mary L. (Eds.) (2002). *Rethinking the DSM: A psychological perspective.* Washington, DC: American Psychological Association.

Beydoun, M. A.; Kaufman, J. S.; Satia, J. A.; et al. (2007). Plasma n-3 fatty acids and the risk of cognitive decline in older adults: the Atherosclerosis Risk in Communities Study. *American Journal of Clinical Nutrition, 85,* 1103–1111.

Beyerstein, Barry L. (1996). Graphology. In G. Stein (Ed.), *The encyclopedia of the paranormal.* Amherst, NY: Prometheus Books.

Bhatarah, Parveen; Ward, Geoff; & Tan, Lydia (2008). Examining the relationship between free recall and immediate serial recall: The serial nature of recall and the effect of test expectancy. *Memory & Cognition, 36,* 20–34.

Bierut, Laura Jean; Stitzel, Jerry A.; Wang, Jen C.; et al. (2008). Variants in nicotinic receptors and risk for nicotine dependence. *American Journal of Psychiatry, 165,* 1163–1171.

Binder, Jens; Zagefka, Hanna; Brown, Rupert; et al. (2009). Does contact reduce prejudice or does prejudice reduce contact? A longitudinal test of the contact hypothesis among majority and minority groups in three European countries. *Journal of Personality and Social Psychology, 96,* 843–856.

Birdwhistell, Ray L. (1970). *Kinesics and context: Essays on body motion communication.* Philadelphia: University of Pennsylvania Press.

Birkhead, Tim (2001). *Promiscuity: An evolutionary history of sperm competition.* Cambridge, MA: Harvard University Press.

Bischof, Matthias, & Bassetti, Claudio L. (2004). Total dream loss: A distinct neuropsychological dysfunction after bilateral PCA stroke. *Annals of Neurology,* published online Sept. 10, 2004. (DOI: 10.1002/ana.20246.)

Bjork, Robert A. (October, 2000). Human factors 101: How about just trying things out? *APS Observer, 13,* 3, 30.

Bjorkland, D. F. (2000). *Children's thinking: Developmental function and individual differences.* Belmont, CA: Wadsworth.

Blackmore, Susan (2001, March/April). Giving up the ghosts: End of a personal quest. *Skeptical Inquirer, 25.*

Blagrove, Mark (1996). Problems with the cognitive psychological modeling of dreaming. *Journal of Mind and Behavior, 17,* 99–134.

Blair, R. D. J.; Jones, L.; Clark, F.; & Smith, M. (1997). The psychopathic individual: A lack of responsiveness to distress cues? *Psychophysiology, 45,* 192–198.

Blakemore, Colin, & Cooper, Grahame F. (1970). Development of the brain depends on the visual environment. *Nature, 228,* 477–478.

Blanton, Hart; Jaccard, James; Klick, Jonathan; Mellers, Barbara; Mitchell, Gregory; & Tetlock, Philip E. (2009). Strong claims and weak evidence: Reassessing the predictive validity of the IAT. *Journal of Applied Psychology, 94,* 567–582.

Blass, Thomas (Ed.) (2000). *Obedience to authority: Current perspectives on the Milgram paradigm.* Mahwah, NJ: Erlbaum.

Blazer, Dan G.; Kessler, Ronald C.; & Swartz, Marvin S. (1998). Epidemiology of recurrent major and minor depression with a seasonal pattern: The National Comorbidity Survey. *British Journal of Psychiatry, 172,* 164–167.

Bleuler, Eugen (1911/1950). *Dementia praecox or the group of schizophrenias.* New York: International Universities Press.

Bliss, T. V., & Collingridge, G. L. (1993). A synaptic model of memory: Longterm potentiation in the hippocampus. *Nature, 361*(6407), 31–39.

Bloom, Mia (2005). *Dying to kill: The allure of suicide terror.* New York: Columbia University Press.

Blow, Charles M. (2009, December 5). Black in the age of Obama. *New York Times,* op-ed.

Blum, Deborah (2002). *Love at Goon Park: Harry Harlow and the science of affection.* Cambridge, MA: Perseus Books.

Boesch, Cristophe (1991). Teaching among wild chimpanzees. *Animal Behavior, 41,* 530–532.

Bogaert, Anthony F. (2006, June 28). Biological versus nonbiological older brothers and men's sexual orientation. *Proceedings of the National Academy of Sciences,* published online June 28, 2006, 10.1073/pnas. 0511152103.

Bogle, Kathleen (2008). *Hooking up: Sex, dating, and relationships on campus.* New York: New York University Press.

Bohannon, John N., & Symons, Victoria (1988). Conversational conditions of children's imitation. Paper presented at the biennial Conference on Human Development, Charleston, South Carolina.

Bolshakov, Vadim Y., & Siegelbaum, Steven A. (1994). Postsynaptic induction and presynaptic expression of hippocampal long-term depression. *Science, 264,* 1148–1152.

Bonanno, George A. (2004). Loss, trauma, and human resilience. *American Psychologist, 59,* 20–28.

Bonanno, George A.; Galea, Sandro; Bucciarelli, Angela; & Vlahov, David (2006). Psychological resilience after disaster. *Psychological Science, 17,* 181–186.

Bond, Meg A.; Punnett, Laura; Pyle, Jean L.; et al. (2004). Gendered work conditions, health, and work outcomes. *Journal of Occupational Health Psychology, 91,* 28–45.

Bond, Rod, & Smith, Peter B. (1996). Culture and conformity: A meta-analysis of studies using Asch's (1952b, 1956) line judgment task. *Psychological Bulletin, 119,* 111–137.

Bonnet, Michael H. (1990). The perception of sleep onset in insomniacs and normal sleepers. In R. R. Bootzin, J. F. Kihlstrom, & D. L. Schacter (Eds.), *Sleep and cognition.* Washington, DC: American Psychological Association.

Booth, Frank W., & Neufer, P. Darrell (2005). Exercise controls gene expression. *American Scientist, 93,* 28–35.

Bootzin, Richard R. (2009, March). Update on the psychological science accreditation system. Association for Psychological Science, *The Observer,* 20–21.

Borch-Jacobsen, Mikkel (1997, April 24). Sybil—The making of a disease: An interview with Dr. Herbert Spiegel. *The New York Review of Books,* 60–64.

Bordo, Susan (2000). *The male body.* New York: Farrar, Straus and Giroux.

Bornstein, Robert F.; Leone, Dean R.; & Galley, Donna J. (1987). The generalizability of subliminal mere exposure effects: Influence of stimuli perceived without awareness on social behavior. *Journal of Personality and Social Psychology, 53,* 1070–1079.

Boroditsky, Lera (2003). Linguistic relativity. In L. Nadel (Ed.), *Encyclopedia of cognitive science.* London: Nature Publishing Group.

Boroditsky, Lera; Schmidt, Lauren; & Phillips, Webb (2003). Sex, syntax, and semantics. In D. Gentner & S. Goldin-Meadow (Eds.), *Language in mind: Advances in the study of language and thought.* Cambridge: MIT Press.

Bosworth, Hayden B., & Schaie, K. Warner (1999). Survival effects in cognitive function, cognitive style, and sociodemographic variables in the Seattle Longitudinal Study. *Experimental Aging Research, 25,* 121–139.

Bouchard, Claude; Tremblay, A.; Despres, J. P.; et al. (1990, May 24). The response to long-term overfeeding in identical twins. *New England Journal of Medicine, 322,* 1477–1482.

Bouchard, Thomas J., Jr. (1995). Nature's twice-told tale: Identical twins reared apart—what they tell us about human individuality. Paper presented at the annual meeting of the Western Psychological Association, Los Angeles.

Bouchard, Thomas J., Jr. (1997a). The genetics of personality. In K. Blum & E. P. Noble (Eds.), *Handbook of psychiatric genetics.* Boca Raton, FL: CRC Press.

Bouchard, Thomas J., Jr. (1997b). IQ similarity in twins reared apart: Findings and responses to critics. In R. J. Sternberg & E. Grigorenko (Eds.), *Intelligence: Heredity and environment*. New York: Cambridge University Press.

Bouchard, Thomas J., Jr. (2004). Genetic influence on human psychological traits: A survey. *Current Directions in Psychological Science, 13,* 148–151.

Bouchard, Thomas J., Jr., & McGue, Matthew (1981). Familial studies of intelligence: A review. *Science, 212,* 1055–1058.

Boudry, Maarten; Termote, Roeland; & Betz, Willem (2010, July/August). Fabricating communication: The case of the Belgian coma patient. *The Skeptical Inquirer, 34,* 12–15.

Bouret, Sebastien G.; Draper, Shin J.; & Simerly, Richard B. (2004). Trophic action of leptin on hypothalamic neurons that regulate feeding. *Science, 304,* 108–110.

Bousfield, W. A. (1953). The occurrence of clustering in the recall of randomly arranged associates. *Journal of General Psychology, 49,* 229–240.

Bowen, Murray (1978). *Family therapy in clinical practice*. New York: Jason Aronson.

Bower, Gordon H., & Forgas, Joseph P. (2000). Affect, memory, and social cognition. In E. Eich et al. (Eds.), *Cognition and emotion*. New York: Oxford University Press.

Bowers, Kenneth S.; Regehr, Glenn; Balthazard, Claude; & Parker, Kevin (1990). Intuition in the context of discovery. *Cognitive Psychology, 22,* 72–110.

Bowlby, John (1969). *Attachment and loss. Vol. 1. Attachment*. New York: Basic Books.

Bowlby, John (1973). *Attachment and loss: Vol. 2. Separation*. New York: Basic Books.

Bowleg, Lisa; Lucas, Kenya J.; & Tschann, Jeanne M. (2004). "The ball was always in his court": An exploratory analysis of relationship scripts, sexual scripts, and condom use among African American women. *Psychology of Women Quarterly, 28,* 70–82.

Bowles, Samuel (2008). Policies designed for self-interested citizens may undermine "the moral sentiments": Evidence from economic experiments. *Science, 320,* 1605–1609.

Brand-Miller, Jennie C.; Fatima, Kaniz; Middlemiss, Christopher; et al. (2007). Effect of alcoholic beverages on postprandial glycemia and insulinemia in lean, young, healthy adults. *American Journal of Clinical Nutrition, 85,* 1545–1551.

Brandt, Allan M. (2007). The Cigarette Century: The rise, fall, and deadly persistence of the product that defined America. New York: Basic Books.

Braun, Kathryn A.; Ellis, Rhiannon; & Loftus, Elizabeth F. (2002). Make my memory: How advertising can change our memories of the past. *Psychology & Marketing, 19,* 1–23.

Braungert, J. M.; Plomin, Robert; DeFries, J. C.; & Fulker, D. W. (1992). Genetic influence on tester-rated infant temperament as assessed by Bayley's Infant Behavior Record: Nonadoptive and adoptive siblings and twins. *Developmental Psychology, 28,* 40–47.

Breland, Keller, & Breland, Marian (1961). The misbehavior of organisms. *American Psychologist, 16,* 681–684.

Brennan, Patricia A., & Mednick, Sarnoff A. (1994). Learning theory approach to the deterrence of criminal recidivism. *Journal of Abnormal Psychology, 103,* 430–440.

Brescoll, Victoria L., & Uhlmann, Eric L. (2008). Can an angry woman get ahead? Status conferral, gender, and expression of emotion in the workplace. *Psychological Science, 19,* 268–275.

Breslau, Naomi; Lucia, Victoria C.; & Alvarado, German F. (2006). Intelligence and other predisposing factors in exposure to trauma and posttraumatic stress disorder. *Archives of General Psychiatry, 63,* 1238–1245.

Brewer, Marilynn B., & Gardner, Wendi (1996). Who is this "we"? Levels of collective identity and self representations. *Journal of Personality and Social Psychology, 71,* 83–93.

Brissette, Ian; Scheier, Michael F.; & Carver, Charles S. (2002). The role of optimism in social network development, coping, and psychological adjustment during a life transition. *Journal of Personality and Social Psychology, 82,* 102–111.

Brockner, Joel, & Rubin, Jeffrey Z. (1985). *Entrapment in escalating conflicts: A social psychological analysis*. New York: Springer-Verlag.

Broks, Paul (2004). *Into the silent land: Travels in neuropsychology*. New York: Grove Press.

Brooks-Gunn, J. (1986). Differentiating premenstrual symptoms and syndromes. *Psychosomatic Medicine, 48,* 385–387.

Brosnan, Sarah F., & de Waal, Frans B. M. (2003). Monkeys reject unequal pay. *Nature, 425,* 297–299.

Brown, Alan S. (2004). *The déjà vu experience: Essays in cognitive psychology*. New York: Psychology Press.

Brown, Alan S.; Begg, M. D.; Gravenstein, S.; et al. (2004). Serologic evidence of prenatal influenza in the etiology of schizophrenia. *Archives of General Psychiatry, 61,* 774–780.

Brown, D.; Scheflin, A. W.; & Whitfield, C. L. (1999). Recovered memories: The current weight of the evidence in science and in the courts. *Journal of Psychiatry and Law, 27,* 5–156.

Brown, G. W. & Harris, T. O. (2008). Depression and the serotonin transporter 5-HTTLPR polymorphism: A review and a hypothesis concerning gene-environment interaction. *Journal of Affective Disorders, 111,* 1–12.

Brown, Gillian R.; Laland, Keven N.; & Mulder, Monique Borgerhoff (2009). Bateman's principles and human sex roles. *Trends in Ecology & Evolution, 24,* 297–304.

Brown, Gregory K.; Ten Have, Thomas; Henriques, Gregg R.; et al. (2005, August 3). Cognitive therapy for the prevention of suicide attempts. *Journal of the American Medical Association, 294,* 563–570.

Brown, Roger (1986). *Social psychology* (2nd ed.). New York: Free Press.

Brown, Roger; Cazden, Courtney; & Bellugi, Ursula (1969). The child's grammar from I to III. In J. P. Hill (Ed.), *Minnesota Symposium on Child Psychology* (Vol. 2). Minneapolis: University of Minnesota Press.

Brown, Roger, & Kulik, James (1977). Flashbulb memories. *Cognition, 5,* 73–99.

Brown, Roger, & McNeill, David (1966). The "tip of the tongue" phenomenon. *Journal of Verbal Learning and Verbal Behavior, 5,* 325–337.

Brown, Ryan P., & Josephs, Robert A. (1999). A burden of proof: Stereotype relevance and gender differences in math performance. *Journal of Personality and Social Psychology, 76,* 246–257.

Brown, Ryan P.; Osterman, Lindsey L.; & Barnes, Collin D. (2009). School violence and the culture of honor. *Psychological Science, 20,* 1400–1405.

Brown, Stephanie L.; Nesse, Randolph M.; Vinokur, Amiram D.; & Smith, Dylan M. (2003). Providing social support may be more beneficial than receiving it: Results from a prospective study of mortality. *Psychological Science, 14,* 320–327.

Browning, James R.; Hatfield, Elaine; Kessler, Debra; & Levine, Tim (2000). Sexual motives, gender, and sexual behavior. *Archives of Sexual Behavior, 29,* 135–153.

Bruck, Maggie (2003). Effects of suggestion on the reliability and credibility of children's reports. Invited address at the annual meeting of the American Psychological Society, Atlanta.

Bruck, Maggie; Ceci, Stephen J.; Francoeur, E.; & Renick, A. (1995). Anatomically detailed dolls do not facilitate preschoolers' reports of a pediatric examination involving genital touching. *Journal of Experimental Psychology: Applied, 1,* 95–109.

Bruder, Carl E. G. E.; Piotrowski, Arkadjusz; Gijsbers, Antoinet A.; et al. (2008). Phenotypically concordant and discordant monozygotic twins display different DNA copy-number-variation profiles. *American Journal of Human Genetics, 82,* 763–771.

Bruner, Jerome S. (1990). *Acts of meaning*. Cambridge, MA: Harvard University Press.

Bryant, Gregory A., & Barrett, H. Clark (2007). Recognizing intentions in infant-directed speech. *Psychological Science, 18,* 746–751.

Bryant, Richard A., & Guthrie, Rachel M. (2005). Maladaptive appraisals as a risk factor for posttraumatic stress. *Psychological Science, 16,* 749–752.

Buchanan, Tony W. (2007). Retrieval of emotional memories. *Psychological Bulletin, 133,* 761–779.

Buck, Linda, & Axel, Richard (1991). A novel multigene family may encode odorant receptors: A molecular basis for odor recognition. *Cell, 65,* 175–187.

Bukowski, William M. (2001). Friendship and the worlds of childhood. In D. W. Nangle & C. A. Erdley (Eds.), The role of friendship in psychological adjustment. *New directions for child and adolescent development, No. 91.* San Francisco, CA: Jossey-Bass.

Burger, Jerry M. (2009). Replicating Milgram: Would people still obey today? *American Psychologist, 64,* 1–11.

Burke, Brian L.; Arkowitz, Hal; & Menchola, Marisa (2003). The efficacy of motivational interviewing: A meta-analysis of controlled clinical trials. *Journal of Consulting and Clinical Psychology, 71,* 843–861.

Burke, Deborah M.; MacKay, Donald G.; Worthley, Joanna S.; & Wade, Elizabeth (1991). On the tip of the tongue: What causes word finding failures in young and older adults? *Journal of Memory and Language, 30,* 237–246.

Burke, Deborah M., & Shafto, Meredith A. (2004). Aging and language production. *Current Directions in Psychological Science, 13,* 21–24.

Burnham, Denis; Kitamura, Christine; & Vollmer-Conna, Uté (2002, May 24). What's new, pussycat? On talking to babies and animals. *Science, 296,* 1435.

Buscemi, N.; Vandermeer, B.; Pandya, R.; et al. (2004). *Melatonin for treatment of sleep disorders.* Evidence Report/Technology Assessment No. 108. (Prepared by the University of Alberta Evidence-based Practice Center.) Rockville, MD: Agency for Healthcare Research and Quality.

Bushman, Brad J., & Anderson, Craig A. (2009). Comfortably numb: Desensitizing effects of violent media on helping others. *Psychological Science, 20,* 273–277.

Bushman, Brad J.; Bonacci, Angelica M.; Pedersen, William C.; et al. (2005). Chewing on it can chew you up: Effects of rumination on triggered displaced aggression. *Journal of Personality and Social Psychology, 88,* 969–983.

Bushman, Brad; Bonacci, Angelica M.; van Dijk, Mirjam; & Baumeister, Roy F. (2003). Narcissism, sexual refusal, and aggression: Testing a narcissistic reactance model of sexual coercion. *Journal of Personality and Social Psychology, 84,* 1027–1040.

Bushman, Brad J.; Ridge, Robert D.; Das, Enny; et al. (2007). When God sanctions killing. *Psychological Science, 18,* 204–207.

Buss, David M. (1994). *The evolution of desire: Strategies of human mating.* New York: Basic Books.

Buss, David M. (1995). Evolutionary psychology: A new paradigm for psychological science. *Psychological Inquiry, 6,* 1–30.

Buss, David M. (2000). The dangerous passion: Why jealousy is as necessary as love or sex. New York: The Free Press.

Buster, J. E.; Kingsberg, S. A.; Aguirre, O.; et al. (2005). Testosterone patch for low sexual desire in surgically menopausal women: a randomized trial. *Obstetrics and Gynecology, 105* (Pt 1), 944–952.

Butcher, James N.; Lim, Jeeyoung; & Nezami, Elahe (1998). Objective study of abnormal personality in cross-cultural settings: The MMPI-2. *Journal of Cross-Cultural Psychology, 29,* 189–211.

Butcher, James N., & Perry, Julia N. (2008). *Personality assessment in treatment planning: Use of the MMPI-2 and BTPI.* New York: Oxford University Press.

Butler, S.; Chalder, T.; Ron, M.; et al. (1991). Cognitive behaviour therapy in chronic fatigue syndrome. *Journal of Neurology, Neurosurgery & Psychiatry, 54,* 153–158.

Button, T. M. M.; Thapar, A.; & McGuffin, P. (2005). Relationship between antisocial behaviour, attention-deficit hyperactivity disorder and maternal prenatal smoking. *British Journal of Psychiatry. 187,* 155–160.

Buunk, Bram; Angleitner, Alois; Oubaid, Viktor; & Buss, David M. (1996). Sex differences in jealousy in evolutionary and cultural perspective: Tests from the Netherlands, Germany, and the United States. *Psychological Science, 7,* 359–363.

Byers-Heinlein, Krista; Burns, Tracey C.; & Werker, Janet F. (2010). The roots of bilingualism in newborns. *Psychological Science, 21,* 343–348.

Cabiya, Jose J.; Lucio, Emilia; Chavira, Denise A.; et al. (2000). MMPI-2 scores of Puerto Rican, Mexican, and U.S. Latino college students: A research note. *Psychological Reports, 87,* 266–268.

Cacioppo, J. T.; Berntson, G. G.; Lorig, Tyler S.; et al. (2003). Just because you're imaging the brain doesn't mean you can stop using your head: A primer and set of first principles. *Journal of Personality and Social Psychology, 85,* 650–661.

Cacioppo, John T.; Fowler, James H.; & Christakis, Nicholas A. (2009). Alone in the crowd: The structure and spread of loneliness in a large social network. *Journal of Personality and Social Psychology, 97,* 977–991.

Cadinu, Mara; Maass, Anne; Rosabianca, Alessandra; & Kiesner, Jeff (2005). Why do women underperform under stereotype threat? Evidence for the role of negative thinking. *Psychological Science, 16,* 472–578.

Cahill, Larry (2005, May). His brain, her brain. *Scientific American, 292,* 40–47.

Cahill, Larry; Prins, Bruce; Weber, Michael; & McGaugh, James L. (1994). β-adrenergic activation and memory for emotional events. *Nature, 371,* 702–704.

Cai, Denise J.; Mednick, Sarnoff A.; Harrison, Elizabeth M.; et al. (2009). REM, not incubation, improves creativity by priming associative networks. *Proceedings of the National Academy of Sciences, 106,* 10130–10134.

Calder, A. J.; Keane, J.; Manes, F.; Antoun, N.; & Young, A. W. (2000). Impaired recognition and experience of disgust following brain injury. *Nature Neuroscience, 3,* 1077–1078.

Callaghan, Glenn M.; Chacon, Cynthia; Coles, Cameron; et al. (2009). An empirical evaluation of the diagnostic criteria for premenstrual dysphoric disorder: Problems with sex specificity and validity. *Women & Therapy, 32,* 1–21.

Camerer, Colin F. (2003). Strategizing in the brain. *Science, 300,* 1673–1675.

Cameron, Judy; Banko, Katherine M.; & Pierce, W. David (2001). Pervasive negative effects of rewards on intrinsic motivation: The myth continues. *Behavior Analyst, 24,* 1–44.

Campbell, Benjamin C.; Pope, Harrison G.; & Filiault, Shaun (2005). Body image among Ariaal men from Northern Kenya. *Journal of Cross-Cultural Psychology, 36,* 371–379.

Campbell, Frances A., & Ramey, Craig T. (1995). Cognitive and school outcomes for high risk students at middle adolescence: Positive effects of early intervention. *American Educational Research Journal, 32,* 743–772.

Campbell, Joseph (1949/1968). *The hero with 1,000 faces* (2nd ed.). Princeton, NJ: Princeton University Press.

Campbell, Susan M., & Collaer, Marcia L. (2009). Stereotype threat and gender differences in performance on a novel videospatial task. *Psychology of Women Quarterly, 33,* 427–444.

Canetto, Silvia S. (1992). Suicide attempts and substance abuse: Similarities and differences. *Journal of Psychology, 125,* 605–620.

Canino, Glorisa (1994). Alcohol use and misuse among Hispanic women: Selected factors, processes, and studies. *International Journal of the Addictions, 29,* 1083–1100.

Cannon, Tyrone D.; Huttunen, Matti O.; Loennqvist, Jouko; et al. (2000). The inheritance of neuropsychological dysfunction in twins discordant for schizophrenia. *American Journal of Human Genetics, 67,* 369–382.

Cannon, Walter B. (1929). *Bodily changes in pain, hunger, fear and rage* (2nd ed.). New York: Appleton.

Cao, Xiaohua; Wang, Huimin; Mei, Bing; et al. (2008). Inducible and selective erasure of memories in the mouse brain via chemical-genetic manipulation. *Neuron, 60,* 353–366.

Capaldi, Deborah M.; Pears, Katherine C.; Patterson, Gerald R.; & Owen, Lee D. (2003). Continuity of parenting practices across generations in an at-risk sample: A prospective comparison of direct and mediated associations. *Journal of Abnormal Child Psychology, 31,* 127–142.

Carnagey, Nicholas L., & Anderson, Craig A. (2005). The effects of reward and punishment in violent video games on aggressive affect, cognition, and behavior. *Psychological Science, 16,* 882–889.

Carskadon, Mary A.; Mitler, Merrill M.; & Dement, William C. (1974). A comparison of insomniacs and normals: Total sleep time and sleep latency. *Sleep Research, 3,* 130 [Abstract].

Cartwright, Rosalind (1977). *Night life: Explorations in dreaming.* Englewood Cliffs, NJ: Prentice-Hall.

Cartwright, Rosalind (2010). *The twenty-four hour mind: The role of sleep and dreaming in our emotional lives.* New York: Oxford University Press.

Cartwright, Rosalind; Agargun, Mehmet Y.; Kirkby, Jennifer; & Friedman, Julie Kabat (2006). Relation of dreams to waking concerns. *Psychiatry Research, 141,* 261–270.

Cartwright, Rosalind D.; Young, Michael A.; Mercer, Patricia; & Bears, Michael (1998). Role of REM sleep and dream variables in the prediction of remission from depression. *Psychiatry Research, 80,* 249–255.

Carver, Charles S., & Baird, Eryn (1998). The American dream revisited: Is it *what* you want or *why* you want it that matters? *Psychological Science, 9,* 289–292.

Carver, Charles S., & Harmon-Jones, Eddie (2009). Anger is an approach-related affect: Evidence and implications. *Psychological Bulletin, 135,* 183–204.

Carver, Charles S., & Scheier, M. F. (2002). Optimism. In C. R. Snyder & S. J. Lopes (Eds.), *The handbook of positive psychology.* New York: Oxford University Press.

Caspi, Avshalom (2000). The child is father of the man: Personality continuities from childhood to adulthood. *Journal of Personality and Social Psychology, 78,* 158–172.

Caspi, Avshalom; McClay, Joseph; Moffitt, Terrie E.; et al. (2002, August 2). Role of genotype in the cycle of violence in maltreated children. *Science, 297,* 851–857.

Caspi, Avshalom, & Moffitt, Terrie E. (1991). Individual differences are accentuated during periods of social change: The sample case of girls at puberty. *Journal of Personality and Social Psychology, 61,* 157–168.

Caspi, Avshalom; Sugden, Karen; Moffitt, Terrie E.; et al. (2003). Influence of life stress on depression: Moderation by a polymorphism in the 5-HTT gene. *Science, 301,* 386–389.

Cassin, Stephanie E.; von Ranson, Kristin M.; Heng, Kenneth; et al. (2008). Adapted motivational interviewing for women with binge eating disorder: A randomized controlled trial. *Psychology of Addictive Behaviors, 22,* 417–425.

Cattell, Raymond B. (1973). *Personality and mood by questionnaire.* San Francisco: Jossey-Bass.

Ceci, Stephen J., & Bruck, Maggie (1995). *Jeopardy in the courtroom: A scientific analysis of children's testimony.* Washington, DC: American Psychological Association.

Cejka, Mary Ann, & Eagly, Alice H. (1999). Gender-stereotypic images of occupations correspond to the sex segregation of employment. *Personality and Social Psychology Bulletin, 25,* 413–423.

Cermak, Laird S., & Craik, Fergus I. M. (Eds.) (1979). *Levels of processing in human memory.* Hillsdale, NJ: Erlbaum.

Cervone, Daniel, & Shoda, Yuichi (1999). Beyond traits in the study of personality coherence. *Current Directions in Psychological Science, 8,* 27–32.

Chabat, Daniel-Robert; Rainville, Constant; Kupers, Ron; & Ptito, Maurice (2007). Tactile-"visual" acuity of the tongue in early blind individuals. *Neuroreport, 18,* 1901–1904.

Chamberlain, Samuel R.; Menzies, Lara; Hampshire, Adam; et al. (2008, July 18). Orbitofrontal dysfunction in patients with obsessive-compulsive disorder and their unaffected relatives. *Science, 321,* 421–422.

Chambless, Dianne L., & Ollendick, T. H. (2001). Empirically supported psychological interventions: Controversies and evidence. *Annual Review of Psychology, 52,* 685–716.

Chambless, Dianne L.; & the Task Force on Psychological Interventions (1998). Update on empirically validated therapies II. *The Clinical Psychologist, 51,* 3–16.

Chan, Brenda L.; Witt, Richard; Charrow, Alexandra P.; et al. (2007). Mirror therapy for phantom limb pain [correspondence]. *New England Journal of Medicine, 357,* 2206–2207.

Chang, Edward C. (1998). Dispositional optimism and primary and secondary appraisal of a stressor. *Journal of Personality and Social Psychology, 74,* 1109–1120.

Charles, S. T., & Carstensen, Laura L. (2004). A life-span view of emotional functioning in adulthood and old age. In P. Costa (Ed.), *Recent advances in psychology and aging* (Vol. 15). Amsterdam: Elsevier.

Charles, Susan T.; Reynolds, Chandra A.; & Gatz, Margaret (2001). Age-related differences and change in positive and negative affect over 23 years. *Journal of Personality and Social Psychology, 80,* 136–151.

Chaves, J. F. (1989). Hypnotic control of clinical pain. In N. P. Spanos & J. F. Chaves (Eds.), *Hypnosis: The cognitive-behavioral perspective.* Buffalo, NY: Prometheus Books.

Chen, Edith; Cohen, Sheldon; & Miller, Gregory E. (2010). How low socioeconomic status affects 2-year hormonal trajectories in children. *Psychological Science, 21,* 31–37.

Chen, Zhansheng; Williams, Kipling D.; Fitness, Julie; & Newton, Nicola C. (2008). When hurt will not heal. *Psychological Science, 19,* 789–795.

Cheney, Dorothy L., & Seyfarth, Robert M. (1985). Vervet monkey alarm calls: Manipulation through shared information? *Behavior, 94,* 150–166.

Chida, Yoichi, & Hamer, Mark (2008). Chronic psychosocial factors and acute physiological responses to laboratory-induced stress in healthy populations: A quantitative review of 30 years of investigations. *Psychological Bulletin, 134,* 829–885.

Chipuer, Heather M.; Rovine, Michael J.; & Plomin, Robert (1990). LISREL modeling: Genetic and environmental influences on IQ revisited. *Intelligence, 14,* 11–29.

Choi, Incheol; Dalal, Reeshad; Kim-Prieto, Chu; & Park, Hyekyung (2003). Culture and judgment of causal relevance. *Journal of Personality and Social Psychology, 84,* 46–59.

Chomsky, Noam (1957). *Syntactic structures.* The Hague, Netherlands: Mouton.

Chomsky, Noam (1980). Initial states and steady states. In M. Piatelli-Palmerini (Ed.), *Language and learning: The debate between Jean Piaget and Noam Chomsky.* Cambridge, MA: Harvard University Press.

Chorpita, Bruce F., & Barlow, David H. (1998). The development of anxiety: The role of control in the early environment. *Psychological Bulletin, 124,* 3–21.

Chrisler, Joan C. (2000). PMS as a culture-bound syndrome. In J. C. Chrisler, C. Golden, & P. D. Rozee (Eds.), *Lectures on the psychology of women* (2nd ed.). New York: McGraw-Hill.

Christakis, Dimitri A.; Zimmerman, Frederick J.; DiGiuseppe, David L.; & McCarty, Carolyn A. (2004). Early television exposure and subsequent attentional problems in children. *Pediatrics, 113,* 708–713.

Christensen, Andrew, & Jacobson, Neil S. (2000). *Reconcilable differences.* New York: Guilford.

Christopher, Andrew N., & Wojda, Mark R. (2008). Social dominance orientation, right-wing authoritarianism, sexism, and prejudice toward women in the workforce. *Psychology of Women Quarterly, 32,* 65–73.

Church, A. Timothy, & Lonner, Walter J. (1998). The cross-cultural perspective in the study of personality: Rationale and current research. *Journal of Cross-Cultural Psychology, 29,* 32–62.

Cinque, Guglielmo (1999). *Adverbs and functional heads: A cross-linguistic approach.* New York: Oxford University Press.

Cioffi, Frank (1998). *Freud and the question of pseudoscience.* Chicago, IL: Open Court.

Clancy, Susan A. (2005). *Abducted: How people come to believe they were kidnapped by aliens.* Cambridge, MA: Harvard University Press.

Clark, Lee Anna, & Watson, David (2008). Temperament: An organizing paradigm for trait psychology. In O. P. John, R. W. Robbins, & L. A. Pervin (Eds.), *Handbook of personality: Theory and research* (3rd ed.). New York: Guilford.

Clark, Rodney; Anderson, Norman B.; Clark, Vernessa R.; & Williams, David R. (1999). Racism as a stressor for African Americans: A biopsychosocial model. *American Psychologist, 54,* 805–816.

Clarke, H. F.; Dalley, J. W.; Crofts, H. S.; et al. (2004, May 7). Cognitive inflexibility after prefrontal serotonin depletion. *Science, 304,* 878–880.

Clarke, Peter, & Evans, Susan H. (1998). *Surviving modern medicine.* Rutgers, NJ: Rutgers University Press.

Cleary, Anne M. (2008). Recognition memory, familiarity, and déjà vu experiences. *Current Directions in Psychological Science, 17,* 353–357.

Cleckley, Hervey (1976). *The mask of sanity* (5th ed.). St. Louis, MO: Mosby.

Cloninger, C. Robert (1990). *The genetics and biology of alcoholism*. Cold Springs Harbor, ME: Cold Springs Harbor Press.

Coan, James A.; Schaefer, Hillary; & Davidson, Richard J. (2006). Lending a hand: Social regulation of the neural response to threat. *Psychological Science, 17*.

Coats, Erik J.; Janoff-Bulman, Ronnie; & Alpert, Nancy (1996). Approach versus avoidance goals: Differences in self-evaluation and well-being. *Personality and Social Psychology Bulletin, 22*, 1057–1067.

Coe, Christopher L., & Lubach, Gabriele R. (2008). Fetal programming: Prenatal origins of health and illness. *Current Directions in Psychological Science, 17*, 36–41.

Cohen, David B. (1999). *Stranger in the nest: Do parents really shape their child's personality, intelligence, or character?* New York: Wiley.

Cohen, Dov (1998). Culture, social organization, and patterns of violence. *Journal of Personality and Social Psychology, 75*, 408–419.

Cohen, Dov; Nisbett, Richard E.; Bowdle, Brian F.; & Schwarz, Norbert (1996). Insult, aggression, and the Southern culture of honor: An "experimental ethnography." *Journal of Personality and Social Psychology, 70*, 945–960.

Cohen, Florette; Jussim, Lee; Harber, Kent D.; & Bhasin, Gautam (2009). Modern anti-Semitism and anti-Israeli attitudes. *Journal of Personality and Social Psychology, 97*, 290–306.

Cohen Kadosh, Roi; Henik, Avishai; Catena, Andres; et al. (2009). Induced cross-modal synaesthetic experience without abnormal neuronal connections. *Psychological Science, 20*, 258–265.

Cohen, Sheldon; Doyle, William J.; Turner, Ronald; et al. (2003). Sociability and susceptibility to the common cold. *Psychological Science, 14*, 389–395.

Cohen, Sheldon; Frank, Ellen; Doyle, William J.; et al. (1998). Types of stressors that increase susceptibility to the common cold in healthy adults. *Health Psychology, 17*, 214–223.

Cohen, Sheldon; Tyrrell, David A.; & Smith, Andrew P. (1993). Negative life events, perceived stress, negative affect, and susceptibility to the common cold. *Journal of Personality and Social Psychology, 64*, 131–140.

Colcombe, Stanley, & Kramer, Arthur F. (2003). Fitness effects on the cognitive function of older adults: A meta-analytic study. *Psychological Science, 14*, 125–130.

Cole, Michael, & Scribner, Sylvia (1974). *Culture and thought*. New York: Wiley.

Collaer, Marcia L., & Hines, Melissa (1995). Human behavioral sex differences: A role for gonadal hormones during early development? *Psychological Bulletin, 118*, 55–107.

Collins, Allan M., & Loftus, Elizabeth F. (1975). A spreading-activation theory of semantic processing. *Psychological Review, 82*, 407–428.

Collins, Barry E., & Brief, Diana E. (1995). Using person-perception vignette methodologies to uncover the symbolic meanings of teacher behaviors in the Milgram paradigm. *Journal of Social Issues, 51*, 89–106.

Collins, Rebecca L. (1996). For better or worse: The impact of upward social comparison on self-evaluations. *Psychological Bulletin, 119*, 51–69.

Comas-Díaz, Lillian (2006). Latino healing: The integration of ethnic psychology into psychotherapy. *Psychotherapy: Theory, Research, Practice, Training, 43*, 436–453

Comuzzie, Anthony G., & Allison, David B. (1998). The search for human obesity genes. *Science, 280*, 1374–1377.

Conroy, John (2000). *Unspeakable acts, ordinary people: The dynamics of torture*. New York: Knopf.

Cook, Joan M.; Biyanova, Tatyana; & Coyne, James C. (2009). Influential psychotherapy figures, authors, and books: An Internet survey of over 2,000 psychotherapists. *Psychotherapy: Theory, Research, Practice, Training, 46*, 42–51.

Cooper, M. Lynne; Frone, Michael R.; Russell, Marcia; & Mudar, Pamela (1995). Drinking to regulate positive and negative emotions: A motivational model of alcohol use. *Journal of Personality and Social Psychology, 69*, 990–1005.

Cooper, M. Lynne; Shapiro, Cheryl M.; & Powers, Anne M. (1998). Motivations for sex and risky sexual behavior among adolescents and young adults: A functional perspective. *Journal of Personality and Social Psychology, 75*, 1528–1558.

Corkin, Suzanne (1984). Lasting consequences of bilateral medial temporal lobectomy: Clinical course and experimental findings in H. M. *Seminars in Neurology, 4*, 249–259.

Corkin, Suzanne; Amaral, David G.; Gonzalez, R. Gilberto; et al. (1997). H. M.'s medial temporal lobe lesion: Findings from magnetic resonance imaging. *Journal of Neuroscience, 17*, 3964–3979.

Corriveau, Kathleen H.; Fusaro, Maria; & Harris, Paul L. (2009). Going with the flow: Preschoolers prefer nondissenters as informants. *Psychological Science, 20*, 372–377.

Costa, Paul T., Jr.; McCrae, Robert R.; Martin, Thomas A.; et al. (1999). Personality development from adolescence through adulthood: Further cross-cultural comparisons of age differences. In V. J. Molfese & D. Molfese (Eds.), *Temperament and personality development across the life span*. Hillsdale, NJ: Erlbaum.

Cota-Robles, S.; Neiss, M.; & Rowe, D. C. (2002). The role of puberty in violent and nonviolent delinquency among Anglo American, Mexican American, and African American boys. *Journal of Adolescent Research, 17*, 364–376.

Council, J. R.; Kirsch, Irving; & Grant, D. L. (1996). Imagination, expectancy and hypnotic responding. In R. G. Kunzendorf, N. K. Spanos, & B. J. Wallace (Eds.), *Hypnosis and imagination*. Amityville, NY: Baywood.

Courage, Mary L., & Howe, Mark L. (2002). From infant to child: The dynamics of cognitive change in the second year of life. *Psychological Bulletin, 128*, 250–277.

Courtney, Kelly E., & Polich, John (2009). Binge drinking in young adults: Data, definitions, and determinants. *Psychological Bulletin, 135*, 142–156.

Couzin, Jennifer (2009). Celebration and concern over U.S. trial of embryonic stem cells. *Science, 323*, 568.

Cowen, Emory L.; Wyman, Peter A.; Work, William C.; & Parker, Gayle R. (1990). The Rochester Child Resilience Project (RCRP): Overview and summary of first year findings. *Development and Psychopathology, 2*, 193–212.

Cowan, Nelson (2010). The magical mystery four: How is working memory capacity limited, and why? *Current Directions in Psychological Science, 19*, 51–57.

Cowan, Nelson, & Chen, Zhijian (2009). How chunks form in long-term memory and affect short-term memory limits. In A. S. Thorn & M. P. Page (Eds.), *Interactions between short-term and long-term memory in the verbal domain*. New York: Psychology Press.

Cowan, Nelson; Morey, Candice C.; Chen, Zhijian; et al. (2008). Theory and measurement of working memory capacity limits. In B. H. Ross (Ed.), *The psychology of learning and motivation*. San Diego: Elsevier.

Cox, Martha J., & Paley, Blair (2003). Understanding families as systems. *Current Directions in Psychological Science, 12*, 193–196.

Cox, W. Michael, and Alm, Richard (2005, February 28). Scientists are made, not born. *The New York Times*, op-ed page (online).

Coyne, James C.; Thombs, Brett D.; Stefanek, Michael; & Palmer, Steven C. (2009). Time to let go of the illusion that psychotherapy extends the survival of cancer patients. *Psychological Bulletin, 135*, 179–182.

Cozolino, Louis (2006). *The neuroscience of human relationships: Attachment and the developing social brain*. New York: Norton.

Craik, Fergus I. M., & Lockhart, Robert (1972). Levels of processing: A framework for memory research. *Journal of Verbal Learning and Verbal Behavior, 11*, 671–684.

Craik, Fergus I. M., & Tulving, Endel (1975). Depth of processing and the retention of words in episodic memory. *Journal of Experimental Psychology: General, 104*, 268–294.

Crair, Michael C.; Gillespie, Deda C.; & Stryker, Michael P. (1998). The role of visual experience in the development of columns in cat visual cortex. *Science, 279*, 566–570.

Cramer, Phebe (2000). Defense mechanisms in psychology today: Further processes for adaptation. *American Psychologist, 55*, 637–646.

Crews, Frederick (Ed.) (1998). *Unauthorized Freud: Doubters confront a legend*. New York: Viking.

Critchlow, Barbara (1986). The powers of John Barleycorn: Beliefs about the effects of alcohol on social behavior. *American Psychologist, 41*, 751–764.

Crits-Christoph, Paul; Wilson, G. Terence; & Hollon, Steven D. (2005). Empirically supported psychotherapies: Comment on Westen, Novotny, and Thompson-Brenner (2004). *Psychological Bulletin, 131,* 412–417.

Critser, Greg (2002). *Supersize.* New York: Houghton-Mifflin.

Crombag, Hans S., & Robinson, Terry E. (2004). Drugs, environment, brain, and behavior. *Current Directions in Psychological Science, 13,* 107–111.

Cronbach, Lee (1990). *Essentials of psychological testing* (5th ed.). New York: Harper & Row.

Cruz, Vitor Tedim; Nunes, Belina; Reis, Ana Mafalda; & Pereira, Jorge Resende (2005). Cortical remapping in amputees and dysmelic patients: A functional MRI study. *NeuroRehabilitation, 18,* 299–305.

Cumming, Geoff; Fidler, Fiona; Leonard, Martine; et al. (2007). Statistical reform in psychology: Is anything changing? *Psychological Science, 18,* 230–232.

Cummings, Brian J.; Uchida, Nobuko; Tamaki, Stanley J.; et al. (2005). Human neural stem cells differentiate and promote locomotor recovery in spinal cord–injured mice. *Proceedings of the National Academy of Science, 102,* 14069–14074.

Cummings, Nicholas A., & O'Donohue, William T. (2008). *Eleven blunders that cripple psychotherapy in America.* New York: Routledge/Taylor & Francis.

Cummings, Nicholas A., & Wiggins, Jack G. (2001). A collaborative primary care/behavioral health model for the use of psychotropic medication with children and adolescents. *Issues in Interdisciplinary Care, 3,* 121–128.

Currie, Janet; DellaVigna, Stefano; Moretti, Enrico; & Pathania, Vikram (2010). The effect of fast food restaurants on obesity and weight gain. *American Economic Journal: Economic Policy, 2,* 32–63.

Curtiss, Susan (1977). *Genie: A psycholinguistic study of a modern-day "wild child."* New York: Academic Press.

Curtiss, Susan (1982). Developmental dissociations of language and cognition. In L. Obler & D. Fein (Eds.), *Exceptional language and linguistics.* New York: Academic Press.

Cypess, A.M.; Lehman, S.; Williams, G.; et al. (2009, April 9). Identification and importance of brown adipose tissue in adult humans. *New England Journal of Medicine, 360,* 1509–1517.

Czeisler, Charles A.; Duffy, Jeanne F.; Shanahan, Theresa L.; et al. (1999). Stability, precision, and near-24-hour period of the human circadian pacemaker. *Science, 284,* 2177–2181.

Dadds, Mark R.; Bovbjerg, Dana H.; Redd, William H.; & Cutmore, Tim R. H. (1997). Imagery in human classical conditioning. *Psychological Bulletin, 122,* 89–103.

Daley, Tamara C.; Whaley, Shannon E.; Sigman, Marian D.; et al. (2003). IQ on the rise: The Flynn Effect in rural Kenyan children. *Psychological Science, 14,* 215–219.

Dalgleish, Tim (2004). Cognitive approaches to posttraumatic stress disorder: The evolution of multirepresentational theorizing. *Psychological Bulletin, 130,* 228–260.

Dalgliesh, Tim; Hauer, Beatrijs; & Kuyken, Willem (2008). The mental regulation of autobiographical recollection in the aftermath of trauma. *Current Directions in Psychological Science, 17,* 259–263.

Dalton, K. S.; Morris, D. L.; Delanoy, D. I.; et al. (1996). Security measures in an automated ganzfeld system. *Journal of Parapsychology, 60,* 129–147.

Daly, Martin, & Wilson, Margo (1983). *Sex, evolution, and behavior* (2nd ed.). Belmont, CA: Wadsworth.

Damasio, Antonio R. (1994). *Descartes' error: Emotion, reason, and the human brain.* New York: Grosset/Putnam.

Damasio, Antonio R. (2003). *Looking for Spinoza: Joy, sorrow, and the feeling brain.* San Diego: Harcourt.

Damasio, A. R.; Grabowski, T. J.; Bechara, A.; et al. (2000). Subcortical and cortical brain activity during the feeling of self-generated emotions. *Nature Neuroscience, 3,* 1049–1056.

Damasio, Hanna; Grabowski, Thomas J.; Frank, Randall; et al. (1994). The return of Phineas Gage: Clues about the brain from the skull of a famous patient. *Science, 264,* 1102–1105.

Damon, William (1995). *Greater expectations.* New York: Free Press.

Danker, Jared F., & Anderson, John R. (2010). The ghosts of brain states past: Remembering reactivates the brain regions engaged during encoding. *Psychological Bulletin, 136,* 87–102.

Danner, Deborah D.; Snowdon, David A.; & Friesen, Wallace V. (2001). Positive emotions in early life and longevity: Findings from the nun study. *Journal of Personality and Social Psychology, 80,* 804–813.

D'Antonio, Michael (2004, May 2). How we think. *Los Angeles Times Magazine,* 18–20, 30–32.

Darley, John M. (1995). Constructive and destructive obedience: A taxonomy of principal agent relationships. In A. G. Miller, B. E. Collins, & D. E. Brief (Eds.), Perspectives on obedience to authority: The legacy of the Milgram experiments. *Journal of Social Issues, 51*(3), 125–154.

Darley, John M., & Latane, Bibb (1968). Bystander intervention in emergencies: Diffusion of responsibility. *Journal of Personality and Social Psychology, 8,* 377–383.

Darwin, Charles (1874). *The descent of man and selection in relation to sex* (2nd ed.). New York: Hurst.

Daum, Irene, & Schugens, Markus M. (1996). On the cerebellum and classical conditioning. *Psychological Science, 5,* 58–61.

Davidson, Richard J.; Abercrombie, H.; Nitschke, J. B.; & Putnam, K. (1999). Regional brain function, emotion, and disorders of emotion. *Current Opinion in Neurobiology, 9,* 228–234.

Davidson, Richard J.; Kabat-Zinn, J.; Schumacher, J.; et al. (2003). Alterations in brain and immune function produced by mindfulness meditation. *Psychosomatic Medicine, 65,* 564–570.

Davis, Christopher G.; Nolen-Hoeksema, Susan; & Larson, Judith (1998). Making sense of loss and benefiting from the experience: Two construals of meaning. *Journal of Personality and Social Psychology, 75,* 561–574.

Davis, Deborah (2010). Lies, *damned* lies, and the path from police interrogation to wrongful conviction. In M. H. Gonzales, C. Tavris, & J. Aronson (Eds.), *The scientist and the humanist: A festschrift in honor of Elliot Aronson.* New York: Psychology Press.

Davis, Michael; Myers, Karyn M.; Ressler, Kerry J.; & Rothbaum, Barbara O. (2005). Facilitation of extinction of conditioning fear by D-cycloserine. *Current Directions in Psychological Science, 14,* 214–219.

Davison, Gerald C. (1976). Homosexuality: The ethical challenge. *Journal of Consulting and Clinical Psychology, 44,* 157–162.

Dawes, Robyn M. (1994). *House of cards: Psychology and psychotherapy built on myth.* New York: Free Press.

Dawson, Neal V.; Arkes, Hal R.; Siciliano, C.; et al. (1988). Hindsight bias: An impediment to accurate probability estimation in clinicopathologic conferences. *Medical Decision Making, 8*(4), 259–264.

Dean, Geoffrey (1992). The bottom line: Effect size. In B. Beyerstein & D. Beyerstein (Eds.), *The write stuff: Evaluations of graphology-The study of handwriting analysis.* Buffalo, NY: Prometheus Books.

de Araujo, Ivan E.; Oliveira-Maia, A.J.; Sotnikova, T.D.; et al. (2008, March 27). Food reward in the absence of taste receptor signaling. *Neuron, 57,* 930–941.

Deci, Edward L.; Koestner, Richard; & Ryan, Richard M. (1999). A meta-analytic review of experiments examining the effects of extrinsic rewards on intrinsic motivation. *Psychological Bulletin, 125,* 627–668.

Deci, Edward L., & Ryan, Richard M. (1985). *Intrinsic motivation and self-determination of human behavior.* New York: Plenum.

Deffenbacher, Jerry L.; Deffenbacher, David M.; Lynch, Rebekah S.; & Richards, Tracy L. (2003). Anger, aggression and risky behavior: A comparison of high and low anger drivers. *Behaviour Research and Therapy, 41,* 701–718.

De Houwer, Jan; Teige-Mocigemba, Sarah; Spruyt, Adriaan; & Moors, Agnes (2009). Implicit measures: A normative analysis and review. *Psychological Bulletin, 135,* 347–368.

Dement, William (1978). *Some must watch while some must sleep.* New York: Norton.

Dement, William (1992). *The sleepwatchers.* Stanford, CA: Stanford Alumni Association.

Dennett, Daniel C. (1991). *Consciousness explained.* Boston: Little, Brown.

Denning, Patt; Little, Jeannie; & Glickman, Adina (2004). *Over the influence: The harm reduction guide for managing drugs and alcohol.* New York: Guilford.

Denny, Dallas (Ed.) (1998). *Current concepts in transgender identity.* New York: Garland Press.

Denson, Thomas F.; Spanovic, Marija; & Miller, Norman (2009). Cognitive appraisals and emotions predict cortisol and immune responses: A meta-analysis of acute laboratory social stressors and emotion inductions. *Psychological Bulletin, 135*, 823–853.

DePaulo, Bella M. (1992). Nonverbal behavior and self-presentation. *Psychological Bulletin, 111*, 203–243.

de Rivera, Joseph (1989). Comparing experiences across cultures: Shame and guilt in America and Japan. *Hiroshima Forum for Psychology, 14*, 13–20.

Desbonnet, L.; Waddington, J. L.; & O'Tuathaigh, C.M. (2009). Mutant models for genes associated with schizophrenia. *Biochemical Society Transactions, 37*(Pt 1), 308–312.

DeValois, Russell L., & DeValois, Karen K. (1975). Neural coding of color. In E. C. Carterette & M. P. Friedman (Eds.), *Handbook of perception* (Vol. 5). New York: Academic Press.

Devlin, B.; Daniels, Michael; & Roeder, Kathryn (1997). The heritability of IQ. *Nature, 388*, 468–471.

de Waal, Frans (2001a). *The ape and the sushi master: Cultural reflections by a primatologist.* New York: Basic Books.

Diamond, Adele, & Amso, Dima (2008). Contributions of neuroscience to our understanding of cognitive development. *Current Directions in Psychological Science, 17*, 136–141.

Diamond, Lisa M. (2004). Emerging perspectives on distinctions between romantic love and sexual desire. *Current Directions in Psychological Science, 13*, 116–119.

Diamond, Lisa (2008). *Sexual fluidity: Understanding women's love and desire.* Cambridge, MA: Harvard University Press.

Diamond, Marian C. (1993, Winter–Spring). An optimistic view of the aging brain. *Generations, 17*, 31–33.

Diamond, M., & Sigmundson, H. K. (1997). Sex reassignment at birth: Long-term review and clinical implications. *Archives of Pediatrics and Adolescent Medicine, 151*, 298–304.

Dick, Danielle M. (2007). Identification of genes influencing a spectrum of externalizing psychopathology. *Current Directions in Psychological Science, 16*, 331–335.

Dick, Danielle M.; Aliev, Fazil; Wang, Jen C.; et al. (2008). A systematic single nucleotide polymorphism screen to fine-map alcohol dependence genes on chromosome 7 identifies association with a novel susceptibility gene ACN9. *Biological Psychiatry, 63*, 1047–1053.

Dickerson, Sally S., & Kemeny, Margaret E. (2004). Acute stressors and cortisol responses: A theoretical integration and synthesis of laboratory research. *Psychological Bulletin, 130*, 355–391.

Dien, Dora S. (1999). Chinese authority-directed orientation and Japanese peer-group orientation: Questioning the notion of collectivism. *Review of General Psychology, 3*, 372–385.

DiFranza, Joseph R. (2008, May). Hooked from the first cigarette. *Scientific American*, 82–87.

Digman, John M., & Shmelyov, Alexander G. (1996). The structure of temperament and personality in Russian children. *Journal of Personality and Social Psychology, 71*, 341–351.

Dijk, Corine; de Jong, Peter J.; & Peters, Madelon L. (2009). The remedial value of blushing in the context of transgressions and mishaps. *Emotion, 9*, 287–291.

Dimberg, Ulf; Thunberg, Monika; & Elmehed, Kurt (2000). Unconscious facial reactions to emotional facial expressions. *Psychological Science, 11*, 86–89.

Dimidjian, Sona, & Hollon, Steven D. (2010). How would we know if psychotherapy were harmful? *American Psychologist, 65*, 21–33.

Dinero, Rachel E.; Conger, Rand D.; Shaver, Phillip R.; et al. (2008). Influence of family of origin and adult romantic partners on romantic attachment security. *Journal of Family Psychology, 22*, 622–632.

Dinges, David F.; Whitehouse, Wayne G.; Orne, Emily C.; Powell, John W.; Orne, Martin T.; & Erdelyi, Matthew H. (1992). Evaluating hypnotic memory enhancement (hypermnesia and reminiscence) using multitrial forced recall. *Journal of Experimental Psychology: Learning, Memory, and Cognition, 18*, 1139–1147.

Dinn, W. M., & Harris, C. L. (2000). Neurocognitive function in antisocial personality disorder. *Psychiatry Research, 97*, 173–190.

Dion, Kenneth L., & Dion, Karen K. (1993). Gender and ethnocultural comparisons in styles of love. *Psychology of Women Quarterly, 17*, 463–474.

Doering, Stephan; Katzlberger, Florian; Rumpold, Gerhard; et al. (2000). Videotape preparation of patients before hip replacement surgery reduces stress. *Psychosomatic Medicine, 62*, 365–373.

Dolnick, Edward (1990, July). What dreams are (really) made of. *The Atlantic Monthly, 226*, 41–45, 48–53, 56–58, 60–61.

Domhoff, G. William (1996). *Finding meaning in dreams: A quantitative approach.* New York: Plenum.

Domhoff, G. William (2003). *The scientific study of dreams: Neural networks, cognitive development, and content analysis.* Washington, DC: American Psychological Association.

Dominguez, Maria de Gracia; Viechtbauer, Wolfgang; Simons, Claudia J. P.; et al. (2009). Are psychotic psychopathology and neurocognition orthogonal? A systematic review of their associations. *Psychological Bulletin, 135*, 157–171.

Donlea, Jeffrey M.; Ramanan, Narendrakumar; & Shaw, Paul J. (2009). Use-dependent plasticity in clock neurons regulates sleep need in *Drosophila*. *Science, 324*, 105–108.

Dovidio, John F. (2009, December 18). Racial bias, unspoken but heard. *Science, 326*, 1641–1642.

Dovidio, John F., & Gaertner, Samuel L. (2008). New directions in aversive racism research: Persistence and pervasiveness. In C. Willis-Esqueda (Ed.), *Motivational aspects of prejudice and racism.* Nebraska Symposium on Motivation. New York: Springer Science + Business Media.

Dovidio, John F.; Gaertner, Samuel L.; & Validzic, Ana (1998). Intergroup bias: Status, differentiation, and a common in-group identity. *Journal of Personality and Social Psychology, 75*, 109–120.

Drevets, W. C. (2000). Neuroimaging studies of mood disorders. *Biological Psychiatry, 48*, 813–829.

Duckworth, Angela L., & Seligman, Martin E. P. (2005). Self-discipline outdoes IQ in predicting academic performance of adolescents. *Psychological Science, 16*, 939–944.

Dumit, Joseph (2004). *Picturing personhood: Brain scans and biomedical identity.* Princeton, NJ: Princeton University Press.

Dunbar, R. I. M. (2004). Gossip in evolutionary perspective. *Review of General Psychology, 8*, 100–110.

Duncan, Paula D.; Ritter, Philip L.; Dornbusch, Sanford M.; et al. (1985). The effects of pubertal timing on body image, school behavior, and deviance. *Journal of Youth and Adolescence, 14*, 227–235.

Dunkel, Curtis S., & Sefcek, Jon A. (2009). Eriksonian lifespan theory and life history theory: An integration using the example of identity formation. *Review of General Psychology, 13*, 13–23.

Dunlosky, John, & Lipko, Amanda R. (2007). Metacomprehension: A brief history and how to improve its accuracy. *Current Directions in Psychological Science, 16*, 228–232.

Dunn, Elizabeth W.; Wilson, Timothy D.; & Gilbert, Daniel T. (2003). Location, location, location: The misprediction of satisfaction in housing lotteries. *Personality and Social Psychology Bulletin, 29*, 1421–1432.

Dunning, David (2005). *Self-insight: Roadblocks and detours on the path to knowing thyself.* New York: Psychology Press.

Dunning, David; Heath, Chip; & Suls, Jerry M. (2004). Flawed self-assessment: Implications for health, education, and the workplace. *Psychological Science in the Public Interest, 5*, 69–106.

Dunning, David; Johnson, Kerri; Ehrlinger, Joyce; & Kruger, Justin (2003). Why people fail to recognize their own incompetence. *Current Directions in Psychological Science, 12*, 83–87.

Duranceaux, Nicole C. E.; Schuckit, Marc A.; Luczak, Susan E.; et al. (2008). Ethnic differences in level of response to alcohol between Chinese Americans and Korean Americans. *Journal of Studies on Alcohol and Drugs, 69*, 227–234.

Dweck, Carol S. (2006). *Mindset: The new psychology of success.* New York: Random House.

Dweck, Carol S. (2008). Can personality be changed? *Current Directions in Psychological Science, 17*, 391–394.

Dweck, Carol S., & Grant, Heidi (2008). Self-theories, goals, and meaning. In J. Y. Shah & W. L. Gardner (Eds.), *Handbook of motivation science.* New York: Guilford.

Dweck, Carol S., & Sorich, Lisa A. (1999). Mastery-oriented thinking. In C. R. Snyder (Ed.), *Coping: The psychology of what works*. New York: Oxford University Press.

Eagly, Alice H., & Wood, Wendy (1999). The origins of sex differences in human behavior: Evolved dispositions versus social roles. *American Psychologist, 54*, 408–423.

Earl-Novell, Sarah L., & Jessup, Donna C. (2005). The relationship between perceptions of premenstrual syndrome and degree performance. *Assessment & Evaluation in Higher Education, 30*, 343–352.

Eaton, Danice; Kann, Laura; Kinchen, Steve; et al. (2008, June 6). Youth Risk Behavior Surveillance—United States, 2007. Centers for Disease Control, 57(SS04);1–131. http://www.cdc.gov/mmwr/preview/mmwrhtml/ss5704a1.htm?s_cid=ss5704a1_e

Ebbinghaus, Hermann M. (1885/1913). *Memory: A contribution to experimental psychology* (H. A. Ruger & C. E. Bussenius, Trans.). New York: Teachers College Press, Columbia University.

Edwards, Kari, & Smith, Edward E. (1996). A disconfirmation bias in the evaluation of arguments. *Journal of Personality and Social Psychology, 71*, 5–24.

Edwards, Robert R.; Campbell, Claudia; Jamison, Robert N.; & Wiech, Katja (2009). The neurobiological underpinnings of coping with pain. *Current Directions in Psychological Science, 18*, 237–241.

Ehrenreich, Barbara (1978). *For her own good: 150 years of the experts' advice to women*. New York: Doubleday.

Ehrenreich, Barbara (2001, June 4). What are they probing for? [Essay.] *Time*, 86.

Ehrensaft, Miriam K.; Moffitt, Terrie E.; & Caspi, Avshalom (2006). Is domestic violence followed by an increased risk of psychiatric disorders among women but not among men? A longitudinal cohort study. *American Journal of Psychiatry, 163*, 885–892.

Eich, E., & Hyman, R. (1992). Subliminal self-help. In D. Druckman & R. A. Bjork (Eds.), *In the mind's eye: Enhancing human performance*. Washington, DC: National Academy Press.

Eigsti, Inge-Marie; Zayas, Vivian; Mischel, Walter; Shoda, Yuichi; et al. (2006). Predicting cognitive control from preschool to late adolescence and young adulthood. *Psychological Science, 17*, 478–484.

Ein-Dor, Tsachi; Mikulincer, Mario; Doron, Guy; & Shaver, Phillip R. (2010). The attachment paradox: How can so many of us (the insecure ones) have no adaptive advantages? *Perspectives on Psychological Science, 5*, 123–141.

Ekman, Paul (2003). *Emotions revealed*. New York: Times Books.

Ekman, Paul; Friesen, Wallace V.; & O'Sullivan, Maureen (1988). Smiles when lying. *Journal of Personality and Social Psychology, 54*, 414–420.

Ekman, Paul; Friesen, Wallace V.; O'Sullivan, Maureen; et al. (1987). Universals and cultural differences in the judgments of facial expression of emotion. *Journal of Personality and Social Psychology, 53*, 712–717.

Elfenbein, Hillary A., & Ambady, Nalini (2003). When familiarity breeds accuracy: Cultural exposure and facial emotion recognition. *Journal of Personality and Social Psychology, 85*, 276–290.

Elliot, Andrew J., & McGregor, Holly A. (2001). A 2 X 2 achievement goal framework. *Journal of Personality and Social Psychology, 80*, 501–519.

Ellis, Albert (1993). Changing rational-emotive therapy (RET) to rational emotive behavior therapy (REBT). *Behavior Therapist, 16*, 257–258.

Ellis, Albert, & Blau, S. (1998). Rational emotive behavior therapy. *Directions in Clinical and Counseling Psychology, 8*, 41–56.

Elmquist, Joel K., & Flier, Jeffrey S. (2004, April 2). The fat-brain axis enters a new dimension. *Science, 304*, 63–64.

Else-Quest, Nicole M.; Hyde, Janet S.; Goldsmith, H. Hill; & Can Hulle, Carol A. (2006). Gender differences in temperament: A meta-analysis. *Psychological Bulletin, 132*, 33–72.

Else-Quest, Nicole M.; Hyde, Janet S.; & Linn, Marcia C. (2010). Cross-national patterns of gender differences in mathematics: A meta-analysis. *Psychological Bulletin, 136*, 103–127.

Emery, Robert E., & Laumann-Billings, Lisa (1998). An overview of the nature, causes, and consequences of abusive family relationships. *American Psychologist, 53*, 121–135.

Emery, Robert E.; Otto, Randy K.; & O'Donohue, William T. (2005). A critical assessment of child custody evaluations: Limited science and a flawed system. *Psychological Science in the Public Interest, 6*, 1–29.

Emmons, Robert A., & King, Laura A. (1988). Conflict among personal strivings: Immediate and long-term implications for psychological and physical well-being. *Journal of Personality and Social Psychology, 54*, 1040–1048.

Emmons, Robert A., & McCullough, Michael E. (2003). Counting blessings versus burdens: An experimental investigation of gratitude and subjective well-being in daily life. *Journal of Personality and Social Psychology, 84*, 377–389.

Englander-Golden, Paula; Whitmore, Mary R.; & Dienstbier, Richard A. (1978). Menstrual cycle as focus of study and self-reports of moods and behavior. *Motivation and Emotion, 2*, 75–86.

Engle, Randall W. (2002). Working memory capacity as executive attention. *Current Directions in Psychological Science, 11*, 19–23.

Epel, Elissa S. (2009). Telomeres in a life-span perspective: A new "psychobiomarker"? *Current Directions in Psychological Science, 18*, 6–10.

Epel, E. S.; Blackburn, E. H.; Lin, J.; et al. (2004, December 7). Accelerated telomere shortening in response to life stress. *Proceedings of the National Academy of Science, 101*, 17312–17315.

Erceg-Hurn, David M., & Miosevich, Vikki M. (2008). Modern robust statistical methods. *American Psychologist, 63*, 591–601.

Erikson, Erik H. (1950/1963). *Childhood and society* (2nd ed.). New York: Norton.

Erikson, Erik H. (1982). *The life cycle completed*. New York: Norton.

Ervin-Tripp, Susan (1964). Imitation and structural change in children's language. In E. H. Lenneberg (Ed.), *New directions in the study of language*. Cambridge, MA: MIT Press.

Escera, Carles; Cilveti, Robert; & Grau, Carles (1992). Ultradian rhythms in cognitive operations: Evidence from the P300 component of the event-related potentials. *Medical Science Research, 20*, 137–138.

Evans, Christopher (1984). *Landscapes of the night* (edited and completed by Peter Evans). New York: Viking.

Evans, Gary W., & Kim, Pilyoung (2007). Childhood poverty and health. *Psychological Science, 18*, 953–957.

Evans, Gary W.; Lepore, Stephen J.; & Allen, Karen Mata (2000). Cross-cultural differences in tolerance for crowding: Fact or fiction? *Journal of Personality and Social Psychology, 79*, 204–210.

Evans, Gary W., & Schamberg, Michelle A. (2009, March 30). Childhood poverty, chronic stress, and adult working memory. *Proceedings of the National Academy of Sciences, 106*.

Ewart, Craig K. (1995). Self-efficacy and recovery from heart attack. In J. E. Maddux (Ed.), *Self-efficacy, adaptation, and adjustment: Theory, research, and application*. New York: Plenum.

Ewart, Craig K., & Kolodner, Kenneth B. (1994). Negative affect, gender, and expressive style predict elevated ambulatory blood pressure in adolescents. *Journal of Personality and Social Psychology, 66*, 596–605.

Eyferth, Klaus (1961). [The performance of different groups of the children of occupation forces on the Hamburg-Wechsler Intelligence Test for Children.] *Archiv für die Gesamte Psychologie, 113*, 222–241.

Fagan, Joseph F., III (1992). Intelligence: A theoretical viewpoint. *Current Directions in Psychological Science, 1*, 82–86.

Fagot, Beverly I. (1993, June). Gender role development in early childhood: Environmental input, internal construction. Invited address presented at the annual meeting of the International Academy of Sex Research, Monterey, CA.

Fagot, Beverly I., & Leinbach, Mary D. (1993). Gender-role development in young children: From discrimination to labeling. *Developmental Review, 13*, 205–224.

Fairholme, C. P.; Boisseau, C. L.; Ellard, K. K.; et al. (2009). Emotions, emotion regulation, and psychological treatment: A unified perspective. In A. M. Kring & D. M. Sloan (Eds.), *Emotion regulation and psychopathology*. New York: Guilford.

Fallon, James H.; Keator, David B.; Mbogori, James; et al. (2004). Hostility differentiates the brain metabolic effects of nicotine. *Cognitive Brain Research, 18*, 142–148.

Fallone, Gahan; Acebo, Christine; Seifer, Ronald; & Carskadon, Mary A. (2005). Experimental restriction of sleep opportunity in children: Effects on teacher ratings. *Sleep, 28,* 1280–1286.

Farooqi, Sadaf; Bullmore, Edward; Keogh, Julia; et al. (2007, Sept. 7). Leptin regulates striatal regions and human eating behavior. *Science, 317,* 1355–1355.

Farooqi, I. Sadaf, & O'Rahilly, Stephen (2004). Monogenic human obesity syndromes. *Recent Progress in Hormone Research, 59,* 409–424.

Fausto-Sterling, Anne (1997). Beyond difference: A biologist's perspective. *Journal of Social Issues, 53,* 233–258.

Feather, N. T. (1966). Effects of prior success and failure on expectations of success and subsequent performance. *Journal of Personality and Social Psychology, 3,* 287–298.

Feeney, Brooke C., & Cassidy, Jude (2003). Reconstructive memory related to adolescent-parent conflict interactions. *Journal of Personality and Social Psychology, 85,* 945–955.

Fehr, Beverley; Baldwin, Mark; Collins, Lois; et al. (1999). Anger in close relationships: An interpersonal script analysis. *Personality and Social Psychology Bulletin, 25,* 299–312.

Fehr, Ernest & Fischbacher, Urs (2003). The nature of human altruism. *Nature, 425,* 785–791.

Fein, Steven, & Spencer, Steven J. (1997). Prejudice as self-image maintenance: Affirming the self through derogating others. *Journal of Personality and Social Psychology, 73,* 31–44.

Feinberg, Andrew P. (2008). Epigenetics at the epicenter of modern medicine. *Journal of the American Medical Association, 299,* 1345–1350.

Feng, Q.; Lu, S. J.; Klimanskaya, I.; et al. (2010, April 28). Hemangioblastic derivatives from human induced pluripotent stem cells exhibit limited expansion and early senescence. *Stem Cells, 28,* 704–712.

Ferguson, Christopher J. (2007). The good, the bad and the ugly: A meta-analytic review of positive and negative effects of violent video games. *Psychiatric Quarterly, 78,* 309–316.

Ferguson, Christopher (2009). Media violence effects: Confirmed truth or just another X-file? *Journal of Forensic Psychology Practice, 9,* 103–126.

Ferguson, Christopher J., & Kilburn, John (2010). Much ado about nothing: The misestimation and overinterpretation of violent video game effects in Eastern and Western nations. *Psychological Bulletin, 136,* 174–178.

Fernald, Anne, & Mazzie, Claudia (1991). Prosody and focus in speech to infants and adults. *Developmental Psychology, 27,* 209–221.

Fernea, Elizabeth, & Fernea, Robert (1994). Cleanliness and culture. In W. J. Lonner & Malpass (Eds.), *Psychology and culture.* Boston: Allyn & Bacon.

Ferrari, Pier Francesco; Rozzi, Stefano; & Fogassi, Leonardo (2005). Mirror neurons responding to observation of actions made with tools in monkey ventral premotor cortex. *Journal of Cognitive Neuroscience, 17,* 212–226.

Feshbach, Seymour, & Tangney, June (2008). Television viewing and aggression: Some alternative perspectives. *Perspectives on Psychological Science, 3,* 387–389.

Festinger, Leon (1957). *A theory of cognitive dissonance.* Evanston, IL: Row, Peterson.

Festinger, Leon; Pepitone, Albert; & Newcomb, Theodore (1952). Some consequences of deindividuation in a group. *Journal of Abnormal and Social Psychology, 47,* 382–389.

Festinger, Leon; Riecken, Henry W.; & Schachter, Stanley (1956). *When prophecy fails.* Minneapolis: University of Minnesota Press.

Fiedler, K.; Nickel, S.; Muehlfriedel, T.; & Unkelbach, C. (2001). Is mood congruency an effect of genuine memory or response bias? *Journal of Experimental Social Psychology, 37,* 201–214.

Field, Tiffany (2009). The effects of newborn massage: United States. In T. Field et al. (Eds.), *The newborn as a person: Enabling healthy infant development worldwide.* Hoboken, NJ: John Wiley & Sons.

Fields, R. Douglas (2004, April). The other half of the brain. *Scientific American,* 54–61.

Fine, Ione; Wade, A. R.; Brewer, A. A.; et al. (2003). Long-term deprivation affects visual perception and cortex. *Nature Neuroscience, 6,* 915–916.

Fischer, Pamela C.; Smith, Randy J.; Leonard, Elizabeth; et al. (1993). Sex differences on affective dimensions: Continuing examination. *Journal of Counseling and Development, 71,* 440–443.

Fischhoff, Baruch (1975). Hindsight is not equal to foresight: The effect of outcome knowledge on judgment under uncertainty. *Journal of Experimental Psychology: Human Perception and Performance, 1,* 288–299.

Fivush, Robyn, & Hamond, Nina R. (1991). Autobiographical memory across the school years: Toward reconceptualizing childhood amnesia. In R. Flacks & S. L. Thomas (1998, November 27). Among affluent students, a culture of disengagement. *Chronicle of Higher Education,* p. A48.

Fivush, Robyn, & Nelson, Katherine (2004). Culture and language in the emergence of autobiographical memory. *Psychological Science, 15,* 573–582.

Flacks, Richard, & Thomas, Scott L. (1998, November 27). Among affluent students, a culture of disengagement. *Chronicle of Higher Education,* p. A48.

Flavell, John H. (1999). Cognitive development: Children's knowledge about the mind. *Annual Review of Psychology, 50,* 21–45.

Fleeson, William (2004). Moving personality beyond the person-situation debate. *Current Directions in Psychological Science, 13,* 83–87.

Flynn, James R. (1987). Massive IQ gains in 14 nations: What IQ tests really measure. *Psychological Bulletin, 95,* 29–51.

Flynn, James R. (1999). Searching for justice: The discovery of IQ gains over time. *American Psychologist, 54,* 5–20.

Fogassi, Leonardo, & Ferrari, Pier Francesco (2007). Mirror neurons and the evolution of embodied language. *Current Directions in Psychological Science, 16,* 136–141.

Folkman, Susan, & Moskowitz, Judith T. (2000). Positive affect and the other side of coping. *American Psychologist, 55,* 647–654.

Forbes, Gordon; Zhang, Xiaoying; Doroszewicz, Krystyna; & Haas, Kelly (2009). Relationships between individualism-collectivism, gender, and direct or indirect aggression: A study in China, Poland, and the US. *Aggressive Behavior, 35,* 24–30.

Forgas, Joseph P. (1998). On being happy and mistaken: Mood effects on the fundamental attribution error. *Journal of Personality and Social Psychology, 75,* 318–331.

Forgas, Joseph P., & Bond, Michael H. (1985). Cultural influences on the perception of interaction episodes. *Personality and Social Psychology Bulletin, 11,* 75–88.

Foulkes, D. (1962). Dream reports from different states of sleep. *Journal of Abnormal and Social Psychology, 65,* 14–25.

Foulkes, David (1999). *Children's dreaming and the development of consciousness.* Cambridge, MA: Harvard University Press.

Fouts, Roger S. (with Stephen T. Mills) (1997). *Next of kin: What chimpanzees have taught me about who we are.* New York: Morrow.

Fouts, Roger S., & Rigby, Randall L. (1977). Man–chimpanzee communication. In T. A. Seboek (Ed.), *How animals communicate.* Bloomington: University of Indiana Press.

Fowler, James H., & Christakis, Nicholas A. (2008, December 4). Dynamic spread of happiness in a large social network: Longitudinal analysis over 20 years in the Framingham Heart Study. *BMJ, 337,* a2338.

Fowles, Don C., & Dindo, Lilian (2009). Temperament and psychopathy: A dual-pathway model *Current Directions in Psychological Science, 18,* 179–183.

Fox, Mary Kay; Pac, Susan; Devaney, Barbara; & Jankowski, Linda (2004). Feeding infants and toddlers study: What foods are infants and toddlers eating? *Journal of the American Dietetic Association, 104,* 22–30.

Fox, Nathan A.; Henderson, Heather A.; Marshall, Peter J.; et al. (2005a). Behavioral inhibition: Linking biology and behavior within a developmental framework. *Annual Review of Psychology, 56,* 235–262.

Fox, Nathan A.; Nichols, Kate E.; Henderson, Heather A.; et al. (2005b). Evidence for a gene–environment interaction in predicting behavioral inhibition in middle childhood. *Psychological Science, 16,* 921–926.

Frankl, Victor E. (1955). *The doctor and the soul: An introduction to logotherapy.* New York: Knopf.

Frans, Emma M.; Sandin, Sven; Reichenberg, Abraham; et al. (2008). Advancing paternal age and bipolar disorder. *Archives of General Psychiatry, 65,* 1034–1040.

Frasure-Smith, Nancy, & Lespérance, Francois (2005). Depression and coronary heart disease: Complex synergism of mind, body, and environment. *Current Directions in Psychological Science, 14,* 39–43.

Frasure-Smith, Nancy; Lesperance, F.; Juneau, M.; Talajic, M.; & Bourassa, M. G. (1999). Gender, depression, and one-year prognosis after myocardial infarction. *Psychosomatic Medicine, 61,* 26–37.

Frayling, Timothy M.; Timpson, Nicholas J.; Weedon, Michael N.; et al. (2007, May 11). A common variant in the *FTO* gene is associated with body mass index and predisposes to childhood and adult obesity. *Science, 316,* 889–894.

Frazier, Patricia A. (2003). Perceived control and distress following sexual assault: A longitudinal test of a new model. *Journal of Personality and Social Psychology, 84,* 1257–1269.

Fredrickson, Barbara L., & Losada, Marcial F. (2005). Positive affect and the complex dynamics of human flourishing. *American Psychologist, 60,* 678–686.

Fredrickson, Barbara L.; Tugade, Michele M.; Waugh, Christian E.; & Larkin, Gregory R. (2003). What good are positive emotions in crises? *Journal of Personality and Social Psychology, 84,* 365–376.

Frensch, Peter A., & Rünger, Dennis (2003). Implicit learning. *Current Directions in Psychological Science, 12,* 13–18.

Freud, Anna (1967). *Ego and the mechanisms of defense* (The writings of Anna Freud, Vol. 2) (rev. ed.). New York: International Universities Press.

Freud, Sigmund (1900/1953). The interpretation of dreams. In J. Strachey (Ed.), *The standard edition of the complete psychological works of Sigmund Freud* (Vols. 4 and 5). London: Hogarth Press.

Freud, Sigmund (1905). Three essays on the theory of sexuality. In J. Strachey (Ed.), *Standard edition* (Vol. 7).

Freud, Sigmund (1920/1960). *A general introduction to psychoanalysis* (Joan Riviere, Trans.). New York: Washington Square Press.

Freud, Sigmund (1923/1962). *The ego and the id* (Joan Riviere, Trans.). New York: Norton.

Freud, Sigmund (1961). *Letters of Sigmund Freud, 1873–1939.* Edited by Ernst L. Freud. London: Hogarth Press.

Fridlund, Alan J. (1994). *Human facial expression: An evolutionary view.* San Diego: Academic Press.

Friedrich, William; Fisher, Jennifer; Broughton, Daniel; et al. (1998). Normative sexual behavior in children: A contemporary sample. *Pediatrics, 101,* 1–8. See also www.pediatrics.org/cgi/content/full/101/4/e9.

Frome, Pamela M., & Eccles, Jacquelynne S. (1998). Parents' influence on children's achievement-related perceptions. *Journal of Personality and Social Psychology, 74,* 435–452.

Frye, Richard E.; Schwartz, B. S.; & Doty, Richard L. (1990). Dose-related effects of cigarette smoking on olfactory function. *Journal of the American Medical Association, 263,* 1233–1236.

Fuchs, C. S.; Stampfer, M. J.; Colditz, G. A.; et al. (1995, May 11). Alcohol consumption and mortality among women. *New England Journal of Medicine, 332,* 1245–1250.

Gable, Shelly L., & Haidt, Jonathan (2005). What (and why) is positive psychology? *Review of General Psychology, 9,* 103–110.

Gable, Shelly L., & Poore, Joshua (2008). Which thoughts count? Algorithms for evaluating satisfaction in relationships. *Psychological Science, 19,* 1030–1036.

Gaertner, Samuel L.; Mann, Jeffrey A.; Dovidio, John F.; et al. (1990). How does cooperation reduce intergroup bias? *Journal of Personality and Social Psychology, 59,* 692–704.

Gagnon, John, & Simon, William (1973). *Sexual conduct: The social sources of human sexuality.* Chicago: Aldine.

Galanter, Eugene (1962). Contemporary psychophysics. In R. Brown, E. Galanter, H. Hess, & G. Mandler (Eds.), *New directions in psychology.* New York: Holt, Rinehart and Winston.

Gallant, Sheryle J.; Hamilton, Jean A.; Popiel, Debra A.; et al. (1991). Daily moods and symptoms: Effects of awareness of study focus, gender, menstrual-cycle phase, and day of the week. *Health Psychology, 10,* 180–189.

Gallo, Linda C., & Matthews, Karen A. (2003). Understanding the association between socioeconomic status and physical health: Do negative emotions play a role? *Psychological Bulletin, 129,* 10–51.

Galotti, Kathleen (1989). Approaches to studying formal and everyday reasoning. *Psychological Bulletin, 105,* 331–351.

Garbarino, James, & Bedard, Claire (2001). *Parents under siege.* New York: The Free Press.

Garcia, John, & Gustavson, Carl R. (1997, January). Carl R. Gustavson (1946–1996): Pioneering wildlife psychologist. *APS Observer,* 34–35.

Garcia, John, & Koelling, Robert A. (1966). Relation of cue to consequence in avoidance learning. *Psychonomic Science, 4,* 23–124.

Gardner, Howard (1983). *Frames of mind: The theory of multiple intelligences.* New York: Basic Books.

Gardner, R. Allen, & Gardner, Beatrice T. (1969). Teaching sign language to a chimpanzee. *Science, 165,* 664–672.

Garmezy, Norman (1991). Resilience and vulnerability to adverse developmental outcomes associated with poverty. *American Behavioral Scientist, 34,* 416–430.

Garry, Maryanne; Manning, Charles G.; & Loftus, Elizabeth F. (1996). Imagination inflation: Imagining a childhood event inflates confidence that it occurred. *Psychonomic Bulletin & Review, 3,* 208–214.

Garry, Maryanne, & Polaschek, Devon L. L. (2000). Imagination and memory. *Current Directions in Psychological Science, 9,* 6–10.

Garven, Sena; Wood, James M.; Malpass, Roy S.; & Shaw, John S., III (1998). More than suggestion: The effect of interviewing techniques from the McMartin Preschool case. *Journal of Applied Psychology, 83,* 347–359.

Gatz, Margaret (2007). Genetics, dementia, and the elderly. *Current Directions in Psychological Science, 16,* 123–127.

Gauthier, Irene; Skudlarksi, P.; Gore, J. C.; & Anderson, A. W. (2000). Expertise for cars and birds recruits brain areas involved in face recognition. *Nature Neuroscience, 3,* 191–197.

Gauthier, Irene; Tarr, M. J.; Anderson, A. W.; et al. (1999). Activation of the middle fusiform "face area" increases with expertise in recognizing novel objects. *Nature Neuroscience, 2,* 568–573.

Gawande, Atul (2009, March 30). Hellhole. *The New Yorker,* 36–45.

Gazzaniga, Michael S. (1967). The split brain in man. *Scientific American, 217*(2), 24–29.

Gazzaniga, Michael S. (1983). Right hemisphere language following brain bisection: A 20-year perspective. *American Psychologist, 38,* 525–537.

Gazzaniga, Michael S. (1988). *Mind matters.* Boston: Houghton Mifflin.

Gazzaniga, Michael S. (1998). *The mind's past.* Berkeley, CA: University of California Press.

Gazzaniga, Michael S. (2005). *The ethical brain.* Washington, DC: Dana Press.

Gazzaniga, Michael S. (2008). *Human: The science behind what makes us unique.* New York: Ecco/Harper Collins.

Geers, Andrew L.; Wellman, Justin A.; & Lassiter, G. Daniel (2009). Dispositional optimism and engagement: The moderating influence of goal prioritization. *Journal of Personality and Social Psychology, 96,* 913–932.

Gelbard-Sagiv, H.; Mukamel, R.; Harel, M.; et al. (2008, October 3). Internally generated reactivation of single neurons in human hippocampus during free recall. *Science, 322,* 96–101.

Gelernter, David (1997, May 19). How hard is chess? *Time,* 72–73.

Gentile, Brittany; Grabe, Shleey; Dolan-Pascoe, Brenda; et al. (2009). Gender differences in domain-specific self-esteem: A meta-analysis. *Review of General Psychology, 13,* 34–45.

Gentner, Dedre, & Goldin-Meadow, Susan (Eds.) (2003). *Language in mind: Advances in the study of language and thought.* Cambridge: MIT Press.

Gerken, Louann A.; Wilson, Rachel; & Lewis, William (2005). Infants can use distributional cues to form syntactic categories. *Journal of Child Language, 32,* 249–268.

Gershoff, Elizabeth T. (2002). Parental corporal punishment and associated child behaviors and experiences: A meta-analytic and theoretical review. *Psychological Bulletin, 128,* 539–579.

Gibson, Eleanor, & Walk, Richard (1960). The "visual cliff." *Scientific American, 202,* 80–92.

Giesbrecht, Timo; Lynn, Steven Jay; Lilienfeld, Scott O.; & Merckelbach, Harald (2008). Cognitive processes in dissociation: An analysis of core theoretical assumptions. *Psychological Bulletin, 134,* 617–647.

Gilbert, Daniel (2006a). *Stumbling on happiness.* New York: Knopf.

Gilbertson, Mark W.; Shenton, Martha E.; Ciszewski, Aleksandra; et al. (2002). Hippocampal volume predicts pathologic vulnerability to psychological trauma. *Nature Neuroscience, 5,* 1242–1247.

Gilestro, Giorgio F.; Tononi, Giulio; & Cirelli, Chiara (2009). Widespread changes in synaptic markers as a function of sleep and wakefulness in *Drosophila. Science, 324,* 109–112.

Gillath, Omri; Shaver, Phillip R.; Baek, Jong-Min; & Chun, David S. (2008). Genetic correlates of adult attachment style. *Personality and Social Psychology Bulletin, 34,* 1396–1405.

Gilmore, David D. (1990). *Manhood in the making: Cultural concepts of masculinity.* New Haven, CT: Yale University Press.

Gladwell, Malcolm (2004, September 20). Personality plus. *The New Yorker,* 42–48.

Gleaves, David H. (1996). The sociocognitive model of dissociative identity disorder: A reexamination of the evidence. *Psychological Bulletin, 120,* 42–59.

Glick, Peter (2006). Ambivalent sexism, power distance, and gender inequality across cultures. In S. Guimond (Ed.), *Social comparison and social psychology: Understanding cognition, intergroup relations, and culture.* New York: Cambridge University Press.

Glick, Peter; Fiske, Susan T.; Mladinic, Antonio; et al. (2000). Beyond prejudice as simple antipathy: Hostile and benevolent sexism across cultures. *Journal of Personality and Social Psychology, 79,* 763–775.

Glick, Peter; Lameiras, Maria; Fiske, Susan T.; et al. (2004). Bad but bold: Ambivalent attitudes toward men predict gender inequality in 16 nations. *Journal of Personality and Social Psychology, 86,* 713–728.

Golden, Robert M.; Gaynes, Bradley N.; Ekstrom, R. David; et al. (2005). The efficacy of light therapy in the treatment of mood disorders: A review and meta-analysis of the evidence. *American Journal of Psychiatry, 162,* 656–662.

Goldin-Meadow, Susan (2003). *The resilience of language.* New York: Psychology Press.

Goldin-Meadow, Susan; Cook, Susan W.; & Mitchell, Zachary A. (2009). Gesturing gives children new ideas about math. *Psychological Science, 20,* 267–272.

Goldman-Rakic, Patricia S. (1996). Opening the mind through neurobiology. Invited address at the annual meeting of the American Psychological Association, Toronto, Canada.

Goldstein, Alan J.; de Beurs, Edwin; Chambless, Dianne L.; & Wilson, Kimberly A. (2000). EMDR for panic disorder with agoraphobia: Comparison with waiting list and credible attention-placebo control conditions. *Journal of Consulting and Clinical Psychology, 68,* 947–956.

Goldstein, Jill M.; Seidman, Larry J.; Horton, Nicholas J.; et al. (2001). Normal sexual dimorphism of the adult human brain assessed by in vivo magnetic resonance imaging. *Cerebral Cortex, 11,* 490–497.

Goldstein, Michael, & Miklowitz, David (1995). The effectiveness of psychoeducational family therapy in the treatment of schizophrenic disorders. *Journal of Marital and Family Therapy, 21,* 361–376.

Goldstein, Noah J.; Cialdini, Robert B.; & Griskevicius, Vladas (2008). A room with a viewpoint: Using social norms to motivate environmental conservation in hotels. *Journal of Consumer Research, 35,* 472–482.

Goldston, David B.; Molock, Sherry D.; Whitbeck, Leslie B.; et al. (2008). Cultural considerations in adolescent suicide prevention and psychosocial treatment. *American Psychologist, 63,* 14–31.

Goldstone, Robert L.; Roberts, Michael E.; & Gureckis, Todd M. (2008). Emergent processes in group behavior. *Current Directions in Psychological Science, 17,* 10–15.

Golinkoff, Roberta M., & Hirsh-Pasek, Kathy (2006). Baby wordsmith: From associationist to social sophisticate. *Current Directions in Psychological Science, 15,* 30–33.

Golub, Sharon (1992). *Periods: From menarche to menopause.* Newbury Park, CA: Sage.

Gonzaga, Gian C.; Turner, Rebecca A.; Keltner, Dacher; et al. (2006). Romantic love and sexual desire in close relationships. *Emotion, 6,* 163–179.

Goode, Erica (2003, May 6). Experts see mind's voices in new light. *The New York Times,* Science Times, pp. D1, D4.

Goodwyn, Susan, & Acredolo, Linda (1998). Encouraging symbolic gestures: A new perspective on the relationship between gesture and speech. In J. Iverson & S. Goldin-Meadow (Eds.), *The nature and functions of gesture in children's communication.* San Francisco: Jossey-Bass.

Gopnik, Alison (2009). *The philosophical baby.* New York: Farrar, Straus and Giroux.

Gopnik, Alison; Meltzoff, Andrew N.; & Kuhl, Patricia K. (1999). *The scientist in the crib.* New York: Morrow.

Gopnik, Myrna; Choi, Sooja; & Baumberger, Therese (1996). Cross-linguistic differences in early semantic and cognitive development. *Cognitive Development, 11,* 197–227.

Gosling, Samuel D.; Kwan, Virginia S. Y.; & John, Oliver P. (2003). A dog's got personality: A cross-species comparative approach to personality judgments in dogs and humans. *Journal of Personality and Social Psychology, 85,* 1161–1169.

Gotlib, Ian H.; Joormann, Jutta; Minor, Kelly L.; & Hallmayer, Joachim (2008). HPA axis reactivity: A mechanism underlying the associations among 5-HTTLPR, stress, and depression. *Biological Psychiatry, 63,* 847–851.

Gottesman, Irving I. (1991). *Schizophrenia genesis: The origins of madness.* New York: Freeman.

Gottesman, Irving; Laursen, T. M.; Bertelsen A.; & Mortensen, P. B. (2010). Severe mental disorders in offspring with 2 psychiatrically ill parents. *Archives of General Psychiatry, 67,* 252–257.

Gottfredson, Linda S. (2002). g: Highly general and highly practical. In R. J. Sternberg & E. I. Grigorenko (Eds.), *The general intelligence factor: How general is it?* Mahway, NJ: Erlbaum.

Gougoux, Frederic; Zatorre, Robert J.; Lassonde, Maryse; et al. (2005). A functional neuroimaging study of sound localization: Visual cortex activity predicts performance in early-blind individuals. *PloS Biology, 3,* 324–333.

Gouin, Jean-Philippe; Kiecolt-Glaser, Janice K.; Malarkey, William B.; & Glaser, Ronald (2008). The influence of anger expression on wound healing. *Brain, Behavior, and Immunity, 22,* 699–708.

Gould, Stephen Jay (1994, November 28). Curveball. [Review of *The Bell Curve,* by Richard J. Herrnstein and Charles Murray.] *The New Yorker,* 139–149.

Gould, Stephen Jay (1996). *The mismeasure of man* (Rev. ed.). New York: Norton.

Grabe, Shelly, & Hyde, Janet S. (2006). Ethnicity and body dissatisfaction among women in the United States: A meta-analysis. *Psychological Bulletin, 132,* 622–640.

Grabe, Shelly; Ward, L. Monique; & Hyde, Janet S. (2008). The role of the media in body image concerns among women: A meta-analysis of experimental and correlational studies. *Psychological Bulletin, 134,* 460–476.

Graham, Jesse; Haidt, Jonathan; & Nosek, Brian A. (2009). Liberals and conservatives rely on different sets of moral foundations. *Journal of Personality and Social Psychology, 96,* 1029–1046.

Graham, Jill W. (1986). Principled organizational dissent: A theoretical essay. *Research in Organizational Behavior, 8,* 1–52.

Grant, Heidi, & Dweck, Carol S. (2003). Clarifying achievement goals and their impact. *Journal of Personality and Social Psychology, 85,* 541–553.

Grant, Igor; Gonzalez, Raul; Carey, Catherine L.; et al. (2003). Non-acute (residual) neurocognitive effects of cannabis use: A meta-analytic study. *Journal of the International Neuropsychological Society, 9,* 679–689.

Gray, Kurt, & Wegner, Daniel M. (2008). The sting of intentional pain. *Psychological Science, 19,* 1260–1261.

Greely, Henry T., & Illes, Judy (2007). Neuroscience-based lie detection: The urgent need for regulation. *American Journal of Law & Medicine, 35.*

Greely, Henry; Sahakian, Barbara; Harris, John; et al. (2008). Towards responsible use of cognitive-enhancing drugs by the healthy. *Nature, 455,* 702–705. [Published online December 10, 2008; doi: 10.1038/456702a; accessed April 30, 2009.]

Greenberg, Jeff; Solomon, Sheldon; & Arndt, Jamie (2008). A basic but uniquely human motivation: Terror management. In J. Shah & W. Gardner (Eds.), *Handbook of motivation science.* New York: Guilford Press.

Greenberger, Dennis, & Padesky, Christine A. (1995). *Mind over mood: A cognitive therapy treatment manual for clients.* New York: Guilford.

Greenberger, Ellen; Lessard, Jared; Chen, Chuansheng; & Farruggia, Susan P. (2008). Self-entitled college students: Contributions of personality, parenting, and motivational factors. *Journal of Youth & Adolescence, 37,* 1193–1204.

Greenfield, Susan A., & Collins, T. F. T. (2005). A neuroscientific approach to consciousness. *Progress in Brain Research, 150,* 11–23.

Greenough, William T. (1984). Structural correlates of information storage in the mammalian brain: A review and hypothesis. *Trends in Neurosciences, 7,* 229–233.

Greenough, William T., & Anderson, Brenda J. (1991). Cerebellar synaptic plasticity: Relation to learning vs. neural activity. *Annals of the New York Academy of Sciences, 627,* 231–247.

Greenough, William T., & Black, James E. (1992). Induction of brain structure by experience: Substrates for cognitive development. In M. Gunnar & C. A. Nelson (Eds.), *Behavioral developmental neuroscience: Vol. 24. Minnesota Symposia on Child Psychology.* Hillsdale, NJ: Erlbaum.

Greenwald, Anthony G.; McGhee, Debbie E.; & Schwartz, Jordan L. K. (1998). Measuring individual differences in implicit cognition: The Implicit Association Test. *Journal of Personality and Social Psychology, 74,* 1464–1480.

Greenwald, Anthony G.; Poehlman, T. Andrew; Uhlmann, Eric L.; & Banaji, Mahzarin R. (2009). Understanding and using the Implicit Association Test: III. Meta-analysis of predictive validity. *Journal of Personality and Social Psychology, 97,* 17–41.

Greenwald, Anthony G.; Spangenberg, Eric R.; Pratkanis, Anthony R.; & Eskenazi, Jay (1991). Double-blind tests of subliminal self-help audiotapes. *Psychological Science, 2,* 119–122.

Gregg, L., & Tarrier, N. (2007). Virtual reality in mental health: A review of the literature. *Social Psychiatry and Psychiatric Epidemiology, 42,* 343–54.

Gregory, Richard L. (1963). Distortion of visual space as inappropriate constancy scaling. *Nature, 199,* 678–679.

Grewen, Karen M.; Girdler, Susan S.; Amico, Janet; & Light, Kathleen C. (2005). Effects of partner support on resting oxytocin, cortisol, norepinephrine, and blood pressure before and after warm partner contact. *Psychosomatic Medicine, 67,* 531–538.

Griffin, Donald R. (2001). *Animal minds: Beyond cognition to consciousness.* Chicago: University of Chicago Press.

Griffiths, R. R.; Richards, W. A.; Johnson, M. W.; et al. (2008). Mystical-type experiences occasioned by psilocybin mediate the attribution of personal meaning and spiritual significance fourteen months later. *Journal of Psychopharmacology, 22,* 621–632.

Grinspoon, Lester, & Bakalar, James B. (1993). *Marihuana, the forbidden medicine.* New Haven, CT: Yale University Press.

Gross, James J. (1998). The emerging field of emotion regulation: An integrative review. *Review of General Psychology, 2,* 271–299.

Gross, James J. (2001). Emotion regulation in adulthood: Timing is everything. *Current Directions in Psychological Science, 10,* 214–219.

Gross, James J., & John, Oliver, P. (2003). Individual differences in two emotion regulation processes: Implications for affect, relationships, and well-being. *Journal of Personality and Social Psychology, 85,* 348–362.

Grossman, Michele, & Wood, Wendy (1993). Sex differences in intensity of emotional experience: A social role interpretation. *Journal of Personality and Social Psychology, 65,* 1010–1022.

Guilford, J. P. (1988). Some changes in the structure-of-intellect model. *Educational and Psychological Measurement, 48,* 1–4.

Gur, R. C.; Gunning-Dixon, Faith; Bilker, Wareen B.; & Gur, Raquel E. (2002). Sex differences in temporo-limbic and frontal brain volumes of healthy adults. *Cerebral Cortex, 12,* 998–1003.

Gur, R. E.; Maany, V.; Mozley, P. D.; et al. (1998). Subcortical MRI volumes in neuroleptic-naive and treated patients with schizophrenia. *American Journal of Psychiatry, 155,* 1711–1717.

Gustavson, Carl R.; Garcia, John; Hankins, Walter G.; & Rusiniak, Kenneth W. (1974). Coyote predation control by aversive conditioning. *Science, 184,* 581–583.

Guthrie, Paul C., & Mobley, Brenda D. (1994). A comparison of the differential diagnostic efficiency of three personality disorder inventories. *Journal of Clinical Psychology, 50,* 656–665.

Guzman-Marin, Ruben; Suntsova, Natalia; Methippara, Melvi; et al. (2005). Sleep deprivation suppresses neurogenesis in the adult hippocampus of rats. *European Journal of Neuroscience, 22,* 2111–2116.

Haber, Ralph N. (1970, May). How we remember what we see. *Scientific American, 222,* 104–112.

Hacking, Ian (1995). *Rewriting the soul: Multiple personality and the sciences of memory.* Princeton: Princeton University Press.

Hahn, Robert; Fuqua-Whitley, Dawna; Wethington, Holly; et al. (2008). Effectiveness of universal school-based programs to prevent violent and aggressive behaviour: A systematic review. *Child: Care, Health, & Development, 34,* 139.

Haier, Richard J.; Jung, Rex E.; Yeo, Ronald A.; et al. (2005). The neuroanatomy of general intelligence: sex matters. *NeuroImage, 25,* 320–327.

Haimov, I., & Lavie, P. (1996). Melatonin—A soporific hormone. *Current Directions in Psychological Science, 5,* 106–111.

Hall, Calvin (1953a). A cognitive theory of dreams. *Journal of General Psychology, 49,* 273–282.

Hall, Calvin (1953b). *The meaning of dreams.* New York: McGraw-Hill.

Hall, Edward T. (1959). *The silent language.* Garden City, NY: Doubleday.

Hall, Edward T. (1976). *Beyond culture.* New York: Anchor.

Hall, Edward T. (1983). *The dance of life: The other dimension of time.* Garden City, NY: Anchor Press/Doubleday.

Hall, Edward T., & Hall, Mildred R. (1987). *Hidden differences: Doing business with the Japanese.* Garden City, NY: Anchor Press/Doubleday.

Hall, Edward T., & Hall, Mildred R. (1990). *Understanding cultural differences.* Yarmouth, ME: Intercultural Press.

Hall, Nathan C.; Perry, Raymond P.; Ruthig, Joelle C.; et al. (2006). Primary and secondary control in achievement settings: A longitudinal field study of academic motivation, emotions, and performance. *Journal of Applied Social Psychology, 36,* 1430–1470.

Hall, G. Stanley (1899). A study of anger. *American Journal of Psychology, 10,* 516–591.

Halpern, Diane (2002). *Thought and knowledge: An introduction to critical thinking* (4th ed.). Hillsdale, NJ: Erlbaum.

Halpern, Diane F. (2008). Psychologists are redefining retirement as a new phase of life. *The General Psychologist, 43,* 22–29.

Hamby, Sherry L., & Koss, Mary P. (2003). Shades of gray: A qualitative study of terms used in the measurement of sexual victimization. *Psychology of Women Quarterly, 27,* 243–255.

Hammen, Constance (2009). Adolescent depression. *Current Directions in Psychological Science, 18,* 200–204.

Han, Jin-Hee; Kushner, Steven A.; Yiu, Adelaide P.; et al. (2009). Selective erasure of a fear memory. *Science, 323,* 1492–1496.

Haney, Craig; Banks, Curtis; & Zimbardo, Philip (1973). Interpersonal dynamics in a simulated prison. *International Journal of Criminology and Penology, 1,* 69–97.

Haney, Craig, & Zimbardo, Philip (1998). The past and future of U.S. prison policy: Twenty-five years after the Stanford Prison Experiment. *American Psychologist, 53,* 709–727.

Hardie, Elizabeth A. (1997). PMS in the workplace: Dispelling the myth of cyclic function. *Journal of Occupational and Organizational Psychology, 70,* 97–102.

Harding, Courtenay M. (2005). Changes in schizophrenia across time: Paradoxes, patterns, and predictors. In L. Davidson, C. Harding, & L. Spaniol (Eds.), *Recovery from severe mental illnesses: Research evidence and implications for practice* (Vol. 1). Boston, MA: Center for Psychiatric Rehabilitation/Boston U.

Hare, Robert D. (1965). Temporal gradient of fear arousal in psychopaths. *Journal of Abnormal Psychology, 70,* 442–445.

Hare, Robert D. (1996). Psychopathy: A clinical construct whose time has come. *Criminal Justice and Behavior, 23*, 24–54.

Haritos-Fatouros, Mika (1988). The official torturer: A learning model for obedience to the authority of violence. *Journal of Applied Social Psychology, 18*, 1107–1120.

Harlow, Harry F. (1958). The nature of love. *American Psychologist, 13*, 673–685.

Harlow, Harry F., & Harlow, Margaret K. (1966). Learning to love. *American Scientist, 54*, 244–272.

Harmon-Jones, Eddie; Peterson, Carly K.; & Harris, Christine R. (2009). Jealousy: Novel methods and neural correlates. *Emotion, 9*, 113–117.

Harris, Gardiner (2003, August 7). Debate resumes on the safety of depression's wonder drugs. *The New York Times*, pp. A1, C4.

Harris, Judith R. (2006). *No two alike: Human nature and human individuality*. New York: Norton.

Harris, Judith R. (2009). *The nurture assumption* (2nd ed.). New York: Free Press.

Harris, Lasana T., & Fiske, Susan T. (2006). Dehumanizing the lowest of the low: Neuro-imaging responses to extreme outgroups. *Psychological Science*, in press.

Hart, A. J.; Whalen, P. J.; Shin, L. M.; et al. (2000). Differential response in the human amygdala to racial outgroup vs. ingroup face stimuli. *NeuroReport, 11*, 2351–2355.

Hart, John, Jr.; Berndt, Rita S.; & Caramazza, Alfonso (1985, August 1). Category-specific naming deficit following cerebral infarction. *Nature, 316*, 339–340.

Haslam, S. Alexander; Jetten, Jolanda; Postmes, Tom; & Haslam, Catherine (2009). Social identity, health and well-being: An emerging agenda for applied psychology. *Applied Psychology: An International Review, 58*, 1–23.

Haslam, S. Alexander, & Reicher, Stephen (2003, Spring). Beyond Stanford: Questioning a role-based explanation of tyranny. *Society for Experimental Social Psychology Dialogue, 18*, 22–25.

Hassett, Janice M.; Siebert, Erin R.; & Wallen, Kim (2008). Sex differences in rhesus monkey toy preferences parallel those of children. *Hormones and Behavior, 54*, 359–364.

Hatfield, Elaine, & Rapson, Richard L. (1996/2005). *Love and sex: Cross-cultural perspectives*. Boston: Allyn & Bacon.

Hatfield, Elaine, & Rapson, Richard L. (2008). Passionate love and sexual desire: Multidisciplinary perspectives. In J. P. Forgas & J. Fitness (Eds.), *Social relationships: Cognitive, affective, and motivational processes*. New York: Psychology Press.

Hauser, Marc (2000). *Wild minds: What animals really think*. New York: Holt.

Haut, Jennifer S.; Beckwith, Bill E.; Petros, Thomas V.; & Russell, Sue (1989). Gender differences in retrieval from long-term memory following acute intoxication with ethanol. *Physiology and Behavior, 45*, 1161–1165.

Hawkins, Elizabeth H.; Cummins, Lillian H.; & Marlatt, G. Alan (2004). Preventing substance abuse in American Indian and Alaska Native Youth: Promising strategies for healthier communities. *Psychological Bulletin, 130*, 304–323.

Hawkins, Scott A., & Hastie, Reid (1990). Hindsight: Biased judgments of past events after the outcomes are known. *Psychological Bulletin, 107*, 311–327.

Hayes, Steven C. (2004). Acceptance and commitment therapy and the new behavior therapies: Mindfulness, acceptance, and relationship. In S. C. Hayes, V. M. Follette, & M. M. Linehan (2004), *Mindfulness and acceptance: Expanding the cognitive-behavioral tradition*. New York: Guilford.

Hayes, Steven C.; Follette, Victoria M.; & Linehan, Marsha M. (Eds.) (2004). *Mindfulness and acceptance: Expanding the cognitive-behavioral tradition*. New York: The Guilford Press.

Hazan, Cindy, & Diamond, Lisa M. (2000). The place of attachment in human mating. *Review of General Psychology, 4*, 186–204.

Hazan, Cindy, & Shaver, Phillip R. (1994). Attachment as an organizational framework for research on close relationships. *Psychological Inquiry, 5*, 1–22.

Headey, Bruce (2008). Life goals matter to happiness: A revision of set-point theory. *Social Indicators Research, 86*, 213–231.

Healy, David (2002). *The creation of psychopharmacology*. Cambridge, MA: Harvard University Press.

Heath, A. C.; Madden, P. A. F.; Bucholz, K. K.; et al. (2003). Genetic and genotype x environment interaction effects on risk of dependence on alcohol, tobacco, and other drugs: new research. In R. Plomin et al. (Eds.), *Behavioral genetics in the postgenomic era*. Washington, DC: APA Books.

Heilig, Markus (2008, December 1). Molecular biology teases out two distinct forms of alcoholism. *The Scientist, 22*. On line at www.the-scientist.com/article/display/55237/.

Heinrichs, R. Walter (2005). The primacy of cognition in schizophrenia. *American Psychologist, 60*, 229–242.

Helson, Ravenna; Roberts, Brent; & Agronick, Gail (1995). Enduringness and change in creative personality and the prediction of occupational creativity. *Journal of Personality and Social Psychology, 6*, 1173–1183.

Helzer, John E.; Wittchen, Hans-Ulrich; Krueger, Robert F.; & Kraemer, Helena C. (2008). Dimensional options for DSM-V: The way forward. In J. E. Helzer, H. C. Kramer, & R. F. Krueger (Eds.), *Dimensional approaches in diagnostic classification: Refining the research agenda for DSM-V*. Washington, DC: American Psychiatric Association.

Henderlong, Jennifer, & Lepper, Mark R. (2002). The effects of praise on children's intrinsic motivation: A review and synthesis. *Psychological Bulletin, 128*, 774–795.

Henggeler, Scott W.; Schoenwald, Sonya K.; Borduin, Charles M.; et al. (1998). *Multisystemic treatment of antisocial behavior in children and adolescents*. New York: Guilford Press.

Hennessy, Michael B.; Schiml-Webb, Patricia A.; & Deak, Terrence (2009). Separation, sickness, and depression. *Current Directions in Psychological Science, 18*, 227–231.

Henrich, Joseph; Boyd, Robert; Bowles, Samuel; et al. (2001). In search of Homo Economicus: Behavioral experiments in 15 small scale societies. *American Economics Review, 91*, 73–78.

Herbert, Alan; Gerry, Norman P.; McQueen, Matthew B.; et al. (2006, April 14). A common genetic variant is associated with adult and childhood obesity. *Science, 312*, 279–283.

Herdt, Gilbert (1984). *Ritualized homosexuality in Melanesia*. Berkeley: University of California Press.

Herek, Gregory M., & Capitanio, J. P. (1996). "Some of my best friends": Intergroup contact, concealable stigma, and heterosexuals' attitudes toward gay men and lesbians. *Personality and Social Psychology Bulletin, 22*, 412–424.

Herman, John H. (1992). Transmutative and reproductive properties of dreams: Evidence for cortical modulation of brainstem generators. In J. Antrobus & M. Bertini (Eds.), *The neuropsychology of dreaming*. Hillsdale, NJ: Erlbaum.

Herman, Louis M.; Kuczaj, Stan A.; & Holder, Mark D. (1993). Responses to anomalous gestural sequences by a language-trained dolphin: Evidence for processing of semantic relations and syntactic information. *Journal of Experimental Psychology: General, 122*, 184–194.

Herman, Louis M., & Morrel-Samuels, Palmer (1996). Knowledge acquisition and asymmetry between language comprehension and production: Dolphins and apes as general models for animals. In M. Bekoff & D. Jamieson et al. (Eds.), *Readings in animal cognition*. Cambridge, MA: MIT Press.

Heron, Woodburn (1957). The pathology of boredom. *Scientific American, 196*(1), 52–56.

Hertzog, Christopher; Kramer, Arthur F.; Wilson, Robert S.; & Lindenberger, Ulman (2008). Enrichment effects on adult cognitive development: Can the functional capacity of older adults be preserved and enhanced? *Psychological Science in the Public Interest, 9*, 1–65.

Herz, Rachel S., & Cupchik, Gerald C. (1995). The emotional distinctiveness of odor-evoked memories. *Chemical Senses, 20*, 517–528.

Hess, Thomas M. (2005). Memory and aging in context. *Psychological Bulletin, 131*, 383–406.

Hess, Ursula; Adams, Reginald B., Jr.; & Kleck, Robert (2005). Who may frown and who should smile? Dominance, affiliation, and the display of happiness and anger. *Cognition & Emotion, 19*, 515–536.

Hess, Ursula, & Thibault, Pascal (2009). Darwin and emotional expression. *American Psychologist, 64*, 120–128.

Hewlitt, Sylvia Ann; Luce, Carolyn B.; & Servon, Lisa J. (2008, June). Stopping the exodus of women in science. *Harvard Business Review,* ePub.

Hilgard, Ernest R. (1977). *Divided consciousness: Multiple controls in human thought and action.* New York: Wiley-Interscience.

Hilgard, Ernest R. (1986). *Divided consciousness: Multiple controls in human thought and action* (2nd ed.). New York: Wiley.

Hill-Soderlund, Ashley L., & Braungart-Rieker, Julia M. (2008). Early individual differences in temperamental reactivity and regulation: Implications for effortful control in early childhood. *Infant Behavior & Development, 31,* 386–397.

Hilts, Philip J. (1995). *Memory's ghost: The strange tale of Mr. M. and the nature of memory.* New York: Simon & Schuster.

Hines, Terence M. (1998). Comprehensive review of biorhythm theory. *Psychological Reports, 83,* 19–64.

Hirsch, Helmut V. B., & Spinelli, D. N. (1970). Visual experience modifies distribution of horizontally and vertically oriented receptive fields in cats. *Science, 168,* 869–871.

Hobson, J. Allan (1988). *The dreaming brain.* New York: Basic Books.

Hobson, J. Allan (1990). Activation, input source, and modulation: A neurocognitive model of the state of the brain mind. In R. R. Bootzin, J. F. Kihlstrom, & D. L. Schacter (Eds.), *Sleep and cognition.* Washington, DC: American Psychological Association.

Hobson, J. Allan (2002). *Dreaming: An introduction to the science of sleep.* New York: Oxford University Press.

Hobson, J. Allan; Pace-Schott, Edward F.; & Stickgold, Robert (2000). Dreaming and the brain: Toward a cognitive neuroscience of consious states. *Behavioral and Brain Sciences, 23,* 793–842, 904–1018, 1083–1121.

Hochschild, Arlie R. (2003). *The Managed Heart: Commercialization of human feeling* (2nd ed.). Berkeley, CA: University of California Press.

Hoffrage, Ulrich; Hertwig, Ralph; & Gigerenzer, Gerd (2000). Hindsight bias: A by-product of knowledge updating? *Journal of Experimental Psychology: Learning, Memory, & Cognition, 26,* 566–581.

Hofstede, Geert, & Bond, Michael H. (1988). The Confucius connection: From cultural roots to economic growth. *Organizational Dynamics,* 5–21.

Holden, Constance (2008, July 11). Poles apart. *Science, 321,* 193–195.

Holden, George W., & Miller, Pamela C. (1999). Enduring and different: A meta-analysis of the similarity in parents' child rearing. *Psychological Bulletin, 125,* 223–254.

Holland, Rob W.; Hendriks, Merel; & Aarts, Henk (2005). Smells like clean spirit: Nonconscious effects of scent on cognition and behavior. *Psychological Science, 16,* 689–693.

Hollon, Steven D.; Thase, Michael E.; & Markowitz, John C. (2002). Treatment and prevention of depression. *Psychological Science in the Public Interest, 3,* 39–77.

Holloway, Renee A.; Waldrip, Amy M.; & Ickes, William (2009). Evidence that a simpático self-schema accounts for differences in the self-concepts and social behavior of Latinos versus Whites (and Blacks). *Journal of Personality and Social Psychology, 96,* 1012–1028.

Homer, Bruce D.; Solomon, Todd M.; Moeller, Robert W.; et al. (2008). Metamphetamine abuse and impairment of social function: A review of the underlying neurophysiological causes and behavior implications. *Psychological Bulletin, 134,* 301–310.

Hooker, Evelyn (1957). The adjustment of the male overt homosexual. *Journal of Projective Techniques, 21,* 18–31.

Hopper, Kim; Harrison, Glynn; Janca, Aleksandar; & Sartorius, Norman (Eds.) (2007). *Recovery from schizophrenia: An international investigation.* New York: Oxford University Press.

Horgan, John (1995, November). Get smart, take a test: A long-term rise in IQ scores baffles intelligence experts. *Scientific American, 273,* 12,14.

Horney, Karen (1926/1973). The flight from womanhood. *The International Journal of Psycho-Analysis, 7,* 324–339. Reprinted in J. B. Miller (Ed.), *Psychoanalysis and women.* New York: Brunner/Mazel, 1973.

Hornung, Richard W.; Lanphear, Bruce P.; & Dietrich, Kim N. (2009). Age of greatest susceptibility to childhood lead exposure: A new statistical approach. *Environmental Health Perspectives, 117,* 1309–1312.

Hotz, Robert Lee (2000, November 29). Women use more of brain when listening, study says. *Los Angeles Times,* A1, A18–19.

House, James S.; Landis, Karl R.; & Umberson, Debra (2003). Social relationships and health. In P. Salovey & A. J. Rothman (Eds.), *Social psychology of health.* New York: Psychology Press.

Houston, Derek M., & Jusczyk, Peter W. (2003). Infants' long-term memory for the sound patterns of words and voices. *Journal of Experimental Psychology: Human Perception & Performance, 29,* 1143–1154.

Houts, Arthur C. (2002). Discovery, invention, and the expansion of the modern *Diagnostic and Statistical Manuals of Mental Disorders.* In L. E. Beutler & M. L. Malik (Eds.), *Rethinking the DSM: A psychological perspective.* Washington, DC: American Psychological Association.

Howard, George S. (1991). Culture tales: A narrative approach to thinking, cross-cultural psychology, and psychotherapy. *American Psychologist, 46,* 187–197.

Howe, Mark L. (2000). *The fate of early memories: Developmental science and the retention of childhood experiences.* Washington, DC: American Psychological Association.

Howe, Mark L.; Courage, Mary L.; & Peterson, Carole (1994). How can I remember when "I" wasn't there? Long-term retention of traumatic experiences and emergence of the cognitive self. *Consciousness and Cognition, 3,* 327–355.

Hrdy, Sarah B. (1988). Empathy, polyandry, and the myth of the coy female. In R. Bleier (Ed.), *Feminist approaches to science.* New York: Pergamon.

Hrdy, Sarah B. (1994). What do women want? In T. A. Bass (Ed.), *Reinventing the future: Conversations with the world's leading scientists.* Reading, MA: Addison-Wesley.

Hrdy, Sarah B. (1999). *Mother nature.* New York: Pantheon.

Hu, H.; Real, E.; Takamiya, K.; et al. (2007). Emotion enhances learning via norepinephrine regulation of AMPA-receptor trafficking. *Cell, 131,* 160–173.

Hu, Peter; Stylos-Allan, Melinda; & Walker, Matthew (2006). Sleep facilitates consolidation of emotional declarative memory. *Psychological Science, 17,* 891–898.

Hu, Wei; Saba, Laura; Kechris, Katharina; et al. (2008). Genomic insights into acute alcohol tolerance. *Journal of Pharmacology and Experimental Therapeutics, 326,* 792–800.

Hubel, David H., & Wiesel, Torsten N. (1962). Receptive fields, binocular interaction and functional architecture in the cat's visual cortex. *Journal of Physiology* (London), *160,* 106–154.

Hubel, David H., & Wiesel, Torsten N. (1968). Receptive fields and functional architecture of monkey striate cortex. *Journal of Physiology* (London), *195,* 215–243.

Huggins, Martha K.; Haritos-Fatouros, Mika; & Zimbardo, Philip G. (2003). *Violence workers: Police torturers and murderers reconstruct Brazilian atrocities.* Berkeley, CA: University of California Press.

Hunsley, John; Lee, Catherine M.; & Wood, James (2003). Controversial and questionable assessment techniques. In S. O. Lilienfeld, S. J. Lynn, & J. M. Lohn (Eds.), *Science and pseudoscience in clinical psychology.* New York: Guilford.

Hupka, Ralph B. (1981). Cultural determinants of jealousy. *Alternative Lifestyles, 4,* 310–356.

Hupka, Ralph B. (1991). The motive for the arousal of romantic jealousy. In P. Salovey (Ed.), *The psychology of jealousy and envy.* New York: Guilford Press.

Hupka, Ralph B.; Lenton, Alison P.; & Hutchison, Keith A. (1999). Universal development of emotion categories in natural language. *Journal of Personality and Social Psychology, 77,* 247–278.

Hwang, Wei-Chin (2006). The psychotherapy adaptation and modification framework: Application to Asian Americans. *American Psychologist, 61,* 702–715.

Hyde, Janet S. (2007). New directions in the study of gender similarities and differences. *Current Directions in Psychological Science, 16,* 259–263.

Hyman, Ira E., Jr., & Pentland, Joel (1996). The role of mental imagery in the creation of false childhood memories. *Journal of Memory and Language, 35,* 101–117.

Iacoboni, Marco (2008). *Mirroring people: The new science of how we connect with others.* New York: Farrar, Straus and Giroux.

Iacono, William G., & Lykken, David T. (1997). The scientific status of research on polygraph techniques: The case against polygraph tests. In D. L. Faigman, D. Kaye, M. J. Saks, & J. Sanders (Eds.), *Modern scientific evidence: The law and science of expert testimony.* St. Paul, MN: West.

Ikonomidou, Chrysanthy; Bittigau, Petra; Ishimaru, Masahiko J.; et al. (2000, February 11). Ethanol-induced apoptotic neurodegeneration and fetal alcohol syndrome. *Science, 287,* 1056–1060.

Impett, Emily A.; Gable, Shelly; & Peplau, Letitia A. (2005). Giving up and giving in: The costs and benefits of daily sacrifice in intimate relationships. *Journal of Personality and Social Psychology, 89,* 327–344.

Impett, Emily A., & Tolman, Deborah L. (2006). Late adolescent girls' sexual experiences and sexual satisfaction. *Journal of Adolescent Research, 21,* 628–646.

International Consensus Conference (2002, June). *Female Androgen Deficiency Syndrome: Definition, Diagnosis, and Classification: International Consensus* Conference, Princeton, NJ. http://www.medscape.com/viewprogram/302.

Inzlicht, Michael, & Ben-Zeev, Talia (2000). A threatening intellectual environment: Why females are susceptible to experiencing problem-solving deficits in the presence of males. *Psychological Science, 11,* 365–371.

Islam, Mir Rabiul, & Hewstone, Miles (1993). Intergroup attributions and affective consequences in majority and minority groups. *Journal of Personality and Social Psychology, 64,* 936–950.

Ito, Tiffany A., & Urland, Geoffrey R. (2003). Race and gender on the brain: Electrocortical measures of attention to the race and gender of multiply categorizable individuals. *Journal of Personality and Social Psychology, 85,* 616–626.

Izard, Carroll E. (1990). Facial expressions and the regulation of emotions. *Journal of Personality and Social Psychology, 58,* 487–498.

Izard, Carroll E. (1994a). Four systems for emotion activation: Cognitive and noncognitive processes. *Psychological Review, 100,* 68–90.

Izard, Carroll E. (1994b). Innate and universal facial expressions: Evidence from developmental and cross-cultural research. *Psychological Bulletin, 115,* 288–299.

Izard, Carroll E. (2007). Basic emotions, natural kinds, emotion schemas, and a new paradigm. *Perspectives on Psychological Science, 2,* 260–280.

Izard, Véronique; Sann, Coralie; Spelke, Elizabeth S.; & Streri, Arlette (2009). Newborn infants perceive abstract numbers. *Proceedings of the National Academy of Sciences, 106,* 10382–10385.

Izumikawa, Masahiko; Minoda, Ryosei; Kawamoto, Karen A.; et al. (2005). Auditory hair cell replacement and hearing improvement by *Atoh1* gene therapy in deaf mammals. *Nature Medicine, 11,* 271–276.

Jackson, Daren C.; Mueller, Corrina J.; Dolski, Isa; Dalton, Kim M.; Nitschke, Jack B.; et al. (2003). Now you feel it, now you don't: Frontal brain electrical asymmetry and individual differences in emotion regulation. *Psychological Science, 14,* 612–617.

Jacobs, Gregg D.; Pace-Schott, Edward F.; Stickgold, Robert; & Otto, Michael W. (2004). Cognitive behavior therapy and pharmacotherapy for chronic insomnia: A randomized controlled trial and direct comparison. *Archives of Internal Medicine, 164,* 1888–1896.

Jacobsen, Paul B; Bovbjerg, Dana H.; Schwartz, Marc D.; et al. (1995). Conditioned emotional distress in women receiving chemotherapy for breast cancer. *Journal of Consulting & Clinical Psychology, 63,* 108–114.

James, William (1890/1950). *Principles of psychology* (Vol. 1). New York: Dover.

James, William (1902/1936). *The varieties of religious experience.* New York: Modern Library.

Jamison, Kay (1992). *Touched with fire: Manic depressive illness and the artistic temperament.* New York: Free Press.

Jamison, Kay (1999). *Night falls fast: Understanding suicide.* New York: Knopf.

Jancke, Lutz; Schlaug, Gottfried; & Steinmetz, Helmuth (1997). Hand skill asymmetry in professional musicians. *Brain and Cognition, 34,* 424–432.

Jang, Kerry L.; McCrae, Robert R.; Angleitner, Alois; et al. (1998). Heritability of facet-level traits in a cross-cultural twin sample: Support for a hierarchical model of personality. *Journal of Personality and Social Psychology, 74,* 1556–1565.

Janis, Irving L. (1982). *Groupthink: Psychological studies of policy decisions and fiascoes* (2nd ed.). Boston: Houghton Mifflin.

Janis, Irving L. (1989). *Crucial decisions: Leadership in policymaking and crisis management.* New York: Free Press.

Jenkins, John G., & Dallenbach, Karl M. (1924). Oblivescence during sleep and waking. *American Journal of Psychology, 35,* 605–612.

Jensen, Arthur R. (1998). *The g factor: The science of mental ability.* Westport, CT; Praeger/Greenwood.

Jobe, Thomas H., & Harrow, Martin (2010). Schizophrenia course, long-term outcome, recovery, and prognosis. *Current Directions in Psychological Science, 19,* 220-225.

Johanek, Lisa M.; Meyer, Richard A.; Friedman, Robert M.; et al. (2008). A role for polymodal C-fiber afferents in nonhistaminergic itch. *The Journal of Neuroscience, 28,* 7659–7669.

Johns, Michael; Schmader, Toni; & Martens, Andy (2005). Knowing is half the battle: Teaching stereotype threat as a means of improving women's math performance. *Psychological Science, 16,* 175–179.

Johnson, Andrew J., & Miles, Christopher (2009). Serial position effects in 2-alternative forced choice recognition: functional equivalence across visual and auditory modalities. *Memory, 17,* 84–91.

Johnson, Marcia K.; Hashtroudi, Shahin; & Lindsay, D. Stephen (1993). Source monitoring. *Psychological Bulletin, 114,* 3–28.

Johnson, Wendy; Turkheimer, Eric; Gottesman, Irving I.; & Bouchard, Thomas J., Jr. (2009). Beyond heritability: Twin studies in behavioral research. *Current Directions in Psychological Science, 18,* 217–221.

Joiner, Thomas (2005). *Myths about suicide.* Cambridge, MA: Harvard University Press.

Jones, Edward E. (1990). *Interpersonal perception.* New York: Macmillan.

Jones, Mary Cover (1924). A laboratory study of fear: The case of Peter. *Pedagogical Seminary, 31,* 308–315.

Joormann, Jutta (2010). Cognitive inhibition and emotion regulation in depression. *Current Directions in Psychological Science, 19,* 161–166.

Joormann, Jutta, & Gotlib, Ian H. (2007). Selective attention to emotional faces following recovery from depression. *Journal of Abnormal Psychology, 116,* 80–85.

Joormann, Jutta; Siemer, Matthias; & Gotlib, Ian H. (2007). Mood regulation in depression: Differential effects of distraction and recall of happy memories on sad mood. *Journal of Abnormal Psychology, 116,* 484–490.

Jost, John T. (2006). The end of the end of ideology. *American Psychologist, 61,* 651–670.

Jost, John T.; Glaser, Jack; Kruglanski, Arie W.; & Sulloway, Frank J. (2003). Political conservatism as motivated social cognition. *Psychological Bulletin, 129,* 339–375.

Jost, John T.; Nosek, Brian A.; & Gosling, Samuel D. (2008). Ideology: Its resurgence in social, personality, and political psychology. *Perspectives on Psychological Science, 3,* 126–136.

Judd, Charles M.; Park, Bernadette; Ryan, Carey S.; et al. (1995). Stereotypes and ethnocentrism: Diverging interethnic perceptions of African American and white American youth. *Journal of Personality and Social Psychology, 69,* 460–481.

Judge, Timothy A. (2009). Core self-evaluations and work success. *Current Directions, 18,* 18–22.

Jung, Carl (1967). *Collected works.* Princeton, NJ: Princeton University Press.

Jusczyk, Peter W. (2002). How infants adapt speech-processing capacities to native-language structure. *Current Directions in Psychological Science, 11,* 15–18.

Jussim, Lee; Cain, Thomas R.; Crawford, Jarret T.; et al. (2009). The unbearable accuracy of stereotypes. In T. Nelson (Ed.), *The handbook of prejudice, stereotyping, and discrimination.* New York: Psychology Press.

Just, Marcel A.; Carpenter, Patricia A.; Keller, T. A.; et al. (2001). Interdependence of nonoverlapping cortical systems in dual cognitive tasks. *NeuroImage, 14,* 417–426.

Kagan, Jerome (1984). *The nature of the child.* New York: Basic Books.

Kagan, Jerome (1997). Temperament and the reactions to unfamiliarity. *Child Development, 68,* 139–143.

Kahn, Arnold S. (2004). 2003 Carolyn Sherif Award Address: What college women do and do not experience as rape. *Psychology of Women Quarterly, 28,* 9–15.

Kahneman, Daniel (2003). A perspective on judgment and choice: Mapping bounded rationality. *American Psychologist, 58,* 697–720.

Kaminski, Juliane; Call, Josep; & Fisher, Julia (2004). Word learning in a domestic dog: Evidence for "fast mapping." *Science, 304,* 1682–1683.

Kanagawa, Chie; Cross, Susan E.; & Markus, Hazel R. (2001). "Who am I?" The cultural psychology of the conceptual self. *Personality and Social Psychology Bulletin, 27,* 90–103.

Kandel, Eric R. (2001). The molecular biology of memory storage: A dialogue between genes and synapses. *Science, 294,* 1030–1038.

Kane, Michael J.; Brown, Leslie H.; McVay, Jennifer C.; et al. (2007). For whom the mind wanders, and when: An experience-sampling study of working memory and executive control in daily life. *Psychological Science, 18,* 614–621.

Kanter, Rosabeth M. (2006). Some effects of proportions on group life: Skewed sex ratios and responses to token women. In J. N. Levine & R. L. Moreland (Eds.), *Small groups. Key Readings in Social Psychology.* New York: Psychology Press.

Kanwisher, Nancy (2000). Domain specificity in face perception. *Nature Neuroscience, 3,* 759.

Karasek, Robert, & Theorell, Tores (1990). *Healthy work: Stress, productivity, and the reconstruction of working life.* New York: Basic Books.

Karlsgodt, Katherine H.; Sun, Daqiang; & Cannon, Tyrone D. (2010). Structural and functional brain abnormalities in schizophrenia. *Current Directions in Psychological Science, 19,* 226-231.

Karney, Benjamin, & Bradbury, Thomas N. (2000). Attributions in marriage: State or trait? A growth curve analysis. *Journal of Personality and Social Psychology, 78,* 295–309.

Karni, Avi; Tanne, David; Rubenstein, Barton S.; Askenasy, Jean J. M.; & Sagi, Dov (1994). Dependence on REM sleep of overnight improvement of a perceptual skill. *Science, 265,* 679–682.

Karpicke, Jeffrey D., & Roediger, Henry L. III (2008, February 15). The critical importance of retrieval for learning. *Science, 319,* 966–968.

Karraker, Katherine H.; Vogel, Dena A.; & Lake, Margaret A. (1995). Parents' gender-stereotyped perceptions of newborns: The eye of the beholder revisited. *Sex Roles, 33,* 687–701.

Karremans, Johan C.; Van Lange, Paul A. M.; Ouwerkerk, Jaap W.; & Kluwer, Esther S. (2003). When forgiving enhances psychological well-being: The role of interpersonal commitment. *Journal of Personality and Social Psychology, 84,* 1011–1026.

Kasser, Tim, & Ryan, Richard M. (1996). Further examining the American dream: Correlates of financial success as a central life aspiration. *Personality and Social Psychology Bulletin, 22,* 280–287.

Katigbak, Marcia S.; Church, A. Timothy; Guanzon-Lapeña, Ma. Angeles; et al. (2002). Are indigenous personality dimensions culture specific? Philippine inventories and the Five-Factor model. *Journal of Personality and Social Psychology, 82,* 89–101.

Kaufman, Joan, & Zigler, Edward (1987). Do abused children become abusive parents? *American Journal of Orthopsychiatry, 57,* 186–192.

Kazdin, Alan E. (2001). *Behavior modification in applied settings* (6th ed.). Belmont, CA: Wadsworth.

Kazdin, Alan E. (2008). Evidence-based treatment and practice: New opportunities to bridge clinical research and practice, enhance the knowledge base, and improve patient care. *American Psychologist, 63,* 146–150.

Keating, Caroline F. (1994). World without words: Messages from face and body. In W. J. Lonner & R. Malpass (Eds.), *Psychology and culture.* Needham Heights, MA: Allyn & Bacon.

Keel, Pamela K., & Klump, Kelly L. (2003). Are eating disorders culture-bound syndromes? Implications for conceptualizing their etiology. *Psychological Bulletin, 129,* 747–769.

Keen, Sam (1986). *Faces of the enemy: Reflections of the hostile imagination.* San Francisco: Harper & Row.

Keizer, Kees; Lindenberg, Siegwart; & Steg, Linda (2008, December 12). The spreading of disorder. *Science, 322,* 1681–1685.

Keller, Heidi; Abels, Monika; Lamm, Bettina; et al. (2005). Ecocultural effects on early infant care: A study in Cameroon, India, and Germany. *Ethos, 33,* 512–541.

Kelman, Herbert C., & Hamilton, V. Lee (1989). *Crimes of obedience: Toward a social psychology of authority and responsibility.* New Haven, CT: Yale University Press.

Keltner, Dacher, & Anderson, Cameron (2000). Saving face for Darwin: The functions and uses of embarrassment. *Current Directions in Psychological Science, 9,* 187–192.

Kemeny, Margaret E. (2003). The psychobiology of stress. *Current Directions in Psychological Science, 12,* 124–129.

Kempermann, Gerd (2006). Adult neurogenesis: Stem cells and neuronal development in the adult brain. New York: Oxford University Press.

Kendall [no first name] (1999). Women in Lesotho and the (Western) construction of homophobia. In E. Blackwood & S. E. Wieringa (Eds.), *Female desires: Same-sex relations and transgender practices across cultures.* New York: Columbia University Press.

Kennedy-Moore, Eileen, & Watson, Jeanne C. (2001). How and when does emotional expression help? *Review of General Psychology, 5,* 187–212.

Kenrick, Douglas T.; Sundie, Jill M.; Nicastle, Lionel D.; & Stone, Gregory O. (2001). Can one ever be too wealthy or too chaste? Searching for nonlinearities in mate judgment. *Journal of Personality and Social Psychology, 80,* 462–471.

Kephart, William M. (1967). Some correlates of romantic love. *Journal of Marriage and the Family, 29,* 470–474.

Kessler, Ronald C.; Sonnega, A.; Bromet, E.; et al. (1995). Posttraumatic stress disorder in the National Comorbidity Survey. *Archives of General Psychiatry, 52,* 1048–1060.

Khan, A.; Detke, M.; Khan, S. R.; & Mallinckrodt, C. (2003). Placebo response and antidepressant clinical trial outcome. *Journal of Nervous and Mental Diseases, 191,* 211–218.

Kida, Thomas (2006). *Don't believe everything you think: The 6 basic mistakes we make in thinking.* Amherst, NY: Prometheus Books.

Kiecolt-Glaser, Janice K.; Loving, T. J.; Stowell, J. R.; et al. (2005). Hostile marital interactions, proinflammatory cytokine production, and wound healing. *Archives of General Psychiatry, 62,* 1377–1384.

Kiecolt-Glaser, Janice K., & Newton, Tamara L. (2001). Marriage and health: His and hers. *Psychological Bulletin, 127,* 472–503.

Kiecolt-Glaser, Janice K.; Page, Gayle G.; Marucha, Phillip T.; et al. (1998). Psychological influences on surgical recovery: Perspectives from psychoneuroimmunology. *American Psychologist, 53,* 1209–1218.

Kihlstrom, John F. (1994). Hypnosis, delayed recall, and the principles of memory. *International Journal of Clinical and Experimental Hypnosis, 40,* 337–345.

Kihlstrom, John F. (1995). From a subject's point of view: The experiment as conversation and collaboration between investigator and subject. Invited address presented at the annual meeting of the American Psychological Society, New York.

Kim, Heejung S.; Sherman, David K.; & Taylor, Shelley E. (2008). Culture and social support. *American Psychologist, 63,* 518–526.

King, Aimee E.; Austin-Oden, Deena; & Lohr, Jeffrey M. (2009, January). Browsing for love in all the wrong places. *Skeptic, 15,* 48–55.

King, Michael, & Woollett, Earnest (1997). Sexually assaulted males: 115 men consulting a counseling service. *Archives of Sexual Behavior, 26,* 579–588.

King, Patricia M., & Kitchener, Karen S. (1994). *Developing reflective judgment: Understanding and promoting intellectual growth and critical thinking in adolescents and adults.* San Francisco: Jossey Bass.

King, Patricia M., & Kitchener, Karen S. (2002). The reflective judgment model: Twenty years of research on epistemic cognition. In B. K. Hofer & P. R. Pintrich (Eds.), *Personal epistemology: The psychology of beliefs about knowledge and knowing.* Mahway, NJ: Erlbaum.

King, Patricia M., & Kitchener, Karen S. (2004). Reflective judgment: Theory and research on the development of epistemic assumptions through adulthood. *Educational Psychologist, 39,* 5–18.

King, Ryan S.; Mauer, Marc; & Young, Malcolm C. (2005). *Incarceration and crime: A complex relationship.* Washington, DC: The Sentencing Project.

King, Suzanne; St-Hilaire, Annie; & Heidkamp, David (2010). Prenatal factors in schizophrenia. *Current Directions in Psychological Science, 19,* 209-213.

Kinoshita, Sachiko, & Peek-O'Leary, Marie (2005). Does the compatibility effect in the race Implicit Association Test reflect familiarity or affect? *Psychonomic Bulletin & Review, 12,* 442–452.

Kinsey, Alfred C.; Pomeroy, Wardell B.; & Martin, Clyde E. (1948). *Sexual behavior in the human male.* Philadelphia: Saunders.

Kinsey, Alfred C.; Pomeroy, Wardell B.; Martin, Clyde E.; & Gebhard, Paul H. (1953). *Sexual behavior in the human female.* Philadelphia: Saunders.

Kirsch, Irving (1997). Response expectancy theory and application: A decennial review. *Applied and Preventive Psychology, 6,* 69–70.

Kirsch, Irving (2004). Conditioning, expectancy, and the placebo effect: Comment on Stewart-Williams and Podd (2004). *Psychological Bulletin, 130,* 341–343.

Kirsch, Irving; Deacon, B. J.; Huedo-Medina, T. B.; et al. (2008). Initial severity and antidepressant benefits: A meta-analysis of data submitted to the Food and Drug Administration. *PLoS Medicine,5,* e45.

Kirsch, Irving, & Lynn, Steven J. (1995). The altered state of hypnosis: Changes in the theoretical landscape. *American Psychologist, 50,* 846–858.

Kirsch, Irving, & Lynn, Steven J. (1998). Dissociation theories of hypnosis. *Psychological Bulletin, 123,* 100–113.

Kirsch, Irving; Silva, Christopher E.; Carone, James E.; Johnston, J. Dennis; & Simon, B. (1989). The surreptitious observation design: An experimental paradigm for distinguishing artifact from essence in hypnosis. *Journal of Abnormal Psychology, 98,* 132–136.

Kitayama, Shinobu, & Markus, Hazel R. (1994). Introduction to cultural psychology and emotion research. In S. Kitayama & H. R. Markus (Eds.), *Emotion and culture: Empirical studies of mutual influence.* Washington, DC: American Psychological Association.

Kitayama, Shinobu; Snibbe, Alana C.; Markus, Hazel R.; & Suzuki, Tomoko (2004). Is there any "free" choice? Self and dissonance in two cultures. *Psychological Science, 15,* 517–533.

Kitchener, Karen S.; Lynch, Cindy L.; Fischer, Kurt W.; & Wood, Phillip K. (1993). Developmental range of reflective judgment: The effect of contextual support and practice on developmental stage. *Developmental Psychology, 29,* 893–906.

Klauer, Sheila G.; Dingus, Thomas A.; Neale, Vicki L.; et al. (2006). *The impact of driver inattention on near-crash/crash risk: An analysis using the 100-car naturalistic driving study data*[pdf]. Performed by Virginia Tech Transportation Institute, Blacksburg, VA, sponsored by National Highway Traffic Safety Administration, Washington, DC, DOT HS 810 594.

Klein, Daniel N.; Schwartz, Joseph E.; Santiago, Neil J.; et al. (2003). Therapeutic alliance in depression treatment: Controlling for prior change and patient characteristics. *Journal of Consulting & Clinical Psychology, 71,* 997–1006.

Klein, Raymond, & Armitage, Roseanne (1979). Rhythms in human performance: 1 1/2-hour oscillations in cognitive style. *Science, 204,* 1326–1328.

Kleinke, Chris L.; Peterson, Thomas R.; & Rutledge, Thomas R. (1998). Effects of self-generated facial expressions on mood. *Journal of Personality and Social Psychology, 74,* 272–279.

Kleinman, Arthur (1988). *Rethinking psychiatry: From cultural category to personal experience.* New York: Free Press.

Klima, Edward S., & Bellugi, Ursula (1966). Syntactic regularities in the speech of children. In J. Lyons & R. J. Wales (Eds.), *Psycholinguistics papers.* Edinburgh, Scotland: Edinburgh University Press.

Klimoski, R. (1992). Graphology and personnel selection. In B. Beyerstein & D. Beyerstein (Eds.), *The write stuff: Evaluations of graphology—The study of handwriting analysis.* Buffalo, NY: Prometheus Books.

Kling, Kristen C.; Hyde, Janet S.; Showers, Carolin J.; & Buswell, Brenda N. (1999). Gender differences in self-esteem: A meta-analysis. *Psychological Bulletin, 125,* 470–500.

Klohnen, Eva C., & Bera, Stephan (1998). Behavioral and experiential patterns of avoidantly and securely attached women across adulthood: A 31-year longitudinal perspective. *Journal of Personality and Social Psychology, 74,* 211–223.

Kluft, Richard P. (1987). The simulation and dissimulation of multiple personality disorder. *American Journal of Clinical Hypnosis, 30,* 104–118.

Koch, Christof (2004). *The quest for consciousness: A neurobiological approach.* Greenwood Village, CO: Roberts & Company Publishers.

Kochanska, Grazyna; Forman, David R.; Aksan, Nazan; & Dunbar, Stephen B. (2005). Pathways to conscience: Early mother-child mutually responsive orientation and children's moral emotion, conduct, and cognition. *Journal of Child Psychology and Psychiatry, 46,* 19–34.

Kochanska, Grazyna, & Knaack, Amy (2003). Effortful control as a personality characteristic of young children: Antecedents, correlates, and consequences. *Journal of Personality, 71,* 1087–1112.

Kohlberg, Lawrence (1964). Development of moral character and moral ideology. In M. Hoffman & L. W. Hoffman (Eds.), *Review of child development research.* New York: Russell Sage Foundation.

Köhler, Wolfgang (1925). *The mentality of apes.* New York: Harcourt, Brace.

Köhler, Wolfgang (1929). *Gestalt psychology.* New York: Horace Liveright.

Kohsaka, Akira; Laposky, Aaron D.; Ramsey, Kathryn Moynihan; et al. (2007). High-fat diet disrupts behavioral and molecular circadian rhythms in mice. *Cell Metabolism, 6,* 414–421.

Kok, Bethany E.; Catalino, Lahnna I.; & Fredrickson, Barbara L. (2008). The broadening, building, buffering effects of positive emotions. In S. J. Lopez (Ed.), *Positive psychology: Exploring the best in people* (Vol. 2). Westport, CT: Praeger Publishers/Greenwood.

Komarraju, Meera, & Cokley, Kevin O. (2008). Horizontal and vertical dimensions of individualism-collectivism: A comparison of African Americans and European Americans. *Cultural Diversity and Ethnic Minority Psychology, 14,* 336–343.

Koocher, Gerald P.; Goodman, Gail S.; White, C. Sue; et al. (1995). Psychological science and the use of anatomically detailed dolls in child sexual-abuse assessments. *Psychological Bulletin, 118,* 199–222.

Kornell, Nate (2009). Metacognition in humans and animals. *Current Directions in Psychological Science, 18,* 11–15.

Kosfeld, Michael; Heinrichs, Markus; Zak, Paul J.; et al. (2005). Oxytocin increases trust in humans. *Nature, 435,* 673–676.

Kosslyn, Stephen M. (1980). *Image and mind.* Cambridge, MA: Harvard University Press.

Kounios, John, & Beeman, Mark (2009). The *Aha!* Moment: The cognitive neuroscience of insight. *Current Directions in Psychological Science, 18,* 210–216.

Koyama, Tetsua; McHaffie, John G.; Laurienti, Paul J.; & Coghill, Robert C. (2005). The subjective experience of pain: Where expectations become reality. *Proceedings of the National Academy of Sciences, 102,* 12950–12955.

Kramer, Arthur F., & Willis, Sherry L. (2002). Enhancing the cognitive vitality of older adults. *Current Directions in Psychological Science, 11,* 173–177.

Krantz, David S.; Olson, Marian B.; Francis, Jennifer L.; et al. (2006). Anger, hostility, and cardiac symptoms in women with suspected coronary artery disease: The women's ischemia syndrome evaluation (WISE) study. *Journal of Women's Health, 15,* 1214–1223.

Krebs, Dennis L. (2008). Morality: An evolutionary account. *Perspectives on Psychological Science, 3,* 149–172.

Kreps, Bonnie (1990). *Subversive thoughts, authentic passions.* San Francisco: Harper & Row.

Krieger, Nancy, & Sidney, S. (1996). Racial discrimination and blood pressure: The CARDIA study of young black and white adults. *American Journal of Public Health, 86,* 1370–1378.

Krimsky, Sheldon (2003). *Science in the private interest.* Lanham, MD: Rowman & Littlefield.

Kring, Ann M., & Gordon, Albert H. (1998). Sex differences in emotion: Expression, experience, and physiology. *Journal of Personality and Social Psychology, 74,* 686–703.

Kripke, Daniel F. (1974). Ultradian rhythms in sleep and wakefulness. In E. D. Weitzman (Ed.), *Advances in sleep research* (Vol. 1). Flushing, NY: Spectrum.

Krueger, Alan B. (2007). *What makes a terrorist: Economics and the roots of terrorism.* Princeton, NJ: Princeton University Press.

Krueger, Robert F.; Hicks, Brian M.; & McGue, Matt (2001). Altruism and antisocial behavior: Independent tendencies, unique personality correlates, distinct etiologies. *Psychological Science, 12,* 397–402.

Kruglanski, Arie W.; Chen, Xiaoyan; Dechesne, Mark; et al. (2009). Fully committed: Suicide bombers' motivation and the quest for personal significance. *Political Psychology, 30,* 331–357.

Krützen, Michael; Mann, Janet; Heithaus, Michael R.; et al. (2005). Cultural transmission of tool use in bottlenose dolphins. *Proceedings of the National Academy of Sciences, 102,* 8939–8943; published online before print as 10.1073/pnas.0500232102.

Kuhl, Patricia K.; Williams, Karen A.; Lacerda, Francisco; et al. (1992, January 31). Linguistic experience alters phonetic perception in infants by 6 months of age. *Science, 255,* 606–608.

Kuhn, Deanna; Weinstock, Michael; & Flaton, Robin (1994). How well do jurors reason? Competence dimensions of individual variation in a juror reasoning task. *Psychological Science, 5,* 289–296.

Kuncel, Nathan R.; Hezlett, Sarah A.; & Ones, Deniz S. (2004). Academic performance, career potential, creativity, and job performance: Can one construct predict them all? *Journal of Personality and Social Psychology, 86,* 148–161.

Kutchins, Herb, & Kirk, Stuart A. (1997). *Making us crazy: DSM. The psychiatric bible and the creation of mental disorders.* New York: Free Press.

Laan, Ellen, & Both, Stephanie (2008). What makes women experience desire? In L Tiefer (Ed.), The New View campaign against the medicalization of sex (Special Issue). *Feminism and Psychology, 18,* 505–514.

LaBerge, Stephen, & Levitan, Lynne (1995). Validity established of DreamLight cues for eliciting lucid dreaming. *Dreaming: Journal of the Association for the Study of Dreams, 5,* 159–168.

Lacasse, Jeffrey R., & Leo, Jonathan (2005, December). Serotonin and depression: A disconnect between the advertisements and the scientific literature. *PloS Medicine,* 2(12):e392. doi:10.1371/journal.pmed.0020392.

Lachman, Margie E., & Weaver, Suzanne L. (1998). The sense of control as a moderator of social class differences in health and well-being. *Journal of Personality and Social Psychology, 74,* 763–773.

Lachman, Sheldon J. (1996). Processes in perception: Psychological transformations of highly structured stimulus material. *Perceptual and Motor Skills, 83,* 411–418.

LaFrance, Marianne; Hecht, Marvin A.; & Paluck, Elizabeth L. (2003). The contingent smile: A meta-analysis of sex differences in smiling. *Psychological Bulletin, 129,* 305–334.

Lahey, B. B.; Pelham, W. E.; Loney, J.; et al. (2005). Instability of the DSM-IV subtypes of ADHD from preschool through elementary school. *Archives of General Psychiatry, 62,* 896–902.

Lai, Hui-Ling, & Good, Marion (2005). Music improves sleep quality in older adults. *Journal of Advanced Nursing, 49,* 234–244.

Landrigan, C. P.; Fahrenkopf, A. M.; Lewin, D.; et al. (2008). Effects of the Accreditation Council for Graduate Medical Education duty hour limits on sleep, work hours, and safety. *Pediatrics, 122,* 250–258.

Landrine, Hope (1988). Revising the framework of abnormal psychology. In P. Bronstein & K. Quina (Eds.), *Teaching a psychology of people.* Washington, DC: American Psychological Association.

Lang, Ariel J.; Craske, Michelle G.; Brown, Matt; & Ghaneian, Atousa (2001). Fear-related state dependent memory. *Cognition & Emotion, 15,* 695–703.

Lang, Frieder R., & Heckhausen, Jutta (2001). Perceived control over development and subjective well-being: Differential benefits across adulthood. *Journal of Personality and Social Psychology, 81,* 509–523.

Langer, Ellen J.; Blank, Arthur; & Chanowitz, Benzion (1978). The mindlessness of ostensibly thoughtful action: The role of placebic information in interpersonal interaction. *Journal of Personality and Social Psychology, 36,* 635–642.

Lanphear, B. P.; Hornung, R.; Ho, M.; et al. (2002). Environmental lead exposure during early childhood. *Journal of Pediatrics, 140,* 40–47.

Lany, Jill, & Gómez, Rebecca L. (2008). Twelve-month-old infants benefit from prior experience in statistical learning. *Psychological Science, 19,* 1247–1252.

Lau, H.; Alger, S.; & Fishbein, W. (2008). Naps and relational memory—a daytime nap facilitates extraction of general concepts. Paper presented at the annual meeting of the Society for Neuroscience, November, Washington DC.

Laumann, Edward O., & Gagnon John H. (1995). A sociological perspective on sexual action. In R. G. Parker & J. H. Gagnon (Eds.), *Conceiving sexuality: Approaches to sex research in a postmodern world.* New York: Routledge.

Laumann, Edward O.; Gagnon, John H.; Michael, Robert T.; & Michaels, Stuart (1994). *The social organization of sexuality.* Chicago: University of Chicago Press.

Lavie, Peretz (1976). Ultradian rhythms in the perception of two apparent motions. *Chronobiologia, 3,* 21–218.

Lavie, Peretz (2001). Sleep-wake as a biological rhythm. *Annual Review of Psychology, 52,* 277–303.

Lazarus, Richard S. (2000). Toward better research on stress and coping. *American Psychologist, 55,* 665–673.

Lazarus, Richard S., & Folkman, Susan (1984). *Stress, appraisal, and coping.* New York: Springer.

LeDoux, Joseph E. (1996). *The emotional brain.* New York: Simon & Schuster.

Lee, Susan J., & McEwen, Bruce S. (2001). Neurotrophic and neuroprotective actions of estrogens and their therapeutic implications. *Annual Review of Pharmacology & Pharmacological Toxicology, 41,* 569–591.

Leib, Rebecca (2008). MMPI-2 family problems scales in child-custody litigants. *Dissertation Abstracts International:* Section B: The Sciences and Engineering. 68(7-B), 4879.

Leibenluft, E., & Rich, B. A. (2008). Pediatric bipolar disorder. *Annual Review of Clinical Psychology, 4,* 163–187.

Leichsenring, Falk, & Rabung, Sven (2008, October 1). Effectiveness of long-term psychodynamic therapy: A meta-analysis. *Journal of the American Medical Association, 300,* 1551–1565.

Leinbach, Mary D.; Hort, Barbara E.; & Fagot, Beverly I. (1997). Bears are for boys: Metaphorical associations in young children's gender stereotypes. *Cognitive Development, 12,* 107–130.

Lemieux, Robert, & Hale, Jerold L. (2000). Intimacy, passion, and commitment among married individuals: Further testing of the Triangular Theory of Love. *Psychological Reports, 87,* 941–948.

Leo, Richard A. (2008). *Police interrogation and American justice.* Cambridge, MA: Harvard University Press.

Leonard, Karen M. (2008). A cross-cultural investigation of temporal orientation in work organizations: A differentiation matching approach. *International Journal of Intercultural Relations, 32,* 479–492.

Lepore, Stephen J.; Ragan, Jennifer D.; & Jones, Scott (2000). Talking facilitates cognitive-emotional processes of adaptation to an acute stressor. *Journal of Personality and Social Psychology, 78,* 499–508.

Lepowsky, Maria (1994). *Fruit of the motherland: Gender in an egalitarian society.* New York: Columbia University Press.

Lepper, Mark R.; Greene, David; & Nisbett, Richard E. (1973). Undermining children's intrinsic interest with extrinsic rewards. *Journal of Personality and Social Psychology, 28,* 129–137.

Leproult, Rachel; Copinschi, Georges; Buxton, Orfeu; & Van Cauter, Eve (1997). Sleep loss results in an elevation of cortisol levels the next evening. *Sleep, 20,* 865–870.

Lerner, Melvin J. (1980). *The belief in a just world: A fundamental delusion.* New York: Plenum.

Lester, Barry M.; LaGasse, Linda L.; & Seifer, Ronald (1998, October 23). Cocaine exposure and children: The meaning of subtle effects. *Science, 282,* 633–634.

Levenson, Robert W. (1992). Autonomic nervous system differences among emotions. *Psychological Science, 3,* 23–27.

Levenson, Robert W.; Ekman, Paul; & Friesen, Wallace V. (1990). Voluntary facial action generates emotion-specific autonomic nervous system activity. *Psychophysiology, 27,* 363–384.

Levenson, Robert W., & Miller, Bruce L. (2007). Loss of cells—loss of self. *Current Directions in Psychological Science, 16,* 289–294.

Levin, Daniel T. (2000). Race as a visual feature: Using visual search and perceptual discrimination tasks to understand face categories and the cross-race recognition deficit. *Journal of Experimental Psychology: General, 129,* 559–574.

Levine, James A.; Eberhardt, Norman L.; & Jensen, Michael D. (1999, January 8). Role of nonexercise activity thermogenesis in resistance to fat gain in humans. *Science, 283,* 212–214.

Levine, Robert V. (2003, May-June). The kindness of strangers. *American Scientist, 91,* 227–233.

Levine, Robert V.; Norenzayan, Ara; & Philbrick, Karen (2001). Cross-cultural differences in helping strangers. *Journal of Cross-Cultural Psychology, 32,* 543–560.

LeVine, Robert A., & Norman, Karin (2008). Attachment in anthropological perspective. In R. A. LeVine & R. S. New (Eds.), *Anthropology and child development: A cross-cultural reader.* Malden: Blackwell.

Levy, Becca. (1996). Improving memory in old age through implicit self-stereotyping. *Journal of Personality and Social Psychology, 71,* 1092–1107.

Levy, David A. (2010). *Tools of critical thinking: Metathoughts for psychology* (2nd ed.). Long Grove, IL: Waveland.

Levy, Jerre; Trevarthen, Colwyn; & Sperry, Roger W. (1972). Perception of bilateral chimeric figures following hemispheric deconnection. *Brain, 95,* 61–78.

Levy, Robert I. (1984). The emotions in comparative perspective. In K. R. Scherer & P. Ekman (Eds.), *Approaches to emotion.* Hillsdale, NJ: Erlbaum.

Lewin, Kurt (1948). *Resolving social conflicts.* New York: Harper.

Lewontin, Richard C. (1970). Race and intelligence. *Bulletin of the Atomic Scientists, 26*(3), 2–8.

Lewontin, Richard C. (2001, March 5). Genomania: A disorder of modern biology and medicine. Invited address at the University of California, Los Angeles.

Lewy, Alfred J.; Ahmed, Saeeduddin; Jackson, Jeanne L.; & Sack, Robert L. (1992). Melatonin shifts human circadian rhythms according to a phase response curve. *Chronobiology International, 9,* 380–392.

Lewy, Alfred J.; Lefler, Bryan J.; Emens, Jonathan S.; & Bauer, Vance K. (2006). The circadian basis of winter depression. *Proceedings of the National Academy of Sciences, 103,* 7414–7419.

Lickona, Thomas (1983). *Raising good children.* New York: Bantam.

Lieberman, J. A.; Stroup, T. S.; McEvoy, J. P.; et al. (2005, September 22). Effectiveness of antipsychotic drugs in patients with chronic schizophrenia. *New England Journal of Medicine, 353,* 1209–1223.

Lieberman, Matthew (2000). Intuition: A social cognitive neuroscience approach. *Psychological Bulletin, 126,* 109–137.

Lien, Mei-Ching; Ruthruff, Eric; & Johnston, James C. (2006). Attentional limitations in doing two tasks at once: The search for exceptions. *Current Directions in Psychological Science, 16,* 89–93.

Liepert, J.; Bauder, H.; Miltner, W. H.; et al. (2000). Treatment-induced cortical reorganization after stroke in humans. *Stroke, 31,* 1210–1216.

Lilienfeld, Scott O. (2007). Psychological treatments that cause harm. *Perspectives on Psychological Science, 2,* 53–70.

Lilienfeld, Scott O.; Gershon, Jonathan; Duke, Marshall; Marino, Lori; & De Waal, Frans B. M. (1999). A preliminary investigation of the construct of psychopathic personality (psychopathy) in chimpanzees (Pan troglodytes). *Journal of Comparative Psychology, 113,* 365–375.

Lilienfeld, Scott O., & Lohr, Jeffrey (2003). Dissociative identity disorder: Multiple personalities, multiple controversies. In S. O. Lilienfeld, S. J. Lynn, & J. M. Lohr (Eds.), *Science and pseudoscience in clinical psychology.* New York: Guilford.

Lilienfeld, Scott O.; Lynn, Steven Jay; & Lohr, Jeffrey M. (Eds.) (2003). *Science and pseudoscience in clinical psychology.* New York: Guilford.

Lilienfeld, Scott O.; Wood, James M.; & Garb, Howard N. (2000). The scientific status of projective techniques. *Psychological Science in the Public Interest, 1,* 27–66.

Liljenquist, Katie; Zhong, Chen-Bo; & Galinsky, Adam D. (2010). The smell of virtue: Clean scents promote reciprocity and charity. *Psychological Science, 21,* 381–383.

Lin, Keh-Ming; Poland, Russell E.; & Chien, C. P. (1990). Ethnicity and psychopharmacology: Recent findings and future research directions. In E. Sorel (Ed.), *Family, culture, and psychobiology.* New York: Legas.

Lin, L.; Hungs, M.; & Mignot, E. (2001). Narcolepsy and the HLA region. *Journal of Neuroimmunology, 117,* 9–20.

Lindquist, Kristen A., & Barrett, Lisa F. (2008). Constructing emotion. *Psychological Science, 19,* 898–903.

Lindsay, D. Stephen; Hagen, Lisa; Read, J. Don; et al. (2004). True photographs and false memories. *Psychological Science, 15,* 149–154.

Linton, Marigold (1978). Real-world memory after six years: An in vivo study of very long-term memory. In M. M. Gruneberg, P. E. Morris, & R. N. Sykes (Eds.), *Practical aspects of memory.* London: Academic Press.

Linton, Simi (1998). *Claiming disability: Knowledge and identity.* New York: New York University Press.

Linton, Simi (2006). *My body politic.* Ann Arbor, MI: University of Michigan Press.

Linville, P. W.; Fischer, G. W.; & Fischhoff, B. (1992). AIDS risk perceptions and decision biases. In J. B. Pryor & G. D. Reeder (Eds.), *The social psychology of HIV infection.* Hillsdale, NJ: Erlbaum.

Lissner, L.; Odell, P. M.; D'Agostino, R. B.; et al. (1991, June 27). Variability of body weight and health outcomes in the Framingham population. *New England Journal of Medicine, 324,* 1839–1844.

Lloyd-Richardson, E. E.; Bailey, S.; Fava, J. L.; Wing, R.; Tobacco Etiology Research Network (TERN) (2009). A prospective study of weight gain during the college freshman and sophomore years. *Preventive Medicine, 48,* 256–261.

LoBue, Vanessa, & DeLoache, Judy S. (2008). Detecting the snake in the grass. *Psychological Science, 19,* 284–289.

Locke, Edwin A., & Latham, Gary P. (2002). Building a practically useful theory of goal setting and task motivation. *American Psychologist, 57,* 705–717.

Locke, Edwin A., & Latham, Gary P. (2006). New directions in goal-setting theory. *Current Directions in Psychological Science, 15,* 265–268.

Loehlin, John C.; Horn, J. M.; & Willerman, L. (1996). Heredity, environment, and IQ in the Texas adoption study. In R. J. Sternberg & E. Grigorenko (Eds.), *Intelligence: Heredity and environment.* New York: Cambridge University Press.

Loftus, Elizabeth F., & Greene, Edith (1980). Warning: Even memory for faces may be contagious. *Law and Human Behavior, 4,* 323–334.

Loftus, Elizabeth F.; Miller, David G.; & Burns, Helen J. (1978). Semantic integration of verbal information into a visual memory. *Journal of Experimental Psychology: Human Learning and Memory, 4,* 19–31.

Loftus, Elizabeth F., & Palmer, John C. (1974). Reconstruction of automobile destruction: An example of the interaction between language and memory. *Journal of Verbal Learning and Verbal Behavior, 13,* 585–589.

Loftus, Elizabeth F., & Pickrell, Jacqueline E. (1995). The formation of false memories. *Psychiatric Annals, 25,* 720–725.

Loftus, Elizabeth F., & Zanni, Guido (1975). Eyewitness testimony: The influence of the wording of a question. *Bulletin of the Psychonomic Society, 5,* 86–88.

Lohr, Jeffrey M.; Montgomery, Robert W.; Lilienfeld, Scott O.; & Tolin, David F. (1999). Pseudoscience and the commercial promotion of trauma treatments. In R. Gist & B. Lubin (Eds.), *Response to disaster: Psychosocial, community, and ecological approaches.* Philadelphia, PA: Brunner/Mazel (Taylor & Francis).

Lohr, Jeffrey M.; Tolin, D. F.; & Lilienfeld, Scott O. (1998). Efficacy of eye movement desensitization and reprocessing: Implications for behavior therapy. *Behavior Therapy, 29,* 123–156.

Lonner, Walter J. (1995). Culture and human diversity. In E. Trickett, R. Watts, & D. Birman (Eds.), *Human diversity: Perspectives on people in context.* San Francisco: Jossey-Bass.

Lonsdorf, Tina B.; Weike, Almut I.; Nikamo, Pernilla; et al. (2009). Genetic gating of human fear learning and extinction: Possible implications for gene-environment interaction in anxiety disorder. *Psychological Science, 20,* 198–206.

López, Steven R. (1995). Testing ethnic minority children. In B. B. Wolman (Ed.), *The encyclopedia of psychology, psychiatry, and psychoanalysis.* New York: Holt.

Lorber, Michael F. (2004). Psychophysiology of aggression, psychopathy, and conduct problems: A meta-analysis. *Psychological Bulletin, 130,* 531–552.

Löw, Andreas; Lang, Peter J.; Smith, J. Carson; & Bradley, Margaret M. (2008). Both predator and prey: Emotional arousal in threat and reward. *Psychological Science, 19,* 865–873.

Lozano, A. M.; Mayberg, H. S.; Giacobbe, P.; et al. (2008). Subcallosal cingulate gyrus deep brain stimulation for treatment-resistant depression. *Biological Psychiatry, 64,* 461–467.

Lu, Luo (2008). The individual-oriented and social-oriented Chinese bicultural self: Testing the theory. *Journal of Social Psychology, 148,* 347–373.

Lubinski, David (2004). Introduction to the special section on cognitive abilities: 100 years after Spearman's (1904) "'General intelligence,' objectively determined and measured." *Journal of Personality and Social Psychology, 86,* 96–111.

Lucchina, L. A.; Curtis, O. F.; Putnam, P.; et al. (1998). Psychophysical measurement of 6-n-propylthiouracil (PROP) taste perception. *Annals of the New York Academy of Sciences, 855,* 816–819.

Luders, Eileen; Narr, Katherine L.; Thompson, Paul M.; et al. (2004). Gender differences in cortical complexity. *Nature Neuroscience, 7,* 799–800.

Luengo, M. A.; Carrillo-de-la-Peña, M. T.; Otero, J. M.; & Romero, E. (1994). A short-term longitudinal study of impulsivity and antisocial behavior. *Journal of Personality and Social Psychology, 66,* 542–548.

Luhrmann, T. M. (2000). *Of two minds: The growing disorder in American psychiatry.* New York: Knopf.

Luria, Alexander R. (1968). *The mind of a mnemonist* (L. Soltaroff, Trans.). New York: Basic Books.

Luria, Alexander R. (1980). *Higher cortical functions in man* (2nd rev. ed.). New York: Basic Books.

Lutz, Catherine (1988). *Unnatural emotions.* Chicago: University of Chicago Press.

Lykken, David T. (1995). *The antisocial personalities.* Hillsdale, NJ: Erlbaum.

Lykken, David T. (1998). *A tremor in the blood: Uses and abuses of the lie detector.* New York: Plenum Press.

Lykken, David T., & Tellegen, Auke (1996). Happiness is a stochastic phenomenon. *Psychological Science, 7,* 186–189.

Lyndon, Amy E.; White, Jacquelyn W.; Kadlec, Kelly M. (2007). Manipulation and force as sexual coercion tactics: Conceptual and empirical differences. *Aggressive Behavior, 33,* 291–303.

Lynn, Steven Jay; Rhue, Judith W.; & Weekes, John R. (1990). Hypnotic involuntariness: A social cognitive analysis. *Psychological Review, 97,* 69–184.

Lytton, Hugh, & Romney, David M. (1991). Parents' differential socialization of boys and girls: A meta-analysis. *Psychological Bulletin, 109,* 267–296.

Maass, Anne; Cadinu, Mara; Guarnieri, Gaia; & Grasselli, Annalisa (2003). Sexual harassment under social identity threat: The computer harassment paradigm. *Journal of Personality and Social Psychology, 85,* 853–870.

MacArthur Foundation Research Network on Successful Midlife Development (1999). Report of latest findings (Orville G. Brim, director; 2145 14th Avenue, Vero Beach, FL 32960).

Maccoby, Eleanor E. (1998). *The two sexes: Growing up apart, coming together.* Cambridge, MA: Belknap Press/Harvard University Press.

Maccoby, Eleanor E. (2002). Gender and group process: A developmental perspective. *Current Directions in Psychological Science, 11,* 54–58.

Mack, Arien (2003). Inattentional blindness: Looking without seeing. *Current Directions in Psychological Science, 12,* 180–184.

MacLean, Paul (1993). Cerebral evolution of emotion. In M. Lewis & J. M. Haviland (Eds.), *Handbook of emotions.* New York: Guilford Press.

Macleod John; Oakes Rachel; Copello, Alex; et al. (2004). Psychological and social sequelae of cannabis and other illicit drug use by young people: A systematic review of longitudinal, general population studies. *The Lancet, 363,* 1568–1569.

Macrae, C. Neil, & Bodenhausen, Galen V. (2000). Social cognition: Thinking categorically about others. *Annual Review of Psychology, 51,* 93–120.

Maddux, James E. (Ed.) (1995). *Self-efficacy, adaptation, and adjustment: Theory, research, and application.* New York: Plenum.

Madsen, Kreesten M.; Hviid, Anders; Vestergaard, Mogens; et al. (2002). A population-based study of measles, mumps, and rubella vaccination and autism. *New England Journal of Medicine, 347,* 1477–1482.

Maguire, Eleanor A.; Gadian, David G.; Johnsrude, Ingrid S.; et al. (2000). Navigation-related structural change in the hippocampi of taxi drivers. *Proceedings of the National Academy of Sciences, 97,* 4398–4403.

Maki, Pauline M.; & Resnick, Susan M. (2000). Longitudinal effects of estrogen replacement therapy on PET cerebral blood flow and cognition. *Neurobiology of Aging, 21,* 373–383.

Malamuth, Neil M.; Linz, Daniel; Heavey, Christopher L.; et al. (1995). Using the confluence model of sexual aggression to predict men's conflict with women: A 10-year follow-up study. *Journal of Personality and Social Psychology, 69,* 353–369.

Malaspina, Dolores (2001). Paternal factors and schizophrenia risk: De novo mutations and imprinting. *Schizophrenia Bulletin, 27,* 379–393.

Mandrusiak, Michael; Rudd, M. David; Joiner Jr., Thomas E.; et al. (2006). Warning signs for suicide on the Internet: A descriptive study. *Suicide and Life-Threatening Behavior, 36,* 263–271.

Marcus, Gary F.; Pinker, Steven; Ullman, Michael; et al. (1992). Overregularization in language acquisition. *Monographs of the Society for Research in Child Development, 57* (Serial No. 228), 1–182.

Marcus, Gary F.; Vijayan, S.; Rao, S. Bandi; & Vishton, P. M. (1999). Rule learning by seven-month-old infants. *Science, 283,* 77–80.

Marcus-Newhall, Amy; Pedersen, William C.; Carlson, Mike; & Miller, Norman (2000). Displaced aggression is alive and well: A meta-analytic review. *Journal of Personality and Social Psychology, 78,* 670–689.

Margolin, Gayla, & Gordis, Elana B. (2004). Children's exposure to violence in the family and community. *Current Directions in Psychological Science, 13,* 152–155.

Markus, Hazel R., & Kitayama, Shinobu (1991). Culture and the self: Implications for cognition, emotion, and motivation. *Psychological Review, 98,* 224–253.

Marlatt, G. Alan, & Rohsenow, Damaris J. (1980). Cognitive processes in alcohol use: Expectancy and the balanced placebo design. In N. K. Mello (Ed.), *Advances in substance abuse* (Vol. 1). Greenwich, CT: JAI Press.

Marsh, Elizabeth J., & Tversky, Barbara (2004). Spinning the stories of our lives. *Applied Cognitive Psychology, 18,* 491–503.

Martin, Carol Lynn, & Ruble, Diane (2004). Children's search for gender cues. *Current Directions in Psychological Science, 13,* 67–70.

Martin, Carol Lynn; Ruble, Diane N.; & Szkrybalo, Joel (2002). Cognitive theories of early gender development. *Psychological Bulletin, 128,* 903–933.

Martin, Garry, & Pear, Joseph (2007). *Behavior modification: What it is and how to do it* (8th ed.). NY: Prentice Hall.

Maruta, T.; Colligan R. C.; Malinchoc, M.; & Offord, K. P. (2000). Optimists vs. pessimists: Survival rate among medical patients over a 30-year period. *Mayo Clinic Proceedings, 75,* 140–143.

Marvan, M. L.; Diaz-Erosa, M.; & Montesinos, A. (1998). Premenstrual symptoms in Mexican women with different educational levels. *Journal of Psychology, 132,* 517–526.

Masand, P. S. (2000). Side effects of antipsychotics in the elderly. *Journal of Clinical Psychiatry, 61*(suppl. 8), 43–49.

Maslach, Christina; Schaufeli, Wilmar B.; & Leiter, Michael P. (2001). Job burnout. *Annual Review of Psychology, 52,* 397–422.

Maslow, Abraham H. (1970). *Motivation and personality* (2nd ed.). New York: Harper & Row.

Maslow, Abraham H. (1971). *The farther reaches of human nature.* New York: Viking.

Masten, Ann S. (2001). Ordinary magic: Resilience processes in development. *American Psychologist, 56,* 227–238.

Masters, William H., & Johnson, Virginia E. (1966). *Human sexual response.* Boston: Little, Brown.

Masuda, Takahiko, & Nisbett, Richard E. (2001). Attending holistically versus analytically: Comparing the context sensitivity of Japanese and Americans. *Journal of Personality and Social Psychology, 81,* 922–934.

Mather, Jennifer A., & Anderson, Roland C. (1993). Personalities of octopuses (Octopus rubescens). *Journal of Comparative Psychology, 197,* 336–340.

Mather, Mara; Shafir, Eldar; & Johnson, Marcia K. (2000). Misremembrance of options past: Source monitoring and choice. *Psychological Science, 11,* 132–138.

Matsumoto, David (1996). *Culture and psychology.* Pacific Grove, CA: Brooks-Cole.

Matthews, Gerald; Zeidner, Moshe; & Roberts, Richard D. (2003). *Emotional intelligence: Science and myth.* Cambridge, MA: MIT Press/ Bradford Books.

Maviel, Thibault; Durkin, Thomas P.; Menzaghi, Frédérique; & Bontempi, Bruno (2004). Sites of neocortical reorganization critical for remote spatial memory. *Science, 305,* 96–99.

Mayer, Jane (2009). *The dark side: The inside story of how the war on terror turned into a war on American ideals* (reprint edition). New York: Anchor.

Mayer, John D., & Salovey, Peter (1997). What is emotional intelligence? In P. Salovey & D. Sluyter (Eds.), *Emotional development and emotional intelligence: Implications for educators*. New York: Basic Books.

Mayou, R. A.; Ehlers, A.; & Hobbs, M. (2000). Psychological debriefing for road traffic accident victims. *British Journal of Psychiatry, 176*, 589–593.

Mazza, James J., & Reynolds, William M. (1999). Exposure to violence in young inner-city adolescents: Relationships with suicidal ideation, depression, and PTSD symptomatology. *Journal of Abnormal Child Psychology, 27*, 203–213.

Mazzoni, Giuliana A.; Loftus, Elizabeth F.; & Kirsch, Irving (2001). Changing beliefs about implausible autobiographical events: A little plausibility goes a long way. *Journal of Experimental Psychology: Applied, 7*, 51–59.

Mazzoni, Giuliana A.; Loftus, Elizabeth F.; Seitz, Aaron; & Lynn, Steven J. (1999). Changing beliefs and memories through dream interpretation. *Applied Cognitive Psychology, 13*, 125–144.

McAdams, Dan P. (2006). *The redemptive self: Stories Americans live by*. New York: Oxford University Press.

McAdams, Dan P. (2008). Personal narratives and the life story. In O. P. John, R. W. Robbins, & L. A. Pervin (Eds.), *Handbook of personality: Theory and research*. New York: Guilford.

McAdams, Dan P., & Pals, Jennifer L. (2006). A new Big Five: Fundamental principles for an integrative science of personality. *American Psychologist, 61*, 204–217.

McClearn, Gerald E.; Johanson, Boo; Berg, Stig; et al. (1997). Substantial genetic influence on cognitive abilities in twins 80 or more years old. *Science, 176*, 1560–1563.

McClelland, David C. (1961). *The achieving society*. New York: Free Press.

McClelland, David C.; Atkinson, John W.; Clark, Russell A.; & Lowell, Edgar L. (1953). *The achievement motive*. New York: Appleton-Century-Crofts.

McClelland, James L. (1994). The organization of memory: A parallel distributed processing perspective. *Revue Neurologique, 150*, 570–579.

McCord, Joan (1989). Another time, another drug. Paper presented at conference on Vulnerability to the Transition from Drug Use to Abuse and Dependence, Rockville, MD.

McCrae, Robert R. (1987). Creativity, divergent thinking, and openness to experience. *Journal of Personality and Social Psychology, 52*, 1258–1265.

McCrae, Robert R., & Costa, Paul T. (2008). The five-factor theory of personality. In O.P. John, R.W. Robbins, & L.A. Pervin (Eds.), *Handbook of personality: Theory and research* (3rd ed.). New York: Guilford.

McCrae, Robert R.; Terracciano, Antonio; & members of the Personality Profiles of Cultures Project (2005). Universal features of personality traits from the observer's perspective: Data from 50 cultures. *Journal of Personality and Social Psychology, 88*, 547–561.

McDaniel, Mark A.; Howard, Daniel C.; & Einstein, Gilles O. (2009). The Read-Recite-Review study strategy: Effective and portable. *Psychological Science, 20*, 516–522.

McDonough, Laraine, & Mandler, Jean M. (1994). Very long-term recall in infancy. *Memory, 2*, 339–352.

McEwen, Bruce S. (1998). Protective and damaging effects of stress mediators. *New England Journal of Medicine, 338*, 171–179.

McEwen, Bruce S. (2000). Allostasis and allostatic load: Implications for neuropsychopharmacology. *Neuropsychopharmacology 22*, 108–124.

McEwen, Bruce S. (2007). Physiology and neurobiology of stress and adaptation: Central role of the brain. *Physiological Review, 87*, 873–904.

McFadden, Dennis (2008). What do sex, twins, spotted hyenas, ADHD, and sexual orientation have in common? *Perspectives on Psychological Science, 3*, 309–322.

McFarlane, Jessica; Martin, Carol L.; & Williams, Tannis M. (1988). Mood fluctuations: Women versus men and menstrual versus other cycles. *Psychology of Women Quarterly, 12*, 201–223.

McFarlane, Jessica M., & Williams, Tannis M. (1994). Placing premenstrual syndrome in perspective. *Psychology of Women Quarterly, 18*, 339–373.

McGoldrick, Monica (2005). Irish families. In M. McGoldrick, J. Giordano, & N. Garcia-Preto (Eds.), *Ethnicity and family therapy* (3rd ed.). New York: Guilford.

McGregor, Ian, & Holmes, John G. (1999). How storytelling shapes memory and impressions of relationship events over time. *Journal of Personality and Social Psychology, 76*, 403–419.

McGue, Matt; Bouchard, Thomas J., Jr.; Iacono, William G.; & Lykken, David T. (1993). Behavioral genetics of cognitive ability: A life-span perspective. In R. Plomin & G. E. McClearn (Eds.), *Nature, nurture, and psychology*. Washington, DC: American Psychological Association.

McGue, Matt, & Lykken, David T. (1992). Genetic influence on risk of divorce. *Psychological Science, 3*, 368–373.

McHugh, Paul R. (2008). *Try to remember: Psychiatry's clash over meaning, memory, and mind*. New York: Dana Press.

McKee, Richard D., & Squire, Larry R. (1992). Equivalent forgetting rates in long-term memory for diencephalic and medial temporal lobe amnesia. *Journal of Neuroscience, 12*, 3765–3772.

McKee, Richard D., & Squire, Larry R. (1993). On the development of declarative memory. *Journal of Experimental Psychology: Learning, Memory, and Cognition, 19*, 397–404.

McKemy, D. D.; Neuhausser, W. M.; & Julius, D. (2002). Identification of a cold receptor reveals a general role for TRP channels in thermosensation. *Nature, 416*, 52–58.

McKinlay, John B.; McKinlay, Sonja M.; & Brambilla, Donald (1987). The relative contributions of endocrine changes and social circumstances to depression in mid-aged women. *Journal of Health and Social Behavior, 28*, 345–363.

McMullin, Darcy, & White, Jacqueline W. (2006). Long-term effects of labeling a rape experience. *Psychology of Women Quarterly, 30*, 96–105.

McNally, Richard J. (2003). *Remembering trauma*. Cambridge, MA: Harvard University Press.

McNally, Richard J.; Bryant, Richard A.; & Ehlers, Anke (2003). Does early psychological intervention promote recovery from posttraumatic stress? *Psychological Science in the Public Interest, 4*, 45–79.

McNeill, David (1966). Developmental psycholinguistics. In F. L. Smith & G. A. Miller (Eds.), *The genesis of language: A psycholinguistic approach*. Cambridge, MA: MIT Press.

Mealey, Linda (2000). *Sex differences: Developmental and evolutionary strategies*. San Diego: Academic Press.

Mednick, Sara C.; Nakayama, Ken; Cantero, Jose L,; et al. (2002). The restorative effect of naps on perceptual deterioration. *Nature Neuroscience, 5*, 677–681.

Mednick, Sarnoff A. (1962). The associative basis of the creative process. *Psychological Review, 69*, 220–232.

Mednick, Sarnoff A.; Huttunen, Matti O.; & Machón, Ricardo (1994). Prenatal influenza infections and adult schizophrenia. *Schizophrenia Bulletin, 20*, 263–267.

Medvec, Victoria H.; Madey, Scott F.; & Gilovich, Thomas (1995). When less is more: Counterfactual thinking and satisfaction among Olympic medalists. *Journal of Personality and Social Psychology, 69*, 603–610.

Meeus, Wim H. J., & Raaijmakers, Quinten A. W. (1995). Obedience in modern society: The Utrecht studies. In A. G. Miller, B. E. Collins, & D. E. Brief (Eds.), *Perspectives on obedience to authority: The legacy of the Milgram experiments. Journal of Social Issues, 51*(3), 155–175.

Mehl, Matthias R.; Vazire, Simine; Ramírez-Esparza, Nairán; & Pennebacker, James W. (2007). Are women really more talkative than men? *Science, 317*, 82.

Meindl, James R., & Lerner, Melvin J. (1985). Exacerbation of extreme responses to an out-group. *Journal of Personality and Social Psychology, 47*, 71–84.

Meissner, Christian A. & Brigham, John C. (2001). Thirty years of investigating the own-race bias in memory for faces: A meta-analytic review. *Psychology, Public Policy, & Law, 7*, 3–35.

Meltzoff, Andrew N., & Gopnik, Alison (1993). The role of imitation in understanding persons and developing a theory of mind. In S. Baron-Cohen, H. Tager-Flusberg, & D. Cohen (Eds.), *Understanding other minds*. New York: Oxford University Press.

Melzack, Ronald (1992, April). Phantom limbs. *Scientific American, 266,* 120–126. [Reprinted in the special issue *Mysteries of the Mind,* 1997.]

Melzack, Ronald (1993). Pain: Past, present and future. *Canadian Journal of Experimental Psychology, 47,* 615–629.

Melzack, Ronald, & Wall, Patrick D. (1965). Pain mechanisms: A new theory. *Science, 13,* 971–979.

Mendoza-Denton, Rodolfo, & Page-Gould, Elizabeth (2008). Can cross-group friendships influence minority students' well-being at historically white universities? *Psychological Science, 19,* 933–939.

Mennella, Julie A.; Jagnow, C. P.; & Beauchamp, Gary K. (2001). Prenatal and postnatal flavor learning by human infants. *Pediatrics, 107,* E88.

Mercer, Jean (2006). *Understanding attachment.* Westport, CT: Praeger.

Mercer, Jean; Sarner, Larry; and Rosa, Linda (2003). *Attachment therapy on trial.* Westport, CT: Praeger.

Merikle, Philip M., & Skanes, Heather E. (1992). Subliminal self-help audiotapes: A search for placebo effects. *Journal of Applied Psychology, 77,* 772–776.

Merskey, Harold (1992). The manufacture of personalities: The production of MPD. *British Journal of Psychiatry, 160,* 327–340.

Merton, Robert K. (1948). The self-fulfilling prophecy. *Antioch Review, 8,* 193–210.

Mesquita, Batja, & Frijda, Nico H. (1992). Cultural variations in emotions: A review. *Psychological Bulletin, 112,* 179–204.

Meston, Cindy M., & Buss, David M. (2007). Why humans have sex. *Archives of Sexual Behavior, 36,* 477–507.

Metcalfe, Janet (2009). Metacognitive judgments and control of study. *Current Directions in Psychological Science, 18,* 159–163.

Meyer, Gregory J.; Finn, Stephen E.; Eyde, Lorraine D.; et al. (2001). Psychological testing and psychological assessment. *American Psychologist, 56,* 128–165.

Mezulis, Amy H.; Abramson, Lyn Y.; Hyde, Janet S.; & Hankin, Benjamin L. (2004). Is there a positivity bias in attributions? *Psychological Bulletin, 130,* 711–747.

Mieda, Michihiro; Willie, Jon T.; Hara, Junko; et al. (2004). Orexin peptides prevent cataplexy and improve wakefulness in an orexin neuron-ablated model of narcolepsy in mice. *Proceedings of the National Academy of Science, 101,* 4649–4654.

Miklowitz, David J. (2007). The role of the family in the course and treatment of bipolar disorder. *Current Directions in Psychological Science, 16,* 192–196.

Mikulincer, Mario, & Shaver, Philip R. (2007). *Attachment in adulthood: Structure, dynamics, and change.* New York: Guilford Press.

Mikulincer, Mario; Shaver, Phillip R.; Gillath, Omri; & Nitzberg, R. E. (2005). Attachment, caregiving, and altruism: Boosting attachment security increases compassion and helping. *Journal of Personality and Social Psychology, 89,* 817–839.

Mikulincer, Mario; Shaver, Phillip R.; & Horesh, Nita (2006). Attachment bases of emotion regulation and posttraumatic adjustment. In D. K. Snyder, J. A. Simpson, & J. N. Hughes (Eds.), *Emotion regulation in couples and families: Pathways to dysfunction and health.* Washington, DC: American Psychological Association.

Milgram, Stanley (1963). Behavioral study of obedience. *Journal of Abnormal and Social Psychology, 67,* 371–378.

Milgram, Stanley (1974). *Obedience to authority: An experimental view.* New York: Harper & Row.

Miller, George A. (1956). The magical number seven, plus or minus two: Some limits on our capacity for processing information. *Psychological Review, 63,* 81–97.

Miller, Greg (2008, April 11). Tackling alcoholism with drugs. *Science, 320,* 168–170.

Miller, Gregory E.; Chen, Edith; & Zhou, Eric S. (2007). If it goes up, must it come down? Chronic stress and the hypothalamic-pituitary-adrenocortical axis in humans. *Psychological Bulletin, 133,* 25–45.

Miller, Inglis J., & Reedy, Frank E. (1990). Variations in human taste bud density and taste intensity perception. *Physiology and Behavior, 47,* 1213–1219.

Miller, William R., & Rollnick, Stephen (2002). *Motivational interviewing: Preparing people for change* (2nd ed.). New York: Guilford Press.

Miller-Jones, Dalton (1989). Culture and testing. *American Psychologist, 44,* 360–366.

Milner, Brenda (1970). Memory and the temporal regions of the brain. In K. H. Pribram & D. E. Broadbent (Eds.), *Biology of memory.* New York: Academic Press.

Milner, J. S., & McCanne, T. R. (1991). Neuropsychological correlates of physical child abuse. In J. S. Milner (Ed.), *Neuropsychology of aggression.* Norwell, MA: Kluwer Academic.

Milton, Julie, & Wiseman, Richard (1999). Does psi exist? Lack of replication of an anomalous process of information transfer. *Psychological Bulletin, 125,* 387–391.

Milton, Julie, & Wiseman, Richard (2001). Does psi exist? Reply to Storm and Ertel (2001). *Psychological Bulletin, 127,* 434–438.

Mineka, Susan, & Zinbarg, Richard (2006). A contemporary learning theory perspective on the etiology of anxiety disorders. *American Psychologist, 61,* 10–26.

Minuchin, Salvador (1984). *Family kaleidoscope.* Cambridge, MA: Harvard University Press.

Minzenberg, Michael J., & Carter, Cameron S. (2008). Modafinil: A review of neurochemical actions and effects on cognition. *Neuropsychopharmacology, 33,* 1477–1502.

Mischel, Walter (1973). Toward a cognitive social learning reconceptualization of personality. *Psychological Review, 80,* 252–253.

Mischel, Walter, & Ayduk, Ozlem (2004). Willpower in a cognitive-affective processing system: The dynamics of delay of gratification. In R. F. Baumeister & K. D. Vohs (Eds.), *Handbook of self-regulation: Research, theory, and applications.* New York: Guilford Press.

Mischel, Walter, & Shoda, Yuichi (1995). A cognitive affective system theory of personality: Reconceptualizing situations, dispositions, dynamics, and invariance in personality structures. *Psychological Review, 102,* 246–268.

Mistry, Jayanthi, & Rogoff, Barbara (1994). Remembering in cultural context. In W. J. Lonner & R. Malpass (Eds.), *Psychology and culture.* Needham Heights, MA: Allyn & Bacon.

Mitchell, David B. (2006). Nonconscious priming after 17 years: Invulnerable implicit memory? *Psychological Science, 17,* 925–929.

Mitchell, Karen J., & Johnson, Marcia K. (2009). Source monitoring 15 years later: What have we learned from fMRI about the neural mechanisms of source memory? *Psychological Bulletin, 135,* 638–677.

Mitte, Kristin (2005). Meta-analysis of cognitive-behavioral treatments for generalized anxiety disorder: A comparison with pharmacotherapy. *Psychological Bulletin, 131,* 785–795.

Mitte, Kristin (2008). Memory bias for threatening information in anxiety and anxiety disorders: A meta-analytic review. *Psychological Bulletin, 134,* 886–911.

Mitterer, Holger, & de Ruiter, Jan Peter (2008). Recalibrating color categories using world knowledge. *Psychological Science, 19,* 629–634.

Modigliani, Andre, & Rochat, François (1995). The role of interaction sequences and the timing of resistance in shaping obedience and defiance to authority. In A. G. Miller, B. E. Collins, & D. E. Brief (Eds.), Perspectives on obedience to authority: The legacy of the Milgram experiments. *Journal of Social Issues, 51*(3), 107–125.

Moffitt, Terrie E. (1993). Adolescence-limited and life-course-persistent antisocial behavior: A developmental taxonomy. *Psychological Review, 100,* 674–701.

Moghaddam, Fathali M. (2005). The staircase to terrorism: A psychological exploration. *American Psychologist, 60,* 161–169.

Mohr, Cynthia; Armeli, Stephen; Tennen, Howard; et al. (2001). Daily interpersonal experiences, context, and alcohol consumption: Crying in your beer and toasting good times. *Journal of Personality and Social Psychology, 80,* 489–500.

Molnar-Szakacs, Istvan; Iacoboni, Marco; Koski, Lisa; & Mazziotta, John C. (2005). Functional segregation within pars opercularis of the inferior frontal gyrus: Evidence from fMRI studies of imitation and action observation. *Cerebral Cortex, 15,* 986–994.

Monahan, Jennifer L.; Murphy, Sheila T.; & Zajonc, R. B. (2000). Subliminal mere exposure: Specific, general, and diffuse effects. *Psychological Science, 11,* 462–466.

Moncrieff, Joanna (2001). Are antidepressants overrated? A review of methodological problems in antidepressant trials. *Journal of Nervous and Mental Disease, 189,* 288–295.

Monroe, Scott M., & Reid, Mark W. (2009). Life stress and major depression. *Current Directions in Psychological Science, 18,* 68–72.

Monroe, Scott M.; Slavich, George M.; Torres, Leandro D.; & Gotlib, Ian H. (2007). Severe life events predict specific patterns of change in cognitive biases in major depression. *Psychological Medicine, 37,* 863–871.

Monti, Martin M.; Vanhaudenhuyse, Audrey; Coleman, Martin R.; et al. (2010, February 3). Willful modulation of brain activity in disorders of consciousness. *New England Journal of Medicine.* Published online at NEJM.org. (10.1056/NEJMoa0905370).

Moore, Robert Y. (1997). Circadian rhythms: Basic neurobiology and clinical applications. *Annual Review of Medicine, 48,* 253–266.

Moore, Timothy E. (1992, Spring). Subliminal perception: Facts and fallacies. *Skeptical Inquirer, 16,* 273–281.

Moore, Timothy E. (1995). Subliminal self-help auditory tapes: An empirical test of perceptual consequences. *Canadian Journal of Behavioural Science, 27,* 9–20.

Moore, Timothy E., & Pepler, Debra J. (2006). Wounding words: Maternal verbal aggression and children's adjustment. *Journal of Family Violence, 21,* 89–93.

Morell, Virginia (2008, March). Minds of their own. *National Geographic, 213,* 36–61.

Morelli, Gilda A.; Rogoff, Barbara; Oppenheim, David; & Goldsmith, Denise (1992). Cultural variation in infants' sleeping arrangements: Questions of independence. *Developmental Psychology, 28,* 604–613.

Moreno, Carmen; Laje, Gonzalo; Blanco, Carlos; et al. (2007). National trends in the outpatient diagnosis and treatment of bipolar disorder in youth. *Archives of General Psychiatry, 64,* 1032–1039.

Morewedge, Carey K., & Norton, Michael I. (2009). When dreaming is believing: The (motivated) interpretation of dreams. *Journal of Personality and Social Psychology, 96,* 249–264.

Morgan, Charles A.; Hazlett, Gary; Baranoski, Madelon; et al. (2007). Accuracy of eyewitness identification is significantly associated with performance on a standardized test of face recognition. *International Journal of Law and Psychiatry, 30,* 213–223.

Morin, Charles M. (2004). Cognitive-behavioral approaches to the treatment of insomnia. *Journal of Clinical Psychiatry, 65*(suppl. 16), 33–40.

Morton, Thomas A.; Postmes, Tom; Haslam, S. Alexander; & Hornsey, Matthew J. (2009). Theorizing gender in the face of social change: Is there anything essential about essentialism? *Journal of Personality and Social Psychology, 96,* 653–664.

Moscovitch, Morris; Winocur, Gordon; & Behrmann, Marlene (1997). What is special about face recognition? Nineteen experiments on a person with visual object agnosia and dyslexia but normal face recognition. *Journal of Cognitive Neuroscience, 9,* 555–604.

Moskowitz, Judith T.; Hult, Jen R.; Bussolari, Cori; & Acree, Michael (2009). What works in coping with HIV? A meta-analysis with implications for coping with serious illness. *Psychological Bulletin, 135,* 121–141.

Moyer, Christopher A.; Rounds, James; & Hannum, James W. (2004). A meta-analysis of massage therapy research. *Psychological Bulletin, 130,* 3–18.

Mozell, Maxwell M.; Smith, Bruce P., Smith, Paul E.; Sullivan, Richard L.; & Swender, Philip (1969). Nasal chemoreception in flavor identification. *Archives of Otolaryngology, 90,* 367–373.

Mroczek, D. K., & Sprio, A., III (2005). Changes in life satisfaction during adulthood: Findings from the Veterans Affairs normative aging study. *Journal of Personality and Social Psychology, 88,* 189–202.

Mueller, Claudia M., & Dweck, Carol S. (1998). Praise for intelligence can undermine children's motivation and performance. *Journal of Personality and Social Psychology, 75,* 33–52.

Mukamal, Kenneth J.; Conigrove, Katherine M; Mittleman, Murray A.; et al. (2003). Roles of drinking pattern and type of alcohol consumed in coronary heart disease in men. *New England Journal of Medicine, 348,* 109–118.

Murphy, Sheila T.; Monahan, Jennifer L.; & Zajonc, R. B. (1995). Additivity of nonconscious affect: Combined effects of priming and exposure. *Journal of Personality and Social Psychology, 69,* 589–602.

Murray, Charles (2008). *Real education: Four simple truths for bringing America's schools back to reality.* New York: Crown Forum.

Myrtek, Michael (2007). Type A behavior and hostility as independent risk factors for coronary heart disease. In J. Jordan et al. (Eds.), *Contributions toward evidence-based psychocardiology: A systematic review of the literature.* Washington, DC: American Psychological Association.

Nakaya, Naoki; Tsubono, Yoshitaka; Hosokawa, Toru; et al. (2003). Personality and the risk of cancer. *Journal of the National Cancer Institute, 95,* 799–805.

Nash, Michael R. (1987). What, if anything, is regressed about hypnotic age regression? A review of the empirical literature. *Psychological Bulletin, 102,* 42–52.

Nash, Michael R. (2001, July). The truth and the hype of hypnosis. *Scientific American, 285,* 46–49, 52–55.

Nash, Michael R., & Barnier, Amanda J. (2007). *The Oxford handbook of hypnosis.* Oxford, UK: Oxford University Press.

Nash, Michael R., & Nadon, Robert (1997). Hypnosis. In D. L. Faigman, D. Kaye, M. J. Saks, & J. Sanders (Eds.), *Modern scientific evidence: The law and science of expert testimony.* St. Paul, MN: West.

Navarrete, Carlos David; Olsson, Andreas; Ho, Arnold K; et al. (2009). Fear extinction to an out-group face: The role of target gender. *Psychological Science, 20,* 155–158.

Needleman, Herbert L.; Riess, Julie A.; Tobin, Michael J.; et al. (1996). Bone lead levels and delinquent behavior. *Journal of the American Medical Association, 275,* 363–369.

Neher, Andrew (1996). Jung's theory of archetypes: A critique. *Journal of Humanistic Psychology, 36,* 61–91.

Neisser, Ulric, & Harsch, Nicole (1992). Phantom flashbulbs: False recollections of hearing the news about *Challenger.* In E. Winograd & U. Neisser (Eds.), *Affect and accuracy in recall: Studies of "flashbulb memories."* New York: Cambridge University Press.

Nelson, Charles A., III; Zeanah, Charles H.; Fox, Nathan A.; et al. (2007). Cognitive recovery in socially deprived young children: The Bucharest early intervention project. *Science, 318,* 1937–1940.

Nelson, Thomas O., & Dunlosky, John (1991). When people's judgments of learning (JOLs) are extremely accurate at predicting subsequent recall: The "delayed JOL effect." *Psychological Science, 2,* 267–270.

Ness, Jose; Aronow, Wilbert S.; & Beck, Gwen (2006). Menopausal symptoms after cessation of hormone replacement therapy. *Maturitas, 53,* 356–361.

Nesse, Randolph M., & Ellsworth, Phoebe C. (2009). Evolution, emotion, and emotional disorders. *American Psychologist, 64,* 129–139.

Newcombe, Nora S.; Drummey, Anna B.; Fox, Nathan A.; et al. (2000). Remembering early childhood: How much, how, and why (or why not). *Current Directions in Psychological Science, 9,* 55–58.

Newland, M. Christopher, & Rasmussen, Erin B. (2003). Behavior in adulthood and during aging is affected by contaminant exposure in utero. *Current Directions in Psychological Science, 12,* 212–217.

Newton, Nicola, & Stewart, Abigail J. (2010). The middle ages: Change in women's personalities and social roles. *Psychology of Women Quarterly, 34,* 75–84.

NICHD Early Child Care Research Network (2006). Infant–mother attachment classification: Risk and protection in relation to changing maternal caregiving quality. *Developmental Psychology, 42,* 38–58.

Nichols, Michael P., & Schwartz, Richard C. (2008). *Family therapy: Concepts and methods* (8th ed.). Boston, MA: Allyn & Bacon.

Nickerson, Raymond S. (1998). Confirmation bias: A ubiquitous phenomenon in many guises. *Review of General Psychology, 2,* 175–220.

Nickerson, Raymond A., & Adams, Marilyn Jager (1979). Long-term memory for a common object. *Cognitive Psychology, 11,* 287–307.

Nisbett, Richard E. (1993). Violence and U.S. regional culture. *American Psychologist, 48,* 441–449.

Nisbett, Richard E. (2009). *Intelligence and how to get it: Why schools and culture count.* New York: W. W. Norton.

Nisbett, Richard E., & Ross, Lee (1980). *Human inference: Strategies and shortcomings of social judgment*. Englewood Cliffs, NJ: Prentice-Hall.

Nolan, Susan A.; Flynn, Cynthia; & Garber, Judy (2003). Prospective relations between rejection and depression in young adolescents. *Journal of Personality and Social Psychology, 85*, 745–755.

Nolen-Hoeksema, Susan; Wisco, Blair E.; & Lyubomirsky, Sonja (2008). Rethinking rumination. *Perspectives on Psychological Science, 3*, 400–424.

Norman, Donald A. (1988). *The psychology of everyday things*. New York: Basic Books.

Nosek, Brian A.; Greenwald, Anthony G.; & Banaji, Mahzarin R. (2007). The Implicit Association Test at 7: A methodological and conceptual review. In J. A. Bargh (Ed.), *Social psychology and the unconscious*. New York: Psychology Press.

Nyberg, Lars; Habib, Reza; McIntosh, Anthony R.; & Tulving, Endel (2000). Reactivation of encoding-related brain activity during memory retrieval. *Proceedings of the National Academy of Sciences, 97*, 11120–11124.

Ó Scalaidhe, Séamas P.; Wilson, Fraser A. W.; & Goldman-Rakic, Patricia S. (1997). A real segregation of face-processing neurons in prefrontal cortex. *Science, 278*, 1135–1138.

Oaten, Megan; Stevenson, Richard J.; & Case, Trevor I. (2009). Disgust as a disease-avoidance mechanism. *Psychological Bulletin, 125*, 303–321.

Oatley, Keith, & Jenkins, Jennifer M. (1996). *Understanding emotions*. Cambridge, MA: Blackwell.

Odgers, Candice L.; Caspi, Avshalom; Nagin, Daniel S.; et al. (2008). Is it important to prevent early exposure to drugs and alcohol among adolescents? *Psychological Science, 19*, 1037–1044.

Offit, Paul A. (2008). *Autism's false prophets: Bad science, risky medicine, and the search for a cure*. NY: Columbia University Press.

Ofshe, Richard J., & Watters, Ethan (1994). *Making monsters: False memory, psychotherapy, and sexual hysteria*. New York: Scribners.

Ogden, Jenni A., & Corkin, Suzanne (1991). Memories of H. M. In W. C. Abraham, M. C. Corballis, & K. G. White (Eds.), *Memory mechanisms: A tribute to G. V. Goddard*. Hillsdale, NJ: Erlbaum.

Öhman, Arne, & Mineka, Susan (2001). Fears, phobias, and preparedness: Toward an evolved module of fear and fear learning. *Psychological Review, 108*, 483–522.

Oliver, Mary Beth, & Hyde, Janet S. (1993). Gender differences in sexuality: A meta-analysis. *Psychological Bulletin, 114*, 29–51.

Olson, James M.; Vernon, Philip A.; Harris, Julie Aitken; & Jang, Kerry L. (2001). The heritability of attitudes: A study of twins. *Journal of Personality and Social Psychology, 80*, 845–850.

Olson, Michael A. (2009). Measures of prejudice. In T. Nelson (Ed.), *The handbook of prejudice, stereotyping, and discrimination*. New York: Psychology Press.

Olsson, Andreas; Ebert, Jeffrey; Banaji, Mahzarin; & Phelps, Elizabeth A. (2005). The role of social groups in the persistence of learned fear. *Science, 309*, 785–787.

Olsson, Andreas, & Phelps, Elizabeth (2004). Learned fear of "unseen" faces after Pavlovian, observational, and instructed fear. *Psychological Science, 15*, 822–828.

Olujic, M. B. (1998). Embodiment of terror: Gendered violence in peacetime and wartime in Croatia and Bosnia-Herzegovina. *Medical Anthropology Quarterly, 12*, 31–50.

Ophir, Eyal; Nass, Clifford; & Wagner, Anthony D. (2009). Cognitive control in media multitaskers. *Proceedings of the National Academy of Sciences*. Epub ahead of print, August 24, doi: 10.1073/pnas.0903620106.

O'Rahilly, Ronan, & Müller, Fabiola (2001). *Human embryology and teratology*. New York: Wiley.

Orbach, Susie (2009). *Bodies*. London: Profile Books.

O'Rourke, Lindsey (2008, August 2). Behind the woman behind the bomb. *The New York Times,* op-ed page.

Ostrovsky, Yuri; Andalman, Aaron; & Sinha, Pawan (2006). Vision following extended congenital blindness. *Psychological Science, 12*, 1009–1014.

O'Sullivan, L. F., & Allgeier, Elizabeth R. (1998). Feigning sexual desire: Consenting to unwanted sexual activity in heterosexual dating relationships. *Journal of Sex Research, 35*, 234–243.

Oyserman, Daphna, & Lee, Spike W. S. (2008). Does culture influence what and how we think? Effects of priming individualism and collectivism. *Psychological Bulletin, 134*, 311–342.

Ozer, Emily J.; Best, Suzanne R.; Lipsey, Tami L.; & Weiss, Daniel S. (2003). Predictors of posttraumatic stress disorder and symptoms in adults: A meta-analysis. *Psychological Bulletin, 129*, 52–73.

Packer, Dominic J. (2008). Identifying systematic disobedience in Milgram's obedience experiments: A meta-analytic review. *Perspectives on Psychological Science, 3*, 301–304.

Packer, Dominic J. (2009). Avoiding groupthink: Whereas weakly identified members remain silent, strongly identified members dissent about collective problems. *Psychological Science, 20*, 619–626.

Pagel, James F. (2003). Non-dreamers. *Sleep Medicine, 4*, 235–241.

Panksepp, Jaak (1998). Attention deficit hyperactivity disorders, psychostimulants, and intolerance of childhood playfulness: A tragedy in the making? *Current Directions in Psychological Science, 7*, 91–98.

Panksepp, Jaak; Herman, B. H.; Vilberg, T.; et al. (1980). Endogenous opioids and social behavior. *Neuroscience and Biobehavioral Reviews, 4*, 473–487.

Park, Denise, & Gutchess, Angela (2006). The cognitive neuroscience of aging and culture. *Current Directions in Psychological Science, 15*, 105–108.

Parker, Elizabeth S.; Cahill, Larry; & McGaugh, James L. (2006). A case of unusual autobiographical remembering. *Neurocase, 12*, 35–49.

Parlee, Mary B. (1982). Changes in moods and activation levels during the menstrual cycle in experimentally naive subjects. *Psychology of Women Quarterly, 7*, 119–131.

Parlee, Mary B. (1994). The social construction of premenstrual syndrome: A case study of scientific discourse as cultural contestation. In M. G. Winkler & L. B. Cole (Eds.), *The good body: Asceticism in contemporary culture*. New Haven, CT: Yale University Press.

Pascual-Leone, Alvaro; Amedi, Amir; Fregni, Felipe; & Merabet, Lotfe B. (2005). The plastic human brain cortex. *Annual Review of Neuroscience, 28*, 377–401.

Pastalkova, Eva; Itskov, Vladimir; Amarasingham, Asohan; & Buzsáki, György (2008, September 5). Internally generated cell assembly sequences in the rat hippocampus. *Science, 321*, 1322–1327.

Patterson, Charlotte J. (2006). Children of lesbian and gay parents. *Current Directions in Psychological Science, 15*, 241–244.

Patterson, David R., & Jensen, Mark P. (2003). Hypnosis and clinical pain. *Psychological Bulletin, 129*, 495–521.

Patterson, Francine, & Linden, Eugene (1981). *The education of Koko*. New York: Holt, Rinehart and Winston.

Paul, Annie M. (2004). *The cult of personality*. New York: The Free Press.

Paul, Pamela (2008). *Parenting, Inc.: How the billion-dollar baby business has changed the way we raise our children*. New York: Henry Holt.

Paul, Richard W. (1984, September). Critical thinking: Fundamental to education for a free society. *Educational Leadership*, 4–14.

Paunonen, Sampo V. (2003). Big Five factors or personality and replicated predictions of behavior. *Journal of Personality & Social Psychology, 84*, 411–422.

Paunonen, Sampo V., & Ashton, Michael C. (2001). Big Five factors and facets and the prediction of behavior. *Journal of Personality and Social Psychology, 81*, 524–539.

Pavlov, Ivan P. (1927). *Conditioned reflexes* (G. V. Anrep, Trans.). London: Oxford University Press.

Payne, Jessica D.; Stickgold, Robert; Swanberg, Kelley; & Kensinger, Elizabeth A. (2008). Sleep preferentially enhances memory for emotional components of scenes. *Psychological Science, 19*, 781–788.

Peabody, Dean (1985). *National characteristics*. Cambridge, England: Cambridge University Press.

Peele, Stanton, & Brodsky, Archie, with Mary Arnold (1991). *The truth about addiction and recovery*. New York: Simon & Schuster.

Peier, A. M.; Moqrich, A.; Hergarden, A. C.; et al. (2002). A TRP channel that senses cold stimuli and menthol. *Cell, 108*, 705–715.

Pennebaker, James W. (2002). Writing, social processes, and psychotherapy: From past to future. In S. J. Lepore and J. M. Smyth (Eds.), *The writing cure:*

How expressive writing promotes health and emotional well-being. Washington, DC: American Psychological Association.

Pennebaker, James W.; Colder, Michelle; & Sharp, Lisa K. (1990). Accelerating the coping process. *Journal of Personality and Social Psychology, 58,* 528–527.

Pennebaker, James W.; Kiecolt-Glaser, Janice; & Glaser, Ronald (1988). Disclosure of traumas and immune function: Health implications for psychotherapy. *Journal of Consulting and Clinical Psychology, 56,* 239–245.

Peplau, Letita Anne (2003). Human sexuality: How do men and women differ? *Current Directions in Psychological Science, 12,* 37–40.

Peplau, Letitia Anne; Spalding, Leah R.; Conley, Terri D.; & Veniegas, Rosemary C. (2000). The development of sexual orientation in women. *Annual Review of Sex Research, 10,* 70–99.

Pepperberg, Irene (2000). *The Alex studies: Cognitive and communicative abilities of grey parrots.* Cambridge, MA: Harvard University Press.

Pepperberg, Irene M. (2002). Cognitive and communicative abilities of grey parrots. *Current Directions in Psychological Science, 11,* 83–87.

Pepperberg, Irene M. (2006). Grey parrot (Psittacus erithacus) numerical abilities: Addition and further experiments on a zero-like concept. *Journal of Comparative Psychology, 120,* 1–11.

Pepperberg, Irene (2008). *Alex and me.* New York: HarperCollins.

Persons, Jacqueline; Davidson, Joan; & Tompkins, Michael A. (2001). *Essential components of cognitive-behavior therapy for depression.* Washington, DC: American Psychological Association.

Pesetsky, David (1999). Introduction to symposium: "Grammar: What's innate?" Paper presented at the annual meeting of the American Association for the Advancement of Science, Anaheim.

Petersen, Jennifer L., & Hyde, Janet S. (2010). A meta-analytic review of research on gender differences in sexuality, 1993-2007. *Psychological Bulletin, 136,* 21–38.

Peterson, Christopher; Seligman, Martin E. P.; Yurko, Karen H.; et al. (1998). Catastrophizing and untimely death. *Psychological Science, 9,* 127–130.

Peterson, Lloyd R., & Peterson, Margaret J. (1959). Short-term retention of individual verbal items. *Journal of Experimental Psychology, 58,* 193–198.

Petkova, Valeria I., & Ehrsson, H. Henrik (2008). If I were you: Perceptual illusion of body swapping. *PLoS ONE, 3:* e3832.doi:10.1371/journal.pone.0003832.

Petrie, Keith J.; Booth, Roger J.; & Pennebaker, James W. (1998). The immunological effects of thought suppression. *Journal of Personality and Social Psychology, 75,* 1264–1272.

Pettigrew, Thomas T., & Tropp, Linda R. (2006). A meta-analytic test of intergroup contact theory. *Journal of Personality and Social Psychology, 90,* 751–783.

Pfungst, Oskar (1911/1965). *Clever Hans (The horse of Mr. von Osten): A contribution to experimental animal and human psychology.* New York: Holt, Rinehart and Winston.

Phillips, Micheal D.; Lowe, M. J.; Lurito, J. T.; et al. (2001). Temporal lobe activation demonstrates sex-based differences during passive listening. *Radiology, 220,* 202–207.

Phinney, Jean S. (1996). When we talk about American ethnic groups, what do we mean? *American Psychologist, 51,* 918–927.

Piaget, Jean (1929/1960). *The child's conception of the world.* Paterson, NJ: Littlefield, Adams.

Piaget, Jean (1952). Play, dreams, and imitation in childhood. New York: W. W. Norton.

Piaget, Jean (1984). Piaget's theory. In P. Mussen (Series Ed.) & W. Kessen (Vol. Ed.), *Handbook of child psychology: Vol. 1. History, theory, and methods* (4th ed.). New York: Wiley.

Pierce, W. David; Cameron, Judy; Banko, Katherine M.; & So, Sylvia (2003). Positive effects of rewards and performance standards on intrinsic motivation. *Psychological Record, 53,* 561–579.

Pika, Simone, & Mitani, John (2006). Referential gesture communication in wild chimpanzees (Pan troglodytes). *Current Biology, 16,* 191–192.

Pillemer, Jane; Hatfield, Elaine; & Sprecher, Susan (2008). The importance of fairness and equity for the marital satisfaction of older women. *Journal of Women and Aging, 20,* 215–229.

Pincus, Tamar, & Morley, Stephen (2001). Cognitive-processing bias in chronic pain: A review and integration. *Psychological Bulletin, 127,* 599–617.

Pinker, Steven (1994). *The language instinct: How the mind creates language.* New York: Morrow.

Piper, August, & Merskey, Harold (2004). The persistence of folly: A critical examination of dissociative identity disorder. Part I: The excesses of an improbable concept. *Canadian Journal of Psychiatry, 49,* 592–600. [Note: Part II (The defence and decline of multiple personality or dissociative identity disorder) appeared in the following issue of the *Canadian Journal of Psychiatry, 49,* 678–683.]

Pittenger, David J. (1993). The utility of the Myers-Briggs Type Indicator. *Review of Educational Research, 63,* 467–488.

Plomin, Robert (1989). Environment and genes: Determinants of behavior. *American Psychologist, 44,* 105–111.

Plomin, Robert; Asbury, Kathryn; & Dunn, Judith F. (2001). Why are children in the same family so different? Nonshared environment a decade later. *Canadian Journal of Psychiatry, 46,* 225–233.

Plomin, Robert, & DeFries, John C. (1985). *Origins of individual differences in infancy: The Colorado Adoption Project.* New York: Academic Press.

Plomin, Robert; DeFries, John C.; McClearn, Gerald E.; & McGuffin, Peter (2001). *Behavioral genetics* (4th ed.). New York: Worth.

Plotnik, Joshua M.; de Waal, Frans B. M.; & Reiss, Diana (2006). Self-recognition in an Asian elephant. *Proceedings of the National Academy of Science,* published online October 30, 10.1073/pnas.0608062103.

Ponitz, Claire C.; McClelland, Megan M.; Matthews, J. S.; & Morrison, Frederick J. (2009). A structured observation of behavioral self-regulation and its contribution to kindergarten outcomes. *Developmental Psychology, 45,* 605–619.

Poole, Debra A., & Lamb, Michael E. (1998). *Investigative interviews of children.* Washington, DC: American Psychological Association.

Pope, Harrison G., Jr.; Poliakoff, Michael B.; Parker, Michael P.; et al. (2007). Is dissociative amnesia a culture-bound syndrome? Findings from a survey of historical literature. *Psychological Medicine, 37,* 22533.

Popkin, Barry M. (2009). *The world is fat: The fads, trends, policies, and products that are fattening the human race.* New York: Avery (Penguin).

Portenoy, Russell K. (1994). Opioid therapy for chronic nonmalignant pain: Current status. In H. L. Fields & J. C. Liebeskind (Eds.), *Progress in pain research and management. Pharmacological approaches to the treatment of chronic pain: Vol. 1.* Seattle: International Association for the Study of Pain.

Posthuma, D.; de Gues, E. J.; Baare, W. F.; et al. (2002). The association between brain volume and intelligence is of genetic origin. *Nature Neuroscience, 5,* 83–84.

Postmes, Tom, & Spears, Russell (1998). Deindividuation and antinormative behavior: A meta-analysis. *Psychological Bulletin, 123,* 238–259.

Postuma, R. B.; Gagnon, J. F.; Vendette, M.; et al. (2008). Quantifying the risk of neurodegenerative disease in idiopathic REM sleep behavior disorder. *Neurology,* published on line December 24, doi:10.1212/01.wnl.0000340980.19702.6e.

Potter, W. James (1987). Does television viewing hinder academic achievement among adolescents? *Human Communication Research, 14,* 27–46.

Poulin-Dubois, Diane; Serbin, Lisa A.; Kenyon, Brenda; & Derbyshire, Alison (1994). Infants' intermodal knowledge about gender. *Developmental Psychology, 30,* 436–442.

Powell, Russell A., & Boer, Douglas P. (1995). Did Freud misinterpret reported memories of sexual abuse as fantasies? *Psychological Reports, 77,* 563–570.

Premack, David, & Premack, Ann James (1983). *The mind of an ape.* New York: Norton.

Presnell, Katherine; Bearman, Sarah Kate; & Stice, Eric (2004). Risk factors for body dissatisfaction in adolescent boys and girls: A prospective study. *International Journal of Eating Disorders, 36,* 389–401.

Pressman, Sarah D., & Cohen, Sheldon (2005). Does positive affect influence health? *Psychological Bulletin, 131,* 925–971.

Principe, Gabrielle; Kanaya, Tamoe; Ceci, Stephen J.; & Singh, Mona (2006). Believing is seeing: How rumors can engender false memories in preschoolers. *American Psychologist, 17,* 243–248.

Prochaska, James O.; Norcross, John C.; & DiClemente, Carlo C. (1994). *Changing for good*. New York: Morrow.

Proffitt, Dennis R. (2006). Distance perception. *Current Directions in Psychological Science, 3*, 131–135.

Pronin, Emily (2008, May 30). How we see ourselves and how we see others. *Science, 320*, 1177–1180.

Pronin, Emily; Gilovich, Thomas; & Ross, Lee (2004). Objectivity in the eye of the beholder: Divergent perceptions of bias in self versus others. *Psychological Review, 111*, 781–799.

Ptito, Maurice; Moesgaard, Solvej M.; Gjedde, Albert; & Kupers, Ron (2005). Cross-modal plasticity revealed by electrotactile stimulation of the tongue in the congenitally blind. *Brain, 128*, 606–614.

Punamaeki, Raija-Leena, & Joustie, Marja (1998). The role of culture, violence, and personal factors affecting dream content. *Journal of Cross-Cultural Psychology, 29*, 320–342.

Pynoos, R. S., & Nader, K. (1989). Children's memory and proximity to violence. *Journal of the American Academy of Child and Adolescent Psychiatry, 28*, 236–241.

Pyszczynski, Tom; Rothschild, Zachary; & Abdollahi, Abdolhossein (2008). Terrorism, violence, and hope for peace: A terror management perspective. *Current Directions in Psychological Science, 17*, 318–322.

Pyter, L.M.; Pineros, V.; Galang, J.A.; et al. (2009, June 2). Peripheral tumors induce depressive-like behaviors and cytokine production and alter hypothalamic-pituitary-adrenal axis regulation. *Proceedings of the National Academy of Sciences, 106*, 9069–9074.

Quinn, Diane M., & Spencer, Steven J. (2001). The interference of stereotype threat with women's generation of mathematical problem-solving strategies. *Journal of Social Issues, 57*, 55–71.

Quinn, Paul, & Bhatt, Ramesh (2005). Learning perceptual organization in infancy. *Psychological Science, 16*, 511–515.

Racsmány, Mihály; Conway, Martin A.; & Demeter, Gyula (2010). Consolidation of episodic memories during sleep: Long-term effects of retrieval practice. *Psychological Science, 21*, 80–85.

Radford, Benjamin (2005, June). Psychic predictions (and rationalizations) fail again. *Skeptical Briefs, 15*, 529.

Radford, Benjamin (2010, March/April). The psychic and the serial killer. *Skeptical Inquirer, 34*, 32–37.

Rahman, Qazi, & Wilson, Glenn D. (2003). Born gay? The psychobiology of human sexual orientation. *Personality and Individual Differences, 34*, 1337–1382.

Raine, Adrian (2008). From genes to brain to antisocial behavior. *Current Directions in Psychological Science, 17*, 323–328.

Raine, Adrian; Lencz, Todd; Bihrle, Susan; LaCasse, Lori; & Colletti, Patrick (2000). Reduced prefrontal gray matter volume and reduced autonomic activity in antisocial personality disorder. *Archives of General Psychiatry, 57*, 119–127.

Raine, Adrian; Meloy, J. R.; Bihrle, S.; et al. (1998). Reduced prefrontal and increased subcortical brain functioning assessed using positron emission tomography in predatory and affective murderers. *Behavioral Science and Law, 16*, 319–332.

Raja, Srinivasa (2008, May 8). From poppies to pill-popping: Is there a "middle way?" Paper presented at the annual meeting of the American Pain Society, Tampa, Fl.

Ramachandran, V.S., & Altschuler, Eric L. (2009). The use of visual feedback, in particular mirror visual feedback, in restoring brain function. *Brain, 132*, 1693–1710.

Ramachandran, V.S., & Blakeslee, Sandra (1998). *Phantoms in the brain*. New York: William Morrow.

Rankin, Lindsay E., & Eagly, Alice H. (2008). Is his heroism hailed and hers hidden? Women, men, and the social construction of heroism. *Psychology of Women Quarterly, 32*, 414–422.

Rapkin, Andrea J.; Chang, Li C.; & Reading, Anthony E. (1988). Comparison of retrospective and prospective assessment of premenstrual symptoms. *Psychological Reports, 62*, 55–60.

Rasch, Björn, & Born, Jan (2008). Reactivation and consolidation of memory during sleep. *Current Directions in Psychological Science, 17*, 188–192.

Rasch, Björn; Büchel, Christian; Gais, Steffen; & Born, Jan (2007). Odor cues during slow-wave sleep prompt declarative memory consolidation. *Science, 315*, 1426–1429.

Rasch, Björn; Pommer, Julian; Diekelmann, Susanne; & Born, Jan (2009). Pharmacological REM sleep suppression paradoxically improves rather than impairs skill memory. *Nature Neuroscience, 12*, 396–397. Epub Oct. 5, 2008, 10.1038/nn.2206.

Rasheed, Parveen, & Al-Sowielem, Latifa S. (2003). Prevalence and predictors of premenstrual syndrome among college-aged women in Saudi Arabia. *Annals of Saudi Medicine, 23*, 381–387.

Ratcliffe, Heather (2000, January 28). Midwest UFO sightings get once-over from scientists. *Detroit News,* Religion Section [online version].

Rathbun, Constance; DiVirgilio, Letitia; & Waldfogel, Samuel (1958). A restitutive process in children following radical separation from family and culture. *American Journal of Orthopsychiatry, 28*, 408–415.

Rauschecker, Josef P. (1999). Making brain circuits listen. *Science, 285*, 1686–1687.

Ravussin, Eric; Lillioja, Stephen; Knowler, William; et al. (1988). Reduced rate of energy expenditure as a risk factor for body-weight gain. *New England Journal of Medicine, 318*, 467–472.

Ray, Wayne A.; Chung, Cecilia P.; Murray, Katherine T.; et al. (2009). Atypical antipsychotic drugs and the risk of sudden cardiac death. *New England Journal of Medicine, 360*, 225–235.

Reber, Paul J.; Stark, Craig E. L.; & Squire, Larry R. (1998). Contrasting cortical activity associated with category memory and recognition memory. *Learning & Memory, 5*, 420–428.

Redd, W. H.; Dadds, M. R.; Futterman, A. D.; Taylor, K.; & Bovbjerg, D. (1993). Nausea induced by mental images of chemotherapy. *Cancer, 72*, 629–636.

Redelmeier, Donald A., & Tversky, Amos (1996). On the belief that arthritis pain is related to the weather. *Proceedings of the National Academy of Sciences, 93*, 2895–2896.

Reedy, F. E.; Bartoshuk, L. M.; Miller, I. J.; Duffy, V. B.; Lucchina, L.; & Yanagisawa, K. (1993). Relationships among papillae, taste pores, and 6-n-propylIthiouracil (PROP) suprathreshold taste sensitivity. *Chemical Senses, 18*, 618–619.

Reichenberg, Abraham; Gross, Raz; Weiser, Mark; Bresnahan, Michealine; et al. (2006). Advancing paternal age and autism. *Archives of General Psychiatry, 63*, 1026–1032.

Reid, R. L. (1991). Premenstrual syndrome. *New England Journal of Medicine, 324*, 1208–1210.

Remick, Abigail K.; Polivy, Janet; & Pliner, Patricia (2009). Internal and external moderators of the effect of variety on food intake. *Psychological Bulletin, 135*, 434–451.

Rensink, Ronald (2004). Visual sensing without seeing. *Psychological Science, 15*, 27–32.

Repetti, Rena L.; Taylor, Shelley E.; & Seeman, Teresa E. (2002). Risky families: Family social environments and the mental and physical health of offspring. *Psychological Bulletin, 128*, 330–366.

Rescorla, Robert A. (1988). Pavlovian conditioning: It's not what you think it is. *American Psychologist, 43*, 151–160.

Restak, Richard M. (1994). *The modular brain*. New York: Macmillan.

Revell, Victoria L., & Eastman, Charmane I. (2005). How to fool Mother Nature into letting you fly around or stay up all night. *Journal of Biological Rhythms, 20*, 353–365.

Reyna, Valerie, & Farley, Frank (2006). Risk and rationality in adolescent decision making. *Psychological Science in the Public Interest, 7*, 1–44.

Reynolds, Brent A., & Weiss, Samuel (1992). Generation of neurons and astrocytes from isolated cells of the adult mammalian central nervous system. *Science, 255*, 1707–1710.

Reynolds, Kristi; Lewis, L. Brian; Nolen, John David L.; et al. (2003). Alcohol consumption and risk of stroke: A meta-analysis. *Journal of the American Medical Association, 289*, 579–588.

Rhoades, Linda, & Eisenberger, Robert (2002). Perceived organizational support: A review of the literature. *Journal of Applied Psychology, 87*, 698–714.

Rice, Mabel L. (1990). Preschoolers' QUIL: Quick incidental learning of words. In G. Conti-Ramsden & C. E. Snow (Eds.), *Children's language* (Vol. 7). Hillsdale, NJ: Erlbaum.

Richardson, John T. E. (Ed.) (1992). *Cognition and the menstrual cycle.* New York: Springer-Verlag.

Richardson-Klavehn, Alan, & Bjork, Robert A. (1988). Measures of memory. *Annual Review of Psychology, 39,* 475–543.

Ridley-Johnson, Robyn; Cooper, Harris; & Chance, June (1983). The relation of children's television viewing to school achievement and I.Q. *Journal of Educational Research, 76,* 294–297.

Rieber, Robert W. (2006). *The bifurcation of the self.* New York: Springer.

Rind, Bruce; Tromovitch, Philip; & Bauserman, Robert (1998). A meta-analytic examination of assumed properties of child sexual abuse using college samples. *Psychological Bulletin, 124,* 22–53.

Risch, N.; Herrell, R.; Lehner, T.; et al. (2009). Interaction between the serotonin transporter gene (5-HTTLPR), stressful life events, and risk of depression: A meta-analysis. *Journal of the American Medical Association, 301,* 2462–2471.

Ro, Tony; Farnè, Alessandro; Johnson, Ruth; et al. (2007). Feeling sounds after a thalamic lesion. *Annals of Neurology, 62,* 433–441.

Roberson, Debi; Davies, Ian; & Davidoff, Jules (2000). Color categories are not universal: Replications and new evidence in favor of linguistic relativity. *Journal of Experimental Psychology: General, 129,* 369–398.

Roberts, Brent W.; Caspi, Avshalom; & Moffitt, Terrie E. (2001). The kids are alright: Growth and stability in personality development from adolescence to adulthood. *Journal of Personality and Social Psychology, 81,* 670–683.

Roberts, Brent W.; Edmonds, Grant; & Grijalva, Emily (2010). It is developmental me, not generation me: Developmental changes are more important than generational changes in narcissism. *Perspectives on Psychological Science, 5,* 97–102.

Roberts, Brent W., & Mroczek, Daniel (2008). Personality trait change in adulthood. *Current Directions in Psychological Science, 17,* 31–35.

Roberts, Brent W.; Walton, Kate E.; & Viechtbauer, Wolfgang (2006). Patterns of mean-level change in personality traits across the life course: A meta-analysis of longitudinal studies. *Psychological Bulletin, 132,* 1–25.

Robins, Lee N.; Davis, Darlene H.; & Goodwin, Donald W. (1974). Drug use by U.S. Army enlisted men in Vietnam: A follow-up on their return home. *American Journal of Epidemiology, 99,* 235–249.

Robinson, Thomas; Wilde, M. L.; Navracruz, L. C.; et al. (2001). Effects of reducing children's television and video game use on aggressive behavior: A randomized controlled trial. *Archives of Pediatric and Adolescent Medicine, 155,* 13–14.

Rodriguez, Paul; Wiles, Janet; & Elman, Jeffrey L. (1999). A recurrent neural network that learns to count. *Connection Science, 11,* 5–40.

Roediger, Henry L. (1990). Implicit memory: Retention without remembering. *American Psychologist, 45,* 1043–1056.

Roediger, Henry L., & McDermott, Kathleen B. (1995). Creating false memories: Remembering words not presented in lists. *Journal of Experimental Psychology; Learning, Memory, & Cognition, 21,* 803–814.

Rofé, Yacov (2008). Does repression exist? Memory, pathogenic, unconscious and clinical evidence. *Review of General Psychology, 12,* 63–85.

Rogers, Carl (1951). *Client-centered therapy: Its current practice, implications, and theory.* Boston: Houghton Mifflin.

Rogers, Carl (1961). *On becoming a person.* Boston: Houghton Mifflin.

Rogers, Ronald W., & Prentice-Dunn, Steven (1981). Deindividuation and anger-mediated interracial aggression: Unmasking regressive racism. *Journal of Personality and Social Psychology, 41,* 63–73.

Rogge, Ronald D.; Bradbury, Thomas N.; Hahlweg, Kurt; et al. (2006). Predicting marital distress and dissolution: Refining the two-factor hypothesis. *Journal of Family Psychology, 20,* 156–159.

Rogoff, Barbara (2003). *The cultural nature of human development.* New York: Oxford University Press.

Ropper, Alan H. (2010). Cogito ergo sum by MRI. *New England Journal of Medicine, 362,* 648–649.

Rosch, Eleanor H. (1973). Natural categories. *Cognitive Psychology, 4,* 328–350.

Rosen, Gerald M.; Glasgow, Russell E.; & Moore, Timothy E. (2003). Self-help therapy: The science and business of giving psychology away. In S. O. Lilienfeld, S. J. Lynn, & J. M. Lohr (Eds.), *Science and pseudoscience in clinical psychology.* New York: Guilford.

Rosenberg, Harold (1993). Prediction of controlled drinking by alcoholics and problem drinkers. *Psychological Bulletin, 113,* 129–139.

Rosenthal, Jack (2006, August 27). Precisely false vs. approximately right: A reader's guide to polls. *The New York Times.* Published online at www.nytimes.com.

Rosenthal, Robert (1994). Interpersonal expectancy effects: A 30-year perspective. *Current Directions in Psychological Science, 3,* 176–179.

Rosenzweig, Mark R. (1984). Experience, memory, and the brain. *American Psychologist, 39,* 365–376.

Roser, Matt E., & Gazzaniga, Michael S. (2004). Automatic brains: Interpretive minds. *Current Directions in Psychological Science, 13,* 56–59.

Ross, Heather E.; Freeman, Sara M.; Spiegel, Lauren L.; et al. (2009). Variation in oxytocin receptor density in the nucleus accumbens has differential effects on affiliative behaviors in monogamous and polygamous voles. *Journal of Neuroscience, 29,* 1312–1318.

Ross, Lee (2010). Dealing with conflict: Experiences and experiments. In M. H. Gonzales, C. Tavris, & J. Aronson (Eds.), *The scientist and the humanist: A festschrift in honor of Elliot Aronson.* New York: Psychology Press.

Ross, Michael; Xun, W. Q. Elaine; & Wilson, Anne E. (2002). Language and the bicultural self. *Personality and Social Psychology Bulletin, 28,* 1040–1050.

Rothbart, Mary K.; Ahadi, Stephan A.; & Evans, David E. (2000). Temperament and personality: Origins and outcomes. *Journal of Personality and Social Psychology, 78,* 122–135.

Rothbaum, Fred; Weisz, John; Pott, Martha; et al. (2000). Attachment and culture: Security in the United States and Japan. *American Psychologist, 55,* 1093–1104.

Rothbaum, Fred M.; Weisz, John R.; & Snyder, Samuel S. (1982). Changing the world and changing the self: A two-process model of perceived control. *Journal of Personality and Social Psychology, 42,* 5–37.

Rothermund, Klaus, & Wentura, Dirk (2004). Underlying processes in the Implicit Association Test: Dissociating salience from associations. *Journal of Experimental Psychology: General, 133,* 139–165.

Rotter, Julian B. (1990). Internal versus external control of reinforcement: A case history of a variable. *American Psychologist, 45,* 489–493.

Roughgarden, Joan (2004). *Evolution's rainbow: Diversity, gender, and sexuality in nature and people.* Berkeley: University of California Press.

Rouw, Romke, & Scholte, Steven S. (2007). Increased structural connectivity in grapheme-color synesthesia. *Nature Neuroscience, 10,* 792–797.

Rovee-Collier, Carolyn (1993). The capacity for long-term memory in infancy. *Current Directions in Psychological Science, 2,* 130–135.

Rowe, Meredith L., & Goldin-Meadow, Susan (2009, February 13). Differences in early gesture explain SES disparities in child vocabulary size at school entry. *Science, 323,* 951–953.

Rowatt, Wade C.; Ottenbreit, Alison; Nesselroade Jr., K. Paul; & Cunningham, Paige A. (2002). On being holier-than-thou or humbler-than-thee: A social-psychological perspective on religiousness and humility. *Journal for the Scientific Study of Religion, 41,* 227–237.

Roy, Mark P.; Steptoe, Andrew; & Kirschbaum, Clemens (1998). Life events and social support as moderators of individual differences in cardiovascular and cortisol reactivity. *Journal of Personality and Social Psychology, 75,* 1273–1281.

Røysamb, Espen; Tambs, Kristian; Reichborn-Kjennerud, Ted; et al. (2003). Happiness and health: Environmental and genetic contributions to the relationship between subjective well-being, perceived health, and somatic illness. *Journal of Personality and Social Psychology, 85,* 1136–1146.

Rozin, Paul; Lowery, Laura; & Ebert, Rhonda (1994). Varieties of disgust faces and the structure of disgust. *Journal of Personality and Social Psychology, 66,* 870–881.

Rozin, Paul; Kabnick, Kimberly; Pete, Erin; et al. (2003). The ecology of eating: Smaller portion sizes in France than in the United States help explain the French paradox. *Psychological Science, 14*, 450–454.

Ruggiero, Vincent R. (2004). *The art of thinking: A guide to critical and creative thought* (7th ed.). Pearson/Longman.

Rumbaugh, Duane M. (1977). *Language learning by a chimpanzee: The Lana project.* New York: Academic Press.

Rumbaugh, Duane M.; Savage-Rumbaugh, E. Sue; & Pate, James L. (1988). Addendum to "Summation in the chimpanzee (*Pan troglodytes*)." *Journal of Experimental Psychology: Animal Behavior Processes, 14*, 118–120.

Rumelhart, David E.; McClelland, James L.; & the PDP Research Group (1986). *Parallel distributed processing: Explorations in the microstructure of cognition* (Vols. 1 and 2). Cambridge, MA: MIT Press.

Rupp, Heather A., & Wallen, Kim (2008). Sex differences in response to visual sexual stimuli: A review. *Archives of Sexual Behavior, 37*, 206–218.

Rushton, J. Philippe, & Jensen, Arthur R. (2005). Thirty years of research on race differences in cognitive ability. *Psychology, Public Policy, and Law, 11*, 235–294.

Rutter, Michael; O'Connor, Thomas G.; & the English and Romanian Adoptees (ERA) Study Team (2004). Are there biological programming effects for psychological development? Findings from a study of Romanian adoptees. *Developmental Psychology, 40*, 81–94.

Rutter, Michael; Pickles, Andrew; Murray, Robin; & Eaves, Lindon (2001). Testing hypotheses on specific environmental causal effects on behavior. *Psychological Bulletin, 127*, 291–324.

Ruys, Kirsten I., & Stapel, Diederik A. (2008). The secret life of emotions. *Psychological Science, 19*, 385–391.

Ryan, Richard M.; Chirkov, Valery I.; Little, Todd D.; et al. (1999). The American dream in Russia: Extrinsic aspirations and well-being in two cultures. *Personality and Social Psychology Bulletin, 25*, 1509–1524.

Rymer, Russ (1993). *Genie: An abused child's flight from silence.* New York: HarperCollins.

Sabattini, Laura, & Crosby, Faye (2009). Work ceilings and walls: Work-life and "family-friendly" policies. In M. Barreto, M. Ryan, & M. Schmitt (Eds.), *The glass ceiling in the 21st century: Understanding barriers to gender equality.* Washington, DC: American Psychological Association.

Sack, Robert L., & Lewy, Alfred J. (1997). Melatonin as a chronobiotic: Treatment of circadian desynchrony in night workers and the blind. *Journal of Biological Rhythms, 12*, 595–603.

Sackett, Paul R.; Hardison, Chaitra M.; & Cullen, Michael J. (2004). On interpreting stereotype threat as accounting for African American-White differences on cognitive tests. *American Psychologist, 59*, 7–13.

Sacks, Oliver (1985). *The man who mistook his wife for a hat and other clinical tales.* New York: Simon & Schuster.

Saey, Tina H. (2008, March 29). Dad's hidden influence. *Science News, 173*, 200–201.

Sagan, Eli (1988). *Freud, women, and morality: The psychology of good and evil.* New York: Basic Books.

Sage, Cyrille; Huang, Mingqian; Karimi, Kambiz; et al. (2005). Proliferation of functional hair cells in vivo in the absence of the retinoblastoma protein. *Science, 307*, 114–118.

Sageman, Marc (2008). *Leaderless jihad: Terror networks in the twenty-first century.* Philadelphia: University of Pennsylvania Press.

Sahley, Christie L.; Rudy, Jerry W.; & Gelperin, Alan (1981). An analysis of associative learning in a terrestrial mollusk: 1. Higher-order conditioning, blocking, and a transient US preexposure effect. *Journal of Comparative Physiology, 144*, 1–8.

Salovey, Peter, & Grewal, Daisy (2005). The science of emotional intelligence. *Current Directions in Psychological Science, 14*, 281–285.

Salthouse, Timothy A. (2006). Mental exercise and mental aging: Evaluating the validity of the "use it or lose it" hypothesis. *Perspectives on Psychological Science, 1*, 68–87.

Sameroff, Arnold J.; Seifer, Ronald; Barocas, Ralph; et al. (1987). Intelligence quotient scores of 4-year-old children: Social-environmental risk factors. *Pediatrics, 79*, 343–350.

Sampson, Robert J; Sharkey, Patrick; & Raudenbush, Stephen W. (2008). Durable effects of concentrated disadvantage among verbal ability of African-American children. *Proceedings of the National Academy of Sciences, 105*, 845–853.

Sanfey, Alan G.; Rilling, James K.; Aronson, Jessica K. (2003). The neural basis of economic decision-making in the Ultimatum Game. *Science, 300*, 1755–1758.

Santelli, John; Ott, Mary A.; Lyon, Maureen; et al. (2006). Abstinence and abstinence-only education: A review of U.S. policies and programs. *Journal of Adolescent Health, 38*, 72–81.

Sarbin, Theodore R. (1991). Hypnosis: A fifty year perspective. *Contemporary Hypnosis, 8*, 1–15.

Sarbin, Theodore R. (1997). The power of believed-in imaginings. *Psychological Inquiry, 8*, 322–325.

Saucier, Deborah M., & Kimura, Doreen (1998). Intrapersonal motor but not extrapersonal targeting skill is enhanced during the midluteal phase of the menstrual cycle. *Developmental Neuropsychology, 14*, 385–398.

Saucier, Gerard (2000). Isms and the structure of social attitudes. *Journal of Personality and Social Psychology, 78*, 366–385.

Savage-Rumbaugh, Sue, & Lewin, Roger (1994). *Kanzi: The ape at the brink of the human mind.* New York: Wiley.

Savage-Rumbaugh, Sue; Shanker, Stuart; & Taylor, Talbot (1998). *Apes, language and the human mind.* New York: Oxford University Press.

Savic, Ivanka; Berglund, Hans; & Lindström, Per (2005, May 17). Brain response to putative pheromones in homosexual men. *Proceedings of the National Academy of Sciences, 102*, 7356–7361.

Savin-Williams, Ritch C. (2006). Who's gay? Does it matter? *Current Directions in Psychological Science, 15*, 40–44.

Saxe, Leonard (1994). Detection of deception: Polygraph and integrity tests. *Current Directions in Psychological Science, 3*, 69–73.

Saxena, S.; Brody, A. L.; Maidment, K. M.; et al. (2004). Cerebral glucose metabolism in obsessive-compulsive hoarding. *American Journal of Psychiatry, 161*, 1038–1048.

Sayette, Michael; Reichle, Erik; & Schooler, Jonathan (2009). Lost in the sauce: The effects of alcohol on mind wandering. *Psychological Science, 20*, 747–752.

Scarr, Sandra (1993). Biological and cultural diversity: The legacy of Darwin for development. *Child Development, 64*, 1333–1353.

Scarr, Sandra; Pakstis, Andrew J.; Katz, Soloman H.; & Barker, William B. (1977). Absence of a relationship between degree of white ancestry and intellectual skill in a black population. *Human Genetics, 39*, 69–86.

Scarr, Sandra, & Weinberg, Robert A. (1994). Educational and occupational achievement of brothers and sisters in adoptive and biologically related families. *Behavioral Genetics, 24*, 301–325.

Schacter, Daniel L. (2001). *The seven sins of memory: How the mind forgets and remembers.* Boston: Houghton Mifflin.

Schacter, Daniel L.; Chiu, C. Y. Peter; & Ochsner, Kevin N. (1993). Implicit memory: A selective review. *Annual Review of Neuroscience, 16*, 159–182.

Schaeffer, Cindy M., & Borduin, Charles M. (2005). Long-term follow-up to a randomized clinical trial of multisystemic therapy with serious and violent juvenile offenders. *Journal of Consulting and Clinical Psychology, 73*, 445–453.

Schafer, Roy (1992). *Retelling a life: Narration and dialogue in psychoanalysis.* New York: Basic Books.

Schaie, K. Warner, & Willis, Sherry L. (2002). *Adult development and aging* (5th ed.). Upper Saddle River, NJ: Prentice Hall.

Schaie, K. Warner, & Zuo, Yan-Ling (2001). Family environments and cognitive functioning. In R. J. Sternberg & E. Grigorenko (Eds.), *Cognitive development in context.* Hillsdale, NJ: Erlbaum.

Schank, Roger, with Peter Childers (1988). *The creative attitude.* New York: Macmillan.

Scharfman, Helen E., & Hen, Rene (2007). Is more neurogenesis always better? *Science, 315*, 336–338.

Schenck Carlos H., & Mahowald Mark W. (2002). REM sleep behavior disorder: Clinical, developmental, and neuroscience perspectives 16 years after its formal identification in SLEEP. *Sleep, 25*, 120–138.

Schlossberg, Nancy K., & Robinson, Susan P. (1996). *Going to plan B*. New York: Simon & Schuster/Fireside.

Schmader, Toni (2010). Stereotype threat deconstructed. *Current Directions in Psychological Science, 19*, 14–18.

Schmelz, M.; Schmidt, R.; Bickel, A.; et al. (1997). Specific C-receptors for itch in human skin. *Journal of Neuroscience, 17*, 8003–8008.

Schmidt, Frank L., & Hunter, John (2004). General mental ability in the world of work: Occupational attainment and job performance. *Journal of Personality and Social Psychology, 86*, 162–173.

Schmidt, Louis A.; Fox, Nathan A.; Perez-Edgar, Koraly; & Hamer, Dean H. (2009). Linking gene, brain, and behavior: DRD4, frontal asymmetry, and temperament. *Psychological Science, 20*, 831–837.

Schmitt, David P. (2003). Universal sex differences in the desire for sexual variety: Tests from 52 nations, 6 continents, and 13 islands. *Journal of Personality and Social Psychology, 85*, 85–104.

Schnell, Lisa, & Schwab, Martin E. (1990, January 18). Axonal regeneration in the rat spinal cord produced by an antibody against myelin-associated neurite growth inhibitors. *Nature, 343*, 269–272.

Schofield, P.; Ball, D.; Smith, J. G.; et al. (2004). Optimism and survival in lung carcinoma patients. *Cancer, 100*, 1276–1282.

Schuckit, Marc A. (1998). Relationship among genetic, environmental, and psychological variables in predicting alcoholism. Invited address presented at the annual meeting of the American Psychological Association, San Francisco.

Schuckit, Marc A.; Smith, Tom L.; Pierson, Juliann; et al. (2007). Patterns and correlates of drinking in offspring from the San Diego Prospective Study. *Alcoholism: Clinical and Experimental Research, 31*, 1681–1691.

Schuckit, Marc A.; Smith, Tom L.; Trim, Ryan; et al. (2008). The performance of elements of a "level of response to alcohol"-based model of drinking behaviors in 13-year-olds. *Addiction, 103*, 1786–1792.

Schulz, Richard; Beach, S. R.; Ives, D. G.; et al. (2000). Association between depression and mortality in older adults: The Cardiovascular Health Study. *Archives of Internal Medicine, 160*, 1761–1768.

Schwartz, Barry (2004). *The paradox of choice: Why more is less*. New York: Ecco Press.

Schwartz, Jeffrey; Stoessel, Paula W.; Baxter, Lewis R.; et al. (1996). Systematic changes in cerebral glucose metabolic rate after successful behavior modification treatment of obsessive–compulsive disorder. *Archives of General Psychiatry, 53*, 109–113.

Schwartz, Seth J.; Unger, Jennifer B.; Zamboanga, Byron L.; & Szapocznik, José (2010). Rethinking the concept of acculturation. *American Psychologist, 65*, 237–251.

Schenck Carlos H., & Mahowald Mark W. (2002). REM sleep behavior disorder: Clinical, developmental, and neuroscience perspectives 16 years after its formal identification in SLEEP. *Sleep, 25*, 120–138.

Schwekendiek, D. (2008). Height and weight differences between North and South Korea. *Journal of Biosocial Sciences, 41*, 51–55.

Seabrook, John (2008, November 10). Suffering souls: The search for the roots of psychopathy. *The New Yorker*, 64–73.

Sears, Pauline, & Barbee, Ann H. (1977). Career and life satisfactions among Terman's gifted women. In J. C. Stanley, W. C. George, & C. H. Solano (Eds.), *The gifted and the creative: A fifty-year perspective*. Baltimore, MD: Johns Hopkins University Press.

Segal, Julius (1986). *Winning life's toughest battles*. New York: McGraw-Hill.

Segall, Marshall H.; Campbell, Donald T.; & Herskovits, Melville J. (1966). *The influence of culture on visual perception*. Indianapolis, IN: Bobbs-Merrill.

Segall, Marshall H.; Dasen, Pierre R.; Berry, John W.; & Poortinga, Ype H. (1999). *Human behavior in global perspective: An introduction to cross-cultural psychology* (2nd ed.). Boston: Allyn & Bacon.

Segerstrom, Suzanne C., & Miller, Gregory E. (2004). Psychological stress and the human immune system: A meta-analytic study of 30 years of inquiry. *Psychological Bulletin, 130*, 601–630.

Segerstrom, Suzanne C., & Sephton, Sandra E. (2010). Optimistic expectancies and cell-mediated immunity: The role of positive affect. *Psychological Science, 21*, 448–455.

Seidenberg, Mark S.; MacDonald, Maryellen C.; & Saffran, Jenny R. (2002). Does grammar start where statistics stop? *Science, 298*, 553–554.

Seifer, Ronald; Schiller, Masha; Sameroff, Arnold; et al. (1996). Attachment, maternal sensitivity, and infant temperament during the first year of life. *Developmental Psychology, 32*, 12–25.

Sekuler, Robert, & Blake, Randolph (1994). *Perception* (3rd ed.). New York: Knopf.

Seligman, Martin E. P., & Csikszentmihaly, Mihaly (2000). Positive psychology: An introduction. *American Psychologist, 55*, 5–14.

Seligman, Martin E. P., & Hager, Joanne L. (1972, August). Biological boundaries of learning: The sauce-béarnaise syndrome. *Psychology Today*, 59–61, 84–87.

Seligman, Martin E. P.; Schulman, Peter; DeRubeis, Robert J.; & Hollon, Steven D. (1999). The prevention of depression and anxiety. *Prevention & Treatment, 2*, electronic posting December 21, 1999 on the website of the American Psychological Association.

Sellbom, Martin; Ben-Porath, Yossef S.; & Bagby, R. Michael (2008). Personality and psychopathology: Mapping the MMPI-2 Restructured Clinical (RC) Scales onto the Five Factor Model of Personality. *Journal of Personality Disorders, 22*, 291–312.

Senghas, Ann; Kita, Sotaro; & Özyürek, Asli (2004). Children creating core properties of language: Evidence from an emerging sign language in Nicaragua. *Science, 305*, 1779–1782.

Senko, Corwin; Durik, Amanda M.; & Harackiewicz, Judith M. (2008). Historical perspectives and new directions in achievement goal theory: Understanding the effects of mastery and performance-approach goals. In J. Y. Shah, & W. L. Gardner (Eds.), *Handbook of motivation science*. New York: Guilford

Serpell, Robert (1994). The cultural construction of intelligence. In W. J. Lonner & R. S. Malpass (Eds.), *Psychology and culture*. Needham Heights, MA: Allyn & Bacon.

Serrano, Peter; Friedman, Eugenia L.; Kenney, Jana; et al. (2008). PKMz maintains spatial, instrumental, and classically conditioned long-term memories. *PLoS Biology, 6*, e318. Doi:10.1371/journal/pbio.0060318. Accessed May 23, 2009.

Shaffer, Ryan, & Jadwiszczok, Agatha (2010, March/April). Psychic defective: Sylvia Browne's history of failure. *Skeptical Inquirer, 34*, 38-42.

Shapiro, Francine (1994). EMDR: In the eye of a paradigm shift. *Behavior Therapist, 17*, 153–156.

Shapiro, Francine (1995). *Eye movement desensitization and reprocessing: Basic principles, protocols, and procedures*. New York: Guilford.

Sharman, Stephanie J.; Manning, Charles G.; & Garry, Maryanne (2005). Explain this: Explaining childhood events inflates confidence for those events. *Applied Cognitive Psychology, 19*, 16–74.

Shatz, Marilyn, & Gelman, Rochel (1973). The development of communication skills: Modifications in the speech of young children as a function of the listener. *Monographs of the Society for Research in Child Development, 38*.

Shaver, Phillip R., & Hazan, Cindy (1993). Adult romantic attachment: Theory and evidence. In D. Perlman & W. H. Jones (Eds.), *Advances in personal relationships* (Vol. 4). London: Kingsley.

Shaver, Phillip R.; Wu, Shelley; & Schwartz, Judith C. (1992). Cross-cultural similarities and differences in emotion and its representation: A prototype approach. In M. S. Clark (Ed.), *Review of Personality and Social Psychology* (Vol. 13). Newbury Park, CA: Sage.

Shaywitz, Bennett A.; Shaywitz, Sally E.; Pugh, Kenneth R.; et al. (1995). Sex differences in the functional organization of the brain for language. *Nature, 373*, 607–609.

Shedler, Jonathan (2010). The efficacy of psychodynamic therapy. *American Psychologist, 65*, 98–109.

Sheldon, Kennon M.; Elliot, Andrew J.; Kim, Youngmee; & Kasser, Tim (2001). What is satisfying about satisfying events? Testing 10 candidate psychological needs. *Journal of Personality and Social Psychology, 80*, 325–339.

Sheldon, Kennon M., & Houser-Marko, Linda (2001). Self-concordance, goal attainment, and the pursuit of happiness: Can there be an upward spiral? *Journal of Personality and Social Psychology, 80*, 152–165.

Shepard, Roger N., & Metzler, Jacqueline (1971). Mental rotation of three-dimensional objects. *Science, 171*, 701–703.

Sherif, Muzafer (1958). Superordinate goals in the reduction of intergroup conflicts. *American Journal of Sociology, 63,* 349–356.

Sherif, Muzafer; Harvey, O. J.; White, B. J.; Hood, William; & Sherif, Carolyn (1961). *Intergroup conflict and cooperation: The Robbers Cave experiment.* Norman: University of Oklahoma Institute of Intergroup Relations.

Shermer, Michael (1997). *Why people believe weird things: Pseudoscience, superstition, and other confusions of our time.* New York: Freeman.

Sherry, John L. (2001). The effects of violent video games on aggression: A meta-analysis. *Human Communication Research, 27,* 409–431.

Sherry, Simon B., & Hall, Peter A. (2009). The perfectionism model of binge eating: Tests of an integrative model. *Journal of Personality and Social Psychology, 96,* 690–709.

Sherwin, Barbara B. (1998a). Estrogen and cognitive functioning in women. *Proceedings of the Society for Experimental Biological Medicine, 217,* 17–22.

Sheth, B. R.; Sandkühler, S.; & Bhattacharya, J. (2009). Posterior beta and anterior gamma oscillations predict cognitive insight. *Journal of Cognitive Neuroscience, 21,* 1269–1279.

Shields, Stephanie A. (2002). *Speaking from the heart: Gender and the social meaning of emotion.* New York: Cambridge University Press.

Shields, Stephanie A. (2005). The politics of emotion in everyday life: "Appropriate" emotion and claims on identity. *Review of General Psychology, 9,* 3–15.

Shih, Margaret; Pittinsky, Todd L.; & Ambady, Nalini (1999). Stereotype susceptibility: Identity salience and shifts in quantitative performance. *Psychological Science, 10,* 80–83.

Shors, Tracey J. (2009, March). Saving new brain cells. *Scientific American,* 46–54.

Shorter, Edward, & Healy, David (2008). *Shock therapy: A history of electroconvulsive treatment in mental illness.* New Brunswick, NJ: Rutgers University Press.

Sidanius, Jim; Pratto, Felicia; & Bobo, Lawrence (1996). Racism, conservatism, affirmative action, and intellectual sophistication: A matter of principled conservatism or group dominance? *Journal of Personality and Social Psychology, 70,* 476–490.

Sidanius, Jim; Van Laar, Colette; Levin, Shana; & Sinclair, Stacey (2004). Ethnic enclaves and the dynamics of social identity on the college campus: The good, the bad, and the ugly. *Journal of Personality and Social Psychology, 87,* 96–110.

Siegel, Jerome M. (2009, August 9). Sleep viewed as a state of adaptive inactivity. *Nature Reviews | Neuroscience.* Advance online publication; doi:10.1038/nrn2697.

Siegel, Ronald K. (1989). *Intoxication: Life in pursuit of artificial paradise.* New York: Dutton.

Siegel, Shepard (2005). Drug tolerance, drug addiction, and drug anticipation. *Current Directions in Psychological Science, 14,* 296–300.

Siegler, Robert S. (2006). Microgenetic analyses of learning. In D. Kuhn & R. S. Siegler (Eds.), *Handbook of child psychology: Vol. 2. Cognition, perception, and language* (6th ed.). New York: Wiley.

Silke, Andrew (Ed.) (2003). *Terrorists, victims, and society: Psychological perspectives on terrorism and its consequences.* New York: Wiley.

Simcock, Gabrielle, & Hayne, Harlene (2002). Breaking the barrier: Children fail to translate their preverbal memories into language. *Psychological Science, 13,* 225–231.

Simon, Herbert A. (1955). A behavioral model of rational choice. *Quarterly Journal of Economics, 69,* 99–118.

Simons, Daniel J., & Chabris, Christopher F. (1999). Gorillas in our midst: Sustained inattentional blindness for dynamic events. *Perception, 28,* 1059–1974.

Simonton, Dean Keith, & Song, Anna (2009). Eminence, IQ, physical and mental health, and achievement domain. *Psychological Science, 20,* 429–434.

Sims, Ethan A. (1974). Studies in human hyperphagia. In G. Bray & J. Bethune (Eds.), *Treatment and management of obesity.* New York: Harper & Row.

Sinaceur, Marwan; Heath, Chip; & Cole, Steve (2005). Emotional and deliberative reactions to a public crisis: Mad cow disease in France. *Psychological Science, 16,* 247–254.

Singer, Margaret T. (2003). *Cults in our midst* (rev. ed.). New York: Wiley.

Singh, Devendra; Vidaurri, Melody; Zambarano, Robert J.; & Dabbs, James M., Jr. (1999). Lesbian erotic role identification: Behavioral, morphological, and hormonal correlates. *Journal of Personality and Social Psychology, 76,* 1035–1049.

Skeem, Jennifer L., & Cooke, David J. (2010). Is criminal behavior a central component of psychopathy? Conceptual directions for resolving the debate. *Psychological Assessment, 22,* 433–445.

Skeem, Jennifer L.; Poythress, Norman; Eden, John F.; Lilienfeld, Scott O.; & Cale, Ellison M. (2003). Psychopathic personality or personalities? Exploring potential variants of psychopathy and their implications for risk assessment. *Aggression and Violent Behavior, 8,* 513–546.

Skinner, B. F. (1938). *The behavior of organisms: An experimental analysis.* New York: Appleton-Century-Crofts.

Skinner, B. F. (1948/1976). *Walden Two.* New York: Macmillan.

Skinner, B. F. (1956). A case history in the scientific method. *American Psychologist, 11,* 221–233.

Skinner, B. F. (1972). The operational analysis of psychological terms. In B. F. Skinner, *Cumulative record* (3rd ed.). New York: Appleton-Century-Crofts.

Skinner, B. F. (1990). Can psychology be a science of mind? *American Psychologist, 45,* 1206–1210.

Skinner, Ellen A. (1996). A guide to constructs of control. *Journal of Personality and Social Psychology, 71,* 549–570.

Skinner, Ellen A. (2007). Secondary control critiqued: Is it secondary? Is it control? *Psychological Bulletin, 133,* 911–916.

Skinner, J. B.; Erskine, A.; Pearce, S. A.; et al. (1990). The evaluation of a cognitive behavioural treatment programme in outpatients with chronic pain. *Journal of Psychosomatic Research, 34,* 13–19.

Slade, Pauline (1984). Premenstrual emotional changes in normal women: Fact or fiction? *Journal of Psychosomatic Research, 28,* 1–7.

Slater, Mel; Antley, Angus; Davison, Adam; et al. (2006). A virtual reprise of the Stanley Milgram obedience experiments. PLoS ONE 1(1): e39. doi:10.1371/journal.pone.0000039.

Slavin, Robert E., & Cooper, Robert (1999). Improving intergroup relations: Lessons learned from cooperative learning programs. *Journal of Social Issues, 55,* 647–663.

Slovic, Paul; Finucane, Melissa L.; Peters, Ellen.; & MacGregor, Donald G. (2002). The affect heuristic. In T. Gilovich, D. Griffin, & D. Kahneman (Eds.), *Heuristics and biases: The psychology of intuitive judgment.* New York: Cambridge University Press.

Slovic, Paul, & Peters, Ellen (2006). Risk perception and affect. *Current Directions in Psychological Science, 15,* 322–325.

Smith, David N. (1998). The psychocultural roots of genocide: Legitimacy and crisis in Rwanda. *American Psychologist, 53,* 743–753.

Smith, Peter B., & Bond, Michael H. (1994). *Social psychology across cultures: Analysis and perspectives.* Boston: Allyn & Bacon.

Smither, Robert D. (1998). *The psychology of work and human performance* (3rd ed.). New York: Longman.

Snodgrass, Sara E. (1992). Further effects of role versus gender on interpersonal sensitivity. *Journal of Personality and Social Psychology, 62,* 154–158.

Snowdon, Charles T. (1997). The "nature" of sex differences: Myths of male and female. In P.A. Gowaty (Ed.), *Feminism and evolutionary biology.* New York: Chapman and Hall.

Snyder, C. R., & Shenkel, Randee J. (1975, March). The P. T. Barnum effect. *Psychology Today,* 52–54.

Solms, Mark (1997). *The neuropsychology of dreams.* Mahwah, NJ: Erlbaum.

Solomon, Robert C. (1994). *About love.* Lanham, MD: Littlefield Adams.

Somer, Oya, & Goldberg, Lewis R. (1999). The structure of Turkish trait-descriptive adjectives. *Journal of Personality and Social Psychology, 76,* 431–450.

Sommer, Robert (1969). *Personal space: The behavioral basis of design.* Englewood Cliffs, NJ: Prentice-Hall.

Sorce, James F.; Emde, Robert N.; Campos, Joseph; & Klinnert, Mary D. (1985). Maternal emotional signaling: Its effect on the visual cliff behavior of 1-year-olds. *Developmental Psychology, 21,* 195–200.

Spalding, K. L.; Arner, E.; Westermark, P. O.; et al. (2008, June 5). Dynamics of fat cell turnover in humans. *Nature, 453,* 783–787.

Spanos, Nicholas P. (1991). A sociocognitive approach to hypnosis. In S. J. Lynn & J. W. Rhue (Eds.), *Theories of hypnosis: Current models and perspectives.* New York: Guilford Press.

Spanos, Nicholas P. (1996). *Multiple identities and false memories: A sociocognitive perspective.* Washington, DC: American Psychological Association.

Spanos, Nicholas P.; Burgess, Cheryl A.; Roncon, Vera; et al. (1993). Surreptitiously observed hypnotic responding in simulators and in skill-trained and untrained high hypnotizables. *Journal of Personality and Social Psychology, 65,* 391–398.

Spanos, Nicholas P.; Menary, Evelyn; Gabora, Natalie J.; et al. (1991). Secondary identity enactments during hypnotic past-life regression: A sociocognitive perspective. *Journal of Personality and Social Psychology, 61,* 308–320.

Spanos, Nicholas P.; Stenstrom, Robert J.; & Johnson, Joseph C. (1988). Hypnosis, placebo, and suggestion in the treatment of warts. *Psychosomatic Medicine, 50,* 245–260.

Spear, Linda P. (2000). Neurobiological changes in adolescence. *Current Directions in Psychological Science, 9,* 111–114.

Spearman, Charles (1927). *The abilities of man.* London: Macmillan.

Spelke, Elizabeth S., & Kinzler, Katherine D. (2007). Core knowledge. *Developmental Science, 10,* 89–96.

Sperling, George (1960). The information available in brief visual presentations. *Psychological Monographs, 74*(498).

Sperry, Roger W. (1964). The great cerebral commissure. *Scientific American, 210*(1), 42–52.

Sperry, Roger W. (1982). Some effects of disconnecting the cerebral hemispheres. *Science, 217,* 1223–1226.

Spitz, Herman H. (1997). *Nonconscious movements: From mystical messages to facilitated communication.* Mahwah, NJ: Erlbaum.

Sprecher, Susan; Schwartz, Pepper; Harvey, John; & Hatfield, Elaine (2008). The businessoflove.com: Relationship initiation at Internet matchmaking services. In S. Sprecher, A. Wenzel, & J. Harvey (Eds.), *The Handbook of Relationship Initiation.*New York: Psychology Press.

Springer, Sally P., & Deutsch, Georg (1998). *Left brain, right brain: Perspectives from cognitive neuroscience.* New York: Freeman.

Squier, Leslie H., & Domhoff, G. William (1998). The presentation of dreaming and dreams in introductory psychology textbooks: A critical examination with suggestions for textbook authors and course instructors. *Dreaming, 8,* 149–168.

Squire, Larry R. (2007, April 6). Rapid consolidation. *Science, 316,* 57–58.

Squire, Larry R.; Ojemann, Jeffrey G.; Miezin, Francis M.; et al. (1992). Activation of the hippocampus in normal humans: A functional anatomical study of memory. *Proceedings of the National Academy of Science, 89,* 1837–1841.

Squire, Larry R., & Zola-Morgan, Stuart (1991). The medial temporal lobe memory system. *Science, 253,* 1380–1386.

Srivastava, Abhishek; Locke, Edwin A.; & Bartol, Kathryn M. (2001). Money and subjective well-being: It's not the money, it's the motives. *Journal of Personality and Social Psychology, 80,* 959–971.

Srivastava, Sanjay; Tamir, Maya; McGonigal, Kelly M.; et al. (2009). The social costs of emotional suppression: A prospective study of the transition to college. *Journal of Personality and Social Psychology, 96,* 883–897.

Staats, Carolyn K., & Staats, Arthur W. (1957). Meaning established by classical conditioning. *Journal of Experimental Psychology, 54,* 74–80.

Stajkovic, Alexander D., & Luthans, Fred (1998). Self-efficacy and work-related performance: A meta-analysis. *Psychological Bulletin, 124,* 240–261.

Stanley, Damian; Phelps, Elizabeth; & Banaji, Mahzarin (2008). The neural basis of implicit attitudes. *Current Directions in Psychological Science, 17,* 164–170.

Stanovich, Keith (2010). *How to think straight about psychology* (9th ed.). Boston: Allyn & Bacon.

Stanwood, Gregg D., & Levitt, Pat (2001). *The effects of cocaine on the developing nervous system.* In C. A. Nelson & M. Luciana (Eds.), *Handbook of developmental cognitive neuroscience.* Cambridge, MA: The MIT Press.

Stattin, Haken, & Magnusson, David (1990). *Pubertal maturation in female development.* Hillsdale, NJ: Erlbaum.

Staub, Ervin (1996). Cultural-social roots of violence. *American Psychologist, 51,* 117–132.

Staub, Ervin (1999). The roots of evil: Social conditions, culture, personality, and basic human needs. *Personality and Social Psychology Review, 3,* 179–192.

St. Clair, D.; Xu, M.; Wang, P.; et al. (2005, August 3). Rates of adult schizophrenia following prenatal exposure to the Chinese famine of 1959–1961. *Journal of the American Medical Association, 294,* 557–562.

Stearns, Peter N. (1997). *Fat history: Bodies and beauty in the modern West.* New York: New York University Press.

Steele, Claude M. (1992, April). Race and the schooling of Black Americans. *Atlantic Monthly,* 68–78.

Steele, Claude M. (1997). A threat in the air: How stereotypes shape intellectual identity and performance. *American Psychologist, 52,* 613–629.

Steele, Claude M., & Aronson, Joshua (1995). Stereotype threat and the intellectual test performance of African-Americans. *Journal of Personality and Social Psychology, 69,* 797–811.

Stein, M. B.; Jang, K. L.; Taylor, S.; Vernon, P. A.; & Livesley, W. J. (2002). Genetic and environmental influences on trauma exposure and posttraumatic stress disorder symptoms: A general population twin study. *American Journal of Psychiatry, 159,* 1675–1681.

Steinberg, Laurence (2007). Risk taking in adolescence. *Current Directions in Psychological Science, 16,* 55–59.

Steinberg, Laurence, & Scott, Elizabeth S. (2003). Less guilty by reason of adolescence. *American Psychologist, 58,* 1009–1018.

Stenberg, Craig R., & Campos, Joseph (1990). The development of anger expressions in infancy. In N. Stein, B. Leventhal, & T. Trabasso (Eds.), *Psychological and biological approaches to emotion.* Hillsdale, NJ: Erlbaum.

Stepanski, Edward, & Perlis, Michael (2000). Behavioral sleep medicine: An emerging subspecialty in health psychology. *Journal of Psychosomatic Research, 49,* 343–347.

Stephan, Walter G.; Ageyev, Vladimir; Coates-Shrider, Lisa; et al. (1994). On the relationship between stereotypes and prejudice: An international study. *Personality and Social Psychology Bulletin, 20,* 277–284.

Sternberg, Robert J. (1988). *The triarchic mind: A new theory of human intelligence.* New York: Viking.

Sternberg, Robert J. (2004). Culture and intelligence. *American Psychologist, 59,* 325–338.

Sternberg, Robert J.; Forsythe, George B.; Hedlund, Jennifer; et al. (2000). *Practical intelligence in everyday life.* New York: Cambridge University Press.

Sternberg, Robert J.; Wagner, Richard K.; Williams, Wendy M.; & Horvath, Joseph A. (1995). Testing common sense. *American Psychologist, 50,* 912–927.

Stevenson, Harold W.; Chen, Chuansheng; & Lee, Shin-ying (1993, January 1). Mathematics achievement of Chinese, Japanese, and American children: Ten years later. *Science, 259,* 53–58.

Stevenson, Harold W., & Stigler, James W. (1992). *The learning gap.* New York: Summit.

Stewart-Williams, Steve, & Podd, John (2004). The placebo effect: Dissolving the expectancy versus conditioning debate. *Psychological Bulletin, 130,* 324–340.

Stice, Eric; Spoor, S.; Bohon, C.; & Small, D.M. (2008, October 17). Relation between obesity and blunted striatal response to food is moderated by *Taq*1A A1 allele. *Science, 322,* 449–452.

Stix, Gary (2008, August). Lighting up the lies. *Scientific American,* 18–19.

Stoch, M. B., & Smythe, P. M. (1963). Does undernutrition during infancy inhibit brain growth and subsequent intellectual development? *Archives of Diseases in Childhood, 38,* 546–552.

Strahan, Erin J.; Spencer, Steven J.; & Zanna, Mark P. (2002). Subliminal priming and persuasion: Striking while the iron is hot. *Journal of Experimental Social Psychology, 38,* 556–568.

Strayer, David L., & Drews, Frank A. (2007). Cell-phone-induced driver distraction. *Current Directions in Psychology, 16,* 128–131.

Strayer, David L.; Drews, Frank A.; & Crouch, Dennis J. (2006). A comparison of the cell phone driver and the drunk driver. *Human Factors, 48,* 381–391.

Streissguth, Ann P. (2001). Recent advances in fetal alcohol syndrome and alcohol use in pregnancy. In D. P. Agarwal & H. K. Seitz (Eds.), *Alcohol in health and disease.* New York: Marcel Dekker.

Streyffeler, Lisa L., & McNally, Richard J. (1998). Fundamentalists and liberals: personality characteristics of Protestant Christians. *Personality and Individual Differences, 24,* 579–580.

Strickland, Bonnie R. (1989). Internal–external control expectancies: From contingency to creativity. *American Psychologist, 44,* 1–12.

Strickland, Tony L.; Lin, Keh-Ming; Fu, Paul; et al. (1995). Comparison of lithium ratio between African-American and Caucasian bipolar patients. *Biological Psychiatry, 37,* 325–330.

Strickland, Tony L.; Ranganath, Vijay; Lin, Keh-Ming; et al. (1991). Psychopharmacological considerations in the treatment of black American populations. *Psychopharmacology Bulletin, 27,* 441–448.

Striegel-Moore, Ruth H., & Bulik, Cynthia M. (2007). Risk factors for eating disorders. *American Psychologist, 62,* 181–198.

Stunkard, Albert J. (Ed.) (1980). *Obesity.* Philadelphia: Saunders.

Suddendorf, Thomas, & Whiten, Andrew (2001). Mental evolution and development: Evidence for secondary representation in children, great apes, and other animals. *Psychological Bulletin, 127,* 629–650.

Sue, Derald W.; Capodilupo, Christina M.; Torino, Gina C.; et al. (2007). Racial microaggressions in everyday life: Implications for clinical practice. *American Psychologist, 62,* 271–286.

Suedfeld, Peter (1975). The benefits of boredom: Sensory deprivation reconsidered. *American Scientist, 63*(1), 60–69.

Suinn, Richard M. (2001). The terrible twos—Anger and anxiety. *American Psychologist, 56,* 27–36.

Suls, Jerry; Martin, René; & Wheeler, Ladd (2002). Social comparison: Why, with whom, and with what effect? *Current Directions in Psychological Science, 11,* 159–163.

Surowiecki, James (2004). *The wisdom of crowds.* New York: Doubleday.

Swartz, M. S.; Perkins, D. O.; Stroup, T. S., et al., & CATIE Investigators (2007). Effects of antipsychotic medications on psychosocial functioning in patients with chronic schizophrenia: findings from the NIMH CATIE study. *American Journal of Psychiatry, 164,* 428–36.

Swenson, Cynthia C.; Henggeler, Scott W.; Taylor, Ida S.; & Addison, Oliver W. (2005). *Multisystemic therapy and neighborhood partnerships: Reducing adolescent violence and substance abuse.* New York: Guilford Press.

Tajfel, Henri; Billig, M. G.; Bundy, R. P.; & Flament, C. (1971). Social categorization and intergroup behavior. *European Journal of Social Psychology, 1,* 149–178.

Tajfel, Henri, & Turner, John C. (1986). The social identity theory of intergroup behavior. In S. Worchel & W. G. Austin (Eds.), *Psychology of intergroup relations.* Chicago: Nelson-Hall.

Takahashi, Kazutoshi; Tanabe, Koji; Ohnuki, Mari; et al. (2007). Induction of pluripotent stem cells from adult human fibroblasts by defined factors. *Cell, 131,* 861–872.

Talarico, Jennifer M., & Rubin, David C. (2003). Confidence, not consistency, characterizes flashbulb memories. *Psychological Science, 14,* 455–461.

Talbot, Margaret (2008, May 12). Birdbrain: The woman behind the world's chattiest parrots. *The New Yorker,* on line archive.

Talbot, Margaret (2009, April 27). Brain gain: The underground world of neuroenhancing drugs. *The New Yorker,* pp. 32–43.

Tangney, June P.; Wagner, Patricia E.; Hill-Barlow, Deborah; et al. (1996). Relation of shame and guilt to constructive versus destructive responses to anger across the lifespan. *Journal of Personality and Social Psychology, 70,* 797–809.

Tarbox, Sarah I., & Pogue-Geile, Michael F. (2008). Development of social functioning in preschizophrenia children and adolescents: A systematic review. *Psychological Bulletin, 34,* 561–583.

Taubes, Gary (2008). *Good calories, bad calories: Fats, carbs, and the controversial science of diet and health.* New York: Anchor.

Tavris, Carol (1989). *Anger: The misunderstood emotion* (Rev. ed.). New York: Simon & Schuster/Touchstone.

Tavris, Carol, & Aronson, Elliot (2007). *Mistakes were made (but not by me).* Orlando, FL: Houghton Mifflin Harcourt.

Taylor, Annette Kujawski, & Kowalski, Patricia (2004). Naïve psychological science: The prevalence, strength, and sources of misconceptions. *Psychological Record, 54,* 15–25.

Taylor, Shelley E. (2006). Tend and befriend: Biobehavioral bases of affiliation under stress. *Current Directions in Psychological Science, 15,* 273–277.

Taylor, Shelley E.; Kemeny, Margaret E.; Reed, Geoffrey M.; Bower, Julienne E.; & Gruenewald, Tara L. (2000a). Psychological resources, positive illusions, and health. *American Psychologist, 55,* 99–109.

Taylor, Shelley E.; Klein, Laura C.; Lewis, Brian P.; et al. (2000b). Biobehavioral responses to stress in females: Tend-and-befriend, not fight-or-flight. *Psychological Review, 107,* 411–429.

Taylor, Shelley E.; Lichtman, Rosemary R.; & Wood, Joanne V. (1984). Attributions, beliefs about control, and adjustment to breast cancer. *Journal of Personality and Social Psychology, 46,* 489–502.

Taylor, Shelley E., & Lobel, Marci (1989). Social comparison activity under threat: Downward evaluation and upward contacts. *Psychological Review, 96,* 569–575.

Taylor, Shelley E.; Repetti, Rena; & Seeman, Teresa (1997). Health psychology: What is an unhealthy environment and how does it get under the skin? *Annual Review of Psychology* (Vol. 48). Palo Alto, CA: Annual Reviews.

Taylor, Steven; McKay, Dean; & Abramowitz, Jonathan S. (2005). Is obsessive-compulsive disorder a disturbance of security motivation? *Psychological Review, 112,* 650–657.

Taylor, Steven; Thordarson, Dana S.; Maxfield, Louise; et al. (2003). Comparative efficacy, speed, and adverse effects of three PTSD treatments: Exposure therapy, EMDR, and relaxation training. *Journal of Consulting and Clinical Psychology, 71,* 330–338.

Terman, Lewis M., & Oden, Melita H. (1959). *Genetic studies of genius: Vol. 5. The gifted group at mid-life.* Stanford, CA: Stanford University Press.

Terracciano, Antonio, & McCrae, Robert R. (2006, February). "National character does not reflect mean personality traits levels in 49 cultures": Reply. *Science, 311,* 777–779.

Thomas, Jennifer J.; Vartanian, Lenny R.; & Brownell, Kelly D. (2009). The relationship between eating disorder not otherwise specified (EDNOS) and officially recognized eating disorders: Meta-analysis and implications for DSM. *Psychological Bulletin, 135,* 407–433.

Thomas, Michael S. C., & Johnson, Mark H. (2008). New advances in understanding sensitive periods in brain development. *Current Directions in Psychological Science, 17,* 1–5.

Thompson, Clara (1943/1973). Penis envy in women. *Psychiatry, 6,* 123–125. Reprinted in J. B. Miller (Ed.), *Psychoanalysis and women.* New York: Brunner/Mazel, 1973.

Thompson, J. Kevin, & Cafri, Guy (Eds.) (2007). *The muscular ideal: Psychological, social, and medical perspectives.* Washington, DC: American Psychological Association.

Thompson, Paul M.; Vidal, Christine N.; Giedd, Jay N.; et al. (2001). Mapping adolescent brain change reveals dynamic wave of accelerated gray matter loss in very early-onset schizophrenia. *Proceedings of the National Academy of Sciences of the USA, 98,* 11650–11655.

Thompson, Richard F. (1983). Neuronal substrates of simple associative learning: Classical conditioning. *Trends in Neurosciences, 6,* 270–275.

Thompson, Richard F. (1986). The neurobiology of learning and memory. *Science, 233,* 941–947.

Thompson, Richard F., & Kosslyn, Stephen M. (2000). Neural systems activated during visual mental imagery: A review and meta-analyses. In A. W. Toga & J. C. Mazziotta (Eds.), *Brain mapping: The systems.* San Diego, CA: Academic Press.

Thompson, Robin; Emmorey, Karen; & Gollan, Tamar H. (2005). "Tip of the fingers" experiences by deaf signers. *Psychological Science, 16,* 856–860.

Thompson-Cannino, Jennifer; Cotton, Ronald; & Torneo, Erin (2009). *Picking Cotton: Our memoir of injustice and redemption.* New York: St. Martin's Press.

Thorndike, Edward L. (1898). Animal intelligence: An experimental study of the associative processes in animals. *Psychological Review Monograph Supplement, 2* (Whole No. 8).

Thorndike, Edward L. (1903). *Educational psychology.* New York: Columbia University Teachers College.

Thornhill, Randy, & Palmer, Craig T. (2000). *A natural history of rape: Biological bases of sexual coercion.* Cambridge, MA: MIT Press.

Tiefer, Leonore (2004). *Sex is not a natural act, and other essays* (Rev. ed.). Boulder, CO: Westview.

Tiefer, Leonore (Ed.) (2008). The New View campaign against the medicalization of sex. Special issue (12 articles). *Feminism and Psychology, 18.*

Timmers, Monique; Fischer, Agneta H.; & Manstead, Antony S. R. (1998). Gender differences in motives for regulating emotions. *Personality and Social Psychology Bulletin, 24,* 974–985.

Tolman, Edward C. (1938). The determiners of behavior at a choice point. *Psychological Review, 45,* 1–35.

Tolman, Edward C., & Honzik, Chase H. (1930). Introduction and removal of reward and maze performance in rats. *University of California Publications in Psychology, 4,* 257–275.

Tomasello, Michael (2000). Culture and cognitive development. *Current Directions in Psychological Science, 9,* 37–40.

Tomasello, Michael (2008). *Origins of human communication.* Cambridge, MA: MIT Press.

Tomlinson, Mark; Cooper, Peter; & Murray, Lynne (2005). The mother–infant relationship and infant attachment in a South African peri-urban settlement. *Child Development, 76,* 1044–1054.

Tomppo, L.; Hennah, W.; Miettunen, J.; et al. (2009). Association of variants in DISC1 with psychosis-related traits in a large population cohort. *Archives of General Psychiatry, 66,* 134–141.

Toomela, Aaro (2003). Relationships between personality structure, structure of word meaning, and cognitive ability: A study of cultural mechanisms of personality. *Journal of Personality and Social Psychology, 85,* 723–735.

Tourangeau, Roger, & Yan, Ting (2007). Sensitive questions in surveys. *Psychological Bulletin, 133,* 859–883.

Tracy, Jessica L., & Robins, Richard W. (2007). Emerging insights into the nature and function of pride. *Current Directions in Psychological Science, 16,* 147–151.

Tracy, Jessica L., & Robins, Richard W. (2008). The nonverbal expression of pride: Evidence for cross-cultural recognition. *Journal of Personality and Social Psychology, 94,* 516–530.

Triandis, Harry C. (1996). The psychological measurement of cultural syndromes. *American Psychologist, 51,* 407–415.

Triandis, Harry C. (2007). Culture and psychology: A history of the study of their relationship. In S. Kitayama & D. Cohen (Eds.), *Handbook of cultural psychology.* New York: Guilford Press.

Trivers, Robert (2004). Mutual benefits at all levels of life. [Book review.] *Science, 304,* 965.

Tronick, Edward Z.; Morelli, Gilda A.; & Ivey, Paula K. (1992). The Efe forager infant and toddler's pattern of social relationships: Multiple and simultaneous. *Developmental Psychology, 28,* 568–577.

Trzesniewski, Kali H., & Donnellan, M. Brent (2010). Rethinking "Generation Me": A study of cohort effects from 1976-2006. *Perspectives on Psychological Science, 5,* 58–75.

Trzesniewski, Kali H.; Donnellan, M. Brent; & Robins, Richard W. (2008). Do today's young people really think they are so extraordinary? An examination of secular changes in narcissism and self-enhancement. *Psychological Science, 19,* 181–188.

Tulving, Endel (1985). How many memory systems are there? *American Psychologist, 40,* 385–398.

Turati, Chiara (2004). Why faces are not special to newborns: An alternative account of the face preference. *Current Directions in Psychological Science, 13,* 5–8.

Turiel, Elliot (2002). *The culture of morality.* Cambridge, England: Cambridge University Press.

Turner, C. F.; Ku, L.; Rogers, S. M.; et al. (1998). Adolescent sexual behavior, drug use, and violence: Increased reporting with computer survey technology. *Science, 280,* 867–873.

Turner, E. H.; Matthews, A. M.; Linardatos, E.; et al. (2008). Selective publication of antidepressant trials and its influence on apparent efficacy. *New England Journal of Medicine, 358,* 252–260.

Turner, Marlene E.; Pratkanis, Anthony R.; & Samuels, Tara (2003). Identity metamorphosis and groupthink prevention: Examining Intel's departure from the DRAM industry. In A. Haslam, D. van Knippenberg, M. Platow, & N. Ellemers (Eds.), *Social identity at work: Developing theory for organizational practice.* Philadelphia, PA: Psychology Press.

Turvey, Brent E. (2008). Serial crime. In B. E. Turvey (Ed.), *Criminal profiling: An introduction to behavioral evidence analysis* (3rd ed.). San Diego: Elsevier Academic Press.

Tustin, Karen, & Hayne, Harlene (2006). A new method to measure childhood amnesia in children, adolescents, and adults. Poster presented at the annual meeting of the International Society for the Study of Behavioural Development, Melbourne, Australia.

Tversky, Amos, & Kahneman, Daniel (1973). Availability: A heuristic for judging frequency and probability. *Cognitive Psychology, 5,* 207–232.

Tversky, Amos, & Kahneman, Daniel (1981). The framing of decisions and the psychology of choice. *Science, 211,* 453–458.

Twenge, Jean (2009). Change over time in obedience: The jury's still out, but it might be decreasing. *American Psychologist, 64,* 28–31.

Twenge, Jean M.; Konrath, Sara; Foster, Joshua D.; Campbell, W. Keith; & Bushman, Brad J. (2008). Egos inflating over time: A cross-temporal meta-analysis of the Narcissistic Personality Inventory. *Journal of Personality, 76,* 875–901.

Tyrer, P.; Oliver-Africano, P.C.; Ahmed, Z.; et al. (2008, January 5). Risperidone, haloperidol, and placebo in the treatment of aggressive challenging behaviour in patients with intellectual disability: A randomised controlled trial. *Lancet, 371,* 57–63.

Uhlhaas, Peter J., & Silverstein, Steven M. (2005). Perceptual organization in schizophrenia spectrum disorders: Empirical research and theoretical implications. *Psychological Bulletin, 131,* 618–632.

Ullian, E. M.; Chrisopherson, K. S.; & Barres, B. A. (2004). Role for glia in synaptogenesis. *Glia, 47,* 209–216.

Unsworth, Nash, & Engle, Randall W. (2007). On the division of short-term and working memory: An examination of simple and complex span and their relation to higher order abilities. *Psychological Bulletin, 133,* 1038–1066.

Updegraff, John A.; Gable, Shelly L.; & Taylor, Shelley E. (2004). What makes experiences satisfying? The interaction of approach-avoidance motivations and emotions in well-being. *Journal of Personality and Social Psychology, 86,* 496–504.

Urry, Heather L.; Nitschke, Jack B.; Dolski, Isa; et al. (2004). Making a life worth living: Neural correlates of well-being. *Psychological Science, 15,* 367–372.

Usher, JoNell A., & Neisser, Ulric (1993). Childhood amnesia and the beginnings of memory for four early life events. *Journal of Experimental Psychology: General, 122,* 155–165.

Uttal, William R. (2001). *The new phrenology: The limits of localizing cognitive processes in the brain.* Cambridge, MA: MIT Press/Bradford Books.

Vaillant, George E. (1983). *The natural history of alcoholism: Causes, patterns, and paths to recovery.* Cambridge, MA: Harvard University Press.

Vaillant, George E. (Ed.) (1992). *Ego mechanisms of defense.* Washington, DC: American Psychiatric Press.

Valenstein, Elliot (1986). *Great and desperate cures: The rise and decline of psychosurgery and other radical treatments for mental illness.* New York: Basic Books.

Valentine, Tim, & Mesout, Jan (2009). Eyewitness identification under stress in the London dungeon. *Applied Cognitive Psychology, 23,* 151–161.

Van Boven, Leaf, & Gilovich, Thomas (2003). To do or to have? That is the question. *Journal of Personality and Social Psychology, 85,* 1193–1202.

Van Cantfort, Thomas E., & Rimpau, James B. (1982). Sign language studies with children and chimpanzees. *Sign Language Studies, 34,* 15–72.

Vandello, Joseph A., & Cohen, Dov (1999). Patterns of individualism and collectivism across the United States. *Journal of Personality and Social Psychology, 77,* 279–292.

Vandello, Joseph A., & Cohen, Dov (2008). U.S. Southern and Northern differences in perceptions of norms about agression: Mechanisms for the perpetuation of a culture of honor. *Social and Personality Psychology Compass, 2,* 652–667.

van den Dries, Linda; Juffer, Femmie; van IJzendoorn, Marinus H.; & Bakermans-Kranenburg, Marian J. (2009). Fostering security? A meta-analysis of attachment in adopted children. *Children and Youth Services Review, 31,* 410–421.

Van Emmerik, Arnold A.; Kamphuis, Jan H.; Hulsbosch, Alexander M.; & Emmelkamp, Paul M. G. (2002, September 7). Single session debriefing after psychological trauma: A meta-analysis. *The Lancet, 360,* 766–771.

Van Gelder, B. M.; Tijhuis, M.; Kalmijn, S.; & Kromhout, D. (2007). Fish consumption, n-3 fatty acids, and subsequent 5-y cognitive decline in elderly men: the Zutphen Elderly Study. *American Journal of Clinical Nutrition, 85,* 1142–1147.

Van Goozen, Stephanie H. M.; Fairchild, Graeme; Snoek, Heddeke; & Harold, Gordon T. (2007). The evidence for a neurobiological model of childhood antisocial behavior. *Psychological Bulletin, 133,* 149–182.

van IJzendoorn, Marinus H.; Juffer, Femmie; & Klein Poelhuis, Caroline W. (2005). Adoption and cognitive development: A meta-analytic comparison of adopted and nonadopted children's IQ and school performance. *Psychological Bulletin, 131,* 301–316.

Van Laar, Colette; Levin, Shana; & Sidanius, Jim (2008). Ingroup and outgroup contact: A longitudinal study of the effects of cross-ethnic friendships, dates, roommate relationships and participation in segregated organizations. In U. Wagner, L. R. Tropp, G. Finchilescu, & C. Tredoux (Eds.), *Improving intergroup relations: Building on the legacy of Thomas F. Pettigrew.* Malden: Blackwell.

van Ommeren, Mark; Saxena, Shekhar; & Saraceno, Benedetto (2005, January). Mental and social health during and after acute emergencies: emerging consensus?. *Bulletin of the World Health Organization, 83,* 71–76.

Van Orden, Kimberly A.; Lynam, Meredith E.; Hollar, Daniel; & Joiner Jr., Thomas E. (2006). Perceived burdensomeness as an indicator of suicidal symptoms. *Cognitive Therapy and Research, 30,* 457–467.

van Schaik, Carel (2006 April). Why are some animals so smart? *Scientific American,* 64–71.

van Tilburg, Miranda A. L.; Becht, Marleen C.; & Vingerhoets, Ad J. J. M. (2003). Self-reported crying during the menstrual cycle: Sign of discomfort and emotional turmoil or erroneous beliefs? *Journal of Psychosomatic Obstetrics & Gynecology, 24,* 247–255.

Varnum, Michael E. W.; Grossman, Igor; Kitayama, Shinobu; & Nisbett, Richard E. (2010). The origin of cultural differences in cognition: The social orientation hypothesis. *Psychological Science, 19,* 9–13.

Vecera, Shaun P.; Vogel, Edward, K.; & Woodman, Geoffrey F. (2002). Lower region: A new cue for figure-ground assignment. *Journal of Experimental Psychology: General, 131,* 194–205.

Vertes, Robert P., & Siegel, Jerome M. (2005). Time for the sleep community to take a critical look at the purported role of sleep in memory processing. *Sleep, 28,* 1228–1229.

Vierbuchen, Thomas; Ostermeier, Austin; Pang, Zhiping P.; et al. (2010, January 27). Direct conversion of fibroblasts to functional neurons by defined factors. *Nature* advance online publication, doi:10.1038/nature08797.

Vila, J., & Beech, H. R. (1980). Premenstrual symptomatology: An interaction hypothesis. *British Journal of Social and Clinical Psychology, 19,* 73–80.

Vita, A. J.; Terry, R. B.; Hubert, H. B.; & Fries, J. F. (1998). Aging, health risks, and cumulative disability. *New England Journal of Medicine, 338,* 1035–1041.

Vogelzangs, N.; Kritchevsky, S. B.; Beekman, A. T.; et al. (2008). Depressive symptoms and change in abdominal obesity in older persons. *Archives of General Psychiatry, 65,* 1386–1393.

Volkow, Nora D.; Chang, Linda; Wang, Gene-Jack; et al. (2001). Association of dopamine transporter reduction with psychomotor impairment in methamphetamine abusers. *American Journal of Psychiatry, 158,* 377–382.

Vroon, Piet (1997). *Smell: The secret seducer* (Paul Vincent, Trans.). New York: Farrar, Straus & Giroux.

Vul, Edward; Harris, Christine; Winkielman, Piotr; & Pashler, Harold (2009). Puzzlingly high correlations in fMRI studies of emotion, personality, and social cognition. *Perspectives on Psychological Science, 4,* 274–290.

Vul, Edward, & Pashler, Harold (2008). Measuring the crowd within. *Psychological Science, 19,* 645–647.

Wade, Carole (2006). Some cautions about jumping on the brain-scan bandwagon. *APS Observer, 19,* 23–24.

Wagenaar, Willem A. (1986). My memory: A study of autobiographical memory over six years. *Cognitive Psychology, 18,* 225–252.

Wager, Tor D.; Rilling, James K.; Smith, Edward E.; et al. (2004). Placebo-induced changes in fMRI in the anticipation and experience of pain. *Science, 303,* 1162–1167.

Wagner, Christopher C., & Ingersoll, Karen S. (2008). Beyond cognition: Broadening the emotional base of motivational interviewing. *Journal of Psychotherapy Integration, 18,* 191–206.

Wagner, Ullrich; Gais, Steffen; Haider, Hilde; et al. (2004). Sleep inspires insight. *Nature, 427,* 304–305.

Wakefield, Jerome C. (1992). Disorder as harmful dysfunction: A conceptual critique of DSM-III-R's definition of mental disorder. *Psychological Review, 99,* 232–247.

Wakefield, Jerome C. (2006). Are there relational disorders? A harmful dysfunction perspective: Comment on the special section. *Journal of Family Psychology, 20,* 423–427.

Wakefield, Jerome C.; Schmitz, Mark F.; First, Michael B.; & Horwitz, Allan V. (2007). Extending the bereavement exclusion for major depression to other losses: Evidence from the National Comorbidity Survey. *Archives of General Psychiatry, 64,* 433–440.

Walker, Anne (1994). Mood and well-being in consecutive menstrual cycles: Methodological and theoretical implications. *Psychology of Women Quarterly, 18,* 271–290.

Walker, David L.; Ressler, Kerry J.; Lu, Kwok-Tung; & Davis, Michael (2002). Facilitation of conditioned fear extinction by systemic administration or intra-amygdala infusions of D-cycloserine as assessed with fear-potentiated startle in rats. *The Journal of Neuroscience, 22,* 2343–2351.

Walker, Elaine, & Tessner, Kevin (2008). Schizophrenia. *Perspectives on Psychological Science, 3,* 30–37.

Walker-Andrews, Arlene S. (1997). Infants' perception of expressive behaviors: Differentiation of multimodal information. *Psychological Bulletin, 121,* 437–456.

Wallace-Wells, Ben (2009, February 5). Bitter pill. *Rolling Stone,* 56–63, 74–76.

Wallbott, Harald G.; Ricci-Bitti, Pio; & Bänninger-Huber, Eva (1986). Non-verbal reactions to emotional experiences. In K. R. Scherer, H. G. Wallbott, & A. B. Summerfield (Eds.), *Experiencing emotion: A cross-cultural study.* Cambridge, England: Cambridge University Press.

Wallen, Kim (2001). Sex and context: Hormones and primate sexual motivation. *Hormones and Behavior, 40,* 339–357.

Waller, Niels G.; Kojetin, Brian A.; Bouchard, Thomas J., Jr.; et al. (1990). Genetic and environmental influences on religious interests, attitudes, and values: A study of twins reared apart and together. *Psychological Science, 1,* 138–142.

Walum, Hasse; Westberg, Lars; Henningsson, Susanne; et al. (2008). Genetic variation in the vasopressin receptor 1a gene (AVPR1A) associates with pair-bonding behavior in humans. *Proceedings of the National Academy of Sciences, 105,* 14153–14156.

Wampold, Bruce (2001). *The great psychotherapy debate: Models, methods, and findings.* Mahwah, NJ: Erlbaum.

Wang, Qi (2008). Being American, being Asian: The bicultural self and autobiographical memory in Asian Americans. *Cognition, 107,* 743–751.

Wansink, Brian (2006). Mindless eating. New York: Bantam.

Warren, Gayle H., & Raynes, Anthony E. (1972). Mood changes during three conditions of alcohol intake. *Quarterly Journal of Studies on Alcohol, 33,* 979–989.

Watanabe, Shigeru (2001). Van Gogh, Chagall and pigeons: Picture discrimination in pigeons and humans. *Animal Cognition, 4,* 1435–9448.

Watkins, Linda R., & Maier, Steven F. (2003). When good pain turns bad. *Current Directions in Psychological Science, 12,* 232–236.

Watson, John B. (1925). *Behaviorism.* New York: Norton.

Watson, John B., & Rayner, Rosalie (1920/2000). Conditioned emotional reactions. *Journal of Experimental Psychology, 3,* 1–14. (Reprinted in *American Psychologist, 55,* March 2000, 313–317.)

Watters, Ethan, & Ofshe, Richard (1999). *Therapy's delusions.* New York: Scribner.

Weaver, Charles N. (2008). Social distance as a measure of prejudice among ethnic groups in the United States. *Journal of Applied Social Psychology, 38,* 778–795.

Webster, Richard (1995). *Why Freud was wrong.* New York: Basic Books.

Wechsler, David (1955). *Manual for the Wechsler Adult Intelligence Scale.* New York: Psychological Corporation.

Wegner, Daniel M., & Gold, Daniel B. (1995). Fanning old flames: Emotional and cognitive effects of suppressing thoughts of a past relationship. *Journal of Personality and Social Psychology, 68,* 782–792.

Wehr, Thomas A.; Duncan, Wallace C.; Sher, Leo; et al. (2001). A circadian signal of change of season in patients with seasonal affective disorder. *Archives of General Psychiatry, 58,* 1108–1114.

Weil, Andrew T. (1974a, June). Parapsychology: Andrew Weil's search for the true Geller. *Psychology Today,* 45–50.

Weil, Andrew T. (1974b, July). Parapsychology: Andrew Weil's search for the true Geller: Part II. The letdown. *Psychology Today,* 74–78, 82.

Weiner, Bernard (1986). *An attributional theory of motivation and emotion.* New York: Springer-Verlag.

Weinstein, Tamara A.; Capitanio, John P.; & Gosling, Samuel D. (2008). Personality in animals. In O.P. John, R.W. Robbins, & L.A. Pervin (Eds.), *Handbook of personality: Theory and research.* New York: Guilford.

Weiss, Alexander; Bates, Timothy C.; & Luciano, Michelle (2008). Happiness is a personal(ity) thing. *Psychological Science, 19,* 205–210.

Weissman, Myrna M.; Markowitz, John C.; & Klerman, Gerald L. (2000). *Comprehensive guide to interpersonal psychotherapy.* New York: Basic Books.

Weisz, John R.; Weiss, Bahr; Han, Susan S.; et al. (1995). Effects of psychotherapy with children and adolescents revisited: A meta-analysis of treatment outcome studies. *Psychological Bulletin, 117,* 450–468.

Wellman, H. M.; Cross, D.; & Watson, J. (2001). Meta-analysis of theory-of-mind development: The truth about false belief. *Child Development, 72,* 655–684.

Wells, Brooke E., & Twenge, Jean (2005). Changes in young people's sexual behavior and attitudes, 1943–1999: A cross-temporal meta-analysis. *Review of General Psychology, 9,* 249–261.

Wells, Gary L., & Olson, Elisabeth A. (2003). Eyewitness testimony. *Annual Review of Psychology, 54,* 277–295.

Wells, Gary L.; Small, Mark; Penrod, Steven; et al. (1998). Eyewitness identification procedures: Recommendations for lineups and photospreads. *Law and Human Behavior, 22,* 602–647.

Wenzel, Amy (2005). Autobiographical memory tasks in clinical research. In A. Wenzel & D. C. Rubin, *Cognitive methods and their application to clinical research.* Washington, DC: American Psychological Association.

Werner, Emmy E. (1989). High-risk children in young adulthood: A longitudinal study from birth to 32 years. *American Journal of Orthopsychiatry, 59,* 72–81.

Wertheimer, Michael (1958/1923). Principles of perceptual organization. In D. C. Beardslee & M. Wertheimer (Eds.), *Readings in perception.* Princeton, NJ: Van Nostrand. [Original work published 1923.]

West, Melissa O., & Prinz, Ronald J. (1987). Parental alcoholism and childhood psychopathology. *Psychological Bulletin, 102,* 204–218.

Westen, Drew (1998). The scientific legacy of Sigmund Freud: Toward a psychodynamically informed psychological science. *Psychological Bulletin, 124,* 333–371.

Westen, Drew; Novotny, Catherine M.; & Thompson-Brenner, Heather (2004). The empirical status of empirically supported psychotherapies: Assumptions, findings, and reporting in controlled clinical trials. *Psychological Bulletin, 130,* 631–663.

Westen, Drew, & Shedler, Jonathan (1999). Revising and assessing axis II, Part II: Toward an empirically based and clinically useful classification of personality disorders. *American Journal of Psychiatry, 156,* 273–285.

Westermeyer, Joseph (1995). Cultural aspects of substance abuse and alcoholism: Assessment and management. *Psychiatric Clinics of North America, 18,* 589–605.

Wethington, Elaine (2000). Expecting stress: Americans and the "midlife crisis." *Motivation & Emotion, 24,* 85–103.

Whaley, Arthur L., & Davis, King E. (2007). Cultural competence and evidence-based practice in mental health services. *American Psychologist, 62,* 563–574.

Wheeler, David L. (1998, September 11). Neuroscientists take stock of brain-imaging studies. *Chronicle of Higher Education,* pp. A20–A21.

Wheeler, Mary E., & Fiske, Susan T. (2005). Controlling racial prejudice: Social-cognitive goals affect amygdala and stereotype activation. *Psychological Science, 16,* 56–63.

Whiting, Beatrice B., & Edwards, Carolyn P. (1988). *Children of different worlds: The formation of social behavior.* Cambridge, MA: Harvard University Press.

Whiting, Beatrice, & Whiting, John (1975). *Children of six cultures.* Cambridge, MA: Harvard University Press.

Whitlock, Jonathan R.; Heynen, Arnold J.; Shuler, Marshall G.; & Bear, Mark F. (2006, August 25). Learning induces long-term potentiation in the hippocampus. *Science, 313,* 1093–1098.

Whooley, Mary A.; de Jonge, Peter; Vittinghoff, Eric; et al. (2008). Depressive symptoms, health behaviors, and risk of cardiovascular events in patients with coronary heart disease. *Journal of the American Medical Association, 300,* 2379–2388.

Whorf, Benjamin L. (1956). *Language, thought and reality.* Cambridge, MA: MIT Press. [Original work published 1940.]

Wicks-Nelson, Rita, & Israel, Allen C. (2003). *Behavior disorders of childhood* (5th ed.). Upper Saddle River, NJ: Prentice Hall.

Widiger, Thomas; Cadoret, Remi; Hare, Robert; et al. (1996). DSM-IV antisocial personality disorder field trial. *Journal of Abnormal Psychology, 105,* 3–16.

Widiger, Thomas, & Clark, Lee Anna (2000). Toward DSM-V and the classification of psychopathology. *Psychological Bulletin, 126,* 946–963.

Widom, Cathy Spatz; DuMont, Kimberly; & Czaja, Sally J. (2007). A prospective investigation of major depressive disorder and comorbidity in abused and neglected children grown up. *Archives of General Psychiatry, 64,* 49–56.

Wiederhold, Brenda K., & Wiederhold, Mark D. (2000). Lessons learned from 600 virtual reality sessions. *CyberPsychology & Behavior, 3,* 393–400.

Williams, Janice E.; Paton, Catherine C.; Siegler, Ilene C.; et al. (2000). Anger proneness predicts coronary heart disease risk. *Circulation, 101,* 2034–2039.

Williams, Kipling D. (2009). Ostracism: Effects of being excluded and ignored. *Advances in Experimental Social Psychology, 41,* 279–314.

Williams, Lisa A., & DeSteno, David (2009). Pride: Adaptive social emotion or seventh sin? *Psychological Science, 20,* 284–288.

Williams, Redford B., Jr.; Barefoot, John C.; & Shekelle, Richard B. (1985). The health consequences of hostility. In M. A. Chesney & R. H. Rosenman (Eds.), *Anger and hostility in cardiovascular and behavioral disorders.* New York: Hemisphere.

Wilner, Daniel; Walkley, Rosabelle; & Cook, Stuart (1955). *Human relations in interracial housing.* Minneapolis: University of Minnesota Press.

Wilson, Sandra Jo, & Lipsey, Mark W. (2007). School-based interventions for aggressive and disruptive behavior: Update of a meta-analysis. *American Journal of Preventive Medicine, 33,* S130–S143.

Wilson, G. Terence, & Fairburn, Christopher G. (1993). Cognitive treatments for eating disorders. *Journal of Consulting and Clinical Psychology, 61,* 261–269.

Wilson, Timothy D.; & Gilbert, Daniel T. (2005). Affective forecasting: Knowing what to want. *Current Directions in Psychological Science, 14,* 131–134.

Wiltermuth, Scott S., & Heath, Chip (2009). Synchrony and cooperation. *Psychological Science, 20,* 1–5.

Winick, Myron; Meyer, Knarig Katchadurian; & Harris, Ruth C. (1975). Malnutrition and environmental enrichment by early adoption. *Science, 190,* 1173–1175.

Winnicott, D. W. (1957/1990). *Home is where we start from.* New York: Norton.

Wirz-Justice, Anna; Benedetti, Francesco; Berger, Mathias; et al. (2005). Chronotherapeutics (light and wake therapy) in affective disorders. *Psychological Medicine, 35,* 939–944.

Wirth, James H., & Bodenhausen, Galen V. (2009). The role of gender in mental-illness stigma: A national experiment. *Psychological Science, 20,* 169–173.

Wisdom, Jennifer P.; Saedi, Goal A.; & Green, Carla A. (2009). Another breed of "service" animals: STARS study findings about pet ownership and recovery from serious mental illness. *American Journal of Orthopsychiatry, 79,* 430–436.

Wispé, Lauren G., & Drambarean, Nicholas C. (1953). Physiological need, word frequency, and visual duration thresholds. *Journal of Experimental Psychology, 46,* 25–31.

Witelson, Sandra F.; Glazer, I. I.; & Kigar, D. L. (1994). Sex differences in numerical density of neurons in human auditory association cortex. *Society for Neuroscience Abstracts, 30* (Abstr. No. 582.12).

Witkiewitz, Katie, & Marlatt, G. Alan (2004). Relapse prevention for alcohol and drug problems: That was Zen, this is Tao. *American Psychologist, 59,* 224–235.

Witkiewitz, Katie, & Marlatt, G. Alan (2006). Overview of harm reduction treatments for alcohol problems. *International Journal of Drug Policy, 17,* 285–294.

Witvliet, Charlotte vanOyen; Ludwig, Thomas E.; & Vander Laan, Kelly L. (2001). Granting forgiveness or harboring grudges: Implications for emotion, physiology, and health. *Psychological Science, 12,* 117–123.

Wolpe, Joseph (1958). *Psychotherapy by reciprocal inhibition.* Palo Alto, CA: Stanford University Press.

Wood, James M.; Nezworski, M. Teresa; Lilienfeld, Scott O.; & Garb, Howard N. (2003). *What's wrong with the Rorschach?* San Francisco: Jossey-Bass.

Wood, Joanne V.; Michela, John L.; & Giordano, Caterina (2000). Downward comparison in everyday life: Reconciling self-enhancement models with the mood-cognition priming model. *Journal of Personality and Social Psychology, 79,* 563–579.

Wood, Wendy; Lundgren, Sharon; Ouellette, Judith A.; et al. (1994). Minority influence: A meta-analytic review of social influence processes. *Psychological Bulletin, 115,* 323–345.

Woodward, Amanda L. (2009). Infants' grasp of others' intentions. *Current Directions in Psychological Science, 18,* 53–57.

Woody, Erik Z., & Bowers, Kenneth S. (1994). A frontal assault on dissociated control. In S. J. Lynn & J. W. Rhue (Eds.), *Dissociation: Clinical, theoretical and research perspectives.* New York: Guilford.

Wu, Shali, & Keysar, Boaz (2007). The effect of culture on perspective taking. *Psychological Science, 18,* 600–606.

Wynne, Clive D. L. (2004). *Do animals think?* Princeton, NJ: Princeton University Press.

Wyrobek, A. J.; Eskenazi, B.; Young, S.; et al. (2006, June 9). Advancing age has differential effects on DNA damage, chromatin integrity, gene mutations, and aneuploidies in sperm. *Proceedings of the National Academy of Sciences, 103,* 9601–9606.

Yalom, Irvin D. (1989). *Love's executioner and other tales of psychotherapy.* New York: Basic Books.

Yang, Chi-Fu Jeffrey; Gray, Peter; & Pope, Harrison G. Jr. (2005). Male body image in Taiwan versus the West: Yanggang Zhiqi meets the Adonis Complex. *American Journal of Psychiatry, 162,* 263–269.

Yapko, Michael (1994). *Suggestions of abuse: True and false memories of childhood sexual trauma.* New York: Simon & Schuster.

Young, Larry J., & Francis, Darlene D. (2008). The biochemistry of family commitment and youth competence: Lessons from animal models. In K. Kline (Ed.), *Authoritative communities: The scientific case for nurturing the whole child.* New York: Springer Science + Business Media.

Young, Malcolm P., & Yamane, Shigeru (1992). Sparse population coding of faces in the inferotemporal cortex. *Science, 256,* 1327–1331.

Young, Terry; Finne, Laurel; Peppard, Paul E.; et al. (2008). Sleep-disordered breathing and mortality: Eighteen-year follow-up of the Wisconsin Sleep Cohort. *Sleep, 31,* 1071–1078.

Yu, Junying; Vodyanik, Maxim A.; Smuga-Otto, Kim; et al. (2007). Induced pluripotent stem cell lines derived from human somatic cells. *Science, 318,* 1917–1920.

Yu, ManSoo, & Stiffman, Arlene R. (2007). Culture and environment as predictors of alcohol abuse/dependence symptoms in American Indian youths. *Addictive Behaviors, 32,* 2253–2259.

Yu, M.; Zhu, X.; Li, J. et al. (1996). Perimenstrual symptoms among Chinese women in an urban area of China. *Health Care for Women International, 17,* 161–172.

Yuan, Sylvia, & Fisher, Cynthia (2009). "Really? She blicked the baby?" Two-year-olds learn combinatorial facts about verbs by listening. *Psychological Science, 20,* 619–626.

Yzerbyt, Vincent Y.; Corneille, Olivier; Dumont, Muriel; & Hahn, Kirstin (2001). The dispositional inference strikes back: Situational focus and dispositional suppression in causal attribution. *Journal of Personality and Social Psychology, 81,* 365–376.

Zajonc, R. B. (1968). Attitudinal effects of mere exposure. *Journal of Personality and Social Psychology, 9,* Monograph Supplement 2, 1–27.

Zalta, Alyson K., & Chambless, Dianne L. (2008). Exploring sex differences in worry with a cognitive vulnerability model. *Psychology of Women Quarterly, 32,* 469–482.

Zhu, L. X.; Sharma, S.; Stolina, M.; et al. (2000). Delta-9-tetrahydrocannabinol inhibits antitumor immunity by a CB2 receptor-mediated, cytokine-dependent pathway. *Journal of Immunology, 165,* 373–380.

Zimmer, Lynn, & Morgan, John P. (1997). *Marijuana myths, marijuana fact: A review of the scientific evidence.* New York: Lindesmith Center.

Zimmerman, F.J.; Christakis, D.A.; & Meltzoff, A.N. (2007). Associations between media viewing and language development in children under age 2 years. *Journal of Pediatrics, 151,* 364–368.

Zone, Nolon; Sue, Stanley; Chang, Janer; et al. (2005). Beyond ethnic match: Effects of client–therapist cognitive match in problem perception, coping orientation, and therapy goals on treatment outcomes. *Journal of Community Psychology, 33,* 569–585.

Zosuls, Kristina M.; Ruble, Diane N.; Tamis-LeMonda, Catherine S.; et al. (2009). The acquisition of gender labels in infancy: Implications for gender-typed play. *Developmental Psychology, 45,* 688–701.

Zubieta, Jon-Kar; Bueller, Joshua A.; Jackson, Lisa R.; et al. (2005). Placebo effects mediated by endogenous opioid activity on μ-opioid receptors. *Journal of Neuroscience, 25,* 7754–7762.

Zucker, Kenneth J. (1999). Intersexuality and gender identity differentiation. *Annual Review of Sex Research, 10,* 1–69.

Zur, Ofer, & Nordmarken, M. A. (2008). DSM: Diagnosing for status and money. *National Psychologist, May/June,* 15.

Zurbriggen, Eileen L. (2000). Social motives and cognitive power-sex associations: Predictors of aggressive sexual behavior. *Journal of Personality and Social Psychology, 78,* 559–581.

Credits

Photos and Cartoons

Photographer; **p. 246,** © David Young-Wolff\Alamy; **p. 247,** Marc Asnin\Queen Esther Production; **p. 250,** Thomas & Pat Leeson\Photo Researchers, Inc; **p. 250,** SuperStock, Inc.; **p. 250,** SuperStock, Inc.; **p. 250,** SuperStock, Inc.; **p. 251,** Janet Mann; **p. 251,** © The New Yorker Collection, 1990. Peter Steiner from cartoonbank.com. All Rights Reserved; **p. 252,** Georgia State University\LRC; **p. 253,** Michael Goldman Photography; **p. 254,** The Granger Collection, New York; **p. 255,** www.CartoonStock.com; **p. 261,** Michael Goldman Photography

Chapter 8: p. 262, HO\Burlington Police Department\AP Wide World Photos; **p. 264,** Corbis RF; **p. 265,** © Landov; **p. 265,** ScienceCartoonsPlus.com; **p. 266,** Wilson and Neff, Inc. Reprinted by permission of Harper Collins Publishers; **p. 267,** © (Photographer)\CORBIS. All Rights Reserved; **p. 268,** Dr. Elizabeth Loftus; **p. 268,** Dr. Elizabeth Loftus; **p. 271,** From "Rudolph the Red-Nosed Reindeer" by Robert L. May. © 1939, 1967 by Robert L. May Company. Published Modern Curriculum Press, an imprint of Pearson Learning Group. Used by permission of Pearson Education, Inc.; **p. 274,** Travis Gering; **p. 274,** Hank deLespinasse\Hank deLespinasse Studios, Inc.; **p. 276,** Jacka Photography; **p. 278,** Jennifer K. Berman; **p. 279,** Fig. 3, from Reber, PJ, Stark, CEL & Squire, LR (1998). Contrasting cortical activity associated with category memory and recognition memory. Learning & Memory, 5, p. 420-428.; **p. 281,** Wasyl Szrodzinski\Photo Researchers, Inc.; **p. 281,** Tom Stewart\CORBIS-NY; **p. 283,** ScienceCartoonsPlus.com; **p. 284,** © Warren Miller\The New Yorker Collection\www.cartoonbank.com. All Rights Reserved; **p. 285,** Karen Preuss\The Image Works; **p. 286,** Loftus EF, Miller DG, Burns HJ, (1978). Semantic integration of verbal information into a visual memory. J. Expt. Psychology; Human Learning and Memory, 4, 19–31; **p. 286,** Loftus EF, Miller DG, Burns HJ, (1978). Semantic integration of verbal information into a visual memory. "Journal of Experimental Psychology"; Human Learning and Memory, 4, 19–31; **p. 287,** ScienceCartoonsPlus.com; **p. 290,** Courtesy of Carolyn Rovee-Collier; **p. 290,** ©The New Yorker Collection from cartoonbank.com. All Rights Reserved; **p. 292,** Chuck Burton\AP Wide World Photos

Chapter 9: p. 298, Redux Pictures; **p. 299,** Dennis MacDonald\PhotoEdit Inc.; **p. 299,** bildagentur-online\Alamy Images; **p. 299,** Adam Woolfitt; **p. 300,** The Granger Collection; **p. 304,** ©Martin Harvey\Photographers Choice\Getty Images, Inc.; **p. 306,** Cameramann\The Image Works; **p. 307,** Michael Newman\PhotoEdit Inc.; **p. 308,** NEIGHBORHOOD © KING FEATURES SYNDICATE; **p. 312,** Joe McNally Photography; **p. 313,** © Charles Barsotti\The New Yorker Collection\www.cartoonbank.com. All Rights Reserved; **p. 314,** Stephen Ferry; **p. 314,** Erik S. Lesser; **p. 314,** ©The New Yorker Collection 1988 Bernard Schoenbaum from cartoonbank.com. All Rights Reserved; **p. 317,** Dennis MacDonald\PhotoEdit Inc.; **p. 318,** bildagentur-online\Alamy Images; **p. 320,** © Lee Lorenz\The New Yorker Collection\www.cartoonbank.com. All Rights Reserved; **p. 322,** Adam Woolfitt; **p. 322,** © Jack Ziegler\The New Yorker Collection\www.cartoonbank.com. All Rights Reserved; **p. 325,** © Capcom\Newscom; **p. 329,** Adam Woolfitt

Chapter 10: p. 330, AP Wide World Photos; **p. 331,** The Yomiuri Shimbun; **p. 331,** AP Wide World Photos; **p. 331,** Syndicated Features Limited\The Image Works; **p. 332,** © Giuliano Colliva\News\Getty Images, Inc.; **p. 333,** Archives of the History of American Psychology - The University of Akron; **p. 333,** Copyright 1968 by Stanley Milgram. Copyright Renewed 1993, Alexander Milgram. From the film OBEDIENCE, distributed by Penn State Media Sales; **p. 333,** Robert Azzi\Woodfin Camp & Associates, Inc.; **p. 334,** Copyright 1965 by Stanley Milgram. From the film OBEDIENCE, distributed by Penn State Media Sales; **p. 335,** © Bettman\CORBIS; **p. 336,** AP Wide World Photos; **p. 339,** © Barbara Smaller\Conde Nast Publications\www.cartoonbank.com; **p. 340,** © Rob Carr\AP Wide World; **p. 341,** AP Wide World Photos; **p. 343,** The Yomiuri Shimbun; **p. 346,** Alex Webb\Magnum Photos, Inc.; **p. 346,** AP Wide World Photos; **p. 346,** ScienceCartoonsPlus.com; **p. 348,** Syndicated Features Limited\The Image Works; **p. 349,** © Tommy Trenchard\Alamy; **p. 349,** Scott J. Ferrell\Congressional Quarterly\Newscom; **p. 351,** David Young-Wolff\PhotoEdit Inc.; **p. 351,** Al-xVadinska\Shutterstock; **p. 351,** Monica Almeida\The New York Times; **p. 353,** © Bryan Denton\The New York Times\Redux; **p. 355,** AP Wide World Photos; **p. 355,** Creators News Service (CNS); **p. 356,** © Tim Boyle\News\Getty Images, Inc.; **p. 356,** National Archives and Records Administration; **p. 356,** Photo by Matthew Trana, courtesy of Houston Community Newspapers; **p. 356,** © Scott B. Rosen\Alamy; **p. 356,** AP Photo\ Community Security Trust, HO; **p. 357,** CORBIS-NY; **p. 357,** National Archives and Records Administration; **p. 357,** Courtesy of the Library of Congress; **p. 357,** Bill Pugliano\Getty Images; **p. 357,** © Jeff Topping\Reuters\Corbis; **p. 360,** Tom Watson\Merrill Education; **p. 361,** AP Wide World Photos; **p. 361,** Yves Herman\CORBIS-NY

Chapter 11: p. 368, Ray Tamarra\Getty Images; **p. 369,** © David Grossman\Alamy; **p. 369,** © Everett Collection; **p. 369,** Paintings by Bryan Charnley\ © Terence Charnley & SANE; **p. 370,** Bojan Brecelj\CORBIS-NY; **p. 370,** Al Campanie\The Image Works; **p. 370,** Elena Dorfman\Redux Pictures;

p. 372, © Bettmann\CORBIS; **p. 374,** Marilyn Volan\Shutterstock; **p. 375,** CORBIS-NY; **p. 377,** David Turnley\CORBIS-NY; **p. 379,** Chet Gordon\The Image Works; **p. 381,** Mick Hutson\Retna Ltd.; **p. 382,** © David Grossman\Alamy; **p. 384,** AP Wide World Photos; **p. 384,** © Evan Agostini\AP Wide World; **p. 386,** © Palm Springs Police Dept.\AP Wide World; **p. 387,** Brookhaven National Laboratory; **p. 388,** © Leland Bobbe\Stone\Getty Images, Inc.; **p. 388,** 1999 Daniel Laine\CORBIS- NY; **p. 389,** Universal Uclick; **p. 390,** © Jordan Strauss\WireImage\Getty Images, Inc.; **p. 392,** © Everett Collection; **p. 394,** © Painting by Bryan Charnley\© Terence Charnley & SANE; **p. 394,** Paintings by Bryan Charnley\© Terence Charnley & SANE; **p. 394,** Paintings by Bryan Charnley\© Terence Charnley & SANE; **p. 394,** Paintings by Bryan Charnley\© Terence Charnley & SANE; **p. 396,** "Courtesy, Dr. Arthur W. Toga, Laboratory of Neuro Imaging"; **p. 403,** Paintings by Bryan Charnley\© Terence Charnley & SANE; **p. 403,** © Painting by Bryan Charnley\© Terence Charnley & SANE

Chapter 12: p. 404, ©St Petersburg Times\Melissa Lyttle\The Image Works; **p. 405,** University of Washington HIT Lab\Mary Levin; **p. 405,** © Fotosearch.com Royalty Free; **p. 407,** Alvin H. Perlmutter Inc.; **p. 407,** Alvin H. Perlmutter Inc.; **p. 407,** © Lee Lorenz\The New Yorker Collection\www.cartoonbank.com. All Rights Reserved; **p. 409,** © Barbara Smaller\The New Yorker Collection\www.cartoonbank.com. All Rights Reserved; **p. 410,** Top two images: Sanjaya Saxena, MD and J.M. Schwartz, M.D.- UCLA Neuropsychiatric Institute (unpublished data, 1996). Bottom two images: Copyright ©1996, American Medical Association, from Schwartz, J.M. et. al, "Archives of General Psychiatry", February 1996, Volume 53, pages 109–113.; **p. 411,** W McIntyre\Photo Researchers, Inc.; **p. 411,** George Ruhe\ The New York Times; **p. 412,** © Fotosearch.com Royalty Free; **p. 413,** IN THE BLEACHERS © Steve Moore. Reprinted with permission of UNIVERSAL PRESS SYNDICATE. All rights Reserved; **p. 414,** University of Washington HIT Lab\Mary Levin; **p. 415,** Shutterstock; **p. 416,** Michael Newman\PhotoEdit Inc.; **p. 417,** Courtesy of Alan Entin, Ph. D., family psychologist; **p. 417,** © Jack Ziegler\The New Yorker Collection\www.cartoonbank.com. All Rights Reserved; **p. 420,** Giuseppe Costantino, Ph.D., Director; **p. 420,** Government of Puerto Rico Economic Development Administration; **p. 422,** AP Photo/Pier Paolo Cito; **p. 423,** © Mike Twohy\The New Yorker Collection\www.cartoonbank.com. All Rights Reserved; **p. 430,** George Ruhe\ The New York Times; **p. 431,** Michael Newman\ PhotoEdit Inc.

Chapter 13: p. 432, © BOB PEARSON\epa\Corbis; **p. 433,** Fred Prouser\CORBIS- NY; **p. 433,** Michael Greenlar\The Image Works; **p. 433,** Juergen Berger, Max-Planck Institute\Science Photo Library\Photo Researchers, Inc.; **p. 435,** Michael Newman\PhotoEdit Inc.; **p. 435,** Erika Stone; **p. 435,** Laura Dwight Photography; **p. 435,** Eric Gay\AP Wide World Photos; **p. 435,** Fred Prouser\CORBIS-NY; **p. 435,** Michael Philip Manheim\ImageState Media Partners Limited; **p. 435,** Itar-Tass\Sovfoto; **p. 435,** Jessica Tracy, University of British Columbia, Tracy, J.L., & Robins, R.W. (2004). Show your pride: Evidence for a discrete emotion expression. Psychological Science, 15, 194–197.; **p. 436,** Heidi S. Mario; **p. 438,** Janice Rubin Photography; **p. 449,** Juergen Berger, Max-Planck Institute\Science Photo Library\Photo Researchers, Inc.; **p. 449,** CartoonStock Ltd.; **p. 450,** Michael Greenlar\The Image Works; **p. 450,** Stephen Agricola Photography\The Image Works; **p. 453,** Bill Varie\CORBIS-NY; **p. 454,** Barry Lewis; **p. 454,** © Barbara Singer\Photonica\Getty Images, Inc.; **p. 456,** Los Angeles Times Photo By Gina Ferazzi; **p. 458,** Chris Haston\Picture Desk, Inc.\Kobal Collection; **p. 459,** Chris Haston\NBCU Photo Bank/AP Images; **p. 460,** Mary Hancock; **p. 461,** BIZARRO (NEW) © DAN PIRARO. KING FEATURES SYNDICATE

Chapter 14: p. 466, ALEXIS C. GLENN\UPI\Newscom; **p. 467,** Nicole Bengiveno\The New York Times; **p. 467,** Victor Englebert\Photo Researchers, Inc.; **p. 467,** Picture Press Bild- und Textagentur GmbH, Munich, Germany; **p. 468,** Dennis Stock\Magnum Photos, Inc.; **p. 468,** Victor Englebert\Photo Researchers, Inc.; **p. 469,** Remi Banali\ZUMA Press - Gamma; **p. 470,** Guang Niu\CORBIS- NY; **p. 472,** CinemaPhoto\CORBIS-NY; **p. 472,** © Chris Pizzello\AP Wide World; **p. 472,** Time Life Pictures\Getty Images; **p. 472,** Carlos Costa\PacificPhotos\Newscom; **p. 473,** Remy de la Mauviniere\AP Wide World Photos; **p. 473,** Jennifer Graylock\AP Wide World Photos; **p. 474,** Picture Press Bild- und Textagentur GmbH, Munich, Germany; **p. 474,** Picture Press Bild- und Textagentur GmbH, Munich, Germany; **p. 475,** David Young-Wolff\PhotoEdit Inc.; **p. 476,** © Robert Weber\The New Yorker Collection\www.cartoonbank.com. All Rights Reserved; **p. 477,** JUMP START reprinted by permission of United Feature Syndicate, Inc.; **p. 478,** Magnum Photos, Inc.; **p. 479,** © Bruce Ayres\Stone\Getty Images, Inc.; **p. 480,** Reprinted by permission of The Kinsey Institute for Research in Sex, Gender, and Reproduction, Inc.; **p. 481,** © The New Yorker Collection 1995 Donald Reilly from cartoonbank.com. All Rights Reserved; **p. 482,** Joseph Van Os\Getty Images, Inc Bridgeman; **p. 482,** C&M Denis Huot\Photolibrary\Peter Arnold, Inc.; **p. 484,** © John

Ferguson\Newscom; **p. 484,** Carol Ford\Getty Images Inc. RF; **p. 485,** Monkey Business Images\Shutterstock; **p. 486,** Jupiter Images PictureArts Corporation\Brand X Royalty Free; **p. 486,** Cassy Cohen\PhotoEdit Inc.; **p. 487,** Nicole Bengiveno\The New York Times; **p. 488,** CORBIS-NY; **p. 488,** Stephanie Diani\The New York Times; **p. 489,** © W.B. Park\The New Yorker Collection\www.cartoonbank.com. All Rights Reserved; **p. 490,** Courtesy of the Library of Congress; **p. 490,** CORBIS-NY; **p. 490,** Flip Schulke\Stock Photo\Black Star; **p. 490,** CORBIS- NY; **p. 491,** © SuperStock\SuperStock; **p. 491,** Marvin Koner\Stock Photo\Black Star; **p. 491,** CORBIS-NY; **p. 491,** Carol Halebian\Carol Halebian Photography; **p. 492,** © Daniel Bosler\Stone\Getty Images, Inc.; **p. 495,** Spencer Grant\Photolibrary.com; **p. 496,** The Far Side® by Gary Larson © 1985 FarWorks, Inc. All Rights Reserved. Used with Permission

Figures and Tables

Chapter 1: p. 2, Tracey Wilkinson, "Mexico City Legalizes Gay Marriage" Copyright © 2010 *Los Angeles Times.* Reprinted with permission; **p. 22,** Figure 1.2a, b, & c, David S. Moore and George P. McCabe. *Introduction to the Practice of Statistics,* Copyright © 2008. Reprinted by permission of W.H. Freeman and Company/Worth Publishers.

Chapter 2: p. 48, Figure 2.1, from *Temperament and personality development across the life span* by Costa et al. Copyright 1999 by Taylor & Francis Group LLC BOOKS. Reproduced with permission of Taylor & Francis Group LLC. Books in the formats Text and Other book via Copyright Clearance Center.; **p. 61,** Figure 2.2, from "Insult Aggression and the Southern Culture of Honor" by Cohen et. al. *Journal of Personality and Social Psychology,* 70. Copyright © 1996 Reprinted by permission in accordance with the American Psychological Association Guidelines.

Chapter 3: p. 86, Figure 3.3, from Renee Ballargeon, "How do infants learn about the physical world?" *Current Directions in Psychology,* 5 Copyright © 1994 Reprinted by permission of SAGE Publications.; **p. 100,** Figure 3.4, from Jeffrey Arnett, "Conceptions of the transition from adulthood from adolescence through mid life" *Journal of Adult Development* 8(2) April, 2001. Copyright © 2001 Reprinted by permission of Kluwer Academic/Plenum.

Chapter 5: p. 158, Figure 5.3, Figure 3 a&b, p. 786 from "Sleep Preferentially Enahances Memory for Emotional Components of Scenes" by J.D. Payne, R. Stickgold, K. Swanberg, and E.A. Kensinger, (2008) *Psychological Science,* 19(8) 781–788. Copyright © 2008 by Association for Psychological Science. Reprinted by permission of Wiley Blackwell.

Chapter 6: p. 208, Figure 6.12, From Figure 2 in "The Subjective Experience of Pain: Where Expectations Become Reality" by T. Koyama et al. *Proceedings of the National Academy of Sciences,* 102(36) September 6, 2005 Copyright © 2005 by the National Academies of Sciences, USA. Reprinted by permission.

Chapter 7: p. 237, Figure 7.2, From "The Effect of Severity of Initiation on Liking for a Group" by E. Aronson and J. Mills (1959) *Journal of Abnormal and Social Psychology,* 59, 177–181 Copyright ©1959 American Psychological Association; **p. 248,** Figure 7.8, Adapted from page 14 in "Get Smart: Take a Test: A Long Term Rise in IQ Scores Baffles Intelligence Experts" by J. Horgan, *Scientific American,* November 1995. Copyright © 1995 Reprinted by permission of Dimitry

Schildlovsky.; **p. 248,** Figure 7.9, Duckworth & Seligman, "Self discipline Outdoes IQ in Predicting Academic Performance of Adolescents" *Psychological Science ,* 16(12), 6. Copyright © 2005 Reprinted by permission of SAGE Publications.

Chapter 8: p. 269, Figure 8.2, From "More Than Suggestion: The Effect of Interviewing Techniques from the McMartin Preschool Class" by S. Garven, J.M. Wood, R.S. Malpass, and J.S. Shaw (1998) *Journal of Applied Psychology,* 83, 347–359. Copyright © 1998 by American Psychological Association.

Chapter 9: p. 319, Figure 9.7, From "Undermining Children's Intrinsic Interest with Extrinsic Rewards" by M.R. Lepper, D. Greene, and R.E. Nisbett (1973), *Journal of Personality and Social Psychology,* 28, 129–137. Copyright © 1973 by American Psychological Association.

Chapter 10: p. 342, Figure 10.2, John R. Alford, Carolyn L. Funk, and John R. Hibbing, "Are Political Orientations Genetically Transmitted?" *American Political Science Review,* 99(2) May, 2005. Copyright © 2005 American Political Science Association. Reprinted with the permission of Cambridge University Press.; **p. 359,** Figure 10.4, From "Can Cross Group Friendships Influence Minority Students' Well being at Historically White Universities?" by R. Mendoza Denton and E. Page Gould (2008) *Psychological Science,* 19, 933–939. Copyright © 2008 by SAGE Publications.

Chapter 11: p. 371, Figure 11.1, DSM IV Copyright © 2000 Reprinted with permission of The American Psychiatric Association.

Chapter 12: p. 422, Figure 12.2, From "Psychological Debriefing for Road Traffic Accident Victims" by R.A. Mayou, A. Ehlers, and M. Hobbs (2000) *British Journal of Psychiatry,* 176, 589–593. Copyright © 2000 by the Royal College of Psychiatrists. Reprinted by permission; **p. 424,** Table 12.3, From "Psychological Treatments That Cause Harm" by Scott O. Lillenfeld, (2007), *Perspectives on Psychological Science,* 2, 53–70. Copyright © 2007 by Wiley Blackwell. Reprinted by permission of the publisher.

Chapter 13: p. 448, Figure 13.3a, Jane Brody, "A Cold Fact: High Stress Can Make You Sick" *New York Times,* November 19, 2007 Copyright © 1997 New York Times Co., Inc. Reprinted by permission. All rights reserved; **p. 454,** Figure 13.4b, "The Health Consequences of Hostility" by Williams, Barefoot, and Shekelle in Margaret A. Chesney and Ray H. Rosenman, *Anger and Hostility in Cardiovascular and Behavior Disorder,* pp. 173–85. Copyright © 1985 Reprinted with permission; **p. 455,** Figure 13.5, From Witvilet, et al. "Granting Forgiveness" *Psychological Science,* 12(2) 7 Copyright © 2001 Reprinted by permission of SAGE Publications.; **p. 458,** Figure 13.6, From James A. Coan, Hillary S. Schaefer, Richard J. Davidson. Lending a Hand: Social Regulation of the Neural Response to Threat, *Psychological Science,* 17(12) 8 Copyright © 2006 Reprinted by permission of SAGE Publications.

Chapter 14: p. 492, Figure 14.2, Adapted from pp. 42–43 in "Praise for Intelligence Can Undermine Children's Motivation and Performance" by C.M. Mueller and C.W. Dweck, *Journal of Personality and Social Psychology,* 75(1998) Copyright © 1998 by the American Psychological Association. Adapted with permission.; **p. 496,** From "Location, Location, Location: The Misprediction of Satisfaction in Housing Lotteries" by E.W. Dunn, D.T. Gilbert, and T.D. Wilson (2003) *Personality and Social Psychology Bulletin,* 29, 1421–1432. Copyright © 2003 by The American Psychological Association.

Name Index

W

Waddington, J. L., 396
Wade, A. R., 211
Wade, Carole, 125
Wade, Elizabeth, 276
Wagenaar, W., 287
Wager, Tor D., 208, 409
Wagner, Anthony D., 226
Wagner, Christopher C., 423
Wagner, Patricia E., 442
Wagner, Richard K., 244
Wagner, Ullrich, 159
Wakefield, Jerome C., 370, 372, 380, 382
Waldfogel, Samuel, 104
Waldrip, Amy M., 349
Walk, Richard, 210
Walker, Anne, 152
Walker, David L., 306
Walker, Elaine, 396
Walker, Matthew, 158
Walker-Andrews, Arlene S., 436
Walkley, Rosabelle, 359
Wall, P., 206
Wallace-Wells, Ben, 406
Wallbott, Harald G., 445
Wallen, Kim, 92, 480, 488
Waller, Niels G., 53
Walton, Kate E., 47
Walum, Hasse, 475
Wampold, Bruce, 420
Wang, Gene-Jack, 172
Wang, Huimin, 140
Wang, Jen C., 387
Wang, P., 396
Wang, Qi, 291
Ward, Geoff, 277
Ward, L. Monique, 472
Warren, Gayle H., 173
Watanabe, Shigeru, 312
Watkins, Linda R., 206
Watson, David, 50, 51
Watson, J., 49, 86, 304
Watson, Jeanne C., 455
Watters, Ethan, 344, 425
Waugh, Christian E., 453
Weaver, Charles N., 356, 358
Weaver, Suzanne L., 451
Weber, Michael, 280
Webster, Richard, 42
Wechsler, David, 238
Weedon, Michael N., 469
Weekes, John R., 164
Wegner, Daniel M., 212, 454
Wehr, Thomas A., 151
Weike, Almut I., 306
Weil, A., 216
Weinberg, Robert A., 245
Weiner, Bernard, 441

Weinstein, Tamara A., 50
Weinstock, Michael, 234
Weiser, Mark, 74
Weiss, Alexander, 53
Weiss, Bahr, 423
Weiss, Daniel S., 377
Weiss, Samuel, 118
Weissman, Myrna M., 382
Weisz, John, 77, 423, 451
Wellman, H. M., 86
Wellman, Justin A., 450
Wells, Brooke E., 483
Wells, Gary L., 267, 291
Wentura, Dirk, 358
Wenzel, Amy, 287
Werker, Janet F., 80
Werner, Emmy E., 104
Wertheimer, Michael, 193
West, Melissa O., 104
Westberg, Lars, 475
Westen, Drew, 42, 48, 412, 420
Westermark, P. O., 469
Westermeyer, Joseph, 389
Wethington, Elaine, 101
Wethington, Holly, 317
Whalen, P. J., 358
Whaley, Arthur L., 419
Whaley, Shannon E., 248
Wheeler, David L., 126
Wheeler, Ladd, 457
Wheeler, Mary E., 358
Whitbeck, Leslie B., 398
White, B. J., 352
White, C. Sue, 375
White, Jacqueline W., 485
Whitehouse, Wayne G., 165
Whiten, Andrew, 251
Whitfield, C. L., 288
Whiting, Beatrice, 59
Whiting, John, 59
Whitlock, Jonathan R., 278
Whitmore, Mary R., 152
Whooley, Mary A., 453
Whorf, B. L., 225
Wicks-Nelson, Rita, 97
Widiger, Thomas, 373, 384
Widom, Cathy Spatz, 317, 381
Wiech, Katja, 208
Wiederhold, Brenda K., 414
Wiederhold, Mark D., 414
Wiesel, T., 190–191
Wiggins, Jack G., 409
Wilde, M. L., 325
Wiles, Janet, 83
Willerman, L., 52
Williams, David R., 448
Williams, G., 469
Williams, Janice E., 453

Williams, Karen A., 80
Williams, Kipling D., 345
Williams, Lisa A., 434
Williams, Redford B., Jr., 453
Williams, Tannis M., 153
Williams, Wendy M., 244
Willie, Jon T., 157
Willis, Sherry L., 101, 103
Wilner, Daniel, 359
Wilson, Anne E., 58
Wilson, Fraser A. W., 191
Wilson, G. Terence, 173, 420, 423
Wilson, Glenn D., 487
Wilson, Kimberly A., 421, 423
Wilson, Margo, 482
Wilson, Rachel, 83
Wilson, Robert S., 102, 103
Wilson, Sandra Jo, 317
Wilson, Timothy D., 495, 496
Wiltermuth, Scott S., 438
Wing, R., 470
Winick, Myron, 247
Winkielman, Piotr, 126
Winnicott, D. W., 44
Winocur, Gordon, 191
Wirth, James H., 397
Wirz-Justice, Anna, 151
Wisco, Blair E., 382
Wisdom, Jennifer P., 426
Wiseman, Richard, 216
Wispé, Lauren G., 211
Witelson, Sandra F., 136
Witkiewitz, Katie, 391, 423
Witt, Richard, 207
Wittchen, Hans-Ulrich, 373
Wittlinger, Roy P., 270
Witvliet, Charlotte vanOyen, 455
Wojda, Mark R., 355
Wolfe, Marilyn, 487
Wolpe, Joseph, 413
Wood, James M., 269, 374, 375, 489
Wood, Joanne V., 451, 457
Wood, Phillip K., 230
Wood, Wendy, 350, 445, 481
Woodman, Geoffrey F., 193
Woodward, Amanda L., 87
Woody, Erik Z., 165
Woollett, Earnest, 485
Work, William C., 104
Worthley, Joanna S., 276
Wu, Shali, 58
Wu, Shelley, 443
Wyman, Peter A., 104
Wynne, Clive D. L., 250, 253
Wyrobek, A. J., 101

X

Xu, Gang, 341

Xu, M., 396
Xun, W. Q. Elaine, 58

Y

Yalom, I., 416
Yamane, Shigeru, 191
Yanagisawa, K., 204
Yang, Chi-Fu Jeffrey, 473
Yapko, Michael, 165
Yeo, Ronald A., 137
Yiu, Adelaide P., 140
Young, A. W., 436
Young, Larry J., 458
Young, Malcolm C., 317
Young, Malcolm P., 191
Young, Michael A., 161
Young, S., 101
Young, Terry, 157
Yu, Junying, 118
Yu, ManSoo, 152, 388
Yuan, Sylvia, 81
Yurko, Karen H., 450
Yzerbyt, Vincent Y., 338

Z

Zagefka, Hanna, 360
Zajonc, R. B., 340, 442
Zak, Paul J., 475
Zalta, Alyson K., 382
Zambarano, Robert J., 488
Zanna, Mark P., 214
Zanni, Giudo, 267
Zatorre, Robert J., 121
Zayas, Vivian, 89
Zeanah, Charles H., 104, 247
Zeidner, Moshe, 244
Zeki, Semir, 475
Zhang, Xiaoying, 58
Zhong, Chen-Bo, 206
Zhou, Eric S., 451
Zhu, L. X., 171
Zhu, X., 152
Zigler, Edward, 57, 104
Zimbardo, Philip G., 335, 336, 337
Zimmer, Lynn, 171
Zimmerman, Frederick J., 23, 80
Zinbarg, Richard, 322, 376
Zola-Morgan, Stuart, 279
Zone, Nolon, 419
Zosuls, Kristina M., 93
Zubieta, Jon-Kar, 208
Zucker, Kenneth J., 487
Zuo, Yan-Ling, 102
Zur, Ofer, 371
Zurbriggen, Eileen L., 485

Subject Index